# WORLD CONGRESS ON NEURAL NETWORKS- SAN DIEGO

1994 International
Neural Network Society
Annual Meeting

Town & Country Hotel
San Diego, California USA
June 5-9, 1994

Volume 4

T0186724

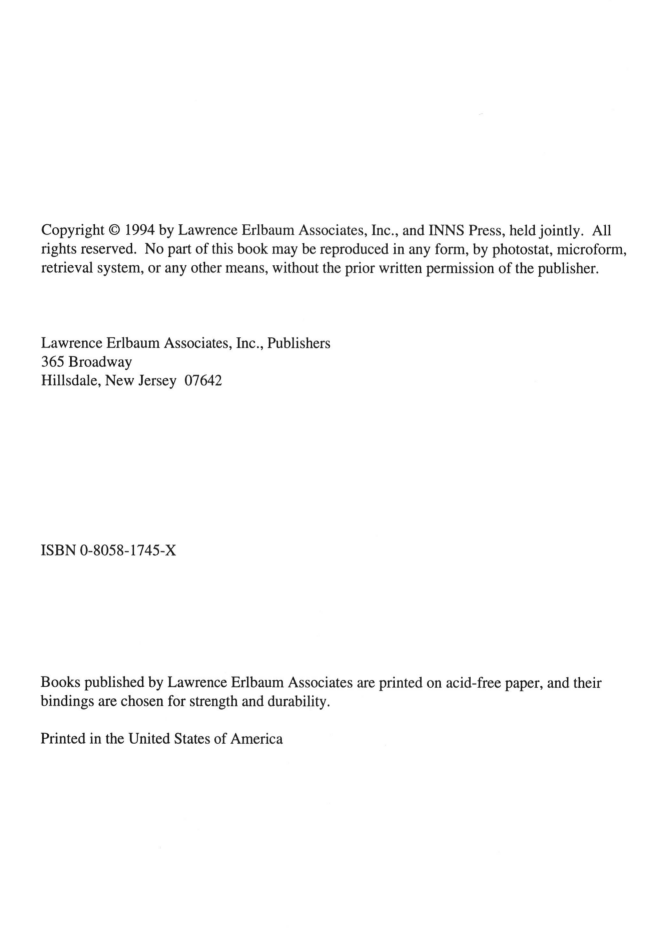

Lawrence Erlbaum Associates, Inc., Publishers
365 Broadway
Hillsdale, New Jersey  07642

ISBN 0-8058-1745-X

Books published by Lawrence Erlbaum Associates are printed on acid-free paper, and their bindings are chosen for strength and durability.

Printed in the United States of America

# WCNN '94 ORGANIZING COMMITTEE

**Paul Werbos**, Chairman, *National Science Foundation*

**Harold Szu**, *Naval Surface Warfare Center*

**Bernard Widrow**, *Stanford University*


# WCNN '94 SPECIAL SESSION CHAIRS

**BIOMEDICAL APPLICATIONS OF NEURAL NETWORKS**
**David G. Brown**, *Center for Devices and Radiological Health,*
*US Food and Drug Administration*
**John N. Weinstein**, *National Cancer Institute*, *US National Institutes of Health*

**COMMERCIAL AND INDUSTRIAL APPLICATIONS OF**
**NEURAL NETWORKS**
**Bernard Widrow**, *Stanford University*

**FINANCIAL AND ECONOMIC APPLICATIONS OF**
**NEURAL NETWORKS**
**Guido J. Deboeck**, *World Bank*

**APPLICATION OF NEURAL NETWORKS IN THE**
**CHEMICAL PROCESS INDUSTRIES**
**Thomas McAvoy**, *University of Maryland*

**MIND, BRAIN, AND CONSCIOUSNESS**
**John G. Taylor**, *King's College London*

# WCNN '94 PROGRAM COMMITTEE

**Daniel Alkon**, *National Institutes of Health*
**Shun-ichi Amari**, *University of Tokyo*
**Richard A. Andersen**, *Massachusetts Institute of Technology*
**James A. Anderson**, *Brown University*
**Kaveh Ashenayi**, *University of Tulsa*
**Andrew Barto**, *University of Massachusetts*
**Horacio Bouzas**, *Geoquest*
**David G. Brown**, *Center for Devices and Radiological Health, US FDA*
**Gail Carpenter**, *Boston University*
**David Casasent**, *Carnegie Mellon University*
**Ralph Castain**, *Los Alamos National Laboratory*
**Chris Darken**, *Siemens Corporate Research*
**Joel Davis**, *Office of Naval Research*
**Judith Dayhoff**, *University of Maryland*
**Guido J. Deboeck**, *World Bank*
**David Fong**, *Photon Dynamics, Inc.*
**Judy Franklin**, *GTE Laboratories*
**Walter J. Freeman**, *University of California at Berkeley*
**Kunihiko Fukushima**, *Osaka University*
**Michael Georgiopoulos**, *University of Central Florida*
**Lee Giles**, *NEC Research Institute*
**Stephen Grossberg**, *Boston University*
**Dan Hammerstrom**, *Adaptive Solutions, Inc.*
**Robert Hecht-Nielsen**, *HNC, Inc.*
**Robert Jannarone**, *University of South Carolina*
**Jari Kangas**, *Helsinki University of Technology*
**Christof Koch**, *California Institute of Technology*
**Teuvo Kohonen**, *Helsinki University of Technology*
**Bart Kosko**, *Signal and Image Processing Institute*
**Clifford Lau**, *Office of Naval Research*
**Soo-Young Lee**, *Korea Advanced Institute of Science and Technology*
**George Lendaris**, *Accurate Automation Corporation*
**Daniel Levine**, *University of Texas - Arlington*
**Alianna Maren**, *Accurate Automation Corporation*
**Kenneth Marko**, *Ford Motor Company*

# WCNN '94 PROGRAM COMMITTEE

**Thomas McAvoy**, *University of Maryland*
**Thomas McKenna**, *Office of Naval Research*
**Larry Medsker,** *American University*
**Erkki Oja**, *Lappeenranta University of Technology*
**Robert Pap**, *Accurate Automation Corporation*
**Barak Pearlmutter**, *Siemens Corporate Research*
**Richard Peterson**, *Georgia Tech Research Institute*
**Gerhardt Roth**, *Brain Research Institute*
**David Rumelhart**, *Stanford University*
**Mohammad Sayeh**, *Southern Illinois University*
**Dejan Sobajic**, *Electric Power Research Institute*
**Harold Szu**, *Naval Surface Warfare Center*
**John G. Taylor**, *King's College London*
**Brain Telfer**, *Naval Surface Warfare Center*
**Shiro Usui**, *Toyohashi University of Technology*
**John N. Weinstein**, *National Cancer Institute*
**Paul Werbos**, *National Science Foundation*
**Bernard Widrow**, *Stanford University*
**Takeshi Yamakawa**, *Kyushu Institute of Technology*
**Lotfi A. Zadeh**, *University of California at Berkeley*
**Mona Zaghloul**, *George Washington University*

# CONGRESS SPONSOR

**The International Neural Network Society (INNS) is the sponsor of WCNN '94 - San Diego.**

PRESIDENT **Walter J. Freeman**, *University of California at Berkeley*
PRESIDENT-ELECT **John G. Taylor**, *King's College London*
PAST PRESIDENT **Harold Szu**, *Naval Surface Warfare Center*
SECRETARY **Gail Carpenter**, *Boston University*
TREASURER **Judith Dayhoff**, *University of Maryland*

## BOARD OF GOVERNORS:

**Shun-ichi Amari**, *University of Tokyo*
**James A. Anderson**, *Brown University*
**Andrew Barto**, *University of Massachusetts*
**David Casasent**, *Carnegie Mellon University*
**Leon Cooper**, *Brown University*
**Rolf Eckmiller**, *University of Bonn*
**Kunihiko Fukushima**, *Osaka University*
**Stephen Grossberg**, *Boston University*
**Mitsuo Kawato**, *Advanced Telecommunications Research Institute*
**Christof Koch**, *California Institute of Technology*
**Teuvo Kohonen**, *Helsinki University of Technology*
**Bart Kosko**, *University of Southern California*
**Christoph von der Malsburg**, *University of Southern California*
**Alianna Maren**, *Accurate Automation Corporation*
**Paul Werbos**, *National Science Foundation*
**Bernard Widrow**, *Stanford University*
**Lotfi A. Zadeh**, *University of California at Berkeley*

# ORDER OF APPEARANCE

# TECHNICAL AREAS  continued

# TABLE OF CONTENTS

Presenting author is listed first.

## VOLUME 1

## Plenaries

## Special Session: Biomedical Applications of Neural Networks

### Oral

# TABLE OF CONTENTS   continued

## Special Session: Commercial and Industrial Applications of Neural Networks

**Oral**

## Special Session: Application of Neural Networks in the Chemical Process Industries

**Oral**

## Special Session: Mind, Brain, and Consciousness

### Oral

## Applications

### Oral

# TABLE OF CONTENTS  continued

# TABLE OF CONTENTS continued

## Machine Vision

### Oral

## Neural Fuzzy Systems

### Oral

### Poster

# TABLE OF CONTENTS   continued

## VOLUME 2

## Neurocontrol and Robotics

# TABLE OF CONTENTS continued

## Prediction and System Identification

**Oral**

**Poster**

## Mathematical Foundations

**Oral**

# TABLE OF CONTENTS continued

# Hardware Implementations

# TABLE OF CONTENTS continued

## Biological Neural Networks

### Oral

### Poster

**VOLUME 3**

## Signal Processing

**Oral**

## Pattern Recognition

**Oral**

# TABLE OF CONTENTS  continued

## Supervised Learning

**Oral**

# TABLE OF CONTENTS continued

# TABLE OF CONTENTS continued

# VOLUME 4

## Associative Memory

**Oral**

**Poster**

## Unsupervised Learning

### Oral

# Biological Vision

# TABLE OF CONTENTS continued

## Circuits and System Neuroscience

### Oral

## Links to Cognitive Science & Artificial Intelligence

### Oral

## Speech and Language

### Oral

# TABLE OF CONTENTS continued

# Cognitive Neuroscience

## Neurodynamics and Chaos

### Oral

# TABLE OF CONTENTS   continued

# Associative Memory

**Session Chairs: John G. Taylor**
**Shiro Usui**

## ORAL PRESENTATIONS

# A perspective of associative learning: Computational models and some applications for color vision models

[1]S.Usui, [1]S.Nakauchi and [2]H.Szu

[1]Department of Information and Computer Sciences,
Toyohashi University of Technology
1–1 Hibarigaoka Tempaku Toyohashi 441, Japan

[2]Naval Surface Warfare Center Dahlgren Division,
Code B44, White Oak, Silver Spring, MD 20903-5640

**Abstract**—We consider associative learning mechanisms and some of the computational "learning" methods for synaptic weight updates. Associativity between an input or several inputs and output is important for self-organization in both biological and artificial neural networks is considered from that perspective. Several applications to color vision models are illustrated.

## 1 Introduction

We consider artificial neural networks (ANN) from the viewpoint of updating synaptic weights. One of the major attributes of ANN that differs from traditional computer architectures is their distributed memory. In fact, the fundamental fault tolerance of ANN is due to the storage method –"write outer products and read an inner product". The most popular model of synaptic plasticity is due to Hebb (1949). He hypothesized that neuronal synaptic plasticity during the learning process results when a pre-synaptic input causes firing of the post-synaptic neuron. Mathematically, this process is commonly denoted as follows:

$$\Delta w_{ij} \propto y_i x_j \tag{1}$$

where the outer product is between the net input $x_j$, the weighted sum over all other neuron outputs $y_i$.

Here, we call attention to the importance of the modelling of the synaptic weights. During the past two decades, increased interest and success in neurobiological studies of learning have revealed relevant biophysical and biochemical mechanisms at several levels: subcellular, cellular and network. The discovery of Synapsin IIb by Paul Greengard and his colleagues at Rockefeller University (Han et al., 1991), adds additional perspective to the development of this fast moving field.

From a network perspective, evidence accumulated in the last decade suggests that a fixed layered architecture and small perturbation bilinear learning, as described by Eq.(1) have limited computational capability and are unlikely to lead us onto the path to full nonlinear animal intelligence. Recent efforts in pruning the interconnections of ANN (e.g. ten papers in IJCNN-93 Nagoya) demonstrate the awareness of the ANN community of the importance of self-organization in layered architectures. For many network architectures, the switching off of existed interconnections is much easier (Szu, 1989) than to build up the network from no connections.

## 2 Computational perspective of associative learning

Hebbian and Hebbian-like learning are popular in the artificial neural network field, despite the growing body of evidence biological associative learning mechanisms are not Hebbian in either invertebrates or mammals. Rather, memory traces in the animal brain appear to be dispersed and stored in specific local aggregates of synaptic sites.

Modeling and simulation studies based on the experimental neurobiological data is now being applied to explore the mechanisms of biologically realistic neural network capable of associative learning (Werness et al., 1992, 1993; Sakakibara et al., 1993). Examples of successful ANN based on these principles include Dystal (Blackwell et al., 1992; Alkon et al., 1990, 1994) and ART and its variants (Carpenter and Grossberg, 1991).

Here, however, we concentrate on traditional simple Hebbian learning and some of its variants.

## 2.1 Simple Hebbian learning

We start by considering a linear neuron model whose output is determined by weighted sum of the incoming signals:

$$y = \sum_{i=1}^{m} w_i x_i = \boldsymbol{w}^t \boldsymbol{x}. \tag{2}$$

The most simple mathematical form for Hebbian learning is described with pre- and post-synaptic activities, as follows:

$$\Delta \boldsymbol{w} = \alpha y \boldsymbol{x}. \tag{3}$$

This rule can be averaged over an ensemble of incoming signals $\{\boldsymbol{x}\}$, assuming the time course of learning is much longer than the time interval of a signal ensemble.

$$\frac{d\boldsymbol{w}}{dt} = <\Delta \boldsymbol{w}> = \alpha Q \boldsymbol{w}, \quad \text{where} \quad Q = <\boldsymbol{x}\boldsymbol{x}^t>; \quad \text{covariance matrix of } \boldsymbol{x}. \tag{4}$$

Viewed another way, the simple Hebbian learning rule updates the connection strength $\boldsymbol{w}$ so as to maximize the output variance because

$$\frac{d\boldsymbol{w}}{dt} \propto \frac{\partial E}{\partial \boldsymbol{w}}, \quad \text{where} \quad E = <y^2> = \boldsymbol{w}^t Q \boldsymbol{w}. \tag{5}$$

One problem with this rule is that the connection strengths can increase without bound.

## 2.2 Hebbian learning that computes principal components

Oja (1989) proposed a Hebbian learning rule for extracting the first principal component vector of the input distribution. Principal component analysis (PCA) is a standard statistical technique for finding a set of linear orthogonal projections in the direction which gives the maximum variation in the input distribution. Extraction the principal component vector is, thus, equivalent to finding $w_i$ which maximize the output variance $<y^2>$, subject to the constraint that the norm of weight vector is one. He analyzed the simple Hebbian learning rule which rescales each updated weight to maintain the norm of the weight vector equal to one:

$$\Delta w_i = \alpha(y x_i - y^2 w_i). \tag{6}$$

He proved that according to this learning rule, the weight vector tends to the first principal component vector of the input distribution if the initial weight vector is not orthogonal to it.

It is noteworthy that PCA is closely related to Infomax principle (Linsker, 1988); the maximum information preservation is achieved through PCA in the case of Gaussian input with Gaussian noise added to each input.

## 2.3 Anti-Hebbian learning

Barlow and Földiák (1989) showed that a network with lateral feedback connections successfully decorrelates the input using anti-Hebbian learning. The output of the decorrelating network $y_i$ is determined by the external input $x_i$ and also by the feedback from other outputs $y_j$ through connections $w_{ij}$:

$$y_i = x_i + \sum_{j=1, j \neq i}^{N} w_{ij} y_j. \tag{7}$$

Feedback connections $w_{ij}$ are updated according to the following anti-Hebbian learning rule except for self-feedback connections $w_{ii}$:

$$\Delta w_{ij} = -\alpha y_i y_j \quad (i \neq j). \tag{8}$$

If $\alpha$ is sufficiently small, the feedback connections will change proportionally to the correlation between the outputs and the network can reach stable state when the outputs are uncorrelated: $< y_i y_j > = 0$.

# 3 Some applications in color vision models

A model of color vision which incorporates both Hebbian learning for PCA and anti-Hebbian learning to decorrelate the output. These learning rules are successfully applied to self-organization of color receptive fields and extracting invariant color information to achieve color constancy.

## 3.1 Self-organization of color receptive fields

Several authors (Field, D.J., 1987; Barrow, H.G., 1987; Linsker, 1988; Atick, J.J. and Redlich, A.N., 1991) have shown that spatial characteristics of self-organized receptive fields depends largely on the spatial correlation between pixels of images in the learning data. In this section, we attempt to explain how the characteristics of color receptive fields relates to the function of the visual system through unsupervised learning process based on Infomax principle (Usui et al., 1993).

We consider a linear network model which consists of two layers. The input layer has three color planes which correspond to two dimensional arrays of red, green and blue cones, respectively. Each output unit connects with all of cones in input layer. As described in section 3.2, if the input and the noise are assumed to have Gaussian distributions, the mutual information between input and output has maximum value when the synapse strengths correspond to the principal vector. We employed GHA (Sanger, 1989) to update the connection strengths. This allows the network to learn a set of the weights which converge precisely to the principal vectors in descending eigenvalue order. We used random color noise images as training data with both spatial and chromatic correlation between three types of cones. Color receptive fields grow depending not only on spatial correlation but also on the chromatic correlation between three kinds of cones. We defined the statistics of random color noise images using the correlation between responses of two cones located at different positions. The spatio–chromatic correlation is described as a multiplication of spatial correlation by chromatic correlation.

Figure 1 shows the synapse strengths self-organized by GHA using 2500 random color noise images. The initial synapse strengths are set randomly, the size of the color plane is $7 \times 7$ pixels and the number of output cells is 15. Number in the figure corresponds to the descending eigenvalue order, that is, the first output cell preserves the most information about the variance of the input. This result suggests that the first output cell preserves the most information based on the achromatic stimuli, that is, achromatic signal contains the most information about the input image. On the other hand, no.2 and 8 can be interpreted as Y-B and R-G chromatic opponent types, respectively. Furthermore, no.5, 6 and 13 can be interpreted as Y-B and R-G color contrast detectors which correspond to double-opponent cells found in blob in V1.

## 3.2 A decorrelating network model for color constancy

Another neural network model, one for color constancy (Usui et al., 1992), decorrelates the triplet of cone responses to colored objects through anti-Hebbian learning.

The model structure and the learning rule are slightly different from the original (Barlow and Földiák, 1989). The network has three bias units with modifiable connections $b_i$ and output units with asymmetric feedback connections $w_{ij}$, as shown in Fig.2. Each external input $x_i$ is transformed into an internal signal

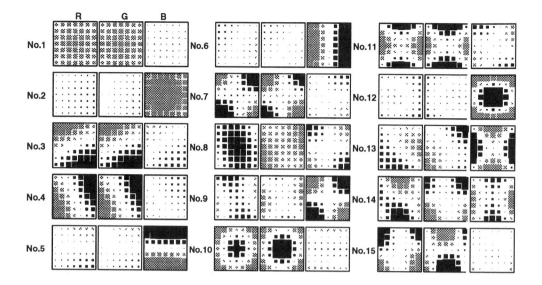

**Fig.1.** Color receptive fields self-organized by GHA using random color noise images. The size of each square indicates the absolute value of connection strengths between an output unit and each cone array in the input layer. Black and gray indicate positive and negative value, respectively. Some units exhibit both chromatic and spatial opponency similar to that of double-opponent cells found in V1.

$y_i = x_i + b_i$ which is fed to the output unit. Each network output $z_i$ is determined by the internal signal $y_i$ and the weighted sum of the outputs of other units as follows:

$$z_i = y_i + \sum_{i \geq j} w_{ij} z_j. \tag{9}$$

In matrix form,

$$z = (x + b) + wz, \tag{10}$$

where $w$ is a lower triangular matrix. After the initial transient, we can write the network output as

$$z = (I - w)^{-1} y, \tag{11}$$

where $I$ is the unit matrix.

All connections are modified according to the anti-Hebbian rule. The external input is transformed into a zero-mean signal by setting the bias connections $b_i$ to the mean value of each input signal. The learning rule for bias connections is

$$\Delta b_i = -\alpha y_i, \tag{12}$$

where $\alpha$ is the learning rate. The feedback connections $w_{ij}$ are modified in order to uncorrelate network outputs:

$$\Delta w_{ij} = \begin{cases} -\dfrac{\alpha}{1 - w_{ii}} y_i y_j, & i > j; \\ -\dfrac{\alpha}{1 - w_{ii}} (y_i^2 - k), & i = j. \end{cases} \tag{13}$$

Note that the modification rule for self-feedback connections $\Delta w_{ii}$ has a constant value $k$ which controls the gain of the network's output; that is, the power of each output approaches to $k$ during learning process.

**Fig.2.** Structure of the network model which has three bias and output units with modifiable connections. The external input is transformed into a zero-mean signal, and feedback connections uncorrelate the network's output through anti-Hebbian learning.

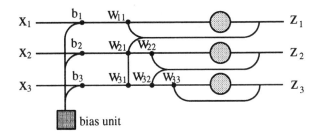

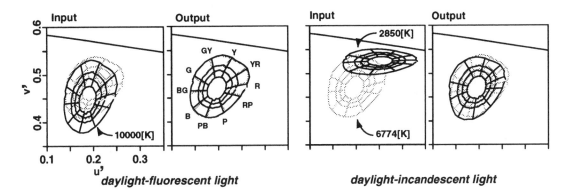

**Fig.3.** Color differences due to the change in illuminant for input and output data (Munsell Value=5) plotted on $u'v'$ chromaticity diagram. Dotted and solid lines show the data for daylight and colored (fluorescent and incandescent) light, respectively. The network removes the effect of change in illuminant color through anti-Hebbian learning which decorrelates the inputs.

To train the network, we used the triplet of red, green and blue cone responses to 1569 Munsell color chips under one white and two colored illuminants: daylight (white), incandescent light (yellowish) and fluorescent light (bluish). We first set the strength of all connections to zero and train the network using white daylight data. We employ the strength of connections of the network after learning the daylight data as an initial condition for other learning simulations; the network is retrained using fluorescent light data or incandescent light data from the initial condition.

After training, each network is adapted to daylight, fluorescent and incandescent light, respectively. In order to evaluate the invariability of color representation by network's output quantitatively, we measure the color differences in input and output space of the network on the CIE $u'v'$ chromaticity diagram between two pairs: daylight–fluorescent lights and daylight–incandescent lights. Figure 3 shows the input and output data of a constant value plane for daylight–fluorescent and daylight–incandescent pairs. Each grid in the figure shows the constant hue and chroma locus. Input distribution strongly depends on the illuminant color, for instance, the input distribution of the fluorescent light shifts to bluish and that of the incandescent light shifts to yellowish from the distribution of the daylight data. By contrast, the output distribution remains almost the same despite the change in illuminant. This means that the network achieved color constancy by decorrelating the cone responses which strongly depend on the illuminant color.

# 4 Conclusion

Several aspects of associative learning have been illustrated from the computational points of view. Our ultimate goal is to obtain insights into biological associative memory; insights that are useful for electronic computing rather for duplicating biological computing. Neuroanatomical investigations have revealed a vast spectrum of biological neurons and a number of different memory mechanisms have been proposed.

Further important discoveries are on the horizon. However, for computationally tractable neuron models and architectures, it is incumbent on the engineer to extract salient features and mechanisms from biology that are not to be replicated slavishly, but rather to serve as the basis for elucidating principles that can be transformed into effective algorithms. It is important that, in this endeavor, we try to captured the simplest possible learning mechanism. We hope that readers will be stimulated to join us in this endeavor.

# References

Alkon, D.L. (1983) Learning in a marine snail, Sci. Am., 249, 70-84

Alkon, D.L., Blackwell, K.T., Vogl, T.P., Werness, S.A. (1993) Biological plausibility of artificial neural networks: Learning by non-Hebbian synapses, In: Associative Neural Memories, M.H. Hassoun, Ed., Oxford University Press

Atick, J.J. and Redlich, A.N. (1991) Predicting ganglion and simple cell receptive field organizations, Int.J.Neural System, 1, 305–315

Barlow, H.B. and Földiák, P. (1989) Adaptation and decorrelation in the cortex, In: The Computing Neuron, chap.4, 54–72, Addison-Wesley

Barrow, H.G. (1987) Learning receptive field, Proc. IEEE ICNN, IV, 115–121

Blackwell, K.T., Vogl, T.P., Hyman, D.S., Barbour, G.S. and Alkon, D.L. (1992) A new approach to hand-written character recognition, Pattern Recognition, 25, 655-666

Carpenter, G.A. and Grossberg, S. (1991) Pattern recognition by self-organizing neural networks, MIT, Cambridge

Field, D.J. (1987) Relations between the statistics of natural images and the response properties of cortical cells, J.Opt.Soc.Am.A, 4, 2379–2394

Han, H., Nichols, R.A., Rubin, M.R., Bahler, M., Greengard, P. (1991) Induction of formation of presynaptic terminals in neuroblastoma cells by Synapsin IIb, Nature, 349, 697–700

Hebb, D.O. (1949) The organization of behavior, In: The first stage of perception: growth of the assembly, xi–xix, 60–78, Wiley, New York

Linsker, R. (1988) Self-organization in a perceptual network, IEEE Computer, 21, 105–117

Oja, E. (1989) Neural networks, principal components, and subspaces, Int.J. Neural Systems, 1, 1, 61–68

Sakakibara, M., Ikeno, H., Usui, S., Collin, C. and Alkon, D.L. (1993) Reconstruction of ionic currents in a molluscan photoreceptor, Biophys. J., 65, 519–527

Sanger, T.D. (1989) Optimal unsupervised learning in a single-layer linear feedforward neural network, Neural Networks, 2, 459–473

Szu, H. (1989) A dynamic reconfigurable neural network, J. Neural Network Computing, 1, Suppl., 1–23, Auerbach, NY

Usui, S., Nakauchi, S. and Miyamoto, Y. (1992) A neural network model for color constatncy based on the minimally redundant color representation, Proc. IJCNN (Beijin), 2, 696–701

Usui, S., Nakauchi, S. and Takahashi, K. (1993) Self-organization of color receptive fields using random color noise images, Proc. WCNN (Portrand), 1, 72–75

Werness, S.A., Fay, S.D., Blackwell, K.T., Vogl, T.P. and Alkon, D.L. (1992) Associative learning in a network model of *Hermissenda crassicornis*, Biol. Cybern., 68, 125–133

Werness, S.A., Fay, S.D., Blackwell, K.T., Vogl, T.P. and Alkon, D.L. (1993) Associative learning in a network model of *Hermissenda crassicornis*, II. Experiments, Biol. Cybern., 69: 19-28

# Using Old Memories To Store New Ones

Dimitrios Bairaktaris
Department of Computing Science and Mathematics
University of Stirling
Stirling FK9 4LA, Scotland
tel: (+44) 786 467426, fax:(+44) 786 464551 e-mail: dib@uk.ac.stir.cs

Joseph P. Levy
Human Communication Research Centre University of Edinburgh
2 Buccleuch Place,
Edinburgh EH8 9LW, Scotland
tel. (+44) 31 6504450, fax:(+44) 31 6504587, e-mail:joe@cogsci.ed.ac.uk

February 14, 1994

## Abstract

This paper describes a connectionist model of the interaction between long and short term memory. The proposed model addresses both issues of old memory utilization and novel memory consolidation. It comprises two different auto-associator network components; one for short term memory (STM) and one for long term memory (LTM). The STM network component uses a Hebbian type fast learning algorithm, while the LTM component uses the relatively slow Mean Field Theory algorithm (Peterson and Hartman 1989). Both components have the same two-layer network architecture comprising an input layer and an hidden layer. Previous modelling attempts put the interaction between LTM and STM at the connection level (e.g. Gardner-Medwin 1989). In this paper we promote the idea that it is more advantageous to define this interaction at the node level using old memory traces to store new ones.

## 1 STM, LTM and Their Interaction Processes

In every day life humans make use of a short term memory store with relatively limited storage capacity. This store is assumed to contain information related to individual events of the near past. Memories from this store contain a high degree of detail and they are stored and accessed relatively quickly. STM memory traces are relatively short lived compared to the bulk of knowledge which refers to the individual's complete record of knowledge. This knowledge is stored in a relatively high capacity long term memory device. STM is assumed to hold event specific information while LTM plays the role of a generalization device, where current information is judged against the complete set of one's past experience. There is a constant flow of information between STM and LTM. In order to interpret and respond to current events, we utilize our past experience. The current stimulus evokes a long term memory response which is bound with the incoming information and creates a temporary new memory trace. We call the flow of information from the LTM to the STM the Binding Process (BP). The information provided by the LTM can be a number of things. For example when a natural language processing application domain is concerned, the LTM trace may contain lexicon related information necessary for the appropriate input categorization. As is mentioned above information in STM is short lived and unless it is transferred into a more permanent store it will be lost. It is therefore reasonable to assume that there is a complement to the BP process, which we call the Consolidation Process (CP), which facilitates flow of information from the STM to the LTM thus enabling incremental LTM learning. Our proposed model relates to previous models in that it uses two sets of synapses, one for STM and one for LTM. Next we describe briefly what we consider to be the two major contributions in this area, we identify their limitations and we discuss specific modelling issues related to the BP and CP processes.

## 2    Doubly Modifiable Synapses

Hinton and Plaut in Hinton and Plaut 1987 describe a network where each synapse has two adaptive weights. One weight changes slowly and reflects storage of long term knowledge, while the other weight is fast changing and stores only temporary knowledge. Their approach focuses on the effects of novel memory acquisition on older memory traces. Adding new memories to a network without re-training on the old ones results in information loss. Their proposed solution uses the fast weights to cancel out the changes on the old memory traces during recent learning. The fast weights serve as a rehearsal device which enables selective retraining on old memories. In our model we also use fast weights as a rehearsal device but to rehearse newly acquired memories. The problem of adding new memories without disturbing the old ones is known as the "catastrophic forgetting" problem and it constitutes a major modelling issue with respect to CP. Gardner-Medwin in Gardner-Medwin 1989 approaches the problem of STM–LTM interaction also using doubly modifiable connections. Each connection is equipped with a temporary and a persistent weight which have a multiplicative effect on the node activation. The proposed model engages a selective consolidation algorithm which enables LTM incremental storage without "catastrophic forgetting" effects, a solution extensively discussed in French 1991. However, the model fails to identify the significance of LTM in STM performance, which becomes almost independent of the amount of LTM experience. It is important to note here, that Hinton and Plaut have chosen to effectively use one learning rule for both sets of their weights as did Gardner-Medwin. Our approach is different, two completely different learning regimes are employed for STM and LTM respectively. Our motivation behind the use of different learning regimes was the understanding that we are effectively modelling two systems with completely different properties. Our understanding of connectionist tools available for the modelling task clearly indicated that a fast, Hebbian type learning rule is required for modelling STM. A repetitive training regime which will enable a network to "discover" hidden regularities in the data domain is necessary for modelling LTM. Our choice of network architecture was a natural consequence of our continuing line of work. Next we describe in turn the LTM and STM components focusing our attention on the issues related to our final modelling goal.

## 3    Incremental Learning in MFT auto-associators

The network architecture of both the LTM and the STM component is shown in Figure 1. It comprises of an input layer fully connected to an hidden layer.

The LTM network is trained to function as an autoassociator device and generalize over a set of input patterns (memories) using the MFT approximation algorithm (Peterson and Hartman 1989). As is the case with back-propagation type auto-associators (French 1991) the LTM network suffers from memory loss when new memories are added without retraining on the old memories. Using an

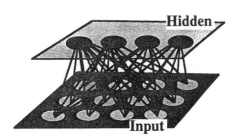

Figure 1: Auto-associator Network with Hidden Layer, Both components of our model have the same architecture.

ABA type learning procedure it is shown in Levy and Bairaktaris 1992 that if there is structure in the A and B memory sets the effects of forgetting can be reduced, but by no means eliminated. Let us now consider the problem within the context of STM-LTM interaction where another possibility is raised. As was mentioned previously, successful interpretation of novel stimuli relies heavily on past experiences. This observation is the basis of our solution to the problem of sequential learning. Consider a network already trained to a set of patterns A. The network is then shown a pattern from a different set B, to which the network will respond erroneously because it has not been trained on set B. The response of the network depends on the formation of a hidden representation which is essentially the network's view of the novel input. If during training with set B we do not disturb this "view", we effectively reduce the interference between old and new memories to a minimum. To test our hypothesis, two sets of patterns A and B were generated. Each set comprised 10 binary vectors each comprising 20 input features. Structure was built into each set by means of correlation between the patterns (Levy and Bairaktaris 1992). The training and testing procedure involved the following steps:

- Test the network's recall performance on set A before any training is done (Stage A).

- Train the network to set A and test its recall performance on set A (Stage B).

- Test the network's recall performance on set B and record the hidden layer representation that corresponds to each pattern in B (Stage C).

- Train the network to set B by forcing it to use the hidden layer representations recorded at stage C and subsequently test its recall performance on set B (Stage D).

- Test the network's recall performance on set A in order to determine the effect of set B on the old memories (Stage E).

When using the standard MFT learning process, the network is allowed to decide freely upon the hidden representations it will use in order to encode the regularities in the domain. In our method, every time the network is trained to a new data set it is forced to use the specific hidden representations that emerge from memories already in store. During our simulations the above procedure was repeated several times for a number of different data sets and network sizes. In all cases the "catastrophic" forgetting effect was reduced significantly. Figure 2 shows the average recall error for sets A and B during stages A through to E, for a network with 30 hidden units and average intra-set correlation of 50%. The average recall error shows the quality of the memory representations in store. It is determined by cueing the network with every memory from the respective data set

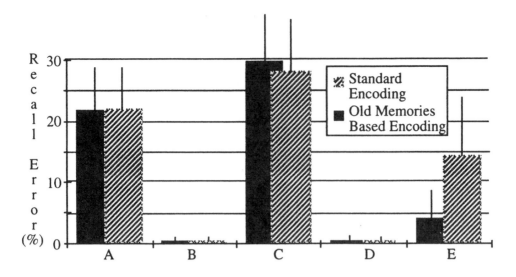

Figure 2: The effect of using previous internal representations on catastrophic forgetting

and computing the average bitwise difference between the memory and the recall pattern. Using the standard MFT training method the "interference" error of set B on the older memories of set A is measured at 14%. This effectively corresponds to a complete elimination of set A from memory given that for the particular network configuration average recall of set A before training was measured at 22%. On the other hand, when using the new method which utilizes older information the effect of learning set B on older memories from set A was measured to an average of 4%.

So far we have made the assumption that set of memory patterns become available instantly. Clearly, this is not the case. Each set is formed gradually and a Short Term store is required where B set and its internal representations can be stored temporarily and at completion rehearsed into LTM. We will use the short term memory component of our model for this purpose.

## 4   Bidirectional Two-Layer Autoassociators

In Bairaktaris 1990 it is shown that bidirectional multi-layer auto-associators combined with Randomized Internal Representation and trained with the "covariance" adaptation rule (Hopfield 1982) can store and recall correlated memory patterns. Each memory vector is associated with a random hidden vector and by means of a bidirectional evaluation process (Kosko 1988) the network functions as an autoassociative memory. Further investigation (Bairaktaris 1993) has shown that the storage capacity of this class of networks is equivalent to the one observed for Hopfield networks. The particular network architecture used for our model is shown in Figure 1. It comprises an input layer of nodes fully connected to a hidden layer. In Levy and Bairaktaris 1991 it was shown that the network's storage and recall performance is not compromised if during encoding the hidden representations emerging from an MFT network were used instead of random internal vectors. Everything is now in place in order to present our model of STM-LTM interaction in detail.

# 5  STM-LTM Interaction

Our complete network model has two sub-network components described in the previous two sections. These two components have the same architecture and they interact using a "copy" function via their internal representations. There are two basic processes fundamental to STM-LTM interaction, the Binding and Consolidation Processes. We will describe them in this order.

## 5.1  The Binding Process

A cue pattern from the environment is received and is submitted to the LTM component. LTM is evaluated in the standard MFT procedure and forms a "view" of the input by means of generating an internal representation. This internal representation is "copied" onto the internal layer of the STM component. At this point weight modifications occurred in STM in order to encode the current pattern. Note that the particular encoding rule used in STM allows incremental learning without "catastrophic" forgetting effects as long as the network's capacity is not exceeded. This "copying" process corresponds to a binding mechanism, during which long term knowledge is associated with current information. This association will become permanent when the memories from the STM component move onto the LTM. In order to avoid duplication of encoding in STM, whenever a previously seen recent input arrives, a novelty detection control device such as the one described in Carpenter and Grossberg 1988 can be employed.

## 5.2  Novel Memory Acquisition

Having a set of memories and their corresponding internal representations stored in the STM component enables us to rehearse them and store them in LTM. The actual internal representations used for storage are the ones LTM itself has provided, thus guaranteeing minimum interference with older memory traces. The use of a bidirectional auto-associator enables us to evoke recently stored STM memory traces in their order of acquisition and without using external stimulation (Kosko 1988). In this way a input pattern and the corresponding internal representation are generated in the STM component and they are both copied onto the corresponding sites in the LTM component. Learning in LTM occurs by clamping both the input and internal node activations and modifying the weights using the MFT algorithm.

# 6  Further Discussion

The model described above is intended to be used as a connectionist modelling tool and it can be applied into a number a domains. For example consider the problem of syntax categorization and novel input acquisition. The LTM component may be used to store information about already known words (e.g. cat–noun, go–verb). When a novel word arrives, the LTM component uses its current knowledge and "context" to categorize the current word into one of the existing categories. This categorization information is represented at the internal representation level. This information is stored in the STM and subsequently moved onto the LTM. There is a further issue which relates to the "copying" processes described above. The architecture of both the STM and the LTM component is identical and in this sense one could describe our model in terms of a single network with doubly modifiable connections which have independent effects, their interaction being at the node level. However, there are a number of synchronization problems involved in such an interpretation which require careful consideration.

# References

Bairaktaris, D. (1990) A model of Auto-Associative Memory that stores and retrieves, Successfully, data regardless of their Orthogonality, Randomness or Size. In *Hawaii International Conference on System Sciences '90*.

Bairaktaris, D. (1993) Multi-layer bidirectional auto-associators. In *Computation and Neural Systems 1992*. Dordrecht: Kluwer Academic Publishers. In press.

Carpenter, G. A. and S. Grossberg (1988) The ART of Adaptive Pattern Recognition by a Self-Organizing Neural Network. *Computer Journal* **21**(3), 77–88.

French, R. M. (1991) Using Semi-Distributed Representations to Overcome Catastrophic Forgetting in Connectionist Networks. In *13th Annual Meeting of the Cognitive Science Society*, pp. 173–178.

Gardner-Medwin, A. R. (1989) Doubly modifiable synapses: a model of short and long term auto-associative memory. *Proc. Royal Society B* **238**, 137–154.

Hinton, G. E. and D. C. Plaut (1987) Using fast weights to deblur old memories. In *Proceedings of the ninth annual conference of the Cognitive Science Society*, pp. 177–186. Lawrence Erlbaum Associates.

Hopfield, J. J. (1982) Neural networks and physical systems with emergent collective computational abilities. *Proceedings of the National Academy of Sciences, USA* **79**, 2554–2558.

Kosko, B. (1988) Bidirectional Associative Memories. *IEEE Transactions on Systems, Man and Cybernetics* **18**(1).

Levy, J. and D. Bairaktaris (1991) A model of the interaction between long and short term memory. In *Proceedings of the International Joint Conference on Neural Networks*, pp. 1741–1746. Singapore: IEEE.

Levy, J. and D. Bairaktaris (1992) Sequential learning in mean field autoassociators. In *International Conference on Artificial Neural Networks*. New York: Elsevier.

Peterson, C. and E. Hartman (1989) Explorations of the Mean Field Theory Learning Algorithm. *Neural Networks* **2**, 475–494.

# The sector conditions and the stability of discrete Hopfield networks

D. Sbarbaro
Department of Electrical Engineering - Casilla 53-C
University of Concepción
Concepción-Chile

### Abstract

A Hopfield network is considered as a linear system with a nonlinear feedback controller. The sufficient conditions for the stability of these nonlinear systems require the feedback nonlinearity to satisfy a certain type of sector condition. This known result is applied to analyse the global asymptotic stability of a Hopfield network, obtaining conditions for testing the stability of the equilibrium points and their regions of attractions. These conditions do not require symmetric interconnection matrices.

## 1  Introduction

The stability properties of Hopfield networks have been studied considering the Lyapunov direct methods [1]. On the other hand, if the Hopfield network is recasted as a linear system with a nonlinear state feedback controller, then some interesting results can be applied to analyse the stabiliiy of the network. It is well known that the sufficient condition for stability of these nonlinear systems requires the feedback nonlinearities to satisfy a certain type of sector condition [2][3]. This paper outline the application of these known results to analyse the stability of the Hopfield networks, obtaining sufficient conditions for the asymptotic stability of its equilibrium points, and some criteria to estimate the size of the stability region.

The paper is organized as follow: Section 2 describes the structure of a Hopfield network. Section 3 describes the sufficient conditions for stability of nonlinear feedback systems. Section 4 describes the results for the Hopfield networks based on the sector conditions, and finally in section 5 some conclusions are given.

## 2  Hopfield Network Structure

The discrete time Hopfield network is defined by a set of $n$ scalar equations described in vector notation as

$$U(k+1) = AU(k) + WG(U(k)) + B \tag{1}$$

where $U = [u_1, \ldots, u_n]^T$, $A = diag[a_1, \ldots, a_n]$, $W \in R^{n \times n}$ (we do not require $W$ to be symetric), and $G = diag[g_1, \ldots, g_n]$.

---

[0]Submitted to the WCNN, San Diego, U.S.A. June-1994

The nonlinear function $g_i(.)$, $i = 1, 2, \ldots, n$ are assumed to satisfy the following conditions:

$$
\begin{aligned}
i) & \quad u_i g_i(u_i) > 0 & \forall u_i \in R \\
ii) & \quad \lim_{|u_i| \to \infty} = sgn(u_i) \\
iii) & \quad \frac{g_i(u_i)}{u_i} \geq \frac{g_i(v_i)}{v_i} & \forall |u_i| \leq |v_i| \\
iv) & \quad g_i'(u_i) = \frac{dg_i(u_i)}{du_i} & \forall u_i \in R
\end{aligned}
\tag{2}
$$

In order for a state $U^* \in R^n$ to be an equilibrium state of the system (1), it is necessary and sufficient that

$$
U^* = AU^* + WG(U^*) + B
\tag{3}
$$

we assume that a given $U^*$ is an isolated equilibrium state, i.e. there exist an $r > 0$ such that the region

$$
B(U^*, r) \subset R^n \ni B = \{U : \|U - U^*\| < r\}
\tag{4}
$$

contains no equilibria other than $U^*$.

For a given equilibrium point $U^*$, with coordinate transformation $X = U - U^*$, equation (1) can be written as

$$
X(k+1) = AX(k) + W\tilde{G}(X(k))
\tag{5}
$$

where $\tilde{G}(X) = G(X + U^*) - G(U^*)$. Obviously, $X = 0$ defines an equilibrium point of (5) and $\tilde{G}(0) = 0$

## 3  The sector conditions in nonlinear discrete systems

Consider the following sequence

$$
x(k+1) = f(x(k))
\tag{6}
$$

and assume that $f(x(k))$ satisfy the *sector conditions*, i.e. $f(x) \in C(R)$, $f(0) = 0$, and $0 < \frac{f(x)}{x} < K$, $\forall x \in R$. If $K < 1$, then the sequence $z(k)$ defined as

$$
z(k+1) = Kz(k)
\tag{7}
$$

converge to zero. Considering $z(0) = x(0)$, and using equations (6) ,(7) and $f(x) < Kx$, the following relationships are obtained

$$
\begin{aligned}
x(1) & = f(x(0)) < Kx(0) = Kz(0) = z(1) \\
x(2) & = f(x(1)) < Kx(1) < Kz(1) = z(2) \\
& \vdots \quad \vdots \\
x(k) & = f(x(k-1)) < Kx(k-1) < Kz(k-1) = z(k).
\end{aligned}
\tag{8}
$$

Thus, as $z(k)$ converges to zero, then $x(k)$ converge to zero. This result can be extended to multivariable nonlinear discrete systems.

A nominal description of a nonlinear discrete system, which consist of linear dynamic elements in the forward path and a memoryless nonlinearity, with multiple non-linearities $f_1, f_2, \ldots, f_m$ composing a vector non-linearity $F$, in the feedback path, is defined by

$$
\begin{aligned}
X(k+1) &= \tilde{A}X(k) + \tilde{B}F(Y(k)) \\
Y(k) &= \tilde{C}X(k)
\end{aligned}
\tag{9}
$$

where $X \in R^n$, $\tilde{A} \in R^{n \times n}$, $\tilde{B} \in R^{m \times n}$, $Y \in R^m$, and $\tilde{C} \in R^{m \times n}$. The nonlinearity $F \in N_K$, where $N_K$ is the family of all non-linearities $f : R^m \to R^m$ with the following properties:

$$
\begin{array}{lll}
i) & F(Y) \in C(R^m) \\
ii) & F(0) = 0 \\
iii) & f_i(y_i)y_i^{-1} \in (0, k_i) \quad \forall y_i \in R, \quad y_i \neq 0 \; \forall i = 1, \ldots, m
\end{array}
\tag{10}
$$

and the motion $\mathcal{X}(k, X_0, F)$ of (9) through $X(0)$ exist, and is defined on $R_+$ and is unique for every $X(0) \in R^n$.

The global stability of the system (9) has been studied by several researchers [2] [3], and the main result can be sumarized in the following theorem, which place no restriction on the derivative of the nonlinearity and gives a sufficient condition for the system to be globally asymptotically stable.

**Theorem 1** *The origen of the nonlinear system (9) is globally asymptotically stable if*

*1) The elements of $K$ satisfy the inequality iii) of (10).*

*2) $\|(\tilde{A} + \tilde{B}K\tilde{C})\|_i < 1$* [1]

*3) $\|\tilde{A}\|_i < 1$*

**Proof:**

Let $F_d = diag\{\frac{f_1(y_1(k))}{y_1(k)}, \ldots, \frac{f_m(y_m(k))}{y_m(k)}\}$, then equation (9) can be written as an autonomous system

$$
X(k+1) = (\tilde{A} + \tilde{B}F_d\tilde{C})X(k)
\tag{11}
$$

If conditions 2) and 3) are satisfy, then $\|(\tilde{A} + \tilde{B}F_d\tilde{C})\|_i < 1$ for all the nonlinearities satisfying condition 1). Thus, the sequence defined by (12)

$$
\|X(k+1)\| \leq \|(\tilde{A} + \tilde{B}F_d\tilde{C})\|_i \|X(k)\|
\tag{12}
$$

converges to zero.$\diamond$

# 4 Verifying the sector conditions in Hopfield networks

The Hopfield network described by (5) is a nonlinear system with $m = n$, $\tilde{A} = A$, $\tilde{C} = I$, $\tilde{B} = W$, and $F = G$.

Thus, applying the results obtained for the autonomous system (9), the following results are obtained for the Hopfield network.

**Theorem 2** *The equilibrium point $U^*$ of the system (5) is globally asymptotically stable if*

$$
\|A + WK\|_i < 1
\tag{13}
$$

*where $K = G'(U^*)$*

**Proof:**

---

[1] $\| \quad \|_i$ is de induced norm of a matrix [4]

The linearized equation of (5) around the equilibrium $X = 0$ is

$$Z(k+1) = AZ(k) + WKZ(k) \tag{14}$$

where $K = \tilde{G}(X)|_{X=0} = G'(U^*)$. Let

$$H(Z(k)) = AZ(k) + WKZ(k), \tag{15}$$

and, $Z_1$ and $Z_2$ be arbitrarly points in a neighborhood of $X = 0$, then

$$\begin{aligned}\|H(Z_1(k)) - H(Z_2(k))\| &< \|A + WK\|_i \|Z_1(k) - Z_2(k)\| \\ &< \rho\|Z_1(k) - Z_2(k)\|, \quad \rho < 1\end{aligned} \tag{16}$$

which implies that $H$ is contraction mapping. Thus, the origen of the linearized system is asymptoticaly stable, then the origen of the system (5) is also a uniformly asymptoticaly stable [4].$\diamondsuit$

**Theorem 3** *For a given equilibrium point $U^*$, there can exist no other equilibrium point of the system defined by (5) in the same quadrant, if*

1) $\|A\|_i < 1$

2) $\|A + WH\|_i < 1$

*where $H = diag[\frac{g_1(u_1^*)}{u_1^*}, \ldots, \frac{g_1(u_1^*)}{u_1^*}]$.*

**Proof:**

The equation of the Hopfield network (5) and equation (9) have the same structure. Let $h_i = \frac{g_i(u_i^*)}{u_i^*}$, this means that

$$0 \le \frac{\tilde{g}_i(x_i)}{x_i} \le h_i, \quad \forall i = 1, \ldots, m \tag{17}$$

for all $x_i$, see figure 1, such that

$$\begin{aligned}-u_i^* \le x_i \le \infty \quad &if \quad u_i^* > 0 \\ -\infty \le x_i \le u_i^* \quad &if \quad u_1^* < 0.\end{aligned} \tag{18}$$

Hence, from Theorem 1, conditions 2) and 1) are sufficient conditions for establishing the asymptotic stability of $X = 0$ in the region defined by (18), i.e. for all $U$ in the same quadrant of the equilibrium point $U^*$. Thus, as $X = 0$ is asymptotically stable in this region, there is no other equilibrium point in it. $\diamondsuit$

The conditions giving by Theorem 2 and Theorem 3 are interrelated because $G'(U^*) \le H$. Thus, if the system meets the condition of Theorem 3, then it satisfy the conditions of Theorem 2 as well.

# 5 Conclusions

In this paper the conditions obtained to analyse the stability of a nonlinear feedback system were applied to analyse the asymptotic stability of the Hopfield network equilibrium points, demonstrating no only the effect of the matrices involved, but also the importance of the nonlinear function. The stability conditions and confinement of the stability region to an especific quadrant are reduced to test the induced norm of a matrix, which depends on the matrices of the discrete time Hopfield networks and the nonlinearties. The conditions obtained can be used in any design procedure.

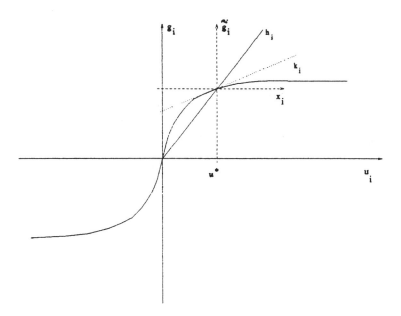

Figure 1: Nonlinearity and the change of coordinates

# References

[1] J. Hopfield, "Neural networks and physical system with emergent collective computational abilities," *Proc. Natl. Acad. Sci.*, vol. 79, pp. 2554–2558, 1982.

[2] Y. Mutoh and P. Nikiforuk, "A method for verifying sector conditions in nonlinear discrete-time control systems," *IEEE Transactions on Automatic Control*, vol. 37, pp. 1505–1509, 1992.

[3] E. Jury, "Sampled-data systems, revised: reflections, recollections and reassessments," in *Joint American Control Conference, San Fransisco, U.S.A, TA-Special Lecture*, 1980.

[4] M. Vidyasagar, *Nonlinear system analysis.* Prentice-Hall International, Englewood Cliffs, New Jersey, 1993.

# A Computationally Verifiable Test for the Complete Recall of All Training Pairs for the BAM

Yee Leung[*], Zong-Ben Xu[‡], Xiang-Wei He[†] and Bai-Li Chen[‡]

[*] Department of Geography and Center for Environmental Studies,
The Chinese University of Hong Kong, Shatin, Hong Kong
[†] Department of Information Engineering, The Chinese University
of Hong Kong, Shatin, Hong Kong
[‡] Department of Mathematics, Xi'an Jiaotong University, Xi'an,
Shaanxi, 710049, China

**Abstract**    A computationally verifiable test is proposed to determine whether or not a given set of heteroassociative pattern pairs can be completely stored and recalled through a bidirectional associative memory (BAM). This test is not only capable of exploring the maximal storage capacity of the BAM, but can also generates automatically a specific symmetric or asymmetric encoding scheme whenever it exists. Theoretical analysis and simulation results all demonstrate that the BAM models deduced from the proposed test outperforms the existing variants of the BAM in terms of storage capacity and error-correction capability.

## 1. Introduction

As well known, bidirectional associative memory (BAM) behaves as a heteroassociative pattern matcher which stores a given set of pattern pairs $\{(X^{(k)}, Y^{(k)}): k=1, 2, ..., P\}$ in the encoding matrices (weight matrices) A and B and then recalls them through the evolution of the system

$$X(t+1) = \text{sgn}(AY(t) - T) \tag{1.1}$$

$$Y(t+1) = \text{sgn}(BX(t) - S). \tag{1.2}$$

Extended on the Hopfield net [1-2], the original BAM [3-4] used the symmetric Hebbian encoding

$$A = \sum_{i=1}^{P} (X^{(i)})(Y^{(i)})^T, \ B = A^T = \sum_{i=1}^{P} (Y^{(i)})(X^{(i)})^T \tag{1.3}$$

for storing pattern pairs. However, such an encoding scheme does not guarantee the recall of all training pairs unless the pattern vectors are orthogonal or the pattern number P is very small.

Over the years, other symmetric encoding schemes [4-7] have been proposed for improving the storage capacity of the BAM. Though these proposed techniques improve the capacity of the BAM to a certain degree, they still do not guarantee the recall of all training pairs.

The requirement of a symmetric encoding scheme limits intrinsically the capacity of the BAM. To enlarge capacity, the BAM with an asymmetric encoding scheme, called the asymmetric bidirectional associative memory (ABAM), which can assure the recall of all linearly independent training pairs has recently been proposed [8]. In that model, the weight matrices are encoded as

$$A = H_P(X, Y), \ B = H_P(Y, X) \tag{1.4}$$

where $H_P(Y, X)$ is an interpolation operator defined recursively by a learning algorithm. Oh and Kothari [9] also suggested the use of a pseudo-relaxation learning algorithm to encode arbitrarily given training patterns.

An outstanding problem of the BAM model, regardless of which encoding scheme we are using, is that not any given set of training patterns can be stored in a BAM. It is thus imperative to know under what conditions a given set of training patterns can be stored. We present in this paper the necessary and sufficient conditions for storing a given set of training patterns in a BAM. In addition, we make such conditions computationally verifiable. Furthermore, whenever a given set of training patterns is justified to be encoded in a BAM, a corresponding encoding scheme will be consequently generated. Without loss of generality, we consider both the asymmetric and symmetric encodings in our discussion.

## 2. Asymmetric and Symmetric Encodings of the BAM

### 2.1. Standard Form of the Asymmetric Encoding

Given a set of training patterns $\{(X^{(k)}, Y^{(k)}): k=1, 2, ..., P\}$, where $X^{(k)} \in \{-1, 1\}^N$ and $Y^{(k)} \in \{-1, 1\}^M$ for any $k$. Suppose this set of patterns can be completely recalled by means of a BAM (1.1)-(1.2). Then each pair $(X^{(k)}, Y^{(k)})$ is a bidirectionally stable state of the BAM. That is,

$$Y_i^{(k)} \left( \sum_{j=1}^{N} b_{ij} X_j^{(k)} - s_i \right) > 0, \quad i = 1, 2, ..., M, \quad k = 1, 2, ..., P \tag{2.1}$$

$$X_i^{(k)} \left( \sum_{j=1}^{M} a_{ij} Y_j^{(k)} - t_i \right) > 0, \quad i = 1, 2, ..., N, \quad k = 1, 2, ..., P \tag{2.2}$$

Thus the consistency of systems (2.1)-(2.2) is the necessary and sufficient condition for a BAM to completely store and recall all pattern pairs $(X^{(k)}, Y^{(k)})$.

To make sure that the consistency of systems (2.1)-(2.2) can be checked by a computational test, particularly the one developed in this paper, we need to rewrite (2.1)-(2.2) into a typical form as follows:

$$\{D_i(Y)X^T\}\tilde{B}_i > 0, \quad i = 1, 2, ..., M \tag{2.3}$$

$$\{D_j(X)Y^T\}\tilde{A}_j > 0, \quad j = 1, 2, ..., N \tag{2.4}$$

where

$$X = \begin{pmatrix} X^{(1)} & X^{(2)} & ... & X^{(P)} \\ -1 & -1 & ... & -1 \end{pmatrix} = [X^{(1)}, X^{(2)}, ..., X^{(P)}]$$

$$Y = \begin{pmatrix} Y^{(1)} & Y^{(2)} & ... & Y^{(P)} \\ -1 & -1 & ... & -1 \end{pmatrix} = [Y^{(1)}, Y^{(2)}, ..., Y^{(P)}]$$

$$D_i(Y) = \text{diag}\{Y_i^{(1)}, Y_i^{(2)}, ..., Y_i^{(P)}\}, \quad i = 1, 2, ..., M$$

$$D_j(X) = \text{diag}\{X_j^{(1)}, X_j^{(2)}, ..., X_j^{(P)}\}, \quad j = 1, 2, ..., N.$$

And

$$(\tilde{A}_j) = ((a_{j1}, a_{j2}, ..., a_{jM}, t_j)^T, \quad j = 1, 2, ..., N.)$$

$$(\tilde{B}_i) = ((b_{i1}, b_{i2}, ..., b_{iN}, s_i)^T, \quad i = 1, 2, ..., M)$$

are respectively the augmented matrices of

$$A = (a_{ij})_{N \times M} \quad \text{and} \quad B = (b_{ij})_{M \times N}.$$

IV-21

To take into account of the robustness and error-correction capability requirement of the model, (2.3) and (2.4) can be constrained by an arbitrarily chosen value $\epsilon \geq 0$ as follows:

$$\{D_i(Y)X^T\}\tilde{B}_i > \epsilon, \ i = 1,2,...,M \tag{2.5}$$

$$\{D_j(X)Y^T\}\tilde{A}_j > \epsilon, \ j = 1,2,...,N. \tag{2.6}$$

## 2.2. Standard Form of the Symmetric Encoding

Extended on the discussion of the asymmetric formulation, the necessary and sufficient conditions for (1.1)-(1.2) to admit a symmetric encoding is that the following inequalities all hold:

$$\{D_i(Y)X^T\}\tilde{B}_i > 0, \ i = 1,2,...,M \tag{2.7}$$

$$\{D_j(X)Y^T\}\tilde{A}_j > 0, \ j = 1,2,...,N \tag{2.8}$$

$$\tilde{B}_i(j) = \tilde{A}_j(i), \ i = 1,2,...,M, \ j = 1,2,...,N \tag{2.9}$$

where $$\tilde{B}_i(j) = b_{ij}, \quad \tilde{A}_j(i) = a_{ji}.$$

It should be noted that (2.9) only refers to those indices i and j such that $i \leq M$ and $j \leq N$, although $\tilde{B}_i(N+1) = s_i$ and $\tilde{A}_j(M+1) = t_j$ have been defined for any $i = 1, 2, ..., M$ and $j = 1, 2, ..., N$.

To rewrite (2.7)-(2.9) as a standard form, we let

$$e_M = (1,1,...,1)^T \in R^M, \ e_N = (1,1,...,1)^T \in R^N$$

and $$X_i = (X_i^{(1)}, X_i^{(2)}, ..., X_i^{(P)})^T, \ i = 1,2,...,N$$

$$Y_j = (Y_j^{(1)}, Y_j^{(2)}, ..., Y_j^{(P)})^T, \ j = 1,2,...,M.$$

Observe that the inequalities (2.7) can be expressed as

$$\begin{pmatrix} \{D_1(Y)X^T\} & 0 & \cdots & 0 \\ 0 & \{D_2(Y)X^T\} & \cdots & 0 \\ \cdot & \cdot & \cdots & \cdot \\ \cdot & \cdot & \cdots & \{D_M(Y)X^T\} \end{pmatrix} \begin{pmatrix} \tilde{B}_1 \\ \tilde{B}_2 \\ \vdots \\ \tilde{B}_N \end{pmatrix} \geq \begin{pmatrix} 0 \\ 0 \\ \vdots \\ \vdots \\ 0 \end{pmatrix} \tag{2.10}$$

and (2.9) implies that

$$\tilde{A}_i = (\tilde{B}_1(i), \ \tilde{B}_2(i), ..., \tilde{B}_N(i), t_i)^T, \ i = 1,2,...,M$$

and consequently, $\{D_j(X)Y^T\}\tilde{A}_j > 0$, for any $j \in [1, N]$ can be written as

$$[\mathbf{0}(D_j(X)Y_1) \quad \mathbf{0}(D_j(X)Y_2) \quad \cdots \quad \mathbf{0}(D_j(X)Y_M) \quad \mathbf{0}(D_j(X)e_P)]\begin{pmatrix} \tilde{B}_1 \\ \tilde{B}_2 \\ \vdots \\ \vdots \\ \tilde{B}_M \\ T \end{pmatrix} \geq 0. \tag{2.11}$$

where, for any $i \in [1, N]$ and $j \in [1, M]$, $\mathbf{0}(D_i(X)Y_j)$ (resp. $D_i(X)e_P$) denotes the $P \times (N+1)$ matrix deduced from the $P \times (N+1)$ zero matrix by replacing its ith column with the vector $D_i(X)Y_j$ (resp. $D_i(X)e_P$). By replacing 0 by the parameter $\epsilon$, the system of inequalities (2.7)-(2.9) then can be written as follows:

$$\begin{pmatrix} \{D_1(Y)X^T\} & 0 & \cdots & 0 & 0 \\ 0 & \{D_2(Y)X^T\} & \cdots & 0 & 0 \\ \cdot & \cdot & \cdots & \cdot & \cdot \\ 0 & 0 & \cdots & \{D_M(Y)X^T\} & 0 \\ \mathbf{0}(D_1(X)Y_1) & \mathbf{0}(D_1(X)Y_2) & \cdots & \mathbf{0}(D_1(X)Y_M) & \mathbf{0}(-D_1(X)e_P) \\ \mathbf{0}(D_2(X)Y_1) & \mathbf{0}(D_2(X)Y_2) & \cdots & \mathbf{0}(D_2(X)Y_M) & \mathbf{0}(-D_2(X)e_P) \\ \cdot & \cdot & \cdots & \cdot & \cdot \\ \mathbf{0}(D_N(X)Y_1) & \mathbf{0}(D_N(X)Y_2) & \cdots & \mathbf{0}(D_N(X)Y_M) & \mathbf{0}(-D_N(X)e_P) \end{pmatrix} \begin{pmatrix} \tilde{B}_1 \\ \tilde{B}_2 \\ \vdots \\ \vdots \\ \vdots \\ \tilde{B}_M \\ T \end{pmatrix} \geq \begin{pmatrix} \epsilon \\ \epsilon \\ \vdots \\ \vdots \\ \vdots \\ \epsilon \\ \epsilon \end{pmatrix}. \tag{2.12}$$

Clearly, once (2.12) is consistent, any of its solutions $(B^*, S^*, T^*)$ gives a symmetric encoding of the BAM (1.1)-(1.2). The consistency of the system (2.12) and a computational test for the complete recall of all training patterns of the BAM in (1.1)-(1.2) are discussed in the following section.

## 3. Consistency Condition and Computational Test for the Complete Recall of All Patterns

In this section, we first state conditions under which the system of inequalities (2.5)-(2.6) associated with the BAM (1.1)-(1.2) is consistent. We then propose a computational test for the complete recall of all patterns in the BAM.

**Theorem 1.** The pattern set $\{(X^{(k)}, Y^{(k)}): k = 1, 2, \ldots, P\}$ can be completely recalled through an asymmetric BAM (resp. a symmetric BAM) if and only if the systems of linear inequalities (2.5)-(2.6) (resp. the system (2.12)) are consistent for some $\epsilon \geq 0$. Moreover, whenever (2.5)-(2.6) (resp. (2.12)) are consistent, every pattern $(X^{(k)}, Y^{(k)})$ can be recalled by the asymmetric BAM encoded as that in (2.3), (2.4) with $\tilde{A}_i$ and $\tilde{B}_j$ being any solution of (2.5)-(2.6) (resp. by the symmetric BAM with $A = B^T$ and $(B, S, T)$ being the solution of (2.12)).

**Theorem 2.** The necessary and sufficient condition for the complete recall of all training pairs $\{(X^{(k)}, Y^{(k)}): i = 1, 2, \ldots, P$ by the BAM (1.1)-(1.2) is that there are no non-negative numbers $\lambda_k, \mu_k$ ($k = 1, 2, \ldots, P$), not all zero, such that

$$\begin{cases} (\lambda_1 Y_i^{(1)})X^{(1)} + (\lambda_2 Y_i^{(2)})X^{(2)} + \cdots + (\lambda_P Y_i^{(P)})X^{(P)} = 0 \\ (\lambda_1 Y_i^{(1)} + (\lambda_2 Y_i^{(2)}) + \cdots + (\lambda_P Y_i^{(P)})) = 0, \quad i = 1, 2, \ldots, P \end{cases} \tag{3.1}$$

$$\begin{cases} (\mu_1 X_i^{(1)})Y^{(1)} + (\mu_2 X_i^{(2)})Y^{(2)} + \ldots + (\mu_P X_i^{(P)})Y^{(P)} = 0 \\ (\mu_1 X_i^{(1)}) + (\mu_2 X_i^{(2)}) + \ldots + (\mu_P X_i^{(P)}) = 0, \quad i=1,2,\ldots,P \end{cases} \qquad (3.2)$$

Whenever $\{X^{(1)}, X^{(2)}, \ldots, X^{(P)}\}$ and $\{Y^{(1)}, Y^{(2)}, \ldots, Y^{(P)}\}$ are both linearly independent, (3.1) and (3.2) certainly have no non-zero solutions $\{\lambda_1, \lambda_2, \ldots, \lambda_P\}$ and $\{\mu_1, \mu_2, \ldots, \mu_P\}$. It implies the well-known fact that any linearly independent training patterns can be completely recalled by the BAM [8].

In this paper our main interest is to offer a computational test (rather than a theoretical test) for the complete recall of all training pairs $\{(X^{(k)}, Y^{(k)}): k=1,2,\ldots,P\}$ of the BAM (1.1)-(1.2). This is certainly important because a theoretical test usually is not so easy to justify for a set of arbitrarily given training pairs.

By a computational test, we mean an algorithm that can verify automatically whether or not the systems (2.5)-(2.6) or (2.12) are consistent, and, whenever they are, the algorithm automatically generates a solution of the systems. In our present case, the computational test will be developed on the basis of a revised ellipsoid algorithm of Shor and Gershovich [10] for linear inequalities problems.

**Computational Test -- Ellipsoid Algorithm:**

**Step 1.** Set $x_0 = 0 \in R^{R+1}$, $B_0 = I$ and $\mu = 0$. Let

$$a_k = M_k, \quad k = 1, 2, \ldots, s.$$

**Step 2.** If for any $k \in \{1,2,\ldots,s\}$, $a_k^T x_\mu \le b_k$, then terminate the algorithm with $x_i = x_\mu$; Otherwise, let $k_0$ be an arbitrary index such that $a_{k_0}^T x_\mu > b_{k_0}$. Compute

$$E(x_{\mu+1}, B_{\mu+1}) = <<E(x_\mu, B_\mu) \cap H(a_{k_0}, b_{k_0})>> \qquad (3.3)$$

according to formula (3.4) in the following lemma [11] with $n := s$.

**Lemma.** Let $a^T x_0 > b$ and

$$\alpha = \frac{a^T x_0 - b}{a^T B a}.$$

Then

$$<<E(x_0, B) \cap H(a, b)>> = \begin{cases} E(x_1, B_1), & \text{if } \alpha < 1 \\ \varnothing, & \text{if } \alpha \ge 1 \end{cases} \qquad (3.4)$$

where
$$\begin{aligned} x_1 &= x_0 - \tau(Ba)/(a^T Ba) \\ B_1 &= \delta[B - \sigma(Baa^T B)/(a^T Ba)] \end{aligned}$$

with
$$\begin{aligned} \tau &= (1 + n\alpha)/(n+1) \\ \sigma &= 2(1 + n\alpha)/[(n+1)(1+\alpha)] \\ \delta &= \{n^2/(n^2-1)\}(1 - \alpha^2). \end{aligned}$$

**Step 3.** Return to **Step 2** with $\mu := \mu + 1$.

The **Ellipsoil Algorithm** now can be directly applied to test consistency of the systems (2.5), (2.6) and (2.12).

Based on the above theoretical results, the following theorem states the condition under which pattern pairs can be completely recalled and a suitable encoding can be generated.

**Theorem 3.** The pattern pairs $\{(X^{(k)}, Y^{(k)}): k=1,2,...,P\}$ can be completely recalled through an asymmetric BAM (resp. a symmetric BAM) if and only if the above algorithm simultaneously applied to

$$\{D_i(Y)X^T\}\tilde{B}_i > 0, \quad i = 1,2,...,M$$

$$\{D_i(X)Y^T\}\tilde{A}_j > 0, \quad j = 1,2,...,N$$

(resp. applied to (2.12) with 0 replacing $\epsilon$) never terminates at a finite number of steps. In this case, the algorithm will generate a specific asymmetric (resp. symmetric) encoding (A,S,B,T) such that all patterns $(X^{(k)}, Y^{(k)})$ can be recalled by the BAM with such encoding.

## 4. Simulation Results and Conclusion

We have proposed a computationally verifiable test — the ellipsoid algorithm, for testing whether or not a given set of pattern pairs can be completely stored and recalled in a BAM network. The algorithm will terminate at a finite number of iterative steps if the given pattern pairs can not be completely memorized by the BAM network. Otherwise, the algorithm will generate automatically a specific asymmetric or symmetric encoding scheme, whichever exists.

To evaluate the effectiveness of the above proposed model, the linear-inequalities asymmetric bidirectional associative memory (LABAM), a series of simulation runs was made to compare its performance with the Hopfield network (HOP), BAM and the asymmetric BAM (ABAM) proposed in [8] in terms of their restorability and error-correction capability. Simulation results of the LABAM with asymmetric and symmetric encoding are also compared. The simulation results demonstrate that LABAM out-performs all other networks. It restores the largest number of patterns (at $\epsilon=0$), an even better performance than the ABAM. Its error-correction capability is similar to that of the ABAM but superior to that of the HOP and the BAM.

## Reference

[1]     Hopfield J J 1982 Neural networks and physical systems with emergent collective computational ability, *Proc. Nat. Acad. Sci. USA* **79** 2554-2558

[2]     Hopfield J J 1984 Neurons with graded response have collective computational properties like those of two-state neurons *Proc. Nat. Acad. Sci. USA* **81** 3088-3092

[3]     Kosko B 1988 Bidirectional associative memories *IEEE Trans. Syst. Man Cybern.* **18** 49-60

[4]     Kosko B 1987 Adaptive bidirectional associative memories *Appl. Opt.* **26** 4947-4960

[5]     Simpson P K 1990 Higher-ordered and intraconnected bidirectional associative memories *IEEE Trans. Syst. Man Cybern.* **20** 637-652

[6]     Wang Y F, Cruz J B Jr and Mulligan J H 1990 Two coding strategies for bidirectional associative memory *IEEE Trans. Neural Networks* **1** 181-192

[7]     Wang Y F, Cruz J B Jr and Mulligan J H 1990 Guaranteed recall of alltraining pairs for bidirectional associative memory *IEEE Trans. Neural Networks* **2** 559-567

[8]     Leung Y, Xu Z B and He X W 1993 An asymmetric generalization of bidirectional associative memories, *Proceedings, World Congress on Neural Networks (Portland, 1993)* **II** 319-322

[9]     Oh H and Kothari S C 1992 A pseudo-relaxation algorithm for bidirectional associative memory, *IJCNN (1992)* **II** 208-213

[10]    Shor N Z and Gershovich V I 1979 Family of algorithms for solving convex programming problems *Kibernetika* **15** 62-67

[11]    Xu Z B and Wolfe M A 1991 Region analysis approach for constructing solutions of nonlinear operator equations *J. Engrg. Math.* **8** 31-45

# Feature based Contraction
# of Sparse Holographic Associative Memory

Javed I. Khan and D. Y. Y. Yun

University of Hawaii at Manoa
Department of Electrical Engineering
Laboratories of Intelligent and Parallel Systems
491 Holmes Hall, 2450 Dole Street, Honolulu, HI-96822
javed@wiliki.eng.hawaii.edu

## Abstract

The paper presents a scheme for reducing memory space of a holographic associative memory for content based learning, searching and retrieval of sparse patterns. Holographic associative memory developed on the properties of complex valued Riemann space is one of the most promising models of associative memory. It has demonstrated 10 to 100 times speedup than most other models of associative memories in learning pattern associations with nearly arbitrary level of complexity. The correlation space of the sparse patterns, is also sparse in information, but representationally dense. Therefore, holograph of sparse patterns (such as images) becomes extremely large. In this paper we describe a holographic memory model which projects the sparse holograph on a reduced memory space along all three of its dimensions by unsupervised learning of the stimulus and response patterns. The resulting holographic model also simultaneously increases the encoding, searching and decoding speed.

## 1 Introduction

Associative computing is expected to play a critical role in the field of intelligent image data-base management. The applications such as content addressable retrieval, query by example, indexing by features; such as color, texture, shape, all these require some form of associative recollection.

Since the advancement of synoptic theory of signal transmission by McCulloch and Pitts (1943), and Hebb (1949) a number of models of artificial associative memories have been developed to mimic the behavior of human brain by researchers such as Marr (1969), Anderson (1989), Willshaw (1971), Kanerva (1988) and many others [Kane88, Will89]. These pioneering models were able to reproduce some of the intriguing behaviors of human brain. Two of the most serious concern with most of these associative memories are their capacity and difficulty in storing arbitrary patterns. However, for image applications, the problem becomes more acute in terms of enormous physical memory requirement. Very few work has been done to make the assosiative memory space efficient.

A typical image pattern generally consists of a large number of pixels, and by nature individually they carry small amount of significant information. As a consequence, the correlation space of the image pattern becomes physically large but sparse in information. The objective of our research is to find ways to extract useful information from this sparseness of the correlation space and to contract the space of associative memory.

Our research is specifically aimed at a model of holographic associative memory proposed by Sutherland [Suth90], which has demonstrated a major break through in speed and capacity. Experiments have revealed speedup of factors 10 to 100 times compared to other paradigms [Souc92,p8]. Multiple pattern associations at nearly arbitrary complexity, without hindered by the linear separability problem, can be enfolded with the holographic memory. Thus, it challenges the principal two limitations of earlier models. The memory operates in complex number domain, in contrast to most other models. The holographic memory itself can be considered as a 3-D volume. The first two dimensions are the stimulus and response pattern elements. The 3rd dimension or the depth represents the bits required to store each of the correlation element. In this paper we present a uniform technique based on the autonomous learning of patterns to contract the holograph along all three dimensions based on the sparseness analysis of the correlation information. The next section presents a background on holographic associative memory. Section 3 presents the contraction model. Finally section 4 provides some performance results from a simulated holograph.

# 2 Background and Mathematical Basis

## 2.1 Bi-Modal Representation

A pattern S is a suit of stimulus elements in the form of $\{s_1, s_2, \ldots s_n\}$. The individual pattern elements are represented as a complex number, where the magnitude of the complex number is representative of the *confidence* in the element and the phase of the complex number enumerates the *content*. Unlike the conventional representation schemes, our model treats information as a bi-modal (confidence:content) notion. Thus a stimulus and response patterns with respectively n and q elements are represented as:

$$S = \{s_1, s_2, \ldots s_n\} = \left\{ \lambda_1 e^{i\theta_1}, \lambda_2 e^{i\theta_2}, \cdots, \lambda_n e^{i\theta_n} \right\} \qquad R = \{r_1, r_2, \ldots r_q\} = \left\{ \gamma_1 e^{i\phi_1}, \gamma_2 e^{i\phi_2}, \cdots, \gamma_n e^{i\phi_q} \right\}$$

The content of each element $(s_j, r_j)$ is transformed to the phase exponent $(\theta_j, \phi_j)$ through some suitable transformation. A sigmoidal transformation can a generate uniform phase distribution if the stimulus elements are distributed normally. $\lambda_j$ is assigned a confidence value between 0 and 1.0.

## 2.2 Holographic Memory Model

Holograph stores a large number of stimulus and response pattern associations in the form of complex correlation matrix. The encoding is performed by super-imposing individual correlations on the same holographic memory substrate. Despite the superimposition, provided with a query stimulus, the holograph can regenerate the closest associated response. An association is encoded as the correlation of the response and the transpose conjugate of the stimulus patterns. (In this paper we will use a superscript T to denote the transpose and the bar to denote transpose).

$$A = R \cdot \overline{S}^T$$

All such (k) associations are enfolded by superimposing them in the holograph.

$$H = \sum_t^k A_t \qquad \qquad \ldots (1a)$$

The learning equation (1a) has been improved to encode only that part of a new association that is new, instead of the whole. The component of a new association which is already learned is not encoded. The following equation forms the differential learning algorithm for the holograph which incorporates this modification.

$$H = H + (R - H \cdot S)\overline{S}^T \qquad \qquad \ldots (1)$$

The differential learning has demonstrate lower saturation and higher capacity of the holograph [Suth90]. To associatively retrieve a pattern, a query pattern $S_Q$ is convolved with the holograph for target response $R_Q$.

$$R_Q = \frac{1}{c} \cdot H \cdot S_Q \qquad \text{where,} \quad c = \sum_{j=1}^n \lambda_j \qquad \qquad \ldots (2)$$

If the query is close to some priori encoded stimulus $S_T$ in the holograph then the target response resembles the corresponding response pattern $R_T$.

The underlying process can be explained through the recovery of a single response element, through (1a). Let the subscripts i and j refer to the element index and t refers to the association index. According to (1a) and (2), the $j^{th}$ element of the query response:

$$r_{(j,Q)} = \frac{1}{c} \sum_i^n \left[ \sum_t^k r_{(j,t)} \overline{S}^T_{(i,t)} \right] S_{(i,Q)}$$

If $S_Q$ is close to some priory encoded stimulus $S_{(t=T)}$, then the above equation can be rewritten as:

IV-27

$$r_{(j,Q)} = \frac{1}{c}\sum_i^n r_{(j,t=T)}\overline{S}^T_{(i,T)}S_{(i,T)} + \frac{1}{c}\sum_i^n\left[\sum_{(l\neq T)}^k r_{(j,l)}\overline{S}^T_{(i,l)}\right]S_{(i,Q)}$$

$$= \frac{1}{c}\sum_i^n r_{(j,t=T)} \mid \overline{S}^T_{(i,T)}S_{(i,T)} \mid + r_{crosstalk}$$

The phase of the first summation term here is exactly equally to the phase of $r_{(j,T)}$. Because, the product $\overline{S}^T_{(i,T)}S_{(i,T)}$ is always a scalar quantity. For symmetrically distributed associations, the second summation contributes as a random walk in the two dimensional vector space, The length of this path grows very slowly with the square root of the number of vectors. Thus, the resulting response phase closely resembles the phase of the correct response.

If both the stimulus and response patterns are identical, then holograph acts as a content addressable auto associative memory. More extensive analysis of this holographic process can be found in [Suth90, KhYu94]. Now we will concentrate on the reduction of physical space required by the holograph H, which is the key.

## 3 Dimension of the Holograph

For stimulus and response patterns respectively with n and q elements, corresponding holograph requires $qn$ complex correlations requiring a large number of physical memory locations. Our objective is to exploit the sparseness of information content in the patterns and to reduce the physical memory space of the holograph. Our principal decomposition strategy is given by the following modified form of (2):

$$R = T_R^{-1}[\ddot{H}T_S[S]] \qquad \qquad ...(3)$$

Where, transformation $T_S[.]$ projects the n-dimensional stimulus pattern is projected on an m-dimensional space, and transformation $T_R^{-1}[.]$ projects the p-dimensional output of the holograph onto q-dimensional response pattern space. The new holograph $\ddot{H}$ has dimension $p\times m$, where both $m<n, p<q$.

### 3.1 Optimum Transformations and Feature Construction

The optimality criterion for the transformations is the faithful reconstruction of the patterns. Now we will concentrate on the computation of the transformations, which can satisfy minimum mean square error (MMSE) transformation criterion.

For a given sparse pattern space, the dense features are be selected from the feature space of the following format, where each of the feature elements is a product of the original pattern elements, each raised to an exponent.

$$y_j = \prod_i^n [s_i]^{d(j,i)} \qquad \qquad ...(4)$$

An infinite number of features can be constructed from this feature space for each unique set of exponents. However, we will choose only $m$ such feature elements. So that the dense pattern will be of the form:

$$Y = \{y_1, y_2, ...y_m\} = \left(\alpha_1 e^{i\beta_1}, \alpha_2 e^{i\beta_2}, ...\alpha_m e^{i\beta_m}\right)$$

Where $\alpha_j$ is the confidence of feature j, and $\beta_j$ is the content of feature j. This feature space is a generalization of the higher order feature space previously proposed by Sutherland to attack the reverse problem of dense pattern [Suth90], where the pattern space is small in comparison to the number of features present in the stimulus pattern. Such situation arises in cases such as decoder problem, x-or problem etc.

The exponents $d(j,i)$, should be chosen to suit the MMSE optimum reconstruction criterion of the information content. For each feature, there should be a set of $n$ such exponents corresponding to each of the pattern elements. There should be $m$ such sets to construct the complete feature set $Y$. We will denote the exponents in the form of matrix $D$. Now, we would like to compute $D$ which will satisfy the criterion of optimum linear reconstruction.

Let, the vector B defines a vector with the exponents (phase components) of $Y$, and vector $\Theta$ defines a vector with the exponents (phase components) of $S$. Then the following iterative equations provide the autonomous learning equation to compute $D$.

$$D = D + \mu \cdot (B \cdot \Theta^T - LT[B \cdot B^T] \cdot D \qquad \ldots(5)$$

Where, $\mu$ is the learning constant for the encoder which is decreasing with time. Operator LT[] refers to the lower triangularization. The reverse transformation is given by (5), which is symmetric to (4) and uses the transposed form $D^T$ as its transformation matrix.

$$\bar{s}_i = \prod_{j}^{m} y_j d(j,i) \qquad \ldots(6)$$

The following two theorems explain the mathematical basis of (4), (5) and (6).

*Theorem 1: If D is assigned random values at time zero, then with probability 1.0 equation (5) will converge and D and $D^T$ will approach to a transformation pair between S and Y planes. The pair ensures MMSE reconstruction of the phase components (content) of the suit S.*

Proof: Using the bi-modal representation, a feature element can be re-written as:

$$y_j = \prod_{i}^{n}(\lambda_i)^{d_{(j,i)}} \cdot \exp\left( i \sum_{i}^{n} d_{(j,i)} \cdot \theta_i \right)$$

$$= \alpha_j \exp(i\beta_j) \qquad \ldots(7)$$

Thus, the transformation (4) in the phase plane (content) can be written in the matrix form as:

$$\begin{bmatrix} \beta_1 \\ \beta_2 \\ . \\ . \\ \beta_m \end{bmatrix} = \begin{bmatrix} d_{(1,1)} & d_{(1,2)} & \cdots & d_{(1,n)} \\ d_{(2,1)} & d_{(2,2)} & \cdots & d_{(2,n)} \\ . & & & \\ . & & & \\ d_{(m,1)} & d_{(m,2)} & \cdots & d_{(m,n)} \end{bmatrix} \begin{bmatrix} \theta_1 \\ \theta_2 \\ . \\ . \\ \theta_n \end{bmatrix}, \quad \text{or } B = D\Theta$$

$\beta_j$ is a linear combination of the individual pattern elements, where $d(j,i)$ are the coefficients. The optimum coefficients for linear reconstruction of the content of S can be found by determining the eigenvectors of the space defined by the auto correlation matrix $Q = E[\Theta\Theta^T]$ of the patterns. Let, the eigenvectors of Q are ordered in the decreasing order of their corresponding eigenvalues. The patterns are spanned in an $n$ dimensional space. Then the subspace spanned by the first m eigenvectors will retain maximum reconstruction information for the suit of *Thata* for a given m. Thus, it will allow reconstruction of the input suit Ss from Ys with minimum mean square error. Sanger [Sang89] has proved for scalar case that the learning algorithm of (5) is doing exactly that. For, bounded magnitude of the elements of $D$, and decreasing $\mu$, irrespective of the initial values, (7) converges in such a manner that the rows of D converges to the eigenvectors of $Q$ in sorted order. Since, the matrix D is an eigenvector matrix, therefore, the reverse transformation is given by transpose of D.$O$

*Theorem 2: The transformation pair specified by (4) and (6), using the transformation matrix D computed through (5) can also reconstructs the magnitude component (confidence) of the pattern suit S.*

Now, we will proof the reconstruction criterion for the magnitude component of S. The forward and reverse transformations are respectively specified by (4) and (6), which can be re-written in the following forms:

$$| y_k | = \prod_{i} [\lambda_i]^{d(k,i)} \qquad \text{and} \quad \tilde{\lambda}_p = \prod_{k} | y_k |^{d(k,p)}$$

Where, $\tilde{\lambda}_p$ is the reconstructed pattern element. Expanding the right hand side of the reverse transformation,

$$\tilde{\lambda}_p = \prod_k \left[ \prod_i [\lambda_i]^{d(k,i)} \right]^{d(k,p)} = \prod_k \prod_i [\lambda_i]^{d(k,i)d(k,p)}$$

$$= \prod_i \prod_k [\lambda_i]^{d(k,i)d^T(p,k)} = \prod_i [\lambda_i]^{\sum_k d^T(p,k)d(k,i)}$$

Since, rows of the matrix $D$ are the eigenvectors, therefore the product of its transpose with itself is an identity matrix of size n.

$$D^T \cdot D = I_{n \times n}, \quad \text{thus,} \quad I(p,i) = \sum_k d(k,p)d(k,i) = 1 \ when, p=i$$

$$= 0 \ otherwise.$$

Thus,

$$\tilde{\lambda}_p = \prod_i (\lambda_i)^{I(p,i)} = (\lambda_p)^1 \prod_{i \neq p} (\lambda_i)^0 = \lambda_p \qquad \qquad \ldots(8)$$

Thus, the above transformation pair also reconstructs the magnitude component of the patterns.$O$

In fact, Sanger's proof can be further generalized for complex valued numbers. The basic assumptions of Oja [Oja83] and Ljung's [Ljun77] theorems (which are the foundation of Sanger's proof) are also valid for complex numbers. Thus, an equation analogous to (5), where B and $\Theta$ are replaced by corresponding $Y$ and $S$ vectors, can directly compute the eigenvector matrix.

There are several other algorithms for computing multiple eigenvectors such as by Brockett (89), Karhunen & Oja (82), Kuusela & Oja (82) [Oja83, Sang89]. However, the advantage of (5) is that it also sorts the eigenvectors, and the computation in (5) can be performed using smaller final and intermediate memory.

### 3.2 Feature Based Associative Memory Model

The following set of equations provide the operational principle of the contracted holograph. First transformation matrices, $D_S$ and $D_R$ are computed from the autonomous learning algorithm given by (5) using the stimulus and response pattern suits. Then (9) is used to enfold the pattern associations onto the contracted holograph $\ddot{H}$. The query into the holograph is performed by (10).

$$\ddot{H} = \ddot{H} + \gamma \cdot T_R (R - T_R^{-1}(\ddot{H}Y))\overline{Y}^T \qquad \qquad \ldots(9)$$

$$R = T_R^{-1}[\ddot{H}T_S[S]] \qquad \qquad \ldots(10)$$

In (9), $Y$ is computed from (4), using $T_S[\cdot]$. The transformations $T_R[\cdot]$, $T_R^{-1}[\cdot]$, and $T_S[\cdot]$ all are computed from (4) using $D_R, D_R^T$, and $D_S$ respectively.

### 3.3 Size of the Contracted Holograph

From the storage perspective, a holograph can be thought as a 3 dimensional volume. Where the first two dimensions respectively represent the stimulus (n) and pattern (q) lengths. The depth dimension represents the number of bits required to store each of the correlation elements. If b bits are used to encode each of the correlation element, then the size of the original holograph is $qnb$ bits.

The proposed contraction method not only contracts the holograph in the first two dimensions, but also it can be used to save space in the 3rd dimension. The eigenvalues for the auto-correlation matrices of stimulus and response patterns can be computed by:

$$D_S E[\Theta\Theta^T]D_S^T = \Delta_S \qquad\qquad\qquad D_R E[\Phi\Phi^T]D_R^T = \Delta_R \qquad \qquad \ldots(11)$$

Where, $\Theta$ and $\Phi$ are the vectors spanned by the phase components of stimulus and response patterns. $\Delta$ are real valued diagonal matrices. $E$ is expectation. Each of the elements in the diagonal represents the eigenvalue corresponding to the eigenvectors arranged in $D$. The eigenvalues of $Q_\Theta$ and $Q_\Phi$ correspond to the estimate of the variance of the patterns along the dimensions spanned by their corresponding first m eigenvectors. Each of the feature contents, therefore need not to be encoded with same number of bits. Each of them can be quantized according to their variance along corresponding dimensions. One way of assignment is to allot bits proportional to the log of variance. In the holograph, each of the correlation terms requires bits equal to the sum of the bits required by the component product terms. Therefore, if $e_1, e_2, \ldots e_m$ are the bits assigned to the stimulus feature elements, and $f_1, f_2, \ldots f_p$ are the bits assigned to the response feature elements, then the bits to quantize the entire holograph is:

$$= p(e_1 + e_2 + \ldots + e_m) + m(f_1 + f_2 + \ldots + f_p) = a \cdot \{p \cdot \log(trace(\Delta_S)) + m \cdot \log(trace(\Delta_R))\} \text{ bits}$$

Where a is some proportionality constant. Physically, as a result of this contraction along the depth $\ddot{H}$ will resemble a rectangular box with four trapezoidal sides and tapered bottom. A Typical holograph for storing 64x64 frame images, requires about 128 megabytes. While the contraction reduces the size to 1.5 megabytes.

### 3.4 Reduction in Computation

**Search and Retrieval:** The holograph query is performed by (10). If we consider, right parenthetical computation in the order as shown in (12):

$$\overset{(qxl)}{R_{target}} = \left[ \overset{(qxp)}{T_R^T} \left[ \overset{(pxm)}{\ddot{H}} \left[ \overset{(mxn)}{T_S} \left[ \overset{(nxl)}{S_{query}} \right] \right] \right] \right] \qquad \ldots(12)$$

The dimensions are shown over each element. Then, evaluation of (12) can be performed by $(pq + mn + 2pm)$ multiplications, $(pq + mn + 2pm)$ additions, and $(pq + mn)$ logarithm evaluation. For, a typical image pattern with 256x256 pixels, $p = m$, $q = n$, and a ratio $n/m = 8$, it means approximately $2^{31}$ multiplications and $2^{30}$ logarithms. On the other hand, the regular uncontracted holograph requires $4qn$ multiplications and $2qn$ additions. For the same typical case it means $2^{34}$ multiplications and half as much additions.

**Holographic Learning:** Similar saving can be attained in the case of encoding too. If we consider a single step evaluation of equation-7 in the parenthetical order shown below:

$$\overset{(pxm)}{\ddot{H}} = \left[ \overset{(pxm)}{\ddot{H}} + \gamma \cdot \left[ \left[ \overset{(pxq)}{T}_R \left[ \overset{(qxl)}{R} - \left[ \overset{(qxp)}{T_R^{-1}} \left[ \overset{(pxm)(mxl)}{\ddot{H} \quad Y} \right] \right] \right] \right] \overset{(lxn)}{\overline{Y}^T} \right] \right] \qquad \ldots(13)$$

A single step iteration including the stimulus pattern transformation requires $2(mn + 2pq + 4pm)$ multiplications, $(mn + 2pq + 5pm)$ additions and $(mn + 2pq)$ logarithms. In contrast, the uncontracted holograph requires $8qn$ multiplications and $(6qn + 2q)$ additions. For the typical case, the contracted case means approximately $3.5 \times 2^{30}$ multiplications and additions, and $3 \times 2^{29}$ logarithms. The uncontracted holograph requires $2^{35}$ multiplications and $3 \times 2^{33}$ additions.

As shown above, despite the additional input and output processing, the contracted holograph model requires less overall computation both, in the enfolding and query process. The saving is approximately given by the $n/m$ ratio. The computations can be performed with high degree of parallelism with pipelined stages. The matrix nature of the computations makes the holographic assosiative model highly scalable of conventional high performance parallel machines. The parallel execution time also reduces by $n/m$ ratio.

## 4 Experiment

The feasibility of the contracted holograph has been demonstrate by implementing a contracted holographic associative memory. Fig-1(a) shows the original image that was stored in the holograph. Fig-1(b) shows the retrieved image from the holograph for 100% frame query. Fig-1(c) shows the retrieved pattern using query with 50% of the full frame. Unlike most other associative memories, holograph has the unique capability to focus at any arbitrary region of the query frame, with small degeneration of the retrieved pattern. Fig-2(a),(b) and (c) shows similar frames for another

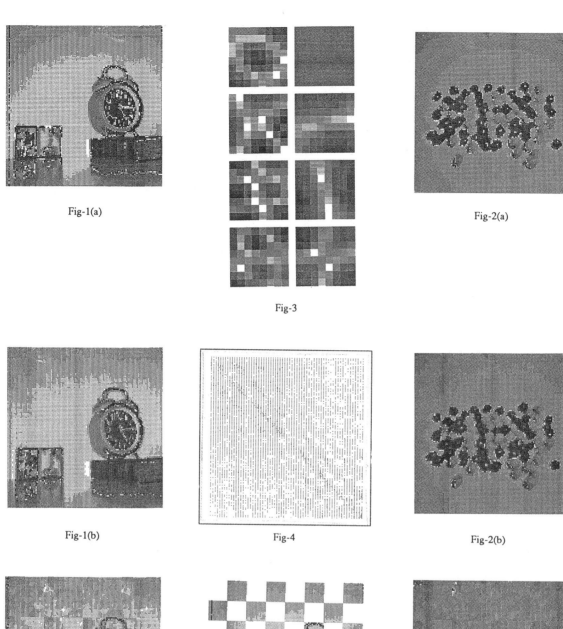

Fig-1(a)

Fig-3

Fig-2(a)

Fig-1(b)

Fig-4

Fig-2(b)

Fig-1(c)

Fig-5

Fig-2(c)

image stored in the same holograph. The 50% frame window is shown in Fig-5. The excitation of the holograph can be seen at the distribution presented in Fig-4, which has 32 images encoded in it. The contraction mask set is shown in Fig-3.

The following table provides the signal to noise (SNR) characteristics among these images. The loss only due to transformation is characterized by the comparison between the original image and retransformed image (18.65 db). The loss due to holographic encoding is shown by the comparison between the retransformed and 100% frame based retrieved images (31.37 db). The loss due to partial frame query is expressed by the comparison of 100% frame with 75% and 25% frame based recovered images (20.39 db and 16.62 db respectively). The table provides a comparative picture of the trade-off, for which our methods provides a mechanism. The result of this table corresponds to 64 times contraction in holograph size, and almost 8 times faster encoding and search speed.

**SNR Characteristics**

| SNR between: | Retranformed Image | Retrieved Image (100% Frame) | Retrieved Image (75% Frame) | Retrieved Image 50% Frame |
|---|---|---|---|---|
| Original | 18.65 db | 18.43 db | 16.47 db | 14.54 db |
| Retranformed | x | 31.37 db | 20.29 db | 16.52 db |
| (100% Frame) | x | x | 20.39 db | 16.62 db |

## 5 Conclusion

The proposed work provides a formal mechanism to perform trade-off between size of space and quality of space for holographic associative memory. As for other search problems, the reduction of search space also simultaneously reduces the search speed. The more is the sparseness of the pattern information, the less is the loss of quality in storage due to this contraction and vice verse. Sutherland has previously proposed a method to increase the feature space for dense patterns [Suth90], however without any optimality consideration.

One of the principal significance of this work is to develop an effective means to construct reversible optimum features for complex valued patterns. We have shown the process of constructing compressed holographs based on autonomous learning of features from the pattern space. The features are not only optimum in MMSE reconstruction sense, but also warrants classification. Because, the m feature dimensions are selected in order of pattern variance along each of them.

## 6 References

[Kane88]    Kanerva, Pentti., Sparse Distributed Memory, MIT Press, Cambridge, 1988.

[KhYu94]    Javed I. Khan & D. Y. Y. Yun, Chaotic Vectors and A Proposal for Multi-Dimensional Associative Network, Proceedings of the IS&T/SPIE 1994 International Symposium of Electronic Imaging, (to be published), San Jose, February 1994.

[Ljun77]    Ljung, L, Analysis of Recursive Stochastic Algorithms, IEEE Trans. on Automatic Control, AC-22, pp551-575, 1977.

[Oja83]    Oja, E., Subspace Methods of Pattern Recognition, John Wiley & Sons, NY, 1983.

[Sang89]    Sanger, T. D., Optimal Unsupervised Learning in a Single-Layer Linear Feedforward Neural Network, Neural Networks, v2, pp459-473, 1989.

[Souc92]    Soucek, B. and The IRIS Group, Fuzzy, Holographic, and Parallel Intelligence, John Wiley & Sons, NY, 1992.

[Suth90]    Sutherland, J. G., A Holographic Model of Memory, Learning and Expression, Journal of Neural Systems, v1, pp259-267, 1990.

[Will89]    Willshaw, D., Holography, Associative memory and Inductive Generalization, Parallel Models of Associative Memory (updated edition), ed- G. E. Hinton, Lawrence Erlbaum Associates, New Jersey, 1989.

# Adaptive Filtering Network for Associative Memory Data Preprocessing

Joel DeWitt

Computer Engineering Department

University of California, Santa Cruz

1156 High Street, Santa Cruz California 95064

## Abstract

A key factor in the performance of an autoassociative memory is the distribution and density of training patterns in the learning space. To provide an improved distribution, an artificial neural network is described here which adaptively learns sets of approximately orthogonal features for many overlapping patches of the input space. This results in the training patterns being projected into an expanded memory space with a randomized distribution. Adaptive feature-filtering is achieved by training units in a filter layer between the input layer and memory layer to become spacial feature-detectors using a principle-component-analysis learning rule. Simulations on a SIMD array show that the network trains rapidly and that cross-talk between stored patterns is reduced.

## Motivation

The concept of an artificial neural network functioning as a correlational associative memory has been in use since 1972 or earlier ([1],[2],[3]). In 1982 Hopfield [4] proposed the use of an energy function in the ANN context, providing a mathematical mechanism to deal with recurrent nonlinear networks. Aspects of the model such as the neural unit's transfer function [5] and dynamics of recall [6] have since been refined to boost the performance and generality of application of the architecture. In spite of these improvements, and the fact that the model is biologically plausible, simple to implement, and to analyze, its application has been limited due to several serious performance deficiencies. Because a primary mechanism of the memory the execution of a parallel search of hamming distances between presented and stored patterns, recall is disturbed if stored patterns have overlap, or if the presented pattern is even slightly transformed in displacement, rotation, or magnification. An approach to overcome these problems is to project the input pattern into a space where such transforms do not produce much variance, and where stored patterns are dispersed as widely as possible.

The standard result of $\approx 0.14n$ being the storage capacity of an autoassociative memory of size $n$ is derived with the condition that a particular bit $s_i^\mu$ of vector $S^\mu$ from training set $P$ has probability 0.5 of being set. The pattern bias $a$ defines the likelihood that a particular pixel of the input pattern is set, where $0 \le a \le 1$. Amari provides a derivation that operating with sparse encoding, where $a$ is small, provides performance benefits in terms of storage capacity, noise tolerance, and reduction of spurious attractors in the memory's state space [7]. In [8], I found this to be true, measuring by simulation that storage capacity of up to 0.7 can be achieved by projecting the input space into a recall space of four times greater dimensionality, using a projection which took advantage of known structure in the training patterns. This report describes a network which is able to discover such a projection without prior knowledge of structure in the training set.

We consider an associative memory of size $n$, storing patterns of bias $a$, so that a particular pattern has $m = an$ bits set. For a given $a$, there are $\binom{n}{m}$ possible patterns, from which sets of $n/m = 1/a$ orthogonal patterns with no common pixels can be constructed. The overlap criterion between any two patterns $\mu$ and $\nu$ from the trainig set is $O = 1/n \sum_i^n s_i^\mu s_i^\nu$, counting the likelihood that there are common pixels between the patterns. If $O = 0$, the patterns are orthogonal, $O = a$, the patterns are identical, and $O = a^2$ is the expected value for uncorrelated patterns. Recall accuracy is maximized with orthogonal patterns, but the set of orthogonal patterns is too small unless $a \to 1/n$, so the uncorrelated case provides the best storage capacity in typical situations. Given a network that allows projection from an input space of size $n$ into a recall space of size $pn$ with $p > 1$, the ideal projection provides $O \approx (a/p)^2$ for any pair of patterns in the recall space.

It is known that the primary visual pathway of many animals includes arrays of spacial feature-detectors sensitive to such structure as line segments and ends, and that layers of such arrays are arranged to respond to more complex and less localized structure in deeper layers [9]. Furthermore, the features to which at least some of these detectors respond are determined by experience. Although the information coding schemes of the brain are still largely unknown, there is at least some indication that sparse codings are present [10]. These facts are the biological inspiration of the network described here.

Linsker formalized the principle of information-maximization for ANN learning in [11], under which units in an ANN spontaneously organize themselves into oriented feature detectors. Units operating under this principle adjust their link-weights to maximize their output variance. This is generalization of principle component analysis (PCA), first cast in ANNs by Oja [12], and written as the generalized Hebb learning rule by Sanger [13]. This rule, operating in a network with $N$ inputs and $M$ outputs $(M < N)$, is designed to find weights for the $M$ output units so that they account for as much as possible of the variance in the $N$ inputs over the training set. This has application for data compression. The same rule is used here, but in a network which has many sets of $M_i$ clusters, where each cluster receives activation from a different but overlapping subset of the $N$ inputs. Once the weights have settled, the network perform a mapping from the $N$ dimensional input space into an $MXN$ dimensional space, for which input patterns are scattered with less overlap than in the input space.

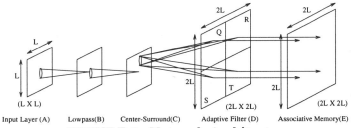

**FIGURE 1. Network Architecture**

## Network Structure

The network being studied is similar to that described in [11], but with a divergence of 4 in deeper layers and with a learning rule modified to explicitly perform PCA as in [13]. It is a stack of five 2-dimensional grids of units. A unit in some layer $L$ receives stimulus from units in a particular region in the previous layer $K$, called its receptive field. Each link has a connection weight $w_{ij}$ which defines the influence of unit $j$ on unit $i$. Topographic mapping due to synaptic density is modeled by calculating a density field which follows a quantized Gaussian distribution $d_{ij} = exp(-r_{ij}^2/r_L^2)/N_M$, where $r_{ij}$ is the distance from $i$ to $j$ in layer $K$, and $r_L$ is a network parameter determining the radius of the receptive field for units in a layer $L$. $N_L$ is an normalization constant such that the total link density received by a unit in $L$ is 1. The units have a linear response function in all layers except $E$. The activity of unit $i$ in layer $D$ for a presentation of a training pattern is given by $F^D = R_a + R_b \sum_j w_j d_j F_j^C$.

The initial layer $A$ operates as an input register. Its state can be set to that of a pattern file. It contains one unit per pixel of the input pattern, a $2D$ binary vector of size $64 \times 64$. When the network is presented with a test pattern $\mu$ from the training set, the state $F_i$ of each unit $i$ is set to bit $i$ from pattern

$\mu$, $F_i^A = S_i{}^\mu$, where the $S_i$ may take values of $\pm 1$. Layer $B$ performs lowpass spacial filtering over layer $A$, by convolving with a $2D$ gaussian weighting with $r_B = 1.5$. Layer $C$ performs a focusing on layer B, by convolving with a $2D$ center-surround weighting with $r_c = 1.5$.

Layer $D$ performs feature detection on layer $C$. Each unit in layer $D$ receives activation through a receptive field centered at some unit in layer $C$, with a gaussian field and $r_D = 3.0$, and links that learn according to (1). For every unit $i$ in layer $C$, there are four units in $D$ with an identical receptive field centered at $i$. The weights to these units will be different due to learning. The learning rule is arranged so that these four units compete for variance within their receptive field.

Finally layer $E$ receives a unity projection from $D$. It contains an associative memory array in the Hopfield style (for design and performance details, see [8]), and data gathering functions, in particular calculation of the overlap metric over the training set.

The learning rule for links between layers $C$ and $D$ is written in (1). This is an embedding of Sanger's PCA rule into Linsker's spacial structuring rule. The parameters $R_a, R_b, K_a, \eta$, and $F_0$ in the learning and unit-function rules allow average link weight ($\bar{w} = \sum_i d_i w_i$) to be programmed to a desired value, while its geometric length ($\sqrt{\sum_i (d_i w_i)^2}$) is normalized to unity. In (1), the index $k$ indicates the location of the unit in its cluster of four with common receptive field.

$$\Delta w_{ij}^{DC} = k_a + \eta(F_i^D - F_0^D)(F_j^C - F_0^C - \sum_k^{\leq 4} w_{kj}^{DC} F_k^D) - \eta w_{ij}^{DC}(F_i^D)^2 \tag{1}$$

Using $k_1 \equiv k_a + \eta(R_a^D - F_0^D)(\bar{F}^C - F_0^C)$, and $k_2 \equiv \bar{F}^C(\bar{F}^C - F_0^C)$, the average value of its incoming connections to a unit becomes $\bar{w} \approx -k_1/k_2$ provided $-1 < -k_1/k_2 < +1$. So it is possible to set the average connection strength by specifying parameters, and leave the spacial structure of the individual saturated weights to be determined by the correlation matrix of layer $C$.

## RESULTS

The network was operated by training on 400 patterns generated with a particular structure, and then calculating the crosstalk of post-processed patterns not in the training set but with the same structure. The learning rate was $\eta = 0.01$, $\bar{w} = 0.1$, and the training procedure involved five passes over the training set.

Figure 2 illustrates a set of weights for the four units in a cluster with common receptive field. In this case, the network was trained on patterns constructed of line segments, each randomly located in the pattern, and one of four possible orientations. The probabilities of each orientation were different, with $P(\backslash) > P(/) > P(|) > P(-)$. When trained on patterns with equal orientation probabilities, the resulting structure of the receptive fields tended to be less clear. A dark dot indicates a link with excitatory weight, and a light dot indicates a link with inhibitory weight.

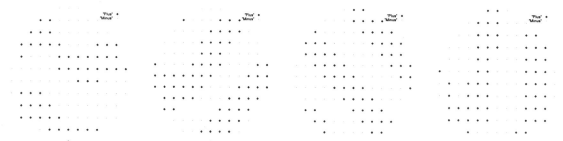

**FIGURE 2. Learned Feature-Filters**

Figure 3 shows the average overlap between pairs of patterns having been projected through a trained filter layer. The horizontal axis is the pattern bias (percentage of pixels set in the input pattern), and the

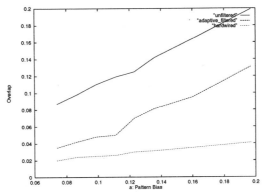

**FIGURE 3. Overlap among Raw, Filtered, and Optimally Filtered Patterns.**

vertical axis is the crosstalk. Three traces are shown, for the raw input patterns, for the patterns after filtering, and for the patterns having been filtered by a hard-wired optimal filter. The raw patterns have the expected overlap of $a$, and the optimal filter achieves close to the expected $a^2$. The performance of the adaptive network, while not reaching $a^2$, is consistently improved over the raw patterns for $a < 0.3$. For larger $a$, the network was not able to learn meaningful feature sets because in this case each line segment in a pattern would intersect many others.

## DISCUSSION

It is established knowledge that associative memories achieve improved performance when trained on sparse patterns. A network that adaptively achieves a sparsification projection allows this improvement to be had even when the raw input patterns are moderately dense. The network described here partially achieves this goal. It has the additional advantage that spurious correlation between pixels in different patterns in the recall space will generally be substantially lower than in the input space, provided the input patterns are produced by some process whose statistical structure the network is able to discover. Because the adaptive process operating in the network requires only local information and no error signal, it is suited to an asynchronous network architecture. This fact allows the scheme to be simulated very rapidly on a SIMD parallel computer (in this case, a MasPar II with $4K$ nodes was used to achieve about 100 training iterations of the network per minute).

There are now many network-based PCA algorithms, only two of which were explored in this study. Linsker suggests wiring inhibitory links between the feature detectors to achieve similar goals as intended here, but this architecture does not guarantee convergence to the principle eigenvectors. Sanger's learning rule has the advantage over Oja's of sorting the eigenvectors by their eigenvalues, but in a linear system this is only a convenience and does not enhance performance. While this network has substantially more layers and units that is explicitly needed to implement Sanger's and Oja's rules, the extra parameters and structure allowed more flexible tuning. In particular, a minimal 3-layer PCA network tended to waste the first unit of a cluster learning the average intensity of the input pattern.

Although the network was able to learn the desired projection, another level of adaptation must be added before it can be expected to perform well with natural data sets. It is not likely that natural data sets will have an even distribution of information over the input space as was the case for the artificial patterns used here. To overcome this I am exploring implementing adaptive receptive-field scaling mechanism to allocate the network's resources to areas of the input with highest activity. Another modification in preparation is a nonlinear unit function in the filter layer to aid noise-cancellation. Nonetheless the architecture described here appears to have the potential to perform an adaptive encoding that improves certain aspects of the data representation for associative memory performance.

# References

[1] Anderson,J.A.(1972). "A simple neural network generating interactive memory." *Mathematical Biosciences*,**14**,197-220.

[2] Amari,S.(1972). "Learning patterns and pattern sequences by self-organizing nets of threshold elements. *IEEE Transactions on Computers*,**C-21**1197-1206

[3] Kohonen,T.(1972) "Correlation matrix memories." *IEEE Transactions on Computers*,**C-21**353-359

[4] Hopfield,J.J. (1982) "Neural networks and physical systems with emergent collective computational abilities." *Proceedings of the National Academy of Sciences*,USA **79**2445-2558

[5] Yoshizawa,S. Morita,M. Amari,S. (1993) "Capacity of associative memory using a nonmonotonic Neuron Model." *Neural Networks* **6** 167-176

[6] Rumelhart,D.E. Hinton,G.E. Williams,R.J. (1986) "Learning and Relearning in Boltzmann Machines." **Parallel Distributed Processing Vol.I**, MIT Press, Cambridge, Massachusetts

[7] Amari,S. (1989) "Characteristics of Sparsely Encoded Associative Memory." *Neural Networks***2** 451-457

[8] DeWitt, J.D. (1993) "Feature-Filtering Improves Associative Memory Performance" *WNN93 Proceedings* SPIE 2204:303-307

[9] Hubel,D.H. (1988) **Eye, Brain, and Vision** Scientific American Press, New York

[10] Rolls,E.T. (1987) "Information representation, processing, and storage in the brain: Analysis at the single neuron level." **The neural and molecular bases of learning**, Changeux & Konishi (Eds.) Wiley, New York

[11] Linsker R (1988) "Self-Organization in a Perceptual Network" *IEEE Computer* 21(3), 105-117

[12] Oja E. (1982) "Neural Networks, principal components, and subspaces" *International Journal of Neural Systems* 1(1):61-68

[13] Sanger T.D. (1989) "Optimal unsupervised learning in a single-layer linear feed-forward neural network" *Neural Networks* 2:459-473

# Improving Adaptive Logic Networks:
# Initialization and Confidence

W Martins[1] and N M Allinson
Image Engineering Group
Department of Electronics
University of York
York, UK, YO1 5DD
e-mail: weber@ohm.york.ac.uk

## Abstract

Logical Neural Networks are gradually becoming known for their low-cost and ease of hardware implementation. Most of improvements have been proposed for specific models [1,2,3] with some exceptions [4]. This paper presents successful results on the combination of two logical neural networks: feed-forward networks of Goal Seeking Neuron, GSN, [5] and Adaptive Logic Networks, ALN [6]. A confidence measure for ALN is also introduced and tested. A confidence measure is a very important metric for Logical Neural Networks because several algorithms, like Kohonen's self-organising maps, use this feature.

GSN one-shot training algorithm is used to initialize the application of the ALN iterative learning algorithm. ALN were designed to implement only monotonic functions and to rely on many inputs per network. The proposed initialization overcomes both limitations. An algorithm is developed to convert GSN into ALN networks. For GSNs, not only performance is improved but speed and ease of implementation. The confidence measure for ALN is based on how well supported is the network output. Through a back-propagation of calls, it is possible to compute how many inputs should be inverted to change the final output.

## 1 Introduction

Starting on the neural level, GSN networks use neurons with universal functionality, i.e., neurons that can implement all logical functions of their inputs. ALN neurons, however, must choose their behaviour only from the non-constant monotonic Boolean functions of two variables: AND, OR, LEFT and RIGHT (where LEFT(x,y) = x and RIGHT(x,y) = y). The number of inputs of a GSN is not limited to two as is the case with ALN. The number of outputs per neuron leads to pyramidal topologies (i.e., a binary tree in ALN) where each pyramid is assigned to one bit of the output code.

The two constraints imposed on ALN neurons (fan-in = 2 and use of non-universal elements) are justified by increasing the insensitivity of such pyramids when changes are made at input level [7]. A consequence of such constraints is that even easier hardware implementation can be undertaken. Software implementations are also speeded up because not all nodes must be analysed. Since the ALN subset of Boolean functions is not able to represent every mapping, some inputs are taken in complemented form.

Another important point in the GSN model is the neuron's ability to store, receive and output 'undefined' values (from now on termed 'u'). By defining deterministic ways of handling the multi-addressing task resulting from receiving those values, GSN overcomes some of the saturation and lack of determinism problems of its predecessor. The 'u' value is output when a neuron does not know whether to answer '0' or '1'. At the beginning of training, every internal position stores 'u'.

The differences between the two models becomes more pronounced as the networks are trained. Feed-forward networks of GSN are characterized by a one-shot training algorithm. The presentation order of examples is the same for all networks to eliminate the need of storing the training data. The ALN training algorithm is iterative and, between iterations, it shuffles all examples to cancel some of the temporal effects in their presentation.

---

[1] On leave from UFG - Escola de Engenharia Elétrica, Caixa Postal 112, Universidade Federal de Goiás, 74000 GO, Brazil. Supported by grant 200291/90-4, CNPq, Brazilian Research Council.

GSN networks use the multi-addressing resulting from the inclusion of the 'u' value to make internal representations more compact and achieve better generalization. A GSN can possess three states: validation, learning and recall. At the validation state, the neuron decides if it is possible to make the desired input-output mapping. The learning itself, which changes the internal contents of the neuron, is carried out during the learning state and priority is given an already occupied address and so improve generalization. If there is no correctly addressed position with the desired output, the neuron uses an unused one (with 'u' content) and changes it. Finally, at the recall state, simple laws are applied (e.g., the neuron outputs the value of the majority of addressed internal positions).

The learning action of GSNs in feed-forward multi-layer networks has some similarity with back-propagation. First, the input pattern is used to provide a "natural" response from the network based on stimulating neurons to answer 'u' if there is an 'u' at some addressed internal position (see Fig. 1), or if there is a '1' and a '0' at addressed positions. If the final output is not the opposite of the desired output, learning can take place. Then, going backwards through the pyramid, each neuron enters the learning state. When the neurons at the output level specify which input addresses they have chosen, the neurons of the previous layer know what answer must be output and are able to enter the learning state as well.

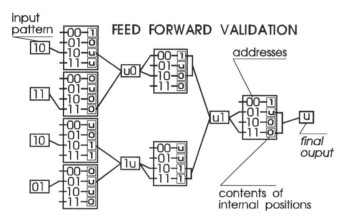

Figure 1: Validation on feed-forward networks of GSN.

The ALN training algorithm is based on a frequency strategy, in a sense that a ALN neuron responds to its modifiable internal positions when the inputs are different from each other, based on what is the most common request for the situation. Two counters are used to control the neuron's behaviour during learning, a left counter, *left_c*, and right counter, *right_c*. A threshold, *t*, is set to state what output the neuron must give. If the left counter is above the threshold the output will be '1' if the left input is '1' without any consideration to the right input. At the beginning, counters are randomly initialized with values near the threshold. The four possibilities for the counters and their associated functions are shown in Fig. 2.

|  | left_c <= t | left_c > t |
|---|---|---|
| right_c <= t | **AND** | **LEFT** |
| right_c > t | **RIGHT** | **OR** |

Figure 2: The way how an ALN neuron defines its function.

As a global strategic, ALN starts to train from the output level towards the input level and just stops when it reaches a situation where both inputs of a neuron are identical to the desired output. Only neurons whose inputs are different from each other are subject to internal modification of their counters. As an iterative process, some performance measure should be inserted to determine when training must finish.

On a system viewpoint, classifiers based on GSN and ALN are similar. First, some choices are required to define the number of inputs per pyramid and the binary code for all (output) classes. For GSN, each positional bit of the output codes corresponds one pyramid and, therefore, the number of pyramids is simply the number of bits in output codes. ALN classifiers uses one positional bit for a group of networks. The driving goal when codes are chosen is to make the Hamming distance between codes as large as possible.

The basic architecture of classifiers is shown in Fig. 3. Inputs are assigned at random to the networks. They are, then, trained independent and individually to perform the mapping required by its associate positonal bit of the output code. Examples are presented to all GSN networks by using the same order in which they are acquired from the environment. ALN shuffles the training set between passes of the training data.

A nearest neighbour rule is used to make the final decision (to which output class the input pattern belongs). More precisely, this rule is slighted changed to cope with possible undefined outputs when GSN networks are used. An undefined output acts like '0.5' (half way between '0' and '1') for similarity measures. The output class with highest similarity is the final output of the system. A rejection occurs when more than one output class share the highest similarity value. ALN classifiers use a majority function to define the group decision before the final nearest neighbour rule is applied.

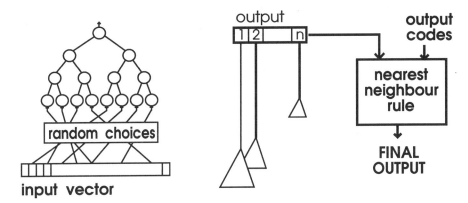

Figure 3: Typical architecture of a classifier based on GSN networks.

## 2 Advantages on Combining GSN with ALN

The advantages of using the ALN learning algorithm on binary trees created from the conversion of GSN networks are clear. The only drawback is that the training time is increased but this is justified by better performance at the evaluation process together with a reduction of complexity on the implementation.

Due to its intrinsic topology (binary trees with inputs randomly chosen), the possibility of ALN to discover non-monotonic relations among inputs is very small. GSN initialization can indicate if these relations are necessary or not. They are generated if needed. Another point is the ability of GSN to use small networks better due to its universal functionality. This property leads to better results in ALN. In fact, ALN discard many sub-trees because of their inadequacy and its own inability to dynamically complement inputs. It should be noted that the GSN's ability to work with fan-ins greater than two enables this possibility to ALN.

## 3 Conversion from GSN to ALN

Suppose that only GSN with fan-in = 2 are used and that, at the end of training, none of the internal positions remains undefined. It is easy to convert this network to a binary tree where only ALN functions are required by proceeding from the output level towards the input level. All negations are pushed backwards in order that they all finish at the input level (see Fig. 4). If a GSN behaviour is an XOR(a,b), for instance, this will require an expansion of the network to implement its equivalent OR(AND(a,NOT(b)), AND(NOT(a),b)). Most of the functions, however, do not require such expansions.

Normally, there are some undefined internal positions after the GSN one-shot learning has been completed. One heuristic is to balance the quantity of internal '0's and '1's since a neuron whose all internal positions are assigned to the same value make no contribution. This heuristic will prefer an XOR behaviour over other possible alternatives. If some choices have still to been made, they can be chosen at random. In the case of fan-in greater than 2, a decomposition is required. Some situations will lead to approximations since they can not be decomposed further. These cases will be analysed in a further paper.

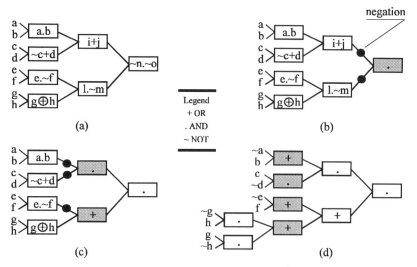

Figure 4: Stages of the Conversion from GSN to ALN: (a) initial GSN network; (d) final ALN.

## 4 Confidence Measure for ALN

Normally, classifiers based on ALN use no confidence measure. A simple confidence measure can be defined as the minimal number of inputs that should be different in order to change the final output. Of course, the computation of this measure introduces a delay for each network, but it is not too costly due to the constraints that ALN imposes on each neuron. The C code of a function that computes this measure is shown in Fig. 5.

```
int EvalCost(tree, ix)            // DATA STRUCTURES
taln *tree;                       // tree : pointer to the top node of a (sub)tree
short ix;                         // ix   : pointer to the current input pattern
{
  switch (tree->b) {              // tree->b    : behaviour of the node
  case ctAND:                     // tree->l/r  : pointer to the left/right node
   if (tree->li == ctZERO)        // tree->li/ri : left/right input to the node
    if (tree->ri == ctZERO)
      return(EvalCost(tree->l,ix) + EvalCost(tree->r,ix));
    else return(EvalCost(tree->l, ix);
   else if (tree->ri == ctZERO)
      return(EvalCost(tree->r, ix));
      else return(MinBetween(EvalCost(tree->l, ix), EvalCost(tree->r, ix)));
  case ctOR:
   if (tree->li == ctONE)
    if (tree->ri == ctONE)
      return(EvalCost(tree->l, ix) + EvalCost(tree->r, ix));
    else return(EvalCost(tree->l, ix));
   else if (tree->ri == ctONE) return(EvalCost(tree->r, ix));
      else return(MinBetween(EvalCost(tree->l, ix), EvalCost(tree->r, ix)));
  case ctRIGHT: return(EvalCost(tree->r, ix));
  case ctLEFT:  return(EvalCost(tree->l, ix));
  case ctLEAF:  return(1);
  }
} /* EvalCost */
```

Figure 5: Implementation of the confidence measure.

## 5 Experiments and Results

Many simulations have been conducted to provide data to confirm the above concepts. Each result displayed in the following table is the average of 100 simulations. Only 25 simulations were undertaken for the confidence measure To make an unbiased comparison, identical (randomly chosen) initial networks are used for standard and optimized training and smaller trees are used as the sub-trees. For instance, 64-input trees are the result of appending new 32-input trees. This seems appropriate for real-world problem tasks where the need is to know how much improvement is possible if current trees are kept as sub-trees to larger ones. Advanced portable random number generators[7] were employed to make repeatable experiments. Results are shown in Fig. 6 and 7.

The training set is composed of 160 16x16 black-white images (of hand-written digits) and the evaluation set is composed of 800 examples. The task is not an easy one since many distance metrics overlappings occur between classes. A simple Hadamard encoding was used to define output codes of 15-bit length where every two codes is 8-bit away from each other. The number of inputs per tree was 32, 64 or 128 and, therefore, it is a subsampling system. The number of trees per positional bit of the output code was 3, 5 or 11. All inputs were randomly assigned to the trees.

| TRAINING SET | | | SITUATION | EVALUATION SET | | |
|---|---|---|---|---|---|---|
| trees per bit / inputs per tree | | | | trees per bit / inputs per tree | | |
| 3 / 32 | 5 / 32 | 11 / 32 | | 3 / 32 | 5 / 32 | 11 / 32 |
| 53.59 | 63.43 | 74.80 | standard GSN | 39.57 | 47.21 | 56.95 |
| 73.46 | 80.76 | 85.08 | standard ALN | 57.98 | 66.76 | 74.20 |
| 80.42 | 89.36 | 96.70 | combination | 61.19 | 71.40 | 83.78 |
| 83.85 | 94.51 | 97.74 | plus confidence | 66.33 | 80.02 | 84.70 |
| 3 / 64 | 5 / 64 | 11 / 64 | | 3 / 64 | 5 / 64 | 11 / 64 |
| 59.04 | 68.84 | 80.63 | standard GSN | 43.78 | 52.25 | 64.35 |
| 81.40 | 84.79 | 87.76 | standard ALN | 67.57 | 72.85 | 77.32 |
| 91.84 | 96.02 | 98.78 | combination | 74.83 | 82.48 | 88.76 |
| 91.63 | 96.71 | 98.58 | plus confidence | 76.59 | 84.91 | 88.08 |
| 3 / 128 | 5 / 128 | 11 / 128 | | 3 / 128 | 5 / 128 | 11 / 128 |
| 66.34 | 75.49 | 85.49 | standard GSN | 47.57 | 56.69 | 68.65 |
| 85.12 | 87.68 | 88.94 | standard ALN | 70.26 | 74.48 | 77.09 |
| 97.21 | 98.71 | 99.51 | combination | 82.03 | 87.25 | 90.53 |
| 95.49 | 98.11 | 99.06 | plus confidence | 84.62 | 89.19 | 90.45 |

Figure 6: Table of percentual recognition rates in training and evaluation sets.

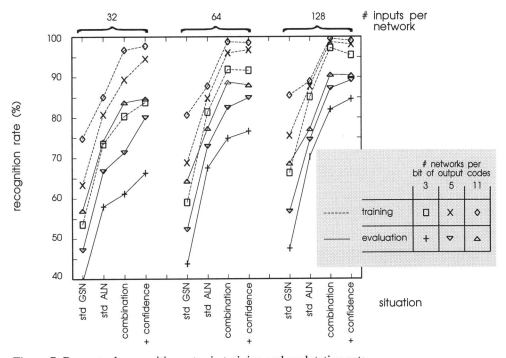

Figure 7: Percentual recognition rates in training and evalutation sets.

The superiority of the combined system is clearly shown by the results. It is interesting to note how GSN performance affects the combined system. The confidence measure, although simple, has displayed improvements for the weakest topologies (with less inputs per tree and/or less trees per positional bit of output codes).

## 6 Conclusions

This paper has presented two improvements for Adaptive Logic Networks. It has shown that in several topologies Goal Seeking Neurons can act as an initialization step and that a simple confidence measure can enhance performance. Moreover, the results are based on a real-world task (recognition of hand-written digits).

The main ideas for the conversion of GSN networks into ALN format were presented. The combined system was shown to be superior to both components and its advantages over them were commented. A confidence measure for networks based on how much the input pattern should change in order to modify final outputs was described. Experiments using this confidence measure have shown its value especially for the weakest topologies.

## References

[1] Bowmaker, R G, and Coghill, G G, 1992, "Improved recognition capabilities for Goal Seeking Neuron", in *Electronic Letters*, vol. 28, No. 3, 220-221.

[2] Martins, W and Allinson, N M, 1993, "Optimization of presentation order in networks of Goal Seeking Neurons", in submission.

[3] Kan, W K, and Aleksander I, 1987, "A probabilistic logic neuron network for associative learning", in *Proc. IEEE First International Conference on Neural Networks*, volume II, 541-548, San Diego, California, USA.

[4] Martins, W and Allinson, N M, 1993, "Two improvements for GSN neural networks", in *Proc. Weighless Neural Network Workshop '93*, 58-63, York, UK.

[5] Bisset, D L et al, 1989, "A comparative study of neural network structures for practical application in a pattern recognition environment" in *Proc. First IEE Interl. Conf. on Artificial Neural Networks*, 378-382, London, UK.

[6] Armstrong, W W et al, 1991, "Learning and generalization in Adaptive Logic Networks", *Artificial Neural Networks*, edited by T Kohonen et al, North Holland.

[7] L'Ecuyer, P, 1988, "Efficient and portable combined random number generators", in *Communications of ACM*, vol 31, 742-749.

# MULTIPLE TARGETS DISCRIMINATION USING NEURAL NETWORK BASED CLUSTERING ALGORITHMS

**Moon W. Kim**

TEW Division

Naval Research Laboratory

4555 Overlook Ave.

Washington, D.C., 20375

## Abstract

The problem of clustering Direction Finding (DF) bearing measurements with multiple targets is studied. The applied clustering algorithms are two Neural Networks, namely the Gram-Charlier Neural Network (GCNN) and Generalized Probabilistic Neural Network (GPNN) classifiers, and the statistical distance measurement method. Performances of these classifiers for bearing measurement clustering are evaluated in terms of probability correctly resolved. These classifiers performed respectably well compared to the statistical distance measurement method. GCNN and GPNN have the advantage of requiring very short training times. Also, these clustering classifiers will be useful in real-time situations.

## I. Introduction

The problem considered in this paper is how to cluster an Electronic Support Measures (ESM) system's bearing measurements against true targets. Typically an ESM system's bearing measurement contains a large error variance especially for a long-range target. The ESM system provides a large set of data for each target. The clustering problem occurs when the ESM system measures for several targets. One of the worst scenarios exists when these targets are flying close to each other at the same angle. Thus, a proper clustering algorithm needs a better estimate of the number of targets within the surveillance volume. In some instances the bearing measurements contain classification information which can be associated with true targets.

Trunk and Wilson [1] considered the problem of associating Direction Finding bearing measurements with radar tracks, using of a statistical distance measurement method. However, in this paper, a different type of clustering problem where limited to clustering the ESM data for the true target's information use of two neural network algorithms, namely Gram-Charlier Neural Network (GCNN) and Generalized Probabilistic Neural Network (GPNN).

## II. Statistical Distance Calculation Method

For each track, calculate the observed square error use of ESM and true target bearing information. The calculation of square error is given by

$$D_j = \sum_{j=1}^{m_j} [\theta_{ei} - \theta_{ti}(j)]^2 / \sigma^2 \qquad (1)$$

Where $\theta_{ei}$ is the $i^{th}$ ESM bearing measurement, $\theta_{ti}(j)$ is the true bearing to target j at the time of the $i^{th}$ bearing measurement, and $\sigma^2$ is a constant variance. In reality, the true bearings $\theta_{ti}(j)$ are unknown. The squared error $D_j$ cannot be used directly since there may be a bias towards making a decision. The cumulative probability $p_j$ of the estimated squared error has a Chi-square density with $m_j$ degrees of freedom since the bearing measurements are Gaussian distributed. Therefore the desired cumulative probability $p_j$ is given by

$$p_j = P_r\{S \geq D_j\} \qquad \text{where } S \approx \chi^2(m_j) \qquad (2)$$

S is Chi-square distributed with m degrees of freedom where the probability S is greater than $D_j$. The Chi-square distribution is given by

$$P_r\{S \geq D_j\} = \int_D^\infty \frac{S^{\frac{n}{2}-1} e^{\frac{-S}{2}}}{2^{\frac{n}{2}} \Gamma(\frac{n}{2})} dS \qquad (3)$$

The decision rule selects the correlation that has the largest probability of $p_j$. Thus it can discriminate the series of bearing inputs from an ESM system.

## III. Principles of Gram-Charlier Neural Network (GCNN) and Generalized Probabilistic Neural Network (GPNN)

Two Generalized Probabilistic Neural Networks are proposed for use as clustering schemes. The first neural network uses Gram-Charlier series expansion to estimate the underlying probability density function (pdf) of the data available for training. These pdfs are then used to form a maximum likelihood classifier. This classifier is further discussed in Reference [2]. The second neural network method uses the Gram-Charlier series expansion with a Parzen's windowing technique to estimate the underlying pdf from the training data. This classifier is further discussed in Reference [2]. The presented Generalized Probabilistic Neural Networks can use any type of pdfs for each class category for classification.

### III.1. Gram-Charlier Neural Network (GCNN)

For this classifier, an estimated that the density function p(x) has zero mean, and $x_i$'s are inputs from the same random variable $x$. Thus, the conditional density function $p(x|H_i)$ of $x$ under the $i^{th}$ hypotheses $H_l$ is given by

$$p(x|H_l) = \frac{1}{(2\pi\sigma^2)^{1/2}} e^{\frac{-x^2}{2\sigma^2}} [1 - c_3[(\frac{x}{\sigma})^4 - 6(\frac{x}{\sigma})^3 + 3]]$$

$$-c_5[(\frac{x}{\sigma})^5 - 10(\frac{x}{\sigma})^3 + 15(\frac{x}{\sigma})] + c_6[(\frac{x}{\sigma})^6 - 15(\frac{x}{\sigma})^4 + 45(\frac{x}{\sigma}) - 15] \quad (4)$$

The coefficients $c_3, c_4, c_5$, and $c_6$ are to be calculated using the inputs of the $i^{th}$ class using equations (reference [2]). The overall functional block diagram of the GCNN classifier is shown in Figure 1. If it is used to classify L classes of hypothesis $H_0, H_1, H_2,..., H_{L-1}$, then the Figure 1 consists of L separate subsections, one for each hypothesis. These subsections have similar architecture and function. Only one of the subsections is described in the following: The Gram-Charlier series coefficients $c_{sl}$, s = 3,4,5, and 6 for the $1^{th}$ class are calculated. We will perform the architecture for realization of $p(x|H)$s the pdf corresponding to class H, where H may be any of the L classes $H_0, H_1, H_2,..., H_{L-1}$. Further details of architecture and training process can be found in Ref. [2].

### III.2. Generalized Probabilistic Neural Network (GPNN) using Gram-Charlier Series Expansion (GCSE) with Parzen's Windowing Technique

The Generalized Probabilistic Neural Network (GPNN) based classifier is presented. The data samples x are assumed to be ergodic so that its ensemble average equals an appropriate time average. The elements of samples x and $x_i$ are independent and identically distributed random variables. For the Generalized Probabilistic Neural Network (GPNN) with a Gram-Charlier series expansion (GCSE), and Parzen's windowing [3]. Thus, the conditional density function $f(x|H_l)$, which is an estimate of the underlying parent density function, is given by

$$f(x|H_l) = \frac{1}{N\sigma} \sum_{i=1}^{N} p(x - x_i) \tag{4}$$

where $p(x - x_i)$ is a density function shifted by $x_i$'s. The following section presents the architecture of a neural network based system that generates the conditional density functions $f(\underline{x}|H_l)$'s according to equation (4) is presented. The conditional density function $f(\underline{x}|H_l)$ in equation (4) involves n training samples $x = x_1, x_2, ..., x_n$ from a random process corresponding to class $H_l$, $l = 0,1,2,...,L-1$. The overall functional block diagram of the Generalized Probabilistic Neural Network (GPNN) classifier is shown in figure 2. To classify L classes of hypotheses $H_0$, $H_1$, ..., $H_{L-1}$ then Figure 2 consists of L separate subsections, one for each hypothesis. These subsections are similar in architecture and function and hence only one such subsection (e.g. the subsection for $H_l$) is described below. In the subsection for hypothesis $H_l$ shown in Fig. 2, the Gram-Charlier coefficients $c_{sl}$ for the class $l$ will be calculated and further realized $p(x - x_i|H_l)$'s. Further details of architecture and training process can be found in Ref. [2].

## IV. Angle Measurement Error Ellipse Calculation

The measurements from an ESM system to a target do not measure range. By combining other information from geographically distributed ESM sites range can be estimated Thus, the location of a target may be measured even though it may not be accurate. Furthermore, the error can be estimated and displayed to create an ellipse shape. If the ellipse is quite large, the measurement accuracy is very low.

The area of ellipse is defined in terms of the mean values and the covariance matrix of a Gaussian density function.The area of the ellipse can be determined. Let's assume that the measured target position $R_t$ at the time t is given by

$$R(t) = \begin{bmatrix} x(t) \\ y(t) \end{bmatrix}$$

where $x(t)$ and $y(t)$ represents x axis and y axis in cartesian coordinate. The covariance matrix $\Lambda$ is a non-negative definite sysmmetric matrix.

$$\Lambda = \begin{bmatrix} \sigma_x^2 & \sigma_{xy} \\ \sigma_{xy} & \sigma_y^2 \end{bmatrix}$$

The bivariate Gaussian density function is given as

$$f(x,y) = \frac{1}{2\pi\sigma_x\sigma_y\sqrt{1-\rho^2}} e^{\frac{-1}{2(1-\rho^2)}\left[\frac{x^2}{\sigma_x^2}+\frac{2\rho xy}{\sigma_x\sigma_y}+\frac{y^2}{\sigma_y^2}\right]} \qquad (6)$$

Thus, the area of ellipse is expressed as

$$-\frac{1}{2(1-\sigma^2)}\left(\frac{x^2}{\sigma_x^2}+\frac{2\rho xy}{\sigma_x\sigma_y}+\frac{y^2}{\sigma_y^2}\right) = A \qquad (7)$$

and the size of ellipe can be calculated as

$$S = 2\pi A\sigma_x\sigma_y\sqrt{1-\sigma^2} = -2\pi\sigma_x\sigma_y\sqrt{1-\sigma^2}\ln(1-P) \qquad (8)$$

where p is the estimated probability within the region and $\rho$ is the correlation coefficient

$$\rho = \frac{\sigma_{xy}}{\sigma_x\sigma_y}, -1 \le \rho \le 1$$

Equation (7) can be rewritten as

$$-\frac{1}{2}Z\Lambda^{-1}Z' = A \qquad (9)$$

where $\quad Z = \begin{bmatrix} x \\ y \end{bmatrix}$, $\Lambda^{-1} = \frac{1}{1-\rho^2}\begin{bmatrix} \dfrac{1}{\sigma_x^2} & -\dfrac{\rho}{\sigma_x\sigma_y} \\ -\dfrac{\rho}{\sigma_x\sigma_y} & \dfrac{1}{\sigma_y^2} \end{bmatrix}$

The covariance matrix $\Lambda$ has two positive eigenvalues $\lambda_1, \lambda_2$ which are orthogonal. Furthermore equation (9) can be rewritten as

$$\frac{U_1^2}{\lambda_1} + \frac{U_2^2}{\lambda_2} = A \qquad (10)$$

where $U_1 = ZZ_1$ and $U_2 = ZZ_2$. Therefore the error ellipse (equation (10)) is centered at the origin of $U_1$ and $U_2$ with major and minor semi-axes at $\sqrt{\lambda_1 m}$ and $\sqrt{\lambda_2 m}$, where m is the degree of freedom.

## V. Simulation Results

From collected data that are assumed to be the true targets, and plotted on Plan Position Indicator (PPI) display, which is shown in figure 3. The data contains longitude, latitude, and an associated error ellipse. Based on this information, a set of ESM data is generated synthetically with the error variance, where not greater than 2.6 degrees. The data file contains bearing measurement $\theta_e$ at the time $t_i$ and typically a large size of different bearing measurements at each time $t_i$. This scenario is limited to 20 true targets.

Table 1. Probability of correct clustering against true targets

| $P_d$ | | | |
|---|---|---|---|
| # of true targets | GCNN | GPNN | Statistical Dis. Cal. |
| 1 | 1.0 | 1.0 | 1.0 |
| 2 | 1.0 | 1.0 | 1.0 |
| 3 | 1.0 | 1.0 | 1.0 |
| 4 | 1.0 | 1.0 | 0.984 |
| 5 | 0.998 | 1.0 | 0.981 |

| | | | |
|---|---|---|---|
| 6 | 0.998 | 0.999 | 0.975 |
| 7 | 0.992 | 0.993 | 0.974 |
| 8 | 0.986 | 0.990 | 0.967 |
| 9 | 0.981 | 0.984 | 0.923 |
| 10 | 0.975 | 0.973 | 0.875 |
| 11 | 0.934 | 0.964 | 0.812 |
| 12 | 0.868 | 0.900 | 0.796 |
| 13 | 0.814 | 0.834 | 0.646 |
| 14 | 0.750 | 0.710 | 0.615 |
| 15 | 0.711 | 0.673 | 0.603 |
| 16 | 0.702 | 0.641 | 0.546 |
| 17 | 0.693 | 0.627 | 0.523 |
| 18 | 0.672 | 0.589 | 0.511 |
| 19 | 0.635 | 0.532 | 0.502 |
| 20 | 0.626 | 0.512 | 0.478 |

Table 1 shows the probabilities of correctly clustering against the true target measurements. Based on Table 1, ESM bearing measurements are synthetically generated for 5 measurements for each target. The total number of measurements of these targets is 100 samples. To be realistic, all measurements tend to mixed, and it does not know which ESM measurement belongs to which true target. The three algorithms described in sections II and III are performed to do clustering. It shows that the GCNN and GPNN performed good compare to the Statistical distance calculation method.

Expressions for the error ellipse, which described in section IV, require variances to be computed for $\sigma_x, \sigma_y$, and $\sigma_{xy}$. These measurements for each clustering region are to be used for calculation of these variances. Once these variances are calculated, then the major and minor semi-axes can be calculated, and can create an error ellipse for the estimated target. This research is still ongoing, and will presents the result in the near future.

## VI. Summary

The multi-target clustering problem using neural network and statistical distance measurement methods has been presented by a combination of analytic, simulation, and experimental techniques. The problem should be correlated against all nearby true targets. Clustering decisions are made based on three clustering algorithms described in sections II and III. First, the statistical distance measurement method is based on the probability that the square error between the ESM bearing measurements and the true target's bearing measurements. Second, neural network based the GCNN and GPNN algorithms have been applied and performed for these same measurements. The correctly clustered probability is observed, and also shown that the GCNN and GPNN algorithms were performed good against true target. This paper presents a preliminary result of ongoing research work. Further study and implementation results will be discussed in the near future.

**Acknowledgment**

Author thanks to Mr. Mike Hsu for generating the PPI display plot.

**References**

1. G.V. Trunk and J.D. Wilson, " Association of DF Bearing Measurements with Radar Tracks"', IEEE Trans. AES, Vol. 4, July 1987.
2. M.W. Kim and M. Arozullah," Generalized Probabilistic Neural Network Based Classifiers,", IEEE IJCNN, June 1992.

3. M.W. Kim and M. Arozullah," Neural Network Based Optimum Radar Target Detection in Non-Gaussian Noise,", IEEE IJCNN, June 1992.
4. M.W. Kim," Handwritten Digit Recognition Using Gram-Charlier and Generalized Probabilistic Neural Networks," WCNN, Portland, Oregon, June 1993.

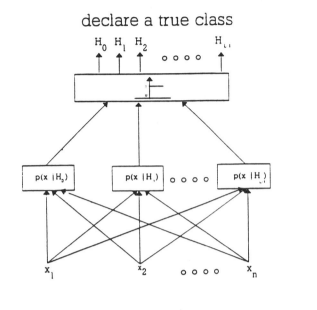

Figure 1. The Gram-Charlier Neural Network overall block diagram

Figure 2. The Generalized Probabilisitic Neural Network overall block diagram

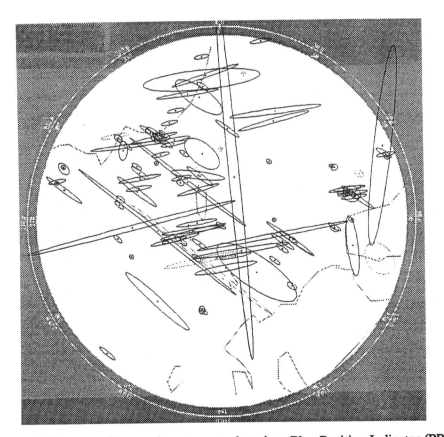

Figure 3. The error ellipses of true targets plotted on Plan Position Indicator (PPI) display

# AN ERROR-CORRECTING LEARNING ALGORITHM USING DOUBLE HYSTERESIS THRESHOLDS FOR ASSOCIATIVE MEMORY

Kenji NAKAYAMA          Katsuaki NISHIMURA

Dept. of Electrical and Computer Eng., Faculty of Tech., Kanazawa Univ.
2-40-20, Kodatsuno, Kanazawa 920 JAPAN
E-Mail: nakayama@haspnn1.ec.t.kanazawa-u.ac.jp

**ABSTRACT**   An associative memory using fixed and variable hysteresis thresholds, $\pm T$ and $\pm T(n)$, in learning and recalling processes, respectively, has been proposed by authors. This model can achieve a large memory capacity and very low noise sensitivity. However, a relation between weight change $\Delta w$ and the hysteresis threshold $\pm T$ has not been well discussed. In this paper, a new learning algorithm is proposed, which is based on an error-correcting method. However, in order to avoid unstable behavior, double hysteresis thresholds are introduced. Unit states are updated using $\pm T$. The error is evaluated using $\pm (T+dT)$ instead of $\pm T$. This means 'over correction'. Stable and fast convergence can be obtained. Relations between $\eta =dT/T$ and convergence rate and noise sensitivity are discussed, resulting the optimum selection for $\eta$. Furthermore, the order of presenting training data is optimized taking correlation into account. In the recalling process, a controlling method for $\pm T(n)$ is proposed in order to achieve fast recalling from noisy patterns. Memory capacity is investigated, which is about 1.6 times the the number of units.

## I INTRODUCTION

An associative memory is one of hopeful applications of artificial neural networks (NNs). Connection weights are adjusted so that patterns are memorized on equilibrium states. Conventional methods, auto-correlation methods and orthogonal methods [1]-[6], assume symmetrical weights, and are effective only for lineally independent patterns or orthogonal patterns. Therefore, memory capacity and noise insensitivity are strictly limited.

Authors proposed an associative memory, and its learning and recalling algorithms [7]-[9]. Fixed and variable hysteresis thresholds were effectively employed in the learning and recalling processes, respectively. It can drastically improve recalling ability from noisy pattens. However, a relation between connection weight change and the threshold was not well discussed. It was determined by experience. Furthermore, control of the variable hysteresis threshold in the recalling process was not optimized.

In this paper, new learning and recalling algorithms are proposed in order to solve the above remaining problems, and to achieve fast convergence, low noise sensitivity and large memory capacity.

## II ASSOCIATIVE MEMORY WITH HYSTERESIS THRESHOLD

The associative memory proposed in [7]-[9] is briefly described here. A unit is connected with all the other units. The weights are not always symmetrical. A self-loop is not used. Let the input and output for the ith unit at the nth cycle be $u_i(n)$ and $v_i(n)$, respectively. The connection weight from the ith unit to the jth unit is expressed $w_{IJ}$. Network transition is formulated as follows:

$$u_J(n) = \sum_{I=1}^{N} w_{IJ}v_I(n), \quad w_{II}=0 \tag{1}$$

$$v_J(n+1) = f(u_J(n)) = \begin{cases} 1, & u_J(n) \geq T(n) & (2a) \\ v_J(n), & |u_J(n)| < T(n) & (2b) \\ 0, & u_J(n) \leq -T(n) & (2c) \end{cases}$$

## III LEARNING ALGORITHM FOR CONNECTION WEIGHTS

### 3.1 Error-Correction with Double Hysteresis Threshold

The proposed learning algorithm is based on an error-correcting method [10]. However, the ordinary error correcting method is very poor in training the mutually connected NNs. This means the learning process is very unstable and oscillation easily occurs. Therefore, in order to prevent such unstable behavior and to achieve fast convergence, double hysteresis threshold is introduced. The learning algorithm is described in the following step by step.

Let P(m), m=1~M, be patterns to be memorized. $p_i(m)$ expresses the ith element of P(m), which takes a binary value, that is 1 or 0.

(1) Initial connection weights are set to zero.

(2) The network state is set to one of the patterns P(m).

(3) Calculate the unit input by Eq.(1). $p_i(m)$ is used instead of $v_i(n)$.

$$u_J(n) = \sum_{I=1}^{N} w_{IJ}(n)p_I(m), \quad p_I(m)=1 \text{ or } 0 \tag{3}$$

(4) Letting $\pm T$ be the hysteresis thresholds, the error is evaluated by

$$\varepsilon_J(n) = p_J(m)[T-u_J(n)] + (1-p_J(m))[T+u_J(n)] \tag{4}$$

(5) If $|u_J(n)|$ cannot exceed T, then $\varepsilon_J(n) > 0$. Thus, $\varepsilon_J(n) \leq 0$ means the output is correct, that is $v_J(n+1)=p_J(m)$. Therefore, the weights are updated by

$$w_{IJ}(n+1) = w_{IJ}(n) + \mu(n)\delta_J(n)p_I(m)S[\varepsilon_J(n)] \tag{5}$$

$$\delta_J(n) = p_J(m)[T+dT-u_J(n)] + (p_I(m)-1)[T+dT+u_J(n)] \tag{6}$$

$$S[\varepsilon_J(n)] = \begin{cases} 1, & \varepsilon_J(n) > 0 \\ 0, & \varepsilon_J(n) \leq 0 \end{cases} \tag{7}$$

$$\mu(m) = \mu_0/(M(m)-1), \quad 0 < \mu_0 \leq 1, \tag{8}$$

$$M(m) \text{ is the number of the units locate on P(m).}$$

In the above equation, T+dT is used instead of T. dT serves as the hysteresis margin. A pair of T and dT is called "double hysteresis thresholds" in this paper. This method makes it possible to stabilize and accelerate the learning process. In the later section, we will compare the learning behavior with dT and without dT through computer simulation. A ratio of dT and T is denoted $\eta$ =dT/T.

(6) The connection weights are simultaneously updated for a pattern P(m).

(7) By replacing P(m) by P(m+1), the above processes (2) through (6) are repeated.

Furthermore, Steps (2) through (7) are repeated until all unit inputs satisfy

$$\text{If } p_i(m) =1, \quad \text{then } u_i(n) \geq T \tag{9a}$$

$$\text{If } p_i(m) =0, \quad \text{then } u_i(n) \leq -T \tag{9b}$$

### 3.2 Relation between dT/T and Convergence Rates

dT is used to stabilize the learning process. If patterns P(i) and P(j) are conflict with each other, then adjusting of the connection weights for P(i) are easily broken by learning P(j) some other time. This cause oscillation, that is unstable learning and slow convergence. In order to avoid this unstable phenomena, dT is introduced. However, if it is small, effect of dT is not sufficient. A large dT is desired to guarantee stable and fast convergence.

### 3.3 Relation between dT/T and Noise Sensitivity

Noise sensitivity is determined by the variance of connection weights. An example is shown here. Two sets of weights are considered here.

$$\mathbf{W}_1 = [1,1,1,1,1], \quad \mathbf{W}_2 = [2,1,1,0.5,0.5]$$

Sums of the weights are the same, that is 5. Suppose the unit state will change if its input change more than 2.5. Using $\mathbf{W}_1$, three units should be changed at least. Let the number of units in the whole network be N. When the noise is added at random, a probability of selecting one unit is given by 1/N. Selection of three units from five units has probability $p_1$ given by Eq.(10a). At the same time, using $\mathbf{W}_2$, probability of changing more than 2.5 is $p_2$ given by Eq.(10b).

$$p_1 = 9(1/N)^4 \tag{10a}$$
$$p_2 \fallingdotseq (1/N)^3 \tag{10b}$$

Usually, N takes a large number (>>9), then $p_1$ is smaller than $p_2$.

On the other hand, variance of $\mathbf{W}_2$ is larger than that of $\mathbf{W}_1$. Thus, the noise sensitivity is proportional to the variance of the connection weights. The variance is highly dependent on $\eta = dT/T$. A large $\eta$ will cause a large variance. Therefore, a small $\eta$ is desirable to achieve robustness for noisy patterns. This direction for $\eta$ is opposite to stable and fast convergence. Therefore, $\eta$ should be optimized taking both the convergence rate and the noise sensitivity into account. This will be further discussed in Sec. V.

### 3.4 Order of Presenting Training Patterns

In the mutually connected NNs, connections from common units for many patterns to the other units are not emphasized. On the contrary, connections from the units, not included in many patterns, to the other units are emphasized, and play an important role in the recalling process. In other words, patterns having high correlation with the other patterns are difficult to be memorized, and to be recalled from noisy patterns.

In the learning process given by Eqs.(5) through (8), the connection weights are adjusted so that the unit inputs just satisfy the threshold pattern by pattern. This adjusting affects the patterns early presented in both positive and negative directions. This negative affection will be readjusted in the next learning. The positive affection will remain. By repeating this learning, the early presented patterns can gain noise margin.

Taking the above discussions into account, highly correlated patterns are early presented to the NN. By this method, noise sensitivity is averaged over all patterns. The correlation is evaluated by Hamming distance as follows:

$$d_H(i,j) = \sum_{k=1}^{M} | p_k(i) - p_k(j) | \tag{11}$$

$$d_H(i) = \frac{1}{M} \sum_{j=1}^{M} d_H(i,j) \tag{12}$$

## IV RECALLING FROM INCOMPLETE PATTERNS

### 4.1 Variable Hysteresis Threshold

After the training completed, all units satisfy Eqs.(9a) and (9b). By adding noise, these conditions are destroyed, and the network changes its state. State changes are transferred through connections to the other units, and cause another state transition. The wrong state change tend to cause another wrong state changes. As a result, the NN fails in recalling the correct memory. Therefore, it is important to select the units, whose input are probably correct, and to change these units first.

For this purpose, we proposed variable hysteresis threshold $\pm T(n)$ in the association process [7]-[9]. Let $e_i(n)$ be an error added to the ith unit. It takes $\pm 1$. In the noisy pattern, the unit input is expressed using $e_i(n)$ as follows:

$$u_J(n) = \sum_i w_{IJ}[p_I(m)+e_i(n)] = \sum_i w_{IJ}p_I(m) + \sum_i w_{IJ}e_i(n) \qquad (13)$$

The first term is the correct component, satisfies Eq.(9). The second term is the error component. If the following condition is held, inaccurate transition is caused. The first and second terms are denoted $U_J(n)$ and $E_J(n)$, respectively.

$$p_J(m)=1: U_J(n) < -T(n), \qquad p_J(m)=0: U_J(n) > T(n) \qquad (14)$$

If we assume for $p_J(m)=1$ and 0, $U_J(n)$ takes T and -T, respectively, the above conditions can be rewritten as,

$$p_J(m)=1: E_J(n) < -T-T(n), \qquad p_J(m)=0: T+T(n) < E_J(n) \qquad (15)$$

$E_J(n)$ is uniformly distributed. The probability of Eq.(15) can be decreased by setting $T(n)$ to much larger than T. Finally, $T(n)$ should approach to T. This is an idea behind the variable hysteresis threshold [7]-[9].

$T(n)$ is chosen to be large enough to T, and is gradually decreased toward T. In the previous work, $T(n)$ was determined by

$$T(n) = T(0) - \alpha n, \qquad \alpha : \text{constant} \qquad (16)$$

$T(0)$ is chosen to larger than T. $T(0)$ and $\alpha$ are also determined by experience.

## 4.2 Optimum Control of Variable Hysteresis Threshold

In this paper, an improved version of controlling $T(n)$ is proposed. The method is described in the following step by step.

(1) The first threshold is determined by

$$T(0) = \max_i \{ \mid u_i(0) \mid \} \qquad (17)$$

$u_i(0)$ is the input of the ith unit at the initial state. The operation $\mid x \mid$ means absolute value of x.

(2) The units, whose input satisfy

$$\mid u_i(0) \mid = T(0) \qquad (18)$$

are updated following Eqs.(1) and (2). $\pm T(0)$ are used until the network state does not change any more.

(3) The next threshold $T(1)$ is determined in the same way as Eq.(17).

$$T(1) = \max_i \{ \mid u_i(n) \mid \} \qquad (19)$$

The same processes in Step(2) are repeated.

Thus, after the network reaches to some sate, the maximum input is adopted as the next threshold. Finally, $T(n)$ can reach T.

## V SIMULATION RESULTS

### 5.1 Convergence Properties

A mutually connected NN, having 8x8=64 units, is used. Training data are generated as random patterns. Half of the units take 1, and the other units take 0. Hamming distances among patterns form normal distribution with mean of 32 and covers from 22 to 44. The learning coefficient $\mu_0$ in Eq.(8) is unity.

Figure 1 shows relation between the number of patterns memorized (horizontal axis) and the number of iterations (vertical axis). Adjusting connection weights using one set of patterns is counted as one iteration. dT/T=0 means the ordinary error-correcting method [10]. The graph with a symbol ◇ indicates that order of training patterns presented is always fixed. The other graph with a symbol + means that the order is randomized at each iteration. dT/T=0.1 and 1 indicate the proposed method.

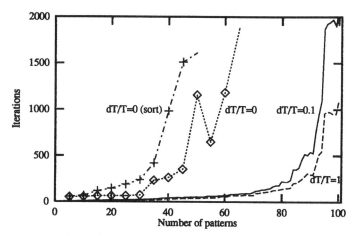

Fig.1 Relations between the number of patterns, which can be memorized, and the number of iterations in learning.

From these results, the error-correcting method without dT is very poor for training mutual connected NNs. Patterns more than 45(+) and 60(◇) cannot be memorized due to unstable behavior. On the contrary, the proposed method is very efficient. As discussed in Sec.3.2, a large $\eta$ =dT/T can provide fast convergence. Memory capacity can be also increased.

## 5.2 Memory Capacity

The memory capacity is dependent on correlation among the patterns. In this paper, random patterns are used. The results of Fig.1 are used for this discussion. The number of iterations gradually increases up to about 80 patterns. After that, it quickly increases. This is a very peculiar phenomenon. The training converged until 100 patterns. The number of the patterns could be increased a little more. However, from the very sharp slope, it is almost limited near by 100 patterns. Thus, the memory capacity is about $100/64 \fallingdotseq 1.56$ times as large as N. This result is much higher than the other models.

## 5.3 Recalling Accuracy for Noisy Patterns

Noisy patterns are generated by adding random error. Units are randomly selected, and their state are reversed. Thirty sets of random numbers are used. Association rates are evaluated in average. Figure 2 shows the simulation results. These results also support the previous discussion given in Sec.3.3. Association rates are inversely proportional to $\eta$ =dT/T. Roughly speaking, around $\eta$ =0.2 is desirable for both convergence speed and recalling accuracy.

## 5.4 Improvement of Association Rates

Effects of the order of presenting the training data, and the control method of the hysteresis threshold are investigated. Since random patterns have almost the same correlation, alphabet patterns, are employed for this purpose. The patterns are expressed with 16x16=256 dots. The network has also 256 units.

Table 1 lists association rates for noisy alphabet patterns. Method A is the original one [8], B improves the hysteresis threshold control, C orders the training patterns based on correlation, and BC combines Methods B and C. Association rate X is of the original pattens, that is 'correct answer', Y is of untrained patterns, that is spurious, and Z is of the other training patterns.

The recalling accuracy form noisy patterns can be improved by 3~5% from the original version. The ordering of the training patterns is more efficient.

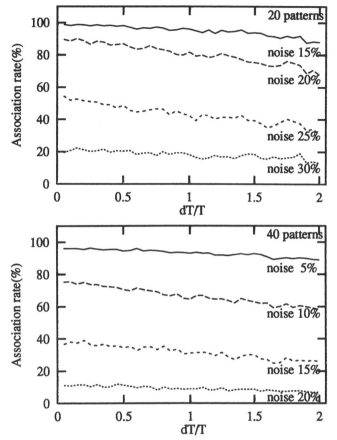

Fig.2 Relations between association rates and dT/T. (a) 20 and (b) 40 patterns are memorized.

Table 1 Association rates for alphabet patterns with random noise.

(a) $\eta$ =0.1, Noise=15%

| Methods | Association rates | | |
|---------|------|------|------|
|         | X    | Y    | Z    |
| A       | 96.3 | 2.8  | 0.9  % |
| B       | 96.4 | 2.6  | 1.0  |
| C       | 97.1 | 2.2  | 0.7  |
| BC      | 97.1 | 2.3  | 0.6  |

(b) $\eta$ =0.1, Noise=20%

| Methods | Association rates | | |
|---------|------|------|------|
|         | X    | Y    | Z    |
| A       | 87.1 | 8.7  | 4.2  % |
| B       | 88.1 | 7.7  | 4.2  |
| C       | 89.1 | 7.5  | 3.4  |
| BC      | 89.5 | 7.1  | 3.3  |

(c) $\eta$ =0.1, Noise=25%

| Methods | Association rates | | |
|---------|------|------|------|
|         | X    | Y    | Z    |
| A       | 71.7 | 17.5 | 10.8% |
| B       | 73.3 | 17.1 | 9.7  |
| C       | 76.6 | 13.9 | 9.5  |
| BC      | 76.8 | 14.6 | 8.6  |

## VI CONCLUSIONS

The error-correcting method using the double hysteresis thresholds has been proposed for the associative memory. Stable and fast learning can be achieved. Large memory capacity is obtained. The proposed ordering the training patterns and the controlling the hysteresis threshold can further improve association rates for noisy patterns.

**REFERENCES**
[1]T.Kohonen, Self-Organization and Associative Memory, 3rd Ed., Springer-Verlag 1989.
[2]K.Nakano,"Associatron-A model of associative memory",IEEE Trans vol.SMC-2,pp.380-388 1972.
[3]S.Amari,"Neural theory of association and concept-formation",Biol.Cybern.,vol.26,pp.175-185,1977.
[4]J.J.Hopfield,"Neural networks and physical system ~",Proc.Natl.Sci.USA,vol.79,pp.2554-2558, 1982.
[5]D.Amit et al,"Storing infinite number of patterns~",Phys.Rev.Lett.,pp.1530-1533,1985.
[6]S.Amari and K.Mginu,"Statistical neurodynamics of~",Neural Networks,vol.1,pp.63-73,1988.
[7]N.Mitsutani and K,Nakayama, IEICE Japan Rep. Tech. Meeting, vol.NC90-89, pp.125-130, March 1991.
[8]K.Nakayama and N.Mitsutani,"An adaptive hysteresis~", Proc. IJCNN'91 Seattle, p. II A-914, 1991.
[9]K.Nakayama et al.,"Memory capacity bound threshold~", Proc. IJCNN'93 Nagoya, pp.2603-2606, 1993.
[10]D.E.Rumelhart and J.L.McClelland,Parallel Distributed Processing, MIT Press, 1986.

# Further Cross Talk Reduction of Associative Memory using Functional Property of Cross Talk

Yukio KUMAGAI

Dept. of Computer Science and Systems Engineering
Muroran Institute of Technology
27-1 Mizumoto-cho, Muroran, 050 Japan

Abstract - The recalling performance of associative memory, whose construction is based on the outer product algorithm and naturally extended to higher order correlation, can be explicitly formalized as a functional form of Hamming distance between the memorized keys and the input key. This functional form is quite similar to the Krawtchouk polynomial, and thus cross talk in associative memory can be efficiently reduced by utilizing the functional properties of the Krawtchouk polynomial. In this paper, it is shown that, by further investigating detailed functional properties of the Krawtchouk polynomial, furthermore advanced effective cross talk reduction can be achieved and thus superior exact data retrieval is substantiated by computer experiments.

## I. Introduction

An associative memory is defined as a mapping from an n dimensional key vector $\mathbf{x} = \text{col} (x_1, x_2, ..., x_n)$ to an m dimensional datum vector $\mathbf{y} = \text{col} (y_1, y_2, ..., y_m)$ associated with the corresponding key $\mathbf{x}$. Usually, the components of these vectors are selected from a set $\{\pm 1\}$, and the realization of this mapping is done by taking an algebraic sum operation of componentwise correlation all over the data and keys to be memorized. This implementation method is called as the outer product algorithm and its recalling performance, including how to apply input key and obtain the recalled output, can be described as follows:

$$\mathbf{z} = F\{(\Sigma_{i=0}^{v} \mathbf{y}^{(i)} \otimes \mathbf{x}^{(i)}) \cdot \mathbf{x}\}, \tag{1}$$

where $\otimes$ denotes the outer product operator, F denotes the signum function which operates componentwise, $\mathbf{y}^{(i)}$ and $\mathbf{x}^{(i)}$ are the i-th datum and key to be memorized among the v kinds of data and keys respectively, and $\mathbf{z}$ and $\mathbf{x}$ are the recalled output and the input key respectively.

So far as the memorization of associative memory is concerned, the most essential feature of associative memory is taking an algebraic sum operation mentioned above, i.e., the superposition, over all the data and keys to be memorized. But we have to notice the significant theoretical background of this simple algorithm that the outer product algorithm is the lowest approximation of converged mathematical results in the two layered neural network trained by Hebbian learning rule which consists of the excitatory and inhibitory neurons [1], [2]. Thus the concept of this superposition has to be common in any extension of neural associative memory or new proposal of the neural network architecture. However, it is well known that, due to the superposition, the storage capacity for the exact recall is much too low and much less than the theoretically possible number. In order to increase this quantity, extensions to the higher order correlation associative memory have been attempted by many researchers, and its recalling performance can be described as follows:

$$\mathbf{z} = F\{(\Sigma_{i=0}^{v} \mathbf{y}^{(i)} \otimes \mathbf{x}_{(\alpha)}^{(i)}) \cdot \mathbf{x}_{(\alpha)}\}, \tag{2}$$

where the notations $\mathbf{x}_{(\alpha)}^{(i)}$ and $\mathbf{x}_{(\alpha)}$ imply the i-th key to be memorized among the v kinds of keys and the input key extended to the higher order correlation up to the $\alpha$-th order, respectively.

The improved results, especially the improved storage capacity, have been calculated, related to the associative memory recently re-examined by Hopfield [3], [5,6,7,8,9]. However, from the quantitative point of view, the essential explanation for this improvement is not always given. And, achieving further improvement of storage capacity, all the results concerned hitherto explicitly or implicitly assumes the necessity of monotonic increment of the degree of higher order correlation to be extended. This is a crucial problem, since it is well known that it causes the combinatorial explosion.

In this paper, we present the functional formularization of recalling performance in the higher order correlational associative memory in terms of Hamming distance between the memorized keys and input key [10]. Based on this formularization, we proposed a new architecture of associative memory which completely removes cross talk due to the memorized keys having odd number Hamming distance between the memorized keys and the input key [11, 12]. And also we pointed out that the formulated result corresponds to the special case of the Krawtchouk polynomial [4], [10]-[12]. Therefore, by utilizing of the functional properties of the Krawtchouk polynomial, a considerably effective reduction method of still remaining cross talk in higher order associative memory is suggested [13] and a new architecture of associative memory employing less number of higher order cross products compared to the conventional one is proposed. Computer simulation has been done and superior ability on exact data retrieval of the proposed associative memory architecture is exemplified.

## II. Performance Formulation of Associative Memory and Construction of New Architecture

Associative memory described by the representation (2) is formalized in terms of Hamming distance between the memorized keys and the input key as follows [10, 11, 12]:

Theorem [1]: Let $\mathbf{x}$ be an arbitrarily chosen input key belonging to the set of the memorized keys. Then the output recalled by this input key can be formularized uniquely in terms of Hamming distance d between the memorized keys and this input key as follows:

$$\mathbf{z} = F\{ \sum_{d=0}^{n} ( \sum_{i_v(d) \in \mathbf{I}^{(d)}} \mathbf{y}^{(i_v(d))} ) \cdot H(d, \alpha; n) \},$$

where

$$H(d, \alpha; n) = \Sigma_{k=0}^{\alpha} h(d, k; n), \quad h(d, k; n) = \Sigma_{\zeta=0}^{d} (-1)^{\zeta} \cdot {}_dC_{\zeta} \cdot {}_{(n-d)}C_{(k-\zeta)},$$

and the Hamming distance d is defined as follows:

$$d = d( \mathbf{x}^{(i)}, \mathbf{x} ) = (1/2) \cdot \Sigma_{j=1}^{n} | x_j^{(i)} - x_j |. \qquad \Box$$

Here, the notation $\mathbf{I}^{(d)} = \{ i_v(d) : i_v(d) \in \mathbf{I}, v = 1, 2, \cdots, v_d \} (d = 0, 1, \cdots, n)$ implies that the index set $\mathbf{I} = \{ i : (\mathbf{y}^{(i)}, \mathbf{x}^{(i)}), i = 1, 2, \cdots, v \} ( \supseteq \mathbf{I}^{(d)} )$ is uniquely partitioned into the mutually disjoint subsets $\{ \mathbf{I}^{(d)} \}_{d=0}^{n}$.

Consequently, if we desire to recall the datum associated with the applied input key from all the superimposed items, both this desired datum and other data are uniquely decomposed depending upon the Hamming distance between the memorized keys and input key, but the recalled output is the mixture of desired datum and other undesirable data. Therefore, the following corollary is easily deduced:

Corollary [1]: Let $\mathbf{x}^{(i^*)}$ be an input key belonging to the set of the memorized keys and $\mathbf{y}^{(i^*)}$ be the corresponding datum. Then the recalled output $\mathbf{z}$ by applying the input key $\mathbf{x}^{(i^*)}$ is uniquely decomposed as follows:

$$\mathbf{z} = F\{ \mathbf{y}^{(i^*)} \cdot H(0, \alpha; n) + \sum_{d \neq 0} ( \sum_{i_v(d) \in \mathbf{I}^{(d)}} \mathbf{y}^{(i_v(d))} ) \cdot H(d, \alpha; n) \}. \qquad \Box$$

The latter quantity described above becomes just cross talk since this would add the disturbance to the first quantity $\mathbf{y}^{(i^*)}H(0, \alpha; n)$ which is the desired one. Thus by using this expression, the quantitative behavior of data retrieval of associative memory can be explicitly explained. Therefore, the investigation of properties of $H(d, \alpha; n)$ is crucial. In the following, we summarize the properties of this function clarified in our study.

Theorem [2]: For $\forall \alpha$, ($\alpha = 0, 1, \cdots, n$), there holds $H(0, \alpha; n) > 0$. $\qquad \Box$

Theorem [3]: For $\forall d \neq 0$, $\alpha \neq 0$, there holds $H(0, \alpha; n) > | H(d, \alpha; n) |$. $\qquad \Box$

Remark [1]: Putting $\alpha = n$ in $H(d, \alpha; n)$, then for $\forall d \neq 0$, there holds $H(d, n; n) = 0$. $\qquad \Box$

Remark [2]: The definition of the Krawtchouk polynomial which is sometimes used in the coding theory is as below [4]:

$$K(d, k; n, q) = \Sigma_{\zeta=0}^{k} (-1)^{\zeta} \cdot {}_dC_{\zeta} \cdot {}_{(n-d)}C_{(k-\zeta)} \cdot (q-1)^{(k-\zeta)}. \qquad \Box$$

Putting $q = 2$, $k \geq d$, we notice the Krawtchouk polynomial : $K(d, k; n, 2)$ is identical with $h(d, k; n)$. Several Properties of this polynomial which is particularly useful in our study have been investigated. Utilizing these properties of the Krawtchouk polynomial we can derive some noticeable properties of cross talk, $h(d, k; n)$ and $H(d, \alpha; n)$ resulting from our computation. The analysis of these properties provides us with important insights on cross talk reduction based on the proposed new associative memory architecture with reduced cross talk using fewer cross products than the conventional one.

Theorem [4]: For $\forall k$, $\alpha$ ( $k, \alpha = 0, 1, \cdots, n$ ), there hold

$$h(n-d, k; n) = (-1)^k h(d, k; n), \quad H(n-d, \alpha; n) = (-1)^{\alpha} H(d, \alpha; n). \qquad \Box$$

$H(d, \alpha; n)$ for $d \neq 0$ strongly dominates the behavior of cross talk. In this meaning, $h(d, k; n)$ has to be called suitably as the component of $H(d, \alpha; n)$. It is worth mentioning that $| h(d, k; n) |$ has symmetricity with respect to d = n/2, while $| H(d, \alpha; n) |$ is symmetric within the interval $[1, n]$ with the center at $d = (n+1)/2$, i.e., in the true cross talk's region, and $H(0, \alpha; n)$ corresponding to the desired datum is always greater than $| H(d, \alpha; n) |$ corresponding to $d \neq 0$.

Theorem [5]: For $\forall d$ ($d = 0, 1, \cdots, n$), there holds $h(d, n-k; n) = (-1)^d h(d, k; n)$. $\qquad \Box$

Corollary [2]: For $\forall$ d (d = 0,1,..., n), there holds $\widetilde{H}(d, n-\alpha; n) = (-1)^d H(d, \alpha; n)$.

where $\widetilde{H}(d, n-\alpha; n) = \Sigma_{k=n}^{n-\alpha} h(d, k; n)$. □

Remark [3]: For $\forall$ k (k = 1,2, ..., n), there holds $h(d, n-k; n) = h(d, n; n) h(d, k; n)$. □

The above theorem [5] and corollary [2] state symmetricity of h(d, k; n) and H(d, $\alpha$; n) with respect to k and $\alpha$ for some fixed d. The first part of the theorem [5] states symmetricity with respect to k for some fixed d. Particular emphasis has to be put on the fact arising due to this symmetricity that the component h(d, k; n) for the extreme low and the corresponding higher order correlation (i.e., k and n - k) have the same magnitude but opposite sign for odd number d, and furthermore both components need equal number of cross products for their realization. Therefore, following the corollary [2] which results from the first part of the theorem [5], we can propose a new architecture that simultaneously includes low and the corresponding extreme high order ( i.e., the simultaneous inclusion of $\alpha$-th and (n-$\alpha$)-th order, n being the highest order), and it is easily shown that this new associative memory architecture completely removes cross talk due to the memorized keys having odd number Hamming distance from the input key. The number of different kinds of cross products attains maximum value for high-order around n/2. Consequently the conventional higher order associative memory architecture, if necessary, might include the cross products for the order around n/2 up to the highest order in order to achieve the desired performance. But those cross products are the last one to be used in the proposed architecture and usually do not need to be included. Thus, compared to the conventional one, the proposed construction extremely reduces the number of cross products to be used and it also greatly facilitates the efforts for constructing the cross products (Remark [3]). In the following, we show these situations in the form of the theorem concretely:

Theorem [6]: For $\forall$ d, k = 0, 1, ..., n, there holds

$$(1/2)\cdot\{h(d, n-k; n) + h(d, k; n)\} = \left\{ \begin{array}{ll} 0 & \text{for odd number d,} \\ h(d, k; n) & \text{for even number d.} \end{array} \right.$$

For d = 1,2, ..., n and $\alpha$ = 0,1, ..., n, there holds

$$(1/2)\cdot\{H(d, n-1-\alpha; n) + H(d, \alpha; n)\} = \left\{ \begin{array}{ll} 0 & \text{for odd number d,} \\ H(d, \alpha; n) & \text{for even number d.} \end{array} \right. \quad □$$

Consequently, the following corollary is derived:

Corollary [3]: For d, $\alpha$ = 0,1, ..., n, there holds

$$(1/2)\cdot\{\widetilde{H}(d, n-\alpha; n) + H(d, \alpha; n)\} = \left\{ \begin{array}{ll} 0 & \text{for odd number d,} \\ H(d, \alpha; n) & \text{for even number d.} \end{array} \right. \quad □$$

Numerical computation results support the theorems, corollaries and remarks state so far. Figure 1(a) and 1(b) demonstrate these, exemplifying h(d,k;n), H(d,$\alpha$;n) normalized by h(0,k;n), H(0,$\alpha$;n), respectively for n = 11. This illustrates the kinds of symmetricity, cross talk cancellation phenomenon, and concrete magnitude of cross talk.

Based on Corollary [3], we deduce the following theorem which describes the architecture of the proposed associative memory that employs less number of higher order cross products compared to the conventional one.

Theorem [7]: Let $\widetilde{\mathbf{x}}^{(i)}_{(n-\alpha)}$, $\widetilde{\mathbf{x}}_{(n-\alpha)}$ be the i-th extended higher order correlational vector and the extended input key vector, constructed from using n to (n-$\alpha$)-th order respectively. Then the associative memory is described by the following expression:

$$\mathbf{z} = F[(1/2)\cdot\{(\Sigma_{i=0}^{v} \mathbf{y}^{(i)} \otimes \mathbf{x}^{(i)}_{(\alpha)}) \cdot \mathbf{x}_{(\alpha)} + (\Sigma_{i=0}^{v} \mathbf{y}^{(i)} \otimes \widetilde{\mathbf{x}}^{(i)}_{(n-\alpha)}) \cdot \widetilde{\mathbf{x}}_{(n-\alpha)}\}], \tag{3}$$

make it possible to reduce completely cross talk due to the memorized keys having odd number Hamming distance between the memorized keys and the input key. □

Figure 2 demonstrates such behavior of cross talk of the proposed architecture, and this substantiates the properties of the theorem [7] and corollary [3].

However, there still remains cross talk due to the memorized keys having even number Hamming distance between the memorized keys and input key. In the next step, we attempt to reduce cross talk due to those memorized keys.

In order to do this, we furthermore investigate another property of H(d,$\alpha$; n) as the Krawtchouk polynomial. Then, we can present the following property:

Theorem [8]: For $\forall$ d, $\alpha$ (d = 1,2, ..., n ; $\alpha$ = 0, 1, ..., n), there holds

$$H(d, \alpha; n) = h(d-1, \alpha; n-1). \quad □$$

Numerical computation illustrated in Fig. 3 exemplifies this relationship for $\alpha$=0 to $\alpha$=4 and n=9. From the values of H(d, $\alpha$; 9) and h(d-1, $\alpha$: 8) shown in the figure, validity of the above relationship is proven, although the mathematical proof is omitted due to the limited space.

In order to apply this property to a new associative memory architecture, it is quite important to understand that the right hand side of the representation in the theorem [8] is described as a function of n-1. Hence, assuming $x_1$ be the component of the memorized keys and input key vectors occurring mismatch, the even Hamming distance between the memorized keys and input key is equivalently transformed into the odd number when excluding $x_1$.

By using this idea, we have presented the following theorem which contributes to reduce still remaining cross talk due to the memorized keys having even number Hamming distance between the memorized keys and the input key [13].

Theorem [9]: The associative memory based on the Theorem [8] is constructed as follows:

$$z = F[(1/2) \cdot \{(\Sigma_{i=0}^{v} y^{(i)} \otimes x_{(\alpha)}^{(i)}) \cdot x_{(\alpha)} + (\Sigma_{i=0}^{v} y^{(i)} \otimes \widetilde{x}_{(n-\alpha)}^{(i)}) \cdot \widetilde{x}_{(n-\alpha)}\}$$

$$- (1/4) \cdot \{(\Sigma_{i=0}^{v} y^{(i)} \otimes x_{1,(\alpha)}^{(i)}) \cdot x_{1,(\alpha)} + (\Sigma_{i=0}^{v} y^{(i)} \otimes \widetilde{x}_{1,(n-\alpha)}^{(i)}) \cdot \widetilde{x}_{1,(n-\alpha)}\} \qquad (4)$$

$$+ (1/4) \cdot \{(\Sigma_{i=0}^{v} y^{(i)} \otimes x_1^{(i)} \cdot x_{1,(\alpha)}^{(i)}) \cdot x_1^{(i)} \cdot x_{1,(\alpha)} + (\Sigma_{i=0}^{v} y^{(i)} \otimes x_1^{(i)} \cdot \widetilde{x}_{1,(n-\alpha)}^{(i)}) \cdot x_1 \cdot \widetilde{x}_{1,(n-\alpha)}\}],$$

where $x_{1,(\alpha)}^{(i)}$, $\widetilde{x}_{1,(n-\alpha)}^{(i)}$ denote two i-th extended memorized keys, each component of which does not contain $x_1^{(i)}$ and consists of higher order cross products from n to (n-$\alpha$)-th order, respectively. And $x_{1,(\alpha)}$, $\widetilde{x}_{1,(n-\alpha)}$ are the input key constructed under the same condition. □

Remark [4]: In this theorem [9], we used $x_1^{(i)}$, $x_{1,(\alpha)}^{(i)}$ and $\widetilde{x}_{1,(n-\alpha)}^{(i)}$ of the component of the memorized keys and $x_1$, $x_{1,(\alpha)}$ and $\widetilde{x}_{1,(n-\alpha)}$ of the input key in order to furthermore reduce cross talk in the proposed architecture represented by (3). But instead of them, we may construct this architecture based on any another component of the memorized keys and input key. □

Remark [5]: The architecture subjected to the representation (4) needs $2 \cdot {}_{(n-1)}C_\alpha$ more higher order cross products compared to the representation (3). □

Remark [6]: In general, there holds ${}_{(n-1)}C_\alpha = \{(\alpha+1)/n\} \cdot {}_nC_{(\alpha+1)}$. Therefore, if n is sufficiently large and $\alpha$ is relatively small, the architecture proposed here implies that the improvement of exact recall is achievable by using less number of higher order cross products rather than the monotonic increment of the degree of higher order correlation. □

Now, in this paper, we extend this idea presented in the theorem [9] as follows:

Let $W = (\omega_{h,j})$ be a matrix consisted of the net outputs $\omega_j = col (\omega_{1,j}, \omega_{2,j}, \cdots, \omega_{m,j})$ (j = 1, 2, ..., n) corresponding to the recalled output $z = col (z_1, z_2, ..., z_m)$, in which the components of $W$ are constructed under the condition that mismatch would be occurred between the memorized key $x^{(i)}_j$ and the input key $x_j$ as follows:

$$\omega_j = (1/2) \cdot \{(\Sigma_{i=0}^{v} y^{(i)} \otimes x_{(\alpha)}^{(i)}) \cdot x_{(\alpha)} + (\Sigma_{i=0}^{v} y^{(i)} \otimes \widetilde{x}_{(n-\alpha)}^{(i)}) \cdot \widetilde{x}_{(n-\alpha)}\}$$

$$- (1/4) \cdot \{(\Sigma_{i=0}^{v} y^{(i)} \otimes x_{j,(\alpha)}^{(i)}) \cdot x_{j,(\alpha)} + (\Sigma_{i=0}^{v} y^{(i)} \otimes \widetilde{x}_{j,(n-\alpha)}^{(i)}) \cdot \widetilde{x}_{j,(n-\alpha)}\} \qquad (5)$$

$$+ (1/4) \cdot \{(\Sigma_{i=0}^{v} y^{(i)} \otimes x_j^{(i)} \cdot x_{j,(\alpha)}^{(i)}) \cdot x_j^{(i)} \cdot x_{j,(\alpha)} + (\Sigma_{i=0}^{v} y^{(i)} \otimes x_j^{(i)} \cdot \widetilde{x}_{j,(n-\alpha)}^{(i)}) \cdot x_j \cdot \widetilde{x}_{j,(n-\alpha)}\},$$

Then we make a decision of the value of output $z$ according to the following rule:

[ decision rule ]: The output $z_h$ for h = 1, 2, ..., m is determined as the sign of the absolute value of net output $\omega_{h,j}$ which takes the nearest value to $\Sigma_{k=0}^{\alpha} {}_nC_k$ among the components $\omega_{h,j}$ for j = 1, 2, ..., n.

Here, it should be noticed that $\Sigma_{k=0}^{\alpha} {}_nC_k$ is the value of net output if cross talk would be completely eliminated.

[Remark 7]: In the above mentioned architecture, the number of cross products to be needed for adding newly to the architecture already proposed by representation (3) is the $2 \cdot {}_nC_\alpha$ next higher order cross products. This number is an intermediate next higher order correlation which is less than that of the conventional next higher order cross product $2 \cdot {}_nC_{(\alpha+1)}$ if $\alpha+1 \le n/2$. □

Exact data retrieval ability of the proposed architecture represented by (5) is compared to the architecture in representation (4).

III. Computer Simulation and Discussions

Computer simulation was carried out in order to compare the ability on exact data retrieval between the proposed architectures by keeping the condition that the total number of cross products used in each architecture is nearly equal. By doing so, we can evaluate the ability on exact data recall with nearly the same cost. The components of the data and keys are randomly generated with the equal probability of +1 or -1 occurring.

The experimental results are illustrated in Figure 4 and 5. Conventional architecture, already proposed architecture represented by (3), proposed architecture using the theorem [9], in Ref. [13], and proposed architecture using decision rule represented by (5) are compared. Figure 4(a) shows performance comparison between the architecture proposed previously and the conventional one in terms of percentage of exact recall and total number of failed pairs, using m=9 and n=11. Especially, in Fig. 4(b) and 4(c), it is shown that the broadness being caused by the differences between the desired output and actually recalled output becomes much wider as the number of memorized pairs is increased. Figure 5 shows the same type of performance comparison using or not using the decision rule proposed. Comparison among the architectures are made with a nearly equal number of cross products used and the proposed architectures use less order of correlation than the conventional one. This makes the comparison to be on a cost performance basis. Comparison shows that the proposed architectures possesses far better retrieval ability than the conventional one, and yields the best retrieval cost performance. Even when the number of memorized pairs is almost equal to the maximum possible number of stored pairs (in this experiment, 500 out of maximum possible 512), the proposed architecture using the decision rule represented by (5) almost perfectly recalled all of the stored pairs [Fig. 5]. The number of failed pairs in this case was only one against among the 490 and 500 memorized pairs. This significant improvement of exact data retrieval performance in the proposed architecture using the decision rule is due to the substantial reduction of cross talk employed in its architecture.

In the theorem [9], the component used in the construction of the proposed architecture is based on $x^{(i)}_1$ and $x_1$. But the component between the memorized keys and input key vectors need not be restricted to these ones and any of components of key vector can be considered. In Figure 5, we illustrate the variation width of experimental results, i.e., the maximum and minimum values in terms of percentage of exact recall, along with the average performance, when $x^{(i)}_j$ and $x_j$, ($j = 1, 2, ..., n$) for different values j is used in the construction of the theorem [9]. Even though the performance varies slightly depending upon which component is considered, the usefulness of the proposed idea, i.e., representation (5) or the introduction of new decision rule into the construction of associative memory is clearly substantiated through our experiments.

## IV. Conclusion

In this paper, we have formulated explicitly cross talk of associative memory as the functional form of Hamming distance between the memorized keys and the input key. And we have elucidated some noticeable properties of cross talk for reducing cross talk by using the Krawtchouk polynomial. The properties described in this paper are not only highly useful for reducing cross talk but also make it quite worthwhile to devise a new architecture for further reducing cross talk. The associative memory architecture proposed in this paper eliminates not only cross talk due to the memorized keys having odd number Hamming distance from the input key but also the still remaining cross talk having even number Hamming distance from the input key. In addition, this proposed architecture considerably reduces the number of cross products to be used compared to the conventional higher order correlational associative memory architectures. It can be highly appreciated that, by utilizing an alternate property of the Krawtchouk polynomial, we have achieved further advanced cross talk reduction and we have achieved almost exact data retrieval in the proposed architecture. As a result of this reduction, we have exemplified experimentally the perfect data recall of 9 dimensional datum vector associated with 11 dimensional key vector. In the conventional way of constructing associative memory, the only way to improve data retrieval performance is to employ the next higher order correlation, or to increase the number of cross products in a single step, and no intermediate range of cross product number can be used. In the architecture proposed in this paper, we do not need to increase the number of cross products in a single step and the intermediate step mentioned earlier can be utilized. The recalling characteristics for the larger data and keys has to be conducted for concrete evaluation of this architecture and is currently being investigated with great enthusiasm.

Acknowledgment

The author is grateful to Prof. K. Honda of Dept. of Mathematics, Muroran Institute of Technology, for helpful discussions, and Mr. O. Takeuchi for helpful numerical computation and simulation.

References

[1] T. Kohonen,"Correlation matrix Memories," IEEE Trans. Compt., 21., pp. 353-359, 1972.
[2] S. Amari, "Neural theory of association and concept formulation," Biol. Cyber., 26., pp. 175-185, 1977.
[3] J.J. Hopfield, "Neurons with graded response collective computational properties like those of two-state neurons," in Proc. Nat. Acad. Scie. (USA), 81., pp. 3088-3092, 1984.
[4] G. Szegoe, Orthogonal Polynomials, Coll. Pub., 23, Amer. Math. Soc.: New York, 1959.
[5] P. Baldi and S.S. Venkatesh, "Number of stable points for spin glasses and neural networks of higher orders," Phys. Rev. Lett., 58., pp. 913-915, 1987.
[6] R.J. McEliece, E.C. Posner, E.R. Rodemich and S.S. Venkatesh, " The capacity of the Hopfield associative memory," IEEE Trans. Inf. Theo., 33., 4., pp. 461-482, 1987.
[7] D. Psaltis, C.H. Park and J. Hong, "Higher order associative memory and the optical implementation," Neur.

Networks, 1., 2., pp. 149-163, 1988.

[8] X. Xu and W.T. Tsai, "Constructing associative memories using neural network," Neur. Networks, 3., 3., pp. 301-309, 1990.

[9] A.N. Michel and J.A. Farrell, "Associative memories via artificial neural networks," IEEE Contr. Syst. Magazine, 10., 3., pp. 6-17, 1990.

[10] Y. Kumagai, et al.,"Artificial cross talk reduction of associative memory," in Proc. of IEEE/INNS Int'l. Joint Conf. on Neural Networks, Baltimore, 2., pp. 153-159, 1992.

[11] Y. Kumagai, et al.,"A novel architecture of high order associative memory with reduced cross talk," Neural Networks 2, I. Alexander and J. Taylor (eds.), 1., pp. 417-420, 1992.

[12] Y. Kumagai, et al., "Further cross talk reduction of associative memory and exact data retrieval," in Proc. of IEEE Int'l. Conf. on Neural Networks, San Francisco, 3., pp. 1371-1378, 1993.

[13] Y. Kumagai, et al., "Exact data retrieval of associative memory based on cross talk formulation," in Proc. of IEEE Int'l. Symp. on Circuits and Systems, Chicago, 4., pp. 2395-2398, 1993.

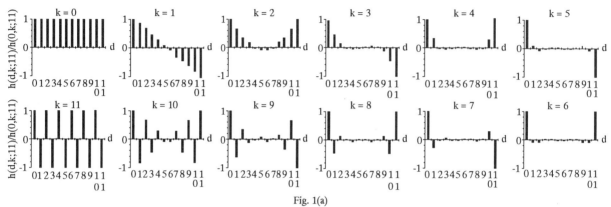

Fig. 1(a)

Fig. 1(a). Normalized h(d, k ; n) by h(0, k ; n) for m=9, n=11. |h(d, k ; n)| is symmetric with respect to d and k . Especially in the latter case, it should be noticed that, for odd d, h(d, k ; n) for k and (n - k) are equal in magnitude but opposite in sign. This property plays an important role in designing higher order correlation associative memory with reduced cross talk.

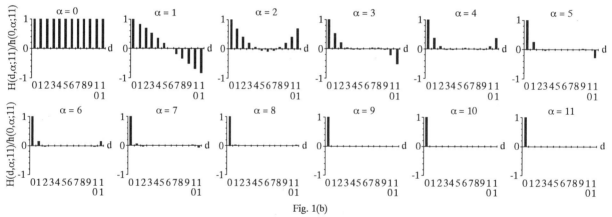

Fig. 1(b)

Fig. 1(b). Normalized H(d, α ; n) by H(0, α ; n) for m=9, n=11. H(0, α; n) > |H(d, α; n)| for any nonzero d and α. |H(d,α; n) | is symmetric with respect to d, attains comparatively lower value for d around n/2 and decreases monotonically with increasing α.

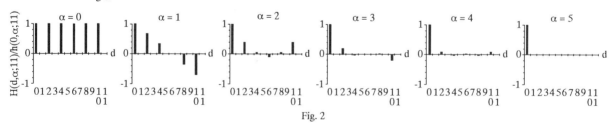

Fig. 2

Fig. 2. Behavior of cross talk of the proposed architecture. This shows the complete elimination of cross due to the memorized keys having odd Hamming distance from the input key.

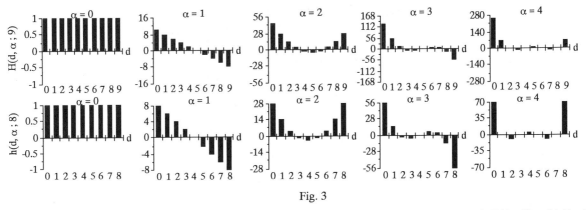

Fig. 3

Fig. 3. Numerical computation exemplifying the property shown in theorem [8] for α=0 to α=4, n=9, H(d,α;9) and h(d,α;8).

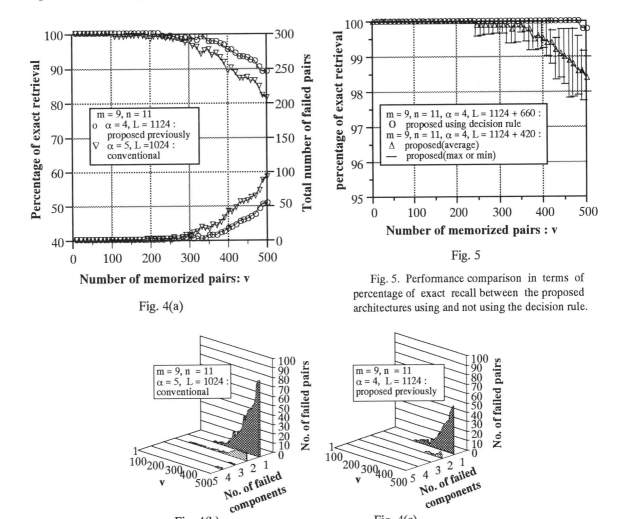

Fig. 4(a)

Fig. 5

Fig. 5. Performance comparison in terms of percentage of exact recall between the proposed architectures using and not using the decision rule.

Fig. 4(b)

Fig. 4(c)

Fig. 4. (a) Comparison of retrieval ability among the two architectures in terms of percentage of exact recall and number of failed pairs. Number of failed components in the failed pairs against memorized pairs: (b) Conventional architecture (c) Previously proposed architecture. α is the order of extension, L is the number of cross products used in each architecture, and v is the number of memorized pairs.

# INFORMATION THEORY ANALYSIS OF
# HEBBIAN-TYPE ASSOCIATIVE MEMORIES (HAMs)

Qi Yu and Thomas F. Krile
Electrical Engineering Department
Texas Tech University
Lubbock, TX 79409

This material is based in part upon work supported by the Texas Advanced Research Program under Grant No.003644-067

## ABSTRACT

A Hebbian-type associative memory with outer-product training is analyzed here. Previous results, giving probability of one-step recall in terms of the number of neurons N, number of stored patterns M, and number of input error bits, b, are used to form an information channel model of the network. With this model, the network's mutual information , I, is derived. From this measure a "channel capacity", indicating optimal performance in terms of N, M, and b is found. The mutual information is obtained for both first and second order systems.

## 1. INTRODUCTION

The concept of applying information theory to the study of neural networks has been promoted by a number of researchers since the seminal work of Linsker [1]. Among these are Takahashi [2], who postulated a new biological model, Jones, et.al. [3] who examined general feedforward networks, and Kamimura [4] who studied competitive learning models.

The work presented in this paper differs in that information theory concepts are applied to Hebbian-type associative memories (HAMs) which are characterized by an outer-product learning rule. We assume a network of N neurons storing M pattern vectors where each vector component is +1 or -1 with equal probability and all components are independent. In order to examine the generalization capability of these networks, a parameter, b, is included which is the number of input vector bit errors. In previous work [5], it was shown that a single signal-to-noise parameter, C, which is a known function of N, M and b, can be used to completely characterize the performance of a HAM. In particular, the one-step probability of correct recall, Pc, can be expressed as a function of C for linear as well as quadratic HAMs.

In this work, we build on these previous results to construct an information channel model for a HAM based on communication channel ideas. We show that the HAM's mutual information $I(X,Y) = Pc*H(X)$ where $H(X)$ is the entropy of the input pattern set. Since Pc is a known function of C and C is itself a known function of N, M and b, we now have a measure of the network information transfer in terms of the network parameters.

## 2. A COMMUNICATION CHANNEL FOR MODELING HAMs

Let V1,V2,... Vm be M prescribed N bit binary patterns to be stored in a first order HAM of size N. Using a signal-to-noise (S/N) analysis, the probability of direct recall is found to be [5] :

$$P ( correct ) = ( 1 - \eta )^N, \tag{1}$$

where $\eta$ is given, as a function of the parameter $C = |S/\sigma_n| \approx (N-2b-1)/\sqrt{(N-1)(M-1)}$ , by :

$$\eta = \frac{1}{\sqrt{2\pi}} \int_C^\infty \exp(-z^2/2)\, dz \ .$$

(2)

Assuming at first that there are no error bits in the test patterns, we can model the HAM as a communication channel as shown in Fig.1.

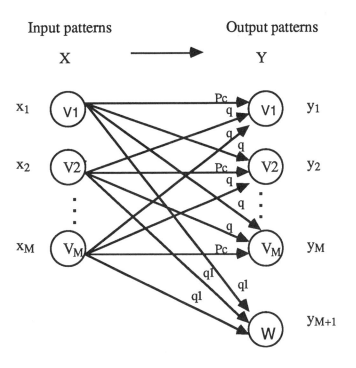

Fig.1 Communication channel model of a HAM

In Fig.1, W includes all possible wrong outputs which do not belong to the M prescribed patterns. Pc = P(correct) is the probability of getting a correct output in one iteration and it is determined by the C parameter, $C = \sqrt{N-1}/\sqrt{M-1}$ [5]. q is the probability of getting an incorrect output where the output is one of the prescribed patterns. q1 is the probability of getting an incorrect output which belongs to the W group.

Because there are $2^N$ possible output patterns, we find that

$$q = \frac{1}{2^N - 1} (1 - Pc) = P(y_i \mid x_j) , \quad i, j = 1, M; \quad i \neq j$$

and

$$q1 = \frac{2^N - M}{2^N - 1} (1 - Pc) = P(w \mid x_i), \quad i = 1, M \ .$$

Now that all the transition probabilities between each input and output pattern in our model are known, we can begin our entropy calculations. Assuming that the input patterns have a uniform distribution (a constraint that will be relaxed later), the source information content is defined as:

$$H(X) = -\sum_{i=1}^{M} P(x_i) \log_2 P(x_i) = \log_2 M \quad . \tag{3}$$

The average uncertainty of the source given the received output is defined as the conditional entropy function:

$$H(X \mid Y) = -\sum_{i=1}^{M} \sum_{j=1}^{M+1} P(x_i, y_j) \log_2 P(x_i \mid y_j) \quad . \tag{4}$$

Because $y_{M+1} = W$, we can rewrite Eq. (4) as:

$$H(X \mid Y) = -\sum_{i=1}^{M} \sum_{j=1}^{M} P(x_i, y_j) \log_2 P(x_i \mid y_j) - \sum_{i=1}^{M} P(x_i, w) \log_2 P(x_i \mid w) \quad . \tag{5}$$

For $1 \leq i, j \leq M$, $i \neq j$, we obtain :

$$P(x_i, y_i) = P(y_i \mid x_i) P(x_i) = \frac{Pc}{M} \quad , \text{ and thus} \tag{6}$$

$$P(x_i \mid y_i) = \frac{P(x_i, y_i)}{P(y_i)} = \frac{P(x_i, y_i)}{\sum\limits_{k=1}^{M} P(y_i \mid x_k) * P(x_k)} = \frac{Pc}{Pc + (M-1)q} \quad . \tag{7}$$

Also, $P(x_i, y_j) = P(y_j \mid x_i) P(x_i) = \dfrac{q}{M}$, from which

$$\tag{8}$$

$$P(x_i \mid y_j) = \frac{P(x_i, y_j)}{P(y_j)} = \frac{P(x_i, y_j)}{\sum\limits_{k=1}^{M} P(y_j \mid x_k) * P(x_k)} = \frac{q}{Pc + (M-1)q} \quad . \tag{9}$$

Finally, $P(x_i, w) = P(w \mid x_i) P(x_i) = \dfrac{q1}{M}$, so

$$\tag{10}$$

$$P(x_i \mid w) = \frac{P(x_i, w)}{P(w)} = \frac{P(x_i, w)}{\sum\limits_{k=1}^{M} P(w \mid x_k) * P(x_k)} = \frac{1}{M} \quad . \tag{11}$$

Substituting Eqs. (6) - (11) into Eq. (5), we find that

$$H(X \mid Y) = -M * \frac{Pc}{M} * \log_2 P(x_i \mid y_i) - M(M-1) * \frac{q}{M} * \log_2 P(x_i \mid y_j) - M * \frac{q1}{M} * \log_2 P(x_i \mid w) \quad . \tag{12}$$

If N is sufficiently large, ie., $2^N \gg M$, $q \to 0$, $q1 \to 1-Pc$, $P(x_i \mid y_i) \to 1$ and $P(x_i \mid y_j) \to 0$ simultaneously, so $H(X \mid Y)$ can be simplified as :

$$H(X \mid Y) = (1 - Pc) \log_2 M = (1 - Pc) H(X) \quad . \tag{13}$$

Mutual information is defined as : $\quad I(X, Y) = H(X) - H(X \mid Y)$,

so in this channel model the mutual information is given by:

$$I(X, Y) = Pc * H(X) = P(\text{correct}) * H(X) \quad . \tag{14}$$

Using Eqs. (14), (1) and (2), we can get the relationship between the C parameter value and information transfer as :

$$I(X,Y) = (1 - \eta)^N \log_2 M$$

$$= \left[ 1 - \frac{1}{\sqrt{2\pi}} \int_C^{\infty} \exp(-z^2/2) \, dz \right]^N \log_2 M \quad . \tag{15}$$

Many computer simulations were performed to check the probability assumptions that were made in the derivation of Eq.(14) . As an example, consider a linear HAM with 50 neurons and 5 input patterns, $(N, M) = (50, 5)$. Using $C = |S/\sigma_n| = \sqrt{N-1}/\sqrt{M-1}$ ( for b=0) , we find that C=3.500, from which P(correct)=0.99 [using Eqs(1-2)].The simulation results for the probability values $P(y_i \mid x_i)$, $P(y_i \mid x_j)$ and $P(w \mid x_i)$ are shown in Table 1.

From this table we can see: $Pc = P(y_i \mid x_i) \rightarrow P(correct)$, $q=P(y_i \mid x_j) \rightarrow 0$, and $q1=P(w \mid x_i) \rightarrow 1-P(correct)$. This means that all the assumptions that were made in the derivation of Eq.(14) agree with this practical case and thus it supports the accuracy of Eq. (14).

## 3. INFORMATION THEORY ANALYSIS FOR MORE GENERAL CASES

We only dealt with the no-input-error bit case in the previous analysis. If error bits are present in the test input patterns, we need to change the previous channel model slightly in order to calculate the information transfer (see Fig.2).

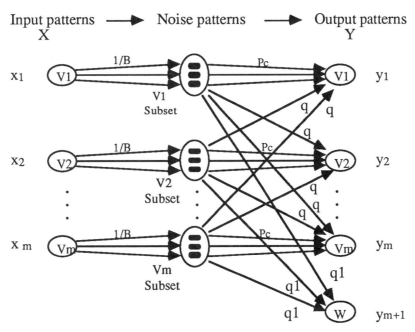

Fig.2 Communication channel model with input error bits

In this model , the number of elements of each noise subset is equal to $B = C_b^N$ , where b is the number of error bits in each test pattern and $C_b^N = N! / b!(N-b)!$ . Assuming that the error bits are uniformly distributed inside each subset, the probability connection between each input pattern and an element of its subset is 1/B. Pc is the transition probability between an element of the ith input subset and the ith stored pattern, q is the transition probability between an element of the ith input subset and the jth stored pattern and q1 is the transition probability between an element of the ith input subset and the wrong output group, W.

As in the previous discussion, Pc = P(correct), which is determined by the C parameter, and

$$q = \frac{1}{2^N - 1}(1 - Pc), \qquad q1 = \frac{2^N - M}{2^N - 1}(1 - Pc).$$

Following a procedure similar to the previous b=0 case, it can be shown that Eqs.(14) and (15) still hold.

It has been shown that the performance of higher order HAMs can also be characterized by a C parameter [6]. Thus the previous information theory analysis can be applied directly to higher order HAMs. Using the same assumptions that were made in the previous proof (if N is sufficiently large, ie., $2^N \gg M$, $q \to 0$, $q1 \to 1\text{-}Pc$, $P(x_i \mid y_i) \to 1$ and $P(x_i \mid y_j) \to 0$ simultaneously), it can be shown that in the second order HAM (QAM) case, $I(X,Y)$ = P(correct) * H(X) as before [7].

Until now, we assumed that the input patterns had a uniform distribution. It has been shown [7] that the relation $I(X,Y)$ = P(correct) * H(X) still holds for any distribution by following a procedure similar to the previous uniform distribution case.

In communication theory, a key parameter is channel capacity, which is defined as $I(X,Y)$ maximized over all possible input probability distributions. For the case of equally likely input patterns, we can now easily find the "channel capacity" equivalent of a HAM (see Figs.3-4) or a QAM (see Fig.5). For fixed N in the HAM case, we find that the value of M which maximizes $I(X,Y)$ for high Pc is approximately 0.1* N, which is the same as the empirically derived rule-of-thumb used for the capacity of first order HAMs. Also, as B increases, $I(X,Y)$ is maximized at lower values of M, which is consistent with the reduction of memory capacity as input errors increase. In these curves, T means theoretical results from Eq.(15) and S means results from computer simulations.

## 5. CONCLUSION

The information theory analysis of HAMs reported here has been shown to accurately predict the performance of networks with varying N, M and b using both first and second order input correlations. This method can be extended to find the network weights which provide the greatest information transfer and thus can be used to design high performance networks with a reduced number of interconnections.

REFERENCE:
1. R. Linsker, "Self-organization in a perceptual network", Computer, Vol. 21, 105-117, March, 1988.
2. T. Takahashi, "An information theoretical interpretation of neuronal activities", IJCNN Proc., Vol. II, Seattle, WA, 1991.
3. R. Jones, C. Barnes, Y. Lee and W. Mead, "Information theoretic derivation of network architecture and learning algorithms", IJCNN Proc., Vol. II, Seattle, WA, 1991.
4. R. Kamimura, "Minimum entropy methods in neural networks: competition and selective responses by entropy minimization", IJCNN Proc., Vol. I, San Francisco, CA, 1993.
5. J.H. Wang, T.F. Krile and J.F. Walkup, "Determination of Hopfield associative memory characteristics using a single parameter ", Neural Networks, Vol.3, No.3, 319 - 331, 1990.
6. J.H. Wang, "Performance Characteristics of Higher Order Neural Network Associative Memories", Ph.D. Dissertation, Dept. of Electrical Engineering, Texas Tech University, Lubbock, TX, May,1991.
7. Qi Yu, "Information theory applied to neural networks", M.S. Thesis, Dept. of Electrical Engineering, Texas Tech University, Lubbock, TX, May,1993.

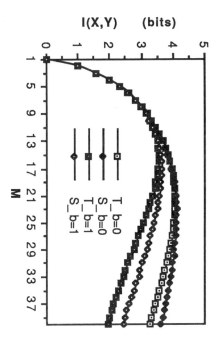

Fig.5 Mutual information I(X,Y) versus M in second order HAM (N=20)

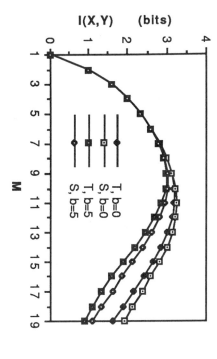

Fig.3 Mutual information I(X,Y) versus M in first order HAM (N=100)

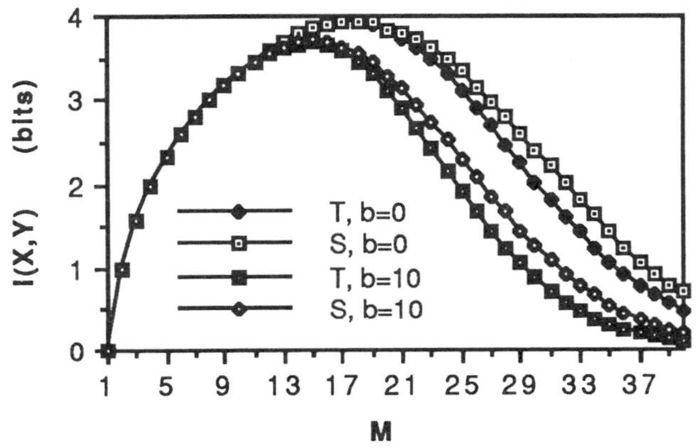

Fig.4 Mutual information I(X,Y) versus M in first order HAM (N=200)

Table 1. Probability connections in the communication model

| Output / Input | V1 | V2 | V3 | V4 | V5 | W |
|---|---|---|---|---|---|---|
| V1 | 0.993 | 0 | 0 | 0 | 0 | 0.007 |
| V2 | 0 | 0.993 | 0 | 0 | 0 | 0.007 |
| V3 | 0 | 0 | 0.993 | 0 | 0 | 0.007 |
| V4 | 0 | 0 | 0 | 0.993 | 0 | 0.007 |
| V5 | 0 | 0 | 0 | 0 | 0.993 | 0.007 |

# An attractor neural network model of associative memory at low spike rates with fast inhibitory interneurons

Anthony N. Burkitt*

*Computer Sciences Laboratory, Research School of Information Sciences and Engineering, Australian National University, Canberra, ACT 0200, Australia*

**Abstract.** The mean field formalism of attractor neural networks described in terms of spike rates and currents is extended to networks of interacting excitatory and inhibitory neurons in which the inhibitory neurons have a *fast* response to the excitatory neurons. Such a network of integrate-and-fire neurons with unstructured inhibition has attractors with uniform low firing rates that correspond to the retrieval of single patterns. Pattern mixtures are suppressed by the network. In the case where there are extensively many patterns, the analysis is carried out in the replica symmetric approximation.

## 1. Introduction

Studies of attractor neural networks [1, 2] have developed to incorporate a number of features that make them increasingly plausible as neurophysiological models. In a series of recent papers Amit and Tsodyks [3, 4] (hereafter referred to as ATI and ATII respectively) investigated a network of noisy integrate-and-fire neurons. They showed that such a description in terms of individual spikes can be converted to an effective description in terms of current dynamics driven by spike rates. The current induces a spike rate described by a neural gain function, thus providing a closed set of dynamical equations for the currents. The network is analysed using mean field theory and allows the retrieval of patterns at low spike rates, while being stable to the admixture of additional patterns. Furthermore, the various approximations involved are quite realistic in typical cortical conditions.

In this paper the above work is extended to describe a coupled excitatory-inhibitory network in which the individual neurons are either excitatory or inhibitory, in contrast to standard Hopfield-type models, in which the neurons do not possess such specificity. In this model information is stored only on the synapses between excitatory neurons, whose cooperative dynamics is thus responsible for the associative storage of the patterns and their recall, in accord with the common view in neuroanatomy [5]. The inhibitory neurons serve to control the activity of the excitatory neurons through a feedback process. In general, such systems cannot be described by an energy function and they allow the existence of a rich dynamical behaviour that is difficult to analyse in any generality. However, in the limit of *fast* inhibitory neurons, in which the characteristic time constant $\mathcal{T}^I$ of the decay of their afferent current is vanishingly small in comparison with that of the excitatory neurons, an energy function is found and an analysis of the behaviour of the model is carried out using the standard techniques involving the free energy [2, 6]. In this approximation the inhibitory neurons are assumed to operate so fast relative to the excitatory neurons that they provide an inhibitory influence that instantanously reflects the activity of the excitatory neurons. This approximation has the twofold advantage that it may be analysed using well known and powerful techniques and also that the fixed points are exactly the same as those of the more general ($\mathcal{T}^I \neq 0$) dynamical equations, and it may therefore provide

---

*email: tony@nimbus.anu.edu.au

some insight into this more complex system. Although an instantaneous reaction time for the inhibitory neurons clearly doesn't correspond to the neurophysiological situation, it may nevertheless partially capture the shorter transmission times for inhibitory signals that results from the more local nature of inhibitory neurons.

This approach of introducing fast inhibition was first adopted in the study of networks with low temporal firing rates [7, 8], where the excitatory connection matrix was of the Hopfield type and the inhibition had a very specific pattern dependent form. This structured inhibition was introduced in order to counterbalance the tendency of the Hopfield excitatory connections to enhance the retrieval of pattern mixtures. In the present work it is shown that such pattern mixtures are suppressed *without* any structure in the inhibition.

Coupled excitatory-inhibitory networks have been investigated in a variety of contexts [9, 10, 11], where the need for structured inhibition was overcome by introducing an excitatory network with a Willshaw synaptic structure [12]. In [10, 11] the neurons had a membrane potential below the spiking threshold, and spikes were generated by noise. Although the coupled network produced low rates of firing, the noise had the effect that the patterns being recalled were not stable. In [9] the inhibition was modelled to act non-linearly and recall was achieved by the relaxation of the network to a limit cycle. However there is some uncertainty about the extent to which the stability of the pattern retrieval was due to the non-linearity or a lingering neural memory caused by the random serial updating procedure [13].

## 2. The model

Following the notation of ATII, the effective network dynamics in terms of the rates $\nu_i^E, \nu_i^I$ of the excitatory and inhibitory neurons and their afferent currents $I_i^E, I_i^I$ is:

$$
\begin{aligned}
\frac{dI_i^E(t)}{dt} &= -\frac{1}{\mathcal{T}^E} I_i^E(t) + \sum_{j=1}^{N_E} J_{ij}^{EE} \nu_j^E(t) + \sum_{j=1}^{N_I} J_{ij}^{EI} \nu_j^I(t) \\
\frac{dI_i^I(t)}{dt} &= -\frac{1}{\mathcal{T}^I} I_i^I(t) + \sum_{j=1}^{N_E} J_{ij}^{IE} \nu_j^E(t) + \sum_{j=1}^{N_I} J_{ij}^{II} \nu_j^I(t)
\end{aligned}
\tag{2.1}
$$

where the $\mathcal{T}^A$ are the time decay constants, $J_{ij}^{AB}$ is the synaptic matrix, and the $N_A$ are the number of neurons of each type ($A = E$ or $I$ for excitatory and inhibitory neurons respectively). The rate is given by the integrate-and-fire relation [3] $\nu_i^A = \phi(I_i^A)$:

$$
\phi_A(I^A) = \left\{ 1 + \tau_A \frac{\sqrt{\pi}}{\sigma_A} \int_0^{\theta_A} dz \exp\left( \frac{(z - I - \mu_A)^2}{\sigma_A^2} \right) \left[ \mathrm{erf}\left( \frac{z - I - \mu_A}{\sigma_A} \right) + 1 \right] \right\}^{-1}
\tag{2.2}
$$

where $\tau_A$ is the time constant for the membrane depolarization, $\theta_A$ is the threshold, and $\mu_A$ and $\sigma_A$ are the mean and RMS of the afferent noise, all of which may be different for the two populations of neurons.

The synaptic matrix is chosen as follows:

$$
\begin{aligned}
J_{ij}^{EE} &= \frac{1}{\mathcal{T}_E N_E} \left( \frac{1}{f} \sum_\mu^p \eta_i^\mu \eta_j^\mu + \lambda_E \right) \quad , \quad i \neq j; \qquad & J_{ii}^{EE} &= 0 \\
J_{ij}^{EI} &= \frac{-\rho_E}{\mathcal{T}_E N_I} \quad , \qquad & J_{ij}^{IE} &= \frac{\lambda_I}{\mathcal{T}_I f N_E} \\
J_{ij}^{II} &= \frac{-\rho_I}{\mathcal{T}_I N_I}, \quad i \neq j; \qquad & J_{ii}^{II} &= 0
\end{aligned}
\tag{2.3}
$$

where the $\eta^\mu$, $\mu = 1, .., p$ are the random $N$-bit memorized patterns on the $N_E$ excitatory neurons, a fraction $f$ of which are one and the remainder of which are zero.

The arrival of the network at an attractor is characterized by a set of neurons remaining quiesent while the remaining neurons fire at a substantially higher rate for some macroscopic time. The quality of retrieval of the patterns is characterized by the similarity of the firing rates $\nu_i$ to the stored patterns $\eta_i^\mu$:

$$m_\mu^+ = \frac{1}{fN_E}\sum_{i=1}^{N_E}\eta_i^\mu < \nu_i^E > \quad , \quad m_\mu^- = \frac{1}{(1-f)N_E}\sum_{i=1}^{N_E}(1-\eta_i^\mu) < \nu_i^E >$$

$$m_\mu = m_\mu^+ - m_\mu^- = \frac{1}{f(1-f)N_E}\sum_{i=1}^{N_E}(\eta_i^\mu - f) < \nu_i^E > \tag{2.4}$$

where $m_\mu^+$ and $m_\mu^-$ are the mean firing rates of the neurons in the foreground and background respectively. The rates are measured as the number of spikes per absolute refractory period. In addition to $m_\mu$ there are also the average firing rates of the two sets of neurons:

$$m_0 = \frac{1}{N_E}\sum_{i=1}^{N_E} < \nu_i^E > \quad , \quad \bar{m} = \frac{1}{N_I}\sum_{i=1}^{N_I} < \nu_i^I > \tag{2.5}$$

## 3. Mean-field equations in the limit $\mathcal{T}_I \to 0$

In the limit of *fast* inhibitory neurons the model can be analysed using the standard techniques [6, 14, 15]. The inhibitory current $I_i^I$ comes instantaneously to equilibrium, providing an inhibition to the afferent current of the excitatory neurons:

$$\frac{dI_i^E(t)}{dt} = -\frac{1}{\mathcal{T}^E}I_i^E(t) + \sum_{j=1}^{N_E}J_{ij}^{EE}\nu_j^E(t) - \frac{\rho_E}{\mathcal{T}^E}\Psi\left(\frac{\lambda_I}{fN_E}\sum_{j=1}^{N_E}\nu_j^E\right) \tag{3.1}$$

where the function $\Psi$ is defined (via its inverse) by the relation

$$\Psi^{-1}(x) = \phi_I^{-1}(x) + \rho_I x \tag{3.2}$$

(a small non-zero noise $\sigma_I$ in eq. (2.2) ensures that $\phi_I^{-1}$, and hence also $\Psi^{-1}$, is single valued). The above dynamical equation for $I_i^E(t)$ can be written in the form

$$\mathcal{T}_E\frac{dI_i^E(t)}{dt} = -\frac{\partial H}{\partial \nu_i^E} \tag{3.3}$$

with the Lyapanov function

$$H = -\frac{\mathcal{T}_E}{2}\sum_{i,j;j\neq i}^{N_E}J_{ij}^{EE}\nu_i^E\nu_j^E + \sum_j^{N_E}G(\nu_j^E) + \rho_E\int_0^{\sum_j^{N_E}\nu_j^E}du\,\Psi\left(\frac{\lambda_I}{fN_E}u\right) \tag{3.4}$$

where $G(\nu) = \int_0^\nu I(\nu')d\nu'$. The free energy and the partition function are defined as usual by (dropping the sub- and super-scripts $E$):

$$F_N(\beta) = -\frac{1}{\beta N}\ln Z \quad , \quad Z = \int \prod_{i=1}^N d\nu_i \exp(-\beta H) \tag{3.5}$$

where the $\nu$-integrals are over the interval $[0,1]$.

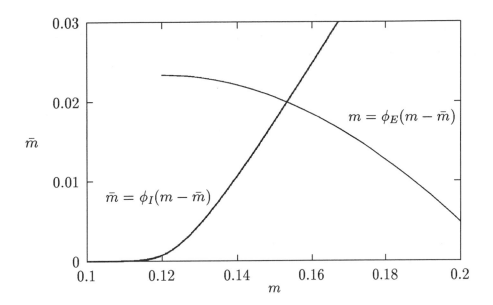

Figure 1: The solution plot of the two mean-field equations with $\tau_{E,I} = 4$, $\theta_{E,I} = 0.25$, $\mu_E = 0.20$, $\mu_I = 0.10$, $\sigma_{E,I} = 0.0125$.

## 3.1 Finitely many patterns

If the number of patterns $p$ remains fixed as $N$ increases (i.e., $\alpha = p/N \to 0$) the free energy may be calculated using standard techniques. The inclusion of the $\Psi$-term is facilitated by introducing a variable $\varepsilon = \frac{1}{N}\sum_i^N \nu_i$ and a momentum $\upsilon$ conjugate to $\varepsilon$, in order to impose this constraint. The free energy is then given by

$$
\begin{aligned}
F(\beta) &= \lim_{N\to\infty} F_N(\beta) = \frac{f}{2}\sum_\mu (m_\mu^+)^2 + \frac{\lambda_E}{2}m_0^2 + \varepsilon\upsilon - \rho_E \int_0^\varepsilon du\,\Psi\left(\frac{\lambda_I}{f}u\right) \\
&\quad - \frac{1}{\beta}\left\langle\!\left\langle \ln\int_0^1 d\nu \exp\beta\left\{\sum_\mu^p m_\mu^+\eta^\mu\nu + \lambda_E m_0\nu + \upsilon\nu - G(\nu)\right\}\right\rangle\!\right\rangle
\end{aligned}
\tag{3.6}
$$

The resulting mean-field equations are

$$
fm_\mu^+ = \langle\!\langle \eta^\mu[\nu]_\eta\rangle\!\rangle \quad,\quad m_0 = \varepsilon = \langle\!\langle [\nu]_\eta\rangle\!\rangle \quad,\quad \upsilon = -\rho_E\Psi\left(\frac{\lambda_I}{f}\varepsilon\right)
\tag{3.7}
$$

with the notation

$$
[\nu]_\eta = \frac{\int_0^1 d\nu\,\nu \exp\beta\left\{\left(\sum_\mu^p m_\mu^+\eta^\mu + \lambda_E m_0 + \upsilon\right)\nu - G(\nu)\right\}}{\int_0^1 d\nu \exp\beta\left\{\left(\sum_\mu^p m_\mu^+\eta^\mu + \lambda_E m_0 + \upsilon\right)\nu - G(\nu)\right\}}
\tag{3.8}
$$

which in the $\beta \to \infty$ (zero temperature) limit becomes

$$
[\nu]_\eta = \phi_E(\sum_\mu m_\mu^+\eta^\mu + \lambda_E m_0 - \rho_E\Psi(\frac{\lambda_I}{f}m_0))
\tag{3.9}
$$

In the pure Hebbian limit ($\lambda_E \to 0$) and for a small noise distribution $\sigma_E$ (so that $\phi_E(-\rho_E\bar{m})$ can be neglected) the mean field equations reduce to

$$
m = \phi_E(m - \rho_E\bar{m}) \quad,\quad m_0 = fm \quad,\quad \bar{m} = \phi_I(\lambda_I m - \rho_I\bar{m})
\tag{3.10}
$$

Each equation gives a solution trajectory in the $m - \bar{m}$-plane, as plotted in figure 1 for $\lambda_I = \rho_E = \rho_I = 1$ and typical parameter values. The mean field solution is given by the point of intersection of the two trajectories.

The mean field equations for the symmetric mixture of two states has been investigated and it is found that such mixture states are suppressed for sparsely coded patterns (small $f$). This result may be understood simply by the fact that the simultaneous activation of two patterns would induce an overall inhibition so large as to suppress all activity in the network.

### 3.2 Extensively many patterns

If the ratio of the number of patterns to the number of neurons remains finite as $N$ increases (i.e., $\alpha = p/N \neq 0$) the free energy per neuron may be evaluated by the replica method [14, 15, 6]. Introducing the conjugate variables $\varepsilon$ and $v$ as before, the free energy in the replica symmetric approximation is

$$
\begin{aligned}
F(\beta) &= \frac{f}{2}\sum_\mu (m_\mu^+)^2 + \frac{\lambda_E}{2}m_0^2 + \varepsilon v - \rho_E \int_0^\varepsilon du\, \Psi\left(\frac{\lambda_I}{f}u\right) \\
&+ \frac{\alpha\beta}{2}(r_0 q_0 - rq) + \frac{\alpha}{2\beta}\left(\ln[1 - \beta(q_0 - q)] - \frac{\beta q}{1 - \beta(q_0 - q)}\right) \\
&- \frac{1}{\beta}\left\langle\!\!\left\langle \ln\int_0^1 dv\, \exp\beta\left\{\left(\sum_\mu^p m_\mu^+\eta^\mu + \lambda_E m_0 + \sqrt{\alpha r}\,z + v\right)v\right.\right.\right. \\
&\left.\left.\left. + \frac{\alpha}{2}(\beta(r_0 - r) - 1)v^2 - G(v)\right\}\right\rangle\!\!\right\rangle
\end{aligned} \tag{3.11}
$$

The resulting mean-field equations are

$$
\begin{aligned}
fm_\mu^+ &= \langle\!\langle \eta^\mu [v]_\eta\rangle\!\rangle & , & & m_0 &= \varepsilon = \langle\!\langle [v]_\eta\rangle\!\rangle \\
q_0 &= \langle\!\langle [v^2]_\eta\rangle\!\rangle & , & & q &= \langle\!\langle [v]_\eta^2\rangle\!\rangle \\
r_0 &= \frac{1}{\beta[1-\beta(q_0-q)]} + \frac{q}{[1-\beta(q_0-q)]^2} & & & & \\
r &= \frac{q}{[1-\beta(q_0-q)]^2} & , & & v &= -\rho_E\Psi\left(\frac{\lambda_I}{f}\varepsilon\right)
\end{aligned} \tag{3.12}
$$

with the notation

$$
[Z(v)]_{\eta,z} = \frac{\int_0^1 dv\, Z(v)\exp[\beta H(v,z)]}{\int_0^1 dv\, \exp[\beta H(v,z)]} \tag{3.13}
$$

$$
H(v,z) = \left(\sum_\mu^p m_\mu^+\eta^\mu + \lambda_E m_0 + \sqrt{\alpha r}\,z + v\right)v + \frac{\alpha}{2}\frac{\beta(q_0-q)}{1-\beta(q_0-q)}v^2 - G(v)
$$

In the $\beta \to \infty$ limit $v$ is determined as the solution of the implicit equation

$$
v_\eta(z) = \phi_E\left(\sum_\mu m_\mu^+\eta^\mu + \lambda_E m_0 + z\frac{\sqrt{\alpha q}}{1-C} + \alpha\frac{C}{1-C}v_\eta(z) - \rho_E\Psi\left(\frac{\lambda_I}{f}m_0\right)\right) \tag{3.14}
$$

### 4. Discussion

The form of the inhibition considered above is *linear* (equation (1)). In order to model such effects as shunting, it is of interest to consider *non-linear* terms in the inhibitory interaction [9]. Such non-linear inhibition can be introduced straightforwardly into the formalism so long as the function is invertible, since it simply has the effect of modifying the form of the function $\Psi$.

In summary, it has been shown that a network of interacting excitatory and inhibitory integrate-and-fire neurons can be analysed using mean field theory in the limit in which the dynamics of the inhibitory neurons is fast in comparison to that of the excitatory neurons. The firing rates remain quite low, with the neurons in the foreground having mean firing rates which are well elevated compared with those in background. Investigations are currently under way to solve the replica symmetric mean field equations, to examine the validity of the replica symmetric approximation, and study the behaviour of the network for non-zero values of $T_I$ by means of simulations.

## References

[1] J.J. Hopfield, "Neural networks and physical systems with emergent collective computational abilities", *Proc. Natl. Sci.* **79** (1982) 2554–2558.

[2] D.J. Amit, *Modeling Brain Function: The world of attractor neural networks*, (Cambridge University Press, 1989).

[3] D.J. Amit and M.V. Tsodyks, "Quantitative study of attractor neural network retrieving at low spike rates: I.", *Network* **2** (1991) 259–273.

[4] D.J. Amit and M.V. Tsodyks, "Quantitative study of attractor neural network retrieving at low spike rates: II.", *Network* **2** (1991) 275–294.

[5] E.R. Kandel and J.R. Schwartz, *Principles of Neural Science*, (Elsevier, Amsterdam, 1985).

[6] D.J. Amit, H. Gutfreund, and H. Sompolinsky, "Statistical mechanics of neural networks near saturation", *Ann. Phys., NY* **173** (1987) 30–67.

[7] D.J. Amit and A. Treves, "Associative memory neural network with low temporal spiking rates", *Proc. Natl. Acad. Sci.* **86** (1989) 7871–7875.

[8] A. Treves and D.J. Amit, "Low firing rates: an effective Hamiltonian for excitaatory neurons", *J. Phys.* **A22** (1989) 2205–2226.

[9] J. Buhmann, "Oscillations and low firing rates in associative memory neural networks", *Phys. Rev.* **40** (1989) 4145–4148.

[10] N. Rubin and H. Sompolinsky, "Neural networks with low local firing rates", *Europhys. Lett.* **10** (1989) 465–470.

[11] D. Golomb, N. Rubin, and H. Sompolinsky, "Willshaw model: Associative memory with sparse coding and low firing rates", *Phys. Rev.* **41** (1990) 1843–1854.

[12] D. Willshaw, "Non-holographic associative memory", *Nature* **222** (1969) 960.

[13] D.J. Amit, M.R. Evans, and M. Abeles, "Attractor neural networks with biological probe records", *Network* **1** (1990) 381–405.

[14] R. Kühn, "Statistical mechanics for networks of analog neurons", In I. Garrido, *Statistical mechanics of neural networks*, (Springer, Berlin, 1990).

[15] M. Shiino and T. Fukai, "Replica-symmetric theory of the nonlinear analogue neural networks", *J. Phys.* **A23** (1990) L1009–L1017.

# Minimizing the Number of Weights for Prescribed Performance in Hebbian-Type Associative Memories

Qi Yu ,Thomas F.Krile

Department of Electrical Engineering

Texas Tech University

Lubbock, Tx 79409

This material is based in part upon work supported by the Texas Advanced Research Program under Grant No.003644-067

Abstract

This paper presents a new approach for the design of first order Hebbian-Type Associative Memory networks using a signal/noise analysis method. We develop a simple algorithm to find the optimal network structure which utilizes a minimum number of interconnection weights when the number of stored patterns , M, and the required one-step recall probability, P, are fixed. It is shown that such optimal networks also retain excellent generalization capabilities.

## 1. Introduction

Hebbian-Type Associative Memories (HAMS) based on the outer product rule have been studied extensively [1- 4]. Generally, in order to get high probability of correct recall, P, the first order HAM's size "N" must be on the order of ten times as large as the number of stored patterns "M" for $P \approx 90\%$. If we increase the number of neurons, "N," we can get higher recall capability, but the number of interconnection weighting terms also increases very fast because there are $O(N^2)$ weighted interconnections.

It is interesting to pose the following question: which network structure will utilize a minimum number of interconnection weights for a prescribed performance? In this paper we use a signal/noise analysis method [2,4] to find the effect of each value of the weights during one recall iteration for a first order HAM. Then we develop a simple algorithm to find the optimal network structure and minimum size when the number of stored patterns, M, and the required one-step recall probability, P, are fixed.

## 2. Relationship of weight values to signal/noise parameter, C

Let $V^1$, $V^2$, ..., $V^M$ be M prescribed N bit binary patterns to be stored in a first order HAM. Hebb's rule is incorporated by a correlation memory matrix " T " where:

$$T_{ij} = \sum_{k=1}^{M} V_i^k V_j^k \quad ; \quad 1 \le i,j \le N \text{ and } i \ne j .$$

(1)

Each bit of $V_i^k$ in Eq.(1) is considered to be an independent identically distributed random variable with equal probabilities of being +1 or -1. If M is an even number, $T_{ij}$ can be 0, $\pm 2$, $\pm 4$, $\pm 6$, ... $\pm M$ , and if M is an odd number, $T_{ij}$ can be $\pm 1$, $\pm 3$,$\pm 5$, $\pm 7$, ... $\pm M$ . $T_{ij}$ has a binomial distribution which can be determined as follows:

$$P(T_{ij} = D) = P(T_{ij} = -D) = \begin{pmatrix} M \\ \frac{M+D}{2} \end{pmatrix} * p^{\frac{M+D}{2}} * q^{\frac{M-D}{2}} \quad (\text{here } p = q = \frac{1}{2})$$

$$\approx \frac{2}{\sqrt{2\pi M}} \exp\left(-\frac{D^2}{2M}\right) \tag{2}$$

Thus, in each row of matrix " T ," the number of weights whose absolute value is D is

$$L_D = \begin{cases} \dfrac{4(N-1)}{\sqrt{2\pi M}} \exp\left(-\dfrac{D^2}{2M}\right) & (0 < D \le M) , \\[4mm] \dfrac{2(N-1)}{\sqrt{2\pi M}} & (D = 0) . \end{cases} \tag{3}$$

Let $V_i^q$ be the $i$ th bit of input vector q. After one step of the recall process:

$$V_i^q(t+1) = F_h\left(\sum_{j=1}^{N} T_{ij} V_j^q\right) \quad \text{where } i \ne j \text{ and } F_h(Y) = 1 \text{ if } Y \ge 0, F_h(Y) = -1 \text{ if } Y < 0.$$

If we only use $|T_{ij}| = D$ and set all other weights equal to zero, then

$$V_i^q(t+1) = F_h\left(\sum_{j_1=1}^{L_D} T_{ij_1} V_{j_1}^q\right) .$$

Here $j_1$ is the index of those $T_{ij}$ whose values are $+D$ or $-D$ . A new variable Y is defined:

$$Y = \sum_{j_1=1}^{L_D} T_{ij_1} V_{j_1}^q . \tag{4}$$

From [4], the absolute mean and standard deviation of Y are

$$|\mu_D| = L_D * \frac{D^2}{M} , \qquad \sigma_D = \sqrt{L_D} * \sqrt{D^2 - \frac{D^4}{M^2}} . \tag{5}$$

These terms have been shown to represent the signal and noise standard deviation values of this reduced network. Wang et al. [2] defined a parameter C=S/N for Hebbian-type associative memories where S is the signal value and N is the noise standard deviation. So in this case, if we only use the connection weights with absolute value equal to D, the C parameter value will be :

$$C_D = \frac{|\mu_D|}{\sigma_D} = \sqrt{L_D} * \frac{D}{\sqrt{M^2 - D^2}} , \tag{6}$$

which can be used to predict the probability of one - step recall [2].

From [2], the C parameter is related to the probability of one-step recall by:

$$\eta = P(\text{incorrect}) = \phi(C) = \frac{1}{\sqrt{2\pi}} \int_C^\infty \exp(-z^2/2) \, dz . \tag{7}$$

where $\eta = P(\text{incorrect})$ is the probability of a neuron being in an incorrect state after a single step update. The probability that all neurons are in a correct state after a single step update is

$$P = (1 - \eta)^N . \tag{8}$$

So by Eqs.(5-8) we can find the effect of each value of the weights during one recall iteration for a first order HAM.

## 3. An algorithm to find optimal network size

From the discussion in Sec. 2 , we know that $|T_{ij}| \geq D_0$ for some $D_0$ is the tail part of the histogram of $|T_{ij}|$ . It contributes only a small fraction of all weights if $D_0$ is large enough compared to M .Our approach is to examine using only this subset of weights to get a smaller network with high recall ability and good generalization capabilities.

In Eq.(6), the C parameter ($C_D$) comes from only using one value of weight with absolute value $|T_{ij}| = D$ . Usually this is not large enough to get high recall capability. Hence we combine the weights in the tail part of the histogram. Since different values of weights are statistically independent , the C=S/N will be:

$$C_{sum} = \left. \sum_{D=D_0}^{M} \mu_D \middle/ \sqrt{\sum_{D=D_0}^{M} \sigma_D^2} \right. \tag{9}$$

Now the only thing we do not know is the optimal $D_0$ , which we can obtain as follows:

Before we design a network, we assume that we know the desired number of stored patterns, M, and the required minimum one-step recall probability, P. For any given network size N, and a given neuron i, $\eta = P \, ( \text{incorrect} ) = 1 - P^{1/N}$. From [2] ,we know that for each $\eta$ there is a corresponding C value ( let's call it $C_0$ ). The relationship is shown by Eq.(7). Thus we can say $C_0 = \phi^{-1}(\eta)$ , and only if $C_{sum} \geq C_0$ can we get the desired or better recall probability P.

Replacing $C_{sum}$ by Eq.(9), we solve this inequality in this way:

Replace $D_0$ by M, M-2, M-4, ..., 2, 0 if M is an even number, or by M, M-2, M-4, ..., 3, 1 if M is an odd number. The largest possible integer solution is the $D_0$ that we need. If the largest possible solution is less than zero, this means that the network size N is not large enough to store M patterns with the required probability of correct recall, P, even if we use all the interconnection weights.

After we get $D_0$ , the total number of weights used in this design is:

$$\text{Number of weights} = \sum_{D=D_0}^{M} L_D \, , \tag{10}$$

where $L_D$ is given by Eq.(3). Varying N for fixed M and minimum recall probability P, we can get a theoretical curve showing the number of weights used in each case. As an example: for M =10, P = 94% , we get curve "T (P=94%)" in Fig.1. We used computer simulations to check the theoretical analysis,and the results are shown by the curve "S (P=96%)" in Fig.1. The theory and simulation results are very close for the same M value and slightly different P values, as will be discussed later.

From Fig.1, theoretically when M = 10 and P = 94%, many different neural network sizes, N, can satisfy the requirements on M and P, but there are some cases (e.g., N=150, N=275 ) which need a relatively small number of weights ( about 7500). In comparison , for M = 10 , P = 94% and a fully interconnected network, we would need N = 125 and 15625 interconnections.

The non-monotonic shape of the curves is due to the discrete property of the $D_0$ value and the distribution of weight values [Eq.(2)]. In Fig.1, when N=125, $D_0$ is equal to 2, we use all the weights with absolute value greater than or equal to 2. Similarly, when $150 \leq N \leq 250$, $D_0$ is equal to 4; when $275 \leq N \leq 500$, $D_0$ is equal to 6. Every time $D_0$ increases, we use a smaller fraction of all weights in the recall procedure.

We also investigated changing M for fixed N and P and got a theoretical curve showing the number of weights used in each case. Here is an example: for N =200, P = 96% , we got curve "T (P=96%)" in Fig.2. We used computer simulations to check the theoretical analysis, and the results are shown by the curves "S (P=98%)" in Fig. 2. The theory and simulation results are very close for the same N value and slightly different P values.

The non-monotonic shape of the curves is again due to the discrete property of the $D_0$ value and the distribution of weight values [Eq.(2)]. In Fig. 2, when M=5, $D_0$ is equal to 5, we only use all the weights with absolute value equal to 5 and the percentage of these weights is $P(|T_{ij}| = 5) \approx 5.8\%$ . When M=6, $D_0$ is equal to 4, we only use all the weights with absolute value greater than or equal to 4 and the percentage of these weights is $P(|T_{ij}| \geq 4) \approx 20.3\%$ . Similarly we can explain all the points of Fig. 2.

In Figs.1-2, the simulation recall probability, P, is higher than in the corresponding theoretical cases by about two percentage points. This constant bias (due to the simplicity of the model for high performance networks) can be built into the design process for obtaining a minimum interconnection network.

Combining the processes used in developing Figs.1-2, we can find a curve showing the minimum requirement for the number of weights vs. the number of stored patterns, M, for a fixed one step recall ability, P. An example is shown in Fig. 3.

In Fig.3 , one step recall ability is set to be P=95%, M goes from 10 to 30, curve "T_weight" is the minimum requirement for the number of weights from our theoretical calculation, and curve " 10M_square " comes from the square of 10M. From these results, we postulate that the total number of interconnections needed to store M patterns with high recall probability is on the order of $(10M)^2$, independent of N. This is consistent with the " rule - of - thumb" that a network with N neurons can store approximately $M \approx 0.1N$ patterns.

So far we have shown how to use our simple algorithm to find the optimal network structure which utilizes a minimum number of interconnection weights when the number of stored patterns , M, and the required one-step recall probability, P, are fixed. Usually a reduced large network can provide a good recall ability and in some cases use less weights than a smaller fully connected network.


4. Error correction ability

To check the error correction ( i.e., generalization ) capability of a HAM when only a small number of weights are used, we did further computer simulations. Some results are shown in the Fig.4 for various numbers of input error bits, B.

In Fig.4 when N=125, $D_0$=2 and the number of weights used is 11686; when N=175, $D_0$=4 and the number of weights used is 10461; when N=325, $D_0$=6 and the number of weights used is 11509. The case N=125, $D_0$=2 corresponds to a smaller fully connected network, the latter two cases correspond to reduced larger networks. Note that B is plotted up to 10% N for each case.

From Fig.4, we can see that the error correction capability holds constant ( in terms of percent of input bits in error ) at a high level when we only use a subset of the possible interconnection weights in the one-step recall iteration. This implies that the basins of attraction maintain the same relative widths as the network size N increases and the fraction of possible interconnections decreases.

## 5.Conclusion

We have used theoretical analysis and computer simulations to show that a first-order associative memory can be realized with an optimal (minimum) set of specially selected interconnection weights, given the number,M, of patterns to be stored and given a prescribed probability of one-step recall, P. There are also several near-optimal solutions with about the same number of interconnections required, but different numbers of neurons, N. All these networks have essentially the same generalization capability, i.e., their basins of attraction scale linearly with N.

It is interesting to see that to make the network provide a good performance, the critical point is not the network size but the actual number of weights used. It looks as if there is a lower bound on the number of weights (about 7500 in Fig.1) that we cannot be below for prescribed M and P values. In other words, there is a minimum-number-of-weights requirement to represent a certain information content at fixed recall capability. From our simulations, it appears that the number of weights is approximately $(10M)^2$, which is consistent with the " rule - of - thumb" that $M \approx 0.1N$ for a good performance in a fully connected network.

### Reference

[1] J.J.Hopfield,"Neural networks and physical systems with emergent collective computational abilities " Proceedings of the National Academy of Science of the United States of America, vol.79,pp.2445-2558,1982.

[2] J.H.Wang, T.F.Krile and J.F.Walkup,"Determination of Hopfield associative memory characteristics using a single parameter," Neural Networks. vol.3, no.3,pp.319-331,1990.

[3] D. Psaltis, C.H. Park and J. Hong, " Higher order associative memories and their optical implementations," Neural Networks, Vol.1, No 2, pp. 149 - 163, 1988.

[4] J.H.Wang and T.F.Krile," Reduction of Interconnection Weights in Higher-Order Associative Memory Networks ", Proc. of International Joint Conf. on Neural Networks, vol 2, 177 - 182, Seattle, 1991.

**Figures:**

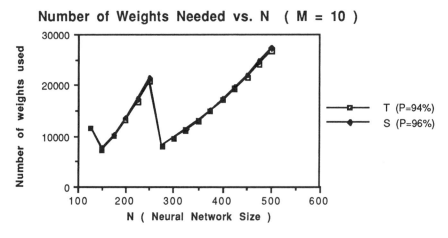

Fig. 1

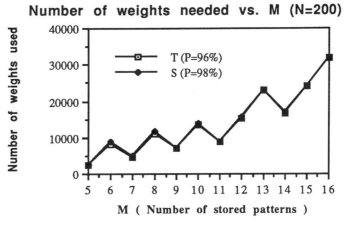

**Number of weights needed vs. M (N=200)**

Fig. 2

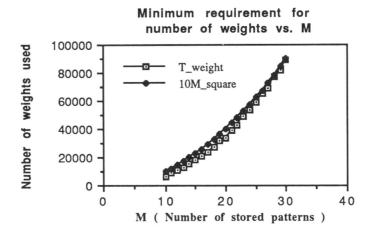

**Minimum requirement for number of weights vs. M**

Fig. 3

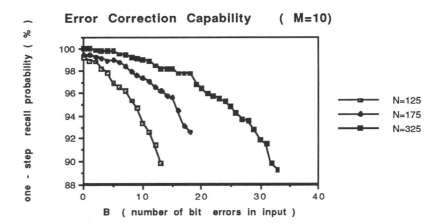

**Error Correction Capability    ( M=10)**

Fig. 4

# Associative Memory

**Session Chairs: John G. Taylor**
**Shiro Usui**

## POSTER PRESENTATIONS

# A Continuous Input Heteroassociative Neural Network Model for Perfect Recall

**Abul L. Haque**
School of Computer Science
University of Oklahoma
Norman, OK 73019, U.S.A.

**John Y. Cheung**
School of Electric Engineering
University of Oklahoma
Norman, OK 73019, U.S.A.

### Abstract

In this paper a model of a Neural Network is developed which is capable of producing perfect recall of the continuous valued training vectors. The model is based on the Linear Associator Neural Network, a number of which are connected in parallel to increase the capacity. It requires that the input to the Linear Associators be all linearly independent to retain the exact recall property. A technique to group all the input vectors as a set of linearly independent vectors is presented. A Kohonen Type Competitive Network (KTCN) is designed to select the best possible output from the set of outputs of the Linear Associator Neural Networks. The performance of the model is then discussed.

## 1 Introduction

The Linear Associator Neural Networks was introduced by Anderson [1] and Kohonen [10, 11] in 1972. It is considered as a heteroassociative memory capable of memorizing a finite number of $(\mathbf{x}_i, \mathbf{y}_i)$ vector pairs. One of its most interesting features is the ability to reproduce the training vectors exactly during recall provided the input $\mathbf{x}_i$ vectors are orthonormal. In this case, the number of pattern pairs $(\mathbf{x}_i, \mathbf{y}_i)$ that it can memorize are limited to the dimensionality of the $\mathbf{x}_i$ vectors. It has been observed that the weight matrix $W$ could be computed without the orthonormality condition, and it simply requires that the vectors be all linearly independent.

Since the criterion of all the input $\mathbf{x}_i$ vectors be linearly independent is not always achievable in a real life situation, many researchers used different techniques to handle this problem and consequently the capability of producing the exact recall by the Linear Associator was lost. Stiles and Deng [14], Murakami and Aibara [13], Casasent and Telfer [3, 4], Cherkassky *et.al* [5], and others used the Moore-Penrose generalized inverse to compute the weight matrix $W$. As a result they introduced a new performance measure for the noise in terms of signal-to-noise ratio (as a ratio of the input and output variances, $\sigma_o^2/\sigma_i^2$) and discussed its effect in various situations.

The other Neural Network that is capable of producing exact recall is the Bidirectional Associative Memories (BAM) developed by Kosko [12]. But this network works only for binary (or bipolar) inputs. The Linear Associator Neural Network does not have any restrictions on the type of input vectors (it even works for complex numbers).

We focus our research by increasing the capacity of the Linear Associator Neural Networks and also keeping its ability to produce perfect recall. We develop a technique that involves connecting a number of Linear Associators in parallel and then ensuring that the input to these Linear Associators be all linearly independent. This is achieved by adding a preprocessor to the model whose only task is to group the input vectors as linear independent sets. Since there are a number of Linear Associators connected in parallel, we have outputs from each of these during recall, and consequently we need to select only one which is the most appropriate as an output. This is done by a postprocessor unit which is added to our model. The idea of our basic model had already been presented in [7] which can be outlined in a diagram as shown in Fig 1. The input and the output of the preprocessor unit is shown in Fig. 2.

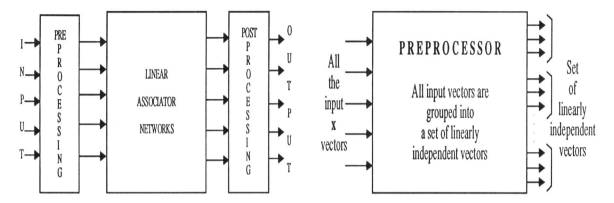

Figure 1: The new model of the Linear Associator Neural Networks with one preprocessor and one postprocessor

Figure 2: The Input and Output of the Preprocessor Block

We organize this paper by presenting a design of the preprocessor and the postprocessor blocks. The preprocessor block groups the input vectors as linearly independent sets. The postprocessor block selects one vector from the outputs of each Linear Associator Neural Network which are connected in parallel. Finally, we discuss the performance of our model.

## 2    Increasing The Capacity

As mentioned earlier, a number of Linear Associators are needed to be connected in parallel to increase the capacity with the capability to produce the exact recall. If there are $M$ such Linear Associators and each network can store $N$ number of input vectors then the capacity can be increased to $M \times N$. This combined network is arranged in such a way so that it acts like a single Linear Associator having a number of input and one output. The number of Linear Associators needed to be combined depends on the number of $(x_i, y_i)$ training pairs available and the dimensionality of the $x_i$ vectors. The next task would be to ensure the inputs to these Linear Associators be all linearly independent. For this purpose we need a preprocessor unit.

## 3    The Design of the Preprocessor

The introduction of the preprocessor unit enables us to manipulate the $x_i$ vectors as desired. It involves the grouping of the input vectors in such a way so that the vectors which are to be input to the Linear Associators be all linearly independent. This process does not change the input vector in any way.

## 3.1  Grouping the Input Vectors

Suppose the dimension of the $\mathbf{x}_i$ vectors is $N$ and the number of input vectors is $L$. Normally $L \gg N$ and we need at least $K$ number of Linear Associators, where $K = \lceil L/N \rceil$. However, the actual number of groups (the number $K$) will be determined by the algorithm that is responsible for making the sets linearly independent. The main objective is to form $K$ groups from these $L$ vectors each containing $N$ number of vectors in a way so that all of these $K$ groups be linearly independent. Fig. 2 illustrates the input/output relations.

## 3.2  Testing for Linear Dependency

The next task of the preprocessor block is to test for linear dependence of each of the $K$ groups. This could be done by evaluating the value of the determinant of each set. If it is zero then the set is linearly dependent; otherwise, it is linearly independent. A methodology presented by Haque *et.al* [6] may be utilized for this purpose since it computes the value of the determinant using Neural Networks. If some of the sets are found to be linearly dependent, then we develop an algorithm to make these sets linearly independent.

Haque and Cheung [8] also developed a Neural Network to test for the linear independence of the input vectors. But their network is limited to only binary inputs vectors of dimension four which restricts its practical usefulness.

## 3.3  Rearranging the Input Vectors

Our investigation reveals that the solution to the problem of making all the sets linearly independent may be done by simply interchanging one or more vectors among the linearly dependent sets. The following example will clarify the concept.

**Example.** *Suppose there are a total of 9 input vectors and there are 3 Linear Associator Neural Networks each needs only 3 input vectors. Let the vectors are:* $\mathbf{x}_1 = (2, 1, -2)$, $\mathbf{x}_2 = (-4, 2, 3)$, $\mathbf{x}_3 = (-8, 8, 5)$, $\mathbf{x}_4 = (1, 3, 5)$, $\mathbf{x}_5 = (2, 4, 0)$, $\mathbf{x}_6 = (3, 1, 7)$, $\mathbf{x}_7 = (3, 0, 2)$, $\mathbf{x}_8 = (2, -1, 1)$, *and* $\mathbf{x}_9 = (5, 2, 4)$.

*Let us divide these vectors into three sets each containing three vectors. They are:* $\mathbf{S}_1 = \{\mathbf{x}_1, \mathbf{x}_2, \mathbf{x}_3\}$, $\mathbf{S}_2 = \{\mathbf{x}_4, \mathbf{x}_5, \mathbf{x}_6\}$, *and* $\mathbf{S}_3 = \{\mathbf{x}_7, \mathbf{x}_8, \mathbf{x}_9\}$.

*We have found that the set* $\mathbf{S}_2$ *is linearly independent whereas the sets* $\mathbf{S}_1$ *and* $\mathbf{S}_3$ *are both linearly dependent. Now we need some regrouping of these vectors so that all the three sets are linearly independent. Since* $\mathbf{S}_2$ *is already linearly independent; therefore, we keep it as it is. We exchange the vectors* $\mathbf{x}_3$ *and* $\mathbf{x}_9$ *between the sets* $\mathbf{S}_1$ *and* $\mathbf{S}_3$ *yielding as:* $\mathbf{S}_1 = \{\mathbf{x}_1, \mathbf{x}_2, \mathbf{x}_9\}$ *and* $\mathbf{S}_3 = \{\mathbf{x}_7, \mathbf{x}_8, \mathbf{x}_3\}$

*We observe that all the three sets* $\mathbf{S}_1, \mathbf{S}_2$, *and* $\mathbf{S}_3$ *are now linearly independent.*

This example outlines the type of processing that is required in the preprocessing unit. It is the grouping process of all the incoming $\mathbf{x}_i$ vectors so that they all form a linearly independent set.

## 3.4  Development of an Algorithm

The above example leads to the following algorithm to group all the input vectors arbitrarily and then to test each set of vectors for linear dependence. The swapping of vectors occurs between the sets that are linearly dependent or between a linearly dependent set and a linearly independent set. Let N be the dimension of each vector.

Step 1. Divide all the input vectors to form K number of sets in such a way that a the number of vectors in each set is N.

Step 2. Test for linear dependence for all K sets.

Step 3. Let Q number of sets become linearly independent and R number of sets become linearly dependent.

Step 4. Swap a number of vectors between these R sets and test them again for linear independence. Suppose S number of sets among the R sets now became linearly independent. Then $Q \leftarrow Q + S$, and $R \leftarrow R - S$.

Step 5. Repeat step 4 a predetermined number of times. If $Q = K$ then stop.

Step 6. Swap one vector at a time between any of the Q set and one of the R set and test for linear independence of both the sets. Unswap if both becomes linearly dependent.

Step 7. Repeat step 6 a predetermined number of times. If $Q = K$ then stop.

Step 8. Assign $N \leftarrow N - 1$. Put all the vectors of the R sets into input list and divide the vectors in K number of sets each having N vectors. If N = 1 then stop, otherwise Goto Step 2.

## 3.5  The Computation of the Weight Matrix W

The above algorithm produces, although not guaranteed, $K$ number of sets with all linearly independent vectors in each set. All the vectors in these sets are now ready to be given as input to each Linear Associator Neural Network as part of training the network.

In the best case scenario, all the $K$ sets form a square matrix and are linearly independent; therefore, the computation of the weight matrix $W$ is done by using the following formula:

$$W = YX^{-1} \tag{1}$$

where $X^{-1}$ is the true inverse of the matrix X and Y is the corresponding output matrix.

In the average case scenario, not all the $K$ sets are a square matrix. For those which form a square matrix, the weight matrix $W$ is computed by using the above formula. Those sets which do not form a square matrix, the weight matrix $W$ is computed by using the pseudoinverse formula [2] as given below:

$$W = YX^{+} \tag{2}$$

Once the network is trained, the output vector is obtained by using the following recall formula:

$$\mathbf{y}_k = W\mathbf{x}_k \tag{3}$$

It can be shown that if the vectors are linearly independent the exact recall is guaranteed [9].

## 4  The Design of the Postprocessor

The postprocessor consists of a number of Kohonen Type Competitive Network (KTCN) connected in parallel and output processing nodes as shown in Fig. 3. The KTCN is a two layer Neural Network in which the first layer consists of the Kohonen Type processing nodes associated with the weight **G**. In our case the winning processing node outputs the input value instead of a 1 as in the case of the Kohonen Neural Network. The second layer is associated with the weight **H** and simply outputs the inputs. The design of KTCN is shown in Fig. 4.

There is no formal training in the postprocessing part. All the weights are fixed and initialized as follows. The weight matrix **H** has the weight all equal to 1. The weight matrix **G** is a $p \times q$ matrix where $p$ is the number of training pairs, and $q$ is the dimension of the **y** vectors. The

G matrix is initialized to $g_1 = y_1, g_2 = y_2, \cdots, g_p = y_p$. Each processing element of the KTCN computes the input intensity $I_i$ in accordance with the following formula:

$$I_i = D(y_i, z) \tag{4}$$

where $z$ is the output from the **LA**, and $D(u,v)$ is the Euclidean distance defined by:

$$D(\mathbf{u}, \mathbf{v}) = |\ \mathbf{u} - \mathbf{v}\ | \tag{5}$$

A competition is then held between all the $I_i$ values of all the KTCN processing elements. The processing unit with the lowest $I_i$ value wins the competition and sends the same input signals through its $q$ channels. If any of the $I_i$ value is zero, then we have a perfect recall.

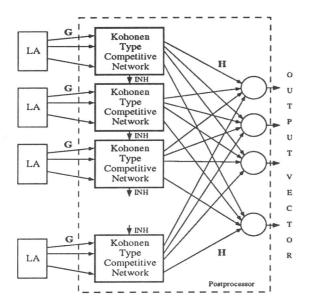

Figure 3: The basic architecture of the postprocessor block

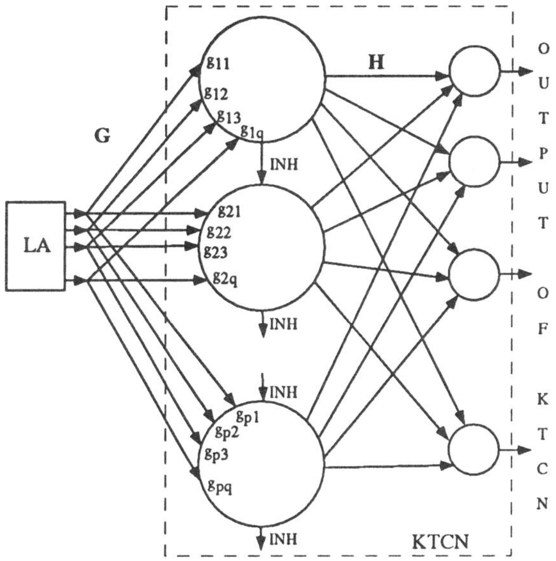

Figure 4: The detailed design of the Kohonen Type Competitive Network (KTCN)

## 4.1 The Competition Rules

Initially, the threshold value of all the Processing Elements (PEs) of all the KTCN are equal to zero. Each PE of the KTCN has a lateral input from the top (except for the top most one). The winning PE inhibits all the PEs below it through an inhibition connection INH as shown in Fig. 4. If there is no winning PE with zero threshold then the threshold value of all the KTCN are increased slightly until we have a winning PE.

## 5   Discussion and Conclusion

We have proposed a new model of a Neural Network that can accept any type of data: binary, bipolar, continuous and even complex numbers having unlimited, but finite, capacity. This increase in the capacity has been attained simply by connecting a number of Linear Associator

Neural Network in parallel and dividing the input vectors into groups. To retain the exact recall property of the Linear Associators we develop a heuristics to arrange the input vectors as a set of linearly independent vectors. A preprocessor is added to perform this task. Our algorithm does not guarantee that the vectors could be grouped as a linearly independent set of vectors and, therefore, needs further improvement. Since there are many Linear Associators connected in parallel we needed to design a postprocessor in order to select the most appropriate output vector. We used the slightly modified version of the Kohonen Neural Network for this purpose.

Theoretically, the new model should perform as indicated. However, extensive simulation with this network has to be performed in order to determine its effectiveness for practical applications. Also the network complexity has to be evaluated and discussed. Our ongoing research has been directed towards these issues.

# References

[1] Anderson, J.A., "A Simple Neural Network Generating an Interactive Memory", *Mathematical Bioscience*, **14**, 1972, 197-220.

[2] Ben-Israel, A., and T.N.E. Greville, *Generalized Inverses: Theory and Applications*, John Wiley & Sons, New York, 1974.

[3] Casasent, D., and B. Telfer, "Associative Memory Synthesis, Performance, Storage Capacity and Updating: New Heteroassociative Memory Results", *SPIE Intelligent Robots and Computer Vision: Sixth in a Series*, Vol 848, 1987, 313-330.

[4] Casasent, D., and B. Telfer, "Key and Recollection Vector Effects on Heteroassociative Memory Performance", *Applied Optics*, Vol 28, No. 2, 1989, 272-283.

[5] Cherkassky, V., K. Fassett, and N. Vassilas, "Linear Algebra Approach and Noise Performance of Neural Classifiers", *IEEE Transactions on Computers*, Vol 40, No. 12, 1991, 1429- 1435.

[6] Haque, A. L., M. A. Abu-Ali, and J. Y. Cheung, "Computation of the Determinant of a Matrix Using Neural Networks", In *Intelligent Engineering Systems Through Artificial Neural Networks - Volume 3*, (Eds. C.H. Dagli, L.I. Burke, J. Ghosh, and B. Fernandez), ASME Press, New York, 1993, 857-862.

[7] Haque, A. L., and J. Y. Cheung, "Linear Associator Neural Network with Larger Capacity", *Proceedings of the World Congress on Neural Networks - Portland*, July, 1993, vol. IV, 363-366.

[8] Haque, A. L., and J. Y. Cheung, "Using Neural Networks to Determine the Linear Dependence of Input Vectors", *Proceedings of the World Congress on Neural Networks - Portland*, July, 1993, vol. I, 642-645.

[9] Hecht-Nielsen, R., *Neurocomputing*, Addison-Wesley, Reading, MA, 1990.

[10] Kohonen, T., "Correlation Matrix Memories", *IEEE Trans. on Computers*, **C-21**(4), 1972, 353-359.

[11] Kohonen, T., *Self-Organization and Associative Memory*, 3rd. Ed., Springer-Verlag, New York, 1989.

[12] Kosko, B., "Bidirectional Associative Memories", *IEEE Transactions on System, Man and Cybernetics*, **SMC-18**, Jan-Feb, 1988, 49-60.

[13] Murakami, K., and T. Aibara, "An Improvement on the Moore-Penrose Generalized Inverse Associative Memory", *IEEE Transactions on System, Man and Cybernetics*, **SMC-17**(4), 1987, 699-707.

[14] Stiles, G.S., and D-L. Deng, "On the Effect of Noise on the Moore-Penrose Generalized Inverse Associative Memory", *IEEE Trans. on Pattern and Machine Intelligence*, **PAMI-7**(3), 1985, 358-360.

# A CLASS OF AUTO-ASSOCIATIVE NEURAL NETWORKS WITH LOW CONNECTIVITY

David D. Vogel, Creighton University, School of Dentistry, Omaha, NE 68178

## ABSTRACT

Two classic problems with the use of auto-associative neural networks to model mammalian memory are the small size of fully connected networks with realistic numbers of connections per neuron, and the small storage capacity of networks with realistic learning algorithms. Much larger networks (P-nets) may be constructed by connecting neurons in patterns that form projective planes (symmetric block designs) or similar structures such as affine planes. The smallest P-net constructed with 1000 connections per neuron contains $2 \times 10^6$ neurons. Implemented with a simple Hebbian learning algorithm, the network stores more than $10^6$ training vectors with 32 active neurons per vector.

## 1 INTRODUCTION

Neural networks have provided useful insights into the mechanisms by which real brains might, in principle, perform certain kinds of information processing. There are, however, well known problems with neural networks as models of memory in mammalian brains. A pyramidal cell may have a few tens of thousands of synapses, but it is unlikely that such cells connect to more than a few thousand other neurons involved in engram formation - there being multiple connections between single pairs of neurons and many connections which must serve functions other than direct encoding of memory (Traub and Miles, 1991). In contrast, large scale cortical synchrony implies the existence of large, functionally integrated regions. While it is possible to use local connections to account for slowly developing synchrony, as is seen in the δ-frequency synchrony of the cortically stimulated thalamus (Steriade, Dossi, and Nunez, 1991), local connectivity seems unlikely to produce the synchronous oscillation of the cat visual cortex (Gray et al. 1989). Still more problematical is the small information storage capacity of fully connected networks (F-nets) with learning rules that might be implemented physiologically. Among networks that use simple learning algorithms, Palm's (1980) auto-associative model has an unusually large information storage capacity. However, the capacity of a network in which each neuron is connected to 1000 other neurons is still only 1300 sets of 20 neurons each which seems too small to account for human cognition. Palm (1980) writes of a "severe problem in regarding [a fully connected network] as a model for the cortex" and adds, "It would be interesting to analyze whether specific arrangements of the storage elements or possible connections... could provide particularly large storage capacities." This paper describes a large class of such arrangements.

## 2 NETWORK ARCHITECTURE

The networks described here are all multilayer networks which conform to the following conditions.

1.  All layers have the same number of neurons.

2.  All neurons in the same layer have the same number of synapses.

3.  If the $i$th neuron of layer p synapses on the $j$th neuron of layer q, then the $j$th neuron of layer q synapses on the $i$th neuron of layer p.

4. Every neuron in the primary layer is linked to every other neuron in the primary layer through exactly one neuron in each secondary layer.

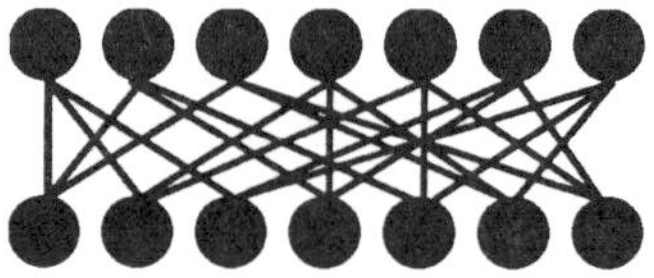

Figure 1. A small P-net. Lines represent both feed forward and feed backward connections.

These additional statements follow from the above conditions.

5. The pattern of synapses of primary neurons on the neurons of each separate secondary layer forms a symmetric block design (projective plane).

6. The pattern of synapses of the neurons of each separate secondary layer on primary neurons also forms a symmetric block design with the property that every secondary neuron is linked to every other secondary neuron through exactly one primary neuron.

Other cognate conditions produce other strongly regular graphs (e.g., those based on affine planes) with similar mnemonic properties.

Some of the P-nets described in this paper have two secondary layers connected to the same primary layer with different block designs. (The second secondary layer is not to be mistaken for a tertiary layer which would be connected to a secondary layer rather than the primary layer.) I refer to P-nets with one secondary layer as "*first-order*" and to P-nets with two secondary layers as "*second-order*."

## 3 ACTIVATION AND LEARNING RULES

During a training phase several sets of randomly selected primary neurons (*training sets*) are activated. During a recall phase the network is stimulated with *recall sets*, each of which contains half the neurons of some training set. Stimulation with a recall set always activates all the neurons in the corresponding training set. In addition, a number of *spurious neurons* which are not part of the training set may become active.

Let $a_i$ denote the activity of the $i$th neuron, and $w_{ij}$ the synaptic weight of j on i. During the first pass of recall, the activation rule is

$$a_i = S \qquad \text{if } \sum_j w_{ij}a_j > S \qquad \text{where S is a saturation.} \qquad (1a)$$

$$a_i = 0 \qquad \text{if } \sum_j w_{ij}a_j < T \qquad \text{where T is a threshold.} \qquad (1b)$$

$$a_i = \sum_j w_{ij}a_j \qquad \text{elsewise.} \qquad (1c)$$

At all other times the activation rule is

$$a_i = S \qquad \text{if } \sum_j w_{ij}a_j - aw > S \qquad (1d)$$

$$a_i = 0 \qquad \text{if } \sum_j w_{ij}a_j - aw < T \qquad (1e)$$

$$a_i = \sum_j w_{ij}a_j - aw \qquad \text{elsewise.} \qquad (1f)$$

where $a$ is the activity of training set neurons when first activated, and w is the untrained synaptic weight. For the primary layer, $S = T = a$.

The learning algorithm is simple. Let $w'$ be the trained synaptic weight.

$$w_{ij} = w \qquad \text{until both pre and post synaptic neurons} \tag{2a}$$
$$\text{are active on the same pass.}$$

$$w_{ij} = w' \qquad \text{thereafter.} \tag{2b}$$

The network is trained in one pass, though it reverberates naturally and may be trained on any pass. Let $n$ and $n'$ respectively be the number of neurons in a training set and a recall set. Appropriate thresholds during training are given by

$$T_1 = (n\text{-}1)w^2 a \qquad \text{for the primary layer,} \tag{3a}$$

and

$$T_2 = wa \qquad \text{for the secondary layer.} \tag{3b}$$

Appropriate thresholds during recall are given by

$$T_1 = n'\,w'^{\,2}a \qquad \text{during the first pass,} \tag{3c}$$

$$T_1 = (n\text{-}1)w'^{\,2}a \qquad \text{during subsequent passes,} \tag{3d}$$

and

$$T_2 = wa \quad . \tag{3e}$$

## 4 SIMULATIONS AND COMPARISONS

The similarity of the activation and training algorithms we have used to those of Willshaw, Buneman, and Longuet-Higgins (1969) or Palm (1980) suggests conducting a mathematical analysis of P-nets analogous to Palm's analysis of F-nets. Unfortunately, the comparable analysis of P-nets leads to numerical equations which must be programmed to calculate impractically large numbers of permutations. However, I next show that the number of spurious neurons in P-nets is bounded well <u>below</u> the number of spurious neurons in F-nets, as connectivity increases.

In the sequel, I use the word "*pathway*" to refer to either a direct connection between neurons of an F-net, or a link through the secondary layer between primary neurons of a P-net. The values of $T_x$ (equation 3) are chosen such that P-nets and Palm-style F-nets have the same condition for a neuron to be spurious at the start of the second cycle of reverberation; namely, that the neuron have trained pathways to each of the recall neurons.

The probability that a randomly chosen neuron, $S$, not a member of the training set, will have a trained pathway to the first neuron of the recall set can be calculated for F-nets as follows. Let $\mathcal{N}_F$ denote the total number of pathways in the network other than those which interconnect the training set, $\mathcal{T}_F$ the number of these pathways that are trained, $\mathcal{P}_F$ their ratio, $u$ the number of neurons per layer, and $k$ the number of synapses per neuron.

$$\mathcal{N}_F = u(u\text{-}1) - n(n\text{-}1) = (k+1)k - n(n\text{-}1) < (k+1)k \quad . \tag{4}$$

The number of pathways trained in a naive F-net by a training set of size $n$ is $n(n\text{-}1)$. However, in a previously trained network some of these pathways may already be trained. Palm (1980) has demonstrated that about half the synapses are trained in a fully trained F-net. Accordingly, the last of L training sets may train roughly $(1/2)n(n\text{-}1)$ pathways. It is unlikely that L training sets would train fewer than $(1/2)n(n\text{-}1)L$ pathways. The lower bound of the probability of $S$ being trained to the first recall neuron, $\mathcal{P}_F$, is thus approximately

$$\mathcal{P}_F = \mathcal{T}_F / \mathcal{N}_F > (1/2)n(n-1)L / [(k+1)k] > (1/2)n(n-1)L / k^{2.1} \qquad (5)$$

for sufficiently large k.

I now calculate an upper bound of the probability, $\mathcal{P}_P$, that a randomly chosen neuron in a P-net, not a member of the training set, has a trained pathway to the first neuron of a recall set. Once again, the number of possible pathways is given by

$$\mathcal{N}_P = u(u-1) - n(n-1) \qquad . \qquad (6)$$

However, for symmetric block designs $u = k^2 - k + 1$, so

$$\mathcal{N}_P = (k^2 - k + 1)(k^2 - k) - n(n-1) > (k-1)^4 \qquad (7)$$

for sufficiently large k.

Again, in a naive P-net, the number of pathways trained by a training set of size n is n(n-1). However, each of the n(n-1) pathways passes through a secondary neuron which synapses onto k-1 primary neurons other than the original training neuron at the start of the pathway. Accordingly, training one new pathway between neurons of a given training set could complete the training of k-1 pathways. However, the pathway from the $i$th to the $j$th training neuron passes through the same secondary neuron as the pathway from the $j$th to the $i$th training neuron, so the <u>maximum</u> number of pathways which could be trained in this way is $(1/2)n(n-1)(k-1)$. Accordingly,

$$\mathcal{P}_P = \mathcal{T}_P / \mathcal{N}_P < (1/2)n(n-1)L / (k-1)^3 \approx (1/2)n(n-1)L / k^3 \qquad (8)$$

for large k. Call the conditions under which S is trained to the first recall neuron "*case 0.*"

For F-nets, the probability that S has a trained pathway to the second neuron of the recall set is independent of the probability that it has a trained pathway to the first (Palm, 1980). For P-nets, however, there are two cases in which S may be trained to the second neuron of the recall set. In <u>case 1</u>, the secondary neuron which links S to the first recall neuron is the same secondary neuron as links the first recall neuron to the second, in which case S also has a trained pathway to the second. In <u>case 2</u>, S has a trained pathway to the second recall neuron through one of the other k-1 secondary neurons which connect to the second recall neuron. An upper bound for case 2 may be constructed along lines which closely resemble case 0. The resulting expression also approaches equation 8 as k becomes large.

For case 1, the probability that the secondary neuron is the neuron which also links the first and second recall neurons is $(k-2)/[(k-1)(k-1)+(k-2)]$. The numerator, k-2, is the number of "available" synapses on the secondary neuron which connects the first and second recall neurons. The denominator is the total number of "available" synapses on secondary neurons that synapse on the second recall neuron. (There are k-1 "available" synapses on each of k-1 other secondary neurons which connect to the second recall neuron). This ratio is always $<1/k$ and approaches $1/k$ as k increases. Thus the probability, $P_2$, that S has a trained pathway to the first recall neuron, and the secondary neuron which links them is the secondary neuron that links the first and second recall neurons is

$$P_2 < (1/2)n(n-1)L / (k-1)^3 k \approx (1/2)n(n-1)L / k^4 \qquad . \qquad (9)$$

For the third recall neuron there are cases which resemble cases 0 through 2 plus a case 3, in which S is connected to the third recall neuron through a secondary neuron which links the first three recall neurons. As we consider additional cases, it is straightforward to show that all such cases have upper bound probabilities for which the negative exponent of k is greater than (say) 3.9.

Comparison of equations 5, 8, and 9 reveals that, for every case applicable to P-nets, the probability of S being trained to a neuron of a recall set falls more rapidly with increasing k than the probability for an F-net of S being trained to a neuron of a recall set. Accordingly, the probability of the union of these cases also falls more rapidly for P-nets than equation 5 for F-nets, and the probability of S being spurious (the probability of the intersection of the events that S is trained to the first through $n$th recall neurons) falls much more rapidly with increasing k for P-nets than F-nets. This demonstrates that P-nets show ever-greater storage capacity relative to F-nets with equal numbers of synapses per neuron as k becomes large.

I now express equations 5, 8, and 9 in terms of the total number of synapses, $\sigma$, instead of k. For either network $\sigma = ku$. For F-nets $u = k+1$, and inequality 5 yields

$$P_F > (1/2)n^2L / \sigma \quad . \tag{10}$$

For P-nets $u = k^2 - k + 1 \approx k^2$, and inequalities 8 and 9 for large k yield

$$P_P \approx (1/2)n^2L / \sigma \tag{11}$$

$$P_2 \approx (1/2)n^2L / \sigma^{4/3} \quad . \tag{12}$$

Equations 10 through 12 give confidence in extrapolated comparisons between P-nets and F-nets with equal numbers of synapses. A simulated first order P-net with 433,344 synapses was found to store 63% of the number of training sets stored by a 433,344 synapse F-net. A lower bound estimate of the storage capacity of a P-net with 1000 connections per neuron is then 63% of the storage capacity of an F-net with equally many synapses (approximately $10^9$ synapses). The estimate is $10^6$ training sets of 32 neurons each.

Empirical studies show other similarities between P-nets and F-nets. The training set size that maximizes information storage increases with network size in both P-nets and F-nets. From 3540 to 433,344 synapses, the optimal training set size for first-order P-nets is essentially the same as for F-nets. For second-order P-nets, the optimal size is very small (6 to 8 neurons). However, second-order P-nets store many more sets than first-order P-nets with equal numbers of neurons per layer regardless of the training set size. (In these studies, *the number of training sets which may be stored by a network* is taken to be the number of training sets which will produce, on recall, a mean number of spurious neurons equal to 1% of the number of neurons in the training sets.)

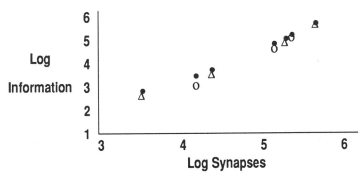

Figure 2. Total number of synapses in a network vs. information stored (with 1% spurious neurons).

    • F-nets         o first-order P-nets         △ second-order P-nets

All trials were run with the training set size optimized for F-nets. If the second-order networks are run with the training set size optimized for second-order networks, the data points are indistinguishable from those of F-nets.

# 5 DISCUSSION

P-net architectures are useful when the number of synapses per neuron is limited. The mammalian brain seems to be such a case. As much as half the surface of the neuronal soma may be occupied by synapses, and it seems likely that evolution has already optimized (in some sense) the connectivity of neurons.

Symmetric block designs only exist when the number of neurons per layer is related to the number of synapses per neuron by $u = k^2 - k + 1$. However, there are several reasons for believing that the evolutionary barrier to networks which resemble P-nets, at least in part, is reasonably low. 1) For any u and k for which there is a symmetric block design, there are many such designs. 2) There are many asymmetric block designs which should provide the same performance as symmetric block designs. 3) I have constructed P-net-like networks (*R-Nets*) in which rule 3 is retained, but the projection of synapses is otherwise completely randomized. These networks still retain 18% of the information storage capacity of P-nets. 4) The reciprocal connections required by rule 3 seem to be a natural consequence of the function of cell adhesion molecules.

In fact, casual inspection of brains and symmetric block designs seems to reveal that brains resemble P-nets more than R-nets. The resemblance lies first in the fact that neurons in one layer of a P-net project with high density to a small region of another layer, and with much lower density to surrounding regions. Additionally, in the most easily constructed block designs (cyclic designs), neurons which are adjacent in one layer project with highest density to adjacent regions of another layer.

Because the structure of F-nets is easily apprehended, we tend to think of P-nets as highly structured, special cases. In fact, the opposite is more nearly the case. An F-net is a zeroeth order P-net in which $u = k+1$. As there is only one such network for a given $u = k+1$, the evolutionary barrier to F-nets is comparatively high.

Like F-nets of the type described by Palm (1980), P-nets require sparse coding. It seems apparent that a substantial part of the initial information processing in real sensory systems is directed toward producing sparse code. What we usually refer to as "feature detection" may be regarded as a sparse coding procedure.

Finally, the large memory capacity of second-order P-nets seems to give form to certain common notions concerning the large scale organization of mammalian memory. In particular, we imagine an indefinitely higher order brain in which memory depends on the cooperation of several sparsely connected regions, and in which any isolated pair of regions would produce an error rate which is higher than that of the larger network.

# 6 REFERENCES

Gray, C.M., Konig, P., Engle, A.K., and Singer, W. (1989). Oscillatory responses in cat visual cortex exhibit inter-columnar synchronization which reflects global stimulus properties. Nature, 338, 334-337.

Palm, G. (1980). On associative memory. Biological Cybernetics, 36, 19-31.

Steriade, M., Dossi, R.C., and Nunez, A. (1991). Network modulation of a slow intrinsic oscillation of cat thalamocortical neurons implicated in sleep delta waves: cortically induced synchronization and brainstem cholinergic suppression. Journal of Neuroscience, 11, 3200-3217.

Traub, R.D., and Miles, R. (1991). Neuronal Networks of the Hippocampus. Cambridge University Press, Cambridge.

Willshaw, D.J., Buneman, O.P., and Longuet-Higgins, H.C. (1969). Non-holographic associative memory. Nature, 222, 960-962.

# The Predictive RAAM: A RAAM That Can Learn to Distinguish Sequences from a Continuous Input Stream

Kenneth A. Hester,
University of South Alabama, School of Computer Science
FCW 20, Mobile, AL 36688
hester@cis.usouthal.edu   (205) 343-3894

Michael J. Bringmann
Quality Micro Systems Inc., Mobile, AL

David Langan
University of South Alabama, School of Computer Science

Marino J. Niccolai
University of South Alabama, School of Computer Science

William J. Nowack
University of South Alabama, College of Medicine

Abstract

Recursive Auto-Associative Memories (RAAM) can encode a sequence of individual data items into a single fixed length representation. Each of these encoded sequences is treated as a single entity by a neural network designed to manipulate the original data stream. Pollack has shown that it is desirable to arrange RAAM-style neural networks hierarchically when the sequences to be encoded contain subsequences. However, during the training phase, each subsequence must be identified by an external observer who determines where one pattern ends and the next begins. These RAAM-style networks can be used to decompose paragraphs (written or spoken) into sentences, words, and finally individual characters, thus providing a mechanism to interpret simple "Tarzan" language constructs.

Elman used a simple recurrent network to predict the next letter in a sequence of words. By analyzing the error of the predicted next letter, he obtained reasonable estimates for the beginning and ending characters of each word. This paper describes the combination of an Elman prediction network with a RAAM, to form a Predictive RAAM, that can be used to discover and encode the most appropriate decomposition of the input data stream into individual atomic structures (words or characters). This approach does not require any prior knowledge of these structures nor does it require an external agent to set the start and end positions of the structure.

## Introduction

Neural networks are easily applied to problems where the data is represented numerically, however much of the reasoning required for speech and text-based reading comprehension is symbolic in nature. Neural networks have not been used extensively to solve problems in this domain. Recurrent Auto-

Associative Memories (RAAM) [Pollack, 1989a] can encode symbolic data into numerical data and in so doing they give the data meaning not necessarily contained in the symbolic form. RAAMs encode data from examples where the individual symbols are only seen in the context of the larger sequence (e.g., words, sentences). The numeric representations that are developed have this contextual information built into their final form. Symbols that are used in closely related contexts will take on similar numeric forms [Chambers, 1990].

There are many problem domains in which the input will contain multiple levels of symbolic data. For example, in speech recognition problems, phrases consist of words and the words are constructed from phonemes. Similarly, for text-based reading comprehension, sentences are decomposed into words separated by blanks, and the words are constructed from non-blank characters. In cases involving multiple symbolic levels, it has been shown [Chambers, 1990] that RAAMs arranged hierarchically produce a more efficient network than does a single RAAM. However, when these hierarchical RAAMs (HRAAM) are trained, at each level of the hierarchy, the individual RAAM must be trained independently and the beginning and end of every subsequence clearly marked. This limits the use of HRAAM in the area of "continuous" symbolic pattern recognition. This paper presents the results of experiments on building new RAAMs that can dynamically discover the end point of subsequences (words, characters). Thus, an HRAAM constructed from these units could be trained together as a single unit rather than training each level separately.

## Recurrent Auto-Associative Memories

The Recurrent Auto-Associative Memory (RAAM) [Pollack, 1989a] is useful in language processing, phoneme processing, and other sequence processing. This network has two forms. The two forms can be used to encode trees and stacks into fixed length vectors. Functionally the architecture consists of two parts: the compressor and the reconstructor. In the tree case, the compressor takes leaves of a tree and compresses them into one vector that is the same size as each of the leaves. The reconstructor takes the compressed representation and expands it back out into the original leaves. The two parts are trained together to form an auto-associative network. The network must be used repeatedly to combine all subtrees into leaves until only one vector remains. The compression of an entire binary tree would start with the end leaves. These would be combined two at a time to

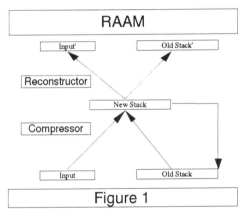

Figure 1

form their parent node. This parent node representation, which is now a leaf itself, is stored externally to the network. When all of the first layer of leaves have been processed, the next layer is encoded, using the compressed representations that we obtained by combining the original leaves. This process is repeated until there is one vector that represents the entire tree. One problem with this form of the RAAM is that the combined representation of the tree is the same size as each of the leaves, thus restricting the combined representation in accuracy and information holding ability. Another disadvantage is that during the compression and decompression, the representations must be stored externally to the network.

In the stack case, the compressor is used to combine an element and a stack into a new stack. The reconstructor expands the new stack back into the original stack and element. (Figure 1) Again this is an auto-associative network. The stack version of the architecture is more generally useful and does not suffer from the problem of having to store intermediate values externally while encoding and decoding the stack. In the stack version the length of the vector representing the encoded structure can be assigned arbitrarily thus not restricting the accuracy and capacity of the encoded structure. [Kwasny, 1993] has shown that trees can effectively be encoded in the stack version of the RAAM. Another reason that the stack style RAAM is preferred over the tree style is that the intermediates values of the stack version of the RAAM need not be stored externally. This means that the architecture can be implemented as a simple recurrent network (SRN). In a simple recurrent network the output of the middle layer, which in this case is the new stack, is copied down to the input layer before each new pattern presentation. This gives the network a degree of recurrence without complicating the training algorithm. When implemented in this form the items to be pushed onto the stack can be presented on successive iterations to a network with an initially empty stack and the resulting representation will be the stack with all of the items pushed onto it.

The RAAM architecture has been used to counter one of the arguments against the use of neural networks for higher level cognitive tasks (e.g. language processing). The question that arises is how to represent symbolic data in the vector format that neural networks are so good at processing. Many attacks on neural networks are based on this representational inadequacy. [Pollack, 1989a] The RAAM architecture is an example of an architecture that can not only represent these symbols, but represent combinations of these symbols that can be acted on as a whole without having to parse the individual items out of the combined representation. [Chalmers, 1990] It is important to note that even though this representation is called a stack, because the method of encoding the combined representation is similar to pushing items onto a stack, it also possesses many of the attributes of arrays and other direct access structures. Items within the structure can be acted on directly without having to pop preceding items off as you would in a stack. Another important characteristic of RAAM encoded structures is that, unlike symbolic data, vectors with similar meaning take on similar values. [Blank, 1991]

In some cases multiple RAAM architectures can be combined hierarchically to exploit the inherent levels of the data. [Pollack, 1991] As an example, one RAAM might be used to encode letters into words. At the next level, another RAAM might be used to encode these resulting words into sentences. Such a combined RAAM is called a Hierarchical RAAM (HRAAM). HRAAMs are trained from the bottom up. Pollack [Angeline, 1991] used a two level HRAAM to first encode point pairs of lines into letters, then letters into words. He achieved better results with the two level approach than with a single RAAM

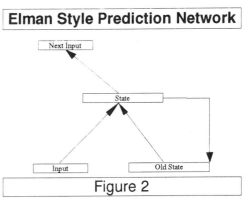

**Elman Style Prediction Network**

Next Input

State

Input        Old State

Figure 2

to encode the point pairs into words. In this example, since the point pairs of each letter are repeating patterns in the input stream, the authors chose them as input into the first level RAAM. If a RAAM is to discover its own modularization of the data it must find the breaks between repeating subpatterns in the input stream.

## Elman Style Prediction Networks

Elman has produced a network that can discover the beginning and end of patterns in an input sequence [Elman, 1990]. He used a simple recurrent network, much like the structure of the RAAM architecture, to predict the next element in a sequence (Figure 2). Like a RAAM network, the middle layer output is copied to part of the input layer after each iteration. In one of Elman's experiments he used letters of words as input, and tried to predict what letter would be next. He found that the error in the prediction of the next letter tended to be high at the beginning of a word and lower as the word progressed. It is this property that we wish to use to determine the end of the sequence to be encoded by the RAAM.

By utilizing two networks, one for RAAM encoding and one for detecting the end of a sequence, we can train a RAAM on sequences of inputs without having to signal the end of a sequence to the network (Figure 3).

## Implementation

A network was designed and built that combines the principles of the RAAM and the Elman prediction network. Both networks are implemented as simple recurrent networks so that no external storage is needed. The RAAM network was implemented as in Figure 1. The middle layer, which represents the stack is initially set to the null stack. Following the example of [Pollack, 1989a], we used a vector with each element set to 0.5 to represent the null stack. As the first element of the sequence is presented to the network, the middle layer "new stack" is copied down to the input layer as the "old stack" (Figure 3). With these two patterns as input, a forward pass is made through the network to compute the activities of all neurodes. The new stack now contains a combination of the old stack and the item that are present in the input layer, which is equivalent to the old stack with the item pushed onto it. Since the network is auto-associative, the error at the output layer can eas-

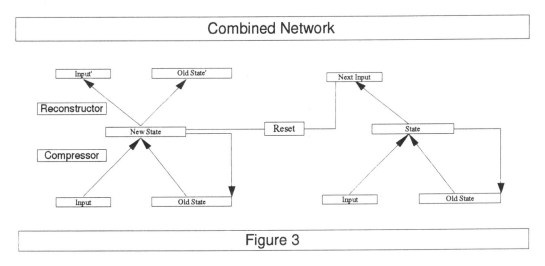

Figure 3

ily be computed as the difference in the output and input of the network. This process is repeated with the next element of the sequence until the end of the sequence is reached. At this time the new state needs to be reset to the null state before beginning the next sequence. The auto-associative nature of this network assures that all of the elements will be contained in the new stack, within the tolerance error used to define training. Since the capacity of this layer is limited in a practical network implementation, the new stack must be cleared.

The decision about whether the end of the sequence has been reached is made by the Elman prediction network. This network was built as in figure 2 above. The middle layer in the Elman prediction network contains the "relevant" history needed to predict the next element. This network can forget elements as they become older and less significant. Because of this, the middle layer or "state" vector does not need to be cleared. The prediction network operates in a manner similar to the RAAM network. Since the network runs continuously with no clearing of the state vector, the system always contains the activity produced by the last element, including the output layer, which was a prediction of what the next element should be. Each time a new element is received, the network first checks to see how close the prediction of this element was. If the error is high the prediction network signals the RAAM network that this is the beginning of a new pattern so that it can clear the stack before processing this element. Using the error just computed, the weights of the system are adjusted using back-propagation. Finally, the prediction network makes a forward pass to predict the next element and prepare for the next iteration.

Using this methodology, the combined network can accept a string of characters and through its predictive ability can encode the stream of characters into distinct words without prior knowledge of where the words begin and end.

Experimental results

As an example, the problem of encoding words from letters was chosen. Letters were encoded into a 5 bit binary number. This 5 bit number was presented to both of the networks' input layers along with their respective previous states. A small sample of words was used for the training set. Words were presented in random order to the network. A sample of 15 words was trained to within 0.05 of the desired output at each neurode with about 10,000 presentations of the words with the network correctly recognizing the end of the words more than 95 percent of the time. With 25 words about 20,000 presentations were required. These results are similar to the results obtained by Elman with his prediction network.

Training of the combined network proceeds in two phases. During the first phase, the prediction network learns the breaks between patterns. During this phase the input stream is broken up into somewhat random subsequences for the RAAM half to process. The training of the RAAM portion is not effective during this phase. After the prediction half of the network begins to predict the end of sequences with some accuracy, the second phase of training begins. In this phase the RAAM learns to encode the sequences while the prediction portion completes training. The majority of the training time is taken up in the first phase. The addition of the prediction network increases the training time required to learn the patterns but does not require the knowledge of where patterns begin and end.

Discussion

The predictive ability of the combined network follow Elman's results. The Predictive RAAM network cannot be used as an absolute determiner of the end of words. It does demonstrate that a RAAM architecture, together with an Elman style SRN to determine end of sequences, can be to form a Predictive RAAM architecture that can find useful subpatterns within a continuous input stream. The network design requires that the end of a sequence must be recognizable when the first letter of the next sequence is received. Because of this design the system has limitations on the sequences that it can recognize. The prediction portion of the network can perform no better than a human can. With many sequences, it is impossible to know whether the next letter is an extension of the current word or the beginning of the next word. As an example consider the sequence of letters T H E Y. Without the rest of the letters we cannot tell whether the is The Y... or They. Thus a more complex scheme for determining the end of words must be used with many patterns.

The ability to learn the end of sequences is an important step in designing HRAAMs that can learn the modularization of the input instead of this modularization having to be assigned manually. In training a Hierarchical RAAM, other authors have not addressed a solution to this modularization problem. In [Angeline, 1991] the authors state "While it is beyond the scope of this study to allow the architecture to discover an appropriate modularization of the data, our future systems will be able to organize their own stable levels according to discovered regularities in the environment. In fact, we feel that the prospect of constructing artificial neural systems with a complexity on par with their biological cousins hinges upon this capability."

If we were designing a system with a level of complexity on par with living beings it would not be possible to train each level of a HRAAM separately because of the complexity of the system. Since our new RAAM can learn the end of patterns, it should be possible to train the whole HRAAM in one training sequence instead of training each layer separately. While this is expected to be computationally more expensive, because of the additional levels of floating symbols, [Pollack, 1989b] the fact that the levels of the problem do not have to be assigned but instead are learned is very valuable to more complex problems.

References

Angeline, Peter J., and Pollack, Jordan B., (1991) *Hierarchical RAAMs: A Modular Approach to Neural Networks*, Dept. of Computer Science, The Ohio State University.

Blank, Douglas S., Meeden, Lisa A., and Marshall, James, B. (1991). *Exploring the Symbolic/Subsymbolic Continuum: A Case Study of RAAM*, Department of Computer Science, Indiana University, May 6, 1991.

Chalmers, D.L. (1990). *Transformations on Distributed Representations.* In Noel Sharkey (ed.), Connectionist Natural Language Processing. Intellect Publishers, Oxford, pp. 46-55.

Doya, Kenji, (1993) *Universality of Fully-Connected Recurrent Neural Networks*, Department of Biology, University of California, San Diego, February 1, 1993.

Elman, J. L. (1990), *Finding Structure in Time*, Cognitive Science, vol. 14 no. 2, April 1990, pp. 179-211.

Kwasny, Stan C., Kalman Barry K., and Chang, Nancy, (1993) *Distributed Patterns as Hierarchical Structures,* in the Proceedings of The World Congress on Neural Networks, 1993, Vol. II, pp. 198-201.

Pollack, Jordan B., (1989a) *Recursive Distributed Representations*, Laboratory for AI Research & computer & Information Science Department, The Ohio State University, 1989.

Pollack, Jordan B., (1989b) *Implications of Recursive Distributed Representations*, Laboratory for AI Research, Ohio State University, 1989.

# Paralleled Hardware Annealing for Optimal Solutions in Multi-Level Recursive Neural Networks

Sa Hyun Bang, Bing J. Sheu, Josephine C.-F. Chang

Department of Electrical Engineering (Electrophysics and Systems)
University of Southern California, Los Angeles, CA 90089-0271

### Abstract

In a multi-level neural network, the output of each neuron is to produce a multi-bit representation. Therefore, the total network size can be significantly smaller than a conventional network. The reduction in network size is a highly desirable feature in VLSI neuroprocessor implementation for large-scale applications. The formulation of the Lyapunov energy function for a multi-level analog-to-digital decision network can be constructed. Due to the nonlinearity associated with the neuron transfer function, multiple local minima exist in the energy function. The procedure for applying hardware annealing by continuously changing the neuron gain from a low value to a certain high value, to reach the globally optimal solution is described. Several simulation results are also presented. The hardware annealing technique, which is the analog electronic version of the mean-field annealing method, can be applied to the neurons in a parallel format, and is much faster than the simulated annealing method on digital computers.

## I. Introduction

A typical neural network for solving optimization problems multiplies input signals with synapse weights, and the summed results are processed by the output neurons. As the number of input signals increases, the number of synapse weights increases accordingly. A large number of synapse weights will complicate the interconnection wiring between neuron layers, and significantly limit the size of a network to be implemented by a very large-scale intergation (VLSI) chip. An m-level neuron can produce output with $2^m$-bit accuracy [1,2]. Therefore, a multi-level neuron is quite desirable for VLSI implementation for complex optimization problems.

The gradient descent method is a conventional approach for optimization. It finds the gradient of the cost function to determine the direction for the next processing step. This method suffers from the inherent problem of possibly converging at a local minimum in the cost function. Recently, Yuh and Newcomb [1] presented a method using a correction logic circuit to obtain the optimal solutions for the multi-level Hopfield networks. Alspector et al. [3] have pioneered in the analog electronic implementation of the Boltzmann machine by adding the uncorrelated noise to find the globally optimal solution. Simulated annealing [4] is another important method for searching for the optimal results on digital computers. It is a stochastic process modeled after the metallurgical annealing. Due to a slow cooling schedule in software execution, the simulated annealing method on digital computers requires a lot of computing time for a complex optimization problem. By constructing a hardware-based parallel annealing technique in analog electronics, the processing speed can be significantly improved.

A high-quality semiconductor crystal can be formed by providing a seed as a guidance in the process of metallurgical annealing. On the other hand, if no seed is provided, the melting semiconductor will be cooled down to an amorphous condition. In hardware annealing, which is the analog hardwared version of the mean-field annealing [5], the external bias voltage provides a similar effect as the seed in metallurgical annealing. During the whole annealing process, the constant external bias directs the outcome of the network. If no bias is applied, the output of the network undergoes influence from residual capacitances of the output nodes initially. These capacitances constitute an initial state of the network. The output of the network becomes unpredictable if the network goes through the annealing process without the external bias. In this paper, an analog-to-digital (A/D) decision network is used to illustrate the properties of multi-level Hopfield networks because the optimal solution of an A/D decision network is always known [6,7].

## II. Multi-Level Neurons

To represent a multi-level neuron with $m$ threshold values, $\theta_0$ to $\theta_{m-1}$, a neuron transfer function of the form [1]

$$M_s(x) = \sum_{j=0}^{m-1} \frac{c_j}{1 + e^{-(x - \theta_j)}} \cdot \tag{1}$$

can be used. The transfer function for each level in (1) is replaced by a widely used sigmoid function. The scaling factor for the $p$-th level is $c_0 + c_1 + \cdots + c_p$. Therefore, the output level has a step size of $\Delta k_p = c_p$. In addition, $\theta_p < \theta_{p+1}$ holds for $0 \le p \le m-1$. The accumulation function $M(x)$ is a monotonically increasing function.

The 1-dimensional A/D decision network is suitable for illustrating the properties of the Hopfield multi-level neural network. In the Hopfield A/D network, a neuron with m-bit resolution is realized by $2^m$ amplifiers connected in parallel with their output currents summed together [1]. The summed current can be converted to the output voltage of the neuron by a current-to-voltage converter. The output voltages are connected back to the neuron inputs through interconnection conductances. An analog input value and a reference voltage are applied to all neurons. Figure 1 shows the schematic diagram of a 6-bit A/D decision network by using three 4-level neurons. The governing equation for the $i$-th neuron in an N-neuron network can be expressed as

$$C_i \frac{du_i(t)}{dt} + G_i u_i(t) = \sum_{j \ne i, j = 0}^{N-1} G_{ij} v_j(t) + G_{ri} x_r(t) + G_{ai} x_a(t) = \sum_{j \ne i, j = 0}^{N-1} G_{ij} v_j(t) + I_i(t) , \tag{2}$$

where $C_i$ and $G_i$ are the equivalent total capacitance and conductance at the input node of the $i$-th neuron, $G_{ij}$ is the conductance between the $i$-th and the $j$-th neurons, $x_r$ is the reference voltage, $x_a$ is the input analog voltage, $G_{ri}$ and $G_{ai}$ are the conductances connecting $x_r$ and $x_a$ to the $i$-th neuron. The voltage at the input node of the $i$-th neuron is $u_i(t)$, and the output voltage of the $j$-th neuron is $v_j(t)$.

The energy function for the network can be expressed as

$$E = -\frac{1}{2} \sum_{i=0}^{N-1} \sum_{j \ne i, j = 0}^{N-1} G_{ij} v_i v_j - \sum_{i=0}^{N-1} I_i v_i + \sum_{i=0}^{N-1} G_i \int_0^{v_i} g_i^{-1}(v) dv , \tag{3}$$

where $g(\cdot)$ is the voltage transfer function of the amplifier.

In a multi-level A/D decision network, the synapse weight values can be determined by minimizing the squared value of the difference between the input analog value and the corresponding digital representation [1],

$$E_o = (x_a - \sum_{i=0}^{N-1} m^i v_i)^2 . \tag{4}$$

After expanding (4) and dropping the constant term $x_a^2$, we obtain,

$$\hat{E}_o = -\frac{1}{2} \sum_{i=0}^{N-1} \sum_{j \ne i, j = 0}^{N-1} (-m^{i+j}) v_i v_j - \sum_{i=0}^{N-1} m^i x_a v_i + \frac{1}{2} \sum_{i=0}^{N-1} m^{2i} v_i^2 . \tag{5}$$

By assuming uniform spacings between the neighboring threshold values and the output levels in the decision network, i.e., $\Delta\theta$ and $\Delta k$ are constants, (3) can be reformulated as

$$E = -\frac{1}{2} \sum_{i=0}^{N-1} \sum_{j \ne i, j = 0}^{N-1} G_{ij} v_i v_j - \sum_{i=0}^{N-1} (I_i - \frac{1}{2} G_i \Delta\theta_i \Delta k_i) v_i + \frac{1}{2} \sum_{i=0}^{N-1} G_i \Delta\theta_i \Delta k_i v_i^2 . \tag{6}$$

By equating corresponding items in (5) and (6), we can obtain

$$G_{ij} = -m^{i+j} , \tag{7}$$

$$I_i = m^i x_a + \frac{1}{2} G_i \Delta\theta_i \Delta k_i = G_{ai} x_a + G_{ri} x_r \, ,$$

and

$$G_i \Delta\theta_i \Delta k_i = m^{2i} \, .$$

Here, $\Delta\theta_i$ is the increment in the threshold value and $\Delta k_i$ is the increment in the output-level value at the $i$-th neuron. The weights, inputs and thresholds for the neurons from (7) are clearly labeled in Fig. 1. The negative conductances $G_{ij}$'s are implemented by taking results from the inverted outputs of the neurons. The $G_{ri}$'s are determined for $x_r$ being one.

Let us carefully examine the transfer function of the A/D decision network. Assume that all neurons are biased in the linear region. In the steady state condition,

$$u_i = \frac{\sum\limits_{j \neq i, j=0}^{N-1} G_{ij} v_j + G_{ri} x_r + G_{ai} x_a}{G_i} \tag{8}$$

and

$$\theta_{i,k} \leq u_i < \theta_{i,k+1} \tag{9}$$

for the $k$-th level at the $i$-th neuron. Substituting (8) into (9), we can obtain

$$\frac{-\sum\limits_{j \neq i, j=0}^{N-1} G_{ij} v_j + G_i \theta_{i,k} - G_{ri} x_r}{G_{ai}} \leq x_a < \frac{-\sum\limits_{j \neq i, j=0}^{N-1} G_{ij} v_j + G_i \theta_{i,k+1} - G_{ri} x_r}{G_{ai}} \, . \tag{10}$$

Figure 2 shows the plot of the transfer function of a three-neuron A/D decision network. All the possible states determined by (10) are included. The output value of each neuron can be classified into one of four distinct levels. Please note that for some analog input values, the network can converge to different digital representations which correspond to multiple local minima in the energy function. For example, when the input value is 19.8, the output value may be 15, 19 or 20 depending on the initial condition of the network.

## III. Hardware Annealing

The Hopfield network is a recurrent network which finds the stable solution through iterations. Due to the nonlinear property of the network, the output could be stable at one of the local minima. Simulated annealing helps to escape from local minima by using the Boltzmann distribution function as the transfer function of a neuron. In hardware annealing, we change the voltage gain of the neurons in a continuous manner to achieve a similar effect as changing temperature in simulated annealing. Recently, some researchers have discussed methods of how to construct a gain-adjustable amplifier [3,8]. A multi-level Boltzmann neuron function [1] can be modified from (1):

$$M_b = \sum_{i=0}^{m-1} \frac{c_i}{1 + e^{-\eta(x - \theta_i)}} \, , \tag{11}$$

where $\eta$ is a gain-controlling factor which controls the slope of a multi-level transfer function. With a large gain value, the slope of the transfer curve around the threshold value is quite steep. A smaller gain value gives a smoother transition. When the threshold values are close to each other as shown in Fig. 3(a), the transfer curve for a high voltage gain still shows distinct levels, while that for a low voltage gain shows no distinct levels. By assigning 1 to $\Delta k_i$, the three threshold values for the least-significant-bit neuron are 1/21, 2/21, and 1/7, respectively. The threshold values for the most-significant-bit neuron are 8/3, 16/3, and 8, respectively, as shown in Fig. 3(b).

When the voltage gain of the neurons is sufficiently large, the sum of eigenvalues of the system matrix **M** of a Hopfield A/D decision network approximates to zero, and the product of eigenvalues is not equal to zero [9]. when the voltage gain of the neurons is sufficiently large. With the constraint that $G_{ij} = G_{ji}$, all eigenvalues will lie on the real axis of the $s$-plane. Thus at least one positive real eigenvalue exists, and the neuron outputs are saturated at digital values. Table 1 lists the eigenvalues for a 6-bit A/D decision network at a very large neuron gain. The single positive value $\lambda_1$ in a conventional two-level neuron decision network is much larger than that in a multi-level neuron decision network. In the multi-level 6-bit case, $\lambda_1 + \lambda_2 + \lambda_3$ is equal to 0, and $\lambda_1 \cdot \lambda_2 \cdot \lambda_3$ is equal to 8,205.

In a conventional Hopfield network, the output of an A/D decision network is stablized at an equilibrium state which corresponds to one of the local minima of the energy function. When the voltage gain is reduced to a critically low value, all neurons operate in the linear condition. The output of the A/D decision network is not fully digital. When the voltage gain reaches

$$A_{N-k} = \max \left\{ \frac{G_i}{\sum\limits_{j=0,j \in S}^{N-1} |G_{ij}|}, \text{ for } 0 \leq i \leq N-1, 0 \leq k \leq N-3 \right\}, \tag{12}$$

where $S$ contains linear-region neurons, only $N-k$ neurons operate in the linear region. As the voltage gain is increased, smaller number of neurons operates in the linear region. When the voltage gain reaches a critically high value,

$$A_2 = \max \left\{ \sqrt{\frac{G_p G_q}{G_{pq} G_{qp}}}, \text{ for } \textit{every } p, q \in [0, N-1], p \neq q \right\}, \tag{13}$$

only two neurons operate in the linear region [10]. When the voltage gain is slightly larger than $A_2$, only one neuron could be in the linear region. Although at this point the neuron output is still an analog value, the digital output of the amplifier can be easily determined. Table 2 lists the different critical voltage gains for a 6-bit A/D decision network. The $A_2$ values for the 4-level neural network are smaller than those for the 2-level network.

## IV. Analysis Results

In metallurgical annealing, a certain high temperature was first applied to highly mobilize the atoms. It is then slowly decreased to allow atoms to fit into lattice sites in a minimum-energy fashion. In our experiment, an A/D decision network which consists of three neurons was analyzed. Each neuron has four distinguishable levels which correspond to the 2-bit accuracy. The analog input has a nominal range of 0 to 64 which can be scaled to the range of 0 to 5 V if electronic hardware implementation is considered. The network output is reconstructed by a D/A converter.

The voltage gain of neurons is decreased first and then gradually increased. The analog input value $x_a$ was chosen to be 7.9 which has one local minimum at digital representation (020) besides the global minimum at (013). When the voltage gain value was low, all neurons operated in the linear region. Then, the voltage gain was increased until all neuron outputs became saturated into digital representation. The input and output values of neurons are shown in Figs. 4 and 5, respectively. Initially, the output state of the A/D decision network was at (013) which corresponds to the local minimum. After the hardware annealing process, the output state changed to (020) which is the desired digital output. The trajectory of the output state is plotted in Fig. 6. Plots of energy surfaces and contours which correspond to different voltage gain values are shown in Figs. 7, 8, and 9. Two energy minima occur when the neuron is at a high voltage gain value of 100. When the voltage gain is reduced to 10, only one energy minimum left. At a low voltage gain value of 2.5, the minimum energy corresponds to a solution which is not a fully digital representation.

## V. Conclusion

The Hopfield network can be equipped with multi-level neurons in order to reduce the size of the synapse matrix. We have applied the hardware annealing technique to the multi-level Hopfield network to quickly search for the optimal solution. The voltage gain of the neurons is gradually increased from a certain low value to a critically high value. The energy surface was modified by the annealing process and the natural gradient-descent operation at various gain values help the solution to reach the optimal state.

## References

[1]  J.-D. Yuh and R. W. Newcomb, "A multilevel neural network for A/D conversion," *IEEE Trans. on Neural Networks,* vol. 4, no. 3, pp. 470-483, May 1993.

[2]  J. Si and A. N. Michel, "Analysis and synthesis of discrete-time neural networks with multilevel threshold functions," *Proc. of IEEE International Symposium on Circuits and Systems,* pp. 1461-1464, Singapore, June 1991.

[3]  J. Alspector, A. Jayakumar, and S. Luna, "Experimental evaluation of learning in a neural microsystems," *Proceedings of Neural Information Processing Systems,* vol. 4, pp. 871-878, 1991.

[4]  S. Kirkpatrick, C. D. Gelatt, Jr., and M. P. Vecchi, "Optimization by simulated annealing," *Science,* vol. 220, no. 4598, pp. 671-680, May 1983.

[5]  C. Peterson, "Mean field theory neural networks for feature recognition, content addressable memory and optimization," *Connection Science,* vol. 3, pp. 3-33, 1991.

[6]  D. W. Tank and J. J. Hopfield, "Simple 'neural' optimization networks: an A/D converter, signal decision circuit, and a linear programming circuit," *IEEE Trans. on Circuits and Systems,* vol. 33, pp. 533-541, May 1986.

[7]  B. W. Lee and B. J. Sheu, "Parallel hardware annealing for optimal solutions on electronic neural networks," *IEEE Trans. on Neural Networks,* vol. 4, no. 4, pp. 588-599, Jul. 1993.

[8]  R. P. Lippmann, "An introduction to computing with neural nets," *IEEE Acoustics, Speech, and Signal Processing Magazine,* vol. 4, pp. 4-21, Apr. 1987.

[9]  B. J. Sheu, J. Choi, and C.-F. Chang, "An analog neural network processor for self-organizing mapping," *Tech. Dig. of IEEE International Solid-State Circuits Conference,* pp. 136-137 and 266, San Francisco, CA, Feb. 1992.

[10]  B. W. Lee and B. J. Sheu, *Hardware Annealing in Analog VLSI Neurocomputing,* Kluwer Academic Publishers: Boston, MA, 1991.

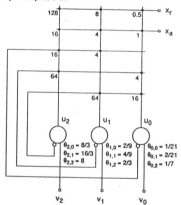

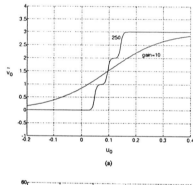

Fig. 1    A Hopfield 4-level neural A/D decision network.

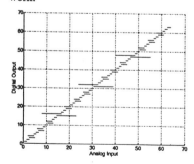

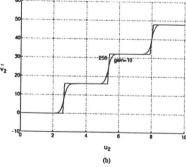

Fig. 2    Transfer function of a 6-bit A/D decision network. Each neuron contains three levels.

Fig. 3    Plots of the 4-level neuron functions with different controlling gains used in a 3-neuron A/D decision network . (a) Least-significant neuron. (b) Most-significant neuron.

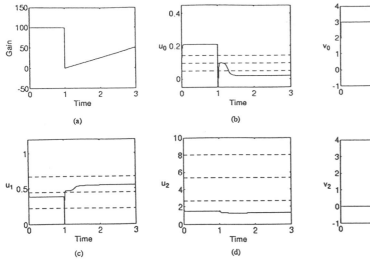

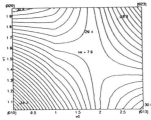

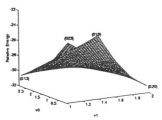

**Fig. 4** Time domain responses of the voltages at the neuron input nodes in the A/D decision network when the analog input value $x_a$ is 7.9. (a) Neuron gain. (b) Neuron 0. (c) Neuron 1. (d) Neuron 2.

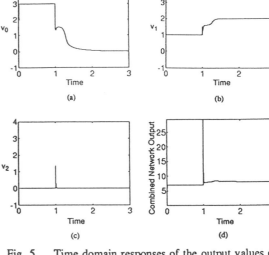

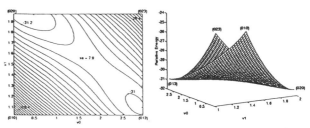

**Fig. 5** Time domain responses of the output values of neurons when the analog input value $x_a$ is 7.9. (a) Neuron 0. (b) Neuron 1. (c) Neuron 2. (d) Combined output.

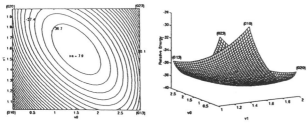

**Fig. 7** The energy contour and the energy surface of the voltage at the input node of neuron $u_2$ is kept as 0. $x_a$ is 7.9 and amplifier gain is 100.

**Fig. 8** The energy contour and the energy surface of the voltage at the input node of neuron $u_2$ is kept as 0. $x_a$ is 7.9 and amplifier gain is 10.

**Fig. 9** The energy contour and the energy surface of the voltage at the input node of neuron $u_2$ is kept as 0. $x_a$ is 7.9 and amplifier gain is 2.5.

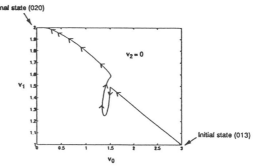

**Fig. 6** The output state trajectory of the A/D decision network.

Table 1 Eigenvalues of a 6-bit A/D decision network

| | I: 6-bit ($2^6$) | II: 6-bit ($4^3$) |
|---|---|---|
| $\lambda_1$ | 668.63 | 67.01 |
| $\lambda_2$ | -534.96 | -65.13 |
| $\lambda_3$ | -104.64 | -1.88 |
| $\lambda_4$ | -22.65 | |
| $\lambda_5$ | -5.19 | |
| $\lambda_6$ | -1.22 | |

I: Conventional Hopfield network
II: Multi-level Hopfield network

Table 2 Critical amplifier gains of a 6-bit A/D decision network

| | I: 6-bit ($2^6$) | II: 6-bit ($4^3$) |
|---|---|---|
| $A_2$ | 44.72 | 10.37 |
| $A_3$ | 20.67 | 2.80 |
| $A_4$ | 8.57 | |
| $A_5$ | 3.73 | |
| $A_6$ | 1.55 | |

I: Conventional Hopfield Network
II: Multi-leveled Hopfield Network

# OPTIMIZATION OF PRESENTATION ORDER IN NETWORKS OF GOAL SEEKING NEURONS

W Martins[1] and N M Allinson
Image Engineering Group
Department of Electronics
University of York
York, UK, YO1 5DD
e-mail: weber@ohm.york.ac.uk

## Abstract

Logical (weighless) neural networks are known for their low-cost and ease of physical implementation. Networks of Goal Seeking Neurons provide an interesting class of logical neural networks and were designed to overcome some problems with Probabilistic Logic Neurons[1], the successor of the very first logical model. Being created to make hardware implementation even easier, special concern was given to ensure that neuronal computations were local, i.e., by using only data directly available and use of an one-shot learning algorithm.

Some promising results have been achieved using GSN networks[2] and some improvements have already been proposed[3],[4]. This paper reports an empirical study on ways to enhance GSN performance by considering the temporal presentation order of examples during learning. Some principles could be useful in improving other learning models based on one-shot training algorithms. Another point is the way nets are usually trained: individually with no consideration on their future roles in a collective task. Considering training as a collective task can lead to a better management of internal locations occupied within networks.

## 1  Introduction

Networks of Goal Seeking Neurons were proposed to overcome problems with Aleksander's Probabilistic Logical Node model[1]. The main difference from PLN is the possibility to output the undefined value 'u'. Therefore, a layer of neurons in a typical feed-forward architecture can address not just one location of the following layer but many. This multiple addressing can join similar patterns, save free space and delay occurance of consequent saturation. Moreover, it suggests an one-shot learning algorithm that rejects pairs of input-output patterns that would disrupt (contradict with) stored information. On the other hand, the recall algorithm does not allow a stochastic behaviour but it provides deterministic ways to define outputs.

The neuron can possess three states: validation, learning and recall. In the validation state, the neuron decides if it is possible to make the desired input-output mapping. The learning itself, which changes the internal contents of the neuron, is done during the learning state and priority is given to use an already occupied address and so improve generalization. If there is no correctly addressed position with the desired output, the neuron uses an unused one (with 'u' content) and changes it. Finally, in the recall state, simple laws are applied (such as the neuron outputs the value of the majority of addressed internal positions).

The learning action of GSNs in feedforward multi-layer networks has some similarity with back-propagation. First, the input pattern is used to provide a *natural* response from the network based on stimulating neurons to answer 'u' (see Figure 1), if there is an 'u' in some addressed internal position, or if there is a '1' and a '0' at addressed positions. If the final output is 'u' or the desired output, learning can take place. Then, propagating from the output level towards the input level, each neuron enters the learning state. When the neurons at the output level specify which input addresses they have chosen, the neurons of the previous layer discern what answer must be output and are able to enter the learning state and so on.

---

[1] On leave from UFG - Escola de Engenharia Eletrica, Caixa Postal 112, Universidade Federal de Goias, 74000 GO, Brazil. Supported by grant 200291/90-4, CNPq, Brazilian Research Council.

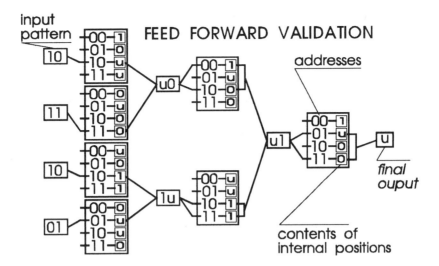

Figure 1:     Validation stage in a GSN multi-layer feed forward network.

Some promising results have been achieved using GSN networks[2] and some improvements have already been proposed on how internal physical locations should be chosen[3], and on how inputs and output codes should be arranged before training takes place[4].

This paper focuses on the optimization of the presentation order used to input examples during training. To avoid the need of storing examples, systems based on GSN have all networks exposed to the examples in the same order (the acquisition order). Since GSN nets do not change internal locations that have been previously assigned, it is to be expected differences in learning due, in part, to the presentation order. Filho[5], on the basis of experimental work, concluded that the best strategy was to use random ordering for classes. He, however, used very few examples and only tested arbitrary class sequences. A dynamic search using example sequences does show significant effects due to presentation order.

Another important point is that nets are usually trained individually with no consideration of their future roles in a collective task.  The advantages of distributed knowledge representation and processing have been raised for many years. Seeing training as a collective task can enhance the system performance because pattern space is better utilized within networks.

Finally, the search for improved sequences leads *naturally* to the recognition of inconsistent (or outlying) examples. These tend to require high priority (i.e., early presentation) in the learning, since they try to teach something *strange* within the whole context. Moreover, their acceptance can prevent the learning for other input examples. This strategy will be analysed in a further paper.

## 2 Algorithms for Optimization of Presentation Order

Once the importance of presentation order is considered, and training is viewed as a group activity, many algorithms appear to be feasible. The essential idea is to compensate the resulting learning from one network with the behaviour of another.  How this *history* is recorded (and transmited) is the main issue.

The first algorithm is relatively straightforward. The presentation order for each network is the result of sorting a global ranking vector[2]. Initially, examples are in a random order and each one has a '0' as its associated ranking. The ranking vector is updated by training of the current network. One family of algorithms is illustrated in Fig. 2 and 3. One simple rule is to increase by '1' the rankings of examples successfully learned.  Despite its simplicity, this strategy can control, depending on how the output codes are prearranged, when the entire training set has been learnt (if every output code is separated by $n$ bits and every ranking is greater than this, then all training examples are learnt). Other update procedures can take into

_____

[2]More precisely, the ranking vector is a 2-dimensional vector used to store the example position in the training set and ranking. As the positional link never changes, just the ranking part is discussed.

account the relative position when a particular example was presented, the number of changed internal locations, etc.

```
1. Ranking ← 0;
2. B ← 1;  { positional bit of output code }
3.      N ← 1;  { number of nets per positional bit }
4.          E ← 1;  { training example }
5.              Teach_and_Update(Ranking[E],B,N);
6.              E ← E + 1;
7.          if E ≤ Number_Of_Examples then Goto 5;
8.          Sort_Ranking;
9.          N ← N + 1;
10.     if N ≤ Number_Of_Nets_Per_Bit then Goto 4;
11.     B ← B + 1;
12. if B ≤ Number_Of_Bits_In_Output_Codes then Goto 3.
```

Figure 2:        Family of sequencial algorithms to optimize the presentation order with full cooperation among networks.

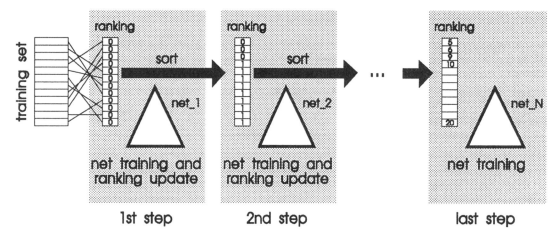

Figure 3:        Visualization of sequential algorithms to dynamically optimize the presentation order with full cooperation among networks.

The extent of collective effort can be imposed explicitly by controlling the context of cooperation. Two obvious contexts are: (a) all networks, and (b) networks that undertake the same mapping or, in other words, related to the same positional bit of output codes. Since this last version involves independent processes, nothing precludes the employment of concurrency to execute it, if a ranking vector is provided for each group. Moreover, it is possible to invert the two innermost controlling loops in order to work with groups of networks, where each group has a network designated to each positional bit of the output code. The four ways to control the temporal path along which networks can be trained are shown schematically in Fig. 4.

For parallel computation, a dynamic sorting and updating of the ranking vector creates further possibilities for more concurrent algorithms. Some auxiliary data structures must be used to ensure a network never attempts to learn an example more than once and to provide an unbiased procedure for assigning examples to networks.

| | |
|---|---|
| **Case 1 (FUL):** Ranking ← 0; for B from 1 to Bmax do; for T from 1 to Tmax do; Teach_and_Update |
| **Case 2 (FU2) :** Ranking ← 0; for T from 1 to Tmax do; for B from 1 to Bmax do; Teach_and_Update |
| **Case 3 (PAR):** for B from 1 to Bmax do; Ranking ← 0; for T from 1 to Tmax do; Teach_and_Update |
| **Case 4 (PA2) :** for T from 1 to Tmax do; Ranking ← 0; for B from 1 to Bmax do; Teach_and_Update |

where B     is the positional bit of the output code
Bmax is the total number of bits in an output code
T      is the network pointer
Tmax is the total number of networks per positional ouput code bit

Figure 4:        Ways to control the temporal path along which networks are trained.

## 3 Experiments

Many simulations have been conducted to provide data to confirm the above concepts. Each result displayed in following figures is the average of 100 simulations. Neurons have only two inputs. To make an unbiased comparison, identical (randomly chosen) initial networks are used for the standard and optimized trainings and smaller trees are used as the sub-trees. For instance, 64-input trees are the result of appending new 32-input trees. This seems appropriate for real-world problem tasks where the need is to know how improvement is possible if current trees are kept as sub-trees to larger ones. Advanced portable random number generators[6] were employed to make the results repeatable.

Initially, a sequential algorithm was tried with the simplest update procedure of adding '1' to rankings of successfully learnt examples (*rule_1*). A more elaborated update procedure was then applied. The relative position inside the ranking vector is considered and used as the value to add to, or subtract from, the current ranking if an example is learnt or not respectively. With this strategy, (*rule_2*) examples presented late tend to maintain their positions when successfully learnt or to be presented earlier if not learnt. Developing this idea (*rule_3*), the complement of the current position in ranking (i.e., quantity of examples yet to be presented) was used to decrement rankings of unsuccessfully learnt examples.

Heuristic strategies were also employed to extend the power of individual networks. Since each network changes itself to learn a 2-class ('0' and '1') mapping, an attempt was made to post-process the sorted ranking vector so that desired outputs of consecutive examples were always different. This approach was termed *static alternation* and gave rise to *rule_4*, *rule_5* and *rule_6* (matching *rule_1*, *rule_2*, and *rule_3* respectively). Another approach is to consider the sorted ranking as a queue. The procedure for choosing examples is dictated by the aim of balancing the amount of learnt examples of both classes. This balance is initialized by the difference of the number of examples in both classes. This heuristic is called *dynamical alternation* and produced *rule_7*, *rule_8* and *rule_9* (matching *rule_1*, *rule_2*, and *rule_3* respectively).

The outcome of these experiments is presented by Fig. 6. In the next section, some conclusions are drawn from these results. The training set is composed of 160 16x16 black-white images and the evaluation set is composed of 800 examples. The task is not an easy one (Fig. 5 shows some statistics from the training and evaluation sets). A simple Hadamard encoding was used to define output codes.

| *average Hamming distance* | *training set* | *evaluation set* |
|---|---|---|
| *intra-class: minimum* | 4.99 (digit 1) | 5.19 (digit 1) |
| *average* | 9.18 | 10.00 |
| *maximum* | 11.72 (digit 8) | 12.89 (digit 8) |
| *inter-class: minimum* | 9.83 (between 1 and 3) | 10.02 (between 1 and 7) |
| *average* | 14.31 | 14.41 |
| *maximum* | 17.31(between 5 and 8) | 17.46 (between 0 and 8) |

Figure 5:        Percentual average Hamming distances in training and evaluation sets.

# 4 Results

Since there many results to present, Fig. 6 employs gray-level images. At the left side, absolute values are shown to give a general impression of how the topologies and algorithms compared. At the right side, the "contrast" for each topology was set to its maximum to provide an improved indication of performance for each topology.

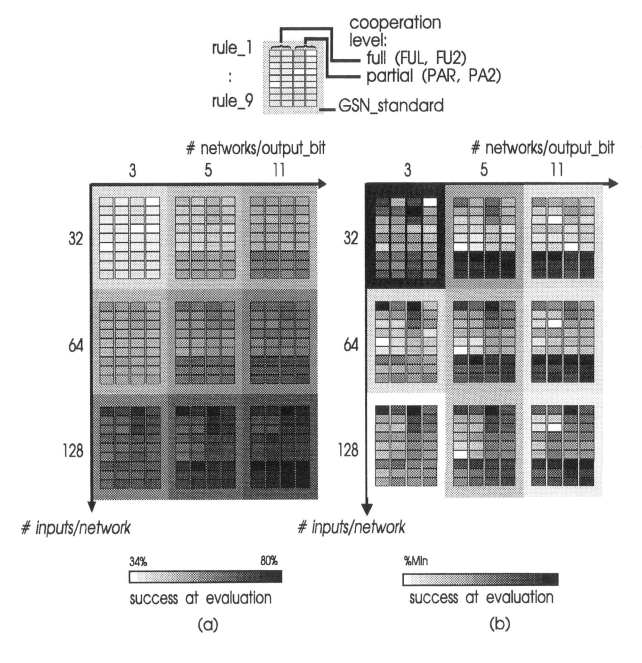

Figure 6:     Success rate at evaluation for all algorithms:
(a) absolute values; (b) maximum contrast.

There is greater advantage in keeping the number of networks constant and increasing the number of inputs per network than vice-versa. Since training algorithms are focused on one network at a time, more representational power is obtained by increasing the number of inputs rather than calling for other networks of the same size to be created.

The first topology, three 32-input networks per positional bit of the output code, is the only one where the standard GSN has performed as well as the best results from any of the proposed algorithms. The proposed algorithms have little space in which to propagate their qualities. On the other hand, it is clear that for this topology maximum performance (38%) is inadequate for most applications. The proposed algorithms surpass the standard one in line with the representational power of the topology, i.e., they become relatively more efficient with the increasing of the number of networks and the number of inputs per network.

For the applied rules, the results show a clear superiority of *rule_1*. This rule is also the simplest to implement. The *dynamic alternation* is specially efficient when the number of networks is high; even though, *rule_1* without any alternation scheme has proved consistent for all topologies.

With respect to the ways of controlling the temporal path in which networks are trained (Fig. 4), the most natural choice of clustering networks (i.e., by the mapping they should implement) is also the best one. As a global strategic, *partial cooperation* gave better results than *full cooperation*. This is important because it reassures the efficiency of concurrent implementations.

## 5 Conclusions

Algorithms for the optimization of presentation order have been described and empirically justified. The various schemes indicated that, since GSN rejects "unlearnable" examples, they should make the presentation order dynamic to take into account the behaviour of the network. In the main, the simplest scheme, *rule_1*, has proved to be the most useful.

As feed-forward networks of GSNs undergo their learning phase before being used for classification, so every possible improvement is important during this learning. The presentation order affects the system because of its one-shot training algorithm. It may be that the principles described play a significant role in similar situations. This study represents the first steps in the recognition of false (or very strange) examples that should perhaps be excluded from the training process.

## 6 References

[1]  Kan, W K and Aleksander I, 1987, "A probabilistic logic neuron network for associative learning", in *Proc. IEEE First International Conference on Neural Networks*, volume II, 541-548, San Diego, California, USA.
[2] Bisset, D L et al, 1989, "A comparative study of neural network structures for practical application in a pattern recognition environment" in *Proc. First IEE Interl. Conf. on Artificial Neural Networks*, 378-382, London, UK.
[3]  Martins, W and Allinson, N M, 1993, "Two improvements for GSN neural networks", in *Proc. Weighless Neural Network Workshop '93*, 58-63, York, UK.
[4] Bowmaker, R G, and Coghill, G G, 1992, "Improved Recognition Capabilities for Goal Seeking Neuron", in *Electronic Letters*, vol. 28, No. 3, 220-221.
[5] Filho, E, 1990, "Investigation of boolean neural network based on a novel Goal-Seeking-Neuron", PhD Thesis, Electronic Engineering Laboratories, University of Kent, UK.
[6] L'Ecuyer, P, 1988, "Efficient and portable combined random number generators", in *Communications of ACM*, vol 31, 742-749.

# A NETWORK PARADIGM TO DETECT SIMILARITIES IN A DATA BASE CONCERNING INDUSTRIAL HEALTH SURVEY

M.R. CONSOLA RIZZO, GNOSIS sarl,2, Rue des Sablons,
                    78400 CHATOU (FRANCE)
M. FALCY, INRS - 30, Rue Olivier Noyer
                    75680 PARIS Cedex 14
A. EMOND, INRS - BP 27 - 54501 VANDOEUVRE

## ABSTRACT

With regard to extract the knowledges from the set of records stored in the medical toxicovigilance data base of the INRS, (French National Institute for Research and Safety), we were looking for an automatic system able to find similarities between records. It's a matter of similarity criteria, closeness evaluation and/or distance valuation. The data base contains, among other items, an "Entry vector" that represents the coded "exposures", including relationship factors, and an "Output vector" that represents the coded "symptoms".

The BAM (Bi-directional Associative Memory) network paradigm has shown the best performance during the tests about some records. Indeed, the network learns each pair of vectors as an "Association" between the "exposures" (Inputs) and the "symptoms" (output). For a shown Association, the network recall procedure tries to find among all the learned Associations, the closest learned Association, i.e. the local minimum of the agregate weight matrix. The "similarity" between the two pairs of Associations is immediately found.

KEYWORDS : Toxicovigilance - Closeness evaluation - Exposures - Symptoms - BAM network paradigm - Energy fonction

## 1. MEDICAL TOXICOVIGILANCE : OBJECT

It is important 1) to explain what we call in French "vigilance industrielle", and 2) to understand the necessity for an intelligent classification system.

We could define "vigilance industrielle" as the surveillance of health events related to occupational problems. This includes not only chemicals-related accidents but also accidents related with physical or infectious agents, even though, at the present time, toxicological observations represent the main data.

Hazardous situations at the workplace are so various that it is actually impossible to study and detect them a priori. For example, a complete toxicological testing is not performed on a substance before its industrial use. Short-term tests are used (acute toxicity, irritation and mutagenicity testing) but not long term ones (carcinogenicity testing...).

Thus, it appears necessary to develop a system for collecting all accident or incident data possibly related to occupational exposures and comparing them to detect as early as possible either a new pathololology (set of symptoms) related to a known industrial process or a pathology induced by new risk factors.

The first problem to be solved is the validation of each observation, the second is the characterization of the informations computerized. Validation is an important step which generally involves a multidisciplinary approach :
        -technical aspect: the materiality of exposure has to be confirmed (by analysis, measurement of physical nuisance...).
        -medical aspect: complementary exams have to be performed in order to confirm the diagnosis.

Through this validation process we ascertain the validity of the observation, but it is not sufficient to prove either the relationship between exposure and symptoms or even the occupational cause of the disease.

This phase, requiring the cooperation of technicians, engineers and physicians, takes necessarily place at the local level.

Once validated, the data must be systematically codified and recorded. Each file includes a complete medico-technical observation: information concerning the injured patient (sex, age, medical history, smoking and drinking habits, use of medications), his or her kind of work (type of industry, precise job, work history) and of course a complete description of the symptoms observed, the results of complementary examination and the exposure assessment (in a qualitative and semi-quantitative way).

At this stage it is necessary to centralize the observations in order to obtain a homogeneous codification process and a sufficient number of observations for comparison purposes.

The computerization is made on a classical relational database system (INGRES) that allows us to perform multicriteria interrogations on all fields of input data. But industrial vigilance also needs an intelligent computational system able to identify as similar two or more similar incidents described in different ways.

This search for proximity or distance ensure a quick detection of related occupational incidents, wich will be investigated later by toxicological and epidemiological studies.

For this purpose, we only take into account exposure and symptom fields, so that these data are coded in a hierarchical way, as described later.

## 2. TRADITIONAL DATA PROCESSING

A way to solve the problem of proximity research was to explore the traditional computer systems, i.e. the approved data processing technologies such as :

    a. Graphical-tree representation (Graph theory)
    b. The fuzzy set theory
    c. The Hamming distance computation

However, in the first case, the combinational logic becomes quickly "explosive" : there is a symptom for each node, the same symptom is a member of several trees and there are thousands of symptoms to schedule.

With regard to the second case, the complex system design difficulty and its complicated implementation compelled us to give up this solution.

In the third solution, the statistical distance computation fulfills the "statistical" proximity, but does not include the "neighbourhood" concept, which is a major element in the SNOMED (Systematized Nomenclature of Medicine) symptoms codification. This codification is a systematized multi-axial nomenclature of medically useful terms, hierarchically organized. A topological information exists in the code nodes, which has to be highlighted.

Lastly, because of the difficulties in implementing these solutions, the neural network technology was explored.

## 3. A SOLUTION BY THE NETWORK PARADIGM : THE BAM MODEL

### 3.1. CONSTRAINTS FOR A NETWORK PARADIGM

Several constraints exist for a network paradigm, i.e., :

    a. Unsupervised learning

There are no "best" incidents or "best" relationship between a set of pattern symptoms and a set of exposures or pattern exposures. So the network must be self-organizing : no external teacher provides the desired response patterns.

    b. Hetero-associative memory

The pattern on recall from the memory (incident x) is purposely different from the input patterns (all other learned incidents).

    c. Non-orthogonal states

With regard to the input-output data matrix, the coded and effectively present information concern approximately twenty percent of the possible information. I.e., the "empty" or dummy values are much more numerous.

d. Neighbouring groups classification

The classification inside exclusive classes is not interesting for our application, because the topological information contained in the code roots would be lost.

Different paradigms, such as the Kohonen "topological maps", the "Kanerva" memory or the Hopfield model were analysed and implemented as breadboard models, with a view to finding the best solution. Finally it is an adaptation of the Grossberg ART model, the BAM network (Bi-directional Associative Memory), which gives the best results.

### 3.2. THE BAM PARADIGM IMPLEMENTATION

The BAM model was developed by Bart KOSKO at Verac Corporation (USA, 1987). It was designed with optical computers in mind. It was inspired by Stephen Grossberg's Adaptive Resonance Theory (ART) and generalizes the Hopfield model to construct a hetero-associative memory.

The network has two central (BAM) layers fully inter-connected in the following way :

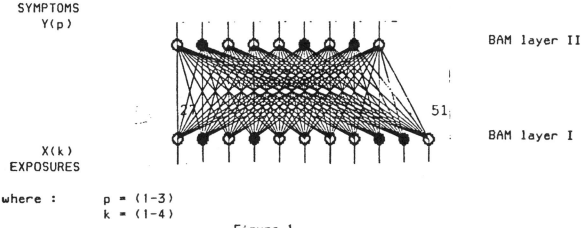

SYMPTOMS
$Y(p)$

BAM layer II

BAM layer I

$X(k)$
EXPOSURES

where :      $p = (1-3)$
          $k = (1-4)$

Figure 1

The double arrows on the BAM layer connections indicate that information can flow in both directions which is what happens during the oscillatory recall process.

Every incident stored in the toxicovigilance data base is composed of a set of "exposures" and a set of "symptoms" linked by a relationship factor. This factor represents the "robustness index" of the relation.

For a given association (incident), the set of Exposures corresponds to the network input vector 'Xi' and the set of Symptoms corresponds to output vector 'Yi'. The incident 'i' is therefore defined by the vector pairs (Xi,Yi).

The network is designed to store the associated pairs of vectors as follows :

a. The input vector (Xi) (the set of EXPOSURES) : the BAM layer I
b. The output vector (Yi) (the set of SYMPTOMS) : the BAM layer II
   (See Fig. 1)


## 3.3. THE DATA CODIFICATION CRITERIA

For the description of symptomatology, SNOMED (Systematized Nomenclature of Medicine) has been chosen. This is a precise codification system established by the College of American Pathologists. It can be described as a multi-axial nomenclature of useful medical terms hierarchically organized. We use five of the six axes defined, each of them being identified by one letter (to represent the name of the axis) and a five-digit code.

The first axis Topography refers to the sick organs or tissues; the second Morphology, corresponds to pathological anatomy; all human functions and functional states are found in the third axis, called Function, and the administrative, preventive, diagnostic and therapeutic actions in the Procedure axis. Disease is the last axis used when the combination of the other axes is equal to a complex disease entity or syndrome.

The classification problem is more difficult to solve in the case of exposures, as no classification systems appear to be satisfying. For example, the Etiology axis of SNOMED is not precise enough in the case of chemical exposures. We only use it for bacteriological and drug exposures. A home-made codification based on the same principles as SNOMED has been developed. It is a three axes, one-letter and five-digit codification system which allows us to define the main type of products or pollutants (ie., mineral fibers, pesticides...), the type of chemicals (beryllium and inorganic beryllium compounds, cyclic aliphatic amines...), the type of physical stressors (mental load, non-ionising radiation...).

This codification system is certainly complex but this is quite necessary for our classification purposes.

EXAMPLE OF EXPOSURE CODIFICATION

    A 20000 Fibers
    A 21000 Mineral fibers
    A 21100 Asbestos


EXAMPLE OF SYMPTOMS CODIFICATION

    Disease Axis :   D 30000 Complex diseases and syndromes of the skeletal
                             system, skin and connective tissues
                     D 35000 Disease or syndrome of skin, Dermatosis
                     D 35400 Urticaria, Hives
                     D 35420 Psychogenic urticaria


EXAMPLE of codification according to SNOMED  classification :

```
   T    +    M    +     E      +   F   =    D
Lung  + Granuloma + Tuberculosis + Fever = Tuberculosis
T28000    M44060      E20010      F03003     D01880
```

The data coding takes the internal structure of data codification into account and this data layout is very interesting for the proximity detection.

Data Organization in accordance with the internal hierarchic structure of the used codification

Example :

EXPOSURES AXIS MATRIX

| A (Materials) | B (Chemical Prod.) | C (Physical Damages) | E (Etiology) |
|---|---|---|---|
| 00000000000100 | 000000000000000000000 | 001000000000000100000 | 0000000100010000 |
| 00000000000001 | 000000000100000010000 | 000000000000000010000 | 0000000100000000 |
| 00000100000000 | 000000000000000000000 | 000010000000000000000 | 0001000000000000 |
| 00000010000000 | 000001000000000000000 | 000100000000000100000 | 0000000100001000 |

SYMPTOMS AXIS MATRIX

| D (Disease) | F (Function) | M (Morphology) | P (Procedure) | T (Topography) |
|---|---|---|---|---|
| 000000000001 | 000000000000000 | 00100000000000010 | 000000010010000 | 000100010000010 |
| 000000000000 | 000000001000001 | 00000000000000001 | 000000010000000 | 000001000000000 |
| 000001000000 | 000000000000000 | 00001000000000000 | 000100000000000 | 000010000000100 |
| 000000100000 | 000001000000000 | 00010000000000010 | 000000100001000 | 000010000000000 |

## 3.4. LEARNING STRATEGY

At the learning stage, for each association the Exposure vector is applied to the first layer and the Symptom vector is applied to the second layer (See Fig.1).

The set of vector pairs is applied to the network once and for all. To simulate the relationship factor, the learning is reinforced in proportion to the factor intensity. For example : for an 'i' association, if the relationship factor is '5', this association is applied to the network 5 times.

IV-121

The learning rule applied to the BAM layers is the bi-polar version of the Hopfield learning rule. (If the desired output and the input are both '1' or '-1', the weight is incremented. If either are zero, the weight isn't changed; otherwise, the weight is decremented.)

The learning rate originally set to '1.0' was changed, because of the non-orthogonal states of the examples. Some different rates were tested, with the aim of increasing the impact of the positive values and reducing the negative values power.

The weighted summation function is the traditional sum of the effective inputs.

The transfer function used by the BAM network is the following :
if the sum is > 0, the value for the transfer is '1'; if the sum is < 0, the value is '-1'; otherwise it is zero.

As soon as the associations are applied to the network, <<the learning process forms an energy surface whose domain is the set of vector pairs defining pattern association; each such association has an energy value>>(9).


### 3.5. THE RECALL PROCEDURE

<<The recall procedure iteratively updates the state of the network so that its energy monotonically decreases to a local minimum.>>(9)

For the energy function of an association :
$$xi * yi$$
the recall procedure tries to find the energy function of the association :
$$xi1 * yi1$$
which corresponds to the closest learned association : i.e., the local minimum of the aggregate weight matrix :

$$W(k) = x(k) * y(k)$$

The aim is to find the association (or the associations) which are the closest to a given vector pair : the search therefore of the best "similar" association.

To get that, a selected incident (association) is applied to the network : the exposures vector to the first BAM layer and the symptoms vector to the second BAM layer. <<The recall is done by oscillating back and forth between the two layers until equilibrium is achieved. The convergence to an equilibrium state is guaranteed by means of an energy function which is reduced at each iteration of the process.>>(9)

Each new association is "seen" as an existing (learned) but noised association; so the recall procedure tries to find the best "similar" vector pair : the local minimum for this association.

Indeed for each learned vector pair the local minimum is this vector pair itself; the other pairs right next to the local minimum are "similar". The aim of this application is not to find the local minimum, but to search for the other pairs very close to this minimum.


## 3.6. THE FIRING RATE

A firing rate, i.e., a restriction to the neurons activation, was introduced in recall.<< In this way the condition for a given neuron to be modified is both that the summation value be non-zero and a uniform random variable has a value greater than the firing rate.>>(9)

Several firing rate values were analysed and implemented either at the breadboard level or at the prototype level. Finally, at the system run level with 200 incidents, we found that low firing rates compel the system to explore all the possible proximities for a given association and avoid falling on a local minimum.

But a firing rate greater than 25 often gives inaccurate results.
A rate of 10 or 15 gives consistent results, but not very rich. Lastly, some similarities are detected with a higher rate.


## 3.7. CONCLUSION : THE BEST PARAMETERS

Many values of the different parameters have been examined and implemented, before reaching the best performance.

a. The bipolar version of the Hopfield learning rule (the Hebb rule) was modified as follows : the momentum term was not used and the input-output values finally agreed were " -0.001" (for the absent values) and " +0.95" (for the present values). The aim was to minimize the dummy values and maximize the real values, because of the non-orthogonal states.

b. We introduce a low firing rate as an option in the recall procedure in order to approximate asynchronous updating of the neuronal state. It seems that this restriction on neuronal updating allows a closer modeling of the asynchronous activity of the brain.
Also, to find all the similar incidents for a given association, it had to be run with two firing rates, one lower (10 or 15) and the other higher (30 or 35) and later to compare the results.


c. In the global processing, the observed proximities are wrong when the data stand around the axis break. So a specific processing, i.e. a scan by each symptom axis largely solves this problem, highlights all the possible proximities per axis and finally reduces the network size.
This partial analysis is very useful and complements the global analysis.
Even if some wrong proximities persist in this pre-selection, they will be detected later in the case by case analysis.

The breadboard models were implemented in the "Neuralworks Explorer",

Neural Ware Inc., Penn Center, USA.

The prototype and the final system were implemented in the "SN2 Software", Neuristique S.A., Paris, France.

### REFERENCES

1. [Meyer] C.Meyer-Bisch,M.Falcy,M.Puzin," Risques professionels, soyons vigilants", Note ND-1501-117-84, INRS, Paris, 1984

2. [Meyer] C.Meyer-Bisch, M.Falcy, "Aspects conceptuels d'un programme automatique d'extraction de la connaissance du système de vigilance industrielle de l'INRS, N°.Etude B.2/3.1.02, INRS, Paris, 1989

3. [Kosko, B87a] Bart Kosko, "Constructing an Associative Memory", BYTE Magazine, Septembre 1987

4. [Kosko, B87b] Kosko, Bart, "Bidirectional Associative Memories", IEEE Trans on Systems, Man and Cybernetics, 1987

5. [Kosko, B87c] Kosko, Bart, "Adaptive Bidirectional Associative Memories" Applied Optics, 1987

6. [Grossberg] Grossberg, Stephen (ed.), The adaptive Brain, Volume I, North-Holland,1986

7. [Jorgensen] Jorgensen, Chuck, Matheus, Chris, "Catching Knowledge on Neural Nets", AI Expert, Décembre 1986

8. [Hopfield JJ82]Hopfield, John J., "Neural Networks and Physical Systems with Emergent Collective Computational Abilities", Procedings of the National Academy of Sciences, USA, Vol.79, pp 2554/2558, 1982

9. [NeuralWorks] NeuralWorks of Neural Ware, Inc., User's Guide, 1988

10. [SN2] A simulator for connectionist models, Reference manual, Neuristique S.A., Paris, France, 1990

# A Model of Neural Electromagnetic Fields

Haibin Liu and Yukinori Kakazu
Dept. of Precision Engineering,Faculty of Engineering
Hokkaido University, N13-W8, Sapporo 060, Japan
Tel:(+81)11-736-3818,Fax:(+81)11-758-1619,E-mail:liu@hupe.hokudai.ac.jp

**Abstract**

In this paper, we construct a mathematical artificial neural network architecture called a neural electromagnetic fields (NEF) model which is a mixture of connection and disconnection models. This NEF model is defined in a four dimensional time-space, and consists of three AUNONs (Artificial Unit Neuron model proposed by introducing magnetic field information into the conventional neuron model (McCulloch-Pitts' neuron model)). These AUNONs are two connected and one unconnected AUNON: $N_1$, $N_2$ and $N_3$, and $N_1$ and $N_2$ which are connected as a network. The dynamics of this NEF model are analyzed mathematically. The analyses show that the function of information processing in the model is realized through the INTERACTION among the AUNONs by both electric and magnetic information. It is clear that this new artificial model has a more powerful capability for information processing than the connection model.

## 1 Introduction

The behavior of a unit neuron in the neural electromagnetic fields was studied and an artificial unit neuron (AUNON) model was proposed [3]. The AUNON model is a nonlinear model and has adaptive and autonomous ability [2]. The learning theorems show that the learning of the AUNON can guarantee the convergence of solution with high speed and has no local minimum problem [4]. However, there is a limitation to the learning capability of just a single AUNON. It is uncertain as to whether or not a learning target can be attained by a single AUNON within a limited time. This is because the changes in synaptic efficiencies $w_i^D$, the memory capacity n, and also the learning time $T_l$ are limited. It is necessary to make a study on several AUNONs in a Neural Electromagnetic Field.

On the other hand, it is important to propose a new architecture different from the famous connection models developed by the PDP research group [6]. We think that the main reason that the PDP models have not achieved the expected goal lies in the architecture called a network of connectivity itself. Therefore, in this paper, by introduction of magnetic field information we attempt to construct a new framework called a neural electromagnetic fields (NEF) model which is a mixture of the connection and disconnection models.

## 2 A model of neural electromagnetic fields

As a case study, it is considered that in the $\Omega$ field(conscious space) in a four dimensional time-space, there are three AUNONs: $N_1$, $N_2$ and $N_3$; $N_1$ and $N_2$ are connected as a network, as illustrated in Fig.1.

$\Omega$(x,y,z) are absolute coordinates. $N_1(x_{N_1}, y_{N_1}, z_{N_1})$, $N_2(x_{N_2}, y_{N_2}, z_{N_2})$, and $N_3(x_{N_3}, y_{N_3}, z_{N_3})$ are relative coordinates. In the $\Omega$ space, the origin of the $N_1$ coordinates is $(x_1, y_1, z_1)$, the origin of the $N_2$ coordinates is $(x_2, y_2, z_2)$, and the origin of the $N_3$ coordinates is $(x_3, y_3, z_3)$. The input information from external to $\Omega$ space is perceptual information: $\mathcal{P} = \{ \boldsymbol{P}, \boldsymbol{P'} \}$, $\boldsymbol{P} = [p_1, p_2, p_3, p_i]$ and $\boldsymbol{P'} = [p'_1, p'_2, p'_j]$. The output information from $\Omega$ space to external space is action information: $\mathcal{O} = \{ O_{u_1}, O_{u_2}, O_{u_3} \}$.

Generally, in a three dimensional space, electromagnetic waves travelling from their origin can be described as

$$\phi_3(x, y, z, t) = \frac{1}{r} f(r - ct) \tag{1}$$

At time t, the coordinates of the observed position of the waves are (x,y,z), and $r = \sqrt{x^2 + y^2 + z^2}$, where c is light speed [1]. The function f(r) shows the shape of the wave function $\phi_3$ at t=0. Waves $\phi_3$ are shown in Fig.2.

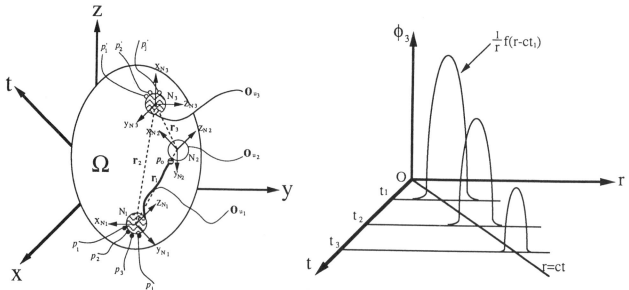

Figure 1. A neural electromagnetic field model. There are three aunons : $N_1$, $N_2$ and $N_3$ in the $\Omega$ field. $N_1$ and $N_2$ are a net. $\Omega$(x,y,z) is absolute coordinates. $N_1(x_{N_1}, y_{N_1}, z_{N_1})$, $N_2(x_{N_2}, y_{N_2}, z_{N_2})$, and $N_3(x_{N_3}, y_{N_3}, z_{N_3})$ are relative coordinates.

Figure 2. Electromagnetic waves travel from the origin in a 3-D space. The function f(r) shows the shape of waves $\phi_3$ at time t = 0, where c is light speed.

Now, in order to define the neural electromagnetic fields (NEF) model, we make the following assumptions.

**Assumption 1** *If an AUNON's excitation time is less than $\tau_e$ and the distances from the other AUNONs are within $\rho_e$, then its activities will be affected by the magnetic field information of those other AUNONs.*

**Assumption 2** *In the $\Omega$ space, at time $t_1$, AUNON $N_1$ which has the input information $\boldsymbol{P}$ and AUNON $N_3$ which has the input information $\boldsymbol{P'}$ are fired almost at the same time. After that, AUNON $N_2$ is fired at time $t_2$.*

**Assumption 3** *The distance between $N_1$ and $N_2$ is defined as $r_1$, and $r_1 \leq \rho_e$. The distance between $N_2$ and $N_3$ is defined as $r_3$, and $r_3 \leq \rho_e$. The distance between $N_1$ and $N_3$ is defined as $r_2$, and $r_2 > \rho_e$. Set $t_2 - t_1 > \tau_e$.*

## 2.1 State equations of AUNONs in the NEF model

**Definition 1** *Learning period(T): In the $\Omega$ space, the time between the beginning time $t_s$ of the first fired AUNON and the finishing time $t_e$ of the last fired AUNON is defined as the Learning Period.*

From assumption 2 we know that at time $t_1$ AUNON $N_1$ and AUNON $N_3$ are fired almost at the same time. Because $r_2 > \rho_e$ by assumption 3, there is no interaction of magnetic fields between $N_1$ and $N_3$ based on assumption 1.

**[1]. The state model of AUNON $N_1$**

For AUNON $N_1$, input information is perceptual information: $\boldsymbol{P} = [p_1, p_2, p_3, p_i]$, the memory consolidation function is $M_{e_{N_1}}(t_1) = A_r + h_{N_1}$, and the output information is action information: $O_{u_1} = A_r$. We understand that AUNON $N_1$ already contains knowledge $A_r$.

Now we can write the AUNON equations [3] of $N_1$ as

$$\tau_{u_{N1}} \frac{du_{N1}(t_{Ni})}{dt_{Ni}} = -u_{N1}(t_{N1}) + \boldsymbol{P}_{N_1} \boldsymbol{W}_{N_1}^D - \mu_{N1} \frac{\partial v_{N1}(x_1, y_1, z_1, t_{N1})}{\partial t_{N1}} - h_{N1} \qquad (2)$$

$$\tau_{v_{N1}} \frac{\partial v_{N1}(x_1, y_1, z_1, t_{N1})}{\partial t_{N1}} = -v_{N1}(x_1, y_1, z_1, t_{N1}) + \epsilon_{N1} \boldsymbol{P}_{N_1} \boldsymbol{W}_{N_1}^D + \epsilon_{N1} u_{N1}(t_{N1}) \qquad (3)$$

And the conscious function(magnetic field function) will be

$$\phi_{N1}(x,y,z,t) = \phi'_{N1}(x_{N1}, y_{N1}, z_{N1}, t_{N1}) = \frac{1}{r_{N1}} O_{v1}(r_{N1} - ct_{N1}) \tag{4}$$

where $r_{N1} = \sqrt{x_{N1}^2 + y_{N1}^2 + z_{N1}^2} = \sqrt{(x-x_1)^2 + (y-y_1)^2 + (z-z_1)^2}$, and $t_{N1}$ is the excitation time of AUNON $N_1$.

**[2]. The state model of AUNON $N_3$**

For AUNON $N_3$, the input information is perceptual information: $\boldsymbol{P'} = [p'_1, p'_2, p'_j]$; the memory consolidation function is $M_{e_{N3}}(t_1) = 0$; and the learning target $A_m$ is desired to be produced as a learning result, that is to say, after learning, new knowledge $A_m$ will be assimilated by AUNON $N_3$.

Now we can write the AUNON equations [3] of $N_3$ as

$$\tau_{u_{N3}} \frac{du_{N3}(t_{N3})}{dt_{N3}} = -u_{N3}(t_{N3}) + \boldsymbol{P}_{N3} \boldsymbol{W}_{N3}^D - \mu_{N3} \frac{\partial v_{N3}(x_3, y_3, z_3, t_{N3})}{\partial t_{N3}} - h_{N3} \tag{5}$$

$$\tau_{v_{N3}} \frac{\partial v_{N3}(x_3, y_3, z_3, t_{N3})}{\partial t_{N3}} = -v_{N3}(x_3, y_3, z_3, t_{N3}) + \epsilon_{N3} \boldsymbol{P}_{N3} \boldsymbol{W}_{N3}^D + \epsilon_{N3} u_{N3}(t_{N3}) \tag{6}$$

And the conscious function(magnetic field function) will be

$$\phi_{N3}(x,y,z,t) = \phi'_{N3}(x_{N3}, y_{N3}, z_{N3}, t_{N3}) = \frac{1}{r_{N3}} O_{v3}(r_{N3} - ct_{N3}) \tag{7}$$

where $r_{N3} = \sqrt{x_{N3}^2 + y_{N3}^2 + z_{N3}^2} = \sqrt{(x-x_3)^2 + (y-y_3)^2 + (z-z_3)^2}$, and $t_{N3}$ is the excitation time of AUNON $N_3$.

**[3]. The state model of AUNON $N_2$**

By assumption 2, AUNON $N_2$ is fired at time $t_2$. After that, because $r_1 \leq \rho_e$, $r_3 \leq \rho_e$, and the excitation time of AUNON $N_2$ is $t_{N2} < \tau_e$, based on assumption 1, the magnetic fields of AUNONs $N_1$ and $N_3$ will affect the activities of AUNON $N_2$. However, for AUNONs $N_1$ and $N_3$, since the excitation time of AUNONs $N_1$ and $N_3$ is $t_2 - t_1 > \tau_e$, the magnetic fields of AUNON $N_2$ will have no effect on their activities.

Therefore, for AUNON $N_2$ the input information is both perceptual information and conscious information. As AUNONs $N_1$ and $N_2$ are connected as a network, the perceptual information is $\boldsymbol{P}_{N_2} = [p_o]$ and $p_o = O_{u1}$. And the conscious information is $\boldsymbol{Q}_{N_2} = [q_1, q_2]$, $q_1 = \phi_{N1}(x_2, y_2, z_2, t) = \frac{1}{r_1} O_{v1}(r_1 - ct_{N1})$, where $r_1 = \sqrt{(x_2-x_1)^2 + (y_2-y_1)^2 + (z_2-z_1)^2}$, and $q_2 = \phi_{N3}(x_2, y_2, z_2, t) = \frac{1}{r_3} O_{v3}(r_3 - ct_{N3})$, where $r_3 = \sqrt{(x_2-x_3)^2 + (y_2-y_3)^2 + (z_2-z_3)^2}$.

Let the memory consolidation function be $M_{e_{N2}}(t_2) = \boldsymbol{P}_{N_2} \boldsymbol{W}_{N_2}^D$.

Now the AUNON equations [3] of $N_2$ can be written as

$$\tau_{u_{N2}} \frac{du_{N2}(t_{N2})}{dt_{N2}} = -u_{N2}(t_{N2}) + \boldsymbol{P}_{N_2} \boldsymbol{W}_{N_2}^D - \mu_{N2} \frac{d(\boldsymbol{Q}_{N_2} \boldsymbol{W}_{N_2}^H)}{dt_{N2}} - \mu_{N2} \frac{\partial v_{N2}(x_2, y_2, z_2, t_{N2})}{\partial t_{N2}} - h_{N2} \tag{8}$$

$$\tau_{v_{N2}} \frac{\partial v_{N2}(x_2, y_2, z_2, t_{N2})}{\partial t_{N2}} = -v_{N2}(x_2, y_2, z_2, t_{N2}) + \epsilon_{N2} \boldsymbol{P}_{N_2} \boldsymbol{W}_{N_2}^D + \boldsymbol{Q}_{N_2} \boldsymbol{W}_{N_2}^H + \epsilon_{N2} u_{N2}(t_{N2}) \tag{9}$$

And the conscious function(magnetic field function) will be

$$\phi_{N2}(x,y,z,t) = \phi'_{N2}(x_{N2}, y_{N2}, z_{N2}, t_{N2}) = \frac{1}{r_{N2}} O_{v2}(r_{N2} - ct_{N2}) \tag{10}$$

where $r_{N2} = \sqrt{x_{N2}^2 + y_{N2}^2 + z_{N2}^2} = \sqrt{(x-x_2)^2 + (y-y_2)^2 + (z-z_2)^2}$.

As is known[4], the Hebbian function is $H_{N2}(t_{N2}) = 2 \frac{d(\boldsymbol{Q}_{N_2} \boldsymbol{W}_{N_2}^H)}{dt_{N2}} + \tau_{v_{N2}} \frac{d^2(\boldsymbol{Q}_{N_2} \boldsymbol{W}_{N_2}^H)}{dt_{N2}^2}$,

and the conscious control function is $C_{e_{N2}}(t_{N2}) = \boldsymbol{Q}_{N_2} \boldsymbol{W}_{N_2}^H$, where $t_{N2}$ is the excitation time of AUNON $N_2$.

# 3 Mathematical analysis of the dynamics of the NEF model

Since there is only perceptual information in the input information of $N_1$, according to the Reflex-learning definition [4], we know the learning of AUNON $N_1$ to be Reflex learning. Moreover, because $M_{e_{N_1}}(t_1) = A_r + h_{N_1}$ and $O_{u1} = A_r$, we can regard the learning of AUNON $N_1$ as a Self-recall process [4]. This means that, when AUNON $N_1$ is being excited at time $t(t > t_1)$, the already-known knowledge $A_r$ which $N_1$ has is recalled and produced as action information:

$$O_{u1} = A_r \tag{11}$$

At the same time, based on the Reflex-learning Formulas [4] the conscious information is

$$O_{v1} = \epsilon_{N1}(2A_r + h_{N1}) \tag{12}$$

and the conscious function(magnetic field function) is

$$\phi_{N1}(x, y, z, t) = \frac{1}{r_{N1}} O_{v1}(r_{N1} - ct_{N1}) \tag{13}$$

Since there is only perceptual information in the input information of $N_3$, we know that the learning of AUNON $N_3$ is Reflex learning [4]. Moreover, because $M_{e_{N3}}(t_1) = 0$ and the learning target $A_m$ is targeted for production, the learning of AUNON $N_3$ can be regarded as a memorization process. The reason for this is that, for AUNON $N_3$, if $A_m$ is desired to be yielded as the learning result, the memory consolidation function $M_{e_{N3}}$ has to be changed, so that new knowledge $A_m$ can be memorized in the learning.

According to the Reflex-learning Formulas [4], after learning$(t > t_1)$, the output information of AUNON $N_3$ is in the forms of:
action information:

$$O_{u3} = A_m + [M_{e_{N3}}(t_1) - h_{N3} - A_m]e^{-\frac{t_{N3}}{\alpha_{N3}}} = A_m - (h_{N3} + A_m)e^{-\frac{t_{N3}}{\alpha_{N3}}} \tag{14}$$

conscious information:

$$O_{v3} = \epsilon_{N3}(2A_m + h_{N3}) + \epsilon_{N3}[M_{e_{N3}}(t_1) - h_{N3} - A_m]e^{-\frac{t_{N3}}{\alpha_{N3}}} = \epsilon_{N3}A_m + \epsilon_{N3}(A_m + h_{N3})(1 - e^{-\frac{t_{N3}}{\alpha_{N3}}}) \tag{15}$$

conscious function:

$$\phi_{N3}(x, y, z, t) = \frac{1}{r_{N3}} O_{v3}(r_{N3} - ct_{N3}) \tag{16}$$

memory consolidation function:

$$M_{e_{N3}}(t) = (h_{N3} + A_m)(1 - e^{-\frac{t_{N3}}{\alpha_{N3}}}) + M_{e_{N3}}(t_1)e^{-\frac{t_{N3}}{\alpha_{N3}}} = (h_{N3} + A_m)(1 - e^{-\frac{t_{N3}}{\alpha_{N3}}}) \tag{17}$$

When AUNON $N_2$ is affected by conscious control information, and if the learning target is undecided, although $N_2$ is fired, the memory consolidation function $M_{e_{N2}}$ does not change(Memory self-protection hypothesis).

Therefore, after learning, i.e. at time $t(t > t_2)$, the output information of AUNON $N_2$ is in the forms of:
action information:

$$O_{u2} = f_u [M_{e_{N2}}(t_2), H_{N2}, C_{N2}, h_{N2}, t_{N2}] \tag{18}$$

conscious information:

$$O_{v2} = \epsilon_{N2}f_v [M_{e_{N2}}(t_2), H_{N2}, C_{N2}, h_{N2}, t_{N2}] \tag{19}$$

conscious function:

$$\phi_{N2}(x,y,z,t) = \frac{1}{r_{N2}} O_{v2}(r_{N2} - ct_{N2}) \tag{20}$$

memory consolidation function:

$$M_{e_{N2}}(t) = M_{e_{N2}}(t_2) \tag{21}$$

$O_{u2}$ and $O_{v2}$ are the solutions of the AUNON equations of AUNON $N_2$(eqns.(8) and (9)).

We set $A_c = O_{u2}$. The learning result $A_c$ is a nonlinear solution and something new related to $A_r$ and $A_m$. The learning of AUNON $N_2$ can be regarded as a Creative process. Although $A_c$ may be a useless, unrealistic concept, it should be stressed that it is still something that has been newly created, something that did not exist before.

If $A_c$ answers the purpose, it can be made into the learning target in a new learning period: that is to say, on the basis of Union-learning theorem [4], $A_c$ can be memorized and turned into long term memory over several new learning periods.

If $A_c$ does not answer the purpose, there are two kinds of ensuing situation: One situation is that, because the memory consolidation function $M_{e_{N2}}$ is unchanged, $A_c$ is only a temporary (momentary) idea and will be forgotten in a short time. This means that the model has a forgetting function. The other is that, if the learning target $A_m$ of AUNON $N_3$ is modified, and if the modified knowledge $A'_m$ is memorized once more, $A_c$ can also be changed during a new learning period. This indicates that, if the subgoals are adjusted, an ultimate goal can be obtained.

Attention should be paid to the fact that, whether the learning result $A_c$ is useless or not, it can be obtained once again in a new learning period under the same conditions as defined above, though the memory consolidation function $M_{e_{N2}}$ remains unchanged. This phenomenon is not the result of the MEMORY (the state) of AUNON $N_2$, but the result of the INTERACTION among the excited AUNONs($N_1$, $N_2$, and $N_3$) in the $\Omega$ space. The dynamics of the information processing in the $\Omega$ space also shows an important and interesting fact that although the state of AUNON $N_2$ is not transformed the output information from AUNON $N_2$ can be changed. There are two reasons: one reason is that since the AUNONs $N_2$ and $N_3$ are not connected, $N_2$ has no change in synaptic efficiency,that is to say,the state of $N_2$ is not changed; the other is that AUNON $N_3$ affects and changes the output of AUNON $N_2$ through magnetic field information only when $N_3$ is fired (we can see this according to the solutions of AUNON $N_2$'s equations: eqns.(8)and(9)). By the traditional network theory [6], it is known that the transformation of state of a system decides the output from the system. In other words, if the state of a system is not transformed the output from the system will be not changed. Based on this point, we argue that the FEM model has a more flexible capability for information processing than the connection models.

Since the memory consolidation function $M_{e_{N2}}$ remains unchanged, the learning of $N_2$ is also a recall process, but different from a Self-recall or a Compound recall process [2]. As the learning result $A_c$ is something new related to $A_r$ and $A_m$, the learning can be defined as an Associative creative process. If $A_c$ has been memorized by AUNON $N_2$, i.e. the memory consolidation function $M_{e_{N2}}$ is changed and AUNON $N_2$ takes possession of $A_c$, even though AUNON $N_3$ is not fired, $A_c$ can be generated(recalled) once more as AUNON $N_2$ is fired.

When one learning period($T_1$) is finished, the output information [4] from the $\Omega$ space is

$$O_{u1} = A_r \tag{22}$$

$$O_{u2} = A_c = f_u[A_r, A_m, t_{N2}] \tag{23}$$

$$O_{u3} = A_m - (h_{N3} + A_m)e^{-\frac{t_{N3}}{\alpha_{N3}}} \tag{24}$$

and the internal state of the $\Omega$ space is

$$M_{e_{N1}}(T_1) = h_{N1} + A_r \tag{25}$$

$$M_{e_{N2}}(T_1) = \boldsymbol{P}_{N_2} \boldsymbol{W}_{N_2}^D \tag{26}$$

$$M_{e_{N3}}(T_1) = (h_{N3} + A_m)(1 - e^{-\frac{t_{N3}}{\alpha_{N3}}}) \tag{27}$$

If $A_c$ answers the purpose and is decided upon as the learning target in another learning period($T_2$), the output information [4] from the $\Omega$ space is

$$O_{u1} = A_r \tag{28}$$

$$O_{u2} = A_c + \left[ M_{e_{N2}}(T_1) - h_{N2} - A_c + \frac{\mu_{N2}}{\alpha_{N2}} \int H_{N2}(t_{N2}) e^{\frac{t_{N2}}{\alpha_{N2}}} dt_{N2} \right] e^{-\frac{t_{N2}}{\alpha_{N2}}} - \mu_{N2} \frac{d[C_{eN2}(t_{N2})]}{dt_{N2}} \tag{29}$$

$$O_{u3} = A_m + [M_{e_{N3}}(T_1) - h_{N3} - A_m] e^{-\frac{t_{N3}}{\alpha_{N3}}} \tag{30}$$

and the internal state of the $\Omega$ space is

$$M_{e_{N1}}(T_2) = h_{N1} + A_r \tag{31}$$

$$M_{e_{N2}}(T_2) = (h_{N2} + A_c)(1 - e^{-\frac{t_{N2}}{\alpha_{N2}}}) + \left[ M_{e_{N2}}(T_1) + \frac{\mu_{N2}}{\alpha_{N2}} \int H_{N2}(t_{N2}) e^{\frac{t_{N2}}{\alpha_{N2}}} dt_{N2} \right] e^{-\frac{t_{N2}}{\alpha_{N2}}} \tag{32}$$

$$M_{e_{N3}}(T_2) = (h_{N3} + A_m)(1 - e^{-\frac{t_{N3}}{\alpha_{N3}}}) + M_{e_{N3}}(T_1) e^{-\frac{t_{N3}}{\alpha_{N3}}} \tag{33}$$

There are three processes that occur in the $\Omega$ space. These are a recall process, a memorization process and a creative process. These processes show that the NEF model is an autonomous system and it has parallel distributed processing functions. Moreover, it is worth noticing that for this NEF model it is unnecessary for the AUNONs to memorize everything: utilizing the interaction among AUNONs which already contain knowledge, it can create something new that satisfies the objective reality by itself. This is one of the special features of this model. In this sense, this model can convey intelligence [5].

## 4    Conclusions

In this paper we present a model of neural electromagnetic fields for the study of neural networks. This model can be regarded as a new type of neural networks architecture. From the analyses of its dynamics, it is clear that this mixture model which is composed of connected and unconnected units has two advantages: one advantage is the increase in the flexibility of information processing, and the other is that the model provides a new mechanism for associative memory. The dynamics of this NEF model also suggests that magnetic field information plays an important role in information processing.

## References

[1] Ingard,K.U.(1988):Fundamentals of waves and oscillations. Cambridge University Press.

[2] Liu,H.,&Kakazu,Y.(1992):A study on new control mechanisms of memory. Proc. of KACC'92-SEOUL, I, 324-329

[3] Liu,H.,&Kakazu,Y.(1993):Introducing magnetic fields into artificial neural networks. Proc. of IJCNN'93-NAGOYA, vol.1, 383-388

[4] Liu,H.,&Kakazu,Y.:Study on the theory of neural electromagnetic fields: Learning rule and learning theorems. Int. Journal of JSPE.(in press)

[5] Rosenfield,I.(1988):The invention of memory:a new view of the brain. New York Press.

[6] Rumelhart,D.E.,McClelland.J.L.,&The PDP Research Group(1986):Parallel distributed processing. Vol.1, The MIT Press.

# Unsupervised Learning

**Session Chairs: Gail Carpenter**
**Robert Jannarone**

## ORAL PRESENTATIONS

# Distributed Recognition Codes
## and Catastrophic Forgetting

Gail A. Carpenter

Center for Adaptive Systems & Department of Cognitive and Neural Systems
Boston University, 111 Cummington Street, Boston, MA 02215 USA

## Abstract

Analysis of catastrophic forgetting by distributed codes leads to the unexpected conclusion that the standard synaptic transmission rule may not be optimal in certain neural networks. The distributed outstar generalizes the outstar network for spatial pattern learning, replacing the outstar source node with a source field, of arbitrarily many nodes, where the activity pattern may be arbitrarily distributed or compressed. Distributed outstar learning proceeds according to a principle of atrophy due to disuse whereby a path weight decreases in joint proportion to the transmitted path signal and the degree of disuse of the target node. During learning, the total signal to a target node converges toward that node's activity level. Weight changes at a node are apportioned according to the distributed pattern of converging signals. Three types of synaptic transmission, the standard product rule, a fuzzy capacity rule, and an adaptive threshold rule, are examined for this system. Only the threshold rule solves the catastrophic forgetting problem of fast learning. Analysis of spatial distributed coding hereby leads to the conjecture that the unit of long-term memory in a spatial pattern learning system may be a subtractive threshold, rather than a multiplicative weight.

## Optimal rules of synaptic transmission

When neural networks became popular in the 1980s, researchers struggled to define *neural network* with words that would include the diverse models in current use. As a step toward constructing such a definition, consider the question: What, if anything, do all the neural networks of the past fifty years have in common? The answer to this question is, most likely, nothing. However, the large majority of neural network models, from the McCulloch-Pitts (1943) neuron to the many biological and engineering models at this year's conferences, do have one element in common, namely, the rule setting the net signal from a source node to a target node equal to a path signal times a synaptic weight. This *product rule* of synaptic transmission is in such universal use that it is almost always treated as a nameless fact rather than a hypothesis, although neurophysiology has so far neither confirmed nor refuted the rule. Why, then has this particular process found such widespread use? One answer is its computational power: the product rule sets the sum of weighted signals equal to the dot product of the signal vector and the weight vector. This dot product provides a useful measure of the similarity between the active path signal vector and the learned weight vector. However, utility and universality do not necessarily imply optimality.

This research was supported in part by ARPA (ONR N00014-92-J-4015), the National Science Foundation (NSF IRI-90-00530), and the Office of Naval Research (ONR N00014-91-J-4100).

The author wishes to thank Cynthia E. Bradford and Robin L. Locke for their valuable assistance in the preparation of the manuscript.

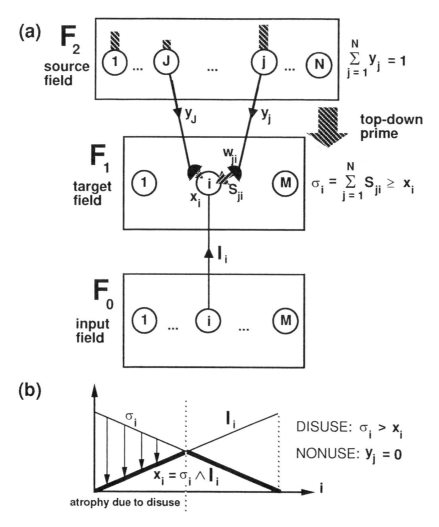

**Figure 1.** (a) Distributed outstar network for spatial pattern learning. During adaptation a top-down weight $w_{ji}$, from the $j^{th}$ node of the coding field $F_2$ to the $i^{th}$ node of the pattern registration field $F_1$, may decrease or remain constant. (b) An atrophy-due-to-disuse learning law causes the total signal $\sigma_i$ from $F_2$ to the $i^{th}$ $F_1$ node to decay toward that node's activity level $x_i$, if $\sigma_i$ is initially greater than $x_i$. Within this context, three synaptic transmission rules are analyzed.

This article describes a neural network learning problem for which the product rule is not computationally optimal. Solution of the learning problem requires a neural network design to support stable distributed codes. One such design is the *distributed outstar* (Figure 1), which solves the distributed code catastrophic forgetting problem when the product rule is replaced by the equally plausible *threshold rule* (Carpenter, 1993, 1994). The threshold rule postulates that the unit of long-term memory (LTM) is a subtractive threshold, rather than a multiplicative weight. In the process of solving a particular learning problem, therefore, computational analysis questions the optimality of a fundamental neural network design hypothesis.

### Outstar learning and distributed codes

An *outstar* is a neural network that can learn and recall arbitrary spatial patterns (Grossberg, 1968). Outstars have played a central role in both the theoretical analysis of cognitive phenomena and the neural models that realize the theories, as well as applications of these systems (Carpenter and Grossberg, 1991). In particular, neural network realizations of adaptive resonance theory (ART models) use outstar learning in the top-down adaptive filter (Carpenter and Grossberg, 1987). An outstar is characterized by one source node that sends weighted inputs to a target field. When the source node is active, weights converge toward the target field activity pattern. During performance, an active path reproduces the learned pattern at the target field. We here consider spatial pattern learning in a more general setting, in which an arbitrarily large source field replaces the single source node of the outstar. This *distributed outstar network* (Figure 1a) is similar to the original outstar when the source field $F_2$ contains a single node. Then, weights in the $F_2 \to F_1$ adaptive filter track the $F_1$ activity pattern when the one $F_2$ node is active.

At first, distributed outstar learning would appear to be modeled already in the ART top-down adaptive filter, since the ART field $F_2$ can have arbitrarily many nodes. However, to date, networks that explicitly realize adaptive resonance assume the special case in which $F_2$ is a *choice*, or *winner-take-all*, network. In this case, only one $F_2$ node is active during learning, so each $F_2$ node acts, in turn, as an outstar source node. The distributed outstar is a spatial pattern learning network that allows the activity pattern at the coding field $F_2$ to be arbitrarily distributed. That is, one, several, or all of the $F_2$ nodes may be active during learning.

One possible distributed outstar design simply implements outstar learning in each active path. However, such a system is subject to catastrophic forgetting that quickly renders the network useless unless learning rates are very slow. In particular, if all $F_2$ nodes were active during learning, all $F_2 \to F_1$ weight vectors would converge toward a common pattern.

A learning principle of *atrophy due to disuse* leads toward a solution of the catastrophic forgetting problem. By this principle, a weight in an active path atrophies, or decays, in joint proportion to the size of the transmitted synaptic signal and a suitably defined "degree of disuse" of the target cell. During learning, the total transmitted signal $\sigma_i$ from $F_2$ converges toward the activity level of the $i^{th}$ target $F_1$ node (Figure 1b). Atrophy due to disuse thereby dynamically substitutes the total $F_2 \to F_1$ signal for the individual outstar weight. This would seem to be a natural step toward spatial pattern learning by a coding source field rather than a single source node. Unfortunately, this development is, by itself, insufficient. The network still suffers catastrophic forgetting if signal transmission from source node to target node obeys a product rule. This rule, now used in nearly all neural models, assumes that the transmitted synaptic signal $S_{ji}$ from the $j^{th}$ $F_2$ node to the $i^{th}$ $F_1$ node is proportional to the product of the path signal $y_j$ and the path weight $w_{ji}$. An alternative transmission process, used in a neural network realization of fuzzy ART (Carpenter, Grossberg, and Rosen, 1991a, 1991b), obeys a *capacity rule* (Table 1). However, catastrophic forgetting is even more serious a problem for the capacity rule than for the product rule.

Fortunately, another synaptic transmission rule solves the problem. This *threshold rule* postulates a transmitted signal $S_{ji}$ equal to the amount by which the $F_2 \to F_1$ signal $y_j$ exceeds an adaptive threshold $\tau_{ji}$. Where weights decrease during atrophy-due-to-disuse learning thresholds increase: formally, $\tau_{ji}$ is identified with $(1 - w_{ji})$. When synaptic transmission is implemented by a threshold rule, weight/threshold changes are bounded and automatically apportioned according to the distribution of $F_2$ activity, with fast learning as

$$\textbf{Product rule}: S_{ji} = y_j w_{ji}$$

$$\textbf{Capacity rule}: S_{ji} = y_j \wedge w_{ji} \equiv \min(y_j, w_{ji})$$

$$\textbf{Threshold rule}: S_{ji} = [y_j - (1 - w_{ji})]^+ = [y_j - \tau_{ji}]^+ \equiv \max([y_j - \tau_{ji}], 0)$$

**Table 1.** Synaptic transmission functions.

well as slow learning. When $F_2$ makes a binary choice, the three synaptic transmission rules (Table 1) are computationally identical, and atrophy-due-to-disuse learning is essentially the same as outstar learning. Thus functional differences between the three types of transmission would be experimentally and computationally measurable only in situations where the $F_2$ code is distributed.

Computational analysis of distributed codes hereby leads unexpectedly to a hypothesis about the mechanism of synaptic transmission: the unit of long-term memory in a spatial pattern learning system is conjectured to be an adaptive threshold rather than a multiplicative path weight. Historically, early definitions of the perceptron specified a general class of synaptic transmission rules (Rosenblatt, 1958, 1962). However, the electrical switching circuit model, which realizes multiplicative weights as adjustable gains, quickly became the dominant metaphor (Widrow and Hoff, 1960). Over the ensuing decades, efficient integrated hardware implementation of the linear adaptive filter has remained a challenge. In optoelectronic neural networks, the adaptive threshold synaptic transmission rule, realized as a rectified bias, may be easier to implement than on-line multiplication (T. Caudell, personal communication). Thus, even in networks where the product rule and the threshold rule are computationally equivalent, their diverging physical interpretations may prove significant, in both the neural and the hardware domains.

The adaptive threshold hypothesis completes the *distributed outstar learning law*. This article includes a summary and an explicit solution of the distributed outstar equations, discussions of the physical unit of memory and a confidence-plasticity tradeoff, and a phase plane example of distributed outstar dynamics.

### Confidence-plasticity tradeoff

Figure 2 illustrates why the product rule and the capacity rule cause catastrophic forgetting and how the threshold rule solves this problem. During atrophy-due-to-disuse learning, if the $i^{th}$ $F_1$ target node is disused ($\sigma_i > x_i$) then the weight $w_{ji}$ will decay in any path that sends a signal to the $i^{th}$ node ($S_{ji} > 0$) (Figure 2a). When $F_2$ makes a choice, each of the three synaptic transmission rules allows weight change in only one path to each target node. However, if $y_j$ is even slightly positive, both the product rule (Figure 2b) and the capacity rule (Figure 2c) allow weights $w_{ji}$ to decay without limit, unless learning rates are very slow. In contrast, the threshold rule (Figure 2d) implies that, even if the $J^{th}$ $F_2$ node is active, the signal $S_{Ji}$ is still zero if the path threshold is large ($\tau_{Ji} \geq y_J$); or, equivalently, if the path weight is small ($w_{Ji} \leq 1 - y_J$). Only the positive signals $S_{Ji}$ sum to $\sigma_i$ and only these signals

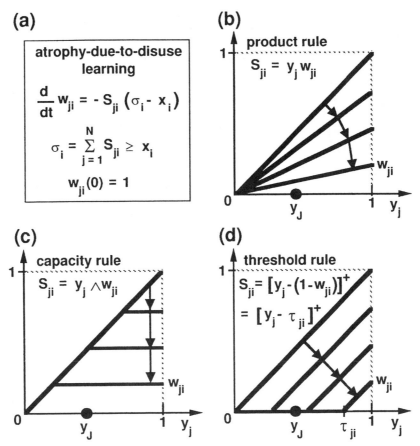

**Figure 2.** (a) Atrophy-due-to-disuse learning causes a weight $w_{ji}$ to decay at a rate proportional to (i) the signal from the $j^{th}$ $F_2$ node to the $i^{th}$ $F_1$ node and (ii) the degree of disuse, which equals to the difference between the total $F_2 \rightarrow F_1$ signal to the $i^{th}$ node and the activity of that node. (b) When the $J^{th}$ $F_2$ node is active, the product rule implies that that signal $S_{Ji}$ to the $i^{th}$ $F_1$ node is positive. All weights $w_{Ji}$ therefore decay when $\sigma_i > x_i$, even if those weights are already small. This causes catastrophic forgetting. (c) The capacity rule leads to catastrophic forgetting for the same reason as the product rule. (d) The threshold rule buffers learned codes against catastrophic forgetting by allowing only paths with sufficiently large weights (small thresholds) to contribute to the recognition code and hence to be subject to change during learning.

can atrophy due to disuse. Threshold $\tau_{Ji}$ remains small, and therefore plastic, if $y_J$ is always small when $\sigma_i > x_i$. If $y_J$ is large, $\tau_{Ji}$ may increase toward 1. Once this occurs, however, $S_{Ji} = 0$ for all $F_2$ codes $\mathbf{y}$ except those which compress most activity at the $J^{th}$ node. Thus in a recognition system that allows an $F_2$ node to become highly active only when it is highly confident of its choice, the threshold rule automatically links confidence to stability. Conversely, when category selection is uncertain, distributed codes retain plasticity.

### Distributed outstar equations

Computational analysis of distributed spatial pattern learning leads to the selection of the adaptive threshold synaptic transmission rule (Carpenter, 1993, 1994). In terms of the threshold $\tau_{ji}$ in the path from the $j^{th}$ $F_2$ node to the $i^{th}$ $F_1$ node, a stable learning law for distributed codes is defined as the:

### Distributed outstar

$$\frac{d\tau_{ji}}{dt} = S_{ji}(\sigma_i - x_i), \tag{1}$$

where $S_{ji}$ is the thresholded path signal $[y_j - \tau_{ji}]^+$ transmitted from the $j^{th}$ $F_2$ node to the $i^{th}$ $F_1$ node and where $\sigma_i$ is the sum:

$$\sigma_i \equiv \sum_{j=1}^{N} S_{ji} = \sum_{j=1}^{N} [y_j - \tau_{ji}]^+. \tag{2}$$

Initially,

$$\tau_{ji}(0) = 0. \tag{3}$$

The $F_2$ path signal vector $\mathbf{y} = (y_1, \ldots y_j, \ldots y_N)$ is assumed to be normalized:

$$\sum_{j=1}^{N} y_j = 1, \tag{4}$$

but is otherwise arbitrary.

In a system such as ART 1 or fuzzy ART, the total top-down signal *primes* $F_1$. In these models, $\sigma_i$ is always greater than or equal to $x_i$, since $x_i = I_i \wedge \sigma_i \equiv \min(I_i, \sigma_i)$. If $\sigma_i \geq x_i$, the distributed outstar equation (1) allows thresholds $\tau_{ji}$ to grow but never shrink. The principle of atrophy due to disuse implies that a threshold $\tau_{ji}$ is unable to change at all unless (i) the path signal $y_j$ exceeds the previously learned value of $\tau_{ji}$; and (ii) the total top-down signal $\sigma_i$ to the $i^{th}$ node exceeds that node's activity $x_i$. In particular, if $\tau_{ji}$ grows large when the node $j$ represents part of a compressed $F_2$ code, then $\tau_{ji}$ cannot be changed at all when node $j$ is later part of a more distributed code, since threshold changes are disabled if $y_j \leq \tau_{ji}$ (Figure 2d).

## Distributed outstar solution

The form of the distributed outstar system (1)–(4) is nearly linear, and the equations can be solved in closed form. The formulas below give an explicit solution for an arbitrary input sequence with either slow or fast learning. An example then illustrates the phase space geometry of this solution.

Assume that an input $\mathbf{I}$ activates a distributed outstar field $F_1$ at some time $t = t_0$ and that $\mathbf{I}$ is held fixed for some ensuing interval. If $\sigma_i \leq x_i$ at $t = t_0$, then $\tau_{ji}$ will remain constant during that interval, for all $j = 1, \ldots, N$. Similarly, $\tau_{ji}$ will remain constant if $y_j \leq \tau_{ji}$ at $t = t_0$. Consider now a fixed $F_1$ index $i$ such that $\sigma_i > x_i$ at $t = t_0$. Let:

$$\Phi_i = \{j : y_j(t_0) > \tau_{ji}(t_0)\} \equiv \{j : S_{ji}(t_0) > 0. \tag{5}$$

For $j \in \Phi_i$,

$$\frac{d}{dt}\tau_{ji} = (y_j - \tau_{ji})(\sigma_i - x_i), \tag{6}$$

until $y_j$ or $x_i$ changes. In a network such as ART 1 or fuzzy ART, $F_1$ activity $\mathbf{x}$ and $F_2$ activity $\mathbf{y}$ remain constant as long as $\mathbf{I}$ is constant.

Geometrically, by (6), the projected vector of $\tau_{ji}$ values with $j \in \Phi_i$ follows a straight line toward the corresponding projected vector of $y_j$ values. If all such $\tau_{ji}$ were to approach $y_j$ then $\sigma_i$ would converge to 0, by (2). Progress halts, however, as the $\tau_{ji}$ vector approaches the set of points where $\sigma_i = x_i$, by (6). Explicitly, for $t \geq t_0$, while $y_j$ and $x_i$ are constant:

$$\tau_{ji}(t) = \tau_{ji}(t_0) + \alpha(t) \frac{[\sigma_i(t_0) - x_i]^+}{\sigma_i(t_0)} [y_j - \tau_{ji}(t_0)]^+, \tag{7}$$

where $\alpha(t)$ is an exponential that goes from 0 to 1 as $t$ goes from $t_0$ to $\infty$.

By (7), $\tau_{ji}(t)$ remains constant if $\sigma_i(t_0) \leq x_i$ or if $y_j \leq \tau_{ji}(t_0)$. If $\sigma_i(t_0) > x_i$ and if $j \in \Phi_i, \tau_{ji}(t)$ moves from $\tau_{ji}(t_0)$ toward:

$$\tau_{ji}(\infty) = \tau_{ji}(t_0) + \frac{(\sigma_i(t_0) - x_i)}{\sigma_i(t_0)} (y_j - \tau_{ji}(t_0)) \tag{8}$$

as $t$ goes from $t_0$ to $\infty$. In particular:

$$\begin{aligned}
\sigma_i(\infty) &= \sum_{j \in \Phi_i} (y_j - \tau_{ji}(\infty)) \\
&= \sum_{j \in \Phi_i} (y_j - \tau_{ji}(t_0)) - \frac{(\sigma_i(t_0) - x_i)}{\sigma_i(t_0)} \sum_{j \in \Phi_i} (y_j - \tau_{ji}(t_0)) \\
&= \sigma_i(t_0) - \frac{(\sigma_i(t_0) - x_i)}{\sigma_i(t_0)} \sigma_i(t_0) \\
&= x_i.
\end{aligned} \tag{9}$$

For the unbiased case where $t_0 = 0$, so all $\tau_{ji}(0) = 0$,

$$S_{ji}(0) \equiv y_j - \tau_{ji}(0) = y_j \tag{10}$$

and:

$$\sigma_i(0) \equiv \sum_j S_{ji}(0) = \sum_j y_j = 1. \tag{11}$$

Thus:

$$\begin{aligned}
\tau_{ji}(t) &= \tau_{ji}(0) + \alpha(t) \frac{[\sigma_i(0) - x_i]^+}{\sigma_i(0)} [y_j - \tau_{ji}(0)]^+ \\
&= \alpha(t)(1 - x_i) y_j,
\end{aligned} \tag{12}$$

$$\begin{aligned}
S_{ji}(t) &\equiv y_j - \tau_{ji}(t) \\
&= y_j - \alpha(t)(1 - x_i) y_j \\
&= y_j(1 - \alpha(t)(1 - x_i)),
\end{aligned} \tag{13}$$

and

$$S_{ji}(t) \rightarrow y_j x_i \tag{14}$$

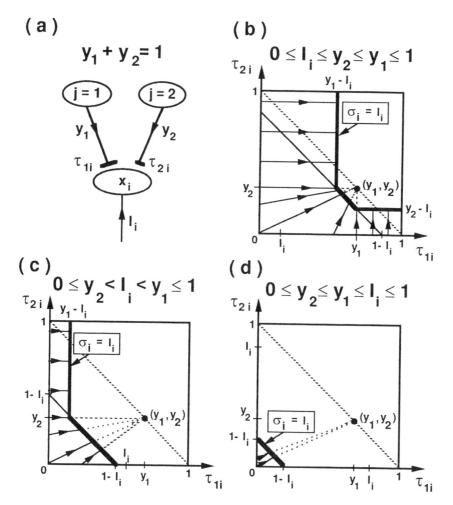

**Figure 3.** (a) A distributed outstar whose coding field $F_2$ has just two nodes ($N = 2$). For each code **y**, $y_1 + y_2 = 1$ and $x_i = I_i \wedge \sigma_i$. When thresholds start out small enough, $\tau_{1i}$ and/or $\tau_{2i}$ increase toward $\{(\tau_{1i}, \tau_{2i}) : \sigma_i = I_i\}$. (b) Threshold changes are greatest for small $I_i$. (c) When $I_i > y_j$, the $j^{th}$ node cannot dominate learning. Here, $I_i > y_2$, so $\tau_{2i}$ can change only when $\tau_{1i}$ also changes. (d) When $I_i$ is large, only small thresholds can change at all.

as $t \to \infty$. By (14), when the system begins with no initial threshold bias, the signal $S_{ji}$ from the $j^{th}$ $F_2$ node to the $i^{th}$ $F_1$ node begins equal to the path signal $y_j$ and converges toward the Hebbian pre- and post-synaptic correlation term $y_j x_i$.

### Distributed outstar dynamics

The dynamics of distributed outstar learning will now be illustrated by means of a low-dimensional example. Consider a coding network with just two $F_2$ nodes (Figure 3a). Two top-down paths, with thresholds $\tau_{1i}$ and $\tau_{2i}$, converge upon each $F_1$ node. Assume that $x_i = I_i \wedge \sigma_i$, as in fuzzy ART, and fix an $F_2$ code $\mathbf{y} = (y_1, y_2)$, with :

$$0 \leq y_2 \leq y_1 \leq 1. \tag{15}$$

By the $F_2$ normalization hypothesis (4), $y_1 + y_2 = 1$. By (1), for $j = 1, 2$:

$$\frac{d}{dt}\tau_{ji} = [y_j - \tau_{ji}]^+[\sigma_i - I_i]^+, \tag{16}$$

**(a)** **multiplicative weight**

$y_j w_{ji}$

**(b)** **fuzzy capacity (sieve)**

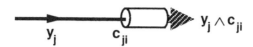

$y_j \wedge c_{ji}$

**(c)** **subtractive threshold**

$[y_j - \tau_{ji}]^+$

**Figure 4.** (a) The product rule implies a physical substrate of memory that is a multiplicative weight (McCulloch and Pitts, 1943). (b) The capacity rule implies a memory unit that is a fuzzy sieve (Zadeh, 1965). (c) The distributed outstar implies a memory unit that is a subtractive threshold.

where, by (2),

$$\sigma_i = [y_1 - \tau_{1i}]^+ + [y_2 - \tau_{2i}]^+. \tag{17}$$

Figures 3b–d show the 2-D phase plane dynamics of the threshold vector $(\tau_{1i}, \tau_{2i})$ for a fixed input $I_i$. In each plot, trajectories that begin in the set of points where $\sigma_i > I_i$ approach the set where $\sigma_i = I_i$. Where $\tau_{1i}(t_0) < y_1$ and $\tau_{2i}(t_0) < y_2$, the point $(\tau_{1i}(t), \tau_{2i}(t))$ moves along a straight line from $(\tau_{1i}(t_0), \tau_{2i}(t_0))$ toward $(y_1, y_2)$, slowing down asymptotically as:

$$\begin{aligned}\sigma_i &= [y_1 - \tau_{1i}(t)]^+ + [y_2 - \tau_{2i}(t)]^+ \\ &= 1 - (\tau_{1i}(t) + \tau_{2i}(t)) \to I_i.\end{aligned} \tag{18}$$

Only if $I_i = 0$ does $(\tau_{1i}, \tau_{2i})$ approach $(y_1, y_2)$. Larger thresholds $\tau_{ji}$, which make $\sigma_i \leq I_i$, are unchanged during learning. A small $I_i$ value allows the greatest threshold changes (Figure 3b). If $I_i = 0$,

$$\tau_{ji} \to y_j \tag{19}$$

as $\sigma_i$ decreases to 0.

Both thresholds grow if both are initially small. However, if one threshold is initially so large as to prevent $F_2 \to F_1$ signal transmission in the corresponding path, the other $F_2$ node "takes over" the code. For example, if $\tau_{2i}(t_0) \geq y_2$ (Figure 3b), there is no signal from the $F_2$ node $j = 2$ to the $i^{th}$ $F_1$ node, and hence no threshold change in that path. If, then, $\tau_{1i}(t_0) < y_1 - I_i$, $\tau_{1i}$ increases until:

$$\sigma_i = y_1 - \tau_{1i} \to x_i = I_i. \tag{20}$$

Larger $I_i$ values permit threshold changes only for smaller initial threshold values. In Figure 3c, $\tau_{2i}$ can change only if $\tau_{1i}$ changes as well, when both are initially small. In contrast, since $y_1$ is greater than $I_i$, $\tau_{1i}$ may increase, by itself, toward $(y_1 - I_i)$ if $\tau_{2i}(t_0) \geq y_2$. Finally, for $I_i$ close to 1 (Figure 3d) adaptive changes can occur only if both $\tau_{1i}$ and $\tau_{2i}$ are initially small, as they are when little learning has taken place.

## The unit of memory

The distributed outstar network derives from a computational analysis of stable pattern learning by distributed codes. In the distributed outstar, the adaptive threshold synaptic transmission rule solves a catastrophic forgetting problem caused by other rules. Since each formal transmission rule corresponds to a physical theory of synaptic transmission, computational analysis implies physiological prediction. Each transmission rule assumes a physical memory unit: a multiplicative weight (Figure 4a), a fuzzy capacity, or sieve (Figure 4b), or a subtractive threshold (Figure 4c). Experiments that probe distributed coding in a living organism may be able to test for the three types of memory unit. Similarly, distributed outstar computations imply distinct physical realizations of optical and electronic neural networks.

## References

Carpenter, G.A. (1993). Distributed outstar learning and the rules of synaptic transmission. **Proceedings of the world congress on neural networks (WCNN–93)**, **II**, 397–404.

Carpenter, G.A. (1994). A distributed outstar network for spatial pattern learning. *Neural Networks*, **7**. Technical Report CAS/CNS TR-93-036, Boston, MA: Boston University.

Carpenter, G.A. and Grossberg, S. (1987). A massively parallel architecture for a self-organizing neural pattern recognition machine. *Computer Vision, Graphics, and Image Processing*, **37**, 54–115.

Carpenter, G.A. and Grossberg, S. (1991). **Pattern recognition by self-organizing neural networks**. Cambridge, MA: MIT Press.

Carpenter, G.A., Grossberg, S., and Rosen, D.B. (1991a). Fuzzy ART: Fast stable learning and categorization of analog patterns by an adaptive resonance system. *Neural Networks*, **4**, 759–771.

Carpenter, G.A., Grossberg, S., and Rosen, D.B. (1991b). A neural network realization of fuzzy ART. Technical Report CAS/CNS TR-91-021, Boston, MA: Boston University.

Grossberg, S. (1968). Some nonlinear networks capable of learning a spatial pattern of arbitrary complexity. *Proceedings of the National Academy of Sciences*, **59**, 368–372.

McCulloch, W.S. and Pitts, W. (1943). A logical calculus of the ideas immanent in nervous activity. *Bulletin of Mathematical Biophysics*, **5**, 115–133.

Rosenblatt, F. (1958) The perceptron: A probabilistic model for information storage and organization in the brain. *Psychological Review*, **65**, 386–408.

Rosenblatt, F. (1962). **Principles of neurodynamics**. Washington, DC: Spartan Books.

Widrow, B. and Hoff, M.E. (1960). Adaptive switching circuits. *1960 IRE WESCON Convention Record*. New York: IRE, pp. 96–104.

Zadeh, L. (1965). Fuzzy sets. *Information Control*, **8**, 338-353.

# CONCURRENT LEARNING ALGORITHM TRENDS

Robert J. Jannarone
Electrical & Computer Engineering Department
University of South Carolina
Columbia, SC 29208
jannaron@ece.scarolina.edu

## Abstract

In the first part of this talk conventional neurocomputing algorithms will be examined from a real-time learning viewpoint. Emphasis will be placed on if and how existing algorithms can learn as fast as information arrives. In the second part of this talk a concurrent information processing system will be contrasted with conventional systems that has provisions for automatic and concurrent learning, monitoring, data reduction and pattern completion. The model is based on reinforced learning and concept formation principles from psychology, Bayes and polynomial regression principles from statistics and a fast Kernel algorithm for concurrent operation. The Kernel algorithm processes records containing 64 features each at the rate of 400 per second on a work station, it processes records containing more features at exponentially increasing rates on sequential computers, it can process records at linearly increasing rates on special-purpose digital computers and it can process records at faster rates on special-purpose analog computers.

## CONCURRENT LEARNING ALGORITHM TRENDS

Neurocomputers can be classified either as conventional systems that learn off line,[1,2] or as concurrent information processing systems that learn on line.[3-15] Conventional systems are important because they were the first functional neurocomputing systems,[2] they are useful when model learning from total ignorance is necessary and they are firmly established.[1] However, conventional use is limited to settings where (a) delays are acceptable between the time learning occurs and the the time learning models are used and (b) input-output relationships are stable from the time learning data are gathered to the time decision functions are calculated.

By contrast with conventional neurocomputers, the concurrent information processing (CIP) system of emphasis for this talk is designed to keep up with changing measurement structures and perceptual worlds as they evolve. The key CIP system attribute is its ability to learn computing relationships automatically as well as concurrently, based on sound principles from psychology, statistics and computational science. Other attributes include available sequential software that can process incoming records at rates from the millisecond range to the second range depending on record size; available parallel algorithms for applications where faster operation is needed; provisions for concurrent learning, missing value imputing and measurement deviance monitoring; and provisions for occasional model refinement and interpretation.

Conventional systems are designed for settings where previously gathered data are analyzed off line to produce predictive models and parameter estimates. Both traditional statistics systems and traditional neurocomputing systems are in the conventional category. The main difference between statistics and neurocomputing systems is that the former require manual model identification by data analysts, while the latter are designed for automatic identification by learning algorithms.

The CIP system does not belong in the conventional category because it is designed for settings where data are gathered, analyzed and processed at once. It does belong in the neurocomputing category, however, because it is designed for automatic rather than manual data analysis. The CIP system also resembles conventional neurocomputing systems because it is based on parallel network structure and psychological learning principles. However, it differs sharply from conventional neruocomputing systems in both modeling and learning algorithm structure. To illustrate CIP and conventional neurocomputing differences, the two alternative models will be contrasted next, after which alternative learning algorithms will be contrasted.

The standard conventional neurocomputing model is the multilayer perceptron (MP),[1] and CIP counterparts to MP models are product feature models like the phoneme recognition model in Figure 1. A corresponding MP model for the same setting is shown in Figure 2, for comparison purposes.

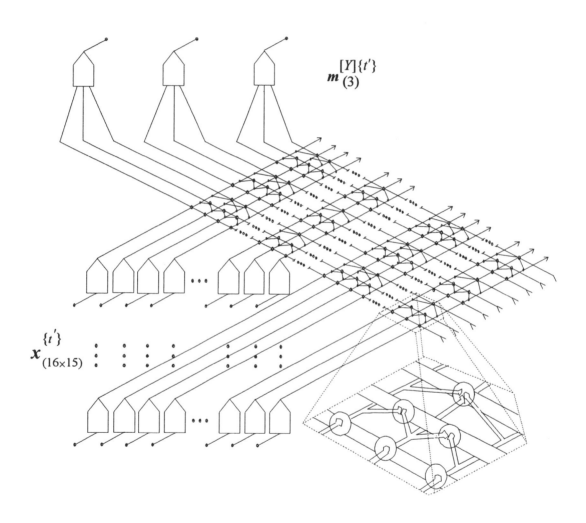

Figure 1. A Concurrent Information Processing Phoneme Recognition Model

Both the Figure 1 CIP model and the Figure 2 MP model are designed for phoneme recognition data, where uttering any of three phonemes "B" "D" or "G" produces an array of 16 audible frequencies at 15 time slices.[11] Both models include 240 inputs giving frequency power levels at different time slices, denoted by $x^{\{t'\}}_{(16\times15)}$ in the two figures. In addition, both models can accept training data during which all $x^{\{t'\}}$ and $m^{[Y]\{t'\}}$ are known, with $m^{[Y]\{t'\}}$ values being either (1, 0, 0), (0, 1, 0) or (0, 0, 1). However, the CIP model is designed to receive a concurrent plausibility vector and a concurrent learning weight with each ($x^{\{t'\}}$, $m^{[Y]\{t'\}}$) record, while the MP model has no such provisions.[15]

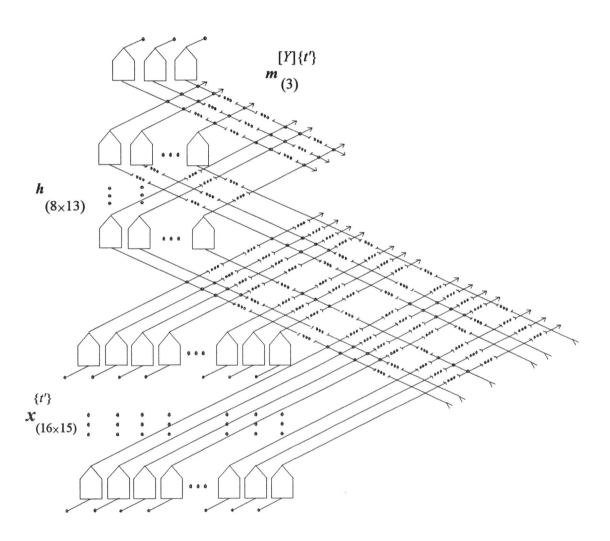

Figure 2. A Multilayer Perceptron Phoneme Recognition Model

Concurrent plausibility and learning weight provisions give CIP models added imputing and learning flexibility. CIP plausibility records allow any of the $x^{\{t'\}}$ or $m^{[Y]\{t'\}}$ values to be imputed from any of the others and from prior learning during each trial. For example, only connections for imputing phoneme types from filter values are shown in Figure 1, but the CIP phoneme model can also impute any of the filter values that might be missing during any trials. Also, concurrent learning weights allow each $(x^{\{t'\}}, m^{[Y]\{t'\}})$ record to have flexible impact on future CIP performance. For example, if identifying a "D" is more important than identifying either a "B" or a "G," CIP learning weights can be set to produce more learning impact for "D" trials than for other trials. Thus, CIP model learning weights and plausibility vectors give them pattern completion and learning flexibility that the MP model does not have.

Besides differing in imputing and learning weight flexibility, CIP models and MP models differ in how they identify connection structures and functions, as shown in Figures 1 and 2. When CIP connections like those in Figure 1 are specified, they identify product features precisely such as the first-order, second-order and third-order features in the Figure 1 detail. By contrast, specifying an MP model only identifies features partially. For example, the Figure 2 phoneme model restricts the number of features to 104, which is the number of elements in $h_{(8 \times 13)}$. It also restricts feature types so that only elements in the first three columns of $x$ can be connected to the first 8 column elements in $h$, only elements in the second through fourth columns of $x$ can be connected to the second column elements in $h$ and so on. However, the MP model allows any of several product features to be linked to each element in $h$ and each such feature can be any product of that element's 48 inputs. This results in a Figure 2 MP model that is much less identified than its Figure 1 CIP counterpart.

CIP features are identified when the model is fixed, so that only feature weights remain to be learned. For example, only the weights connecting each of the first-order through third-order features to each of the 3 output phonemes in Figure 1 can vary during fixed CIP model learning. By contrast, features as well as their connection weights must be determined during MP learning, because features are not identified when the MP model is specified. For example, if only one of the 48 weights for $h_{11}$ is nonzero then $h_{11}$ will be a first-order feature; if two such weights are nonzero then it will be a second-order feature and so on. (Product MP features result from additive Figure 2 connections to $h$ elements because they are combined using exponential functions.[11,15]) Thus, CIP models fix features and allow their weights to be learned while MP models allow both features and their weights to be learned.

Turning finally to learning contrasts, the most widely used conventional neuro-computing learning algorithm is backpropagation (BP).[1,2] CIP learning and BP learning differ mainly because CIP operation requires on-line adaptability but conventional operation does not. To accomplish on-line adaptability along with model learning flexibility, CIP operation breaks learning down into immediate concurrent learning and slower model refinement. During concurrent learning the CIP Kernel algorithm updates connection weights for fixed models of the Figure 1 type immediately after each record arrives.[15] During model refinement, CIP feature combining, removing and creating procedures operate more slowly after concurrent learning has been going on for some time.[15] By contrast, the BP algorithm both establishes input-to-feature connections and sets feature-to-output connection weights during a combined learning operation, starting with MP models that are less identified than their CIP counterparts.

Due to less MP model identification, BP learning is more open-ended than CIP learning, but it comes at an added cost. BP learning requires waiting for iterative programs that make multiple passes at training data to converge, waiting for training data to be gathered off line and waiting for learned models to be implemented off line. Instead, CIP concurrent learning is fully identifiable (in the statistical sense[6,10,18]), permitting real-time, adaptive operation.

Open-ended BP learning carries other costs that are not linked to concurrent operation. Because MP models are not identifiable and MP start values are randomly assigned, the BP algorithm may produce different results from the same data, it may converge to local solutions or it may not converge at all.[1,2,16-17] Learned MP connection weights are also difficult to interpret in terms of how much each input affects each output.[11] By contrast, the CIP learning algorithm is based on a statistical theory foundation that guarantees convergence to optimal learning as information is processed, without requiring iterative learning or producing poor solutions along the way. Also, input feature effects on output CIP variables are easy to assess by examining multiple, partial and reduced correlations.[15]

The MP model and BP learning algorithm are historically important because they have inspired information processing researchers, including this speaker, to produce automatic learning systems. Moreover, the MP-BP system remains very popular because it is firmly established and it produces automatic, open-ended learning. The MP-BP system understandably comes up short for concurrent learning, however, because it was never designed for that purpose.

## References

1. P. Wasserman, *Advanced Methods in Neural Computing,* Van Nostrand Reinhold, New York, 1993.

2. P.W. Werbos, *Beyond Regression: New Tools for Prediction and Analysis in the Behavioral Sciences,* Unpublished Ph.D. Dissertation, Harvard University, 1974.

3. R.J. Jannarone, "Conjunctive Item Response Theory Kernels," *Psychometrika,* Vol. 51, pp. 357-373, 1986.

4. R.J. Jannarone, K.F. Yu, and Y. Takefuji, "Conjunctoids: Statistical Learning Modules for Binary Events," *Neural Networks,* Vol. 1, pp. 325-337, 1988.

5. R.J. Jannarone, K.F. Yu, and J.E. Laughlin, "Easy Bayes Estimation for Rasch Type Models," *Psychometrika,* Vol. 55, pp. 449-460, 1990.

6. R.J. Jannarone, "Conjunctive Measurement Theory: Cognitive Research Prospects," in M. Wilson (Ed.), *Objective Measurement: Theory Into Practice,* Ablex, Norwood, NJ, 1991.

7. Y. Hu, "Automated Real-Time Neural Computing for Defense Waste Processing," *Proceedings of the International Topic Meeting on Nuclear and Hazardous Waste Management,* American Nuclear Society, Inc., La Grange Park, IL, Vol. 1, pp. 534-540, 1992.

8. Y. Takefuji, *Neural Network Parallel Computing,* Kluwer, Boston, 1992, Ch. 16.

9. R.J. Jannarone, K. Ma, K.F. Yu, and J.W. Gorman, "Extended Conjunctoid Theory and Implementation: a General Model for Machine Cognition based on Categorical Data," *Progress in Neural Networks,* Vol. 3, in press.

10. R.J. Jannarone, "Local Dependence: Objectively Measurable or Objectionally Abominable?" in M. Wilson (Ed.), *Objective Measurement: Theory Into Practice,* Vol. 2, Ablex, Norwood, NJ, in press.

11. G. Tatman, R.J. Jannarone & C.M. Amick, "Neural Networks for Speech Recognition: Contrasts Between a Traditional and a Parametric Approach," *IEEE Transactions on Neural Networks,* in revision.

12. Y. Hu, "Hypercube Implementation of a Concurrent Information Processing Kernel Algorithm," *Journal of Parallel and Distributed Computing,* in review.

13. K.V. Ananthakrishnan & R.J. Jannarone, "A Concurrent Information Processing Coordinator Package," *Software Practice and Experience,* in review.

14. R.J. Jannarone, "Measuring Quickness and Correctness Concurrently: a Conjunctive IRT Approach," in M. Wilson & G. Engelhard Jr. (Eds.), *Objective Measurement: Theory Into Practice,* Ablex, Norwood, NJ, Vol. 3, to appear.

15. R.J. Jannarone, *Concurrent Information Processing: A Psycho-Statistical Model for Real-Time Neurocomputing,* Van Nostrand Reinhold, to appear.

16. K.J. Aström & T.J. McAvoy, "Intelligent Control: an Overview and Evaluation," in D.A. White & D.A. Sofge (Eds.), *Handbook of Intelligent Control,* Van Nostrand Reinhold, New York, 1992.

17. P.J. Werbos, T. McAvoy, & T. Su, "Neural Networks, System Identification, and Control in the Chemical Process Industries," in D.A. White & D.A. Sofge (Eds.), *Handbook of Intelligent Control,* Van Nostrand Reinhold, New York, 1992.

18. E.L. Lehmann, *Theory of Point Estimation,* Wiley, New York, 1983.

# Self-organization of Temporal Pattern Generation Based on Anticipation

DeLiang Wang[†‡] and Budi Yuwono[†]

[†]Department of Computer and Information Science, [‡]Center for Cognitive Science
The Ohio State University, Columbus, Ohio 43210-1277, USA

## Abstract

*A neural network model of complex temporal pattern generation is proposed and investigated analytically and by computer simulation. Temporal pattern generation is based on recognition of the contexts of individual components. Based on its acquired experience, the model actively yields system anticipation, which then compares with the actual input flow. A mismatch triggers self-organization of context learning, which ultimately leads to resolving various ambiguities in producing complex temporal patterns. We show analytically that the network model can learn to generate any complex temporal pattern. Multiple patterns can be acquired sequentially by the system, manifesting a form of retroactive interference. The model is consistent with cognitive studies of sequential learning.*

## 1. Introduction

The ability to learn and generate temporal patterns is one of the most important characteristics of an intelligent system. Such an ability enables the systems to perform tasks, ranging from a simple behavior of limb movement to abstract temporal reasoning. This paper presents a neural network model of learning and generating complex temporal patterns by self-organization. The basic idea for self-organization is an *anticipation mechanism* where the system actively anticipates the next component in a sequence and compares its anticipation with the next input component. With this mechanism, we analytically show that the network can learn any complex temporal patterns.

We assume discrete temporal patterns, or temporal sequences. A continuous temporal pattern can usually be sampled into a discrete pattern before processing. Following the terminology introduced by Wang and Arbib [11], a sequence $S$ of length $N$ is defined as $p_1$-$p_2$-...-$p_N$, where each $p_i$ is a component (static pattern) of $S$. Any part of $S$ is called a subsequence of $S$. Generally, in order to unambiguously produce a component, a prior subsequence is required to be detected. For instance, in the sequence $R$-$E$-$F$-$E$-$R$-$E$-$E$, the prior subsequence $E$-$R$-$E$ of the last $E$ is required to determine the $E$, since $R$-$E$ is a recurring subsequence in the sequence. Thus we define the *context* of a component $p_i$ as the shortest subsequence which unambiguously determines $p_i$, and its length is called the *degree* of $p_i$. The *degree of a sequence* is the maximum degree of its components. Thus, a *simple* sequence is a degree 1 sequence, whereas a *complex* sequence has a degree greater than one.

Neural networks to learn and generate temporal sequences have been investigated by a number of investigators [2, 4, 6, 5]. One of the main problems with the proposed methods lies in producing complex sequences. High-order networks have been proposed to fix the problem [1, 4]. However, the number of connections in a high-order network grows exponentially with the order of the network. Another difficulty is that unless the degree of the sequence is known in advance, a fixed network cannot guarantee unambiguous production of an arbitrary sequence. Recently, Wang and Arbib [11, 12] proposed a model for complex temporal sequence learning. Complex temporal sequences are acquired through a form of supervised learning. The present model differs from the earlier models of Wang and Arbib [11, 12] in several major aspects. First, the selection of context detectors is done by competitive learning in this model whereas the previous models need the system to assign and remember appropriate context detectors. Second, active anticipation is missing from the previous models. Also a much more extensive analytical investigation has been undertaken for the present model.

## 2. Model Specification

As a basic idea, this model generates a sequence $S$ by successively predicting component $p_i$ based on the context of $p_i$. More specifically, the model is designed to detect the context of $p_i$ first, and then associate this detection with $p_i$, thus producing $p_i$ once its context occurs from the input. Since a context is, by definition, also a sequence, recognizing the contexts of sequence components can be done by means of a set of sequence detectors, each of which is uniquely associated with a component. In the following discussions, we assume that each symbol, or static pattern, is uniquely represented by an input unit.

In order to learn a complex sequence, each input component must be associated with successive components beyond its immediate successor. This can be achieved with a short-term memory (STM) model. A decay-based STM model is used in this model, with each input unit being extended to a local network, called a *shift-register assembly*. A shift-register assembly is a group of units, which are serially linked one after another, forming a chain like the outstar avalanche [2]. Each assembly is triggered by a unique input *terminal* which is directly activated by external stimulation or by a modulator unit (to be discussed shortly) during generation. Each terminal represents a unique input symbol. With such a STM model in place, a single detector layer is introduced for detecting different contexts. Each unit in this layer receives inputs from all the shift-register units (SR units) and this layer can be trained to associate its units with the input subsequences corresponding to different contexts. Figure 1 shows the architecture of this model. A detector in the network is said to be *committed* if it is tuned to a particular input subsequence, i.e., the detector unit will be activated when the subsequence is presented. We use a winner-take-all mechanism for the detector layer as described by Grossberg [3]. Due to winner-take-all dynamics, there is at most one detector unit activated at any time.

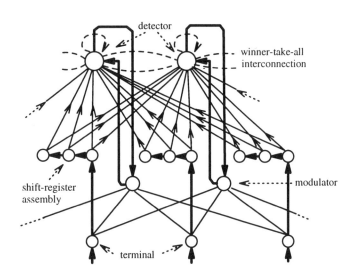

**Figure 1**. The architecture of the overall network model. Thin lines denote modifiable connections, while thick lines and dashed lines denote fixed connections.

The system anticipates the next component and compares it with the external input through the modulator layer. As shown in Fig. 1, there is one modulator associated with each detector in the network. Each modulator unit receives upward connections from every individual terminal. In addition, it receives a downward connection from its respective detector. An active detector enables its modulator in the next time step. Once enabled, the modulator performs one-shot (one step) learning to update its upward connection weights. Since only one terminal corresponding to the current input component can be active, one-shot learning leads to one-to-one connection from an active terminal to a triggered modulator. Basically, this one-shot learning establishes the association between a context detector and the next input component. If they do not match next time, the anticipated activation of the corresponding modulator will be absent, and this mismatch will be detected by the modulator, which in turn sends a signal to its respective detector to expand the context that the detector is supposed to recognize. We provide more detailed neural dynamics and learning in the following.

Assume that each assembly has $r$ SR units. The activity of detector $i$ at time $t$, $E_i(t)$, is defined as:

$$E_i(t) = g(\sum_{j,k} W_{i,jk} V_{jk}(t), \theta_i) \qquad (1)$$

where $g(x, y) = $ x if $x \geq y$, or 0 otherwise. $W_{i,jk}$ is the connection weight from the $k$th SR unit of assembly $j$ to detector $i$. $V_{jk}(t)$ is the activity of this SR unit at time $t$. $\theta_i$ is an adjustable threshold for the detector, set to the current value of $E_i$ when unit $i$ is activated  As shown in the next section, the adjustable $\theta_i$ never decreases. The activity $V_{jk}(t)$ is defined as follows,

$$V_{jk}(t) = \begin{cases} I_j(t) & \text{if } k = 1 \text{ (head unit)} \\ \max[0, V_{j,k-1}(t-1)-\delta] & \text{otherwise} \end{cases} \qquad (2)$$

where $I_j(t)$ is the binary input at terminal $j$. Due to the nature of sequential input, at most one terminal has its $I(t)$ equal to 1. $\delta$ is a decay parameter. Eq. 2 provides an implementation of the decay-based STM model described earlier, i.e., an input activity is held for a short time and decays gradually in a shift-register assembly. Apparently, the input cannot be held longer than $r$ steps, the limit of STM capacity.

The learning rule for each detector $i$ is a Hebbian rule plus normalization to keep the overall weight a constant, denoted as a *normalized Hebbian rule*,

$$\hat{W}_{i,jk}(t+1) = W_{i,jk}(t) + \alpha\, O_i(t)\, g(V_{jk}(t), A_i) \tag{3a}$$

$$W_{i,jk}(t+1) = \frac{\hat{W}_{i,jk}(t+1)}{\alpha\, C + \displaystyle\sum_{j,k} \hat{W}_{i,jk}(t+1)} \tag{3b}$$

where $\alpha$ is a gain parameter or learning rate. A large $\alpha$ makes training fast. It is easy to see that a large $\alpha$ results in approximate one-shot learning. To indicate the outcome of winner-take-all competition in the detector layer while omitting the details of competitive dynamics, we introduce $O_i(t)$ which equals 1 if detector $i$ is the winner of the competition, or 0 otherwise. Function $g$ in (3a) serves as a gate to let in the influences of only those SR units whose activities are greater or equal to $A_i$. $A_i$ is the sensitivity parameter of unit $i$. The lower the sensitivity parameter the more SR units can be sensed by a winning detector. Thus more connections of the detector can be modified according to (3a). Furthermore, the sensitivity parameter $A_i$ is adaptive by itself, following the rule below,

$$A_i = \begin{cases} 1 & \text{if } d_i = 0 \\ \max[0,\, 1-\delta(d_i-1)] & \text{if } d_i > 0 \end{cases} \tag{4}$$

where $d_i$, called the *degree parameter* of detector $i$, is a non-negative integer, initialized to 0. According to (4) and (3a), when $d_i$ increases, more SR units can be sensed, and except when $d_i = 0$, $d_i$ is equal to the number of units that can be sensed by unit $i$. The role of constant $C$ in (3b) will become clear in the next section.

A modulator receives both top-down connection from its corresponding detector and bottom-up connections from input terminals (Fig. 1). More specifically, the activity of modulator $i$ is defined as,

$$M_i(t) = O_i(t-1) \sum_{j=1}^{n} R_{ij}\, I_j(t) \tag{5}$$

where $R_{ij}$ is a binary-valued weight of the connection from terminal $j$ to modulator $i$. If $O_i(t-1) = 1$ and $M_i(t) = 0$ then the modulator sends a feedback signal to its detector. Upon receiving this feedback signal, the detector increases its degree parameter, thus lowering its sensitivity parameter $A_i$ (see Eq. 4). We refer to this situation where $O_i(t-1) = 1$ and $M_i(t) = 0$ as a *mismatch*. A mismatch occurs when an anticipated next component in the sequence does not appear.

Finally, one-shot learning is performed on the bottom-up connection weights of the modulator of a winning detector $z$, $R_{zj} = I_j(t)$. This learning rule sets the connection weights of modulator $z$ to the current activities of the input terminals. The training steps are repeated at each following time step. After all sequence components have been presented, the entire cycle of training, referred to as a *training sweep*, is repeated. The training phase is completed when there is no mismatch occurring during the last training sweep.

During sequence generation (reproduction), the connections from the input terminals to the modulators in the model are reversed (see Fig. 1), which can be neurally implemented by introducing bidirectional connections between the two layers and assuming identical training for the two-way connections. Since only one bottom-up link from the terminals to a modulator is non-zero, once reversed a modulator triggers only one terminal. The generation process of a learned sequence starts from the presentation of the beginning component of the sequence. The beginning component will trigger an appropriate context detector, which in turn activates its respective modulator, thus leading to the activation of the second component in its corresponding terminal. The activated terminal joins the beginning component to activate another context detector, which again triggers its respective modulator and thus the third input component. This process continues until the entire sequence is generated.

# 3. Analytical Results and Computer Simulation

We have formally analyzed the above model for sequence generation. Due to space limitation, we can only list the major conclusions without proofs. The interested reader can find the details in Wang and Yuwono [13]. Before presenting the conclusions, let us define the following functions,

$$E(d) = \sum_{i=1}^{d} [1-(d-i)\delta]; \qquad \text{and } h(d) = \sum_{i=1}^{d} [1-(d-i)\delta]^2 / (C+E(d))$$

1°. *The learning rule of Eq. 4 with a proper choice of parameter C guarantees that the detector of sequence S is preferred to the detectors of all subsequences of S.*

In other words, when sequence $S$ occurs, the detector that recognizes $S$ masks those detectors that recognize the subsequences of $S$. We call this property of the learning rule *temporal masking*.

2°. *Initial training of a detector results in only one non-zero weight, which equals $1/(1+C)$. Also, the activity of the unit equals $h(1)$ and the threshold increases to $h(1)$.*

3°. *Except for $d = 0$ (initial training), an activated detector of degree d has u non-zero weights which have the distribution, $[1-(u-i)\delta]/[C+E(u)]$, for $i = 1,..., u$, where $u \leq d$. The activity and the threshold of the unit are both equal to $E(u)$.*

4°. *(a). The threshold of an activated unit never decreases; (b). At any time, a detector can be triggered by only a single sequence; (c). Except for initial training, once a unit is activated by sequence S, it can only be activated by S or S plus a prior subsequence.*

Based on the above conclusions, we provide the major theoretical result of this paper.

**Theorem 1.** *A model defined in Sect. 2 with r SR units for each shift-register assembly can learn to produce an arbitrary sequence S of degree $\leq r$.*

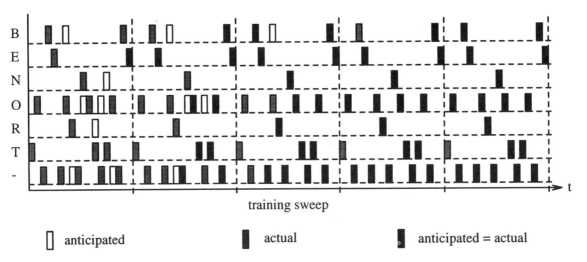

training sweep

□ anticipated    ▮ actual    ▮ anticipated = actual

**Figure 2**. Training and generation of the sequence <TO-BE-OR-NOT-TO-BE>. Shown in the figure are the activity traces of the input terminals of a simulated network. The parameters used in the simulation are : $\alpha = 0.2$, $\delta = 0.1$, and $C = 3.0$.

To illustrate the model, we carried out the following computer simulation. The network has 24 detector units, each of which is associated with one modulator unit, 24 terminals each of which is connected to one shift-register assembly, and 6 SR units for each shift-register assembly (144 register units in total). See the figure legend for the other parameter values used in the simulation. Figure 2 shows the activity trace of the network from a simulation run with input sequence <TO - BE - OR - NOT - TO - BE>. Symbol '-' here is treated as a distinct symbol separating meaningful words instead of a component separator. The network learned the sequence in 5 training sweeps. In the last training sweep, the system correctly anticipated every component of the sequence, as shown in the last column of the figure. After this training, the entire sequence can be correctly generated by the presentation of its first component, $T$ in this case, and the activity trace will be the same as the last sweep of training. The degree of the sequence is 6. Once one sequence is learned, a part of it can also be reproduced from a middle point of the sequence. For instance, with symbol $R$ as the initial input the network correctly produced the remaining part of the sequence <- *NOT - TO - BE>*.

## 4. Other Model Properties

**Efficiency of Training.** The number of training sweeps the model takes to learn a sequence largely depends on how complex the sequence is. We can derive a upper bound on the number of training sweeps for a sequence of degree $k$. Again, the detailed derivation can be found in Wang and Yuwono [13]. An upper bound $\mu$ of the training algorithm satisfying,

$$\mu = k(k+1)/2 \qquad (6)$$

The above upper bound is not a tight one at all. In fact, a more realistic estimate should be about $k$ training cycles.

**Multiple Sequences.** The network is capable of storing multiple input sequences. Multiple sequences can be learned simultaneously. In simultaneous training, all input sequences are presented one after another during each training sweep. Interestingly, multiple sequences can also be trained sequentially, meaning that new ones can be learned after some sequences have been stored into the network. If a new sequence to be learned has no component in common with the stored ones, it can be trained and stored as if nothing were already stored in the network. The more interesting situation is that a new sequence has subsequences which also occur in the stored ones. In this case, as should be expected from the learning algorithm, some previous links between modulators and input terminals will be altered. In this sense, the previous memory is interfered as a result of learning new sequences. This effect, however, conforms with a well-known psychological phenomenon, called *retroactive interference*. The critical question is whether the interference can be overcome with a little retraining or not. In our model, the answer is yes. The committed detectors which are interfered are only those which have been tuned to a subsequence that occurs in the new sequence. With a little retraining, the degrees of appropriate detectors will be increased to differentiate the interfered old subsequences and the new one.

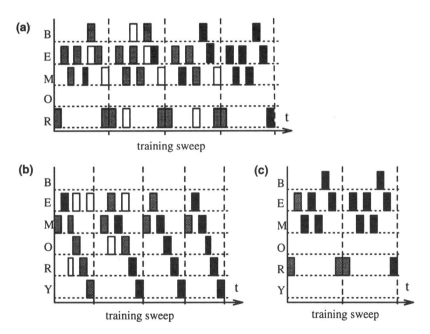

**Figure 3.** Sequential training of two temporal sequences. The figure notations are the same as in Fig. 2. (a) Training of the network to generate sequence $S_3$. (b) Training of the same network to generate sequence $S_4$. (c) The network was retrained to generate $S_3$. The parameter values used are the same as in Fig. 2.

To demonstrate a typical situation of retroactive interference, the same network simulated in Sect. 2 was used to learn sequentially two sequences, $S_3$: R-E-M-E-M-B-E-R and $S_4$: M-E-M-O-R-Y. $S_3$ was trained first, and the network took 4 sweeps to learn it, as shown in Fig. 3a. After that, $S_4$ was presented for training, and the network also took 4 sweeps to learn it (Fig. 3b). Because of common subsequences in the two sequences, acquisition of $S_4$ interfered with the memory of $S_3$. The network needs to be retrained in order to correctly generate $S_3$. In the simulation, the network took two more sweeps to regain $S_3$, as shown in Fig. 3c. After this relatively brief retraining to overcome retroactive interference, the network stored both sequences with no interference between them.

The above demonstration clearly shows that this model does not suffer from the so called *catastrophic interference* as exhibited in backpropagation learning of multilayer perceptrons [9]. Catastrophic interference refers that training of new associations destroys previously learned associations. On the contrary, the present model exhibits the kind of retroactive interference similar to the limitations that people have in sequential learning.

## 5. Discussion

Although our discussion so far focuses on temporal sequence generation, the model with some straightforward revision can also serve for sequence recognition. This is because the model has a component of context recognition which can be extended to arbitrary sequence recognition. The temporal masking mechanism leads to the desirable property that a detector tuned to a sequence will win the competition over those detectors tuned to the subsequences of the sequence.

In this model, we have demonstrated how anticipation may be used to learn to generate complex temporal behaviors. The idea of anticipation-based learning seems to be consistent with psychological evidence about human learning of sequential behaviors. It is observed that in learning temporal sequences human subjects can even be explicitly aware of the temporal structure of a sequence, and predict what comes next in the sequence [10].
The present model argues from the computational perspective for the chaining theory of temporal behavior as rejected by Lashley [7], echoing more recent psychological theories of serial order organization [8]. Simple associative chaining between adjacent sequence components is unlikely to be true. However, as demonstrated in this work, if chaining between remote components and chunking of subsequences into high-order components are allowed, much more complex temporal behaviors can be realized with the basic idea of associative chaining, going beyond what was discussed by Lashley [7].

**Acknowledgments:** The work described in this paper was supported in part by NSF grant IRI-9211419 and ONR grant N00014-93-1-0335.

## References

[1] T. Dehaene, J.P. Changeux, and J.P. Nadal, "Neural networks that learn temporal sequences by selection," *Proc. Natl. Acad. Sci. USA*, vol. 84, pp. 2727-2731, 1987.

[2] S. Grossberg, "Some networks that can learn, remember, and reproduce any number of complicated space-time patterns, I," *J. Math. Mechan.*, vol. 19, pp. 53-91, 1969.

[3] S. Grossberg, "Adaptive pattern classification and universal recoding: I. Parallel development and coding of neural feature detectors," *Biol. Cybern.*, vol. 23, pp. 121-134, 1976.

[4] I. Guyon, L. Personnaz, J.P. Nadal, and G. Dreyfus, "Storage and retrieval of complex sequences in neural networks," *Phys. Rev. A*, vol. 38, pp. 6365-6372, 1988.

[5] M.J. Healy, T.P. Caudell, and S.D.G. Smith, "A neural architecture for pattern sequence verification through inferencing," *IEEE Trans. Neural Networks*, vol. 4, pp. 9-20, 1993.

[6] T.M. Heskes and S. Gielen, "Retrieval of pattern sequences at variable speeds in a neural network with delays," *Neural Networks*, vol. 5, pp. 145-152, 1992.

[7] K.S. Lashley, "The problem of serial order in behavior," in *Cerebral mechanisms in behavior*, L.A. Jeffress, Ed.. New York: Wiley & Sons, pp. 112-146, 1951.

[8] S. Lewandowsky and B.B. Murdock, Jr., "Memory for serial order," *Psychol. Rev.*, vol. 96, pp. 25-57, 1989.

[9] M. McCloskey and N.J. Cohen, "Catastrophic interference in connectionist networks: The sequential learning problem," *Psychol. of Learning and Motivat.*, vol. 24, pp. 109-165, 1989.

[10] M.J. Nissen and P. Bullemer, "Attentional requirements of learning: Evidence from performance measures," *Cognit. Psychol.*, vol. 19, pp. 1-32, 1987.

[11] D.L. Wang and M.A. Arbib, "Complex temporal sequence learning based on short-term memory," *Proc. of IEEE* , vol. 78, pp. 1536-1543, 1990.

[12] D.L. Wang and M. A. Arbib, "Timing and chunking in processing temporal order," *IEEE Trans. Syst. Man Cybern.*, vol. 23 (4), 1993.

[13] D.L. Wang and B. Yuwono, "An anticipation-based neural network model for temporal pattern generation," Technical Report, Department of Computer and Information Science, Ohio State University, 1993.

# Representation of Temporal Order with the Sequential Memory with ART Neural Network

## JAMES VOGH

vogh@park.bu.edu
Graduate Program in Cognitive and Neural Systems
Boston University, 111 Cummington Street, Boston, MA 02215

*Abstract - A sequential memory with ART (SMART) model is presented which represents temporal order with both the associative chain and spatial patterns forms of representation. Such a combination of representations allows the SMART neural network to reproduces results from a variety a psychological and physiological data.*

## 1. Introduction

This paper will describe a new version of the sequential memory adaptive resonance theory architecture (SMART) which was introduced in Vogh (1993). Attention will be paid to the form of representation used and how that form of representation affects the implementation of the SMART network.

The SMART neural network combines the associative chain and spatial pattern forms of temporal order representation with the adaptive resonance theories (ART) of self-organized learning capabilities (Grossberg, 1976a. 1976b). By combining the two theories of temporal order representation SMART is able to explain psychological and neurological data which neither theory alone can explain and provide an effective solution to problems involving temporal order recognition like 3D object recognition. The representation of temporal order used by SMART will be described in the following section and other sections will describe how the SMART architecture is implemented and how it relates to the adaptive resonance theories of Grossberg.

## 2. SMART: Representation of Temporal Order

Figure 1 illustrates the method of temporal order representation used by SMART. Each of the nodes illustrated represents temporally associated items. For example, if the sequence *ABCD* is represented then a single node will represent *A*, another node will represent *B*, etc. Temporally associated nodes are interconnected with long term memory (LTM). The node representing *A* is connected to the node representing *B*, for example (see Figure 2a). Connection strength between nodes is a function of how temporally associated two items are. For example, *A* is more associated with *B* than *C* so that the connection strength between the node for *A* and the node for *B* is greater than the connection

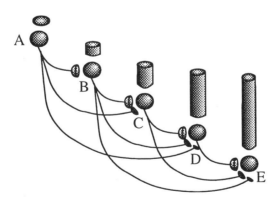

**Figure 1.** The representation of serial order used by SMART. Each node, which is illustrated as a circle, represents an item, such as a letter, from a sequence of items. Each node has an activity associated with it and temporally associated nodes are connected with long term memory. The greater the temporal distance, the weaker the connection.

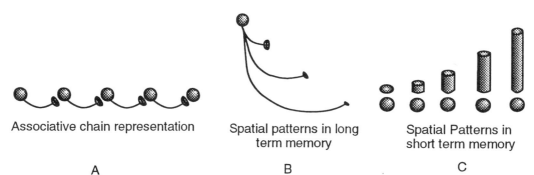

Associative chain representation

Spatial patterns in long term memory

Spatial Patterns in short term memory

A  B  C

**Figure 2.** Three forms of serial order representation used by SMART. (A) The Associative chain form of representation connects temporally associated nodes with long term memory. (B) The spatial patterns in long term memory represent temporal order by the strength of the long term memory. (C) The spatial pattern in short term represents temporal order as spatial patterns in the activity of the nodes.

strength between the node for $A$ and the node for $C$. The result of different connection strengths is a spatial pattern of LTM as illustrated in Figure 2b. This pattern of activity is the result of a decreasing sampling signal at the sampling nodes. These decreasing activities make up a STM spatial pattern that represents recency of activation of the node, see Figure 2c.

Let's look at little more closely at SMART's method of representing temporal order. The associative chain form of representation as illustrated in Figure 1 and Figure 2a provides precise serial order information which allows accurate recall and recognition of sequences. Traditional disadvantages of the associative chain representation are that no direct serial order information is provided.

The spatial patterns in LTM, see Figure 2b, provides second, third, etc. order information for the network as described by both Kenerva (1988) and Wang and Arbib (1990). Second order and above information allows a network to learn a sequences which have a limited number of repeated items and not use multiple nodes like the STORE 3 model does (Bradski, Carpenter, &Grossberg 1992).

The spatial patterns in STM, see Figure 1 and Figure 2c, give direct information on the serial order of a sequence. With this information a separate system can compare items and determine both relative temporal order and temporal distance.

The SMART model is a modification of the adaptive resonance theory (ART) models described by Grossberg (1976a, 1976b) and Carpenter & Grossberg (1987). These models are very good at self-organizing and self-stabilizing recognition codes in response to input patterns. However, these models include no method of associating recognition codes produced in the $F_2$ layer with each other. Sequential memory requires the ability to associate recognition codes.

The design of the SMART architecture had to satisfy a number of special design principles. I will now describe these principles and SMART's solution to the problems they present.

### 3. The SMART Architecture

The SMART network, illustrated in Figure 3, is composed of two layers: the $F_1$ layer which matches input and the $F_2$ layer which categorizes the input. The $F_1$ layer matches the input being sent to the network to the categorization made by the $F_2$ layer. If the network's categorization does not match the input then the categorization of the network is changed.

The $F_2$ layer categorizes the input and is composed of two different types of layers. The first type of layer is the sub-layer which contains categorization nodes. Typically only one node in a sub-layer is active at a time so that only one category is active at once. The sequential memory aspect of SMART is accomplished by interconnecting these nodes with modifiable connections. A connection between a node $A$ and a node $B$ will be increased if node $B$ is activated soon after node $A$ is active. Once a node is connected to another node, it will be able to improve the chances of the other node becoming active. In other words, after $A$ is active it will improve the chances of $B$ becoming active.

The second type of layer in the $F_2$ layer is the region select layer. The region select layer summates activity from

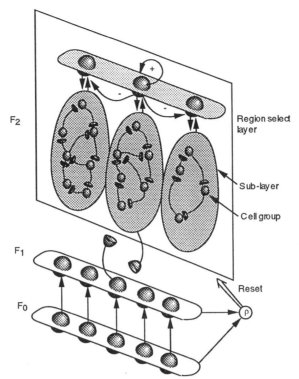

**Figure 3.** The SMART architecture. The $F_2$ layer of ART has been modified by spliting it into sub-layers. Nodes within the sub-layers are both interconnected with long term memory and interconnected in a on-center/off-surround manner so that each node competes for activity. The most active node will become the only active node in the sub-layer. Different sub-layers are selected by the region select layer. The sub-layer sends input to the region select layer nodes which in turn select the most active sub-layer.

the sub-layers and selects either single or multiple sub-layers which have the most activity. One node in the region select layer corresponds to each sub-layer in the $F_2$ layer and when that node is active the corresponding sub-layer becomes fully active while other sub-layers are deactivated. Input the region select layer nodes only comes from sub-layers which the region select layer node can activate.

In order for a connection to form between two nodes, both nodes must have some activity at the same time. However, since typically only one sub-layer and only one node in that sub-layer can be active at the same time, two nodes can not be active at once. This problem is overcome by introducing fast and slow activity for each node. Fast activity corresponds to node activation. Slow activity reflects previous fast activity. The slow activity slowly decreases during several item presentations after the node was active. This slow activity is therefore the basis of SMART's STM spatial pattern form of representation.

Figure 4 illustrates the presentation of the sequence of patterns $A,B,C$ to the SMART network. When $A$ is presented the first cell in the region select layer starts to become active (due to random factors) and the first sub-layer is selected. Once the first sub-layer is active, the first cell in the sub-layer wins the competition and becomes active. The next input, $B$, is presented and the first sub-layer remains active due to continued input from the node representing A. By random chance, the second cell in the first sub-layer is selected. Since the node representing A is still active, a connection between the node representing $A$ to the node representing $B$ is formed. When $C$ is presented the first region select layer cell remains active and the third node is activated. A connection is then formed between the node for $B$ to the node for $C$ and a weaker connection is formed from the node for $A$ to the node for $C$.

Each of the components of SMART described above and the interconnection to ART will now be described in more detail.

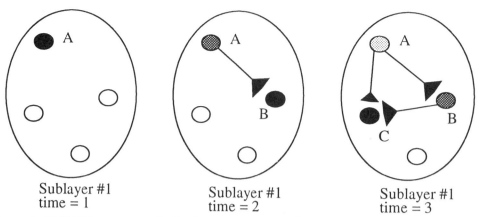

**Figure 4.** Example SMART's response to the input sequence *ABC*. When A is presented a sub-layer representing the sequence and a node representing A are selected. When B is presented a new node in the same sub-layer is selected. Activity in the cell representing A allows a long term memory connection to form between the node representing A and the node representing B. When C is presented a new node is selected and a strong connection forms between the B node and the C node and a weak connection forms between the A node and the C node because the activity at the A node has decayed.

## 3.1. SMART Sub-Layers

The SMART sub-layer is illustrated in Figure 3. The nodes within a sub-layer are connected in a on-center off-surround manner so that each node excites itself and inhibits all other nodes in the sub-layer. The result is that either the node with the most input becomes the only active node in the sub-layer or it becomes much more active than the other nodes. In the typical SMART network the individual sub-layers represent different sequences. Seperating the sequences provides for a simple recognition mechanism (the region select layer) and ensures that shared items in different sequences are represented by different nodes.

In addition to representing individual sequences, the sub-layers in $F_2$ serve several other useful roles. If every node in every sub-layer can have a connection to every other node in every other sub-layer and if the number of items is large then the number of connections can be very large. The number of connections can be reduced by limiting connections to sub-layers which are close or keeping all connections within sub-layers.

Clumping of similar patterns into the same sub-layer is a extra benefit provided by the sub-layers. Similar patterns will be placed into the same sub-layer since the sub-layer is more strongly activated by the input and sends this activity to the region select layer. Even if the pattern does not match any patterns previously classified in the sub-group, a reset will place the new input in the same sub-layer.

## 3.2. Cell Groups

As described above, each node in the sub-layers needs both fast and slow activity. For this reason, the nodes within the sub-layers are made up of groups of cells called *cell-groups* which are composed of groups of cells with different properties (Figure 5). The basic design of the SMART cell group has three nodes. The principle component of the cell group is the *activity cell* which provides fast activity. This cell samples activity of the $F_1$ layer and competes with the other cells in the sub-layer to become the active cell. Since the activity cell is in a competitive network it cannot maintain sustained activity after another node has been selected. The *forward cell* provides the slow activity by remaining on for many input presentations after it is activated and forms the basis for SMART's STM spatial pattern form of representation. The forward cell is activated by the combination of a *forward* signal and the activity of the activity cell. The forward signal is similar to the reset signal and is generated when a new pattern is presented to the network.

The *backward cell* is the remaining cell in the cell group. It receives input from forward cells in other cell-groups and sends this input to the activity cell. The backward cell is separated from the activity cell for several reasons. The most obvious reason is that this cell should stay on for a fixed period of time as opposed to the variable amount of time the activity cell is on (due to the variable amount of time an input pattern could be present). The time has to be fixed

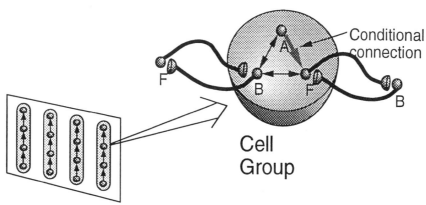

**Figure 5.** The SMART cell group. The cell group is the node which the sub-layers are composed of. It is composed of three different cells. The A cell represents the activity of the cell group and is connected with outer A cells in the same sub-layer to form the competitive network. The F cell maintains activity after a cell group is activated and samples activity of subsequently activated cell groups. The B cell remains on for a fixed period after the cell group is activated and receives input from F cells from other cell groups. An optional backward connection from the B cells to the F cells.

so that other cell groups have a fixed sampling time which results in weights which are not a function of item duration. If weights were a function of item duration then a sequence could become disconnected if an input pattern remained on for a shorter period than the rest of the patterns.

Two additional cells are also used in the cell group. These cells separate functions out from the activity cell and the forward cell. The reason for separating these functions is to simplify both the definition of these cells and the algorithmic simulator.

The *sustained activity* cell is separated out from the forward cell. It provides the source of sustained activity and allows the forward cell to act as a simple outstar. If a spatial pattern of temporal order is being kept then the forward cell would need to be on for almost the entire duration of a sequence. While the forward cell is on it is forming connections to active backward cells and sending output to nodes it is connected to. The result is a lack of contrast in the backward and activity cells of the entire system which can prevent correct learning, recall, and recognition of sequences. The sustained activity cell sends input to the forward cell via a non-linear function which thresholds the activity of the sustained activity cell resulting in a forward cell which remains active for a few item presentations and a sustained activity cell which remains active for many item presentations.

The remaining additional cell is the *sampling cell*. The sampling cell is separated out from the activity cell and performs many of the functions that the traditional ART $F_2$ node does. The sampling cell samples the pattern of activity at $F_1$ and produces an activity level which corresponds to how well the cell's LTM matches the pattern at $F_1$.

### 3.3. Subliminal loop

The associative chain form of representation used by SMART allows the activity of one item in a sequence to subliminally activate other items in the sequence (subliminal activity here refers to low level activity, perhaps 20% of full activity). This subliminal activity is spread by connections between items (Figure 6). As soon as one node in the sequence becomes active it sends input to nodes which it is connected to. These nodes in turn send activity to nodes they are connected to. Activity at nodes farther from the source is less because each node only passes along only part of the activity it receives. Subliminal activity provides several benefits such as: an explanation of Miyashita (1988) results, a measure of match between stored and presented sequences, and a priming of items which occur next in the sequence.

In the SMART architecture subliminal activity is provided by establishing a weak connection between the backward and forward cells of the same cell-group. Thus when a backward cell receives input it can only send a fraction of that input to the forward cell and the forward cell only becomes subliminally active. In addition, overall $F$ cell activity modulates how the $B$ cells respond to input. If Many $F$ cells are active then a $B$ cell requires a very strong input to become subliminally active and if few $F$ cells are active a weak signal can subliminally activate a $B$ cell.

For one directional sequences such as the sequence of letters in a word and the sequence of notes in music the

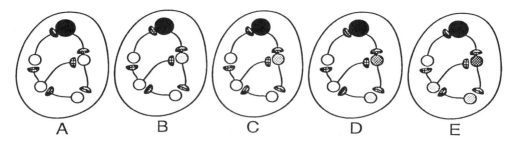

**Figure 6.** An example of the spread of subliminal activity from one node. Over time the activity spreads and is strongest at nodes connected to the active one.

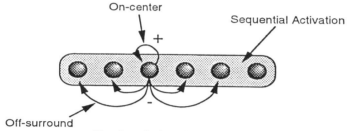

**Figure 7.** The SMART region select layer. The region select layer is a on-center/off-surround competitive network which selects the node which receives the most input.

subliminal activity will only spread in the forward direction. In most cases this is desirable, but in some cases it may not be. For these cases bidirectional connections have become an optional part of SMART. With bidirectional connections the $B$ cells sample the activity of active $F$ cells. Subliminal activity is therefore allowed to flow in both a backward and a forward direction.

### 3.4. Region Select Layer

The region select layer, see Figure 7, is responsible for selecting the active sub-layer within $F_2$. It is a competitive layer with a cell which corresponds to each sub-layer in $F_2$. Activity from the cell groups within a sub-layer is summated at the region select layer cell corresponding to that sub-layer. The cell at the most active sub-layer wins the competition and then sends feedback to the sub-layer(s) which it is associated with. That sub-layer (or sub-layers) then becomes the only active sub-layer(s) in the $F_2$ layer.

The primary purpose of the region select layer (RSL) is to select the sub-layer whose stored sequence best matches the presented sequence. Since sequences are presented over time and different sequences can only be separated over time, the RSL must have the following characteristics:

**1.** Slow competition that produces contrast enhancement during the early part of sequential pattern presentation. The region select layer makes a decision slowly and will leave several sub-layers active for awhile if the sub-layers appear to represent the presented pattern well.

**2.** Sensitivity to changes in input from the sub-layer which is greater at the beginning of the presentation of a sequence. Different sub-layers might represent parts of a sequence well but not provide as good as overall match as another sub-layer. Since the RSL is performing contrast enhancement it could easily have made the wrong choice at first. If it is still very sensitive to change at the beginning of the sequence then it could still change. After a large amount of a sequence has been presented the RSL should not

Note that the presence of distributed activity in the sub-layers is implied here. When more than one RSL node is active at once the corresponding sub-layers can also be active. Within these sub-layers competition is occurring and active nodes are being selected. When a forward signal occurs $S$ cells are activated. However, at any time only one RSL node and only one sub-layer node has full activity and it is only at these locations that learning can occur. The purpose of the distributed activity is to allow sub-layers to compete with each other while a sequence is being presented.

## 3.5. Top Down Activation of Sequences

One desirable property of sequential memory system is the ability to recall a sequence when only a high level representation is used as a cue. Suppose for example, that you want to recall the sequence of notes that make up a song when you are given only the title of the song. This is equivalent to activating a region select layer in SMART and recalling the sequence stored in the associated sub-layer. The SMART network presented so far does not have a mechanism to reliably recall the sequence from the first item to the last. The SMART system could potentially start anywhere in the sequence.

Several solutions to this problem exist. Subliminal loop activity could be exploited to activate the first item of the sequence or a top down modifiable connection from the region select layer could be used. The solution selected for SMART uses modifiable connections from the region select layer. The connection are from a cell which is most active at the beginning of the sequence. When the first item is presented to the network the cell is most active and the connection strength to the first item is large. As other items are presented the activity of the cell decays and connection strengths are less. When a sequence is recalled the cell is highly active at first and sends a strong signal to the first item of the sequence. As the sequence is recalled the cells strength decreases and has less influence.

## 3.6. Interconnection to ART

Figure 3 illustrates how the SMART architecture is interconnected to the ART architecture. All elements of ART are unmodified except for the $F_2$ layer. In the $F_2$ layer the sampling cell acts very much like the traditional $F_2$ layer node of ART. The difference is that the competition is taking place in both the activity cells and the region select layer. The activity cells are biased by intra-layer connections in $F_2$ and the region select layer is biased towards sub-layers whose nodes match the input well. The amount of bias can be controlled by using faster than linear inputs to activity cells.

Since the primary difference between ART and SMART is the location where competition occurs, different types of ART architectures can be used. These ART architectures can be used with SMART by making the ART F2 nodes into SMART M nodes and allowing the competition to occur in the SMART A nodes instead of the M nodes. With a small number of modifications, ART 1, ART 2, and Fuzzy ART architectures can be used with SMART.

## 3.7. Reset of $F_2$ nodes and $F_2$ regions

A primary component of all ART models is the ability to deactivate an active node when a mismatch occurs. For the ART 3 system (Carpenter & Grossberg, 1990), depletable transmitters were used to reduce activities at nodes. The SMART model also uses depletable transmitters to deactivate nodes.

The activity cells receive excitatory input from three sources: the backward cell, the $F_1$ layer, and the region select layer nodes. In order to prevent an activity cell from becoming active the activity cell must not receive inputs from any of the three sources. The inputs from the forward cell, $F_1$, and the region select layer can be gated by a depletable chemical transmitter. When a node becomes active the transmitter is depleted and the node will have a small chance of winning the competition.

If a sub-layer has recently miscategorized a sequence then it should be inhibited so that it won't incorrectly classify the sequence again. If input to the RSL cells is gated by depletable transmitters then the RSL cells can be inhibited and misclassification can be avoided.

## 3.8. Sub-layer Reset

If a sub-layer is incorrectly categorizing a sequential pattern then the network should force a new categorization. The SMART architecture has a two stage method of enforcing correct categorization. The first method is the traditional ART reset mechanism. If a particular item in a sequence does not match any item in a stored sequence then the ART reset mechanism via the search process will force a different sub-layer to be chosen (new nodes in a sub-layer become more difficult to allocate as the sub-layer learns the sequence over many presentations). For example, after a sub-layer has been presented with a sequence many times one or two new nodes may be temporarily allocated but any more presentations of items not stored in the sub-layer will force a new sub-layer to be chosen.

However, if a sequential pattern being presented and a stored sequence share common elements the traditional

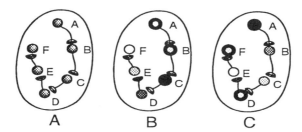

**Figure 8.** An example of how to detect sequence mismatches with subliminal loop activity. (A) The sub-layer has learned the sequence *ABCDEF*. (B) When the sub-sequence ABC is presented, the subliminal activity at C is very large while subliminal elsewhere is smaller. (C) The sequence DFA is presented and subliminal activity is small both overall and at C.

ART reset mechanism will not work as well. For example consider the stored sequence *ABCDEF* and the presented sequence *DFACEB*. Both sequences have the same items but the items are in a different order. The second stage of the SMART reset mechanisms is designed to detect this type of mismatch.

Figure 8a illustrates a sub-layer which has learned the sequence *ABCDEF*. The connection strengths are quite large because the sequence has been presented many times. In Figure 8b the sequence ABCDEF is presented to the network. Note how the subliminal activity spreads and builds as the sequence is presented. Subliminal activity is always stronger at the nodes close to the current one. Now look at Figure 8c where the sequence DFACEB is presented. Subliminal activity spreads somewhat but never builds very much because neighboring nodes are not activated together. In particular, note the subliminal activity at each node when the node is activated. The subliminal activity at a newly activated node is less in comparison to the subliminal activity elsewhere. In contrast, the subliminal activity is much greater at newly activated nodes when the correct sequence is presented (Figure 8b). This difference in subliminal activity forms the basis of the SMART sub-layer reset mechanism.

To perform a sub-layer reset the subliminal activity at a newly activated node is divided by the average subliminal activity of cell groups with subliminal activity. The resulting value is compared to a vigilance parameter and the reset occurs if the value is less than the vigilance parameter. The reset is applied to the active sub-layer and the associated RSL node. The MTM in the effected nodes is reduced and a new sub-layer will be selected if enough MTM is lost. Several resets may be necessary to force the selection of a new sub-layer.

## 3.9. Stability of Coding and the Forward Signal

The SMART network is designed to learn continuous sequences of input. In such a sequence the pattern can be continuously varying and it is up the network to differentiate one part of the sequence from another. In such a sequence two network features are needed to maintain stability of coding: reset for mismatch of categorization and input, and continuous competition among categorization nodes for activity. The reset mechanism assures that the input pattern matches the pattern stored by the node but it does not assure that the node provides the best match. Continuous competition, on the other hand does assure that the node provides the best match since at any time all nodes in $F_2$ are competing with each other. The requirement for continuous competition in the $F_2$ layer presents two problems to SMART; how is a forward signal generated when the categorization changes without a reset and how is stability of coding maintained when competition is based on both bottom-up input and intra-layer input.

Basing the $F_2$ competition on both intra-layer and bottom-up inputs could be a potential problem under the following situation: Suppose a constantly changing input is being presented, the input is changing in one direction, learning is very fast, the reset level is low. Under these circumstances a single node might encode the entire sequence during the first presentation. During the second presentation a new node is selected and also encodes the entire sequence. When the end of the sequence is reached the original node is not selected because the second node is still receiving intra-layer input from the first node and now encodes the pattern almost as well as the first node due to the learning speed. As the sequence is presented new nodes are generated and each node categorizes only the final pattern of the sequence. An endless number of nodes will be created and the nodes will never learn the sequence.

Fortunately a solution exist for the above dilemma. The solution uses the non-linear connections to the activity cell and a buffering of the continuous input. The non-linear connections are faster than linear connections between both the backward cell and the sampling cell to the activity cell. The input from a perfect match at the sampling cell is therefore much greater than a close match. Inputs to the activity cell are balanced so that a perfect match at the sampling cell will always cause the cell group to win.

The SMART architecture uses a buffering system to segment continuous inputs into sequences of discrete inputs. Input which is sent to the SMART architecture comes from a buffer which is refreshed each time the input to the buffer and the buffer contents vary by too much (an ART like mechanism determines when this has occurred).

The following summarizes the components of SMART which provide stability:

**1.** ART reset mechanism. This mechanism ensures that the input pattern and learned pattern adequately match

**2.** Continuous competition. This mechanism ensures that the node categorizing the input provides the best match.

**3.** Faster than linear input to the activity cell. This mechanism ensures that a perfect match overrides sequential memory influences.

**4.** Buffering of input. This mechanism ensures that the input patters vary by a sufficient amount so that the above mechanisms will work. If this mechanism was not provided then a single node could remain on for the entire duration of a sequence.

**5.** Sub-layer reset mechanism. This mechanism ensures that input sequences match stored sequences.

## 4. Discussion

The SMART architecture has been introduced. The representation used by SMART is a combination of both the spatial pattern theories and the associative chain theories of temporal order representation. The resulting architecture consist of sets of sub-layers which represent individual sequences and a region select layer which selects between the different sub-layers. Recognition of sequential patterns is aided by the presence of subliminal activity within sub-layers. When subliminal activity is high, the sub-layer matches the current sequence and when it is low, the sub-layer does not match the sequence. With the addition of reset mechanisms, more stable learning of both single inputs and entire sequences is provided.

## 5. References

Bradski, G, Carpenter, G. and Grossberg, S. (1992). *Store working memory networks for storage and recall of arbitrary temporal sequences.* (Tech. Rep.) CNS/CAS-TR-92-028. Boston, MA:Boston University.

Carpenter, G. and Grossberg, S.. (1987). A Massively Parallel Architecture for a Self-organizing Neural Pattern Recognition Machine. *Computer Vision, Graphics, and Image Processing, 37.* 54-115.

Carpenter, G. and Grossberg, S. (1991). ART 3: Hierarchical search using chemical transmitters in self-organizing pattern recognition architectures. *Neural Networks, 3.* 129-152.

Grossberg., S. (1976a). Adaptive Pattern Recognition and Universal Recoding, I: Parallel Development and Coding of Neural Feature Detectors. *Biological Cybernetics, 23.* 121-134.

Grossberg, S. (1976b). Adaptive Pattern Recognition and Universal Recoding, II: Feedback, expectation, olfaction, and illusions . *Biological Cybernetics, 23.* 187-202.

Kanerva, P. (1988). *Sparse Distributed Memory.* Cambridge, MA, The MIT Press.

Miyashita, Y. (October 1988). Neuronal correlate of visual associate long-term memory in the primate temporal cortex. *Nature, 335* (27), 817-820.

Vogh, J. (1993). Sequential memory with ART: A self-organizing network capable of learning sequences of patterns. World Congress on Neural Networks, Portland, OR.

Wang, D., & Arbib, M. A. (1990). Complex temporal sequence learning based on short-term memory. *Proceedings of the IEEE, 78* (9), 1536-1543.

# Sequence Prediction and Cognitive Mapping by a Biologically Plausible Neural Network

Colin Prepscius and William B Levy
Department of Neurological Surgery
University of Virginia Health Sciences Center
Charlottesville, VA 22908

*Cognitive mapping involves encoding a representation of an environment in memory. A cognitive map can be formed from collections of sequences of representations of environmental features that change in time. Sequence prediction is important to this theory because it enables efficient searching of the map. We propose a neural network inspired by the hippocampus that, by virtue of a recurrent hidden layer, predicts sequences at a faster rate than they are originally presented.*

## I. Introduction

### Cognitive Mapping

The role of the hippocampus in cognitive mapping has been studied extensively (see, for example, O'Keefe and Nadel, 1978). These studies propose that the hippocampus recodes and retains information about an organism's environment in such a way that this information can be used to navigate the real world (the rat in the maze being the classic example). According to Tolman (1932), a cognitive map enables an organism with three properties: 1) The ability to navigate between any two points, 2) The ability to find a detour when the most efficient path is blocked, and 3) The ability to find short cuts if better routes are suddenly opened.

Both Saypoff, Muller and Kubie (1992) and Schmajuk and Thieme (1992) treat cognitive mapping essentially in terms of graph theory; both use discrete (and orthogonal) representations of "places" and "views", in which the firing of each neuron represents a different single place or graph vertex. Adjacencies between places, or *edges* between graph *vertices* (in Schmajuk's case), or distances between them (in Saypoff's case) are represented by synaptic connections between neurons. During maze navigation with these models, all possible paths from the starting point to the goal point are mentally explored, until the shortest path is found. We propose that this is an essentially un-neural-like method of solving the problem, for the following reason : although this method may work well for small graphs (or small mazes), because the number of edges increases with the square of the number of vertices in a graph, in the real world exploring all possible paths would be difficult. Another limit on this method is that searching is carried out no faster than the rate of learning; because point B in the maze is encountered directly after point A during exploration, during mental navigation (or *prediction*), point B is not arrived at any faster from point A. Faster searches of the cognitive map are clearly desirable from the point of view of an animal's survival.

### Sequence Prediction

The role of sequence prediction in cognitive mapping is now clear. A succession of points or places an animal visits during exploration of its environment is a *sequence* which the animal needs to remember and recall later during mental navigation of the environment. Many sequences make up a cognitive map - this could be considered a generalization of Tolman's learning of expectancies (stimulus-response-stimulus sets).

The ability of neural networks to remember and recall sequences of varying degrees of difficulty has been studied extensively (see, for example, Mozer 1993). Biologically plausible networks of the type studied here (see below) also effectively recall a wide variety of sequences (Minai, Barrows and Levy, 1993, Minai and Levy 1993a). Several aspects of sequence learning have not been previously explored, to our knowledge : First, a truly fast-time prediction mechanism would not just recall a sequence in the order in which it is presented, but would predict the end of a sequence (or better yet, any arbitrary point in the sequence) by skipping over or compressing intervening points. Second, we propose that sequences in the real world change slowly in comparison to an animal's physical movement, or exploration of its environment. Thus, an animal would not encounter place A and then immediately place B, but would instead see a more or less continuous progression between the two. Third, an even more powerful ability for a neural network, based on these latter two abilities, is *temporal feature extraction*, which would enable an animal's cognitive map to mentally navigate between the most prominent patterns in a sequence, providing both a faster-than-real-time method of prediction, and a method of encoding these features into a cognitive map.

A neural network capable of fast-time prediction on a slowly-changing sequence is described below.

## II. Description of Neural Network

The network described here is illustrated in Figure 1, and is inspired by the architecture of the hippocampus (Levy 1989). The input layer, roughly corresponding to the entorhinal cortex, projects to two different layers, corresponding to the CA3 and CA1 layers of the hippocampus. The CA3 layer projects both back onto itself and onto the CA1 layer. The CA1 layer gives the final output.

The network studied is small; the CA3 region contains 512 neurons, and the CA1 region 100 (more CA1 neurons could be used but are not necessary for the inputs used here). By virtue of the recurrent connections between CA3 neurons, CA3 can recode each input pattern not only for each independent time-step but also in the context of its immediate history of neuron firings. This aspect of contextual recoding of an input signal has been studied by Minai, Levy, and Barrows, (1993) who found it be a key factor in the remembrance of ambiguous sequences. This recoding property will also be important in the studies presented here.

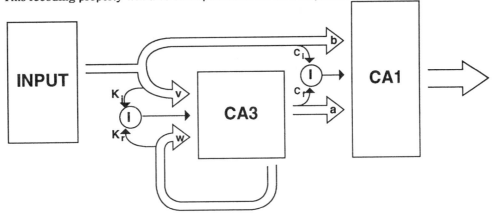

*Figure 1* - *Block diagram of the neural network inspired by the CA1 & CA3 regions of the hippocampus. Arrows represent projections between layers (connections). The small circles labelled I represent single inhibitory neurons.*

Another important and biologically valid feature of the network is sparse, random connectivity. The recurrent CA3 projection (arrow w of Figure 1) is only 5% connected; neurons will therefore have connections to 25 other neurons in the CA3 layer. Connectivity from CA3 to CA1 (arrow a of Figure 1) is also 5%. Inputs project from the input layer to the CA3 (arrow v of fig.1) with a 1-2 connectivity, so if a total of 30 neurons are used in the input data, only 60 neurons in the CA3 are directly activated. Each neuron in the CA1 is connected to one input (arrow b of Figure 1). Each input connection is strong enough to guarantee that its postsynaptic neurons will fire (input designated by x in equations 1 and 2). The input is modulated via shunting inhibition through a single interneuron for each layer. The excitation, $y_j$, of a CA3 neuron, and $p_k$ from a CA1 neuron, is thresholded at a value ß=0.9. Activity for the CA3 and CA1 neurons is described by (1, 2), where $z_i(t)$ is the binary output of neuron i in the CA3 layer at time t, and $q_k(t)$ is the output from a CA1 neuron, and h(x) denotes the Heaviside function.

**CA3 activation function** $: y_i(t) = \dfrac{v x_{\lceil \frac{i}{2}\rceil}(t) + \sum_j w_{ij} z_j(t-1)}{\sum_j w_{ij} z_j(t-1) + K_r \sum_j z_j(t-1) + K_f \sum_j x_j(t)}$ $\qquad(1)$

$$z_i(t) = h\left(y_i(t) - \beta\right) \qquad\qquad 0 < \beta < 1$$

**CA1 activation function** $: p_k(t) = \dfrac{b x_k(t) + \sum_j a_{kj} z_j(t-1)}{\sum_j a_{kj} z_j(t-1) + C_k \sum_j z_j(t-1) + C_f \sum_j x_j(t)}$ $\qquad(2)$

$$q_k(t) = h\left(p_k(t) - \beta\right) \qquad\qquad 0 < \beta < 1$$

## III. Sequence Prediction

**How sequence prediction is accomplished**

Sequence compression by the CA3 layer is illustrated below. A sequence consisting of three temporally overlapping patterns (A, B, C) is presented to the network repeatedly. After the network modifies its weights according to some associative scheme, the original sequence occurs during recall. That is, presentation of pattern A to the network would result in the recall of pattern B at a later time which would, in turn, recall pattern C at an even later time. However, the network does not necessarily end up conserving the original time course of the sequence. Any associative weight modification between A and B will be used during the next presentation of the sequence at the start of pattern A. Thus, pattern A will immediately recall a fraction of B. During training, this fraction grows until A effectively predicts the onset of B. Patterns B and C will exhibit the same behavior except that, eventually, pattern C will be predicted while pattern A is still occuring. That is, pattern A will immediately predict pattern C.

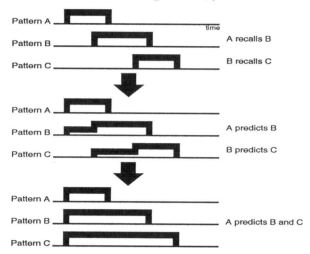

*Figure 2 - Graphical representation of sequence compression.*

Because we are running our networks discretely in time, a relevant question might be: how do these patterns persist for more than one time step? Because the CA3 layer is recurrently connected to itself, any pattern presented at time step 1 will persist with a decreasing representational strength and a different code at time step 2. This is, in fact, the contextual recoding explained above.

In these simulations, another factor assisting sequence compression is slowly-changing sequences - sequences of patterns that overlap spatially and thus give smooth transitions between patterns. Spatial overlap is, however, equivalent to temporal overlap. Other processing element characteristics that would support this overlapping effect include capacitance and delay lines, but they were not included in our model. Another relevant question might be: how can intervening patterns (such as pattern B above) be skipped entirely to avoid too much activity in the network? This is achieved through attractor properties of the network and through inhibition. Because pattern C ends up being presented to the network the most, it becomes a self-exciting "fixed point" - it is the end of the sequence - and consequently has the strength to inhibit the other patterns.

**Results**

One illustrative sequence the network was trained on is 40 patterns in length. Each pattern contains eight on-bits, represented by the firing of 8 input neurons. The Hamming distances between successive patterns is 2 - any pattern will be missing 1 bit from the previous pattern and will also contain 1 additional on-bit. The network is presented with the entire sequence for 100 trials and allowed to modify its weights according to the postsynaptic learning rule (equ. 3) (Levy, Colbert and Desmond, 1990). The value $\mu$, the learning rate, is generally kept small in the model here, but Minai and Levy (1993a) have studied higher learning rates.

**Post-Synaptic Learning Rule :** $\quad w_{ij}(t) = w_{ij}(t-1) + \mu z_i(t)[z_j(t-1) - w_{ij}(t-1)]$ (3)

Before each trial, the network is reset randomly. During recall, the network is given the first pattern in the sequence as a prompt and allowed to relax.

When the network is given just the first pattern in the sequence at time step 1, the network exhibits one of two modes of behavior. In the first mode, the network exhibits *sequential recall*: it presents the patterns in the sequence in order at roughly the same rate as the patterns were presented (albeit with added noise), before settling at the last pattern (apparently a fixed point). The other mode is *predictive recall*, wherein the network converges to the last pattern at a significantly faster rate than when the sequence was presented. In all networks, predictive recall appears at values of inhibition (modulated through the interneurons) lower than the inhibition the network was trained at, and sequential recall appears at generally higher values of inhibition.

The speed of recall can be viewed graphically using the Hamming measure for distance between vectors. By plotting the distance from the current pattern to the last pattern as a function of time, the two different modes of recall can be distinctively pictured. Data for a typical network is given below (figure 3), for both the CA3 and CA1 layers, at different inhibition levels.

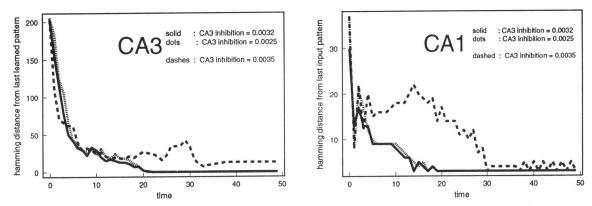

*Figure 3 - Recall of a length 40 sequence by a network at different CA3 inhibition levels in the CA3 (left) and CA1 (right) layers. The dashed lines illustrate sequential recall, the other two lines of each graph show predictive recall. Plotted in each graph is the Hamming distance of the representation at time t from the last pattern in the sequence.*

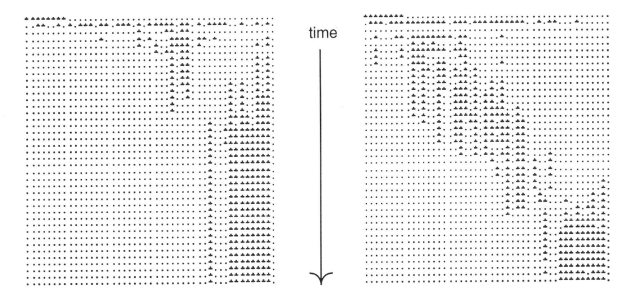

*Figure 4 - Firing patterns of CA1 (presented as Hamming distances in Fig 3, right) illustrate predictive (left figure) and sequential (right figure) recall. Each * represents the firing of a neuron. Each row represents the entire state of the CA1 at a particular point in time. Rows further down represent states at later times. Thus, the evolution of the CA1 layer through time can be traced directly.*

Predictive and sequential recall can also be viewed directly by looking at the actual firings of the neurons over time (Figure 4). In fact, by doing so, several additional features of the representations pictured during recall become apparent: After the initial prompting input to the network, consisting of the first pattern in the sequence, at the next time step (the second timestep, that is) nearly all of the neurons involved in all subsequent patterns turn on, and then turn off at the third time step. This rapid change in activity levels is due to the inhibition not stabilizing the network quickly enough, and indicates, in one sense, that compression of the sequence has in fact progressed as far as possible- the first pattern does recall the last pattern (and all intervening patterns). The potential usefulness of this property is discussed in part IV. Following this initial burst, the network then recalls the sequence in predictive or sequential fashion as outlined above.

## IV. Discussion

### Inhibitory Control

Inhibition plays a vital role in controlling the speed of recall. Minai and Levy (1993b) found that for a similar network (sparsely connected, recurrent) which underwent no synaptic modification, inhibition was the controlling factor in setting the activity level of the network as it relaxed from a random initial starting point (see also Amari, 1972). In brief, low inhibition levels, when not allowing the network to completely turn on (a non-interesting fixed point), led to high-activity, high-frequency activity patterns. High levels of inhibition led to low-activity, low-frequency activity patterns. Although the authors of this paper pointed out that these analyses were not applicable generally to networks which undergo synaptic modification, and no similar study has been made of such networks, the same ideas seem applicable here.

On a macroscopic scale, inhibition in the CA3 controls the rate at which recurrent feedback decays. At low inhibition levels, at any given time-step, a larger number of context neurons is likely to turn on. This increases the chance that a portion of the last context pattern will be present. Since the last pattern is a fixed point of the system and reinforces itself through self-excitation, even a small portion of this pattern will quickly recall the rest of the pattern, inhibit the other previous intervening patterns, and lead to predictive recall. Higher inhibition levels reduce the chance of the last pattern appearing at any given time, and lead to sequential recall through learned patterns, rather than fast convergence.

### Sequence Prediction and Cognitive Mapping

Although these studies are preliminary, sequence prediction promises to be an important factor in cognitive mapping. An animal is hypothesized to explore its environment, coding afferent information in the context of its history. This information, in the form of temporal sequences, is later recalled during mental navigation of the assembled cognitive map. Based on various prompts, including the actual position of the animal and its desired position (driven perhaps by other hypothesized mechanisms, such as hunger and thirst), an appropriate sequence is recalled. The animal would need to vary the strength of inhibition (perhaps using one of the modulatory systems projecting to the hippocampus and perhaps reflected in theta rhythm) to affect the speed of recall. The networks studied here have the property that at the time step directly after the initial prompt, they recall a mixture of subsequent patterns in the sequence. This brief burst facilitates predictive recall due to the mechanism described above, but it is unclear whether there must be such a step. The usefulness of this single time-step can be readily imagined, however.

## V. Conclusion

The network studied here, while conserving biological plausibility, introduces an effective method for dealing with the memory and recall of time-varying sequences. Predictive recall is a property, first introduced by Levy (1989), that provides a useful mechanism for navigating cognitive maps. The complete cognitive mapping properties as defined by Tolman have not been realized so far, but will be explored in future work.

The theoretical framework for making additional steps in this direction, including learning of sequences that change at varying rates, learning multiple sequences, extraction and convergence to temporal features, and fast learning (Minai and Levy, 1993a), has been begun.

## Acknowledgements

This research was supported by the following grants: NIMH MH00622; NIMH MH48161; NSF MSS-9216372; and EPRI RP8030-08. It was also supported by the Department of Neurosurgery, University of Virginia, Dr. John A. Jane, Chairman.

## References

Amari S. 1972. "Characteristics of Random Nets of Analog Neuron-Like Elements," *IEEE Transactions on Systems, Man, and Cybernetics*, VOL.SMC-2, No.5, November.

Levy W. 1989. "A Computational Approach to Hippocampal Function," in Computational Models of Learning in Simple Neural Systems (R.D.Hawkins & G.H.Bower, eds.) [The Psychology of Learning and Motivation, vol. 23] San Diego: Academic Press, 243-305.

Levy W, Colbert C, Desmond N. 1990. "Elemental Adaptive Processes of Neurons and Synapses: A Statistical/Computational Perspective," in: Neuroscience and Connectionist Theory, M. Gluck & D. Rumelhart (eds.), Hilldale, NJ, Lawrence Erlbaum Associates, 187-230.

Minai A, Barrows G, Levy W. 1993. "Disambiguation of Pattern Sequences with Recurrent Networks," (in submission to *World Congress on Neural Networks*).

Minai A, Levy W. 1993a. "Sequence Learning in a Single Trial," *Proceedings of the World Congress on Neural Networks*, Vol II.

Minai A, Levy W. 1993b. "The Dynamics of Sparse Random Networks," *Biological Cybernetics*, in press.

Mozer M. 1993. "Neural Net Architectures for Temporal Sequence Processing," (to appear in : A. Weigend & N. Gershenfeld (Eds.), Predicting the Future and Understanding the Past. Redwood City, CA: Addison Wesley Publishing).

O'Keefe J, Nadel L. 1978. The Hippocampus as a Cognitive Map. Clarendon Press, Oxford.

Saypoff R, Muller R.U, Kubie J.L. 1992. "How Place Cells Connected by Hebbian Synapses can Solve Spatial Problems," *Soc. Neurosci. Abstr*. 2. 1211.

Schmajuk N, Thieme A. 1992. "Purposive Behavior and Cognitive Mapping: A Neural Network Model," *Biological Cybernetics*, 67, 165-174.

Tolman EC. 1932. Purposive Behavior of Animals and Men. Irvington, New York.

# An Unsupervised Network for Speech Recognition

C.K. Lee, C.H. Chung

Department of Electronic Engineering, Hong Kong Polytechnic,

Hung Hom, Hong Kong.

Email:encklee@hkpcc.hkp.hk

*Abstract*

In this paper, we shall describe the development of a kind of neural networks for speech recognition. This network uses an unsupervised learning algorithm, which is namely called learning by experience (LBE). It is based on the past learnt experience to recognize or classify patterns. Here, we have applied it for recognizing pre-recorded speech of single words. Various experimental results have demonstrated its feasibility in this aspect.

## 1. Introduction

A commonly used algorithm for speech recognition is template matching[5]. In template matching, the recognition process compares a test pattern with a set of standard templates to give the similarity measure. Usually, a set of parameters for each speech is extracted as the template and then a distance measure is used to classify or recognize. Here, we use the linear prediction codes as the feature extracted from the recorded speech. The LPC prediction coefficients, are then used to measure the similarity between a test pattern and a reference pattern based on *log area ratios*[4, 5]. Given a reference set of prediction coefficients $a'_k$ and another set of parameters $a_k$, which corresponds to the matching pattern with an autocorrelation value, $R_i$, the distance measure between these two sets of parameters is defined as

$$d = \log \frac{\sum_{i=-p}^{p} b'_i R_i}{\sum_{i=-p}^{p} b_i R_i} \tag{1}$$

where $b'_i$ and $b_i$ are obtained from $a'_k$ and $a_k$ by using the autocorrelation equation

$$b_i = \sum_{k=0}^{p-i} a_k a_{k+i}, \qquad a_0 = 1, \ 0 \le i \le p \tag{2}$$

When the distance, $d$, between the two patterns is smaller than a preset value, the two patterns can be classified to the same class. However, in this paper, we propose the use of an unsupervised neural network, the LBE network[6] for speech recognition. In our method, we use the *reflection coefficients* of the LPC as the input patterns to the LBE network. This network will then classify those patterns with difference which is smaller than a preset *mean square error* into the same class. An advantage of this network is that it uses much simpler arithmetics than those of the *log area ratio* test. Therefore, it will be much easier to be implemented.

This paper is divided into 5 sections. In Section 2, we first describe the structure of the LBE network and its learning algorithm. Then the linear prediction coding method for feature extraction is described in Section 3. In Section 4, we illustrate a way to map the prediction error of the LPC to the *mean square error* of the LBE network. Finally, some experimental results will be presented.

## 2. Learning By Experience (LBE) Network

### 2.1 Structure of the LBE network

Unlike other unsupervised learning neural networks, the main idea of LBE network is not how to update the weigths of the winner, but instead, is how to use *memory* to let output neurons know whether the applied input pattern belonging to the stored patterns or not. In fact, it employs the competitive learning as the updating rule for the winner.

First, a memory is added to each output neuron to store the strength, $SS_i$. This strength is used to compare the current input pattern with the stored pattern. As analog signals are applied to the network, the strength function is represented by the mean square error between the input pattern and the weight. Therefore, the lower the strength, the closer is the 2 compared patterns. The structure of the LBE network is shown in Fig. 1.

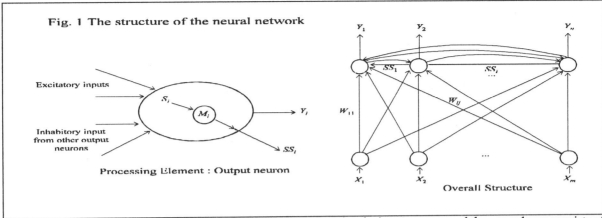

It is a two-layer, feed forward type network. The lower layer contains the input neurons and the upper layer consists of the output neurons. The connections among the lower layer and the upper layer store the weights, $W_{ij}$, which in turn store the learnt patterns. The connections within the upper layer indicate the output neurons, each receiving $SS_i$ as the inhibitory input, from all the other output neurons. Also, each output neuron has a memory to store its experience. Once the output neuron has become the winner, the current strength $SS_i$ will be stored into its memory. This memory is used to determine whether any applied pattern is associated to this output neuron.

When an input pattern is applied to the network, $X_i$ will be equal to $P_i$, the input pattern. Then $S_i$ will be built up through the network connections. When $S_i$ is obtained, it will be compared with the strength stored in its internal memory $M_i$ to work out $SS_i$. Finally the output neuron which has the minimum strength will become the winner, and its internal memory and the weights will be updated only.

*2.2 The Learning Algorithm:*

Step 1 - the initialization phase

All weights, $W_{ij}$, are set to 0. All memory locations, $M_i$, are set to $N + 1$, where $N$ is the number of input neurons. The *learning rate* can be set to any value from 0 to 1. The *mean square error* can be set to any value from 0 to 1. This is the maximum allowable error between two input patterns to be classified to the same class.

Step 2 - the weight updating phase

Apply the pattern to the input neuron $X_i$ of the network, then $S_i$ is calculated as

$$S_i = \sum_{j=0}^{M} \frac{(W_{ij} - X_i)^2}{N} \tag{3}$$

The final strength $SS_i$, for competition within the upper layer is obtained as

$$SS_i = \begin{cases} S_i & \text{if } S_i \le M_i + mean\ square\ error \\ \infty & otherwise \end{cases} \tag{4}$$

The winner is searched among all the output neurons, and it is the one which has the minimum strength. Two cases will occur. They are, (1) *normal case* -- the winner with $SS_i$ not equal to $\infty$. This means the input pattern is recognized; ( 2) *memory full case* -- the winner with $SS_i$ equal to $\infty$. This means that there is no pattern stored in this network matched with this pattern and the network has no more unused output neuron to store this new pattern, which is a memory catastrophe.

For the normal case, the internal memory and the weights of the winner are updated as:

If $M_i = N + 1$ then

$$W_{ij} = X_i,$$ (5)

else

$$W_{ij} = W_{ij} + L \times (X_i - W_{ij})$$ (6)

where $j$ = index of the winner

$L$ = learning rate

Next, we compute the $S_j$ again and use these new weights, $W_{ij}$, to update the memory $M_j$ as

$$M_j = S_j$$ (7)

and the output is given as

$$Y_j = \begin{cases} 1 & \text{if } j = \text{index of winner} \\ 0 & \text{otherwise} \end{cases}$$ (8)

## 3. Linear Predictive Coding

The linear predictive coding (LPC) is based on the assumption that a speech sample can be approximated as a linear combination of previous speech samples[2]. It models the speech as a linear all pole filter having the system function

$$H(z) = \frac{G}{1 + \sum_{k=1}^{p} a_p(k)z^{-k}}$$ (9)

where $p$ is the number of poles, $G$ is the filter gain, and $a_p(k)$ are the parameters that determine the poles. On a short time basis, voiced speech is periodic with a fundamental frequency $F_o$, or a pitch period $1/F_o$, which depends on the speaker. Thus voiced speech can be generated by exciting the all pole filter model by a periodic impulse train with a period equal to the desired pitch period. For unvoiced speech, sound is generated by exciting the all pole filter model by the output of a random noise generator. This model is shown in Fig. 2

Fig. 2 LPC generated voice

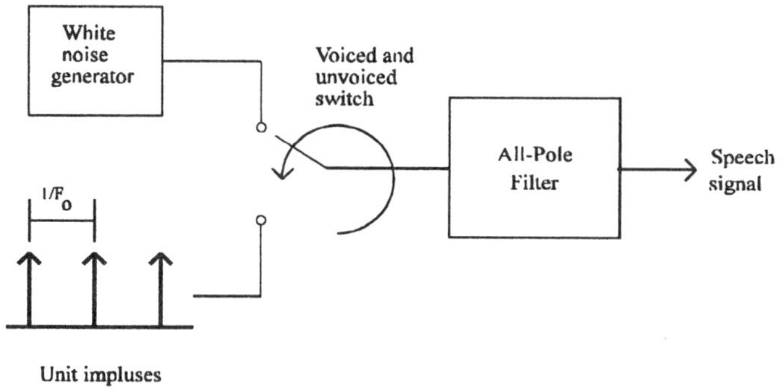

The parameters of the all pole filter can be determined from the speech samples by means of linear prediction. The output of the filter is

$$s_1(n) = -\sum_{k=1}^{p} a_p(k)s(n - k)$$ (10)

and the corresponding error between the observed samples $s(n)$ and the estimate $s_1(n)$ is the sum of squared errors given as

$$E = \sum_{n=0}^{N} e^2(n) = \sum_{n=0}^{N} [s(n) + \sum_{k=1}^{p} a_p(k)s(n-k)]^2 \qquad (11)$$

By minimizing $E$, we can determine the pole parameters $a_p(k)$ of the model. The result of differentiating $E$ with respect to each of the parameters and equating it to zero, is a set of $p$ linear equations

$$\sum_{k=1}^{p} a_p(k)r_{ss}(m-k) = -r_{ss}(m), \qquad\qquad m = 1, 2, 3, ..., p \qquad (12)$$

where $r_{ss}(m)$ is the autocorrelation of the sequence $s(n)$ defined as

$$r_{ss}(m) = \sum_{n=0}^{N} s(n)s(n+m) \qquad (13)$$

These equations can be solved recursively by using the Levinson-Durbin algorithm. The recursive equations are

$$a_m = K_m = -\frac{r_{ss}(m) + \sum_{k=1}^{m-1} a_{m-1}(k)r_{ss}(m-k)}{E_{m-1}}, \qquad m = 1, 2, ..., p \qquad (14)$$

$$a_m(k) = a_{m-1}(k) + K_m a_{m-1}(m-k), \qquad k = 1, 2, ..., m-1 \qquad (15)$$

$$E_m = E_{m-1}(1 - K_m^2) \qquad (16)$$

$$E_0 = r_{ss}(0) \qquad (17)$$

where $K_m$ are the reflection coefficients in the equivalent lattice filter. The prediction coefficients in the all pole model are $a_p(k)$ and the residual prediction squared error is $E_p$. The reflection coefficients are applied to the LBE network as the input pattern. This set of reflection coefficients is chosen because it has a smaller dynamic range, $|K| \leq 1$.

To find $K_i$, we first digitize the voiced speech using 8 bit PCM codes at 11KHz sampling rate. Then the voiced speech is subdivided into eleven 20 millisecond windows which each has 220 sample data. The LPC coefficients are obtained by the Levinson-Durbin recursion equations[3]

$$k'_i = \frac{r_s(i) - \sum_{j=1}^{i-1} a_j r_s(i-j)}{E} \qquad (18)$$

$$a'_i = k'_i \qquad (19)$$

$$a'_j = a_j - k'_i a_{i-j}, \qquad\qquad j = 1, 2, ... i-1 \qquad (20)$$

$$E' = (1 - (k'_i)^2)E \qquad (21)$$

where $k_i$ are the negative values of the reflection coefficients of the all-pole filter,

$a_i$s are the prediction coefficients,

$r_s(i)$ is the autocorrelation value of the input signal,

$E$ is the average squared prediction error between the actual input and predicted input.

While the autocorrelation function of the input signal $s(n)$ is found by

$$r_s(k) = \sum_{m=0}^{N-1-k} s(m)s(m+k) \qquad (22)$$

where $N$ is the number of input signals in the window.

$E$ is initialized to $r_s(0)$ first. Then Equ. 18 - 21 are solved recursively for $i = 1$ to $P$, where $P$ is the number of coefficients. In each iteration, Equ. 18 & 19 yield another $k$-value and $a$-value. In Equ. 20, all previously calculated $a$-values are recalculated using the new $k$-value. Finally, Equ. 21 gives a new value for $E$. Then the $k$-values are multiplied by -1, and stored to a file. The $E$-value of each small window is saved to another error file for comparison with the *mean square error* of the LBE network. The above process is repeated for all the remaining windows.

The prediction errors over each 20 ms. windows are then summed together, and the sum is then square rooted to give the total prediction error over the whole sample speech. In experiment 3, this total prediction error is then subtracted by the prediction error of a reference speech. The result is the error between the sample speech and the reference speech. This error is then compared with the *mean square error* (*MSE*) of the LBE network. This *MSE* is obtained by applying the reference speech and the sample speech to the network and adjusting the minimum allowable *MSE* until the network classifies these two speeches as the same class.

### 4. Simulation and experiment results

Several experiments have been tried to test the feasibility of the LBE network for speech recognition. In the first two experiments, some recorded speeches are applied to the LBE network to check its classification capability. In experiment 3, a mapping between the LPC prediction error and the *mean square error* of the LBE network has been performed.

*4.1 Data acquisition*

The voiced speech is first recorded and digitized by using a Sound Blaster Pro adapter card on a 80386 PC. The PCM codes obtained are 8 bit and at a 11kHz sampling rate. The voiced data file are then applied to the LPC encoder. A program is written in C language to find the reflection coefficients using the Levinson-Durbin recursion equations. Each voiced speech is about 200ms long. Therefore, there are total 11 windows in each speech. In each windows, there are 220 sample data, and only 7 coefficients are obtained. Then these 77 coefficients are applied to the LBE network for learning. Also, the residual prediction squared error $E_p$ of each window is obtained. From these prediction squared errors, the total prediction error is then calculated as explained previously. A block diagram of this experimental setup is shown in Fig. 3.

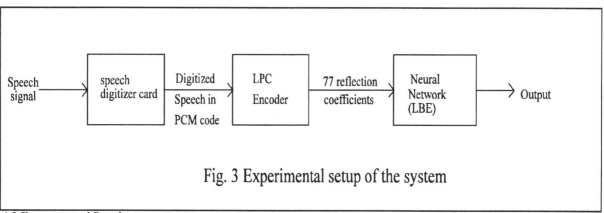

Fig. 3 Experimental setup of the system

*4.2 Experimental Results*

*Experiment 1*

In this experiment, we try to distinguish between several words using the LBE network. A sequence of "One", "Two", "Three", "Four", and "Five" is recorded. Each voice is about 220ms in length. Each word is then compressed using LPC to give 77 reflection coefficients for the input of the network. The network is set up as having 77 input neurons, 5 output neurons, and the mean square error is set to 0, which allows no error between two patterns which will be classified as the same class. The result shows that the network fires all the 5 output neurons, i.e. 5 different classes.

*Experiment 2*

In this experiment a "One" is added between "Two" and "Three" of the above sequence. This time, the network is set up as having 77 input neurons, 5 output neurons, and the *mean square error* is set to 0.000134. The network fires the same output neurons for speech 1 and 3, whereas the other four speeches fire the remaining 4 output neurons. Hence, the network successfully classifies speech 1 and 3 as the same class; whereas the others as 4 different classes.

*Experiment 3*

In this experiment, 10 "One" of different variations are recorded. One of them is selected as the reference speech; while the other 9 "One" are then applied individually to compare with the standard "One". We vary the *mean square error* until the LBE network classifies them as the same class, and this *mean square error* is the minimum allowable error between the two speeches. From the LPC process, the residual prediction error is also obtained from each window. Hence, the *mean square error* is compared with the LPC prediction error. The results of these comparisons are tabulated in Table 1, and plotted in Fig. 4. Here, we shall expect a linear curve, instead of the plotted one. The peak indicates that the test waveform is slightly different from the reference one, as it is revealed from the large *MSE* of the LBE network. A large *MSE* occurs because the test waveform is shorter than the reference one. The LPC prediction error is just the comparsion difference between the predicted waveform to the actual waveform, and there is no indication of the degree of deviation from the 2 waveforms. Therefore, when finding the LPC, we shall detect the silent period in order to avoid this discrepancy.

Table 1

| Mean Square Error of LBE network | LPC prediction error |
|---|---|
| 0.004067 | 0.054510 |
| 0.000076 | 0.000941 |
| 0.000093 | 0.021255 |
| 0.000016 | 0.021294 |
| 0.000023 | 0.046314 |
| 0.001435 | 0.096471 |
| 0.000037 | 0.026588 |
| 0.000958 | 0.089176 |
| 0.000974 | 0.094863 |

## 5. Conclusion

In the paper, we have illustrated applications of an unsupervised network for speech recognition. From the experimental results, it shows that the LBE network can successfully classify different spoken words into different classes, and similar words into the same class. In addition, we have established a way of mapping the *mean square error of* the LBE network to the LPC prediction error.

Common methods for voice recognition use distance measurement - a metric standard, and they will involve complicated functions such as logarithmic calculation as in *log area ratio* method. For this network, only simple mathematical calculations are involved. Therefore, it is much easier to be implemented for speech recognition.

**References**

1. Bart Kosko, *Neural Networks for Signal Processing*, Prentice Hall, 1992.
2. R. J. Higgins, *Digital Processing in VLSI*, Prentice Hall, 1990.
3. A. Mar (edited), *Digital Signal Processing Applications Using the ADSP-2100 Family*, Prentice Hall, 1990.
4. D. Raj Reddy, *Speech Recognition*, Academic Press, 1975
5. Michael Allerhand, *Knowledge-Based Speech Pattern Recognition*, Kogan Page, 1987.
6. C. K. Lee, K. F. Yeung, "An Unsupervised Learning Algorithm for Character Recognition and Classification," *WCNN '93*, 11-15 July, 1993, vol. 2, pp. 427-430, Portland, USA.

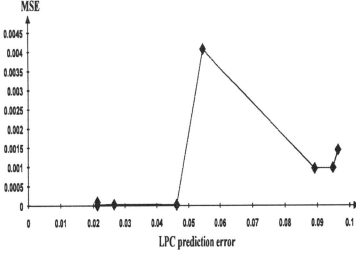

**Fig. 4 MSE of LBE vs LPC error**

# Disambiguation of Pattern Sequences with Recurrent Networks

*Ali A. Minai*
*Dept. of Electrical and Computer Engg.*
*University of Cincinnati*
*Cincinnati, OH 45221-0030*

*Geoffrey L. Barrows*
*Department of Electrical Engineering*
*Stanford University*
*Stanford, CA 94305*

*William B. Levy*
*Department of Neurosurgery*
*University of Virginia*
*Charlottesville, VA 22908*

## Abstract

Recently, there has been great interest in using neural networks to learn sequences of patterns. This is obviously very important from a cognitive point of view. In this paper, we show how a simple network with a hippocampal-like structure can be used to learn complex stimulus sequences. Specifically, we train the system, which has a one-step recurrent dynamics, to disambiguate sequences with temporal overlaps of more than one step. Usually, this is done either through delay lines or by means of capacitive effects. We show that a significant population of unforced, recurrently activated neurons in the system can enable the system to disambiguate quite well over several time steps.

## 1. Introduction

Recurrently connected networks of neuron-like elements have been widely used for associative storage of pattern sequences (Amari, 1972; Fukushima, 1973; Sompolinsky & Kanter, 1986; Kleinfeld, 1986; Buhmann & Schulten, 1987; Coolen & Gielen, 1988; Bauer & Krey, 1990; Jordan, 1986; Mozer, 1989; Elman, 1990; Reiss & Taylor, 1991; Heskes & Gielen, 1992; Bartholomeus & Coolen, 1992). The ability to learn sequences is obviously important in the cognitive context where the brain must constantly process time-varying information. In this paper, we consider the problem of disambiguating stimulus sequences with temporal overlap. Learning such sequences requires that context information be remembered over an extended period. We show that a simple network, inspired by the structure of the mammalian hippocampus, can learn sequences with long temporal overlap without any explicit memory mechanism beyond one-step recurrence.

We consider sequences with one pattern per step and use a sparsely connected recurrent network with modified hebbian learning. However, we *do not* force all neurons externally, allowing a portion of them to fire freely depending on the recurrent activation. As we discuss below, this is a key feature of the system

## 2. First-Order and Higher-Order Sequences

An important issue for sequence learning is that of order: how many previous states does a transition depend on? In the simplest case, each pattern has a unique successor, giving a first-order finite-state machine. A more interesting situation arises when the same pattern (or sub-sequence) can have different successors depending on several previous states. This creates a higher-order finite-state machine and leads to the problem of *disambiguation*: learning the correct transition when it depends on more than just the current state (Fukushima, 1973; Reiss & Taylor, 1991).

Problems involving higher-order situations have typically been solved using two devices: an explicit multiplicity of delays (Fukushima, 1973; Coolen & Gielen, 1988; Heskes & Gielen, 1992; Bartholomeus & Coolen, 1992); or capacitive effects (Reiss & Taylor, 1991). In both situations, the aim is to provide information from the past in order to facilitate the decision at the current transition point. We show that the same effect can be obtained by allowing a small amount of unforced recurrent activity in the network, provided that a sizeable proportion of neurons is never directly activated by any pattern in the sequence.

## 3. The Biological Motivation

Our study of sequence learning in neural systems was motivated largely by a desire to understand the mammalian hippocampus. We have previously suggested (Levy, 1989; Minai & Levy, 1993b) that the hippocampus might be involved in the storage, recall, and prediction of sensory sequences. In the context of this hippocampal hypothesis, we constructed a three layer system: an input layer, corresponding roughly to the entorhinal cortex and the dentate gyrus; a recurrent associative layer, corresponding to the CA3 region; and an output layer analogous to the CA1. The input layer provided strong reinforcement to the CA1 and stimulated *some of the neurons* in CA3. It also sent non-specific inhibitory signals to both layers to act as a normalization mechanism. The CA3 layer sent specific, randomly placed excitatory and non-specific inhibitory connections to itself and to the CA1 layer (see Figure 1).

The input layer provided stimulus sequences to the CA3-CA1 system. The CA3-CA3 and the CA3-CA1 excitatory weights were modified via an associative rule to learn the sequences. The system's goal was to complete a learned sequence given an initial fragment. Sequence learning occurred primarily in the CA3 layer, which constructed an encoding of the dynamics implicit in the stimulus. The CA3 neurons not directly stimulated by the input were left free to encode contextual representations. The CA1 layer acted essentially as a pattern recognition/categorization layer, recovering the original sequence patterns from the CA3 recodings.

## 4. Network Specification and Problem Definition

We used a network model which builds on one that we have previously investigated (Minai & Levy, 1993 a,b,c). A network had $N$ inputs and outputs and consisted of three layers of binary neurons: an input layer, $I$; a recurrent CA3 layer; and a CA1 output layer. The input layer consisted of $N$ dummy units which simply distributed the $N$ network inputs to the other two layers. Thus, the output, $x_i$, of the $i$th input layer neuron was equal to the $i$th network input. The recurrent layer consisted of $n \geq N$ binary (0/1) primary neurons with identical firing thresholds, $\theta$. The neurons were interconnected via a Bernoulli process: each neuron $i$ had probability $p$ of receiving a modifiable excitatory connection from each neuron $j$ in the recurrent layer. The presence of such a connection was indicated by the binary variable $c_{ij}$. Neurons 1 through $N$ also received strong one-to-one excitatory inputs, $x_i$, from the input layer through a synapse of fixed strength $v$. Inhibition was mediated by a single interneuron that received input from all primary neurons in the layer and all inputs, $x_i$, and then provided an identical shunting conductance proportional to its input to all primary neurons. At time $t$, taking $w_{ij}(t)$ as the excitatory weight from neuron $i$ to $j$, $K_I$ as the fixed inhibitory weight from the input layer, $K_R$ as the fixed weight for feedback inhibition, $m(t)$ as the number of active neurons in the recurrent layer, and $s(t)$ as the number of active inputs, the excitation $y_i$ of neuron $i$ was given by:

$$y_i(t) = Input_i(t) + \sum_{j \in R} c_{ij} w_{ij} z_j(t-1) - [\, K_I s(t) + K_R m(t-1)\,] \tag{1}$$

where $Input_i(t) = vx_i(t)$ if $1 \leq i \leq N$ and 0 otherwise. We defined $y_i(t) = 0$ for all $i$ if $s(t) = m(t-1) = 0$. The output of the neuron was calculated as:

$$z_i(t) = \begin{cases} 1 & \text{if } y_i(t) \geq \theta \\ 0 & otherwise \end{cases} \tag{2}$$

It was assumed that input weight $v$ was strong enough that $x_i(t) = 1 \Rightarrow z_i(t) = 1$. However, neurons with no external input were *not* forced to the zero state and could be fired through feedback connections.

The CA1-like output layer consisted of $N$ primary neurons which received random modifiable connections, $a_{ij}$, from the recurrent layer and strong, non-modifiable, one-to-one connections of magnitude $b$ from the input layer. They also got feed-forward inhibition via an interneuron that received input from the recurrent and input layers. The equations for neurons in the output layer were:

$$y_i(t) = bx_i(t) + \sum_{j \in R} c_{ij} a_{ij} z_j(t) - [\, C_I s(t) + C_R m(t)\,] \tag{3}$$

$$z_i(t) = \begin{cases} 1 & \text{if } y_i(t) \geq \phi \\ 0 & otherwise \end{cases} \tag{4}$$

where $C_I$ and $C_R$ were inhibitory weights from the input and CA3 layers, respectively, and $\phi$ was the firing threshold. The CA3-CA1 weights began at zero so that, initially, the learning from the recurrent to the output layer was driven by the network input. The purpose of the output layer was to recover the original patterns from the context-dependent representations developed by the recurrent layer, effectively implementing an inverse mapping.

## 5. The Problem

The task investigated was to learn to disambiguate two higher-order sequences of $n$-dimensional binary patterns. Temporal overlap was created between the sequences by including identical sub-sequences in both. The length of this overlap was varied from 0 to 4 to evaluate disambiguation performance. The sequences were constructed from a repertoire of 20 mutually orthogonal patterns, labeled A through T, as follows:

**0 step overlap:** ABCDEFGH and IJKLMNOP
**1 step overlap:** ABQDEFGH and IJQLMNOP
**2 step overlap:** ABQREFGH and IJQRMNOP
**3 step overlap:** ABQRSFGH and IJQRSNOP
**4 step overlap:** ABQRSTGH and IJQRSTOP

At least the first two and the last two patterns in each sequence pair were distinct and mutually orthogonal. The network was evaluated by its ability to reproduce the final pattern of a sequence at step 8 given the initial pattern at step 1.

## 5.1. The Basic Premise

The basic premise of this investigation was that simple one-step associative learning could imprint higher-order sequences in recurrent networks if some neurons not directly stimulated by patterns were also allowed to fire. This *auxiliary activity* creates distinguishable, context-dependent secondary representations of the stimulus patterns and allows the correct transitions to be learned. In essence, auxiliary activity plays the same role as hidden neurons do in a supervised learning situation. It allows the received dynamics of the input stimulus to be mapped to a higher-dimensional space where degeneracies can be distinguished in the extra dimensions. Auxiliary activity can come from noise added to patterns in off-line training, or be produced through excitatory feedback if the training is on-line. The very long transients produced through recurrence (Minai & Levy, 1993 a,b,c) can be used to this end.

## 5.2. The Training Process

For training, the network was repeatedly stimulated by the two sequences and the CA3-CA3 and CA3-CA1 synapses were allowed to modify. We tried two different learning rules in the *CA*3 layer:

Postsynaptic Rule: $w_{ij}(t) = w_{ij}(t-1) + \varepsilon z_i(t) [z_j(t-1) - w_{ij}(t-1)]$

Presynaptic Rule: $w_{ij}(t) = w_{ij}(t-1) + \varepsilon z_j(t-1) [z_i(t) - w_{ij}(t-1)]$

where $\varepsilon$ was a small learning rate parameter. Only the presynaptic rule was used for the CA1 layer. The relative pros and cons of the rules are discussed in Sections 5.4 and 6. Both rules are biologically plausible (see Levy (1982); Levy, Colbert & Desmond (1990) for the postsynaptic rule and Fujii et al (1991); Dudek & Bear (1992); Mulkey and Malenka (1992) for the presynaptic.) At the beginning of each sequence presentation, the state of the network was reset to 0, so that the sequences did not merge together.

## 5.3. Performance Evaluation

To test recall, all neurons were reset to 0 and the system was then stimulated with the first pattern of a learned sequence. The network was then allowed to relax without further input for 7 time steps; its output over the final step of the sequence (step 8) was compared with the corresponding true pattern in the sequence to evaluate performance on that sequence. The process was then repeated with the other sequence. The completion performance on a sequence was judged by calculating two measures:

1) The number of correct neurons on        2) The number of incorrect neurons on.

Each measure was averaged over both sequences and over ten networks, each with different, randomly generated CA3-CA3 and CA3-CA1 connection matrices. It should be noted that the patterns used were very sparse (10 active bits in each), so the correct number of active neurons at any step was far lower than the number that should have remained inactive. Thus, in a 10-out-of-100 pattern, if 9 correct neurons were active and 9 incorrect ones, the *proportion* of correct to incorrect firing would be 9 : 1, not 1 : 1. We chose to plot absolute numbers rather than proportionate values because they represent a more exacting criterion.

## 5.4. Choice of Learning Rules

Two different situations were investigated in our simulations. In the first set of experiments, the CA3-CA3 weights were modified using the pre-synaptic rule, while in the second series, the post-synaptic rule was used. The pre-synaptic rule was used in both cases for the CA3-CA1 weights. The reason can be appreciated by considering the difference between the two rules, which is basically in their depressive aspects. Suppose two pre-synaptic patterns, V and W, map into the same post-synaptic pattern, X. If a post-synaptic rule is used, it sets up *competition* between the synapses used by V and those used by W: when the V-X pair is active, the W-X synapses are depressed, and vice-versa when W-X is active. The result is that neither V nor W gets properly associated with X, whereas both should have. With the pre-synaptic rule, the competition is not between candidate pre-synaptic patterns but between prospective post-synaptic ones, i.e., if X elicits Y or Z in different situations, the X-Y and X-Z synapses compete. For synapses from CA3 to CA1, the latter situation should not arise, since the CA3 should not form identical representations for two distinct input/output patterns. The former situation, however, occurs routinely, since two convergent sub-sequences (e.g., ABQ and IJQ) will usually lead to different CA3 patterns but should both elicit Q in CA1. It is, therefore, clear that the pre-synaptic rule is the rule of choice for CA3-CA1 synapses. However, this is not so clear for the CA3-CA3 synapses where the association is temporal, and it is possible to have convergent (ABQ and IJQ) and divergent (TGH and TOP) situations.

### 6. Simulation Results and Discussion

The results from the simulations are shown in Figure 2 (a & b). In each case, the CA3 layer was 200 neurons wide and each neuron received excitatory connections from 40 other randomly chosen neurons. The input bus was also 200 neurons wide, but its effective size depended upon the number of different patterns in the two sequences. At most 160 neurons were used (in the 0-overlap situation) and at least 120 (in the 4-overlap case). The CA1 mirrored the input layer, with 200 neurons and a variable effective size. The input layer projected in a 1-1 manner to the CA3 and the CA1 with powerful "sure-fire" synapses. The CA3 projected to CA1 randomly with a 40% chance of connection between two specific neurons. The CA3-CA3 weights were initially set to values that allowed some recurrently generated CA3 activity. However, the CA3-CA1 weights were initially zero so that the CA1 learned only through reinforcing input layer activity. Each data point was averaged over both sequences in the corresponding pair and over ten random networks.

The results show several interesting features. The most notable is that our system, without any explicit long delay memory mechanism, is able to disambiguate quite well across several steps of overlap. This is especially true with the pre-synaptic rule. In this case, even an overlap of 4 activates about 45% of the correct neurons and only 2% of the incorrect ones.

Another notable feature is the manner in which the two learning rules affect the error with increasing temporal overlap. The pre-synaptic rule degrades in terms of correct neurons on but holds the number of spurious firings down. The post-synaptic rule does the opposite. This can be explained by considering the point of decision in the network's task. Since performance is judged by the ability to reach the correct one of two possible terminations, the critical point is when the system emerges from the temporal overlap and opts for one terminal direction or the other. For example, in the ABQREFGH/IJQRMNOP situation (overlap = 2), the critical decision is made at the $R \rightarrow E/R \rightarrow M$ transition. This is also where the effect of temporal overlap is maximal and the CA3 representations of the two contexts most alike. Let X be the final pattern in a temporal overlap of length $q$, to be followed by Y or Z. Since X can be arrived at in two contexts, it will have two CA3 representations, one of which should elicit Y and the other Z. Call these representations $X_1$ and $X_2$, respectively, and let $X'$ be their intersection. Then the size of $X'$ is an increasing function of $q$. Now, the post-synaptic rule, at this point, associates $X_1$ with Y and $X_2$ with Z. More importantly, the active bits in $X'$ are associated *equally strongly* with *both* Y and Z, without competition. As the temporal overlap becomes longer, $X'$ approaches both $X_1$ and $X_2$. Thus, there will be an increased tendency to elicit *both* Y and Z regardless of context, leading to the situation in Figure 2(b). Note also that this problem cannot be fixed simply by using a competitive firing mechanism like firing the 10 most excited neurons.

In the presynaptic case, however, there is competition at the point of decision, so that synapses from $X'$ to Y and Z are kept relatively weak, while synapses from $X_1 - X_2$ to Y and from $X_2 - X_1$ to Z are strengthened. Thus, the decision is made on the basis of the *differentiated* parts of the two CA3 representations rather than on the entire representations as in the post-synaptic case. In this sense, the pre-synaptic rule is the logically correct choice for learning disambiguation. However, since the differentiated parts of the CA3 representations become smaller with increasing $q$, the total activity in the network also declines. This effect is apparent in Figure 2(a). However, this situation can be improved by a competitive firing mechanism.

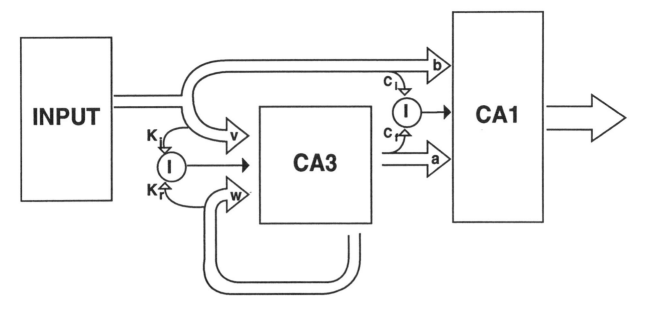

**Figure 1:** Schematic of the system components and connections. The wide arrows indicate specific connections, and the thin line arrows indicate non-specific inhibitory pathways feeding into and out of interneurons (I). Open arrowheads are excitatory synapses, and solid ones are inhibitiory synapses. Only connections **w** and **a** are modifiable.

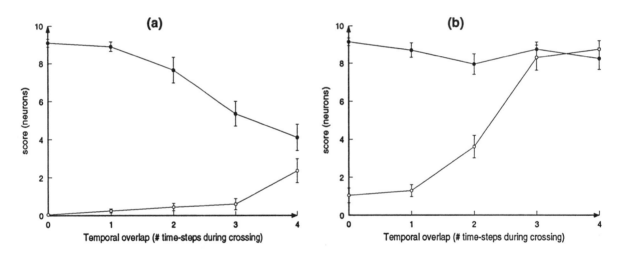

**Figure 2:** The performance of the system on sequences with different temporal overlaps. The filled circles indicate the number of correctly firing neurons and the open circles show the number of spurious firings. Each data point is averaged over ten randomly generated networks and over the sequence pair. Error bars show one standard deviation. Every network was trained with 200 passes over both sequences. Graph (a) depicts the case where CA3 weights were modified by the pre-synaptic rule. Good parameter settings were found by trying different combinations on the 3-step overlap. These settings were then used for all cases. CA3 weights were initially set to 0.36. The learning rate for all weights was 0.02. Graph (b) shows the results for the case where CA3 weights were trained with the post-synaptic rule. Attempts to find good parameter settings with 3-step overlap case failed in this case because the network did very poorly on this problem. Thus, the 2-step overlap case was used to find good parameter values. The initial CA3 weight was 0.48, and the learning rate was 0.02.

**Acknowledgements:** This research was supported in part by the following grants to WBL: NIMH MH00622; NIMH MH48161; NSF MSS-9216372; and EPRI RP8030-08. It was also supported by the Department of Neurosurgery, University of Virginia, Dr. John A. Jane, Chairman. The authors would like to thank Dawn Adelsberger-Mangan for her constructive comments and Colin Prepscius for his help with the manuscript.

S. Amari (1972) "Learning Patterns and Pattern Sequences by Self-Organizing Nets of Threshold Elements", *IEEE Trans. on Computers*, C-21, 1197-1206.

M. Bartholomeus & A.C.C. Coolen (1992) "Sequences of Smoothly Correlated Patterns in Neural Networks with Random Transmission Delays", *Biological Cybernetics*, 67, 285-290.

K. Bauer & U. Krey (1990) "On Learning and Recognition of Temporal Sequences of Correlated Patterns", *Z. Phys. B - Condensed Matter*, 79, 461-475.

J. Buhmann & K. Schulten (1987) "Noise-Driven Temporal Association in Neural Networks" *Europhys. Lett.*, 4, 1205-1209.

A.C.C. Coolen & C.C.A.M. Gielen (1988) "Delays in Neural Networks", *Europhys. Lett.*, 7, 281-285.

S.M. Dudek & M.F. Bear (1992) "Homosynaptic Long-Term Depression in Area CA1 of Hippocampus and Effects of N-Methyl-D-Aspartate Receptor Blockade", *Proc. Nat. Acad. Sci. USA*, 89, 4363-4367.

J.L. Elman (1990) "Finding Structure in Time", *Cognitive Science*, 14, 179-211.

S. Fujii, K. Saito, H. Miyakawa, K. Ito & H. Kato (1991) "Reversal of Long-Term Potentiation (Depotentiation) Induced by Tetanus Stimulation of the Input to CA1 Neurons of Guinea Pig Hippocampal Slices", *Brain Res.* 555, 112-122.

K. Fukushima (1973) "A Model of Associative Memory in the Brain" *Kybernetik*, 12, 58-63.

T.M. Heskes & S. Gielen (1992) "Retrieval of Pattern Sequences at Variable Speeds in a Neural Network with Delays", *Neural Networks*, 5, 145-152.

M.I. Jordan "Attractor Dynamics and Parallelism in a Connectionist Sequential Machine", *Proc. 8th Ann. Conf. of the Cog. Sci. Soc.*, 531-546.

D. Kleinfeld (1986) "Sequential State Generation by Model Neural Networks", *Proc. Natl. Acad. Sci. USA*, 83, 9469-9473.

W.B. Levy (1982) "Associative Encoding at Synapses", *Proc. Fourth Ann. Conf. Cognitive Sci. Soc.*, 135-136.

W.B. Levy, C.M. Colbert & N.L. Desmond (1990) "Elemental Adaptive Processes of Neurons and Synapses: A Statistical/Computational Perspective", in: Neuroscience and Connectionist Theory, M. Gluck & D. Rumelhart (eds.), Hillsdale, NJ, Lawrence Erlbaum Associates, 187-235.

A.A. Minai & W.B. Levy (1993a) "Predicting Complex Behavior in Sparse Asymmetric Networks", in: Advances in Neural Information Processing Systems 5, S.J. Hanson, J.D. Cowan & C.L. Giles (eds.), San Mateo, CA, Morgan Kaufmann, 556-563.

A.A. Minai & W.B. Levy (1993b) "The Dynamics of Sparse Random Networks", *in press*.

A.A. Minai & W.B. Levy (1993c) "Setting the Activity Level in Sparse Random Networks", *in press*.

M.C. Mozer (1989) "A Focused Backpropagation Algorithm for Temporal Pattern Recognition", *Complex Systems*, 3, 349-381.

Mulkey, R.M. & Malenka, R.C. (1992). Mechanisms underlying induction of homosynaptic long-term depression in area CA1 of the hippocampus, *Neuron,* **9**: 967-975.

M. Reiss & J.G. Taylor (1991) "Storing Temporal Sequences", *Neural Networks*, 4, 773-787.

H. Sompolinsky & I. Kanter (1986) "Temporal Association in Asymmetric Neural Networks", *Physical Rev. Lett.*, 57, 2861-2864.

# ON THE STABILITY OF RECEPTIVITY-BASED ADAPTIVE SYNAPTOGENESIS

*Hakan Deliç and William B. Levy*
Department of Neurological Surgery
Health Sciences Center Box 420
University of Virginia
Charlottesville, Virginia 22908

**Abstract:** We investigate the stability properties of the receptivity-based adaptive synaptogenesis process. We show that, following convergence, synaptogenesis enters an oscillatory state unless a switching mechanism is employed for its termination. Algorithms that detect changes in the statistics of the input environment can then be used to regulate the resumption of the process.

## 1 Adaptive Synaptogenesis and Receptivity

Adaptive synaptogenesis is a biologically plausible process of making synaptic connections in an initially unconnected network [4]. In this theory, synaptic connections between a postsynaptic neuron and potential presynaptic neurons are gradually formed until the postsynaptic neuron either quits making chemotacticly mediated requests or denies sites, for new innervation.

The postsynaptic neuron $j$'s receptivity to new innervation is represented by the functional $R_j(\overline{y}_j(t))$ where $\overline{y}_j(t)$ is the average postsynaptic activity at time $t$. A neurally acceptable receptivity functional $R_j(t) \equiv R_j(\overline{y}_j(t))$ must satisfy the following conditions:

1) $R_j(t) \geq 0, \forall t$.

2) It is continuous but not necessarily differentiable.

3) It is bounded.

4) There exists a constant $\mu_y$ such that $R_j(t) = 0$ whenever $\overline{y}_j(t) \geq \mu_y$. This cut-off value is typically some preset or desired postsynaptic activity level, and it is assumed that $\mu_y \leq E[y_j]$.

Let $t_j^0$ be the time point when the connectivity of the postsynaptic neuron $j$ becomes fixed; that is, $t_j^0 = \min t : \overline{y}_j(t) \geq \mu_y$. At time $\max_j t_j^0$, synaptogenesis is terminated for all postsynaptic neurons and the entire network converges to some fixed state.

Let $P_{ij}(t) \equiv P_{ij}(\overline{y}_j(t))$ be the probability of input neuron $i$ making a connection with output neuron $j$ at time $t$. This probability is in fact defined as a functional of the average postsynaptic activity [1]:

$$P_{ij}(\overline{y}_j(t)) = \gamma R_j(\overline{y}_j(t)) \tag{1}$$

where $\gamma$ is a constant that controls the convergence rate of the synaptogenesis process. Clearly, $R_j(t) \leq 1/\gamma, \forall t$. From equation (1), synaptogenesis terminates for postsynaptic neuron $j$ when $P_{ij}(t_j^0) = 0$, and hence the condition (4) above.

The calculation of the average postsynaptic activity is performed through a running averager such as

$$\overline{y}_j(t + 1) = (1 - \epsilon)\overline{y}_j(t) + \epsilon y_j(t + 1) \tag{2}$$

where $0 < \epsilon < 1$ [1]. The constant coefficient $\epsilon$ eliminates any counting requirements for the neuron. Moreover, for large $\epsilon$, recent observations carry more weight in the calculation of equation (2); hence the running averager is capable of handling small nonstationarities in $y_j(t)$ as well.

## 2 Neuronal Properties and Associative Synaptic Modification

All input neurons are assumed to produce $\{0, 1\}$-binary outputs corresponding to {not firing, firing}, respectively. At time step $t$, the activity $y_j(t)$ of the postsynaptic neuron $j$ is determined according to the inner product

$$y_j(t) = f\left\{\sum_{i \in S_j}^{N} x_i(t)w_{ij}(t)\right\} \tag{3}$$

where $x_i(t)$ is the activity of the input neuron $i$ and $w_{ij}(t)$ is the synaptic weight between the input neuron $i$ and the output neuron $j$, both at time $t$. $S_j$ is the set of input neurons that are connected to neuron $j$. The threshold function $f$ is defined as

$$f(\zeta) = \begin{cases} 1, & \text{if } \zeta \geq \theta \\ 0, & \text{otherwise,} \end{cases} \tag{4}$$

where $\theta$ is a suitable threshold. Hence, $y_j(t) \in \{0, 1\}, \forall j$.

The weights of the existing connections in equation (3) are adjusted via an adaptive process called the associative synaptic modification. One synaptic modification rule with desirable convergence properties is the following:

$$w_{ij}(t + 1) = w_{ij}(t) + \varepsilon y_j(t)[x_i(t) - w_{ij}(t)]. \tag{5}$$

The positive constant $\varepsilon$ controls the modification rate. In this paper, we will set $\varepsilon = 0.05$ to ensure that the synaptic weights converge very slowly.

# 3   Stability of Receptivity-Based Adaptive Synaptogenesis

Naturally, it is desirable that synaptogenesis be a stable process. That is, the network should converge to a stationary state of connectivity and stay in that state as long as the input environment does not change. Unfortunately, the simple running averager in equation (2) may drive the synaptogenesis process to instability. Consider Example 1 to see this point:

**Example 1:** Let $y_j(t) \in \{0, 1\}, \forall t$, and suppose $\overline{y}_j(t_j^0) = 0.52$. When $\mu_y = 0.5$ and $\epsilon = 0.05$, then $\overline{y}_j(t_j^0 + 1) < \mu_y$ if $y_j(t_j^0 + 1) = 0$, and thus synaptogenesis would restart after only one time step.

More formally, the following lemma establishes the instability of a running averager-based synaptogenesis mechanism.

**Lemma 1:** Let $\delta$ be the amount of overshoot of $\overline{y}_j(t_j^0)$ above $\mu_y$. Suppose synaptogenesis is terminated at time $t_j^0$ for postsynaptic neuron $j$, and assume that $\mu_y \gg \delta$ and $\epsilon \ll 1$. Synaptogenesis will resume in finite time with non-zero probability. $\square$

**Proof of Lemma 1:** For the sake of simplicity, let $t_j^0 = 0$. That is, let $\overline{y}_j(0) = \mu_y + \delta$. Assume further that $\overline{y}_j(t) \geq \mu_y, \forall t > 0$, with probability one. Then,

$$\overline{y}_j(t) = \epsilon^t(\mu_y + \delta) + \sum_{k=1}^{t} \epsilon(1 - \epsilon)^{t-k} y_j(k) \geq \mu_y.$$

The above equation implies that

$$\underbrace{\sum_{k=1}^{t}(1 - \epsilon)^{t-k} y_j(k)}_{h(\{y_j(k)\}_{k=1}^{t})} \geq \frac{\mu_y - \epsilon^t(\mu_y - \delta)}{\epsilon} \gg 1$$

with probability one. But $h(\{y_j(k)\}_{k=1}^{t}) < 1$ with non-zero probability for some $t > 0$, and hence, the assumption that $\overline{y}_j(t) \geq \mu_y, \forall t > 0$, with probability one is false by contradiction. $\square$

It is important to quantify how the instability of synaptogenesis affects the formation of new synapses. If synaptogenesis turns back on very rarely, the chances of new connections being made will be low. Then one may claim that the instability issue is not critical enough to cause any disturbances in the overall balance of the system.

We need the following basic result first.

**Proposition 1:** Suppose that the learning constant $\varepsilon$ in equation (5) is small enough so that the synaptic weights converge very slowly and they can be assumed constant in the steady-state. Let $\bar{y}_j(0) = 0$, and let the running averager be defined as in equation (2). Then $\bar{y}_j$ is asymptotically normal with mean $E[y_j]$ and variance $\eta_\epsilon^2 \sigma_y^2$, where $E[y_j]$ and $\sigma_y^2$ are respectively the mean and the variance of the postsynaptic activity $y_j$, and

$$\eta_\epsilon = \sqrt{\frac{\epsilon}{2 - \epsilon}}. \quad \Box$$

**Proof of Proposition 1:** The recursion in equation (2) is equivalent to

$$\bar{y}_j(t) = \epsilon^t \bar{y}_j(0) + \sum_{k=1}^{t} \epsilon(1 - \epsilon)^{t-k} y_j(k). \tag{6}$$

Because $\bar{y}_j(0) = 0$ and the weights are slowly varying, the right-hand side of equation (6) reduces to the sum of independent postsynaptic firing activities. The result then follows from the central limit theorem. $\Box$

Notice that the asymptotic distribution of $\bar{y}_j$ is tightly centered around $E[y_j]$. However, since $\bar{y}_j(t)$ converges only in the mean, it is clear that synaptogenesis will oscillate between on- and off-states with non-zero probability.

**Lemma 2:** Suppose that all the conditions in Lemma 1 are valid. Let $\nu_j$ denote the ratio of the number of times when synaptogenesis is on over the number of times when synaptogenesis is off, after convergence is achieved for postsynaptic neuron $j$. Then,

$$\nu_j = \frac{\Phi\left(\frac{\mu_y - E[y_j]}{\eta_\epsilon \sigma_y}\right)}{1 - \Phi\left(\frac{\mu_y - E[y_j]}{\eta_\epsilon \sigma_y}\right)}, \tag{7}$$

where $\Phi(\zeta)$ is the cumulative distribution function of the zero-mean, unit-variance Gaussian random variable at point $\zeta$. $\Box$

**Proof of Lemma 2:** The proof follows directly from Lemma 1. $\Box$

Interestingly enough, $\nu_j = 1$ for $\mu_y = E[y_j]$. That is, synaptogenesis is on half of the time. Below we give a more general example.

**Example 2:** Let $\mu_y = 0.5$ and $\epsilon = 0.05$. By equations (3) and (4), $y_j(t)$ is a stationary Bernoulli process, and let $p_y$ denote the corresponding Bernoulli parameter. Then, $E[y_j] = p_y$ and $\sigma_y^2 = p_y(1 - p_y)$. The following receptivity functional is employed in all simulations:

$$R_j(t) = \max\{-2\bar{y}_j(t) + 1, 0\}, \ 0 \leq \bar{y}_j(t) \leq 1, \ \forall\, t. \tag{8}$$

From equation (7), one can see that, for $0 < \mu_y < 1$, $\nu_j \to \infty$ as $p_y \to 0$ since more synapses are required to reach the desired activity level when the output (and hence the input) firing probability is small. For similar reasons, $\nu_j \to 0$ as $p_y \to 1$. In fact, for this particular example, $\nu_j > 10,000$ for $p_y < 0.2$ and $\nu_j < 1.0 \times 10^{-4}$ for $p_y > 0.8$.

For the same example, we also carried out one set of numerical experiments with 64 input neurons receiving 64 distinct input patterns. The threshold $\theta$ in equation was set to 2. $p_y$ was controlled by varying the input activity level. The simulations were run for 409,600 time steps, for ten different input environments. We started keeping track of the running averager as soon as synaptogenesis stopped for the first time. Table 1 lists averages of the theoretical (equation(7)) and experimental values for $\nu_j$, as well as the number of new synapses accrued due to the instability of synaptogenesis, for various values of $p_y$.

We ignored trivial situations where $p_y < \mu_y$. The relative discrepancy between the theoretical and experimental $\nu_j$ values is due to the extremely tight asymptotic distribution of $\overline{y}_j$. As the table indicates, the number of new synapses formed during on-times (following convergence) is not negligible when the cut-off value $\mu_y$ is close to the average postsynaptic activity, and thus a regulatory mechanism is necessary.

Table 1: Theoretical and experimental values of $\nu_j$ as a function of $p_y$, for $\mu_y = 0.5$ and $\epsilon = 0.05$. Numbers in table are averages over ten distinct input environments.

| $p_y$ | $\nu_j$ (theoretical) | $\nu_j$ (experimental) | New synapses accrued |
|---|---|---|---|
| 0.50 | 1.000 | 1.002 | 8 |
| 0.58 | 0.185 | 0.168 | 11 |
| 0.63 | 0.048 | 0.040 | 2 |
| 0.64 | 0.036 | 0.016 | 1 |

# 4   Stabilizing Mechanisms

In this section, we propose two alternatives to regulate synaptogenesis after convergence. Both methods turn off synaptogenesis as soon as the receptivity functional becomes zero, and then start monitoring the running averager to detect a change in the input environment. (A change in the statistics of the input environment will result in a change in the output firing level.) In particular, we model the latter change by a drop in the neurons' firing probability as there is ample biological evidence in support of this premise. The first mechanism uses a statistical change detection algorithm due to Page [6], while the second one is based on tracking the number of times the running averager falls below the cut-off threshold $\mu_y$.

**Page's Stopping Rule**

This approach is based on the fact that any change in the Bernoulli parameter of the input firing distribution will manifest itself in a somewhat delayed variation in the Bernoulli parameter of the output firing distribution (see equations (3) and (4)). An efficient method to detect a change in the mean (which is the Bernoulli parameter in our model) is Page's stopping rule [3, 6], which is shown to minimize the expected delay of detection for a fixed and non-zero false alarm rate [5]:

Suppose it is necessary to detect a possible change from a Bernoulli process whose parameter is $p$ to a Bernoulli process whose parameter is $q$ where $p > q$, based on the observation sequence $y_j(t)$. Then the test has the following form [7]:

Detect a drop in the mean at the first instant $t > t_j^0$ such that $g_j(t) \geq \lambda$ where

$$g_j(0) = 0, \tag{9}$$

$$g_j(t) = \max\{0, g_j(t-1) - y_j(t) - \eta(\overline{y}_j(t_j^0), \overline{y}_j(t))\}, \tag{10}$$

$$\eta(p, q) = \frac{\log \frac{1-q}{1-p}}{\log \frac{q(1-p)}{p(1-q)}}. \tag{11}$$

In engineering applications, the threshold $\lambda > 0$ is optimized so as to meet a prespecified upper bound on the false alarm probability. However, the detection performance is not very sensitive to the particular choice of this threshold [3].

In our biological model, the change parameter that is monitored by the detector is the average postsynaptic activity. The change detector will activate at time $t_j^0 + 1$, and the Bernoulli parameter $p$ at the time of convergence of synaptogenesis will have already been calculated by the running averager; that is, $p = \overline{y}_j(t_j^0)$. A change in the input environment will result in a change in the value of the running averager after convergence; hence, $q = \overline{y}_j(t)$, $t > t_j^0$.

The change detector in equations (9), (10) and (11) is biologically plausible because only local information is used. The algorithm is recursive and does not require tracking time steps.

**Example 3:** Consider the adaptive synaptogenesis and synaptic modification rules described earlier, and let the receptivity functional be as defined in equation (8). Let $\mu_y = 0.5$, $\epsilon = 0.05$ and $\theta = 2$. Two sets of input environments represented by 64 and 128 distinct 64-bit input patterns were created. In each case, the input patterns were randomly fed to the network over 10 times the number of input patterns time steps. The input firing level was brought down from 0.30 to 0.25 in order to simulate the change in the input environment. Synaptogenesis terminated at time $t_j^0$ as soon as $\overline{y}_j(t_j^0) \geq \mu_y$, and it was turned back on when a change in the input environment was detected for the first time.

Table 2 displays the detection delays for Page's stopping rule under various scenarios.

Table 2: Detection delay of Page's stopping rule as a function of $\lambda$ and the number of 64-bit input patterns, for $\mu_y = 0.5$ and $\epsilon = 0.05$. The delays are determined by calculating the number of time steps between the occurrence of the change and the first time the change is detected. The numbers in the table are averages over ten distinct input environments.

| $\lambda$ | 64 patterns | 128 patterns |
|---|---|---|
| 2 | 15 | 3 |
| 3 | 16 | 5 |
| 4 | 18 | 6 |

As Table 2 demonstrates, Page's algorithm detects any changes in the Bernoulli parameter very rapidly. One reason is that the drop in input Bernoulli parameter is amplified by the input-output relation in equation (3) into a larger difference, making the parameter shift more detectable; hence the advantage of monitoring the running averager. Our simulations also verify the claim that the algorithm's performance is relatively independent of the threshold $\lambda$. Finally, we notice that the detection delay is smaller for larger number of input patterns.

A simpler, and perhaps more intuitive, method is the following algorithm which is based on monitoring the status of synaptogenesis directly.

**Tracking the Threshold Crossings of the Running Averager**
Define

$$r(t) = \begin{cases} 1, & \text{if } \overline{y}_j(t) < \mu_y \\ 0, & \text{otherwise,} \end{cases}$$

for $t \geq t_j^0$. In other words, $r(t)$ valuates the event $\overline{y}_j(t) < \mu_y$ over the time interval $(t_j^0, t]$. The average of this quantity can be calculated recursively by means of the running averager

$$\overline{r}_j(t) = (1 - \xi)\overline{r}_j(t - 1) + \xi r(t),$$

where $0 < \xi < 1$. When the average number of times $\overline{y}_j(t)$ is less than $\mu_y$ exceeds a threshold $\omega$, synaptogenesis restarts.

At the time when a change in the input environment is detected, receptivity will be zero. Therefore the running averager has to be reset to some value smaller than $\mu_y$ in order to restart synaptogenesis. That is, $\overline{y}_j(t_j^c + 1) = \mu_c$ where $t_j^c$ is the time when the change is detected and $\mu_c < \mu_y$ is the reset value for the running averager.

# 5 Summary and Discussion

Adaptive synaptogenesis, when controlled solely by the receptivity of postsynaptic neurons, is unstable in the sense that the process may oscillate indefinitely, resulting in unwanted or unnecessary synaptic connections. In this paper, we introduced a modified model where synaptogenesis is turned off as soon as convergence is achieved, and the postsynaptic activity is subsequently monitored to detect any changes in the input environment. Synaptogenesis is then turned on again in order to cope with these changes.

One definite conclusion of this paper is that receptivity alone may not be enough to regulate synaptogenesis. Future research should include avidity and synapse removal [2] functions in explaining the dynamics of synaptogenesis. On the other hand, one can certainly argue that once the input neuron set $S_j$ has reached fixed connectivity with output neuron $j$, it is not desirable to break up the existing configuration because the subject may face the same input environment in the future. So, perhaps, there exists some intra-neuronal mechanism where output neuron $j$ calls upon other output neurons to form connectivity in order to learn the new environment.

Ultimately, context-dependent synaptogenesis which requires a very large network may provide the best explanation.

# 6 Acknowledgments

This research was supported by the grants NIH RR07864, NIMH MH00622, NIMH MH48161, NSF MSS-9216372 and EPRI RP8030-08, and the Department of Neurological Surgery, University of Virginia Health Sciences Center, Dr. John A. Jane, Chairman.

# References

[1] D. M. Adelsberger-Mangan and W. B. Levy (1993): "Adaptive Synaptogenesis Can Construct Networks Which Maintain Information and Reduce Statistical Dependence", *Biological Cybernetics*, in press.

[2] D. M. Adelsberger-Mangan and W. B. Levy (1993): "The Influence of Limited Presynaptic Growth and Synapse Removal on Adaptive Synaptogenesis", *Biological Cybernetics*, submitted.

[3] M. Basseville (1988): "Detecting Changes in Signals and Systems- A Survey", *Automatica*, vol. 24, pp. 309-326.

[4] W. B. Levy and N. L. Desmond (1985): "Associative Potentiation/Depression in the Hippocampal Dentate Gyrus", in *Electrical Activity of the Archicortex*, G. Buzsaki and C. H. Vanderwolf, Editors, Budapest, Hungary: Akademiai Kiado, pp. 359-373.

[5] G. M. Moustakides (1986): "Optimal Procedures for Detecting Changes in Distributions", *Annals of Statistics*, vol. 14, pp. 1379-1387.

[6] E. S. Page (1954): "Continuous Inspection Schemes", *Biometrika*, vol. 41, pp. 100-115.

[7] P. Papantoni-Kazakos (1979): "Algorithms for Monitoring Changes in Quality of Communication Links", *IEEE Transactions on Communications*, vol. 27, pp. 682-693.

# THE MEDIAN LEARNING ALGORITHM
# FOR ROBUST UNSUPERVISED LEARNING

Duane DeSieno
Logical Designs Consulting, Inc.
2015 Olite Ct.
La Jolla, CA 92037

## Abstract

Unsupervised learning algorithms characteristically have difficulty in two areas. These are the effective utilization of resources and the sensitivity to outliers. Algorithms make use of techniques such as a neighborhood function, conscience mechanism, vigilance or a growing technique to improve the utilization of resources. This paper will present the median learning algorithm as an effective means of controlling both utilization and outliers. Using daily price movements for the SP500 stock future, a comparison will be made of the median learning algorithm and unsupervised learning with the conscience mechanism.

## INTRODUCTION

Unsupervised learning algorithms are typically used for vector quantization and clustering. While the desired output is not known for a given training input pattern, unsupervised learning attempts to minimize the squared distance between the winning processing elements weights and the input vector. The distance measure can be expressed by

$$d_i^2(t) = \sum_{j=1}^{m}(x_j(t) - w_{ji}(t))^2 \tag{1}$$

where $x_j$ is the jth of m inputs, and $w_{ji}$ is the associated weight of the ith processing element. The output of the jth processing element is determined by the following competition.

$$y_j(t) = 1 \quad \text{if } d_j^2(t) \le d_i^2(t) \ \forall \ j \ne i$$
$$y_j(t) = 0 \quad \text{otherwise} \tag{2}$$

The error function which is calculated over all training patterns p is defined by

$$E = \tfrac{1}{2}\sum_{t=1}^{P} d_i^2(t)y_i(t). \tag{3}$$

This error function can be minimized by using the following weight adjustment rule,

$$w_{ji}(t+1) = w_{ji}(t) + \alpha(x_j(t) - w_{ji}(t))y_i(t) \tag{4}$$

where $\alpha$ is the learning rate.

When successfully trained, a network using the above algorithm will have the characteristic that the winning processing elements weights are located at the center of mass of the training points for which that processing element is the winner.

This basic form of unsupervised learning suffers from several problems. The frequencies with which processing elements win the competition will not be equal. The weights can become trapped in local minima, where a processing element never wins the competition in equation (2). The algorithm is sensitive to outliers in the same fashion that standard back propagation is. This is due to the squared distance in the error function.

Several methods have been developed to deal with the problems described above. The topology-preserving feature map of Kohonen (1984) used a neighborhood function to bring inactive processing elements into the competition. In the ART1 architecture, Carpenter and Grossberg (1988) used the concept of vigilance to control the region for which a processing element, on the F2 layer, could win the competition. Grossberg (1987) also suggested a method in which a processing element becomes more or less sensitive based on the frequency of winning and similarly adapts the learning rate. DeSieno (1988) introduced the conscience mechanism to control the frequency of winning of the processing elements and to increase the speed of training. Ahalt (1990) described frequency-sensitive competitive learning in which the distance measure in (2) is replaced by

$$d_i^*(t) = d_i^2(t)u_i(t) \tag{5}$$

where $u_i(t)$ is the total number of times that processing element i has won during training.

While there are many ways to modify the competition to improve utilization, it should be noted that any method that modifies the basic form of unsupervised learning will increase the squared error E of the trained network. Experiments with the conscience mechanism show that if the mechanism is turned off after initial training of a network, that additional training will decrease E. If conscience is reintroduced, additional training will then increase E. To achieve a minimum squared error result, methods modifying the competition should gradually decrease their effect during training. Kohonen's topology preserving feature map decreases the effects of the neighborhood function with time.

When using unsupervised learning to develop typical daily price movements from SP500 stock future data, each trained network would contain a processing element that reflected the extreme price swing that occurred in the October 1987 crash. This was an undesirable effect of the basic form of unsupervised learning. There were two alternative approaches that could be taken to correct this problem. The first was to simply eliminate the data point from the training set and retrain the network. This is not an acceptable choice since it relies on the users expert knowledge to modify the training set. Furthermore, there may be other outliers, that the user is unaware of, that would remain in the solution. The second option was to use a method like the conscience mechanism to decrease the effects of outliers by forcing equiprobable regions. What is needed is a weight adjustment rule that works directly on the effects of outliers without imposing other constraints on the solution.

The median learning algorithm described below appears to provide a more robust method of unsupervised learning.

## ITERATIVE EVALUATION OF THE MEDIAN

From statistics we have seen that the median of a distribution is much less sensitive to outliers than the mean of the distribution. For a given set of data, the median is not effected by the movement of a data point far from the median while the mean is effected more by points far from the mean then by the ones close to it.

To iteratively find the median M of a one dimension continuous distribution, the following method can be used where $\varepsilon$ is a small positive increment amount.

$$
\begin{aligned}
M(t+1) &= M(t)+\varepsilon \quad \text{if } X(t) > M(t) \\
M(t+1) &= M(t)-\varepsilon \quad \text{if } X(t) < M(t)
\end{aligned}
\tag{6}
$$

Using a one dimensional skewed distribution generated by the product of two uniform random variables on the range of 0 to 1 for X(t), and $\varepsilon$ of 0.00001 the above procedure produced M(1000000) = 0.1875, while the mean value for this distribution was 0.2500.

## MEDIAN LEARNING ALGORITHM

By modifying the error function (3) it is possible to produce an algorithm that resembles the iterative calculation of the median in equation (6) that would be less sensitive to outliers. The new error function uses the absolute value of the distance instead of the square of the distance and can be conveniently written as follows.

$$
E = \sum_{t=1}^{P} \sqrt{d_i^2(t)} y_i(t)
\tag{7}
$$

The resulting unsupervised learning algorithm will not effect the calculation of the winning processing element since the processing element with the minimum squared distance will also have the minimum absolute value distance. Therefore, equation (2) is still valid in the median learning algorithm. Only the weight adjustment equation (4) will be effected. The conscience mechanism will be included in the algorithm to guarantee proper utilization of processing elements. The median weight adjustment equation is given by

$$
w_{ji}(t+1) = w_{ji}(t)+\alpha(t)\frac{(x_j(t)-w_{ji}(t))z_i(t)}{\sqrt{d_i^2(t)}} \quad .
\tag{8}
$$

For the one dimensional case (m=1) this equation reduces to equation (6). The learning rate $\alpha(t)$ is made a function of time and should gradually decrease to provide the most efficient learning. One possible schedule for the learning rate is

$$
\alpha(t) = \alpha(0)/\sqrt{t} .
\tag{9}
$$

The winning processing element is replaced by $z_j(t)$ which represents the biased winning processing element at time t for the purposes of weight adjustment ($y_i(t)$ is still used for forward calculations). The bias term $b_j(t)$ is the means by which the conscience mechanism modifies the competition. Then,

$$z_j(t) = 1 \quad \text{if } d_j^2(t) - b_j(t) \le d_i^2(t) - b_j(t) \quad \forall \ j \ne i$$
$$z_j(t) = 0 \quad \text{otherwise} \tag{10}$$

where,

$$b_j(t) = C(t)(\tfrac{1}{n} - p_j(t)) \tag{11}$$

The factor $C(t)$ represents the time varying bias factor and n is the number of processing elements in the competitive layer. $C(t)$ determines the maximum distance a losing processing element can reach in order to win the competition. This distance should gradually decrease with time unless equiprobable regions are desirable. $C(0)$ / n should be no larger than the maximum distance between any two training examples. Let $p_j(t)$ represent the fraction of time that processing element j has won the competition. An effective means of evaluating this probability during training is:

$$p_j(t+1) = p_j(t) + B(z_j(t) - p_j(t)) \tag{12}$$

where B is the probability smoothing constant. B should normally be set to a value smaller than the reciprocal of the number of items in the training set.


## SP500 FUTURE APPLICATION

The goal in training a network on the SP500 future data was determine on a daily basis, typical trading patterns. The training data used in this test was derived from 1266 days of price data from April 1985 to December 1990. Each training example consisted of inputs representing the change in the price of the future relative to the open at 50 evenly spaced points during the trading day. Using the difference of current price from the opening price eliminates the effects of price trends seen over the 1266 days of data.

Two networks were trained so that the effects of median learning could be compared. For the purposes of this report, each network contained only 15 processing elements. Both networks started with the same initial weights and similar settings for the conscience mechanism. The first "normal" network used equation (4) for weight adjustments and the second "median" network used equation (8) for weight adjustments but left $\alpha(t)$ and $C(t)$ constant during the training. An initial training run of 20,000 passes through the training data was made with each network with the conscience bias factor $C(t)$ set to 50000 for the normal network and 2000 for the median network. The median network requires less bias to achieve equiprobable regions. The probability smoothing constant B was 0.0002 for both networks. At the end of training, both networks had stabilized.

Training was then continued without the conscience mechanism. The root mean squared error showed a greater decrease in the normal than the median networks when the conscience mechanism was turned off, as seen in table 1.

| Network | RMS Error | Mean Error | Median Error |
|---|---|---|---|
| Normal Initial Training | 10.703162 | 5.787240 | 4.297020 |
| Median Initial Training | 11.219157 | 5.727911 | 4.162272 |
| Normal Final Training | 8.164830 | 5.582677 | 4.562539 |
| Median Final Training | 10.974318 | 5.619861 | 4.272989 |

Table 1. Error results for the normal and median trained networks.

This effect is due to the fact that the conscience mechanism attempts to form equiprobable regions pulling the normal processing elements away from the outliers. When conscience is removed (final training) some processing elements are pulled back toward the outliers to lower the squared error. The comparison of root mean squared error and median error provide an effective means of comparing the two algorithms. The median learning algorithm consistently produced lower median error regardless of the use of the conscience mechanism, while the use of conscience consistently increased the RMS error. The comparison of the mean error statistic to the median error shows the skew caused by the outliers in the training data. The median error was lower when median learning and the conscience mechanism were used in combination than when either were used alone. Therefore, if minimum median error is the goal of training, the conscience mechanism should always be used.

The final weights of the two networks are plotted in figure 1 and figure 2. Each line segment in the figure shows a plot of the 50 weights of a processing element, and represents a plot of a typical price movement during a trading day.

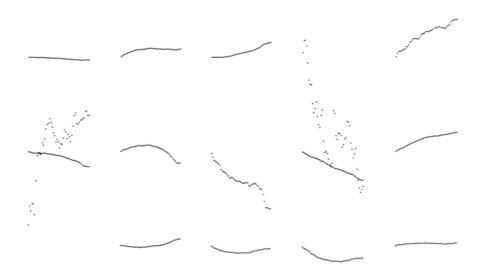

Figure 1. Weights of normal network (15 processing elements 50 inputs).

It is easy to see the effects of outliers on the processing elements of the normal network. The 4th processing element shows the crash. When the number of processing elements in the network is increased, the effects of outliers become more pronounced.

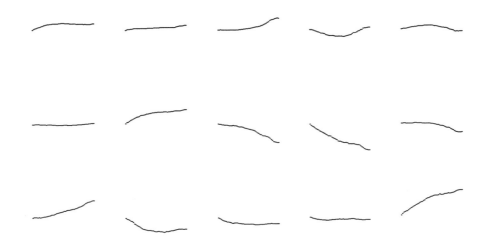

Figure 2. Weights of median network (15 processing elements 50 inputs).

## CONCLUSION

The combination of median learning and the conscience mechanism appear to be an effective method for controlling the influence of outliers in unsupervised learning. The implementation of median learning is simple and could be used as an alternative in most unsupervised learning algorithms.

The results of training on the SP500 future data illustrate the importance of tailoring of the learning algorithm to meet the requirements of the learning task. The small number of processing elements used here made illustration of the concepts easier. Increasing the number of processing elements produces more distinct features in trained networks. Work with the SP500 data is continuing to determine if the trading patterns produced by median learning can be used to predict price movements.

## REFERENCES

Ahalt, S., Krishnamurthy, A., Chen, P. and Melton, D. (1990). Competitive Learning Algorithms for Vector Quantization. *Neural Networks*, **3**, pp. 277-290.
Carpenter, G. and Grossberg, s. (1988). The ART of Adaptive Pattern Recognition by a Self-Organizing Neural Network. *IEEE Computer*, March, pp. 77-88.
DeSieno, D. (1988) Adding a Conscience to Competitive Learning. *IEEE International Conference on Neural Networks*, pp. I117-I124.
Grossberg, S. (1987) Competitive Learning: From Interactive Activation to Adaptive Resonance. *Cognitive Science*, **11**, pp. 23-63.
Kohonen, T. (1984) *Self-Organization and Associative Memory*, Springer-Verlag, New York.

# Assemblies of neural elements with adaptively expanding structure.

Simon A. Katz

Alex S. Katz

Multi Spectrum Technologies, 914 Arizona Ave, #1, 90401

(310) 576-0419

## Abstract

A new class of neural net type structures that can adaptively expand, increasing their complexity, is described and tested on medical and rock mechanics data. These are two-layer structures with the first layer presented as an assembly of the neural elements. Each element may be a one node perceptron or a multi-node neural net. Each element has its own cost function. The elements of the assembly interact with each other in such a way that the procedure of the assembly synthesis is reduced to the consecutive synthesis of individual neural elements. The accuracy of an individual neural element in the assembly is described by its output error. The output error of each neural element is cascading to the next element, where it becomes the expected output. The whole assembly is characterized by the global error. Given a set of neural elements and a rule for their initialization , a number of the neural elements in the assembly increases until an estimate of the global error decreases to such a level that it satisfies a predefined condition.

## Introduction

The aim of this paper is to introduce a class of neural net type structures, aimed at prediction of values of unknown parameter or at pattern recognition. These structures will be called here "cascading assemblies of neural elements". Their building blocks, called "neural elements", are either one-node perceptrons or multi-node neural nets with partially predefined structure (predefined in terms of a number of layers and number of nodes in each layer, but not in terms of weights defining interconnections between nodes). The synthesis of the assembly is understood as a problem of calculation of a number of elements in the assembly and synthesis of these elements (e.g. estimation of interconnection weights in the neural elements included in the assembly). The main advantage of this methodology is that the neural elements in the assembly interact with each other in such a way that the synthesis of the assembly is reduced to solution of a sequence of two problems: (a) synthesis of the current neural element under condition that elements preceding it in the assembly are fixed, and (b) formation of a desired output for the neural element that should be synthesized at the next step.

The standard feed-forward backpropagation neural net is synthesized by minimization of the estimate of its squared output error

$$\varepsilon(\mathbf{v}) = \sum_{\mathbf{x}_i \subset \Omega} (F(\mathbf{x_i}, \mathbf{v}) - y_i)^2 \tag{1}$$

Here, $\mathbf{v}$ is a vector of parameters of the neural element,

$\mathbf{x_i}$ is the input data-vector, which belongs to the training data-set $\Omega$,

$y_i$ is a desired output corresponding to the input $x_i$.

Backpropagation of the error (1) allows for optimization of the linear weights defining the interconnections and for estimation of optimal parameters of activation functions in the nodes of the neural net. Such important parameters of the neural net as the total number of nodes in each layer and the number of layers are usually defined in advance, before the process of minimization of th error (1) starts. This may lead to two kinds of complications when neural nets are applied to real life data: (a) If the structure of the neural net is too simple with an insufficient total number of nodes, it may perform poorly on the data from the training set and have large approximation error (1). This is the problem of underfitting. (b) If the total number of the nodes in the neural net is too large, the approximation error (1) may be very small, while the neural net may perform poorly on data that do not belong to the training set, thus leading to the problem of overfitting.

In the design of the cascading assembly of neural elements the accuracy of each neural element is described by its output error, which is cascading to the next element, where it becomes the expected output. The whole structure of the cascading assembly is characterized by the global error, which is the error of the last neural element.

The main advantage of this design is that its complexity is not fixed in advance. The assembly starts with a single neural element that may be underfitting and then proceeds with the consecutive inclusion of additional neural elements to decrease the global output error to a desired level. Importantly, the total number of elements in the assembly is not fixed and is defined during the process of the assembly synthesis.

## Number of neural elements in the assembly

The cascading assembly is presented as a two-layer structure with the neural elements included in the first layer. The scheme of the cascaded assembly consisting of three neural elements is shown in the Figure 1. The neural elements in the assembly are indexed from 1 to $P+1$ and the accuracy of the neural element with index p is characterized by its cost function

$$\varepsilon_p(\mathbf{v}) = \sum_{\mathbf{x}_i \subset \Omega} (F(\mathbf{x}_i, \mathbf{v}_p) - y_{i,p})^2 \tag{2}$$

Where $y_{i,p}$ is the desired output for the neural element with index p and input $\mathbf{x}_i$.

According to (2), all neural elements in the assembly are synthesized using the same set of input data-vectors, but a desired output for different elements vary from one element to another. According to the Fig. 1, the desired output for the neural element with index $p+1$ is the output error of the element with the index $p$.

The accuracy of the whole assembly is characterized by its global error

$$\delta(\mathbf{v}_1, \ldots, \mathbf{v}_{P+1}) = \sum_{\mathbf{x}_i \subset \Omega} (A(\mathbf{x}_i, \mathbf{v}_1, \ldots, \mathbf{v}_{P+1}) - g_i)^2 \tag{3}$$

where $A(\mathbf{x_i}, \mathbf{v}_1, \ldots, \mathbf{v_{P+1}})$ is the output of the assembly consisting of P+1 elements, $\mathbf{x_i}$ is the input data-vector, $g_\mathbf{i}$ is the desired output of the assembly, corresponding to $\mathbf{x_i}$. Equations (2) and (3) show the fundamental difference between a neural net with the cost function (1) and an cascading assembly of neural elements. The accuracy of a neural net is defined by its cost function (1). Its vector of parameters is obtained via minimization of this cost function. Individual nodes in the neural net do not have quality characteristics. As for the cascading assembly of the neural elements, each of its neural elements has its own quality characteristics. It will be shown further that the cascading assembly may be synthesized via minimization of the cost functions (2) describing the accuracy of the individual neural elements of the assembly. To synthesize an accurate cascading assembly the index P in (3) is increased and for each value of P a minimum of the cost function (3) is to be found. This process is to be continued iteratively until conditions of the type

$$\delta(\mathbf{v}_1, \ldots, \mathbf{v_{P+1}}) \leq \sigma_0 \tag{4}$$

or

$$\delta(\mathbf{v}_1, \ldots, \mathbf{v_P}) - \delta(\mathbf{v}_1, \ldots, \mathbf{v_{P+1}}) \leq \sigma_1 \tag{5}$$

are met.

A minimal value of the index P for which (4) or (5) holds is the desired number of the neural elements in the cascading assembly. The exact structure of the assembly and the number of its neural elements is not determined in advance, but rather defined during the process of the assembly synthesis and minimization of its global error (4).

Increase of the index P in Eqs. (4) or (5) means inclusion of additional elements in the assembly. It will be shown in the following section, that interaction of the neural elements may be organized in such a way that in order to increase the number of elements in the assembly by one, one only has to synthesize a neural element with the index P+1, while the elements with indexes $p \leq P$ are kept unchanged.

**Global error of the cascading assembly**

We consider here a two-layer structure of neural elements, where all of the neural elements are in the first layer. The output of the first layer is the vector of outputs of the neural elements

$$O_{i,p} = F(\mathbf{X_i}, \mathbf{V_p}) \tag{6}$$

The output of the second layer is the output of the assembly and is of the form

$$A_i = \sum_{p=1}^{P+1} O_{i,p} \tag{7}$$

The assembly starts with a single neural element, the cost function of which is defined as

$$\varepsilon(\mathbf{v}_1) = \sum_{\mathbf{x_i} \subset \Omega} (F(\mathbf{x_i}, \mathbf{v}) - y_{\mathbf{i},1})^2 \tag{8}$$

where

$$y_{\mathbf{i},1} = g_i, \tag{9}$$

$g_i$ is the desired output of the cascading assembly for the input data-vector $\mathbf{x_i}$.
The desired output of the neural element with index p is defined as follows

$$y_{i,p+1} = y_{i,p} - O_{i,p} \tag{10}$$

and its cost function is defined by (2).

According to (9), the desired output for the neural element with index p+1 is the output error of the neural element with index p.

It follows from (9) and (10) that the output of the assembly (7) may be written in the form

$$A_i = g_i - y_{i,2} + \sum_{p=2}^{P+1} (y_{i,p} - y_{i,p+1}) \tag{11}$$

Therefore, we have

$$A_i = g_i - y_{i,P+1} \tag{12}$$

where, according to (10)

$$y_{i,P+1} = y_{i,P} - O_{i,P} \tag{13}$$

Hence, the global error of the cascading assembly may be written as

$$A_i = g_i - \delta g_i \tag{14}$$

$$\delta g_i = y_{i,P} - O_{i,P} \tag{15}$$

where $g_i$ is the desired output of the cascading assembly, $\delta g_i$ is the global error of the assembly resulting from the input vector $\mathbf{x}_i$. The global squared error of the assembly, according to (3) and (14) is

$$\sigma(v_1,\ldots,v_{P+1}) = \sum_{\mathbf{x_i}} \delta g_i^2 \quad \sigma(v_1,\ldots,v_{P+1}) = \sum_{\mathbf{x_i}} \delta g_i^2 \tag{16}$$

**Synthesis of the cascading assembly**
The final structure of the cascading assembly is obtained as the result of the multistep optimization, in which the cost functions of all the neural elements are minimized sequentially. The vector of parameters of the *p*-th neural element is obtained from the characteristic equation

$$\varepsilon_{p+1}(\mathbf{v}_{p+1}) = \min_{\mathbf{v}} \sum_{\mathbf{x_i} \subset \Omega} (F(\mathbf{x_i}, \mathbf{v}) - y_{i,p+1})^2 \tag{17}$$

According to (9). (10) and (17), after the *p*-th neural element is synthesized and optimized, its error is cascaded to the neural element *p+1*, where it becomes the desired output.

## Examples of application of the neural assemblies to problems in medical science and rock mechanics

Figs. 2 and 3 show two examples of pattern recognition and prediction based on the use of the assemblies of neural elements. Fig. 2 shows medical application of the neural asembly. At this figure we show the results of classification of a group of patients in two groups - low and high post-operative risk, basing on pre-operative data. Fig. 3 is a geological application. It shows the results of prediction of porosity of rock samples, when measurements of seismic velocities and information on lithology of the rock were used as input data. Threshold for classification (Fig. 2) is shown by a solid line at the level 0.55. Samples 1 -60 and 61 to 62 are respectively from high and low risk group. Correct classification for the samples 1 -60 - the output is larger than threshold, for the samples 61 - 120, the correct output is smaller than threshold. In the case of porosity prediction - continuous line is actual porosity, dashed line is prediction. In the both cases, the neural elements in the assembly were taken in the form of one node perceptrons. In total, five elements were used in the assemblies.

## Conclusions

A new type of a neural system called cascading assembly of neural elements was developed and tested on medical and geological data. The new system is constructed as a two-layer structure, The first layer consists of indexed neural elements, for which any type of a neural network may be used. It also is responsible for cascading of the approximation approximation error where the error of one neural element becomes the desired output for the next one. When the error, that propagates from one neural element to another, becomes sufficiently small, the neural structure stops growing. Therefore, the value of the propagating error itself defines the necessity of expansion for the cascading assembly and the complexity of the resulting structure. The benefit of the system is in the simplicity of the system's expansion where at each step only one neural element of a simple predefined structure needs to be optimized. Additionally, the system stops expanding when adequate levels of approximation are reached.

## References

Domay, E. Van Hemman J. L., Shulten, K. S., 1991. Models of neural networks. Springer-Verlag

Katz, A. , Katz S. , Wickman E., Quijano R. C., 1993. Prediction of Valve related complications for artificial heart valves using adaptive neural networks. J. Heart Valve Dis. Vol. 2, No 5: 504-508

Katz, S., and Aki, K., 1992. Experiments with a neural net based earthquake prediction. Proceedings of Int. AGU meeting. 73, 43:366

Kosko, B., 1992. Neural networks for signal processing. Prentice Hall

Yoh-Han Pao, 1989. Adaptive Pattern Recognition in Neural Networks. Addison Wesley Publ. Co., Inc.

# Cascading Assembly of Neural Elements

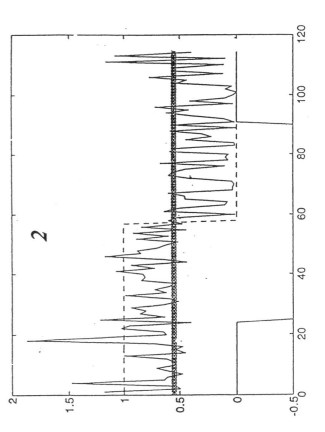

*1*

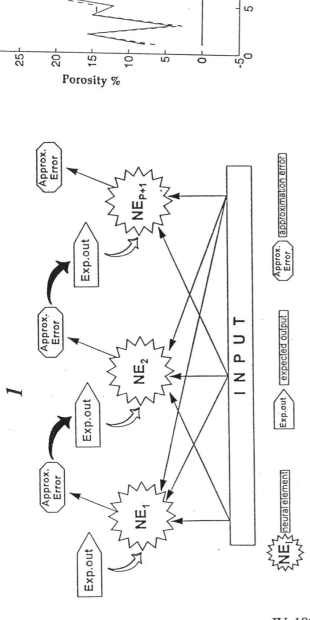

*2*

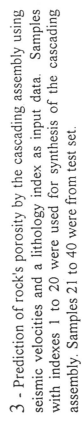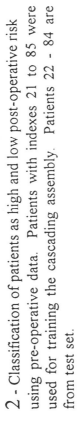

*3*

2 - Classification of patients as high and low post-operative risk using pre-operative data. Patients with indexes 21 to 85 were used for training the cascading assembly. Patients 22 - 84 are from test set.

3 - Prediction of rock's porosity by the cascading assembly using seismic velocities and a lithology index as input data. Samples with indexes 1 to 20 were used for synthesis of the cascading assembly. Samples 21 to 40 were from test set.

# Unsupervised Learning with the Soft-Means Algorithm

Chris Thornton
Cognitive and Computing Sciences
University of Sussex
Brighton BN1 9QN
Email: Chris.Thornton@cogs.susx.ac.uk

December 7, 1993

## Abstract

This note describes a useful adaptation of the 'peak seeking' regime used in unsupervised learning processes such as competitive learning and 'k-means'. The adaptation enables the learning to capture low-order probability effects and thus to more fully capture the probabilistic structure of the training data.

Relevant areas: automated discovery, neural networks

## 1 Introduction

Unsupervised learning involves discovering the underlying structure of a dataset without knowing how the individual data items are classified. This has been recognized as a hard problem in machine learning [1]. Many unsupervised learning methods operate by trying to find the 'prototypes' of the dataset. The usual approach here is to search for the density peaks in the distribution of training data. This can be done by explicit clustering [2], say, or by some iterative method such as competitive learning [3] or k-means clustering [4, 5].

Methods which seek out density peaks effectively sample the probabilistic structure of the data. However, they are only sensitive to, and can therefore only exploit, the $n$th-order structure of the data (where $n$ is the number of inputs variables), i.e., the probabilities associated with *complete* data items. However, there are other aspects of the probabilistic structure which may be captured. In particular, there are the various $m$th-order probabilities (where $m < n$, $m > 0$), all of which may appear in both conditional and unconditional forms.

Consider the following dataset:

| x1 | x2 | x3 | x4 | x5 |
|----|----|----|----|----|
| 0 | 1 | 0 | 0 | 1 |
| 0 | 1 | 0 | 1 | 1 |
| 0 | 1 | 1 | 0 | 1 |
| 0 | 1 | 1 | 1 | 1 |
| 1 | 0 | 1 | 0 | 0 |
| 1 | 0 | 1 | 0 | 1 |
| 1 | 0 | 1 | 1 | 0 |
| 1 | 0 | 1 | 1 | 1 |
| 1 | 1 | 0 | 0 | 1 |
| 1 | 1 | 0 | 1 | 1 |
| 1 | 1 | 1 | 0 | 0 |
| 1 | 1 | 1 | 0 | 1 |
| 1 | 1 | 1 | 1 | 0 |
| 1 | 1 | 1 | 1 | 1 |

This is based on five binary variables, x1, x2, x3, x4 and x5. The dataset shows very little $n$th-order structure, which is to say there are no obvious density peaks. This is confirmed by the dendrogram produced from a conventional, hierarchical clustering process (see Figure 1) applied to the training data. The leaf nodes in the dendrogram are the numbers (subscripts) of individual data items and the internal nodes are the maximum distances for items in the relevant cluster. Note the general homogeneity of the structure and, in particular, how all the internal distances [6] for the initial clusters are the same.

Of course, the apparent absence of density peaks in a dataset does not mean that it has no probabilistic structure. In the present case, variables x2 and x5 are, in fact, conditionally related, as are variables x1 and x3, since

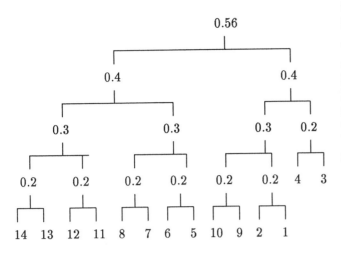

Figure 1:

```
P(x2=1|x5=1) = 1
P(x1=1|x3=1) = 1
```

and

```
P(x5=1|x2=1) = 1
p(x3=1|x1=1) = 1
```

In addition to these conditional effects there are various unconditional effects to be taken into account. For example, P(x1=1) substantially exceeds the chance value for a binary variable. These conditional and unconditional $m$th-order probabilities are not necessarily reflected in the $n$th-order statistics and therefore are not exploited by methods that looks solely for density peaks. However, they form an important aspect of the probabilistic structure of the data and may be vital for purposes such as prediction, data compression or classification.

## 2  The soft-means algorithm

The contribution of the present paper is to show that a subclass of the peak-seeking methods can be adapted so as to take into account the 'low-order' aspects of the probabilistic structure. The subclass includes all methods which operate by moving 'centres' towards density peaks (e.g., competitive learning and k-means clustering). The adaptation involves associating each component of each centre with a confidence weight which

is then allowed to converge on the 'accuracy' value for that component.

We can illustrate the adaptation using a variant of competitive learning. In its simplest form competitive learning works with some prespecified set of centres. Each of these is a vector $V$ of $n$ components. The response of a particular centre to a particular input vector is just the negated sum of absolute differences between the input components and the vector components:

$$-\sum |X_i - V_i|$$

For each input vector, the algorithm selects the centre with the highest response and then changes each component of the vector by

$$r(X_i - V_i)$$

where $r$ is the learning rate.

To sensitize the method to lower-order probabilistic structure we associate each centre with a vector $W$ of confidence weights. We modify the response function so that the response of a centre to an input is

$$-\sum W_i(|X_i - V_i|)$$

and arrange for the weight vectors to be updated at the end of each training epoch so that each $W_i$ moves towards the normalized accuracy of the corresponding $V_i$. The unnormalized accuracy value for the $i$th component of a particular centre is just

$$\sum |X_i - V_i|$$

With this adaptation in place, the confidence weights for each centre are adapted as the centres converge towards the density peaks. Due to the effective decay of confidence weights on low-quality peak components (i.e., components providing relatively inaccurate estimates of input values) the process is able to discover density peaks in subspaces of the input space. This enables it to capture $m$th-order probability effects in an $n$-dimensional input space ($m < n$).

A graphical illustration of the adapted learning process is provided in Figure 2. The top box in this figure represents a 3-dimensional input space. The small circles are data points (training inputs) and the Xs are the centres. Within a conventional peak-seeking regime, the relatively compact clusters might be expected to successfully attract centres to their peaks. However, the cluster situated in the front-left of the space, which is distributed uniformly in the vertical dimension, would pose a problem since it has no obvious density peak.

The adapted competitive learning regime copes gracefully with this scenario. The vertical distribution of the problematic cluster would produce low accuracy values for the 'vertical' component of any nearby centre. This would lead to the weight on that component decaying which would, in turn, lead to the cluster being 'compressed' vertically, giving it a more distinct peak. The general form of this process is illustrated in the middle and bottom boxes in Figure 2.

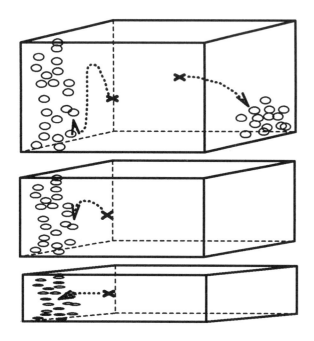

Figure 2:

## 3  Applications

I use the term 'soft-means algorithm' to label the modified peak-seeking regime described above. The following two examples illustrate the behaviour of this algorithm. In the first example the algorithm is applied to the training data from above:

```
x1 x2 x3 x4 x5
 0  1  0  0  1
 0  1  0  1  1
 0  1  1  0  1
```

```
0  1  1  1  1
1  0  1  0  0
1  0  1  0  1
1  0  1  1  0
1  0  1  1  1
1  1  0  0  1
1  1  0  1  1
1  1  1  0  0
1  1  1  0  1
1  1  1  1  0
1  1  1  1  1
```

The behaviour of the algorithm is illustrated by the listing below. This shows the behaviour of the centres through the first ten epochs of processing. Each segment of the listing is headed with the relevant epoch number and contains just two lines. The first line shows the state of centre 1 (in the relevant epoch). The second line shows the state of centre 2. The bracketed part of each line shows the components and weights of the relevant centre. Each colon separates one component/weight pair. The component value appears before the colon; the weight comes after. Both values are real numbers in the range 0-1 but only the first two decimal places are shown. (1.00 always appears as '99').

```
Epoch 1
1  {99:50 99:50 00:50 99:50 99:50}
2  {00:50 99:50 99:50 00:50 99:50}

Epoch 2
1  {90:56 99:67 20:64 87:53 99:67}
2  {79:65 70:52 97:73 43:56 54:56}

Epoch 3
1  {65:41 99:81 19:67 72:47 99:81}
2  {94:76 72:35 99:89 56:39 57:30}

Epoch 4
1  {53:33 99:90 28:54 60:32 99:90}
2  {99:89 71:20 99:95 60:23 56:18}

Epoch 5
1  {50:24 99:95 30:38 57:22 99:95}
2  {99:95 71:12 99:98 61:14 56:11}

Epoch 6
1  {49:16 99:97 31:25 56:15 99:97}
2  {99:98 71:08 99:99 61:09 56:07}

Epoch 7
1  {49:11 99:98 31:17 56:11 99:98}
```

```
2  {99:99 71:05 99:99 61:06 56:05}

Epoch 8
1  {49:07 99:99 31:11 56:08 99:99}
2  {99:99 71:03 99:99 61:04 56:03}

Epoch 9
1  {49:05 99:99 31:08 56:06 99:99}
2  {99:99 71:02 99:99 61:02 56:02}

Epoch 10
1  {49:03 99:99 31:05 56:04 99:99}
2  {99:99 71:01 99:99 61:02 56:01}
```

Note how the two centres rapidly 'capture' the two main probabilistic effects in the training data, namely

$$P(x2=1|x5=1)/P(x5=1|x2=1) = 1$$
$$p(x1=1|x3=1)/P(x3=1|x1=1) = 1$$

# 4  Supervised learning with soft-means

The soft-means algorithm's sensitivity to low-order probabilistic effects often enables it to reproduce the functionality associated with *supervised* learning processes. To elicit supervised learning from soft-means, we form a set of vectors by appending each input from the relevant training set to its corresponding output. We then feed these to the algorithm as pure input vectors. To test the algorithm's 'output' on a test input, we present the algorithm with the test input appended to a null output (which is ignored by the algorithm) and then return the output component from the most strongly responsive unit.

In many cases, this approach enables the algorithm to produce performance on supervised learning problems comparable to fully supervised algorithms. For example, consider the algorithm's performance on the benchmark problem known as the 'third MONKS problem' [7]. The underlying rule for this problem is as follows.

```
   (attribute_5 = 3 and attribute_4 = 1)
 or (attribute_5 != 4 and attribute_2 != 3)
 (with "!=" denoting inequality).
```

A small sample of the training set (which contains 5% misclassifications) is as follows.

```
1 1 1 1 1 2  -->   1
1 1 1 1 2 1  -->   1
1 1 1 1 2 2  -->   1
1 1 1 1 3 1  -->   0
1 1 1 1 4 1  -->   0
1 1 1 2 1 1  -->   1
1 1 1 2 2 2  -->   1
1 1 1 2 4 2  -->   0
1 1 2 1 2 2  -->   1
1 1 2 1 4 2  -->   0
1 1 2 2 2 2  -->   1
1 1 2 2 4 1  -->   0
```

The initial two centres generated by the soft-means algorithm applied to these training data are as follows.

```
Epoch 2
1  {98:83 93:72 83:38 51:35 62:27 69:12 00:99}
2  {98:93 28:62 50:26 76:50 56:59 60:23 99:98}
```

Using the output-generation procedure described above, these produce a classification accuracy on the testing data of 87%. This is comparable to the accuracy produced by several of the supervised algorithms in the original MONKS study.

# 5  Summary

The paper has described an enhancement of the 'peak-seeking' regime for unsupervised learning. As far as the author has been able to ascertain, this enhancement has not yet been investigated by the community. Its main advantage is that it enables the regime to capture probabilistic structure involving low-order probabilistic effects (i.e., effects which impact sub-spaces of the input space). A secondary advantage is that it enables the reproduction of supervised-learning functionality without necessitating the explicit classification of training inputs. The algorithm would appear to have possible applications in any task requiring unsupervised learning and to suggest a possible form for a novel neural-network learning method.

# References

[1] Duda, R. and Hart, P. (1973). *Pattern Classification and Scene Analysis*. New York: Wiley.

[2] Van Ryzin, J. (1977). *Classification and Clustering*. London: Academic Press.

[3] Rumelhart, D. and Zipser, D. (1986). Feature discovery by competitive learning. In D. Rumelhart, J. McClelland and the PDP Research Group (Eds.), *Parallel Distributed Processing: Explorations in the Microstructures of Cognition. Vol I* (pp. 151-193). Cambridge, Mass.: MIT Press.

[4] Darken, C. and Moody, J. (1990). Fast adaptive k-means clustering: some empirical results. *Proceedings of IJCNN, San Diego*.

[5] Selim, S. and Ismail, M. (1984). K-means-type algorithms: a generalized convergence theorem and characterization of local optimality. *IEEE Transactions on Pattern Analysis and Machine Intelligence, 6*, No. 1 (pp. 81-87).

[6] Everitt, B. (1974). *Cluster Analysis*. London: Heinemann.

[7] Thrun, S., Bala, J., Bloedorn, E., Bratko, I., Cestnik, B., Cheng, J., De Jong, K., Dzeroski, S., Fisher, D., Fahlman, S., Hamann, R., Kaufman, K., Keller, S., Kononenko, I., Kreuziger, J., Michalski, R., Mitchell, T., Pachowicz, P., Reich, Y., Vafaie, H., Van de Welde, W., Wenzel, W., Wnek, J. and Zhang, J. (1991). The MONK's problems - a performance comparison of different learning algorithms. CMU-CS-91-197, School of Computer Science, Carnegie-Mellon University.

# Local Stochastic Competition for Vector Quantification of Images

M. Graña, A. D´Anjou, A. I. Gonzalez, F.X. Albizuri, M. Cottrell*
Dept. CCIA Univ. Pais Vasco/EHU[1]
Aptdo 649, 20080 San Sebastián, España
e-mail: ccpgrrom@si.ehu.es
* SAMOS Univ. Paris I

**Abstract**: We propose a distributed stochastic procedure for the Vector Quantization of images with a given codebook. We call this procedure Local Stochastic Competition (LSC). The main feature of LSC is that it would allow an almost fully parallel implementation of the image codification process. Empirical evidence on image codification show that LSC can be easily tuned to behave as a good approximation to the usual NN (Nearest Neighbour) rule for codification. Besides that two new algorithms somehow based on LSC (Isodata-LSC and Local Stochastic Learning Rule) for codebook design are empirically tested. Isodata-LSC is a perturbed version of the classical Isodata clustering algorithm (GLA in VQ literature), where the random component is introduced by the LSC codification rule. Local Stochastic Learning Rule (LSLR) is a corruption of the Soft-Competition learning rule. In essence it consists in the local updating of the set of winning codevectors selected via LSC. More detailed definitions can be found elsewhere [18]. A key set of parameters in the LSC procedure and related VQ design algorithms are the assumed temperatures at which the codification is attempted. These temperatures are proportional to the assumed variances of the clusters around the codevectors. In some experiments an empirical estimation of these parameters is used. Also the ability of Soft-Competition and LSLR to provide useful estimates of them has been tested.

# Experimental details

The experiments were programmed in C on a SUN machine. Experimental data consists on a set of 24 images of (512,768) pixels. Each pixel was quantified by 256 grey levels. The experiments were aiming to reach a 1/8 compression, giving an information rate of 1bit per pixel. Vector decomposition of the images were obtained taking row vectors of 8 pixels.

The euclidean distance was used and the space considered was $\mathbb{R}^8$. The codebook design algorithms were applied to samples of (320,320) pixels obtained by extracting the central square of each image. The codebook design algorithms provide one codebook for each image.

The percentage of degradation induced by the LSC procedure is given for each case. For the SNR this degradation is computed as $(SNR_{NN}-SNR_{LSC}) / SNR_{NN}$, while for the distortion is computed as $(Distorsión_{LSC}-Distorsión_{NN}) / Distorsión_{LSC}$. This distinction is

---

[1]This work is being supported by a research grant from the Excma. Diputación de Guipuzcoa

due to the nature of each measure: While SNR is an increasing measure of the codification goodness, distortion is a decreasing measure of it.

The initial codebooks were obtained by assignement of the n-th sample vector to the mod(n,256)-th partition or codevector. This procedure gives relatively poor initial estimations of the codebook, which provide better contrast of the relative abilities of the codebook design algorithm to avoid local minima in the search for the best codebook.

# Codification using Local Stochastic Competition

Local Stochastic Competition (LSC) is a *local* approach to the codification of input vectors with a given codebook. The procedure is local in the sense that the decision of which region the input is assigned is performed *concurrently* and using only local information (without reference to other codevectors) for all the codevectors in the codebook. Each codevector samples independently a Bernouilli random variable of parameters $\left(p_n(i), 1 - p_n(i)\right)$:

$$P[x_n \in R_i] = p_n(i) = e^{-\frac{d(x_n - y_i)}{\sigma_i^2}} \qquad i \in \{1..N\}$$

These quantities imply that regions $R_i$ are roughly modelled by hiperspheres of radius $\sigma_i^2$ and center $y_i$, an asumption near to the hypothesis of $P(x)$ being a mixture of normal densities with diagonal covariance matrices. The Nearest Neighbour (NN) decisión procedure is the optimal Bayes decision function in the case of equal variances, and LSC is intended as an stochastic aproximation to it. Taken together the $p_n(i)$ probabilities do not form a probability distribution (in general $\sum_{i=1}^{N} p_n(i) \neq 1$). Some algorithms, such as Soft-Competition, normalize these probabilities. This normalization implies the use of non-local information. As our aim is to obtain a fully distributed procedure in wich each codevector performs a decision independently, we avoid normalization. By avoiding nornnalisation we are, roughly, computing and sampling the "a posteriori" probabilities of the codevector classes as if they were isolated one-class classification problems. When an input vector is presented three situations may occur:

> 1- Only one codevector gets a positive outcome of the sampling: the input is unambiguously codified.
> 2- No codevector gives a positive outcome: the input is a *wildshot* . The collection of isolated one-class problems does not cover properly the classification problem, clusters are very sparse or far away from the input vector
> 3- Several codevectors get a positive outcome: there are potential ambiguities in the codification. Clusters overlap upon the input vector, and some extra (random) decision rule is needed.

Figure 1 gives an algorithmic specification of the LSC decision rule. In this procedure, $x_n$ is the input vector, from the sample X, being codified, $k$ is the number of attempts made to codify $x_n$, Y is the codebook, and $\sigma_i$ are the assumed nominal values of the standard deviations of the clusters around the codevectors. Step 4 detecs the occurrence of a wildshot, dealing with it involves increasing the counter $k$, and retrying the classification. Increasing $k$ has the effect of augmenting the clusters variances modeled by $t_i(k)$ for the new attempt. Step 5 detects the occurrence of ambiguities: more than one codevector claims the input vector. This situation is solved by applying a random decision rule over the set $S_k$ of "winning" codevectors.

---

0- $k=0$
1- Built up the probability vector $\mathbf{p}=(p_n(i,k)\ i=1..N)$ computed as follows:

$$p_n(i,k) = e^{-\frac{d(x_n - y_i)}{t_i(k)}}$$

$$t_i(k) = f(k)\sigma_i^2$$

2- Obtain $(u_1,...,u_N)$ random numbers uniformly distributed in $[0,1)$
3- Sample the probabilities in $\mathbf{p}$: Built up the set

$$S_k = \left\{ y_i \in Y \middle| p_n(i,k) \geq u_i \right\}$$

4-If $|S_k| = 0$ a wildshot has occurred, increase $k$ by 1 and go to step 1
5- If $|S_k| > 0$ perform a random selection with equal probabilities in the set $S_k$. If codevector $y_i$ is chosen the codification is its index $i$:

$$C_{LSC}(x_n) = i$$

---

Figure 1 LSC procedure for an input vector $x_n$

In the actual sequential simulation of LSC used in the experiments reported in this paper, the variance increase function used is $f(k)=2^k$. So the occurence of a wildshot has the effect of doubling the assumed variances of the clusters around the codevectors. These variances are reset to their nominal values each time an input vector is presented for classification ($k=0$). In our sequential simulations, the random selection of step 5 is performed by taking as winner the first codevector of $S_k$: that is, the one with the lesser index.

In the experiments reported, we distinguish two versions of the implementations of LSC: LSC1 and LSC2. LSC1 uses a common nominal value for the variance parameter $\sigma_i^2 = \sigma^2$. LSC2 uses local estimations of the codevector nominal cluster variances, usually provided by the VQ design algorithm (Soft-Competition or LSLR).

The mean time employed by an ideal harware implementation to codify an input vector will be proportional to the mean number of attempts needed to clasify an input vector. A sequential NN clasifier will need a time proportional to the codebbok size: o(N). Therefore, we consider $\hat{s} = N/\langle k \rangle$ as an estimation of the speedup (acceleration factor) that an ideal hardware implementation of LSC would obtain against a NN sequential clasifier.

It is easy to verify that the LSC procedure eventually clasifies an input vector. The probability of a wildshot at the $k$-th attempt to classify the input vector $x_n$ can be computed as:

$$P\left[wildshot(x_n,k)\right] = \prod_{i=1}^{N}\left(1 - p_n(i,k)\right) = \prod_{i=1}^{N}\left(1 - e^{-\frac{d(x_n - y_i)}{t_i(k)}}\right)$$

Obviously, as the number of attempts increase, $t_i(k)$ grows and the wildshot probability decreases to 0. The function $f(k)$ determines the speed with which this probability vanishes. The exponential expression used in this paper provides a fast decreasing to zero, but increases the risk of erroneous codifications. We consider as probability of erroneous codification the probability of LSC giving a code other than the NN code $(C_{LSC}(x_n) \neq C_{NN}(x_n))$. Let it be $C_{NN}(x_n)=m$, that is, $y_m$ is the nearest neighbour codevector to the input $x_n$. The probability of getting in the k-th LSC attempt to classify $x_n$ a code other than $m$ is:

$$P\left[error(x_n,k)\right] = P\left[y_m \notin S_k\right] + P\left[y_m \in S_k\right]P\left[C_{LSC} \neq m \,|\, y_m \in S_k\right] = 1 - \frac{p_n(m,k)}{\langle|S_k|\rangle}$$

Is easy to see that as $t_i(k)$ grows this probability converges to $1-1/N$, which means equiprobable selection of the codevector. The conflictive nature of the definition of $f(k)$ becomes evident. Fast increasing functions provide less wildshots, (faster codifications) at the expense of more risk of erroneous codifications. Despite this, we stand with our choice of $f(k)=2^k$ for our simulations, because our aim is to emphasize the acceleration that can be obtained with LSC, and, therefore, our prime desire is to minimize the number of attemps needed to clasify each input vector.

Obviously, good codebooks and good estimations of the cluster variances will increase the probability of "first-shot" codifications, decreasing both the error and the wildshots. Along the paper several algorithms have been used to compute the codebooks (some also giving estimations of the cluster variances) and it becomes clear that good codebooks improve the performance of LSC. In our experiments we have used some empirical values for the cluster variances and, when available, estimations provided by the codebook design algorithm. Fine tuning of the cluster variances seems to be more difficult and less critical that can be expected.

# Summary of results, conclussions and further work

Table 1 gathers together all the results obtained, showing the mean values obtained for the diverse codebook design algorithms, codification methods over the set of images used for the experiments. The figures in this table can be read in several ways. First as a comparison between the codification quality of NN and LSC, it can be said that the degradation of LSC with respect to NN codifications for the SNR measure remains always below the 20%. This degradation could be visually acceptable for some applications. As a comparison tool, the distortion measure has been of little utility in this work, and has produced some extravagant figures. In all the cases the expected speedup that a distributed implementation of LSC could give remains above 64 in our experiments.

Second, as a comparison between codebook design algorithms, it can be said that Isodata-LSC seems to be a fortunate finding, it is easy to implement and it is quite robust. It must be remembered that the initial codeboks were of little quality. Our bare implementation of Soft-Competition performs also quite well. Finally, LSLR could be worth of more study, despite the bad results reported here. The promise of great speedups in the codebok design process is worth some more experimentation and expending of efforts in its numerical tuning. One of the ways of making LSLR useful maybe applying it to the refinement of medium quality initial codebooks, obtained through more elaborate procedures than the plain sample partition used in the experiments in this paper.

Third, the LSC procedure appears to be quite insensitive (with respect to the qualitative measures) to the values of the variances associated to the codevectors, be them local or global. We are working in the definition of expressions for these variances to obtain them from the codebook itself, in order to avoid the empirical determination of their value. Although the mentioned insensitivity to $\sigma$, the use of these expressions could be a source of improvement for the behavior of LSLR.

Our inmediate future work will be addressed to further experimentation of the codebook design algorithms, testing initial codebok design procedures, higher compression ratios, and other code structures (i.e. matrix codes). Further research is intended in the application of LSC and related codebook design algorithms to the vector quantification of sound.

| MEDIDAS | ALGORITMOS | NN | LSC 1 | | LSC 2 | |
|---------|------------|-----|------|------|------|------|
| | | | $\sigma 8$ | % degr. | | % degr. |
| SNR (mean) | Isodata | 20.93 | 17.71 | 15.7 | | |
| | Iso_lsc $\sigma=8$ | 21.69 | 18.97 | 12.85 | | |
| | Softcomp $\sigma=8$ | 20.51 | 17.57 | 14.75 | 17.28 | 16.20 |
| | LSLR | 14.73 | 12.37 | 16.74 | 11.95 | 17.74 |
| Distortion (mean) | Isodata | 1149 | 3763 | 64.73 | | |
| | Iso_lsc $\sigma=8$ | 1277.1 | 2317.2 | 39.68 | | |
| | Softcomp $\sigma=8$ | 1149.8 | 3354.8 | 61.25 | 3117.4 | 50.15 |
| | LSLR | 505.9 | 10730.9 | 93.45 | 1536.8 | 150.27 |
| Expected Speedup $\hat{s}$ | Isodata | | 90.78 | | | |
| | Iso_lsc $\sigma=8$ | | 106.67 | | | |
| | Softcomp $\sigma=8$ | | 97.71 | | 87.37 | |
| | LSLR | | 78.77 | | 84.49 | |

Table 1 Mean results for the codebook design algorithms and codification methods

# References

[1] Ahalt S.C., A.K. Krishnamurthy, P. Chen, D.E. Melton (1990) "Competitive Learning Algorithms for Vector Quantization" Neural Networks 3 pp.277-290

[2] Duda R.O., P.E. Hart (1973) "Pattern Clasification and Scene Analysis" Wiley

[3] Gray R.M. (1984) "Vectort Quantization" IEEE ASSP 1pp.4-29

[4] Gersho A. (1982) "On the structure of vector quantizers" IEEE Trans. Inf. Th. 28(2) pp.157-166

[5] Johnson D.S., Aragon C.R. , McGeoch L.A. , Schevon C. (1989). "Optimization by simulated annealing: an experimental evaluation; part 1, graph partitioning". Oper. Res. 37(6), pp.865-892.

[6] Kirpatrick S., Gelatt C.D. Jr., Vecchi M.P. (1983). "Optimization by simulated annealing". Science 20, pp.671-680.

[7] Kohonen T. (1984) (1988 2nd ed.) "Self-Organization and associative memory" Springer Verlag

[8] Laarhoven P.J.M., Aarts E.H.L. (1987). "Simulated annealing: Theory and Applications". Kluwer, Dordrecht, Neth.

[9] Linde Y., A. Buzo, R.M. Gray (1980) "An algorithm for vector quantizer design" IEEE TRans. Comm. 28 pp.84-95

[10] Nasrabadi NM, Y. Feng (1988) "Vector Quantization of images based upon the Kohonen Self-Organizing feature maps" IEEE Int. Conf. on Neural Net. San Diego pp.1101-1108

[11] Naylor J., K.P. Li (1988) "Analysis of neural network algorithm for vector quantization of speech parameters" Proc. First Ann. INNS Meet. Pergamon Press p.310-315

[12] K. Rose, E. Gurewitz, G.C. Fox "Vector Quantization by Deterministic Annealing" IEEE Trans. Inf. Th. 38(4) pp.1249-1257

[13] Yair E., K. Zeger, A. Gersho (1992) "Competitive Learning and Soft Competition for Vector Quantization" IEEE Trans. Sign. Proc. 40(2) pp.294-308

[14] Zeger K., J. Vaisey, A. Gersho (1992) "Globally Optimal Vector Quantizer design by stochastic relaxation" IEEE Trans. Sign. Proc. 40(2) pp.310-322

[15] Tomassini, L. (1993) "Apprentissage d'une representation statistique et topologique d'un environment" PhD Thesis, Ecole Nationale Superieure de l'Aeronautique et de l'Espace.

[16] M. Graña, A. D'Anjou, F.X. Albizuri, F.J. Torrealdea, M.C. Hernandez (1993) "Local Stochastic Competition and Vector Quantification" in J. Mira, J. Cabestany, A. Prieto (eds) New trends in Neural Computation, LNCS 686, Springer Verlag pp.216-222

[17] N.B Venkateswarlu, P.S.V.S.K. Raju (1993) "Fast Isodata clustering algorithms" Pattern Recognition 25(3) pp.335-342

[18] M. Graña, A. D'Anjou, A. I. Gonzalez, F.X. Albizuri, M. Cottrell "Local Stochastic Competion and Vector Quantification of images" Dept. CCIA Internal Report in progress

# A Neural Architecture for 3-D Object Recognition from Multiple 2-D Views

Gary Bradski † and Stephen Grossberg ‡

Department of Cognitive and Neural Systems,
Boston University, 111 Cummington Street, Boston, Massachusetts 02215

†Supported in part by the National Science Foundation (NSF IRI-90-24877) and the Office of Naval Research (ONR N00014-92-J-1309).

‡Supported in part by the Air Force Office of Scientific Research (AFOSR F49620-92-J-0499), ARPA (AFOSR 90-0083 and ONR N00014-92-J-4015) and the Office of Naval Research (ONR N00014-91-J-4100).

## Abstract

The recognition of 3-D objects from sequences of their 2-D views is modeled by a neural architecture, called VIEWNET, that uses View Information Encoded With NETworks. VIEWNET processes 2-D views of 3-D objects using the CORT-X 2 filter, which discounts the illuminant, regularizes and completes figural boundaries, and removes noise from the images. A log-polar transform is taken with respect to the centroid of the resulting figure and then re-centered to achieve 2-D scale and rotation invariance. The invariant images are coarse coded to further reduce noise, reduce foreshortening effects, and increase generalization. These compressed codes are input into a supervised learning system based on the fuzzy ARTMAP algorithm. Evidence from sequences of 2-D views is accumulated to improve object recognition. Recognition is studied with noisy and clean images using slow and fast learning. VIEWNET is demonstrated on an MIT Lincoln Laboratory database of 2-D views of jet aircraft with and without additive noise. A recognition rate of 90% is achieved with one 2-D view category and of 98.5% correct with three 2-D view categories.

## 1 Introduction

Much research on 3-D visual object recognition relies on appearance based approaches. Appearance based approaches use input imagery to construct 3-D object models. Koenderink and van Doorn (1979) created *Aspect Graphs* consisting of 2-D views of a 3-D object along the nodes of the graph, with legal view transitions indicated by the arcs among nodes. For Koenderink and van Doorn, 2-D views and view transitions are equally important for recognizing the object. Seibert and Waxman (1990a,1990b,1991,1992) have developed a neural network architecture that self-organizes aspect graph representations of 3-D objects from 2-D view sequences. Images of rotating jets were binarized and points of high curvature and the object centroid were found using a reaction-diffusion process. A log-polar transform around the object centroid was used to remove 2-D rotation and scale variations. The result was coarse coded (compressed to 5x5 pixels from 128x128) using Gaussian filters. The coarse codes (25 data points) were fed into an ART 2 (Carpenter and Grossberg 1987b) network for clustering and categorization. These "categorical" 2-D views were then fed into a series of cross-correlation matrices, or view graphs, one for each possible 3-D object, so that views and view transitions could be learned by a 3-D object categorization layer. The 3-D categorization layer incorporated "evidence accumulation" nodes which integrate activations that they receive from learned connections to the correlation matrix. The node receiving maximal evidence in the 3-D layer is chosen as the network's recognition of the 3-D object being viewed.

Seibert and Waxman's approach of automatically generating aspect graphs directly from 2-D imagery comes at a cost: Given $N$ 2-D views and $M$ objects, the architecture must have the potential to encode on order of $M \times N^2$ 2-D view transitions. Another potential problem is that an error in identifying a 2-D view may introduce a spurious 2-D view transition. Finally, unless one presumes a 2-D view frame capture rate fast enough to capture the highest speed movement that an object can make, view transitions may be skipped inadvertently by fast object motion.

As reported in Seibert and Waxman (1992), 75% of the 2-D jet images were ambiguous to some degree. That is, 75% of the 2-D view categories formed by ART 2 gave evidence for more than one type of jet. Even if several views are ambiguous, the transitions between them may unambiguously identify a particular 3-D object. Thus, view transitions are critically important in the Seibert and Waxman architecture, which may then incur the cost of needing up to $M \times N^2$ view transitions.

This paper further develops the perspective that, although multiple views may facilitate recognition, view transitions, as such, may not be needed to achieve high recognition accuracy from one or more views. A neural network architecture, called **VIEWNET**, for **Vi**ew **I**nformation **E**ncoded **W**ith **NET**works is proposed that can categorize individual views with high accuracy, in accord with the human experience that many objects can be identified with a single view, except when they are observed from an unfamiliar perspective or from a perspective that reduces the objects apparent dimension. Single view recognition accuracy of up to 90% is achieved by this architecture on the Seibert and Waxman database.

As diagrammed in Figure 1, the architecture consists of three parts: an image preprocessor, a supervised self-organizing recognition network, and a network to accumulate evidence over multiple views. It is assumed that the figure to be recognized is separated from its background. Neural networks for figure-ground separation that use computations consistent with those in the preprocessors are described in Grossberg (1993) and Grossberg and Wyse (1992). The image figure is then processed by a feedforward network, called the CORT-X 2 filter (Carpenter, Grossberg, and Mehanian, 1989; Grossberg and Wyse, 1991, 1992) that suppresses image noise while it completes and regularizes a boundary segmentation of the figure. The noise-suppressed boundary segmentation is made invariant under 2-D rotation, translation, and scale invariance by a centering, log-polar, centering operation (Schwartz, 1977). The resulting spectra are coarse coded to gain some insensitivity to 3-D deformation effects and to reduce memory requirements. This coarse-coded, invariant spectrum of a noise-suppressed boundary segmentation defines the input vectors to the self-organizing neural network classifier. Fuzzy ARTMAP (Carpenter, Grossberg, Markuzon, Reynolds and Rosen, 1992) was used to categorize the output spectra. Fuzzy ARTMAP can use supervised learning to rapidly fit the number, size, and shape of input categories to the statistical demands of the environment. Each category codes a range of target views. Storage of several learned categories in working memory, followed by a voting procedure, leads to high recognition rates on the test set. Whereas a single view category leads to up to 90% recognition accuracy, voting with two view categories achieves up to 94%, and of three views up to 98.5%.

## 2 Data

The image database used to test the architecture described below consists of multiple 2-D images images of three jets [1]. Video images were taken of 3 jet models: an F-16, an F-18, and an HK-1. Each jet was painted black and suspended by string against a light background to aid in segmentation. The camera was mounted anywhere in an arc around the jets that started at 0.0 degrees above horizontal and went in increments of 4.5 degrees to a maximum of 72.0 degrees above horizontal. For each camera angle, the jets were spun and frames covering one full revolution (an average of 88 frames) were retained resulting in 1200 to 1400 images per object. The images themselves were 128x128 pixel gray scale. The images were then thresholded and binarized into a SUN raster format to form the "raw" database. For our processing, data was turned into a floating point format scaled between 0.0 and 1.0 and an additive noise process was introduced. The noise consisted of a $128 \times 128$ pixel images with each pixel taken from a uniform distribution between 0.0 and 1.0 scaled by a constant $C \geq 0.0$. These scaled, $128 \times 128$ noise images were then added to the $128 \times 128$ jet images prior to preprocessing. Thus, both noise-free and noisy 2-D views covering a half-sphere surrounding the 3-D object were collected, keeping their spatial relationships intact.

Even numbered rotation images from each camera angle were taken as the training set with the odd numbered images forming the test set. The system was trained using random walks over the half-sphere of training images. Testing was done using random walks over the half-sphere of test images so that the paths taken and views seen were never the same between the training and test sets.

---

[1] Special thanks to Michael Seibert, Alan Waxman and MIT Lincoln Laboratory for their assistance and use of their data.

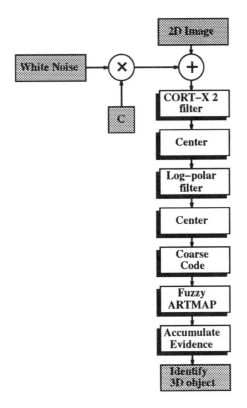

Figure 1: The image processing flow chart of the VIEWNET system from presenting a 2-D image in the image database till the read out of the predicted 3-D object.

## 3  Coarse coding

Coarse coding, or data reduction, reduces memory requirements as it helps to compensate for modest inaccuracies of figural alignment, 3-D viewpoint specific foreshortening, and self-occlusions. On the other hand, too much coarse coding can obscure critical input features and thereby harm recognition performance. Our analysis shows how to balance these effects to maximize the benefits of coarse coding.

Coarse coding of the 2-D images used a spatial averaging method. Spatial averaging consists of convolving the original image $I$ with a function $\Psi$ and then sampling the resultant image with delta functions spaced every $T$ pixels: $\delta(x - nT, y - kT)$. For simplicity, in 1D this is

$$(I * \Psi) \cdot \sum_{n=-\infty}^{\infty} \delta(x - nT). \tag{1}$$

If the Fourier transform of $I$ is $\hat{I}$, and that of $\Psi$ is $\hat{\Psi}$, then the Fourier transform of equation (1) is

$$(\hat{I} \cdot \hat{\Psi}) * \frac{2\pi}{T} \sum_{k=-\infty}^{\infty} \delta(\Omega - k\Omega_s), \tag{2}$$

where $\Omega_s = 2\pi/T$, and $T$ is the sampling period in pixels. If $\Omega_N$ is the highest frequency in the image, then for the image to be uniquely determined by its samples, we must have by the Nyquist sampling theorem that

$$\Omega_s = \frac{2\pi}{T} > 2\Omega_N. \tag{3}$$

Two simple spatial averaging functions $\Psi$ are: (1) uniform averaging of the input image so that all pixels in a window of some width are summed and divided by the number of pixels in the window; (2) Gaussian averaging of the input image so that a normalized, Gaussian weighted sum of all pixels is taken over a window of some width. Both approaches were investigated in this paper.

Method (1) has the problem that uniform averaging is a rectangular filter in the space domain and a sinc function in the frequency domain which introduces high frequency aliasing ("ringing") in the resultant

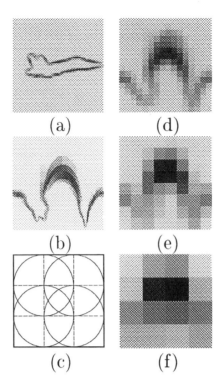

Figure 2: Preprocessing summary. (a) Output of CORT-X 2 preprocessing. (b) Centered log-polar image. (c) Gaussian coarse coding pattern. (d-f) Coarse coding reduction from $128 \times 128$ pixels down to $16 \times 16$, $8 \times 8$, and $4 \times 4$ pixels.

image. The Gaussian function of method (2) is a "smoother" low pass filter and so does not suffer from this problem. A Gaussian is also an eigenfunction of a Fourier transform, which simplifies calculation.

To best set the standard deviation $\sigma$ of the Gaussians, we define two standard deviations away from the Gaussian midpoint to be essentially zero. The cutoff frequency of such a low pass filter is then $\pi/2\sigma$, which by equation (3) yields at equality:

$$\sigma = \frac{T}{2}. \tag{4}$$

Thus, the zero point of each Gaussian just touches the center of the next Gaussian. Figure 2 summarizes the preprocessing: 2(a) shows the output of CORT-X 2, 2(b) the centered log polar transform of (a), 2(c) depicts Gaussian coarse coding according to equation (4), and 2(d-f) show coarse coding down to $16 \times 16$, $8 \times 8$, and $4 \times 4$ pixels.

## 4  Learning and recognition using Fuzzy ARTMAP

A simplified version of the Fuzzy ARTMAP network discussed in Carpenter *et al.* (1992) is used here consisting of a Fuzzy ART module (Carpenter, Grossberg, and Rosen 1991) $ART_a$ and a field of output nodes $F^b$ linked together by an associative memory $F^{ab}$ that is called the *Map Field*. Fuzzy ARTMAP was modified to allow for on-line slow learning from $ART_a$ $F_2^a$ to the Map Field nodes. A maximal $ART_a$ vigilance level, $\bar{\rho}_{max}$ is introduced such that an error at the Map Field triggers match tracking only if match tracking leads to a vigilance $\rho_a \leq \bar{\rho}_{max}$. If $\rho_a > \bar{\rho}_{max}$, learning takes place instead of memory search. By setting the Map Field learning rate $\beta_{ab}$, baseline ($\bar{\rho}$) and maximal ($\bar{\rho}_{max}$) vigilance levels appropriately, weights from $F_2^a$ nodes to the Map Field approximate the conditional probability of the true class given the selected $F_2^a$ category. A related approach to slow probability learning is described in Carpenter, Grossberg, and Reynolds (1993).

| CORT-X 2 filter set | Data presentation | Coarse code using spatial avg / Gaussian avg | | |
|---|---|---|---|---|
| | | 4x4 | 8x8 | 16x16 |
| Small | Ordered | 81.0/83.1 | 84.4/86.4 | 86.7/90.5 |
| Small | Unordered | 80.3/83.9 | 84.9/86.5 | 86.8/89.3 |
| Large | Ordered | 76.8/78.7 | 79.0/81.6 | 79.1/80.1 |
| Large | Unordered | 77.4/79.7 | 80.5/81.5 | 77.1/80.5 |

Table 1: Recognition results on a noise free database ($C = 0$). In the table, "Large" refers to the run with the larger set of CORT-X 2 oriented filters, "Small" refers to the run with the smaller set of filters. Views were presented either in natural order or in random order. Data was coarse coded from 128x128 down to 4x4, 8x8, or 16x16 using simple spatial averaging or Gaussian averaging. Recognition scores refer to the percent of 2-D views correctly associated with a 3-D object.

| % noise surviving CORT-X 2 filtering and Coarse Coding: | | |
|---|---|---|
| | Large CORT-X 2 filters (16x8, 10x5) | Small CORT-X 2 filters (10x5, 6x3) |
| | 1.79 | 2.42 |
| After Gaussian coarse coding from 128x128 down to: | | |
| 16x16 | 0.33 | 0.34 |
| 8x8 | 0.23 | 0.29 |
| 4x4 | 0.19 | 0.26 |
| After spatial average coarse coding from 128x128 down to: | | |
| 16x16 | 0.40 | 0.40 |
| 8x8 | 0.28 | 0.30 |
| 4x4 | 0.21 | 0.28 |

Table 2: Percent of additive white noise surviving processing by CORT-X 2 and coarse coding.

# 5   Simulation results

A computer simulation on the jet airplane database was done using the CORT-X 2 filter with a larger and a smaller pair of oriented filters in order to compare recognition results at different scales. Coarse coding was done with both simple spatial averaging and Gaussian averaging, reducing the image down to $16 \times 16$, $8 \times 8$, and $4 \times 4$ pixels from an original size of $128 \times 128$.

The data were presented to the network in two different ways: (1) 2-D views were presented in the "natural" order in which they would appear if viewing the actual object in motion; (2) 2-D views were presented in random order. This was done to test whether presenting views in natural order helps recognition scores. Training in natural order consisted of 160 runs of from 1 to 50 views over each object. Training in random order consisted of a series of 40 runs of 100 training set views over each object. Recognition scores are taken as an average of fifteen separate training-testing cycles.

## 5.1   Fast learning without noise

No clear advantage results from ordered presentation as compared to unordered presentation using noise-free data ($C = 0$) and fast learning, as shown by the results in Table 1. It can be seen that the smaller CORT-X 2 filter set resulted in better recognition performance overall and did better given more detail (less coarse coding).

## 5.2   Fast learning simulation with noise

The system was next tested with noisy data using additive white noise scaled by $C = 1.0$. Table 2 shows what percent of the additive noise survives processing by CORT-X 2 alone, and by CORT-X 2 and coarse coding together. The percent noise surviving these transformations was measured by the following formula:

$$\max_{\forall (x,y)} \left[ \frac{\Psi(\mathbf{I} + \mathbf{N}) - \Psi(\mathbf{I})}{C} \right] \times 100, \qquad (5)$$

| CORT-X 2 | Data | Coarse code using spatial avg / Gaussian avg | | |
|----------|------|------|------|------|
| filter set | presentation | 4x4 | 8x8 | 16x16 |
| Small | Ordered | 80.1/83.3 | 84.5/85.9 | 84.2/89.1 |
| Small | Unordered | 79.4/83.2 | 83.9/86.4 | 84.3/88.0 |
| Large | Ordered | 76.6/79.4 | 79.3/80.8 | 75.8/79.3 |
| Large | Unordered | 76.0/79.7 | 78.4/80.7 | 75.5/79.0 |

Table 3: Recognition results on noisy data ($C = 1$) with fast learning ($\beta_{ab} = 1.0$). These results differ little from the noise-free results in Table 1 (no noise condition) with the exception of some consistent reduction in scores for the 16x16 coarse coding.

| CORT-X 2 | Data | Coarse code using spatial avg / Gaussian avg | | |
|----------|------|------|------|------|
| filter set | presentation | 4x4 | 8x8 | 16x16 |
| Small | Ordered | [172, 184]/[165, 169] | [77, 73]/[70, 73] | [34, 33]/[33, 35] |
| Small | Unordered | [191, 198]/[175, 179] | [76, 77]/[73, 76] | [34, 35]/[35, 36] |
| Large | Ordered | [168, 179]/[160, 162] | [71, 68]/[67, 71] | [31,33 ]/[30, 31] |
| Large | Unordered | [183, 192]/[169, 174] | [73, 75]/[69, 72] | [32, 32]/[33, 32] |

Table 4: Average number of $ART_a$ categories formed during training for the simulations of Table 1 (no noise) and Table 3 (noise). The format in the table is as follows: [spatial avg.]/[Gaussian avg.] = [No noise, Noise]/[No noise, Noise].

where $\mathbf{I}$ is the image, $\mathbf{N}$ is the noise image, $\Psi$ is the CORT-X 2 filter, $C > 0$ is the noise scaling parameter and $(x, y)$ is the pixel index in the images. Table 2 represents the average results from ten measurements using equation (5). With such noise reduction, the recognition results shown in Table 3 were similar to those for the noise-free case in Table 1, except for some falling off of recognition scores at the lowest level of coarse coding (the $16 \times 16$ case).

Table 4 shows the number of nodes created by the network after training for the no noise (left entry) and noise (right entry) results reported above. Noise causes a small increase in the number of categories formed on average as the network attempts to correct a greater number of noise-induced errors during supervised training.

## 5.3 Slow learning simulation with noise

For the next set of computer simulations, the network was run on the noisy data using slow learning to the Map Field ($\beta_{ab} = 0.2$). Fast learning was still used within the $ART_a$ module itself ($\beta_a = 1.0$). Note that for $\bar{\rho}_{max} = 1.0$, the results for slow learning and fast learning to the Map Field are equivalent. They are equivalent because with Map Field vigilance set to $\rho_{ab} = 1.0$, the slightest mismatch at the Map Field will invoke match tracking and a new category will be created. To derive benefit from slow learning in the case $\rho_{ab} = 1.0$, we set $\bar{\rho}_{max} = 0.95$. Table 5 records the results using slow learning in large amplitude noise ($C = 1$). Where noise levels after preprocessing were very small, the results were approximately the same as in the fast learning case shown in Table 3. Slow learning begins to help when the noise level increases, as with the $16 \times 16$ coarse coding. Table 6 records the average number of categories formed for the noisy data case using fast learning and slow learning. Slow learning with $\bar{\rho}_{max} = 0.95$, caused approximately 10% fewer categories to be formed than with $\bar{\rho}_{max} = 1.0$, since noise-induced errors do not always cause the formation of a new category in the former case.

## 6 Voting versus view transitions

For the jet data set as processed by VIEWNET, it was found that the average overall length of an error sequence was 1.31 2-D views with a standard deviation of 0.57 views. Thus, when an error occurs, collecting evidence from (or voting over) two more views will usually be sufficient to correct the error. This can be done in VIEWNET by adding an integration field ($F^{int}$) between the Map Field ($F^{ab}$) and the winner-take-all field ($F^{wta}$). The equation for the integrator field is stepped once each time $ART_a$ chooses a

| CORT-X 2 filter set | Data presentation | Coarse code using spatial avg / Gaussian avg | | |
|---|---|---|---|---|
| | | 4x4 | 8x8 | 16x16 |
| Small | Ordered | 79.9/83.1 | 84.0/85.6 | 84.7/89.9 |
| Small | Unordered | 78.8/83.3 | 83.2/85.7 | 84.9/89.1 |
| Large | Ordered | 76.3/78.2 | 78.5/81.5 | 77.0/78.8 |
| Large | Unordered | 77.4/80.2 | 79.6/80.41 | 75.8/79.2 |

Table 5: Recognition results on noisy data ($C = 1$) with slow learning to the Map Field ($\beta_{ab} = 0.2$, $\bar{\rho}_{max} = 0.95$). Due to the low levels of noise surviving preprocessing, the recognition results here are not substantially different than those found using fast learning in noise in Table 3 except where noise was highest as in the 16x16 coarse coding. As noise increases, slow learning becomes more important for maintaining good recognition scores.

| CORT-X 2 filter set | Data presentation | Coarse code using spatial avg / Gaussian avg | | |
|---|---|---|---|---|
| | | 4x4 | 8x8 | 16x16 |
| Small | Ordered | [184, 165]/[169, 150] | [73, 67]/[73, 66] | [33, 30]/[35, 32] |
| Small | Unordered | [198, 180]/[179, 163] | [77, 69]/[76, 70] | [35, 32]/[36, 33] |
| Large | Ordered | [179, 160]/[162, 147] | [68, 61]/[71, 66] | [33 , 30]/[31, 29] |
| Large | Unordered | [192, 175]/[174, 160] | [75, 69]/[72, 67] | [32, 30]/[32, 30] |

Table 6: Average number of nodes formed during training for the simulations of Tables 3 (noise with fast learning) and 5 (noise with slow learning). The format in the table is as follows: [spatial avg.]/[Gaussian avg.] = [fast learning, slow learning]/[fast learning, slow learning]. It can be seen that slow learning reduced the number of nodes formed by approximately 10%.

category:

$$(x_k^{int})^{new} = \beta_{int}x_k^{ab} + (1 - \beta_{int})(x_k^{int})^{old}, \tag{6}$$

where $x_k^{int}$ is an integrator node for the $k^{th}$ object, $\beta_{int}$ is the integration rate each time the equation is stepped, and $x_k^{ab}$ is the $k^{th}$ Map Field category. The maximal integration node is chosen by the winner-take-all field ($F^{wta}$) as the network's identification of the 3-D object.

Figure 3 shows the average recognition scores for voting with $\beta_{int} = 0.2$ over one, two, and three views under CORT-X 2 preprocessing with large and small scale filter sets and Gaussian coarse coding to $4 \times 4$, $8 \times 8$ and $16 \times 16$ pixels. Voting over 3 frames improves recognition results by an average of ten percent with the best results being 98.5% correct for small scale filtered $16 \times 16$ Gaussian coarse coded data.

## 6.1 Do view transitions lead to better recognition?

The advantage of voting over using 2-D view transitions is that given $N$ 2-D views, the $O(N^2)$ cost for learning view transitions is avoided. To compare how well voting over view sequences does to using view transitions, the architecture described in Bradski, Carpenter, and Grossberg (1991) (Section 1) that incorporates 2-D views and 2-D view transitions for recognition was simulated.

In Figure 3, the black circles and squares represent the recognition scores using view transitions for preprocessing with the large and small scale CORT-X 2 filters respectively. Recognition scores from view transitions and from evidence accumulation are similar. Since evidence accumulation does not require the $O(N^2)$ nodes needed for learning 2-D view transitions, evidence accumulation over view transitions seems preferable for this application.

## 7 Discussion

Using the smaller set of CORT-X 2 filters, a 3-D object recognition rate of approximately 90% may be achieved from single 2-D views alone without recourse to more elaborate methods of generating aspect graph models of the 3-D objects. When evidence integration or voting over a sequence of views is added, recognition rates reach 98.5% within three views. Voting over two views did as well as using view transitions

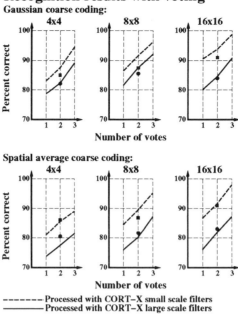

**Recognition results with voting**

Figure 3: Recognition results for voting with an integration rate of $\beta_{int} = 0.2$. The graphs show the recognition results after gathering evidence over one, two and three 2-D views for data preprocessed using large (solid line) and small (dotted line) scale CORT-X 2 filters. Results from both Gaussian and spatial averaging coarse coding are shown where the images were reduced from $128 \times 128$ down to $4 \times 4$, $8 \times 8$ and $16 \times 16$ pixels. The circles and squares represent recognition scores resulting from using view transitions discussed in Section 6.1.

on this database, but without the drawback of needing to learn $O(N^2)$ view transitions given $N$, 2-D views. In addition, it was shown that the above recognition rates can be maintained even in high noise conditions using the preprocessing methods described here.

These high recognition rates were achieved by using a different preprocessor and supervised learning to create more optimal category boundaries than in the Seibert and Waxman studies. As reported in Seibert and Waxman (1992), their unsupervised clustering of coarse coded maximal curvature data created general categories that unambiguously selected for the correct 3-D object only 25% of the time. In so doing, their network created 41 categories during training. In order to overcome the ambiguity of their general ART 2 categories, Seibert and Waxman used 2-D view category transitions to help identify the 3-D objects. Even if two 3-D objects shared the 2-D view categories of ART 2, they might not share the particular 2-D view category transitions that could then be used to distinguish one object from the other at the cost of needing to represent $O(N^2)$ transitions. Seibert and Waxman's network must then be able to represent possible cross-correlations between every categorical 2-D view in its view transition matrices, one for each object, even if no correlations are eventually found between some of the categories. Thus, their algorithm needed to represent the possible correlations between each of the 41 2-D view categories that were generated. The total number of correlations were then $(41^2 - 41)/2 = 820$, since transitions and their reverse are equivalent and there are no self-transitions. This is done for each object for a total representation of $820 \times 3 = 2460$ possible correlations. In actual practice, the view transition matrices were sparse. For example, 70 view transitions were actually learned during training for the F-16. In contrast, Tables 1 and 4 show that VIEWNET obtained its best recognition results over all three jets using a total of 33 2-D view categories without any representation of view transitions.

# References

Bradski, G., Carpenter, G., & Grossberg, S. (1991). Working memory networks for learning multiple groupings of temporally ordered events: Application to 3-D visual object recognition. In *Proceedings of the IJCNN-91, Seattle, WA.*, Vol. 1, pp. 723–728. Piscataway, NJ: IEEE Service Center.

Carpenter, G., & Grossberg, S. (1987b). ART 2: Self-organization of stable category recognition codes for analog input patterns. *Applied Optics, 26,* 4919–4930.

Carpenter, G., Grossberg, S., Markuzon, N., Reynolds, J., & Rosen, D. (1992). Fuzzy ARTMAP: A neural network architecture for incremental supervised learning of analog multidimensional maps. *IEEE Transactions on Neural Networks, 3,* 698–713.

Carpenter, G., Grossberg, S., & Mehanian, C. (1989). Invariant recognition of cluttered scenes by a self-organizing ART architecture: CORT-X boundary segmentation. *Neural Networks, 2,* 169–181.

Carpenter, G., Grossberg, S., & Reynolds, J. (1993). Fuzzy ARTMAP, slow learning and probability estimation. Tech. rep. CAS/CNS-TR-93-014, Boston University, Boston, MA: Boston University.

Carpenter, G., Grossberg, S., & Rosen, D. (1991). Fuzzy ART: Fast stable learning and categorization of analog patterns by an adaptive resonance system. *Neural Networks, 4.*

Grossberg, S. (1993). 3-D vision and figure-ground separation by visual cortex. Tech. rep. CAS/CNS-TR-92-019, Boston University, Perception and Psychophysics, in press.

Grossberg, S., & Wyse, L. (1991). A neural network architecture for figure-ground separation of connected scenic figures. *Neural Networks, 4,* 723–742.

Grossberg, S., & Wyse, L. (1992). A neural network architecture for figure-ground separation of connected scenic figures. In Pinter, R., & Nabet, B. (Eds.), *Nonlinear Vision: Determination of Neural Receptive Fields, Function, and Networks* (1 edition)., chap. 21, pp. 516–543. CRC Press, Inc.

Koenderink, J., & van Doorn, A. (1979). The internal representation of solid shape with respect to vision. *Biological Cybernetics., 32,* 211–216.

Schwartz, E. (1977). Spatial mapping in primate sensory projection: analytic structure and relevance to perception. *Biological Cybernetics, 25,* 181–194.

Seibert, M., & Waxman, A. (1992). Adaptive 3-D-object recognition from multiple views. *IEEE Transactions on Pattern Analysis and Machine Intelligence, 11,* 107–124.

Seibert, M., & Waxman, A. (1990a). Learning aspect graph representations of 3-D objects in a neural network. In *Proceedings of IJCNN-90, Washington, D.C.*, Vol. 2, pp. 233–236.

Seibert, M., & Waxman, A. (1990b). Learning aspect graph representations from view sequences. In Touretzky, D. (Ed.), *Advances in Neural Information Processing Systems 2*, pp. 258–265. San Mateo, CA: Morgan Kaufmann publishing.

Seibert, M., & Waxman, A. (1991). Learning and recognizing 3-D objects from multiple views in a neural system. In Wechsler, H. (Ed.), *Neural Networks for Perception,.*, Vol. 1. New York, NY: Academic Press.

# USING THE BINARY DIAMOND NEURAL NETWORK
# IN THE CLASSIFICATION OF SATELLITE IMAGES

by Yehuda Salu

Based on: Classification of Multispectral Image Data by the Binary Diamond Neural Network and by Nonparametric, Pixel-by-Pixel Methods. By Yehuda Salu and James Tilton. IEEE Transactions on Geoscience and Remote Sensing, Vol 31, pp 606-617, 1993.

## Abstract

Artificial neural networks are widely used in classification tasks, in which an item has to be assigned to one of a given set of classes, based on the features that the item possesses. Presented here is a new neural network, the Binary Diamond, which is especially suited to perform classifications. The network learns the classification rules in an unsupervised way from a provided training set. Each example in the training set consists of an item, its features, and its class. An example has to be provided just once for the network to correctly learn the implicit classification information that it contains. The network is of the multi-layer, feed-forward kind, and it classifies new items in a straight-forward, non-iterative process. The network has been tested in classification of 90,000 land pixels, based on their reflection spectra, that had been recorded by a satellite. The network performed well when compared to backpropagation neural net, and to a nearest neighbor algorithm.

# Unsupervised Learning

**Session Chairs: Gail Carpenter**
**Robert Jannarone**

## POSTER PRESENTATIONS

# ANALYSIS OF LONG-TERM BEHAVIORAL DYNAMICS
# OF AN UNSUPERVISED PATTERN CLASSIFICATION SYSTEM

R. Athinarayanan and M. R. Sayeh

Department of Electrical Engineering

Southern Illinois University at Carbondale

Carbondale, Illinois 62901-6603

## ABSTRACT

In this paper we analyze the LYAM system, an unsupervised classifier whose dynamics describe the competitive interaction of pattern classes. We will investigate its limiting behaviour defined for all $t \geq 0$, in which case its highly nonlinear classifier dynamics can effectively be replaced by that of a much simpler one. The study of this simpler analogue dynamics, allowed us to identify the $2^M$ equilibrium states of the system, which would otherwise be quite impossible.

## Introduction

In the study of nonlinear dynamical systems, we hope that all trajectories converge to an equilibrium point or asymptotically approach a closed orbit. Hence the most obvious question is what is the long-term behaviour of its trajectories. An effective analysis is to study its $\omega$ −limit set $\omega(\phi)$; the set of points which are limits of sequences $\phi(t_k)$ where $t_k \rightarrow \infty$. The $\omega$ −limit set can consist of equilibrium points, equilibrium points and orbits joining them, or periodic orbits. In this work however, we are not interested in studying the limiting behaviour of the individual trajectories, but to globally characterize the LYAM[1] dynamics for large values of time $t$.

The classifier state dynamics in [1] is derived from the minimization of an energy function represented as

$$L = \left( \gamma - \sum_{j=1}^{M} z_j x_j \right)^2 + \beta \sum_{i=1}^{M} \sum_{\substack{j=1 \\ j \neq i}}^{M} z_i x_i z_j x_j$$

The overall network dynamics is summarized as

$$\frac{dz_j}{dt} = c_j x_j \left[ z_j (1 - z_j) \right]^2$$

$$\frac{dw_{ij}}{dt} = c_j x_j z_j (1 - x_j)(u_i - w_{ij})$$

$$\frac{du_i}{dt} = \left( \gamma - \sum_{j=1}^{M} z_j x_j \right) \sum_{j=1}^{M} D_{ij}$$

where

$$c_j = \left[ \gamma - z_j x_j - (1 + \beta) \sum_{k \neq j}^{M} z_k x_k \right], \quad D_{ij} = z_j x_j (1 - x_j)(w_{ij} - u_i)$$

and $x_j = f\left( r^2 - \|U - W_j\|^2 \right)$. $f(\alpha) = (1 + e^{-\lambda \alpha})^{-1}$ is the logistic or sigmoid function, and $\|.\|$ is the Euclidean norm.

In the forthcoming section we provide a detailed study of the long-run behaviour of the LYAM dynamics, from which we extract information pertaining to identifiying its limiting characteristics. As a consequence of this result, in Section 2 we study a much simpler analogue of the actual dynamics that will allow us to trivially identify the critical states which is otherwise rendered as being quite impossible.

## 1. Limiting Analysis of the LYAM Dynamics

In this analysis we devote considerable interest to the description of the equilibrium states on the $L$-energy surface. We focus attention on the quantity $\phi(t) = x(t)z(t)$, due to the nature of signals affecting the $L$-energy surface. We will then show that the dynamics of the signal $\phi(t)$ to be the single most important information pertaining to the construction of the $L$-energy surface which can be represented by

$$L = \left( \gamma - \sum_{j=1}^{M} \phi_j \right)^2 + \beta \sum_{i=1}^{M} \sum_{j \neq i}^{M} \phi_i \phi_j$$

It is however quite impossible to explicitly extract the state-space dynamics of the signal $\phi(t)$ from the LYAM dynamics. Nevertheless characterization of the dynamics can be realized by $\overset{\circ}{\phi}(t) = z(t)\overset{\circ}{x}(t) + x(t)\overset{\circ}{z}(t)$ where $x = f(U, W)$. The activation of the various memory clusters, $\phi(t)$, are governed by the set of equations

$$d\phi_j \Big/ dt = -\partial L \Big/ \partial \phi_j \left[ \frac{x_j}{z_j} - \eta(t) \left( \frac{d \big/ dt \, (u - w_j)^2}{(\gamma - \phi_j - (1 + \beta) \sum_{k \neq j}^{M} \phi_\cdot)} \right) \right] \tilde{\eta}(t) \phi_j$$

where $j = 1, 2, \ldots, M$ and $\eta(t) > 0$, $\tilde{\eta}(t) > 0$, $\forall t \geq 0$.

The convergence or the divergence of the cluster centers $W_j$, upon arrival of an input information $U$ can be represented by

$$\left( \overset{\circ}{u} - \overset{\circ}{w}_j \right) = -a_j(t)\left( u - w_j \right) + \sum_{k \neq j}^{M} \alpha_k(t)(u - w_k) \qquad (1)$$

where $a_j(t) = A(t)\left[ \gamma - \phi_j - (1 + \overline{\beta}) \sum_{k \neq j}^{M} \phi_k \right]$, $\alpha_k(t) = \left( \gamma - \sum_{j=1}^{M} \phi_j \right)\phi_k(1 - x_k)$, $\beta > \overline{\beta}$, and

$A(t) \geq 0 \; \forall t > 0$.

Then by the continuity of $U$ and $W_j$, we represent the solution in the integral form as

$$(u - w_j)(t) = e^{-\int_0^t a_j(q)dq} (u - w_j)^{(0)} + \int_0^t e^{-\int_\tau^t a_j(q)dq} \sum_{k \neq j}^{M} \alpha_k(\tau)(u - w_k)(\tau)d\tau$$

From the above equation, it is evident that for $a_j(t) < 0$, $\lim_{t \to \infty}|u - w_j| = \infty$.

However if we now define $\tilde{a}_j = A(t)\left[ \gamma - \phi_j - (1 + \beta) \sum_{k \neq j}^{M} \phi_k \right]$, the dynamics of the *jth*. cluster center

can now be represented by

$$\left( \overset{\circ}{u} - \overset{\circ}{w}_j \right) \leq -\overline{a}_j(t)\left( u - w_j \right) + \sum_{k \neq j}^{M} \alpha_k(t)(u - w_k) \qquad (2)$$

Taking the absolute value of the quantity $(u - w_j)$, the solution can be written as

$$\left| u - w_j \right| \leq e^{-\int_0^t \overline{a}_j(q)dq} \left| u - w_j \right|^{(0)} + \int_0^t e^{-\int_\tau^t \overline{a}_j(q)dq} \left| \sum_{k \neq j}^{M} \alpha_k(\tau)(u - w_k)(\tau) \right| d\tau$$

The quantity $\left| \sum_{k \neq j}^{M} \alpha_k(u - w_k) \right| \leq B$, and also let $\left| e^{-\int_0^t \tilde{a}_j(s)ds} \right| \leq K\left| e^{-\int_0^t \rho ds} \right|$ for some $K > 0$ and

$|\rho| < \infty$. Rewriting the equation we obtain

$$\left| u - w_j \right| \leq Ke^{-\int_0^t \rho dq} \left| u - w_j \right|^{(0)} + \int_0^t Ke^{-\int_\tau^t \rho dq} Bd\tau \quad j = 1, 2$$

It is then obvious that for any $\rho > 0$, $\lim\limits_{t \to \infty} |u - w_j| = 0$.

From the above analysis we can conclude that for any cluster center $j$, $\lim\limits_{t \to \infty} \alpha_j (u - w_j) = 0$,

hence $\lim\limits_{t \to \infty} \sum\limits_{k=1}^{M} \alpha_k (u - w_k) = 0$. Based on these results we now consider two separate cases.

<u>Case 1</u> Multiplying both sides of equation (1) by the quantity $(u - w_j)$, and taking the limits as

$t \to \infty$, we obtain

$$\lim_{t \to \infty} \frac{d}{dt} (u - w_j)^2 = - \lim_{t \to \infty} a_j(t)(u - w_j)^2 + \lim_{t \to \infty} \sum_{k \neq j}^{M} \alpha_k (u - w_k)(u - w_j)$$

For $a_j(t) < 0 \Rightarrow \left[ \gamma - \phi_j - (1 + \beta) \sum\limits_{k \neq j}^{M} \phi_k \right] < 0$, $\lim\limits_{t \to \infty} |u - w_j| = \infty$. Since the second limit on

the R.H.S of the above equation approaches zero, hence $\lim\limits_{t \to \infty} \frac{d}{dt} (u - w_j)^2 > 0$.

<u>Case 2</u> Performing the similar operation as in case 1 for equation (2), we obtain

$$\lim_{t \to \infty} \frac{d}{dt} (u - w_j)^2 \leq - \lim_{t \to \infty} \overline{a}_j(t)(u - w_j)^2 + \lim_{t \to \infty} \sum_{k \neq j}^{M} \alpha_k (u - w_k)(u - w_j)$$

We saw that for any $\rho > 0$, i.e. $\left[ \gamma - \phi_j - (1 + \beta) \sum\limits_{k \neq j}^{M} \phi_k \right] > 0$, $\lim\limits_{t \to \infty} |u - w_j| = 0$. Since both the

limits on the R.H.S. approaches zero, we can conclude that $\lim\limits_{t \to \infty} \frac{d}{dt} (u - w_j)^2 \leq 0$.

Hence from the equation that governs the dynamics of the memory clusters, we conclude that

$$\lim_{t \to \infty} sgn\left[ \frac{d}{dt} (u - w_j)^2 \right] \neq \lim_{t \to \infty} sgn\left[ \gamma - \phi_j - (1 + \beta) \sum_{k \neq j}^{M} \phi_k \right]$$

for both the cases considered above.

## 2. The Analogue of LYAM dynamics

From the preceeding analysis, the limiting behaviour of the LYAM system characteristics can

essentially be modelled after $\frac{d\phi_j}{dt} = \left( -\nabla_j L \right) \phi_j$, i.e.

$$\frac{d\phi_j}{dt} = \left[ \gamma - F(\phi) - \beta \sum_{k \neq j}^{M} \phi_k \right] \phi_j \quad ; \quad j = 1, 2, \ldots, M$$

$F(\phi) = \sum_{j=1}^{M} \phi_j$ represents a linear combination of activation signals of the $M$ pattern clusters. We now

seek to find the equilibrium states of the above *Mth.* order system. By inspection these are solution to the

set of equations

$$0 = \left[ \gamma - \left( F(\bar{\phi}) + \beta \sum_{k \neq j}^{M} \bar{\phi}_k \right) \right] \bar{\phi}_j, \quad j = 1, 2, \ldots, M$$

where $\bar{\phi}_j$ represents the equilibrium states. We first assume the case when $\phi_j(t) \neq \phi_k(t), \ k \neq j$.

For each such equation above we distinguish cases $\bar{\phi}_j \rangle 0$ and $\bar{\phi}_j = 0$. If $\bar{\phi}_j \rangle 0$ for some $j$, it

follows that

$$F(\bar{\phi}) = \frac{\gamma + \beta \bar{\phi}_j}{1 + \beta}$$

Based upon the assumption made above, the expression for $F(\phi)$ can hold for at most one index $j$ since

otherwise $F(\phi)$ would supposedly have two different values. Therefore when $\phi_j(t) \neq \phi_k(t)$,

$k \neq j$, at most one cluster can have nonzero cluster activation in an equilibrium state. Suppose that

$\bar{\phi}_j$ is the single positive equilibrium component, its value can be found from the above equations to yield

$$\bar{\phi}_j = \gamma, \quad \bar{\phi}_k = 0, \quad k \neq j$$

In view of the above assumption, it is interesting to note that the $L$-energy surface has at most

$M+1$ equilibrium states; i.e. the zero state $\bar{\phi} = [0, 0, \ldots, 0]$, and the $M$ equilibria corresponding to a

single positive cluster activation,

$$\bar{\phi} = \{ (\gamma, 0, \ldots, 0), (0, \gamma, \ldots, 0), \ldots, (0, 0, \ldots, \gamma) \}$$

If we now consider the possible case when any two cluster centers having the same activations,

i.e. $\phi_i(t) = \phi_j(t) > \phi_k(t), \ k \neq i, j$ and $\bar{M} = 2$, then the equilibrium states can be realized as

$$\bar{\phi} = \left\{ \left[ \frac{\gamma}{\overline{M} + (\overline{M} - 1)\beta}, \frac{\gamma}{\overline{M} + (\overline{M} - 1)\beta}, 0, \dots, 0 \right], \left[ \frac{\gamma}{\overline{M} + (\overline{M} - 1)\beta}, 0, \frac{\gamma}{\overline{M} + (\overline{M} - 1)\beta}, 0, \dots, 0 \right], \dots, \left[ 0, 0, \dots, 0, \frac{\gamma}{\overline{M} + (\overline{M} - 1)\beta}, \frac{\gamma}{\overline{M} + (\overline{M} - 1)\beta} \right] \right\}$$

i.e. there exists $\dfrac{M!}{(M-2)!\,2!}$ equilibrium states. More generally for any $\overline{M} \leq M$, we have

$\dfrac{M!}{(M - \overline{M})!\,\overline{M}!}$ critical points for the system. Thus for an *Mth.* order system, there are precisely

$$1 + \sum_{\overline{M}=1}^{M} \frac{M!}{(M - \overline{M})!\,\overline{M}!} = 2^M \text{ equilibrium states.}$$

## Conclusion

In this work we characterized the long term behaviour of the LYAM by a much simpler analogue of the actual dynamics, which led us to the identification of its $2^M$ equilibrium states. It however remains to be seen the limits behaviour of the individual trajectories $\phi_j(t_k)$ where $t_k \rightarrow \infty$, which requires extensive study of the $\omega$-limit set of the LYAM dynamics.

## REFERENCES

[1]     M. R. Sayeh , A. Ragu, and H. H. Szu, "Design of an Unsupervised Classifier," *IJCNN*, Seattle, WA, pp. II417-II422, 1991.

[2]     M. W. Hirsch, "Systems of Differential Equations Which are Competitive or Cooperative. I: Limit Sets," *SIAM Journal of Mathematical Analysis*, Vol. 13, No. 2, pp. 167-179, 1982.

[3]     M. A. Cohen, "The Construction of Arbitrary Stable Dynamics in Nonlinear Neural Networks," *Neural Networks*, Vol. 5, pp. 83-103, 1992.

[4]     D. G. Luenberger, *Introduction to Dynamical Systems, Theory, Models and Applications*, Wiley, 1979

# Redundancy Reduction by Unsupervised Boltzmann Machines

*G. Deco and L. Parra*
*Siemens AG, Corporate Research and Development, ZFE ST SN 41*
*Otto-Hahn-Ring 6, 81739 Munich, Germany*

### Abstract

Unsupervised features extraction through a stochastic neural network can be defined as maximization of the transmitted information from the input layer to the output by simultaneously minimization of the redundancy between the elements of the output layer. The minimization of the redundancy can be achieved by minimization of the mutual information between the units in the output layer. With this two constraints we define a novelty learning algorithm for Boltzmann Machines. Simulation demonstrates the performance of this method.

## 1.0 Introduction

One of the brains's most important task is to detect "statistical coincidences" in any combination of sensory stimuli. Barlow (1989) related this problem with unsupervised learning by redundancy reduction. The aim of unsupervised learning is to find a set of features (symbols) to represent the messages such that the occurrence of each feature is independent of the occurrence of any of the others. This kind of learning is called factorial learning. Parallel, Linsker (1988) applied a well known concept from the information theory. He has proposed an optimization principle, called infomax, according to which synaptic weights develop in such a way that the mutual information between input and output layers of a cortical network is maximized under constrained boundary conditions. It has been proved that statistically salient input features can be optimally extracted from a noisy input by maximizing the mutual information. The aim of the present work is to define for the Boltzmann Machine (Ackley et al, 1985) an unsupervised learning paradigm based on the maximization of the mutual information between input and output layer by simultaneously factorization of the extracted features, i.e. redundancy minimization. In this way we extend the infomax principle for probabilistic non-linear neurons and for recurrent networks. The learning algorithm yields an interesting weighted combination of Hebbian and anti-Hebbian rule. The weighted coefficients can be interpreted by the infomax principle and the redundancy reduction principle (Barlow, 1989).

## 2.0 Theoretical Formulation

A Boltzmann Machine can be defined as a neural network composed by stochastic binary units $S_i$, taking output value $S_i = 1$ with probability $p$ and value $S_i = -1$ with probability $1 - p$. The probability $p$ is given by,

$$p = \frac{1}{1 + e^{(-2\tau \sum_j w_{ij} S_j)}} \tag{2.1}$$

Equation 2.1 defines the Glauber dynamic for a system of Ising spins. The parameter $\tau$ in equation 2.1 is related with the inverse of the temperature. If the connections $w_{ij}$ between the neurons are symmetric, than an energy function can be defined and the Boltzmann-Gibbs distribution from the statistical mechanics gives the probability of finding the system in a determined state $\{S\}$. Let us label the states of the input units by $\gamma$, of the output units by $\alpha$. We ignore the hidden neurons in order to do the presentation more clear (The extension of the formalism for hidden units is straightforward). Then the Boltzmann-Gibbs distribution of the states of the output neurons states for a fixed input pattern $\gamma$ can be written as,

$$P_{\alpha/\gamma} = \frac{e^{-\tau H^{\alpha/\gamma}}}{Z_\gamma} \qquad Z_\gamma = \sum_\alpha e^{-\tau H^{\alpha/\gamma}} \tag{2.2}$$

where $Z_\gamma$ is the partition function and $H^{\alpha\beta/\gamma}$ the energy function,

$$H^{\alpha/\gamma} = -\frac{1}{2}\sum_{ij} w_{ij} \cdot S_i^{\alpha/\gamma} \cdot S_j^{\alpha/\gamma} \tag{2.3}$$

In order to implement factorial learning the information contained in the input distribution should be completely transmitted to the outputs layer and the probability distribution of the output neurons should be statistically decorrelated. The first fact is assured by maximizing the transfer of information from the input neurons to the output neuron. That means that a message $\gamma$ coded in the input layer should be transmitted through the stochastic neurons so that the code given by the averaged thermal value of the output neurons contains the most information included in the original message $\gamma$. A measure of the transmitted information is given by the "Mutual Information" (Shannon, 1948) that in our case can be written as,

$$MIV = \sum_\gamma P_\gamma \sum_\alpha P_{\alpha/\gamma}\log(P_{\alpha/\gamma}) - \sum_\gamma P_\gamma \sum_\alpha P_{\alpha/\gamma}\log\left(\sum_\gamma P_\gamma P_{\alpha/\gamma}\right) \tag{2.4}$$

where $P_\gamma$ is the probability distribution of the input patterns and $P_{\alpha/\gamma}$ is the probability distribution of the possible configurations of the output neurons given that pattern $\gamma$ is presented at the input (Conditional probability).

The second fact is the constraint that the output code should be factorial. A factorial code implies that the occurrence of each symbol (output) is independent of the occurrence of any of the others. This statistical independence between the output units can be expressed as,

$$P_\alpha = \prod_j (\alpha_j P_j + (1-\alpha_j)(1-P_j)) \tag{2.5}$$

which is equivalent to (Atick and Redlich, 1992),

$$MIH = \sum_j H(j) - H(\alpha) = 0 \tag{2.6}$$

where $\alpha_j$ is the state of the output unit "j" in the output configuration $\alpha$. Equation 2.5 express the condition of factorial code by setting the "Horizontal Mutual Information" (MIH) equal to zero. The MIH is defined as the difference between the sum of the entropy of each output "j" ($H(j)$) and the entropy of the joint output states $H(\alpha)$. This two entropies are defined as,

$$H(j) = P_j \log P_j + (1 - P_j) \log(1 - P_j) \tag{2.7}$$

$$H(\alpha) = \sum_\alpha P_a \log P_\alpha \tag{2.8}$$

This means that a factorial code (eq. 2.5) is obtained by minimizing the horizontal mutual information, which is a measure of the grade of correlation between the outputs. The unsupervised learning that we introduce in this paper for a stochastic network described by equation 2.2 consists in maximizing MIV and minimizing MIH. The cost function that we choose is,

$$C = (H(\gamma) - MIV) + MIH \tag{2.9}$$

If we minimize this cost function then we maximize the MIV and minimize the MIH, due to the fact that both mutual information are always positive and the maximum value of MIV is the input entropy $H(\gamma)$. In order to minimize C we perform gradient ascendent corrections on the weights. This yields following learning rule,

$$w_{ij}^{new} = w_{ij}^{old} - \eta \cdot \frac{\partial C}{\partial w_{ij}} \tag{2.10}$$

where $\eta$ is a learning constant.

The derivative in eq. 2.10 can be calculated after some algebra,

$$\Delta w_{ij} = \eta \frac{\tau}{2} \sum_\gamma P_\gamma \sum_\alpha \left[ \log\left(\frac{P_{\alpha/\gamma}}{P_\alpha}\right) - \log\left(\frac{P_\alpha}{\prod_j (\alpha_j P_{j/\gamma} + (1 - \alpha_j)(1 - P_{j/\gamma}))}\right) \right] (s_i^{\alpha/\gamma} s_j^{\alpha/\gamma} - \langle s_i s_j \rangle) \tag{2.12}$$

where the symbol $\langle x \rangle$ denotes the average value of $x$. The interpretation of the obtained unsupervised learning rule is interesting. A Hebbian term is given by the $s_i^{\alpha/\gamma} s_j^{\alpha/\gamma}$ in equation 2.12 and is the actual correlation between the neurons in the state $\alpha$ given that $\gamma$ is presented at the input. The second term $-\langle S_i S_j \rangle_\gamma$ is an anti-Hebbian term given by the averaged correlation between the neurons. These terms are the weighted sum over all possible states, where the weighting factor is the difference between the information transmitted from input to output and the redundancy in the output layer.

## 3.0  Results and Simulations

We have applied the herein introduced learning paradigm to two problems: a) A simple Boolean recoding and b)The real world problem of eliminating redundancy in the ASCII-code (Barlow et al, 1989).

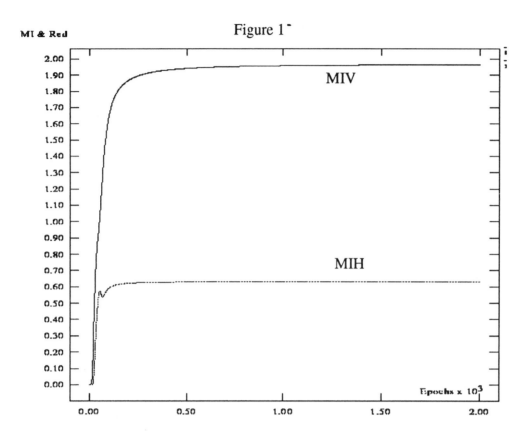

Figure 1

In the first example we used four patterns: 0 0 1; 0 1 1; 1 1 0 and 1 1 1 with probabilities 0.2, 0.3, 0.3, 0.2 respectively as input for a Boltzmann Machine with 3 inputs and 3 outputs (without hidden units). The initial bit entropy is 2.85 (see eq.1 of Barlow et al (1989)) and the entropy of the patterns distribution is 1.97. Figure 1 shows the evolution of the vertical mutual information a nd horizontal mutual information when only the MIV is maximized. All the information is transmitted (MIV=1.97) but the code associated at the output is still redundant, then the bit entropy of the output is 2.60. When MIH is also minimized (eq.2.9 and 2.12), i.e. we reduce redundancy, a factorial code is found at the output. The bit entropy of the output is 1.97 correspond to the minimum of MIH. In this case MIH=0 (corresponding to the absolute suppression of redundancy) the bit entropy of the output have to be equal to the pattern entropy of the input, which is the minimum possible. Figure 2 shows the evolution of MIV and MIH for this case.

In the second example taken from (Barlow et al, 1989) we generated with our algorithm a minimum redundancy code for the ASCII-code for the english language. The initial bit entropy (ASCII) is 5.5 (redundancy=25%, see Barlow et al (1989) for a definition of %-redundancy) and the entropy of the characters is 4.34. At the end of training with the present model we generated at the output a binary code with reduced bit entropy that approximates a factorial code, i.e. eliminates the high redundancy contained in the ASCII-code.

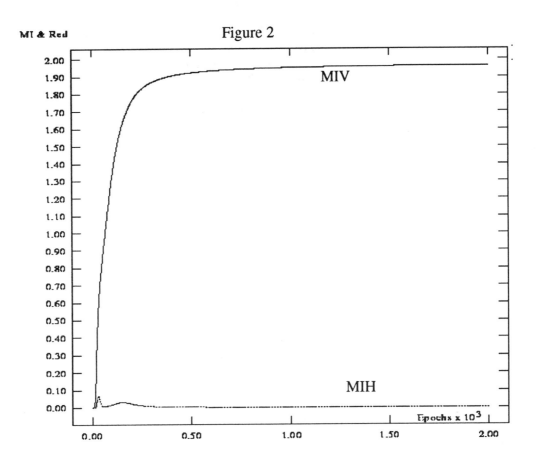

Figure 2

**References:**

- Ackley D., Hinton G. and Sejnowski, 1985,"A Learning Algorithm for Boltzmann Machines", Cognitive Science, **9**, 147-169.
- Atick J. and Redlich A., 1992, " What Does the Retina Know about Natural Scenes?", Neural Computation, **4**, 196-210.
- Barlow H., 1989, "Unsupervised Learning", Neural Computation, **1**, 295-311
- Barlow H., Kaushal T. and Mitchison G., 1989, "Finding Minimum Entropy Codes", Neural Computation, **1**, 412-423.
- Linsker R., 1988, "Self-organization in a perceptual network", Computer, **21**, 105.
- Shannon C., 1948, "A mathematical theory of communication", Bell System Technical Journal, **7**, 379-423.

# Weight Shifting Technique For Recovering Faulty Self-Organizing Neural Networks[1]

*C. Khunasaraphan, T. Tanprasert*
The Center for Advanced Computer Studies
The University of Southwestern Louisiana
Lafayette, LA 70504, U.S.A.

*C. Lursinsap*
Department of Mathematics, Faculty of Science
Chulalongkorn University
Bangkok 10330, Thailand.

## Abstract

A fault tolerant technique of feed-forward neural networks called *weight shifting* and its analytical models are proposed. The technique is applied to recover a self-organized network when some faulty links and/or neurons occur during the operation. If some input links of a specific neuron are detected faulty, their weights will be shifted to healthy links of the same neuron. On the other hand, if a faulty neuron is encountered, then we can treat it as a special case of faulty links by considering all the output links of that neuron to be faulty. The aim of this technique is to recover the network in a short time without any retraining and hardware repair.

## 1. Introduction

The advancement in VLSI technology makes it possible to implement a neural network on a VLSI chip. We assume that the weight of each link is computed during the training period by a software program. After obtaining the weights, the computed network is implemented on a chip with the appropriate weight set for each link. There are two possible faults of a network worth considered: faulty links and faulty neurons. The proposed models are applied to recover the faulty links and/or neurons while the networks are in the operational period.

The weight shifting technique for the sum of products of input and weight vectors has been proposed in [7]. In this paper, we propose a new weight shifting technique which is applied to the networks using the distance between input and weight vectors as their computing basis. There are some neural networks which their computation do not based on the sum of products. One good example is Kohonen's self-organizing feature map network.

The problem of designing a fault tolerance network has been studied as reported in [1,2,4,5,6]. There are several techniques to repair the fault which are (1) readjusting the weight and the threshold value based on the pre-specified sensitivity [2], (2) adding the weight function to the error function [4], and (3) pruning the network while training the network [2]. All these techniques are impractical if the network is implemented by a chip where retraining can not be executed. Unlike these techniques, which use redundancy and retraining, the weight of a faulty link is shifted to the other links. The shifting mechanism can be implemented as a small part of the network. The goal of our technique is to avoid retraining when the network is inaccessible such as when operated in the space. The weight adjustment must be

---

[1]The work is supported in part by National Science Foundation under grant number NSF-ADP-04. and partially supported by The Development and Promotion of Science and Technology Talents Project from Thailand.

executed inside the network itself not outside by any host computer.

The most prior step to the fault-tolerant process is to detect whether there is an error occurring. The error that we consider in this paper is when link $w_i$ changes to some other values different from the original value obtained during training. The fault detection or self-testing techniques using coding techniques [3] can be employed for this matter.

## 2. Weight Shifting Concept

We would like to propose the *weight shifting* techniques for fault tolerance of networks which apply the distance between weight vector and input vectors in order to compute the outputs. There are two methods of weight shifting: single weight shifting and multiple weight shifting. The faults can be faulty neurons and/or faulty links. For each input vector $\mathbf{X}_p$ of the $p^{th}$ pattern with the weight vector $\mathbf{W}$, it generates distance according to the equation:

$$d_k = \sqrt{\sum_{i=1}^{i=n}(w_{ki} - x_{i,p})^2} \tag{1}$$

where $d_k$ is distance between weight vectors from node $k$ to all $n$ input nodes of pattern $p^{th}$. When some weight $w_{ki}$ is changed to a new value $w'_{ki}$, we need to compensate this change so that the value $d_k$ will not be changed or be minimum changed. We will try to compensate the fault by transferring it to other healthy links such that $|d_k - d'_k|$ for all pattern $p$'s will be minimum.

For the single weight shifting of $w_{ki}$, the changed value will be added to the $w_{kj}$ where $j$ is one of the healthy links of neuron $k$. The multiple weight shifting of $w_{ki}$ is performed by breaking $w_{ki}$ into a set of $(\delta_1, \delta_2, \ldots, \delta_m)$, where $\sum_{j=1}^{j=m} \delta_j = w_{ki}$, and adding each $\delta_j$ to other weights $w_{kj}$'s where $w_{kj}$ are the healthy links of neuron $k$.

There are three possible kinds of fault; faulty links, faulty neurons, and faulty links and neurons in the network. Since there is a limit of space, we will explain only the derivation of equations for faulty links, the equations of other two cases can be derived by the similar method.

### Recovery of Faulty Links

Let $k$ be a neuron with a faulty input link $i$ and $\delta_j$ be the partial weight that must be added to link $j$ to compensate the weight change of the link $i$. Also, let $w'_{ki}$ be the new weight of link $i$ when it is faulty, let $S_l$ be the set of faulty input links of neuron $k$, and $S_h$ be the set of healthy input links of neuron $k$. The fault tolerance of the neuron $k$ will occur if the output value of $k$ is not changed after one or more links are faulty. Thus, the condition that we must preserve, for any pattern $p$, is as follows:

$$\sum_{l=1}^{l=n}(w_{kl} - x_{l,p})^2 = \sum_{j \in S_h} ((w_{kj} + \delta_j) - x_{j,p})^2 + \sum_{l \in S_l} (w'_{kl} - x_{l,p})^2 \tag{2}$$

where $|S_h| + |S_l| = n$ where $n$ is the total number of input nodes. After shifting the weights $\delta_j$, the distance $d_k$ must remain consistent as before for a given pattern. Let $E_p$ be the error function for pattern $p$ and be defined as follows.

$$E_p = \frac{1}{2} \left( \sum_{l=1}^{l=n}(w_{kl} - x_{l,p})^2 - \sum_{j \in S_h} ((w_{kj} + \delta_j) - x_{j,p})^2 - \sum_{l \in S_l} (w'_{kl} - x_{l,p})^2 \right)^2 \tag{3}$$

IV-235

The total error for all patterns in set $P$ is equal to

$$E = \frac{1}{2} \sum_P \left( \sum_{i \in S_l} (w_{ki}^2 - w_{ki}'^2 - 2w_{ki}x_{i,p} + 2w_{ki}'x_{i,p}) - 2 \sum_{j \in S_h} \delta_j(w_{kj} - x_{j,p}) - \sum_{j \in S_h} \delta_j^2 \right)^2 \tag{4}$$

The value of $\delta_j$ that gives minimum error $E$ can be found by differentiating equation (4). Let $L_p$ be equal to $\sum_{i \in S_l} (w_{ki}^2 - w_{ki}'^2 - 2w_{ki}x_{i,p} + 2w_{ki}'x_{i,p})$. We can compute $L_p$ since the value of $w_{ki}$, $w_{ki}'$, and $x_{i,p}$ are known. Differentiating the error function with respect to $\delta_j$, we have

$$\frac{\partial E}{\partial \delta_j} = \sum_P \left( (L_p - 2\sum_{j \in S_h} \delta_j(w_{kj} - x_{j,p}) - \sum_{j \in S_h} \delta_j^2 \right)\left(2x_{j,p} - 2w_{kj} - 2\delta_j\right) \tag{5}$$

Setting $\frac{\partial E}{\partial \delta_j}$ to zero, we have

$$2\sum_P L_p(w_{kj} - x_{j,p}) = -2\delta_j \sum_P L_p - \sum_P \sum_{l \in S_h} (2\delta_l w_{kl} - 2\delta_l x_{l,p} + \delta_l^2)(2x_{j,p} - 2w_{kj} - 2\delta_j) \tag{6}$$

If we consider the single weight shifting technique, the value of $\delta_j$ can be derived by setting $\delta_k$'s to zero where $k \in S_h$, and $k \neq j$. Therefore, the value of $\delta_j$ is derived from

$$\sum_P L_p(w_{kj} - x_{j,p}) = -\delta_j \sum_P L_p + \sum_P (2\delta_j w_{kj}^2 - 4\delta_j x_{j,p}w_{kj} + 2\delta_j x_{j,p}^2 + 3\delta_j^2 w_{kj} - 3\delta_j^2 x_{j,p} + \delta_j^3) \tag{7}$$

Since we know the value of $w_{kj}$, $x_{j,p}$, and $L_p$, substitute them in the equation (7) to find the value of $\delta_j$. The value of $\delta_j$ is added to selected healthy link $j$ to compensate the error that causes by the faulty link $i$.

In the case of multiple weight shifting, the value of each $\delta_j$ can be computed by differentiating the error function in equation (4) with respect to each $\delta_j$ and solving the following equations.

$$\frac{\partial E}{\partial \delta_j} = \sum_P \left( L_p - 2\sum_{l \in S_h} \delta_l(w_{kl} - x_{l,p}) - \sum_{l \in S_h} \delta_l^2 \right)\left(2x_{j,p} - 2w_{kj} - 2\delta_j\right) = 0 \tag{8}$$

for all $1 \leq j \leq n$, $j \neq i$, $i \in S_l$.

The above equation can be solved by Gaussian elimination method easily. The number of equations and the number of unknown are equal to $n - |S_l|$. If there are no solution for the above equation, the single weight shifting in equation (7) will be applied for recovering the faulty links. The condition that we must preserve for recovery of faulty neurons is slightly different from equation (2), i.e.

$$\sum_{i=1}^{i=n} (w_{ki} - x_{i,p})^2 = \sum_{j \in S_h} ((w_{kj} + \delta_j) - x_{j,p})^2 - \sum_{l \in S_n} (w_{kl} - x_{l,p}')^2 \tag{9}$$

Furthermore, the condition of recovery of faulty links and neurons case is

$$\sum_{i=1}^{i=n} (w_{ki} - x_{i,p})^2 = \sum_{j \in S_h} ((w_{kj} - x_{j,p})^2 + \sum_{l \in S_l} (w_{kl}' - x_{l,p})^2 + \sum_{n \in S_n} (w_{kn} - x_{n,p}')^2 \tag{10}$$

where $S_n$ is the set of faulty neurons connect to neuron $k$.

# 3. Recovery Procedures

In this section, an implementation of these recovery concepts is discussed. The proposed recovery procedures are based on the following assumptions:

    1. All weights are known after the training period.

    2. All faulty situations occur during the operational period.

    3. Retraining the network is not permitted once the network is operating.

In this paper, we will consider only the fault tolerance design for faulty link situation. The other two situations, (1) faulty neuron and (2) faulty link and neuron, can be achieved by applying the similar algorithms. The values of each link weight, and bias weights are computed prior to the hardware implementation of the network. The compensatory value $\delta_j$ are computed when an error occurs.

The recovery algorithm is activated immediately after an error is detected. If the error occurs because of some faulty links then apply the equations in Section 2 to compute $\delta_j$. We should consider the multiple weight shifting scheme first. Compute the value of each $\delta_j$ if there is a solution. If there is no solution for multiple weight shifting scheme, then compute $\delta_j$ of single weight shifting scheme. Then add $\delta_j$ to the weights according to the techniques corresponding to each error type.

# 4. Experimental Results

Without loss of generality, we experimented our weight shifting theory only with the faulty link situation to demonstrate the merit and the practicality of the theory. Kohonen's self-organizing feature map network is applied in our experiments since its basic computing is based on the distance between input and weight vectors. The set of data is a set of points in 2-D space. So we can see pictures of positions of data easily and clearly.

During the training period, we have found that the order of data is very important for the learning process. If the data is prepared in random order, the learning outputs are usually wrong. It means that the order of training is very significant for the right classification. This can be explained by each data has an effect on the average weight of the class which it is assigned to. We should not feed the input vectors of the same class close to each other to the network. Because the average weight of each class will be shifted from the right positions.

We experiment with several sets of 2-D data. In this paper, we will show only two sets of them. Figure 1 shows the structure and name of Kohonen's self-organizing feature map network using in the experiments. Figure 2 shows the positions of training and testing data. Table 1 and 2 illustrates the tolerant ranges with and without weight shifting technique for data set 1, 2, respectively. For example, when the link from output node (1,0) to input node 0 is faulty, the weight of the link will be shifted to link from the same output node to input node 1. In Table 1, the link has original training weight equal to 2.475. With weight shifting technique, this weight can be changed to the other value in the range (1.3, 7.7) and the output still correct for all testing patterns. The tolerant range is only (1.6, 4.0) without weight shifting technique. The tolerant range width of table 1 is wider than range of table 2 because locations of classes in data set 1 are farther away from one another than those of classes in data set 2, as can be seen in Figure 2.

We do not need to perform the multiple weight shifting technique in the 2-D classification problem since there is only two weight links for each output node. When one link of an output node $k$ is faulty, we have to shift the weight to the other link of the output node $k$.

The result shows that weight shifting technique usually expand the tolerant ranges of the Kohonen's self-organizing network. When the tolerant range from weight shifting technique is shorter, it usually expand the tolerance to the other way of the tolerance of the network without weight shifting technique. So this method is a useful technique for the fault tolerance concept of neural networks.

## 5. Conclusion

We have proposed a technique to recover faulty links and/or neurons. In addition, we have conducted experiments, and their results support the merit of this technique. The technique can be used in real time operations. Although our experiment substantiates our concept and hypothesis, we can not apply this technique to recover the faulty neurons in the top layer. To overcome this deficiency, one possible solution is to apply the triple modular redundancy (TMR) [3] design.

## References

[1]   L. Chu and B. Wah, "Fault Tolerant Neural Networks with Hybrid Redundancy", pp. II-639-649, IJCNN 1990.

[2]   C.H. Sequin and R. D. Clay, "Fault Tolerance in Artificial Neural Networks", pp. I-703-708, IJCNN 1990.

[3]   J. Wakerly, "Error Detecting Codes, Self-Checking Circuits and Applications", North-Holland Publishing, 1982.

[4]   C. Neti, M.H. Schneider, and E.D. Young, "Maximally Fault Tolerant Neural Networks", IEEE Transactions on Neural Networks, January 1992, pp.14-23.

[5]   J. Kim, C. Lursinsap, and S. Park, "Fault_Tolerant Artificial Neural Networks", Internation Joint Conference on Neural Networks, Vol. II, pp.II-A-951, 1991.

[6]   R. Clay and C. Sequin, "Limiting Fault-Induced Output Errors in ANN's", International Joint Conference on Neural Networks, Vol. 2, pp.II-A-965, 1991.

[7]   C. Khunasaraphan, K. Vanapipat, and C. Lursinsap, "Weight Shifting Technique for Self-Recovery Neural Networks", accepted to be published in IEEE Transactions on Neural Networks.

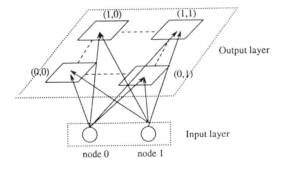

Figure 1. Shows the structure and name of Kohonen's self-organizing network

using in our experiments.

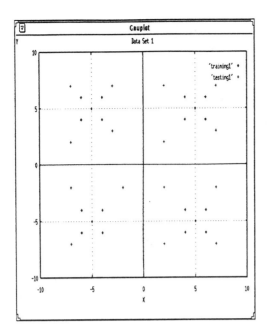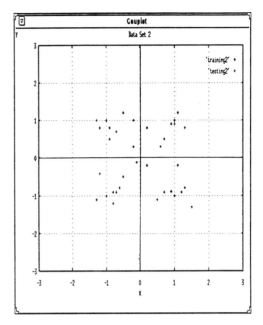

Figure 2. Shows the positions of training and testing patterns.

| Input node | Output node | Original weight | With/without weight shifting | Tolerant range of weights | Range width |
|---|---|---|---|---|---|
| 0 | (0,0) | -0.824 | w | (-5.9,-0.1) | 5.8 |
|   |       |        | w/o | (-1.6,4.9) | 6.5 |
| 0 | (0,1) | -4.126 | w | (-6.9,-4.0) | 2.9 |
|   |       |        | w/o | (-4.3,-2.3) | 2.0 |
| 0 | (1,0) | 2.475 | w | (1.3,7.7) | 6.4 |
|   |       |       | w/o | (1.6,4.0) | 2.4 |
| 0 | (1,1) | -2.475 | w | (-2.6,-1.0) | 1.6 |
|   |       |        | w/o | (-4.4,-2.4) | 2.0 |
| 1 | (0,0) | 2.557 | w | (2.1,5.0) | 2.9 |
|   |       |       | w/o | (0.6,3.0) | 2.4 |
| 1 | (0,1) | 2.557 | w | (-0.1,2.7) | 2.8 |
|   |       |       | w/o | (2.5,5.0) | 2.5 |
| 1 | (1,0) | -4.263 | w | (-5.1,-2.2) | 2.9 |
|   |       |        | w/o | (-7.2,-3.3) | 3.9 |
| 1 | (1,1) | 0.851 | w | (0.7,5.8) | 5.1 |
|   |       |       | w/o | (-5.0,1.0) | 6.0 |

Table 1. Illustrates the range of tolerant weights of data set 1.

| Input node | Output node | Original weight | With/without weight shifting | Tolerant range of weights | Range width |
|---|---|---|---|---|---|
| 0 | (0,0) | 0.101 | w | (-2.1,0.7) | 2.8 |
|   |       |       | w/o | (-0.2,1.5) | 1.7 |
| 0 | (0,1) | -0.332 | w | (-1.0,-0.1) | 0.9 |
|   |       |        | w/o | (-0.7,-0.2) | 0.5 |
| 0 | (1,0) | 0.245 | w | (-0.6,2.1) | 2.7 |
|   |       |       | w/o | (0.2,1.8) | 1.6 |
| 0 | (1,1) | -0.327 | w | (-0.7,-0.1) | 0.6 |
|   |       |        | w/o | (-0.5,-0.1) | 0.4 |
| 1 | (0,0) | -0.412 | w | (-1.4,-0.1) | 1.3 |
|   |       |        | w/o | (-2.0,0.1) | 2.1 |
| 1 | (0,1) | -0.256 | w | (-0.5,0.3) | 0.8 |
|   |       |        | w/o | (-0.8,0.0) | 0.8 |
| 1 | (1,0) | 0.647 | w | (0.2,1.2) | 1.0 |
|   |       |       | w/o | (-0.3,1.5) | 1.8 |
| 1 | (1,1) | -0.023 | w | (-0.9,0.2) | 1.1 |
|   |       |        | w/o | (-0.2,1.3) | 1.5 |

Table 2. Illustrates the range of tolerant weights of data set 2.

# Generalized ART2 Algorithms

Magnús Snorrason, & Alper K. Caglayan

Charles River Analytics Inc.

55 Wheeler St., Cambridge, MA 02138

mss@cra.com

**Abstract** - This paper introduces a class of Adaptive Resonance Theory (ART) algorithms based on generalizations of the ART2-A algorithm, collectively known as GEN-ART. While retaining the overall framework common to all ART systems (bottom up competitive filtering combined with top down template matching and reset mechanism), it is possible to use other forms of interaction between input patterns and stored weights than the Euclidean inner product. Benefits of this new class of algorithms include the use of different distance metrics (L1, L2, max-norm, etc.) to tailor the algorithm to the input domain, or to make the algorithm more efficient on a given hardware platform (for example by eliminating multiplication from inner loops to speed up processing on digital CPUs). Another benefit is the ability to handle input vectors with non-scalar elements through the use of customized distance metrics. Examples of related clustering algorithms, such as Fuzzy-ART and GEC, which are not in the GEN-ART class are also discussed.

## 1. Introduction

The concept of a feedforward layered network with weights attached to the inter-layer connections is at the very basis of neural network computation. This concept is grounded in neuronal signal transmission: the weights model synaptic transmission and the convergence of multiple connections to a single node models the physical branching of dendritic trees. By it self, this concept does not specify the type of interaction between inputs and weights. The weight/input interaction used in ART, and most other neural networks, is the Euclidean inner product. This involves a single scalar multiplication at each connection followed by a single scalar addition at each node for each connection that leads to it. Alternatively, for a single node with $n$ connections fanning in to it, this can be thought of as one vector multiplication of $n$ dimensional vectors followed by one summation of $n$ scalars. This choice of processing is biologically inspired although it is clear that modelling synaptic transmission as multiplication and dendritic convergence as summation is an extreme simplification.

Our work examines the use of other methods for weight/input interactions within the framework of ART neural networks. The intent is not just to improve the model of synaptic transmission, as was done in ART3 (Carpenter and Grossberg, 1990) and in (Carpenter, 1993), but rather to expand the domain of applicability for ART-style clustering by generalizing the weight/input interactions. We have chosen the algorithmic version of ART2, known as ART2-A (Carpenter, Grossberg, and Rosen, 1991), as our starting point. The result is a class of algorithms, collectively known as GEN-ART, for "GENeralized Adaptive Resonance Theory".

A block diagram of ART2-A (figure 1) shows that computation is performed in four distinct blocks. To summarize the algorithm, the main equations for each block are listed below (see Carpenter, Grossberg, and Rosen, 1991 for details of parameter ranges).

NORMALIZE & THRESHOLD:

$$I = N(F_\theta(N(I^0))) \tag{1}$$

$$N(x) = x \ / \ \|x\|_e , \text{ where } \| \cdot \|_e \text{ represents the Euclidean norm} \tag{2}$$

$$F_\theta(x) = [(F_\theta(x))_i], \ (F_\theta(x))_i = \begin{cases} x_i, \ x_i > \theta \\ 0, \text{ otherwise} \end{cases} \tag{3}$$

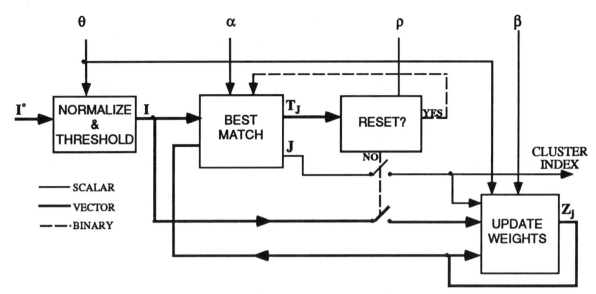

*Figure 1: Block diagram of the ART2-A algorithm.*

BEST MATCH:

$$T_J = \max_j(T_j) \tag{4}$$

$$T_j = \begin{cases} \langle \mathbf{I}, \mathbf{z}_\alpha \rangle_e, & y_j = 0 \\ \langle \mathbf{I}, \mathbf{z}_j \rangle_e, & y_j = 1 \end{cases}, \text{ where } < \cdot >_e \text{ represents the Euclidean inner product} \tag{5}$$

Where $\mathbf{z}_\alpha$ is a vector of initial weights with every element equal to $\alpha$. The weights associated with cluster node $j$ are represented by vector $\mathbf{z}_j$. The binary variable $y_j$ represents the status of node $j$, "0" for uncommitted (no previously coded inputs), and "1" for committed.

RESET:

$$\text{"Yes" if } T_J < \rho \text{ and } y_J = 1, \text{"No" otherwise} \tag{6}$$

A reset cancels the present index of best match, $J$, and forces the new choice of $J$ to be an uncommitted node. Only then (or if no reset occurred in the first place) is $J$ recorded as the index of the cluster which the given input belongs to, and the weights representing that cluster are updated.

WEIGHT UPDATE:

$$\mathbf{z}^{new}{}_J = \begin{cases} N(\beta \cdot N(\Psi) + (1-\beta) \cdot \mathbf{z}^{old}{}_J), & y_J = 1 \\ \mathbf{I}, & y_J = 0 \end{cases} \tag{7}$$

$$\Psi = [\Psi_i], \ \Psi_i = \begin{cases} I_i, & z^{old}{}_{Ji} > \theta \\ 0, & \text{otherwise} \end{cases} \tag{8}$$

In the next three sections of this paper we will show three levels of generalization to this algorithm:

1. Drop the Euclidean assumption: Choose an arbitrary inner product and use $\|x\|_\lambda = (\langle x,x\rangle_\lambda)^{1/2}$ for norm.

2. Drop the inner product assumption: Choose an arbitrary norm and use $d_\mu(x,y) = \|x-y\|_\mu$ for distance metric.

3. Drop the normed vector space assumption: Choose an arbitrary distance metric and use no norm.

## 2. Allowing Arbitrary Inner Products

The first level of generalization is to drop the requirement that the inner product in the "Best Match" block be Euclidean. This is done by allowing an arbitrary inner product, which is defined as follows:

Let X be a vector space (Real or Complex). Then inner product $\lambda$ is defined for $x,y,z \in X$ and $\alpha,\beta \in R$ as:

$$\langle x,y\rangle_\lambda: X\times X \to R \text{ such that } \begin{cases} \langle x,y\rangle_\lambda = \overline{\langle y,x\rangle_\lambda} \\ \langle \alpha x +\beta y,z\rangle_\lambda = \alpha\langle x,z\rangle_\lambda + \beta\langle y,z\rangle_\lambda \\ \langle x,x\rangle_\lambda \geq 0 \;\; \forall\, x \in X \\ \langle x,x\rangle_\lambda = 0 \;\Leftrightarrow\; x = \varnothing \end{cases} \tag{9}$$

Every inner product can generate a vector norm as follows:

$$\|x\|_\lambda = (\langle x,x\rangle_\lambda)^{1/2} \tag{10}$$

Consequently, only equations (2) and (5) change in the ART2-A algorithm:

$$N(x) = x\,/\,\|x\|_\lambda \tag{11}$$

$$T_j = \begin{cases} \langle I,z_\alpha\rangle_\lambda, y_j = 0 \\ \langle I,z_j\rangle_\lambda, y_j = 1 \end{cases} \tag{12}$$

Examples of useful non-Euclidean inner products:

$$\langle x,y\rangle_{\lambda 1} = E(x,y)\,, \quad \text{where x and y are random variables and } E(\bullet) \text{ is the expected value.}$$

$$\langle f(x),g(x)\rangle_{\lambda 2} = \int_a^b f(x)g(x)dx\,, \quad \text{where } f(x) \text{ and } g(x) \text{ are functions defined on the interval } [a,b]$$

$$\langle x,y\rangle_{\lambda 3} = \int_0^T xy\varphi(t)dt\,, \quad \text{where } \varphi(t) \text{ is a fixed weighting function, defined on the interval } [0,T]$$

## 3. Allowing Arbitrary Vector Norms

The second level of generalization is to drop the requirement that the distance between input vectors and weights in the "Best Match" block be computed by taking an inner product. This can be accomplished by allowing an *arbitrary* vector norm, rather than being limited by norms which are derived from inner products (as in the previous case). An arbitrary vector norm is defined as follows:

Let X be a vector space (Real or Complex). Then vector norm $\mu$ is defined for $x,y \in X$ and $\alpha \in R$ as:

$$\|x\|_\mu: X \to R \text{ such that } \begin{cases} \|\alpha x\|_\mu = |\alpha| \cdot \|x\|_\mu \\ \|x+y\|_\mu \leq \|x\|_\mu + \|y\|_\mu \\ \|x\|_\mu \geq 0 \quad \forall\, x \in X \\ \|x\|_\mu = 0 \iff x = \emptyset \end{cases} \tag{13}$$

A distance metric can be derived from every vector norm as follows:

$$d_\mu(x,y) = \|x-y\|_\mu \tag{14}$$

Again, equations (2) and (5) in the ART2-A algorithm are affected:

$$N(x) = x\, /\, \|x\|_\mu \tag{15}$$

$$T_j = \begin{cases} d_\mu(I,z_\alpha), & y_j = 0 \\ d_\mu(I,z_j), & y_j = 1 \end{cases} \tag{16}$$

But now equation (4) must also change. The closest weight vector is no longer represented by the largest $T_j$, but rather the smallest one:

$$T_J = \min_j(T_j) \tag{17}$$

Examples of useful norms include L1 (Hamming), L2 (Euclidean), L$i$ with $i \geq 3$, and max-norm.

## 4.    Allowing Arbitrary Distance Metrics

The third level of generalization is to allow an arbitrary distance metric in computing the distance between input vectors and weights in the "BEST MATCH" block. This is more general then the previous level because a metric space (i.e. a space where a distance metric is defined) is not necessarily a normed vector space. An arbitrary distance metric is defined as follows:

Let S be an arbitrary set. Then distance metric $\delta$ is defined for $x,y,z \in S$ as:

$$d_\delta(x,y): S \times S \to R \text{ such that } \begin{cases} d_\delta(x,y) = d_\delta(y,x) \\ d_\delta(x,z) \leq d_\delta(x,y) + d_\delta(y,z) \\ d_\delta(x,y) \geq 0 \quad \forall\, x,y \in S \\ d_\delta(x,y) = 0 \iff x = y \end{cases} \tag{18}$$

Equation (5) in the ART2-A algorithm changes as expected:

$$T_j = \begin{cases} d_\delta(I,z_\alpha), & y_j = 0 \\ d_\delta(I,z_j), & y_j = 1 \end{cases} \tag{19}$$

However, since it is not possible to derive a vector norm for an arbitrary distance metric, the ART2-A algorithm must now be modified to work with out norms. In particular, the thresholding performed on the input is no longer meaningful if the input elements are not normalized. Not thresholding the input is of course equivalent to setting $\theta = 0$,

IV-243

and hence a special case of the original ART2-A algorithm. By eliminating normalization and thresholding, all processing has been removed from the "NORMALIZE AND THRESHOLD" block, replacing equations (1), (2), and (3) with:

$$I = I^0 \tag{20}$$

Also, since inputs and weights are no longer required to be real (or complex), vectors operations such as addition and multiplication by a scalar are no longer defined. The weight update rule must therefore be limited to the ART2-A "fast learning" case where $\beta = 1.0$, replacing the "WEIGHT UPDATE" equations (7 and 8) with:

$$z^{new}_j = I \tag{21}$$

Examples of useful distance metrics which do not induce vector norms come up in clustering patterns with elements from multiple sources. In image processing for example, it is often useful to consider as a pattern the triad $\{x, y, I(x,y)\}$ where $x$ and $y$ are coordinates and $I(x,y)$ is the intensity at that coordinate. Given this form of input patterns, a distance metric can be constructed which is insensitive to spatial noise (local shifts and rotations) in both $x$ and $y$ directions. In fact, this operation can be performed by an arbitrarily complex convolution kernel, so long as the requirements in equation (18) are met.

Since distance is a function of both input patterns and weight patterns, it also allows for context dependent effects which can be learned as the network weights change. For example, the size of a convolution kernel could vary with the size of the weights or even with the index of the weights, allowing attentional priming in a similar manner to the dynamically changing receptive field sizes which have been recorded in primates (Desimone, 1992). This is an advantage of having a processing kernel built into the distance metric, rather than applied during preprocessing,

## 5. GEN-ART Level 2 With Hamming Norm vs. Fuzzy-ART

Another reason to change the form of weight/input interaction in ART2-A is to make the algorithm more efficient on a given hardware platform. For example, the conventional digital CPU performs the operation of addition many times faster then multiplication. By switching from the Euclidean inner product to the Hamming norm induced distance metric, all multiplications are replaced by additions and comparisons in the innermost loops of the "BEST MATCH" block (and one square root operation per vector is also eliminated). This can lead to significant performance speedup, especially for high dimensional inputs.

Fuzzy-ART (Carpenter, Grossberg, and Rosen, 1991) also uses additions and comparisons rather then multiplications in its innermost loops. The "BEST MATCH" computation is based on the Hamming norm of the *fuzzy set theory conjunction* of the input and the weight vectors, rather then the Hamming norm of the *vector difference* as in equation (14). Fuzzy-ART falls outside the class of algorithms defined by GEN-ART because fuzzy set theory conjunction violates the last requirement for a distance metric in equation (18), however, it shows the same performance improvement over ART2-A as does GEN-ART with Hamming norm and its clustering of inputs is qualitatively similar. In addition to not using a distance metric, most implementations of Fuzzy-ART also differ from GEN-ART by complement coding of inputs such that both the presence and absence of a feature is coded.

## 6. GEN-ART Level 3 vs. Generalized Equality Clustering

Another algorithm which allows the use of an arbitrary distance metric is the Generalized Equality Clustering (GEC) algorithm introduced in (Caglayan and Snorrason, 1993) and based on work by (Lorczak, Caglayan, and Eckhardt, 1989). The algorithm is summarized as follows:

Let $X = \{x_1, x_2, \dots, x_n\}$ denote the set of $n$ patterns fto be clustered and let $(X, d)$ be a metric space with the distance metric $d$. Generalized Equality Clustering constructs $k$ clusters $S_1, S_2, \dots, S_k$ such that $S_1, S_2, \dots, S_j, \dots, S_k$ is maximal with respect to the property that for *any* x and y in $S_j$ $d(x, y) \leq e$, where $k$ is not predetermined. The GEC algorithm can be implemented as follows:

1)     select a distance metric $d$ and a threshold $\varepsilon$

2)     let the cluster index $j = 1$

3)     select any element $x_i$ from $X$

4)     let cluster $S_j = \{x_i\}$

5)     select any element y from $X-S_j$

6)     let $S_j = S_j \cup \{y\}$ if $d(y, x_i) \leq \varepsilon$ for all $x_i$ in $S_j$

7)     repeat steps 5 and 6 until no new elements are added to $S_j$

8)     replace $X$ with $X-S_j$

9)     if $X$ is the empty set then stop, else increment $j$ and return to step 3

As demonstrated in (Caglayan and Snorrason, 1993), this algorithm can produce very similar clustering results as ART2-A, with significant improvement in speed when using the Hamming distance (for the same reasons as discussed in the previous section).

The GEC algorithm does not fit in the class of algorithms defined by GEN-ART for two reasons. First, GEC does not use weight vectors to determine cluster membership, instead it requires every pair of elements in a cluster to be within a given distance from each other (see step 6 in the algorithm). This requirement implies the necessity for having all inputs available at the same time, while GEN-ART class algorithms can operate with incremental input presentation. Second, there is no "BEST MATCH" *optimization* using either the min(•) or max(•) functions, instead the *first* cluster which fulfills the requirement in step 6 is chosen. This is an obvious advantage for speed but a disadvantage for "accuracy" in terms of minimizing total within-cluster mean-squared-error. However, since all the algorithms discussed in this paper give different clustering results based on the order of input presentation, it is likely that in most applications this difference in accuracy is insignificant.

## 7.    Summary

A class of clustering algorithms, called GEN-ART, has been developed by generalizing the ART2-A algorithm. The first two levels of generalization retain all aspects of ART2-A other then the form of weight/input interaction, which is generalized to all inner products (level 1) or to all distance metrics which can be derived from vector norms (level 2). The third level of generalization limits processing to the "fast learning" case with no thresholding or normalization of inputs, but generalizes weight/input interactions to include all distance metrics. Further work is currently being done in developing specific algorithms in GEN-ART and in studying issues of stability.

## References

Caglayan, A.K. and Snorrason, M. 1993. "On the Relationship between Generalized Equality Clustering and ART 2 Neural Networks." *WCNN'93*, Portland, OR.

Carpenter, G.A. 1993. "Distributed Outstar Learning and the Rules of Synaptic Transmission" *WCNN'93*, Portland, OR.

Carpenter, G.A. and Grossberg, S. 1990. "ART3: Hierarchical Search Using Chemical Transmitters in Self-Organizing Pattern Recognition Architectures." *Neural Networks*, Vol. 3, pp. 129-152.

Carpenter, G.A., Grossberg, S. and Rosen, D.B. 1991a. "ART2-A: An Adaptive Resonance Algorithm for Rapid Category Learning and Recognition." *Neural Networks*, Vol. 4, pp. 493-504.

Carpenter, G.A., Grossberg, S. and Rosen, D.B. 1991b. "Fuzzy ART: Fast Stable Learning and Categorization of Analog Patterns by an Adaptive Resonance System" *Neural Networks*, Vol. 4, pp. 759-771.

Desimone, R. 1992. "Neural Circuits for Visual Attention in the Primate Brain." In Carpenter, G.A. and Grossberg, S, (Eds.), *Neural Networks for Vision and Image Processing*, Ch. 12, pp. 343-364, MIT Press, Cambridge, MA.

Lorczak, P.R., Caglayan, A.K. and Eckhardt, D.E. 1989. "A Theoretical Investigation of Generalized Voters for Redundant Systems." *FTCS 19*. Chicago, IL.

# Fuzzy ART and morphological image processing

N. Sungar
*Department of Physics,*
*California Polytechnic State University,*
*San Luis Obispo, CA 93407*

J. P. Sharpe and K. M. Johnson
*Optoelectronic Computing Systems Center,*
*University of Colorado at Boulder,*
*Boulder, CO 80309*

## Abstract

The connection between adaptive resonance theory (ART) and image morphology is explored. We show how ART can be used to generate morphological kernels for the hit-or-miss transform and thus permit detection of classes or clusters of objects.

## 1 Introduction

Mathematical morphology is a technique that can be used to describe and manipulate images and signals [1] [2]. Since it has its basis in set theory and is inherently nonlinear, it differs significantly from linear systems theory as a formalism, but permits treatment of images and signals in regimes where conventional methods find it difficult (e.g. in the presence of impulse or multiplicative noise). Mathematical morphology has also found application in many industrial machine vision systems since it is well suited to shape and size inspection and is amenable, through specialized hardware, to rapid electronic implementation. It is also interesting to note that mathematical morphology had as part of its background an attempt to mathematically quantify the ideas of the gestalt psychologists [1].

Although a great deal of work has been done on image morphology since its inception as a discipline in the 1960s, there seems to have been little done in the area of adaptation or self learning in morphological systems. In this paper we point out the similarities between a self organizing neural network model (adaptive resonance theory or ART) and image morphology. Specifically, we will be concerned with the morphological hit-or-miss transformation (HoM) which is conventionally defined as [3]

$$A \otimes B = (A \ominus X) \cap [A^c \ominus (W - X)] \tag{1}$$

where B denotes the set comprised of the object X (to be detected) and its background and W is a window surrounding X. $\ominus$ is morphological erosion, superscript c represents set complementation and $\cap$ is set intersection. The HoM in effect detects the *presence* of the target object in the scene and the *absence* of the object in the complementary (video reversed) scene. The HoM is also open to a somewhat broader interpretation where the hit and miss kernels need not be simple inverses of each other and where we wish to detect not a single object but a class of objects.

For example, let us assume we have a number of objects, $O_1, O_2 \cdots O_n$ and we wish to detect a subset of these objects. The restriction we shall put on the objects to detect are that they fall in a certain size range. That is, we want to ignore objects bigger and smaller than certain bounds. In terms of the HoM we wish to find kernels or structuring elements H and M such that

$$S \otimes < H, M > = (S \ominus H) \cap (S^c \ominus M) \tag{2}$$

is true for that subset. If we assume that the subset of objects are the same shape and differ by a scale factor such that $O_x \subseteq O_{x+1} \subseteq O_{x+2} \cdots \subseteq O_{x+m}$ then it is easy to see that hit and miss kernels to perform the detection operation are given by $H = O_x$ and $M = O_{x+m}^c$ so we have

$$S \otimes < H, M > = (S \ominus O_x) \cap (S^c \ominus O_{x+m}^c) \tag{3}$$

or using the duality relation of morphology

$$S \otimes < H, M > = (S \ominus O_x) - (S \oplus O_{x+m}^c) \tag{4}$$

where $\oplus$ is dilation so that the HoM is the set difference between the erosion of the image by the smaller object and the dilation by the larger object. Although it is easy to see the types of kernels required for detection when we have the above simple constraint, it is not so obvious what kernels to use if we have irregular and partially overlapping sets. We shall see later how the required morphological kernels arise naturally in a complement coded fuzzy ART system.

Although we could first derive the equations for the case of binary images we will go directly to the case of grayscale by treating the images as fuzzy subsets. In section 2 we outline the theory of fuzzy ART theory as detailed in reference [4] and show the conditions under which different clusters are formed. We also show that the distance metric which naturally arises from this treatment has a useful set-theoretic interpretation. In section 3 we show how, through complement coding, the hit and miss kernels are automatically generated. In the process we also show that the definitions of distance in morphology, although they appear strange at first, do in fact fit within the context of ART.

## 2 Fuzzy ART

Although the full implementation of ART is described by a set of coupled differential equations [5], under certain conditions known as fast learning the implementation reduces to a simple clustering algorithm [6] [7] as shown in figure 1. Here the $Is$ are (binary) input vectors, the $Ts$ are stored templates, $\rho$ is the vigilance parameter which determines the coarseness of categorization and $\beta$ is a constant.

ART was also originally defined for binary input patterns and, although later extended (as ART2) to incorporate analog patterns [8], the original ART can be used if the ANDing operation is replaced with the fuzzy minimum operation [4]. In fact, the transition from ART to fuzzy ART can be made in a more natural fashion if we consider the analog patterns as coded in a "stack" representation where the analog value is coded as a stack of binary elements. So, for example, if we want to represent numbers in the range 0 to 256 we set aside a vector of length 256 for each number. Then if we wish to represent the number of value $m$ we fill up the vector to $m$ with the value 1 and leave the rest zero. This is implicitly carried out in [4] but the concept of a stack preserves the "pattern" of the input (which does not occur with other binary representations of analog values) and also permits a direct extension of ART without the seemingly *ad hoc* approach of set fuzzification.

We now show the criteria under which similar patterns are clustered using fuzzy ART. For notational convenience we will consider the components of the M-dimensional vectors we discuss as accessed by a single coordinate.

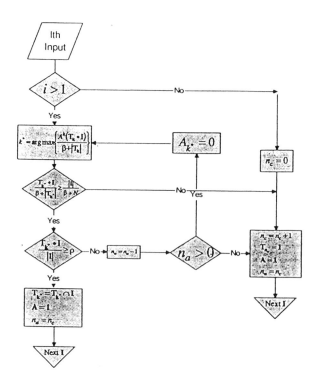

Figure 1: Algorithmic form of ART1, after Moore 1989 and Caudell 1992.

Consider the $N$ M-dimensional vectors $I'_i$ where the components of $I'_i$ lie in the range [0,1] and $i = 1 \cdots N$. We want to show under what conditions the fuzzy ART algorithm can categorize these N vectors in the same cluster and what is the form of the generated weight vectors.

As in reference [4] we will use complement coded input vectors so that the actual input vectors are $I_i = (I'_i, I'^c_i)$ where $I'_i$ is the original vector and the components of $I'^c_i$ are $I'^{c}_{ij} = 1 - I'_{ij}$ where $I'_{ij}$ is the $jth$ component of vector $I'_i$. In this way the input vectors are automatically normalized so that $|I_i| = M$ where $|I_i| = \sum_j I_{ij}$ and this coding also prevents the phenomenon of "template proliferation"[4]. The initial network weights are also set to 1. Then, following [4], we define the choice and match functions as

$$T_j = \frac{|I_i \wedge w_j|}{\beta + |w_j|} \tag{5}$$

and

$$\frac{|I_i \wedge w_j|}{|I_i|} \geq \rho, \tag{6}$$

respectively where $\wedge$ is fuzzy intersection which is implemented as a minimum operation i.e. $|I_i \wedge w_j| = \sum_k min(I_{ik}, w_{jk})$ and $w_{jk}$ is the $kth$ element of the $jth$ stored weight vector.

Since the initial weights are set to one, presentation of the first input, $I_1$, results in this input being copied as the first weight vector (template). Any subsequent presentation of another input vector $I_i$ can be analysed as follows: the choice function is

$$T_1 = \frac{|I_i \wedge w_1|}{\beta + |w_1|} = \frac{|I_i \wedge I_1|}{\beta + |I_1|} = \frac{|(I_i', I_i'^c) \wedge (I_1', I_1'^c)|}{\beta + M} \tag{7}$$

and using the distributivity of the min operation and $I_a^c \wedge I_b^c = (I_a \vee I_b)^c$ we get

$$T_1 = \frac{|(I_i' \wedge I_1'), (I_i' \vee I_1')^c|}{\beta + M} \tag{8}$$

where $\vee$ is the max operation. For any other uncommited node the choice function is $M/(\beta+2M)$ so that if $T_1 \geq M/(\beta + 2M)$ then no new cluster will be generated and we can proceed to the matching criterion. If

$$\frac{|I_i \wedge w_i|}{|I_i|} = \frac{|(I_i', I_i'^c) \wedge (I_1', I_1'^c)|}{M} \geq \rho \tag{9}$$

then

$$w_1^{new} = I_i \wedge w_1 = ((I_i' \wedge I_1'), (I_i' \vee I_1')^c) \tag{10}$$

which shows that some of the entries of $w_1(= I_1)$ will be replaced by entries of $I_i$ iff $I_{ij} < I_{1j}$ and in the complement part iff $I_{il} > I_{1l}$. Therefore, in order for any subsequent inputs to be categorized together we require

$$\frac{|(I_i' \wedge I_j'), (I_i' \vee I_k')^c|}{\beta + |w_1^{new}|} \geq \frac{M}{\beta + 2M} \tag{11}$$

and, of course, satisfaction of the matching criterion for any inputs $I_i', I_j', I_k'$. Note that after we have presented all the inputs the weights will have assumed the final form $w^{final} = (u, v^c)$ where $u_k = min(I_{ik}')$ and $v_k = max(I_{ik}')$, $i = 1, ...N$ and $k = 1, ...M$. Also, $|w^{final}| \leq M$. Therefore the numerator of equation 11 will be greater than or equal to $|min(I_i'), (max(I_i')^c)|$ and the denominator will always be less than or equal to $(\beta + M)$. So, if

$$\frac{|min(I_i'), (max(I_i'))^c|}{\beta + M} \geq \frac{M}{\beta + 2M} \tag{12}$$

then equation 11 will always be satisfied. The matching criterion is satisfied as well if

$$\frac{|min(I_i'), (max(I_i'))^c|}{M} \geq \rho \tag{13}$$

which can be written as

$$\sum_k min(I_{ik}') + M - \sum_k max(I_{ik}') \geq M\rho \tag{14}$$

or

$$\sum_k (max(I_{ik}') - min(I_{ik}')) \leq M(1 - \rho). \tag{15}$$

Performing a similar manipulation on equation 12 gives

$$\sum_k (max(I_{ik}') - min(I_{ik}')) \leq \frac{M^2}{\beta + 2M}. \tag{16}$$

Equations 15 and 16 give the criteria for similar clustering with the ART algorithm. If we examine equations 11 and 12 in their binary form we see that the distance metric defined by them is equivalent to

$$Card[A \cup B - A \cap B] \tag{17}$$

where A and B are binary sets and $Card$, $\cup$, $\cap$ and $-$ denote set cardinality, union, intersection and difference respectively. This distance, which is equivalent to the Hamming distance of we consider A and B as binary vectors, has been introduced previously in mathematical morphology [9] as the set difference distance function (SDDF) for quantitative comparison of images.

## 3 Fuzzy Morphology using ART generated kernels

In order to make the transition from binary morphology to grayscale, Sinha and Dougherty [10] decided to fuzzify set inclusion. For this purpose they defined membership and index functions where the membership function, $\mu$, takes values in the range [0,1] and we may interpret it as the grayscale of any pixel, $j$, such that $0 \leq \mu(j) \leq 1$. We can then define an index function, $K$, which denotes the degree to which a set A is a subset or part of a set B.

$$K(A, B) = \min_j \min[1, 1 + \mu(j)_B - \mu(j)_A] \tag{18}$$

where $\min_j$ means the minimum over all $j$. In consonance with our previous notation $\mu(j)_{I_i}$ is equivalent to $I_{ij}$, that is the gray value of the $jth$ element of the set or input vector $I_i$. As a measure of distance or similarity, equation 18 looks strange in that a change in just one pixel can greatly change the index function. We can now also define fuzzy erosion of the set A by the set B as

$$\mu(j)_{A \ominus B} = K(\tau(B, j), A) \tag{19}$$

where $\tau(B, j)$ is the translate of $B$ to pixel $j$. And we can finally define fuzzy hit-or-miss such that

$$S \otimes < H, M > = (S \ominus H) \wedge (S^c \ominus M) \tag{20}$$

Now consider a class of objects $I_i, i = 1, \cdots N$. Using fuzzy ART with complement coding we can generate a kernel that can be used to detect an object from the class using fuzzy HoM. This is because the kernel for the hit will be such that $\mu(j)_H = \min_j(\mu(j)_{I_i})$ and the miss kernel such that $\mu(j)_M = 1 - \max_j(\mu(j)_{I_i})$. Now, if any member of the set of objects (say $I_x$) is within a scene presented for the HoM the scene is first eroded with the hit kernel to give

$$\mu(j)_{I_x \ominus H} = \min_k \min[1, 1 + \mu(k)_{I_x} - \mu(k - j)_H] \tag{21}$$

and we must have detection when the kernel is coincident with the object (j=0) since at this position we are sure that the kernel is entirely contained within all of the training examples. For the miss kernel we have

$$\mu(j)_{I_x^c \ominus M} = \min_k \min[1, 1 + \mu(k)_{I_x^c} - \mu(k - j)_M] \tag{22}$$

which becomes

$$\mu(j)_{I_x^c \ominus M} = \min_k \min[1, 1 - \mu(k)_{I_x} - \mu(k - j)_M] \tag{23}$$

from the definition of complementation. Since we have $\mu(k)_M = 1 - max(\mu(k)_{I_i})$ we can also see that there will again be at least one point (j=0) for which the miss kernel will be completely within the (complementary) object to be detected. Valid detection for any patterns or objects within the original group is thus achieved. Note that since the ART algorithm "learns" by a process of erosion, in effect creating a minimum sized prototype or exemplar for the hit kernal for a particular class, noise is removed from the exemplar and only statistically significant kernel contours remain.

# 4 Summary

We have proved that by using adaptive resonance theory it is possible to produce a set of kernels which may be used in the morphological hit-or-miss transform for object detection. By considering the cases of fuzzy ART and fuzzy morphology we have also been able to go directly to the case of grayscale images. Future work includes extension to the case where the objects are corrupted by noise. We are also presently implementing a system based on the above algorithm for the detection of cancerous cells in Pap smears [11].

# References

[1] J. Serra. *Image analysis and mathematical morphology.* Academic Press, London, 1982.

[2] C. R. Giardina and E. R. Dougherty. *Morphological Methods in Image and Signal Processing.* Prentice Hall International, Englewood Cliffs, NJ, 1988.

[3] R. C. Gonzalez and R. E. Woods. *Digital Image Processing.* Addison-Wesley, 1992.

[4] G. A. Carpenter, S. Grossberg, and D. B. Rosen. Fuzzy art: fast stable learning and categorization of analog patterns by an adaptive resonance system. *Neural Networks*, 4:759–771, 1991.

[5] G. A. Carpenter and S. Grossberg. A massively parallel architecture for a self-organizing neural pattern recognition machine. *Computer Vision, Graphics, and Image Processing*, 37:54–115, 1987.

[6] B. Moore. Art1 and pattern clustering. In *Proceedings of 1988 Connectionist Models Summer School*, pages 174–185. Morgan Kauffman Publishers, 1988.

[7] T. P. Caudell. Hybrid optoelectronic adaptive resonance theory neural processor, art1. *Applied Optics*, 31:6220–6229, 1992.

[8] G. A. Carpenter and S. Grossberg. Art2: Self organization of stable category recognition codes for analog input patterns. *Applied Optics*, 26:4919–4930, 1987.

[9] D. Schonfeld and J. Goutsias. Optimal morphological pattern restoration from noisy binary images. *IEEE Transactions on Pattern Analysis and Machine Intelligence*, 13(1):14–29, 1991.

[10] D. Sinha and E. R. Dougherty. Fuzzy mathematical morphology. *Journal of Visual Communication and Image Representation*, 3(3):286–302, 1992.

[11] R. Narayanswamy, J. P. Sharpe, R. J. Stewart, L. Mckeogh, I. Bar-Tana, S. Goggin, P. Black, and K. M. Johnson. Optoelectronic information processing for diagnostic cytology. OCS Technical Report 94-05, University of Colorado at Boulder, 1994.

# An Algorithmic implementation of Sequential Memory with ART

JAMES VOGH

vogh@park.bu.edu
Graduate Program in Cognitive and Neural Systems
Boston University, 111 Cummington Street, Boston, MA 02215

*Abstract - This paper presents of algorithmic version of the sequential memory ART neural network. The algorithmic implementation replaces the competitive interactions in the network with algorithms and allows faster simulation. The detailed design of both the region select layer and the cell group is presented. Based on these details, the algorithm is presented in a pseudo-code format.*

## 1. Introduction

The SMART network presented in Vogh (1994) and introduced in Vogh (1993) has been algorithmicly implemented. Figure 1 illustrates the SMART architecture described in Vogh 1994. The SMART neural network is a network which expands the ART architectures described in Grossberg (1976a, 1976b) and Carpenter & Grossberg (1987) to memory for sequences of events. Sequential memory is implemented as both a short term memory pattern of activity and a long term memory pattern of connections between $F_2$ nodes. The purpose of the algorithm is to bypass the competitive interactions which exist within the SMART architectures. These competitive interactions exist within both the sub-layers and region select layer and can result in very long simulation times. Substituting algorithms results is similar behavior and much shorter simulation times.

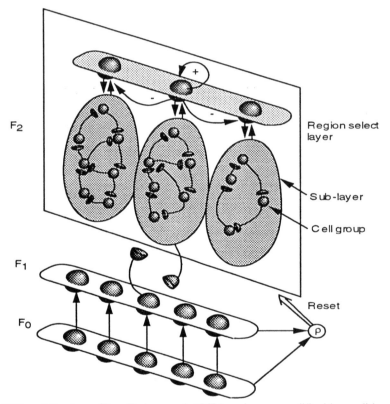

**Figure 1.** The SMART architecture. The $F_2$ layer of ART has been modified by splitting it into sub-layers. Nodes within the sub-layers are both interconnected with long term memory and interconnected in a on-center/off-surround manner so that each node competes for activity. The most active node will become the only active node in the sub-layer. Different sub-layers are selected by the region select layer. The sub-layer sends input to the region select layer nodes which in turn select the most active sub-layer.

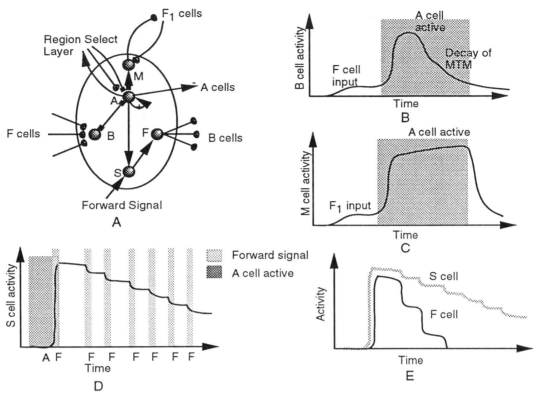

**Figure 2.** The full SMART cell group. (A) The cell group is composed of the Activity cell, *A*, the sampling cell, *S*, the Backward cell, *B*, the sustained activity cell, *S*, and the Forward cell, *F*. (B)The *B* cell receives input from the *B* cells of other cell groups. Input from the *A* cell is gated through medium term memory which causes the *B* cell to be highly active for a fixed period of time. (C) The *M* cell seres as the ART $F_2$ cell. (D)The *S* cell is activated by the coactivation of the *A* cell and the forward signal. *S* cell activity is decreased when the *Forward* signal is present while the *A* cell is not active. (E) The *F* cell activity is a thresholded faster-than-linear function of *S* cell activity.

## 2. The SMART cell group

The SMART cell-group is illustrated in Figure 1. The cell group consist of the following five types of cells: the *M* (saMpling) cell which sums LTM gated signals from the $F_1$ layer, the *F* (Forward) cell which samples activity of sub-sequently activated B cells, the *S* (Sustained) cell which maintains sustained activity after a cell group is deactivated, the *A*(Activity) cell which receives input from the *S* and *M* cells and forms a recurrent competitive field with other *A* cells in its $F_2$ sub-layer, and the *B* (Backward) cell which receives input from the *F* cells.The addition of subliminal activity has required the addition of a connection between the forward cell and the backward cell in the same cell group.

The sustained activity *S* cell maintains activity for long periods of time and is activated by the combination of the forward signal and *A* cell activity. The *S* cell loses activity when the forward signal is active and the activity cell is not. Since the forward signal corresponds to the presentation of a new input pattern, the *S* cell at the active node will be activated and the *S* cell activity at other nodes will decrease.

The *F* cell serves three purposes: it samples the activity of other cell groups which are subsequently activated, it aids in the recall of a sequence by sending input to the these nodes, and it is responsible for the spreading of subliminal

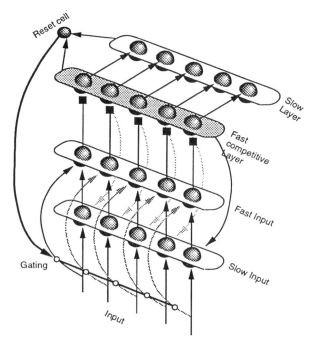

**Figure 3.** The region select layer. The region select layer is composed of the input stage and the competitive stage. Both stages have fast and slow activity.

activity. In order to prevent too many LTM connections between nodes, the $F$ cell needs to stay on for a shorter period of time than the $S$ cell. Since the $S$ cell is suppling the sustained activity to the $F$ cell, the input function from the S cell to the $F$ cell is both faster than linear and thresholded. A weak connection from the $B$ cell to the $F$ cell exist to spread subliminal activity.

In addition to representing the probability of the cell-group being the next item in the sequence, the $B$ cell forms part of the subliminal loop if a network has bi-directional connections. The $B$ cell receives input from LTM gated $F$ cells in other cell groups and MTM gated input from the $A$ cell in the same cell group. When the A cell is active, it sends MTM gated input to the B cell so that the B cell remains on for a constant amount of time after node activation regardless of the duration of the input pattern.

The characteristics of the $M$ cell depend on what type of ART module is being used. The purpose of the $M$ cell is to receive bottom-up input from $F_1$ and send a signal to the $A$ cell which represents the amount of match between the bottom-up input and the bottom-up filter.

The $A$ cells form a recurrent competitive field, RCF, with the other $A$ cells in the same $F_2$ sub-layer. The RCF uses a faster than linear function so that choice occurs, see Grossberg (1973). Each $A$ cell receives input from the $B$, $M$ and, $L$ cells (the $L$ cell is part of the region select layer and is discussed below). The inputs from the $B$ and $M$ cells control which cell group becomes active and the functions $f(x_S)$ and $g(x_M)$ control how the cell group is selected. These functions are faster than linear and are adjusted so that a perfect match to the input overrides intra-layer input.

## 3. The SMART region select layer

The region select layer (RSL) of SMART is illustrated in Figure 7. The SMART RSL is divided into two parts. The first part receives input from the sub-layer and sends an output to the competitive stage. The second part, the competitive stage, contrast enhances the input and forms a choice. Both parts of the RSL have been separated into fast and slow parts.

The input section of the RSL provides fast response time at the beginning of a sequence presentation and slow response time otherwise. The input section consist of three parts: the slow layer input (*SI*), fast layer input (*FI*), and the RSL reset cell. The slow layer averages both sub-layer and RSL activity over times. The *FI* and RSL reset cell act together to provide the varying rates of response speed. The *SI* layer is directly connected to the *FI* layer and the RSL reset cell modulates a direct connection from the sub-layers to the *FI* layer. When the RSL reset cell is active direct sub-layer input is strong and the RSL responds quickly and when it is inactive time averaged sub-layer input primarily effects the RSL. Activity of the RSL reset cell is controlled by the competitive stage.

The competitive stage of the RSL consist of the fast competitive layer, *FL*, and the slow averaging layer, *SL*. The layer which is competitive, the *FL* layer, performs contrast enhancement of MTM gated input from the *FI* layer and the averaging layer, the SL layer, averages the activity of the competitive layer. The averaged activity is compared to the current activity of the competitive layer by the RSL reset cell. If the difference between the two layers is too large then the RSL reset cell is activated.Although the *SI* layer has an time average of sub-layer and RSL activity it can not be used for the comparison because it does not have the same contrast enhanced activity pattern that the *SL* layer does. The difference between the *SI* and the *SL* layers would cause the RSL to constantly reset.

# 4. How to set up SMART

The initial values for the short term memory (STM), medium term memory (MTM), and long term memory (LTM) are set by using the following rules.

**1.** Set LTM interconnection strength of $F_2$ nodes to zero.

**2.** Set categorization of $F_2$ nodes so that each node categorizes a wide range of inputs.

**3.** Set MTM to maximum values.

**4.** Set activity of all nodes to zero.

# 5. Learning of Sequences by SMART

The following pseudo-code describes the SMART algorithm. Since SMART functions with various types of ART architectures the ART equations are not specified. See Carpenter, Grossberg, & Rosen (1991) paper for an example of these types of equations.

**1.** While the currently presented input pattern is not being classified

    **1.a.** Present input pattern to the $F_1$ layer using ART equations.

    **1.b.** Activate all of the M cells using ART equations. M cell activity is equivalent to ART $F_2$ node activity.

    **1.c.** Calculate A cell activity with the following equation:

$$x_{i,j}^A = A_A \left( y_{i,j}^{MA} x_{i,j}^M \right)^{m_A} + B_A \left( y_{i,j}^{BA} x_{i,j}^B \right)^{n_A} \tag{EQ 1}$$

    **1.d.** Spread subliminal loop activity (see section 8.).

    **1.e.** Calculate RSL activity (see section 9.).

    **1.f.** Select active node within sub-layer.

    If choice is being used then set activity of most active A cell to 1.0 and set all other A cells to 0.0. It contrast enhancement is being used then calculate A cell activity with the following equation:

$$x_{i,j}^A = \frac{\left( A_A \left( y_{i,j}^{MA} x_{i,j}^M \right)^{m_A} + B_A \left( y_{i,j}^{BA} x_{i,j}^B \right)^{n_A} + C_A \left( y_{i,j}^{LA} x_i^{FL} \right)^{p_A} \right)^{q_A}}{\sum_{k=1}^{N_i} \left( A_A \left( y_{i,k}^{MA} x_{i,k}^M \right)^{m_A} + B_A \left( y_{i,k}^{BA} x_{i,k}^B \right)^{n_A} + C_A \left( y_{i,k}^{LA} x_i^{FL} \right)^{p_A} \right)^{q_A}}, \tag{EQ 2}$$

Where $q_A$ specifies the amount of contrast enhancement. As $q_A$ gets very large Equation 2 begins to make a choice.

**1.g.** Spread subliminal activity

**1.h.** Check for an ART reset using ART equations and perform an ART reset if necessary (see section 6.).

**1.i.** Check for a sub-layer reset. The sub-layer reset signal is responsible for detecting a mismatch between the presented sequential pattern and the stored sequential pattern. A mismatch is detected by comparing over-all subliminal activity to the subliminal activity at a newly activated $F_2$ node. The following equation is applied just after a $F_2$ node becomes active:

$$R_2 = \begin{cases} 1 & \text{if } \dfrac{x_{i,j}^B \sum\limits_{k=1}^{N} f(x_{i,k}^B)}{\sum\limits_{k=1}^{N} [x_{i,k}^B - C]^+} > \rho_2 \\ 0 & otherwise \end{cases} \tag{EQ 3}$$

$$f(x) = \begin{cases} 1 & \text{if } x > C \\ 0 & otherwise \end{cases}, \tag{3a}$$

where $i$ is the number of the active sub-layer and $j$ is the number of the active node. C is a threshold for subliminal activity. Nodes with subliminal activity below this threshold are no considered. A reset is performed if necessary (see section 6.).

**1.j.** If a previously active node has been deactivated then do the following:

**1.j. i.** Activate the S cell of the previously active node and use the following equation to decrement the F cell activity in other nodes:

$$x_{i,j}^F(t + \Delta t) = \begin{cases} A_F x_{i,j}^F(t) & \text{if } (A_F x_{i,j}^F(t)) > Min_F \\ 0 & otherwise \end{cases} \tag{EQ 4}$$

**1.j. ii.** Spread subliminal activity (see section 8.).

**2.** Perform steady state modifications

**2.a.** Modify F2 intra-layer LTM

The intra-layer LTM is modified with a the following equation:

$$z(t + \Delta t) = e^{-b\Delta t}(z(t) - x^F) + x^F, \tag{EQ 5}$$

$$b = \begin{cases} -C_{OFF} x^B & \text{if } x^B > D \text{ and } z > x^F > D \\ C_{ON} x^B & \text{if } x^B > D \text{ and } z \le x^F \text{ and } x^F > D \\ 0 & otherwise \end{cases}, \tag{EQ 6}$$

where $\Delta t$ is the time increment, $x^F$ is the activity of the $F$ cell in another cell group, and $x^B$ is the activity of the $B$ cell in the cell group. $D$ is a threshold value and $C_{ON}$ controls the speed of learning and $C_{OFF}$

IV-256

controls the speed of forgetting.

**2.b.** Modify the $F_1$ to $F_2$ and $F_2$ to $F_1$ weights using ART equations.

**2.c.** Adjust MTM using steady state variables (see section 7.).

## 6. ART and sub-layer Reset

**1.** Adjust MTM. Adjust sub-layer MTM if an ART reset and adjust sub-layer and RSL MTM if a sub-layer reset.

**2.** If steady state had been reached at node then activate the S cell of the active node and decrement activity of active S cells in other cell groups. Use the Equation 3 to decrement the F cell activity:

**3.** Deactivate active node.

**4.** Spread subliminal activity (see section 8.).

## 7. Adjust MTM

Three different sets of variables are used to modify the MTM. The difference between the different variables depends on what type of reset is occurring and how long the MTM is being adjusted. The following table summarizes the variables which are used:

### Table 1: MTM adjustment values

| Type of Event | Sub-layer reset level | RSL reset level | time |
|---|---|---|---|
| ART or sub-layer reset after steady state | R | F | $t_R$ |
| ART or sub-layer reset after reclassification | R | R | $t_F$ |
| Steady State | 0 | 0 | $t_S$ |

The MTM of SMART is adjusted by using solutions of MTM equations. All of the MTM equations have the same form which is as follows:

$$y_{ij}(t + \Delta t) = e^{-b\Delta t}(y(t) - \frac{A}{b_{ij}}) + \frac{A}{b_{ij}}, \tag{EQ 7}$$

$$b_{ij} = 1 + x_i x_j (B + R), \tag{EQ 8}$$

where A is the maximum value for the MTM (usually 1.0) and B is the decay rare. $R$ is the reset signal which is described in Table 1. The value of $R$ is the same for all MTM in the sub-layers and a different value is used for all MTM in the RSL.

## 8. Spread Subliminal Activity

**1.** For several iterations do the following:

**1.a.** Calculate input to the B cell using the following equation:

$$I_{i,j}^B = f_{i,j}(\sum_{k \neq j} z_{(i,k),(i,j)}^{FB} x_{i,j}^F) + A_A (x_{i,j}^B)^{n_{AB}} y_{i,j}^{AB}, \tag{EQ 9}$$

where $f_{i,j}(x)$ is defined in Equation 9.

**1.b.** Calculate input to the F cell using the following equation:

$$I_{i,j}^F = f_{i,j} \left( \sum_{k \neq j} z_{(i,k),\,(i,j)}^{BF} x_{i,j}^F \right) + B_F \left[ (x_{i,j}^S)^2 - C_F \right]^+ \qquad \text{(EQ 10)}$$

**1.c.** Calculate activity of the B cell with the following equation:

$$x_{i,j}^B(t + \Delta t) = e^{-b\Delta t} \left( x_{i,j}^B(t) - \frac{a_{i,j}^B}{b_{i,j}^B} \right) + \frac{a_{i,j}^B}{b_{i,j}^B} \qquad \text{(EQ 11)}$$

$$a_{i,j}^B = \begin{cases} B_B I^B + E_B F_B x_{i,j}^F & \text{if } I^B \geq 0 \\ -B_B I^B + E_B F_B x_{i,j}^F & \text{otherwise} \end{cases} \qquad \text{(11a)}$$

$$b_{i,j}^B = \begin{cases} A + I^B + F_B x_{i,j}^F & \text{if } I^B \geq 0 \\ A - I^B + F_B x_{i,j}^F & \text{otherwise} \end{cases} \qquad \text{(11b)}$$

**1.d.** Calculate activity of the F cell with the following equation:

$$x_{i,j}^F(t + \Delta t) = e^{-b\Delta t} \left( x_{i,j}^B(t) - \frac{a_{i,j}^F}{b_{i,j}^F} \right) + \frac{a_{i,j}^F}{b_{i,j}^F} \qquad \text{(EQ 12)}$$

$$a_{i,j}^F = \begin{cases} B_F I^F + F_F G_F x_{i,j}^B & \text{if } I^F \geq 0 \\ -B_F I^F + F_F G_F x_{i,j}^B & \text{otherwise} \end{cases} \qquad \text{(12a)}$$

$$b_{i,j}^F = \begin{cases} A + I^F + G_F x_{i,j}^B & \text{if } I^F \geq 0 \\ A - I^B + G_F x_{i,j}^B & \text{otherwise} \end{cases} \qquad \text{(12b)}$$

## 9. Calculate region select layer activity

**1.** Calculate activity of the fast input layer by using the following equation:

$$x_i^{FI}(t + \Delta t) = \sum_j x_{i,j}^A(t). \qquad \text{(EQ 13)}$$

**2.** Calculate activity of the slow input layer using the following equation:

$$x_i^{SI}(t + \Delta t) = e^{-B_{SL}\Delta t} \left( x_i^{SI}(t) - \frac{a_i^{SI}}{B_{SI}} \right) + \frac{a_i^{SI}}{B_{SI}}, \qquad \text{(EQ 14)}$$

where $a_i^{SI}$ is defined as follows:

$$a_i^{SI} = A_{SI} x_i^{FI} + C_{SI} x_i^{FL} y_i^L, \qquad \text{(EQ 15)}$$

and $A_{SI}$, $B_{SI}$, and $C_{SI}$ are parameters.

**3.** Calculate the slow layer activity with the following equation.

$$\dot{x}_i^{SL}(t+\Delta t) = e^{-B_{SL}\Delta t}\left(x_i^{SL}(t) - \frac{A_{SL}x_i^{FL}(t)}{B_{SL}}\right) + \frac{A_{SL}x_i^{FL}(t)}{B_{SL}} \tag{EQ 16}$$

**4.** Calculate the fast layer activity with the following equation:

$$x_i^{FL}(t+\Delta t) = \frac{\left(A_{FL}x_i^{FL}(t) + B_{FL}x^R(t)x_i^{FI}(t)\right)^{C_{FL}}}{\sum_j \left(A_{FL}x_j^{FL}(t) + B_{FL}x^R(t)x_j^{FI}(t)\right)^{C_{FL}}} \tag{EQ 17}$$

**5.** The activity of the most active *FL* cell is set to 1.0 and the other *FL* cells are set to 0.

**6.** The RSL reset cell activity is modified using the following equation:

$$x^R(t+\Delta t) = \begin{cases} 1 & \text{if } (x_{active}^{FL} - x_{active}^{SL} > A_R) \\ e^{-B_R\Delta t}(x^R(t) - \frac{1}{B_R}) + \frac{1}{B_R} & otherwise \end{cases} \tag{EQ 18}$$

## 10. Recall of patterns

Recall can be performed either with or without inputs. When no input is present the network is prompted with a single input and it recalls the sequence it associates with that input. When input is present the network tries to match both the inputs and learned sequences. When no inputs are being presented during recall the *forward* signal is used to advance the network to the next category.

## 11. Discussion

The algorithm presented above has been implemented and the algorithmic version of SMART is fast and retains the desirable properties of SMART. The presented algorithm uses a combination of solutions to differential equations and algorithmic control to implement the ART network.

## 12. References

Carpenter, G. and Grossberg, S.. (1987). A Massively Parallel Architecture for a Self-organizing Neural Pattern Recognition Machine. *Computer Vision, Graphics, and Image Processing, 37*. 54-115.

Carpenter, G., Grossberg, S., and Rosen, D. (1991). ART 2A: An adaptive resonance algorithm for rapid learning and recognition. *Neural Networks,* Vol. *4* .

Grossberg, S.. (1973). Contour enhancement, short-term memory, and constancies in reverberating neural networks. *Studies in Applied Mathematics.* **52**. 217-257.

Grossberg., S. (1976a). Adaptive Pattern Recognition and Universal Recoding, I: Parallel Development and Coding of Neural Feature Detectors. *Biological Cybernetics, 23*. 121-134.

Grossberg, S. (1976b). Adaptive Pattern Recognition and Universal Recoding, II: Feedback, expectation, olfaction, and illusions . *Biological Cybernetics, 23*. 187-202.

Vogh, J. (1993). Sequential memory with ART: A self-organizing network capable of learning sequences of patterns. World Congress on Neural Networks, Portland, OR.

Vogh, J. (1994). Representation of Temporal Order with the Sequential Memory with ART Neural Network. Submitted to World Congress on Neural Networks, San Diego.

# NEURAL NETWORKS IN THE FORMER SOVIET UNION

Donald C. Wunsch II
Texas Tech University
Department of Electrical Engineering
Lubbock, TX  79409-3102
dwunsch@coe2.coe.ttu.edu

## Abstract

The neural network community is all too familiar with the struggles of the field's development in the United States.  A decrease in funding of neural network activities in favor of symbolic artificial intelligence lasted from the late 1960's until the 1980's.  In what was then the Soviet Union, various sources continued to aggressively fund neural network research.  Most American scientists have not found out about this work for reasons including secrecy, travel costs, and language barriers.  However, the current economic and political situation motivates greater openeness among Russian scientists.  The extraordinary opportunity to see this research is not unique to neural networks--many fields aggressively pursued by Russians are now, for the first time, being shared with western scientists.  However, neural networks are special in that the Russians generously supported the field during decades in which there was a recession in the field in the United States.  Some of the work is described here.[5]

## References

1.  Few sources yet exist for Western scientists to access Russian neural network research. Aside from this paper, one excellent source is: *Proc. RNNS/IEEE Symposium on Neuroinformatics and Neurocomputers*, Rostov-on-Don, Russia, IEEE, 1992.

2.  This paper is based on:
 Wunsch, Donald C., "Neural Networks in the Former Soviet Union,"  Proc. AIAA Computing in Aerospace Conference, October 20, 1993.

# NEURAL NETWORKS IN THE FORMER SOVIET UNION

Donald C. Wunsch II
Texas Tech University
Department of Electrical Engineering
Lubbock, TX 79409-3102
dwunsch@coe2.coe.ttu.edu

## Introduction

The neural network community is all too familiar with the field's struggles in the United States. The publication of Perceptrons [1] in 1969 led to a decrease in funding of neural networks in favor of symbolic artificial intelligence. Rapid progress in certain subfields of AI seemed to support emphasizing it at the expense of neural networks in order to quickly meet the needs of defense industries. However, later AI development was not as rapid, with many interesting problems stubbornly refusing to yield to symbolic approaches. This and several other issues led to a powerful re-emergence of neural networks in the 1980's. [2,3,4] Of course, much of the funding for both fields' activities came from aerospace and other defense communities that needed the advanced computational abilities they offered.

In what was then the Soviet Union, the aerospace industry and other sources continued to aggressively fund neural network research. For this reason the field thrived there, and many useful ideas were developed. American scientists for the most part have not found out about this work for reasons including classification of the results and economics. Many Russian scientists find it difficult to travel to the United States, and they also usually publish in their own Russian-language journals. However, their current economic situation motivates them to discuss their research more openly, and the current political situation also allows greater opportunities for openness. Exchange programs and jointly-held conferences also improve opportunities for learning from each other. The extraordinary opportunity to have a peek at this research is not unique to neural networks--many fields aggressively pursued by Russians are now, for the first time, being opened up for communication with western scientists. However, neural networks are special in that the Russians generously supported the field during decades in which there was a recession in the field in the United States. Their consistent investment in neural networks has paid off. Much of their work in this field is definitely of a world-class caliber, and will certainly have historic and business implications. Some of the work is described in this paper. This is of necessity a preliminary and incomplete description--the subject could easily occupy several volumes. (In fact it already does, in Russian.)

Some general comments apply to much of the Russian research in the field. Because of American export control laws, it was difficult for Russian scientists to obtain the computing power that we take for granted. This forced them to do one of two things: build their own custom hardware (if they could afford it), or devote extra attention to efficiency issues in their software engineering. Most scientists did a little of both. This puts collaborative efforts into a whole new realm--either to obtain unheard-of results by combining their painstaking innovations with our superior hardware, or to get reasonable performance out of systems we now consider obsolete. Both questions are of interest to the aerospace industry. The former idea is needed because we are still facing challenges for which our best software and hardware still are inadequate. The latter idea has the potential to solve one of the most vexing problems of aerospace manufacturers, the legacy systems problem. Legacy systems are the delivery platforms for computing solutions to manufacturing problems. Often a factory floor is equipped with systems that are obsolete by the standards of software developers, but which are necessary for the daily manufacturing functions. Stopping the factory to install a new system would be prohibitively expensive, not to mention the cost of the new equipment itself. Furthermore, a political resistance to change permeates many factories. Therefore, innovations that would allow old systems to behave like modern high-performance ones would be attractive.

Another observation is that the Russian educational system is different than our own. They have research institutes that do not offer courses but, like universities, have the power to confer graduate degrees. Students typically enter college one year earlier but are better prepared due to a rigorous secondary school curriculum. They spend five years to get their "Diplom", which requires a thesis, and frequently a publication and is roughly similar to our M.S. degree. Students continuing will pursue the "Candidat" degree, which requires multiple journal publications and is like our Ph.D. except that the Candidat degree has a requirement that the work be applied to a real-world problem. Most students stop at this point. A few will return, usually after several years or even more than a decade of working, to finish a "Doktor" degree. The status of this is similar to that of a full Professor or an industry Fellow here. They may supervise several Candidat thesis projects. Finally, a small percentage of Doktors will be elected to the Academy of Sciences and achieve the title "Academician". This is more than a peer recognition award, but more like a super-endowed chair, with funding for subordinates, political power, chauffeured cars, posh offices, and similar perks. The Academy of Sciences directly chooses a large fraction of the membership of the Congress of Peoples Deputies.

The result of this huge hierarchy is that it is not unusual to find scientists with a reasonable ability to stick to a line of research despite the force of the current scientific fashion. Most institutes have at least a few student laborers, and various levels of researchers. The low cost of their activities, from our point of view, has made research there attractive for American industry, as evidenced by significant projects by Boeing, Lockheed, TRW, Sun Microsystems, DEC, and many others. This trend is likely to continue in coming years, in spite of our domestic economic difficulties. This is not necessarily purely from a desire to inexpensively obtain high-quality research. The former Soviet Union represents a significant market opportunity in the long term, and the companies that establish collaborations early will have a relatively inexpensive introduction to the complexities of doing business there, and build a substantial base of goodwill among potential customers in the process.
The rest of this paper is organized by geographic region, starting with Moscow, and proceeding roughly counterclockwise.

## Research Activities

**Moscow**

Perhaps the best-funded Russian neural network researcher is Professor Alexander Galushkin of the Russian Academy of Sciences, who runs the Scientific Center for Neurocomputing, which has done extensive work on transputer-based implementation of neural networks, and many other neural network topics.[5,6,7] He has been working the field since the late 1960's and is completing a comprehensive three-volume encyclopedia of neural networks. It has details about many neural network models including Western ones. He has a voluminous work of his own material, much of which is unique. A few of the other materials appear to be along similar lines of thought as in the United States, but much earlier. In 1974 he implemented neural models by adding nodes in the hidden layers during the learning process. This gives rise to error curves with non-linearities that occur at the time of adding nodes. The Center has several interesting transputer-based implementations, notably one that had 32 transputers on a board to be plugged into a workstation to achieve a claimed 320 MIPS performance. They also have done systems with many Intel I-860 processors for high-speed graphics and pattern recognition applications.

This Center also designed systems that implement continual neural networks, in order to do classifications of a continuous signal without the need for sampling.[8] To do this, a continuous signal is fed into the neural network. The weights are loaded from RAM and are fed through a digital to analog converter and are multiplied by the continuous signal. One then sends the signal into time integrating device such as a capacitor and this then modulates that signal with some other weights, and then adds a fixed bias. It then goes through a digital to analog converter, so the output will be of the form of an expression of an integral of continuous signals (that represent the weights) times the continuous signal that represents the input signal. This yields the desired output for a continuous neural network.

Stanislav Z. Seleznev, Director of Iris Ltd., and Dmitriy O. Scobelev, Vice Director, developed neural net hardware accelerators for personal computers.[9] They got into this business in the area of synthetic aperture radar, and realized that it was a small step to move from that to getting into neural networks. The synthetic aperture radar application was perhaps even more interesting than the neural net hardware; they claimed similar performance to the best published systems, even though they had to use inferior hardware. This work was done under a military contract through the Russian Academy of Sciences Research Institute of VLSI CAD Systems..

Edward A. Manykin, Chief of the Optical Implementations Department at the I. B. Kurchatov Institute of Atomic Energy has a group that applied the photon echo effect in photorefractive materials to various neural network implementations.[10] Specific photorefractive materials exist that display a photon echo effect at cryogenic temperatures. This effect allows an additional dimension of information processing, a fourth dimension, because the systems respond to information that is coded in the direction of time in addition to the three dimensions of space. They also have a mathematician, Dr. Irina Surina, who is looking at neural network models with an eye to finding ones that are easily applied in optical hardware. She will soon publish a new model.

The Moscow State University, Department of Computer Mathematics and Cybernetics is the site of a major laboratory sponsored by Sun Microsystems. The leader of their parallel processing efforts is Russian L. Smeliansky, Associate Professor, Head of Computer System Laboratory. One of his students, Nickolay Umnov is developing optimal NN model choosing methods for concrete applications; analyzing model complexity (e.g. number of neurons and hidden layers) and investigating questions of neural network applications for control of nonlinear dynamical objects. Umnov has also done some neural network hardware design research [11]. The lab has a group of about 30 people very experienced with theoretical issues and analysis of parallel processing problems, but also with the programming. They have developed models for how a program executes on a multiprocessor machine. It's more difficult to deal with things on a multiprocessor machine because one can't guarantee that the same program will execute in the same amount of time in different processors on such machines. Thus models are required of how to synchronize them or how to make them run well even when they are not synchronized.

## St. Petersburg (formerly Leningrad)

Adil Timofev and Danil Prokhorov, of the St. Petersburg Institute of Informatics and Automation have developed a higher-order polynomial network that uses binary weights and results in a logical expression for the network's activity. [12, 13] They are applying this work to pattern recognition and control problems. Their work bears certain similarities to those of and Donald Specht [14]. Prokhorov is now working on application of adaptive critic networks to nonlinear control problems.

Also in St. Petersburg is the famous Vavilov State Optical Institute, the largest optics laboratory in the world. [15] Yuri Mazurenko has designed four dimensional holographic optical interconnects for neural network implementation by using frequency multiplexing. They have several other neural network projects of an applied nature. It is best to arrange well in advance before attempting to visit.

## Kiev

The V. M. Glushkov Institute of Cybernetics in Kiev, Ukraine is a military research institute. Getting permission to visit is best done with some advance notice because of their security requirements. They have a Department of Neural Information Processing Systems headed by Ernst Kussul, who has been active in the field since 1967. His main deputy, Alexander Goltsev, has been active since 1971. They have been developing a neural network model called adaptive projection neural networks. It is based on globally interconnected networks of nodes on each layer with one-to-one mappings between layers with simple on/off interconnections. Also, instead of using a single neuron to do recognition, they operate with large subsets of the neuron population, and these subsets code a particular recognition. They also use binary links and a probabilistic weight change law. These large populations and the law of large numbers make the processing work. They also have a parameter for the number of populations that will win a competition for recognition of a particular pattern. It's possible to have only a single population win, but it is better to have multiple population groups win in a competition. These population groups can be read off in decreasing order of importance. The way this is done is to change the parameter for number of winning activations back down to 1 and then after reading off the winner, inhibit that, and continue reading off the populations in decreasing order of importance until the desired number of winning populations are read out. Training is relatively fast.

Until recently much of their work has been classified, and hardware constraints have prevented them from implementing all of their many designs. They now have limited access to good hardware through a Japanese collaboration, but they generate ideas faster than their ability to implement them. They have applied this work [16] to problems such as brightness-based image segmentation, texture-based image segmentation, speech recognition, intelligent databases, automated rule base system generation, handwritten character recognition, handwritten number recognition, logical inference object recognition, and others. This department has about 20 people, mostly scientists. They have very little administrative overhead.

**Taganrog**

The Taganrog Radio-Engineering Institute after V. D. Kalmykov has a department called the Research Institute for Multiprocessor Computer Systems, which has for many years been a major contributor to Russian parallel processing techniques, and more recently has turned its attention to neural networks. In addition to developing their own neural models [17], they have implemented a parallel backpropagation accelerator [18].

**Rostov-on-Don**

The Neurocybernetics Institute at Rostov State University has a system that does target tracking.[19] This is a sparse memory that models the weights of the Purkinje cells. They have a system that shows the activations of these cells at the same time that the target tracking is being conducted. They also are doing face recognition based on a trajectory that started with the eyes. They developed a graphics program for visually analyzing the dynamics of neural networks in simulation. The effects of the dynamics are visible in streams across the screen with color coding to indicated activation. They also use sound to help analyze. The sound refers to the number of active neurons. There are many different ways of visualizing the neural net activations and organizing those visualizations based on whether one wants to put the active neurons together or do some other things.

They also have conducted experiments on whiskers of rats to show a relationship to the cell structures in the brain. They made many detailed measurements of how different stimulations of these whiskers result in different activations in the rat cortex. Different portions of the brain from the periphery to the cortex are mapped from certain stimulations of these whiskers. These experiments carry over into motor activity as well as sensory activity and they have implications that can carry over into other species as well, such as insights in tactile sensory processing. Some of the conclusions from this carry over to other species including humans as well.

They also have a department of robots and vision, and a department studying the function of the human brain which has several laboratories researching the capability to monitor pilot states and feed that information into the plane's black box. They are working together with Tubolev to implement this system. They have noted that pilot error is a major problem in safety and so by better monitoring and control of the pilot state they feel that they can significantly enhance aircraft safety.

## Krasnoyarsk

The Computing Center of the Krasnoyarsk AMSE Center is run by Prof. A. N. Gorban. Despite his geographical isolation, he is widely known in Russia for theoretical biophysics and a variety of creative neural models. He has a supervised network that uses gradient error updates in a short batch mode, together with feedback connections from the output nodes to the hidden nodes. This network is known for similar performance but much faster training than backpropogation. [20] He has also developed a multi-expert approach to neural architectures [21] and various other approaches.

## Conclusion

This paper has only scratched the surface of neural networks activities in the former Soviet Union that have potential aerospace applications. The opportunities for collaborations offer hope for accelerated progress in the field.

## References

1. Minsky, Marvin and Papert, Seymour, Perceptrons: An Introduction to Computational Geometry, MIT Press, 1969

2. Cohen, Michael A., and Stephen Grossberg, "Absolute stability of global pattern formation and parallel memory storage by competitive neural networks," *IEEE Trans. on Systems, Man and Cybernetics*, Vol. 13, pp 815-826, 1983.

3. Hopfield, John J., "Neural networks and physical systems with emergent collective computational abilities," *Proc. National Acad. Sci.*, Vol. 74, pp. 2554-2558, 1982.

4. Rumelhart, David E., and James L. McLelland (Eds.), Parallel Distributed Processing: Explorations in the Microstructures of Cognition, MIT Press, 1986.

5. Galushkin, Alexander Igorovich, "Neurocomputers and Neuromathematics," *Proc. RNNS/IEEE Symposium on Neuroinformatics and Neurocomputers*, Rostov-on-Don, Russia, IEEE, 1992

6.	Galushkin, Alexander Igorovich, "Continual models of pattern recognition multilayer systems," *Automatics and Computer Science*, No. 2, Riga, 1974

7.	Galushkin, Alexander Igorovich, and D. V. Kirsanov, "Custom-made digital neurochip," *Proc. RNNS/IEEE Symposium on Neuroinformatics and Neurocomputers*, Rostov-on-Don, Russia, IEEE, 1992

8.	Galushkin, Alexander Igorovich, "Continual Neural Networks," *Proc. RNNS/IEEE Symposium on Neuroinformatics and Neurocomputers*, Rostov-on-Don, Russia, IEEE, 1992

9.	Grebenkin, O. A., Stanislav Z. Seleznev, and Dimitri O. Scobolev, "A model of wave associative processing," *Proc. RNNS/IEEE Symposium on Neuroinformatics and Neurocomputers*, Rostov-on-Don, Russia, IEEE, 1992

10.	Manykin, Edward A., and M. N. Belov, "Higher order neural networks and photon echo effect," Neural Networks, Vol. 4, p. 417, 1991

11.	Umnov, Nickolay, "Digital neurochip for fully-connected neural network," *Proc. RNNS/IEEE Symposium on Neuroinformatics and Neurocomputers*, Rostov-on-Don, Russia, IEEE, 1992

12.	Timofeev, Adil, and Danil Prokhorov, "Neural network processing systems in recognition and control problems," *Proc. RNNS/IEEE Symposium on Neuroinformatics and Neurocomputers*, Rostov-on-Don, Russia, IEEE, 1992

13.	Timofeev, Adil, and Danil Prokhorov. Personal communication.

14.	D.F.Specht, "Probabilistic Neural Networks and the Polinomial Adaline as Complementary Techniques for Classification," *IEEE Trans. Neural Networks*, vol.1, pp. 111-121, Mar.1990

15.	Hyde, W. Lewis, "The biggest institute of optics in the world," *Optics and Photonics News*, Vol. 1, No. 3, March 1990, pp. 17 - 21

16.	Goltsev, Alexander D., "Adaptive neuron-like network for a textual segmentation of images," *Proc. RNNS/IEEE Symposium on Neuroinformatics and Neurocomputers*, Rostov-on-Don, Russia, IEEE, 1992

17.	Stadnikov, Ie. N., "Reflector neural network model,"*Proc. RNNS/IEEE Symposium on Neuroinformatics and Neurocomputers*, Rostov-on-Don, Russia, IEEE, 1992

18.	Galuyev, G. A., "Parallel neurocomputer realization of the back propagation algorithm," *Proc. RNNS/IEEE Symposium on Neuroinformatics and Neurocomputers*, Rostov-on-Don, Russia, IEEE, 1992

19.  Chalakhjan, L. M., L. I. Chudakov, W. L. Dunin-Barkowski, M. B. Kozhemjakin, N. M. Zhoukovska, "Synaptic interaction of granule cells and climbing fibre on purkinje cell," *Proc. RNNS/IEEE Symposium on Neuroinformatics and Neurocomputers*, Rostov-on-Don, Russia, IEEE, 1992

20.  Alexander N.Gorban, Cory Waxman, "How many neurons are sufficient to elect the U.S.A. President? Two! (Siberian neurocomputer forecasts results of U.S.A. Presidential elections)," Preprint #191 , RUS, Siberian Brunch, Institute of Biophysics, Krasnoyarsk, 1992.

21.  Gilev, S. Ye, A. N. Gorban, Ye. M. Mirkes, "Internal conflicts in neural networks," *Proc. RNNS/IEEE Symposium on Neuroinformatics and Neurocomputers*, Rostov-on-Don, Russia, IEEE, 1992

# Self-Organizing Surfaces and Volumes - An Extension of the Self-Organizing Map

Andreas Zell, Harald Bayer, Henri Bauknecht

University of Stuttgart,
Institute for Parallel and Distributed High Performance Systems (IPVR),
Applied Comp. Science - Computer Vision
Breitwiesenstr. 20-22, D-70565 Stuttgart, Germany

E-mail: {zell,bayer,bauknecht}@informatik.uni-stuttgart.de

**Abstract:** We here introduce an extension of the self-organizing map. The extension replaces the local grid with a parallel distance calculation on arbitrary topologies. This technique was first developed as an efficient implementation technique of self-organizing maps on massively parallel computers. However, it has given rise to a conceptual extension of the self-organizing map in several ways: The network topology can now be an arbitrary non-convex and even disconnected area. The extension can use real-valued neuron positions and allows for a change of the position of the neurons in the topology. It also gives rise to new network visualization techniques. It very naturally allows for an efficient dynamic change of the network size and density. The algorithm is demonstrated by mapping handwritten digits to a non-convex 10-pointed star and to 10 unconnected circular regions.

## 1    Introduction and Motivation

The self-organizing map (SOM), also called Kohonen map [Kohonen82], [Kohonen89] [RiMaSch91] is currently one of the most popular artificial neural networks for unsupervised clustering and visual grouping of input data. It consists of a number of neurons, say $m$ neurons, whose $n$-dimensional weight vectors are adapted with an unsupervised learning procedure in such a way that they approximate the probability density distribution of the input vectors. The neurons of the self-organizing map possess a special neighborhood relation. Usually the neighborhood is a two-dimensional rectangular grid, a two-dimensional hexagonal grid, a three-dimensional grid or a one-dimensional grid (a line). Most often 2D or 3D rectangular grids are used, because they can be implemented easily as arrays on sequential computers. Depending on the application the grid may be open at the borders or closed, resulting in a circle, a cylinder or a torus. Fig. 2 displays the most popular network topologies. The network of neurons is regarded as rigid, the weight vectors of the neurons can be modified.

During learning the n-dimensional input vector $X = (x_1,..., x_n)$ is compared in parallel with all weight vectors $W_j = (w_{1j},..., w_{nj})$ in an arbitrary metric. Usually the euclidian norm is used or, in the case of normalized vectors, the dot product. The neuron c with smallest distance to the input vector (or the largest dot product for normalized vectors) is the winner neuron

$$\|X - W_c\| = \min_j (\|X - W_j\|) \tag{1}$$

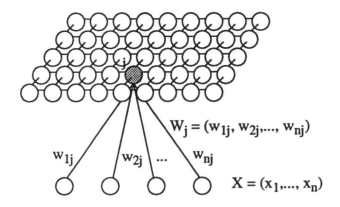

**Fig. 1:** Self-organizing map. Each input neuron is connected with each Kohonen neuron, $W_j$ is the weight vector of neuron j. The neighborhood of the neurons here is a 2D grid.

The weight vectors of the winner neuron and its neighbors on the grid are adapted by moving them in the direction of the input vector, thus making them more similar to the input vector.

$$W_j(t+1) = W_j(t) + \eta(t) h_{cj}(t) [X(t) - W_j(t)] \tag{2}$$

The shape and size of the neighborhood function can vary over time, usually one starts with a large neighborhood (e.g. all neurons of the grid) and reduces it slowly over time. Here $h_{cj}(t)$ is the distance function on the grid of neurons, also called *neighborhood kernel* and $\eta(t)$ is a time varying learning rate which monotonously decreases from 1 to 0 over time.

$$h_{cj}(t) = h(\|pos(c) - pos(j)\|, t) = h(z, t) = h'(z, d) \tag{3}$$

Often a distance parameter d is used instead of the time parameter t for the neighborhood function, with $d \rightarrow 0$ as $t \rightarrow \infty$

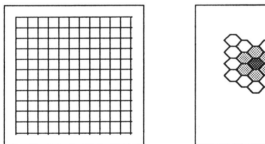 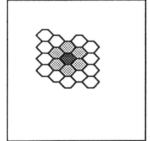 

**Fig. 2:** Popular self-organizing map topologies: 2D-grid, hexagonal grid, 2D-torus

## 2 Implementation of Self-Organizing Maps on Massively Parallel SIMD-Computers - The Key to Self-Organizing Surfaces

In the process of devising an efficient implementation of self-organizing maps on a massively parallel SIMD computer, an implementation technique has been devised by one of the authors [KNet92] which is the key to the extension of the self-organizing map:

The Kohonen neurons are not mapped to an array or to another grid structure but to an unordered set of physical processors. Each neuron is associated with a coordinate in this space of neuron coordinates. This neuron coordinate space need not be a grid, but can be an arbitrary topology. For example, the position of neurons can be chosen on the surface of a sphere, with random neuron positions or with equidistant positions. In fact, the positions of neurons can be on any arbitrary surface and in any volume.

The learning algorithm for self-organizing maps with this implementation technique is nearly identical to the original algorithm, with the exception of the distance calculation. It is given here as a parallel algorithm:

1. For each neuron j do in parallel: compute the distance between the input vector X and the weight vector $W_j$, i.e. $\| X - W_j \|$. This can be done in time O(k), where k is the dimension of the input vector.

2. Choose the winning neuron c by a parallel minimum search. This can be done in time O(log n) by a parallel minimum search on a linear array of processors.

3. Broadcast the position pos(c) of the winning neuron c to all other neurons. This can be done in time O(1).

4. For each neuron j do in parallel: compute the distance between the winner neuron position pos(c) and the current position pos(j) in the norm of the neuron coordinate space, i.e. $z = \| pos\,(c) - pos\,(j) \|$. If $z < d$, the weight vector of neuron j is adapted by the formula

$$W_j\,(t+1) \; = \; W_j\,(t) + \eta\,(t)\,h_{cj}\,(t)\,[X\,(t) - W_j\,(t)] \qquad (4)$$

This can be done in time O(n+m).

This algorithm is extremely efficient for **SIMD** machines with a large number of processors and for large networks, because there is no communication between neurons except for the logarithmic minimum search. It is rather inefficient on serial workstations compared with the self organizing map implementation on a grid, especially if the neighborhood kernel is small. A parallel self organizing map simulator (KNet) on a 16K MasPar MP-1 system obtains up to 50 MCUPS for SOM learning [KNet92] compared with 0.10 MCUPS for our sequential implementation on a Sun SparcStation 2. However, the point here is the conceptual change.

## 3  Self-Organizing Surfaces (SOS)

Self organizing maps (SOM) realize a topology preserving mapping from an n-dimensional input space $A = \mathbf{R}^n$ to a k-dimensional integer-valued grid B of neuron positions.

Self organizing surfaces (SOS) or self-organizing volumes (SOV) represent a topology preserving mapping from an n-dimensional metric input space $A = \mathbf{R}^n$ to a k-dimensional metric space $B \subset \mathbf{R}^m$ of neuron positions. The important concept is a separation of logical neuron position in the k-dimensional neuron space B and physical position of the neurons and weight vectors, as described in the parallel implementation above (see Fig. 3).

Non-convex, disconnected surfaces and volumes pose no problem for the extended algorithm. This is because there is no rigid grid but the topology is given by a distance calculation. It is rather easy to enforce empty space around disconnected areas by initially distributing the positions of neurons only in allowed areas and setting the distance of points in non-connected areas of neuron positions to large values. Then in each disconnected area only a local adaptation takes place.

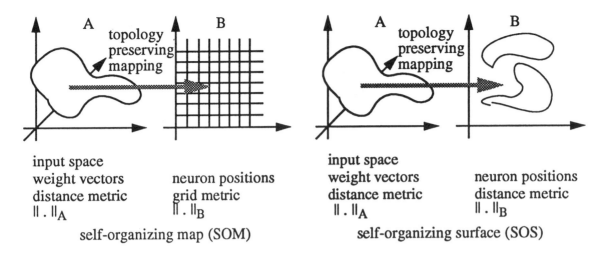

**Fig. 3:** Extending the self organizing map to self-organizing surfaces (SOS)

Note also that in self organizing surfaces no topologic defects can occur, as they are often seen in self-organizing maps. This is because the links between adjacent neurons are not fixed but dynamically computed from the position of neurons.

## 4 Moving the Positions of Neurons

The positions of the neurons in neuron position space may be changed during learning as well. In this further extension, the rigid regular space grid of neurons of the self-organizing map becomes elastic itself. Here, the positions of the neurons are changed together with the weights. This poses some interesting questions. First, how can the neuron position be changed? As the input space is different from the neuron position space, the winner neuron has no external preference for a movement, since there is no target position, no energy gradient etc. Similarly, the movement of a non-winner may only be in the direction of the winner or away from it, unless other information, like class information, is available.

In the model given so far, if close non-winners are moved in the direction of the winner, neurons with positions at the borders of the neuron position distribution have no compensating force to pull them outward. Thus the neuron positions would all converge to their common center of gravity. The opposite, an diverging of neuron positions, would occur with only repulsive forces. There are several ways to deal with this problem, currently all untested:

1. If a rigid and easily defined outside border for the neuron positions is given, a compensating pulling force from the border could compensate the contracting forces for the neurons. One could use a force that decreases as the square of the distance to the border. However, taking the border into account opens up new questions as how to define that force and how to compute it efficiently. One short-cut might be to only take the closest border point.

2. The attracting force between neurons could be defined such that a minimum distance of the neurons is guaranteed, e.g. by a function similar to the inverse "mexican hat" function.

3. The sign and strength for neuron position movements could be varied depending on the hit rate of the winner in comparison to its neighbors. If the winner wins too often, the neighbors may be attracted to the winner, otherwise they may be repelled.

It might be argued that the distribution of neurons in neuron position space is irrelevant in comparison to the weight distribution of the neurons. But the amount of weight change a single neuron performs during training depends not only on its own weight vector (being changed as a winner neuron) but also strongly on the position of the neuron in neuron position space. Its weight vector is also changed if the neuron's position is close to the position of another winner neuron. Regarding it that way, changing the position of neurons is an additional or complementary effect to changing the weights of neurons.

## 5    New Visual Representation Methods of the SOS

The new concept of neighborhood by distance in an arbitrary topology demands new visual display techniques of the networks. The following modifications and extensions to the well-known self-organizing map displays come to mind:

1.  Display of the neuron positions. This is especially interesting if the positions of the neurons are also changed during training.

2.  Display of the weight vectors in the input space in a web in which each neuron j is connected with a link to k neighboring neurons, those neurons which have the smallest distance to j in neuron position space.

3.  Display of the weight vectors in the input space in a web in which each neuron j is connected to all other neurons which have a distance z less or equal than d. The standard self-organizing map display as seen in Fig. 5 is a special case of this display where the neuron positions are not moved and the distance z = 1.

## 6    Dynamic Change of the Network Topology

A dynamic change of the number of neurons is very easy in this model, because no neighborhood relation has to be preserved. This is in contrast to approaches like growing cell structures [Fritzke92] which have to preserve the topology of adjacent triangles. The process of removing single neurons in these structures may involve removing additional neurons to preserve the topology of triangles. This may lead to severe learning problems [Fritzke93]. We also do not need to update a spanning tree topology as in [KaKoLa90].

Adding new neurons in the self-organizing surface is extremely easy. They just have to be given a neuron position and starting weight and can immediately take place in the learning. The well-known concept of a *hit counter* or *conscience factor* can be used to decide when to add additional neurons in the neighborhood of frequently hit neurons. The deletion of neurons is easier still, no neuron topology has to be preserved.

A special implementation technique for additions and deletions of neurons can be used, which is especially useful for SIMD computers: The number of neurons is not changed but a redefinition of existing neurons replaces a simultaneous insertion and deletion of a neuron. The neuron, which was hit least frequently is deleted, a new neuron is generated in an area of high input vector density. This can be done with a local replacement of position and weight vector of a single neuron, without weight vector change. As a further modification the creation and deletion of new neurons can even be done in batches of several or many neurons. This again is especially useful on SIMD computers minimizing operations on individual processors.

It is interesting to note the similarity of this batch creation and deletion of neurons with the selection operator of evolution algorithms and genetic algorithms.

# 7    Examples

As examples we show two (artificial) clustering problems. In both examples we trained 1000 normalized handwritten digits (0 to 9), each pattern a 256-dimensional real vector. In the first example we mapped the digits to a 10-pointed star, showing that non-convex regions pose no problem for the algorithm. In the second example we map the same digits to 10 circles, showing the ability of the SOS to deal with separated regions.

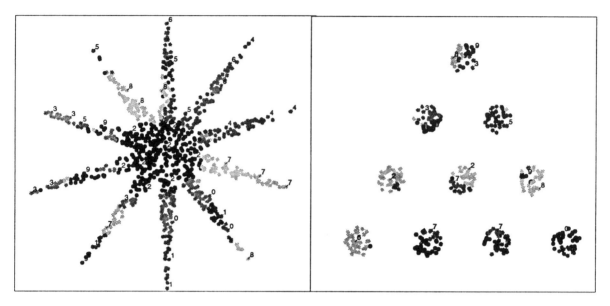

**Fig. 4:** Neuron positions of 1000 handwritten digits (256-dimensional) trained to form a sharp 10-pointed star (left) or falling into one of 10 circles (right). Because in print different classes are mapped to the same grey values, the class names are indicated additionally.

# 8    Literature

[Fritzke92] B. Fritzke: Growing cell structures - a self-organizing network in k dimensions, Artificial Neural Networks II, I. Aleksander, J. Taylor (eds.), North Holland, 1992, pp. 1051-1056

[Fritzke93] B. Fritzke: Vector Quantization with a Growing and Splitting Elastic Net, Proc. ICANN 93, pp. 580-585, 1993

[KaKoLa90] J. A. Kangas, T. K. Kohonen, J. T. Laaksonen: Variants of Self-Organizing Maps, IEEE Trans. on Neural Networks, Vol. 1. No.1, March 1990, pp. 93-99

[KNet92] H. Bayer: KNet user manual, unpublished

[Kohonen82] T. Kohonen: Self-Organized formation of topologically correct feature maps, Biolog. Cybernetics, Vol. 43, pp. 59-69, 1982

[Kohonen89] T. Kohonen: Self-Organization and Associative Memory, 3rd ed., Springer, 1989

[RiMaSch91] H. Ritter, T. Martinetz, K. Schulten: Neuronale Netze, Springer, 1991

# Biological Vision

**Session Chair: Stephen Grossberg**
**Heiko Neumann**

## ORAL PRESENTATIONS

# Why Bright Kanizsa Squares Look Closer: Consistency of Segmentations and Surfaces in 3-D Vision

Stephen Grossberg†
Center for Adaptive Systems
and
Department of Cognitive and Neural Systems
Boston University
Boston, Massachusetts 02215 USA

## 1. Introduction: The Need for Boundary-Surface Consistency

When a human observer views a Kanizsa square under appropriate viewing conditions, the bright square appears to be closer than its inducing pac man wedges (Figure 1). Much experimental evidence suggests that the square's apparent brightness and depth covary relative to those of the picture background (Bradley and Dumais, 1984; Kanizsa, 1955, 1974; Purghé and Coren, 1992). This interaction between the illusory contours that frame the square, the brightness percept that fills it in, and the depthful pop-out of the square from its background illustrate in a dramatic way how fundamentally different are biological vision processes from those of traditional machine vision algorithms. The present article sketches an explanation of this percept as part of a larger theory of biological vision that develops a solution of the classical figure-ground problem (Grossberg, 1993, 1994).

A key property of the theory, called *boundary-surface consistency*, suggests how only those boundary segmentations that are capable of supporting filled-in surface representations survive in the final 3-D percept. Feedback signals between boundary and surface representations are needed to ensure boundary-surface consistency. These feedback signals help to pop-out the brighter Kanizsa square so that it appears in front of its background.

## 2. Interscale and Interstream Interactions

The theory is called FACADE Theory because it suggests how representations of **F**orm-**A**nd-**C**olor-**A**nd-**DE**pth are generated in extrastriate cortex, notably area V4. FACADE theory describes the neural architecture of two parallel subsystems, the Boundary Contour System (BCS) and the Feature Contour System (FCS). The BCS generates an emergent 3-D boundary segmentation of edges, texture, shading, and stereo information at multiple spatial scales, whereas the FCS compensates for variable illumination conditions and fills-in surface properties of brightness, color, and depth among multiple spatial scales. See Grossberg (1994) for a self-contained exposition of the theory and its explanations of other data.

In its original form (Grossberg, 1987a, 1987b), FACADE Theory did not posit interactions between the different spatial scales of the BCS and the FCS, or from the FCS to

† This research was supported in part by ARPA (ONR N00014-92-J-4015) and the Office of Naval Research (ONR N00014-91-J-4100). The author wishes to thank Cynthia E. Bradford and Diana J. Meyers for their valuable assistance in the preparation of the manuscript.

**Figure 1.** A Kanizsa square.

the BCS. Such interactions were not needed to explain the data analysed in previous articles. Grossberg (1994) shows how interactions within and between BCS and FCS scales lead to explanations of a much wider body of data about 3-D visual perception than could be handled before.

The theory posits the existence of seven types of interactions that complement, and are consistent with, previously defined BCS and FCS mechanisms (Figure 2). These interactions clarify how the visual system can generate globally unambiguous 3-D surface representations from image data which contain several different types of local ambiguities. In these interactions, larger scales tend to influence smaller scales, and larger disparities tend to influence smaller disparities. Thus the new interactions tend to be *partially ordered* across scale and disparity.

The first new interaction takes place among the complex cells of the BCS. Model complex cells with large receptive fields can binocularly fuse more disparities than cells with small fields. Inhibitory competitive interactions occur between complex cells that code different disparities at the same position and size scale. These interactions are called *BB Intrascales.* Typically, active BCS complex cells that code larger disparities inhibit complex cells that code smaller disparities—an example of partial ordering. This competition sharpens the disparity tuning curves of the BCS complex cells, and selects those complex cells whose disparity tuning best matches the binocular disparities derived from an image.

Interactions called *BB Interscales* are excitatory cooperative interactions from bipole cells to hypercomplex cells that code the same disparity and position, across all scales. Each such CC Loop network is called a *BCS copy.* Each BCS copy generates its own emergent boundary segmentations corresponding to a prescribed disparity range, or relative depth from the observer. Each segmentation forms the best spatial compromise between all the scales that are sensitive to its disparity range. Due to the combined effect of these cooperative interactions and of competitive interactions among BCS hypercomplex cells, the larger scales tend to inhibit the smaller scales within each BCS copy in the manner reported in psychophysical data (Tolhurst, 1972; Watt, 1987; Wilson, Blake, and Halpern, 1991). These interactions are predicted to include the Interstripes in cortical area V2.

Each disparity-sensitive 3-D boundary segmentation in a BCS copy interacts with a Monocular FIDO, or Filling-In-DOmain, of the FCS. These BCS signals select those monocular brightness and color signals that are consistent with the binocular BCS segmentation, and suppress the rest. These BCS → FCS interactions are called *BF Intracopies* because each BCS copy selects binocularly consistent monocular data from a corresponding FCS copy.

Thus the illuminant-discounted monocular FCS representation is transformed into multiple FCS copies, or Monocular FIDOs, one for each BCS copy. This one-to-many transformation carries out two functions. First, it maps the monocular positions of FCS signals into the binocular positions of the corresponding BCS copy. It is hypothesized that the BF Intracopy signals act as teaching signals to realign the FCS → FCS pathways based on their mutual correlation during visual experience. This adaptive process was used to help explain monocular McCollough effect data in Grossberg (1987b). Second, this one-to-many transformation enables monocular FCS signals that do not positionally match binocular BF Intracopy signals in a given FCS copy to be suppressed. The same monocular FCS signals may be selected for further processing in a different FCS copy where they do positionally match the corresponding BF Intracopy signals. This one-to-many transformation is called *Monocular FF Intercopies*.

In addition, reciprocal interactions exist from the FCS to the BCS. They are called *FB Intercopies*, and ensure boundary-surface consistency. These FCS output signals are derived from those filled-in FCS regions at the monocular FIDOs that are surrounded by connected boundaries. These filled-in connected domains, which represent those monocular surface representations that are binocularly consistent, are used to build up the final 3-D surface representation at the Binocular FIDOs. In particular, the filled-in connected FCS regions activate contrast-sensitive FCS → BCS pathways that generate FCS output signals at the edges of the filled-in connected regions. These outputs excite BCS cells corresponding to the same disparity and position at its BCS copy while inhibiting BCS cells corresponding to smaller disparities at that position. The FB Intercopy signals hereby inhibit the BCS boundaries of any occluded region that occur at the same positions as the boundaries of an occluding region.

Possible neural loci for these BF Intracopies and FB Intercopies are suggested by the neural interpretation of the BCS in terms of the Interblob cortical stream and of the FCS in terms of the Blob parvocellular stream. Within cortical area V2, Thin Stripes should be investigated as possible Monocular FIDOs, with Interstripe-to-Thin Stripe pathways as the BF Intracopies, Blob-to-Thin Stripe pathways as the Monocular FF Intercopies, and Thin Stripe-to-Interstripe pathways as the FB Intercopies.

In addition to these FF, BF, and FB interactions, *Binocular FF Intercopies* are predicted to occur. Both excitatory and inhibitory output signals are generated, as in the case of FB Intercopies. The excitatory signals from each eye activate Binocular FIDOs that correspond to the same disparity and position. The inhibitory signals suppress Binocular FIDOs corresponding to smaller disparities at the same position. These interactions obliterate the

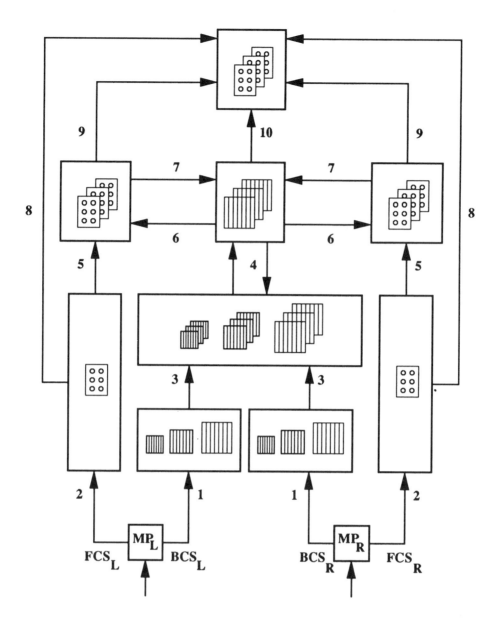

**Figure 2.** Macrocircuit of monocular and binocular interactions of the BCS and FCS: Left eye and right eye monocular preprocessing stages ($MP_L$ and $MP_R$) send parallel pathways to the BCS (boxes with vertical lines, designating oriented responses) and the FCS (boxes with three pairs of circles, designating opponent colors). Output signals from $MP_L$ and $MP_R$ activate BCS simple cells with multiple receptive field sizes via pathways 1. $MP_L$ and $MP_R$ outputs are also transformed into opponent FCS signals via pathways 2. Pathways 3 generate multiple cell pools that are sensitive to multiple disparities and scales. BB Intrascales are at work among the resultant cells. Pathways 4 combine the multiple scales corresponding to the same depth range into a single BCS copy via BB Interscales. Multiple copies exist corresponding to different (but possibly overlapping) depth ranges. Pathways 5 are the Monocular FF Intercopies. Pathways 6 are the BF Intracopies. Pathways 7 are the FB Intercopies. Pathways 8 are the excitatory Binocular FF Intercopies. Pathways 9 are the inhibitory Binocular FF Intercopies. Pathways 10 are the BF Intercopies. See the text for further details.

brightness and color signals that could otherwise erroneously fill-in surface representations of occluded objects in the regions where they are occluded. The surviving excitatory signals from both eyes are binocularly matched to trigger the filling-in of the 3-D surface representation. These Binocular FF Intercopies occur within the Blob cortical stream. The *excitatory* Binocular FF Intercopies arise from the same source of illuminant-discounted FCS signals as the Monocular FF Intercopies. In contrast, the *inhibitory* Binocular FF Intercopies arise from the edges of the filled-in connected regions within the Monocular FIDOs, as do the FB Intercopies. The excitatory Binocular FF Intercopies form a one-to-many map to the Binocular FIDOs. They are positionally aligned among the Binocular FIDOs using BCS → FCS boundary signals as teaching signals. These are the BF Intercopies that were used in Grossberg (1987b) to help explain data about binocular transfer of the McCollough effect. The positions of the inhibitory Binocular FF Intercopies are defined by the binocularly shifted BF Intracopies that define the filled-in domains whose edges activate them. The inhibitory FF Intercopies also converge upon the Binocular FIDOs, where they suppress FCS signals that would otherwise trigger filling-in of occluded regions.

The final interactions are called *BF Intercopies*. These are BCS → FCS boundary signals from a given disparity and position that add to the BCS boundaries of all smaller disparities at that position in order to prevent all nearer occluding surfaces from appearing transparent due to filling-in of their positions by the brightness and colors of farther occluded surfaces.

### 3. Boundary-Brightness-Depth Interactions in Kanizsa Square Percepts

The percept of closer depth and enhanced brightness induced by a Kanizsa display may be explained by these mechanisms. Consider the percept under conditions of binocular viewing. BB Interscales of the CC Loop form an illusory contour around the Kanizsa square. This square boundary encloses a connected region. Within each copy of the BCS, there is a largest disparity at which the complex cells can induce the formation of such a connected square. BB Interscales hereby form multiple copies of the square boundary within multiple BCS copies, where each copy is capable of binocularly fusing a different range of non-zero disparities. These illusory boundaries are no stronger than the boundaries that are formed around the pac man inducers themselves by a similar process.

The connected BCS boundaries use BF Intracopies to form filling-in domains within the monocular FIDOs via the pathways labelled 6 in Figure 2. The discounted feature contour signals from the monocular preprocessing stages then trigger filling-in of the connected regions. The interior of the Kanizsa square has a higher level of filled-in activity than the background due to the spatial distribution of these feature contour signals. As a result, the contrast between the filled-in activity of the Kanizsa square and the pac man figures is greater than the contrast between the filled-in activity of the background and the pac man figures. This contrast difference is one of the key properties in the explanation.

A second key property concerns the way FB Intercopies respond to this contrast difference. In particular, contrast-sensitive FB Intercopy signals via the pathways labelled 7 in Figure 2 excite BCS boundaries corresponding to the same disparity and position, but inhibit BCS boundaries corresponding to smaller disparities at that position. Due to this excitatory FB feedback, the illusory BCS boundaries of the Kanizsa square become stronger than the (remaining) BCS boundaries of the pac man figures. Using competitive BCS interactions at the hypercomplex cells, these strengthened Kanizsa square boundaries can now cause gaps in the boundaries, called end cuts, to form where the pac man boundaries join the square boundary. The boundaries around the pac man regions are no longer connected. Consequently they cannot contain the filling-in process within the corresponding monocular FIDO. Activity hereby diffuses out of the pac man figures.

This excitatory FB feedback and end cutting take place in the BCS copy corresponding to the largest disparity that can respond to the image. The escape of activity from the corresponding pac man FIDO eliminates FB Intercopy signals from the pac man boundaries, both excitatory and inhibitory. Removing the inhibitory FB Intercopy signals from the pac man boundaries enables the BCS copies that are sensitive to smaller disparities to form pac man boundaries. Pac man boundaries do not, however, form at the common edge of any pac man with the square, because FB Intercopy signals from the square region of the largest disparity copy inhibit the BCS square boundaries at all smaller disparities. With the square boundaries out of the way, the pac man boundaries can complete an (almost) circular boundary within the BCS copies of the smaller disparities. In all, a square boundary is completed at a BCS copy corresponding to a nearer depth, while (almost) circular boundaries are completed at a BCS copy corresponding to a slightly farther depth. When these segmentations are input to the Object Recognition System in temporal cortex, they lead to recognition of a Kanizsa square in front of circular regions.

Why do we see a square surface in front of the unoccluded surfaces of the pac men? Why are the boundaries that are completed behind the square *recognized* but not *seen*? BF Intercopies add larger disparity boundaries to smaller disparity boundaries. FF Intercopies transmit the filling-in generators of the high contrast square to the largest disparity binocular FIDO, while they inhibit the filling-in generators of the square at smaller disparity binocular FIDOs. The filling-in generators of the background and of the pac man figures are not inhibited at these smaller disparity FIDOs. The resultant FACADE representation fills-in a brighter surface representation of the square at a larger disparity binocular FIDO. The pac man figures and their background fill-in at a smaller disparity binocular FIDO, but cannot fill-in behind the square, due to the action of BF Intercopies. Consequently, the brighter Kanizsa square looks closer than the background. In addition, the pac man figures are recognized, but not seen, behind the occluding square surface.

At bottom, this interaction between boundary, brightness, and depth percepts is a consequence of the surface filling-in that compensates for variable illumination, the use of connected monocular surfaces to reinforce consistent boundary segmentations which thereupon control the formation of binocular surface representations, and the use of end cuts to detach the boundaries of nearer surfaces from those of farther surfaces to facilitate figure-ground pop-out.

# References

Bradley, D.R. and Dumais, S.T. (1984). The effects of illumination level and retinal size on the depth stratification of subjective contour figures. *Perception*, **13**, 155–164.

Grossberg, S. (1987a). Cortical dynamics of three-dimensional form, color, and brightness perception, I: Monocular theory. *Perception and Psychophysics*, **41**, 87–116.

Grossberg, S. (1987b). Cortical dynamics of three-dimensional form, color, and brightness perception, II: Binocular theory. *Perception and Psychophysics*, **41**, 117–158.

Grossberg, S. (1993). A solution of the figure-ground problem for biological vision. *Neural Networks*, **6**, 463–483.

Grossberg, S. (1994). 3-D vision and figure-ground separation by visual cortex. *Perception and Psychophysics*, in press.

Kanizsa, G. (1955). Margini quasi-percettivi in campi con stimolazione omogénea. *Rivista di Psicologia*, **49**, 7–30.

Kanizsa, G. (1974). Contours without gradients or cognitive contours. *Italian Journal of Psychology*, **1**, 93–113.

Purghé, F. and Coren, S. (1992). A modal completion, depth stratification, and illusory figures: A test of Kanizsa's explanation. *Perception*, **21**, 325–335.

Tolhurst, D.J. (1972). Adaptation to square-wave gratings: Inhibition between spatial frequency channels in the human visual system. *Journal of Physiology*, **226**, 231–248.

Watt, R.J. (1987). Scanning from coarse to fine spatial scales in the human visual system after the onset of a stimulus. *Journal of the Optical Society of America*, **4**, 2006–2021.

Wilson, H.R., Blake, R., and Halpern, D.L. (1991). Coarse spatial scales constrain the range of binocular fusion on fine scales. *Journal of the Optical Society of America*, **8**, 229–236.

# Rules for the Cortical Map of Ocular Dominance and Orientation Columns

Stephen Grossberg and Steven J. Olson
Department of Cognitive and Neural Systems, Boston University
111 Cummington St., Rm. 244, Boston, MA 02215
December 7, 1993

**Abstract -** *Three computational rules are sufficient to generate model cortical maps that simulate the interrelated structure of cortical ocular dominance and orientation columns: a noise input, a spatial band pass filter, and competitive normalization across all feature dimensions. The data of Blasdel from optical imaging experiments reveal cortical map fractures, singularities, and linear zones that are fit by the model. In particular, singularities in orientation preference tend to occur in the centers of ocular dominance columns, and orientation contours tend to intersect ocular dominance columns at right angles.*

Since the classical work of Hubel and Wiesel (1974) many experimental neurobiologists have studied how two key structural attributes of primary visual cortex develop in the neonate and are functionally organized in the adult. These attributes are the ocular dominance columns whereby visual inputs from the left and right eyes are juxtaposed to facilitate binocular vision, and the orientation columns whereby oriented edges, textures, and shading in an image can selectively activate some cells more than others. The anatomical coordination of these attributes was first conceptualized in the hypercolumn model of Hubel and Wiesel (1974). Much subsequent experimental work has revealed a more complex organization of these interwoven attributes, one that includes a mesh of singularities, fractures and linear zones. Blasdel (1992a, 1992b) has described five general characteristics of ocular dominance and orientation maps: (1) there exist regions of smooth change in orientation preference (linear zones), (2) there exist rapid changes in orientation along one direction (fractures), (3) there exist regions at the centers of swirls of orientation preference in which all orientation preferences are present (singularities), (4) singularities tend to lie within the centers of the ocular dominance columns, and (5) linear zones intersect the edges of ocular dominance columns nearly orthogonally. Figure 1 shows the each of these five characteristics in a map of orientation preference and ocular dominance columns obtained by optical dye recordings.

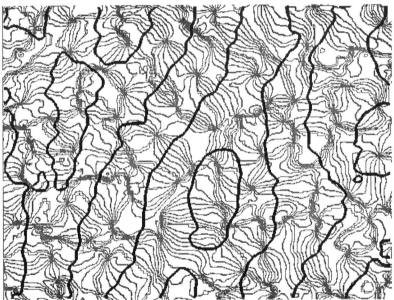

**FIGURE 1. Characteristics of orientation and ocular dominance maps, revealed by optical imaging (Obermayer and Blasdel, 1993). Five key properties of cortical maps are illustrated: (1) regions of smooth change in orientation preference (linear zones), (2) regions in which orientation changes rapidly along one direction (fractures), (3) regions at the center of swirls of orientation where all orientations are present (singularities), (4) singularities tend to lie within the centers of ocular dominance columns, (5) linear zones tend to intersect ocular dominance columns nearly orthogonally.**

This explosion of neural data has led to a correspondingly vigorous development of neural network models to simulate and explain them (Bienenstock *et al*, 1976; Grossberg, 1976a, 1976b, 1976c; Linsker 1986, 1990; Miller *et al*, 1989; Obermayer *et al*, 1992; von der Malsburg, 1973; Willshaw and von der Malsburg, 1976). These models have tended to mix two goals: to understand the functional organization of columnar structures in primate visual cortex, and to understand how this columnar organization forms through a self-organizing developmental process.

Although each of these neural models shares a number of features in common, such as associative learning and competitive decision rules, their very numbers and continued proliferation indicates that no one model has yet definitively been accepted. To facilitate this process, the present article identifies three computational properties that are sufficient to explain data concerning the adult organization of ocular dominance and orientation columns. These properties identify a universal computational substrate that may subserve neural models of these structures.

In their simplest form, the three computational properties are (1) a source of noise that energizes the map formation process; (2) a spatial band pass filter that organizes the noise into a spatial map structure; and (3) a normalization rule that constrains how multiple visual features are competitively allocated across the two-dimensional map surface. These rules extend the key observation of Rojer and Schwartz (1990) that rules (1) and (2) may be used to generate the map structure of ocular dominance columns, and the related insight of Erwin *et al* (1993) that neural models of cortical maps possess ring-shaped Fourier power spectra, given isotropic connection rules.

Taken together, rules (1)-(3) allow us to simulate the spatial organization of both cortical ocular dominance columns and orientation columns, as well as their mutual overlap, as these properties have been revealed by experiment using optical imaging techniques (Blasdel, 1992a, 1992b; Obermayer and Blasdel, 1993).

## Band Pass Filters

Although all band pass filters that we examined produced qualitatively similar maps, the Difference of Gaussians (DOG) filter is of particular interest since DOG filters and their approximations are used to carry out competitive decision making in essentially all the neural network models. The DOG filter is defined as the Fourier transform of a two dimensional DOG spatial convolution kernel:

$$DOG(\omega_x, \omega_y) = 2\pi \left( s_1^2 e^{-\frac{s_1^2\omega_x^2}{2} - \frac{s_1^2\omega_y^2}{2}} - s_2^2 e^{-\frac{s_2^2\omega_x^2}{2} - \frac{s_2^2\omega_y^2}{2}} \right) \tag{1}$$

Figure 2 shows the result of applying this band pass filter to a noise source.

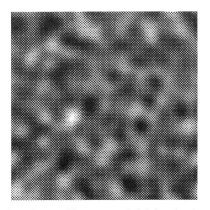

**FIGURE 2. Application of a DOG band pass filter to an initial noise image.**

## Competitive Normalization across Feature Dimensions

A competitive normalization property is found, either explicitly or implicitly, in each of the neural network models mentioned above. The models of Linsker (1986), Miller *et al* (1989), and von der Malsburg (1973) include explicit normalization of the adaptive weights that undergo learning. Grossberg (1976), Kohonen (1989), and Obermayer *et al* (1992) present models which obtain normalization as an emergent network property due to inhibitory interactions. Normalization is necessary to prevent unbounded weight growth and helps the network to learn a feature map in a stable way.

A normalization constraint can be rationalized in higher dimensional systems if the various feature inputs or "dimensions" interact via a mass action or shunting competitive interaction (Grossberg, 1973, 1982). Competitive normalization is shown below to generate a key relationship in the physiological data (Blasdel, 1992): spatial loci that correspond to large values of one dimension correspond to small values of the competing dimension(s). This relationship is expressed by the following equation:

$$\sum_{k=1}^{n} f_k(x_k) = K \tag{2}$$

where each function $f_k(x)$ is an increasing function of $x$, and $K$ is the maximum response.

## Simulations of cortical maps

To simulate cortical maps of orientation and ocular dominance columns we let the number of dimensions $n=3$, select the transfer function

$$f_k(x) = x^2, \tag{3}$$

and choose $K = 1$. By (2) and (3),

$$x_1^2 + x_2^2 + x_3^2 = 1 \tag{4}$$

which is equivalent to requiring each vector $(x_1, x_2, x_3)$ to lie on the unit sphere. Using these parameters we generate simulated cortical maps with the following procedure (depicted graphically in Figure 3):

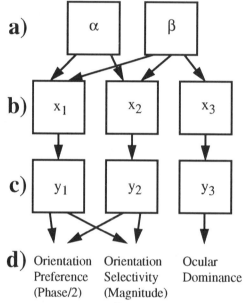

**FIGURE 3. a) Two maps of random angles ($\alpha$ and $\beta$) uniquely determine a map of vectors on the unit sphere. b) The cartesian coordinates ($x_1, x_2, x_3$) of each vector are computed from the maps of $\alpha$ and $\beta$. c) A spatial band pass filter is applied to each of the coordinate maps to generate maps of simulated response vectors ($y_1, y_2, y_3$). d) Maps $y_1$ and $y_2$ are combined to yield maps of orientation preference and orientation selectivity; map $y_3$ is interpreted as ocular dominance.**

- Select two maps of uniformly-distributed angles ($\alpha, \beta$) which together uniquely determine a single point on the surface of the unit sphere (see Figure 4).
- Coordinates ($\alpha, \beta$) correspond to coordinates $x_1$, $x_2$ and $x_3$ such that
$$x_1 = \cos\alpha\cos\beta; \quad x_2 = \sin\alpha\cos\beta; \quad x_3 = \sin\beta \tag{5}$$
  on the unit sphere.
- Each image $x_1$, $x_2$, and $x_3$ is band pass filtered to yield simulated response maps $y_1$, $y_2$, and $y_3$. Specifically, each image $x_i$ is transformed into the frequency domain with a Fast Fourier Transform (FFT) (Press *et al*, 1992), multiplied by the annular-shaped two-dimensional band pass filter, and transformed back into the spatial domain using the inverse FFT.
- We interpret these maps much as Blasdel (1992b) interpreted his physiological data of visual cortex. We take $y_1$ and $y_2$ to represent orientation preference and orientation selectivity. At a unique horizontal and vertical

position there exists a single scalar value (pixel) in each of the $y_1$ and $y_2$ maps, $y_1(h,v)$ and $y_2(h,v)$. The magnitude of the 2-dimensional vector $[y_1(h,v), y_2(h,v)]$,

$$M(h,v) = \sqrt{y_1(h,v)^2 + y_2(h,v)^2}$$

represents orientation selectivity at a given position, and half of the angle of the vector,

$$\theta(h,v) = \arctan\left(\frac{y_1(h,v)}{y_2(h,v)}\right)$$

represents orientation preference. We restrict the angle to lie between $-\pi/2$ and $\pi/2$ because orientation preference is defined only on this range.

- Similarly, we take $y_3$ to represent eye dominance. We interpret positive values of $y_3(h,v)$ to represent preference for one eye, and negative values to represent preference for the other eye. Values of $y_3(h,v)$ near 0 represent an absence of eye preference.

- Figure 5 shows a simulated ocular dominance map. The range $[-1,1]$ of the $y_3$ map is shown as a grey-scale image. Light regions correspond to map values near 1 and to regions that "prefer" input from one eye. By contrast dark regions correspond to map values near -1 and to regions that prefer input from the other eye. Grey regions correspond to values near 0 and prefer input from neither eye.

One-half of the angle of the vector $[y_1(h,v), y_2(h,v)]$ represents orientation preference in our simulations. Contours of iso-orientation preference of a simulated orientation preference map are shown in Figure 6. This map is qualitatively similar to contour maps of physiologically-measured orientation preference, shown in Figure 1. In particular notice the existence in the simulated maps of the features of physiological maps identified earlier: (1) linear zones, (2) fractures, and (3) singularities. In addition note that (4) the singularities in the orientation preference map tend to correspond to the centers of the ocular dominance columns, as shown in Figure 7. This is equivalent to the observation that the singularities in the orientation preference map tend to correlate with regions of low binocularity. Finally, Figure 7 shows (5) the tendency of orientation contours to intersect the edges of ocular dominance columns at right angles.

Singularities, fractures, and linear zones are determined by the topology of the interaction of all three components. The $x_1$ and $x_2$ maps are selected from orthogonal components of a map of random angles. After filtering, high spatial frequencies are removed, resulting in local spatial correlation. Thus small regions which contain vectors with similar angles will form sharply-tuned regions of a specific orientation preference after filtering. By contrast, vectors

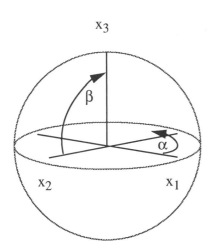

FIGURE 4. Two angles $\alpha$ and $\beta$ uniquely determine a vector $(x_1, x_2, x_3)$ on the surface of the unit sphere.

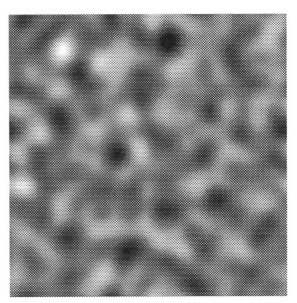

FIGURE 5. Simulated ocular dominance map $y_3$ generated by applying DOG filter to normalized random map $x_3$ (see text). Dark regions correspond to preference for one eye, light regions to preference for the other eye.

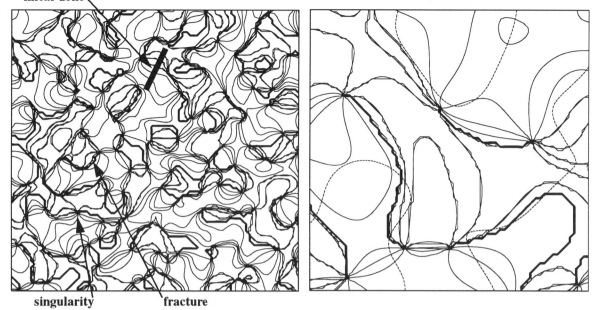

**FIGURE 6.** Simulated orientation preference map extracted from DOG-filtered maps. Orientation preference is defined as half the angle determined by each two-dimensional vector in the map $(y_1, y_2)$. Contours lines are drawn along regions of constant orientation. Examples of a singularity, a fracture, and a linear zone are indicated.

**FIGURE 7.** Simulated orientation preference contours superimposed on simulated ocular dominance column boundaries show the tendency of the contours to intersect the boundaries at right angles. Solid lines show iso-orientation contours, dashed lines show boundaries of ocular dominance columns.

in small regions with many different angles tend to cancel with one another as a result of filtering, yielding small regions in which the vectors all have small magnitude and many orientations. In a contour plot of orientation preference, these regions show up as singularities, and correspond to regions of low orientation selectivity. Removal of low frequencies leads to a spatial anti-correlation of slightly-more-distant regions, and increases the regularity of the spatial pattern.

Linear zones and fractures develop according to similar principles. It is helpful to think about fractures and linear zones as the endpoints of a continuum. Similar nearby regions in the initial angular map interact to form regions in the final map with a range of rates of spatial orientation change. Nearby regions with slightly different orientation preferences yield linear zones. Nearby regions with drastically different initial orientation preference form fractures. The initial distribution of angular differences produces the wide range orientation changes, punctuated by linear zones and fractures, that is seen in simulated maps.

The physiologically-observed tendency of orientation preference singularities to lie at the centers of ocular dominance columns is explained by the normalization constraint. Vectors near the centers of ocular dominance columns have large $y_3$ coordinates and small $y_1$ and $y_2$ coordinates; vectors with a small $y_3$ coordinate have $[y_1, y_2]$ sub-vectors with large magnitudes. Thus vectors near the centers of orientation columns have small orientation selectivity, a necessary condition for singularities in the orientation preference map. Conversely, vectors away from the centers of orientation columns have larger orientation selectivity: therefore singularities as a rule do not lie away from the centers of the ocular dominance columns.

As described above, orientation contour lines run between pairs of singularities. Since singularities show a strong tendency to line up with the centres of ocular dominance columns, these contour lines are constrained to run from the center of one ocular dominance column to the center of a neighboring column, or roughly along the center line of a single ocular dominance column: orientation contours that intersect ocular dominance column borders therefore do so at approximately orthogonal angles.

## Conclusion

This conceptually and computationally simple class of models is capable of explaining the key observations made by physiological imaging of primary visual cortex with 2DG and optical recordings. The qualitative structures of the orientation preference, orientation selectivity, and ocular dominance columns emerge, as do the observed topographical relationships among these maps.

The similarity between the synthetic and the experimental maps suggests that cortex performs a band pass filter of noisy input and competitive normalization across feature dimensions. Such mechanisms could be due to neural interactions. This is the type of explanation given by all the neural network models reviewed above. On the other hand, other types of mechanisms with similar computational properties could also generate the observed results. In one of the foundational articles on self-organizing cortical feature maps, Grossberg (1976a) noted that model neural mechanisms of postnatal feature map tuning share computational properties with model morphogenetic mechanisms of prenatal feature map formation. These computational homologs enable postnatal map tuning to refine prenatally developed maps in a computationally consistent way. For example, in the morphogenetic models, morphogens cooperate and compete among cells that obey mass action reaction-diffusion equations, thereby achieving competitive normalization. In addition, feature tuning by postnatal mechanisms of activity-dependent synaptic modification obey mathematical rules like those that model prenatal growth of intercellular connections. Similar morphogenetic signals and growth rules are also capable of modeling a variety of non-neural developmental data (Grossberg, 1978).

Our simulation results suggest that whatever combination of genetically and environmentally controlled mechanisms for cortical mapping exist, it needs to incorporate computations that behave like a noise input, a spatial band pass filter, and competitive normalization across feature dimensions. The computational similarity of neural and morphogenetic models also suggest that some of these same properties may be sought in examples of non-neural morphogenetic maps.

## References

Bienenstock, Cooper, & Munro (1982) Theory for the development of neuron selectivity: Orientation specificity and binocular interaction in visual cortex. *The Journal of Neuroscience*, 2, 32-48.

Blasdel, G. G. (1992a). Differential imaging of ocular dominance and orientation selectivity in monkey striate cortex. *The Journal of Neuroscience*, *12*(8), 3115-3138.

Blasdel, G. G. (1992b). Orientation selectivity, preference, and continuity in monkey striate cortex. *The Journal of Neuroscience*, *12*(8), 3115-3138.

Erwin, E., Obermayer, K., & Schulten, K. (1992). A Comparison of Models of Visual Cortical Map Formation. Technical Report UIUC-BI-TB-92-16, The University of Illinois.

Grossberg, S. (1976a). On the development of feature detectors in the visual cortex with application to learning and reaction-diffusion systems. *Biological Cybernetics*, *21*, 145-159.

Grossberg, S. (1976b). Adaptive pattern classification and universal recoding I: Parallel development and coding of neural feature detectors. *Biological Cybernetics*, *23*, 121-134.

Grossberg, S. (1976c). Adaptive pattern classification and universal recoding II: Feedback, expectation, olfaction, and illusions. *Biological Cybernetics*, *23*, 187-202.

Grossberg, S. (1978). Communication, memory, and development. In R. Rosen and F. Snell (eds.) *Progress in Theoretical Biology*. Volume 5, New York: Academic Press.

Hubel, D. H. & Wiesel, T. N. (1974) Sequence regularity and geometry of orientation columns in the monkey striate cortex. *J. Comp. Neurol.*, *158*:267-293.

Kohonen, T. (1989). *Self-Organization and Associative Memory* (Third edition). Springer-Verlag.

Linsker, R. (1986). From basic network principles to neural architecture: Emergence of spatial-opponent cells. *Proceedings of the National Academy of Sciences*, 7508-7512.

Linsker, R. (1990). Perceptual neural organization: Some approaches based on network models and information theory. *Annual Review of Neuroscience*, *13*:257-281.

Miller, K., Keller, J., & Stryker, M. (1989). Ocular dominance column development: Analysis and simulation. *Science*, *245*, 605-615.

Obermayer, K., & Blasdel, G. G. (1993). Geometry of Orientation and Ocular Dominance Columns in Monkey Striate Cortex. *The Journal of Neuroscience*, *13*(10), 4114-4129.

Obermayer, K., Blasdel, G. G., & Schulten, K. (1992). Statistical-mechanical analysis of self-organization and pattern formation during the development of visual maps. *Physical Review A*, *45*(10), 7568-7589.

Press, W. H., Teukolsky, S. A., Vetterling, W. T., & Flannery, B. P. (1992) *Numerical Recipes in C*. Cambridge University Press, Cambridge.

Rojer, A., & Schwartz, E. (1990). Cat and monkey cortical columnar patterns modeled by bandpass-filtered 2d white noise. *Biological Cybernetics*, *62*, 381-391.

von der Malsburg, C. (1973). Self-organization of orientation sensitive cells in the striate cortex. *Kybernetik*, *14*, 85-100.

Willshaw, D.J. & von der Malsburg. C. (1976). How patterned neural connections can be set up by self-organization. *Proceedings of the Royal Society of London (B)*, *194*, 431-445.

# A Simple Cell Model with Multiple Spatial Frequency Selectivity and Linear/Non-Linear Response Properties

Heiko Neumann[†,‡1] and Luiz Pessoa[§2]

† Center for Adaptive Systems and
§ Department of Cognitive and Neural Systems,
Boston University, 111 Cummington Street, Boston, MA 02215, USA

‡ Universität Hamburg, FB Informatik, AB Kognitive Systeme,
Bodenstedtstr.16, D-22765 Hamburg, Germany

### Abstract

A model is described for cortical simple cells. Simple cells are selective for local contrast polarity, signaling light-dark and dark-light transitions. The proposed new architecture exhibits both linear and non-linear properties of simple cells. Linear responses are obtained by integration of the input stimulus within subfields of the cells, and by combinations of them. Non-linear behavior can be seen in the selectivity for certain features that can be characterized by the spatial arrangement of activations generated by initial on- and off-cells (center-surround). The new model also exhibits spatial frequency selectivity with the generation of multi-scale properties being based on a single-scale band-pass input that is generated by the initial (retinal) center-surround processing stage.

## 1. Introduction

Although the stimulus-response properties of cells at early stages of visual processing (along the retino-cortical pathway) have been investigated successfully, the underlying mechanisms as well as their functionality are by now not fully understood. For example, the generation of orientation selectivity in cortical simple cells is still a matter of debate. The same holds for the mechanisms underlying the measurement of local contrast.

In this paper, we introduce a neural circuit that attempts to clarify several important properties of simple cells. The model is derived from well documented experimental results as well as previous computational studies. Specifically, the new model *i)* makes explicit local contrast changes of specific polarity; *ii)* shows linear and non-linear response properties producing selectivity to certain feature-like input configurations (potentially allowing for the generation of significant responses not directly related to contrast); and *iii)* incorporates multiple spatial frequency (scale) selectivity.

## 2. Empirical Evidence and Functionality of Simple Cells

The retino-cortical pathway is divided in on and off processing streams, or channels, that remain segregated until area V1 ([25]). The axonal projections of LGN cells terminate in layer 4 of V1, whereby the precise spatial arrangement of the segregated on- and off-pathways differs between species (see [32] for a discussion).

---

[1] Supported in part by the German BMFT, grant 413-5839–01 IN 101 C/1.
[2] Supported in part by CNPq and NUTES/UFRJ, Brazil.

Simple cells in layer 4 can be characterized by their preference for orientation, local contrast polarity, spatial frequency, as well as other attributes. The mechanisms that generate orientation selectivity are still not fully understood, but evidence exists for orientation selectivity being generated by the spatially aligned inputs of on- and off-channel LGN cells ([5, 4]). Utilizing the framework of Fourier and linear system's theory, it is assumed that the visual input is processed in separate channels, each of which is selective to a band of spatial frequencies ([31, 30]). An important question is to where spatial frequency selectivity first arises. Data suggest that spatial frequency channels are a property of the visual cortex alone; physiological and morphological studies failed to show selectivity for cells in retina and LGN ([23]). The corresponding scatter of receptive field sizes to make cells responsive to spatial frequency has, however, been revealed to exist at the level of V1 ([23, 29], see [1] for a discussion of functional implications).

The receptive fields of simple cells can be divided into subfields and an important issue is how the inputs to the different subfields combine. With respect to the combination, both linear and non-linear properties have been shown. Moreover, the structure of the input has been revealed as converging on-LGN afferents to on-subfields and off-LGN afferents to off-subfields ([5, 6, 25]). Let us briefly review the debate concerning linear/non-linear simple cell mechanisms. Simple cells have been shown to exhibit a sum-to-threshold linearity in the integration of its inputs ([26]), a finding used as evidence against non-linear gating-type combinations of subfields as suggested in some computational models (see below). However, non-linear (suppressive) interaction between subfields for reverse-contrast stimulation has been demonstrated by [13] (see also [2]), a fact suggestive of gating-like mechanisms. None of these non-linear interactions occur at the level of dendritic spines ([3]), indicating that cellular interactions account for these phenomena. A contrast dependent non-linearity lead [28] (see also [17, 14]) to the hypothesis of push-pull interactions of on/off inputs to simple cell subfields. FERSTER ([6]) provided evidence for a partial overlap of on and off subfields in simple cells (see also [14]) and suggested that competition between simple cells of opposite contrast polarity at each spatial location occurs (see also [18]).

Further information on the combination of on/off information in simple cells has been obtained by blocking studies. By blocking the on-channel it has been shown that *i)* the orientation selectivity is maintained ([25, 27]) and *ii)* a decline in cortical responsiveness occurs that amounts to more than 50% decrease in response strength ([15]). The latter finding is highly suggestive of non-linear mechanisms.

Computational models of simple cells have employed, for example, AND-gating non-linearities operating on the outputs of center-surround operators as a decision-mechanism determining the existence of contrast edges ([19, 24]). Recently, the analysis of the differential structure of image curves and contrast outlines lead IVERSON AND ZUCKER ([16]) to propose a syntactic scheme defining a language of logical/linear operators. Herein, operators composed of tangentially separated subfields were defined to selectively respond to contrast ("edge") and line features while enabling the operators to automatically suppress "false" responses. A similar functional scheme has been described in [8, 9], in which deviations from co-occurring on- and off-channel activations are penalized, yielding a reduction in activity.

## 3. Model Circuit for Odd-Symmetric Simple Cells

The above review can be summarized into the key computational elements of our simple cell circuit: *i)* on- and off-contrast channels feed into simple cell on- and off-subfields, respectively; *ii)* spatial frequency selectivity; *iii)* push-pull interactions; and *iv)* competition between opposite

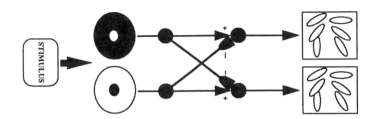

Figure 1: *Sketch of initial center-surround filtering utilizing shunting (membrane) interactions (large circles) and subsequent reciprocal inhibitory cross-channel interaction.*

polarity cells. Moreover, the AND-gating like mechanism employed by several models in the literature is an emergent property of the network proposed here, and therefore rationalizes how it can be obtained with cellular interactions.

A model related to the one introduced here has been described in [11]. In this model, on-cells and spatially displaced off-cells in a multiscale filter excite target simple cells. Simple cells of opposite contrast polarity compete at each position and their rectified output signals converge on target complex cells.

**Center-surround Antagonism and On- and Off-channels.** The initial processing of the input luminance utilizes isotropic center-surround interactions. Response characteristics of on- and off-cells are described by membrane equations of the type used by [12]. The generated responses for on- and off-filtering are denoted by $y_i^+$ and $y_i^-$, respectively. It has been shown in [21, 22] that on- and off-channel activities contain DC components that represent compressed and low-pass transformed versions of the luminance distribution. The segregation of local contrast information in the on- and off-contrast channels is accomplished by reciprocal cross-channel inhibition to generate activations $c_i^+ = [y_i^+ - y_i^-]^+$ and $c_i^- = [y_i^- - y_i^+]^+$ ($[x]^+ = \max[x, 0]$), respectively. An outline of the scheme is sketched in Fig. 1. For further details and overview see [22].

**Simple Cell Responses.** The inputs to simple cells are generated in the circuit outlined in Fig. 1. Following the suggestion in [6], oriented inputs are generated by blurring the activity distribution in the on- and off-contrast channels by utilizing elongated Gaussian weighting functions (represented in Fig. 1 by the "ellipses"). Multiple spatial frequency selectivity is generated by using weighting functions of different orientations, each with different spatial extent in length and width. This stage is operationalized by computing $p_i^{S+} = \sum_j c_j^+ \lambda_{ji}^S$ and $p_i^{S-} = \sum_j c_j^- \lambda_{ji}^S$ where $\lambda_{ji}^S$ denotes an oriented elongated Gaussian weighting function of scale $S^3$.

Figure 2a sketches the circuit of a simple cell with light-dark polarity. The circuit itself has 4 stages and contains two streams, or channels, namely on and off. The first stage receives the blurred contrast activities in the on- and off-channel, $p_i^{S+}$ and $p_i^{S-}$, respectively. The second stage

---

[3]Since so far only a 1-D version of the model has been investigated, the explicit labeling of orientations has been omitted.

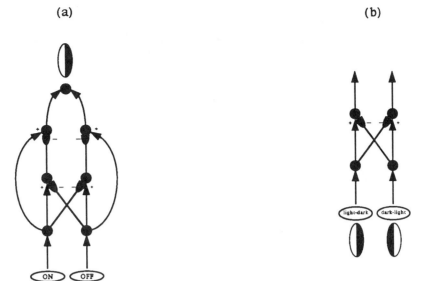

Figure 2: *(a) Circuit for an odd-symmetric simple cell sensitive to light-dark contrast polarity. (b) Final competition of simple cells of opposite contrast polarity at each spatial location.*

contains an opponent interaction of the on- and off-channels as well as direct excitatory inputs from each subfield. The third receives channel-specific inputs from both the first (excitatory) and second (inhibitory) stages. Finally, on and off channels are pooled producing the final response in stage four. The opponent inhibition associated with the within-channel inhibition provides a mechanism for *disinhibition*. As a consequence, the output of the circuit will be large only when the inputs from *both* channels are strong — since disinhibition of activation in each subfield occurs. The self-inhibition/disinhibition mechanisms therefore realize the functionality of a "smooth" AND-gate ([16]).

The model employs both light-dark and dark-light simple cells. These are obtained by collecting contrast information from spatially different branches. For a light-dark cell at position $i$, on-information originates from the "left" and off-information from the "right" (referring to the "symmetry axis" centered at $i$). To simplify the notation below we use the convention $l = i - \sigma_S$ and $r = i + \sigma_S$, where $l$ and $r$ are the "left" and "right" spatial offsets with $\sigma_S$ as a scale-dependent constant[4]. Simple cell responses are computed in two steps, with intermediate variables $q_i^+$ (stage 2) and $z_i^+$ (stage 3) for the on-channel (on-subfield) and $q_i^-$ and $z_i^-$ for the off-channel (off-subfield) (see Fig. 2a). The equations for the on-channel are

$$\dot{q}_i^+ = -\alpha q_i^+ + p_l^+ - \beta p_r^- q_i^+ \tag{1}$$
$$\dot{z}_i^+ = -\gamma z_i^+ + p_l^+ - \delta q_i^+ z_i^+ \tag{2}$$

---

[4]To simplify the notation the spatial scale index, $S$, will not be used in the following; however, all stages further described are computed for multiple scales.

and for the off-channel

$$\dot{q}_i^- = -\alpha q_i^- + p_r^- - \beta p_l^+ q_i^- \tag{3}$$

$$\dot{z}_i^- = -\gamma z_i^- + p_r^- - \delta q_i^- z_i^- \tag{4}$$

where $\alpha$, $\beta$, $\gamma$, and $\delta$ are constants. All the above processes are assumed to reach equilibrium fast and are thereby computed at equilibrium. The final response for a light-dark simple cell is computed as

$$Z_i^{ld} = z_i^+ + z_i^-. \tag{5}$$

The dark-light response, $Z_i^{dl}$, is obtained in a similar manner.

**Mutual Inhibition of Simple Cells.** Simple cells of opposite polarity and same spatial location are postulated to undergo mutual inhibition ([6, 18], see Fig. 2b). Therefore, final light-dark responses are computed as

$$x_i^{ld} = [Z_i^{ld} - Z_i^{dl}]^+ \tag{6}$$

and dark-light responses as

$$x_i^{dl} = [Z_i^{dl} - Z_i^{ld}]^+. \tag{7}$$

The assumption of subtractive inhibition in equations 6 and 7 is not central to the model's functionality; alternatively, a shunting inhibition scheme could have been employed.

**Complex Cell Responses.** Complex cell responses are, *in vivo*, insensitive to direction of contrast ([7]) and are obtained in the model, for simplicity, by pooling (i.e., adding) light-dark and dark-light simple cell responses.

## 4. Computer Simulations

The behavior of the model has been assessed through a set of computer simulations. In all, simple cell responses are shown after mutual inhibition ($x_i^{ld}$ and $x_i^{dl}$). Figure 3 shows the model's behavior when presented with a square wave. For the smaller scale, strong polarity specific "edge" responses are visible; activity is decreased for the coarser scale. In Fig. 4 the input is again a square wave, but now the on channel has been inactivated. As found experimentally, activities are greatly reduced (decreasing to less than 50% of the total activity). Figure 5 illustrates the behavior when the input is a trapezoidal wave. Note the simple cell responses of the larger scale, which respond maximally in the middle of the ramp ("small" local contrast). Finally, Fig. 6 shows the responses to a sine wave. At the proper scale, the corresponding cells respond maximally and in a quasi-linear fashion.

## 5. Summary

A neural circuit is described that realizes the functionality of odd-symmetric simple cells. The internal self-inhibition of activity in each separate channel reduces the level of cell activation generated in the case of input from one channel alone. Via disinhibition, cells respond more selectively to prominent features, such as contrast edges and ramp transitions of certain maximum width. Contrast edges and ramps are represented through correlated activity distributions in the on- and off-contrast channel. The circuit has therefore the capacity to produce strong activations for significant luminance features (such as "edges") as well as for gradual luminance variations. The response to gradual changes in luminance allows for the generation of boundary webs that may

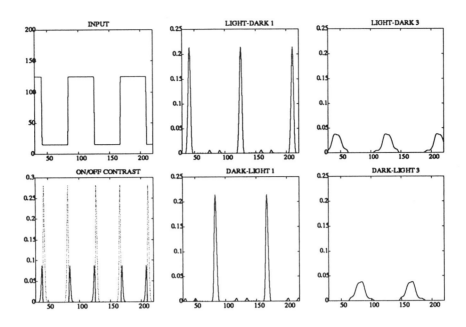

Figure 3: *Square wave: Input activities and on- (solid) and off-contrast (dotted) channels (left column); final responses, $x_i^{ld}$, and $x_i^{dl}$, after mutual inhibition for two different scales (middle and right column).*

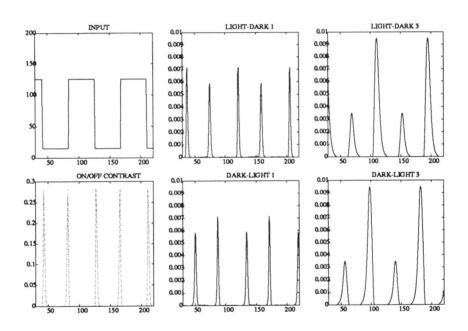

Figure 4: *Square wave processed with inactivated on-path: The overall activity distribution is reduced in amplitude; cells of opposite polarity now become co-activated for reverse contrasts.*

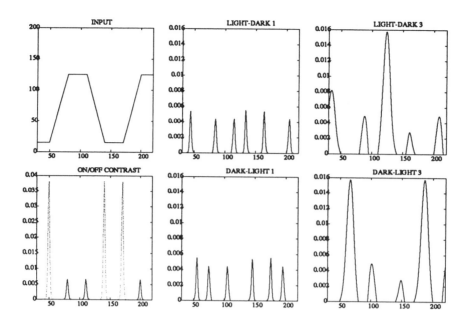

Figure 5: *Trapezoidal wave: Initial on- and off-contrast activations are generated at top and bottom "knee-points" of each individual ramp. Smallest scale responses are located within subfield offset. Maximal responses are generated for a coarser scale with locations of maxima in the center of the ramps.*

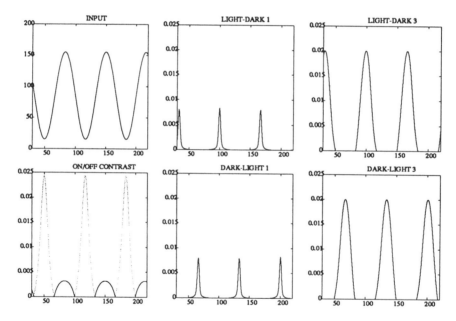

Figure 6: *Sine wave: Spatial frequency selectivity of the model is demonstrated by increasing activation for a coarser scale that matches the spatial frequency of the input. The cells with receptive fields of proper size (coarser scale) also show linear response behavior, although the processing cascade is non-linear.*

underly the generation of 3D surface layout ([10]) and brightness perception([20]). Multiple spatial frequency characteristics of the circuit have been demonstrated for the ramp-shaped transition and for the sine wave input with the cells generating maximal response having receptive fields of the proper scale.

The model so far has been developed to incorporate odd-symmetric cells only. Even-symmetric cells can be incorporated by either cascading the odd-symmetry model or, alternatively, by extending the circuit through a triple-channel version. Both versions will be investigated in the future. In addition, a full 2D version of the model is also envisaged.

# References

[1] V. Braitenberg. Reading the structure of brains. *Network*, 1:1 – 11, 1990.

[2] R.A. Brookes and K.A. Stevens. Symbolic grouping versus simple cell models. *Biological Cybernetics*, 65:375 – 380, 1991.

[3] C. Dehay, R.J. Douglas, K.A.C. Martin, and C. Nelson. Excitation by geniculocortical synapses is not 'vetoed' at the level of dendritic spines in cat visual cortex. *Journal of Physiology*, 440:723 – 734, 1991.

[4] R.J. Douglas, K.A.C. Martin, and D. Whitteridge. An intracellular analysis of the visual responses of neurones in cat visual cortex. *Journal of Physiology*, 440:659 – 696, 1991.

[5] D. Ferster. Origin of orientation selective EPSPs in simple cells of cat visual cortex. *Journal of Neuroscience*, 7(6):1780 – 1791, 1987.

[6] D. Ferster. Spatially opponent excitation and inhibition in simple cells of the cat visual cortex. *Journal of Neuroscience*, 8(4):1172 – 1180, 1988.

[7] K.H. Foster, J.P. Gaska, M. Nagler, and D.A. Pollen. Spatial and temporal frequency selectivity of neurones in visual cortical areas V1 and V2 of the macaque monkey. *Journal of Physiology*, 365:331 – 363, 1985.

[8] A. Gove, S. Grossberg, and E. Mingolla. Brightness perception, illusory contours and corticogeniculate feedback. In *Proc. World Conference on Neural Networks (WCNN-93), Vol. I-IV*, pages (I) 25 – 28, Portland (Oreg./USA), July 11 - 15 1993.

[9] A.N. Gove. *A Neural Network Model of Visual Segmentation: Illusory Contour Formation, Brightness Induction, and Grouping of Scenic Elements*. PhD thesis, Boston University, Graduate School, Dept. of Cognitive and Neural Systems, 1994.

[10] S. Grossberg and E. Mingolla. Neural dynamics of surface perception: Boundary webs, illuminants, and shape-from-shading. *Computer Vision, Graphics, and Image Processing*, 37(1):116 – 165, 1987.

[11] S. Grossberg, E. Mingolla, and J. Williamson. Synthetic aperture radar processing by a multiple scale neural system for boundary and surface representation. TR CAS/CNS-94-001, Boston University, Center for Adaptive Systems and Dept. of Cognitive and Neural Systems, 1993. (submitted).

[12] S. Grossberg and D. Todorovic. Neural dynamics of 1-d and 2-d brightness perception: A unified model of classical and recent phenomena. *Perception and Psychophysics*, 43(3):241 – 277, 1988.

[13] P. Hammond and D.M. MacKay. Influence of luminance gradient reversal on simple cells in feline striate cortex. *Journal of Physiology*, 337:69 – 87, 1983.

[14] P. Heggelund, S. Krekling, and B.C. Skottun. Spatial summation in the receptive field of simple cells in the cat striate cortex. *Experimental Brain Research*, 52:87 – 98, 1983.

[15] J.C. Horton and H. Sherk. Receptive field properties in the cat's lateral geniculate nucleus in the absence of on-center retinal input. *Journal of Neuroscience*, 4(2):374 – 380, 1984.

[16] L.A. Iverson and S.W. Zucker. Logical/linear operators for measuring orientation and curvature. TR TR-CIM-90-06, McGill University, McGill Research Centre for Intelligent Machines, Computer Vision and Robotics Laboratory, 1990.

[17] L.D. Jacobson, J.P. Gaska, H.-W. Chen, and D.A. Pollen. Structural testing of multi-input linear-nonlinear cascade models for cells in macaque striate cortex. *Vision Research*, 33(5/6):609 – 626, 1993.

[18] Z. Lui, J.P. Gaska, L.D. Jacobson, and D.A. Pollen. Interneuronal interaction between members of quadrature phase and anti-phase pairs in the cat's visual cortex. *Vision Research*, 32(7):1193 – 1198, 1992.

[19] D. Marr and E. Hildreth. Theory of edge detection. *Proceedings of the Royal Society of London*, 207(Series B):187 – 217, 1980.

[20] E. Mingolla, L. Pessoa, and H. Neumann. A multi-scale network for brightness perception. In *Proc. World Conference on Neural Networks (WCNN-94)*, San Diego (Calif./USA), June 4 - 9 1994. (submitted).

[21] H. Neumann. Toward a computational architecture for unified visual contrast and brightness perception: I. Theory and model. In *Proc. World Conference on Neural Networks (WCNN-93), Vol. I-IV*, pages (I) 84 – 91, Portland (Oreg./USA), July 11 - 15 1993.

[22] H. Neumann. An outline of a neural architecture for unified visual contrast and brightness perception. TR CAS/CNS-94-003, Boston University, Center for Adaptive Systems and Dept. of Cognitive and Neural Systems, 1994. (submitted).

[23] L. Peichl and H. Wässle. Size, scatter and coverage of ganglion cell receptive field centres in the cat retina. *Journal of Physiology*, 291:117 – 141, 1979.

[24] T. Poggio. Visual algorithms. In O.J. Braddick and A.C. Sleigh, editors, *Physical and Biological Processing of Images*, pages 128 – 153. Springer, Berlin, 1983.

[25] P.H. Schiller. The ON and OFF channels of the visual system. *Trends in Neuroscience*, 15(3):86 – 91, 1992.

[26] R.A. Schumer and J.A. Movshon. Length summation in simple cells of cat striate cortex. *Vision Research*, 24(6):565 – 571, 1984.

[27] H. Sherk and J.C. Horton. Receptive field properties in the cat's area 17 in the absence of on-center geniculate input. *Journal of Neuroscience*, 4(2):381 – 393, 1984.

[28] D.J. Tolhurst and A.F. Dean. The effects of contrast on the linearity of spatial summation of simple cells in the cat's striate cortex. *Experimental Brain Research*, 79:582 – 588, 1990.

[29] R.B.H. Tootell, M.S. Silverman, S.L. Hamilton, E. Switges, and R.L. DeValois. Functional anatomy of macaque striate cortex. V. Spatial frequency. *Journal of Neuroscience*, 8(5):1610 – 1624, 1988.

[30] H.R. Wilson. Psychophysical evidence for spatial channels. In O.J. Braddick and A.C. Sleigh, editors, *Physical and Biological Processing of Images*, volume 11 of *Springer Series in Information Sciences*, pages 88 – 99. Springer, Berlin, 1983.

[31] H.R. Wilson and J.R. Bergen. A four mechanism model for threshold spatial vision. *Vision Research*, 19:19 – 32, 1979.

[32] K.R. Zahs and M.P. Stryker. Segregation of ON and OFF afferents to ferret visual cortex. *Journal of Neurophysiology*, 59(5):1410 – 1429, 1988.

# A MULTI-SCALE NETWORK MODEL OF BRIGHTNESS PERCEPTION

Ennio Mingolla,[†,‡1] Heiko Neumann[†,§2] and Luiz Pessoa[‡3]

and

† Center for Adaptive Systems and
‡ Department of Cognitive and Neural Systems,
Boston University, 111 Cummington Street, Boston, MA 02215, USA

§ Universität Hamburg, FB Informatik, AB Kognitive Systeme,
Bodenstedtstr.16, D-22765 Hamburg, Germany

### Abstract

A neural network model of brightness perception is developed to account for a wide variety of difficult data, including the classical phenomenon of Mach bands and nonlinear contrast effects associated with sinusoidal luminance waves. The model builds upon previous work by Grossberg and colleagues on filling-in models that predict brightness perception through the interaction of *boundary* and *feature* signals. Model equations are presented and computer simulations illustrate the model's potential.

## 1 Introduction

Brightness phenomena are a rich source of information on how the visual system encodes luminance changes in the world. In this paper we develop a neural network for brightness perception in the tradition of filling-in theories (Cohen and Grossberg, 1984; Gerrits and Vendrick, 1970). Our simulations implement a number of refinements already described in the development of Grossberg's (1987, 1994) Form-And-Color-And-DEpth (FACADE) theory, which though conceived as part of the theory, were not implemented in the simulations of Grossberg and Todorovic (1988). These include: a) ON and OFF channels with separate filling-in domains; b) multiple spatial scales; c) computations for simple and complex cells; and d) boundary computations that engage a recurrent competitive circuit. Simulations of the present system of equations account for human's perception of a wide variety of stimuli, including ones whose brightness contains shallow spatial gradients.

## 2 Smooth Brightness Gradients within the BCS/FCS Theory

A fundamental idea of the BCS/FCS theory is that *boundaries* are used to generate filling-in compartments where *featural* quality (e.g., "brightness" in our case) is diffused, or spread. The final diffused activities in the FCS correspond to the model's predicted brightness, which is the outcome of interactions between boundaries and featural quality, whereby boundaries control the process of filling-in by forming gates of variable resistance to diffusion.

Note that while it may seem natural to assume that boundary signals only exist in locations corresponding to discontinuities of luminance ("edges"), Grossberg and Mingolla (1987) showed that "boundary webs" can form in regions of *luminance* gradients, whereby the process of diffusion

---

[1]Supported in part by the Air Force Office of Scientific Research (AFOSR-F49620-92-J-0334), the Northeast Consortium for Engineering Education (NCEE-A303-21-93), and the Office of Naval Research (ONR N00014-91-J-4100).

[2]Supported in part by the German BMFT, grant 413-5839–01 IN 101 C/1.

[3]Supported in part by CNPq and NUTES/UFRJ, Brazil.

may be totally or partially blocked within extended regions, yielding a percept of spatially gradual changes in brightness. Boundary signals work to *contain* diffusion; large boundary values do not allow a featural value at a given spatial position to affect a neighboring one. In regions with zero boundary activity, featural quality is free to diffuse, while in regions containing spatially dense boundary signals, little diffusion of featural quality throughout a large area may occur. In other words, featural quality cannot be spread, and the corresponding predicted brightness will be similar to the profile of featural quality derived by the initial filtering of the scenic input (image) at those spatial positions. In this sense, extended boundaries of sufficient amplitude can be thought of as *print signals*, that is, signals that simply replicate the filtered input to the filling-in stage.

## 2.1  Boundary Computations

Analysis of several brightness stimuli indicates that stimuli with abrupt luminance transitions (e.g., luminance steps) generally require sharp boundary signals to create spatially abrupt barriers between regions of discretely differing brightness levels, while stimuli containing smooth luminance modulations will require smoother boundaries to be able to trap (at least some of) the modulation that is present in the convolved input (featural quality) to create smoothly varying brightness distributions. How then can the visual system, or a model of it, decide without a homunculus — rules invoked by *other* processes — whether or not to sharpen boundary signals?

What differentiates the situations requiring sharp and extended boundary signals? Consider a system where the input waveform is filtered by both ON and OFF center-surround operators. The solution originates from the observation that sharp transitions of luminance produce strong responses in both the ON and OFF channels. In other words, in the region surrounding an "edge," there will be strong ON-activity (at the "light" region) and strong OFF-activity (at the "dark" region). On the other hand, waveforms with more gradual variations of luminance lead to a different distribution of ON and OFF responses.

The above analysis indicates that ON and OFF responses can be used to guide the computation of boundaries: ON/OFF spatial coincidence (Gove, 1993; Grossberg, 1994; Grossberg, Mingolla, and Williamson, 1993; Iverson and Zucker, 1989) should eventually lead to sharp boundaries while ON/OFF separation should produce spatially shallow signals. We propose a two stage process for achieving the computational competencies necessary to generate the proper activity distribution within the BCS: 1) initial boundary responses to stimuli with ON/OFF coincidence should be large; and 2) responses that are "large" relative to neighboring ones are sharpened while those that are (absolutely) small or near in size to neighboring ones are not.

## 3  Multiple Scale Contrast and Brightness System

Recently, Neumann (1993, 1994) presented an analysis that clarified how the double-opponent subtraction of ON/OFF signals for brightness computation (Grossberg, 1987, 1994; Grossberg and Wyse, 1992) can be thought of as "factored" into the computation in parallel of "*contrast*" and "*luminance-derived*" signals. The current model combines the work of Grossberg and Todorovic (1988) and of Neumann (1993, 1994) and modifies them in several ways (see Introduction). The full description of the model follows (Figure 1). The implementation employed is 1-D, i.e., stimuli of interest are actually slices through full 2-D stimuli with 1-D symmetry. As far as possible the parameters of the model have been kept constant across scales; spatial parameters that vary according to scale have an index $S$. Variables that are computed in multiple scales also contain the index $S$.

The input pattern to the model is a spatial pattern given by $I_i$.

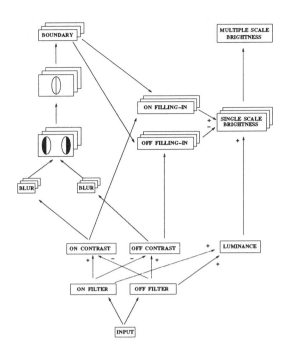

Figure 1: Diagram of model components. Stages that perform multiple scale computations are specified by several "shifted boxes". Simple and complex cells are indicated by polarity specific and direction of contrast insensitive "cells", respectively. The final output is given by the stage "Multiple Scale Brightness". The names employed are indicated in parenthesis in the formal description of the model stages.

**Center-surround Antagonism and On- and Off-channels** (ON/OFF filter). The input pattern is processed by both ON- and OFF-cells in a way similar to retinal ganglion cells. This is accomplished with membrane equations (Grossberg and Todorovic, 1988).

**Segregation of Contrast and Brightness Systems** (ON/OFF contrast and luminance). Call the above ON and OFF filtering responses by $Y_i^+$ and $Y_i^-$, respectively. As proposed by Neumann (1993, 1994), the representation of "contrast" signals is obtained via inhibitory interactions between ON and OFF channels as in

$$c_i^+ \;=\; [Y_i^+ - Y_i^-]^+ \tag{1}$$
$$c_i^- \;=\; [Y_i^- - Y_i^+]^+ \tag{2}$$

where $[x]^+ = \max(x, 0)$. "Baseline", or luminance-driven, activity is obtained by pooling the output of ON and OFF channels, obtaining a low-pass filtered and non-linearly compressed version of the input

$$s_i = Y_i^+ + Y_i^-. \tag{3}$$

**Simple and Complex Cell Responses.** Simple and Complex cells are the first major stage leading to the computation of boundaries. Before feeding into simple cells, ON- and OFF-contrast signals ($c_i^+$ and $c_i^-$) are first blurred by Gaussian kernels producing the signals $p_i^{S+}$ and $p_i^{S-}$, where $S = 1, \ldots, k$, and $k$ is the number of scales.

The model employs both light-dark and dark-light simple cells. These are obtained by collecting contrast information from spatially different branches. Consider a simple cell at position $i$. For a light-dark cell, ON-information originates from the "left" and OFF-information from the "right" (with respect to position $i$). To simplify the notation below we use the following convention:

$l = i - \sigma_S$ and $r = i + \sigma_S$, where $l$ and $r$ are the "left" and "right" spatial offsets and $\sigma_S$ is a scale-dependent constant. Responses are assumed to reach equilibrium fast and are computed in two steps. A light-dark cell involves the following computations for the left branch (fed by the ON channel)

$$q_i^{S+} = \frac{p_l^{S+}}{\alpha + \beta p_r^{S-}} \qquad z_i^{S+} = \frac{p_l^{S+}}{\gamma + \delta q_i^{S+}} \tag{4}$$

where $\alpha$, $\beta$, $\gamma$, and $\delta$ are constants. Similarly for the right branch (fed by the OFF channel) the equilibrated values are

$$q_i^{S-} = \frac{p_r^{S-}}{\alpha + \beta p_l^{S+}} \qquad z_i^{S-} = \frac{p_r^{S-}}{\gamma + \delta q_i^{S-}} \tag{5}$$

The final simple cell response is $z_i^{S+} + z_i^{S-}$. A dark-light cell is obtained by reversing the inputs for the "left" and "right" branches.

Complex cell responses, $x_i^S$, are insensitive to direction of contrast and are obtained by summing light-dark and dark-light simple cell responses. It was assumed that the complex cell output was a scaled-thresholded version as in $X_i^S = \kappa[x_i^S - T]^+$, where $[x]^+ = \max(x, 0)$; $\kappa$ and $T$ are constants.

**Boundaries: Feedback Competition of Complex Cell Responses** (boundary). Boundaries are obtained by processing complex cell responses through a recurrent competitive network. The system sharpens strong inputs and leaves small signals largely unmodified. The nonlinear feedback network is modeled after the work of Grossberg and Marshall (1989) and is given by

$$\frac{dw_i^S}{dt} = -Aw_i^S + (L - w_i^S)(F_i^{S+} + B_i^{S+}) - (M + w_i^S)(F_i^{S-} + B_i^{S-}). \tag{6}$$

where $A$, $L$ and $M$ are constants; see Grossberg and Marshall (1989) for more details. Equation 6 is solved using fourth order Runge-Kutta until the activities equilibrate; the computations are similar to those of the "first competitive stage" of the Cooperative-Competitive (CC) loop of Grossberg and Mingolla (1985).

**On and Off Feature Filling-in** (ON/OFF filling-in). Filling-in is performed for both ON and OFF domains (Gerrits and Vendrick, 1970; Grossberg, 1987, 1994; Grossberg and Wyse, 1992). Diffusive filling-in for the ON domain is implemented as

$$\frac{dv_i^{S+}}{dt} = -Kv_i^{S+} + \sum_{j \in N_i}(v_j^{S+} - v_i^{S+})P_{ji}^S + c_i^{S+} \tag{7}$$

where $K$ is a constant and $N_i$ specifies the neighborhood of influence of node $i$. Term $c_i^+$ is the on contrast that is supplied to the diffusion stage; a similar equation regulates the OFF domain ($v_i^{S-}$), with $c_i^-$ as the contrast input. Diffusion is limited to nearest neighbors so that $N_i = (i - 1, i + 1)$. The diffusion coefficients, $P_{ji}^S$, regulate the magnitude of cross influence of location $j$ on location $i$ and depend on boundary signals as

$$P_{ji}^S = \frac{\rho}{1 + \epsilon(w_i^S + w_j^S)}, \tag{8}$$

where $\rho$ and $\epsilon$ are constants. For simulations, Equation 7 is solved with fourth order Runge-Kutta until activities equilibrate.

**Single Scale Brightness Prediction** (single scale brightness). The filled in activities in the ON and OFF domains are used in conjunction with the low pass luminance to determine the single scale brightness prediction, $u_i^S$. The basic idea is that the low pass luminance ($s_i$ in Equation 3) provides a baseline of activity that can be modified by the equilibrated ON and OFF contrasts ($v_i^{S+}$ and $v_i^{S-}$ in Equation 7). The interactions are governed by the following differential equation

$$\frac{du_i^S}{dt} = -Fu_i^S + s_i + Gv_i^{S+} - Hu_i^S v_i^{S-} \tag{9}$$

which is computed at equilibrium; $F$, $G$, and $H$ are constants.

**Multiple Scale Brightness Pooling** (multiple scale brightness). As implemented in Grossberg, Mingolla, and Williamson (1993), the final brightness percept is obtained by averaging the outputs of the different spatial scales:

$$U_i = \frac{1}{k} \sum_S u_i^S \tag{10}$$

where $k$ is the number of scales being employed. $U_i$ is the final output of the model.

## 4   Simulations

The model correctly predicts the appearance of Mach bands on a trapezoidal wave and Figure 2 shows several model stages (3 spatial scales were used). In the bottom row the input ($I_i$) is shown to the left of the final multiple scale brightness prediction ($U_i$). The input luminance is initially filtered by ON and OFF channels and the results generate "contrast" and "luminance" information; the second row shows ON/OFF filtering ($Y_i^+$ and $Y_i^-$), ON/OFF contrasts ($c_i^+$ and $c_i^-$), and the low-pass luminance ($s_i$). Contrasts are used for multi-scale computations of complex cells and boundaries. At the same time they are used as featural inputs to ON/OFF diffusion leading to single scale brightness predictions. The contrasts fed to diffusion are trapped by the spatially extended boundaries and provide the activities that will generate the corresponding bands for the single scale predictions; for scale 1 some of the complex cell responses are sharpened, though. Rows 3-5 show these multi-scale computations for the trapezoidal wave. Column 1: complex cells ($X_i^S$); column 2: boundaries ($w_i^S$); column 3: equilibrated ON and OFF filling-in ($v_i^{S+}$ and $v_i^{S-}$); column 4: single scale brightness ($u_i^S$). The final multiple scale brightness prediction is obtained by averaging the single scale results and, as mentioned, is shown in the first row ($U_i$). The model also correctly predicts the existence of Mach bands on triangular waves (see Ross *et al.*, 1989).

Other stimuli that the model can account for include (Figure 3) a) the square-wave; b) the high contrast missing fundamental (MF), which is perceived more or less veridically; c) the low contrast MF, which is perceived as a square wave; and d) a high contrast sine wave, perceived with compression. This set of data was chosen so as to illustrate the model's ability to generate sharp or extended boundaries as a function of the input luminance; the square wave and low contrast MF necessitate sharp boundaries while the high contrast MF and sine wave require extended signals. Finally, it should be emphasized that all of our simulations, including ones not shown in this paper, employ the same set of parameters.

## 5   Conclusion

We have presented an implementation of a neural network model of brightness perception that can account for some challenging data involving slow variations in brightness; as well as sharp transitions. The model can account for the classical phenomenon of Mach bands as well as other stimuli (e.g., brightness contrast). Finally, the model should be compared to alternative approaches attempting to explain similar sets of brightness data. For example, while the local energy model of Burr and Morrone obtains rather good quantitative fits to Mach bands (Ross *et al.*, 1989), it does not account for several of the stimuli simulated here (e.g., sine wave). The MIDAAS model of Kingdom and Moulden (1992) accounts for the 1-D phenomena investigated here but does so by employing symbolic interpretation rules (homunculus) that, we feel, are bound to yield contradictions requiring appeal to other rules in a 2-D implementation. The present implementation of ideas from FACADE theory (Grossberg 1987, 1994), on the other hand, has a natural extension to a 2-D implementation. Indeed an implementation of a related multi-scale network for processing large images has already been described in Grossberg, Mingolla, and Williamson (1993).

# Reference

Cohen, M., & Grossberg, S. (1984). Neural dynamics of brightness perception: Features, boundaries, diffusion, and resonance. *Perception & Psychophysics*, **36**, 428-456.

Gerrits, H. & Vendrick, A. (1970). Simultaneous contrast, filling-in process and information processing in man's visual system. *Experimental Brain Research*, **11**, 411-430.

Gove, A. (1994). A neural network model of visual segmentation. Unpublished PhD dissertation. Dept. of Cognitive and Neural Systems, Boston University.

Grossberg, S. (1987). Cortical dynamics of three-dimensional form, color, and brightness perception: II. Binocular theory. *Perception & Psychophysics*, **41**, 117-158.

Grossberg, S. (1994). 3-D vision and figure-ground separation by visual cortex. *Perception & Psychophysics*, **55**, 48-120.

Grossberg, S., & Mingolla, E. (1985). Neural dynamics of perceptual grouping: Textures, boundaries, and emergent features. *Perception & Psychophysics*, **38**, 141-171.

Grossberg, S., & Mingolla, E. (1987). Neural dynamics of surface perception: Boundary webs, illuminants, and shape-from-shading. *Computer Vision, Graphics, and Image Processing*, **37**, 116-165.

Grossberg, S., & Todorovic, D. (1988). Neural dynamics of 1-D and 2-D brightness perception: A unified model of classical and recent phenomena. *Perception & Psychophysics*, **43**, 241-277.

Grossberg, S., & Marshall, J. (1989). Stereo boundary fusion by cortical complex cells: A system of maps, filters, and feedback networks for multiplexing distributed data. *Neural Networks*, **2**, 29-51.

Grossberg, S., & Wyse, L. (1991). Figure-ground segregation of connected scenic figures: Boundaries, filling-in, and opponent processing. *Neural Networks*, **4**, 732-742.

Grossberg, S., Mingolla, E., & Williamnson, J. (1993). Processing of synthetic aperture radar images by a multiscale boundary contour system and feature contour system. Technical Report CAS/CNS-93-024, Dept. of Cognitive and Neural Systems, Boston University.

Iverson, L., & Zucker, S. (1990). Logical/Linear Operators for Measuring Orientation and Curvature. Technical Report TR-CIM-90-06, Computer Vision and Robotics Laboratory, McGill University.

Kingdom, F., & Moulden, B. (1992). A multi-channel approach to brightness coding. *Vision Research*, **32**, 1565-1582.

Neumann, H. (1994). An outline of a neural architecture for unified visual contrast and brightness perception. Technical Report CAS/CNS-94-003, Dept. of Cognitive and Neural Systems, Boston University.

Neumann, H., & Pessoa, L. (1994). A simple cell model with multiple spatial frequency selectivity and linear/non-linear response properties. Submitted to *WCNN, San Diego, June 4-9, 1994*.

Ross, J., Morrone, M., & Burr, D. (1989). The conditions under which Mach bands are visible. *Vision Research*, **29**, 699-715.

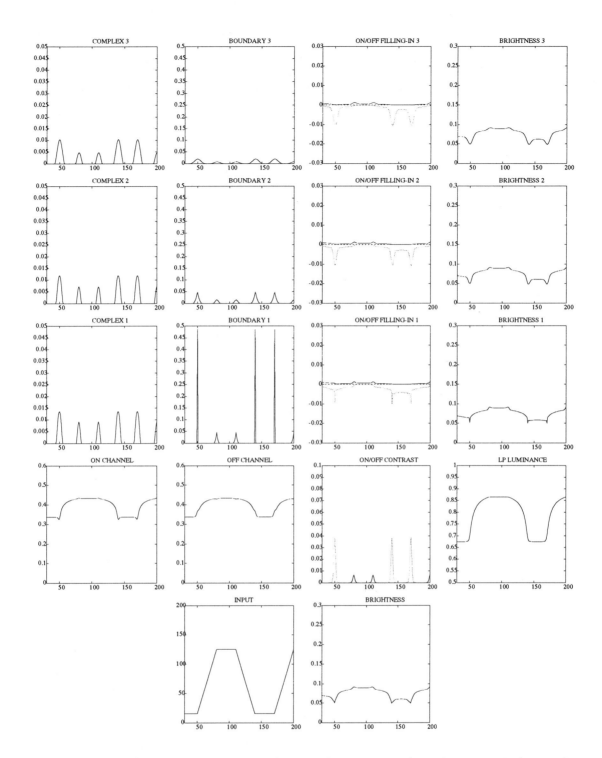

Figure 2: Simulation of a trapezoidal wave. Graphs show activity (in arbitrary units) as a function of spatial position $i$. Bottom row: Input and multi-scale brightness. Second row: ON/OFF filtering, ON (solid) /OFF (dotted) contrast, and low-pass (LP) "luminance". Rows 3-5: Multi-scale computations (3 scales); OFF filling-in (dotted) shown with negative values for illustration only.

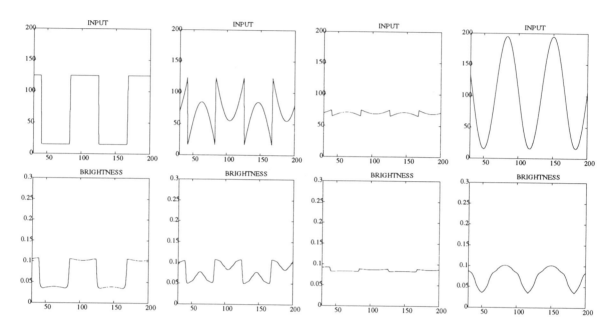

Figure 3: Simulations of square wave (left), high contrast missing fundamental (second column), low contrast missing fundamental (third column), and high contrast sine wave (right). All four simulations display the input luminance (top) and the final multiple scale brightness (bottom). All simulations use the same set of parameters.

# Processing Ultrasound and Night-Vision Images by the Boundary Contour - Feature Contour Model of Biological Vision

Udantha R. Abeyratne*, Bahram Nabet* and William K. Krebs†

*Biomedical Engineering and Science Institute, Drexel University,
Philadelphia, PA 19104

† Naval Aerospace Medical Research Laboratory, NAS Pensacola, FL 32508

In many aspects, biological vision is superior to man-made vision systems in existence today. Most living creatures effortlessly carry out visual tasks such as motion detection, target tracking and figure-ground separation under varying environmental conditions. Hence it is intriguing to see if computational models of biological vision can provide us with useful tools to attack such hard image processing problems, which defy solution despite decades of research. As a first step in that direction, we apply the Boundary Contour/Feature Contour Model , BCS/FCS [1] on ultrasound and night vision images. In medical ultrasound, random scatterers produce grainy image features. Although the speckle statistics are sometimes used to advantage in tissue characterization problems, speckle also compromises the visibility of structures being imaged. Here, our target is to investigate the speckle reduction capabilities of the BCS/FCS model. In processing images obtained from Night Vision Devices (NVD), BCS/FCS's properties of discounting the illumination and edge enhancement are put to the test. BCS/FCS model derives feature(FCS) and boundary(BCS) representations from the original image. They are, in-turn, interacted to reconstitute the final image; a number of parameters have to be set properly. Preliminary computer simulations showed that, by iterating through the algorithm several times with different parameters, it was possible to generate a BCS representative of larger structures in the speckled ultrasound image. By using a 'heavy' diffusion at the BCS-FCS interaction stage, it was possible to "diffuse-out" speckles and reconstitute the image, while keeping larger objects intact and boundaries sharp. However, this also wiped out smaller structures of interest. The output of the algorithm is very sensitive to the parameters. Each different image may have different 'good' parameters, making the tuning of parameters task-specific. Gaps in the boundaries pose another problem; especially in this application because of heavy diffusions leading to a massive leak-out of features. Computer resource requirements are also intense. These considerations elucidate the importance of accelerating these algorithms and implementing them in optics/VLSI technology while keeping enough flexibility in parameter changing. With night vision images, the objective was to eliminate the effects of uneven illumination, smoothly varying patches of specular reflections, and, to enhance the image. The FCS can be made to possess all these characteristics. FCS is easy to derive from the input image. The operator involved is similar to the on-center-off-surround receptive fields in biological vision. It may be fabricated in VLSI technology, using simple MOSFET components [2]. The resulting circuit will posses: real-time operational ability, portability, robustness and graceful degradation. We have processed night vision images through FCS/BCS algorithm, remembering to consider the FCS stage as the final output. Where input images were degraded by noise and inherent limitations of the vision device to a extent such that a simple FCS enhancement would not suffice, we applied the whole algorithm as in the case of ultrasound image, but with no iterative processing, and with 'minimal' diffusion. Results of the BCS/FCS processing of ultrasound and night vision images will be presented, with particular attention to the ramification for Optoelectronic/VLSI implementations.

[1] S. Grossberg and Lonce Wyse, Figure Ground Separation of Connected Scenic Figures: Boundary, Filling-in and Opponent Processing, in Neural Networks for Vision and Image Processing, G. A., Carpenter and S. Grossberg (Eds.), MIT Press, 1992.
[2] B. Nabet, Electronic Hardware for Vision Modeling, in Nonlinear Vision, R.B.Pinter, B.Nabet(Eds), CRC Press, 1992

# Summary

In many aspects, vision systems found in nature are superior to the most sophisticated man-made system in existence today. Visual tasks such as motion detection, target tracking and figure-ground separation are fundamental to the survival of most living creatures, and, are faithfully carried out quite effortlessly under tremendously varying environmental conditions. Hence it is intriguing to see if computational models of biological vision can provide us with useful tools to attack hard image processing problems, which defy solution despite decades of research.

In this work, as a first step in that direction, we attempt to apply the Boundary Contour/Feature Contour Model [1, 2, 3] of biological vision on (1) medical ultrasound images and (2) low-light night images captured through Night Vision Devices (NVDs). In ultrasound, which is one of the most widely used medical imaging techniques, random scatterers in the tissues produce grainy features in the output image. Although the speckle statistics are sometimes used to advantage in tissue characterization problems, speckle can be a problem in that it compromises the visibility of structures being imaged. Here, our target is to investigate the speckle reduction/segmentation capabilities of the Boundary Contour/Feature Contour ( BCS/FCS) model. In processing Night Vision Device images, BCS/FCS properties of discounting the illumination and edge enhancement are put to the test. Biology based techniques such as BCS/FCS, if successful, promise to provide a foundation for very high speed, reliable processing of such images, because (a) they are amenable to analog implementations and (b) they generally show graceful degradation in adverse environments.

The fundamental functional unit of the BCS/FCS model has been derived in analogy to the lateral shunting interaction mechanisms prevalent in the biological vision. Computational layers are interconnected so that the resulting architecture complies with some of the known facts from neuroanatomy and psychophysics. We used both a CORTEX-filter[3] based version of the BCS/FCS, and the basic model derived in [1]. Both are free from feedback loops, and the former promises boundary completion capabilities in noisy environments, while the latter is blessed with relative simplicity.

In the CORTEX-related algorithm, the input image is passed, in parallel, through on-center-off-surround(ON cell) and off-center-on-surround(OFF cell) receptive field stages, in order to discount the effects of ambient illumination. The output of this stage, is an improved featural representation, (FCS), of the original image. Next, edge segments are extracted from the FCS image by convolving it with elongated, orientation and direction-of-contrast sensitive kernels, followed by appropriate thresholding. Each of these kernels respond maximally to image edge segments lying parallel to its orientation, and, the polarity of contrast. Kernels of two spatial scales, "large" and "small" , operate on both ON-cell and OFF-cell produced FCS, resulting in four intermediate output images. In the third stage, processing is geared towards producing a direction-of-contrast insensitive, spatial scale sensitive edge segment representations. Then, the image passes spatial and orientation competition stages as a mechanism to generate a "thinned-edge-representation" with appropriate end-cuts [3]. So far, the algorithm kept "small" scale processing and "large" scale processing separate. In the next few stages, intermediate results from both stages interact. This promises to produce a noise tolerant, contiguous boundary representation, which is taken as the BCS, of the original image. In the final stage, ON-cell featural representation image FCS is allowed to diffuse freely in all directions, within boundaries defined by BCS, to get the reconstituted image. We can consider this image or any other intermediate one as our output, depending on the task at hand. The algorithm contains a large number of parameters that have to be set properly.

Our preliminary computer simulations showed that, by iterating through the algorithm several times with different parameter values ( feeding a version of the BCS as the input to the next round), it was possible to generate a BCS signal that is representative of larger, coherent structures in the speckled ultrasound image. With such BCS signals, and by setting a heavy diffusion rate at the final stage, it was possible to "diffuse-out" speckles and reconstitute the image, while keeping larger boundaries/objects intact. This generates an output image where larger features stand-out in a field of minimal speckle phenomena ( cf. Figure 1). However, this process also wiped out smaller structures and surface details together with speckles. The output of the algorithm is very sensitive to the parameter magnitudes. In addition, the fact that there is a large number of parameters involved and each different image may have different 'good' parameters, makes the tuning of parameters a challenge. The unavailability of an objective measure to quantify the performance as a function of parameters adds to the problem. Being a method heavily dependent on deriving contiguous boundaries, gaps in the boundaries pose a serious problem; especially in this application because of heavy diffusions. Heavy diffusion leads to a massive leak-out of features, resulting in output distortions. CORTEX-based algorithm performs better than the basic Grossberg-Todorovic version in that respect. Both algorithms require huge computer memory( and time), because, in each stage, we have to keep several copies of intermediate results, each of the size of the original image; in addition, diffusion stage requires the inversion of a $N^2 \times N^2$ matrix ( N = Number of Pixels in the input image ). Since the Grossberg-Todorovic algorithm involves fewer stages, it demands less memory and processing time, but the absence of mechanisms to suppress noise and to complete boundaries makes its performance inferior under such situations. These considerations elucidate the importance of simplifying these algorithms and implementing them in optics/VLSI technology while keeping enough flexibility in parameter changing.

In the case of night vision images, the objective was to get rid of the adverse effects of uneven illumination, smoothly varying patches of specular reflections and to enhance edges and image contrast in general. The FCS signal of the BCS/FCS algorithm possesses all these characteristics. FCS signal is the result of the first stage of the BCS/FCS algorithm, and , is relatively easy to derive from the input image. The operator involved is similar to the the the on-center-off-surround receptive fields in biological vision. This operator may be fabricated in VLSI technology, using simple MOSFET components [4]. The resulting circuit will posses: real-time operational ability, portability, robustness and graceful degradation, all of which are expected of a system in this application. We have processed night vision images through FCS/BCS algorithm, remembering to consider the FCS stage as the final output. With some input images which were degraded by noise and inherent limitations of the vision device, to a extent such that a simple FCS enhancement would not suffice, we applied the whole algorithm as in the case of ultrasound image, but with no iterative processing, and with 'minimal' diffusion.

Figures( 2) demonstrate the applicability of the FCS processing to enhance general images. In figure 2(a) details of the eyes, nose and mouth areas are obscure; there is a patch of specular light reflection on the bridge of the nose. FCS processing supresses the specular patch and also makes the details around the eyes, mouth etc. clearer.

Results of our BCS/FCS processing of ultrasound and night vision images will be presented at the conference, with particular attention to the ramification in Optoelectronic/VLSI implementations.

[1] S. Grossberg and D. Todorovic, Neural Dynamics of 1-D and 2-D Brightness Perception: a Unified Model of Classical and Recent Phenomena, in Neural Networks and Natural Intelligence, S.Grossberg (Ed), MIT Press, 1988

[2] S. Grossberg, E. Mingolla and D. Todorovic, A Neural Network Architecture for Preattentive Vision, IEEE Transactions on Biomedical Engineering, Vol 36, No.1, Jan. 1989, pp. 65-83

[3] S. Grossberg and Lonce Wyse, Figure Ground Separation of Connected Scenic Figures: Boundary, Filling-in and Opponent Processing, in Neural Networks for Vision and Image

Processing, G. A., Carpenter and S. Grossberg (Eds.), MIT Press, 1992.

[4] B. Nabet, Electronic Hardware for Vision Modeling, in Nonlinear Vision, R.B.Pinter, B.Nabet(Eds), CRC Press, 1992

## **Figure Captions:**

Figure (1)  (a) Input image, ultrasound scan of a human breast.
      (b) Boundary Contour Signal
      (c) Output signal, after the diffusion stage.


Figure(2) (a) Input image, with specular reflections in the bridge of the nose. Note that the details around the eye and mouth areas are not easily seen.

      (b) Enhanced image, FCS signal level.  Specular reflections have been reduced. Eye and mouth areas has become clearer.

Figure(3)  Edge representations at the simple cell level. The frames shown here are the output of one of a horizontal edge detecting receptive fields. "Large" and "small" scale processing and "On-cell" and "Off-cell" procesing have been used.

Figure 01

Input, Breast01, linear gray(512)

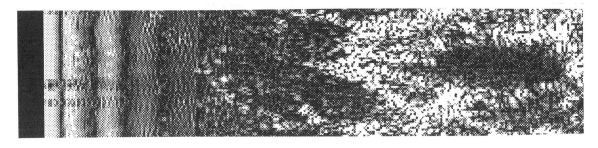

Edges: Linear Gray 512

Output: Linear Gray 512: Breast01

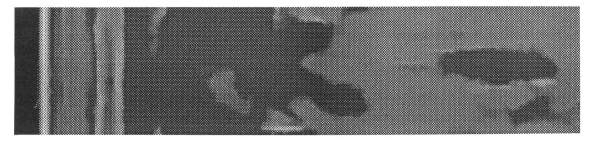

Figure 02

Input Image

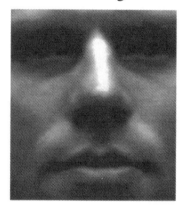

Enhanced Image: Stage 2: On Cell

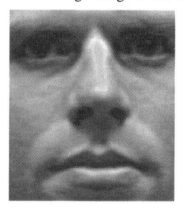

Figure 03

Simple Cells: on, small

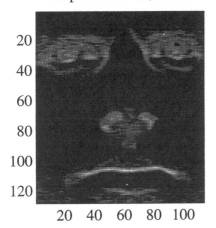

Simple Cells: on, large

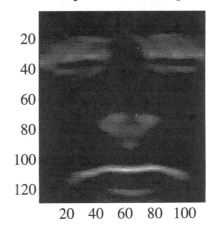

Simple Cells: off, small

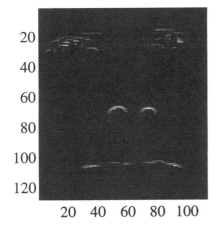

Simple Cells: off, large

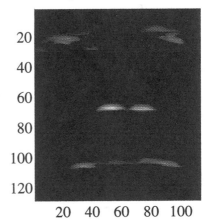

# A Neural Architecture that develops a Chromatic Visual Model for Perceptual Segmentation and Recognition

F. Díaz Pernas, J. López Coronado

Dept. of Control System Engineering, University of Valladolid

Valladolid, Spain

## 1   Introduction

This article takes account of the importance of color and texture in processes dealing with visual information. Our neural architecture processes color images representing scenes made up of a mixture of textured regions. To achieve this, it develops a chromatic visual model that generates a perceptual segmentation of the image and afterwards, it does two types of recognition processes according to its type of functioning mode.

The visual model developed is based on the perceptual aspects of the BCS/FCS model [11] and on the recognition models of the adaptive resonance theory (ART) [1] [2]. These models are widely based on neurofisiological and psychological investigations about the perception-cognition aspects of the human visual system.

Our architecture offers a model of certain functions of the visual system, dealing on color and texture information processing [8]. In particular, the network maintains the global architecture associated with the visual pathway:

*Retinal ganglion cells* → *LGN* → *V1* → *V2* → *V4* → *Inferior Temporal Cortex.*

At the level of the ganglion cells, our architecture proposes a model for *color opponent* processes. It has been proved that these processes are the base of color perception [15] [20].

The architecture includes two functioning modes, preattentive and attentive, that determine the processing characteristics. These two modes have been detected in the visual system. In the preattentive mode, the processing extends to the whole visual field (scene), is highly parallel and has wide receptive fields. On the contrary, the attentive mode is sequential and is caused by the focalization of the attention on small visual field areas [13] [10] [12].

The information the architecture processes comes from an RGB (red, green and blue) output color camera.

## 2   Neural architecture structure

The proposed architecture is made of four main modules (figure 1 -a), called: Color Opponent System (COS), Chromatic Segmentation System (CSS), MultiSignal Recognition System (MSRS) and ATtentive Recognition System (ATRS).

There are two functioning modes in the proposed architecture: preattentive and attentive. First, there is a preattentive functioning in the system formed by the COS, CSS and MSRS, where whole visual field (scene) perceptual segmentation and recognition take place. The preattentive system produces a recognition signal, $k$ signal of the *scene-selector* in figure 1 -a, that shows what scene we are analysing, at the same time that controls the attentive process.

Next, the attentive system, ATRS, focuses the attention on small parts of the scene and recognizes them in sequential order. This focalization is caused by a reduction of the size of the receptive fields. The attentive recognition is done depending on the values obtained in the perceptual segmentation and according to the preattentive recognition signal.

Adaptive processes take place in both recognition stages. Global structures (preattentive recognition) and positional values (attentive recognition) of the segmentations generated in processed scenes, are learned in adaptive processes.

## 3   Color opponent system

In the preattentive processing, the COS generates three signals (see figure 1 -a), two of them chromatic and one achromatic, as the result of two opponent processes: red-green, blue-yellow and a wideband process: white-black channel. This system includes our model [8] [9] of the antagonist mechanisms with *ON-center/OFF-surround*

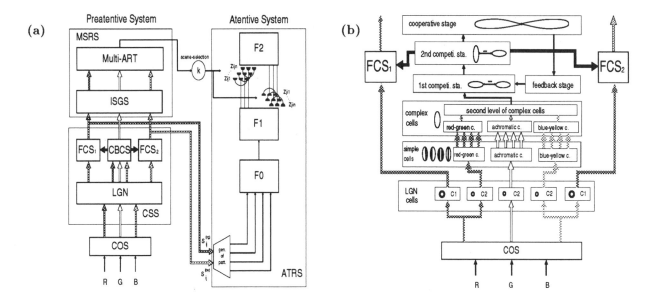

Figura 1: **(a)**: Modular diagram of the proposed architecture. In the preattentive system, white arrows represent the achromatic channel, thickly dotted arrows represent the red-green opponent channel and thinly dotted arrows show the blue-yellow opponent channel. The chromatic features spread control signals are shown by black arrows that connect the BCS Color module with FCS stages. **(b)**: Detailed diagram of the Chromatic Segmentation System (CSS).

structure of signals from spectrally different cones. These mechanisms generate the *color opponent processes* that take place in retinal ganglion cells [15] [20].

Each color opponent process is modelled by a bidimensional field with *shunting ON-center/OFF-surround* interactions, according to the following equation:

$$\frac{d}{dt}x_{ij} = -Ax_{ij} + (B - x_{ij})\sum_{k,l} t_{1kl}C_{klij} - (x_{ij} + D)\sum_{k,l} t_{2kl}S_{klij} \tag{1}$$

where,

$x_{ij}$ is the process activity, excited by a signal $t_{1ij}$ and inhibited by a signal $t_{2ij}$. Coefficients $C_{klij}$ y $S_{klij}$ represent the excitation and inhibition signals weighting coefficients and define the cell receptive field profile.

The achromatic signal is written as the sum of the signals coming from the three photoreceptor types:

$$x_{ij} = R_{ij} + G_{ij} + B_{ij} \tag{2}$$

and,

$R_{ij}$, $G_{ij}$ y $B_{ij}$ are the red, green and blue signals respectively.

## 4   Chromatic segmentation system

The three signals generated in the previous module are processed in a parallel way by the CSS, as shown in figure 1 -a. The CSS module develops our chromatic version of the BCS/FCS model [11] for color signal processing and it does a preattentive segmentation of the scene. The CSS system is made of a LGN stage, a Color BCS (CBCS) stage, and two FCS stages.

The LGN stage enhances the information that comes from the previous module and distributes the signals to the following stages according to the type of processing (see figure 1 -b). In this stage, the signals participate in competitive *ON-center/OFF-surround* processes where the information enhancing takes place. The ON-center/OFF-surround feature with a white inner circle (excitation) and a black circular ring (inhibition) is shown in figure 1 -b.

In this stage, we consider two types of cells, $C1$ y $C2$, and five processing pathways grouped in three parallel channels.

$C1$ cells are distinguished by:

- Sending its signals to a FCS stage.

- Having fairly wide receptive fields, which means a lower resolution.

On the other hand, $C2$ cells:

- Send their information to the Color BCS stage.

- Have relatively small receptive fields, that is to say, a higher resolution.

The reason for proposing these two types of cells is:

The Color BCS stage is in charge of contour extraction. Therefore, in order not to lose textural information or contour position precision, $C2$ cells receptive fields are quite small relatively.

On the other side, chromatic features spread in FCS stages. Relatively wide receptive fields for $C1$ cells will favour this spreading.

We suggest that $C1$ cells belong to the parvocellular-blobs system, while $C2$ cells are part of the parvocellular-interblobs system.

The Color BCS stage has two processing phases (see figure 1 -b). In the first phase, the simple cell stage extracts real contours from the three signals. Therefore, simple cells detect those areas of the scene where textural and chromatic feature changes take place. We propose that these cells have four types of receptive fields, that make up two opposed polarity Gabor filter pairs (the four receptive fields are shown in figure 1 -b). Experiments about receptive fields in striate visual cortex simple cells (cortical area V1) have shown that Gabor filter profiles aproximate these receptive fields perfectly [17] [6] [5] [16] [18]. Besides, receptive fields associated in opposed pairs actually exist in the visual system [17].

Thanks to its two cellular layers, the complex cell stage adds the information from the previous stage, generating a signal containing all the real contours existing in the three channels.

In the second phase, the feedback cycle, made up by a first competitive stage, a second competitive stage, a cooperative stage and a feedback stage, extracts illusory contours and completes real contours using perceptual groupings according to the *emergent features*. In this stage, first the contour signal takes part in competitive processes that enhance contour information. Secondly, illusory contours are generated and real contours are completed by means of cooperative and feedback processes.

The Color BCS stage output is formed by the total contour map appearing from both of these processes and we take it from the second competitive stage.

On the other hand, each FCS stage processes a chromatic channel (red-green or blue-yellow). These FCS stages activate two *filling-in* processes [11], regulated by the spread control signal or contour map, sent by the Color BCS stage. Each filling-in process happens because of a chromatic features spread in all directions, except in those where it finds a strong contour signal. This spread makes that contour limited regions, tend to have a uniform chromatic value. The segmentation of each chromatic channel takes place as a result from it.

## 5 Multisignal recognition system

The preattentive recognition system (MSRS) has two stages: Invariant Signal Generating System (ISGS) and a Multi-ART recognition architecture [7] [19] (see figure 1 -a).

The ISGS generates traslation, rotation and scale invariance signals for the three processing channels. This stage uses the Fourier-Mellin transform [3] [4] to achieve these invariances. An invariance generating process is necessary in a scene recognition process, so that an object visual stimulus and the same turned, translated or scaled object stimulus are considered to be the same one. There is evidence that the human visual system generates these invariances [4].

The Multi-ART architecture recognizes the scene according to the invariant signals coming from the ISGS.

The preattentive recognition is done paying attention to the perceptual contour map and to the chromatic segmentations. That is to say, patterns formed by signals coming from different processing channels, in short, of different magnitude and nature, will participate in the recognition stage. This fact advises using a recognition architecture suitable for categorizing this kind of patterns. Multi-ART architectures categorize this type of patterns satisfactorily, because they process independently each information channel in their first stages [7] [19].

Categorization means the selection of a cell representing a certain input. The inputs contain the chromatic and textural features of the object included in the visual stimulus. Therefore, each recognition cell is activated by a certain scene. There are studies proving the existence of Inferior Temporal cortex (IT) cells in charge of complex form recognition [14]. Besides, there is evidence that the IT does the recognition processes from different processing channels [20] [14]. We suggest that the MSRS system is in IT areas.

## 6 Attentive recognition system

After the preattentive process, the neural architecture changes to its attentive functioning mode.

The receptive fields used in the attentive mode shrink to their minimum size, involving just one image position. This simplification causes a positional image recognition. This recognition is done paying attention to the positional values of the chromatic segmentations obtained in the FCS stages. The attentive recognition system, ATRS, is made of a sequential pattern generator and a recognition architecture, called Multi-scene ART-2 (see figure 1 -a).

The pattern generator moves sequentially along the image and it generates a pattern in every position from the signals coming from both FCS. Each generated pattern is sent to the recognition network for its categorization.

The Multi-scene ART-2 architecture is a modification of the ART-2 model [1]. The changes are in the adaptive connections $F_1 \rightarrow F_2$ y $F_2 \rightarrow F_1$. As we can see in figure 1 -a, $n$ *bottom-up* and $n$ *top-down* adaptive pathways have been included; in short $n$ pathways pairs (bottom-up, top-down).

Every pair (bottom-up, top-down) is associated to the learning of the segmentation values of an image processed by the architecture. Therefore, the architecture will be able to recognize attentively $n$ different images.

The selection of the adaptive pair (bottom-up, top-down) is controlled by the recognition signal coming from the preattentive system Multi-ART architecture (see figure 1 -a). If the node selected by the Multi-ART architecture is node $k$, we will know that we are analysing scene $k$ from the $n$ different images. Next, adaptive pair $k$ will be selected, in which the learning of the scene chromatic segmentation positional values will take place. Once the adaptive pair is selected, the Multi-scene ART-2 functioning is the same as that of the original network.

In this sequential functioning, the Multi-scene ART-2 categorizes every positional pattern in a node that codifies the type of region it belongs to. At the same time, the ATRS generates an image in which every position contains the label of the node where its pattern has been classified. In short, an output image is generated, in which every position has a label of the type of region it belongs to. This image represents the output of the proposed architecture.

## 7 Results

This architecture has been implanted and images of a real industrial application belonging to the EUREKA PROJAM 398 project have been processed. Satisfactory results, as can be seen in [9], have been obtained.

Figure 2 shows the result of the recognition of a scene (figure 2 -a) made up of a piece of meat on a conveyor belt. The recognition has been done using the three types of regions in the scene. They are: background belonging to the conveyor belt, fat matter areas of the piece and muscle areas. These regions appear in the recognition image (figure2 -b) in three different gray levels. Dark gray zones represent the recognition of background regions. Intermediate gray belongs to the recognition of fat matter and light gray matches the recognition of muscle areas.

## 8 Conclusions

This article takes account of the importance of color and texture in processes dealing with visual information. Up to this date, multiple image segmentation and recognition models have been suggested, but, few of them include color and texture informations together.

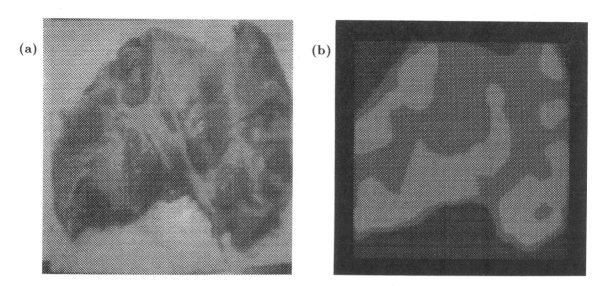

Figura 2: Results obtained with the architecture after processing a real image. **(a):** Original image of the scene. It shows a piece of meat on a conveyor belt. **(b):** Architecture output: recognition image. Dark gray areas belong to areas recognized as background (conveyor belt), intermediate gray areas belong to fat matter areas and light gray regions belong to the recognition of muscle areas

We have introduced a neural architecture that develops a chromatic visual model. In the first place, it does a perceptual segmentation of the image and afterwards, it does two adaptive recognition processes according to the functioning mode.

Similarly to the visual system, the architecture includes two functioning modes, preattentive and attentive, that decide the processing characteristics.

We include the processing of a real scene, showing satisfactory results and the usefulness of the architecture in solving real problems.

# Referencias

[1] Carpenter G. A., and Grossberg S. (1987): "ART2: Self-organization of stable category recognition codes for analog input patterns". *Applied Optics*, **26**, *(23), 4919-4930, 1987.*

[2] Carpenter G.A. (1989): "Neural network models for pattern recognition and associative memory". *Neural Networks*, **2**, *243-257.*

[3] Casasent D. & Psaltis D. (1976): "Position, rotation, and scale invariant optical correlation". *Applied Optics*, **15**, *No. 7, 1795-1799.*

[4] Cavanagh P. (1978): "Size and position invariance in the visual system". *Perception*, **7**, *167-177.*

[5] Daugman J.G. (1980): "Two-Dimensional Spectral Analysis of Cortical Receptive Field Profiles". *Vision Research*, **20**, *847-856.*

[6] Daugman J.G. (1988): "Complete Discrete 2-D Gabor Transforms by Neural Networks for Image Analysis and Compression". *IEEE Transactions on Acoustics, Speech, and Signal Processing*, **36**, *No. 7, 1169-1179.*

[7] Díaz Pernas F., Zalama E., Dimitriadis Y.A. & López-Coronado J. (1992): "Multi-ART architectures: An engineering extension for processing features of different nature". *Proceedings of the Research Conference: Neural Network for Learning, Recognition, and Control, Boston, USA, 14-16 May,1992.*

[8] Díaz Pernas F. & López Coronado J. (1993): "A Neural Architecture for Textured Color Image Segmentation and Recognition". *International Conference On Artificial Neural Networks ICANN '93, Amsterdam, Netherlands, 13-16 September, 1993.*

[9] Díaz Pernas F. (1993): "Arquitectura Neuronal para la segmentación y el reconocimiento de imagenes texturadas en color, usando un modelo visual cromático". *Ph.D.,School of Industrial Engineering, University of Valladolid, Spain, 1993.*

[10] Van Essen D.C. & Anderson C.H. (1990): "Information Processing Strategies and Pathways in the Primate Retina and Visual Cortex". In Zornetzer S.F, Davis J.L. & Lau C. (eds.): *An Introduction to Neural and Electronic Networks, chap. 3, 43-72. San Diego:Academic Press. 1990.*

[11] Grossberg S. & Mingolla E. (1985): "Neural Dynamics of Perceptual Grouping: Textures, Boundaries, and Emergent Segmentations". In Grossberg S. (ed.) : *The Adaptive Brain II. chap. 3. Amsterdam:North-Holland. 1988.*

[12] Iwai E. (1985): "Neuropsychological Basis of Pattern Vision in Macaque Monkeys". *Vision Research,* **25,** *No. 3, 425-439.*

[13] Julesz B. & Bergen R. (1987): "Textons,The Fundamental Elements in Preattentive Vision and Perception of Textures". In Fischer & Firschen (eds.): *Readings in Computer Vision, 243-256, 1987.*

[14] Kandel E.R. (1991): "Perception of Motion, Depth, and Form". In Kandel E.R., Schwartz J.H. & Jessel T.M. (eds.): *Principles of Neural Science, chap. 30. New York:Elsevier. 1991.*

[15] Livingstone M.S. & Hubel D.H. (1984): "Anatomy and physiology of a color system in the primate visual cortex". *Journal of Neuroscience,* **4,** *309-356.*

[16] Marcelja S. (1980): "Mathematical description of the responses of simple cortical cells". *Journal of the Optical Society of America,* **70,** *No. 11, 1297-1300.*

[17] Pollen D.A. & Ronner S.F. (1983): "Visual Cortical Neurons as Localized Spatial Frequency Filters". *IEEE Transactions on Systems, Man, and Cybernetics,* **SMC-13,** *No. 5, 907-916.*

[18] Webster M.A. & De Valois R.L. (1985): "Relationship between spatial-frequency and orientation tuning of striate-cortex cells". *Journal od the Optical Society of America, A,* **2,** *No. 7, 1124-1131.*

[19] Zalama E., Díaz-Pernas F., Dimitriadis Y.A. & López-Coronado J. (1993): "A New Adaptive Resonance Theory architecture, able to categorize input patterns that contain information of different nature". *Journal of Systems Engineering,* **3,** *89-109.*

[20] Zrenner E., Abramov I., Akita M., Cowey A., Livingstone M., & Valberg A. (1990): "Color Perception: Retina to Cortex". In Spillmann L. & Werner J.S. (eds.): *Visual Perception: The Neurophysiological Foundations. chap. 8. Academic Press. San Diego. 1990.*

# The EDANN concept: A Modular Artificial Neural Network model for biological vision and image processing

## Marc M. VAN HULLE and Guy A. ORBAN

Laboratorium voor Neuro- en Psychofysiologie,
Faculteit Geneeskunde, K.U.Leuven,
Campus Gasthuisberg, Herestraat,
B-3000 Leuven, BELGIUM

## Abstract

In this presentation, we will report on the preliminary simulation results obtained with our hierarchy of Entropy Driven Artificial Neural Network (EDANN) modules on real images. The images were obtained by scanning black-and-white pictures by means of a CCD camera (courtesy of the ESAT division of the K.U.Leuven). The results show how **both** line- and edge detection and texture segregation can proceed from a common spatial filtering stage and how line- and edge detection can be **distinguished pre-attentively** from texture segregation. The EDANN-based model is the same as the one used before in case of synthetic images [1], such as broadband noise- and micropattern textures, but now extended with a gain control mechanism [2]. In this presentation, an overview will be given of both the EDANN concept with the newly developed gain control mechanism and the preliminary results on real images. The results are discussed together with an outlook on future work.

## References

[1] Van Hulle, M.M., & Tollenaere, T. (1993). A Modular Artificial Neural Network Model for Texture Processing. *Neural Networks*, 6, 7-32.

[2] Van Hulle, M.M. (1993). An Unsupervised Learning Rule for Vector Normalization and Gain Control. *Proc. 1993 IEEE Int'l Conf. on Neural Networks, San Francisco*, 1202-1206.

# HUMAN VISUAL SYSTEM NEURAL APPROACH TO IMAGE COMPRESSION

*Filippo Passaggio, Rodolfo Zunino, and Davide Anguita*

DIBE - Department of Biophysical and Electronic Engineering
University of Genoa - V. Opera Pia 11a - 16145 GENOVA - Italy

**Abstract** - *In this paper a new kind of neural approach to image compression based on Human Visual System (HVS) is presented. Because of MSE difficulty of tracking the subjective (human) quality assessments, HVS models have been tried in this study for suitably forcing a traditional BP to learn to realize an input data redundancy reduction on, not the objective (MSE), but the subjective (visual) distorsion minimization basis. Several MTFs are presented and discussed, together with a brief introduction to the HVS models application theory, and a particular attention to the preferred Chitprasert-Rao one. Next, two different approaches to the problem (HVS in cost function and HVS in patterns) are pointed out. The results seem to indicate this approach to be able to remarkably reduce the overall spread noise and to avoid, at the same time, low-pass and blurring kind of effects too. Hardware implementation could be a promising feature for the future.*

## I. INTRODUCTION

Numerous "lossy" image-compression techniques have been developed over these years. By results, it is generally recognized that the orthogonal-transform-based approaches to the problem are certainly the most effective methods for obtaining large compression ratios and yet a good visual quality too. In particular, cosine-transform-based techniques have been found to obtain the best results in many digital image compression applications.

Recently, instead of classical ones, new different approaches have been tried. In particular, because of their characteristics and flexibility, neural networks (NNs) have begun to be profitably used for image compression purposes. In 1987, Cottrel, Munro and Zipser studied a first kind of approach to the problem, developing an algorithm based on back propagation [1]. By means of this approach it is possible to realize the principal component analysis (PCA) of input information [2], obtaining a sort of correlation reduction, and, then, an efficient way for data compressing [3][4]. The technique has been proved to be equivalent, in some way, to the Karhunen-Loeve transform (KLT) approach, the statistically optimal transform for the information packing.

With regard to image compression issue, a lot of studies [5][6][7] has pointed out, in these years, the importance of visual fidelity of coding techniques, because of beeing the final target an human eye. It has been proved that the objective quality of a compressed picture is not always strictly related with his visual appearence, which is, on the contrary, the real target. For all these reasons, several studies have been tried for modeling the human eye and for applying these models to image compression techniques, in order to properly select and weight the visual information on a subjective basis.

In this work, an hybrid approach, where the flexibility and self-organizing capability of NNs and the advantages of introducing a suitable model of the human visual system (HVS) for properly weighting the visual information are merged, is presented. For this purpose, a particular implementation of the back propagation algorithm, based on a distributed approach, has been used. Because of computational complexity of the problem during the training phase, it has been needed a new structured version of the back propagation algorithm, able to optimize, first, the learning time on a single machine, and then to extend it to the multiprocessor case. This approach is named Distributed Matrix Back Propagation (DMBP).

First of all, an overview of different HVS models developed by means of psychovisual experiments is proposed, followed by some consideration about the used one. In the next part, it is presented the approach which has been followed for the experimets and the parameters used in tests. A brief description of the DMBP algorithm, together with the effects of this on the compression issue, is also included. Finally, they are reported the results obtained by the experiments in comparison with the spatial Cottrel-Munro-Zipser approach, and some qualitative and quantitative consideration on these ones too.

## II. HUMAN VISUAL SYSTEM MODELS

The image quality measure which is most often used in image compression applications is the Mean Square Error (MSE), or some strictly related parameter, such as Normalized MSE (NMSE), and Signal/Noise Ratio (SNR). The MSE is also the parameter used in the traditional neural approach (Cottrel-Munro-Zipser) as reference point for the gradient operation of the back propagation learning phase. In other words, back propagation tends to minimize the quadratic deviation.

Now, unfortunately it has been proved [8] that the MSE is not always perfectly correlated with subjective quality assessments, and, more, that it spreads degradations all over the image. In fact, MSE does not adequately track some kind of degradations or artifacts caused by the image compression techniques (such as the tile effect), and it is not able to adequately reproduce what the human visual system does in assessing image quality too[9].

Using the symplifying assumption that the HVS is isotropic, Mannos and Sakrison [8] modeled it as a nonlinear point transformation, followed by a multiplicative transfer function (MTF) of the form

$$H(f) = a(b + cf)e^{-(cf)^d} \qquad (1)$$

where $f$ is the radial frequency in cycles/degree of the visual angle subtended, and $a$, $b$, $c$, $d$, are constants.

By psychovisual experiments, they fixed these values, using a DFT (Discrete Fourier Transform) domain, applied to an entire frame. Other researches preferred to work in a more suitable DCT (Discrete Cosine Transform) domain, applied to non-overlapping small subblocks [10][11]. With regard to this, several MTFs, as reported in Table 1, have been developed, introducing a properly multiplicative function $A(f)$, in order to translate $H(f)$ towards positive frequencies. This results, since, in the cosine transform domain, the higher spatial frequencies play a more important role in the corresponding human-observed image quality, than they do in the Fourier transform one.

| Mannos-Sakrison | DFT | - | $H(f) = 2.6(0.0192 + 0.114f)e^{-(0.114f)^{1.1}}$ |
| Nill | DCT | $A(f)$ | $H(f) = 2.5(0.08 + 0.18f)e^{-(0.18f)}$ |
| Ngan | DCT | $A(f)$ | $H(f) = 2.379(0.13 + 0.29f)e^{-(0.29f)}$ |

Table 1. Three different HVS models

Nevertheless, by the experiments, the best approach for this kind of applications is resulted the Chitprasert-Rao one [12]

$$H(f) = 2.46(0.1 + 0.25f)e^{-(0.25f)} \qquad (2)$$

where a simple convolution-multiplication property, derived by the authors for the DCT [13], is also used. Assuming that the subscripts $c$ and $F$ denote DCT and DFT sequences respectively, in a monodimensional case (if the impulse response of a filter $h(n)$ is real and even, so that its DFT $H_F(k)$ is real and even too, such as exactly in the specific case of the MTF of HVS model), it is proved that, if

$$Y_c(k) = X_c(k)H_F(k), \qquad k = -N, -N+1, ..., N-1 \qquad (3)$$

then

$$y(n) = \hat{x}(n) * h(n), \qquad n = 0, 1, ..., N-1 \qquad (4)$$

where $\hat{x}(n)$ is a symmetrical or folded (about $n = -\frac{1}{2}$) sequence, defined as follows

$$\hat{x}(n) = \begin{cases} x(n) & n = 0, 1, ..., N-1 \\ x(-1-n) & n = -N, -N+1, ..., -1 \end{cases} \qquad (5)$$

For all these reasons, passing to the two dimensional case, the weighting function will have, assuming the model to be isotropic, the following structure

$$H_c(k,m) = H_F(f), \qquad f = \frac{\sqrt{k^2 + m^2}}{2N} f_s \qquad (6)$$

where $f$ indicates the spatial frequency in cycles/degree, and $f_s$ (named "sampling density" by Ericsson [14]) depends upon the viewing distance and in this application results to be of 64 pels/degree (using an HP standard display with a pixel size $W=0.027cm$, the fixed viewing distance has been $D=1m$).

The four MTFs are shown in Fig.1. The Nill's and the Ngan's ones are reported together with the multiplicative factor $A(f)$, in order to obtain the exact mutual relation

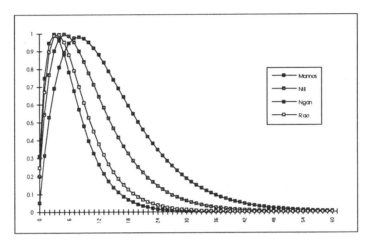

Fig. 1. Human Visual System MTFs

In a first approximation, it is possible to semplify the visual model by eliminating the first stage nonlinearity, the intensity-brightness transformation.

In order to properly modify the importance of different frequencies, it is possible to improve the subjective quality of the neural compression process by moving the working domain to the spectral one and by introducing an HVS weighting operation in the cost function of the back propagation process. The idea, in other words, has been of forcing the neural network to learn which visual information was most important and which was not, by the side of the final target, the human eye. With regard of this, it is possible to note how all the HVS models introduced are provided of shapes able to rightly follow the well known visual effects of spectral compression techniques process, where a low-frequences harsh thresholding and quantising causes blocking effects, while a same operation on the higher ones results in a loss of resolution and blurring.

## III. HVS MODEL IN NEURAL APPROACH TO IMAGE COMPRESSION

Two different approaches have been tried for forcing the network to learn compressing images on a HVS basis and distributing the binary resources in the visually optimum way.

First of all, it is to be noted as, by the experiments, the DC coefficient of DCT transform, because of its importance, needs to be coded indipendently, out of neural approach. As it is well known, the DC coefficient is related to the mean value of the subblock, and contains most of energy of subblock itself. Because of its representing, then, a not-negligible part of information, it has been noted by the experiments the necessity of better preserving this particular factor. With regard to this, the DC coefficient in this study has always been coded, as in classical DCT approach, by means of DPCM technique.

In the first approach, a HVS weighted cost function has been used for learning phase. As presented by Nill [10], working on a intra sub-image distorsion basis (i.e. disregarding tile and blocking effects), a quality measure more accurately tracking human assessments can be stated in spatial frequency domain (i.e. in a cycles/degree space) for a single $j$-$th$ subblock of $M \times N$ linear dimensions as

$$MSE_j^{HVS} = \frac{Wj}{K} \sum_{u=0}^{M-1} \sum_{v=0}^{N-1} \left[ H^2(f) \left( F_j(u,v) - \hat{F}_j(u,v) \right)^2 \right] \tag{7}$$

where $W_j$ indicates the $j$-$th$ subimage structure weighting factor, proportional to subimage's intensity level variance ($1.0$ for maximum and $0.0$ for minimum structure subimage), $K$ is a normalization factor (such as total energy), $H(f)$ the rotational symmetric spatial frequency response of HVS, and the two $F_j(u,v)$ the DCT transform of processed and unprocessed $j$-$th$ subimage. The logarithmic or power function, usually introduced as nonlinear preprocessing stage into HVS models, is not taken into account because of the particular type of images considered (using as target quite low-contrast images it is possible to assume to be working in a linear region of the nonlinearity).

The compression/quality ratios obtained with this approach have been quite interesting. Nevertheless, the best results have been obtained by the second technique. In this kind of approach the HVS weighting factor has been introduced not in the cost function, but, rather, as preprocessing stage for the learning phase. A particular training set has been built, first, for this purpose, taking the blocks of the original pictures and filtering them by means of the HVS-based MTF. These patterns, instead of the original ones, have been given to the neural network (a standard Multiple Layer Perceptron with just an hidden - compressed - layer) for the training phase, with a normal MSE-based cost function.

As illustrated in the next section, with the spectral approaches, both the quantitative measures and the subjective evaluations have shown sharp improvements in comparison with the traditional spatial Cottrel-Munro-Zipser ones.


## IV. RESULTS


For the simulations, a classical BP algorithm with *by epoch* approach and VOGL acceleration [15] has been used. With regard to the network configuration, the best results have been obtained by means of 16×16 masks, as good compromise between processing precision (i.e. quality) and compression quantity. In practice, all the reported tests have been realized with a two layers network, having 255-k-255 units for layer respectively (the input and output layers are characterized by one less unit, in comparison with the number of the input mask pels; this is due, as seen in the previous section, to the DPCM approach used for the DC coefficient). The $k$ number of the hidden units depends on desired quality and necessary compression level.

Of course, for the hidden units, in order to obtain a real data compression it is then necessary, during the validation phase, a quantisation stage, able to map the "continuous" hidden units space in a "discrete" one. With regard to this, a uniform approach has been tried, with all a series of tests, varying the levels number between a maximum of 256 and a minimun of 8 (8 and 3 bits, respectively). From these tests, it is pointed out as the best compromise between quality and compression is realized by something like 5-4 bits. In any case, the uniform one it is not the only approach that is possible to apply. A non-uniform one is actually beeing studied, and it could be able to remarkably improve the whole compression level. Taking into account the quantisation stage, the Compression Ratio (CR) parameter will obviously result to be

$$CR = \frac{N^2 b}{(k+1)q} \tag{8}$$

where $N$ is the monodimensional size of a single subblock, $b$ is the number of bits/pel of the original picture, $k$ is the hidden units number, and $q$ the number of bits used for the quantisation stage.

Because of beeing the neural network applications generally characterized by requiring a remarkable computational power, in particular during the first and most important training phase (in image compression field, this problem is made even more actual by the involved amount of data and by the necessity of large training sets for the learning phase), a new, distributed approach to the BP from the computational point of view has been used. With regard to these applications, in fact, a cluster of traditional workstations can result a competitive solution to the problem compared with supercomputer or dedicated architectures, a kind of approach able to guarantee at the same time computational power and memory space. This has been recently realized by Anguita et al. by means of a Distributed Matrix Back Propagation (DMBP).

DMBP is based on Parallel Virtual Machine (PVM) [16], a free-licence, distributed, low-level software, able to trasparently hide the intrinsic differences between non-homogeneous architectures. On PVM environment it is built the DMBP application.

First, a static mapping of the back propagation learning algorithm is performed on workstations cluster, so that the load distribution results planned once and for all, at the beginning. This feature allows the user to easily model the available computational power, to quickly determine an optimal mapping and to forecast the communication network behaviour. The network speed is guaranteed to be kept constant, for sufficiently large packets, thanks to PVM.

The problem of a non-homogeneous cluster, composed by workstations of different computational power, can be circumvented modeling each machine as a sub-cluster of identical *virtual* workstation, whose computational power is the l.c.m of all the cluster workstations. Obviously, the communication time between virtual workstations that compose a single real workstation must be considered as null (for more details on MBP algorithm see [17]).

For simulations, a database of six grayscale (8 bits/pel) 512×512 pictures, generally used in literature for this kind of applications (the original ones are available on network in standard USC database), have been taken. Several tests have been tried for evaluating the performances of this approach and discovering the parameters for the best compromise between quality and compression. Some of the obtained quality quantitative results are reported in Table 2. In particular, a comparison between the traditional spatial approach and the new spectral one is presented. In the first case, the used configuration for the network has been 256-16-256, with local mean value extraction (one for each subblock), and direct transmission of it with a 4 bits uniform quantisation (16 quantisation levels). In the second, a neural network configuration of 255-16-255 units have been used, with a 4 bits uniform quantisation of hidden units and DC coefficients. The Compression Ratio is easily obtained, from the (8), by substituting the right values ($N=16$, $b=8$, $k=16$, $q=4$), and it results equal to 30.12 (the same, as in the spatial case, such as it is easily verifiable).

| | Spatial Domain | | | Spectral Domain | | |
|---|---|---|---|---|---|---|
| | MSE | PSNR | SNR | MSE | PSNR | SNR |
| Lenna | 82.22 | 29.01 | 23.47 | 75.33 | 29.39 | 23.85 |
| Airplane | 122.37 | 27.29 | 23.98 | 94.14 | 28.43 | 25.11 |
| Baboon | 381.51 | 22.35 | 16.63 | 350.98 | 22.71 | 17.00 |
| Peppers | 82.43 | 29.00 | 23.00 | 64.03 | 30.10 | 24.09 |
| Sailboat | 171.94 | 25.81 | 20.57 | 136.88 | 26.80 | 21.31 |
| Tiffany | 53.87 | 30.85 | 28.67 | 41.49 | 31.99 | 29.80 |
| MEAN | 102.56 | 28.40 | 23.88 | 82.37 | 29.34 | 24.83 |

Table 2. Results of the two different learning approaches for Cr=30.12 (255-16-255, q=4)

The visual quality is improved in the second case. Not only the low-pass and blurring effects are greatly reduced in comparison with the spatial kind of approach, but also the noise, spread all over the image, and the graines effect (characteristic of the traditional approach, in particular, in the smoothest regions) are seldom noticeable. On the contrary, nevertheless, with the spectral approach some blocking effect, in particular in the most active areas, is sometimes visible.

## V. CONCLUSIONS

By introducing a simplified HVS model into the neural approach to image compression, a new kind of approach to the problem has been developed and tested. An optimal MTF, the Chitprasert-Rao one, has been chosen, which tends to preserve the middle frequencies information, cutting off the highest one and smooths the noise in the low-activity regions. Two different methods for compressing with a neural network approach, a spatial and a spectral one, have been presented and placed in comparison. From tests and results reported, it has been proved as the second one is able to achieve the best performances, from an objective and a subjective point of view too. The HVS model use has highly improved not only the definition, but also the compressed image neatness.

The neural approach to the image compression has the great advantage of implementation easiness. After a really computational heavy stage due to the learning phase, but able to be realized ex-ante (i.e. off-line), in fact, the neural approach appears to be quick and low-cost. For these reasons, it seems to be mostly suitable for an hardware implementation, in particular in real-time coding kind of applications. With regard to this, future works will be set for trying neural approaches to motion pictures and for porting them into a multiprocessor, parallel architecture based on DSPs.

## REFERENCES

[1]     Cottrel G.W., Munro P., Zipser D., "Image Compression by back propagation: an example of extensional programming", in SHARKEY, N. E. (Ed.): "Advances in cognitive science" (Ablex, Norwood, NJ, 1988).

[2]     Oja E., "A semplified neuron model as a principal component analyser", J. Math. Biol., N. 15, pp. 267-273, 1982.

[3]     Mougeot M., Azencott R., Angeniol B., "Image Compression With Back Propagation: Improvement of the Visual Restoration Using Different Cost Functions", Neural Networks, Vol. 4, pp. 467-476, 1991.

[4]     Sartori G., Carrato S., Sicuranza G.L., "Linear Neural Networks With Hierarchical Structures For Image Compression", Proc. 4th It. Work. on Parallel Arch. and Neural Networks, Vietri sul Mare, Salerno, May 1991.

[5]     Netravali A.N., Limb J.O., "Picture Coding: A Review", Proc. IEEE, Vol. 68, pp. 366-406, Mar. 1980.

[6]     Jain A.K., "Image Data Compression: A Review", Proc. IEEE, Vol. 69, pp. 349-389, Mar. 1981.

[7]     Tescher A.G., "Transform Image Coding", in Advances in Electronics and Electron Physics, Suppl. 12, W.K. Pratt, Ed. Academic, ch. 4, pp. 113-155, 1979.

[8]     Mannos J.L., Sakrison D.J., "The effects of a visual fidelity criterion on the encoding of images", IEEE Trans. Inform. Theory, Vol. IT-20, pp. 525-536, July 1974.

[9]     Miyahara M., Kotani K., Block distorsion in orthogonal transform coding - analysis, minimization, and distorsion measure", IEEE Trans Commun., Vol. COM-33, pp. 90-96, Jan. 1985.

[10]   Nill N.B., "A visual model weighted cosine transform for image compression and quality assessment", IEEE Trans. Commun., Vol. COM-33, pp. 551-557, June 1985.

[11]   Ngan K.N., Leong K.S., Singh H., "Adaptive cosine transform coding of images in perceptual domain", IEEE Trans. Acoust., Speech, Signal Processing, Vol. ASSP-37, N. 11, pp. 1743-1749, Nov. 1989.

[12]   Chitprasert B., Rao K.R., "Human visual weighted progressive image transmission", IEEE Trans. Commun., Vol. 38, N. 7, pp. 1040-1044, July 1990.

[13]   Chitprasert B., Rao K.R., "Discrete cosine transform filtering", Signal Processing, Vol. 19, N. 3, pp. 233-245, Mar. 1990.

[14]   Ericsson S., "Frequency weighted interframe hybrid coding", Rep. TRITA-TTT-8401, Telecommun. Theory, Royal Inst. Technol., Stockholm, Sweden, Jan. 1984.

[15]   Vogl T.P., Mangis J.K., Rigler A.K., Zink W.T., Alkon D.L., "Accelerating the convergence of back-propagation method", Biological Cybernetics, Vol. 59, pp. 257-263, 1988.

[16]   Geist A. et al., "PVM 3 user's guide and reference manual", May 1993.

[17]   Anguita D., Parodi G.C., Zunino R., "An efficient implementation of back-propagation on RISC-based workstations", Neurocomputing, N.5, pp. 1-9, 1993.

# "Tailored" Neural Networks to Improve Image Classification

Lerner, B., Guterman, H., Dinstein, I. and Romem, Y.*
Department of Electrical and Computer Engineering
Ben-Gurion University of the Negev
Beer-Sheva, Israel 84105

* The Institute of Medical Genetics, Soroka Medical Center
Beer-Sheva, Israel 84105

## Abstract

The concept of "tailored" neural network is inspired by the concept of grouping in the visual cortex of the mammalian brain. This biological animated concept was implemented to develop "tailored" neural networks for image classification improvement. Each "tailored" network was specialized to classify a different class of vectors. This was done by employing separate training and using specific features in each class. Image classification improvement was tested by the chromosome classification application. For chromosome classification, the probability of correct classification using the "tailored" networks was 2.5% higher than the probability achieved by a conventional neural network (97.6% versus 95.1%). This improvement was found to be higher when lower quality features were employed. It is expected that the improvement will increase whenever the image classification task will become more and more complicated.

## 1. Introduction

Image classification using multilayer perceptron (MLP) neural networks has become widespread in the computer vision and neural networks communities. The neural network classifier has the advantage of being fast (highly parallel), easily trainable and capable of creating arbitrary partitions of feature space. However, image classification using an MLP depends on a series of various procedures generally held according to practical considerations. In most vision applications these stages precede the classification itself and are motivated by a mathematical analysis and/or engineering concepts. Even the MLP classifier itself, when applied to a complicated classification task fails very often to correctly classify the input data. The mammalian visual cortex seems not to suffer from this kind of problems. It simply does not function as our classical image classifiers do. Image projected from the retina onto the visual cortex parallelly spread among a series of cell clusters, each of which performs its own special analysis and synthesis. Each retinal area is analyzed over and over again, column after column, and again in neighboring cortical regions, with respect to a number of different variables such as position, orientation and color [2]. From a large series of experiments, it became apparent that in area 17 simple and complex neurons with similar receptive field axis orientation are neatly stacked on top of each other in discrete columns. *Separate* columns exist for each axis orientation. Other functional variables are also grouped in columnar aggregates of cells. In cortical areas of the monkey beyond area 17 of the visual cortex, there exist columns of cells with well-defined color sensitivity and other columns in which the direction of movement of the visual stimulus is important. Cortical structure and functional organization go hand in hand [2].

---

# This work was supported in part by the Paul Ivanier Center for Robotics and Production Management, Ben-Gurion University, Beer-Sheva, Israel.

This study suggests imitating several aspects of the mammalian visual cortex structure and functions in order to improve image classification. We introduce the "tailored" neural network that gains class separability by both extracting specific class features and by tuning the training to a specific class only. The discrete cortex columns are implemented through the discrete "tailored" neural networks.

To implement the suggested concept we have used the chromosome classification task as a model for image classification. The chromosome classification task is well known, yet without satisfying solutions [1], [10], [13]. Several studies on chromosome classification using neural networks were held in the last two years, most of them relate to feature extraction and selection [3]-[6] and other relate to the performance and the optimization of the MLP NN as chromosome classifier [7]-[9]. Therefore, this study can be also regarded as a continuation study, in the way to establish a neural network classifier for human chromosome.

## 2. The "tailored" network

The "tailored" network tries to mimic the outlined biological concept and to optimize its performance. By training an MLP NN to classify *only* vectors of *one* class we enable (and actually force) it to employ all the relevant information of this class feature data in order to perfectly distinguish between the class and the rest of the classes. The network does not need to distinguish vectors of several classes but only "the" class vectors compare to "other" classes vectors. By training several networks, each of them specialized on vectors of a different class, we can get a special network for each class. When a test vector will be introduced to *all* the "tailored" networks, the network with the highest output value will indicate the correct classification of this vector (a kind of "winner-take-all" mechanism). Decomposition of the task to several simpler tasks makes the solution easier and yields better performance, in *vivo,* as well as, while solving difficult engineering problems. Furthermore, it is known that a large network may perform perfectly on the training set but fails to interpolate as well as a smaller network.

One step further in the trail to mimic the visual cortex functioning could be training and testing the network using the best selected features of each class. In a similar way to the visual cortex (e.g., area 17) [2], we can extract features, optimize their selection and train, for a specific task, a network based on these features. This work examined the use of the "knock-out" algorithm [12] to select the best features to represent each class. Each class was represented by a *different* set of *optimal* (in the sense of the "minimum variance" [12]) features. Every vector, in each specific class, either a training or a test vector, was represented by this set of specific optimal features of *its* class. Training and testing the "tailored" networks was done based on these "class optimized" sets of features.

## 3. The methodology

Our data set included 481 chromosome images of types "2", "4", "13", "19" and "x". The features that were used for the classification were based on the density profile of the chromosomes. The density profile extracts the typical banded structure of the chromosomes and yields a suitable representation for the classification [1], [5], [6], [10]. The density profile was normalized both in length (64-dimensional) and in value to the [-0.5,0.5] range [6].

Each "tailored" network is based on a two-layer feedforward neural network trained by the backpropagation (bp) learning algorithm [11]. The number of input units was set by the feature space (64-dimensional) while the number of output units was determined by the number of classes to be classified (5-dimensional). The number of hidden units of the network was set according to the Principal Component Analysis (PCA), applied to the feature vectors. The number was set to be the number of the largest eigenvalues, the sum of which accounts for more than a pre-specified percentage of the sum of all the eigenvalues. In all the simulations, this number was set according to a pre-specified percentage of 90%.

Optimization of the neural network parameters regarding the chromosome data was made elsewhere [7]-[8]. Learning rate ($\mu$) was set to be 0.026, momentum constant ($\alpha$) to be 0.97 and the training cycle was set to be 4000 epochs.

Figure 1 sketches the procedure we have developed to examine "tailored" network performance. First, we used the "knock-out" algorithm to select the optimal features (in the sense of "minimum variance") in *each* class. We chose the best 40 features, although even a smaller number of features is adequate to represent the chromosomes without performance degradation [5]. Second, we partitioned the chromosome feature data set into training and test sets, where 80% of the vectors were chosen randomly to be in the training set. Then, we trained separately the 5 different networks based on the specific class features. Each training vector had 5 different representations each of them was used in the specific network. The desired output of training vectors belonged to the correct specific class was set to "1" while this output for *all* the rest of the vectors was set to "0". After training, vectors from the test set were tested by *all* the networks at once (test vectors had 5 different representations, as well). The largest output among these networks indicates the right class of the tested vector (winner-take-all). All the simulations were repeated 3 times, with the same network parameters but with different sets of randomly chosen training vectors, and the results were averaged. This procedure yields specialized networks we have, therefore, called "tailored" networks.

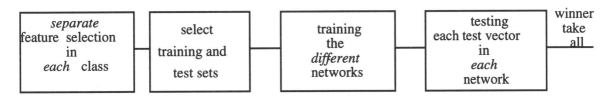

Figure 1. Implementation of a "tailored" network.

## 4. Simulation results

Figure 2 and Figure 3 show, respectively, the probability of correct training set classification and the probability of correct test set classification of the "tailored" networks. Training, as expected, is perfect in (almost) all the classes. Non-perfect training exists in classes with small training sets and/or in classes with considerable variations of image representation. In Figure 3, each network tests vectors according to the optimal features of the class it represents. The only significant columns in the Figure are the highest ones (winner-take-all), where there is an agreement between network type and the tested vector representation.

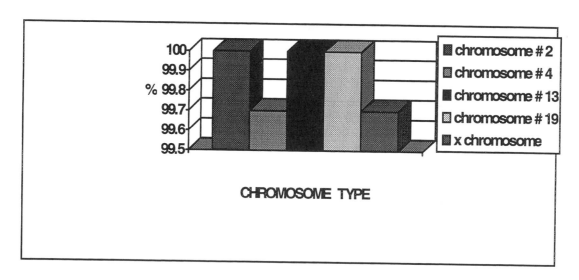

Figure 2. The probability of correct training set classification using the 5 "tailored" networks.

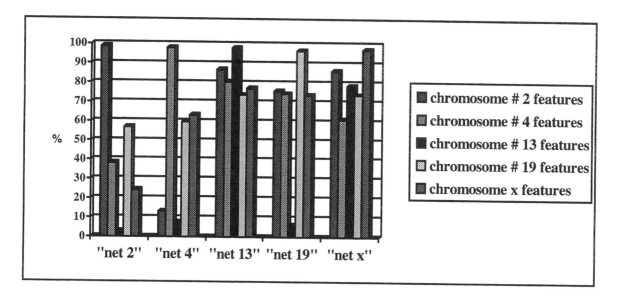

Figure 3. The probability of correct test set classification using the 5 "tailored" networks.

We have compared the classification results using these nets to the results when only *one* MLP network is trained to classify the chromosomes and the features are *common* to all classes. The 5 "tailored" networks yielded *average* probability of correct training set classification of 99.88% compare to 99.3% of the "one" network [6] and 97.6% with the test set compares to 95.1% of the "one" network [6]. When the simulation was repeated on slightly better features, the improvement due to the use of "tailored" networks, was slightly lower. Therefore, the advantage of using "tailored" networks is greater whenever "low quality" features are considered. The superiority of the "tailored" networks comparing to the "one" MLP NN is assumed to become even higher when the classification task will be complicated. Consequently, when all the 24 chromosome types will be considered, the "tailored" networks are believed to perform even better. However, not to be forgotten, that time and memory requirements are multiplied by the number of classes to be classified.

# 5. Discussion

The concept of "tailored" neural networks to improve image classification performance is introduced. Each "tailored" neural network is specialized to classify vectors of a different class. This was done by employing separate training and using specific features in each class. For chromosome classification, the probability of correct classification using the "tailored" networks was 2.5% higher than the probability achieved by a conventional neural network that uses common features in all the classes (97.6% versus 95.1%). This improvement was found to be higher when lower quality features were employed. It is expected that the improvement will increase whenever the image classification task will become more and more complicated.

# 6. References

1. Groen, F.C.A., ten Kate, T.K., Smeulders, A.W.M. & Young, I.T. (1989). Human chromosome classification based on local band descriptors. *Pattern Recognition Letters*, **9**, 211-222.
2. Kuffler, S.W, Nicholls, J.G & Martin, A.R. (1984). *From neuron to brain*. Sinauer Associates Inc.
3. Lerner, B., Guterman, H. & Dinstein, I. (1992). On classification of human chromosomes. *Neural Networks for Learning, Recognition and Control*, a research conference at Boston University, May 14-16.
4. Lerner, B., Guterman, H., Dinstein, I. & Romem, Y. (1993). Classification of human chromosomes by two-dimensional Fourier transform components. *WCNN'93*, Portland, July 11-15, 793-796.
5. Lerner, B., Levinstein, M., Rosenberg, B., Guterman, H., Dinstein, I. & Romem, Y. (1993). Feature selection and chromosome classification using an MLP neural network. (Submitted to *ICNN'94*).
6. Lerner, B., Guterman, H., Dinstein, I. & Romem, Y. (1993). Medial Axis Transform based features and neural network classifier for human chromosome classification. (Submitted for publication).
7. Lerner, B., Guterman, H., Dinstein, I. & Romem, Y. (1993). Human chromosome classification using multilayer perceptron neural network. (Submitted for publication).
8. Lerner, B., Guterman, H., Dinstein, I. & Romem, Y. (1993). Learning curves and optimization of multilayer perceptron neural network for chromosome classification. (Submitted to *WCNN'94*).
9. Lerner, B., Guterman, H., Dinstein, I. & Romem, Y. (1993). A Comparison of Multilayer Perceptron Neural Network and Bayes Piecewise Classifier for Chromosome Classification. (Submitted to *ICNN'94*).
10. Piper, J., Granum, E., Rutovitz, D. & Ruttledge, H. (1980). Automation of chromosome analysis. *Signal Processing*, **2**, 203-221.
11. Rumelhart, D.E., Hinton, G.E. & Williams, R.J. (1986). Learning internal representations by error propagation. In Rumelhart, D.E., McClelland, J.L. and the PDP research group, *Parallel Distributed Processing*, vol. 1, chap. 8, Cambridge: MIT Press.
12. Sambur, M.R. (1975). Selection of acoustic features for speaker identification. *IEEE Transactions on Acoustics, Speech and Signal Processing*, **ASSP-23**, 176-182.
13. Wu, Q., Suetens, P. & Oosterlinck, A. (1987). Toward an expert system for chromosome analysis. *Knowledge-Based Systems*, **1**, 43-52.

# Receptive Fields by Implicit Partial Differentiation: Bifurcations in a CAVLI Model

Harold H. Szu
Naval Surface Warfare Center
Code R44
Silver Spring, Maryland 20903

Frank E. McFadden
Department of Computer Science
University of Maryland
College Park, Maryland 20742

*For neural models defined by differential equations, the relationship between stimulus and response is generally implicit and nonlinear, so that the receptive fields of these models cannot be easily derived analytically. The present article shows that these models can be analyzed by means of implicit partial differentiation, and the technique is applied to a novel model for the role of inhibition in cortical processing, proposed in (Reggia et al., 1992). Sensitivity analysis of the differential receptive field structure reveals previously unremarked bifurcations in the model, and variations in the structure of the sidebands.*

## 1  Biological Background

Ideally, a neural model of perception should make the best possible marriage between the state-of-the art of biological knowledge and its mathematical representation. Even in the restrictive case of the quantitative structure of receptive fields of simple cells in the visual cortex, however, some very basic questions have not been answered definitively. These include the linearity of the summation process (Heggelund, 1985), the precise shape of receptive fields, (Jones, Stepnoski, and Palmer, 1987) vs. (Hawken and Parker, 1987), and the role of inhibition. We review some recent work on inhibition because it is relevant to the model studied in this paper.

Inhibitory effects are difficult to study because activity must be induced before suppression can be measured. The hypothesis of cross-orientation inhibition in the visual cortex is a possible explanation for the sharpness of orientation tuning, and neural network models of visual cortex generally utilize some kind of mechanism to achieve cross-orientation inhibition, but biological research has not fully revealed the underlying structures that would confirm a theory, e.g., one based on direct lateral inhibitory connections. (Sillito, 1985) and (Creutzfeldt and Ito, 1968) demonstrated that chemical blocking of the inhibitory neurotransmitter GABA in the cortex caused cortical cells to loose their orientation selectivity. This led to the supposition that orientation must be caused by direct lateral inhibition, but (Ferster, 1986) measured excitatory postsynaptic (EPSP) and inhibitory postsynaptic (IPSP) potentials separately, and found that the same stimulus evokes maximal EPSPs and IPSPs, i.e., that tuning was not sharpened by combining EPSP and IPSP. Ferster's work cast more doubt on the hypothesis that orientation tuning could be explained by direct lateral inhibition. More recently, (Crook et al., 1989, 1991) applied GABA through four pipettes, arranged radially about the recording site in order to suppress the cells that might otherwise be expected to inhibit the response of the recorded cell, according to the hypothesis of cross-orientation inhibition. They observed that orientation tuning was significantly broadened, which tends to support the hypothesis of cross-orientation inhibition. In summary, the biological understanding of inhibitory mechanisms in cortex is incomplete, and experimental results have been inconclusive.

## 2  Analytical Approach

For a neural model defined by differential equations, its receptive field is defined by the effect on the STM equilibrium of a small change in the external input. For an equation with the form

$$\dot{\mathbf{y}} = \mathbf{f}(\mathbf{y}(t), \mathbf{E}), \tag{1}$$

with external input vector $\mathbf{E}$. We shall denote the STM equilibrium response of the system by the vector $\mathbf{Y}$. This is typical of a layered network characterized by competition among the $\mathbf{y}$ nodes, where the activation vector of the previous layer, denoted by $\mathbf{x}$, can be assumed to stabilize in a manner that is unaffected by further changes in $\mathbf{y}$. Because $\mathbf{Y}$ is an equilibrium, we must have

$$\mathbf{f}(\mathbf{Y}, \mathbf{E}) = 0, \tag{2}$$

and it is possible to determine the change in the equilibrium value of $\mathbf{Y}$ in response to a change in $\mathbf{E}$ by implicit partial differentiation of equation (2). This is analogous to regarding $\mathbf{E}$ as a vector of parameters.

In mathematical terms, the differential receptive field is defined by the Jacobian matrix $(\partial\mathbf{Y}/\partial\mathbf{E})$. Differentiation of (1) with respect to $\mathbf{E}$, while holding $\dot{\mathbf{y}} = 0$, gives us

$$\left(\frac{\partial\mathbf{f}}{\partial\mathbf{y}}\right)\left(\frac{\partial\mathbf{y}}{\partial\mathbf{E}}\right) + \left(\frac{\partial\mathbf{f}}{\partial\mathbf{E}}\right) = 0. \tag{3}$$

Taking the limit as $t \to \infty$ and assuming that $(\partial\mathbf{f}/\partial\mathbf{Y})$ is nonsingular, we get the practical formula

$$\left(\frac{\partial\mathbf{Y}}{\partial\mathbf{E}}\right) = -\left(\frac{\partial\mathbf{f}}{\partial\mathbf{Y}}\right)^{-1}\left(\frac{\partial\mathbf{f}}{\partial\mathbf{E}}\right), \tag{4}$$

which can be applied directly to calculate $(\partial\mathbf{Y}/\partial\mathbf{E})$. This is consistent with the basic methodology for measuring receptive fields in biological research, and is an instantaneous form of methods often used in neural network simulations, which does not require interative computations. This effectiveness of this technique will be demonstrated in the next section for a relatively complex model.

# 3 The Competitive Distribution Model

## 3.1 Basic Definitions

The basic model used in (Reggia et al., 1992) will be described and analyzed, but with a modified notation. The first layer represents the thalamus, and the second layer represents a sensory area of the cortex. The thalamic layer will be represented by the activation vector $\mathbf{x}$, and the cortical layer by the activation vector $\mathbf{y}$. Individual components will be subscripted. Thalamic activation dynamics are given by

$$\dot{x}_j = e_j(M - x_j) + c_s x_j, \tag{5}$$

where $e_j$ is external input and $c_s < 0$ is inhibitory self-decay.[1]

It is possible to simplify the specification and to regard all thalamic nodes as fixed in a steady state. Equation (5) has the general solution

$$x_j(t) = \frac{e_j M}{e_j - c_s} + \left[x_j(0) - \frac{e_j M}{e_j - c_s}\right]e^{-(e_j - c_s)t}, \tag{6}$$

so that $x_j(t)$ approaches $e_j M/(e_j - c_s)$ in the limit regardless of its initial value. The denominator is positive because $c_s$ is negative by assumption. Since we are considering the network to be primarily dependent on the external input term, no generality is lost in the subsequent analysis by simply assuming that

$$x_j(t) = E_j, \tag{7}$$

with $\mathbf{E}$ constant. This is because the equilibrium values at the thalamic layer are governed by equation (6), independent of the dynamics of the cortical layer. After the thalamic layer has approached equilibrium, the limiting dynamics of the cortical layer will depend only on the equilibrium values of the input from the thalamic layer. With this simplification, it is clear that the network has the form of equation (1).

---

[1] In the source article, a bias term $b_j$ was added to the external input, but it was generally assumed that $b_j = 0$ for all thalamic nodes.

Cortical nodes follow the equation:

$$\dot{y}_i(t) = in_i(M - y_i(t)) + c_s y_i(t), \tag{8}$$

where $y_i$ is the activation of the $i$th cortical node, $in_i$ is input to the node, $c_s$ is inhibitory self-decay, and $M$ is the maximum activation that a node can have. Input in turn is given by the equation

$$in_i = \sum_{r \in N_i(1)} w_{ir}^C y_r + \sum_{r \in T_i} w_{ir}^T x_r + b_i, \tag{9}$$

where $b_i$ is a positive bias term. The first sum is from cortical connections to cortical node $i$ and the second sum is from thalamic input. The neighborhoods $N_i(1)$ and $T_i$ depend on the network topology, which is a 2D connection structure based on hexagonal neighborhoods. $N_i(r)$ is the set of all subscripts of nodes that lie within the hexagonal radius of $r$ from a central node at location $i$. There are 6 nodes subscripts in the set $N_i(1)$, there are 12 in the set $N_i(2)$, and so on, according to the recursion $|N_i(r+1)| = |N_i(r)| + 6$. Each node of $N_i(1)$ is directly connected to node $i$ in the cortex. $T_i$ is the arborization set, which represents the projection of the thalamus to the cortex. This set consists of the subscripts[2] of cortical nodes that are directly connected to thalamic node $i$. The set $T_i$ includes $i$ together with the subscripts of all nodes within a hexagonal radius of 3 from node $i$. The basic hypothesis for this formulation is that each thalamic node sends out a group of dendrites that is most concentrated near a central point in the cortex, and progressively less dense as one moves away from the central point in cortex. $w_{ir}^T$ are the strengths of connections from the thalamus to the cortex, defined by

$$w_{ir}^T = \frac{(y_i + q)p_{ir}}{\sum_{k \in T_r}(y_k + q)p_{kr}}, \tag{10}$$

where $p_{kr}$ are auxilliary weight parameters that depend on the distance between node locations $k$ and $r$. This equation is characteristic of the types of models that were referred to as competitive activation models based on virtual lateral inhibition, or CAVLI models, in (McFadden, 1993). $q$ is a parameter that helps to prevent the denominators from approaching zero. This parameter appears to be unnecessary based on some initial analysis, but the computer analysis in a later section will show that $q$ *does* affect the shapes of the receptive fields of the model. Based on the hexagonal radial distance, starting with 0, the auxilliary weight values used in the simulations ranged from 0.199 for $p_{ii}^T$ to 0.176, 0.121, through 0.065 for radial distance 3, based on a normal density function with a standard deviation of 2, so that the denominator of equation (10) could be viewed as the expected activation at cortical center $r$, if the center were only known to be identified up to a normal standard deviation of 2 in a bivariate normal distribution. In image processing terms, this denominator can be seen to be a convolution of the cortical data with center $r$. As is usual in such models, the structure of the $p_{kr}$ weights is designed to model the arborization of dendritic connections from one neural layer to the next, where it is typically assumed that connections are denser near the center of a projection, and thin out as one moves farther away. Intracortical connections, represented as $w_{ir}^C$, are defined in a similar way.

$$w_{ir}^C = w_p \frac{y_i + q}{\sum_{k \in N_r(1)}(y_k + q)}. \tag{11}$$

## 3.2   Receptive Fields at Resting Level

The case where the system is at "resting level," i.e., at equilibrium in the absence of external input, is particularly susceptible to precise mathematical analysis. The scope of this article does not permit a fully detailed derivation, but this can be found in (McFadden, 1993). First of all, the resting level of each cortical neuron is calculated, resulting in the formula.

$$\bar{y} = \frac{1}{2c_p}(Mc_p + c_s - b + \sqrt{b^2 + c_p^2 M^2 + c_s^2 + 2bc_p M - 2bc_s + 2Mc_s c_p}\ ). \tag{12}$$

---

[2]This notation differs from that of (Reggia et al., 1992) Thus, $T_i$ can be used to refer to either cortical or thalamic nodes, by their subscripts.

Next, the Jacobians are calculated, with boolean expressions used to simplify the algebra, as in the C computer language. For example, the expression $(j \in T_i)$ equals 1 if it is true, and 0 if it is false.

$$\left(\frac{\partial f_i}{\partial E_j}\right) = w_{ij}^T (M - \bar{y})(j \in T_i), \tag{13}$$

where

$$w_{ir}^T = \frac{p_{ir}}{\sum_{k \in T_r} p_{kr}}. \tag{14}$$

Finally, the matrix $(\partial f_i / \partial y_j)$ can be expressed as the sum of a diagonal matrix

$$\left[\frac{c_p (M - \bar{y})\bar{y}}{(\bar{y} + q)} + (c_s - c_p \bar{y} - b)\right] I,$$

plus the matrix

$$\frac{c_p (M - \bar{y})}{36} \left[ -\frac{\bar{y}|N_j(1) \cap N_i(1)|}{\bar{y} + q} + 6(j \in N_i(1)) \right] \tag{15}$$

$$= \frac{c_p (M - \bar{y})}{36(\bar{y} + q)} \left[ \{6(j \in N_i(1)) - |N_j(1) \cap N_i(1)|\}\bar{y} + 6q(j \in N_i(1)) \right], \tag{16}$$

where the structure of the matrix is based on the connection structure of the network.

# 4  Numerical Results

## 4.1  Differential Receptive Fields

In this section, the mathematical analysis of the preceding sections is illustrated numerically. The computational requirements for differential analysis are significantly less than those for the methods based on iterative computations. The computation is based on the inversion of a sparse matrix with a symmetrical connection structure. Accordingly, the computation time is $O(N^4)$, where $N$ is the number of nodes on one side of a square patch of cortex. The fast processing time of the present method made it possible to explore the model online and in some cases to make precise iterative computations of bifurcation points that might have taken much longer if it had been necessary to use iterative methods for the computation of receptive fields within the search for bifurcation points.

In the 3D figures, The "ground level" plane, displayed in perspective, represents the spatial dimensions of the neural field, corresponding to a patch of cortex, and the vertical direction represents the activation differential, that is, the partial differential of the STM equilibrium value of the activation with respect to the change in external input caused by the application of a point stimulus applied to the center of the input field. More precisely, the receptive field should be determined by varying the *stimulus* over different input positions, but the symmetry of the model makes it clear that this would lead to equivalent results in all of the simulations reported here. A 33x33 network is used in order to assure that the toroidal wraparound of the network has only limited effects, and also to explore the impulse propagation properties of the network over a wide range..

The primary model described in the preceding sections will be studied for its sensitivity to variations in the parameters of two of the important parameters of the system. One of these is $q$, which in some ways appears to be unnecessary in the model. The other is the $b$ parameter, which affects the "resting level" of the system, as can be seen from formula (12). From equation (9) it is clear that $b$ affects $in_i$ additively. Accordingly, the level of background activity is directly influenced by the value of $b$. It will become apparent that a value of $q$ away from the origin must be chosen in order to assure that the differential receptive fields will not pass through bifurcations as the $b$ parameter varies.

## 4.2 Receptive fields with $q$ near 0

This series of tests is designed to determine whether the $q$ parameter is really needed in the model. With $q = 0$, the sensitivity to variations in $b$ is analyzed systematically.[3] On the basis of these simulations, it becomes clear that even though a positive $b$ parameter should eliminate zero activations and thereby prevent zero denominators in the connection weight formulas, values of $q$ away from zero are necessary in order to assure that anomalous behavior is prevented.

The results are shown in Figure 1. There are two bifurcation ranges, within which the receptive field undergoes dramatic changes. In Figure 1, when $b$ changes from .0002 to .0009, the OFF center pattern of the differential receptive field actually changes to an ON center pattern, but with peaks that show no attenuation away from the center. When $b$ reaches .002, the receptive field pattern has become closer to that of a Mexican hat pattern with ON center, and several sidebands, but the pattern becomes inverted once again when $b$ reaches .006. Finally, as $b$ grows beyond .007, the pattern inverts again and settles into a consistent Mexican hat pattern, with sideband, as when $b = .03$. Bifurcations in the differential receptive fields were also observed when $q = .001$ or $q = .005$ were chosen. The inversions of the receptive field patterns across different levels of background activity imply that the models with $q$ near 0 would not be suitable for perceptual processing.

## 4.3 Sidebands for $q = .01$

For $q = .01$, the entire range of possible values of $b$ was examined for bifurcations, but none were found; accordingly, the model with $q = .01$ could be considered as a suitable candidate for a perceptual model. In Figure 2, with $q = .01$, shape changes in the differential receptive fields do occur as the intensity level is varied, but thes appear primarily as variations in the inhibitory sidebands. At the lowest levels of stimulus intensity, inhibitory subfields, indicative of virtual lateral inhibition (VLI), are almost imperceptible. As $b$ is increased, VLI becomes more pronounced and sidebands develop, with secondary sidebands showing up when $b = .003$. More secondary waves are noticeable for $b = .01$, frame (c) of Figure 2. This pattern persists for a range extending to .005, where the more distant waves are less pronounced, until approximately $b = .02$. At $b = .025$, there is a sideband plus one secondary VLI effect, as in the figure for $b = .003$. By the time $b$ reaches the .1 level, the sideband is greatly diminished, until $b = 1.$, when there is very little VLI. In summary, receptive field shape is reasonably consistent, but the extent of VLI and the number of secondary waves varies considerably over the intensity range.

# 5 Conclusions

1. Implicit partial differentiation proved to be an effective technique for analyzing the receptive fields of the model.

2. Robustness of the Competitive Distribution model is a concern, and the limited range of parameters under which bifurcation do not occur appears to be a drawback. It is possible, however, that these The problem could be solved by considering alternative forms for the activation equation.

3. Another concern is with the biological plausibility. Traditional models based on lateral inhibition are at least partly supported by biological data, although the extensive use of inhibitory connections in such models, e.g., for cross-orientation inhibition in models of visual cortex, goes well beyond what has been confirmed biologically. In the case of the Competitive Distribution model, this possibly excessive use of inhibitory connections is avoided, but at the cost of building in the inhibitory effects through an allocative mechanism similar to that used in competitive learning. While allocational competition is prevalent in social and economic behavior, the means by which columnar groups of neurons might be constrained to compete for activation are very unclear. The interesting observations of (Crook et al., 1989, 1991) tend to support the presence of cross-orientation inhibition, but would not permit a choice between the two alternative hypothesis of direct lateral inhibition vs. the virtual lateral inhibition of the Competitive Distribution model. Further

---

[3] (McFadden, 1993) explores the sensitivity of receptive fields to variations in the other parameters.

work, both biological and theoretical, is required before the mechanisms of cortical inhibition can be better understood.

## References

Creutzfeldt, O. and Ito, M. 1968, Functional synaptic organization of primary visual cortex neurones in the cat. *Exp. Brain Res.*, **6**, 324-352.

Crook, J., Eysel, U., and Machemer, H. 1989, Cross-orientation inhibition contributes to the orientation selectivity of cells in cat striate cortex. In *Dynamics and Plasticity in Neuronal Systems*, N. Elsner and W. Singer, eds., p. 345. Georg Thime Verlag.

Crook, J., Eysel, U., and Machemer, H. 1991, Influence of GABA-induced remote inactivation of the orientation tuning of cells in area 18 of feline visual cortex: a comparison with area 17. *Neurosci.*, **40(1)**, 1-12.

Ferster, D. 1986, Orientation selectivity of synaptic potentials in neurons of cat primary visual cortex. *J. Neurosci.*, **6(5)**, 1284-1301.

Hawken, M. and Parker, A. 1987, Spatial properties of neurons in the monkey striate cortex. *Proc. Roy. Soc. London, B*, **231**, 251-288.

Heggelund, P. 1985, Receptive field organization of simple and complex cells. In *Models of the Visual Cortex*, D. Rose and V. Dobson, eds., pp. 358-365. NY: Wiley.

Jones, J., Stepnoski, A., and Palmer, L. 1987, The two-dimensional spectral structure of simple receptive fields in cat striate cortex. *J. Neurophys.*, **58**, No. 6, 1212-1232.

McFadden, F. 1993, *Competitive Learning and Competitive Activation in Cortical Map Formation*, Ph.D. thesis, University of Maryland, College Park.

Reggia, J., D'Autrechy, C., Sutton, G., and Weinrich, M. 1992, A competitive distribution theory of neocortical dynamics. *Neural Comp.*, **4**, 287-317.

Sillito, A. 1985, Functional considerations of the operation of GABAergic inhibitory processes in the visual cortex. In *Cerebral Cortex, Vol. 2*, A. Peters, and E. Jones, eds., pp. 91-117. NY, Plenum.

Ts'o, D. and Gilbert, C. 1988, The organization of chromatic and spatial interactions in the primate striate cortex. *J. Neurosci.*, **8**, 1712-1727.

Ts'o, D., Gilbert, C., and Wiesel, T. 1986, Relationships between horizontal interactions and functional architecture of cat striate cortex as revealed by cross-correlation analysis. *J. Neurosci.* **6(4)**, 1160-1170.

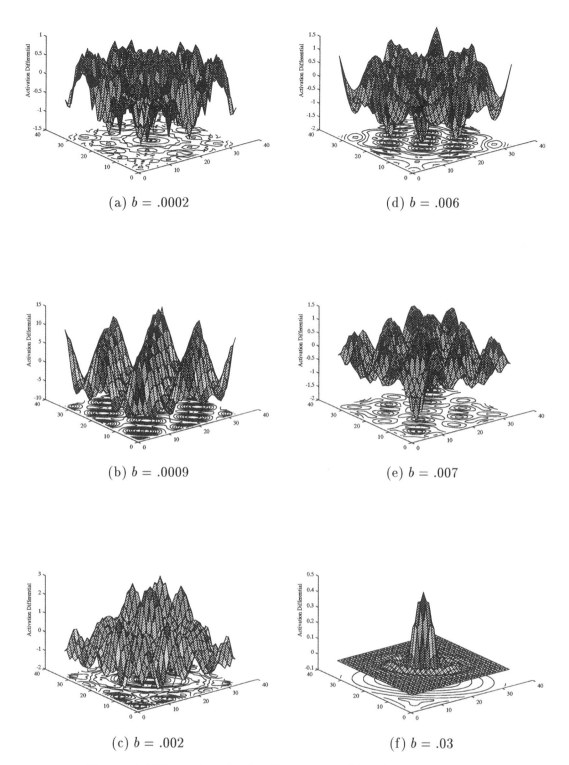

(a) $b = .0002$

(d) $b = .006$

(b) $b = .0009$

(e) $b = .007$

(c) $b = .002$

(f) $b = .03$

Figure 1: Bifurcations in the Competitive Distribution Model with $q = 0$

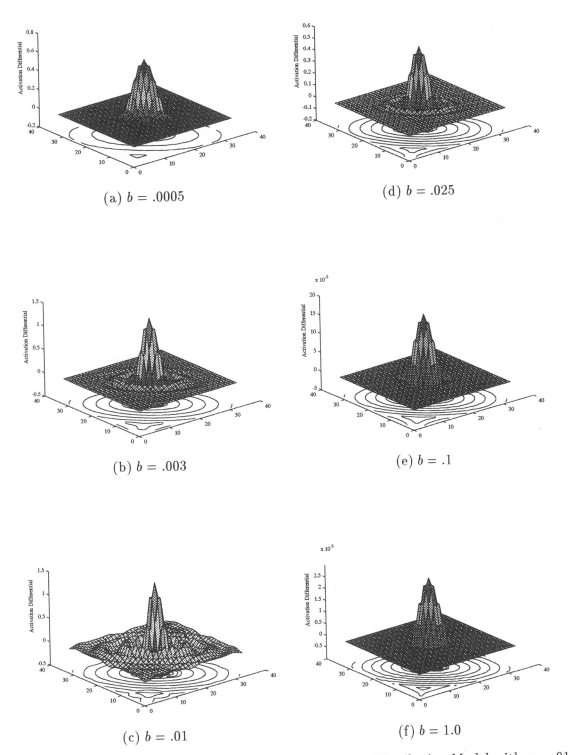

(a) $b = .0005$

(d) $b = .025$

(b) $b = .003$

(e) $b = .1$

(c) $b = .01$

(f) $b = 1.0$

Figure 2: Sideband Variation in the Competitive Distribution Model with $q = .01$

# Parallel processing in the visuomotor system of amphibians

Ursula Dicke and Gerhard Roth

Brain Research Institute, Center for Cognitive Sciences, University of Bremen
PO Box 330440, 28344 Bremen, Germany

## Abstract

The visual system of amphibians is widely believed to be organized according to the feature detector and command neuron concept. Based on behavioral experiments, we demonstrate instead that amphibians use multiple features (e.g., size, shape, velocity, movement pattern) for prey identification in an opportunistic manner. In addition, neurophysiological and neuroanatomical data give evidence that the amphibian visual and visuomotor system is composed of at least four different pathways for processing of visual information, one for figure-ground discrimination and depth perception; a second for perception of shape and color, a third for motion perception, and a fourth for detection of large objects and changes in general illumination. The latter three pathways extend from the retina to premotor and motor centers; interaction between the respective neurons in the tectum (as well as in premotor centers) is likely. Thus, the feature detector and command neuron concept does not apply to the visual system of amphibians.

Concepts of visual object recognition were long dominated by the idea of detector cells or "gnostic units". Such types of neuron were assumed to reside on top of a processing hierarchy and to be activated exclusively by a particular object (prey, face, grandmother) or object feature relevant for behavior (cf. Konorski, 1967). The activity of these neurons was seen as the internal representation of the object under consideration. Some authors believed that these detector or "gnostic" neurons, either singly or in combination with other such neurons, acted more or less directly onto the motor system. For invertebrates as well as "lower" vertebrates" (fishes, amphibians), these neurons were seen as "command neurons" or as members of a command neuron system (Kupfermann and Weiss, 1978).

During the last two decades, evidence has accumulated that the visual system of mammals contains largely separate anatomical and functional pathways for visual information processing. These regard object features such as shape, color and movement (Spillmann and Werner, 1990). Visual objects and processes are represented in the brain in a distributed manner, with local networks processing the different detailed aspects (orientation, disparity, color, form, contrast, movement, etc.) as well as the meaning of these entities. At the same time, the visual system of "lower" vertebrates (as well as invertebrates), particularly in the context of object recognition, is still widely believed to be organized according to the detector and command neuron concept, and this alleged difference to mammals usually is interpreted as reflecting stages in the evolution of the vertebrate visual system.

Barlow (1953) was the first to develop a detector concept in amphibians. He started from the assumption that in frogs "there is no indication of any form discrimination", and speculated that "'on-off' units [later called class-3 retinal ganglion cells] seem to possess the whole of the discriminatory mechanism needed to account for this rather simple behavior. The receptive field of an 'on-off' unit would be nicely filled by the image of a fly at 2 inches in distance and it is difficult to avoid the conclusion that the 'on-off' units are matched to this stimulus and act as 'fly detector'" (p. 86). In addition, 'off' units [class-4 RGC] seemed most suited for localization of prey. The conclusion was that "the retina is acting as a filter rejecting unwanted information and passing useful information" (p. 87).

Lettvin and co-workers (1959, 1960), on the basis of their study of *Rana pipiens*, extended this concept of "early" (i.e. retinal) object recognition. They arrived at a description of five "natural" classes of RGC, which transform the pointlike information of photoreceptors about the distribution of brightness into "meaningful" information about size, shape, illumination, contrast, movement and position. Most importantly, RGC identify properties of objects that are <u>constant</u> in a changing environment. According to the authors, a good deal of object recognition and prey-enemy discrimination already takes place in the retina (e.g. prey is identified by class-1 and class-2 RGC, and enemies are identified by class-3 RGC). This implies that activity of retinal ganglion cells already resembles behavior, and that these behavioral responses are primarily determined by one class or maximally two classes of RGC.

However, a few years later, Grüsser and Grüsser- Cornehls (1968) and Ewert and Hock (1972) showed that retinal ganglion cells are not sufficiently specific in their response patterns to reliably "identify" behaviorally relevant objects. As Grüsser and Grüsser-Cornehls stressed, a complete representation of prey or predator is constituted only at later stages in the visual centers. The authors conducted only preliminary investigations on central visual neurons describing qualitatively seven tectal response types T1 - T 7 (Grüsser and Grüsser-Cornehls, 1968, 1976).

J.P. Ewert was the first to develop more detailed ideas about prey and enemy recognition in amphibians, particularly in the toad *Bufo bufo* (Ewert 1989). According to Ewert, in the nervous system of a toad, prey objects are identified by a three-stage system of filters that preferentially respond to "wormlike" prey configuration; the more "wormlike" a stimulus, the higher the probability that a toad will orient to it and eventually snap at it. The first stage of the system is represented by two kinds of retinal ganglion cell (class 2/R2 and class 3/R3 cells), one type of pretectal neuron (TH 5 cells) and several types of tectal neuron (the T 5.1, T 5.2 and T 5.3 cells). Of these, T 5.2 cells play a particular role, because their response properties are said to resemble most closely the observed behavioral prey preferences. T 5.2 receives excitatory inputs from T 5.1 and is inhibited by T 5.3 and TH 5. In this context, Ewert (1989) adopted the Kupfermann and Weiss command neuron concept. However, for Ewert, T 5.2 cells are no command neurons in the strict sense, because the simultaneous and consecutive activity of a number of other types of tectal neuron are required for the occurrence of orienting, approach and snapping; rather, T 5.2 neurons are necessary members of this ensemble and are, accordingly, called <u>command elements</u>, which "tell" the nervous system: this object is a prey! Inside the tectum, T 5.2 neurons integrate the information about the nature of the prey and act as the only tectal output cell in the context of prey recognition (Fig. 1A).

Although Ewert and his co-workers concentrated their work on the toad *Bufo bufo*, it was always understood that these findings could be generally applied to neural guidance of feeding in amphibians. However, there is a substantial amount of data showing that this concept is applicable neither to the toad nor to any other frog or salamander.

First, it is evident from a priori reasoning that the detector concept can be applied only for cases, where the relevant stimulus has simple and highly invariant properties, e.g., when everything that is "wormlike" and moves <u>is</u> prey. A detector system breaks down, if prey objects have properties that can change. This is indeed the case for object features like size, shape, contrast, and velocity.

Second, there is <u>no</u> close correspondence between the behavioral preferences of the toad and the response of the T 5.2 neuron to wormlike objects. Compact stimuli are often as good as elongated ones in eliciting feeding. Also, T 5.2 cells cannot reliably "distinguish" between wormlike and compact or even "antiwormlike" (i.e., vertically oriented) prey, as clearly derives from Ewert's own data. Rather, the response properties of T 5.2 cells are highly equivocal with respect to a variety of object parameters. Third, T 5.2 cells (as all tectal visual cells) respond only to <u>angular</u> size, while the toad clearly reveals size constancy. Finally, some amphibians, while preferring wormlike prey, do not possess T 5.2-like neurons (cf. Roth, 1987), and the majority of amphibians does not prefer wormlike prey at all.

In order to determine how different visual features are used by amphibians for identification of prey, we conducted behavioral studies in a number of frog and salamander species (*Bombina bombina, Discoglossus pictus, Plethodon jordani, Bolitoglossa subpalmata, Hydromantes italicus*).

Among prey object parameters, <u>size</u> turned out to be the least specific; it can vary within a wide range without affecting the intensity of prey catching behavior. <u>Contrast</u> is likewise of low importance; the visual system of most amphibians is well suited for prey identification and localization at very low illumination and contrast levels. <u>Shape</u>, <u>contour</u> and <u>color</u> are used for object identification mostly at higher illumination levels (daylight), particularly for telling favorable from noxious or distasteful prey. Normally, <u>motion</u> is a necessary prerequisite of prey objects to elicit feeding, although amphibians can learn to feed on stationary prey. <u>Velocity</u> is important, because many amphibians have distinctly different velocity preferences. <u>Movement</u> <u>pattern</u> seems to be the most specific parameter for prey identification. Even under very dim light, most prey can be accurately recognized by the way they move. However, it requires a complex identification network which is at least partially based on learning.

The prey parameters mentioned have different significance and are used in different combinations depending on internal motivational state of the animal and the ambient condition. The more motivated a frog or salamander, the less specific a stimulus parameter need be: in a highly motivated amphibian, any moving object that is not too large will elicit prey catching. Furthermore, at higher illumination level, size and shape are important parameters, whereas at very dim light, velocity and movement pattern are the only cues for detection of prey. Thus, like the mammalian visual system, the amphibian visual system basically works in an <u>opportunistic</u> fashion. This alone refutes any simple detector concept.

In opposition to the detector concept, we proposed a network model for prey recognition (Roth, 1987). According to this model, the tectum contains numerous recognition "modules" consisting of a minimal set of neurons, each of which responds differently (although in an overlapping fashion) to the different features of a prey. For example, it comprises a number of neurons, each exhibiting a preference for edges of a particular orientation (similar to the orientation-specific "simple cells" in the mammalian primary cortex) and for a particular velocity range. Such a module may act as a universal "prey analyzer": any prey object will activate all (or nearly all) components of this network, due to the fact that the response properties of the components vastly overlap, but different objects will activate the module differently. Their <u>simultaneous</u> activity, then, encodes the prey object with regard to some relevant features.

At the same time, this module cannot act as a true "prey detector" network, because it is incapable of determining absolute size and, therefore, cannot reliably distinguish between a near prey and a distant predator of similar shape. This concept also does not imply, that the module has just one output line (i.e., the axon of an output cell) to the motor or premotor centers. So far, no neuron has been found in any amphibian tectum that encodes in its activity the <u>full</u> information about prey and, as a command neuron, sends this information to the premotor and motor centers. Rather, most tectal response types involved in prey recognition project to the premotor and motor region in a <u>parallel</u> fashion (Satou and Ewert, 1985). Thus, the idea has to be abandoned that, with respect to prey recognition, a "command neuron" or "command element" exists in the amphibian tectum and that the tectum is the site of "complete" object recognition.

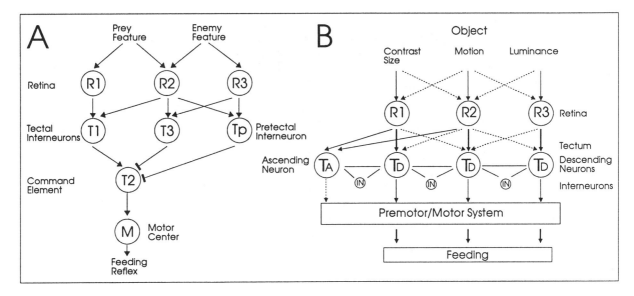

Fig. 1 A. The feature detector concept according to Ewert (1989). T1, T2, T3 and Tp correspond to T 5.1, T 5.2, T 5.3 and TH 5 in the text. B. Model for parallel processing in object recognition

In the following, we propose a model (Fig. 1B) for parallel processing in the visual and visuomotor system of amphibians. This model is based on the assumption that three basic classes of RGC exist in amphibians:

1. Small-field "edge-detector" cells responding either to moving or non-moving objects and requiring relatively high visual contrast. They are represented in frogs by class-1 and class-2 cells, in toads by R2 cells and by layer-1 cells in salamanders. They exhibit low conduction velocity. They may include several subclasses differing in color sensitivity and response to light ON/OFF. These cells are comparable to X-cells in cats and to P-cells in primates.

2. Medium field "movement-detector" or "ON-OFF" cells, which respond to small changes in contrast and small dislocations of edges. They are represented by class-3 RGC in frogs, R3 cells in toads and layer-2 cells in salamanders. They do not respond to non-moving objects and exhibit high conduction velocity. They correspond to Y-cells in cats and M cells in primates.

3. Large-field, "dimming-detector", "OFF"-cells. They respond best to large objects and to changes in illumination in large parts of the visual field. These cells are represented by class-4 and R4 cells in frogs and toads, respectively, and layer-3 cells in salamanders. They show high conduction velocity. They may be involved in predator detection, optomotor behavior or detection of changes in overall illumination. They may correspond to the diverse class of W cells in cats and P-gamma cells in primates.

The axons of RGC terminate in different layers within the optic tectum, where they make contact with tectal cells, with fibers from small-field RGC contained in the most superficial layer, followed by those from medium- and large-field RGC. Below these layers of retinal afferents and directly above the periventricular cellular layers, a layer containing afferent fibers from other parts of the brain and efferent tectal fibers is situated.

In order to further clarify the question, how tectal visual information is transferred to premotor and motor centers, we conducted combined intracellular electrophysiological and neuroanatomical experiments in a number of salamander species, and our findings are highly consistent with those obtained in frogs (Lázár et al., 1983).

The tectum of all amphibians studied so far contains four major types of neuron distinguished by their morphology. The first type is represented by small pear-shaped cells. These cells have small dendritic trees, which arborize predominantly in layer 1 or in layer 1 and 2. Most cells either have no axon or project to the nucleus isthmi, the prectectum or thalamus. Very few project to premotor or motor centers.

The other types are characterized by axons <u>descending</u> to premotor and motor centers, although some of them possess <u>ascending</u> axon collaterals to diencephalic and telencephalic centers as well. One type has a candelabre-shaped dendritic tree that strongly arborizes in the superficial layer of fibers originating from small-field RGC, and its axon descends to the <u>contralateral</u> medulla oblongata and cervical spinal cord in a medial position. Another type has a wide dendritic tree arborizing within the intermediate layer of fibers arising from medium-field RGC; its axon descends <u>ipsilaterally</u> in a <u>lateral</u> position. The last type of efferent tectal cell has very flat dendritic trees that arborize in the deepest tectal fiber layer containing nonretinal afferent and efferent fibers, with some dendrites extending into the deepest layer of retinal afferents originating from large-field RGC; the axon descends <u>ipsilaterally</u> in a <u>medial</u> position. One type of descending tectal neuron constitutes the crossed tecto-bulbo-spinal pathway, and the other two types the uncrossed pathways (Fig. 2). These three pathways are separated down to spinal levels and make separate contacts with neurons from the reticular formation or even directly with motor neurons involved in prey capture (Dicke, in preparation).

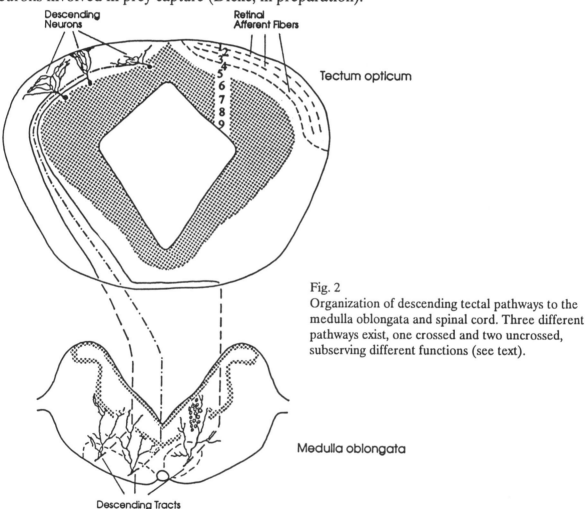

Fig. 2
Organization of descending tectal pathways to the medulla oblongata and spinal cord. Three different pathways exist, one crossed and two uncrossed, subserving different functions (see text).

We interpret our data in the following way. Tectal cells with axons projecting to the nucleus isthmi and diencephalic (pretectal and thalamic) centers are involved in figure-ground discriminiation and depth perception. Tectal cells with axons descending within the crossed tract receive small-field retinal afferents and are, therefore, involved in the shape/color pathway; tectal cells with axons descending within the lateral uncrossed tract receive medium-field RGC and are involved in the motion pathway; and tectal cells with axons descending in the medial uncrossed tract receive large-field RGC afferents and are involved in the detection of large objects and the perception of ambient illumination.

At present, our knowledge about the interaction between the efferent tectal neurons inside the tectum is still scarce. Intracellular recordings from these cells indicate multisynaptic processing of retinal afferent information as well as modulation by nonretinal visual and nonvisual (i.e., auditory, somatosensory) input to the tectum.

In conclusion, there is no fundamental difference in the functional organization of the visual system between amphibians and mammals. While it is simple at a gross anatomical level, the visual system of amphibians evidently is not organized according to the feature detector and command neuron concept. Like that of mammals, it contains largely separate pathways for processing different object features. Surprisingly, these separate pathways do not or not substantially converge inside the tectum as the main visual center, but extend through premotor and motor centers. This latter has not been verified in the mammalian visuomotor system, but we predict its existence even there.

Literature

Barlow, H.B. Summation and inhibition in the frog's retina. J. Physiol. (London) 119: 69-88 (1953).

Ewert, J.-P.: The release of visual behavior in toads: stages of parallel/hierarchical information processing. In: J.-P. Ewert and M. A. Arbib (eds.): Visuomotor Coordination, Amphibians, Comparisons, Models, and Robots. Plenum Press, New York-London, pp. 39-120 (1989).

Ewert, J.-P. and F.J. Hock: Movement-sensitive neurones in the toad's retina. Exp. Brain Res. 16: 41-59 (1972).

Grüsser, J. and U. Grüsser-Cornehls: Neurophysiologische Grundlagen visueller angeborener Auslöse-mechanismen beim Frosch. Z. vergl. Physiol. 59: 1-24 (1968).

Grüsser, J. and U. Grüsser-Cornehls: Neurophysiology of the anuran visual system. In: R. Llinás and W. Precht (eds.): Frog Neurobiology. Springer, Berlin, pp. 297-385 (1976).

Konorski, J.: Integrative Activity of the Brain. Univ. of Chicago Press, Chicago (1967).

Kupfermann, I., and K.R. Weiss. The command neuron concept. Behav. Brain Sci. 1: 3-39 (1978).

Lázár, G., P. Toth, E. Csank and E. Kicliter: Morphology and location of tectal projection neurons in frogs: a study with HRP and cobalt filling. J. Comp. Neurol. 215: 108-120 (1983).

Lettvin, J.Y., H.R. Maturana, W.S. McCulloch and W.H. Pitts: What the frog's eye tells the frog's brain. Proc. Inst. Radio Eng. NY 47: 1940-1951 (1959).

Maturana, H. R., J.Y. Lettvin, W.S. McCulloch and W.H. Pitts: Anatomy and physiology of vision in the frog (Rana pipiens). J. Gen. Physiol. (Suppl. 2) 43: 129-175 (1960).

Roth, G.: Visual Behavior in Salamanders. Springer, Berlin-Heidelberg-New York (1987).

Satou, N. and J.-P. Ewert: The antidromic activation of tectal neurons by electrical stimuli applied to the caudal medulla oblongata in the toad Bufo bufo L. J. Comp. Physiol. 157: 739-748 (1985)

Spillmann, L. and J.S. Werner: Visual Perception. The Neurophysiological Foundations. Academic Press, San Diego (1990).

# Circuits & System Neuroscience

**Session Chairs: Judith Dayhoff**
**Christof Koch**

**ORAL PRESENTATIONS**

# TEMPORAL ANALYSIS FOR NEUROBIOLOGICAL SIGNAL PROCESSING

Judith Dayhoff
Institute for Systems Research
University of Maryland
College Park, MD 20742

## Abstract

Neurobiological signal processing includes rich complexity not found in traditional artificial neural networks. Neurons are continuous-time signal processing and signal generation devices, with particular interconnection topologies and with computational properties subserved by protein-molecular structures and dynamics. Neurons communicate by nerve impulse trains in which timing of impulses is vitally important to their information-carrying capabilities. Here we examine the possibility that the frequency of near-synchronous firing of neural ensembles could be used to represent and encode information. Synchronous activity of neural ensembles provides a putative code for sensory and motor activity as well as a representational mode for feature detection. With synchrony codes, an assembly of $n$ neurons can encode many more than $n$ signals simultaneously. Synchrony frequencies at signal and background levels depend on the firing properties of the synchronous ensemble and the number of neurons that participate in the synchrony. An in-depth analysis of these relationships requires the use of probability calculations as well as pairwise correlations combined with techniques that detect synchronies in more than two neurons at the same time. Current recording technology is dramatically improving to allow capability of collecting action potential activity from assemblies of neurons, to enable the search for ensemble codes in simultaneously active neurons.

# 1 INTRODUCTION

Signals between neurons consist of action potentials, which do not vary in amplitude or duration, so must convey information solely by the placement of the impulses over time. Information can be represented and encoded in such pulsed signals, by alternative pulsed coding schemes, including firing rate codes, interval / pattern codes, and ensemble synchrony codes. In a rate coding scheme, different firing rates represent different information about stimuli or output patterns. Firing rates are the simplest scheme, but take time to be interpreted and have low capacity for distinctions between different levels of firing rate. Interval / pattern codes consist of two or more pulses spaced by particular timing intervals, and allow for large numbers of coded words. Patterns can be comprised of segments of multiunit or single unit impulse trains, but require special post-processing circuits. Ensemble synchrony codes, in which multiple units fire in near-synchrony, can allow $n$ units to carry more than $2^{n/2}$ signals. Special circuits are not required to detect synchronies.

# 2   ENSEMBLE CODES

Neurons are natural detectors of synchronies, because of their post-synaptic processes, membrane potentials, and connection configurations. The post-synaptic potential that results from an excitatory action potential has a peak that appears shortly after the arrival of the action potential at a pre-synaptic site. As a result, the near-synchronous arrival of two or more impulses causes a high rise in post-synaptic potential. Since the target neuron fires at threshold, the most effective way to reach threshold is the near-synchronous arrival of multiple action potentials. The target neuron is then a synchrony-detector, responding by firing to an above-threshold rise in post-synaptic potential.

Stimuli have many features to encode, including the nature and presence of the stimulus, its modality, and its properties. An ensemble synchrony scheme allows a set of n neurons to encode many signals and features simultaneously. Each unit has a firing rate, which can be used as a rate code ($f_A$, $f_B$, ... ). Synchronies can occur between pairs, triples, or groups of $k$ units at any time in the impulse trains. Let $f_{AB}$ be the rate of coincidental firing between units A and B, let $f_{ABC}$ be the rate of near-synchronous firing between units A, B, and C, and in general let $f_S$ be the rate of synchronous firing of set $S$ of units. Each of these rates can be used to represent a different feature of a stimuli, or the presence and properties of different stimuli. Motor signals, too, could be simultaneously represented in this fashion.

The capacity of a synchrony code depends on the number of possible groups of neurons that could be engaged in synchronous activity. The number of possible subsets of $n$ neurons is $2^n$, including individual units and the empty set. Thus there are $2^n - n - 1$ groups of 2 or more units plus $n$ individual firing rates. So, the value of $f_S$ can be used for $2^n - 1$ possible sets $S$. However, some sets are included within other sets, which could allow for confusion. The number of sets that are available without confusion by such set inclusions is at least $2^{n/2}$.

Synchronies from one group can take place at different times from the synchronies of another group. Furthermore, the same neuron could participate in more than one synchrony during the same time interval. However, that neuron's action potentials would at some times by in near-synchrony with one group, and at other times be in near-synchrony with other groups.

As an example, suppose there are five neurons simultaneously recorded (neurons

$A, B, C, D$, and $E$. Suppose also that a synchrony code is to be used to encode these stimulus features from the visual field: (1) presence of a circle (2) color red on the circle (3) presence of a square, (4) color green of the square, (5) presence of a triangle, (6) color yellow of the triangle, and (7) background color purple. Suppose next that the following frequencies represent each of those features, respectively: $f_A$, $f_D$, $f_{ABD}$, $f_{AC}$, $f_{AE}$, $f_{BC}$, and $f_{CE}$. The individual unit rates $f_A$ and $f_D$ would be considerably higher than the pairwise or 3-way synchrony rates, and hence could easily be modulated by themselves, to represent the strength of features (1) and (2). The other rates involve subsets that are not themselves subsets of each other, and hence each subset would make a distinct synchrony and could be modulated alone to represent the corresponding feature.

Detection of synchronies in simultaneously recorded data depends on the frequency of occurrence of the synchronous events. Pair-wise synchronies can be detected by the cross-correlation method, in which a peak is observed when a synchrony is present. This peak shows the presence of pair-wise synchronous behavior that is more frequent than the background frequency observed at delays. Thus pairwise synchronies are identified when their frequency of occurrence exceeds that expected at random.

Significant synchronies from groups of more than two neurons could fail to appear in a cross-correlogram. For a synchrony of $k$ neurons to occur more than expected at random, only a small number of occurrences may be required, especially for larger values of $k$. This small number of occurrences may be lost in the noise of a pairwise cross-correlogram.

For example, suppose there is a multiunit recording of five neurons over a period of five seconds. After dividing this recording into 1000 time windows, the probability of a single cell firing per window is found to be 0.3. Then the probability of two cells firing at once is 0.09, and all five cells is 0.00024. Using the binomial distribution to calculate the probability of finding each number of occurrences of pairwise and 5-way synchronies, we find that at random, the number of pairwise occurrences varies from 72 to 109, whereas the number of 5-way synchronous events varies from 0 to7. Thus the pairwise range is 37 whereas the 5-way range is 7. When 5-way synchronies are excessive ($> 7$), they could be lost in the noise if the analysis were limited to pairwise correlations.

A gravitational clustering method has been developed to detect synchronous groups from multiunit recorded data, and used to identify synchronous group activity in biological recordings from the brainstem [2-6]. This method represents neurons as points on a screen, and moves them towards one another when simultaneous activity occurs. Neurons that tend to fire in synchrony then appear as clusters. Neurons may move apart when synchronies stop and new synchronies begin. Although the original algorithm was time-consuming, a recent improvement has considerably reduced computation time [1].

# 3  DISCUSSION

Biological synapses have a natural means for detecting synchronies. Near-synchronous firing from incoming lines produces rapid excitation to threshold. Thus, no special circuitry is required to interpret an encoding scheme based on ensemble synchronies. Furthermore, the synchrony detection can happen quickly after the synchronous instance, and does not have to wait until a firing rate is averaged or computed over time. Information representation as well as network processing via synchrony codes appears feasible in models of neural networks, and the capacity of multiple impulse trains to carry synchrony codes is higher than firing rate codes.

# 4   REFERENCES

1. J. E. Dayhoff, 1994. Synchrony detection in neural assemblies. To appear, Biological Cybernetics.

2. G. L. Gerstein and A. M. H. J. Aertsen (1985) Representation of cooperative firing activity among simultaneously recorded neurons. J. Neurophys. 54 (6): 1513-1528.

3. G. L. Gerstein, D. H. Perkel and J. E. Dayhoff (1984) Cooperative firing activity in simultaneously recorded populations of neurons: Detection and measurement. J. Neuroscience 5 (4): 881-889.

4. B. G. Lindsey, Y. M. Hernandez, K. F. Morris, R. Shannon, and G. L. Gerstein (1992) Respiratory-related neural assemblies in the brain step midline. J. Neurophys. 67 (4): 905-922.

5. B. G. Lindsey, Y. M. Hernandez, K. F. Morris, R. Shannon, and G. L. Gerstein (1992) Dynamic reconfiguration of brain step neural assemblies: respiratory phase-dependent synchrony versus modulation of firing rates. J. Neurophys. 67 (4): 923-930.

6. B. G. Lindsey, R. Shannon, and G. L. Gerstein (1989) Gravitational representation of simultaneously recorded brainstem respiratory neuron spike trains. Brain Research 483: 373-378.

# 5   ACKNOWLEDGEMENTS

The author would like to gratefully acknowledge Dr. Margaret Mortz for contributing to identification of the potential and importance of this research topic. This work was funded by the Army Strategic Defense Command (SBIR DASG 60-89-C-0118), the Systems Research Center of the University of Maryland, the National Science Foundation (NSF BIR 9309169 and NSFD CD 8803012), and the Naval Research Laboratory (N00014-93-K-2019).

# Temporal Analysis of Spike Patterns in Monkeys and Artificial neural Networks.

Christof Koch

Professor of Computation and Neural Systems

California Institute of Technology

The findings regarding the existence and the relevance of oscillations in the neuronal responses of neurons in cat visual cortex in the 30 to 70 Hz region has lead to a general theoretical and experimental re-examination of the detailed temporal discharge patterns of neurons. To what extent can these ``40 Hz" oscillations be seen in cells in the awake and behaving monkey? What about temporal synchronization among cortical cells? How reproducible are the detailed temporal discharge patterns in cortical cells? How noisy and variable are individual cells? What about 1/f-like patterns? To what extent can fractal behavior be observed in the spike discharge patterns of individual neurons and over what time scales? We will review some answers to these questions, in particular by evaluating neuronal discharges from cortical cells in the monkey as well as from simple integrate-and-fire neural networks models.

# Neural Networks for Learning Space Trajectories Based on the Quasi-Newton Method

Oscal T.-C. Chen,  Bing J. Sheu

Department of Electrical Engineering
Center for Neural Engineering
University of Southern California, Los Angeles, CA 90089-0271

**Abstract -- A three-layered feedforward network using the quasi-Newton method can successfully learn a circle. After the training process, the network is connected into a recurrent network. Any point of the circular trajectory can be used as the starting point. According to computer simulation, the whole circular trajectory can be reconstructed by the recurrent network with a mean-squared error of 0.000261 at a starting point (0.5, 1.0). With different starting points which can be inside or outside of the circular trajectory, the trained network also generates a circular trajectory. It indicates that the recurrent network has very good curvature attraction. In another example, one half of symbol eight trajectory can also be reconstructed by this network configuration. The proposed learning procedure for a feedforward network without the time-delay elements can be suitable for learning trajectories without crossovers.**

## I. Introduction

Recurrent neural networks [1,2] and time-delay neural networks [3-5] have been used to learn the space trajectories such as circular and symbol-eight trajectories. In the biological study, recurrent networks are very commonly found in the brain. The recurrent neural networks are capable of holding memories in the network loops. The learning methods [1,2,6] for recurrent networks are required to integrate the information in the previous iterative stages. This learning operation is more complicated than that of feedforward network.

Time-delay feedforward networks have been successfully applied to speech recognition [7,8]. Based on the back-propagation learning method, the adaptive time-delay neural network in the continuous-time mode has been reported in [9]. To learn spatiotemporal topology by using adaptive time-delay neural networks was proposed by Dayhoff et al. [3-5]. They used a gradient decent method for training a feedforward network on the discrete-time mode. The training strategy is to map the current input data to the next incoming data. After the training process, the network is connected into a recurrent network so that the number of input neurons are the same as that of the output neurons. Before a trajectory is reconstructed from a time-delay neural network, a segment of the seed data are required to fill in the delay buffers. According to their simulation results [3], a quarter of a complete circle was used as the network input in order to generate the complete circle. Possible applications of time-delay neural networks include time-series analysis and prediction.

This paper describes multilayer feed-forward networks for learning space trajectories by using the quasi-Newton method. The network without any feedback connection is used to learn the mapping from the input vector to the next incoming vector. After the training process, the network is connected into a recurrent network and only one starting point is provided to reconstruct the complete trajectory. The most common feed-forward networks are static, having no internal delays and responding to a particular input by immediately generating a specific output. This type of networks is suitable for learning trajectories without crossovers. One limitation of static networks is their inability to respond to temporal patterns in the hidden node outputs. To respond to these patterns, the network must have delay elements within its layers.

## II. Quasi-Newton Method

The learning process of a feedforward network, in which the network connection strengths are modified so that the response of the network progressively approximates the desired response, can be structured as a nonlinear optimization problem. The network performance is improved by minimizing the cost function,

$$E(\mathbf{W}) = \frac{1}{2} \sum_{i=1}^{N} (\mathbf{d_i} - \mathbf{y_i})^2, \tag{1}$$

where $\mathbf{W}$ is a synaptic weight matrix, N is the total number of input vectors, $\mathbf{d_i}$ and $\mathbf{y_i}$ are the desired and actual output vector, respectively, corresponding to the $i^{th}$ input vector $\mathbf{x_i}$. By using the truncated Taylor series expansion, $E(\mathbf{W})$ around $\mathbf{W}^{(k)}$ can be described as

$$E(\mathbf{W}^{(k)} + \boldsymbol{\delta}) \approx q^{(k)}(\boldsymbol{\delta}) = E(\mathbf{W}^{(k)}) + \mathbf{g}^{(k)^T}\boldsymbol{\delta} + \frac{1}{2}\boldsymbol{\delta}^T\mathbf{G}^{(k)}\boldsymbol{\delta}, \tag{2}$$

where $\mathbf{g}$ is the first derivative term of $E(\mathbf{W})$, $\mathbf{G}$ is the second derivative term of $E(\mathbf{W})$, $\boldsymbol{\delta}$ is equal to $\mathbf{W} - \mathbf{W}^{(k)}$, and $q^{(k)}(\boldsymbol{\delta})$ is the resulting quadratic approximation at the $k^{th}$ iteration. The $\mathbf{W}^{(k+1)}$ in Newton's method is simply $\mathbf{W}^{(k)} + \boldsymbol{\delta}^{(k)}$, where the correction $\boldsymbol{\delta}^{(k)}$ is used to minimize the value of $q^{(k)}(\boldsymbol{\delta})$. The method requires zero, first and second derivatives of E to be available at any point. The $k^{th}$ iteration of Newton's method can be performed in the following procedures,

(a) solve $\mathbf{G}^{(k)}\boldsymbol{\delta} = -\mathbf{g}^{(k)}$ for $\boldsymbol{\delta} = \boldsymbol{\delta}^{(k)}$, and $\qquad\qquad$ (3)

(b) set $\mathbf{W}^{(k+1)} = \mathbf{W}^{(k)} + \boldsymbol{\delta}^{(k)}$.

The second derivative of the cost function with respect to the synaptic weights provides information about the curvature of the error surface. By using the first and second derivative information, the network can be trained to reach the minimum of the cost function. Since the computation complexity of the second derivative is very high, the quasi-Newton method can be applied by using an iterative approximation scheme for the inverse second derivative term. This approach avoids the direct computation of second derivative, and computational complexity is reduced by a factor of O(N) [10]. The basic quasi-Newton algorithm consists of the following steps:

(a) set a search direction $\mathbf{s}^{(k)} = -\mathbf{H}^{(k)} \cdot \mathbf{g}^{(k)}$,

(b) let $\mathbf{W}^{(k+1)} = \mathbf{W}^{(k)} + \eta\mathbf{s}^{(k)}$, and $\qquad\qquad$ (4)

(c) update $\mathbf{H}^{(k)}$ to $\mathbf{H}^{(k+1)}$,

where $\mathbf{H}$ is the approximate inverse second derivative matrix, $\mathbf{s}$ contains weight-change information, $\eta$ is the learning rate constant, and k is the iteration index. The key feature of the algorithm is the updating strategy for the approximate inverse second derivative matrix. The Broyden, Fletcher, Goldfarb and Shanno (BFGS) technique [10] can be applied,

$$\mathbf{H}^{(k+1)} = \mathbf{H}^{(k)} + (1 + \frac{\boldsymbol{\gamma}^{(k)^T}\mathbf{H}^{(k)}\boldsymbol{\gamma}^{(k)}}{\boldsymbol{\delta}^{(k)^T}\boldsymbol{\gamma}^{(k)}})\frac{\boldsymbol{\delta}^{(k)}\boldsymbol{\delta}^{(k)^T}}{\boldsymbol{\delta}^{(k)^T}\boldsymbol{\gamma}^{(k)}} - \frac{\boldsymbol{\delta}^{(k)}\boldsymbol{\gamma}^{(k)^T}\mathbf{H}^{(k)} + \mathbf{H}^{(k)}\boldsymbol{\gamma}^{(k)}\boldsymbol{\delta}^{(k)^T}}{\boldsymbol{\delta}^{(k)^T}\boldsymbol{\gamma}^{(k)}},$$

$$\boldsymbol{\gamma}^{(k)} = \mathbf{g}^{(k+1)} - \mathbf{g}^{(k)}, \text{ and} \tag{5}$$

$$\boldsymbol{\delta}^{(k)} = \eta\mathbf{s}^{(k)} = \mathbf{W}^{(k+1)} - \mathbf{W}^{(k)}.$$

The initial matrix $\mathbf{H}^{(0)}$ is usually selected to be an unity matrix. In the quasi-Newton method, the BFGS formula is suitable because it can provide a better performance than the other formulas such as the rank-one formula and DFP formula [10].

### III. Computer Analysis Results

A three-layered feedforward network for learning circular trajectory was configured with 2 input units, 6 hidden units, and 2 output units. Figure 1 shows the schematic diagram of the neural network. The hidden and output neurons have the transfer function,

$$F(S) = \frac{1}{1 + e^{-S}},\tag{6}$$

where S is the summed value of synaptic signals and bias signal for each neuron. The original circular trajectory is sampled at 128 reference points which become the training data. These points can be defined as

$$a(n) = \frac{1}{2}\left(\sin(\frac{\pi}{64}n) + 1\right), \text{ and}\tag{7}$$

$$b(n) = \frac{1}{2}\left(\cos(\frac{\pi}{64}n) + 1\right), \text{ for } 0 \le n \le 127.$$

The quasi-Newton method based on the BFGS scheme is used for the feedforward network learning. If the input vector is (a[n], b[n]), then the desired output vector is (a[n+1], b[n+1]). The network learning is performed by optimizing Eq. (1). If an initial synaptic weight matrix is selected, the cost function E will be updated based on the information of its first and second derivatives. After 15,000 iterations, a mean-squared error of 0.000010 can be achieved. Table 1 lists the initial values of the synaptic weights and the values after the training process. This trained network is connected into a recurrent network. Only one initial input vector is required to be the network input. Figure 2 shows the plots of the desired and reconstructed trajectories with the starting point (0.5, 1.0). The mean-squared error is increased to 0.000261 because the distortion is accumulated in the reconstruction process of the recurrent network. Any point of the desired circular trajectory can serve as a network input datum. Figure 3 shows the reconstruction performance versus the different input data. The worst case is the mean-squared error of 0.000859, and the plot of its reconstructed circle is shown in Fig. 4. This reconstructed circle is still very similar to the desired circular trajectory. Figures 5 shows the plots of two reconstructed trajectories for the input vectors, (1.0, 1.0) and (0.5, 0.5), which are not on the desired circle. It indicates that the recurrent network memorizes the topology of a circular trajectory and is not sensitive to the noise added to the input signals.

One half of the symbol eight trajectory is used for the network learning. The same three-layered feedforward network shown in Fig. 1 is used. The original trajectory is sampled at 64 reference points which can be defined as

$$a(n) = \frac{1}{2}\left(\sin(\frac{\pi}{32}n) + 1\right), \text{ and}\tag{8}$$

$$b(n) = \frac{1}{2}\left(\sin(\frac{\pi}{64}n) + 1\right), \text{ for } 0 \le n \le 63.$$

The network was trained by using the quasi-Newton method. The initial and final values of the synaptic weights are listed in Table 1. The mean-squared error between the original and reconstructed trajectories is 0.000038 at the 10,000 iterations for the feedforward network. After the training process, the network is connected into a recurrent network. Figure 6 shows the plots of the reconstructed and desired trajectories for the initial input vector (0.5, 0.5). The mean-squared error is increased to 0.000501. Figure 7 shows the plots of two reconstructed trajectories for the input vectors, (1.0, 0.5) and (0.5, 0.75), which are not on the desired trajectory. In such a case, a very good reconstruction performance can also be achieved.

A three-layered feedforward network for learning a symbol eight trajectory was configured with 2 input units, 12 hidden units, and 2 output units. After 20,000 iterations, the mean-squared error between the original and reconstructed trajectories is 0.000059 for the feedforward network. If the trained network is connected to a recurrent network, the mean-squared error is increased to be 0.275 for the input vector (0.5, 0.5). Figure 8 shows the plots of the desired and reconstructed trajectories. In the intersection point (0.5, 0.5) of the symbol-eight trajectory, there are four possible moving directions. Here, the recurrent network only remembers one direction in the intersection point so that one half of symbol eight trajectory is reconstructed. In order to determine the correct direction, the network is required to keep the information of the previous curvature positions as in the time-delay neural networks. Our future studies will include the use of the quasi-Newton method in the time-delay neural networks.

## IV. Conclusion

A three-layered feedforward network without the time-delay elements by using the quasi-Newton method can successfully learn space trajectories without crossovers, such as a circle. Only one input vector is required for the trajectory reconstruction. One half of symbol-eight trajectory can also be reconstructed through its recurrent network. According to the computer simulation, the trained recurrent network has very good curvature attraction for the different initial input vectors.

## V. Acknowledgment

Valuable discussions, guidance, and support from Dr. Robert Hecht-Nielsen and Dr. Geoffrey J. Hueter of HNC Inc. are highly appreciated.

## Reference

[1]   F. J. Pineda, "Generalization of back-propagation to recurrent neural networks," *Physical Review Letters,* vol. 59, no. 19, pp. 2229-2232, Nov. 1987.

[2]   B. A. Pearlmutter, "Learning state space trajectories in recurrent neural networks," *Proc. of IEEE Inter. Joint Conf. on Neural Networks,* vol. 2, pp. 365-372, Washington, 1989.

[3]   D.-T. Lin, J. E. Dayhoff, P. A. Ligomenides, "Learning with the adaptive time-delay neural network," *Technical Report,* Systems Research Center, University of Maryland, College Park, Aug. 20, 1993.

[4]   D.-T. Lin, P. A. Ligomenides, J. E. Dayhoff, "Learning spatiotemporal topology using an adaptive time-delay neural network," *Proc. of World Congress on Neural Networks,* vol. 1, pp. 291-294, Portland, July 1993.

[5]   D.-T. Lin, J. E. Dayhoff, P. A. Ligomenides, "Trajectory recognition with a time-delay neural network," *Proc. of IEEE Inter. Joint Conf. on Neural Networks,* vol. 3, pp. 197-202, Baltimore, 1992.

[6]   K. Doya, S. Yoshizawa, "Adaptive neural oscillator using continuous-time back-propagation learning," *Neural Networks,* vol. 2, pp. 375-385, 1989.

[7]   A. Waibel, T. Hanazawa, G. Hinton, K. Shikano, K. Lang, "Phoneme recognition: neural networks versus hidden markov models," *Proc. of IEEE Inter. Conf. Acoustics, Speech, and Signal Processing,* vol. 1, pp. 107-110, April 1988.

[8]   A. Waibel, T. Hanazawa, G. Hinton, K. Shikano, K. Lang, "Phoneme recognition using time-delay neural networks," *IEEE Trans. on Acoustics, Speech, and Signal Processing,* vol. 37, no. 3, pp. 328-339, March 1989.

[9]   S. P. Day, M. R. Davenport, "Continuous-time temporal back-propagation with adaptive time delays," *IEEE Transactions on Neural Networks,* vol. 4, no. 2, pp. 348-354, March 1993.

[10]  R. Fletcher, *Practical Methods of Optimization* John Wiley & Sons: New York, 1991.

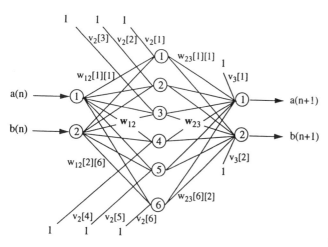

Fig. 1 A three-layered feedforward network.

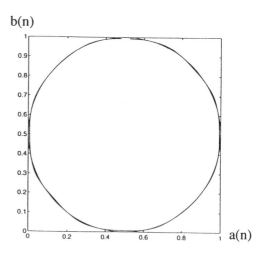

Fig. 2 Desired circle and reconstructed circle at the initial vector (0.5, 1.0).

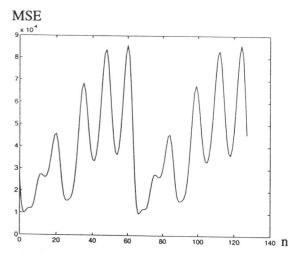

Fig. 3 Reconstruction performance versus the different initial inupt vectors.

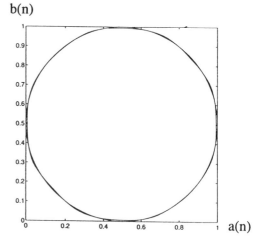

Fig. 4 Desired circle and reconstructed circle at the initial vector (0.4025, 0.9904).

Table 1 Initial and final values of synaptic weights in the network learning process.

| Parameters \ Trajectories | Circle | | Half of Symbol Eight | |
|---|---|---|---|---|
| | Initial values | Values after learning | Initial values | Values after learning |
| $w_{12}[1][1]$ | 0 | 0.544248 | 0.01 | 108.705109 |
| $w_{12}[1][2]$ | -0.1 | -1.137178 | 0.11 | 13.532946 |
| $w_{12}[1][3]$ | -0.2 | 0.297521 | 0.21 | 13.730892 |
| $w_{12}[1][4]$ | -0.3 | -13.857540 | 0.31 | 9.937679 |
| $w_{12}[1][5]$ | -0.4 | -7.225531 | 0.41 | -7.202008 |
| $w_{12}[1][6]$ | -0.5 | -8.704819 | 0.51 | -3.682197 |
| $w_{12}[2][1]$ | 0.1 | 7.402815 | 0.11 | -225.270814 |
| $w_{12}[2][2]$ | 0 | -8.803381 | 0.21 | 1.006211 |
| $w_{12}[2][3]$ | -0.1 | 0.325854 | 0.31 | 1.107231 |
| $w_{12}[2][4]$ | -0.2 | -21.140343 | 0.41 | -3.340440 |
| $w_{12}[2][5]$ | -0.3 | -1.231747 | 0.51 | 8.306527 |
| $w_{12}[2][6]$ | -0.4 | -2.036010 | 0.61 | -5.938786 |
| $v_2[1]$ | 0.6 | -3.973548 | 0.06 | 233.852427 |
| $v_2[2]$ | 0.5 | 4.970312 | 0.05 | -11.980174 |
| $v_2[3]$ | 0.4 | -0.311386 | 0.04 | -12.202378 |
| $v_2[4]$ | 0.3 | 86.556376 | 0.03 | -7.210039 |
| $v_2[5]$ | 0.2 | 4.228620 | 0.02 | 4.803599 |
| $v_2[6]$ | 0.1 | 5.370400 | 0.01 | 6.025146 |
| $w_{23}[1][1]$ | 0 | -50.949602 | 0 | -50.667400 |
| $w_{23}[1][2]$ | 0.1 | -0.556510 | -0.2 | 71.708155 |
| $w_{23}[2][1]$ | 0.1 | -43.244068 | 0.2 | -24.470570 |
| $w_{23}[2][2]$ | 0.2 | 0.808666 | 0 | -409.162616 |
| $w_{23}[3][1]$ | 0.2 | 86.445135 | 0.4 | 24.583345 |
| $w_{23}[3][2]$ | 0.3 | 86.806539 | 0.2 | 403.962532 |
| $w_{23}[4][1]$ | 0.3 | -19.116559 | 0.6 | 7.168182 |
| $w_{23}[4][2]$ | 0.4 | -17.499458 | 0.4 | 1.288556 |
| $w_{23}[5][1]$ | 0.4 | 0.620213 | 0.8 | 4.386206 |
| $w_{23}[5][2]$ | 0.5 | 46.727134 | 0.6 | -2.509051 |
| $w_{23}[6][1]$ | 0.5 | 0.767747 | 1.0 | -1.073878 |
| $w_{23}[6][2]$ | 0.6 | -38.912368 | 0.8 | -3.706801 |
| $v_3[1]$ | 0 | 22.290375 | 0 | 47.079564 |
| $v_3[2]$ | 0.1 | -29.943770 | 0.01 | -65.883203 |

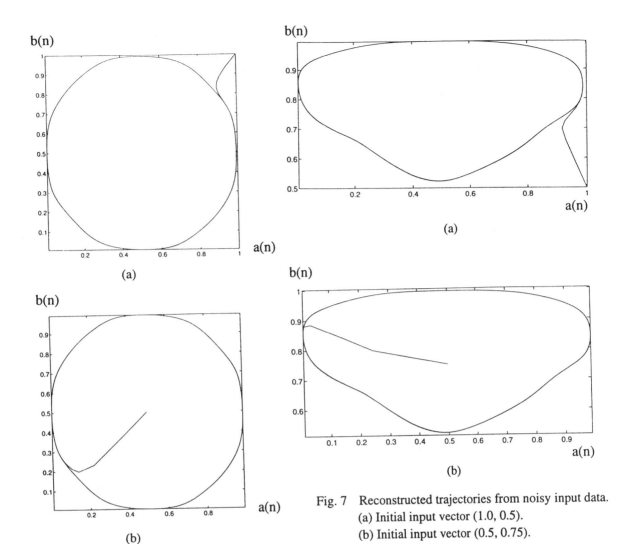

(a)

(a)

(b)

(b)

Fig. 7   Reconstructed trajectories from noisy input data.
(a) Initial input vector (1.0, 0.5).
(b) Initial input vector (0.5, 0.75).

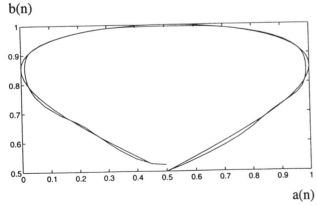

(b)

Fig. 5   Reconstructed trajectories from noisy input data.
(a) Initial input vector (1.0, 1.0).
(b) Initial input vector (0.5, 0.5).

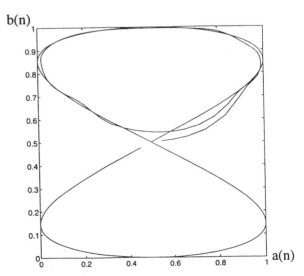

Fig. 6   Desired trajectory and reconstructed trajectory
at the initial vector (0.5, 0.5).

Fig. 8   Desired trajectory and reconstructed trajectory
at the initial vector (0.5, 0.5).

# Weber-Fechner transduction: a logarithmic compressive nonlinearity is a generic property of integrate and fire neurons

Doron Tal and Eric Schwartz

Department of Cognitive and Neural Systems
Boston University, 111 Cummington St., Boston, MA 02215

### Abstract

A logarithmic relationship between neuron firing density and input has been proposed in many computational, physiological and psychophysical contexts. Such a relationship allows multiplication via summation of neural output and has been proposed as the basic element in models of gain compression, motion, correlation, and illumination invariance. However, this logarithmic characteristic has never been fully analyzed in terms of the biophysical properties of single neurons, but has usually been motivated by experimental observations in physiological studies of sensory neurons and in psychophysical studies of threshold responses. In the present paper, we show that the logarithmic property appears in numerical simulations of the Hodgkin-Huxley equations, but that it is in fact a generic property of the integrative action of neuronal membrane. It is not determined by the details of the dynamics of the Hodgkin-Huxley equations, but rather is determined by the "integrate and fire" aspect of the model. We examine the relationship of this property to membrane resistance and capacitance, and also compute the utility of it in terms of the dynamic range and precision of a simple two neuron multiplier. Over the dynamic range imposed by the maximum firing rate of typical neurons, we show that the compressive nonlinearity that is intrinsic to the integrate and fire neuron is sufficient to provided a fairly accurate multiplication function.

## Introduction

A well known fact stated by Ratliff in his book on Mach bands, is that "often the relation between external stimulus and neural response is approximately logarithmic" (Ratliff, 1965, p. 129). As shown in Figure 1, such a relation is observed in simulations based on the Hodgkin-Huxley membrane equations (Hodgkin & Huxley, 1952) where a step-current of varying amplitudes is applied to a single neuron. In psychophysics, logarithmic neural transduction has been used to explain the Weber-Fechner law (Cornsweet, 1970; Land, 1977). In the computational literature, a logarithmic transfer function is also common. For example, Koch and Poggio (1992) offer a simple mechanism for performing multiplication with neurons that have a logarithmic transfer function, and the Cepstrum, a neural theory of disparity calculation in striate cortex, relies on logarithmic processing in single neurons (Yeshurun & Schwartz, 1989). Despite the widespread usage of logarithmic processing, the single neuron literature lacks a biophysical justification for this computation. Rather, logarithmic processing has often been justified by allusion to "common" experimental observation, as Ratliff does in his statement above. Moreover, there has been no analysis of the practical utility of this mechanism in terms of the dynamic range and precision it provides.

The purpose of this paper is to examine biophysical aspects of the repetitive firing process necessary for producing an approximately logarithmic current-frequency relation. Although a Hodgkin-Huxley model is sufficient for producing such a relation, it is not necessary. Rather, we show that there are only two simple requirements necessary to produce the log-property:

- An integrate and fire (IAF) mechanism, in which the integration of input current by membrane capacitance fires the neuron when threshold is reached.

- The existence of an absolute refractory period.

*This work supported by NIMH 5R01MH45969-04.

Since these are common properties in the nervous system, it follows that an approximately logarithmic current-frequency relation is likely to be a ubiquitous neural property. In terms of a simple IAF model, we show that the degree of approximation to a logarithmic characteristic is determined by the ratio of refractory period duration to membrane time constant. By varying this ratio, it is possible to produce a range of firing characteristics which vary from quasi-linear to quasi-logarithmic. We then quantify the utility of a "quasi-logarithmic" function by examining its use as a multiplier, and we quantify the precision of the multiplicative application over the range of typical firing rates. We also conclude that Weber-Fechner behavior is generic, in so far that a simple temporal IAF model of a neuron is valid, and that Weber-Fechner law is not merely a property of sensory neurons, but can appear in central neurons as well. Logarithmic processing may therefore provide a convenient computational support for a variety of functions related to multiplication and correlation with neurons.

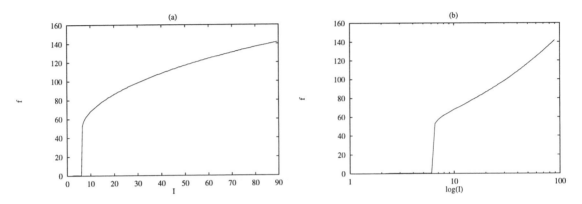

**Figure 1.** (a) Current-frequency curve resulting from uniform depolarization of a membrane modeled by the Hodgkin-Huxley equations, using the giant squid axon parameters (Hodgkin & Huxley, 1952); (b) semi-log plot of the curve in (a). Current (abscissa) is measured in $\mu Acm^{-2}$, frequency (ordinate) is measured in Hz.

# Biophysical basis of the approximately logarithmic current-frequency relation

Agin (Agin, 1964) appears to be the first to briefly relate simulations of a uniformly polarized membrane governed by the Hodgkin-Huxley equations to what he calls "the logarithmic law of sensory physiology". The curve in Figure 1 is a replication of Agin's simulation. Agin fit this curve to the equation

$$f = 27 \log (I + 1), \tag{1}$$

where $f$ is the neuron's firing frequency and $I$ is the applied current. Agin did not explain why the Hodgkin-Huxley equation should have this property, but merely presented a figure similar to Figure 1.

Stein's (1967) analysis of the IAF model provides such an explanation, because this model produces the log-like current-frequency relation under certain ranges of meaningful physical parameters. The membrane resistance and capacitance that provide the time constant for the integrate-and-fire model are also present in the Hodgkin-Huxely model. Thus, we believe that the rationale for Agin's observation is linked to an integrate-and-fire regime inherent in the Hodgkin-Huxely simulation, rather than to its potentially complex dynamics, as we shall discuss further below.

Stein rejected the idea that the logarithmic characteristic of the IAF or the Hodgkin-Huxley model provides a basis for the Weber-Fechner law. His reasoning was that the parameter space of the IAF model produced a good fit to a logarithm only over certain parameter ranges. We provide a detailed analysis of this issue below, and show that the question of "goodness" of fit to a logarithm is less relevant than performance in a computational task. We quantify the "goodness" of the logarithm in terms of multiplication error, and demonstrate that the compressive nonlinearity which is intrinsic to the IAF neuron is sufficient to perform multiplication with reasonable precision.

In Stein's IAF model, a steady current source, $I$, uniformly depolarizes the membrane causing an exponential increase in its potential, $V$. When the membrane potential reaches a threshold, $V_{\text{Th}}$ a spike occurs (at this point we shall assume the spike to take an infinitesimal amount of time). At the spike onset, the membrane capacitance discharges instantaneously and the membrane potential is reset to the resting potential. This firing process repeats for as long as the input current is on and is illustrated in Fig. 2.

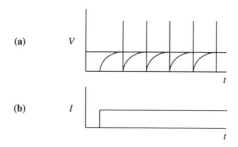

Figure 2. (a) Membrane voltage vs. time in an RC-circuit IAF model; the step-current input is shown in (b).

Stein used a resistor and a capacitor in parallel to model the membrane's charging process. This RC circuit and the relationship of its components to physiological quantities are shown in Fig. 3. The

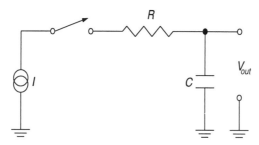

Figure 3. RC circuit used to model charging of a neuron's membrane from its resting potential to $V_{\text{Th}}$. $C$ corresponds to the membrane capacitance, $R$ corresponds to the membrane resistance and $I$ corresponds to an excitatory input such as a current injection or a steady current produced by a train of excitatory postsynaptic potentials.

RC integrator of the IAF model relates membrane potential to input current via the usual exponential charging relationship:

$$V = IR[1 - e^{-t/\tau}] \tag{2}$$

where $\tau = 1/RC$ is the membrane time-constant. The time $t_{\text{isi}}$ (the time it takes the membrane to reach $V_{\text{Th}}$), also called the interspike interval, can be calculated by setting $V = V_{\text{Th}}$, $t = t_{\text{isi}}$ in Eqn. 2, and solving for $t_{\text{isi}}$:

$$t_{\text{isi}} = -\tau \ln \left( 1 - \frac{V_{\text{Th}}}{IR} \right). \tag{3}$$

The rheobasic current, $I_{\text{Rh}}$, is defined as the smallest value of current that can drive the membrane potential to $V_{\text{Th}}$:

$$I_{\text{Rh}} = \frac{V_{\text{Th}}}{R}. \tag{4}$$

Substituting Eqn. 4 for $I$ in Eqn. 3,

$$t_{\text{isi}} = -\tau \ln \left( 1 - \frac{I_{\text{Rh}}}{I} \right). \tag{5}$$

The cell's firing frequency $f$ is the reciprocal of the period of each action potential. Since an action potential is considered to have infinitesimally small duration, the period of each action potential is just the interspike interval (Eqn. 5). The firing frequency as a function of current is therefore

$$f = \frac{1}{-\tau \ln(1 - I_{Rh}/I)}. \tag{6}$$

From the plot of Eqn. 6 in Figure 4, we see that the firing frequency approaches a *linear* function of the input current in Eqn. 6. In fact, Stein has shown that the current-frequency relation becomes linear for large $I$ by replacing the logarithmic term in Eqn. 6 by its power series:

$$\begin{aligned} f &= \frac{1}{-\tau[(I_{Rh}/I) + \frac{1}{2}(I_{Rh}/I)^2 + \frac{1}{3}(I_{Rh}/I)^3 + \cdots]} \\ &= \frac{1}{\tau}\left[(I/I_{Rh}) - \frac{1}{2} - \frac{1}{12}(I/I_{Rh})^{-1} - \cdots\right]. \end{aligned} \tag{7}$$

From Eqn. 7, we see that as $I$ grows larger than $I_{Rh}$, the frequency becomes proportional to the line with

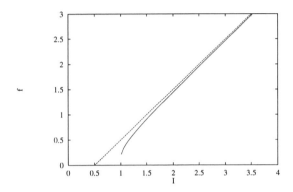

**Figure 4. A plot of Eqn. 6 (solid line) and of the straight line $f = I - 0.5$ (dotted line).**

slope $RC$ intersecting the abscissa at $1/2$.

A linear current-frequency relation does not agree with the logarithmic response observed both experimentally and in simulations that use the Hodgkin-Huxley equations (see Fig. 1). As shown by Stein, however, if we take into account the fact that an action potential has an absolute refractory period then the current-frequency relation becomes log-like. The reason for this is that at low input currents, the firing rate follows a linear curve, but at high firing rates, there must be saturation caused by the absolute refractory period. The joint effect of these two asymptotic regimes is "quasi-logarithmic" for a range of parameters.

In order to take into account the absolute refractory period in the above model, let the absolute refractory period take $t_0$ time; the interspike interval in Eqn. 3 is then $t + t_0$, and the frequency is

$$f = \frac{1}{t_0 + t} = \frac{1}{t_0 - \tau \ln(1 - I_{Rh}/I)} \tag{8}$$

Note that as $I$ grows arbitrarily, $f$ in Eqn. 6 grows without bound while in Eqn. 8 $f$ remains bounded at $1/t_0$. This boundedness compresses high $I$ values and yields a log-like response. The larger $t_0$ is in Eqn. 8, the more $f$ is compressed. The current-frequency relation expressed by Eqn. 8 maintains the same shape when the ratio $t_0/\tau$ remains constant. Figure 5(a) shows plots of Eqn. 8 for different ratios $t_0/\tau$. Of the curves in Figure 5(b), we see that the one for $t_0/\tau = 0.25$ best approximates a log, since it produces the straightest line on the semi-log plot.

In summary we conclude that the log-like response of neurons depends on two properties of the IAF model: (a) the neuron's time constant (i.e. the product of membrane resitance and capacitance) yields an integrative behavior and (b) action potential firing rate which must saturate, due to the refractory period. We can now see why the Hodgkin-Huxley equations also produce a log-like behavior. The underlying passive circuit in the Hodgkin-Huxley model is an RC circuit , with an active component that represents voltage dependent conductances. Although it is difficult to make qualitative statements about the detailed behavior of the Hodgkin-Huxley dynamics, it appears that the logarithmic behavior observed by (Agin, 1964), and replicated in Figure 1 is accounted for by the passive integrative component alone, i.e. is captured by the simple IAF model.

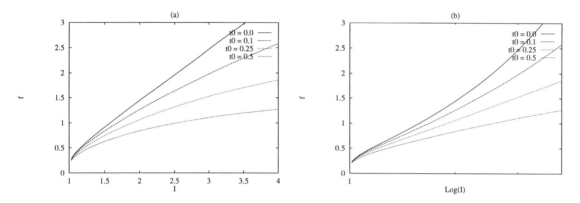

Figure 5. (a) A plot of Eqn. 8 for different values of the ratios $t_0/\tau$. The current $I$ is measured in units of the rheobasic current $I_{\mathrm{Rh}}$ (thus we replaced the term $I_{\mathrm{Rh}}/I$ in Eqn. 8 by $1/I$). $\tau$ was held constant at 1.0, while $t_0$ was varied from 0.0 to 0.5; (b) same plots as in (a), shown on semi-log scale.

## Precision and dynamic range

The firing rate of neurons typically extends from a few Hertz to a few hundred Hertz at the maximum. The utility of any numerical function dependent on firing rate is thus limited to this range. We have examined the precision of a multiplier that is constructed from two summed quasi-logarithmic IAF neurons. We used the IAF transfer function (Eqn. 8), for a range of different $t_0/\tau$, (as plotted in Figure 5) and defined the error by "multiplying" several thousand combinations of input currents. This was done by summing the corresponding "quasi-log" firing rates using the IAF curve, and comparing this method of multiplication with the correct numerical answer. We defined error by the average relative error, i.e. we defined the error $\delta$ in this multiplier as

$$\delta = 1/N \sum_{i=1}^{N} \frac{\left| (\overline{a_i b_i} - a_i b_i) \right|}{a_i b_i}, \tag{9}$$

where $a_i$ and $b_i$ are two "input" currents that we wish to multiply. The estimate of their product $\overline{a_i b_i}$ is obtained by summation of the "quasi-logarithmic" IAF transfer function as follows: Let $f_{\mathrm{IAF}}(I)$ be the frequency-current relation expressed by Eqn. 8. We first generated a number of random current value pairs $\{a_i, b_i\}$. Multiplication of each pair was performed by the equation

$$f_{\mathrm{IAF}}^{-1}\left(f_{\mathrm{IAF}}(a) + f_{\mathrm{IAF}}(b)\right). \tag{10}$$

The products obtained by Eqn. 10 were then fitted using linear interpolation to the "real" numerical products $a_i b_i$, obtaining an equation for a straight-line, $L(I)$. [†] We then generated a new set of products

---

[†]Note that this linear regression is simply to rescale the output in order to compare it to numerical multiplication. In neuronal terms, this implies a gain and offset at the summing neuron that would need to be specified if actual numerical

in the same manner as above, only now we rescaled each IAF product to the scale of the "real" products. The rescaling is done by substituting the result obtained in Eqn. 10 for $I$ into $L(I)$. The interpolated IAF product is $\overline{a_i b_i}$ in Eqn. 9. Figure 6 shows the average relative error of the IAF products as a function of $t_0/\tau$ This error, expressed as a percentage, is around 5% for $0.13 < t_0/\tau < 0.23$, indicating that in this input range the "quasi-logarithmic" IAF transfer function is useful as an approximate multiplier.

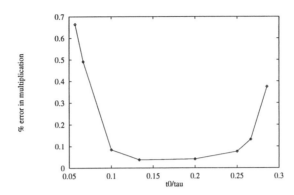

**Figure 6. A plot of the average relative error of the IAF products as a function of $t_0/\tau$ (see text for discussion).**

## Implications for theories neural function

If the input to some neuron is a linear function of the current flowing across the neuron's membrane, and if the neuron's output is its firing frequency, then the above discussion implies that the input-output relation of this neuron is approximately logarithmic. Interestingly, many theories of neural function can be explained by, or specifically require, a logarithmic input-output relationship in single neurons. These include theories of reflectance and brightness processing in vision (Land, 1977), Weber Law (or what Agin called the "logarithmic law" of sensory physiology), neuronal multiplication, stereo matching, adaptive gain control and adaptation (Grossberg, 1983).

In this section we shall mention three theories of neural function that rely on or can be explained by logarithmic processing: Weber's law, multiplying with neurons, and a stereo algorithm based on the use of the cepstrum as a correlational tool.

### Weber's law

Weber's law states that the difference threshold, $\Delta I$ – the minimum amount by which stimulus intensity must be changed to produce a noticeable change in sensation – remains proportional to the stimulus intensity, $I$, or

$$\frac{\Delta I}{I} = c. \tag{11}$$

Since Fechner (1860) introduced Weber's law (termed after it's discoverer, Ernst Weber) numerous psychophysical experiments have demonstrated this law (see, for example, ). Cornsweet (1970) and later Land (1977) have both proposed that Weber's law can be implemented with logarithmic processing. If we start with the assumption that neural transduction is logarithmic, that is,

$$f = \log(I), \tag{12}$$

---

multiplication were desired in a particular model. However, without this, the simple model of summing of the output of two "logarithmic" neurons provides a result which is proportional (with an offset) to the desired numerical (log)product over the entire dynamic range of the neuron.

then, differentiating, we get

$$\frac{df}{dI} = \frac{1}{I}, \;\Rightarrow\; \frac{dI}{I} = df. \tag{13}$$

## Multiplying with neurons

Koch and Poggio (1992) suggest several ways in which multiplication could be performed by neurons or synapses. The simplest scheme they mention involves neurons with a logarithmic transfer function that excite or inhibit each other additively or subtractively. Under these assumptions, if $x_1$ is the input to neuron A and $x_2$ is the input to neuron B, and the outputs of both neurons A and B add, then the output of the sum is

$$\log(x_1) + \log(x_2) = \log(x_1 x_2) \tag{14}$$

which is a multiplicative relation.

## Cepstral stereo matching

(Yeshurun & Schwartz, 1989) show that an estimate of the power spectrum of the log power spectrum, which is called the cepstrum in signal processing, provides a simple model for estimating stereo disparity when applied to an image data structure such as the ocular dominance column system of primate visual cortex. The logarithmic characteristic here is also required by any model dependent on spatial frequency estimation, since the power spectrum tends to be strongly weighted towards low frequencies so that it is unusable if not pre-processed with a compressive non-linearity. In the case of the cepstrum, the logarithm is the correct form of compressive non-linearity to maximize the performance of "echo-dection", which is, in spatial terms, the problem of disparity estimation. The IAF model neuron therefore has the right compressive non-linearity for this, or any other model in which power-spectral estimation is required.

# Conclusions

The integrative properties of the neuronal membrane resistance and capacitance, in a simple integrate-and-fire model, provides an approximate logarithmic transfer function of current input to firing rate output. The parameter range over which this property holds is determined by the ratio of absolute refractory period to membrane time constant. When used as a multiplier, by summing the firing rates that correspond to different inputs, the precision of multiplication is roughly 5%, over a dynamic range constrained by the maximum and minimum firing rates. Because the Weber-Fechner like behavior is dependent only on passive membrane properties and a simple IAF model, we expect it to be generic throughout the nervous system, not just in sensory neurons as is often cited. In computational terms, this property is sufficient to provide a basic mechanism for a wide variety of models, including situations in which multiplication, correlation, motion, stereo, illumination constancy and gain compression are required. Finally, since the behavior of the IAF transfer function ranges from "quasi-linear" to "quasi-logarithmic", adaptive control of the membrane time constant would allow a single neuron to change its transfer function from linear to logarithmic by adjusting its membrane resistance (and hence its time constant $\tau$). This could be accomplished by modifying the membrane permeability with voltage or ligand gated ion channels. Thus, those models which require a multiplicative function can achieve this function without anything more exotic than integrate-and-fire behavior at the single neuron level.

# Reference

Agin, D. (1964). Hodgkin-huxley equations: logarithmic relation between membrane current and frequency of repetitive activity. *Nature, 201*, 625–626.

Cornsweet, T. N. (1970). *Visual perception*. Academic Press, New York.

Fechner, G. T. (1860/1966). *Elements of Psychophysics*. Holt, Rinehart and Winston, New York. Howes, D. H. and Boring, E. G., Eds.; Adler, H. E. (trans.).

Grossberg, S. (1983). The quantized geometry of visual space: The coherent computation of depth, form, and lightness. *The Behavioral and Brain Sciences, 6*, 625–692.

Hodgkin, A. L., & Huxley, A. F. (1952). A quantitative description of membrane current and its application to conduction and excitation in nerve. *Journal of Physiology, 117*, 500–544.

Koch, C., & Poggio, T. (1992). Multiplying with synapses and neurons. In McKenna, T., Davis, J., & Zornetzer, S. F. (Eds.), *Single Neuron Computation*, chap. 12, pp. 315–345. Harcourt Brace Jovanovich, San Diego, CA.

Land, E. H. (1977). The retinex theory of color vision. *Scientific American, 237*, 108–128.

Ratliff, F. (1965). *Mach bands: Quantitative studies on neural networks in the retina*. Holden-Day, New York.

Yeshurun, Y., & Schwartz, E. L. (1989). Cepstral filtering on a columnar image architecture: a fast algorithm for binocular stereo segmentation.. *IEEE Trans. Pattern Analysis and Machine Intelligence, 11*(7), 759–767.

# A neuron model with variable ion concentrations

Alexander Grunewald*

Department of Cognitive and Neural Systems, Boston University

111 Cummington Street, Boston, MA 02215

## Abstract

Many neuron models exist, but usually the voltage is the central feature of those models. Recently interest in long-term potentiation (LTP) has surged, due to the fact that it is linked to learning. It has been shown that LTP is accompanied by an increase of the internal calcium concentration. Thus models with variable calcium concentration have been proposed. Since the calcium concentration is very low, this has a negligible effect on the membrane potential. In the present model all ion concentrations are variable due to ionic current and due to ion pumps. It is shown that this significantly increases the complexity of neural processing, and thus variable ion concentrations cannot be ignored in neurons with high firing frequency, or with very long depolarizations.

## 1    Introduction

Most physiological studies use the voltage at a neuron as an indicator of neural activity. In intracellular recordings the membrane potential is measured directly, and in extracellular recordings the presence of spikes is detected. Using these methods it has been possible to show that the postsynaptic activity due to a presynaptic signal can be enhanced using brief high frequency stimulation. This effect is called long-term potentiation (LTP), since it has been shown to persist for days. It is now commonly accepted that an initial stage of the induction of LTP is based on an increased calcium concentration in the postsynaptic region (Bliss & Collingridge, 1993). Thus several studies have now focussed on measuring the calcium concentration in neurons (Regehr & Tank, 1992).

The concentration of ions is affected by ionic currents across the membrane. Two forces, which may oppose each other or cooperate lead to these ionic currents (Hille, 1992). On the one hand there is the concentration gradient between the concentration of an ion inside the membrane ($[S]_i$) and outside the membrane ($[S]_o$). This force is ion specific. On the other hand, the concentration gradients of all ions together cause a voltage drop across the

---

*This research was conducted at the Sandoz Research Institute Berne and supported in part by AFOSR F49620-92-J-0225 and AFOSR F49620-92-J-0334.

membrane. The current density $i_S$ for an ion $S$ across the membrane is given by (Skinner, Ward, & Bardakjian, 1993):

$$i_S = P_S z_S^2 \frac{E_m F^2}{RT} \frac{[S]_i - [S]_o \exp(-z_S F E_m / RT)}{1 - \exp(-z_S F E_m / RT)} \qquad (1)$$

where $E_m$ is the membrane voltage, $P_S = g p_S$, where $g = 10^{-14}$, is the permeability of the membrane to the ion $S$, $F$ is Faraday's constant, $R$ is the gas constant, and $T$ is the temperature. The ionic current $I_S$ is then given by $I_S = i_S A_m$. By convention the ionic current flows against the potential gradient.

The underlying reason for the membrane potential is the sum of all concentration gradients between the inside and the outside of the neuron. In steady state the Goldman equation gives a good approximation to the membrane voltage, provided that the concentrations are known:

$$E_m = \frac{RT}{F} \ln \frac{P_K [K^+]_o + P_{Na} [Na^+]_o + P_{Cl} [Cl^-]_i}{P_K [K^+]_i + P_{Na} [Na^+]_i + P_{Cl} [Cl^-]_o}. \qquad (2)$$

Thus far many models have assumed that the ionic concentrations both inside and outside of the neuron are affected only marginally by ionic currents, and hence ionic concentrations have been assumed to be constant. While this may be true for concentrations outside of a neuron due to the big volume of the external region, and due to the lack of any compartmentalization of the exterior of neurons, it is not clear that this holds for ion concentration inside of neurons. In fact recently a number of models have been proposed to include the effect of changing $[Ca^{2+}]_i$, but these models only attempt to show that the concentration inside of a neuron can grow, thus explaining how LTP could be obtained (Gamble & Koch, 1987; R.Holmes & Levy, 1990). The effect of the changes of ionic concentrations inside the neuron on the voltage has thus far not been studied.

In this study it is addressed what the effect of variable ion concentrations is, and in how far the assumption of constancy of ion concentrations leads to deviations from these results.

## 2   A model with variable concentrations

A single synapse is modeled, specifically one postsynaptic compartment. The compartment is assumed to be homogeneous, and diffusion across the compartment is assumed to be instantaneous. The volume of the compartment is $V_m$. The area $A_m$ through which current flows is only the area abutting the synapse. In the present model four ion species have been included: $Ca^{2+}, Cl^-, K^+, Na^+$. The choice for these ions is based on the fact that all but $Ca^{2+}$ are recognized as major contributors to the membrane voltage. $Ca^{2+}$ was included for consistency with previous studies, and also to allow future investigations to address the effect of variable ion concentrations on LTP. To study the effect of variable ion concentrations a model was used that included two dynamic equations. The first dynamic equation expresses the voltage as a function of the total membrane current:

$$\frac{dE_m}{dt} = -\frac{I_m}{C_m} \qquad (3)$$

where $C_m$ is the membrane capacitance and $I_m$ is the total membrane current, i.e.

$$I_m = I_{Ca} + I_{Cl} + I_K + I_{Na}. \tag{4}$$

A second dynamic equation governed the concentrations of each of the ions. That equation depends only on the ionic current $I$ of ion species $S$, and on a pump that passively brings the ion concentration $K = [S]_i$ back to its equilibrium value:

$$\frac{dK}{dt} = \epsilon \frac{A_m}{zFV_m}(I_0 - I) + \delta(K_0 - K) \tag{5}$$

where $I_0$ is the ionic current of $S$ at rest, and $K_0$ is the concentration of $S$ at rest. The factors $\epsilon$ and $\delta$ indicate at which rates the ionic current and the ion pumps respectively affect the concentration. These factors were chosen to avoid oscillatory behavior of the model.

In simulations of the model initially the model was in steady state conditions, i.e. the there was no net membrane current, the voltage did not change, and nor did the concentrations. To model synaptic activity the permeability of the membrane was changed. This was a step change, which is physiologically implausible. However, it was opted for step changes instead of a more dynamic change of permeabilities to simplify the ensuing dynamics. This proved essential to keep the focus on the effects of variable ion concentrations.

## 3 Simulations

The initial conditions were as shown in table 1. The parameters of the compartment were as follows: $A_m = 1\mu m^2, V_m = 1\mu m^3, C_m = 1\mu F$. The size of the compartment was chosen to be within a plausible range, but in the present study no efforts were undertaken to understand the precise effects of these parameters. The parameter $\epsilon$ was set to $10^5$, and the ion pump strength $\delta$ was set to 0.01 for all ions, except for the Calcium pump, which was set to 10. This high value is necessary due to the very high concentration gradient. This choice ensured stable dynamics.

| Ion $S$ | $[S]_i$ (mmol) | $[S]_o$ (mmol) | resting $p_S$ | active $p_S$ | activation time |
|---------|----------------|----------------|---------------|--------------|-----------------|
| $Ca^{2+}$ | $10^{-4}$ | 1.5 | 1 | 10 | 10 |
| $Cl^-$ | 4.2 | 123 | 10 | 75 | 60 |
| $K^+$ | 155 | 4 | 25 | 50 | 60 |
| $Na^+$ | 12 | 145 | 1 | 10 | 10 |

Table 1: The initial ion concentrations. The resting permeabilities and the active permeabilities are also shown. Permeabilities are calculated by $P_S = gp_S$, where $g = 10^{-14}$.

The standard units were $F = 96480C/Mol$, $R = 8.315VC/(KMol)$ and the temperature was $T = 310K$. In the simulations all the units were converted into MKS units. Integration was performed using a fourth order Runge-Kutta method, with a timestep of 0.1ms.

In figure 1 the resulting voltage is shown when the permeability was activated for 20ms. It can be seen that the influence is marginal. In another set of simulations the permeabilities were activated for significantly longer periods of time (70ms). In this case the resulting trace is very different. Figure 2 shows the corresponding trace for voltage.

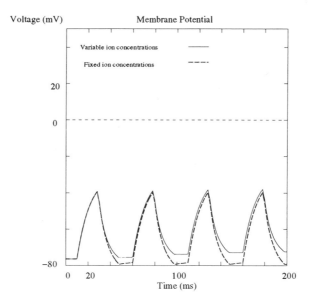

Figure 1: The membrane voltage as a function of time during brief permeability changes.

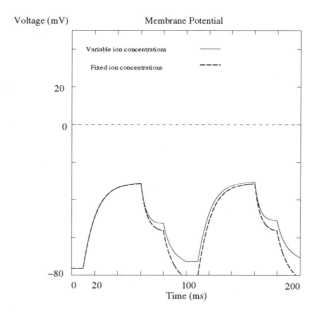

Figure 2: The membrane voltage as a function of time during long permeability changes.

# 4   Conclusion

The results of the simulations are very clear: small ionic currents have a negligible effect, while bigger ionic currents can have an important effect. The effect is stronger for inhibitory currents than for excitatory currents. Moreover, currents that last for a long time have strong effects, while brief currents do not. The influence of the currents is due to the interaction of two different time scales. A rapid timescale of currents and changes in voltage, and a slower timescale of changes in ionic concentrations. The relation between these two timescales is determined by the size of the postsynaptic volume, a factor that remains even if the big volume is subdivided into smaller compartments. Other constant contributing factors are the membrane area, the capacitance, and the pump strength to renormalize the concentrations.

This study indicates that the current simplification to exclude variations in ion concentrations is valid in many contexts, but that it may have to be revised when firing is at high frequencies, or last for prolonged periods of time. The levels of complexity added be including ionic concentrations (Segev, 1992) may be offset by the fact that including ionic dynamics in the model enhances the repertoire of neural dynamics, and thus a simplification may be easier to achieve.

# Reference

Bliss, T. V. P., & Collingridge, G. L. (1993). A synaptic model of memory: long-term potentiation in the hippocampus. *Nature, 361*, 31–39.

Gamble, E., & Koch, C. (1987). The dynamics of free calcium in dendritic spines in response to repetitive synaptic input. *Science, 236*, 1311–1315.

Hille, B. (1992). *Ionic channels of excitable membranes* (2nd edition). Sinauer Associates, Sunderland.

Regehr, W. G., & Tank, D. W. (1992). Calcium concentration dynamics produced by synaptic activation of CA1 hiipocampal pyramidal cells. *Journal of Neuroscience, 12*(11), 4202–4223.

R.Holmes, W., & Levy, W. B. (1990). Insights into associative long-term potentiation from computational models of NMDA receptor-mediated calcium influx and intracellular calcium concentration changes. *Journal of Neurophysiology, 63*(5), 1148–1168.

Segev, I. (1992). Single neuron models: oversimple, cmplex and reduced. *Trends in Neurosciences, 15*(11), 414–421.

Skinner, F. K., Ward, C. A., & Bardakjian, B. L. (1993). Permeation in ionic channels: a statistical rate theory approach. *Biophysical Journal, 65*, 618–629.

# INTERDISCIPLINARY STRATEGIES FOR ANALYZING DATA RECORDED FROM BIOLOGICAL AND SIMULATED ENSEMBLES OF NEURONS

I. Espinosa E., H. González G.*, J. Quiza T., J.J. González F.,
J.M. Gómez G., R. Arroyo A., and F. Santamaría P.

Laboratorio de Cibernética
*Laboratorio de Biofísica

Departamento de Física, Facultad de Ciencias, México National University (UNAM),
Ciudad Universitaria, México, D.F. 04510
fax: 011 52 (5) 622 4841
e-mail: espin@redvax1.dgsca.unam.mx

## ABSTRACT

We describe with examples the application of different methodologies to the analysis of the electrical activity (spikes trains) of real and simulated multiple recordings. An analytical platform as here described is needed to produce a robust interpretation of the complex data obtained from such types of experiments and simulations.

## INTRODUCTION

Technological advances are making possible the simultaneous extracellular recording from many neurons in anesthetized or awake and behaving animals. MacNaughton(21) has been recording from 48 channels at a time, Nicolelis(17) from 8 to 16 channels and other groups record less than that but with the same idea in mind. All these works show that the time has finally come for this type of approach since the technology is ready and up to certain point affordable. However, such experiments produce enormous amounts of data and it is not clear now what should be the way of analyzing and interpreting them. For many years now the groups of Gerstein(4,8,9,14) and Abeles(1) have been facing this problem and some solutions have been suggested although the problem remains open for new ideas.

In our lab we are making multiple recording in rat's hippocampus and using as a platform for analysis and interpretation what we have learned from Abeles, Gerstein, Lindsey(14), and Bloom(4). In a platform for analysis and interpretation of data from recordings made with microelectrode arrays and bundles, many tools are needed to manipulate the data in such a way that significant information could be extracted. One is the facility to build such arrays and bundles as well as the headstages associated with them(9).

One of the tools is simulation, that is, the availability of programs that are capable of simulating an interacting group of neurons. The simulators should produce an output similar to the one obtained from real extracellular recordings. When this is available the same tools can be used to analyze real and synthetic data. In our opinion this is an important tool because it allows to study a wide sample of simulations which otherwise are not possible in real experiments. Also, the simulators work as trainers for the use of analytical tools. As we briefly show below, two types of simulators are usually available, one in which a big network can be modeled even if with limited biological detail but which produces results in a short time, and another with more biological detail but where results are obtained in a long time. For the first case we use MacGregor's(16) simulators and in the second case we use variations of Chay(5) and Kowalsky(12) approaches. In Gerstein's lab they have always had simulations and experiments but in other labs this is a new approach as for example in the case of Simons' simulation(13) of whisker barrels.

As for the analytical tools many could be incorporated in the platform. In our case we are using autocorrelation and crosscorrelation as described by Abeles(1), and Gerstein and Aertsen(2,11,18), gravitational analysis as developed by Gerstein(11) and Lindsey(14), spectral analysis of the type possible with LYSIS(15) and the methods of Sclabassi(20) and nonlinear dynamics as used by Rinzel(19), and Freeman(22). Here we are establishing a standard for all the files that are produced whether they come from experiments or from simulations. These tools allow us to characterize individually the neurons in a cluster as well as to infer the functional connectivity among the neurons which could lead to the construction of a functional diagram that could serve as a complement of diagrams of firing activity and receptive fields.

Another important tool for this study is the spike sorter. Gerstein and Abeles have developed sorting machines and there are at least three more in the market. However, much remains to be done in this very important tool for multiple recording especially in the area of real-time sorting.

One new tool in this analytical platform is the use of artificial neural networks (ANN). We use it for research about spike recognition and sorting(3,6,7,10), even though we are far away of being able to use it in real time but we believe that the effort is worthwhile. On the other hand ANN simulations are very informative about collective behavior in groups of neurons and that helps considerably for interpreting real data and testing the tools for analysis that we mentioned above.

And lastly and certainly the most difficult is the choice of a behavioral paradigm related to the multiple recording in an awake and behaving animal. Many workers have chosen one(1,8,9,13,14,17) but it is still necessary to design a common framework to analyze and interpret the data so that a consistent body of knowledge could be built. It is in that direction that we are aiming our work.

## RECORDING, SIMULATION AND ANALYSIS

### DISPLAYING THE RECORDING

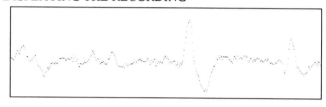

One channel in a multiple recording. We observe that two spikes are easily separable but a third one could not be because its size is comparable to the noise present. The recording is from rat's CA1.

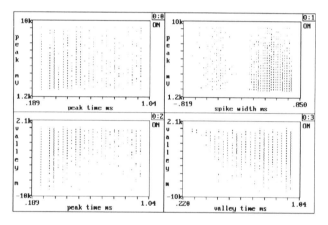

Here we show another recording from rat's hippocampus where bursting activity is observed and two spike widths are in it. This is another way of displaying a multiple recording to facilitate the sorting of the individual contributions from the neurons in the spike train.

### SIMULATION AND ANALYSIS OF LARGE NETWORKS

Our study of dynamic oscillations in artificial neural nets is based in basic modules as shown in figure 1. Using these nets allows a better control over the dynamic variables (in this case the weights) as well as construction and characterization of more complex architectures in such a way that the behavior of the net is associated with the type of synaptic connections between neurons.

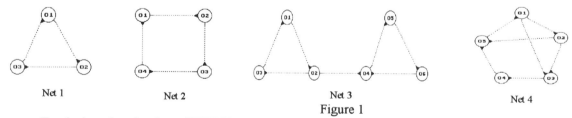

Net 1          Net 2          Net 3          Net 4

Figure 1

Employing the simulator NEURORED, inspired in the simulator programs of MacGregor(16), we describe the qualitative features of oscillations in neurons of Net 1 shown in figure 1 where the black dots in the connections mean an inhibitory weight. In NEURORED each neuron is activated with a fixed excitatory fiber (not shown in figure 1).

The firing shown in figure 2 results from changing the connection weights between the elements of Net 1. In these neurons the bursting rhythmical activity is generated with inhibitory weights and after a certain threshold is reached.

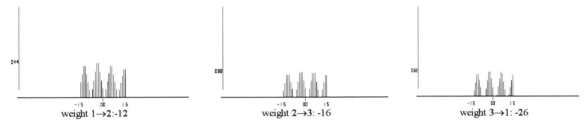

Figure 2

Figure 3 shows the cross-correlation histograms for Net 1. These graphics are typical of the bursting patterns shown in figure 2.

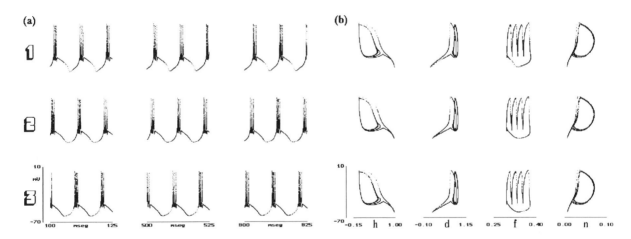

weight 1→2:-12          weight 2→3: -16          weight 3→1: -26

Figure 3

## SIMULATION AND ANALYSIS OF SMALL NETWORKS

The dynamics of Net 1 shown in Figure 1 is described in this section, using the models proposed by Chay(5), and Kowalski(12). The model consists of 18 ordinary differential equations, 5 for each neuron and one for each connection. It is shown that this system can present chaotic behavior even without external perturbations when the time constant $\overline{\tau}_h$, related to a fast inward current carried either by $Na^+$ or $Ca^{2+}$ ions, is changed.

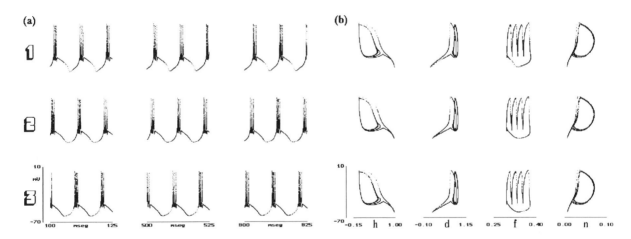

Figure 4. $\overline{\tau}_h$=300 ms. (a) Synchronized temporal series of the membrane potentials for Net 1 shown in Figure 1, with identical Chay's neuron(5). The numbers on the vertical axis correspond to the different neurons. The initial conditions are -50, -55, and -60 mV, respectively. (b) Projections on the V-h, V-d, V-f, and V-n planes for the same neurons; h, d, f, and n are the probabilities of channels opening that are functions of voltage and time.

With $\overline{\tau}_h$=300 ms, the different temporal series (membrane potential vs. time) show three synchronous modes, Figure 4(a), one for each neuron; this means that the system has, at least, three periodic attractors. The oscillations on the V-h, V-d, V-f, and V-n planes appear in Figure 4(b). These synchronized oscillations are similar between them and the 4 spikes of the bursts can be seen more clearly on the V-f plane.

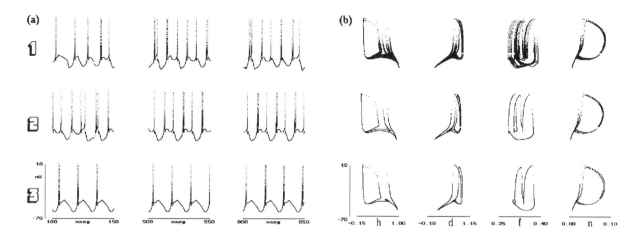

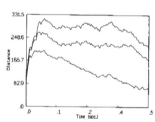

Figure 5. $\bar{\tau}_h$=800 ms. (a) Same as Figure 4(a), but now neurons 2 and 3 presents a synchronized mode and, apparently, the activity of neuron 1 is chaotic. From 100 to 150 ms the activity of neuron 2 shows a transient state. (b) Same as Figure 4(b).

Figure 5 shows the results when $\bar{\tau}_h$=800 ms. In this case, neurons 2 and 3 have periodic attractors. Neuron 1 apparently have a chaotic attractor, or at least, a long chaotic transient due to the presence of a homoclinic orbit. The route to chaos is by period doubling, Chay(5). In order to determine the existence of a chaotic attractor it is necessary to calculate the Lyapunov exponents; with this purpose, we are employing a method based on Gallant and White's results.

These results indicate that a group of similar interconnected neurons may exhibit a great variety of active states, from periodic oscillations to chaos, on each of its different neurons. The changes in the synaptic interactions, the connectivity of the net, and the internal parameters of each neuron are responsible for the gamut of different behaviors of the system. From here it becomes clear that it is necessary to develop efficient methods to evaluate if the activity is chaotic or not.

## SIMULTANEOUS ANALYSIS OF SPIKE TRAINS

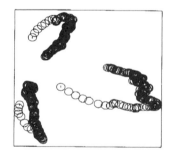

Gravitational representation of spike trains. The plot on the left shows the successive positions of the 3 particles that represent the neurons in Net 1 (figure 1). The labeled circles are the final positions. The plot on the right is the distance between all particles as a function of time. The decreasing distance shows the existence of direct interactions in Net 1.

## APPLYING ARTIFICIAL NEURAL NETWORKS

Input sweeping is a technique in pattern recognition for achieving translation invariance, Espinosa & Quiza(6, 7) designed an ANN using it and trained the network with backpropagation. That network used the logistic sigmoid function, we made a change that substitutes the logistic function by a biological function(3) (BF). We show some problems to demonstrate the performance against the original net.

Two things were done to implement the net, a) change of the activation function and b) discretization of its values. The number of iterations is remarkably less in almost all of the examples using Retro2 as shown below. Presently we are working in linear output layer networks based on Funahashi's theorems(10).

The biological probability of a neuron to fire at maximum rate is given by the following Gaussian distribution,

$$\Pr(U_i = U) = \frac{1}{\sqrt{2\pi\delta^2}} exp\left[-\frac{(U - \overline{U}_i)^2}{2\delta^2}\right]$$

So if we want to know the probability to get a pulse we have to integrate from the action potential to infinity, which in symbols is

$$\Pr(S_i = 1) = \int_{T_i}^{\infty} dU \, \Pr(U_i = U) = \frac{1}{2}\left[1 + erf(\frac{\overline{U}_i - T_i}{\delta\sqrt{2}})\right], \qquad erf(x) \equiv \frac{2}{\sqrt{\pi}} \int_0^x dt \, e^{-t^2}$$

Retro1 is the program with the common logistic function, Retro 2 is the BF. We compare different architectures versus number of iterations to reach a total error less than 0.001. The argument of the error function is x/2.

The numbers that are between the rows in the tables define the architecture of each net, the meaning of these numbers is: Input Nodes, Output Nodes; Nodes per Group, Swept Nodes, Overlapped Nodes; Speed, Momentum. We compare final error and number of iterations for each program.

SPIKE: The problem is to classify eight different patterns irrespective of its translation variance.

| Program | Final Err | Iterations | Final Err | Iterations |
|---|---|---|---|---|
| 128,8;1,32,24;0.2,0.0 | | | 128,8;2,32,24;0.2,0.0 | |
| Retro1 | 0.009998 | 85 | 0.014397 | 100 |
| Retro2 | 0.021507 | 100 | 0.009995 | 30 |
| 128,8;1,32,20;0.15,0.0 | | | 128,8;2,32,20;0.15,0 | |
| Retro1 | 0.008029 | 500 | 0.009968 | 206 |
| Retro2 | 0.018141 | 500 | 0.009997 | 92 |
| 128,8;1,32,26;0.3,0.0 | | | 128,8;2,32,26;0.3,0.0 | |
| Retro1 | 0.022074 | 100 | 0.00991 | 94 |
| Retro2 | 0.009885 | 68 | 0.009713 | 49 |

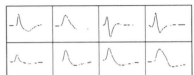

Spikes used. We built a train of 240 spikes with random noise added.

DECODER: The problem is to make the output equal to the input.

| Program | Final Err | Iterations | Final Err | Iterations | Final Err | Iterations |
|---|---|---|---|---|---|---|
| 4, 4; 2, 3, 4;0.7,0.0 | | | 4, 4; 2, 4, 0, 0.7 ,0.0 | | 4, 4; 3, 4, 1; 0.7, 0.0 | |
| Retro1 | 1.695757 | 100 | 1.697550 | 100 | 1.696432 | 100 |
| Retro2 | 0.008756 | 10 | 0.009407 | 36 | 0.007489 | 10 |

XOR: The classic problem.

| Program | Final Err | Iterations | Final Err | Iterations | Final Err | Iterations |
|---|---|---|---|---|---|---|
| 3, 1; 3, 3, 0; 0.5, 0.3 | | | 3, 1; 3, 3, 0; 0.4, 0.6 | | 3, 1; 3, 3, 0; 0.3, 0.5 | |
| Retro1 | 0.451578 | 100 | 0.45146 | 100 | 0.451563 | 100 |
| Retro2 | 0.004456 | 14 | 0.004279 | 14 | 0.002235 | 24 |

**CONCLUSION**

Some aspects of an analytical platform for multiple recordings from ensembles of neurons have been shown where the goal is to enrich the modeling process and give versatility to the analysis in such a way that a robust interpretation can be produced.

**ACKNOWLEDGEMENTS**
The authors wish to thank I. Domínguez, J. Ruiz, R. Serna, and A. Sierra for their help on this research. This work is being supported by DGAPA IN-100593-UNAM.

# REFERENCES

1.- ABELES, M., "Corticonics: Neural Circuits of the Cerebral Cortex", Cambridge Univ. Press, 1991.

2.- AERTSEN, A.M.H.J., AND GERSTEIN, G.L., "Dynamic Aspects of Neuronal Cooperativity: Fast Stimulus-Locked Modulations of Effective Connectivity", In J. KRUGER (Ed.), "Neuronal Cooperativity", Springer Verlag, 1991. pp. 52-67.

3.- AMIT, D.J., "Modeling Brain Function", Cambridge Univ. Press, 1989.

4.- BLOOM, M.J., "Neuronal interactions in the auditory cortex of cats during binaural simulation of sound movement", Ph.D. Thesis, University of Pennsylvania, 1985.

5.- CHAY, T.R. AND LEE, Y.S., "Bursting, Beating, and Chaos by Two Functionally Distinct Inward Current Inactivations in Excitable Cells", Annals of the New York Academy of Sciences 591: 328-350, 1990.

6.- ESPINOSA E., I. AND QUIZA T., J., "Classification of noisy action potentials (APs) by means of a neural network employing back-propagation", Soc. Neurosci. Abstr., vol. 16, p. 1092, 1990.

7.- ESPINOSA E., I. AND QUIZA T., J., "Off-line sorting of spikes using an artificial neural network", Soc. Neurosci. Abstr. Vol. 17, p. 124, 1991.

8.- ESPINOSA E., I., "Connectivity in the observed portion of an auditory neuronal network", en CAUDILL, M.(ed), Theory Track, Neural&Cognitive Sciences Track of the Proceedings of the International Joint Conference on Neural Networks, vol. I, pp. I-66 a I-69, Lawrence Erlbaum Associates, Inc., Publ., 1990.

9.- ESPINOSA, I.E. AND GERSTEIN, G.L., "Cortical auditory neuron interactions during presentation of 3-tone sequences: Effective connectivity", Brain Research 450: 39-50, May 1988.

10.- FUNAHASHI, K., "On the approximate realization of continuous mappings by neural networks", Neural Networks 2: 183-192, 1989.

11.- GERSTEIN, G. AND AERTSEN, A., "Representation of cooperative firing activity among simultaneously recorded neurons", J. Neurophys. 54: 1513-1528, 1985.

12.- KOWALSKI, J.M., ALBERT, G.L., RHOADES, B.K., AND GROSS, G.W., "Neuronal Networks With Spontaneous, Correlated Bursting Activity: Theory and Simulations", Neural Networks 5: 805-822, 1992.

13.- KYRIAZI, H.T. AND SIMONS, D.J., "Thalamocortical response transformations in simulated whisker barrels", J. Neuroscience 13(4): 1601-1615, 1993.

14.- LINDSEY, B.G., SHANNON, R., AND GERSTEIN, G.L., "Gravitational representation of simultaneously recorded brainstem respiratory neuron spike trains", Brain Research 483: 373-378, 1989.

15.- LYSIS V, Biomedical Simulations Resource, School of Engineering, University of Southern California.

16.- MACGREGOR, R.J., "Neural and Brain Modeling", Academic Press, 1987.

17.- NICOLELIS, M.A.L., LIN, R.C.S., WOODWARD, D.J., AND CHAPIN, J.K., "Induction of immediate spatiotemporal changes in thalamic networks by peripheral block of ascending cutaneous information", Nature 361: 533-536, 1993.

18.- PALM, G., AERTSEN, A.M.H.J., AND GERSTEIN, G.L., "On the significance of correlations among neuronal spike trains", Biol. Cybern. 59: 1-11, 1988.

19.- RINZEL, J. AND ERMENTROUT, G.B., "Analysis of neural excitability and oscillations", in C. KOCH and I. SEGEV(eds.), "Methods in Neuronal Modeling", MIT Press, 1989.

20.- SCLABASSI, R.J., ERIKSSON, J.L., PROT, R.L., ROBINSON, G.B., AND BERGER, T.W., "Nonlinear system analysis of the hippocampal perforant path-dentate projection. I. Theoretical and interpretational considerations", J. Neurophysiol. 60: 1066-1076, 1988.

21.- WILSON, M.A. AND McNAUGHTON, B.L., "Dynamics of the hippocampal ensemble code for space", Science 261: 1055-1058, 1993.

22.- YAO, Y. AND FREEMAN, W.J., "Model of Biological Pattern Recognition With Spatially Chaotic Dynamics", Neural Networks 3: 153-170, 1990.

# NEURONAL GROUP SELECTION THEORY:
## STEPS TOWARDS A HIPPOCAMPAL MODEL

Jorge Quiza T. and Ismael Espinosa E.

Laboratorio de Cibernética
Departamento de Física, Facultad de Ciencias,
Mexico National University (UNAM), Ciudad Universitaria,
México, D.F., 04510

fax: 011 52 (5) 622 4841
e-mail: espin@redvax1.dgsca.unam.mx

**ABSTRACT**

A computational model, using reasonably realistic neurons, of the hippocampal formation is proposed. The importance of the relationship between simulation and experimentation is stressed through the discussion of the problems faced to analyze and interpret the data obtained during multineuron recordings in rat's brain.

**INTRODUCTION**

Even if a complex structure such as the mammalian brain can be seen as the result of the relatively simple activity of many elements, the anatomical evidence suggests that brain structures involved in sensory perception, motor responding, and information storage are probably mediated by interactions among neurons within large networks. Several hypotheses have been proposed to explain how perception, memory, and learning are coded by these neuronal networks in the brain.

Hebb (1949) stated the hypothesis of cell assemblies, which are groups of neurons with strong excitatory internal connectivity that activate each other. The changes in synaptic strenghts, from neuron to neuron, organize the groups of neurons into functional units. The connectivity between the neurons in the same group and the amount of overlap among the groups are as important as the size of the groups themselves for the understanding of how the cell assemblies represent brain activity (Palm, 1990).

Edelman (1978) proposed his neuronal group selection theory (NGST) to explain the neurophysiological function of the brain as a Darwinian system involving variation and selection. The basic idea is that groups of neurons, structurally varied as a result of evolutionary and developmental processes, constitute a population from which are selected those groups whose function serves to improve the behavioral responses of the organism.

Other related ideas, such as modules, columns, and motor pools are discussed in Gerstein *et al.* (1989).

The experimental evidence for the concepts of cell assemblies or neuronal groups may be obtained by modern imaging techniques like PET or functional MRI and/or recording simultaneously the activity of many individual neurons in freely behaving animals and looking for signs of dynamic interactions in their activities. Although the recording technologies and methods of analysis have considerably improved during the last years (Gerstein *et al.* 1983; Krüger 1991), the complexity of many brain regions exceeds by far the capacities of these techniques. By reason of this, it is valid to use computer simulations to study different brain structures.

The hippocampus is one of the brain structures of which much of what is known about its function has been obtained by monitoring the simultaneous activity of its neuron (for example, Bostock *et al.* 1991; Buzsáki *et al.* 1992; Wilson & McNaughton 1993). Its role is fundamental in cognition, specially in learning and memory encoding the internal representation of space (O'Keefe & Nadel 1978).

We propose here the steps for a model of the function of the hippocampal formation based on the principles of the NGST, using both realistic neuronal models derived from the programs of MacGregor (1987) and multiple recording in rat's hippocampus.

## NEURONAL GROUP SELECTION THEORY

The premises on which the NGST rest are that the unit of selection is a neuronal group of 50-10,000 cells, with specific connections between the neurons of a same group and a great variability of connections between the neurons of different groups, and that the nervous systems with this kind of organization are able to adapt to changing environments not experienced previously by the organism (Edelman 1978).

Three are the fundamental claims of the theory (Edelman 1987):

1.- During the development of the brain in the embryo, a highly variable pattern of connections is formed between neurons. This process gives rise to a *primary repertoire* of cell groups.

2.- After birth, as the organism experiences its environment, certain combination of connections are selected over others as a result of the stimuli the brain receives through the senses. Such groups, chosen from the primary repertoire, are more likely to be used in the future, and form the *secondary repertoire.*

3.- The secondary repertoires communicate to one another back and forth by means of connections arranged in sheets or maps. This notion, called *reentry*, allows for the creation of categories of objects and events.

Neuronal groups receive inputs either from sensory receptors or from other neuronal groups and respond to specific activity patterns. When a stimulus pattern occurs several times, there is a selective modification in the strength of the synaptic connections between the neurons belonging to the groups that respond to such estimulus. In this way, the collection of neuronal groups that recognize the stimulus becomes better defined every time it happens to be present. The responses of the different repertoires must be specific enough to recognize a given stimulus, but, at the same time, adaptable enough to ensure that similar stimuli can also be identified. This guarantees that the system can adequately match a wide range of inputs.

A set of neuronal groups organized in a way that preserves the pattern of relationships between a sheet of neural tissue and one of sensory receptors or between two sheets of neural tissue is called a map. Merzenich's findings on the variation and rearrangement of sensory maps in the brain of monkeys (Merzenich *et al.* 1983), have given a strong support to the NGST.

The concerted activity of maps and nonmapped regions that correlate sensorial inputs and motor responses forms the bases for categorization, memory, and learning (Edelman 1987). This system is called a global mapping.

These principles of selection have been used to design a series of automatons (Reeke *et al.* 1990) that can manipulate objects present in their environment and for the control of a two-link robotic manipulator (Donnett & Smithers 1990).

## HIPPOCAMPAL FORMATION

In contrast with other cortical areas, the hippocampus is relatively simple, with most of its cellular elements aligned in a narrow layer, the layer of pyramidal cells. The hippocampal formation is composed of the entorhinal cortex, dentate gyrus, hippocampus proper (CA1-CA3), and subiculum. A transverse section shows that a trysinaptic circuit provides the route for information passing through the hippocampal formation. This circuit is a purely feedforward network with the following sequence: Fibers of the perforant path synapse onto granule cells of the dentate gyrus; these cells send mossy-fiber axons to the pyramidal neurons of CA3; these neurons send their axons (Schaffer collaterals) to the CA1 region. It should be noted, however, that there are also important pathways in the direction of the long axis of the hippocampus (Amaral & Witter 1989; Braitenberg & Schüz 1991).

The hippocampal formation contains additional projection systems that connect one of the major outputs of the hippocampus back to its main sensory input. The subiculum and the entorhinal cortex receive axons from CA1 pyramidal cells. The subiculum projects heavily to layers V and VI of the entorhinal cortex, which, in turn, projects to the superficial layers of itself. Since the perforant path originates in these latter layers of the entorhinal cortex, the input to the dentate gyrus is approximately in the same area that the outputs from CA1.

The hippocampus represents the highest level of association cortex in mammalians (McNaughton & Nadel 1990). Numerous hypotheses have been advanced to explain the hippocampal formation function. Most of them sustain that the hippocampus and its related structures participate in some kinds of memory and learning, for example, O'Keefe & Nadel (1978) proposed that the hippocampus functions as a cognitive map and is a spatial memory structure. These ideas have been used to develop connectionist models that try to understand how the basic neuronal circuit produces a particular behavior (Gluck & Myers 1993; Schmajuk *et al.* 1993).

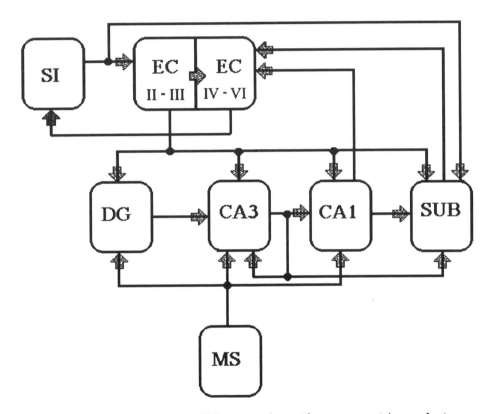

Figure 1. Schematic diagram illustrating the connections between cortex, medial septum, and different structures in hippocampal formation. DG, dentate gyrus; EC, entorhinal cortex; MS, medial septum; SUB, subiculum; SI, sensory inputs from cortex.

In a large system such as a global mapping for sensorimotor coordination (see Figure 8.5 of Edelman 1987), the hippocampal formation must play an important role in modulating sensory aspects of perception. The arrangement of the trysinaptic circuit would be adequate to link sequentially, with a strong temporal component, the activity between sensory system maps in the cortex and between such maps and other ones in the motor system. The synaptic changes among the different maps of the cortex, induced by the sequencing coordinated by the hippocampus, establish a long term memory in which succession can be a derived property (Edelman 1987). Thus, the hippocampus may be considered as a map nontopographically arranged, that combines the relations among the perceptually different parts of a global mapping (Eichenbaum 1993).

Figure 1 outlines the connections among differents components of the model. Some groups receive inputs from cells in other groups in the same structure (for example, the dentate gyrus) or from cells in the same group (CA3), while others (entorhinal cortex, subiculum) receive inputs from extrinsic sources. There are reentry connections between the enthorhinal cortex and CA1. The entorhinal cortex receives the outputs of the primary sensory cortex, several thalamic nuclei, and the amygdala, among others. The entorhinal cortex sends inputs to the dentate gyrus, hippocampus proper and subiculum. A second input to the hippocampal formation comes from the medial septal nucleus. This input may be relevant in regulating the excitability of the hippocampus. A major output of the hippocampus returns to the deep layers of the entorhinal cortex. Other outputs, not shown, go to the septal complex, the mammillary bodies, the hypothalamus, and the thalamus. For a more complete anatomical description see, for example, Amaral & Witter (1989) and Brown & Zador (1990).

The neurons used are based on those with compartmentalized dendritic trees NEURN31 (MacGregor 1987). This model has four state state variables for the soma compartment and four more for each of the dendritic compartments. Although there are more elaborated models for hippocampal neurons, for example the one employed by Traub & Miles (1991), MacGregor's model is fairly realistic and, computationally, less expensive.

In spite of the fact that Edelman uses non-Hebbian rules to modify synaptic strengths, we are using a Hebb-type rule. Simulations carried out by Grajski & Merzenich (1991) show up this kind of synaptic plasticity rule can guaranteed that intergroup connectivities will be stronger than intragroup ones and that neurons belonging to one group will fire together more often than those of different groups.


## STEPS TOWARDS A MODEL

We intend to combine simulation and experimentation in such a way that feedback between them be beneficial to our understanding of how neural groups interact in a behaving context. We want to use as our interpretational framework the NGST. For doing this we will have to go through several stages of simulation, experimentation and analysis. At this moment we are in the early stages of this project.

Simulation was initiated with a simulator that uses concentrated parameters and without learning algorithms. In these days we are starting to use a similar simulator where Hebbian learning is possible and in the near future we will move towards a simulator with distributed parameters and Hebbian learning. All these will be MacGregor's simulators (MacGregor 1987), although we will also consider other simulators as well as different models for neural networks. With these simulators we will model basic modules of the hippocampus and their interactions and will analyze the spike trains as if they were coming out from real neuronal assemblies. We will incorporate into the simulation the cross-correlation maps found in the experimentation results. The results of the interaction between simulation and experimentation will be interpreted in terms of the NGST.

As for experimentation, we will study spontaneous activity of the hippocampus in the first place and then will gradually move to multiple recording in awake rats and from there to behaving rats in structured and non-structured environments. We consider these stages because we started our lab from scratch just recently.

Our main tool for analysis will be the cross-correlation technique. We are considering here three stages at least. One will be the classical visual inspection of cross-correlation histograms for inferring the functional connectivity diagrams and then we will move to using the gravitational representation (Gerstein & Aertsen 1985; Gerstein *et al.* 1985) for the same reason that in the classical stage and finally we will translate our simulations and analysis to supercomputing where it is likely that we will find new ways of visualizing and analyzing the data.

Right now we are recording with two microelectrodes spontaneous activity in rat's hippocampus and are planning to gradually increase the number of electrodes as the resources permit. The crosscorrelation technique allows to infer the functional connectivity diagram for recordings from pairs of neurons. We are using this method with few microelectrodes but as soon as we use more that four we will work with the gravitational representation developed by Gerstein. With this method we expect to find intra-modular and inter-modular distributed maps of correlated activity. These maps are poorly known at this time and the most interesting ones will certainly be those associated with a specific behavior. Our goal is to work with awake and behaving rats as soon as our installation enables us to do so.

## CONCLUSIONS

The simulation of the distinctive functions assigned to the hippocampal formation with a realistic model will provide a fruitful interlacing between experimental and theoretical studies of the hippocampus. Computational models founded upon sound theoretical bases may not only reproduce but also predict the characteristics of the data to be ascertained experimentally. On the other hand, new experimental findings may shed light on hitherto unaccounted for organizational principles which will lead, in turn, to a reconsideration of the original model.

## ACKNOWLEDGMENT

This project is being supported by DGAPA IN-100593-UNAM.

## REFERENCES

Amaral, D.G., & Witter, M.P. (1989). The three-dimensional organization of the hippocampal formation: A review of anatomical data. *Neuroscience*, **31**, 571-591.

Bostock, E., Muller, R.U., & Kubie, J.L. (1991). Experience-dependent modifications of hippocampal place cell firing. *Hippocampus*, **1**, 193-206.

Braitenberg, V., & Schüz, A. (1991). *Anatomy of the cortex*. Berlin: Springer-Verlag.

Brown, T.H., & Zador, A.M. (1990). Hippocampus. In G.M. Shepherd (Ed.), *The synaptic organization of the brain*, (pp. 346-388). New York: Oxford University Press.

Buzsáki, G., Horváth, Z., Urioste, R., Hetke, J., & Wise, K. (1992). High-frequency network oscillation in the hippocampus. *Science*, **256**, 1025-1027.

Donnett, J., & Smithers, T. (1989). Neuronal group selection theory: A grounding in robotics. In D. Touretzky (Ed.), *Advances in neural information processing systems*, Vol. 2 (pp. 308-315). San Mateo, CA: Morgan Kaufmann.

Edelman, G.M. (1978). Group selection and phasic reentrant signaling: A theory of higher brain function. In G.M. Edelman and V.B. Mountcastle (Eds.), *The mindful brain: Cortical organization and the group-selective theory of higher brain function*, (pp. 51-100). Cambridge, MA: The MIT Press.

Edelman, G.M. (1987). *Neural Darwinism: The Theory of Neuronal Group Selection*. New York: Basic Books.

Eichenbaum, H. (1993). Thinking about brain cell assemblies. *Science*, **261**, 993-994.

Gerstein, G.L., & Aertsen, A.M.H.J. (1985). Representation of cooperative firing activity among simultaneously recorded neurons. *J. Neurophysiol.*, **54**, 1513-1528.

Gerstein, G.L., Bedenbaugh, P., & Aertsen, A.M.H.J. (1989). Neuronal assemblies. *IEEE Trans. Biomed. Eng.*, **36**, 4-14.

Gerstein, G.L., Bloom, M.J., Espinosa, I.E., Evanczuk, S., & Turner, M.R. (1983). Design of a laboratory for multi-neuron studies. *IEEE Trans. Syst. Man and Cybern.*, **13**, 668-676.

Gerstein, G.L., Perkel, D.H., & Dayhoff, J.E. (1985). Cooperative firing activity in simultaneously recorded populations of neurons. *J. Neurosci.*, **5**, 881-889.

Gluck, M.A., & Myers, C.E. (1993). Hippocampal mediation of stimulus representation: A computational theory. *Hippocampus, 3*, 491-516.

Grajski, K.A., & Merzenich, M.M. (1990). Hebb-type dynamics is sufficient to account for the inverse magnification rule in cortical somatotopy. *Neural Computation, 2*, 71-84.

Hebb, D. (1949). *The organization of behavior*. New York: Wiley.

Krüger, J.(Ed.) (1991). *Neuronal cooperativity*. Berlin: Springer- Verlag.

MacGregor, R.J. (1987). *Neural and brain modeling*. New York: Academic Press.

McNaughton, B.L., & Nadel, L. (1990). Hebb-Marr networks and the neurobiological representation of action in space. In M.A. Gluck & D.E. Rumelhart (Eds.), *Neuroscience and connectionist theory*, (pp. 1-63). Hillsdale, NJ: Lawrence Erlbaum.

Merzenich, M.M., Kaas, J.H., Wall, J.T., Nelson, R.J., Sur, M., & Felleman, D.J. (1983). Topographic reorganization of somatosensory cortical areas 3a and 1 in adult monkeys following restricted deafferentation. *Neuroscience, 8*, 33-55.

O'Keefe, J., & Nadel, L. (1978). *The hippocampus as a cognitive map*. Oxford, UK: Clarendon.

Palm. G. (1990). Cell assemblies as a guideline for brain research. *Concepts in Neuroscience, 1*, 133-147.

Reeke Jr., G.N., Sporns O., & Edelman G.M. (1990). Synthetic neural modelling: The "Darwin" series of recognition automatas. *Proceedings of the IEEE, 78*, 1498-1530.

Schmajuk, N.A., Thieme, A.D., & Blair, H.T. (1993). Maps, routes, and the hippocampus: A neural network approach. *Hippocampus, 3*, 387-400.

Traub, R.D., & Miles, R. (1991). *Neuronal networks of the hippocampus*. New York: Cambridge University Press.

Wilson, M.A., & McNaughton B.L. (1993). Dynamics of the hippocampal ensemble code for space. *Science, 261*, 1055-1058.

# A new algorithm for unsupervised classification:
## Expectant Hebbian Learning

Terje G. Vold*
Department of Physics and Astronomy
Swarthmore College
Swarthmore, PA 19081

Abstract. A new algorithm for unsupervised classification of probabilistically characterized input data, Expectant Hebbian Learning, is described. It differs from classical Hebbian learning by a) replacing the presynaptic potential with the presynaptic potential minus the exponential of the weight, b) learning an additional weight for each synapse associated with the output neuron being off, c) including a similar learning algorithm for the bias, and d) adding a weight adjustment that maintains a normalization condition for any group of mutually exclusive (inhibitory) input neurons. Numerical simulations that could correspond to olfaction and multimodal sensory fusion show that it performs well.

## 1. Introduction

We consider the problem of unsupervised classification of samples of valuations of a set $x$ = $\{x_i\}$ of input variables $x_i$ indexed by $i$, each of which ranges over a finite set of discrete values, into one of a finite set of classes identified by the discrete output variable $y$. We sparsely encode the variables $x_i$ and $y$ with sets $\{x_{in}\}$ and $\{y_m\}$ of mutually exclusive binary variables $x_{in}$ and $y_m$ indexed by $n=0,1,...,N$ and $m=0,1,...,M$, corresponding to groups of N or M mutually inhibitory neurons; we let $x_{i0}=1$ and $y_0=1$ represent the states of all neurons off in the associated group. We assume that the value of $x$ depends *probabilistically* on the value of $y$ by conditional probabilities $p(x_{in}|y_m)$, and that the value of y is characterized by probabilities $p(y_m)$. We describe a biologically plausible learning algorithm that allows unsupervised learning of these probabilities and optimal network response, even when the "signal strength," or RMSD of the conditional probabilities, is small.

## 2. The Solution

Given $p(x_{in}|y_m)$ and $p(y_m)$, the "best" probability distribution $p(x,y)$ as determined by the principle of maximum entropy (Jaynes 1983) can be written as

$$p(x,y) = \exp\left(-\Omega + \sum_m b_m y_m + \sum_{i,n,m} w_{inm} x_{in} y_m\right)$$

(1)

where the parameters $b_m$ and $w_{inm}$ are related to probabilities by

$$p(x_{in} \mid y_m) = \exp(w_{inm})$$

(2)

and

$$p(y_m) = \exp(b_m) ,$$

(3)

where we have choose arbitrary normalization constants by requiring

$$1 = \sum_n \exp(w_{inm})$$

(4)

for all input groups $i$ to each output $m$.

Given any particular valuation of inputs $x = \{x_{in}\}$, a series of output valuations of $y=\{y_m\}$ drawn from the associated optimal conditional probability distribution $p(y|x)=p(x,y)/p(x)$ will be generated if each output neuron always stays on for some fixed period, say $\tau \approx 5$ msec, and turns on with a probability per time period $\tau$ of

$$\frac{p(y_m = 1 \mid x)}{p(y_m = 1 \mid x) + p(y_0 = 1 \mid x)} = \frac{1}{1 + \exp(S_m)}$$

(5)

if all neurons are off ($y_0=1$), where

$$S_m = (b_m - b_0) + \sum_{i,n} (w_{inm} - w_{in0}) x_{in}$$

(6)

This algorithm can be easily implemented by each neuron $y_m$ within group of mutually inhibitory neurons $y = \{y_m\}$. This is a simple Boltzmann Machine (Ackley et. al. 1984) with strong inhibition between neurons within one group. The special case of one neuron per group has been described (Ackley et. al. 1983; MacKay 1991).

If the network is correctly classifying its input, the actual frequency of occurrence of $x_{in}=1$ for a given output $y_m=1$ will equal the expectation value, $p(x_{in}|y_m=1) = \exp(w_{inm})$. In this case the average value of the product $x_{in}y_m$ will equal the average value of the product $p(x_{in}|y_m)y_m$. To correct this discrepancy between input observation and expectation, we propose an "expectant" Hebbian learning algorithm for the weight $w_{inm}$,

$$\Delta w_{inm} = \varepsilon\left(x_{in} - e^{w_{inm}}\right) y_m$$

(7)

A similar argument motivates a learning algorithm for the bias $b_m$,

$$\Delta b_m = \varepsilon\left(y_m - e^{b_m}\right).$$

(8)

These must be accompanied by changes that maintain normalization within each group $i$ of inputs indexed by $n$ and going to output neuron $m$, but are independent of learning:

$$\Delta w_{inm} = \frac{1 - \sum_{n'} e^{w_{in'm}}}{\sum_{n'} e^{w_{in'm}}} \quad \text{for all } i, m$$

(9)

One can show that the learning rate parameter $\varepsilon$ can be interpreted as approximately equal to one over the number of times that $x_{in}y_m = 1$ during some characteristic time, say T, for learning—that is, $\varepsilon \approx 1/[T p(x_{in}y_m = 1)]$.

This algorithm works well if the network parameters $b_m$ and $w_{inm}$ are already approximately correct. This allows the network to "fine tune" its parameters or to "track" slowly changing probabilities. We illustrate this with a model of olfaction.

## 3. Olfaction Simulation

W suppose there are 10 categories of odors $y_m$, $m=1,2,...,10$, and 100 receptor cells, $x_{in}$, $i=1,2,...,100$, with each receptor cell represented in this formalism by two redundant binary variables $x_{in}$, $n=0,1$, such that $x_{i0}+x_{i1}=1$. Each receptor cell $x_{in}$ has some fixed probability $p(x_{in}|y_m)$ to respond to odor $y_m$. For simplicity we set these probabilities to either of two previously chosen values $phi$ or $plo$, randomly choosing $phi$ for some fraction F of receptor cells. Typical values are $plo = 10\%$, $phi = 50\%$, and F = 20%. One output cell is associated with each category $y_m$ and each output cell has inputs from all receptor cells $x_{in}$. We first set the network parameters $b_m$ and $w_{inm}$ according to these probabilities using equations (2) and (3). We then repeatedly generated odor identities and receptor cell responses according to these probabilities, and have output cells generate responds $y_m$ according to equation (5) and learn according to (7), (8), (9). As long as the difference $phi-plo$ is not too small, the network responds with a very low error rate.

We now assume that each receptor cell has a finite average lifetime, after which it is replaced by a new receptor cell with completely new, randomly chosen response characteristics unknown to the classifying cells $y_m$. We crudely model this by periodically replacing the response probabilities $p(x_{in}|y_m)$ for half of the the receptor cells with new, randomly chosen values, and letting the output cell learn the corresponding new values of weights $w_{inm}$, without supervision as always in these studies. Even after doing this several times on alternate halves of the set of input cells $x$, representing several turnovers of receptor cells, the network continues to classify well, with an error rate comparable to the initial low error rate with weights and biases set according to

(2) and (3).

## 4. Learning with poor initial values

If we do not have good initial values for network parameters, this learning algorithm does not work perfectly: It finds the correct global solution only occasionally, most often learning to respond to two or more input classes with one output value. However, this problem is eliminated with the variety of projection pursuit (Freund and Haussler, 1992) described below.

If the network parameters are correct, then $S_m$ will have a Gaussian distribution in the limit of a large number of inputs; the network will perform poorly and $S_m$ will be distributed with non-Gaussian tails if the network weights and biases are not correct. We assume that the network performance is worse when $S_m$ is in the tail. This suggests that each output unit $y_m$ keep running averages $A_m = <S_m>$ and $\sigma_m^2 = <(S_m-A_m)^2>$ and learn only if $S_m$ is within $\approx \sigma_m$ of $A_m$. We do this by multiplying the the weight and bias changes of equations (7) and (8) by the Gaussian,

$$\exp\left(-\frac{(S_m - A_m)^2}{2\sigma_m^2}\right).$$

$$(10)$$

With this modification, we find in numerical simulations that the network always learns the correct global solution if all parameters $b_m$ and $w_{inm}$ initialized to random values and if the "signal strength" $phi-plo$ is not too small. If the signal strength is subsequently reduced, the network can learn to distinguish very fine differences. If the signal strength is initially small, the network may still incorrectly learn to lump two or more classes together.

An example of this is given below. In this simulation we had three output neurons $y_m$, $m=1,2,3$, representing four possible states, $m=0,1,2,3$, and 30 groups of 3 mutually exclusive input neurons $x_{in}$, $i=1,2,...,30$, $n=1,2,3$, with each group also representing four possible states, $n=0,1,2,3$. The outputs $y_m$ might correspond, for example, to position cells in the hippocampus, while the inputs could correspond to multimodal sensory data. We generated input data $x$ after randomly choosing values of $p(x_{in}|y_m)$ with an average of 0.25 and a fixed RMSD of a few percent, and setting $p(y_m) = 0.25$. All network weights $w_{inm}$ were initialized to random values in the same range, and all biases $b_m$ were initialized to zero. Valuations of input variables $x_{in}$ were generated according to these fixed probabilities, while for each input valuation, the network output variables $y_m$ were selected according to equation (5) and network weights and biases were learned according to equations (7) and (8), and adjusted according to (9).

Below is a graph of the results of numerical simulations for the log of the error rate versus number of input valuations, for two different RMSDs of the conditional probabilities. For a fixed RMSD equal to 0.08, corresponding to very weak, barely distinguishable structure in the input data, the lowest possible error rate—when the weights and bias' are set according to (2) and (3)— is about 26%, only slightly better than the chance rate of 75%; for and RMSD of 15%, this lowest possible error rate is about 1.5%. The error rate was measured after various periods of learning using a set of 1000 input valuations with learning turned off. After starting with an error rate approximately equal to chance as expected, the network learns to respond with an error rate approaching or equal to the best possible error rate.

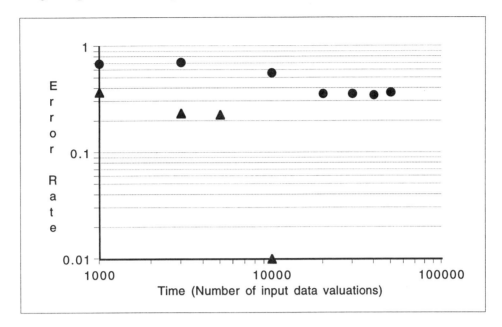

Figure 1. Error Rate versus learning time for unsupervised learning of four probabilistically characterized categories. Circles are for a case of small differences in conditional probabilities, $p(x_{in}|y_m) \approx 25 \pm 8\%$, and triangles are for a case of larger differences, $p(x_{in}|y_m) \approx 25 \pm 15\%$. In both cases the network response approaches or exceeds optimal behavior (26% and 1.5%, respectively) after a long enough learning period.

This algorithm is not perfect: if the weights are initialized to zero rather than random values, the network usually learns to incorrectly lump together two input classes, and even with random initial weight values, the network will often make this mistake if the signal strength is small (this was the effect that increased the error rate to about 35% from the best possible rate of 26% in the small difference data of Figure 1). These and other factors such as the learning rate affect the network performance and are being studied now.

## 5.  Biological  Plausibility

We note here that although this algorithm allows the qualitatively new capability of unsupervised classification, it is different from classical Hebbian learning in only minor, biologically plausible ways:
a)  The learning rules have a "saturation" term in the presynaptic factor.  This could easily implemented by a local biochemical mechanism.
b)  Learning rules are applied to the bias as well as the weights; also, each neuron $y_m$ must learn weights $w_{in0}$ corresponding to input probabilities when $y_0=1$, or equivalently, when $y_m=0$ for all output neurons $m=1,2,...,M$.  Again, these could easily be implemented by local mechanisms.
c)  The weights $w_{inm}$ associated with a group $i,m$ of mutually exclusive inputs $x_{inm}$, $n=0,1,...,N$, to any particular output neuron $y_m$, must be normalized.  This should not be a problem, since such a group would be physically localized and so correspond to some

normalization mechanism in one dendritic branch of each neuron $y_m$. This normalization is algebraically simple with the same normalization offset added to all weights $w_{inm}$, $n=0,1,...,N$ within the group labeled by $i,m$. It is not critically time dependent, but can occur continuously independently of learning.

It is worth noting that these same characteristics that make a biological implementation plausible also allow simple implementations with distributed electronic circuits.

## 6. Conclusion

Unsupervised classification is a process with many potential areas of applications in biology and engineering, including olfaction, position sensing, speech recognition, visual processing, and the generation of multimodal representations. We have given a simple, biologically plausible algorithm for unsupervised classification of probabilistically characterized input data, Expectant Hebbian Learning, that performs well in preliminary numerical simulations.

*References and notes*

* email address: tvold1@cc.swarthmore.edu

Freund, Y., and D. Haussler. 1992. Unsupervised learning of distributions on binary vectors using two layer networks. In *Advances in Neural Network Processing Systems 4,* edited by J. Moody, S.J. Hanson, and R.P. Lippmann. Morgan Kaufmann, San Mateo, C.

Hinton, G.E. and T.J. Sejnowski. 1983. Optimal Perceptual Inference. *Proc. IEEE conference on computer Vision and Pattern Recognition,* 448-453.

Hinton, G.E., T.J. Sejnowski, and D.H. Ackley. 1984. Boltzmann Machines: constraint satisfaction networks that learn. Tech. Rep. CMU-CS-84-119, Pittsburgh: Carnegie-Mellon University, Dept. of Computer Science.

Jaynes, E.T. 1983. *Papers on Probability, Statistic, and Statistical Physics,* edited by R.D. Rosenkrantz, Reidel, Boston.

MacKay, D.J.C. 1991. Maximum entropy connections: neural networks. In *Maximum Entropy and Bayesian Methods,* W.T. Grandy, Jr. and L.H. Schick, eds, 237-244. Kluwer, Boston.

# Generation Mechanism of Integrative Potential in Axon Hillock of a Single Neuron and Noise Feedback Pulse Coding

Jong-Han Shin

Research Department
Electronics and Telecommunication Research Institute
P.O. Box 8, Daeduk Science Town, Daejeon, Korea
(FAX)82-42-860-5033, (E-mail)jhshin@ard.etri.re.kr

## Abstract

This paper describes simplified axon hillock modeling and presents novel concept that pulse encoding in axon hillock of a single neuron is a kind of noise feedback pulse coding. Experimental results, tested in an artificial electronic axon hillock circuit based on the proposed model, shows output signals similar to integrative potential and action potential generated in biological neurons. As a result, the role of the integrative potential is to increase efficiency of the pulse coding in axon hillock through noise feedback.

## 1 Introduction

Recently various neural network models have been proposed and demonstrated to be suitable for pattern recognition, finding approximate solutions to optimization problems, for constraint satisfaction processing, etc. However the neural models which were used in such applications were so simple that these networks have been restricted to small-scale applications. Therefore we have to explore latent abilities of the biological neural system to make a breakthrough in the artificial neural networks [1].

Specially the development of more sophisticated neuron models will lead to generate the brain-type functions of living beings. A simple sophistication introduced in neuron modeling by several researchers is to make the neuron output oscillatory. This means that the output of a neuron becomes a sequence of pulses to express the information of neuron body into frequency, provided that the spacial and temporal summation of the incoming signals exceeds a certain threshold [2,3].

On the other hand, Von der Malsburg and Schneider proposed an interesting feature binding mechanism based on synchronization of nerve pulses(action potentials). Recent experimental findings support this idea, and many theoretical models ensued from the experimental findings to explain the phase locking phenomena in the brain [4,5,6].

There are another trends which make use of chaotic characteristics in biological neural system for information processing. Herald Szu proposed the fuzzy reasoning method using chaotic neurons [7].

As a result, we think that the oscillation, synchronization and chaos characteristics in the biological neural system play important roles in information processing with being linked together, or independently, and the oscillation output of the single neuron can serves as basic element in a novel information processing system using oscillation, synchronization and chaos.

In this paper, we will present a novel model for the generation mechanism of the integrative potential to be generated in relation to occurrence of oscillation output in the axon hillock of the single neuron, and address the hidden role of the integrative potential of the axon hillock in information-processing view.

## 2 Transformation of information in biological neuron

Fig.1 shows various types of spiking-neurons, such as sensory neuron, local interneuron, projection interneuron, motor neuron and the like. However, regardless of size, shape, transmitter biochemistry, or behavioral function, almost all neurons can be described by a generalized model neuron that has four types signals at four different sites as shown in Fig. 1 : an input signal at neuron body( called a receptor potential in the sensory neuron, and a synaptic potential in the interneuron or motor neuron), an integration signal at axon hillock, a conducting signal at axon, and an output signal at axon terminal.

Fig.2 shows the four types of signals, when a stretch stimulus is applied to the sensory neuron [9].

# 3 Novel simplified axon hillock modeling and noise feedback pulse coding

The integrative potential generation mechanism in the axon hillock can be explained by using Hodgkin-Huxley axon equations, which describe action potential generation mechanism in squid axon [10].

From the Hodgkin-Huxley axon equations, we see that the input potential in the neuron body is encoded to a pulse stream in the following form : the input currents I flowing through resistance of the axon hillock from the neuron body are integrated by the membrane capacitance of the axon hillock. When the integrated voltage reaches the threshold voltage of the axon hillock, the sodium current flows into the membrane to be depolarized, and After a finite delay, the potassium current flows out the membrane to be repolarized. As a result, an action potential or nerve pulse is generated by the inrushed sodium current, and the difference between the input current I(t) and the delayed potassium current is integrated by capacitance of the axon hillock, then the integrative potential is produced.

If the input current of the axon hillock is relatively large, the integrative potential will be produced with the train of the action potential, where the amplitude and duration are determined by the cell characteristics constantly and not by the input signals. At this time, the number of the action potentials and separation are dependent on the input.

On the other hand, since the axon is very resistive, the input current I(t) does not flow far from the axon hillock. Therefore, the integrative potential is generated only in the axon hillock and in the axon the action potential only is generated.

The block diagram which simplify the mechanism in the axon hillock is shown in Fig. 3, and expressed by the following equations:

$$C\frac{dV}{dt} = I_{in} - I_r = \frac{X(t)}{R_1} - \frac{Y(t-\tau)}{R_2} \tag{1}$$

$$if \ \ V(t') > V_{th} \ \ then \ Y(t) = \begin{cases} 1 & t' < t < t' + t_d \\ 0 & t' + t_d < t < t' + 2t_d \end{cases} \tag{2}$$

$$if \ \ V(t) < V_{th} \ \ then \ Y(t) = 0. \tag{3}$$

Where X(t) is the input voltage, the Y(t) is the single pulse output with a finite duration $t_d$, $\tau$ is a delay time, $R_1$ represents the axon hillock resistance, $R_2$ represents the potassium channel resistance and $t'$ is the time that V(t) exceeds the threshold voltage. The output pulse density is proportional to the amplitude of the input signal X(t), which can be reconstructed by a low pass filtering contained in the temporal summation function of the neuron body of postsynaptic neurons. In addition, the equation (1) can be described by the following normalized difference equations:

$$v(k) = v(k-1) + (x(k) - y(k-1)). \tag{4}$$

On the other hand, a noise feedback pulse coding is a noise reduction technique which feeds back the coding noise and subtracts it from the next input [11,12]. The block diagram of this technique is shown in Fig. 4. The system input $x(k)$ [−1, 1] and bilevel output $y(k)$ is related by the following nonlinear recursive equations:

$$v(k) = x(k) - e(k-1) \tag{5}$$
$$y(k) = q(v(k)) \tag{6}$$
$$e(k) = y(k) - v(k). \tag{7}$$

The corrected value $v(k)$ is encoded to $y(k)$ by the nonlinear sign function q, thus $y(k) = \pm 1$ depending on whether or not $v(k)$ is positive. The encoder error $e(k)$ (= $q(v(k)) - v(k)$) influences future coding decisions. In other words, it will be subtracted from the actual input value of the next sample to create a

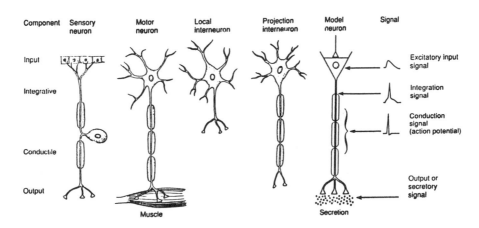

Fig. 1 Four functional components in most neurons.

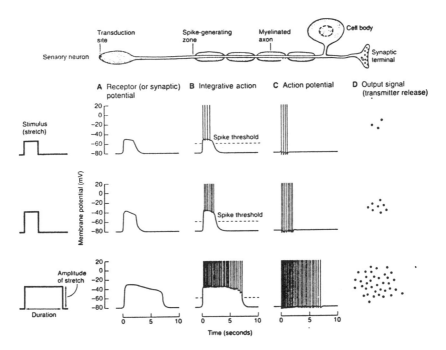

Fig. 2 Transformations of information within a neuron.

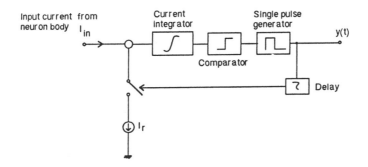

Fig. 3 The block diagram of novel axon hillock modeling.

new corrected value, which will in turn be encoded to generate a new output and a new encoder error, and so on. From equations (5) and (7)

$$e(k) \quad - \quad e(k-1) \quad = \quad y(k) - x(k) \tag{8}$$
$$v(k) \quad = \quad v(k-1) + (x(k) - y(k-1)). \tag{9}$$

Taking the z-transform of both sides of equation (8), the coding noise transform E(z) is obtained as

$$E(z) = \frac{Y(z) - X(z)}{1 - Z^{-1}}. \tag{10}$$

Where E(z) = z-transform of $e_n$, etc: equation (10) suggests that the coding noise decreases in the low frequency band due to high pass filtering and the coding noise in the high frequency band can be removed by low pass filter. As a result, further large signal-to-noise ratio is produced due to the noise feedback pulse coding.

By the way, since equations (4) and (9) are identical with each other, we see that the block diagram of Fig. 5 is equivalent to the one of Fig.4. Therefore, in this paper we insist that the noise feedback pulse coding is performed in the biological axon hillock, which allows to increase efficiency of the nerve pulse coding, and that the integrative potential is a signal accompanied with the noise feedback pulse coding.

# 4 Electronic axon hillock circuit

Fig. 5 shows an electronic axon hillock circuit based on the block diagram of Fig. 3, in which the RC network acts as an integrator and the input current I(t) is integrated in capacitor C. The integrated signal is compared with the threshold voltage $V_{th}$ of a comparator, and the output of the comparator is fed to a single pulse generator which generates a delayed single pulse. The single pulse output is applied to the reference voltage switch, which feeds back the reference voltage $-V_{ref}$ to the other input terminal of integrator. Then the capacitor C integrates the current difference I(t)$-I_r$.

In the electronic axon hillock circuit, X(t) represents the input component of the biological neuron, the capacitor voltage $V_c$ represents the integrative component of the biological neuron, and the output of the single pulse generator represents the conductile component(action potential) of the biological neuron.

The axon hillock circuit of Fig. 5 was built on a test protoboard, using two discrete resisters, a discrete capacitor, a LM311N comparator, a HD74S175P D-type flip flop, and CD4007UB analog switches.

Fig. 6 shows three waveforms observed in experiments, where two different test input signals are used; waveform (1) shows the test input pulse which act as the input component as shown in Fig. 2. (2) shows the integrative potential for the input signal, and (3) shows action potentials for the test input. With the results, we see that the output signals are similar to the integrative potential and action potentials generated in biological neurons.

# 5 Conclusions

In this paper, the novel simplified model for the generation mechanism of the integrative potential in the axon hillock of the biological neuron is presented, and the role of the integrative potential in information-processing view is addressed.

The integrative potential is produced as the result of the noise feedback pulse coding to be performed by the input current flowing from the neuron body to the axon hillock, the current caused by the potassium ion, the current caused by the sodium ion, and the membrane capacitance of the axon hillock.

The noise in the low frequency band, which is generated during the pulse coding in axon hillock, is pushed to the high frequency band by noise feedback operation, and when the pulse train is transmitted to other neurons, the noise in the high frequency band is removed due to the low pass filtering by the temporal summation function of the neuron body. Then the reconstructed signal having large signal-to-noise ratio can be obtained, compared with the case without the noise feedback operations.

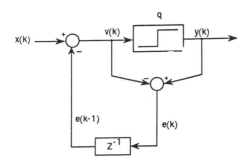

Fig. 4 The block diagram of noise feedback pulse coding.

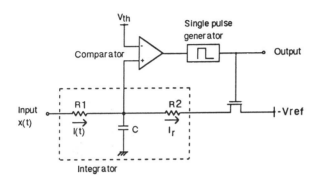

Fig. 5 An electronic axon hillock circuit based on the proposed axon hillock model.

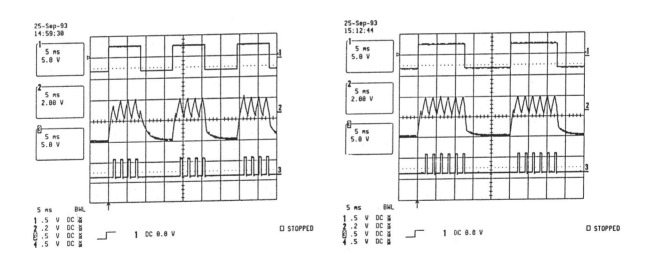

Fig. 6A Experimentally observed waveforms
(duration of test input = 8ms)

Fig. 6B Experimentally observed waveforms
(duration of test input = 12.5ms)

As a result, the role of the integrative potential is to increase efficiency of the pulse coding in axon hillock through noise feedback.

## Acknowledgement

I would like to thank Dr. El Hang Lee for his continuing encouragement.

## References

[1] J. Dayhoff, "Temporal and molecular structures in neural systems", in World Congress on Neural Networks, vol. I, 1993, pp. 105-109.

[2] A. F. Murray, D. D. Corso, and L. Tarassenko, "Pulse-stream VLSI neural networks mixing analog and digital techniques", IEEE Transactions on Neural Networks, vol. 2, 1991, pp.193-204.

[3] B. L. Barranco, E. S. Sinencio, A. R. Vazquez, and J. L. Huertas, "A CMOS implementation of Fitzhugh-Nagumo neuron model", IEEE J. of Solid-State Circuits, vol. 26, 1991, pp.956-965.

[4] C. von der Malsburg, and W. Schneider, "A neural cocktail–party processor", Biol. Cybern., no. 54, 1986, pp.29-40.

[5] P. König, and T. B. Schillen, "Stimulus-dependent assembly formation of oscillatory responses", vol.3, 1991, pp.155-178.

[6] J. S. Jang, "Oscillatory neural network for integrated segmentation and recognition of patterns", in World Congress on Neural Networks, vol. I, 1993, pp.33-35.

[7] H. Szu, "Spaciotemporal chaos information processing in neural networks-electronic implementation", in World Congress on Neural Networks, vol. VI, 1993, pp. 758-762.

[8] C. A. Mead, Analog VLSI and Neural Systems. MA : Addison-Wesley, 1989.

[9] E. R. Kandel, Principles of Neural Science. New York:Elsevier Science Publishing Co., 1991.

[10] A. Hodgkin, and A. F. Huxley, "A quantitative description of membrane current and its application to conduction and excitation in nerve", Journal of Physiology, vol. 117, 1952, p.500.

[11] N. S. Jayant, and P. Noll, Digital Coding of Waveforms, New Jersey : Prentice-Hall, 1984.

[12] J. H. Shin, "Novel neural circuits using stochastic pulse coding and noise feedback pulse coding, International Journal of Electronics, vol. I, 1993, pp.33-35.

# Neural Phase-Locked Loop

## Ju-Seog Jang

Department of Telematics Engineering
National Fisheries University of Pusan
599-1 Daeyun-Dong, Nam-Gu, Pusan, Korea
(FAX) 82-51-628-7433

## Abstract

In this paper, it is explained that a single neuron with a self-feedback path can act as a phase-locked loop, when the synaptic coupling of the feedback is multiplicative. A simulation was carried out to show that this simple neural phase-locked loop can efficiently retransmit incomming signals to another neuron with little signal distortion.

## 1. Introduction

The most common neural models have been usually described by the firing rates of the neurons and the additive synaptic couplings between them. Recent research results, however, have shown that relative phase of neural oscillations can be also an important parameter in information representation and processing [1]-[6].

In this paper, I explain a neural phase-locked loop (NPLL) in which relative phase of nerve impulse trains plays an important role. For an impulse-generating neuron to be a PLL, there should be a self-feedback through the multiplicative synaptic coupling. Many authors have studied the multiplicative coupling in the sigma-pi unit [7], and also utilized it, for example, in the motion detector models [8]. The multiplicative coupling element can be viewed as a logical AND unit. Good candidates of such an element are excitable dendritic spines [9] and axo-axonic synapses [10].

In general, a frequency modulated signal can be demodulated with high fidelity by the PLL device [11]. Let us call the device electronic PLL (EPLL) to distinguish it from NPLL. The same story can be applied to the NPLL. Suppose a pulse-frequency-modulated signal is to be transmitted to other neurons in different areas. Simple demodulation by dendritic integration usually distorts the original signal somehow. To make matters worse, the optimal neural parameters for a good demodulation are dependent upon the input signal frequency. Therefore, as a complex signal passes through just a few neurons, lots of the information can be lost. On the contrary, if signals are transmitted through the NPLLs, the high signal fidelity can be guaranteed as far as the signals are within the NPLL lock range.

The function of monkey somatosensory cortex in texture analysis seems to be based on a PLL-like action as hypothesized by Ahissar and Vaadia [12]. They assumed that the coupled thalamic and cortical neurons can be a PLL. The feedback path from the cortical neuron to the thalamic neuron is inhibitory in their PLL implementation. In this paper, a PLL itself, which is a single neuron with a multiplicative excitatory self-feedback, is studied in detail.

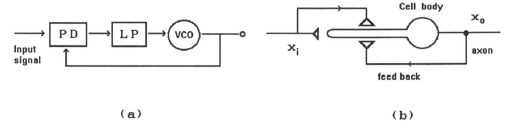

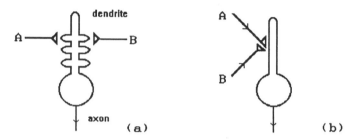

Figure 1: (a) Block diagram of phase-locked loop. See text for abbreviations. (b) A neural phase-locked loop.

Figure 2: Multiplicative synaptic coupling between A and B. (a) Excitable dendritic spines [9]. (b) Axo-axonic synapse.

## 2. Neural phase-locked loop

Three components of the EPLL are a phase detector (PD), a loop filter (LF), and a voltage-controlled oscillator (VCO), as depicted in Fig. 1(a). The input is a frequency-modulated sinusoidal wave. The PD is a kind of analog multiplier that detects phase difference between the input signal and the VCO output. The LF filters out high frequency components of the multiplied signals. The VCO produces a sinusoidal wave output whose frequency is proportional to the output voltage of the LF. The output frequency of VCO for zero voltage is called the free running frequency.

Fig. 1(b) depicts an NPLL, in which the dendrite, axon hillock, and multiplicative synapse map to the LF, VCO, and PD of the EPLL, one by one. Two possible implementations of the multiplicative synaptic coupling, *i.e.*, excitable dendritic spine [9] and axo-axonic synapse [13], are shown in Fig. 2(a) and (b), respectively. Both can detect the coincidence of two arriving nerve impulses. In other words, one impulse alone cannot change the postsynaptic potential significantly.

There is also slight difference between NPLL and EPLL. The input of NPLL is unipolar impulses, while the input of EPLL is a bipolar sinusoidal wave. In addition, without any bias input to the neuron, there is no free running oscillation in the NPLL. In spite of these differences, Fig. 1(b) can work as a PLL as explained below.

Let us assume each nerve impulse is the Dirac delta function $V_0\delta(t)$. In Fig. 1(b), the incoming input impulse train $x_i(t)$ with interspike interval $T_i$ can be written as $x_i(t) = \sum_{k=-\infty}^{\infty} \delta(t - kT_i)$ where $V_0$ is simply set to 1. Its frequency domain representation becomes $x_i(t) = f_i + 2f_i \sum_{n=1}^{\infty} \cos 2\pi n f_i t$ where $f_i = 1/T_i$. If this impulse train arrives at an additive synaptic contact, only two most significant components (dc component and fundamental frequency component) will be considered as a postsynaptic potential in the dendrite near that contact, *i.e.*,

$$u_a(t) = W^a(f_i + 2f_i \cos 2\pi f_i t) \tag{1}$$

where $W^a$ is a coupling coefficient of the additive synapse. Suppose the input $x_i$ and the feedback impulse train $x_o$ with frequency $f_o$ arrive at a purely multiplicative synaptic contact. Let us assume the dendritic postsynaptic potential in the vicinity of the contact becomes simple product of the two potentials of Eq. (1). That is,

$$\begin{aligned} u_m(t) = \ & W^m\{f_i f_o + 2f_i f_o \cos[2\pi(f_i - f_o)t - \phi] \\ & + 2f_i f_o \cos 2\pi f_i t + 2f_i f_o \cos(2\pi f_o t + \phi) \\ & + 2f_i f_o \cos[2\pi(f_i + f_o)t + \phi]\} \end{aligned} \tag{2}$$

where $\phi$ is the phase difference between $x_i$ and $x_o$, and $W^m$ is a coupling coefficient of the multiplicative synapse. The dendritic potentials given in Eq. (1) and (2) are assumed to be further filtered through dendritic trunk. Then, almost dc components will be effective at the axon hillock. Especially when $f_i \approx f_o$, the total postsynaptic potential at the axon hillock becomes

$$u_o(t) \approx W^a f_i + W^m(f_i f_o + 2f_i f_o \cos \phi) \tag{3}$$

The first two terms in Eq. (3) can be viewed as a bias term and the last term as a phase detection term. It is noteworthy that the last term is inversely proportional to a small phase variation $\Delta\phi$, for example, when $\phi = \pi/2$, since $\cos(\pi/2 + \Delta\phi) \approx -\Delta\phi$. This term constructs a negative feedback through the self-feedback loop and thus it can compensate small phase variations in the external input impulses. Note that $\phi = 2n\pi + 3\pi/2$ ($n$ = any integer) are unstable points. The feedback loop can be completed via an additional inhibitory neuron in the NPLL. In this case, $W^m$ will be simply replaced with $-W^m$ in Eq. (3). Then the stable point will shift, for example, from $\phi = \pi/2$ to $\phi = 3\pi/2$. Therefore, whether the feedback loop is excitatory or inhibitory is not important in principle.

To examine whether the NPLL will work in a more practical condition, a simulation was carried out.

## 3. Computer simulations

The Hindmarsh-Rose model for nerve impulse generation [14] was used for the VCO of NPLL. The model, which shows a good linear current-frequency relationship, has two first-order differential equations,

$$\begin{aligned} \dot{x} &= a(-cx^3 + dx^2 + ex + h + y - \theta + I) \\ \dot{y} &= b(cx^3 - dx^2 - ex - h - qe^{rx} + s - y) \end{aligned} \tag{4}$$

where $x$ and $y$ are the membrane potential and an intrinsic current, respectively. The parameter values are as follows: $a = 5400$, $b = 30$, $c = 0.000017$, $d = 0.001$, $e = 0.01$, $h = 0.1$, $q = 0.024$, $r = 0.088$, and $s = 0.046$. A constant $\theta$ is introduced to change the threshold level, $-0.026$, to a positive value. Here, $\theta = 0.04$. Thus the repetative firing occurs when the input current $I$ is greater than 0.014.

The dendrite is simulated by three-stage RC low-pass filter as shown in Fig. 3. The

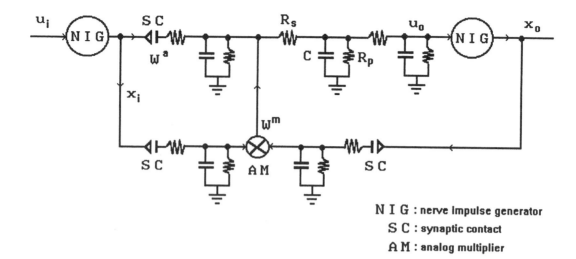

N I G : nerve impulse generator
S C : synaptic contact
A M : analog multiplier

Figure 3: Model of neural phase-locked loop.

multiplicative synapse is modeled as an analog multiplier whose input impedance and the output impedance are both infinite. The gain of the analog multiplier is $W^m$. It is assumed that the synaptic contacts pass the positive part of the impulses to the resistor $R_s$. The coupling coefficient of the additive synapse is $W^a$, while that of multiplicative synapses is unity as a reference. It is also assumed that $u_o$ is directly converted to the input current $I$ of Eq. (4). The parameter values used here are $W^m = 0.09$, $W^a = 0.005$, $R_s = 1$, $R_p = 3$, and $C = 1$. The PLL neuron is biased just below the threshold level.

Two typical simulation results are given in Fig. 4. The modulating signal $u_i$ is a step function in Fig. 4(a), and it is a sinusoidal wave in Fig. 4(b). The demodulated signal $u_o$ in the NPLL converge to $u_i$ quickly in a time average sense. The capture process is clearly seen. The corresponding input and output impusles $x_i$ and $x_o$ are also displayed. After about ten interspike-interval time, the phase of $x_o$ is locked to that of $x_i$. The result with additive synapse alone, $i.e.$, without PLL loop, is also given in Fig. 4(c) for the sake of comparison. To get a good demodulated signal $u_o$, $W^a$ was set to 0.1 instead of 0.005 in Fig. 4(c).

## 4. Discussion

The capture process in the NPLL can fail like an EPLL when $u_i$ changes faster than a certain limit. The limit is determined by the time constant of dendrite and the term $2W^m f_i f_o \cos \phi$ in Eq. (3). Another capture-failing element is the magnitude of $u_i$. Since the analog multiplier and the RC low-pass filter of NPLL do not constitute an ideal PD, there will be additional low-frequency noise terms, which do not appear in Eq. (3). Thus the excitatory self-feedback provides some positive feedback effect, when the approximation of Eq. (3) is violated. This effect was observed when the magnitude of $u_i$ is greater than a certain large value in the simulation. This limit can be improved if an inhibitory neuron is introduced to regulate the NPLL activity.

Note that Fig. 1(b) is not the only way of NPLL implementation. The scheme where an inhibitory neuron is involved in the feedback loop was briefly mentioned in Section 2.

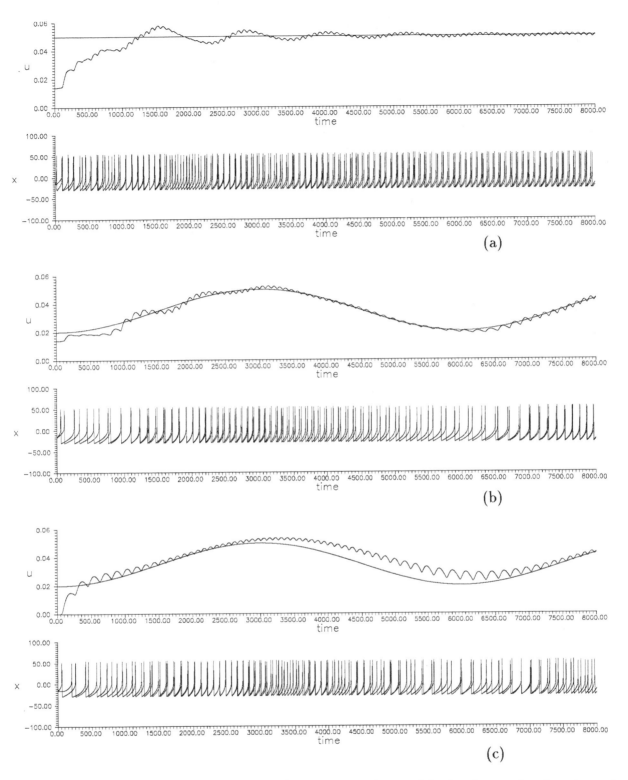

Figure 4: Simulation results. The smooth curves are the modulating input signals $u_i$'s, and the crooked curves are the demodulated waveforms $u_o$'s in the NPLL. Corresponding impulse trains $x_i$'s and $x_o$'s are also displayed. (a) When $u_i$ is a step function. (b) When $u_i$ is a sinusoidal function. (c) Without feedback loop. In this case, $W^a = 0.1$.

Another neural circuit that looks like a PLL is a mitral cell in the olfactory bulb of higher animals. The cell usually has an axonic self-feedback path through a dendritic branch of an inhibitory granule cell. The granule cell has no axon and thus it has dendro-dendritic contact with the mitral cell [15]. (See Fig. 8.4 in [15].) If the dendro-dendritic interaction is modulated by the feedback axon in a multiplicative way, it is possibe to show that a PLL-like action is present in the mitral-granule cell interaction.

## 5. Conclusion

It has been shown that a single neuron can be a PLL. For the neuron to be a PLL, two critically important requirements should be satisfied: the multiplicative synapse and the self-feedback loop through that synapse. It seems that the two elements are found commonly and ubiquitously in any nervous system. Thus the existence of PLL-like action in real nervous systems is highly probable. It has also been found that the phase information, which has been conventionally neglected in common neural network models, is very important when neurons are coupled nonlinearly, for example, through multiplicative synapses.

## References

[1] C. von der Malsburg and W. Schneider, *Biol. Cybern.* **54**, 29-40 (1986).

[2] R. Eckhorn, R. Bauer, W. Jordan, M. Brosch, W. Kruse, M. Munk, and H. J. Reitboeck, *Biol. Cybern.* **60**, 121-130 (1988).

[3] C. M. Gray, P. König, A. K. Engel, and W. Singer, *Nature* **338**, 334-337 (1989).

[4] F. Crick and C. Koch, *Seminars in the Neurosciences* **2**, 263-275 (1990).

[5] O. Sporns, G. Tononi, and G. M. Edelman, *Proc. Natl. Acad. Sci. USA* **88**, 129-133 (1991).

[6] J.-S. Jang and C.-D. Lim, *Proceedings of World Congress on Neural Networks*, Vol. I, pp. 33-35, Portland, Oregon, July 11-15, 1993.

[7] R. J. Williams, in D. E. Rumelhart, J. L. McClelland, and the PDP Research Group (Eds.), *Parallel Distributed Processing* Vol. 1: Foundations (MIT Press, MA, 1986), Chap. 10.

[8] A. Borst and M. Egelhaaf, *Trends Neurosci.* **12**, 297-306 (1989).

[9] G. M. Shepherd and R. K. Brayton, *Neuroscience* **21**, 151-165 (1987).

[10] T. J. Sejnowski and G. Tesauro, in J. H. Byrne and W. O. Berry (Eds.), *Neural Models of Plasticity* (Academic Press, CA, 1989), pp. 94-103.

[11] P. Horowitz and W. Hill, *The Art of Electronics* (Cambridge Univ. Press, Cambridge, 1980).

[12] E. Ahissar and E. Vaadia, *Proc. Natl. Acad. Sci. USA* **87**, 8935-8939 (1990).

[13] T. J. Carew, R. D. Hawkins, and E. R. Kandel, *Science* **219**, 397-400 (1983).

[14] J. L. Hindmarsh and R. M. Rose, *Nature* **296**, 162-164 (1982).

[15] G. M. Shepherd, *The Synaptic Organization of the Brain* (Oxford Univ. Press, Oxford, 1979).

# Learning to Generate a Sinewave with an Autonomous Recurrent Two-Neuron Network

Jyh-Ming Kuo, Jose C. Principe
Computational NeuroEngineering Laboratory
University of Florida

## Abstract

A training procedure to generate a sinewave of a prescribed frequency from a two neuron autonomous recurrent neural network is proposed. Through an analysis of the role of the processing elements, we are able to identify the role of each network parameter in this task. The parameters of one of the neurons are pre-selected analytically such that the adaptation of the connection weights and the parameters of the other neuron can be significantly eased. Experimental results show that using the proposed method we not only can successfully train the network to generate a desired sinewave, but also can significantly reduce the size of required data samples and the number of training epochs.

## 1. Introduction

Not enough is known about learning temporal patterns with autonomous recurrent neural networks. A benchmark task in this area is to train a network to generate a sinewave. Both time domain or state space methods have been proposed [1][2][3]. Neural oscillators have been shown to produce several complex waveforms (including chaotic signals) when a control parameter is changed [4]. Therefore the problem is not one of being able to generate a sinewave with a recurrent neural network, but how to harness this power. Understanding what is the role of each one of the processing units may lead to parsimonious neural architectures, and also to faster ways to train recurrent systems, which is an on-going research goals in the theory of recurrent adaptive systems.

In this paper, we study an autonomous two-processing-element (PE) network and propose a method to decompose the task of determining the network parameters. The theoretical analysis and experimental results show that this network can indeed be trained to produce a sinewave of a desired frequency. Compared with the training methods proposed by other research groups, our method yields an adaptation that converges very fast. Besides, the shape and the phase of the target signal can be preserved quite well in the network. Of most importance in the proposed method is the identification of the roles of the network parameters and the prediction of some of their values.

## 2. Analysis for Sinewave Generation

A two PE, fully connected, network is shown in Figure 1. The fundamental idea of the analysis is to *divide the network into two parts* and identify the role of each PE. On the left-hand side, the dynamics of PE #1 are governed by

$$S_1(n) = \sigma_1(\beta_1(S_1(n-1) + S_2(n-1) + \theta_1)) \tag{1}$$

where $S_1(n)$ and $S_2(n)$ are the output and the input of PE #1 respectively, and $\beta_1$ and $\theta_1$ are the gain and the bias of a nonlinear squashing function, $\sigma_1()$. The most popular squashing functions for neural networks include the logistic function ($1/(1+e^{\beta x})$) and the hyperbolic-tangent function ($\tanh(x)$). Since the self-excitatory feedback and the input of PE#1 can be weighted differently by adjusting $w_{12}$, we can set the weight $w_{11}$ (self-excitatory connection) to 1 without loss of generality.

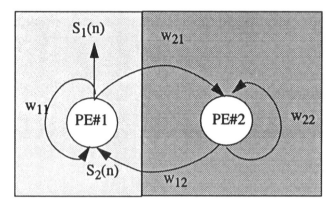

Figure 1. A two-neuron network

Since our task is to generate a target sinewave, the output $S_1(n)$ is assumed known at all times. The required input signal $S_2(n)$ can be determined by the following procedure.

a. Choose $\beta_1$ and $S_2(0)$.

b. Compute $\theta_1$

$$\theta_1 = \frac{1}{\beta_1}\sigma_1^{-1}(S_2(1)) - S_1(0) - S_2(0) \tag{2}$$

c. Compute the sequence $S_2(n)$ iteratively

$$S_2(n) = \frac{1}{\beta_1}\sigma_1^{-1}(S_1(n+1)) - S_1(n) - \theta_1 \tag{3}$$

From eq. 2 and eq. 3, we note that the wave shape of $S_2(n)$ is uniquely determined by the selection of $\beta_1$. The selection of $S_2(0)$ affects only the dc component of the resulting sequence $S_2(n)$. Once we compute the sequence $S_2(n)$, *the parameters on the right-hand side of the network can be determined adaptively.* The sequence $S_1(n)$ becomes the input signal, and $S_2(n)$ is the target signal. Any trajectory learning algorithm (real time recurrent learning (RTRL) [5] or back-propagation through time (BPTT) [6]) can be applied to train the weights $w_{12}$, $w_{21}$, $w_{22}$, and $\theta_2$, $\beta_2$. The advantage of this proposed method is that the size of the training problem is reduced. *The adaptation of an autonomous two-neuron network is converted into the adaptation of a single neuron with external input.* As long as the external input and the target signal have similar waveforms, this approach will ease the adaptation.

## 3. Some Considerations in the Proposed Training Method

Since there are only two PEs, the number of mappings that can be modeled by the network through learning is limited. To ease the adaptation of the right-hand side of the network, we recommend tuning the gain of the activation function of PE#1 to a value such that $S_1(n)$ and $S_2(n)$ have similar wave shapes (a state space analysis of the PE will be presented in a forthcoming paper). This requirement can be achieved easily as long as the first PE is designed to work in the linear region of its activation function.

Therefore, *the main task of the right-hand side of the network is to yield a necessary phase shift between its input ($S_1(n)$) and its output ($S_2(n)$).* We note that the input of a PE always leads its output in phase if we try to preserve the shape of the waveform. Since $S_1(n)$ and $S_2(n)$ are the output and the input of the first PE, the phase of $S_2(n)$ must lead the phase of $S_1(n)$. The leading phase can be up to 180 degrees. This argument can be verified by using a linear approximation of eq. 3 and analyzing the phase response in the frequency domain. The right-hand side of the network consists of one PE(PE#2), two inter-neuron connections (i.e. $w_{21}$ and $w_{12}$), and a self recurrent connection $w_{22}$. *In training, we expect either $w_{12}$ or $w_{21}$, but not both, to have a negative sign such that the input of PE#2 can lead its output in phase.* Thus, assuming a phase difference between $S_2(n)$ and $S_1(n)$ of $\phi$ degrees, the required phase difference between the input and the output of PE #2 becomes 180 - $\phi$ degrees.

To reduce the sensitivity of each PE to the output of the other PE, we need to keep both $\beta_1$ and $\beta_2$ small. A large phase shift requires a large gain. Therefore, we can choose $\beta_1$ such that $\phi$ is about 90 degrees. This setting can be done experimentally or analytically (from the linear approximation of eq. 3). We verified in our experiments that a successful adaptation of the right-hand side of the network should result in a $\beta_2$ very close to $\beta_1$. This is because with this selection of $\beta_1$ the phase difference of the input and the output of the PE#2 is also about 90 degrees. The generation of a 90-degree phase shift between the input and the output of a PE may require a large gain if the target signal, $S_1(n)$, is sampled at a high rate (i.e. if the number of samples per period is large). Therefore, we may need to reduce the sampling rate of the desired signal to relax the requirement of a large gain. Large gains affect the frequency stability of the output sinewave.

To summarize, a successful training of the network to produce a sinewave should result in one and only one inhibitory inter-neuron connection. When we select $\beta_1$ such that the phase shift between $S_1(n)$ and $S_2(n)$ is close to 90 degrees, the adaptation of $\beta_2$ should converge to a value near $\beta_1$. The sampling frequency of the target signal should be selected properly to relax the high gain requirement.

## 4. Experimental Results

A 20-Hz sinewave was sampled at 220 Hz and used as the target signal for the following experiment. The signal is given is Figure 2. We select a hyperbolic-tangent function as the activation function of each PE and set $\beta_1$ equal to 1. The sequence $S_2(n)$ is computed accordingly and also shown in Figure 2. The first 200 samples of $S_1(n)$ and $S_2(n)$ are used for training purposes. The right-hand side of the network was trained using the RTRL algorithm without teacher forcing. The momentum term is included in each recursive update formula. Figure 3 shows the learning curve during the training. We note that the adaptation converges very fast (within 12 training epochs). In Table 1, the parameters of the network after the training are listed. We notice that there is only one inhibitory inter-neuron connection, and $\beta_1$ and $\beta_2$ are almost the same.

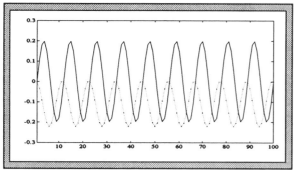

Figure 2. Waveforms for $S_1$(solid line) and $S_2$(dashed line)

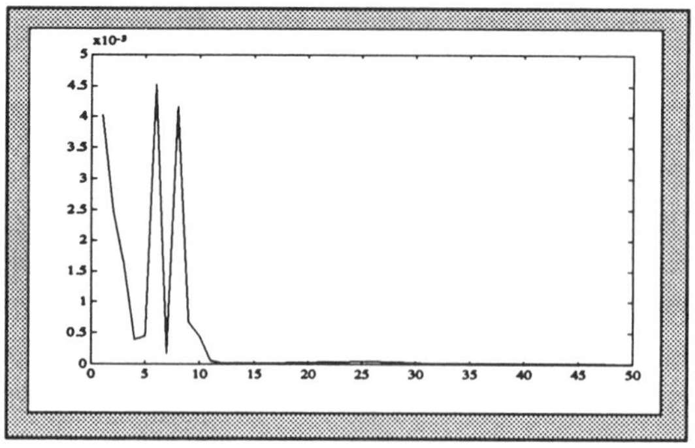

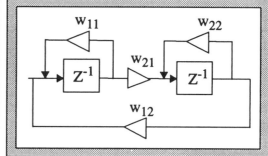

Figure 3. Learning curve.

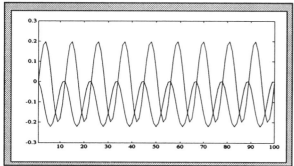

Figure 4. Outputs of neurons (dashed line) and their target signals (solid line).

Figure 5. Linear approximation of the network

**Table 1: Parameters of the Resulting Network**

|  | Preselected parameters | Adaptive parameters |
|---|---|---|
| Gain | $\beta_1 = 1$ | $\beta_2 = 0.9710$ |
| Weights | $w_{11} = 1$ | $w_{12} = -0.4012$ <br> $w_{21} = 0.9053$ <br> $w_{22} = 0.7874$ |
| Bias | $\theta_1 = 0.1086$ | $\theta_2 = 0.0858$ |

After this training, the network weights were frozen and it was relaxed from the initial condition

(0,0). The input and the output of the first PE are plotted with their target signals in Figure 4. This result shows that the network can successfully approximate a sinewave of the desired frequency and phase. Since we designed the network to operate in its linear region, we can validate the resulting network from its linear approximation model as shown in Figure 5. This linear model has poles at $0.8937 \pm 0.5932$ i, which are, as expected, located on the unit circle of the z-plane.

## 5. Conclusions

This paper shows that it is possible to analyze simple recurrent nonlinear circuits, and use this knowledge to improve the efficiency of learning. In fact, an in-depth analysis of the two-neuron network identified the resources necessary to generate a target sinewave. The result shows that the network can indeed approximate the sinewave very well, and with a very efficient training. This conclusion contrasts with the experiments presented in [1] and in [2]. To ease the adaptation and avoid a large value for $\beta_2$, the selection of $\beta_1$ should result in a phase shift between the input and the output of the first PE close to 90 degrees. This turns out to be equivalent to the requirement of equal gains for both PEs. The generation of a 90-degree phase shift with small gain may be difficult when the signal is sampled at a high rate (i.e. when there are a lot of samples in one period).

In our analysis $S_2(n)$ was analytically computed from the knowledge of $\theta_1$ and $\beta_1$. But in fact a simple circuit implementing eq. 3 can generate $S_2(n)$ from the desired signal, thus avoiding the pre-computation of $S_2(n)$, and enabling an on-line implementation.

## Acknowledgments

This work was partially supported by NSF grant ECS #920878.

## References

[1] Williams, R.J. and D. Zipser, Experimental Analysis of the Real-time Recurrent Learning Algorithm, Connection Science, vol. 1, no. 1, pp.87-111, 1989.

[2] Pearlmutter, B.A., Learning State Space Trajectories in Recurrent Neural Networks. IJCNN(Washington 1989), vol. II, pp365-372, 1989.

[3] Tsung, F-S., Learning in Recurrent Finite Difference Networks, Proceedings of the 1990 summer school, ed. by D. S. Touretzky, J. L. ELman, T. J. Sejnowski, and G. E. Hinton, pp.124-130, Morgan Kaufmann, San Mateo, CA, 1990.

[4] Chapeau-Blondeau, F. and G. Chauvet, Stable, Oscillatory, and Chaotic Regimes in the Dynamics of Small Neural Networks With Delay, Neural Networks, vol. 5, pp735-743, 1992.

[5] Williams, R.J. and D. Zipser, A Learning Algorithm for Continually Running Fully Recurrent Neural Networks, Neural Computation 1, pp270-280, 1989.

[6] Werbos, P.J., Backpropagation through time: what it does and how to do it, Proceedings of the IEEE, vol. 78, no. 10, 1990.

# The Role of Short Term Memory for Temporal Processing with Neural Networks

Jose C. Principe

Computational NeuroEngineering Laboratory
University of Florida, FL 32611

The processing of time varying signals with neural networks requires the extension of static architectures such as the multilayer perceptron (MLP) with short term memory structures. The most common memory structure is the tap delay line, which is utilized in the Time Delay Neural Network. However, other memory structures based on local recurrent system exist, with potential advantages.

This presentation addresses a general model for short term memories based on a linear model. It will also define parameters such as memory depth and memory resolution. It will also compare the available types of memory used in connectionist networks. The core of the talk is contained in the paper "The gamma model: a new neural model for temporal processing" published in Neural Networks, vol 5, pp 565-576, 1992. It will be extended with recent results.

# Links to Cognitive Science and Artificial Intelligence

**Session Chairs: James A. Anderson**
**Larry Medsker**

# Neural Network Connections to Expert Systems

Larry Medsker

Department of Computer Science and Information Systems
The American University
Washington, DC 20016-8116

## Abstract

The complementary features of neural networks and expert systems make hybrid systems an important approach for practical applications. The combination of these two technologies produces more powerful systems than can be built with either of the two alone. Models and guidelines for choosing and developing appropriate hybrid systems are emerging as successful applications appear. This paper summarizes current issues in the research, theory, and development of integrated neural network and expert systems.

## I. Characteristics of Expert Systems and Neural Networks

Expert systems and artificial neural networks represent complementary approaches: the logical, cognitive, and mechanical nature of the expert system approach and the numeric, associative, self-organizing, biological nature of neural networks. Thus, expert systems are especially good for closed systems for which inputs are literal and precise, leading to logical outputs. The value of neural network technology includes its usefulness for pattern recognition, learning, classification, generalization and abstraction, and the interpretation of incomplete and noisy inputs. Neural network components can provide solutions for some of the problems that have proven difficult for expert system developers. Current work shows promising results for hybrid approaches in which expert systems and neural networks are used in various combinations to solve problems in a fashion more consistent with human intelligence [5,24,29].

**Expert System** technology provides a powerful way to capture human expertise into computing systems, and many applications are now in use [18,24,28,33]. Expert systems perform reasoning using previously-established rules for a well-defined and narrow domain. They combine knowledge bases of rules and domain-specific facts with the information from users about specific instances of problems in the knowledge domains of the expert systems. An important advantage of expert systems is the ease with which knowledge bases can be modified as new rules and facts become known. This is a result of the architecture that separates the knowledge base from the inference engine. Also, most expert system development tools allow the creation of explanation systems to help the user understand questions being asked or conclusions that are rendered.

For stable applications with well-defined rules, expert systems can be easily developed to provide good performance. Such systems can take advantage of the wealth of techniques developed in AI and expert system research to perform different types of reasoning using very efficient, systematic techniques. People are able to inspect and understand these systems because they have familiar structures similar to the logical frameworks humans use. Another advantage of expert systems is the number and variety of commercial development systems that have become available over the last several years. With these tools and associated techniques, knowledge engineers can use rapid prototyping for exploratory studies and system design. Prototypes are especially useful in gaining the interest and attention of experts so that the knowledge acquisition process is more efficient and effective.

A fundamental limitation of the expert system approach arises from the fact that experts do not always think in terms of rules. Another problem is the knowledge acquisition bottleneck, and while development tools have become very sophisticated and effective, expert systems still require extensive effort for eliciting knowledge from humans as well as from written material. Knowledge acquisition is still primarily a human-intensive activity requiring the usual system analysis abilities plus additional interviewing and interpersonal skills that are tailored to interacting with human experts. Furthermore, human experts may be too busy or otherwise difficult to deal with, so that a whole project may be threatened or delayed. Another difficulty with expert systems is in the area of large systems development, and for real-world applications, the development process becomes difficult to manage. Working with experts and dealing with the complexity of large systems leads to prolonged, expensive development and delivery times. Furthermore, validation and verification of systems becomes difficult, if not impossible, as many lines of reasoning must be checked. More work is needed on how to represent commonplace knowledge, which humans deal with so well and so often. Also, expert systems do not automatically benefit from experience with their use and thus do not learn from failures or their use with novel examples.

**Neural Networks** rely on training data to adjust the system to solve specific problems, learning in a way that allows generalization during operations on future input data. Neural network components can be useful when rules are not known, either because the topic is too complex or no human expert is available. If training data can be generated, the system may be able to learn enough information to function as well as, or better than, an expert system. This approach also has the benefit of easy modification to a system by retraining with an updated data set, thus eliminating programming changes and rule reconstruction. The data-driven aspect of neural networks allows adjustments to changing environments and events. Another advantage of neural network components is the speed of operation after the network is trained, which will be enhanced dramatically as neural chips become readily available. However, because knowledge is represented as numeric weights, the rules and reasoning process inherent in neural networks are not readily explainable. Neural networks have the potential to provide some of the human characteristics of problem solving that are difficult to simulate using the logical, analytical techniques of expert system and standard software technologies. For example, neural networks can analyze large quantities of data to establish patterns and characteristics in situations where rules are not known and can in many cases make sense of incomplete or noisy data. These capabilities have thus far proven too difficult for the traditional symbolic/logic approaches.

## II. Hybrid Systems Research

The emerging need for hybrid connectionist and symbolic systems is currently motivating important research and development work. In terms of the individual technologies, connectionist systems can represent the perceptual aspect of intelligence while symbolic systems provide the cognitive features. In addition to the practical aspect, systems that perform both perceptual as well as cognitive types of tasks are interesting also for expanding the AI effort to better understand human cognition and model it in computer systems. The areas of research and development include fundamentals of hybrid systems, both theoretical issues and practical integration techniques [1,2,7,8,18,24,33,35,36,38].

As discussed in [13], four approaches to systems with cognitive and perceptual features are
1) develop AI systems that can handle well perceptual, pattern recognition, and image and signal processing tasks;
2) discover a method for connectionist systems to handle high-level symbol-processing tasks;
3) develop another paradigm other than the symbolic and connectionist approaches;
4) produce hybrid systems that exploit the strengths of the current generation of connectionist and symbolic technologies.

Although the fourth approach has its own research and development challenges, recent advances in the design and use of hybrid systems are encouraging. Several successful applications have been developed, and hybrid system development tools and environments are becoming commercially available. The hybrid approach also makes sense in terms of modelling human intelligence, which has quite diverse aspects and capabilities (e.g., in tasks involving planning or language). Computer simulations of intelligence should take advantage of any appropriate technologies in order to reflect that diversity.

For the purpose of this paper, the term hybrid refers to systems that consist of two or more integrated subsystems, each of which may have a different representation language and inference technique. The subsystems are assumed to be tied together semantically and influence each other. The coupling can be to such a degree that any given operation may be difficult to classify as symbolic or subsymbolic. On the other hand, loose couplings join distinct components and regulate the flow of information between them.

Hybrid systems research areas include translation of data from neural networks for use by expert systems, identifying appropriate problems for hybrid system, communication protocols for symbolic/subsymbolic interfaces, and multiple processor architectures (see, e.g., [1,7,18,33]). The intelligent components can also use techniques such as genetic algorithms and fuzzy logic, as well as neural networks and expert systems.

Current hybrid systems research can be grouped into four areas (for more detail, see [24]):
**Language Understanding** -- Research in this area seeks to add connectionist components to improve the effectiveness of traditional AI techniques for language recognition and understanding. As part of this work, fundamental aspects of the linkage between symbolic and subsymbolic components are investigated.
**Representation Issues** -- This areas includes frameworks and architectures for integrating intelligent components. Design principles are investigated and structures and processes are developed and tested to gain insight

into the problems and solutions for providing processing, learning, and controlling tasks in hybrid systems. Work in this area addresses distributed control structures that coordinate, switch between, choose, etc. the actions of independent subsystems. In the area of performance, better symbolic to subsymbolic mappings can allow the use of subsymbolic systems that were determined *a priori* and reduce the amount of learning during operational use of the hybrid system.

**Logic and Reasoning** -- In this area, researchers look at the ways to implement reasoning using connectionist models. An important issue is whether connectionist components can deal with aspects of reasoning that are difficult or inefficient to do with symbolic techniques. One approach is to have connectionist nodes correspond to components of the symbolic system. Hybrid system research also addresses ways to increase the efficiency of deduction by reducing search space in logic systems. Work also seeks to enhance the understanding of reasoning by analyzing the performance of experimental hybrid systems for problem solving and other logic operations.

**Coupling Mechanisms** -- This areas includes various interface issues, including communication between subsystems. Also in this category is the practical aspect of linking symbols with connectionist system components. Research into systems design aims both at useful tools for efficient and effective development of systems, but also fundamental principles that can be gained from understanding how hybrid systems work.

The goals of hybrid system research include techniques to increase the efficiency, expressive power and reasoning power of intelligent systems. Some of the work on efficiency makes use of specialized reasoners strategically called by control or supervisor modules that decide which reasoners to use at different times. A general goal is to create hybrid systems that are significantly more powerful, with less development effort, than systems that use symbolic or subsymbolic methods alone. Hybrid systems are able to address some practical problems that have thus far alluded traditional AI approaches. From the perspective of fundamentals, hybrid systems may also give further insight into cognitive mechanisms and models.

Much of the current research in hybrid systems was discussed at the 1992 AAAI Workshop on Integrating Neural and Symbolic Processes (see [35,36]). The focus of this workshop was the architectural approaches that relate to cognitive modeling. Issues include the types of appropriate problems, outstanding integration issues, cognitive plausibility of the architectures, appropriate representational techniques, and the interaction with learning. Four basic architectures were identified. The localist approach implements symbolic structures in a network, e.g., each node representing a concept. This demonstrates the logical or rule-based capability of neural networks. The distributed approach is pure connectionism in which the network is functionally equivalent to symbolic processing. This is especially useful for natural language processing. The combined approach makes use of a set of separate modules with various degrees of coupling. Other architectures include the incorporation of neural networks into symbolic structures; the system is basically symbolic but has connectionist components. Some major issues identified at the workshop include the interaction between the representation. Complex representations usually make learning more difficult. Guidelines are needed on what type to choose, how to build it, and how to know the constraints on learning. Overall, two viewpoints seem to prevail. One is to integrate symbolic structures into connectionist architectures, using representations and techniques from each to tackle problems neither can solve alone; for example, modeling cognition that requires the ability to reason and the ability to perceive. The other viewpoint is to eliminate symbolic aspects altogether, and use only connectionist techniques.

Research on hybrid systems includes the study of obstacles to and solutions for the representation of symbolic and subsymbolic models so that they can function together. This requires mechanisms for communicating data and control signals and developing strategies for monitoring and controlling the symbolic and subsymbolic components. This includes issues in distributed AI for communication protocols among cooperating intelligent agents. Other work in hybrid system involves the creation of useful tools and development environments and the identification of the range of appropriate applications for hybrid systems.

## III. Models and Guidelines for Application Design

Several techniques for integrating expert systems and neural networks have emerged over the past few years, ranging from the primarily independent to the highly interactive. While there are different approaches to categorizing these integration techniques, five different integration strategies have been identified [25,27]:

**Stand-Alone Models** of combined expert system and neural network applications consist of independent software components. These components do not interact in any way. They can provide a direct means of comparing the problem-solving capabilities of the two techniques or, used in parallel, can provide redundancy for validating the prior development process.

**Transformational Models** are similar to stand-alone models in that the end result of development is an independent model that does not interact with another. What distinguishes the two types of models is that transformational systems begin as one type of system (e.g., a neural network), and end up as the other (e.g., an expert system). Determining which technique is used for development and which is used for delivery is based on the desirable features that the technique offers. Neural networks that are transformed into expert systems can be used for data analysis and preliminary knowledge engineering. The neural networks are transformed into expert systems for reasons such as knowledge documentation and verification, the desire for stepwise reasoning, and for explanation facilities.

**Loosely-Coupled Models** are the first true form of integrating expert systems and neural networks. The application is decomposed into separate neural network and expert system components that communicate via data files. Among the variations of loosely-coupled models are preprocessors, post-processors, co-processors, and user interfaces. In preprocessing loosely-coupled models, the neural network serves as a front-end that conditions data prior to passing it on to the expert system. Uses for this type of model include having the neural network perform data fusion, remove errors, identify objects, and recognize patterns. The expert system component can then use this information to solve problems in classification, identification, scene analysis, and problem solving. In post-processing, the expert system produces an output that is passed via a data file to the neural network. In this type of architecture, the expert system can perform data preparation and manipulation, classify inputs, and make decisions. The neural network component then performs functions such as forecasting, data analysis, monitoring, and error trapping. Loosely-coupled models are relatively easy to develop with commercially available expert system and neural network software, which reduces the programming burden on the developers. For examples, see [3,12,21].

**Tightly-Coupled Models** pass information via memory resident data structures rather than external data files. This improves the interactive capabilities of hybrid systems in addition to enhancing their performance. Tightly-coupled models can function under the same variations as loosely- coupled models, except that the tightly-coupled versions of pre-, post-, and coprocessors are typically faster. Variations unique to tight coupling include blackboards, cooperative, and embedded systems.

The SCRuFFy system by Hendler [16] uses a tight-coupling model of integrating expert systems and neural networks. The system includes a temporal pattern matcher that mediates between the two and provides a mapping from acoustic signals to symbols for reasoning about changes in signals over time. SCRuFFy uses a backpropagation neural network and an OPS5-based expert system that communicate via a blackboard architecture, which allows for future expansion to include other sensors or other types of processing modules besides expert systems and neural networks.

One application of this system is the control of the temperature of an underwater welding robot. Signals from acoustic measurements of the welder are inputs to a digital signal processor that creates input to the neural network. The network is pretrained to give four numbers indicating relative classification of either normal welding or three error conditions. The symbolic analysis module tracks the changes over time in the signal classifications by the neural network and produces symbolic information describing the time course of the acoustic signal. This information can be used by the reasoning module to recommend corrective actions early before more extreme, expensive measures are required.

Embedded systems are another variation of tightly-coupled models that use modules from one technique to help control the functioning of the other technique. For example, neural networks can be embedded inside expert systems to control the inferencing process. Embedded neural network components are used to focus the inferencing, guide searches, and perform pattern matching. Expert system components can be used to interpret the results of neural network, to provide internetwork connectivity, and to provide explanation facilities. Applications of embedded systems exist in the areas of robotics, education, and classification.

Tight coupling has the benefits of reduced communications overhead and improved runtime performance, when compared to loose coupling. Several commercial packages are suitable for developing tightly-coupled models, assisting developers to develop and maintain modular expert system and neural network components. Overall, tight coupling offers design flexibility and robust integration.

**Fully-Integrated Models** share data structures and knowledge representations. Communication between the different components is accomplished via the dual nature (symbolic and neural) of the structures. Reasoning is accomplished either cooperatively or through a component designated as the controller. Several variations of fully-integrated systems exist, including connectionist systems, the utilization of I/O nodes, subsymbolic to symbolic connectivity, and integrated control mechanisms.

The most common variation of fully integrated models is the connectionist expert system [9,10]. These systems often rely on local knowledge representations, as opposed to the distributed representation of most neural networks, and reason through spreading activation. Connectionist expert systems represent relationships between pieces of knowledge with weighted links between symbolic nodes. Applications of connectionist expert systems exist in medical diagnosis, information retrieval and analysis, and pattern classification.

Other variations of the fully integrated model are utilizing the input and output nodes of a neural network as facts within an expert system; linking subsymbolic to symbolic computing by connecting nodes and patterns of activation within the hidden layer of a neural network to symbols within an expert system; and integrated control, which differs from embedded tightly-coupled systems in that the expert systems and neural networks are no longer maintained as independent modules.

The benefits of full integration include robustness, improved performance, and increased problem solving capabilities. Robustness and performance improvements stem from the dual nature of the knowledge representations and data structures. In addition, there is little or no redundancy in the development process, because the systems can leverage off of each other. Full integration has limitations caused by the increased complexity of the inter-module interactions. First, there is the complexity of specifying, designing, and building fully-integrated models. Second, there is a distinct lack of tools on the market that facilitate full integration. Finally, there are important questions in verifying, validating, and maintaining fully-integrated systems.

## IV. Hybrid System Applications and Development Tools

Several hybrid systems are being built either as research projects or actual applications that are in use. The following are a few of the examples:

- LAM is a hybrid system used by Du Pont to assist in the design of window glazing [12,24]. The system consists of independent modules that communicate via a common fact file that passes computational results and control parameters form one module to the next. The rule-based system can pass a structured query to the neural network and can use the results back form the neural network to make further inferences. The neural network takes the place of several rules by interpreting engineering data on solar and sound properties.
- Nuclear power plant monitoring system and multiple target recognition system (in [24]). These systems are tightly coupled systems linked via the HyperTalk commands in the NueX development environment. Their rules make use of neural network interpretations of detector data and sensor data. In the first case, the neural network determines plant operating states including normal and off-normal conditions. The expert system uses prediction knowledge to provide plant operators with intelligent recommendations. In multiple target recognition, the neural network is a classifier learning spatiotemporal attributes of target trajectories. The neural network offers robust pattern recognition performance, fault tolerance, and parallel processing capabilities. The expert systems provide symbolic processing and the overall decision making, management, and coordination functions.
- The chemical tank control hybrid system [24,39] demonstrates the use of the Conncert development concept [39], a general facility for embedding neural networks in software systems. The network takes as input the history of PID controller input values and tank pH values and outputs expected pH values for later time steps. The expert system avoids over control by deciding when predicted outcomes are actually to be included in the controlling equation. The expert system uses a combination of temporal pattern matching and rules.
- Image interpretation via fusion of sensors [17,24] with the InFuse system uses a tightly-coupled hybrid system in which neural networks interpret textural descriptors obtained from imagery. The expert system verifies the neural network decisions using data from a spatial database and domain specific knowledge about sensor behavior.

These and many other recent cases provide detailed descriptions of working hybrid neural network and expert systems from which to draw guidelines. The information about the applications and the data used in them allows a good understanding of the problems and opportunities involved in the development of hybrid systems. Many more applications should be forthcoming as development experiences are shared and more and better development tools become available. For further details see [3,8,9,12,18,24,26,29,31,32,33,36].

Several development systems have recently become available for building expert systems or neural networks [5,10,24,28]. Many of these can be used to create loosely-coupled hybrid systems. NueX, by Charles River Analytics, Inc., is the first commercial system for developing hybrid neural network and expert systems [24,28]. Now that hybrid system development tools are starting to emerge, a surge in applications should occur.

## V. Summary

The characteristics of expert systems and neural networks can complement each other to make more powerful systems than could be accomplished using either technology alone. Expert systems contribute symbolic reasoning and explanation systems that help the user understand questions being asked or conclusions and reasoning processes. Neural networks can support expert systems when rules are not known, either because the topic is too complex or no human expert is available, and modifications are made by retraining with an updated data set, thus eliminating programming changes and rule reconstruction. Another advantage of the neural network component is the speed of operation after the network is trained; the use of parallel systems and neural chips will enhance this aspect dramatically.

Hybrid systems take advantage of the synergy associated with the strengths of expert systems and neural networks to produce useful, effective systems. Guidelines for choosing appropriate applications for hybrid neural network and expert systems are starting to emerge. The integration of these and other intelligent components with conventional software systems and with neurocontrol systems [37,38] will continue to be an important area for intelligent systems research and development.

## References

[1] AAAI (1990), "Integrating Symbolic and Neural Processes," Workshop Notes from the AAAI Eighth National Conference on Artificial Intelligence, Boston, 1990.

[2] Barnden, J. (ed) (1991), *Advances in Connectionist and Neural Computation Theory*, Ablex.

[3] Benachenhou, D., Cader, M., Szu, H., Medsker, L., Wittwer, C., and Garling, D. (1990), "Neural networks for computing invariant clustering of a large open set of DNA-PCR primers generated by a feature-knowledge based system." *Proc.IJCNN-90*, San Diego, CA, vol ii, pp. 83-89.

[4] Brachman, R. J., Gilbert, V. P., Levesque, H. J. (1985), "An essential hybrid reasoning system: knowledge and symbol level accounts of KRYPTON," *Proceedings of the Ninth International Joint Conference on Artificial Intelligence*, Los Angeles, pp. 532-539.

[5] Caudill, M. (1990), "Using neural nets: hybrid expert networks," *AI Expert*, vol 5, no. 11, pp. 49-54.

[6] Foss, R. V., and Droste, D. H. (1990), "An expert system for window glazing design," *ASHRAE Transactions*, vol 96, part 2, pp. Atlanta, 563-569.

[7] Frisch, A. M. and Cohn, A. (1991), "Thoughts and afterthoughts on the 1988 workshop on principles of hybrid reasoning," *AI Magazine*, vol 11(5), pp. 77-83.

[8] Frisch, A. M. and Scherl, R. B. (1991), "A bibliography on hybrid reasoning," *AI Magazine*, vol 11(5), pp. 84-87.

[9] Gallant, S. I. (1988), "Connectionist expert systems," *Communications of the ACM*, vol 31, pp. 152-169.

[10] Gallant, S. I. (1993), *Neural Network Learning and Expert Systems*, MIT Press, Cambridge, MA.

[11] Gutknecht, M., Pfeifer, R., and Stolze, M. (1991), "Cooperative hybrid systems." *Institut fur Informatik Technical Report*, Universitat Zurich.

[12] Hanson, M. A. and Brekke, R. L. (1988), "Workload management expert system - combining neural networks and rule-based programming in an operational application," *Proc. Instrument Society of America*, vol 24, pp. 1721-26.

[13] Hendler, J. (1989), "On the need for hybrid systems," *Connection Science*, vol 1, no. 3, pp. 227-229.

[14] Hendler, J. (1989), "Marker-passing over microfeatures: towards a hybrid symbolic/connectionist model," *Cognitive Science*, vol 13, no. 1, pp. 79-106.

[15] Hendler, J. (1991), "Developing hybrid symbolic/connectionist models," in [Barnden, 1991] at pp. 165-179.

[16] Hendler, J., and Dickens, L. (1991), "Integrating neural network and expert reasoning: an example," *Proc. AISB Conf. on Developments of Biological Standardization*, Leeds, United Kingdom, 1991.

[17] Kanal, L. and Raghavan, S. (1992), "Hybrid Systems - A key to intelligent pattern recognition," *Proc. of the IJCNN*, Baltimore, Part IV, pp. 177-183.

[18] Kandel, A., and Langholz, G. (eds) (1992), *Hybrid Architectures for Intelligent Systems*, CRC Press, Boca Raton.

[19] Kuncicky, D. C., Hruska, S. I., and Lacher, R. C. (1991), "The equivalence of rule- based expert system and artificial neural network inference," *International Journal of Expert Systems*, vol 4, no. 1, pp 281-297.

[20] Kwasny, S. C., and Faisal, K. A. (1991), "Rule-based training of neural networks," *Expert Systems with Applications*, vol 2, no. 1, pp. 47-58.

[21] Labate, F. and Medsker, L. (1993), "Employee skills analysis using a hybrid neural network and expert system," *Proceedings of the IEEE International Conference on Developing and Managing Intelligent System Projects*, Washington, DC, 1993, pp. 205-211.

[22] Lacher, R. C., Hruska, S. I., and Kuncicky, D. C. (1992), "Backpropagation learning in expert networks," *IEEE Trans. on Neural Networks*, vol 3(1), pp 62-72.

[23] Maren, A., Harston, C. T., and Pap, R. (eds.) (1990), *Handbook of Neural Computing Applications*, Academic Press, San Diego.

[24] Medsker, L.R., (1994), *Hybrid Neural Network and Expert Systems*, Kluwer Academic Publishers, Boston.

[25] Medsker, L. (1993), "Models and Techniques for Developing Hybrid Neural Network and Expert Systems," *Journal of Computer & Software Engineering*, Summer.

[26] Medsker, L. R. (ed.), (1991), Special Issue of *Expert Systems with Applications: An International Journal*, vol 2, no. 1.

[27] Medsker, L., and Bailey, D. (1992), "Models and guidelines for integrating expert systems and neural networks," in [Kandel and Langholz, 1992] at pp. 154-171.

[28] Medsker, L. and Liebowitz, J. (1994), *Design and Development of Expert Systems and Neural Networks*, Macmillan Publishing Company, New York.

[29] Medsker, L. and Turban, E. (1994), "Integrating expert systems and neural computing for decision support," *Expert Systems with Applications*, vol 7, no. 4.

[30] Minsky, M. (1991), "Logical versus analogical or symbolic versus connectionist or neat versus scruffy," *AI Magazine*, vol 12, no. 2, pp. 35-51.

[31] Schley, C., Chauvin, Y., and Mittal-Henkle, V. (1991), "Integrating optimal control with rules using neural networks," Proc. of the IJCNN, vol. II, Seattle, pp. 759-763.

[32] Schreinemakers, J.F., and Touretzky, D.S., (1990), "Interfacing a neural network with a rule-based reasoner for diagnosing mastitis," *Proc. IJCNN* , vol II, Washington, DC, pp. 487-491.

[33] Soucek, B., and the IRIS Group (eds) (1991), *Neural and Intelligent Systems Integration*, John Wiley and Sons, New York.

[34] Sun, R. (1992), "Connectionist models of rule-based reasoning," in [Sun, Bookman, and Snekhar, 1992] at pp. 91-97.

[35] Sun, R. and Bookman, L. (1993), "How do symbols and networks fit together," AI Magazine, vol 14, no. 2, pp. 20-23.

[36] Sun, R., Bookman, L. A., and Shekhar, S. (eds.) (1992), *Integrating Neural and Symbolic Processes: The Cognitive Dimension*, Working Notes from the AAAI-92 Workshop Program, San Jose, CA, July 12-16, 1992.

[37] Werbos, P. (1990), "Neurocontrol and related techniques," in [Maren, Harston, and Pap, 1990] at pp. 345-380.

[38] Werbos, P. (1993), "Brain-like intelligence in artificial models: how can we really get there?" *INNS Above Threshold*, vol 2, No. 2, pp 8-12.

[39] Wilson, A., and Hendler, J. (1993), "Linking symbolic and subsymbolic computing," *Technical Research Report TR 93-12*, Institute for Systems Research, University of Maryland.

# A NEURAL NETWORK FOR ANALOGICAL REASONING

by: Yehuda Salu.

Department of Physics and CSTEA. Howard university, Washington DC, 20059

*ABSTRACT:*   Analogical reasoning is one of the fundamental mental processes. It is a multi-step procedure that involves retrieval and manipulation of stored information, and generation of new inferences. Presented here is a model neural network, that encodes and stores information, so that it can be easily accessed in analogical reasoning processes. Learning rules that the network uses for incorporating new inferences are formulated. The interactions between the network and an external controller, that controls the execution of the various steps of the analogical reasoning process, are described, and an example that illustrates how these principles operate in a typical analogical reasoning problem is given.   Some of the learning rules that the network employs are different from those currently utilized in other connectionist models of the brain. Whether the brain really employs these new learning rules is an intriguing open question.

## 1. INTRODUCTION

### 1.1 ANALOGIES

Since ancient times, humans have been relying on analogies to guide their reactions to the environment. Old scriptures from different cultures contain analogies, that offer insights to given situations based on previously-experienced unrelated events. Analogies are commonly used, consciously and subconsciously, in a variety of mental activities, and they are one of the tools that AI employs in problem solving. One dictionary definition of analogy is: "inference that if two or more things agree with one another in some respects they will probably agree in others." (1). Another definition, aimed at the utilization of analogies by machines, states: "Analogy is a **mapping** between elements of a **source** domain and a **target** domain,.... Analogy becomes useful in some context when a reasoner is familiar with the source, and can map familiar elements or relations from the source into unfamiliar (or unknown) elements or relations in the target. These mapped elements are **analogical inferences**..." (2).

There are many forms of reasoning by analogy, but they all consist of the same three basic steps: First, gaining access to an (appropriate) analog; second, mapping some part of the information from that analog source to the target; and third, the side effects of analogical reasoning in terms of the production of more general rules and representations (3).

### 1.2 KNOWLEDGE REPRESENTATION

These three steps are operations on a data structure whose elements may be regarded as having two roles: concepts and factors. **Concepts consist of factors**. A factor may belong to several concepts. A concept may be a factor of other concepts. A data structure that consists of concepts and factors can be represented by a layered semantic network. This report introduces one such network. The nodes of the network represent factors and concepts. The arcs of the network connect pairs of nodes; an arc from node **A** in a lower layer to node **B** in a higher layer indicates that **A** is a factor of **B**.

1.2.1 BASIC FACTORS: **Basic factors** are innate to the system. There are two kinds of basic factors; basic features and basic relations. A **basic feature** cannot be decomposed into other factors. It is represented by a node that can only be activated by causes from the outside of the network. A **basic relation** is represented by a node that can be activated by a combination of other nodes, but the specification of that combination is pre-determined. For example, in a network that models the visual system, a retinal rod cell is a basic feature. It can only be activated by light from the outside. A complex cell in the primary visual cortex, that responds to a light bar in a specific orientation, is a basic relation. It is pre-wired to respond to a specific combination of light points. There are, presumably, other neurons that represent basic relations, such as 'spatial-sameness-neurons', that fire when two spatial stimuli at different parts of the retina are 'the same', or 'temporal-sameness-neurons', that fire when the 'same' event occurs at different times. The basic features and the basic relations are the innate building blocks with which the network constructs its concepts and its perception of the external world. Together with the learning rules and the retrieval mechanisms, these basic factors determine the mental capabilities of the network.

1.2.2 EXEMPLARS AND PROPERTIES: There are several **conditional relationships** between factors and concepts that are captured by the network. A factor may be an **exemplar** of a concept, or a **property** of a concept.

*DEFINITION:* Let node **A** be a factor of node **B**. **A** is an **exemplar** of **B** if **B** was active whenever **A** was active. In other words, **A** has been a sufficient condition for **B**. When **B** has several exemplars that have been active at different times, it is called the **class** or the **label** to which **A** belongs.

A may become an exemplar of class **B** in three ways. First, by arbitrary assignment. Second, due to a property; **A** contains a property, due to which it qualifies as a member of **B**. Third, by association; **A** has been associated with a key concept **C**. This association makes **A** eligible to belong to **B**.
Examples:
1. Arbitrary assignment: Inanimate nouns in some languages (e.g. French, Hebrew) belong to one of two gender classes. These affiliations are arbitrary.
2. By property: The class of green objects. Each member has the color green.
3. By association: The class of cigarette smokers. Each member has been associated with cigarette smoking.
Except for cases of arbitrary assignment, a concept is assigned to a class if the concept has any one of a list of properties or associations that defines that class. If a class has just one defining property or association, this property or association is also a necessary condition for each exemplar of the class.

*DEFINITION:* Let node **A** be a factor of node **B**. **A** is a **property** of **B** if whenever **B** was active **A** was active. In other words, **A** has been a necessary condition for **B**.

A property may be also a sufficient condition for its concept. More commonly, a group of properties, as a whole, is a sufficient condition to a concept, while any part of this group is not a sufficient condition. Such a group of properties will be called **a specific clue**. A specific clue is represented by a node, placed in between the properties and their concept. The properties send their arcs to the specific clue, and the specific clue sends an arc to the concept.

Properties, as factors, are necessary conditions for their concepts. If **A** is a property of **B**, and **B** is a property of **C**, then **A** is also a property of **C**. However, **A** will have an arc only to **B**, and not to **C**.
A chain of classes is a sequence of classes in which each member is an exemplar of the next member. When a concept is an exemplar of a chain of classes, the arcs of the network only record its membership in the directly superior class. e.g. there will be arcs between 'dove' and 'bird', and between 'bird' and 'animal', but not between 'dove' and 'animal'. If a chain of classes has a common defining property, this property will have an arc only to the class at the top of the chain, e.g. 'breathing' will have an arc to 'animal' but not to 'bird' or 'dove'. This arcs management method saves on 'network material' without compromising the contents of the stored information.
If **A** is a factor of **B**, **A** may be an exemplar, a property, or an exemplar and a property of **B**. The arc that connects nodes **A** and **B** encodes the relationship between them.

## 2. THE REASONER

The reasoner is capable of performing a variety of reasoning tasks, such as generalization and reasoning by analogy. It consists of two components: The semantic neural network, which learns and stores the semantic information, and the controller, which manipulates these data according to the specific reasoning task. The controller activates the nodes that represent the initial state, activates the data retrieval processes, evaluates the retrieved data, decides on the termination of the reasoning process, and initiates recruitment of nodes to represent new concepts, that are the outcome of analogical reasoning. The network's structure and dynamics facilitate the operation of the controller.

### 2.1 THE NEURAL NETWORK

2.1.1 STRUCTURE:   The nodes of the network, that represent concepts and factors, are arranged in layers. There are two kinds of nodes; innate and recruited. The innate nodes consist of the basic feature nodes, the basic relation nodes, and innate specific-clue nodes. The basic feature nodes fill the first (bottom) layer. Arcs connect the appropriate innate nodes. All the other nodes and arcs are recruited into the network, as the external world is experienced and learned. Information can flow in two directions: from factors to concepts (up), and from concepts to factors (down). Connected nodes are linked by two directional arcs, one in the up and the other in the down direction. The direction of information flow in the network at any given time is determined by the external controller. All nodes act like standard artificial neurons. Their firing status is determined by the weighted sum of their input signals, and by the threshold, which is 1 for all the nodes.

2.1.2 DYNAMICS:   The weights of the two directional arcs that connect a factor node and its concept node encode the conditional relationships that exist between the nodes. The weight between an exemplar and its directly superior class is set to 1. The weight between a concept and its directly inferior feature is 1. Since all the firing thresholds are set to 1, these weights ensure that when information flows up, each exemplar will activate its class labels, and when information flows down, each concept will activate its features. The other weights are set in such a way, that when the entire set of factors that define a concept is present, this concept will be activated. When only a part of this set of factors is present, the appropriate concept may be retrieved by **vector completion.** In vector completion, the controller gradually **modulates** the intensity of the signals, till previously silent nodes fire. The modulation can be accomplished by increasing the strengths of the signals, increasing the weights of the arcs, or decreasing the thresholds. The network has to be constructed in a special way that makes modulation by the controller possible. More details about modulation are given in (4,5).

### 2.2 THE CONTROLLER:

The controller has a repertoire of basic operations that it can exercise on the data base. The starting point of any reasoning process is activating the nodes that represent the input factors. These nodes constitute the initial condition of the problem. Then, information flows in the network as directed by the weights, and  activates the concepts that are made of the input factors. The controller then decides whether the retrieved information is satisfactory, or there is a need for a reasoning process, such as vector completion. Vector completion is a simple reasoning process, which is accomplished by modulation, as explained above.

2.2.1 MAPPING AND SOURCE SELECTION.  Analogical  reasonings  are  more  complicated processes, and they consist of cycles of basic operations. In some problems only the target is given, while in others both the target and the source are given. In both cases, the controller first activates the nodes that represent the initial state of the particular problem.

Then, the controller has to define the mappings between factors of the two concepts. A pair of mapped factors must have a common feature or a common relation. In other words, the two factors must belong to the same class. So, the controller starts with a factor of the target, finds its class, and then activates other members of that class. These members are potential mappings of the original target's factor. A way to achieve this retrieval in the network is to enable information flow up, starting at the factors of the target. This will result in the retrieval of the class labels. Then, information flow is enabled in the down direction, retrieving other exemplars of these classes. These exemplars are possible mappings of the original target's factors. When both the source and the target are given, some of the retrieved factors, which do not belong to the given source, are eliminated. If the source is not given, enabling information flow in the up direction, with or without modulation, will activate concepts that contain these retrieved factors. One of these activated concepts may be selected as the analogical source to the given target.

The controller has means for determining which is the most appropriate source when several sources are retrieved, and which are the most appropriate mappings between the factors of the source and the target. These determinations may be based on the distance between the retrieved and the target entities, and they vary from one analogical reasoning process to another (2).

2.2.2 LEARNING AND INFERENCES.  In learning the external world, the brain receives patterns of factors, parses them, and records the information in its network as inter-connected concepts. In the network presented here, learning is accomplished by two mechanisms: 1. changing weights of arcs, including adding new arcs between existing nodes, and 2. recruiting new nodes and their arcs. A node that represents a class label can always add new exemplars, and a node that represents a property can add more concepts to which it belongs. However, once a concept node is defined as the representation of a conjunction of a given set of factors, it cannot add any new factors to its original set, because that will change its meaning. More details about these learning mechanisms are given in (5,6), where a new network, the Binary Diamond, is described. The Binary Diamond learns the environment one event at a time, and forms its concepts in a way similar to that of the brain. The Binary Diamond recruits its nodes and arcs so that the precise conditional relationships between factors and concepts are recorded. Its structure and dynamics facilitate regular data retrieval, and vector completion by modulation. In analogical reasoning, inferences are made based on retrieved analogical mappings.  In addition to the learning rules that are used to form concepts from information that comes from the outside (5,6), learning rules for consolidating analogical inferences are also needed.

Once the final mappings are determined, the controller recruits nodes and arcs to represent new concepts. These concepts embody the inferences that are the product of the analogical reasoning process. This may be viewed as the learning phase of the analogical reasoning process, since changes in the network occur now. There are three basic mechanisms that are used for recording the inferred information, and they are very similar to those used by (4,5,6).

Let **T** indicate a factor of the target, and **S** indicate its mapped factor in the source.
1.  If **S** is an exemplar of class **C**, then also **T** becomes an exemplar of class **C**. This is accomplished by establishing the appropriate arc between **T** and **C**.
2.  If **P** is a property of **S** then **P** becomes also a property of **T**. This is accomplished by establishing the appropriate arc between **T** and **P**.
3.  If **S**, together with **A** and **B**, are the factors of the concept **C** in the source, then a new concept **N** is recruited in the target. The factors of **N** are **A**, **B**, and **T**. The new concept **N** is the analog of **C**.
Figure 1. illustrates these three basic mechanisms.
All three mechanisms rely on the mapping between **T** and **S**. **S** acts as a pointer to the nodes of the source that will become associated with node **T**. Mechanisms 1 and 2 are of the Hebbian type, and they are reminiscent to classical conditioning. Mechanism 3 is a non-Hebbian recruitment mechanism.

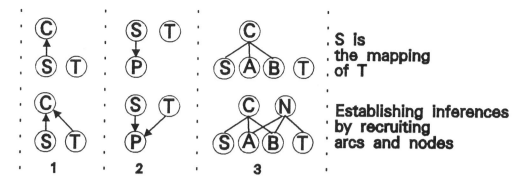

Figure 1. The three inference mechanisms. Arrows indicate weights of 1 in the corresponding direction. In 1 and 2 only arcs are recruited, while in 3 a node and arcs are recruited.

### 3. EXAMPLE

As an example that illustrates the data structure of the network and the operation of the controller in an analogical reasoning process, consider the following situation. The network already stores information about a hammer pushing a nail into a wall, and a knife cutting bread. The target is to push a hook into the wall. A solution is found by analogical reasoning, employing a controller and a semantic neural network. Figure 2 depicts the network. An arrow indicates a relationship between an exemplar and its class label. A solid line indicates an old relationship between a concept and its feature. Dashed lines indicate information that the network acquires during the process of analogical reasoning. The basic properties in this network are: [knife], [hook], [nail], [hammer], [wall], and [bread]. The basic relations are: [cut], [knock], [cause], [to_two], and [into]. The analogical reasoning is carried out in steps as follows (where: [a] --> [b] indicates that concept [a] activated concept [b]. The notation [a] <--> [b] indicates that [a] and [b] are analogs):

1. The initial condition is activated; nodes [hook], [into], and [wall] are activated. A node representing [hook into wall] is recruited and connected to its three factors.

2. Information is allowed to propagate up, and the class labels are activated: [hook] --> [sharp]; [into] --> [shape change]; [wall] --> [flat].

3. Information is allowed to propagate down, modulation takes place, and exemplars of the previously activated class labels are now retrieved: [sharp] --> [nail], [knife], [hook]; [change] --> [into], [to-two]; [flat] --> [wall], [bread]. Possible analogical mappings are stored: [hook] <--> [knife], [nail]; [into] <--> [to-two], [cause]; [wall] <--> [bread].

4. Information is allowed to propagate up. Several nodes are activated. [knife], [cut], [bread] --> [knife cut bread]; [nail], [into], [wall] --> [nail into wall].

5. The controller selects [nail into wall] over [knife cut bread] due to its greater similarity to the target.

6. Information is allowed to propagate up in vector completion. Another concept is activated: [nail into wall] --> [hammer knock nail cause nail into wall].

6 Information is allowed to propagate down, and features are retrieved. [hammer knock nail cause nail into wall] --> {[cause]}, {[hammer knock nail] --> [hammer], [knock], [nail]}, {[nail into wall] --> [nail], [into], [wall]}.

7. Recruitment takes place, and a selected solution is constructed using the inference rules of 2.2.2. In this example rule 3 is used three times. [hammer knock nail], [hammer], [knock], and [nail] <--> [hook] recruits [hammer knock hook]. [nail into wall], [into], [wall], and [nail] <--> [hook] recruits [hook into wall]. and [hammer knock nail cause nail into wall], [cause], [hammer knock nail] <--> [hammer knock hook], and [nail into wall] <--> [hook into wall] recruit [hammer knock hook cause hook into wall], which is a solution to the problem.

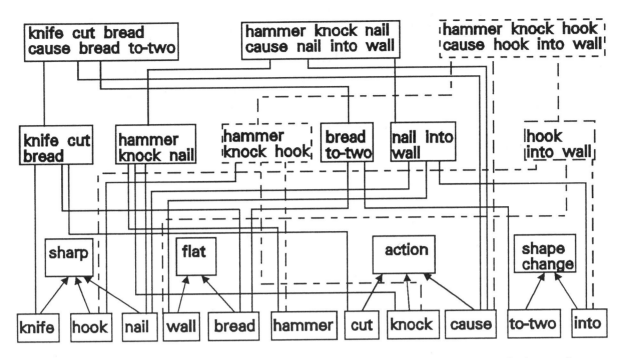

Figure 2. Solid lines = old information. Dashed lines = information gained by analogical reasoning.

## 4. DISCUSSION

There is a school of thought that models the brain as a connectionist network, in which neurons represent concepts, and mental activities are represented by the activation of patterns of neurons. Analogical reasoning is a fundamental process that the brain employs in a wide variety of mental activities. The work presented here illustrates how analogical reasoning can be implemented in a neural network. It uses an architecture and learning mechanisms, that have been found to be effective in other neural network applications. The work suggests that in advanced reasoning processes, the system may need to have two distinct components; memory and controller. This work concentrates on the memory component, while the controller is treated in an ad-hoc manner. It should be possible to implement the controller too in a neural network. The biological actuality of the basic principles of the model have to be tested in biological systems.

## 5. REFERENCES

1. Webster's New Collegiate Dictionary, 1975.
2. R.P. Hall, Computational approaches to analogical reasoning: A comparative analysis. Artificial Intelligence, 39, pp 39-120, 1989.
3. S. Vosniadou and A. Ortony. Similarity and analogical reasoning: a synthesis. in S. Vosniadou and A. Ortony (eds.) Similarity and Analogical Reasoning,Cambridge University Press, pp1-15, 1989.
4. Y. Salu A neural network that stores and retrieves information like the brain. in Cotterill R.M. (ed) Models of Brain Function. Cambridge University Press. pp 553-561. 1989
5. Y. Salu and J. Tilton. Non-parametric analysis of LANDSAT maps using neural nets and parallel computers. SPIE Vol 1623 AIPR Workshop, pp 174-183, 1991.
6. Y. Salu and J. Tilton. Classification of multispectral image data by the binary diamond neural network and by non-parametric, pixel-by-pixel methods. IEEE Transactions on Geoscience and Remote Sensing, Vol 31, pp 606-617, 1993.

# Extracting Shapes and Segmenting Images using Constrained Networks

Raqui Kane    Maurice Milgram

Laboratoire de Robotique de Paris
Université Pierre et Marie Curie
4, place Jussieu
75252 Paris cedex 05 - France.

### Abstract

In this paper we present two methods to analse images. The first one enables us to predict missing components of an image whereas the second one is a segmentation technique. The main point of these approaches is to use constrained networks; indeed, during the training, we constrain networks to build two kinds of units: logical-numerical (resp numerical) units which hold the logical (resp numerical) information of the training data set. Using these approaches, we can also extract information from trained networks, which enables us to control what happens inside networks. Simulation results are reported.

## 1  Introduction

Recent studies in the neural networks field have opened up new alternatives to conventional computer vision and pattern recognition. Examples include compression and images analysis [1], [2] and texture segmentation [3]. This paper describes two methods in images analysis. The first one consists of predicting missing components of an image whereas the second one is focused on images segmentation. During the training, the network is constrained to build two kinds of units: logical-numerical units and numerical units. The constrained networks are developed in [4]. The logical-numerical units hold the logical information of the networks, whereas the numerical units hold the numerical information. Using these approaches, we can control what happens inside trained networks and extract information from them.

This paper is organized as follows: first, we explain how to build constrained networks. Second, we describe the predicting and segmenting approaches. Finally, we report simulation results.

## 2  The constrained networks

It is mainly to specify the task of the units during the training, namely to build two kinds of units: units holding respectively some logical and numerical information.

Consider a unit $i$ with $n$ inputs $u_1^i, \cdots, u_n^i$. The output $o_i$ of unit $i$ is defined by the equation:

$$o_i = f(\sum_{j=1}^{n}(w_{ij} \star u_j^i - \theta_i) = f(a_i) \tag{1}$$

Where

f is a sigmoid function ($f(u) = tanh(u)$)

$w_{ij}$ is the weight of the connection between units $j$ and $i$

$\theta_i$ is the bias of unit $i$ and $a_i$ its activation.

A condition for $i$ to be a logical operator is:

$\forall u_1^i, \cdots, u_n^i \in S = \{-1(false), 1(true)\}^n$, $o_i \in \{-1, 1\}$.

A method to build logical units is developed in [5]. We will extend it to get logical-numerical operators. We define a logical-numerical operator $i$ as a unit such that:

$\forall\, u_1^i, \cdots, u_n^i \in [-1,1]^n,\ o_i \in \{-1, 1\}.$

To get a logical-numerical unit, we constrain its output to be in $\{-1, 1\}$ during the training by adding a penalty term $P(W)$ to the standard error function $E(W)$ of the backpropagation. The function to minimize becomes $E'(W) = E(W) + \lambda P(W)$; $\lambda$ is an adjustable parameter.

Then given a network, we can decide which units should be logical-numerical operators and therefore constrain them during the training to get this property.

*Note 1*

Analyzing equation (1), we notice that $sign(o_i) = sign(f(a_i)) = sign(a_i)$, where $sign$ is the function sign. A logical-numerical unit $i$ is a unit such that whatever the inputs of $i$, its output $o_i$ is in $\{-1, 1\}$. Then for a logical-numerical unit, we obtain the following property:
$o_i = +1\ if\ a_i \geq 0.0$ and $o_i = -1\ if\ a_i < 0.0.$

# 3 Predicting components of images

The model chosed to predict missing components of an image is given by:

$$u(i) \quad = \quad F(W_i, U(i-1)) \tag{2}$$

where
$u(i)$ is a pixel of the image.
$U(i-1) = [u(i-1), u(i-2), \cdots, u(i-k)]$ is a vector of pixels. This vector has $k$ elements.
$W_i$ is the weight vector of the training network.
$F(.,.)$ is a vector function representing the network.
This model enables us to build the training data set of a given image. The data set being submitted to a network will be the set of the elements $(U(i-1), u(i))$, where $U(i-1)$ (resp $u(i)$) will be a network input (resp output).

The data set $D$ obtained from an image is subdivided in two sets $T$ and $P$. $T$ is the training set and $P$ is the predicting set. The network is not any more trained with elements of $P$, just a test is done with these elements to measure the performance of the predicting tool. Indeed, each element of $P$ is presented once to the trained network so that it computes its corresponding output. Let us take an example of this model.

*Example*

Here is an example of the model with the parameter $k = 4$ (see Figure 1). We obtain for example:

$$u(5) \quad = \quad F(W_5, U(4))$$

with $U(4) = [u(4), u(3), u(2), u(1)]$.

To build the data set, we slide the dotted window in all the training area. We slide it aternatively from left to right and from top to bottom. The vector of pixels taken from the picture are normalized before being submitted to the network.

Figure 1: The data set $D$

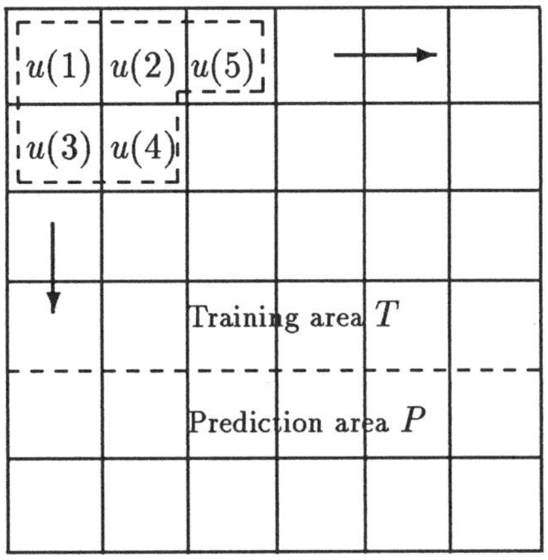

# 4  The Architecture of the networks

We choose multi-layer feed-forward networks, some units are constrained to be logical-numerical operators. Figure 2 shows an example of a network. The architecture of the network is: 4 - 2 - 2 - 1 namely 4 layers with respectively 4, 2, 2 and 1 units. The units of the second layer are constrained to be logical-numerical operators.

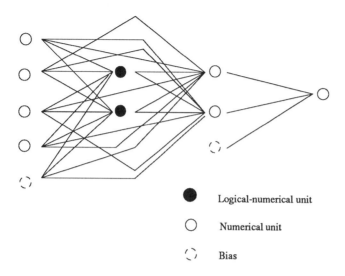

- Logical-numerical unit
- Numerical unit
- Bias

Figure 2: Architecture of a network

# 5  Segmenting images

The goal is here to segment images. The main features of the method follow:

- Training the network

  We train a constrained network to predict shapes. At the end of the training, the output of the constrained units are in $\{-1, +1\}$. This property will be quite important for the images segmentation. We notice here that the main property in the training phase is to constrain networks to build logical-numerical units.

- Classification of the samples

  Once we have trained a network using constrained units, we present all the samples or elements of $D$ (see section 4) to the trained network in oder to classify them according to the outputs of the constrained units. The samples that produce the same outputs for the constrained units are included in the same class. Namely, for example if the network has one logical-numerical unit, we will obtain two classes corresponding respectively to the samples that produce -1 or +1 for the logical-numerical unit. If the network has $n$ logical-numerical units, we will obtain $2^n$ classes. For the experiments on images, we assign the same gray-level value for pixels or samples of a class.

  This approach shows successful results in connectivity and edges detection. We obtain very performant simulation results.

# 6  Rule extraction

Using constrained neworks, we are able to extract rules from trained networks. This step is very important as it is possible to understand what happens inside the network. The main features of the rules extraction method follow:

- Find the property of each unit

  It is mainly to seek logical-numerical units of the network. This step is very simple as we decide before the training which units should be logical-numerical operators and constrain them to get this property.

- Local extraction

  It consists of extracting from each hidden or output unit the realized rule.

- Global extraction

  We have to substitute rules extracted from units by their value inside the network to get the global rule extracted from the network.

*Example*

Let us take a 3 - 2 - 1 trained network. Some units are constrained to be logical-numerical operators to hold the logical information of the training set. The unconstrained units hold the numerical information of the network. Let us extract rules from this trained network.

We use the notation of section 2, then $f$ is the sigmoid function of each unit, $w_{ij}$ is the weight of the connection between units $j$ and $i$, $\theta_i$ is the bias of unit $i$, $o_i$ its output and $a_i$ its activation; for this network $u_1$, $u_2$ and $u_3$ are the inputs units, $\theta_4$, $\theta_5$ and $\theta_6$ the bias , $w_{41}$, $w_{42}$, $w_{43}$, $w_{51}$, $w_{52}$, $w_{53}$, $w_{64}$ and $w_{65}$ the weights, $u_4$, $u_5$ the outputs of the hidden units and $u_6$ is the ouput unit.

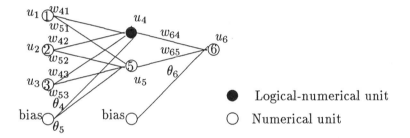

Figure 3: Extracting rules from a sample constrained neural network

Using equation(1), we obtain the following equations:

$$u_4 = f(\sum_{j=1}^{3} w_{4j} \star u_j - \theta_4) = f(a_4) \tag{3}$$

$$u_5 = f(\sum_{j=1}^{3} w_{5j} \star u_j - \theta_5) = f(a_5) \tag{4}$$

$$u_6 = f(\sum_{j=4}^{5} w_{6j} \star u_j - \theta_6) = f(a_6) \tag{5}$$

- Local extraction

  - Extracting dependencies from unit 4

  Unit 4 is contrained to be a logical-numerical unit, then $\forall\, u_1, u_2, u_3 \in [-1,1]^3$, $u_4 \in \{-1,1\}$: $u_4$ is in the saturated part of the sigmoid. One consequence of constraining a unit to be a logical-numerical operator is to lead the weights connected to this unit to get great absolute values. Therefore, using Note (1) and equation (3), we obtain the following relations:

  $IF\ \sum_{j=1}^{3} w_{4j} \star u_j - \theta_4 \geq 0.0\ THEN\ u_4 = +1.0$

  $IF\ \sum_{j=1}^{3} w_{4j} \star u_j - \theta_4 < 0.0\ THEN\ u_4 = -1.0.$

- Extracting dependencies from unit 5

Unit 5 is an unconstrained and numerical unit, then $\forall\ u_1, u_2, u_3 \in [-1,1]^3$, $u_5$ is in the linear part of the sigmoid. Therefore, $u_5$ is simplified and becomes:

$u_5 = \sum_{j=1}^{3} w_{5j} \star u_j - \theta_5$.

- Extracting dependencies from unit 6

Unit 6 is an unconstrained and numerical unit, then $u_6$ is also in the linear part of the sigmoid. Therefore, $u_6$ is simplified and becomes:

$u_6 = \sum_{j=4}^{5} w_{6j} \star u_j - \theta_6$.

- Global extraction

   - Extracting dependencies from the network

The rule extracted from the network is recursively obtained by substituing rules of hidden units in the outputs units. The relation extracted from unit 6 is given by:

$u_6 = w_{64} \star u_4 + w_{65} \star (\sum_{j=1}^{3} w_{5j} \star u_j - \theta_5) - \theta_6$.

Therefore, substituing $u_4$ and $u_5$ by their value, we obtain for the network the relations:

$IF\ \sum_{j=1}^{3} w_{4j} \star u_j - \theta_4 \geq 0.0\ THEN\ u_6 = w_{64} + w_{65} \star (\sum_{j=1}^{3} w_{5j} \star u_j - \theta_5) - \theta_6$

$IF\ \sum_{j=1}^{3} w_{4j} \star u_j - \theta_4 < 0.0\ THEN\ u_6 = -w_{64} + w_{65} \star (\sum_{j=1}^{3} w_{5j} \star u_j - \theta_5) - \theta_6$

# 7   Simulation

## 7.1   Predicting components of images

We train the network to learn a large variety of images. We obtain successful results. We report here an example of a cut muscle.

Figure 4 shows the reference image and figure 5 the image obtained using the predictive approach. We notice two areas in figure 5. In area $T$, we test the training performance of the network. In area $P$, the network is not any more trained, just a test is done to measure the predicting performance; namely each element of $P$ is presented once to the trained network so that it computes the corresponding output. We notice that the missing shapes are well predicted and the image obtained is also less noisy than the reference one.

## 7.2   Segmenting images

Here is an example of a network trained to predict shapes and segment images. The network architecture is 4 - 1 - 2 - 1, namely four layers with respectively 4, 1, 2 and 1 units. It is a full connected network, the units of the first layer are also connected to the units of the third layer. The unit of the second layer is constrained to be a logical-numerical operator (see section 4).

We use the segmentation method described in section 5. All the samples are presented once to the trained network so that it computes the output of the constrained unit. The samples for which the constrained unit produces -1 (resp +1) are coloured in black (resp white). This leads to figure 6.

We notice the ability of the method to detect connectivity and edges. We obtain performant results on a large variety of images.

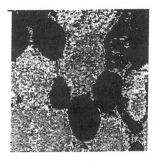

Figure 4: Reference image                    Figure 5: Image obtained by prediction

Figure 6: Image obtained by segmentation

## 8  Conclusion

In this paper, we have proposed two images analysis approaches. This first approach allows to predict missing shapes of an image, whereas the second one enables us to segment images. These two approaches rely on constrained networks. In the constrained neworks are two kinds of units: units constrained to hold the logical information and units holding the numerical information of the training data set. These approaches allow also to extract easily information from network, therefore to control what happens inside networks. We have obtained successful experimental results with a large variety of images. Similar approaches on images analysis are under study.

## References

[1] J. G. Daugman, " Complete discrete 2-D Garbor transformations by neural networks for image analysis and compression," in *IEEE Trans. on Acoustics, Speech and Signal Processing* 1988.

[2] G. Burel and J. Y. Catros, "Image Compression using Topological Maps and MLP," in *Proceedings of ICNN, San Francisco CA 1993*.

[3] B. S. Manjunath, T. Simchony and R. Chellapa, "Stochastic and deterministic networks for texture segmentation," in *IEEE Trans. on Acoustics, Speech and Signal Processing* 1990.

[4] R. Kane and M. Milgram, "Logical and linear dependencies extraction from trained neural networks," in *5th IEEE International Conference on Tools with Artificial Intelligence* Boston 1993.

[5] R. Kane and M. Milgram, "Extraction of semantic rules from trained neural networks," in *Proceedings of ICNN, San Francisco CA 1993*.

# Interactive Knowledge Discovery through Self-Organising Feature Maps

*G Cheng and X Liu*
Department of Computer Science,
Birkbeck College, University of London
Malet Street, London WC1E 7HX, United Kingdom

*J X Wu*
Department of Preventive Ophthalmology,
Institute of Ophthalmology[1], University of London
Bath Street, London EC1V 9EL, United Kingdom

**Abstract**

We have applied the self-organising feature maps to a newly introduced computer controlled visual function test in order to obtain a deep understanding of its characteristics. An interactive procedure is employed which involves the use of self-organising feature maps for extracting features in the data, visualisation methods for displaying features, and experts for guiding the discovery process. By combining the features represented by the maps and the fundamental knowledge about ophthalmological anatomy, a variety of knowledge has been established which is useful in improving test strategies and the diagnosis of visual function diseases.

## Introduction

The Motion Sensitivity Perimetry (MSP) [10] is a newly introduced, computer controlled visual function test to resolve the difficulty in detecting early visual function diseases such as glaucoma. Although the MSP has shown to be a high sensitivity and specificity test in both community and clinical practice [9], there is still limited understanding of the test characteristics as well as the expertise in interpreting the test results.

We propose a method of knowledge acquisition by combining the fundamental domain knowledge and the data feature detection with a self-learning technique. We applied the self-organising feature maps (SOFM) to the MSP test data from glaucoma patients and suspects. The features of the data are extracted, illustrated, and then analysed by the experts. Using an interactive procedure of feature analysis, various kinds of knowledge regarding the test properties have been derived. They have been found useful not only in improving the test strategy but also in diagnosis of visual function diseases.

## The Motion Sensitivity Perimetry (MSP)

The MSP examines the sensitivity of six locations within the central 20 degree region of visual field. All these six locations are measured by four different displacement amplitudes, using vertical bars

---

[1]Associated with the Moorfields Eye Hospital, London.

on the computer screen (Figure 1). During the test, each location is tested with all four amplitudes and the test is repeated ten times. If the stimulus is seen, the patient presses a button as a response. After the test, a sensitivity matrix with six locations by four amplitudes is produced by counting the percentage of responses. The higher value corresponds to higher sensitivity at one particular test location at a certain amplitude [8].

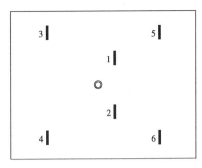

◎ The visual focus point

Figure 1: MSP test locations in the visual field

## Apply SOFM to MSP Data

The self-organising feature maps are organised in ways that reflect the physical characteristics of the training data. Kohonen's self-supervised competitive learning algorithm is capable of training the neurons specialised to detect intrinsic features existing in the set of input data. At the same time, the same topological orders, as in the input data, are preserved in the maps [5].

Assume that the input data $x_j$ have a certain stationary density function $p(x)$. The vectors of connection weights between input and output neurons is represented by $w_i (i = 1, 2, ..., M)$ where $M$ is the number of output neurons. The $\alpha$ is a monotonical decay function with time (gain value) and $\gamma$ is the neighbourhood function. The equation (1) represents a smoothing adaptation process for $w_i$:

$$\frac{dw_i}{dt} = \alpha(t)\gamma(i, t)(x_j - w_i), \tag{1}$$

The distribution of the asymptotic $w_i$ values can be shown to approximate the density function $p(x)$, therefore the map optimally represents a hierarchical clustering graph with respect to the statistics of the input data [6].

We have used the equation (1) as our learning algorithm, and

$$\frac{d\alpha(t)}{dt} = -a \cdot e^{-bt}, \tag{2}$$

$$\gamma(i, t) = c \cdot e^{-\frac{d^2(i, I)}{k\alpha^2(t)}}, \tag{3}$$

Where $a, b, c$ and $k$ are some positive constants, $d(i, I)$ is the distance between the learning neuron $i$ and the current winner neuron $I$ on the output map.

For each test record, the six by four sensitivity matrix with the values within the interval of $[0, 1]$ are given as the input vectors. A two-dimensional 96 neurons are used as the target map.

There are two important characteristics of the learning algorithm. 1) *Feature Representation*: output neurons are used to represent different classes of input patterns, and the weight vector of each neuron represents the centre of each class. The features in the input data would be represented by the distribution of weight vectors in the SOFM. 2) *Neighbourhood Smoothing*: the representation of input patterns would be laterally affected by their neighbours. Therefore the features represented by the SOFM would be formed, not only by typical input patterns but also the most probable ones. Some unusual input patterns, though they actually appear in the input data, would be "smoothed" by others.

The first characteristic is obviously required in our application as we want that the features represented by the SOFM reflect the nature of input data. The second one is also appropriate for our application because the test data, collected from patients, necessarily contain noise caused by various behavioral factors such as fatigue and inattention [7]. The "smoothing" effect of the learning law would be helpful in reducing the magnitude of noise. Vector quantilisation error and the topographical product [1] have been used as measurements for achieving those two characteristics, and trying to minimise both of them has been the convergence criterion for our implementation.

One of the principle features we want to extract are the relations between test behaviour at different test locations. This can be achieved as follows. First, the weight vectors (96 in our case) associated with output neurons are used to form a new vector of 96 elements for each location. This is done by taking each element from each weight vector which is corresponding to the test location. Vectors associated with any two test locations can then be used to draw their correlative behaviour plot.

Figure 2(a) is such a plot for locations 3 and 5, where the weights are around a near-linear fitted line, below the dashed line $f(x) = y$. Two interesting features can be observed from this diagram. First, the test behaviour of location 3 and location 5 are strongly dependent. Second, the sensitivity of locations 3 is higher than that of location 5 when both locations' sensitivity is low (e.g., below 0.7). As a contrast, Figure 2(b) shows another relationship between locations 3 and 4 which is rather weak.

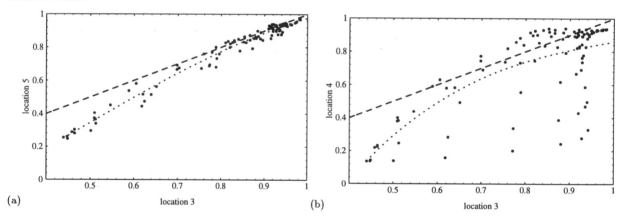

Figure 2: Correlative plot of test behaviour between different locations at the second amplitude

Various kinds of diagrams for the same data can be drawn using different visualisation methods, one of which has been shown above. The features in the diagram can then be observed and analysed by experts. Armed with the fundamental knowledge about ophthalmological anatomy, the experts can decide whether more specific data selection or other alternatives should be made to train the maps again, or something interesting has been discovered. This interactive procedure is carried out until a full picture of the test and its associated diagnostic knowledge has been obtained, and verified if possible (Figure 3).

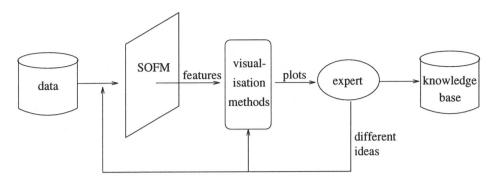

Figure 3: The interactive procedure of knowledge acquisition

## Results

We have chosen 601 test records from glaucoma patients and suspects collected from the Glaucoma Unit, Moorfields Eye Hospital London. In particular, we use the concept of *repeatability* to see whether the features produced from one group of data are reproduced by another group, based on the assumption that true features are more repeatable than false ones. Therefore the data are divided into two groups and analysed separately.

Using the above proposed method, we have discovered different kinds of knowledge which were previously unknown, though many were suspected to be the case. The discovered knowledge can be classified into two categories. One is those that can be supported by clinical evidence and (or) medical knowledge and the other is those that display interesting phenomenon, which do not have concrete support yet, but can be used as a guide to the researchers or clinicians to investigate the matter further. Knowledge from both of these categories have the potentials in improving the test strategy and the diagnosis of visual function losses. For the sake of brevity, we present one example from each category.

We have found that the second amplitude in the MSP is effective in detecting early glaucomatous visual function damage. Observing the relationship between different locations at the amplitude, we found a strong correlation among locations 1, 3, 5 and 2, 4, 6. In fact, the unbalanced horizontal hemifields (1 3 5 versus 2 4 6, see Figure 1) are known as the early sign of glaucoma defined by conventional visual field test methods where *different* kinds of stimuli are used [4]. This phenomenon can be supported by anatomical [3] and clinical evidence [2].

After a detailed study of the relationships at all amplitudes, we found that different amplitudes behave differently. For example, at the first amplitude, the sensitivity values in the central region (locations 1 and 2) are higher than peripheral region (rest of the locations) and little relationship between these two regions is found. An implication of this finding is that different amplitudes may be used to test different visual functions of human eyes. Therefore, fewer amplitudes would be required to design a specific test strategy for detecting a particular type of disease. Consequently, test duration can be reduced and the patients would be less likely to feel tired. More work is needed for the researchers to find out how various kinds of diseases manifest themselves on those amplitudes and test locations.

## Conclusion

In this paper we propose an interactive procedure of knowledge acquisition from data. This is accomplished by first, objectively detecting hidden features in the data, second, displaying features to emphasise different properties, and then interactively inferring to obtain the explicitly expressed knowledge. The combination of self learning, visualisation methods and the use of fundamental knowledge from experts shows to be a satisfactory way in knowledge discovery from data. A variety of knowledge concerning the properties of the test has been derived, which may contribute to both test strategy design and diagnostic expertise.

## Acknowledgements

This work is partly supported by the International Glaucoma Society and British Council for Prevention of Blindness. We would like to thank Steve Councel for reading and commenting on early drafts of the paper.

## References

[1] H-U Bauer and K R Pawelzik. Quantifying the neighborhood preservation of self-organizing feature maps. *IEEE Transactions on Neural Networks*, 3(4):570–579, July 1992.

[2] A Sommer *et al.* Screening for glaucomatous field loss with automated perimetry. *American Journal of Ophthalmology*, 103:681–684, 1987.

[3] D O Harrington and M V Drake. *The Visual Fields Text and Atlas of Clinical Perimetry.* The CV Mosby Co., 6th edition, 1990.

[4] A Heijl. *Some Characteristics of Glaucomatous Visual Field Loss.* Glaucoma Update (IV). Springer-Verlag, 1991.

[5] T Kohonen. *Self-Organization and Associative Memory.* Springer Series in Information Sciences. Springer-Verlag, 3rd edition, 1989.

[6] T Kohonen and K Mäkisara. Representation of sensory information in self-organizing feature maps. In *AIP Conference Proceedings 151, Neural Networks for Computing*, pages 271–276, 1986.

[7] X Liu, G Cheng, and J X Wu. Identifying the measurement noise in glaucomatous testing: an artificial neural network approach. *to appear in Artificial Intelligence in Medicine*, 1994.

[8] J X Wu. *Visual Screening for Blinding Diseases in the Community Using Computer Controlled Video Perimetry.* PhD thesis, University of London, 1993.

[9] J X Wu, F Fitzke, D Poinoosawmy, R Hitchings, and G Johnson. Variability in glaucomatous visual damage measured with motion detection. *Investigative Ophthalmology & Visual Science*, 34(4):1475, 1993.

[10] J X Wu, R Wormald, F Fitzke, D Poinoosawmy, S Nagasubramanian, and R Hitchings. Laptop computer perimetry for glaucoma screening. *Investigative Ophthalmology & Visual Science*, 32(4):810, 1991.

# Improving learning abilities of a coupled connexionist-rules based system

Laurent Condamin [1,2,3]
Patrick Naïm [1,3]
Christian Nottola [2]

(1) Ecole Centrale Paris, Applied Mathematics Laboratory
Grande Voie des Vignes, 92290 Chatenay Malabry, FRANCE

(2) Artificial Intelligence Center of Banque de France
2 av. Pierre Mendes-France, 77186 Noisiel, FRANCE

(3) Elseware
75 rue de Lourmel, 75015 Paris, FRANCE

### Abstract

*In this paper we point out some problems a system coupling connexionism and rules based reasoning has to overcome to learn good classification. We insist on the idea that such a system has to use its rules set to improve its learning abilities and highlight that under these conditions, the coupling system is often more efficient than the using of two independant modules (connexionist and rules based ones).*

**keywords** : *coupled system, rules based system, neural networks, learning.*

## 1. Introduction

When one deals with a classification problem, one has usually two types of knowledges :

* The Theorical Knowledge (TK) is generally a set of rules and properties which have been extracted in former studies.
* The Empirical Knowledge (EK) is rather a set of patterns which are examples of classification.

For example, at Banque de France [Cond] [Nott1] [Nott2], on one hand experts have rules enacted by central departments to assess french firms for credit ratings (TK) and on the other hand large volumes of previously rated firms (EK) are available.

In this general framework, two opposite situations can be found :

* We only have samples of classification (EK) and a machine supposed to classify patterns will have to learn somehow the knowledge embedded in the sample set. Such a machine is an empirical one. Neural Networks and Case Based Reasoning Systems are empirical machines.
* We know all the theory which rules the problem (TK) and a machine which have to classify don't have to learn anything, it only needs to apply rules. The machine is a theorical one. Any Rules Based System belongs to this category of machines.

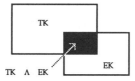

*fig 1 : Theorical and Empirical Knowledge*

But in real problems we often have both empirical knowledge and theorical knowledge, so the classification machine must have learning abilities profiting by theory and examples : it should be able to learn new knowledge all the easier since it possesses a basic theorical corpus. Futhermore empirical and theorical knowledge are not necessarily independant (see fig. 1) : an example of EK can be explained by a rule of TK. This last fact is the starting point of our studies.

In this paper we are interested in a particular case of system coupling a multi-layered neural network and a set of rules. We analyse the difficulties of learning such a system and propose a method to improve learning by using theorical corpus.
At first we describe some notations and introduce some concepts.

## 2. Notations

*Classification*
The classification denoted *Class()* is an application from $R^n$ (RxRx...xR, R denotes the real number set) onto *[1,m]* (integers between *1* and *m*, *m* denotes the number of classes). Different class areas are separed by hypersurfaces.
*Set of Rules*
Let $\mathcal{R}$ be the function which returns the class computed by the set of rules. $\mathcal{R}$ is an application from $R^n$ onto *[1,m+1]* where *m+1* is the index of the class *'unknown'* (if an example doesn't match any rule of $\mathcal{R}$ its class is *m+1*).
*Neural Network*
Let $\mathcal{N}$ be the function which returns the class computed by the neural network. $\mathcal{N}$ is an application from $R^n$ onto *[1,m]*.
*Coupling System*
Let $S$ be the function which returns the class computed by the coupling system $\mathcal{N}^\wedge\mathcal{R}$.
*Rule*
A rule is a couple *(p,c)* which means :
　　　IF *p(x) IS TRUE  THEN Class(x) = c*
*p* is a cunjunction of conditions $x_i \in I_i$ where $I_i$ is a convex part of R.
if *r = (p,c)* denotes a rule we shall designate by *F(r) = {x ∈ $R^n$ / p(x) is true}* the field of *r*. It is a parallelepiped or a degenerate parallelepiped.
*Examples Set*
Let $\mathcal{B}$ be the set of all the examples we have to train the system.
Let $\mathcal{L}$ be the set of examples with which we train the neural network.
Let $\mathcal{T}$ be the set of examples with which we test the system.
*Error Signal*
E($\mathcal{B}$) denotes the mean square error of the network computed on the set $\mathcal{B}$.
Err($\mathcal{N}$) denotes the error back-propagated through the neural network $\mathcal{N}$.

## 3. Some particular rules

If *d* denotes a distance on $R^n$, the distance between $x \in R^n$ and a part S of $R^n$ is denoted *d(x,S)*.
　　*d(x,S) = min d(x,y), y ∈S.*
If X and S denote two parts of $R^n$ the distance between X and S is denoted *d(X,S)* :
　　*d(X,S) = min d(x,S), x ∈X.*
If P denotes the probability distribution on space $R^n$, |. $|_P$ denotes the volume on $R^n$.
*"Buffer" Zone*
If ε denotes a positive real number, we define the ε-"buffer" zone of a part S of $R^n$ as
　　*BZ(S,ε) = {x ∈$R^n$ / d(x,S) < ε)*
*"Bufferness" of a part*
We define the ε-"bufferness" *RBZ(X,S,ε)* of a part X bounded by a hypersurface *Sx* in relation to the hypersurface *S*, where *Sx* doesn't cross *S*, as the volume of the intersection between *BZ(S,ε)* and X :
　　*RBZ(X,S,ε) = |BZ(S,ε) ∩ X|$_P$*
*Partial Rule*
A rule *r* is said to be a partial rule if there exists a part *F'* defined as follows :
　　*F(r) ⊂ F' and Class(F') = Class(F(r))*
A partial rule represents a partial knowledge : we know the class of an example which belongs to an area which is included in another same class area.

IV-436

### Exception Rule

A rule *r* is said to be a partial rule if there exists a part *F'* defined as follows :

$F(r) \subset F'$ and $Class(F') \# Class(F(r))$

An exception rule often represents exception examples, ie examples which are surrounded by different class examples.

### Buffer Rule and Perfect Buffer Rule

A rule *r* is said to be a ε-"buffer" rule in relation to the discriminant hypersuface *S* if :

$RBZ(F(r),S,\varepsilon) > 0$

We say that *r* is a perfect "buffer" rule if it is a 0-"buffer" rule.

When ε is chosen "small enough" ε-"buffer" rules rule examples which are close to the discrimination hypersurfaces. The greater their "bufferness" the more numerous the examples they rule.

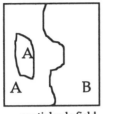 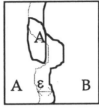 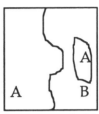

partial rule field    buffer rule field    exception rule field

two classes problem : A and B

*fig 2 : different types of rules*

## 4. Description of the coupled system

As we've mentioned it, it is constituted by a multi-layer neural network (three layers at most) $\mathcal{N}$ and a set of rules $\mathcal{R}$.

The rules are supposed to be consistent and reliable; in particular we can have the following situation :

*r and r' are two rules and  $F(r) \cap F(r')$ and $Class(F(r)) \# Class(F(r'))$*

Let's consider the answer of the coupling system $\mathcal{R}^\wedge\mathcal{N}$ (see fig.3) :

if *x* is an example,
  either $R(x) = m+1$ (unknown class) and $\mathcal{R}^\wedge\mathcal{N}(x) = \mathcal{N}(x)$
  or $\mathcal{R}^\wedge\mathcal{N}(x) = \mathcal{R}(x)$

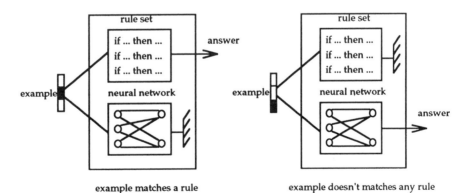

example matches a rule          example doesn't matches any rule

*fig 3 : answer of the coupling system*

## 5. Learning of the coupling system

In this chapter we analyse the hardships we have to face when learning this coupled system. At first let's say that $\mathcal{N}$ will be trained by classical back-propagation algorithm [Rum].

When you intend to learn such a system, the first idea is to consider $\mathcal{N}$ and $\mathcal{R}$ as if they were independant : the training of $\mathcal{N}$ is processed with all examples of $\mathcal{B}$ and the classical mean square error over $\mathcal{B}$. This approach, as we'll highlight it, is not always successful because it doesn't profit by $\mathcal{N}$-$\mathcal{R}$ interaction which should improve learning.

Another approach is to move from the learning set all the examples of $\mathcal{B}$ which are ruled by $\mathcal{R}$:

$$\mathcal{L} = \mathcal{B} \setminus \cup F(r)$$

The network would be used to learn the empirical knowledge only. In this case the network will have sometimes difficulties to find good discrimination hypersurfaces because of partial knowledge included in $\cup F(r)$.

In the following paragraphes we dwell on the difficulties we've just pointed out and propose a method to overcome these hardships.

## 5.1. $\mathcal{R}$ doesn't interact with learning

Here $\mathcal{L} = \mathcal{B}$ and $Err(\mathcal{N}) = E(\mathcal{B})$.

Let's suppose that one of the rules is an exception rule. Since the field where this rule's premices are true is surrounded by an area which elements have a different class, it will be difficult for the network to find the fitting discrimination between $F(r)$ and the surrounding area. One could reply that if the complexity of the network is high enough (increasing the size of tthe hidden layer for example) such a discrimination is theorically possible. To reject this objection we can put forward at least 3 points :

* at first neural network architecture is defined *a priori*, thus it can't fit exactly the discrimination complexity since we generally don't know anything about it,
* then, even if we chose a very complex network the well-known problem of overfitting would arise [**Vap**],
* and finally, since the system $\mathcal{R}$ can rule these exception examples, it is not necessary to waste neural resources to learn them.

To remedy this situation the best solution is to avoid the learning of exception ruled examples. One solution to satisfy this condition is described below.

## 5.2. The learning set is ruled examples free

Here $\mathcal{L} = \mathcal{B} \setminus \cup F(r)$ and $Err(\mathcal{N}) = E(\mathcal{B} \setminus \cup F(r))$.

We have eliminated all ruled examples from the learning set. For this reason we sometimes have to face another hardship due to partial knowledge : the classification learned by $\mathcal{N}$ doesn't take account for partial ruled examples which may be problematical if these partial rules are also "buffer" rules. Indeed if $r$ is a $\varepsilon$-"buffer" rule for $\varepsilon$ small enough, as we 've stressed it before, the greater $RBZ(F(r),S,\varepsilon)$ the more likely you are to have examples in $F(r)$ which is close to the discrimination hypersurface $S$. If you choose an example near a "buffer" ruled zone but not included in it is likely to be ill classed (see fig. 4). Consequently examples of $F(r)$ are very important to learn good discrimination surfaces.

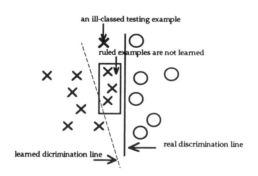

*fig 4 : example of ill learning*

### 5.3. The tradeoff : a differentiated back-propagated error signal

We can sum up the former problems :

> either we take account for ruled examples and we cause the learning to be difficult because of exception rules, or we process a ruled examples free learning and the discrimination computed by the neural network might be unefficient because of unseen buffer zones.

If we had meta-knowledge on the problem we could extract only exception examples from the examples set and process learning, but generally we do not have enough knowledge on the problem to separe exception rules from partial buffer rules. To overcome this difficulties we propose a method based on the following idea :

> *The neural network of the coupled system is to learn most of examples of the examples set, but if it can't learn a ruled example the penality it should get for such a error must be lesser than the penality it would get for an ill classed unruled example.*

To implement this idea we subdivide the back-propagated error into 2 terms :

$$Err(\mathcal{N}) = E(\mathcal{B} \setminus \mathcal{F}(r)) + \alpha * E(\mathcal{B} \cap (\mathcal{F}(r))) \qquad \text{where } \alpha \text{ is a real number in } [0,1].$$

$\alpha$ is the penality we apply to ruled examples.

if $\alpha = 0$ : none of the ruled examples belong to the learning set

if $\alpha = 1$ : all examples are equitably penalised, so the neural network and the ruled based system are independant during learning.

if $\alpha < 1$ : ruled examples are less penalised than unruled examples.

Since the weight increment during learning is computed as $\Delta W = -\lambda \partial Err(\mathcal{N})/\partial W$ , the introduction of $\alpha$ allows us to fit the learning rate when we have ruled examples :

> $\lambda$ for unruled examples
>
> $\lambda \alpha$ for ruled examples

If some exception rules fields have a high volume we must decrease $\alpha$ to compensate the influence of exception ruled examples in $Err(\mathcal{N})$.

If some partial "buffer" rules field have a high volume we must increase $\alpha$ to make the influence of examples which are close to discrimination surfaces higher.

So we can see that fitting $\alpha$ allows us to control the effect of ruled examples on learning.

## 6. Simulations

These simulations have to highlight whether there exists an optimal value for $\alpha$ , that is a value which makes the network find a good discrimination in several situations :

> $\mathcal{R}$ contains only exception rules
>
> $\mathcal{R}$ contains only partial rules
>
> $\mathcal{R}$ contains both partial and exception rules

We make our simulations on a very simple classification problem (see fig. 5).

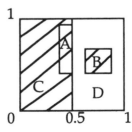

*fig.5 : an example of two class discrimination problem*

**The set of examples**
$\mathcal{B}$ and $\mathcal{T}$ contain 512 examples are picked up from the square [0,1]x[0,1].

**The input space**
In this square we can see 4 areas :

A is the square [0.375 , 0.5]x[0.375 , 0.875]. *Class*(A)=1

B is the square [0.625 , 0.875]x[0.375 , 0.625]. *Class*(B)=1

C is the area $[0 , 0.5] \times [0 , 1] \setminus A$. *Class*(C) = 1

D is the area $[0.5 , 1] \times [0 ,1] \setminus B$. *Class*(D) = 2

*Sa, Sb, Sc, Sd, Ss* denote the surface of A, B, C, D and $[0,1] \times [0,1]$.

Over each of this area the surfacic density of examples is uniform. These densities are denoted *Da, Db, Dc, Dd* and *Ds*.

Da Sa+Db Sb+Dc Sc+Dd Sd = Ds Ss.

### The rules

A can be seen as the field of the partial "buffer" rule $r_a$:

if $x \in [0.375 , 0.5]$ and $y \in [0.375 , 0.875]$ then class(x,y)=1

B can be seen as the field of the exception rule $r_b$:

if $x \in [0.625 , 0.875]$ and $y \in [0.375 , 0.625]$ then class(x,y)=1

Here the discrimination surface is the line $x = 0.5$.

$RBZ(A,x=0.5,\varepsilon) = 0.5 * \varepsilon * Da$ if $\varepsilon < 0.125$, $RBZ(A,x=0.5,\varepsilon)$ is in proportion with *Da*.

The influence of the rule $r_b$ can be computed by $0.25 * 0.25 * Db$ ( $= |B|_{Db}$ ) and is consequently in proportion with *Db*.

### The neural network

The neural network is three layered :
* input layer : 2 cells (x and y)
* hidden layer : 9 cells so that the network can theorically separate all the areas (4 for A , 4 for B, 1 for C against D)
* output layer : 1 cell (class 1 or 2)

The *a priori* complexity of the network is compensated by a systematical decreasing of weights during learning [Chau].

### The performance evaluation

Let's say how we evaluate the learning classification : we compute the proportion of examples of $\mathcal{T}$ which are well classed by the system $\mathcal{R}^\wedge \mathcal{N}$.

### first experiment : R contains only exception rules

A is included in C, there are only three areas (C,B and D).

Dc (Sc+Sa)+Db Sb+Dd Sd = Ds Ss.

We increase the influence of the exception area by increasing *Db* and for each value of *Db* we check the learned classification with $\alpha = 1$ and we try to get the maximal value of $\alpha$ for which the learned classification is good.

The following table presents the results :

| DbSb/DsSs | 10% | 20% | 30% | 40% |
|---|---|---|---|---|
| * $\alpha_{max}$ | 0.2 | 0.1 | 0.06 | 0.02 |
| * %success on a 512 sample testing set | 98% | 95% | 96% | 97% |
| * %success on a 512 sample testing set for $\alpha = 1$ | 98% | 89% | 71% | 56% |

### second experiment : R contains only partial "buffer" rules

B is included in D, there are only three areas (A, C and D).

Da Sa+Dc Sc+Dd (Sb+Sd) = Ds Ss.

We increase the bufferness of the buffer area by increasing *Da* and for each value of *Da* we check the learned classification with $\alpha = 0$ and we try to have the minimal value of $\alpha$ for which the learned classification is good.

The following table presents the results :

| DaSa / DsSs | 10% | 20% | 30% | 40% |
|---|---|---|---|---|
| * $\alpha_{min}$ | 0.2 | 0.1 | 0.06 | 0.02 |
| * %success on a 512 sample testing set | 99% | 97% | 98% | 98% |
| * %success on a 512 sample testing set for $\alpha = 0$ | 98% | 85% | 78% | 71% |

_**third experiment : R contains both exception and buffer rules**_
We only test 2 cases :

$Da=Dc=Db=Dd=Ds$ : uniform density over the whole square $[0 , 1] \times [0 , 1]$

For $\alpha = 1$ the percentage of well classed examples over a 512-examples testing set is 84%, where as for $\alpha = 0.1$ this percentage is 97%.

$Da=Db > Ds > Dc=Dd$ : lots of examples are ruled by exception or buffer rules.

For $\alpha = 1$ the percentage of well classed examples over a 512-examples testing set is 75% and we've not found any $\alpha$ to improve this performance rate.

In the 2 cases we have tried to fit $\alpha$ to obtain a better classification as the one obtained for $\alpha = 1$ (independance of $\mathcal{N}$ and $\mathcal{R}$).

## 7. results

In the two first experiments we always find a fitting value for $\alpha$; this value is all the lower since there are more exception ruled examples and is all the higher since there are less buffer ruled examples.

When the learning set contains both exception and buffer rules examples you can find a value for $\alpha$ in normal situations (uniform distribution) with a simple network architecture but when there are lots of exception and buffer rules examples the network is forced to use all its neurons and the classification is not improved if we compare it to the one obtained when $\alpha = 1$ ($\mathcal{N}$ and $\mathcal{R}$ are independant).

## 8. Conclusion :

The point we've stressed in this paper is that a connexionist/symbolic system has to profit by its rules to improve its learning abilities when faced to a classification. The method we proposed reaches partly this goal, but it is limited by the fact we can't distinguish exception rules from partial rules _a priori_. However it would be possible to extract topological properties (eg by clustering and computing distance between clusters) of the examples set and so to get more knowledge about the "bufferness" or the "exceptionality" of examples. This meta-knowledge would allow us to define more fitting error signals for the network and so to increase interaction between the theorical corpus and the network during learning.

## References

[**Chau**] Chauvin, Y. A back-propagation algorithm with optimal use of hidden units. in _Advances in Neural Information Processing Systems 1_. D Touretsky (Ed.). Palo Alto, CA : Morgan Kaufman.

[**Cond**] Condamin, L., Nottola, C. Concept Extraction from a Neural Network. In _Proceedings of WCNN Portland '93_.

[**Nott1**] Nottola, C., Condamin, L., and Naïm, P. On the Use of Hard Neural Networks for Symbolic Learning : application to company evaluation. In _Proceedings of IJCNN Singapore '91_.

[**Nott2**] Nottola, C., Condamin, L., and Naïm, P. Hard Neural Networks applied to Rule Extraction : a methodological approach applied to company evaluation. In _Proceedings of Neuro-Nîmes '91_.

[**Rum**] Rumelhart, D.E.; Hinton, G.E., and Williams. R. J. Learning intenal represenattions by error propagation. In _Parallel Distributed Processing : Explorations in the microstructure of cognition_. Vol. 1, pages 318-363. MIT Press, Cambridge.

[**Vap**] Vapnik, V.N. _Estimation of Dependencies Based on Empirical Data_. Springer-Verlag, New-York. 1982.

# A HYBRID SYSTEM FOR CASE-BASED REASONING*

Baogang Yao, Yongbao He
Department of Computer Science, Fudan University
Shanghai 200433, P.R.China

## ABSTRACT

This paper introduces a hybrid system (CASIE for short) for blast furnace material surface shape analysis. Neural networks are combined with tradition artificial intelligence techniques to provide a flexible solution of this problem. In CASIE, a back propagation network is used as case retriever to retrieve stored case corresponding to its input data, and the retrieved case is tuned by the case validation. Traditional knowledge system and mathematical models are combined together in case validator to tune the retrieved surface shape for a more accurate material surface description. Simulation results illustrate the feasibility and advantage of neural network as the case retriever in case-based reasoning system.

Keywords: Neural Network, Artificial Intelligence, Case-Based Reasoning, Hybrid System, Blast Furnace

## 1. Introduction

In iron-making process, the distribution of the raw material inside the blast furnace(BF) is a crucial factor for the BF operators to make decisions. Yet the accurate analysis of the material surface shape is very difficult because of the lack of direct detecting means. Operators could only take actions based on their approximate estimate of the internal material shape, which is induced mostly from their experience.

Several models for raw material distribution have been put forward based on the research and experiments on the standard 1:10 experimental blast furnace model. But the experimental conditions are quite different with actual working conditions, therefore these material distribution models could only be treated as a raw estimation. The operators should modify these estimation based on their own experience to result in a better and more accurate estimation.

To provide more accurate raw material surface analysis automatically, the knowledge with which the operators make their decisions should be integrated with the mathematical models. Besides, blast furnace sensor data also provide useful information about the raw material distribution, therefore the operators' knowledge in analysing these sensor data should also be incorporated.

However, knowledge acquisition of this problem is much more difficult than that in developing diagnostic expert systems. In a diagnostic system such as medical consultant, expertise are represented in rule forms, and each rule is a (premise conclusion) pair. Conclusions in these systems are mostly an assessment about a parameter. However, in estimating the material surface shape, we cannot represent the operators' experience in rule forms, because it will be very difficult, almost impossible, to describe the surface shape in a rule's conclusion. Therefore we abandoned the rule-based approach and introduced the case-based reasoning system in stead.

Case-based reasoning system is very appropriate for applications in which the experts' knowledge is very difficult to extract and represent. In CASIE, a hybrid system which

---

* This work is partly supported by the Climbing Programme-National Key Project for Fundamental Research in China , Grant NSC 92097, and Shanghai Natural Science Foundation 93 JC 14003.

incorporated both case-based reasoning and neural networks, we store representative sensor data and their correspondent internal material surface shape in a case base. The on-line sensor data are compared with the cases stored inside the case base and a most similar case will be retrieved. The correspondent surface shape of the retrieved case is then provided to the case validator which modifies this shape with the historical data and thus results in the final shape description. Neural network, due to its learning capability and error tolerance, is introduced in our approach as the case-retriever. Real-time sensor data are provided to the neural network to retrieve the most similar case.

In the following sections, we will firstly give a brief introduction to the technological processing flow of material replenish, then we will concentrate on the architecture and principle of CASIE's hybrid reasoning system.

## 2. Technological Processing Flow

In blast furnace operation, raw materials, which are mainly composed of ore and core, are replenished from the top of the furnace through a turning trough. The trough keeps turning at different angles, therefore the raw material are replenished at different position on the top of the blast furnace. The replenished material forms certain distribution surface which has very importain effect for the blast furnace working status. See Fig.1a and 1b for an illustation of the trough and a possible distribution of raw material within the blast furnace.

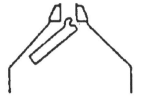
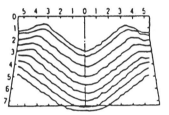

Fig.1a Illustration of the material replenish trough     Fig1b. Material distribution display

Operators could adjust the angle of the trough and the cycling number of the trough at that angle to to control the distribution of the new replenished material. However, to maintain an optimum material distribution within the blast furnace is a very difficult task and demand rich experiences of the blast furnace operators. If the ore and coke are replenished into a container with fixed base, the surface could be easily calculated. However, this is an impracticable assumption because inside the blast furnace, violent physical and chemical reactions keep going on and the material inside the blast furnace are in an ebullient status. To determine the possible surface shape, a system should consider not only the material replenish parameters, but also the real-time and historical blast furnace sensor data.

## 3. Hybrid Reasoning System

The structure of CASIE's hybrid reasoner is illustrated in Fig.2.

CASIE's case-based reasoning system consists of two main components: a case retriever and a case validator. The case retriever is implemented using neural network, and the case validator are implemented using traditional artificial intelligent techniques.

### 3.1. Case Retrieval

Our former approach for case retrieval is an traditional case matching scheme. The case retriever compared its input with all cases stored in the case base and retrieved the most similar

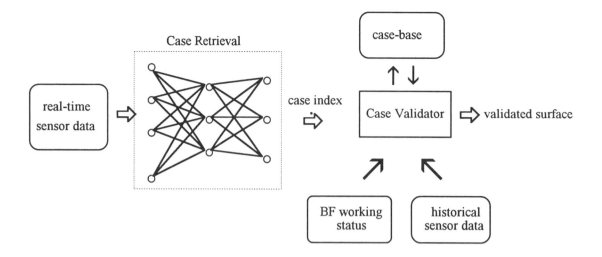

Fig.2 Structure of CASIE's reasoner

one. The problem was how to decide the similarity of two cases. Various criteria could be chosen, such as nearest-neighbour and so on. However, the disadvantage of this approach is its incapability in dealing with incomplete or continuous input. Although we can incorporate fuzzy membership functions into the matching process to describe the similarity of two cases, the decision of fuzzy membership function is also very difficult.

Neural network approach, because of its capability of processing ambiguous input and converting numerical data to symbols, is a more attractive approach in this case. The neural network model we adopted is BP network, which has demonstrated its advantages in many successful applications. The BP network accept blast furnace sensor data as its input and, on the output layer generates the index of the stored case which is most similar to its input. Output of·the network is a continue number which is treated as the similarity degree between this two cases. This number could be used in the case validator for fine modification of the retrieved surface.

The BP network is trained off-line using seed-cases stored inside the case base. Input to the neural network includes the raw-material replenish parameters and sensory data which are closely related the raw material distribution such as blast furnace permeability, top pressure and cross temperature etc. The number of output nodes of the neural network is determined by the cases stored in the case base. Each output node corresponds to one specific case. Therefore during training, the output node corresponding to the index of the specified surface shape is set to 1 and other output nodes are set to zero. After the training, this BP neural network can be used as the case retriever.

### 3.2. Case Validation

The retrieved material surface is only a partial solution. Because the violent reactions carrying on inside the blast furnace, the material surface could vary a lot even if the detected sensor data are quite similar (due to the lack of the most crucial detection sensor). Therefore the retrieved surface shape could only be treated as a reference, a very important reference, though.

The case validator also takes the following two factors into its consideration: the blast furnace(BF) working status and historical sensor data. These information are combined together to tune the retrieved material surface. The BF status assessment, achieved by another rule-based model, is a very important reference to raw material distribution. If the material inside the BF is in an ideal distribution, then the BF should work under a very stable status.

Otherwise, if the material replenished into the BF is ill-distributed, the BF working status could not be good. Therefore, by the analysis of the real-time as well as the historical BF working status assessment, we can tune the retrieved surface shape into a more accurate one. Besides, the surface shape inferred by the mathematical model, and the latest estimated surface shape are all major factors which should be combined to improve our reasoning result.

## 4. Maintenance of the Seed Case-Base

### 4.1. Case representation

Cases stored in the case-base are represented in vector forms. Material replenish parameters, the relative sensor data and the corresponding surface shape are combined as one record. The shape is described in a series of discrete pixels coordinates. These pixels can be linked into a smooth curve. See Fig.3 for an example.

Fig.3 Surface shape representation

### 4.2. Case-base Construction

The seed case-base is acquired during the simulation experiments. These experiments are carried out in a 1:10 scale simulated blast furnace. The model furnace is designed mainly for the analysis of the material distribution. These simulation experiments are sorted and classified, and the most typical one are treated as seed cases and are stored in the seed case-base after modification based on operator's experience.

The surface shape acquired from simulated experiments are used as references for blast furnace operators. In dealing with actual situation, the operators may describe the surface shape corresponding to a certain material replenish parameters and sensor output by one of these seed cases. These are then combined together to form a record in the case base.

After the generation of the seed case base, the neural network is trained. The training data are formed from the case-base.

The case base is not constant and should be improved during on-line working. If the case retriever gives low output value for all its output node, then this case should be added to the case base because it must be a new situation. Consequently the number of output and hidden nodes of the neural network should be modified, and the network should be trained again to adapt to the modified case base.

## 5. Simulation

We have done some simulation experiments based on the proposed approach. Ten typical BF material surface distribution and their corresponding parameters and sensor data are combined together to form ten cases inside the case base. Therefore the network we used has ten output nodes. The input to the neural network is composed of the following parameters: four of the input nodes correspond to the material replenish data. Each node stands for one angle and the input of this node stands for the number of circles the trough turned at this angle. For other six input nodes we chose six closely related sensor output.

The neural network is trained using the simulated cases and is then used as a case retriever.

## 6. Conclusions

In this paper, we have introduced a hybrid approach for case-based reasoning which has been applied to the blast furnace material distribution analysis. The proposed approach achieved very satisfactory results with simulated data. We are now improving our approach by applying CASIE the actual BF sensor data.

However, our simulation results have illustrated the feasibility and advantage of neural network as a case retriever in case-based reasoning system. Retrieving of the most similar case, when using traditional case comparison approach, demand the retriever to scan the whole case base and for each stored case, a similarity degree should be calculated, and then the system should choose the case with the greatest similarity degree. Two difficulties exist during this process: one is how to compare the similarity between two cases, and the other one is how to deal with ambiguous or incomplete input. With the neural network approach, such difficulties can be eliminated and more robust results could be achieved.

## 7. References

[1] "Development and applications of blast furnace material distribution simulation models for large scale blast furnaces", World Iron & Steel, Vol. 2, 1993

[2] Francois F. Ingrand et al, "An Architecture for Real-Time Reasoning and System Control", IEEE Expert, Vol. 7, No. 6, 1993

[3] Daniel Hennessy et al, "Applying Case-Based Reasoning to Autoclave Loading", IEEE Expert, Vol.7, No.5, 1993

[4] S.K.Pal, S.Mitra, "Multilayer Perceptron, Fuzzy Sets, and Classification", IEEE Trans. on Neural Networks, Vol.3, No.5,1992.9

# A Model of Recurrent Neural Networks that Learn State-Transitions of Finite State Transducers

Itsuki NODA

Electrotechnical Laboratory

1-1-4 Umezono, Tsukuba, Ibaraki 305, JAPAN

noda@etl.go.jp

## Abstract

A model, called the 'SGH' model, and its learning method are proposed. While simple recurrent networks (SRN) and finite state transducers (FST) have similar structures, their learning are quite different, so that SRNs can not acquire suitable state-transitions through conventional learning. The proposed model and method construct an SRN that has suitable state-transitions for a given task. In order to derive the model and the method, a procedure to construct an FST from examples of input-output is composed using the state-minimization technique. This procedure consists of three steps, the 'keeping input history' step, the 'grouping states' step, and the 'constructing state-transitions' step. Then each step is reconstructed as learning of a neural network. Finally, three networks are combined into the 'SGH' model. Experiments show that the 'SGH' model can learn suitable state transitions for given tasks. Experiments also show that it increases the ability to process temporal sequences with LDDs by SRNs.

## 1 Introduction

One of characteristics of simple recurrent networks (SRN) is the correspondence with finite state transducers (FST). On the other hand, in processing by an FST, structures of information are represented by state transitions of the FST. Many researchers focused on this point. They tried to analyze pattern transitions of SRNs as state-transitions of FSTs in order to extract structures of processing that the SRNs learned. In these works, there remains an open problem that SRNs do not entirely acquire suitable state transitions. This problem comes from a lack of correspondence between learning of SRNs and one of FSTs. In order to solve this problem, Noda and Nagao[5] proposed the PEX model, whose learning corresponded to learning of FSTs. The correspondence, however, is not exact, so that a PEX model can not acquire accurate state-transitions.

In this article, I propose a new model, called an SGH model, which is derived from revised idea of the PEX model.

## 2 SRN and FST

### 2.1 Simple Recurrent Networks (SRN)

Consider an SRN as shown in Fig. 1. An SRN consists of input, previous-state, state and output layers, Sigma-Pi-type links [2] from input and previous-state layers to the state layer, and Sigma-type links from the state layer to the output layer. Moreover, the network has recurrent links to copy patterns of state layer to the previous-state layer with 1 time delay.

This network works in discrete time. In each time step, an external input pattern is set into the input layer and a previous pattern of the state layer is set into the previous-state layer. Then patterns of state and output layers are calculated in the manner of typical feed-forward networks.

Note that it is not necessary to use Sigma-Pi-type links among input, previous-state and state layers. It is only for avoiding a limitation of transitions of SRN [2]. We can have a same discussion in the rest of this article in the case of using Sigma type links instead of Sigma-Pi type link.

There are two strategies to train an SRN to learn a given sequential task. One strategy is to use the 'back-propagation through time (BPTT)' method to minimize output error. BPTT is powerful, but it requires to

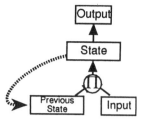

Figure 1: Simple Recurrent Network with Sigma-Pi Link.

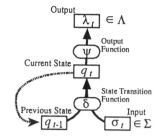

Figure 2: Finite State Transducer.

record whole status of networks during processing. Such a mechanism is not plausible biologically. Another strategy is to use the back-propagation simply within one time step (called a simple BP, or SBP). A merit of this strategy is that learning is simple and plausible biologically. But a demerit is that it has poor ability to learn complex sequential tasks [1].

In these strategies, I take a later one for learning an SRN.

## 2.2 Finite State Transducer (FST)

In the automata theory, an FST is defined by a 6-tuple $< Q, \Sigma, \Lambda, \delta, \psi, q_0 >$, where $Q$ is a set of states, $\Sigma$ is a set of input symbols, $\delta$ is a state-transition function, $q_0$ is an initial state, $\Lambda$ is a set of output symbols, and $\psi$ is an output function. Fig. 2 shows a schema of state transitions of an FST.

When a set of examples of input-output sequences is given, we can construct an FST that performs these input-output sequences with minimum states. This is based on the state-minimization technique of FSTs. The procedure is as follow :

S1 Make states each of which corresponds to a possible input history.

S2 Assign an output value to each state according to examples. Then group states into groups according to outputs of states.

S3 Group states in a group into sub-groups according to groups of next states after transitions from the states. Repeat this sub-categorization until no more group are generated.

S4 Put states belonging a same group together into a state, and construct state transitions and outputs of each state.

## 2.3 Correspondence between SRN and FST

As shown in Fig. 1 and Fig. 2, it is easy to consider a correspondence between an SRN and an FST. On the other hand, learning of SRNs described in section 2.1 does not correspond to learning of FSTs. Therefore, it is not sure that SRNs acquire suitable state transitions as FSTs. As a result of acquiring unsuitable state transitions, the ability of SRNs decrease and also it becomes difficult to analyze patterns of the state layer.

In the next section, in order to solve this problem, I propose a new network model and its learning method, which corresponds to learning of FSTs and builds an SRN that has suitable state transitions.

# 3 SGH Model

## 3.1 Network Architecture

Fig. 3 shows an overview of the network architecture of a proposed model, called the 'SGH model'. The SGH model consists of 'SRN', 'grouping' and 'history' modules. In learning phase, the history module is trained first, the grouping module second, and the SRN module third. After learning, the SRN module works alone as an SRN. In other words, grouping and history modules are used only for learning.

The history module learns pattern representation in which information of input histories is represented by patterns effectively. This learning corresponds to the step S1 of the FST learning algorithm. After learning, this module outputs patterns representing input histories to the grouping module as input patterns. The

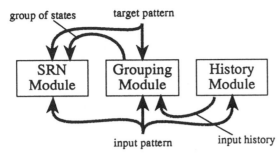

Figure 3: Whole Network Architecture.

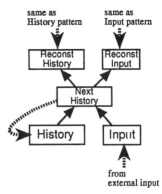

Figure 4: History Module.

grouping module classifies patterns of input histories into groups according to required outputs and next states. This classification is performed through learning. This learning corresponds to the step S2 and the step S3. After learning, this module outputs patterns representing groups of states to the SRN module as teacher patterns. The SRN module learns final state-transitions and an output function according to patterns of state-groups from the grouping module and required output patterns from external teachers. This learning corresponds to the step S4. After learning, a part of this module works alone as an SRN. Note that the learning procedure used in this model is the SBP method.

## 3.2 History Module

The learning of the history module corresponds to the step S1 in the FST learning, that is, making states corresponding to histories of input data. In order to realize this, I use a network, called an X model [4], shown in Fig. 4. This network is trained to minimize the following penalty:

$$E_{\text{history}} = < \left| x_{\text{RI}}^t - x_{\text{I}}^t \right|^2 + \left| x_{\text{RH}}^t - x_{\text{H}}^t \right|^2 > \tag{1}$$

where $x_{\text{RI}}^t$, $x_{\text{I}}^t$, $x_{\text{RH}}^t$ and $x_{\text{H}}^t$ are respectively pattern vectors of reconst-input, input, reconst-history and history layers at time step $t$. Through this learning, information of input histories becomes to be represented by patterns of the history layer. These patterns can be seen as states correspond to input histories. After learning, this module outputs these patterns of the history layer to the grouping module as patterns of states correspond to input histories.

## 3.3 Grouping Module

Fig. 5 shows details of the grouping module. In each time step, a pattern of the history layer in the history module is set on the history layer, a current external input pattern is set on the input layer, a next external input pattern is set on the next-input layer, and a randomly-generated pattern is set on the random-input layer. As teacher signals, a required output pattern is given to the output layer, a pattern of the temporary-group layer at the next time step is given to the next-group layer, and the same pattern of the random-input layer is given to the random-output layer. The network is trained to minimize the following penalty:

$$E_{\text{grouping}} = < \left| x_{\text{O}}^t - x_{\text{T}}^t \right|^2 + \left| x_{\text{NG}}^t - x_{\text{TG}}^{t+1} \right|^2 + \left| x_{\text{RO}}^t - x_{\text{RI}}^t \right|^2 > \tag{2}$$

where $x_{\text{O}}^t$, $x_{\text{NG}}^t$, $x_{\text{RI}}^t$ and $x_{\text{RO}}^t$ are respectively pattern vectors of output, next-group, random-input and random-output layers at time step $t$, $x_{\text{TG}}^{t+1}$ is a pattern vector of the temporary layer at time step $t + 1$, and $x_{\text{T}}^t$ is a required output pattern vectors at time step $t$. Note that weights of links to the temporary-group layer are copied from corresponding links to the group layer at long enough intervals compared with a time scale of weight learning (in experiments in the next section, each 5000 ~10000 epochs). Therefore patterns of the temporary-group layer is almost same as those of the group layer, but is stable. This layer is used for providing stable teacher patterns for the next-group layer.

The learning of this module corresponds to the step S2 and the step S3. In other words, this module groups states according to the output and the next state after transitions. This operation is realized in the following manner.

IV-449

When a 3-layered network is trained to output different patterns for two different input patterns, hidden patterns for two inputs become different. In other words, such learning groups input patterns into groups represented by hidden patterns according to the output patterns. In the context of the grouping module, inputs to the network are patterns of the history layer, which indicate states that correspond to input histories. Moreover, outputs of the module are patterns of the output layer and of the next-group layer. Target patterns of the output layer are required outputs of the states. Target patterns of the next-group layer are the next patterns of the temporary-group layer, which indicate groups of the next states after transitions from the given states. Therefore learning of the grouping module groups states into groups represented by patterns of the group layer according to required outputs and the next states of the states.

However, such learning generally generates redundant groups, because it is not guaranteed that hidden patterns for two different inputs become same when a network is trained to output the same patterns for the inputs. In order to avoid this redundant grouping, the overload learning (OLL) method [3] is used. In this method, a network learns an additional task together with an original task. The OLL method will inhibit redundant grouping because the OLL method has an effect to decrease redundant pattern representation of hidden layers.

After learning, this module outputs patterns of the group layer to the SRN module as patterns of groups of states.

## 3.4 SRN Module

The SRN module constructs reduced state transitions by using information of groups of states from the grouping module. In order to do this, a network like Fig. 6 is considered. This network is same as a SRN in Fig. 1 except for the current-group layer. This layer is trained to output patterns of the group layer in the grouping module. Therefore this network is trained to minimize the following penalty:

$$E_{\text{SRN}} = < \left| x_\text{O}^t - x_\text{T}^t \right|^2 + \left| x_\text{CG}^t - x_\text{G}^t \right|^2 > \tag{3}$$

where $x_\text{CG}^t$ is a pattern vector of the current-group layer at time step $t$. Moreover, in order to avoid generating redundant states, the OLL method is used on the state layer. By the effect of the second term of the right side of (3), each pattern of the state layer becomes to have one-to-one correspondence to a pattern of the group layer in the grouping module. This means that each state of the SRN part corresponds to a group of states that have a same output and same next states. The module also constructs an output function by minimizing the first term.

# 4 Experiments

## 4.1 Learning Flip-flop

The first experiment is learning the same state transitions as of a flip-flop like Fig. 7. A task a network learns is that the network receives a random binary ('0' or '1') sequence followed by a terminal symbol ('s'), and then outputs a parity of the number of '1' in the sequence. In this experiment, each of history, next-history and reconst-history layers consists of 30 units, each of group, previous-group, temporal-group, next-group, state, previous-state and current-group layers consists of 10 units, each of input layers consists of 3 units and each of output layers consists of 2 units.

After learning, I analyzed patterns of the state layer by principle components analysis (PCA). Fig. 8 shows an example of a result of PCA. In this figure the first and second principle components of a pattern of the state layer at each time step are plotted. This figure means the SRN module of the network acquired the same state-transitions as Fig. 7.

For comparison, I also trained SRNs with 60 hidden units by SBP, SRNs with 10 hidden units by BPTT and X models with 50 hidden units to learn the same task. Fig. 9 shows average output errors of each model for various lengths of binary input sequences. We can see that errors of SRNs by SBP and X models increase suddenly when input sequences become long, while errors of SGH models and SRN by BPTT are kept small even for long input sequences. The cause of this advantage of SGH models and SRNs by BPTT is that these networks acquire same state-transitions as Fig. 7. Note that SGH models use the SBP method rather than back-propagating error information through time like the BPTT method.

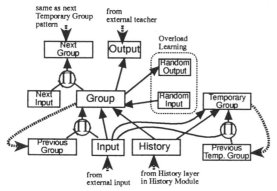

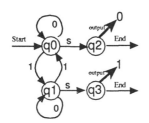

Figure 5: Actual Grouping Module.

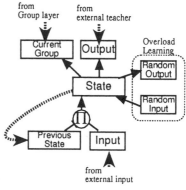

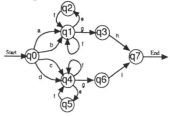

Figure 6: SRN Module.

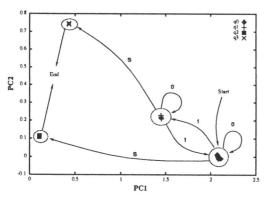

Figure 7: Flip Flop.

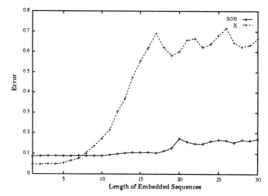

Figure 10: State Transition with Embedded Loop.

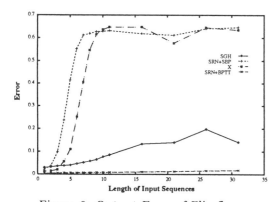

Figure 8: Example of State Transition of Flip-flop.

Figure 11: Prediction Error after Embedded Sequences.

Figure 9: Output Error of Flip-flop.

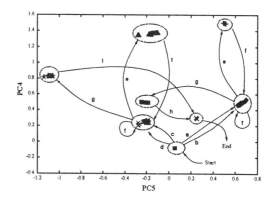

Figure 12: Example of State Transition after Learning.

## 4.2 Learning of Processing with Long Distance Dependency

In the field of natural language processing, one of important problems is how to deal with long distance dependencies (LDD). For example, agreements of between subjects and main verbs hold even if subordinate clauses are embedded between them like "*A dog* that chased cats *is* mine." We tested the ability of SGH models to maintain LDDs by learning a sequence prediction task using sequences generated by an automaton that has state-transitions shown in Fig. 10. If the first data of the sequence is 'a' or 'b', the last data of the sequence is 'i'. Conversely, the first data is 'c' or 'd', the last data is 'j'. Between these correspondences, I interposed embedded sequences generated by automaton whose state-transition has loops. In order to predict the last data of the sequence correctly, the network must keep information about first data in it through embedded sequences. One solution of keeping such information is to acquire the same state-transitions as Fig. 10.

In this experiment, each of history, next-history and reconst-history layers consists of 60 units, each of group, previous-group, temporal-group, next-group, state, previous-state and current-group layers consists of 15 units and each of input and output layers consists of 9 units. I also train an X model with 75 hidden units for comparison. Fig. 11 shows average output errors of both models at predicting last data. We can see that errors of X models increase for longer embedded sequences, while errors of SGH models are kept small. Fig. 12 shows an example of state transitions which SRN modules of an SGH model acquired. This transition map is same as Fig. 10. This means that SGH models learned correct state transitions for this task and became to be able to predict last data correctly even if embedded sequences become long.

## 5 Conclusion

In this article, a model and its learning method to acquire suitable state-transitions are proposed. The method is derived a procedure to construct a finite state transducer from input-output examples using the state-minimization technique. The algorithm consists of three steps. Three network modules and learning methods for them are reconstructed from these three steps and combined into a SGH model.

The proposed method has following features:

- The learning procedure used in this method is simple back-propagation method, in which error signal may not back-propagate through time. Moreover, proposed learning methods are independent from the learning procedure, because only penalty functions to minimize are modified. Therefore it is easy to apply another learning procedure to this method.

- Penalties used in learning are calculated by signals that generated in the network itself except for required outputs. Therefore no other teachers or observers are required for learning.

These features are fit for biological models of brains and also suit for implementing into hardwares.

## References

[1] Axel Cleeremans, David Servan-Schreiber, and James L.MacClelland. Finite State Automata and Simple Recurrent Networks. *Neural Computation*, Vol. 1, pp. 372–381, 1989.

[2] C. L. Giles, G. Z. Sun, H. H. Chen, Y. C. Lee, and D. Chen. Higher Order Recurrent Networks & Grammatical Inference. In *NIPS2*, pp. 380–387. Morgan Kaufmann, 1990.

[3] Itsuki Noda. Learning Method by Overload. In *IJCNN'93-Nagoya*, pp. 1357–1360, Oct. 1993.

[4] Itsuki Noda and Makoto Nagao. Learning Methods for Simple Recurrent Networks Based on Minimizing Information Loss (in Japanese). *Trans. of The Institute of Electronics, Information and Communication Engineers*, Vol. J74-D-II, No. 2, pp. 239–247, 1991.

[5] Itsuki Noda and Makoto Nagao. A Learning Method for Recurrent Networks Based on Minimization of Finite Automata. In *IJCNN'92-Baltimore*, pp. I-27–32, Jun. 1992.

# Cognitive and Semantic interpretation of a NN classifier using prototypes

Christine Decaestecker & Thierry Van de Merckt
IRIDIA - Université Libre de Bruxelles
50 Av. F. Roosevelt, Brussels 1050, Belgium

**Abstract—** In this paper, we present a hybrid neural-symbolic system, called GEM. The neural part learns concepts in a Continuous Attribute Space using optimised prototype locations. Then symbolic descriptions are produced resulting from the Internal Prototypical Representation of the Neural Net. This hybrid system is discussed following two aspects: (i) a cognitive interpretation of the prototypical representation regarding the "Modern view" emerging in Cognitive Science and (ii) a semantic interpretation (using symbolic classification rules) of the encoded knowledge in the neural net.

## I. INTRODUCTION

In the Cognitive Science community, there has been a considerable evolution of ideas about models of concepts, where a central question is "what theories of concepts best account for how people understand the world around them" [6]. The earliest models, called the *Classical view*, assume that concepts have well-defined borders and can be represented by singly necessary and jointly sufficient conditions (for a historical review, see [11]). The inadequacy of the classical view to account for phenomena as "flexible" concepts (where the borders are not clearly defined) and for "typicality effects" of graded concepts (patterns being more or less representative of their class) [14] favoured the emergence of the *Modern* view, i.e., the Prototypical- and the Exemplar-based approaches [10][5]. In these models, concepts are believed to be represented by typical examples or prototypes, that is, objects (observed or abstracted) which are clear cases of their category. A given pattern is then classified with respect to its "distance" from those clear cases that are stored in the long term memory. Hence, the exact matching requirement of the classical view has been relaxed in favour of a partial matching mechanism that entails a measure of similarity between patterns (for a review, see [1]). Additionally to the question of how people represent their concepts "*in Mind*", another issue relates to how people communicate this information to other people. This concept description task is made by introducing a human understandable language and cognitive description constraints (as simplicity) that constitute a common semantic ground shared by all people. It is widely recognised that concept description entails some kind of reduction in both complexity and efficiency. For example, we can easily recognise patterns of the concept of *friendship* but it is difficult to give classification rules for it. Hence, a concept description is never exactly equivalent to our "perception" of it.

In this paper, we analyse a hybrid neural-symbolic system, called GEM, which uses a prototype-based *Knowledge Model*[1] and is able to produce symbolic descriptions reflecting "the encoded knowledge" of the target concept. In first part, we show how the neural part of GEM may constitute a valid computational model of the Modern Cognitive view. In a second part, we show how the symbolic engine using cognitive description biases[2], produces a "communicable" approximation of the *internal concept representation* (ICR) of the neural net.

## II. GEM KNOWLEDGE MODEL

GEM uses a prototype-based Knowledge Model implemented through a neural network, called NNP (Neural Network using Prototypes, a detailed presentation may be found in [2]). NNP uses a three-layer, fully connected, feedforward net. The hidden layer stands for a set of Prototypes whose locations are to be optimised. The weights of the input-to-hidden units are the prototype vector descriptions (location in the pattern space). The hidden-to-output weights are binary and *fixed*: they indicate the class of each prototype. Only the weights of the hidden (prototype) units are trained.

---

[1] In Cognitive Sciences, *Knowledge Models* designate the way an agent encodes its knowledge (e.g., logical rules, exemplars, prototypes, .etc.) as well as the specific way of being used (logical matching by modus ponens, similarity matching by proximity metrics, etc.).

[2] In Machine Learning, a *bias* is a **constraint** used in an algorithm to reduce the search space.

First NNP uses an initialisation strategy that estimates the number of prototype units and good initial weight values for the network. Then NNP aims to globally optimise the location of prototypes in order to minimise the classification error rate. Hence, the vector descriptions of prototypes are adapted through a gradient procedure which minimises an original error function. A deterministic annealing procedure is introduced to avoid local minima and to distribute the prototypes in each class, while finally minimising the total error classification rate. At the end of this process, the optimised network works as a nearest neighbour classifier based on the prototypes and thus produces piecewise-linear decision boundaries. The initialisation strategy as well as the optimisation process are biased (or constrained) in order to provide the minimum number of classification errors on the training set with the minimum number of prototypes (simplicity bias). Hence, redundant prototypes are eliminated and remaining prototypes are forced to cover the largest area in the pattern space.

Each prototype draws in the pattern space a convex decision surface called "Prototypical Region" (PR), resulting from the nearest neighbour competitive process. Each output unit implements a disjunction between these individual regions to build a final region for the corresponding class. The "Diamond" example (Fig.1&2) shows the prototype locations found by NNP and the resulting PRs. The difference between the real frontier and the decision surface produced by NNP results from the lack of training patterns in some places of the pattern space.

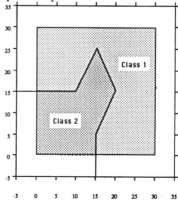

Fig.1: The Diamond Problem

From a cognitive point of view, the semantic signification of a prototype is still an open question, "but it seems to consist of the features of either a typical or an "ideal" category member, rather than invariant features common to every member" [7]. However, in case of their use in classification functions, Medin & Barsalou [8] see prototypes as a special case of reference points for which they associate an interpretation regarding their location in the pattern space. They distinguish three kinds of location: (i) discriminant: located near category boundaries, it provide a salient basis for dividing category exemplars; (ii) central: located at the centre of its category, a prototype represents a central tendency; (iii) ideal: located at an ideal position, a prototype represents an ideal exemplar that may be never observed ("things to eat on a diet" is referenced to a zero calorie food which is ideal but impossible).

Formally, within NNP, a *prototype* is an abstract object in the pattern space whose location (and hence, its values for the attributes) optimises the recognition of concept patterns with respect to the competitive nearest neighbour classification rule. Semantically, the interpretation of NNP prototypes perfectly fits the view of Medin & Barsalou as it can be seen on Fig.2: P4 & P5 are *central* prototypes while P2 & P3 are clear cases of

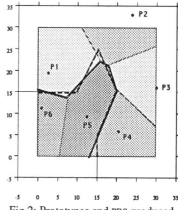

Fig.2: Prototypes and PRS produced by NNP

*ideal* prototypes (they are located outside the range of possible values along both dimensions) and P1 & P6 are rather *discriminant* prototypes that encode the separation line between their decision surface. It is interesting to remark that initial prototypes are issued from a k-means and thus mainly belong to central prototypes (see [2]). The fact that optimised prototypes represent the three types of reference points is a good indication that the process nicely adapts the internal concept representation (ICR) to the nature of the data. This was confirmed by experimental results on various data sets (see [2]).

### III. SYMBOLIC DESCRIPTION OF THE NEURAL ICR

*A. Biases of the Description Algorithm*

Each prototype draws a *convex* decision surface in the pattern space, called Prototypical Region (PR). The region in the pattern space which is allocated to a class by the classifier is the union of the PRs corresponding to the prototypes belonging to this class. We assume that the number of PRs is minimum because of NNP's bias for simplicity which reduces the number of prototypes. In Machine Learning, these individual regions are called "disjuncts" of the class. They are translated in the symbolic description as a logical disjunction. Therefore, to produce a symbolic description of the concept underlined by the ICR (i.e., the prototypes), a *description of each individual PR* will be searched for, each of them being a disjunct of the class description.

In GEM, we use Disjunctive Normal Forms (DNF) to describe a concept, i.e., implication rules where the precondition part contains disjunctive sets of conjunctive predicates and where the conclusion part specifies the resulting class. In continuous space, each conjunctive predicate has one of the following forms: [X<a] or [X>b] where X is a variable (or attribute) of the pattern space and a, b are cut-point values. Hence a conjunction of these predicates determines in the pattern space an orthogonal hyperbox which can be open in some directions. Finally a DNF describes a union of these hyperboxes in the pattern space.

The descriptional algorithm approximates each PR by one or more hyperboxes (a DNF with one or more terms), e.g., the PR of prototype P6 in Fig.2 can be described by the rule: "IF ([x<7] ∧ [x>0] ∧ [y<15] ∧ [y>0]) THEN pattern (x,y) belongs to class-of P6". The whole concept description is then simply the union of all disjunctive terms resulting from the PR approximations. However, this *"Disjunctive view"* is *relaxed when looking at near boundary regions of two adjacent PRs of the same class*. Indeed, prototypes also implicitly draw boundaries separating two adjacent PRs of the same class (called adjacent disjunctive PRs) whose locations are arbitrary. These locations result from the inductive biases used to produce the ICR rather than from some necessity dictated by the target concept (see for example on Fig.2 the border line between P5 and P6). These frontiers may be further inadequate for representing the concept using the orthogonal bias used within the descriptions. Therefore, describing the PRs individually accommodates a relaxing facility near adjacent disjunctive PR boundaries.

Another assumption made by the descriptional algorithm is that noise has been correctly treated by NNP when producing the ICR, i.e., that a pattern whose class is different from the one associated with the PR is a noisy pattern. Therefore, patterns that are wrongly covered by a PR are discarded regarding the description search.

### B. Preference criteria

To generate symbolic descriptions, a number of preferences must be determined: (i) the simplicity of the concept description (related to the level of approximation of the ICR's decision surface); (ii) the consistency and the completeness of the descriptions.

(i)   *Simplicity* - More than one hyperboxes may have to be used to correctly approximate the decision surface drawn by one single Prototype. The number of hyperboxes to be used depends on the adequacy of the orthogonality bias regarding the target concept. The simplicity preference fixes the number of disjunctive rules (hyperboxes) describing a single PR. In the current state of GEM implementation, there are two simplicity levels available: one box per prototype and a free number of boxes, which results in producing "perfect" approximations of the target concept.

(ii)  *Consistency and Completeness* - Given the Disjunctive view adopted, consistency and completeness are related to each PR. A PR description (using hyperboxes) has a x% level of completeness if x% of the *PR-patterns*[3] are included in the corresponding hyperboxes; a x% consistency means that among the patterns included in the hyperboxes, there are x% which belongs to the same class as the one assigned to the PR. Given a level of simplicity, consistency and completeness are related: once a level of consistency for the descriptions has been chosen, the level of completeness is given as a result of the inductive search and inversely. Descriptions may therefore be oriented towards characteristic (100% complete) or discriminant (100% consistent). Any level between 0 and 100% may be asked to the system for consistency or completeness.

Given a level of simplicity and a 100% consistent preference, the level of completeness gives information on the adequacy of the symbolic hyperbox' shape towards the domain. Increasing complexity is a mean to produce "closer" complete and consistent descriptions and hence, simplicity is no longer a bias to avoid overfitting, as usually in symbolic learning, but *it is used for adjusting biased descriptions (hyperboxes) to the underlying shape of the target concept*.

---

3   By *PR-patterns* we mean all patterns that are correctly covered by the PR (with the same class label). The others are assumed to be noise and discard from the symbolic search. (see §A).

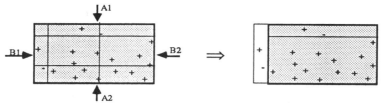

Fig.3: One step of the deflation process (one-complexity algorithm).

### C. The Description Algorithm

Given the preceding considerations, the Symbolic Description Engine starts from the ICR and the training set to produce explicit symbolic descriptions. Two different algorithms have been implemented (for algorithm details see [13]), one that produces a description with one box per prototype, and another one, based on ID3 [9], which produces minimal descriptions of unconstrained complexity. Two important processes are common to the two algorithms: the *Filtering* process for the treatment of noisy data and the *Re-Labelling* process that implements the Disjunctive view (see §A).

*The Filtering procedure* - Given the training set and the ICR, it eliminates from the training all wrongly covered patterns regarding the ICR. It then returns a list of PR-patterns organised into clusters, one per prototype. These filtered ICR_clusters will be further used to build the symbolic description of the target concept.

*The Re-Labelling procedure* - This process creates a new attribute for each filtered pattern, called the *ICR_class*, that tells to which PR they belong. Real classes given by the training set are called *Training-classes*.

*The one-complexity algorithm* - A PR may be described by two extreme boxes: a *characteristic Hyper-Box* (characteristic-HB) and a *discriminant Hyper-Box* (discriminant-HB). The characteristic-HB is uniquely determined by the *smallest* hyperbox covering all PR-patterns (least generalisation strategy). A discriminant-HB is a *100%-consitent* hyperbox (containing no training patterns of another class) *included* in the characteristic-HB which covers the *largest* number of PR-patterns. Once the ICR_clusters have been built, producing the characteristic-HB of one PR is straightforward. It consists in the list of intervals defined by the minimum and maximum values observed among PR-patterns for each attribute[4]. The characteristic-HB is the starting point of the algorithm. To generate an HB of consistency $X$, a deflation of the current characteristic-HB is done. The algorithm performs a hill climbing search constrained to *maximise the cover* in terms of completeness

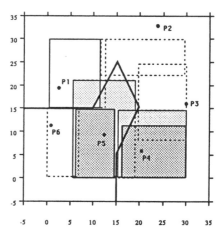

Fig.4: Complete- and discriminant-HB (darker ones) descriptions for the Diamond problem.

and volume (to keep a maximum of positive examples as well as a maximum of the initial characteristic-HB volume). Starting from the characteristic-HB and the filtered ICR_clusters, an iterative procedure excludes *one single* negative example per step, by shrinking the characteristic-HB along one single direction. To choose among all possible directions, two heuristics are used: the direction that minimises the number of positive patterns excluded is chosen and in case of equality, the one that minimises the reduction in volume is chosen (Fig.3). Patterns belonging to adjacent disjunctive PRs are considered as positive by the deflation heuristic, relaxing the Disjunctive view near frontier regions (see §A). Fig.3 shows one step of the deflation process. The 4 directions for deflation are presented: A2 & B2 directions are directly eliminated (too much positive examples are losed for excluding just one negative example). To choose among A1 & B1 (equivalent regarding the loss of positive examples), the minimum generalisation volume loss is used, selecting B1. Fig.4 shows the results of the one-complexity algorithm on the Diamond problem: the characteristic-HBs and discriminant-HBs are presented.

---

[4] Due to the lack of training patterns, some regions in between two adjacent disjunctive PRs may be uncovered by characteristic-HBs. To avoid this problem, characteristic-HBs are slightly extended, in each direction, towards the closest pattern belonging to an adjacent disjunctive PR if it exists (no new negative patterns should be included in the box extension).

It shows that the deflation is high in the areas where the orthogonal bias is inadequate to approximate the concept boundary (see P4, P5). However no deflation is necessary in regions where the bias is adequate (P6) or where there is (nearly) no contact with the Diamond boundary (P2, P3).

*The free-complexity Algorithm* - This algorithm allows to produce characteristic and consistent descriptions of the concept encoded in the ICR. It uses a Decision Tree technique similar to ID3 [9] but in this case the training set has been first Filtered and Re-Labelled. A DT is grown on the filtered patterns *using the ICR_class*, that is, a partition of the PRs is produced. After this first stage, the relaxation of the Disjunctive bias is done by a simple pruning mechanism: a subtree is pruned if all its children are leaves of the same Training_class. This pruning mechanism merges small hyperboxes of same real class that have been separated due to the disjunctive view bias. Each leaf is viewed as a disjunctive rule describing a PR. A rule is the conjunction of the predicates tested at each node on the path from the root to the leaf. Fig.5 shows the result obtained on the Diamond problem. It can be seen that most of the consistent boxes found by the one-complexity algorithm are

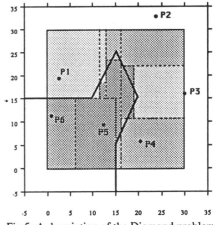

Fig.5: A description of the Diamond problem with a free complexity.

also produced by the free-complexity one (P1, P4, P5 and P6). As a consequence, the main tendency provided by each prototype is preserved and represented by the largest box associated with it, while smaller ones are specialisations in complex shape regions.

## IV. EMPIRICAL EVALUATION

Experiments did not focus on the efficiency of the classification part (NNP) of GEM that has been largely tested against other algorithms and has proven its high performance in [2] and [3]. Instead, the experiences have been done in order to evaluate the quality of the issued descriptions as a means to communicate the concept encoded in the ICR. For this, we used the descriptions as classification rules and compared their results to the classification performed by the ICR (generated by the neural part NNP) on the same data sets. These tests aim to appreciate how the descriptions may represent the central tendencies of the concept and localise "safe" areas (in term of classification) in the pattern space. In a more extended study [13], two others aspects have been explored which concern the treatment of noise through the Filtering effect and the capacity to evaluate the adequacy of the description biases regarding the target concept. Experiments have been made on seven data sets, only average results concerning the one-complexity algorithm are presented here (for details about data &

results see [13]). Two aspects have been taken into account: the noise dependence (each data set has been tested before and after noise addition) and the scarce training dependence (tests have been done with small and large training sets). Fig.6 compares the classification performances of the ICR and discriminant descriptions produced by the one-complexity algorithm (HB), for each type of training (averaged over all data sets). They are evaluated in terms of accuracy (% of correct classifications), omission error (% of no-decisions) and commission error (% of incorrect classifications). Three main observations may be done from this chart:

(i)    On average (except on small noisy ones) *simple* descriptions (one HB by PR) correctly cover a large part of the concept (about 70%). This is mainly due to the disjunctive view bias of GEM.

(ii)   The omission rate depends on the size of the training and on the level of noise. Noise affects the level of omission especially when it introduces a dispersion of

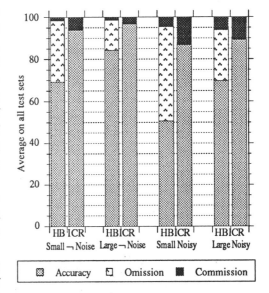

Fig.6: Average results of consistent-HBs

the patterns in the space and therefore decreases the statistical representativeness of the training.

(iii) The commission error rate of descriptions is always less than the ICR, particularly on small training sets. This difference may be explained by the opposite generalisation strategies. The one-complexity algorithm is biased by a least generalisation strategy in order to produce "safe" descriptions adversely to NNP which uses a greatest generalisation strategy. In cases of scarce or noisy data, NNP has not enough data in some pattern space regions and performs "best guess" generalisation, resulting in higher chances to perform errors.

These results confirm that the issued descriptions, while being more or less incharacteristic, depending on the size of the training and the level of noise, correctly capture the major semantic trends of the concepts.


## V. CONCLUSIONS

We have presented an Hybrid Neural-Symbolic Learning algorithm which uses two different inductive engines: one for building an Internal Concept Representation optimised regarding accuracy, and the other for producing symbolic concept description optimised for comprehensibility. This "double" approach has shown two main advantages. Firstly, it allows an optimisation of each task: from the classification point of view, the inductive learning may be optimised without the interference of "human-oriented" biases, and from the concept description point of view, stronger cognitive biases may be used (as accepting omission due to a least generalisation strategy). Secondly, it allows to evaluate the cost of being explicit and human understandable by looking on the omission level produced by the description on the training set. This cost evaluation is not possible if biased class descriptions are directly produced and used for classification. This is the case for most of Symbolic learning systems and for several neural net algorithms [12][4]. It is a main advantage of a hybrid neural-symbolic system as GEM not sacrificing performance as a classifier (by using NNP regarding accuracy) while being able to produce symbolic descriptions on which some reasoning concerning their adequacy for the target concept may be performed.

## REFERENCES

[1] Barsalou L.W. & Hale C.R. (1993) Components of Conceptual Representation: From Feature Lists to Recursive Frames, *Categories & Concepts: Theoritical Views & Inductive Data Analysis*, Academic Press, Cognitive Science Series, pp.97-144.

[2] Decaestecker C. (1993) NNP: a neural net classifier using prototypes, *Proceedings of the IEEE International Conference on Neural Networks*, San Fransisco.

[3] Decaestecker C. & Van de Merckt T. (1993) An unifying framework for analysing bias in Similarity Based Learning, Submitted to Machine Learning - TR Iridia, Université Libre de Bruxelles.

[4] Goodman R.M., Higgins C.M. & Miller J.W. (1992) Rule-based neural networks for classification & probability estimation, *Neural Computation Vol.4 n°6*, pp.781-804.

[5] Hampton J. (1993) Prototype Models of Concept Representation, *Categories & Concepts: Theoritical Views & Inductive Data Analysis*, Academic Press, Cognitive Science Series, pp. 67-95.

[6] Hampton J. & Dubois D. (1993) Psychological Models of Concepts:Introduction, *Categories & Concepts: Theoritical Views & Inductive Data Analysis*, Academic Press, Cognitive Science Series, pp. 11-33.

[7] Harnard S. (1987) Psychological & Cognitive Aspect of Categorical Perception: A Critical Overview, *Categorical Perception: The Groundwork of Cognition*, Ed. by Stevan Harnard, Cambridge University Press, pp. 1-25.

[8] Medin D.L. & Barsalou L.W. (1987) Categorization Processes & Categorical Perception, *Categorical Perception: The Groundwork of Cognition*, Ed. by Stevan Harnard, Cambridge University Press, pp. 455-490.

[9] Quinlan J.R. (1986) Induction of Decision Trees. *Machine Learning Vol 1, n°1*, Kluwer Academic Publishers.

[10] Rosh E. & Mervis C.B. (1975) Family Resemblances: Studies in the Internal Structure of Categories, *Cognitive Psychology 7*, pp. 573-605.

[11] Sutcliffe J.P. (1993) Concept, Class, and Category in the Traditions of Aristotle, *Categories and Concepts: Theoritical Views and Inductive Data Analysis*, Academic Press, Cognitive Science Series, pp. 35-65.

[12] Tschichold N., Ghazvini M. & Diez D. (1992), M-RCE: a self configuring ANN with rule extraction capabilities, *Proceedings of the International Conference on Artificial Neural Networks ICANN'92*, Brighton.

[13] Van de Merckt T. & Decaestecker C. (1993) Concept Learning using Hybrid Systems: The Two Functional Model. IRIDIA-Technical Report-93-19, Université Libre de Bruxelles.

[14] Van Mechelen I., Hampton J., Michalski R.S. & Theuns P. (1993) *Categories & Concepts: Theoritical Views & Inductive Data Analysis*, Academic Press, Cognitive Science Series.

# Use of a Neural Network to Diagnose Student Errors in an Intelligent Tutoring System

Uta M. Ziegler
Department of Computer Science
Western Kentucky University
Bowling Green, KY 42101
Ziegler@wkuvx1.wku.edu

## Abstract

This paper presents some ideas and preliminary results about the use of expert networks for the error diagnosis in intelligent tutoring systems (ITS).

The diagnosis of the student error is driven by two complimentary knowledge sources: 1) knowledge about potential incorrect rules which might be applied by students and 2) knowledge about which correct rules can lead to the incorrect student answer.

Both types of knowledge are incorporated in the neural network. Both types of knowledge identify nodes and connections which might help in the diagnosis of the student error. Since there might be more than one explanation of the student error, a competition among the network representation of the various explanations is necessary. The competition identifies the explanations which use the least and most likely incorrect rules.

## Introduction

This paper presents some ideas and preliminary results about the use of expert networks for the error diagnosis in intelligent tutoring systems (ITS).

ITS generally contain a module which represents the domain expertise. In many cases this expertise is captured in an expert system. Since it is quite time-consuming to develop an expert system, attempts have been made [1, 2] to replace the expert system with a neural network which can acquire the domain expertise from examples. However, an ITS must not only show a student how to solve a problem, but it must also be able to explain the solution process as well as determine/explain which underlying misconceptions lead to the student's error. Such a verbalization of knowledge is easier if a symbolic representation is used as in expert systems, rather than the sub-symbolic representation of neural networks.

Recent research has shown that the processing of expert systems and neural networks is similar [3]. From a given (and potentially imprecise) expert system, a neural network can be derived. That neural network can mimic the processing of the expert system, but it can also improve on the expert system's performance, since it can learn from examples [4].

This paper describes how such a expert network can be used to diagnose the underlying cause for a student error. It will first give a short overview of expert networks, followed by a general and then detailed discussion of the error diagnosis and its implementation. The paper concludes with the presentation of results.

## Expert Networks

Each rule of an expert system is translated into one connection from a node representing the antecedent of the rule to the consequence of the rule. The strength of the connection is given by the certainty factor of the translated rule.

Since the antecedent of a rule can contain logical operators (AND, OR, and NOT), special nodes which represent these antecedents are included in the network as well as connections to the anatecedent nodes. For example, the rule *IF A and B then C (cf)* is translated into the following three network connections: a connection from *A* to *A&B* with weight 1, a connection from *B* to *A&B* with weight 1, and a connection from *A&B* to *C* with weight cf. The input and output of these special nodes is determined in a manner which exactly matches the way these logical operators are dealt with in the underlying expert system. The expert network discussed in [3, 4] has three different type of nodes (AND-nodes, NOT-nodes and REGULAR-nodes), each with its own method of determining its combined input and output. For more information see [3] and [4].

## Student Error Diagnosis using Expert Networks

The expert system of the ITS is translated into an expert network. The information about the current situation is provided as input to the network. If the network output differs from the result determined by the student, the diagnosis process which attempts to determine the underlying cause for the student error is started.

The objective of the diagnosis is to determine an explanation of how the student generated the incorrect answer from the given input and the application of correct as well as incorrect rules. In the expert network, an explanation is represented by a set of nodes and connections, which together form paths from the given input nodes to the node representing the incorrect student answer. This explanation will pinpoint the incorrect knowledge used as well as the context in which it was applied.

The diagnosis of the student error is driven by two complimentary knowledge sources. The first is knowledge about potential incorrect rules which might be applied by students. This knowledge is applied in a data-driven, bottom-up manner. Incorrect rules are either added to the expert network, by encoding them using the same method as for encoding the correct rules or can be learned by the expert network [4].

The second source is knowledge about which correct rules can lead to the incorrect student answer. This knowledge is applied in a top-down manner. The knowledge is implicitly contained in the expert network and can be activated by propagating activation from the output layer towards the input layer.

During the error diagnosis, both knowledge sources are applied. The nodes of the expert network which are activated through both become the crystallization points for the explanation of the student error.

However, there might be several crystallization points, indicating that there might be several explanations for the error. The different explanations then must compete amongst each other to optimize some criterion which measures the quality of an explanation.

## Details about the Error Diagnosis using the Neural Network

Even though expert networks can be built for expert systems which employ non-crisp rules (certainty factors), the research presented here is - as of now - restricted to expert systems which only use crisp rules, that is, all certainty factors are 1. However, the weights for the incorrect rules can be any value between 0 and 1. Furthermore, it is assumed that each possible answer is represented by one output node.

All the nodes which were activated during the feed-forward processing of the network, remain activated throughout the error diagnosis. In the remainder of the paper, this activation is referred to as actual activation (AA). The connections which were added to represent incorrect rules are referred to as out-weights (connections for correct rules are sometimes referred to as in-weights). The value of an out-weight indicates how likely it is that students apply this incorrect rule. In terms of the neural network involved, the explanation of a student error is a subset of the augmented expert network (augmented with out-weights).

**Bottom-up activation:** All the nodes with actual activation spread activation along out-weights, thus activating nodes which might contribute to the explanation of the student error. This activation is called out-activation (OA). The OA of a node is determined in exactly the same manner as the actual activation. If the OA at a node exceeds a certain threshold, than that node itself can spread activation along out-weights.

**Top-down activation:** Activation is spread backwards through the network, from the incorrect student answer towards nodes with actual activation or out-activation. Activation thus spread to nodes is referred to as back-propagated activation (BA). The higher the level of BA at a node, the larger the chance that the node belongs to the subnet explaining the student error. A positive (or negative) BA indicates that the node must be active (or not active) in order to contribute to the explanation. The back-propagation of activation stops at nodes where the actual activation agrees with the back-propagated activation. The back-propagation of activation must differentiate between the various types of nodes in the expert network.

<u>NOT-Node</u>: If H is a node with AA(H)=x, and K is a NOT node which has H as its only predecessor and which received a BA(K)=y, then

$$BA(H) = \begin{cases} -y & \text{if } (y > 0 \wedge x = 1) \vee (y < 0 \wedge x = 0); \\ 0 & \text{otherwise.} \end{cases}$$

<u>AND-Node</u>: IF $H_1$, $H_2$, ... $H_n$ are nodes connected to the AND node K, BA(K)=y, and a is the number of active $H_i$, then

$$BA(H_j) = \begin{cases} (L*y)/(L-1+(n-a)) & \text{if } y > 0; \\ -y & \text{if } y < 0. \end{cases}$$

The above formula assigns the new BA values based on the number of elements among which the y must be distributed. It is very similar to the weight update formula used in ART1 [5].

<u>REGULAR-Node</u>: IF $H_1$, $H_2$, ... $H_n$ are nodes connected to the REGULAR node K, BA(K)=y, and a is the number of active $H_i$, then

$$BA(H_j) = \begin{cases} y \ if \ y > 0; \\ -(L*y)/(L-1+(n-a)) \ if \ y < 0. \end{cases}$$

**Crystallization Points and Competition:** Nodes which receive both, out-activation and back-propagated activation are essential to the error diagnosis. In most cases, there are several crystallization points. The crystallization points might be part of the same subnetwork connecting the given inputs with the incorrect student output, and/or the same crystallization point might be part of several subnetworks. A good subnet (and thus a good explanation) is then selected based on a competition among these subnetworks.

The competing subnets are the parts of the network which received backpropagated activation, including all the nodes at which the backpropagation of activation stopped. The weights (in-weights as well as out-weights) which were used during the backpropagation of activation are included in the subnets. Since crisp weights are used, all the predecessors of an AND-node must contribute to the same solution, but only one of the predecessors of each OR-node is needed. Therefore, competitive weights are added among the predecessors of each OR-node in the subnet.

At the start of the competition, each node is assigned a competition value. That value is based on the highest combined value of back-propagated activation and out-activation at any node in the subnets. Highly active nodes (actual activation) are assigned a competition value slightly below the highest combined value. The competition value of the other nodes of the subnets are set to 0.

The competition itself starts in an interactive-activation manner, to spread competitive activation to all the nodes involved in the competition [6]. After that, directly competing nodes select a winner. The competitive value of the OR-node is based on the competitive value of the winning node as well as the weight of the connection from the winning node to the OR-node. In this manner, a subnet which contains a lot of out-weights will produce a smaller competitive value (and loose) to a subnet which contains fewer out-weights. Thus the competition will automatically settle on a subnet which can explain the student error while attempting to minimize the number of incorrect rules as well as the number of unlikely rules (with low out-weights) involved. For a simple example network, see Figure 1.

**Results**

A very simple expert network was tested out. The expert network has 32 nodes, 13 of which are input nodes and 5 of which are output nodes. Up to 8 different out-weights were added with different strengths. In all cases did the network correctly identify the best explanation for the student mistake.

This is an encouraging beginning, but more tests using more elaborate expert systems must be performed. Also, the addition of incorrect rules as well as the judgement of whether the "best" (or one of the best) explanations has been identified should be done under the supervision of a domain expert and tutor.

## Conclusions

The method discussed here can not only be used to diagnose input/output errors which encompass the entire processing power of the expert system. The expert network and the diagnosis process can be used to help the student debug certain facts/rules by "redefining" the input and output nodes. Thus, the ITS can tutor the student on solving sub-problems, if necessary.

The diagnosis take into account individual strengths and weaknesses of the student, if the neural network stores information about his or her performance, that is, if the neural network is used as a student model. For example, if a student is likely (or unlikely) to use an incorrect rule, then the out-weight of that rule should be increased (decreased).

The discussed neural network can successfully determine good explanations for student errors in a simple domain. The current work must be extended to take advantage of the ability of many expert systems to deal with uncertainty (use certainty factors for weights rather than crisp weights).

## References

[1] S. MENGEL & W. LIVELY (1991). On the Use of Neural Networks in Intelligent Tutoring Systems, Journal of Artificial Intelligence in Education, Vol. 2, No. 2, p 43-56.

[2] S. V. SHANKAM & D. H. COOLEY (1991). A Neural Network Implementation for Expert Systems, Journal of Artificial Intelligence in Education, Vol. 2, No. 4, p 33-49.

[3] D. C. KUNCICKY, S. I. HRUSKA & R. C. LACHER (1993). Hybrid Systems: The Equivalence of Rule-Based Expert Systems and Artificial Neural Network Inference, International Journal of Expert Systems.

[4] R. C. LACHER, S. I. HRUSKA & D. C. KUNCICKY (1992). Back-Propagation Learning in Expert Networks, IEEE Transactions on Neural Networks, Vol. 3, No. 1, p 62-72.

[5] G. A. CARPENTER & S. GROSSBERG (1987). A Massively Parallel Architecture for a Self-Organizing Neural Pattern Recognition Machine, Computer Vision, Graphics, and Image Processing, 37,54-115

[6] J. L. MCCLELLAND & D. E. RUMELHART (1986). Explorations in Parallel Distributed Processing, MIT Press, Massachusetts.

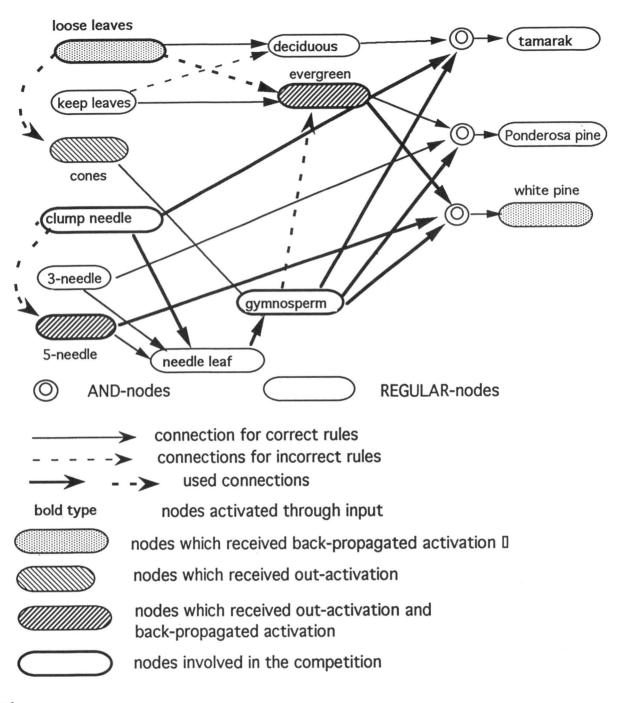

**Figure 1: An example of the error diagnosis.**
The student incorrectly answers "white pine". The example here
shows two crystallization points (evergreen and 5-needle) which
belong to the same explanation. There are two ways of activating
evergreen in the example (from gymnosperm and from loose leave).
Which of the two rules wins the competition depends on the strength
of those out-weights.

# EVOLUTIONARY STRUCTURING OF MAX-MIN PROPAGATION NETS

Pablo A. Estévez *  and Yoichi Okabe
RCAST, University of Tokyo
4-6-1 Komaba, Meguro-ku,  Tokyo 153, Japan
e-mail: pablo@okabe.rcast.u-tokyo.ac.jp

## Abstract

A genetic algorithm is used to guide the evolution of both architectures and connection weights of max-min propagation nets.  A particular node can assume one of three expressions:  linear weighted sum, weighted maximum or weighted minimum.  The prototype bit string or chromosome directly encodes the number of layers,  type and number of units, connectivity pattern and low-precision weights, using binary representations. The procedure allows to find the topology structure along with a good set of initial weights  given a set of input-output examples. Following the evolutionary global search, a fine tuning local search is performed  by a gradient descent algorithm. An application example to the modeling of the normal cardiac rhythm in electrocardiograms, which takes into account real data with 5 inputs and 16 patterns,  is provided.

## 1.  Introduction

Designing an appropriate network architecture given a particular set of examples to be learned is a major problem in neural networks. Several approaches have been taken to alleviate this problem, among them constructive [1], pruning [2] and genetic algorithms [3].  A constructive algorithm starts with a minimal network and adds new layers, nodes and connections if necessary during training. On the contrary, a pruning algorithm starts with a big net and deletes unnecessary layers, nodes and connections during training. In genetic algorithm layers, nodes and connections can be added or deleted during the evolutionary process.

In this paper we consider max-min propagation nets composed of weighted sum units and weighted switching operators such as maximum (Max) and minimum (Min). The term 'propagation' indicates that the largest (smallest) activation magnitude is passed through Max (Min) units towards the output, and not only the label as in "winner-takes all" nets. Two learning algorithms of gradient descent type have been derived elsewhere  to train these networks [4]. It has also been shown that these networks can exactly represent any mapping from a binary string to arbitrary values in the unit interval, i.e., functions of the kind $F : \{0,1\}^n \to [0,1]$, including all Boolean functions [5].

To find an appropriate architecture of a max-min propagation net for a given task, we need to select the number of layers and the  number and type of  nodes besides the pattern of connectivity. Every node can take one of three expressions: weighted Max, weighted Min or weighted sum. This makes the problem more difficult due to the combinatorial explosion of possible architectures. Held [6] has addressed this problem by a trial and error procedure, based on an exhaustive search of solutions of systems of linear equations, but the method is only suitable for very small size problems. The method was applied to synthesize a model of normal electrocardiograms for screening purposes [6,7]. We have implemented elsewhere a genetic algorithm to partially synthesize the structure of a piecewise-linear neural network [8]. This procedure allows to find the weights and location of every linear weighted sum but left unsolved the switching nodes.

In what follows a genetic search is implemented to find a complete suitable architecture to represent a given set of input-output patterns, and a good set of initial weights. After the evolutionary global search  any of the two gradient descent learning algorithms described in [4] can be applied to perform local search starting from these initial weights. The proposed method is applied to the

---

* Also with the Department of Electrical Engineering, University of Chile

modeling of the normal cardiac rhythm in electrocardiograms (EKG), which takes into account real data.

## 2. The Synthesis Problem

The goal is to find an appropriate network architecture and good initial weights given a set of input-output patterns of the form

$$(X_0, X_1, ...., X_N; Y)_p \quad , \tag{1}$$

where $X_i$, $i=1,...N$, represent inputs taking values in $[0,1]$; $Y$ is the output, also in $[0,1]$ (a single output is considered without any loss of generality), and $p=1,..,P$ is the set of examples.

By assumption every node in a max-min propagation net can take one of the following three expressions:

$$Y = \Sigma W_i X_i + \theta, \tag{2}$$

$$Y = Max(W_i X_i), \quad \text{or,} \tag{3}$$

$$Y = Min(W_i X_i), \tag{4}$$

where $Y$ is the output; $X_i$, $W_i$ and $\theta$ for $i=1,..,N$, represent inputs, weights and bias (threshold), respectively.

In practice Max and Min operators can be weightless, i.e. weights can be reduced to the weighted sum nodes only, when different types of nodes are combined. However, since we do not know beforehand the type of each node, it is convenient to assign a set of weights to every unit. This is also useful to attain precision despite using discrete weights, through multiplication of weights in different layers.

A shortcut connectivity pattern is considered, where every unit in layer i is connected with every unit in all upper layers j with j > i, thus connections between non-adjacent layers are allowed.

### 2.1 Genetic Algorithm

We implemented a simple genetic algorithm based on Goldberg's SGA [9]. A prototype solution or chromosome is represented in Fig. 1. In the first part of the chromosome the number of layers, units per layer, and type of each unit are directly encoded using binary representations. The second part of the string consists of the pattern of connectivity represented by coefficients that take the value 1 or 0 depending on whether there is a connection or not. The third and final part of the string encodes the weights using a few bits. The idea is to keep the searching space at a moderate size and at the same time being able to find a good initial set of weights.

Due to the constraint of a chromosome of fixed length, we encode a maximal network although not all individuals will read all genes. An upper bound in the number of layers, units and type of units is required to determine the chromosome's length, but a particular individual can have a smaller number of layers or units, and reads only a part of the chromosome to implement its phenotype.

| No. of Layers | No. Units per layer | Type of units | Connectivity pattern | Weights encoding |
|---|---|---|---|---|
| L bits | U bits | T bits | C bits | W bits |

Fig. 1 Prototype bit string (chromosome) representation of a max-min propagation net architecture and weights. Total length = (L+U+T+C+W) bits.

Algorithm
1. Start with a population of I randomly initialized chromosomes.
2. Evaluate fitness as the L1 norm of the error over the whole set of patterns,

$$\text{Fitness}[i] = \sum_p \left| Y_{pi} - T_p \right|, \tag{5}$$

where Y and T represent the real output and target, respectively. Index p=1,..., P represent the p-th input-output pattern, and index i=1,.., I represent i-th individual in the population. Of course other norms can be used as fitness measurements. We chose norm L1 because we are interested in problems where the errors are small.
3. Roulette wheel selection is used for mating and crossover of offspring and mutations are performed with probability pcross and pmut, respectively. The cross point is selected randomly. This procedure is repeated until generate a complete new population, except that the best two individuals are always kept within the population (elitist criteria).
In the next section a full example is given to illustrate the synthesis procedure of a max-min propagation net.

## 3. Results
A model of the normality of electrocardiograms for screening purposes has been reported [7]. Decision elements such as wave amplitude and duration were measured on 110 real EKG records. Table 1 shows a list of 16 different patterns found among the 110 patients in relation to the normality of the cardiac rhythm. The decision criteria considered are as follows:

X1 : P wave > 0 mv. in leads D1 or D2.
X2:  P duration $\leq 0.12$ sec. in D1 or D2.
X3:  Difference between successive RR < 30%
X4:  Bradycardia
X5:  Tachycardia

Inputs X1 to X3 take values in {0,1} and inputs X4 and X5 in [0,1]. A value of 1 expresses normality.

Table 1.  Degree of Normality of Cardiac Rhythm (Y). Data taken from [6].

| Pattern | X1 | X2 | X3 | X4 | X5 | Y |
|---------|----|----|----|----|----|----|
| 1 | 1 | 1 | 1 | 1 | 1 | 1.0 |
| 2 | 1 | 1 | 1 | 0.8 | 1 | 0.9 |
| 3 | 1 | 1 | 1 | 0.7 | 1 | 0.9 |
| 4 | 1 | 1 | 1 | 0.6 | 1 | 0.9 |
| 5 | 1 | 1 | 1 | 1 | 0.6 | 0.9 |
| 6 | 1 | 1 | 1 | 0.4 | 1 | 0.8 |
| 7 | 1 | 1 | 1 | 0.2 | 1 | 0.8 |
| 8 | 1 | 1 | 1 | 1 | 0.2 | 0.8 |
| 9 | 1 | 1 | 1 | 0 | 1 | 0.8 |
| 10 | 1 | 1 | 0 | 1 | 1 | 0.6 |
| 11 | 1 | 1 | 0 | 1 | 0.2 | 0.6 |
| 12 | 1 | 1 | 0 | 1 | 0 | 0.6 |
| 13 | 0 | 1 | 0 | 1 | 1 | 0.6 |
| 14 | 0 | 1 | 0 | 0.8 | 1 | 0.6 |
| 15 | 0 | 1 | 0 | 1 | 0 | 0.5 |
| 16 | 0 | 1 | 0 | 0 | 1 | 0.3 |

In order to find an appropriate architecture to represent the data shown in Table 1 we implemented the algorithm described above with the following parameters:

L = 1 (Number of layers can be 2 or 3, thus a single bit is required),

U = 6 (At most 4 units (2 bits) per layer , and 1 unit at the output layer: i.e. a 4-4-1 structure with a total of 9 units),

T = 18 (9 units x 2 bits to codify max, min and weighted sum , the latter twice),

C = 78 (1 bit per coefficient, shortcut connectivity implies 9x6 + 4x5 + 4 = 78 connections),

W = 244 (78 connections x 3 bits),

which gives a chromosome's length of (L+U+T+C+W)= 337 bits. The initial size population consisted of 50 random initialized binary strings of 337 bits each. The probability of crossover and mutation were chosen at pcross = 0.6 and pmut = 0.01, respectively.

For the weights codification we used 8 real values (encoded with 3 bits) in the range [-1, 1], mapping integers from 0 to 7 onto the set {-1.0, -0.75, -0.5, -0.25, 0.25, 0.5, 0.75, 1.0}. The value 0 is not needed because a nil weight is equivalent to non-connection, and is already coded in the connectivity coefficient.

After 500 generations a solution was found with a fitness of 0.513 as shown in table 2. The overall error was further reduced by post-evolutionary learning. The two gradient descent algorithms described in [4] were independently applied to perform a fine tuning training phase. Fig. 2 shows the topology and weights found by the genetic algorithm after cleaning up (eliminating unnecessary units or weights) and performing post-evolutionary learning. Although it is difficult to get a better matching than that shown in Table 2 for such a tight net, the approximation is good enough for practical purposes.

Table 2.  Overall error obtained by the genetic algorithm (GA), and post-evolutionary learning by gradient descent methods for the training set given by Table 1.

| Method | L1-norm of error | Square Error | Maximum Error |
|---|---|---|---|
| GA | 0.513 | 0.0225 | 0.062 |
| GA + Mean Square Gradient Descent | 0.152 | 0.0042 | 0.0368 |
| GA + Chebyshev Gradient Descent | 0.1815 | 0.0048 | 0.0312 |

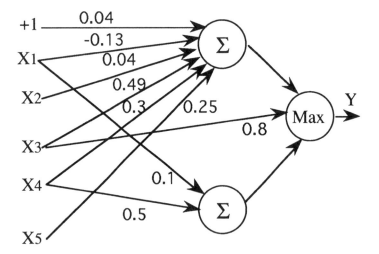

Fig. 2  Model of the Normality of the Cardiac Rhythm (Y)  Synthesized by a Genetic Algorithm from the Data of Table 1.

# 4. Discussion and Conclusions

We have implemented a genetic algorithm to find an appropriate max-min propagation net architecture given a set of input-output patterns, and a good set of initial weights. The prototype bit string or chromosome directly encodes the number of layers, type and number of units, connectivity pattern and low-precision weights. Units can assume one of three types: maximum, minimum or weighted sum.

The method has been successfully applied to solve a non-linearly separable problem of 5 inputs (although it can be reduced to 4 inputs with the current data) and 16 patterns corresponding to a model of the normal cardiac rhythm in the electrocardiogram.

Furthermore hybrid learning, i.e. the combination of global search genetic algorithms and local search gradient descent methods has proven useful in obtaining an approximate solution.

Further research is needed in order to get good scalability, perhaps using some kind of indirect encoding scheme as proposed by Kitano [10]. Other problems such as equivalent nets with permuted labels and the cleaning-up of unnecessary weights or nodes, such as a winless units within a maximum, should be addressed too.

One of the motivations to study max-min propagation nets is that allow a simple network representation that can be easily analyzed for a better understanding of the problem or for giving explanation of the internal representations. We believe that this line of research can provide further insight on problems of human reasoning where slight non-linearities are involved, such as many medical decision-making problems.

## REFERENCES

[1] Fahlman, S. E. and C. Lebiere, "The Cascade-Correlation Learning Architecture", in Advances in Neural Information Processing Systems 2, ed. D. S. Toureztky (Morgan Kauffman, San Mateo, CA, 1990), pp. 524-532.

[2] Reed, R., "Pruning Algorithms - A Survey", IEEE Trans. Neural Networks, Vol. 4, nº 5, Sept. 1993, pp. 740-747.

[3] Yao, X., "Evolutionary Artificial Neural Networks", International J. Neural Systems, Vol.4, nº 3, Sept. 1993, pp. 203-222.

[4] Estévez, P.A. and Y. Okabe, "Max-Min Propagation Nets: Learning by Delta Rule for the Chebyshev Norm", IJCNN'93, Nagoya, Japan, V. I, pp. 524-527.

[5] Estévez, P.A. and Y. Okabe, "Representation Capabilities of Piecewise-Linear Neural Networks", IJCNN'92, Beijing, China, Nov. 1992, V. III, pp. 668-673.

[6] Held, C., "Synthesis of a Medical Diagnosis Model" (in Spanish), Master Thesis, Dept. of Electrical Engineering, Univ. of Chile, 1990.

[7] Holzmann, C., U. Hasseldieck, E. Rosselot, P.Estévez, A. Andrade, and G. Acuña, "Interpretation Module for Screening Normal ECG", Medical Progress through Technology, 16, 1990, pp.163-171.

[8] Estévez, P.A. and Y. Okabe, "Genetic Synthesis of Piecewise Linear Neural Networks", (submitted)

[9] Goldberg, D.E., Genetic Algorithms in Search, Optimization & Machine Learning, Addison-Wesley, 1989.

[10] Kitano, H., "Designing neural networks using genetic algorithms with graph generation system", Complex Syst. 4, 1990, pp. 461-476.

# Neural Network Automata

**Chun-Hsien Chen and Vasant Honavar**
Computer Science Department
Iowa State University
Ames, Iowa 50011

## Abstract

Artificial neural networks (ANN), due to their inherent parallelism and potential fault tolerance offer an attractive paradigm for robust and efficient implementations of functional modules for symbol processing. This paper presents designs of such ANN modules for simulating deterministic finite automata (DFA) and deterministic pushdown automata (DDPA). The designs use an implementation of a class of partially recurrent ANN (modified Elman networks) constructed using a general-purpose binary mapping module (BMP) which in turn is synthesized from multi–layer perceptrons. The paper also discusses some relevant mathematical properties of multi-layer perceptrons that facilitate automated synthesis of BMP modules and points out several potential applications of ANN implementations of DFA and DDPA.

## 1. Introduction

Artificial neural networks (ANN), due to their inherent parallelism and fault tolerance offer an attractive paradigm for fast and robust implementations of functional modules for a variety of applications. Of particular interest are ANN modules for symbol processing [2], [12], [13] & [14]. This paper focuses on the efficient designs for neural network automata for regular and context-free language recognition. Such modules have a variety of practical applications in computer science, linguistics, systems modeling and control, artificial intelligence, and structural pattern recognition. The proposed designs are facilitated by the binary mapping properties of perceptrons. The rest of the paper is organized as follows:

- Section 2 reviews some of the key concepts and definitions that will be used in the rest of the paper.
- Section 3 presents a technique for automating the synthesis of a general–purpose *binary mapping perceptron* (BMP) module.
- Section 4 describes efficient ANN implementations of deterministic finite state automata (NNDFA) and deterministic pushdown automata (NNDDPA).
- Section 5 concludes with a summary of the key points of the paper and a brief discussion of related ongoing research.

## 2. Review

### 2.1 Perceptron

A 1-layer Perceptron has $n$ input neurons, $m$ output neurons and 1 layer of weights. The output $y_i$ of output neuron $i$ is given by $y_i = f_h(\sum_{j=1}^{n} w_{ij}x_j - \theta_i)$. $w_{ij}$ denotes the weight on the link from input neuron $j$ to output neuron $i$, $\theta_i$ is the threshold of output neuron $i$, $x_j$ is input value at input neuron $j$, and $f_h$ is hardlimiter function.

$$f_h(x) = \begin{cases} 1 & \text{if x} > 0 \\ 0 & \text{otherwise} \end{cases}$$

It is well known that such a 1-layer perceptron can implement only linearly separable functions from $\mathbf{R}^n$ to $[0,1]^m$ [Minsky & Papert, 1969]. A 2-layer Perceptron has one hidden layer of $k$ hidden neurons (and hence 2 layers of weights with each hidden neuron being connected to every input neuron as well as every output neuron). In this paper, we use 2-layer perceptrons in which each hidden neuron uses a hard-limiter function (as described above). The output of a neuron $i$ in the output layer is given by $y_i = f_o(\sum_{l=1}^{k} w_{il}z_l)$ where $z_l$ is the output of hidden neuron $l$.

### 2.2 Binary Mapping Function

Given a set $U$ of $k$ input binary vectors $u_1,...,u_k$ of dimension $m$ and a set $V$ of $k$ output binary vectors $v_1,...,v_k$ of dimension $n$, want to find a binary mapping function $g : U \rightarrow V$ such that $g(u_i) = v_i$ for $1 \leq i \leq k$. In this paper we restrict function $g$ to be a many-to-one function.

The realization of binary mapping function by neural networks has been investigated in a number of different contexts by several researchers over last few years [Baum 1988, Grossberg 1988, Hao, Tan & Vandewall 1990 & 1992, Kwon 1992, Ramacher & Wesseling 1989, and Ruján 1989].

### 2.3 Deterministic Finite Automata (DFA)

A *finite automaton* $M_{FA}$ is a 5-tuple $(Q, \Sigma, \delta, q_0, F)$ [Hopcroft & Ullman, 1979], where $Q$ is a finite set of *states*, $\Sigma$ is a finite *input alphabet*, $q_0 \in Q$ is the *initial state*, $F \subseteq Q$ is the set of *final states*, and $\delta$ is the *transition function* mapping from $Q \times \Sigma$ to $Q$. A finite automaton is deterministic if there is at most one transition that is applicable for each combination of state and input symbol. We denote a DFA by $M_{DFA}$.

### 2.4 Deterministic Pushdown Automata (DPDA)

A *pushdown automaton* $M_{PDA}$ is a 7-tuple $(Q, \Sigma, \Gamma, \delta, q_0, Z_0, F)$ [Hopcroft & Ullman, 1979], where $Q$ is a finite set of *states*, $\Sigma$ is a finite *input alphabet*, $\Gamma$ is a finite *stack alphabet*, $q_0 \in Q$ is the *initial state*, $Z_0 \in \Gamma$ is a particular stack symbol called the *stack start symbol*, $F \subseteq Q$ is the set of *final states*, and $\delta$ is the *transition function* mapping from $Q \times (\Sigma \cup \{\epsilon\}) \times \Gamma$ to finite subsets of $Q \times \Gamma^*$. A pushdown automaton is deterministic if there is at most one transition that is applicable for each combination of state, input symbol and stack top symbol. We denote a DPDA by $M_{DPDA}$.

## 3. Binary Mapping Perceptron Module (BMP)

### 3.1 Linearly Separable Binary Vectors

**Theorem 1** : Any single binary pattern is is linearly separable from the set of *all* other binary patterns of same dimension.

This theorem has been proved by Huang & Huang [1991] and Tan & Vandewalle [1992] by finding a linear hyperplane separating a binary vertex from all other vertices in a binary hypercube. Here we examine the spatial distribution and linear separability of binary vertices in a binary hypercube from geometrical perspective. We prove Theorem 1 by locating a set of linear hyperplanes which separate a binary vertex from all other vertices in a binary hypercube. This proof allows us to locate a separating hyperplane that permits an efficient hardware implementation of the corresponding 1-layer Perceptron. Such perceptrons can be used to synthesize a BMP module for any desired binary mapping.

**Proof** : Let $v$ be a binary vector of dimension $n$, i.e., $v = <v_1, ..., v_n>$ where $v_i \in \{0, 1\}$ for $1 \leq i \leq n$. Then we can view $v$ as a binary vertex of an n-dimensional hypercube. Hereafter, we will use binary vertex and binary vector interchangeably. Figure 1 shows a 3-dimensional hypercube.

Let $\overline{v} = <\overline{v}_1, ..., \overline{v}_n>$ be the complement binary vector of $v$, i.e., $v_i + \overline{v}_i = 1$ for $1 \leq i \leq n$; and $v - \overline{v} = v^{ref_v} = <v_1^{ref_v}, ..., v_n^{ref_v}>$. Note that $v_i^{ref_v} \in \{1, -1\}$ *for* $1 \leq i \leq n$. Let $S_k^v$ be the set of $n$-dimensional binary vertices which are located at a Hamming distance equal to $k$ from the vertex $v$; $0 \leq k \leq n$. Then every binary vertex $u \in S_k^v$ falls on a hyperplane $H_k^v$ which is perpendicular to the vector $v^{ref_v}$. Let $H^v = \{H_k^v; 0 \leq k \leq n\}$. Then the hyperplanes in $H^v$ are mutually parallel. Figure 2 shows this situation.

Let $u$ be a binary vertex in $S_k^v$, $u - \overline{v} = u^{ref_v} = <u_1^{ref_v}, ..., u_n^{ref_v}>$ and $l_u^v$ be the length of the projection of $u^{ref_v}$ onto the direction of $v^{ref_v}$. Note that $u_i^{ref_v} = 0$ or 1 if $v_i^{ref_v} = 1$, and $u_i^{ref_v} = 0$ or -1 if $v_i^{ref_v} = -1$ for $1 \leq i \leq n$.

Note also that there are $k$ components $u_i^{ref_v}$ of $u^{ref_v}$ such that $u_i^{ref_v} = 0$ and $(n - k)$ components of $u^{ref_v}$ such that $u_j^{ref_v} = 1$ $or -1$, where $1 \leq j \leq n$. Then

$$l_u^v = \frac{1}{|v^{ref_v}|} v^{ref_v} (u^{ref_v})^T \tag{1}$$

$$= \frac{1}{|v^{ref_v}|} \sum_{i=1}^{n} v_i^{ref_v} u_i^{ref_v} \tag{2}$$

$$= \frac{1}{|v^{ref_v}|} \left( \sum_{u_i^{ref_v}=1 or -1}^{n-k} v_i^{ref_v} u_i^{ref_v} + \sum_{u_i^{ref_v}=0}^{k} v_i^{ref_v} u_i^{ref_v} \right) \tag{3}$$

$$= \frac{1}{\sqrt{n}} (n - k) \tag{4}$$

$where (u^{ref_v})^T$ is the *transpose* of $u^{ref_v}$. Thus, $\forall u \in S_k^v$ the length of the projection of $u^{ref_v}$ in the direction of $v^{ref_v}$ is $(n - k)/\sqrt{n}$. That is, all binary vertices in $S_k^v$ lie on the same hyperplane $H_k^v$ which is perpendicular to the vector $v^{ref_v}$ and has a distance $(k - n)/\sqrt{n}$ to vertex $\overline{v}$. Note that every hyperplane in the set $H^v$ of hyperplanes $H_k^v$'s, $1 \le k \le n$, is parallel to every other hyperplane in the set. Among them, $H_1^v$ is the hyperplane which is closest to the binary vertex $v$ in the n-dimensional space. So there exists at least one separating hyperplane $H_S^v$ between $H_1^v$ and the binary vertex $v$ ($v$ is on $H_0^v$), which linearly separates the binary vertex $v$ from all other $n$-dimensional binary vertices which are all on the other $H_k^v$'s, where $1 \le k \le n$. ............ □□

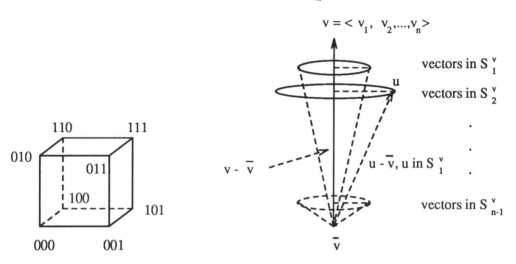

Figure 1. A 3-dimensional hypercube

Figure 2. Parallel-layered partitions of n-dimensional vertices and their reference vector v - $\overline{v}$

The ability of hyperplane $H_S^v$ separating binary vertex $v$ from all other binary vertices in a same dimensional hypercube can be implemented by an 1-layer Perceptron with 1 output neuron. Now let us find the expression defining the separating hyperplane $H_S^v$. Let x be a point on hyperplane $H_S^v$. Then

$$(n-1)/\sqrt{n} < \frac{1}{|v^{ref_v}|} v^{ref_v} (x^{ref_v})^T < (n-0)/\sqrt{n} \tag{5}$$

$$\Rightarrow \quad (n-1) < (v - \overline{v})(x - \overline{v})^T < n \tag{6}$$

Equation (5) follows from the fact that $H_S^v$ is in between $H_0^v$ and $H_1^v$. So the projection length of $x^{ref_v}$ in the direction of $v^{ref_v}$ is less than the projection length of the reference vector of any binary vertex on $H_1^v$ and is greater than that of the reference vector of any binary vertex on $H_0^v$. Equation (6) says that there are infinite number of such separating hyperplanes $H_S^v$'s that point $x$ could be on. To efficiently implement the separating hyperplane $H_S^v$ in a 1-layer Perceptron, let us choose $(v - \overline{v})(x - \overline{v})^T = n - 1$ as the expression defining the separating hyperplane $H_S^v$. Note that in this case $(v - \overline{v})(w - \overline{v})^T \le (n - 1)$ for any binary vertex $w$ of dimension n except binary vertex $v$. Then

$$H_S^v \equiv (v - \overline{v})(x - \overline{v})^T = (n - 1) \tag{7}$$

$$\equiv \quad (v - \bar{v})x^T - (v - \bar{v})\bar{v}^T - (n - 1) = 0 \tag{8}$$

$$\equiv \quad (v - \bar{v})x^T - (n - |\bar{v}|^2 - 1) = 0, \quad note \ |v|^2 + |\bar{v}|^2 = n \tag{9}$$

$$\equiv \quad (v - \bar{v})x^T - (|v|^2 - 1) = 0 \tag{10}$$

$$\equiv \quad (v_1 - \bar{v}_1)x_1 + ... + (v_n - \bar{v}_n)x_n - (|v|^2 - 1) = 0 \tag{11}$$

$$\equiv \quad (2v_1 - 1)x_1 + ... + (2v_n - 1)x_n - (|v|^2 - 1) = 0 \tag{12}$$

$$\equiv \quad (\sum_{i=1}^{n}(2v_i - 1)x_i) - (|v|^2 - 1) = 0 \tag{13}$$

So the separating hyperplane $H_S^v$ can be efficiently implemented by a 1-layer Perceptron whose output neuron has a threshold of $|v|^2 - 1$ and the connection weights on the input links are given by $2v_i - 1$ for $i \le i \le n$.

Note that the value of $2v_i - 1$ is either 1 or -1, $x_i$ is either 1 or 0, $(2v_i - 1)x_i$ is either 1, 0 or -1, and $|v|^2$ is integer. So in the hardware implementation of this Perceptron, only integer adder is needed. Note also that the maximal summation value at output neuron is 1 and minimal value is $-(n - 1)$, since the separating hyperplane $H_S^v$ is defined as $(v - \bar{v})(x - \bar{v})^T - (n - 1) = 0$, the maximal value of $(v - \bar{v})(x - \bar{v})^T$ is $n$, and the minimal value of $(v - \bar{v})(x - \bar{v})^T$ is 0. If zero is used as the initial value in the summation operation at the output neuron, $-n$ is the minimal and $n$ the maximal value appearing in the whole summation process. If $-(|v|^2 - 1)$ is used as the initial value in the summation operation at the output neuron, $-(n - 1)$ is the minimal and 1 the maximal value appearing in the whole summation process. In both cases, an m-bit integer adder is needed where $m = \lceil \log_2(2n + 1) \rceil$ for the former and $m = \lceil \log_2(n + 1) \rceil$ for the latter. Furthermore, the hardware complexity of the the latter implementation is lower since the summation operations executed at the output neuron only involve *increment* and *decrement* operations. So, in the latter case the integer adder could be replaced by a simpler module, *counter*, to execute the summation operation.

### 3.2 Synthesis of General-purpose Binary Mapping Perceptron Module

Given a set $A$ of $k$ input binary vectors $a_1,...,a_k$ of dimension $m$, where $a_h = < a_{h1}, ..., a_{hm} >$ and $a_{hi} \in \{0, 1\}$ for $1 \le h \le k$ & $1 \le i \le m$, and a set $D$ of $k$ desired output binary vectors $d_1,...,d_k$ of dimension $n$, where $d_h = < d_{h1}, ..., d_{hn} >$ and $d_{hj} \in \{0, 1\}$ for $1 \le h \le k$ & $1 \le j \le n$. No two $a_i$'s are equal. Let $\mathbf{B}^m$ denotes the universe of $m$-dimensional binary vectors and $0^n$ the $n$-dimensional binary vector of all zeros. We want to find a binary mapping function $g : \mathbf{B}^m \rightarrow (D \cup \{0^n\})$ such that $g(a_h) = d_h$ for $1 \le h \le k$ and $g(x) = 0^n$ for $x \in (\mathbf{B}^m - A)$. Note that we restrict function $g$ to be a many-to-one function.

A 2-layer BMP module for any desired binary mapping function $g$ can be synthesized using the 1-layer Perceptron (defined in section 3.1) as follows: The BMP module has $m$ input, $k$ hidden and $n$ output neurons. For each binary mapping ordered pair $(a_h, d_h)$, where $1 \le h \le k$, we create a hidden neuron $h$ with threshold $|a_h|^2 - 1$. The connection weight from input neuron $i$ to this hidden neuron is $2a_{hi} - 1$ ($= a_{hi} - \bar{a}_{hi}$) and that from this hidden neuron to output neuron $j$ is $d_{hj}$. The threshold for each of the output neurons is set to zero. Figure 3 shows the implementation. The activation function $f_o$ at output neuron is identity function, i.e., $f_o(x) = I(x) = x$ and that $f_h$ at hidden node is hardlimiter function, i.e.,

$$f_h(x) = \begin{cases} 1 & \text{if x} > 0 \\ 0 & \text{otherwise} \end{cases}$$

Note that for input binary vector $a_h$, only the hidden neuron $h$ produces an output of 1, and the output values from all other hidden neurons are 0 in our BMP module. So the value at output neuron $j$ is $d_{hj}$, and hence the output binary vector will be $< d_{h1}, ..., d_{hn} > = d_h$. Since only one of the hidden neurons has output value 1 and others have output value 0 in the computation at hidden layer, the computation at output layer can be seen as being *enabled* by one of the hidden neurons. So, in hardware implementation it is not necessary to use summation operation to compute the output value from each output neuron. (Note that in this case we have to use *preset* and *synchronization control* to handle case when $g(x) = 0^n$ for $x \in (\mathbf{B}^m - A)$.)

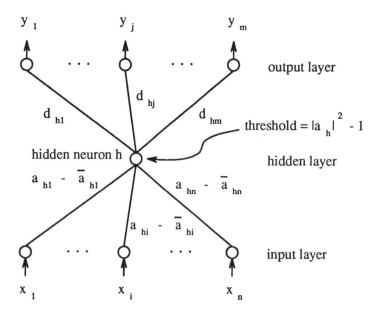

Figure 3. Perceptron implementation for binary mapping pair (a $_h$, d $_h$ )

## 4. Neural Network Automata

The prerequisites for a neural network implementation of automata are: an encoding for the set $Q$ of finite states, an encoding for alphabets including the set $\Sigma$ of input alphabet, the set $\Gamma$ of stack alphabet (only for PDA) and tape alphabet (only for Turing Machines), a representation for transition function, and a neural network architecture for continuous execution of an automaton. In this paper we restrict ourselves to neural network implementations of DFA and PDA. In this case, the first two requirements can be met by a binary coding, the third by using a binary mapping Perceptron module, and the fourth by adding a synchronization mechanism in modified Elman networks [Elman, 1988].

Let us encode the set $Q$ of finite states into a set $S$ of binary values of dimension $m$, the set $\Sigma$ of input alphabet into a set $I$ of of binary values of dimension $n$ and the set $\Gamma$ of stack alphabet into a set $K$ of binary values of dimension $k$. Let $0^m \in S$ denote the encoded binary value of *dead state* (*garbage state*), a state which is not a final state and has transitions to itself on all input symbols. To standardize the implementation we let $1^m \in S$ denote the encoded binary value of initial state. Then $m = \lceil \log_2(|Q| + 1) \rceil$, $n = \lceil \log_2 |\Sigma| \rceil$, and $k = \lceil \log_2 |\Gamma| \rceil$, where $|Z|$ denotes the cardinality of set $Z$. In the BMP module simulating the transition function, the number of needed hidden nodes equals the number of different transitions of the transition function.

### 4.1 NN Deterministic Finite Automata (NN DFA)

Figure 4 shows the neural network architecture for simulating a DFA. Let $0,1,2,...,t$ denote a succession of points along the discrete time line. $State(t)$ denotes current state and $state(t+1)$ denotes next state. $Input(t)$ denotes current input symbol. This NN DFA module consists of two BMP modules, one *accepting state trapping module* (AST module) and three buffers. One buffer stores current state $state(t)$, another stores input symbol $input(t)$ and the other stores next state $state(t+1)$. The first two buffers operate under synchronization control. The *reset* link resets the NN DFA to initial state. The synchronization control enforces discrete time $0,1,...,t$.

BMP module 1, called *transition BMP module*, simulates the transition function of a DFA. The transition BMP module represents each state transition as an ordered pair of binary vectors. Suppose $p, q \in Q, a \in \Sigma, \delta(p, a) = q$ is a valid transition, and $p$, $q$ and $a$ are encoded as binary vectors such that $p = <p_1, ..., p_m>, q = <q_1, ..., q_m>$ and $a = <a_1, ..., a_n>$ where $p_i, q_i, a_j \in \{0, 1\}$ for $1 \le i \le m$ and $1 \le j \le n$. Then the state transition $\delta(p, a) = q$ is a binary mapping ordered pair $(<p_1, ..., p_m, a_1, ..., a_n>, <q_1, ..., q_m>)$ implemented in transition BMP module using the algorithm for the synthesis of a BMP module (see section 3.2). $<p_1, ..., p_m>$ represents the encoded binary value of current state (state($t$)), $<a_1, ..., a_n>$ represents the encoded binary value of current input symbol (input($t$)), and $< q_1, ..., q_m >$ represents the encoded binary value of next state (state($t+1$)). The AST module is optional and can be implemented by AND/OR gates or a BMP module. It enables BMP module 2 to produce an output only when the NN DFA goes into an accepting state. There might need a connection from the AST module to upper-layer control to tell a rejection when the AST module traps rejecting states, i.e., when this NN DFA goes into rejecting states. If the AST module is omitted, this NN DFA simulates a *Moore machine* (Hopcroft & Ullman, 1979), a super-class automaton of finite automaton which produces output depending on current state. BMP module 2 is optional, and it allows the output of the NN DFA to be remapped from the output of BMP module 1. Note that any unspecified transition will automatically have the next state coded as $0^m$ as a consequence of our design of the transition BMP module. This simplifies the implementation of DFA, since any transition to rejecting state does not need to be implemented using a hidden neuron in the transition BMP module.

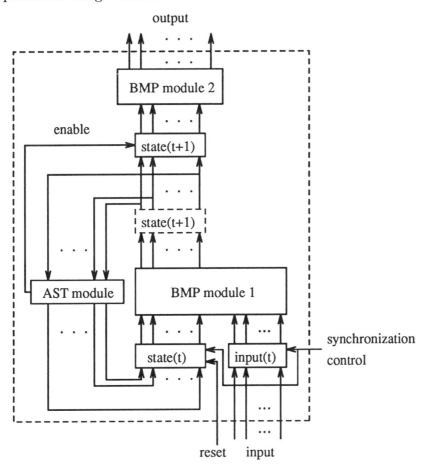

Figure 4. Neural network DFA. The dotted box labeled with state(t+1) exists only logically but not physically.

## 4.2 NN Deterministic Pushdown Automata (NN DPDA)

Figure 5 shows the neural network architecture for simulating a DPDA. *State*($t$) denotes current state and *state*($t + 1$) denotes next state. This NN DPDA module consists of three BMP modules, one AST module, one stack mechanism module and four buffers. One buffer stores current state *state*($t$), one stores input symbol *input*($t$), another stores stack top symbol $stack_{top}$ and the other stores next state *state*($t + 1$). The first three buffers operate under synchronization control. The *reset* link resets the NN DPDA to initial state. The synchronization control enforces discrete time $0,1,...,t$.

BMP module 1 (the transition BMP module) simulates the transition function of a DPDA. Each state transition is coded as an ordered pair of binary mapping vectors.

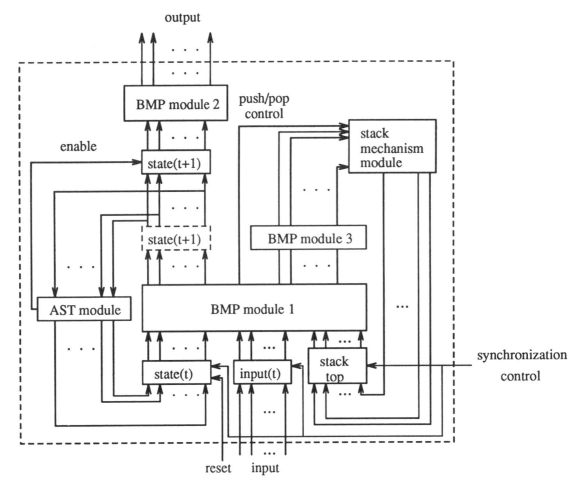

Figure 5. Neural network DPDA. The dotted box labeled with state(t+1)
exists only logically but not physically.

Suppose $p, q \in Q, a \in (\Sigma \cup \{\epsilon\}), \alpha, \beta \in \Gamma, s \in \{pop, \ push\}, \delta(p, a, \alpha) = [q, s, \beta]$ is a valid transition, and $p, q, a, \alpha, \beta$ and $s$ are encoded into binary vectors such that $p = < p_1, ..., p_m >$, $q = < q_1, ..., q_m >$, $a = < a_1, ..., a_n >$, $\alpha = < \alpha_1, ..., \alpha_k >, \beta = < \beta_1, ..., \beta_k >$ and $s = < s_1 >$ where $p_i, q_i, a_j, \alpha_l, \beta_l, s_1 \in \{0, 1\}$ for $1 \leq i \leq m$, $1 \leq j \leq n$, and $1 \leq l \leq k$. Note that our representation of a transition of a DPDA is different from the conventional representation in that we express pop/push action explicitly. Then transition $\delta(p, a, \alpha) = [q, s, \beta]$ is represented as the binary mapping ordered pair $(< p_1, ..., p_m, a_1, ..., a_n, \alpha_1, ..., \alpha_k >, < q_1, ..., q_m, s_1, \beta_1, ..., \beta_k >)$ to be implemented in the transition BMP module. $< p_1, ..., p_m >$ represents the encoded binary value of current state $state(t)$, $< a_1, ..., a_n >$ represents the encoded binary value of current input symbol $input(t)$, $< \alpha_1, ..., \alpha_k >$ represents stack top symbol $stack_{top}$, $< q_1, ..., q_m >$ represents the encoded binary value of next state $state(t + 1)$, $< s_1 >$ represents the pop/push action in the transition, and $< \beta_1, ..., \beta_k >$ represents the produced stack symbols in the transition. There is a *push/pop* connection from BMP module 1 to the stack mechanism module. This link informs the stack mechanism module whether to pop or push. Stack mechanism module can be implemented by sequence memory, memory read-write head and buffer, and a register (*counter*) for storing pointer pointing to the stack top. A push action increments the pointer (counter) and a pop action decrements the pointer (counter). The special symbol $stack_{bottom}$ is stored at the beginning of the memory. The AST module is optional and can be implemented by AND/OR gates or a BMP module. It enables BMP module 2 to produce output only when the NN DPDA goes into accepting states. There might need a connection from the AST module to upper-layer control to tell a rejection when the AST module traps rejecting states, i.e., when this NN DPDA goes into rejecting states. BMP module 2 is optional, and it allows the output from the NN DPDA to be remapped from the output of BMP module 1. BMP module 3 is optional and provides remapping of stack symbol produced from BMP module 1. Note that any unspecified transition will have the next state $0^m$ given our implementation of the transition BMP module.

## 5. Discusion

In this paper we present an algorithm for automating the synthesis of general-purpose binary mapping module in the form of a 2-layer Perceptron. We also present efficient NN architectures for simulation of finite state and pushdown automata. Such designs can be used in a variety of tasks that require the integration of symbol processing capabilities into neural networks (for examples of such applications, see Shastri [12], Smolensky [13], Sun [14].) Other applications of NN automata include efficient hardware implementations of lexical analyzers and parsers used in compilers (Chen & Honavar [2]) and natural language processing, and language recognizers used in syntactic pattern recognition.

## References

[1] E. B. Baum, On the Capabilities of Multilayer Perceptron, *Journal of Complexity*, vol. 4, pp. 193-215, 1988.

[2] C. Chen and V. Honavar, Modularized Neural Networks for Lexical Analyzer and Grammar Parser. *To appear.*

[3] J. L. Elman, Finding Structure in Time, *Technical report, Center for Research in Language (CRL) UCSD*, April 1988.

[4] S. Grossberg, Nonlinear neural networks: Principles, mechanisms, and architectures, *Neural Networks*, vol. 1, pp. 17-61, 1988.

[5] J. Hao, S. Tan and J. Vandewalle, A Geometric Approach to the Structural Synthesis of Multilayer Perceptron Neural Networks, *Proceeding of 1990 International Joint Conference on Neural Networks*, vol. 2, pp. 881-885.

[6] J. E. Hopcroft and J. D. Ullman, Introduction to Automata Theory, Languages, and Computation, Addison-Wesley, 1979.

[7] S. C. Huang and Y. F. Huang, Bounds on the Number of Hidden Neurons in Multilayer Perceptrons, *IEEE Transactions on Neural Networks*, vol. 2, no. 1, pp.47-55, January 1991.

[8] M. Minsky and S. Papert, Perceptrons: An Introduction to Computational Geometry, MIT Press, 1969.

[9] T. M. Kwon, A Guaranteed Training of Binary Pattern Mappings Using Gaussian Perceptron Networks, *IEEE International Joint Conference on Neural Networks*, vol. 3, pp. 614-619, Baltimore, 1992.

[10] U. Ramacher and M. Wesseling, A Geometrical Approach to Neural Network Design, *Proceeding of International Joint Conference on Neural Networks*, vol. 2, pp. 147-153, 1989.

[11] P. Ruján, A Geometric Approach to Learning in Neural Networks, *Proceeding of International Joint Conference on Neural Networks*, vol. 2, pp. 105-109, 1989.

[12] L. Shastri, A Connectionist Approach to Knowledge Representation and Limited Inference, *Cognitive Science*, 12, pp. 331-392, 1988.

[13] P. Smolensky, On Variable Binding and Representation of Symbolic Structure, *Tech Report*, University of Colorado, Boulder, CO, 1987.

[14] R. Sun, Logics and Variables in Connectionist Models: A Brief Overview, *Symbolic Processors and Connectionist Networks for Artificial Intelligence and Cognitive Modeling*, Academic Press, New York, 1994.

[15] S. Tan and J. Vandewalle, Efficient Algorithm for The Design of Multilayer Feedforward Neural Networks, *IEEE International Joint Conference on Neural Networks*, vol. 2, pp. 190-195, Baltimore, 1992.

# The Generation of the Logic Neural Network for Decision Making (Test Strategy Planning)

Zhengrong Yang

Shanghai Institute of Metallurgy, Academia Sinica, 865ChangNing Rd., Shanghai, P. R. CHINA, 200050

## Abstract

*The logic neural network is a new kind neural network, which is constructed by the logic deduction without large training time and results in simpler structure. This kind neural network plays an important role in the field of decision making. A method of generating logic neural network for decision making is presented in this paper. Its application to test strategy planning is presented.*

## 1. Introduction

The rapid development of the research on parallel computers and brain sciences has speeded up the research into neural networks. Neural networks may be characterised by their ability to carry out parallel computation on data and distribute the knowledge inherent in the training data across the net, this process has been termed as the parallel distributed processing [18]. Neural networks have been successful in the application of the classification [8], control [3], diagnosis [2], [12], [14], decision making [7], [8], and prediction [6], [10], [11]. A neural network may be used in decision making. This may be thought as a spreading of the expert's knowledge across the neural network. A fully trained neural network can be treated as a knowledge base. Many researchers have studied decision making methods using neural networks and have enabled them to carry out applications in AI.

For example, *Lee* [6] presented a prediction method of the composition stock price index using a recurrent neural network. *Takagi* [17] and *Yu* [7] proposed an inference structures using a multiple-network structures. *Gallant* [14], *Fu* [13] and *Murty* [15] utilised a type of sparse inferring neural networks. *Sethi* [16] developed a method to construct a neural network from a decision tree. Most of the traditional neural networks were constructed by training the fixed structures, although some sparse structures have been presented.

It is interest to ask if we need to use this kind structure into the decision making? This is the arguement we discuss in this paper. Our goal is to construct a neural network by logic deduction. This kind neural network is called the logic neural network. If the logic neural network can be realised, large training time can be avoided. To catagorise neural networks, we define trained neural networks as analogue neural networks. Our research on the logic neural network has been applied to the test strategy planning. The advantage of logic neural network is its simple structure and its ability avoiding time-consuming training phase.

## 2. The structure of the analogue neural network

An analogue neural network is constructed by training the net with a group of training patterns. These training patterns are pairs of input patterns and target output patterns. Where, training may be thought of as forcing a neural network to memorizing the training data. After training, the neural network has learned the required mapping or desired knowledge from the training data, which can be used as a knowledge base for the decision making. The advantage of this training method is that the neural network can work without any expert or with less expert assistant. There are three drawbacks of the training method. The first, training time are often very long and many researchers have reported applications which require 10000 training iterations. Secondly, it is hard to determine the number of units in the hidden layer, although *David* [4], *Richard* [5], and *Yves* [9] presented some guideline methods. The third drawback is that the structure of these nets may become too complex, which leads to serious problem. It is interesting to ask why analogue neural networks have complex structure? Firstly one should remember that the neural network are parallel distributed processing systems and the knowledge is stored in a distributed manner. In analogue network, there are many "redundent" weights, which have a complementary effects on the whole network. Our research has verified that over-simplified neural networks do not have the required generalization ability when one uses these training method. For example, if a decision tree is used to produce a neural network, its structure will be over-simplified and has no "redundent" weights to attain the required knowledge base. This results in non-optimal generalization. This is depicted in table 1, which arguments this conclusion. The percentage figures in table 1 relate the generalization values. In table 1, there are three kinds of networks, the first deduces the minimum value among three values, the second sorts three values from the largest to the smallest, the third partitions the plane points into two fields, which is an example given by *Sethi* [16]. The from the decision tree, (2) "fully" indicates training a fully-connected network, whose hidden neurals are same as the "sparse" structure, and (3) "extension" represents training a network, which has more hidden units than the "fully" structure.

Table 1

| Network | Sparse | Fully | Extension |
|---------|--------|-------|-----------|
| 1 | 90% | 95% | 100% |
| 2 | 70% | 98% | 100% |
| 3 | 80% | 90% | 98% |

## 3. The logic neural network and its generation

By contrast with the analogue neural network, the logic neural network utilised more knowledge about the process. In these networks, it is not necessary to prepare the training patterns. The complete expert's knowledge is needed and this knowledge should be compiled into a set of logic relations. One should use hard limiting activative function in logic neural network. When a neural network is used to represent expert knowledge, the logical statements may be written as:

$$IF \quad (antecedent \Leftrightarrow P) \quad THEN \quad (conclusion \Leftrightarrow A) \quad ELSE \quad (conclusion \Leftrightarrow B)$$

where, the conclusion $A$ can be represented by $T$ and the conclusion $B$ can be represented by $F$. The antecedent $P$ is an operation on antecedent set $\{p_i\}$:

$$P = \Theta(p_1, p_2, ..., p_n)$$

where, $\Theta = \{\&, \#, \bar{\ }\}$ and "&", "#", and "$\bar{\ }$" represent AND, OR, and NOT operations. So, the expert knowledge can be represented as:

$$T = \Theta \quad (\quad p_1, \quad p_2, \quad ..., \quad p_n \quad)$$
$$F = \bar{\Theta} \quad (\quad p_1, \quad p_2, \quad ..., \quad p_n \quad)$$

The expert knowledge can be generalized in this manner. Figure 1 gives the basic logic operators for logic neural network.

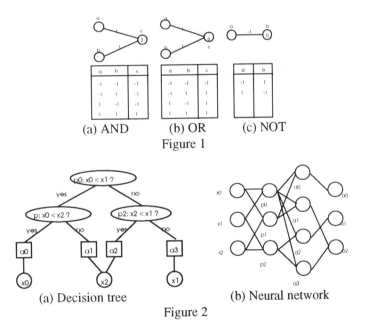

(a) AND          (b) OR          (c) NOT

Figure 1

(a) Decision tree                    (b) Neural network

Figure 2

Previous research by *Sethi* [16] proposed a method of constructing a sparse neural network from a decision tree. Unfortunately, he still trained this sparse netwotk with a group of training patterns. The illustration in figure 2 (a) depicts a decision tree, whose task is to find one minimum value among three values. The sparse neural network developed by this decision tree is shown in figure 2 (b). If the training method is used on this sparse structure, the generalization value is 90%, which means there are 10% decisoin makings in fail, see table 1. If we add more weights on this skeletonized net, the structure will obtain better generalization, 95% or 100%, see table 1.

Inorder to construct a logic neural network one should have a detailed logic analysis of the system.

The first step is to produce a partition set $\Phi_{Partition} = \{p_0, p_1, ..., p_n\}$ which should be generated on the partition space. The second step is to compile a mapping set, which maps the partitioned results into the outputs:

$$\Phi_{Map} = \{o_0, o_1, ..., o_k\} = \{\Theta p_{s_0}, \Theta p_{s_1}, ..., \Theta p_{s_k}\}$$

For example, there is a partition:

$$\Phi_{Partition} = \{p_0, p_1, p_2\} = \{x_0 < x_1, x_0 < x_2, x_1 < x_2\}$$

If we hope that $x_0$ is a minimum value and mark this output with $o_0$, the mapping from partition to output $o_0$ is:

$$\Phi_{Partition} \rightarrow o_0 \Rightarrow o_0 = p_0 \& p_1 = x_0 < x_1 \& x_0 < x_2$$

Here, it should be noted that $p_0 \& p_2 \subset p_0 \& p_1$. So, $p_0 \& p_2$ can not be selected. If we hope that $x_1$ is a minimum value and mark this output with $o_1$, the mapping from partition to output $o_1$ is:

$$\Phi_{Partition} \rightarrow o_1 \Rightarrow o_1 = \overline{p_0} \& p_2 = x_1 \leq x_0 \& x_1 < x_2$$

If we hope that $x_2$ is a minimum value and mark this output with $o_2$, the mapping from partition to output $o_2$ is:

$$\Phi_{Partition} \rightarrow o_2 \Rightarrow o_2 \overline{p_1} \& \overline{p_2} = x_2 \leq x_0 \& x_2 \leq x_1$$

So, the mapping set is

$$\Phi_{Map} = \{o_0, o_1, o_2\} = \{p_0 \& p_1, \overline{p_0} \& p_2, \overline{p_1} \& \overline{p_2}\}$$

The logic neural network developed is shown in figure 3. The structure in figure 3 is simpler than figure 2 (b).

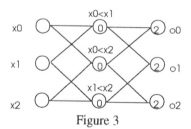

Figure 3

### 4  The application

We have applied the logic neural network to test strategy planning problem. The test strategy planning is a kind of decisoin making problem. There are two kinds of enhancing methods. One is defined as 'testability' enhancing. This method will improve the "testability" and improve the 'accessibility' to a certain degree. The other is defined as 'accessibility' enhancing method. This method only enhances the 'accessibility'. Each enhancement method has its a particular cost when related to a special application. In the test strategy planning, one object is to both enhance the 'testability' and 'accessibility' of a VISL chip. The other object of the test strategy planning is to minimise the testability design cost appended to a VLSI chip. The final goal of the test strategy planning is to select some suitable enhancement methods to a VLSI chip with minimum cost. There are two kinds of problem. One is the 0/1 'accessibility' problem. The other is the leveled 'accessibility' problem.

## 4.1 The test strategy planning with 0/1 'accessibility' enhancing

The 0/1 'accessibility' enhancing is a simplified model of the realistic problem. This model was used by *Dislis* [1]. Here, '0' means a 'testability' enhancing can not improve 'accessibility', '1' means a 'testability' enhancing can improve 'accessibility' to 100%. Given there are three 'testability' enhancing methods and one 'accessibility' enhancing method for a block under the test planning. Each 'testability' enhancing method has the possibility of enhancing the 'accessibility' to this block or not. The problem is how to choose the minimum cost and enhance both the 'testability' and 'accessibility'. These three 'testability' enhancing methods and their costs are marked with $T_1$, $T_2$, $T_3$ and $TC_1$, $TC_2$, $TC_3$. The 'accessibility' enhancing method and its cost are marked with $A$ and $AC$. Given: $TC_1 > TC_2 > TC_3$. then the expert's knowledge can be represented as follows:

if "$T_3$ enhances the accessibility" then "use $T_3$ "

else if "$T_2$ enhances the accessibility" and "$TC_2$ is less than $TC_3$ plus $AC$ " then "use $T_2$ "

else if "$T_1$ enhances the accessibility" and "$TC_1$ is less than $TC_3$ plus $AC$ " then "use $T_1$ "

else "use both $T_3$ and $A$ "

The generalization is important to any system. It is helpful for setting up the knowledge base. Now, some generalizations are made:

**Antecendents**:

$T_3$ enhances the accessibility $\Leftrightarrow A$ ;

$T_2$ enhances the accessibility $\Leftrightarrow B_1$ ;

$T_1$ enhances the accessibility $\Leftrightarrow C_1$ ;

$TC_2$ less than $TC_3$ plus $AC \Leftrightarrow B_2$ ;

$TC_1$ less than $TC_3$ plus $AC \Leftrightarrow C_2$ .

**Conclusions:**

use $T_3 \Leftrightarrow o_0$ ;

use $T_2 \Leftrightarrow o_1$ ;

use $T_1 \Leftrightarrow o_2$ ;

use $T_3$ and $A \Leftrightarrow o_3$ .

Then, three sets can be obtained:

$$\Phi_{Partition1} = \{B_2, C_2\} = \{TC_3 + AC > TC_2, TC_3 + AC > TC_1\}$$

$$\Phi_{Partition2} = \{p_0, p_1, p_2\} = \{A, B_1 \& B_2, C_1 \& C_2\}$$

$$\Phi_{Map} = \{o_0, o_1, o_2, o_3\} = \{\overline{p_0}, \overline{p_0} \& p_1, \overline{p_0} \& \overline{p_1} \& p_2, \overline{p_0} \& \overline{p_1} \& \overline{p_2}\}$$

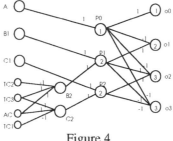

Figure 4

Figure 4 shows the logic neural network developed. Table 2 shows some decision results using this logic neural network.

Table 2

| No | $TC_1$ | $TC_2$ | $TC_3$ | AC | $TA_1$ | $TA_2$ | $TA_3$ | Decision |
|----|--------|--------|--------|------|--------|--------|--------|----------|
| 1 | 0.95 | 0.53 | 0.17 | 0.7 | 0 | 0 | 1 | $T_3$ |
| 2 | 0.39 | 0.28 | 0.08 | 0.37 | 0 | 0 | 0 | $T_3$ & A |
| 3 | 0.78 | 0.77 | 0.65 | 0.82 | 1 | 1 | 1 | $T_3$ |
| 4 | 0.91 | 0.52 | 0.35 | 0.40 | 0 | 1 | 0 | $T_2$ |
| 5 | 0.97 | 0.86 | 0.67 | 0.12 | 1 | 0 | 0 | $T_3$ & A |
| 6 | 0.65 | 0.40 | 0.04 | 0.68 | 1 | 0 | 0 | $T_1$ |

### 4.2 The test strategy planning with leveled 'accessibility' enhancing

The last section described 0/1 'accessibility' enhancing. In a realistic problem, no 'testability' enhancing method can enable itself to enhance the 'accessibility' to 100%. The enhancing values are continuous values. Now, if a block under the test planning has two 'testability' enhancing methods, $T_1$ and $T_2$, with their costs $TC_1$ and $TC_2$. Their 'accessibility' enhancing capabilties are $TAP_1$ and $TAP_2$. This block has two 'accessibility' enhancing methods, $A_1$ and $A_2$, with their costs $AC_1$ and $AC_2$. Their 'accessibility' enhancing capabilties are $AP_1$ and $AP_2$. If the 100% 'accessibility' enhancing is wanted, then the problem is described as follows:

$$\min\{c_1, c_2, c_3, c_4, c_5, c_6\}$$

$$c_1 = TC_2 \quad if(TAP_2 = 1)$$

$$c_2 = TC_2 + AC_2 \quad if(TAP_2 + AP_2 \geq 1)$$

$$c_3 = TC_2 + AC_1 \quad if(TAP_2 + AP_1 \geq 1)$$

$$c_4 = TC_1 + AC_1 \quad if(TAP_1 + AP_1 \geq 1)$$

$$c_5 = TC_1 + AC_2 \quad if(TAP_1 + AP_2 \geq 1)$$

$$c_6 = TC_1 \quad if(TAP_1 = 1)$$

The logic neural network can be constructed as figure 5.

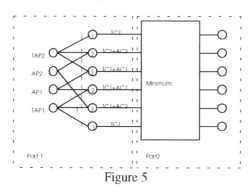

Figure 5

Here, all the system is divided into two parts. In the first parts, two sets are shown as follows:

$$\Phi_{Partition} = \{p_0, p_1, p_2, p_3, p_4, p_5\} = \{TAP_2, TAP_2 \& AP_2, TAP_2 \& AP_1, TAP_1 \& AP_1, TAP_1 \& AP_2, TAP_1\}$$

$$\Phi_{Map} = \{x_0, x_1, x_2, x_3, x_4, x_5\}$$

$$= \{TC_2 * p_0, (TC_2 + AC_2) * p_1, (TC_2 + AC_1) * p_2, (TC_1 + AC_1) * p_3, (TC_1 + AC_2) * p_4, TC_1 * p_5\}$$

In the second part, two sets are shown as follows:

$$\Phi_{Partitoin} = \{p_0, p_1, ...., p_{14}\} = \{x_0 < x_1, x_0 < x_2, x_0 < x_3, x_0 < x_4, x_0 < x_5, x_1 < x_2, x_1 < x_3,$$

$$x_1 < x_4, x_1 < x_5, x_2 < x_3, x_2 < x_4, x_2 < x_5, x_3 < x_4, x_3 < x_5, x_4 < x_5\}$$

$$\Phi_{Map} = \{o_0, o_1, o_2, o_3, o_4, o_5\} = \{p_0 \& p_1 \& p_2 \& p_3 \& p_4, \overline{p_0} \& p_5 \& p_6 \& p_7 \& p_8, \overline{p_1} \& \overline{p_5} \& p_9 \& p_{10} \& p_{11},$$

$$\overline{p_2} \& \overline{p_6} \& \overline{p_9} \& p_{12} \& p_{13}, \overline{p_3} \& \overline{p_7} \& \overline{p_{10}} \& \overline{p_{12}} \& p_{14}, \overline{p_4} \& \overline{p_8} \& \overline{p_{11}} \& \overline{p_{13}} \& \overline{p_{14}}\}$$

## 5. Summary

The logic neural network and its generation have been developed for decision making in this paper. Some simulations have shown the potential of using logic neural network for test strategy planning. It is belived that the logic neural network presents a promising approach to the decision-making problem.

## Acknowledgement

*The author would like to thank **Professor G. Musgrave** (head of dept. of EE & E, brunel university) for his guidance, thank **Dr. Richard Neville** (Dept. of EE & E, Brunel university) for his helpful discussion and support during the wrtting of this paper and thank **Dr. C. Dislis, Dr. I. Dear, and Prof. A. Ambler** (Dept. of EE & E, Brunel university) for their kindly suggestion.*

## Reference

1. C. dislis, "A financially based automated advisor for design for test strategy generation", Phd thesis, brunel university, 1992

2. C. Rodriguez, et al, "A modular approach to the design of neural networks for fault diagnosis in power systems", 1992 International joint conference on neural networks, ppIII-16-23

3. Paul J. Werbos, "Backpropagation through time: what it does and how to do it", Proceedings of the IEEE, vol 78, no. 10, october, 1990, pp1550-1560

4. David S. Touretzky, et al, "What's hidden in the hidden layers?", Byte, august 1989, pp227-233

5. Richard P. Lipmann, "An introduction to computing with neural nets", IEEE ASSP magzine, april 1987, pp4-22

6. Chong Ho Lee, et al, "Prediction of monthly transition of the composition    stock price index using recurrent back-propagation", Artificial neural networks, Vol. 2, 1992, pp1629-1632

7. He Yu, et al, "Knowledge acquisition and resoningbased on neural network - the research of a bridge bidding system",1990 International neural network conference, pp416-423

8. Scott E. Fahiman, et al, "Connectionist architectures for artificial intelligence", Computer, January 1987, pp100-109

9. Yves Chauvin, et al, "A back-propagation algorithm with optimal use of hidden units", Advances in neural informationa processing systems  Vol. 1, 1989, pp519-526

10. Ah Chung Tsoi, "Application of neural network methodology to the modelling of the yield strength in a steel rolling plate mill", Advances in neural informationa processing systems  Vol. 4, 1992, pp698-705

11. Richard Fozzard, et al, "A connectionist expert system that actually works", Advances in neural informationa processing systems  Vol. 1, 1989, pp248-255

12. Yoichi Hayashi, "A neural expert system with automated extraction of fuzzy if-then rules and its application to medical diagnosis", Advances in neural informationa processing systems  Vol. 1, 1991, pp578-584

13. Li Min Fu, "Knowledge-based conectionism for revising domain theories", IEEE trans. on sytems, man, and cybernetics, Vol 23, No. 1, January 1993, pp173-182

14. Stephen I. Gallent, "Perceptron-based learning algorithms", IEEE trans. on neural networks, Vol 1, No. 2, June 1990, pp179-191

15. Venkataesh V. Murty, "Sparse neural networks for system identification", 1993 International neural network conference, ppIII-305-309

16. Ishwar K. Sethi, "Entropy Nets: From decision tree to neural networks", Proc. IEEE 1990, pp1605-1613

17. Hideyuki Takagi, et al, "Neural networks designed on approximate reasoning architechture and their applications", IEEE trans. on neural networks, Vol. 3, No. 5, September 1992, pp752-760

18. D. E. Rumelhart, "Parallel distributed processing, vol. 1, foundations", Cambridge, MA:MIT press, 1986

# Adaptive Fuzzy Cognitive Maps in Virtual Worlds

Julie A. Dickerson and Bart Kosko
Department of Electrical Engineering—Systems
Signal and Image Processing Institute
University of Southern California
Los Angeles, CA, 90089-2564

**Abstract**

*Fuzzy cognitive maps can structure virtual worlds that change with time. A FCM links causal events, actors, values, goals, and trends in a fuzzy feedback dynamical system. A FCM lists the fuzzy rules or causal flow paths that relate events. It can guide actors in a virtual world as the actors move through a web of cause and effect and react to events and to other actors. Experts draw FCM causal pictures of the virtual world. Complex FCMs can give virtual worlds with "new" or chaotic equilibrium behavior. Simple FCMs give virtual worlds with periodic behavior. A FCM limit cycle repeats a sequence of events or a chain of actions and responses. In nested FCMs each causal concept can control its own FCM or fuzzy function approximator. FCM matrices sum to give a combined FCM virtual world for any number of knowledge sources. Adaptive FCMs change their fuzzy causal web as causal patterns change and as actors act and experts state their causal knowledge. Neural learning laws change the causal rules and the limit cycles. Actors learn new patterns and reinforce old ones.*

## 1    Fuzzy Virtual Worlds

What is a virtual world? It is what changes in a "virtual reality" [12] or "cyberspace" [6]. A virtual world links humans and computers in a causal medium that can trick the mind or senses. At the broadest level a virtual world is a dynamical system. In the simplest case only the user moves in the virtual world. In general both the user and the virtual world change and they change each other.

Change in a virtual world is causal. Actors cause events to happen as they move in a virtual world. They add new patterns of cause and effect and respond to old ones. In turn the virtual world acts on the actors or on their physical or social environments. The virtual world changes their behavior and can change its own web of cause of effect. This feedback causality between actors and their virtual world makes up a complex dynamical system that can model events, actors, actions, and data as they unfold in time.

Virtual worlds are fuzzy as well as fedback. Events occur and concepts hold only to some degree. Events cause one another to some degree. In this sense virtual worlds are fuzzy causal worlds. They are fuzzy dynamical systems.

How do we model the fuzzy feedback causality? One way is to write down the differential equations that show how the virtual "flux" or "fluid" changes in time. This gives an exact model. The Navier-Stokes equations [2] used in weather models show how clouds or tornadoes form and dissolve in a changing atmosphere or how an airplane flies through pockets of turbulence. The inverse kinematic equations of robotics [4] show how an actor moves through or grasps in a virtual joint space. Such math models are hard to find, hard to solve, and hard to run in realtime. They paint too fine a picture of the virtual world.

Fuzzy cognitive maps (FCMs) form causal pictures. They do not state equations. They state concept nodes and link them to other nodes. The FCM system turns each picture into a matrix of fuzzy rule weights. The system weights and adds the FCM matrices to combine any number of causal pictures. More FCMs tend to sum to a better picture of the causal web with rich tangles of feedback and fuzzy edges even if each expert gives binary (present or absent) edges. This makes it easy to add or delete actors or to change the background of a virtual world or to combine virtual worlds that are disjoint or overlap. We can also let a FCM node control its own FCM to give a nested FCM in a hierarchy of virtual worlds. The node FCM can model the complex nonlinearities between the node's input and output. It can drive the motions, sounds, actions, or goals of a virtual actor as in Figure 1.

The FCM itself acts as a nonlinear dynamical system. Like a neural net it maps inputs to output equilibrium states. Each input digs a path through the virtual state space. In simple FCMs the path ends in a fixed point or limit cycle. In more complex FCMs the path may end in an aperiodic or "chaotic" attractor.

In contrast an AI expert system [18] models a system as a binary rule tree with graph search. Each input fires one rule or a few rules and the search spreads down the tree branch to a leaf or leaves  The lack of feedback loops allows the tree search. But each serial inference uses only a small part of the stored knowledge. Each FCM input fires all the rules to some degree. In this way FCMs model the "circular causality" [13] of real and virtual worlds.

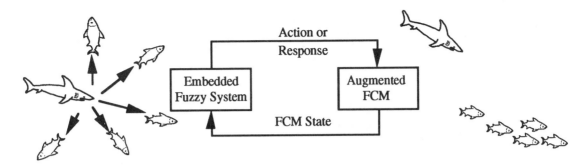

Figure 1. Fuzzy cognitive maps can structure virtual worlds. Embedded fuzzy systems drive lower level fuzzy systems for animation, sounds, and other virtual world outputs. Here a shark finds a school of fish. The shark attacks and the fish flee.

## 2    Fuzzy Cognitive Maps

Fuzzy cognitive maps (FCMs) are fuzzy signed digraphs with feedback [9,10]. Nodes stand for fuzzy sets or events that occur to some degree. The nodes are causal concepts. They can model events, actions, values, goals, or lumped-parameter processes.

Directed edges stand for fuzzy rules or the partial causal flow between the concepts. The sign (+ or –) of an edge stands for causal increase or decrease. The positive edge rule

states that a survival threat increases runway. It is a positive causal connection. The runaway response grows or falls as the threat grows or falls. The negative edge rule

states that running away from a predator decreases the survival threat. It is a negative causal connection. The survival threat grows the less the prey runs away and falls the more the prey runs away. The two rules define a minimal feedback loop in the FCM causal web:

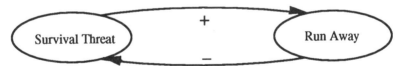

A FCM with $n$ nodes has $n^2$ edges. The nodes $C_i$(t) are fuzzy sets and so take values in [0, 1]. So a FCM state is the *fit* (fuzzy unit) vector $C(t) = (C_1(t), \dots , C_n(t))$ and thus a point in the fuzzy hypercube $I^n = [0, 1]^n$. A FCM inference is a path or point sequence in $I^n$. The FCM can only "forward chain" [18] to answer what-if questions. Nonlinearities do not permit reverse causality. FCMs cannot "backward chain" to answer why questions.

The FCM nonlinear dynamical system acts as a neural network. For each input state $C(0)$ it digs a trajectory in $I^n$ that ends in an equilibrium attractor $A$. The FCM quickly converges or "settles down" to a fixed point, limit cycle, limit torus, or chaotic attractor in the fuzzy cube. The output equilibrium is the answer to a causal what-if question: What if $C(0)$ happens? In this sense each FCM stores a set of global rules of the form "If $C(0)$, then equilibrium attractor $A$." Figure 2 shows three attractors or global rules for a 2-D dynamical FCM.

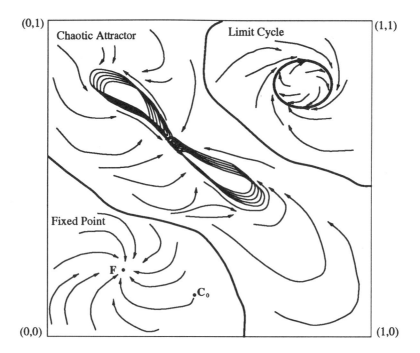

Figure 2. The unit square is the state space for a FCM with two nodes. The system has at most four fuzzy edge rules. In this case it has three fuzzy meta-rules of the form "If input state vector **C** then attractor **A**." The state $\mathbf{C_0}$ converges to a fixed point **F**. Other inputs may converge to a limit cycle or chaotic attractor.

## A.    Simple FCMs

Simple FCMs have bivalent nodes and trivalent edges. Concept values $C_i$ take values in $\{0,1\}$. Causal edges take values in $\{-1,0,1\}$. So for a concept each simple FCM state vector is one of the $2^n$ vertices of the fuzzy cube $I^n$. The FCM trajectory hops from vertex to vertex. $I^n$ ends in a fixed point or limit cycle at the first repeated vector.

We can draw simple FCMs from articles, editorials, or surveys. Most persons can state the sign of causal flow between nodes. The hard part is to state its degree or magnitude. We can average expert responses [10,16] as in equation 3 below or use neural systems to learn fuzzy edge weights from data. The expert responses can initialize the causal learning or modify it as a type of forcing function.

Figure 3 shows a simple FCM for a virtual dolphin. It lists a causal web of goals and actions in the life of a dolphin [15]. The connection matrix $\mathbf{E_D}$ states these causal relations in numbers:

$$\mathbf{E_D} =$$

|        | $D_1$ | $D_2$ | $D_3$ | $D_4$ | $D_5$ | $D_6$ | $D_7$ | $D_8$ | $D_9$ | $D_{10}$ |
|--------|-------|-------|-------|-------|-------|-------|-------|-------|-------|----------|
| $D_1$    | 0     | -1    | -1    | 0     | 0     | 1     | 0     | 0     | 0     | 0        |
| $D_2$    | 0     | 0     | 0     | 0     | 1     | 0     | 0     | 0     | 0     | 0        |
| $D_3$    | 0     | 0     | 0     | 1     | 1     | -1    | -1    | 0     | 0     | -1       |
| $D_4$    | 1     | 0     | -1    | 0     | 0     | -1    | -1    | 0     | 0     | -1       |
| $D_5$    | 0     | 0     | 1     | 0     | 0     | 0     | 0     | 0     | -1    | 0        |
| $D_6$    | 0     | 0     | 0     | 0     | -1    | 0     | 1     | 0     | 0     | 0        |
| $D_7$    | 0     | 0     | 0     | 0     | 0     | 0     | 0     | 1     | 0     | 0        |
| $D_8$    | -1    | 1     | -1    | 0     | 1     | 0     | 0     | 0     | 0     | 0        |
| $D_9$    | 0     | 0     | 0     | -1    | 1     | -1    | -1    | -1    | 0     | 1        |
| $D_{10}$ | -1    | -1    | 1     | 0     | -1    | -1    | -1    | -1    | -1    | 0        |

The $i$th row lists the connection strength of the edges $e_{ik}$ directed out from causal concept $D_i$ and the $i$th column lists the edges $e_{ki}$ directed into $D_i$. Row 1 shows how the concept HUNGER changes the other concepts. Column 1 shows the concepts that change HUNGER.

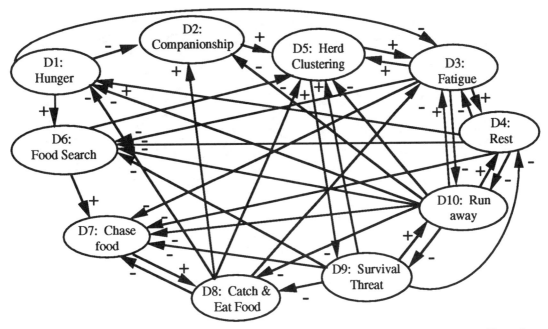

Figure 3. Trivalent fuzzy cognitive map for the control of a dolphin actor in a fuzzy virtual world. The rules or edges connect causal concepts in a signed connection matrix.

*B. FCM Recall*

FCMs recall as the FCM dynamical system equilibrates. Simple FCM inference thresholds a matrix-vector multiplication [9,11]. State vectors $C_n$ cycle through the FCM adjacency matrix $E$: $C_1 \rightarrow E \rightarrow C_2 \rightarrow E \rightarrow C_3 \rightarrow \ldots$ . The system nonlinearly transforms the weighted input to each node $C_i$ [11]:

$$C_i(t_{n+1}) = S\left[\sum_{k=1}^{N} e_{ki}(t_n) C_k(t_n)\right] \tag{1}$$

Here $S(x)$ is a bounded signal function. For simple FCMs $S(x)$ is a threshold function:

$$S(y) = \begin{cases} 1 & \text{for } y \geq a \\ 0 & \text{for } y < a \end{cases} \tag{2}$$

Simple threshold FCMs quickly converge to stable limit cycles or fixed points [13,14]. These limit cycles show "hidden patterns" in the causal web of the FCM. Each node in a simple FCM turns actions or goals on and off. Each node can control its own FCM, fuzzy control system, goal-directed animation system, force feedback, or other input-output map. The FCM can control the temporal associations or timing cycles that structure virtual worlds. These patterns establish the rhythm of the world. "Grandmother" nodes can control the time spent on each step in a FCM "avalanche" [7]. This can change the update rate and thus the timing for the network [7].

We can model a feeding cycle with the dolphin FCM as an input to $D_1$. $C_0$ is the initial input state of the dolphin FCM:

$C_0 = [\,1\ 0\ 0\ 0\ 0\ 0\ 0\ 0\ 0\ 0\,]$.

Then

$C_0\,E_D = [\,0\ \text{-}1\ \text{-}1\ 0\ 0\ 1\ 0\ 0\ \ 0\ 0\,] \rightarrow C_1 = [\,0\ 0\ 0\ 0\ 0\ 1\ 0\ 0\ 0\ 0\,]$,

The arrow stands for a threshold operation with 1/2 as the threshold value. Then they begin to search for food $(C_1, C_2)$. They eat $(C_3)$ and then they socialize and rest $(C_4, C_5, C_6)$. This makes them hungry and the feeding cycle repeats. The FCM converges to the limit cycle $C_0 \rightarrow C_1 \rightarrow C_2 \rightarrow C_3 \rightarrow C_4 \rightarrow C_5 \rightarrow C_6 \rightarrow C_7 \rightarrow C_0 \ldots$ :

$C_1\,E_D = [\,0\ 0\ 0\ \ 0\ \text{-}1\ 0\ 1\ 0\ 0\ 0\,] \rightarrow C_2 = [\,0\ 0\ 0\ 0\ 0\ 0\ 1\ 0\ 0\ 0\,]$,
$C_2\,E_D = [\,0\ 0\ 0\ \ 0\ 0\ 0\ 0\ 1\ 0\ 0\,] \rightarrow C_3 = [\,0\ 0\ 0\ 0\ 0\ 0\ 0\ 1\ 0\ 0\,]$,
$C_3\,E_D = [\text{-}1\ \ 1\ \text{-}1\ \ 0\ 1\ 0\ 0\ 0\ 0\ 0\,] \rightarrow C_4 = [\,0\ 1\ 0\ 0\ 1\ 0\ 0\ 0\ 0\ 0\,]$,
$C_4\,E_D = [\,0\ 0\ \ 1\ \ 0\ 1\ 0\ 0\ 0\ \text{-}1\ 0\,] \rightarrow C_5 = [\,0\ 0\ 1\ 0\ 1\ 0\ 0\ 0\ 0\ 0\,]$,
$C_5\,E_D = [\,0\ 0\ \ 1\ \ 1\ 1\ \text{-}1\ \text{-}1\ 0\ \text{-}1\ \text{-}1\,] \rightarrow C_6 = [\,0\ 0\ 1\ 1\ 1\ 0\ 0\ 0\ 0\ 0\,]$,

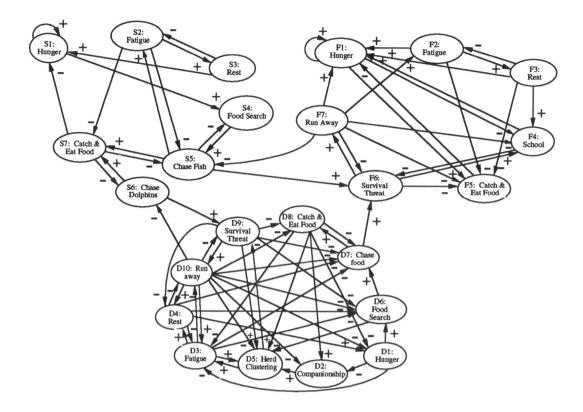

Figure 4. Augmented FCM for different actors in a virtual world. The actors interact through linked common causal concepts such as chasing food and avoiding a threat.

$$\mathbf{C}_6\,\mathbf{E}_D \;=\; [\,1\ 0\ 0\ \ 1\ 1\ \text{-2}\ \text{-2}\ 0\ \text{-1}\ \text{-2}\,] \;\rightarrow\; \mathbf{C}_7 \;=\; [\,1\ 0\ 0\ 1\ 1\ 0\ 0\ 0\ 0\ 0\,],$$
$$\mathbf{C}_7\,\mathbf{E}_D \;=\; [\,1\ \text{-1}\ \text{-1}\ 0\ 0\ \ 0\ \text{-1}\ 0\ \text{-1}\ \text{-1}\,] \;\rightarrow\; \mathbf{C}_0 \;=\; [\,1\ 0\ 0\ 0\ 0\ 0\ 0\ 0\ 0\ 0\,],$$

### C. Augmented FCMs

FCM matrices additively combine to form new FCMs [10]. This allows combination of FCMs for different actors or environments in the virtual world. The new (augmented) FCM includes the union of the causal concepts for all the actors and the environment in the virtual world. If a FCM does not include a concept, then those rows and columns are all zero. The sum of the augmented (zero-padded) FCM matrices for each actor forms the virtual world:

$$\mathbf{F} \;=\; \sum_{i=1}^{n} w_i\,\mathbf{F}_i \qquad\qquad (3)$$

The $w_i$ are positive weights for the $i$th FCM $\mathbf{F}_i$. The weights state the relative value of each FCM in the virtual world and can weight any subgraph of the FCM.

The FCM sum (3) helps knowledge acquisition. Any number of experts can describe their FCM virtual world views and (3) will weight and combine them. In contrast an AI expert system [18] is a binary tree with graph search. Two or more trees need not combine to a tree. Combined FCMs tend to have feedback or closed loops and that precludes graph search with forward or backward "chaining."

Figure 4 shows an augmented FCM for an undersea virtual world. It combines fish school, shark, and dolphin herd FCMs with (3): $\mathbf{F} = \mathbf{F}_{\text{fish}} + \mathbf{F}_{\text{shark}} + \mathbf{F}_{\text{dolphin}}$. The new links among these FCMs are those of predator and prey where the larger eats the smaller. The actors chase, flee, and eat one another. A hungry shark chases the dolphins and that leads to a limit cycle. Augmenting the FCM matrices gives a large but sparse FCM since the actors respond to each other in few ways.

The output of a simple FCM is a binary limit cycle that describes actions or goals. This holds even if the binary concept nodes change state asynchronously. Each output turns a function on or off as in a robotic neural net

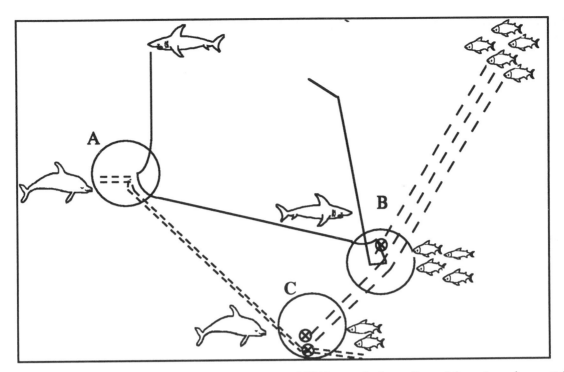

Figure 5. FCMs control the virtual world. The augmented FCM controls the actions of the actors. In event A the hungry shark forces the dolphin herd to run away. Each dashed line stands for a dolphin swim path. In event B the shark finds the fish and eats some. Each dashed line stands for the path of a fish in the school. The cross shows the shark eating a fish. In event C the fish run into the dolphins and suffer more losses. The solid lines are the dolphin paths. The dashes are the fish swim paths. The cross shows a dolphin eating a fish.

[1]. This output can control smaller FCMs or fuzzy control systems. These systems can drive visual, auditory, or tactile outputs of the virtual world. The FCM can control the temporal associations or timing cycles that structure virtual worlds. The FCM state vector drives the motion of each character as in a frame in a cartoon. Simple equations of motion or fuzzy systems can move each actor between the states.

We used a simple update equation for position:

$$\mathbf{p}(t_{n+1}) = \mathbf{p}(t_n) + \Delta t \mathbf{v}(t_n) \tag{4}$$

The velocity $\mathbf{v}(t)$ does not change at time step $\Delta t$. The FCM finds the direction and magnitude of movement. The magnitude of the velocity depends on the FCM state. If the FCM state is RUN AWAY, then the velocity is FAST. If the FCM state is REST, then the velocity is SLOW. The prey choose the direction that maximizes the distance from the predator. The predator chases the prey. Each state moves the actors through the sea.

The result is a complex dance among the actors as they move in a 2-D ocean. Figure 5 shows these movements. The forcing function is a hungry shark. The shark encounters the dolphins who cluster and then flee the shark. The shark chases but cannot keep up. The shark still searches for food and finds the fish. It catches a fish and then rests with its hunger sated. Meanwhile the hungry dolphins search for food and eat more fish. Each actor responds to the actions of the other.

### D. Nested FCMs

FCMs can endow virtual worlds with goals and intentions as they define dynamic physical and social environments. The FCM can combine simple actions to model "intelligent" behavior [1,3]. Each node in turn can control its own simple FCM in a *nested* FCM. Complex actions emerge from networks of simple reflexes. FCM nesting extends to any number of fuzzy sets for the inputs. A concept can divide into smaller fuzzy sets or subconcepts. The edges or rules link the sets. This leads to a discrete multivalued output for each node. Enough nodes allow this feedforward system to approximate any continuous function [8].

The FCM edges or rules map one subconcept to another. These subconcept mappings form a fuzzy system or set of fuzzy if-then rules that map inputs to outputs. Each mapping is a fuzzy rule or state-space patch that links fuzzy sets. The patches cover the graph of some function in the input-output state space. The fuzzy system then averages the patches that overlap to give an approximation of a continuous function [11]. Subconcepts can map to different responses in the FCM. This gives a more varied response to changes in the virtual world.

For example we can model the effects of different threats on a fish school. For that we need a nested FCM:

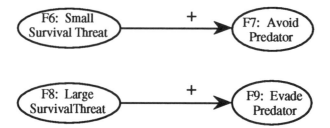

The small survival threat may be a slow-moving predator that has not seen or decided to attack the fish. The large survival threat may be a fast predator such as a barracuda or shark that swims towards the center of the school. We can insert this new sub-FCM into the Fish FCM in Figure 4 in place of $F_6$ SURVIVAL THREAT and $F_7$ RUN AWAY. Different limit cycles appear for different degrees of threat. For a small threat ($F_6$) the fish avoid the predator ($F_7$) as they move out of the line-of-sight of the predator. Large threats ($F_8$) cause the fish to scatter quickly to evade the predator ($F_9$). This leads to fatigue and rest ($F_2$ and $F_3$).

These threat responses cause the "fountain effect" and the "burst effect" in fish schools [14,18] as each fish tries to increase its chances of survival. The fountain effect occurs when a predator moves towards a fish school and the school splits and flows around the predator. The school re-forms behind the predator. In the burst effect the school expands in the form of a sphere to evade the predator.

## 3    Adaptive Fuzzy Cognitive Maps

An adaptive FCM changes its causal web in time. The causal web learns from data. The causal edges or rules change in sign and magnitude. The additive scheme (3) is a type of causal learning since it changes the FCM edge strengths. In general an edge $e_{ij}$ changes with some first-order learning law:

$$\dot{e}_{ij} = f_{ij}\left(e_{ij}, C_i, C_j, \dot{C}_i, \dot{C}_j\right) + g_{ij}(t)$$

(5)

Here $g_{ij}$ is a forcing function. Data fires the concept nodes and in time this leaves a causal pattern in the edge. Causal learning is local in $f_{ij}$. It depends on just its own value and on the node signals that it connects:

The differential Hebbian learning law [11] correlates concept changes or velocities:

$$\dot{e}_{ij} = -e_{ij} + \dot{C}_i(x_i)\dot{C}_j(x_j)$$

(6)

So $\dot{C}_i(x_i)\dot{C}_j(x_j) > 0$ iff concepts $C_i$ and $C_j$ move in the same direction. $\dot{C}_i(x_i)\dot{C}_j(x_j) < 0$ iff concepts $C_i$ and $C_j$ move in opposite directions. In this sense (6) learns patterns of causal change. The first-order structure of (6) implies that $e_{ij}(t)$ is an exponentially weighted average of paired (or lagged) changes. The most recent changes have the most weight. The *discrete* change $\Delta C_i(t) = C_i(t) - C_i(t-1)$ lies in $\{-1,0,1\}$. Discrete differential Hebbian learning can take the form

$$e_{ij}(t+1) = \begin{cases} e_{ij}(t) + c_t\left[\Delta C_i(x_i)\Delta C_j(x_j) - e_{ij}(t)\right] & \text{if } \Delta C_i(x_i) \neq 0 \\ e_{ij}(t) & \text{if } \Delta C_i(x_i) = 0 \end{cases}$$

(7)

Here $c_t$ is a learning coefficient that decreases in time [11]. $\Delta C_i \Delta C_j > 0$ iff concepts $C_i$ and $C_j$ move in the same direction. $\Delta C_i \Delta C_j < 0$ iff concepts $C_i$ and $C_j$ move in opposite directions. E changes only if a concept changes. The changed edge slowly "forgets" the old causal changes in favor of the new ones. This causal law can learn higher-order causal relations if it correlates multiple cause changes with effect changes.

We used differential Hebbian learning to encode a feeding sequence and a chase sequence in a FCM. The concepts in the $i$th row learn only when $\Delta C_i(x_i)$ equals 1 or -1. We used $c_i(t_k) = 0.1\left[1 - {}^{t_k}\!/_{1.1N}\right]$. The training data came from the dolphin FCM in figure 3. This gave the $\mathbf{E}_D$:

$$\mathbf{E}_D =$$

|        | $D_1$ | $D_2$ | $D_3$ | $D_4$ | $D_5$ | $D_6$ | $D_7$ | $D_8$ | $D_9$ | $D_{10}$ |
|--------|-------|-------|-------|-------|-------|-------|-------|-------|-------|----------|
| $D_1$    | 0.0 | 0.0 | -0.1 | -0.6 | -0.5 | 0.6 | -0.6 | 0.0 | 0.0 | 0.0 |
| $D_2$    | 0.0 | -0.5 | 0.5 | -0.5 | 0.0 | 0.0 | 0.0 | 0.0 | 0.0 | 0.0 |
| $D_3$    | 0.0 | 0.0 | 0.0 | 0.9 | 0.5 | 0.0 | 0.0 | 0.0 | -0.1 | -0.1 |
| $D_4$    | 0.8 | 0.0 | -0.4 | 0.0 | 0.0 | -0.2 | 0.0 | 0.0 | -0.2 | -0.1 |
| $D_5$    | 0.4 | -0.3 | 0.3 | -0.1 | -0.2 | -0.2 | 0.0 | 0.0 | -0.1 | 0.1 |
| $D_6$    | 0.0 | 0.0 | 0.0 | 0.0 | 0.0 | -0.5 | 1.0 | -0.6 | 0.0 | 0.0 |
| $D_7$    | 0.0 | -0.6 | 0.0 | 0.0 | -0.5 | 0.0 | -0.5 | 1.0 | 0.0 | 0.0 |
| $D_8$    | 0.0 | 1.0 | -0.5 | 0.0 | 0.5 | 0.0 | 0.0 | -0.5 | 0.0 | 0.0 |
| $D_9$    | -0.5 | 0.0 | 0.5 | 0.0 | 0.5 | 0.0 | 0.0 | 0.0 | 0.0 | 0.5 |
| $D_{10}$ | -0.2 | 0.0 | 0.7 | 0.3 | -0.2 | 0.0 | 0.0 | 0.0 | 0.3 | -0.3 |

This learned edge matrix $\mathbf{E}_D$ resembles the FCM matrix in Figure 3. The causal links it lacks between $D_{10}$ and $\{D_6, D_7, D_8\}$ were not in the training set. The diagonal links terms for self-inhibition of each concept. This occurs since each concept is on for one cycle before the matrix transitions to the next state. The hunger input $\mathbf{CL}_0 = [\,1\ 0\ 0\ 0\ 0\ 0\ 0\ 0\ 0\ 0\,]$ with a threshold of 0.5 now leads to the limit cycle:

$\mathbf{CL}_0\ \mathbf{E}_D = [\,0.0\ 0.0\ -0.1\ -0.6\ -0.5\ 0.6\ -0.5\ 0.0\ 0.0\ 0.0\,] \rightarrow \mathbf{CL}_1 = [\,0\ 0\ 0\ 0\ 0\ 1\ 0\ 0\ 0\ 0\,]$,
$\mathbf{CL}_1\ \mathbf{E}_D = [\,0.0\ 0.0\ 0.0\ 0.0\ 0.0\ -0.5\ 1.0\ -0.6\ 0.0\ 0.0\,] \rightarrow \mathbf{CL}_2 = [\,0\ 0\ 0\ 0\ 0\ 0\ 1\ 0\ 0\ 0\,]$,
$\mathbf{CL}_2\ \mathbf{E}_D = [\,0.0\ -0.6\ 0.0\ 0.0\ -0.5\ 0.0\ -0.5\ 1.0\ 0.0\ 0.0\,] \rightarrow \mathbf{CL}_3 = [\,0\ 0\ 0\ 0\ 0\ 0\ 0\ 1\ 0\ 0\,]$,
$\mathbf{CL}_3\ \mathbf{E}_D = [\,0.0\ 1.0\ -0.5\ 0.0\ 0.5\ 0.0\ 0.0\ -0.5\ 0.0\ 0.0\,] \rightarrow \mathbf{CL}_4 = [\,0\ 1\ 0\ 0\ 1\ 0\ 0\ 0\ 0\ 0\,]$,
$\mathbf{CL}_4\ \mathbf{E}_D = [\,0.4\ -0.8\ 0.8\ -0.6\ -0.2\ -0.2\ 0.0\ 0.0\ -0.1\ 0.1\,] \rightarrow \mathbf{CL}_5 = [\,0\ 0\ 1\ 0\ 0\ 0\ 0\ 0\ 0\ 0\,]$,
$\mathbf{CL}_5\ \mathbf{E}_D = [\,0.0\ 0.0\ 0.0\ 0.9\ 0.5\ 0.0\ 0.0\ 0.0\ -0.1\ -0.1\,] \rightarrow \mathbf{CL}_6 = [\,0\ 0\ 0\ 1\ 1\ 0\ 0\ 0\ 0\ 0\,]$,
$\mathbf{CL}_6\ \mathbf{E}_D = [\,1.2\ -0.3\ -0.1\ -0.1\ -0.2\ -0.4\ 0.0\ 0.0\ -0.3\ 0.0\,] \rightarrow \mathbf{CL}_0 = [\,1\ 0\ 0\ 0\ 0\ 0\ 0\ 0\ 0\ 0\,]$,

This resembles the sequence of rest, eat, play, and rest from section 2. Figure 6a shows the hand-designed limit cycle from section 2. Figure 6b shows the limit cycle from FCM found with differential Hebbian learning. The DHL limit cycle is one step shorter. Both FCMs have just one limit cycle and the null fixed point in the space of $2^{10}$ binary state vectors.

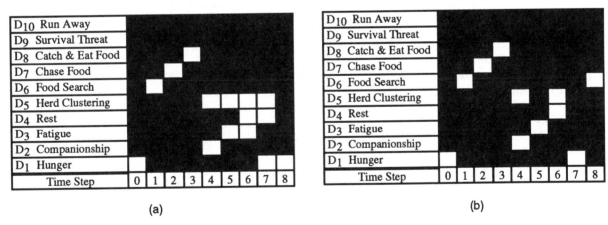

(a)                                                                 (b)

Figure 6. Limit cycle comparison between the hand-designed system and the FCM found with differential Hebbian learning. Each column is a binary state vector. (a) Rest, feed, play, rest limit cycle for the FCM in Figure 3. (b) Limit cycle for the FCM found with (7).

# 4. Conclusions

Fuzzy cognitive maps can model the causal web of a virtual world. The FCM can control its local and global nonlinear behavior. The local fuzzy rules or edges and the fuzzy concepts they connect model the causal links within and between events. The global FCM nonlinear dynamics give the virtual world an "arrow of time." A user can change these dynamics at will and thus change the causal processes in the virtual world. FCMs let experts and users choose a causal web by drawing causal pictures instead of by stating equations.

FCMs can also help visualize data. They show how variables relate to one another in the causal web. The FCM output states can guide a cartoon of the virtual world. The cartoon animates the FCM dynamics as the system trajectory moves through the FCM state space. This can apply to models in economics, medicine, history, and politics [16] where the social and causal web can change in complex ways that may arise from changing the sign or magnitude of a single FCM causal rule or edge.

More complex FCMs have more complex dynamics and can model more complex virtual worlds. Each concept node can fire on its own time scale and fire in its own nonlinear way. The causal edge flows or rules can have their own time scales too and may increase or decrease the causal flow through them in nonlinear ways.

A FCM can model these complex virtual worlds if it uses more nonlinear math to change its nodes and edges. The price paid may be a chaotic virtual world with unknown equilibrium behavior. Some users may want this to add novelty to their virtual world or to make it more exciting. A user might choose a virtual world that is mildly nonlinear and has periodic equilibria. At the other extreme the user might choose a virtual world that is so wildly nonlinear it has only aperiodic equilibria. Think of a virtual game of tennis or raquetball where the gravitational potential changes at will or at random. Fuzziness and nonlinearity are design parameters for a virtual world. They may give a better model of a real process. Or they may be just more fun to play with.

# References

[1] Brooks, R. A., "A Robot that Walks: Emergent Behaviors from a Carefully Evolved Network," *Neural Computation*, Volume 1, Number 2, 253-262, Summer 1989.

[2] Brown, R.A., *Fluid Mechanics of the Atmosphere*, Academic Press, 1991.

[3] Connell, J.H., *Minimalist Mobile Robotics: A Colony-style Architecture for an Artificial Creature*, Academic Press, Harcourt Brace Jovanovich, Publishers, 1990.

[4] Craig, J.J., *Introduction to Robotics*, Addison-Wesley, Reading, MA, 1986.

[5] Dickerson, J. A., Kosko, B., "Fuzzy Function Approximation with Supervised Ellipsoidal Learning," *World Conference on Neural Networks (WCNN'93)*, Volume II, 9-17, Portland, July 1993.

[6] Gibson, W., *Neuromancer*, Ace Books, New York, 1984.

[7] Grossberg, S., *Studies of Mind and Brain*, Reidel, Boston, 1982.

[8] Hornik, K., Stinchcombe, M., White, H., "Multilayered Feedforward Networks are Universal Approximators," *Neural Networks*, Volume 2, Number 5, 359-366, 1989.

[9] Kosko, B., "Fuzzy Cognitive Maps," *International Journal Man-Machine Studies*, Volume 24, 65-75, 1986.

[10] Kosko, B., "Hidden Patterns in Combined and Adaptive Knowledge Networks," *International Journal of Approximate Reasoning*, Volume 2, 337-393, 1988.

[11] Kosko, B., *Neural Networks and Fuzzy Systems: A Dynamical Systems Approach to Machine Intelligence*, Prentice-Hall, Englewood Cliffs, 1992.

[12] Kreuger, M., *Artificial Reality II*, Second Edition, Addison-Wesley, 1991.

[13] Minsky, M.L., *The Society of Mind*, Touchstone Book, Simon & Schuster, 1985.

[14] Partridge, B.L., "The Structure and Function of Fish Schools," *Scientific American*, Volume 246, Number 6, 114-123, June 1982.

[15] Shane, S.H., "Comparison of Bottlenose Dolphin Behavior in Texas and Florida, with a Critique of Methods for Studying Dolphin Behavior," in *The Bottlenose Dolphin*, S. Leatherwood, R.R. Reeves (editors), 541-558, Academic Press, 1990.

[16] Taber, W. R., "Knowledge Processing with Fuzzy Cognitive Maps," *Expert Systems with Applications*, Volume 2, number 1, 83-87, 1991.

[17] Weihs, D., Webb P. W., "Optimal Avoidance and Evasion Tactics in Predator-Prey Interactions," *Journal of Theoretical Biology*, Volume 106, 189-206, 1984.

[18] Winston, P.H., *Artificial Intelligence, 2nd Edition*, Addison-Wesley, Reading, MA, 1984.

# Speech and Language

**Session Chairs: David Rumelhart**
**Richard Peterson**

# COMPUTATIONAL PSYCHOLOGY APPROACH
## to
## HUMAN FACIAL LANGUAGE COMMUNICATION TO ROBOTS

Jinghua Ding
Department of Computer and Mathematical Sciences
Graduate School of Information Sciences, Tohoku University
Email: lchj@ibis.iamp.tohoku.ac.jp

## ABSTRACT

Ekman's human facial expressions that have six emotional states distributed over three facial regions are coded mathematically in a multi-layer perceptron designed with an optimum number of hidden nodes and initial weights in the way of logically analyzing internal representations of features in a face. The performance is benchmarked against other approaches, showing the promise of such a computational psychology in understanding human emotion by face reading. This emotional reading neural net when combined with linguistic-syntactic-semantic neural networks for spoken language can potentially enhance the understanding of the verbal and facial communication to robots.

## 1. INTRODUCTION

Recently, computational psychology has made a great advancement in solving the continuous sound/speech recognition problems[1]. It can solve one of the most challenging problems of a continuous speech segmentation. For example, Rumelhart et al. used a time-dependent transient spectra whose area slices become the input training vector $\{X(t)i\}$ i=1,2,3,...,25 channels and 11 time point t. They have demonstrated a real time operation in less than 10 milliseconds on a SUN SPARK Station I for noisy beep, chirp, double pulses, etc. 6 classes.

Meanwhile, it is known that the sound is often involved with the emotional feeling expressed by the speaker facial expression. For example, a sentence like "I do not know" spoken with a doubt expression, has a completely different meaning from that spoken with a contempt expression. Actually, some human feelings are apt to be expressed in nonverbal language, especially facial expressions, while some are apt to be expressed in verbal language. Communication between humans is based on the combination of both methods. In order to improve the interaction between human and machines, the techniques for understanding both of them should be developed simultaneously.

In this preliminary work of applying back-propagation networks[2], the author wish to report the progress she made after the former researches[3] following P. Ekman's work[4] and wish to demonstrate the efficiency of the strategies initiated by Rumelhart for developing effective neural network applications[5]. The improvement of the efficient design of the hidden layer and the initiation of weights (for off-line training and on-line adaptation for real time noisy system operation) by analyzing the internal representations are emphasized in this work. However, the syntheses of both language understanding and facial expression will be reported in the future investigation.

## 2. Pattern Recognition Subsystems

In this research, the facial expressions are recognized according to facial feature extraction and change detection. Similar to the strategy used commonly in real time video games, the facial feature estimation could be performed after the change detection for a selected set of prominent regions on the facial movement. In principle, such an automatic selection strategy can efficiently avoid processing a quarter million irrelevant pixels, and handle nicely the occlusion problem when the speaker turns away slowly. The current analysis was performed in two steps: first each image frame of a video sequence was selectively processed by a researcher to detect prominent feature regions, then the features were matched between frames to determine their changes. In the future system, the real time image processing algorithm could be automated--change detection following feature extraction like video games. As the kernel of the system, three back-propagation networks are called "subnets" used to recognize the expressions according to the displacements at those characteristic locations. The design of recognition system flow chart is shown in Figure 1.

Since a face can be divided into three basic "eigen regions"--eyes, brows and the mouth of which independent expressions can be computed in each regions. In principle, our design strategy utilized three artificial neural networks (ANN), or subnets. The strategy can fuse better not only the expressions recognized from the movements of each regions but also the sizes of each ANN's can be reduced significantly. It so happened that a smaller size ANN is faster and can generalize better than an over-sized one. The key is to estimate the degree of freedom in the problem and evaluate the performance goal to be achieved. The unnecessary large ANN tends to overly specify those weights associated with hidden nodes. During the training phase, a lot of data used can inadvertently produce the undesirable overfitting. We anticipate that would be detrimental to the final stage synthesis by means of a master ANN responsible for the subsequent fusion among facial feature data with the language understanding ANN's.

Another important but more specific reason for such a subnet approach is due to the emotional feeling of happiness and disgust which are rarely expressed in brows and eyes regions and rather in the mouth region. Using the subnet approach, we can train and distinguish them only in the mouth network. Therefore, both the brows and the eyes networks have four output nodes corresponding to surprise, fear, angry and sadness expressions, and the mouth network has six output nodes corresponding to all six expressions. Some experience has been learned about the data size itself as follows.

The inputs to the neural networks are movements of characteristic points which can be obtained from 2-D image processing. If the pixels are too few, it will be impossible to classify all expressions. On the other hand, too many redundant pixels will cause the complexity of movie image processing algorithm, the cost of training time and the sensitivity to the noise, etc. Therefore, the operator experience in selecting the characteristic points efficiently becomes important in the design of subnet's input. Our finding of a few characteristic feature points is still consistent with the usual rule of thumb known to image processing scientists---the so-called Johnson Criterion for the minimum size about 4x5 raw image pixels for a possible pattern classification, e.g. approaching vehicle versus tank, after the initial single hot pixel target detection in the FLIR imaging over the desert storm horizon. Figure 2 shows a suggestion according to the comprehensive analysis of Facial Action Coding System (FACS), by which necessary and sufficient points have been found out. In order to simplify conditions, we suppose that the studied expressions are symmetrical and characteristic points are only defined for the left half face--one brow, one eye and half mouth.

3.     Facial Expression Features Models
        Given three facial regions with different expressions simultaneously,
we can analyze each regions separately and build up three features
models corresponding to each regions (brows, eyes and mouth)
respectively according to the rules of the facial expressions described
in Ekman's FACS.[3] These models can be used in the simulation to test
the performance of the neural networks.
        According to the Ekman's observation, almost all facial movements can
be described by Action Units (AUs), and the relationship between the
facial expressions and AUs can be clearly identified.  Since not all
AUs are involved in common facial expressions,  Table 1 lists the
necessary AUs which affect the eyes shape corresponding to four
expressions--sad, surprise, fear, and angry.  In an automatic image
processing this AUs will be derived from a few characteristic feature
points over the regional whose pixel numbers shall be slightly bigger
than the aforementioned Johnson criterion.

Table 1. Expressions and Action Units in the Eyes Region

| Expressions | Action Units |
| --- | --- |
| sadness eyes | inner brow raiser |
| surprise eyes | upper lid raiser |
| fear eyes | upper lid raiser; low lid tightener and raiser |
| angry eyes | brow lowerer; low lid tightener and raiser |

        In the eyes region, it is reasonable that the movements only happen in
the Y direction in the local X-Y Cartesian coordinate system fixed along
the vertical face direction. Corresponding to the AUs in Table 1, the
movement values of the characteristic points should be changed in the way
shown in Table 2.

Table 2. Action Units and Movements in the Eyes Region

| Action Units | Movement values |
| --- | --- |
| inner brow raiser | 1y+ |
| upper lid raiser | 1y+, 2y+ |
| lower lid tightener and raiser | 3y+, 4y+, 5y+ |
| brow lowerer | 1y-, 2y- |

(* Ny+: the movement value in the Y direction of
the point N in Figure 1 is positive.)
        Table 1 illustrates the relationship between expressions and AUs and
Table 2 gives the relationship between AUs and movements of the
characteristic points which allow us to construct our features models.
Merge Table 1 and Table 2 into Figure 3, we plot the dotted lines to
indicate the brow-lowerer-AU corresponding to the negative movement
values of points 1 and 2 above the right eye. Likewise, the solid line
indicates positive AU-value. Thus, Fig. 3 reveals the mechanism how our
model generates the characteristic points in the eyes' region. In the
sight of surprise, one tends to increase the verbal pitch and also
widen ones upper eye lid. Thus, the upper-lid-raiser-AU at the
characteristic points #1 and #2 should give the positive values in the
Y direction, while the other AU value may be set to a relative zero
value. In case of angry, one tightens facial muscles and consequently

shrinks the eye lids giving the negative value for the downward movement at the points #1 and #2 at the upper eye lid while the positive value for the upward movement points #3, #4 and #5 at the lower eye lid.

In the same way, the other two models for the brows region and the mouth region can be built up, too.

4.    Neural Network Architecture

As described in Section 2, both the brows subnet and the eyes subnet have four output nodes corresponding to surprise, fear, angry and sadness expressions, and the mouth subnet has six output nodes corresponding to all six expressions.

Inputs to three subnets are the values of the movement of the characteristic points at three regions shown in Figure 1. In the training set of data, these movement values can be obtained from the three features models which have been described in Section 3. The analysis in Section 3 reveals that Ekman's action units can be considered as the internal representations of the hidden nodes, i.e. the so-called Grand Mother cells in the computational psychology (See Figure 3). If we define hidden nodes corresponding to the necessary AUs, then the number of the hidden nodes of the networks follows exactly. Therefore, there are eight, five and ten input nodes and four, four and seven hidden nodes in brows, eyes and mouth subnets, respectively.

Using these three subnets, and recognizing expressions respectively, we can synthesize a lookup table which can define the relationship between the set of desired results for each subnet and the set of actual results obtained by the final judged expression classes (See Fig. 1).

Figure 3 also brings forth an idea of how to initialize the weights logically in the networks. If there is a solid line between two nodes in Figure 3, we set a positive value for that weight. On the contrary, if there is a dotted line between two nodes, we set a negative value for that weight. The other weights are set with very small random values. Let's suppose that there is an angry sample, in which 1y and 2y are negative values and the other inputs are positive. Because the ''brow lowerer''hidden node has two negative weights connecting 1y and 2y and a positive weight connecting 5y, it can be turned on by a high weighted sum. Moreover, because the ''lower lid tightener'' hidden node connects 3y and 4y with positive weights, it also can be turned on. Consequently, the angry eyes output node will surely obtain a large weighted sum from these two hidden nodes. In other words, the output node corresponds to the expression class, while the current input is from the largest weighted sum, and then before the training data is presented, the classification hyper-space has been already divided into hyper-cubes. Note that it always takes a regular back-propagation a long time to obtain the same situation. Of course, the fine tuning of the final decision boundaries, which depend on the weights and thresholds, are obtained by the training set using the regular back-propagation algorithm.

This tuning by training is still necessary because not all relationship between AUs and the characteristic point movements are known, nor all the inverse relationship between the expressions and AUs are known, except a few special case in the mouth region for example. In case that the a priori connection does not exist absolutely, we must set the initial weight with a certain value smaller than those connection weight known a priori absolutely. In this way, the initial subnets can be set up in a balanced fashion.

5.     Simulation Results
     Using our features models described in Section 2, we examined the
networks by error calculation. The error is defined as follows:

\rm error=\sum_{i}\sum_{j}\Bigl|O_d(i,j)-O_c(i,j)\Bigr|

where Od(i,j) is the desired value and Oc(i,j) is the
calculated value of the jth output node of the ith class of expression.
     The simulation results will now be analyzed in two cases as follows:

[Case 1] Initializing all weights with small random values:
     When the number of hidden nodes is more than that of the necessary AUs
we have defined, no improvement has been found according to error sums
(shown in Figure 4). When the number of hidden nodes is less than that
of the necessary AUs, sometimes the networks can succeed to recognize all
expressions but sometimes the local minimum problem occurs. As a result,
some expressions can not be recognized and the reliability of the networks
is degraded seriously.

So our method to determine the number of hidden nodes is certified by
these error bounds.

[Case 2] Initializing weights as we have described in Section 4:
     In this case, the number of the hidden nodes is determined by the
necessary AUs and the initial weights are set in the way described in
Section 4.  Compared with Case 1, the error sums of the six expression
patterns are reduced quickly(See Figure 5).
     Although the values of the final weights  may be different from the
weights logically initialized, the algebraic signs (positive or
negative) remains the same. The fact verifies the correctness of our
method to divide the hyper-space by setting initial weights. We believe
that the final weights accurately indicating the strength of the
relationship among the note of three layers, which reveals the further
investigation direction for the language-feeling fusion work with a
super-net.
     Although the weight-initialization method using the correct algebraic
signs may raise the sensitivity to input perturbation [3], this problem
might be eliminated by using the training set with added random noise,
similar to the Boltzmann machine of Hinton and Sejnowski but based on
Cauchy color noise generating both random walks and random flights
for a fast simulated annealing [6,7].

6.     Conclusions
     In order to design human-robot communication automation, the
often-neglected emotional content of human spoken language may be
remedied by analyzing the speaker's facial expressions. Thus, we have
proposed three back-propagation ANN's for one face reading--brows,
eyes, and mouth---one for each region, and each has 6 emotional
states--angry, fear, happiness, sadness, surprise and disgust. One of
the main conceptual contributions is using smaller subnet approach to
the face-reading, and then a necessary fusion gives more complex facial
expression.  Such small set of ANN's are desirable both to speed the
classification processing and to avoid overfitting the classifier to
the training set.
     According to the simulation results, the sufficient number of the

hidden nodes can be found out by our analysis and weight initialization. The simulation result not only indicated the validity of our method to accelerate convergence of the networks but also enlightened that the qualitative analysis of facial displays may be developed into quantitative analysis by the proposed method of computational psychology so that the strength of the relations between action units and expressions can be obtained accurately.

Toward the mid-term goal of human-robot voice communication, this paper has taken the first step investigation of the component of human facial emotion reading. The method to synthesize both verbal language understanding and facial expression recognition will be reported in the future investigation. For example, one could follow the Reference [1] the space-time generalization of current work employing the time-delayed subnet approach to the case----- winking one eye for joking.

REFERENCES
[1]     C. S. Weaver, K. D. Branch, D. E. Rumelhart, J. S. Ostrem, (Maxim Tech. Inc. Santa Clara, CA)"Acoustic Classification with Neural Networks," available by Defense Technical Information Center, Cameron, Alex. Va, AD-A219 464, March 19, 1990 [Approved for Public Release Distribution Unlimited].
[2]     D. E. Rumelhart, "Parallel Distributed Processing," Vol. 1, MIT Press, 1986.
[3]     Jinghua Ding, M. Shimamura, H. Kobayashi, T. Nakamura,(Computer, Tohoku U.)"Neural Network Structures for Expression Recognition," IJCNN-93 Nagoya, pp.1430-1433, Oct 25-29, 1993.
[4]     P. Ekman (ed.)"Emotion in Human Face," Cambridge Univ. Press 1982.
[5]     D. E. Rumelhart,"Strategies for Developing Effective Neural Network Applications" Keynote Lecture of IJCNN-93 Nagoya, Oct 25-29, 1993.
[6]     H. Szu, R. Hartley,"Fast Simulated Annealing," Phys. Letters A Vol 122, pp.157-162, June 8, 1987.
[7]     H. Szu, "(Cauchy) Color Noise Annealing Benchmark using Exhaustive Search in Solving Traveling Salesman Problem," IJCNN-90, pp.I-317, I-320, Jan. 15-18, 1990.

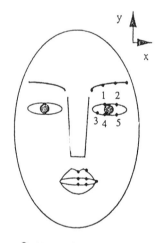

Figure 2  Charactistic Points of a Face

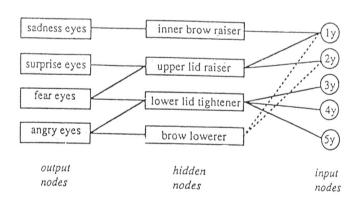

Figure 3. Expressions, AUs and Movements of Charactistics

(eyes region)

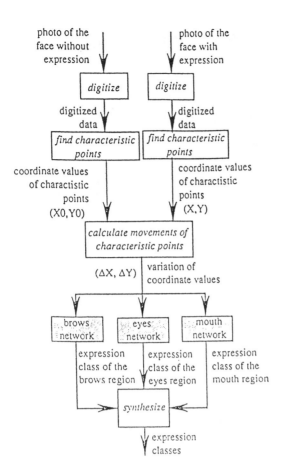

Figure 1 Flowchart of the Facial Expression Recognition System

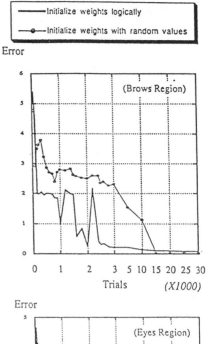

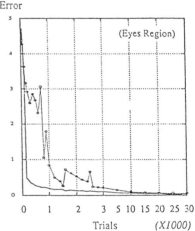

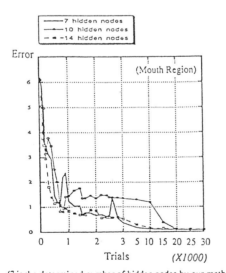

(7 is the determined number of hidden nodes by our method)

Figure 4. Comparison of Error Sums for the NN's
with Different number of Hidden Nodes

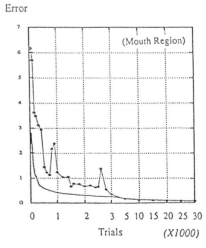

Figure 5. Comparison of Error Sum of NN Using Logically Initialized
Weights with that of NN Using Random Initial Weights

# Word Spotting with the Gamma Neural Model

Jose C. Principe, Larry A. Turner

Computational NeuroEngineering Lab
University of FLorida, Gainesville, FL 32611

## Abstract

This work reports on the use of the focused gamma model as a word spotter. Several modifications in the original gamma model implementation are tested. The preliminary results show that they improve the original model, and demonstrate the importance of appropriate structures for feature representation in complex classification problems such as speech recognition.

## Introduction

The time delay neural network (TDNN) [1] is one of the most widely utilized neural network topologies for speech recognition. The power of TDNN comes from the fact that it utilizes a memory structrue that brings past information to the classification of speech. Unfortunately, the memory structure in TDNN is not very versatile. It is built around a finite impulse response structure, and as such the size of the memory dictates how far into the past the memory can reach. Another characteristic is that the signal past is recalled with maximal resolution, because every sample of the signal up to the length of the FIR is stored. There are alternate memory structures that can potentially improve on the linear combiner characteristics. We have been working with the gamma memory, a feedforward struture with local recursion [2]. The gamma memory is a generalization of the FIR filter, and it has the ability to trade "reach" for resolution [3]. In this paper we compare the performance of the gamma memory with an FIR filter for isolated word recognition. We show that a focused gamma model performs better than a TDNN with the memory layer restricted to the input. The gamma model not only learns faster the pattern classes, but also achieves a smaller mean square error, meaning that it learns more about the input pattern classes. In this work we allowed the tap-to-tap resolution to vary, effectively creating a memory structure that can handle some forms of time warping.

## Preprocessing for the Gamma Model

The gamma memory is a recursive system, therefore the processing can be done one sample at a time. As such, preprocessing models that do not segment speech are very appropriate. Instead of hte more traditional FFT or cepstral coefficients, we built a bank of 14 constant Q bandpass filters (Q=4) in quarter-octave-distribution from 200 to 3,638 Hz [4]. Each filter output is squared, lowpass filtered by a Kaiser window, and decimated to obtain a segment of 30 samples [4]. Each word is therefore represented as a time frequency pattern of size 14x30. In our vocabulary the words sizes were different, so the decimation rate (and the correponding filtering) were dynamically set and in the range [50, 90]. A simple amplitude threshold was used to determine the begining and end of each word. No further hand alignment was performed. Each pattern was normalized over the range [-1, 1] [4].

## Gamma Model Implementation

Unlike previous experiments with the gamma memory for speech recognition, here we allowed the feedback parameter, $\mu_k$, to adapt locally. The gamma memory has an input to tap k transfer function given by :

$$H_{\mu 0k}(z) = \prod_{i=1}^{k} H_{\mu i-1 i}(z) = C^k \prod_{i=1}^{k} \frac{\mu_i}{z - (1 - \mu_i)} \qquad k \to [1, N_\mu] \qquad (1)$$

$$h_{\gamma k}(n) = \frac{C^k (n-1)!}{(k-1)!(n-k)!} (1 - \gamma_k)^k \gamma_k^{n-k} u(n-k) \qquad \begin{matrix} k \to [1, N_\lambda] \\ |\gamma_k| < 1 \end{matrix} \qquad (2)$$

Here each stage can have a different $\mu_k$, yielding a composite effective memory depth, $\mathfrak{S}$, and resolution, $\mathfrak{R}$.

$$\mathfrak{I}_{\mu 0k} \equiv -z\frac{d}{dz}H_{\mu 0k}(z)\big|_{z=1} = -C^k z\frac{d}{dz}\prod_{i=1}^{k}\frac{\mu_i}{z-(1-\mu_i)}\bigg|_{z=1} \tag{3}$$

$$\mathfrak{I}_{\mu i-1i} = C\mu_i^{-1} \qquad i \to [1, N_\mu] \tag{4}$$

$$\mathfrak{I}_{\mu 0k} = C^k\mu_1^{-1} + C\mathfrak{I}_{\mu 1k} = C^{k-1}\mathfrak{I}_{\mu 01} + C\mathfrak{I}_{\mu 1k} = C^{k-1}\sum_{i=1}^{k}\mathfrak{I}_{\mu i-1i} \tag{5}$$

$$\mathfrak{R}_{\mu 0N_\mu} \equiv N_\mu\mathfrak{I}_{0N_\mu}^{-1} = N_\mu C^{-N_\mu+1}\left(\sum_{i=1}^{N_\mu}\mathfrak{I}_{\mu i-1i}\right)^{-1} \tag{6}$$

The value of $\mu_k$ controls the location of the pole, hence the phase of each stage, which means also the delay. The parameter $\mu_k$ is learned during training, using real time recurrent learning (RTRL) according to :

$$\upsilon_k(n) = (1-\mu_k)\upsilon_k(n-1) + C\mu_k\upsilon_{k-1}(n-1) \tag{7}$$

$$\delta_k(n) = \frac{\partial}{\partial\gamma_k}\upsilon_k(n) = (1-\mu_k)\delta_k(n-1) + C\mu_k\delta_{k-1}(n-1) + \upsilon_k(n-1) - C\upsilon_{k-1}(n-1) \tag{8}$$

$$e_{kj}(n) = (d_{kj}(n) - y_{kj}(n))N_{Fk}^{-1} \tag{9}$$

$$\mu_k(n) = -\eta_\mu\frac{\partial}{\partial\gamma_k}e_{mse_k}(n) = -\eta_\mu\frac{\partial}{\partial\gamma_k}\sum_{j=0}^{N_j-1}e^2_{kj}(n) \approx \eta_\mu\sum_{j=0}^{N_j-1}e_{kj}(n)\delta_{kj}(n)\varpi_{kj}(n \tag{10}$$

The step size, $\eta_\mu$, was kept constant at $10^{-3}$. In this experiment the number of taps, $N_\mu$, was experimentally set at 10 (see results). Another modification from previous designs is the fact that an amplification factor C was included in each filter. The reason can be found in the attenuation that each stage produces in the input signal. Experimentally we found that a gain of 1.5 per tap keeps the signal potential at the taps, $\upsilon_k$, within reasonable values and gives good results (Figure 2).

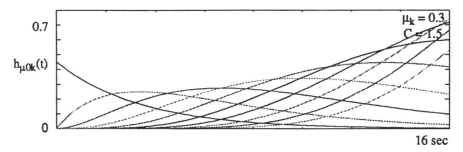

Figure 1. Gamma array continuous dispersive delay kernels for k→[1, 10].

The classification part of the network is built from a multilayer perceptron. The hidden layer has 24 processing elements, and the output layer has 11 processing elements, one for each class. Straight backpropagation with adaptive step size was utilized to train the spatial weights [4]. This is possible since the recurrent portion of the net is restricted to the input layer.

Local, neural cell-level step sizes, $\eta_k$, were adapted with $N_O$ and $N_U$ fixed at 5 and 10, respectively.

$$\Delta\eta_k(n) = \begin{cases} -0.1\eta_k(n-1) & \left(\sum_{m=0}^{N_o-1} \text{sgn}\,(\Delta\delta_k(n-m))\right) \geq N_O \\[2em] 0.1\eta_k(n-1) & \left(\sum_{m=0}^{N_U-1} \text{sgn}\,(\Delta\delta_k(n-m))\right) \leq -N_U \\[2em] 0 & else \end{cases} \tag{11}$$

The cost function utilized in this study was the inverse hyperbolic tangent as proposed by Fahlman [5] with $\varepsilon=0.45$ and hyperbolic tangent activations, $\sigma(\beta x)$, in all neural cells limiting the output layer potential range to [-1, 1]. Output and hidden layer cell relations are denoted by subscript $_O$ and $_H$, respectively.

$$\delta_{Ok} = \tanh^{-1}(\varepsilon\,(P^\rho_k - O^\rho_k)) \qquad \varepsilon \to [0, 0.5) \tag{12}$$

$$\delta_{Hk} = \left(\sum_{m=0}^{N_{Fk}-1} \delta_{Om}\varpi_{mk}\right)\sigma'\left(\sum_{m=0}^{N_{Bk}-1} \varpi_{k\mu}\upsilon^\rho_\mu - \varphi_{Hk}\right) \tag{13}$$

$$\Delta\varpi_{Okm, Hkm}(n) = \eta\delta_{Ok,Hk}\upsilon^\rho_m + \alpha\Delta\varpi_{Okm, Hkm}(n-1) \qquad \alpha \to [0, 1) \tag{14}$$

This cost function effectively weights the larger errors, and serves as an approximation to the $L^\infty$ norm. Training also utilized momentum set in the range [0.6, 0.9]. After the net was trained, the patterns for each class were propagated through the net and the maximum error for the class stored. This vector was used to set the recognition threshold during testing, and created automatically a class of unrecognized patterns.

## Results

A set of 11 words (up, down, left, right, top, bottom, center, home, end, pause, continue) was spoken 10 times by the same person, digitized at 11.025 kHz, and preprocessed as explained above. Figure 2 shows the mean square error during learning for the gamma model and TDNN with the same number of taps. Observe that the gamma model learns faster and more of the input patterns.

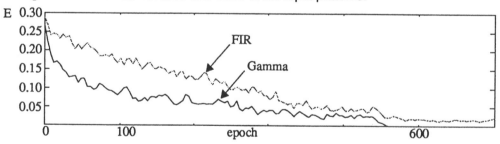

Figure 2. Gamma memory layer ANN vs. TDNN learning curves.

Table 1: Gamma memory layer ANN vs. TDNN performance.

| memory | $epoch_f$ | $E_f$ |
|--------|-----------|-------|
| FIR | 700 | 0.0321 |
| Gamma | 463 | $2.81 \times 10^{-8}$ |

An increase of the memory size of TDNN to 30 did not improve the performance. We explain this result by the added capability of the gamma memory to span a longer time span without increasing the number of degrees of freedom of the net, or the number of weights. For speech recognition it seems that due to the intrinsic variability of the patterns for each word (time warping) there is no point of providing maximal resolution in the memory traces. A coarser sampling makes the system less sensitive to alignment, and so may avoid the need for full blown dynamic warping algorithms. This is particularly the case when the memory structure has the flexibility to choose the tap-to-tap feedback parameter, because it is already creating a distortion in the time axis. Figure 3 depicts the post-convergence effective memory depth surface and intra-channel effective memory depth, respectively. Notice that there are certain channels where the feedback parameter is uniform, but others where it peaks early on in the memory structure. Another interesting experiment was conducted during learning. We restricted the fan in of the frequency channels, $N_{bk}$, of the hidden layer neural cells. Only three neighborhood channels connect to each hidden layer neural cell, with one shared channel between adjacent cells. This decreased tremendously the number of net weights, (from 3948 to 449 weights) and did not affect appreciably the performance of the net. It seems that local frequency information is sufficient to classify words, by preserving spatio-frequency mappings in the pattern set. Varying the gamma memory size affects the MSE and rate of convergence. Nine kernels seem to be the best compromise depth/resolution for this set of words. A remarkable compression of 3:1 was achieved. A fully-connected trained ANN was tested with the training set with 100% recognition. A similar sparsely-connected ANN performed at 98.5%. Test set performance was 95% and 90% for the fully-connected and the sparsely-connected ANN, respectively. All errors were reported as unrecognized exemplars, due to the vectored threshold technique employed.

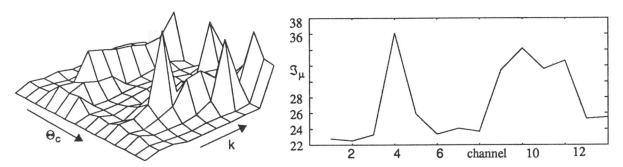

Figure 3. Gamma memory layer surface and intra-channel effective memory depth, k→[1, 10].

# References

1 Waibel, A., T. Hanazawa, G. Hinton, K. Shikano, and K. Lang. 1988. "Phoneme Recognition Using Time-Delay Neural Networks." Readings in Speech Recognition. Morgan Kaufmann. 393-404.

2 De Vries, B. and J. C. Principe. 1992. "The Gamma Model - A New Neural Model for Temporal Processing." IEEE Neural Network Journal, 5, 565-576.

3 Principe, J. C., B. De Vries, and P. G. Oliveira. 1993. "The Gamma Filter - A New Class of Adaptive IIR Filters with Restricted Feedback." IEEE Transactions on Signal Processing, 42:2, 649-656.

4 Turner, L. A. 1993. "Feed-Forward Neural Networks with Adaptive Memory Layers and Applications in Isolated Word Recognition." Master of Engineering Thesis, University of Florida.

5 Fahlman, S. E. 1989. "Fast-Learning Variations on Backpropagation : An Empirical Study." Proceedings of the 1988 Connectionist Models Summer School, Pittsburg. eds. Touretzky, D., G. Hinton, and T. Sejnowski. Morgan Kaufmann. 38-51.

# Dependency Analysis: Assessing the Functional Relationships among Processing Units in Artificial Neural Networks

Steven L. Small

Tran Nguyen

Cognitive Modelling Laboratory
Department of Neurology and Intelligent Systems Program
University of Pittsburgh
325 Scaife Hall
Pittsburgh, PA 15261-2003
Phone: (412) 648-2022
Facsimile: (412) 648-1239
Email: small@cortex.neurology.pitt.edu

**Abstract**: Dependency analysis is a new method of studying the internal representations of neural networks. The technique assesses the functional dependencies among network processing units, and helps to understand how a network evolves during the training period. Dependency analysis is particularly useful in studying the most complex neural networks, because it is an empirical technique rather than an analytical one, and thus depends on the functional properties of the network and not its structural details. Through an example network that performs object identification from semantic representations, the paper demonstrates the use of the technique to understand the contributions of the individual (semantic feature) units in the input layer to the classification represented by the (physical object) units of the output layer.

## Introduction

Cognitive models using connectionist techniques have greater scientific value when their internal behavior can be understood. Dependency analysis (DA) represents an empirical method to analyze neural networks that augments existing techniques. It has particular relevance for feedforward networks with hidden layers and for recurrent networks, which typically perform non-linear transformations that are opaque to direct examination.

Dynamic analysis of unit activation values sometimes explains network performance. In Hinton's family tree network [Hinton, 1986], individual hidden units became specialized for certain family relations. Reuckl et al [1989] demonstrated receptive fields corresponding to high order features of the input "retina" (e.g., diagonal lines). Zipser and Anderson [1988] demonstrated emergent representations in a model of spatial encoding by the parietal lobe, leading to hypotheses about its anatomical structure.

Mathematical manipulation of certain vectors of network unit activations can also be revealing. Elman [1989] performed a principal components analysis [Fukunaga, 1972] on the hidden unit activations of a simple recurrent network to learn a context free grammar, and found syntactic and semantic regularities. Both hierarchical clustering analysis [Tou and Gonzalez, 1974] and contribution analysis [Sanger, 1989] have led to a better understanding of the NetTalk database [Sejnowski and Rosenberg, 1987]. Le Cun et al [1990] describe how to prune connectionist networks with minimal loss of information, a method that involves significant network analysis.

Dependency analysis measures how small changes in the activations of particular network units affect the activation value of some other network unit. It does this dynamically, and does not depend on (a) the shape of the network; (b) the locations of the units in the network; or (c) the specific connectivity among the units. We use dependency analysis with classification networks to evaluate how each classification (i.e., a specific output unit) relates to changes in particular features of the object to be classified (i.e., input layer).

This paper is organized as follows: First we motivate the method of DA with discussion of object

| Object \ Feature | grasshopper | wrench | helicopter |
|---|---|---|---|
| LIMBS | 6 | 0 | 4 |
| COLOR | green | silver | variable |
| SIZE | <1ft | <1 ft | >2 yd |
| CROSS-SECTION | circular | rectangular | circular |
| FORM | cylindrical | rectangular | winged |
| MADE-OF | animal | metal artificial | wood metal glass artificial plastic |
| TEXTURE | smooth | smooth | smooth |
| NOISE | on-own | none | with-input |
| FUNCTIONS | waste reproduces | repairs | transport |
| LOCATION | yard woods farm | basement | air |
| MOVEMENT | self propelled grows | propelled | none with-fuel |

Table 1: Semantic features (properties) of several physical objects in the study corpus.

identification, a classification task performed by the human temporal lobe in many cognitive processing contexts. Second, we provide a formal description of the technique of dependency analysis. Finally, we use DA to analyze an example network that performs object identification, and show how it teaches us both about the task and potentially about the brain mechanisms that might be employed in performing it.

### Object Identification

To use language, people must be able to identify and name objects from their visual, tactile, auditory, and functional properties. As part of a long term study of semantic representations in the brain, we have been using computational techniques to investigate the task of object identification from semantic properties [Small and Holland, 1991]. Given the representation of a physical object in terms of semantic features (properties), and the goal of identifying the object based on this representation, we constructed several connectionist networks to perform the task in different ways.

It was hoped that formal analyses of these networks would shed light on the underlying brain representations and mechanisms. In fact, direct examination of hidden units as well as their principal components revealed the presence of implicit semantic categories [Small et al, 1993], and suggested how the brain might encode verbal knowledge [Hart and Gordon, 1992]. Interestingly, the existence of such categories in the brain has been suggested by empirical research with patients [Hart et al, 1985; Sartori and Job, 1988; Warrington and Shallice, 1984], but not explained. Nonetheless, it remained unclear which elements of the semantic feature vector were the most important in leading the network to make its classification of each object.

A simple identification network is shown in Figure 1. The input vector consists of one unit for each semantic feature known to the system (e.g., blue, smooth texture). In this semantic feature vector, multiple units are active simultaneously, with each active unit indicating a semantic property held by a particular object. The semantic feature vector thus encodes the meaning of an object. Table 1 shows this meaning representation (i.e., the active units in the semantic feature vector) for three example objects. The output vector consists of one unit for each object (e.g., motorcycle, dolphin). This object identification vector has a unit/value representation [Feldman and Ballard, 1982] with one active unit for the identification of a particular object.

The network of Figure 1 was trained using gradient descent to perform the correct mapping [Rumelhart *et al*, 1985] [Fahlman, 1988]. But how does the resulting network achieve this result? The internal functioning of the network is a product of the connections from input units to intermediate units to output units. Understanding the networks requires analysis of the preprogrammed input codes, the connection weights, and the emergent hidden unit activations.

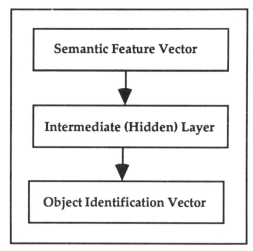

Figure 1: Feedforward network for object identification.

### Dependency Analysis

For each physical object in the corpus, certain features appeared to play a particularly important role in determining its identification. Dependency analysis of the object identification network of Figure 1 revealed, for example, that whereas the semantic representation of a typical object consists of a dozen or more semantic features (e.g., "dolphin" has fourteen features as shown in Table 2), very few of them play a major role in identification. Each object differs in the particular features most important for its identification.

Dependency analysis thus provides a way to understand how a network evolves during the training period, with particular processing units dependent more on the activations of some units than others, despite static connectivity patterns that are similar. It is particularly useful in studying the most complex neural networks, because as an empirical rather than analytical technique, it depends on the functioning rather than the structural details of the network. In multilayer neural networks, it allows the user to study how each unit in a given layer affects each unit in any successive layer, thus revealing information not straightforwardly available from the weights themselves (which would give the same information in systems without hidden layers). In recurrent networks, any unit can be analyzed with respect any number of other units to assess the strength of their dependencies.

The dependency index of output $j$ to an input $i$, $DI_{ji}$ is the measurement of how sensitive output $j$ is to the change in input $i$. In other words, it represents the *dependency* of the final state of output $j$ upon changes in the value of input $i$.

To obtain $DI_{ji}$ we first train a network using the training input and output patterns, the *standard* sets of values. After the network has converged, we then present it with new test patterns to obtain new output patterns, the *new* sets of values. The new test patterns are generated by taking each input pattern and varying input $i$ over the range of $\{y_{io}, y_{in}\}$ while keeping the rest of the input units constant.

LIMBS-0
COLOR-blue
SIZE->1-foot-and-<2-yards
CROSS-SECTION-circular
FORM-cylindrical
MADE-OF-from-animal
TEXTURE-smooth
NOISE-makes-on-its-own
FUNCTION-makes-waste
FUNCTION-esthetic
FUNCTION-reproduces
LOCATION-sea
MOVEMENT-self-moving
MOVEMENT-grows

Table 2: Semantic features representing the concept for "dolphin".

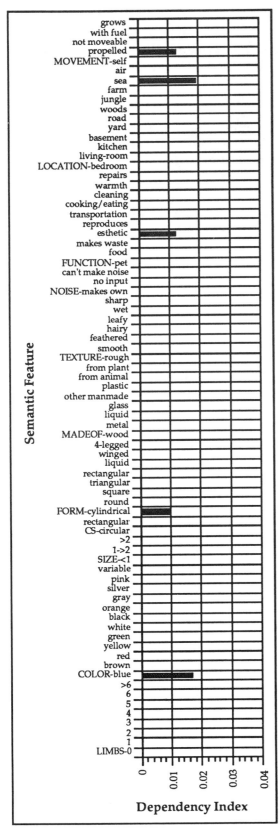

**Figure 2: Dependency indices for input units to output unit "dolphin".**

For input pattern $p$, $DI_{ji}^{p}$ is calculated as the mean of the ratio of the percentage change in output $j$ to the percentage change in input $i$, or

$$DI_{ji}^{p} = \frac{\sum_{x=0}^{x=n} \frac{(y_{jx} - y_{js})/y_{js}}{(y_{ix} - y_{is})/y_{is}}}{n}$$

where $y_{ix}$ is the new value of input $i$, $y_{jx}$ is the new value of output $j$ obtained using the modified input pattern $p$ that contained $y_{ix}$, and $y_{js}$ and $y_{is}$ are the standard values of output $j$ and input $i$ for input pattern $p$, respectively. Finally, the mean of $DI_{ji}^{p}$ over all input patterns is calculated to give us the final value of $DI_{ji}$,

$$DI_{ji} = \overline{DI_{ji}^{p}}$$

## Dependency Analysis of Object Identification Network

For the object identification task, 52 line drawings of physical objects were encoded in terms of 77 semantic features in the style of representation of Hinton and Shallice [1991]. The semantic features included the objects' colors, appendages, sizes, functions, types of movement, textures, external shapes, cross-sectional shapes, compositions, sounds, and locations. The features were designed by John Hart (personal communication) based on his work with patients with semantic memory impairments [Hart *et al*, 1985; Hart and Gordon, 1992]. As described, the object identifications consisted of 52 orthogonal unit vectors.

Figure 2 plots the dependency indices of output unit "dolphin" to the 77 input units (i.e., semantic features) from the network. The network made its decision based primarily on the following features:

COLOR = "blue"
FORM = "cylindrical"
FUNCTION = "esthetic"
LOCATION = "sea"
MOVEMENT = "propelled"

The results clearly indicated that out of the 77 input features, the network recognized 5 semantic features to be the most indicative of object "dolphin". Nine additional features composing the full semantic representation of "dolphin" do not arise at this level of analysis. While the feature MOVEMENT = "propelled" was not one of the positive features encoded in the input pattern for output "dolphin", the

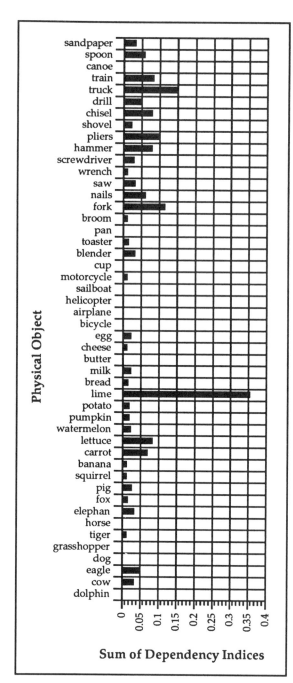

**Figure 3: Sums of dependency indices from all "TEXTURE" input units.**

network takes into consideration both negative and positive features of the object for identification purposes. Thus, analysis of the object identification network with Dependency analysis provides a way to determine the most characteristic and discriminating features of particular entities, given the specific task requested. The characteristic features identified by DA and those found through empirical study [Rosch, 1975] may have some theoretical relationship.

Dependency analysis can be turned around to examine the individual features used to identify the objects. By grouping the features into classes (e.g., TEXTURE), associated with verbal system instantiations of particular perceptual, motor, or cognitive modalities, this method can ascertain the most important feature types (and by inference, modalities) in identifying the individual objects. In object recognition, for example, the question might be which objects depend most on "rough texture" or "blue color" or "size" to identify?

Figure 3 shows the dependency analysis for all TEXTURE features with respect to each object in the output set. The ordinate of this graph is the sum of all the dependency index values from input units representing textures to each output object. Note that the household objects that are typically manipulated manually, as well as certain fruits and vegetables depend more on texture than do other classes of objects, such as transportation items and animals. This is certainly in accordance with both intuition and psychological data about category specificity.

## Conclusions

Dependency analysis is a technique to study the internal representations of connectionist networks. Such an analysis examines the effects of any one unit on any other unit in the network, and can easily be applied to recurrent networks and unsupervised neural networks as it only depends on the relative values in one set of units with respect to any other. Furthermore, DA may have a role in reducing the size of a set of input units or in constructing a smaller network from an existing network.

## Acknowledgments

The authors would like to thank the following individuals for help with the research described here and/or the manuscript: Margie Forbes, Barry Gordon, John Hart, Jr., Gloria Hoffman, Audrey Holland, Steven Phillips, and Nga Thai. We appreciate the financial support of the University of Pittsburgh School of Medicine and of the National Institute of Deafness and other Communication Disorders under grant #DC-00044. A preliminary version of this paper was presented at Midwest Connectfest 1992.

## References

Elman JL (1989) *Representation and Structure in Connectionist Models*. Report #CRL-TR-8903. University of California, San Diego.

Fahlman SE (1988) Faster-learning Variations on Back-propagation: An Empirical Study. In: *Proceedings of 1988 Connectionist Models Summer School*. San Mateo, California: Morgan Kaufmann Publishers, pp. 38-51.

Feldman JA, Ballard D (1982) Connectionist Models and their Properties. *Cognitive Science*, 6, 205-254.

Fukunaga K (1972) *Introduction to Statistical Pattern Recognition*. New York: Academic Press.

Hart J Jr., Berndt RS, Caramazza A (1985) Category-Specific Naming Deficit following Cerebral Infarction. *Nature*, 316, 439-440.

Hart J Jr., Gordon B (1992) Neural Subsystems for Object Knowledge. *Nature*, 359, 60-64.

Hinton GE (1986) Learning Distributed Representations of Concepts. In: *Proceedings of the Eighth Annual Meeting of the Cognitive Science Society*. Lawrence Erlbaum Associates, Hillsdale, New Jersey, pp. 1-12.

Hinton GE, Shallice T (1991) Lesioning an Attractor Network: Investigations of Acquired Dyslexia. *Psychological Review*, 98, 74-95.

Le Cun Y, Denker JS, Solla SA (1990) Optimal Brain Damage. In: *Advances in Neural Information Processing Systems 2*. Edited by Touretzky DS. San Mateo, California: Morgan Kaufmann Publishers, pp. 598-605.

Rosch E (1975) Cognitive Representations of Semantic Categories. *Journal of Experimental Psychology: General*, 104, 192-233.

Rueckl JG, Cave KR, Kosslyn SM (1989) Why are "What" and "Where" Processed by Separate Cortical Visual Systems? A Computational Investigation. *Journal of Cognitive Neuroscience*, 1, 171-186.

Rumelhart DE, Hinton GE, Williams RJ (1985) *Learning Internal Representations by Error Propagation*. Report #ICS-8506. University of California San Diego.

Sanger D (1989) *Contribution Analysis: A Technique for Assigning Responsibilities to Hidden Units in Connectionist Networks*. Report #CU-CS-435-89. University of Colorado at Boulder.

Sartori G, Job R (1988) The Oyster with Four Legs: A Neuropsychological Study on the Interaction of Visual and Semantic Information. *Cognitive Neuropsychology*, 5, 105-132.

Sejnowski TJ, Rosenberg CR (1987) *NETtalk: A Parallel Network that Learns to Read Aloud*. Report #13. The Johns Hopkins University.

Small SL, Hart J Jr., Nguyen T, Gordon B (1993) Distributed Representations of Semantic Knowledge in the Brain (abstract). *Society for Neuroscience Abstracts*, 1, 884.

Small SL, Holland AL (1991) Towards a Computational Model of Picture Naming. In: *Annual Meeting of the Academy of Aphasia*. Rome, Italy: .

Tou JT, Gonzalez RC (1974) *Pattern Recognition Principles*. New York: Addison Wesley Publishing Company.

Warrington EK, Shallice T (1984) Category Specific Semantic Impairments. *Brain*, 102, 43-63.

Zipser D, Anderson RA (1988) A Back Propagation Programmed Network that Simulates Response Properties of a Subset of Posterior Parietal Neurons. *Nature*, 33, 679-684.

# NEURAL NETWORK CODE BOOK SEARCH FOR DIGITAL SPEECH SYNTHESIS

Xingkang Li, Mohammad Bodruzzaman[1] and Harold Szu[2]

Department of Electrical Engineering
Vanderbilt University
Nashville, TN 37235

[1]Center for Neural Engineering
Tennessee State University
Nashville, TN 37209

[2]Naval Surface Warfare Center Dahlgren Division, Code R44
Silver Spring, MD 20903

## Abstract

In this paper, an efficient and fast method for code-excited linear prediction (CELP) speech coding is proposed where neural network technique is employed. In this method, the speech signal to be coded is first clustered into a small set of neighbouring signals and then the neural network based encoder is used to find the associated best matching code sequences in the code book. This set is then used as a candidate set and an exhaustive search is performed within this set to find a optimal code sequence which minimizes the perceptual error between the original speech signal and the synthetic signal. Since the candidate set is usually much smaller than the whole code book, a big saving of computation is achieved.

## 1 Introduction

Digital speech coding, data transmission and speech decoding procedure consists of designing a system that minimizes the data transmission rate (bits/second) while maintaining a certain quality of the speech. Recently, stochastic or code-excited linear predictive (CELP) coders for digital speech coding at low bit rates have been widely studied in the literature [1-6]. The CELP coders synthesize speech by filtering selected white Gaussian innovation sequences through a time-varying linear filter. The innovation sequences are selected in short blocks by exhaustive search through a code book of random sequences. Most of the complexity in the CLEP coders comes from the search used used to select an optimal innovation sequence from the code book. This CELP coders has also demonstrated the potential for producing high quality synthetic speech at bit rates as low as 4.8 kb/second [1, 4, 5]. The basic CELP coding procedure can be conveniently depicted as shown in Figure 1 [6]. The encoder consists basically of two time-varying linear recursive filters, namely, long delay predictor and short delay predictor. The transfer function of the long delay predictor can be specified by

$$P_l(z) = \frac{1}{1 + b_1 z^{-q+1} + b_2 z^{-q} + b_3 z^{-q-1}} \tag{1}$$

where $\{b_i\}$ designate the predictor coefficients and $q$ represents a delay in the range of 2-15 ms, which generally corresponds to a pitch period. Sometimes, the long delay filter can be simplified to be [2, 3]

$$P_l(z) = \frac{1}{1 + \beta z^{-L_p}}. \tag{2}$$

The short delay predictor can be represented in the z-domain as

$$P_s(z) = \frac{1}{1 + a_1 z^{-1} + \cdots + a_p z^{-p}} \tag{3}$$

where $p$ is the order of the short delay predictor and $\{a_i\}$ are the short delay predictor coefficients. Besides the prediction filter, a perceptual error weighting filter is introduced in the encoder to provide a subjectively meaningful error measure, by attenuating the frequencies where the error is perceptually less important and amplifying those frequencies where the error is perceptually more important. The transfer function of the weighting filter is expressed in terms of the short delay predictor coefficients as follows:

$$W(z) = \frac{1 + a_1 z^{-1} + \cdots + a_m z^{-m}}{1 + a_1 \gamma z^{-1} + \cdots + a_m \gamma z^{-m}} \tag{4}$$

where $\gamma$ is a parameter that controls the weighting as a function of the frequency. A $\gamma$ less than one increases the bandwidths of the poles of $W(z)$ and produces sharp dips in the weighting function in the formant regions. The parameter $\gamma$ can also be expressed as [6]

$$\gamma = e^{-2\pi\delta/f_s} \tag{5}$$

where $\delta$ is the increase in the pole bandwidths and $f_s$ is the sampling frequency. Best perceptual results have been obtained with $\delta$ between 100 and 400 Hz, which corresponds to $\gamma$ between 0.73 and 0.92 [6].

During the encoding process the parameters of both filters are adapted in a period $T_f$ of 10-25 ms [2]. Then for each prespecified $T_c$, usually 4-6 ms, an optimal excitation is selected from a code book of white Gaussian sequences to achieve the minimum perceptual error between the original speech signal and the synthetic signal generated by the prediction filter [4], [2]. The index of the optimal code, together with the scale factor and the coefficients of the prediction filter, are then transmitted over the channel to the receiving decoder where signal is reconstructed in aa inverse procedure.

## 2 Problem Specification

The main difficulty with the CELP coders is the required computation to perform the exhaustive search to select the optimal excitation from the code book which amounts to 120-160 million operations per second (MOPS) [2]. The search procedure can be briefly stated as follows: given a code book $C$ of $L$ possible code sequences $\{c_i\}$, each of length $N$, choose the one which, when properly scaled and convolved with the impulse response of the prediction filter, will approximate the original signal $s$ with the minimum perceptual error. Let $\{h(n)\}$ and $\{w(n)\}$ designate the impulse responses of the prediction filter and the perceptual error weighting filter respectively, then the perceptual error between the original speech signal and the synthetic signal generated by passing the $i^{th}$ code sequence $c_i$ through the prediction filter can be specified by

$$\epsilon_i = \|Ws - \mu_i W H c_i\|_2^2 \tag{6}$$

where $W$ and $H$ are $N \times N$ lower triangular Toeplitz matrices defined respectively by

$$W = \begin{bmatrix} w(0) & 0 & \cdots & 0 \\ w(1) & w(0) & \cdots & 0 \\ \vdots & \vdots & \ddots & 0 \\ w(N-1) & w(N-2) & \cdots & w(0) \end{bmatrix} \tag{7}$$

and

$$H = \begin{bmatrix} h(0) & 0 & \cdots & 0 \\ h(1) & h(0) & \cdots & 0 \\ \vdots & \vdots & \ddots & 0 \\ h(N-1) & h(N-2) & \cdots & h(0) \end{bmatrix}. \tag{8}$$

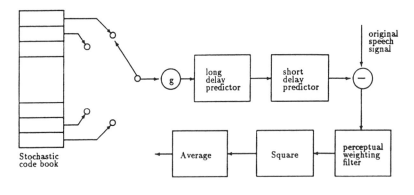

ENCODER

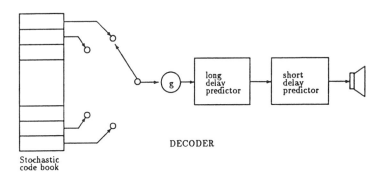

DECODER

Figure 1: CELP block diagram.

The optimal scale factor $\mu_i$ that minimizes $\epsilon_i$ can be determined by setting $\partial\epsilon_i/\partial\mu_i = 0$, which is given by

$$\mu_i = \frac{\underline{s}^T W^T W H \underline{c_i}}{\|W H \underline{c_i}\|_2^2} \tag{9}$$

and this leads to

$$\epsilon_i = \|W\underline{s}\|_2^2 - \frac{(\underline{s}^T W^T W H \underline{c_i})^2}{\|W H \underline{c_i}\|_2^2} \tag{10}$$

With this in mind, the best matching code sequence can then be obtained by either solving the problem

$$\min_{\underline{c_i}} \{\|W\underline{s}\|_2^2 - \frac{(\underline{s}^T W^T W H \underline{c_i})^2}{\|W H \underline{c_i}\|_2^2}\} \tag{11}$$

or the equivalent problem

$$\max_{\underline{c_i}} \frac{(\underline{s}^T W^T W H \underline{c_i})^2}{\|W H \underline{c_i}\|_2^2}. \tag{12}$$

The large computational complexity comes from the presence of the convolution operation represented by $W$ and $H$. An exhaustive search can result in more than twenty thousand operations per sample which is much beyond the processing capabilities of the present digital signal processors for real time operation [6]. Thus, it is interesting to improve the efficiency of code search procedure.

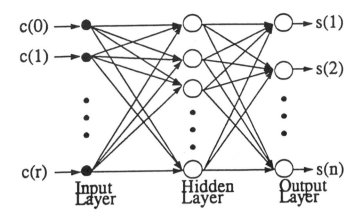

Figure 2: Standard Two-Layer Feedforward Neural Network

## 3  The Proposed Neural Network Based Encoder

A standard one hidden layer feed forward neural network is trained as a mean squared error encoder for a particular code book. The activation function of the neural network is simply selected to be the sigmoid function

$$g(x) = a\frac{1}{1 + e^{-bx}} \tag{13}$$

where both $a$ and $b$ are constants. For a code book $C$ of $L$ white Gaussian code sequences $\{c_i\}$ with length $N$, The number of the input nodes of the neural network is chosen to be $N$ and the number of the output nodes is selected to be the integer $M \geq log_2 L$. Given any normalized sequence $s$ of length $N$, the neural network is required to output an $M$ digits binary sequence representing the index of the best matching code sequence which minimized the mean squared error

$$\epsilon_i = \|s - c_i\|_2^2 \quad \text{for } i = 1, 2, \cdots, L. \tag{14}$$

It should be noted that each code sequence in the code book is normalized such that

$$\|c_i\|_2 = 1 \quad \text{for } i = 1, 2, \cdots, L. \tag{15}$$

To train the neural network, the code sequences in the code book are used as the input vectors and their indices are used as the targets. The training pairs can be formally specified by

$$c_i \Longrightarrow i_b \quad \text{for } i = 1, 2, \cdots, L. \tag{16}$$

where $i_b$ is a binary sequence of length $M$, representing the index $i$. The neural network can be further trained by any set of normalized white Gaussian sequences of length $N$. For each of these sequences, a best matching code sequence and the associated index can be found by exhaustive searching. Then the training pairs can be constructed in the same way as defined in relationship (16). This pretrained neural network is then ready to be used on line for real time encoding.

## 4  Random Code Search Algorithm

With the neural network based encoder described in the last section, an efficient and fast algorithm can be developed for the code search procedure. The basic idea is to define a small candidate set in the code book and search only the code sequences within this set instead of the whole code book. In this algorithm, the original speech signal is first clustered into a small set of neighbouring signals and then the neural network based encoder is used to find the associated best matching code sequences in the code book. This set can then be used as a candidate set and an exhaustive search is performed within this set to find a optimal code sequence which minimizes the mean squared error defined by (6). Since the candidate set is usually much smaller than the whole code book, a big saving of computation is achieved.

A given piece of original signal $\underline{s}$ can be considered as the convolution of an excitation or residual $\underline{x}$ with the impulse response of the prediction filter. The normalized residual $\underline{x}$ can be represented by

$$\underline{x} = \frac{H^{-1}\underline{s}}{\|H^{-1}\underline{s}\|_2} \tag{17}$$

The index of the best matching code sequence for $\underline{x}$ can be found directly by the neural network based encoder and the code itself can be obtained by addressing the code book. Let $\underline{c}_j$ designate this best matching code, then the perceptual error between $\underline{s}$ and $H\underline{c}$ is specified by

$$\epsilon = \|W\underline{s}\|_2^2 - \frac{(\underline{s}^T W^T W H\underline{c}_j)^2}{\|WH\underline{c}\|_2^2} \tag{18}$$

Usually, $\epsilon$ is not the minimum error and a smaller error is wanted. With $\epsilon$ as the radius, an $\epsilon$-ball can be generated around the point $W\underline{s}$. By randomly selecting $K$ points on the surface of the $\epsilon$-ball, we can obtain a set of neighbouring points of $W\underline{s}$ which are expressed as

$$W\underline{s} + \epsilon\underline{v}_i \quad \text{for } i = 1, 2, \cdots, K \tag{19}$$

where $\{\underline{v}_i\}$ are normalized white Gaussian sequences of length $N$. These sequences can be randomly selected from the code book. The normalized residuals for the signals $\{\underline{s} + \epsilon_j W^{-1}\underline{v}_i\}$ can be similarly represented by

$$\underline{x}_i = \frac{H^{-1}\underline{s} + H^{-1}W^{-1}\underline{v}_i}{\|H^{-1}\underline{s} + H^{-1}W^{-1}\underline{v}_i\|_2} \quad \text{for } i = 1, 2, \cdots, K \tag{20}$$

and their associated best matching code sequences can be found by using the neural network based encoder and the code book. These code sequences, designated by $\{\underline{c}_i\}$, can be considered as candidates for the code search, since the other code sequence will in general be farer away from $\underline{x}$ and produce larger perceptual error.

To test the proposed algorithm, a code book of 1024 white Gaussian sequences of length 40 was generated using MATLAB. The codes and their indices of this code book were used as the input vectors and targets for the training of a standard one hidden layer feed forward neural network. This neural network has 40 input nodes, 30 hidden nodes and 10 output nodes. To accelerate the training speed, a multi-direction search training algorithm is employed [7]. The mean squared training error is 0.5This trained neural network was then used as a mean squared error encoder as proposed. The speech signals were simulated by filtered white Gaussian sequences of length 40. For each simulated signal, a candidate set of 20 code sequence was generated by randomly perturbing the signal in a small scale. Upon 100 trails, the algorithm reached the minimum perceptual error 83 times. An example of a real speech signal and the CELP synthetic speech signal is shown in Figure 3.

# 5 Conclusion

In this paper, the well developed neural network technique is applied to the application of digital speech coding and it results in a very efficient code search algorithm. Although the result is not

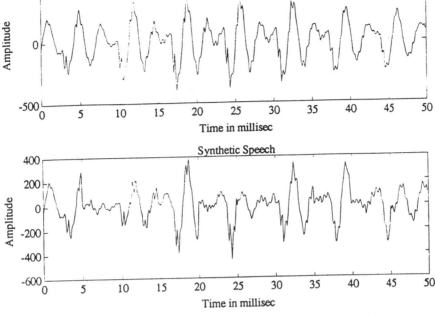

Figure 3: Spech Waveform: Original and Synthetic.

yet perfect (83% success rate), we think it is intersting to continue the investigation. Using neural network can make a larger code book possible and therefore improve the speech coding and systhesis technology.

# References

[1] B. Atal and M. Schroeder, "Stochastic coding of speech signals at very low bit rates," in proceedings of IEEE International Conference on Communication –ICC'84, Amsterdam, The Netherlands, 1984, part 2, pp. 1610-1613.

[2] M. Ahmed and M. Al-Suwaiyel, "Fast Methods for Code Search in CELP," IEEE Transactions on Speech and Audio Processing, vol. 1, no. 3, pp. 315-325, Jan. 1993.

[3] R. Ramachandran and P. Kabal, "Pitch prediction filters in speech coding," IEEE Transactions on Acoustics, Speech, and Signal Processing, vol. ASSP-37, pp. 467-478, Apr. 1989.

[4] M. Schroeder and B. Atal, "Code-excited linear prediction (CELP): high-quality speech at very low bit rates," in Proceedings of the International Conference on Acoustics, Speech, and Signal Processing, vol. 2, pp. 937-940, Mar. 1985.

[5] M. Schroeder and B. Atal, "Stochastic coding of speech signals at very low bit rates: the importance of speech perception," Speech Communication, vol. 4, pp. 155-162, Aug. 1985.

[6] I. Trancoso and B. Atal, "Efficient Search procedures for selecting the optimal innovation in stochastic coders," IEEE Transactions on Acoustics, Speech, and Signal Processing, vol. ASSP-38, pp. 385-395, Mar. 1990.

[7] C. Wang, M. Bodruzzaman, and X. Li,, "Multi-directional search learning algorithms for the modified feed forward neural network," Proceedings of Canadian Conference on Electrical & Computer Engineering, Toronto, Ontario, TM6.12.1, Sept. 1992.

# CONCEPT PREDICTION FOR SPONTANEOUS SPEECH RETRANSCRIPTION

Adélaïde Stévenin, Patrick Gallinari

LAFORIA IBP- UA CNRS 1095
Tour 46-00, Case 169
Université Pierre et Marie Curie
4 Place Jussieu - 75252 Paris cedex 05 - France
stevenin@laforia.ibp.fr, gallinari@laforia.ibp.fr

**Abstract**

The paper investigates the potential of recurrent neural networks for the decoding of semantic concepts from word sequences. We have designed a system for dealing with spontaneous sentences on domain limited tasks, and tests have been performed on an Air Travel Information System decoding task. We analyse the behavior of the network on these ungrammatical queries, and discuss its robustness against incomplete or erroneous inputs.

# 1. Introduction

Predictive Neural Network (NN) systems have been used for sequence processing tasks in different domains. Most applications consist in training NN as production systems for modelizing the unknown process underlying the sequence. Such systems have shown good performances for low level modelization, e. g. time series prediction [1] or speech production [2]. On the other hand, their accuracy usually drops out when processing higher level knowledge sources, e.g. words.

We are interested here in developping NN sub-systems for language processing. Real-life applications raise difficult problems in natural language. Grammatically incorrect sentences or speech recognizer errors are difficult to handle. Being trained from observable data, NN may deal with real situations without involving specialized analysis or relying on grammars. When used alone, they can only handle tasks of limited complexity for language processing, but they sometimes present advantages over more complex classical approaches and offer good performances while avoiding linguistic expertise. Also, they may be used as specialized modules in more complex systems. Last, NN offer a unified formalism for different levels in language processing, allowing the integration of e.g. speech and language processing steps.

We will deal here with concept decoding and prediction in word sequences corresponding to spontaneous sentences. Our application concernes non grammatical queries for flight ticket reservation. Although language involves much more than prediction, it plays an important role. Correct prediction relies on the discovering of regularities (e.g. lexical categories, grammatical or semantic structure) in the temporal structure of sentences. Recurrent NN are natural candidates for these applications and are surprisingly powerful tools for dealing with simple tasks. They have shown their ability to learn lexico-semantic form classes and simple constituant structure markers [3]. They have been used for filling-in unaltered word patterns into slots [4] or implementing a surface-to-semantic transducer [5], i.e. for mapping sequence of words to their corresponding semantic representation. Recently [6] used a simple recurrent network for converting acoustic or orthographic representations of large numbers into convenient semantic representations. Networks with local recurrent connections are only able to build short term representation of past events [7] and are rather poor at word prediction. This is not such a severe limitation since accuracy measures are not always significant for the task and we believe that such systems are capable of extracting useful information.

Let us discuss a simple example of the flight reservation task. When hearing the beginning of a user's request, e.g. "I would like to go ..." one can infer that the next word will probably be "to" or "from". One step further, we can decide whether what follows will indicate the origin or destination of the flight, i.e. we have insights of what might be said next, but not on the exact formulation. Only few concepts may be associated to the next few words of such sentences. They are defined through structural constraints imposed by the temporal sequence. Although they may represent broad categories they are specific, e.g. "john" cannot be an instance of any of these concepts. Thus, we can guess the class or concept corresponding to forthcoming words even when the particular instance of the class is not.

It seems that the conceptual domain constrains syntactic form to be motivated by the conceptual structure it conveys. Though ungrammatical, the data has an oriented structure determined both by syntactic needs (go will determine the next word to be a preposition) and task goals (fill in a reservation form).

The paper is organized as follows : we describe the task we are dealing with in 2 , we present our system in 3 and in 4 tests on a text database.

## 2.. The decoding task

The application deals with the limited domain of airline reservation from a retranscription of spontaneous speech requests. This task corresponds to a part of the standard evaluation domain ATIS (Air Travel Information System) chosen by DARPA for spoken language systems [8]. It deals with general problems such as generic database query and interactive problem solving. Our data comes from the EEC SUNDIAL project which is aimed at task oriented dialogues. We have used the French part of the database, which has been gathered for a flight reservation task. The same approach could be used for designing modules for other ATIS subtasks. It relies on the following hypothesis :

- the sentence meaning can be reduced to a sequence of basic meaning units
- the correspondance between these units and the underlying word sequence respects the sequentiality.

The flight reservation task amounts at extracting from spontaneous speech requests relevant information to fill in reservation forms. We have proceeded in two steps. First, we produce a segmentation of the sentence into conceptual labels. We then exploit the constraints which are inherent to each segment to extract in a second step instances which are relevant for the task. We will deal here only with the first step which produces an intermediate conceptual representation of the sentence.

Consider a typical sentence like : "I would like to go from boston to chicago with a departure on october the 20th, early morning and a return on next saturday. My name is <name>." A conceptual segmentation of the sentence would be :

| | |
|---|---|
| **Query :** | *I would like to go* |
| **Origin :** | *from* <city-name> |
| **Destination :** | *to* <city-name> |
| **Departure Date :** | *with a departure on* october the 20th, early morning |
| **Return Date :** | *and a return on* next saturday |
| **Identity :** | *My name is* <name> |

This representation is the basis for extracting a set of attribute-value pairs needed for the reservation form, e.g (origin, <city-name>) (destination, <city-name>).

Our system has been conceived both for the association of concepts to words and for prediction of concepts (see Figure 1 a). While our goal is word-concept association, prediction can be used to reduce the effective search space during acoustic decoding.

## 3.    System architecture

A system for conceptual decoding should be able to take both word and concept contexts into account. It must deal with the simultaneous use of information from different knowledge levels and time dependent data.

Predictive systems with local recurrent connections may build a short memory of past inputs and outputs and are therefore good candidates for this. Although they do have limited capabilities, they offer a good compromise between time processing abilities and computational efficiency.

Our system uses past output (concept) as well as current input (words) to compute the current output (fig.1). Recurrent connections in this system implement a nonlinear recursive filter upon the output of the feedforward network. To include the recursive property, a weighted sum of the past outputs is used. The corresponding general formula (1) with f(k) an input signal at time k, and g(k) the corresponding output is :

$$g_m = \sum_{n=1}^{N} b_n f_{m-n} - \sum_{n=0}^{N} a_n g_{m-n} \qquad (1)$$

Training has been performed via back-propagation through time [9], i.e. the recurrent network is unfolded in time and feed forward connections corresponding to the same recurrent connection share common weights. Sentence length determines the size of the network spread-out. The same system has been used for longer sequences in other applications and should be able to handle e.g. phoneme strings extracted from speech data.

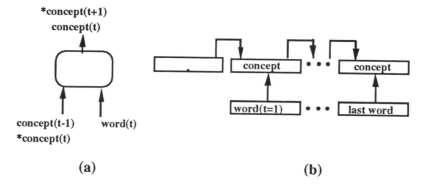

**(a)**            **(b)**

*Figure 1 : system architecture, (a) shows inputs and outputs for prediction and association tasks. They differ by the rank of the conceptsassociated to the word inputs ,(\*) holds for prediction task. (b) is an unfolded description of the recurrent architecture. The empty leftmost box corresponds to initial conditions. The system is completely unfolded before weight modification . The corresponding recurrent connections act as a short term memory.*

# 4. Tests

## 4.1 Classical coding scheme

Our system has been tested on a conceptual segmentation and prediction task. The data comes from a text re-transcription of the french SUNDIAL database. The corpus of this database was built from 300 transcribed dialogues, involving utterances from 26 users, and 16 concepts for the representation of the task-knowledge. We have considered utterances corresponding to the system open question "Formulate your demand" which amounts to about 200 utterances from the 26 users and the 16 concepts. There are no constraints on the user except his need to complete the task, and he can give any information, in any order : the question does not determine the structure of the answer. The sentences are preprocessed using classical choices in the ATIS domain [10]. Some words are simplified (verbs are taken as infinitives), others are clustered (articles and the following word), compound expressions are converted into hyphenated compound expressions (en date du -> endatedu). In order to limit vocabulary during testing, we grouped under labeled variables the parameters whose values are subject to unpredictable changes (proper nouns).

Two thirds of the database was used for learning after manual segmentation, and one third for testing. Keeping for each output the N best scores allows to build a lattice of candidates. Because previous events in the sentence impose strong constraints on current labels, the number of concepts may be kept small (2 or 3) for each time step. The local memory due to the recurrent connections takes into account these constraints. It is however often impossible to give a preference to one concept at a given time. This ambiguity will be resolved later by considering upcoming predictions and searching the lattice.

| k-first candidates | Association word(t) - concept(t) | | Prediction word(t) - concept(t+1) | |
|---|---|---|---|---|
| | correct % | C. I. 95% | correct % | C.I. 95% |
| 1 | 88.24% | [86.99,89.38] | 84.20% | [82.76,85.55] |
| 2 | 94.15% | [93.22,94.96] | 93.26% | [92.24,94.15] |
| 3 | 96.22% | [95.45,96.87] | 95.42% | [94.55,96.15] |

*Table 1: Results of cross validation for association and prediction. Different performances have been computed by considering the answer correct if among the k highest output for k = 1..3. C. I. holds for confidence interval.*

Table 1 shows the performances of our system for both association and prediction tasks. The high accuracy shows that for these un-grammatical sentences, the system can indeed extract symbolic information from low level data without using domain expertise. For a limited domain task, regularities extracted from word sequences allow to infer semantic information. The structure of each request is subordinated to task semantic, which is usually used to set up strong expectations for particular sentence structures. Structural connections between the syntactic structure and the semantic one provide a way of selecting among competing analyses.

The architecture reflects the imbrication of the word-context and the concept-context structure, and uses both type of information through recurrent connections. Without recurrent connections the system reaches a peak around 70% for the best candidate.

## 4.2 Sensitivity to input coding

Up to now, the coding we have used supposes we have been able to :

      1. identify lexical elements (verbs)
      2. label city and person names as proper names
      3. label days and months as dates.
      4. identify numerical data as such.

Although 1 to 4 are classical hypothesis for such systems [10], they are invalidated in many real speech or text systems. We have tested the influence of these hypothesis on the behavior and performances of the system. This allows to evaluate the resistance of the system to corrupting noise, transcription or identification errors and to investigate how accurate word identification should be. In order to do this, we have used different word encodings which relax the above hypothesis.

Consider the simple sentence shown in table 2. In a first coding (code 1) proper nouns (city and person) and indexed words (date) are replaced with a single code *, i.e. the only distinction left is with numbers. In a second coding, hypothesis 2 to 4 are identified under a single code without distinction. Only the structure of the sentence and word context differentiate among them.

| Original | *name *name must go to *city on *date *num *num at *num hour with flight *num |
|---|---|
| Code 1 | * * must go to * on * *num *num at *num hour with flight *num |
| Code 2 | * * must go to * on * * * at * hour with flight * |

*Table 2 : first row represents the original coding used for experiments in §4.1. Codes 1 and 2 eliminate the distinction between several word classes and are less informative about word nature.*

|  | original (1000 iterations ) | code 1 (1500 iterations) | code 2 (1500 iterations) |
|---|---|---|---|
| **Association** | 90.34 % | 84.69 % | 83.54% |
| **Prediction** | 87.68 % | 81.26 % | 80.39 % |

*Table 3 : Performances for the three word codings for association and prediction tasks. We have reported here best results instead of cross-validation as in table 1.*

Results for association appear in table 3. Compared to the original coding the system is resistant to the loss of information and performances only degrade slightly for such an important loss. This shows that the system is robust to errors which may occur in previous text or speech processing steps. Also, because we only need a raw labeling of the data for our system, these processing steps may be simplified.

A closer look at the local errors (fig. 2) shows that many peaks occur during transitions between concepts. Syntactical markers usually determine these transitions. Though important for the processing and the passage from one concept to the other, they will not be used as form fillers and will not be considered as relevant for the second step. Such decoding errors during the first step are thus not important for the extraction of useful information and being unable to predict these particular instances is not limitative for this task driven system. We aim at extracting the values needed to fill in the target representation and not at reasoning with the knowledge contained in the linguistic expressions.

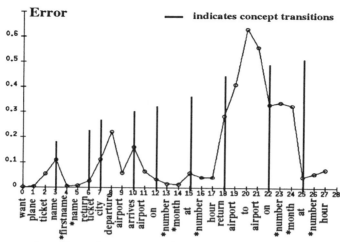

Figure 2 : local errors for each word-concept association on a coded sentence from the database. Bars indicate concept transitions.

Results in table 4 show the error for task filler words. Because concept transition are subject to higher error rates and relevant words for the task seldom appear on transitions, system performances slightly increase when considering only these words.

| Performances on : | Prediction (origin code) | Association (origin code) |
|---|---|---|
| all words | 85.34 % | 88.60% |
| relevant words | 87.069% | 90.77% |
| other words | 84.29% | 87.28% |

Table 4 : Comparison between performances on task-relevant words and the others depending on the task (association or prediction) and the type of coding.

# 5.. Discussion

This paper describes the use of predictive NNs whose recurrent part has a non linear recursive filter structure, for a conceptual clustering task. It validates a new approach to concept extraction which may be an alternative or a complement to more traditional developments. [10] proposes a speech understanding system based on statistical representation of task specific semantic knowledge which uses Hidden Markov Models. Both systems rely on statistical feature extraction and allow the integration of successive processing levels for speech understanding. Our approach takes the context into account more easily, and performs accurate prediction with a much smaller number of parameters. The conceptual approach presents advantages : ambiguities can be avoided since some interpretations do not make sense for the task, each parameter can only be filled-in once syntactic issues which do not affect the task can be ignored.

Implementation in a larger system would require more informations. The linguistic properties of coherent discourse could provide additional mechanisms for focusing. As the structure of our task-oriented discourse typically mirrors the structure of the task, we are thinking of choosing a kind of best path among the output probabilities.

A second property of coherent discourse is that dramatic changes of focus are usually signaled explicitly with phrases. In a way, the various prepositions play that role, taking place at the transitions between concepts. If we focus on task information, we don't need to label these phrases even though they determine the changes, which is a good point since the curves of the local-error rate by word for each sentence show peaks at the transitions .

We are currently working on the integration of the system outputs for choosing the best coherent request.

*Acknowledgments : we would like to thank Cap Gemini Innovation for allowing us to use the text version of the SUNDIAL french database for test purposes , and Neuristique SA for their simulator.*

# 6.. References

1    **Lapedes A., Farber R.**(87)-*"Nonlinear signal processing using neural networks: prediction and system modelling"*, preprint, LA-UR-87-2662,

2    **Mellouk A., Gallinari P.**(93)-*"A discriminative neural prediction system for speech recognition"*, ICASSP 93.

3    **Elman J.**(1988)- *"Finding Structure in Time"*, UCSD report.

4    **Mikkulainen R., Dyer M.**(1989)*3A modular neural network architecture for sequential paraphrasing of script-based stories"*, IJCNN 89.

5    **Stolcke A.**(1988)- *"Learning feature-based semantics with Simple Recurrent Networks"*, ICSI T-R 90-015, April 1990.

6    **Castana M.A, Vidal E., Casacuberta F.**(1988)- *"Learning direct acoustic-to-semantic mapping"*, ICSI T-R 90-015, April 1990

7    **Frasconi P., Gori M., Soda G.**(1988)*"Local Feedback Multilayered Networks"*, ICSI T-R 90-015, April 1990.

8    **Price P.J.**(1990)-*"Evaluation of Spoken Language Systems : The ATIS domain"* Proc. 3rd DARPA Workshop on Speech and Natural Language.

9    **Rumelhart D.E., Hinton G.E., Williams R.J.**(1986)- *"Learning internal representations by error propagation"*, PDP, chap 8.

10   **Pieraccini R., Tzoukermann E., Gorelov Z., Gauvain J.L, Levin E., Lee C.H, Wilpon J.G**(92)-*"A Speech Understanding System Based on Statistical Representation of Semantics"*, ICASSP 92, San Francisco CA.

# Recognizing Norwegian Vowels
# using
# Neural Network

Åge J. Eide and Terje Lindén
Ostfold College
N-1759 Halden

Thomas Lindblad
Manne Siegbahn Institute of Physics
Stockholm

**Abstract**: A speaker dependent neural network system that recognize the nine Norwegian vowels has been developed. The system generates a FFT frequency spectrum of the speech sound, bins this spectrum and uses the amplitudes of the bins as input to the neural network. The network is correct in more than 99 % of the trials, following the training.

## 1. Introduction

Speech recognition is a topic that is easy to understand, but difficult to define. The problem of definition is basically a two-level problem. The human intelligence is related to the "upper level", while the "lower level" problem is a problem of establishing parameters, etc. These parameters are needed to describe the speech sound, or rather an "average" speech sound. To establish the permissible deviation from these "average" values, the subjective "upper level", i.e. the human intelligence has to be approached. How much will any of the parameters be allowed to deviate from their "average" value, before the sound become "unacceptable", and do these limits depend upon each other?

Generally speaking, there seems to be two techniques applied to speech recognition experiments today. Those are the Hidden Markov Model (HMM), and Neural Networks (NN). A review of the use of neural network in speech recognition, as well as reference to works using other methods, up to 1989, may be found in ref [1], as well as details in refs [2-8]. For the HMM and other approaches, the reader is referred to refs. [9-24]. The developed systems deals with recognition of the relative simple sound of phonemes (vowels, or single letters) [2 -6, 23, 24], isolated words, digits [2,7,8,10-13,15-19,21,22]. The systems may be speaker dependent [2-5,14,21,23] or speaker independent [6-8,10-13,15-19,22,24].

A salient feature of speech sound, is the dynamics involved. With that we mean that in ordinary speech, a specific phoneme, a specific vowel, lasts a very short time span, and, most of the speech sound consists of the *changes* from one phoneme to the next. The phonemes themselves is clearly present for only say 10 % of the time. The dynamics in speech sound have received quite a bit of attention in recent works [3, 5,6,8,19].

In this experiment we aim at establishing a very simple neural network system for recognizing Norwegian vowels. The knowledge to be gained in this development, is intended to be used as a platform to dynamic systems, recognizing more complex speech sound. Details will be given on the experimental set-up, testing and results.

## 2. Experimental set-up

### 2.1 GENERAL

The hardware used in the present work consists of a 386/387 microcomputer, and a laboratory microphone, with amplifier connected to an 8 kHz A/D converter with 16 bits resolution. The relatively low frequency may be said to correspond to that of a telephone system. The digitalized amplitudes values are read by a signalprocessor (ZPB32-HS), on a card equipped with 56 kb memory. The signal processor performs the FFT, and presents the real and imaginary part of the frequency spectrum to the microcomputer buss. The microcomputer then performs the processing through the neural network.

The software may be divided into three parts. The first part takes care of the sampling of the sound, performs the FFT, and arranges the results for the next step. This is all done in the assembly language of the signal processor, using factory provided FFT routines. The results may now be used either to train the neural network (second part of the software) or to serve as arguments for a processing network (part 3).

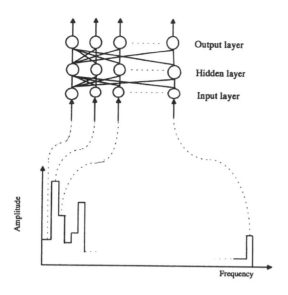

*Figure 1.*

*The input to the neural network is given by the amplitude of each bin in the frequency spectrum. The output layer had 9 nodes, one for each vowel. In the final version, 64 nodes were used in the input layer, one node for each bin.*

The neural network employed here is of the feedforward type with one hidden layer (cf. fig. 1). The input layer is arranged in such a way that there is one input node for each bin in the frequency spectrum. By varying the bin width, the number of bins, and hence the number of inputs nodes, are changed. In the present investigation, the numbers are varied by 64 to 512. The DA converter has a fixed sample rate of 8 kHz, representing a cut in frequency well above all dominant frequencies in speech sound. The minimum bin width provided from the software in this set-up was 8 Hz. Each input node will receive a value corresponding to the amplitude of the pertinent bin. The number of outputs is determined by the number of vowels. As there are 9 vowel in the Norwegian language, there are 9 output nodes in the neural network, each representing one of the vowels. The number of nodes in the hidden layer is determined by the "thumb rule", i.e. the average value of the nodes in the input and the output layers. The transfer function in the nodes is chosen to be a sigmoid function, $f(x) = 1/(1+e^{-x})$. The output will thus range from small positive values, to a value close to unity.

The training of the neural network (part 2 of the software) follows the standard back propagation algorithm. We found it beneficial to start out with a relatively "large" learning rate, 2 or 3 say, and in the end, when approaching convergence, to decrease the learning rate bye a factor 10 say, to 0.2 or 0.5. The training is stopped when all the right classes have outputs greater than 0.9, whereas all the other outputs are smaller than 0.1. The network is then considered to be fully trained and ready to operate in feedforward mode (part 3 of the software).

## 2.2 MOTIVATION FOR EXPERIMENTAL PROCEDURES

In this experiment we have chosen to work with Norwegian vowels. The Norwegian vowels are all steady state, like the English "e". This means that they all generate a set of fairly similar spectra. An example of such a spectrum is shown in figure 2. Here the first periods of the vowel "o" is shown as pressure amplitude *versus* time. The periods of such a vowel, as shown in figure 2, stay very similar throughout the whole utterance, as this figure indicate, where about the first 10 periods are shown. This fact is illustrated in Figure 3, where one period, 19, is compared with different periods through the utterance, from period 19 to period 61.

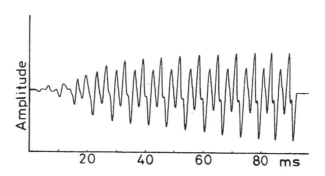

*Figure 2*

*Pressure amplitude versus time of the steady state Norvigian vowel "o".*

We emphasize that these vowels are spoken with what might be called a stable voice. A person with a "trained ear", or with a natural ability, is able to repeatedly reproduce the same patterns for the vowels. However, if the vowels are spoken differently they will, of course, also look different in the time domain, as illustrated in figure 4. In this figure is shown one period from 4 different utterances of the Norwegian vowel "o", and the vowel "i", by the same person. In both cases are shown utterances ranging from high frequencies (a) to low frequencies (d), with the "normal ones" in between (b and c).

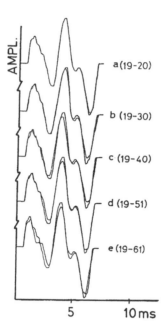

*Figure 3*

*An illustration of the stability which may exist in speech sound. Period 19 is compared with later periods, from period 20 to period 61, in the utterance of the steady state Norwegian vowel "o".*

It is quite clear from these figures that inputs to the network, from the time domain, is not a good solution. Firstly, for many vowels it is very difficult to establish where a period starts, which makes it difficult to obtain unique combinations to the input nodes. Secondly, as shown in figure 4, even if the start of a period is known, there is a very large set of alternatives a neural network must recognize, depending upon the utterance of the vowel.

On the other hand, if we were to use a frequency spectrum as input to the neural network, the amount of possible input data to the neural network would be reduced significantly. It may be seen from figure 2, that rather few frequencies would be present for a specific vowel. Furthermore, and as may be clear from figure 3, the spectrum would practically be the same, no matter where the sampling was performed in the time domain. Only in the "extreme" cases (a and d of fig. 4) will the frequency peaks be shifted (fig. 4) and new peaks appear (fig. 5).

We would like to stress that to achieve a good result for the neural network application, it is very important to understand how the frequencies in this spectrum appear. Only when the number of input nodes is balanced against the bin width in the frequency spectrum, the shift in the frequencies, etc, do we obtain optimum results.

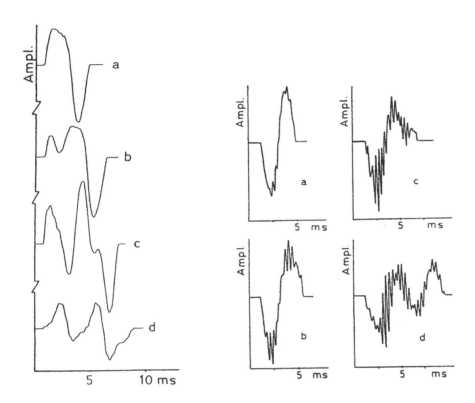

*Figure 4.*

*One period from the speech sound from 4 different utterances of the Norwegian vowels "o" (left) and "i". Figure a) show a high frequency utterance from a male speaker, whereas figure d) show the "lowest" possible from this person. Figure b) and c) is in between, and more "normal".*

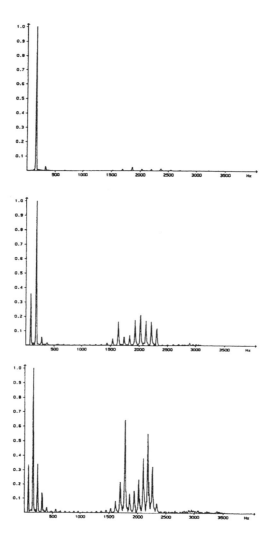

*Figure 5.*

*The frequency spectrum of the Norwegian vowel "i", as calculated by our set-up. The top spectrum represents an utterance like the one in figure 4a, and the next two like the ones in figure 4b, and d, respectively.*

## 2.3 EXPERIMENTAL DETAILS

In spite of the problems related to the lack of definitions, an experiment was attempted that would be reproducible. Furthermore, we decided to perform the experiment in an ordinary laboratory, where other activities were going on at the same time, creating some "general" noise. As we already were in a situation of subjective judgement about such important parameters as quality of the speech sound, it was felt that one might as well stay on this empirical level, as far as background noise was concerned.

### 2.3.1 Designing the neural network

Before data is presented to a neural network it is very important to study the data in detail. The reason is that training algorithms do depend on the data. In back propagation the change or adjustment of the weights is proportional to the input value of the node. This implies that, if the input to a node is zero, or close to zero, no adjustment of those related weights are performed during the training. Hence, the weights will not be the subject to any constraints. If this is also the case during operation, there will be no problems. However, if the network instead is fed with non-zero values to those input nodes that during training always received zero input, one may easily end up with wrong results. The usual ability of neural network to handle a reasonable amount of "slack" in operation, and still end up with the correct result is thus reduced somewhat for the situations, where one has many zero inputs. As can be seen from fig. 5, this is just what we have in our case.

If was found that the best way to overcome this problem was to increase the bin width. Then a shift in the frequency peaks would usually keep the peak within the same bin. In our case we reduced the number of bins from 512 to 64. This corresponds to an increase of the frequency interval of each bin from 8 Hz to 64 Hz. Reducing the number of bins below 64 made it difficult to separate the vowels. This method was also found more promising than the alternative, which was to increase the number of training vectors to insure that most of the frequency bins had been "seen" in the training. Using this latter approach, it was difficult to train the network.

### 2.3.2 Training the neural network.

The training system consists of two parts. The first part deals with establishing the training vectors, the frequency spectra of the vowels, for the neural network. The second part is related to the use of these vectors as input to a back propagation code. In this way we will establish a set of weights in the neural network, that make proper functioning possible. The salient features c the above mentioned first part were four fold:

*i) Pronounce a randomly chosen vowel.*

We found that it was possible to remember the way a sound is pronounced. We also feel it is possible that the way one pronounces a vowel may depend upon what was said previously. In view of this, a computer program told the participant which vowel should be pronounced. There was also a pause of 20 seconds between each utterance.

*ii) Frequency spectrum, calculation and storing.*

The frequency spectrum was calculated, and stored in the memory, immediately after the utterance of the vowel. This was performed without noticeable delay. The frequency spectrum is now referred to as the input vector. It has 64 elements, representing amplitudes in 64 frequency intervals, between 0 and 4000 Hz.

*iii) Stop for the day - if 25 vowels are reached.*

To avoid effects due to the participant getting bored, or even tired, we decided to perform only a few registrations each day. Hence, the experiment was stopped when 25 registrations had been performed and resumed, at the earliest, one day later.

*iv) Stop the registrations - when 250 vowels are reached.*

Following some testing it was concluded that it was sufficient with about 10 training vectors for each vowels were sufficient. We thus stopped the registration when 250 training vectors had been registered. These were now stored in computer memory, and constituted the complete set of training vectors. We note that these training vectors were established without any possibility for the participant to interfere, and so avoided biases.

### 2.3.3 Testing the neural network

The testing of the neural network followed essentially the procedure mentioned above for the training. The vowel to be tested was generated by the computer system at random, and the participant was "asked" to pronounce that specific vowel, by means of a message on the computer screen. When the participant responded, the system sampled the sound, preformed the FFT, and feed the result to the neural network. The result from the neural network output is then compared to the vowel just being asked for, and the result is stored in the "statistical part" of the code. This recording consists mainly of storing two numbers for each test, and each vowel: the best output, and the largest of the outputs that belongs to a "wrong" class.

## 3. Experimental results

Over some extended period of time, test series were carried out with about 200 to 500 randomly chosen instances of these vowels. It should be mentioned that the same person is used for both the training and testing samples. In all these test series there were correct results in more than 99% of the cases. Figure 6 shows the results for about 75 tests. On the y-axis is shown the test numbers, whereas on the x-axis two values are recorded, the output from the node representing the vowel being tested, and the output from the node among the wrong alternatives, which had the largest output. As the node function is a sigmoid, and the network trained as described above, ideally these two value should be close to 1 and close to 0, respectively. The difference between these two values indicate how well the neural network is doing. We note that the results shown in figure 6 are typical for the performance of the system.

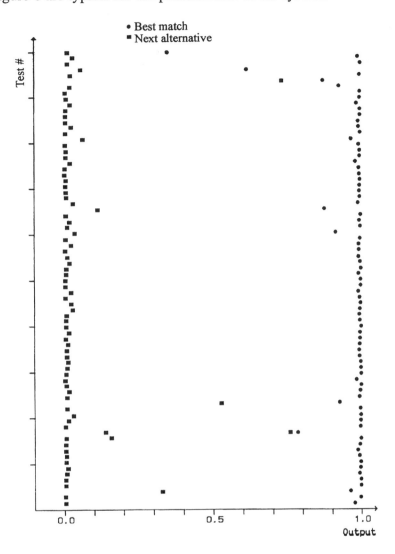

*Figure 6.*

*The two largest output values from the neural network, in the x-direction. The correct output should be as close to 1.0 as possible, whereas all the others should be as close to 0.0 as possible. The number of the tests (about 75) in the y-direction.*

Figure 7 shows the results from a complete series of 270 tests. We have here split the results into groups representing the different vowels. For each vowel there are 3 possible bins, representing:

- a correct result (defined as an output > 0.95 for the correct class, and all other outputs < 0.05) shown in the left bin in fig. 7

- a "fairly correct" result (the output which is the largest correspond to the correct one) shown in the middle bin in fig. 7
- a wrong result (the output node, representing the spoken vowel, did not have the largest output value) shown in the right bin in fig. 7

In this series, with results shown in figure 7, we had 2 wrong classifications.

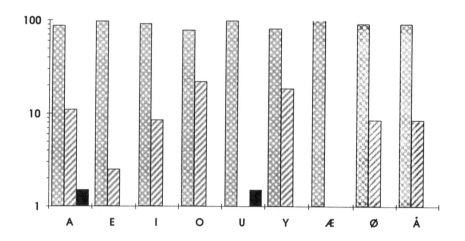

*Figure 7.*

*The results of a test series of 270 randomly chosen vowels, with results of each vowel shown separately. There are 3 columns for each vowel, with the two leftmost columns both representing correct results. The leftmost column represent those cases where the correct outputs were larger the 0.9, and at the same time all the other alternatives had output less than 0.1. The next column from left represents those cases where the solutions were correct, but where the correct output was only the largest of the alternatives. The third column from the left represents the wrong results.*

# 4. Summary and Discussion

In this experiment we have shown that neural network is a convenient tool for recognizing patterns from steady state speech sound, like Norwegian vowels. We have emphasized the importance of matching the network to the data, to optimize the performance of the network. The results show that the network has a very stable performance, with a very clear distinction between a correct and wrong answer. It may be concluded from fig. 7 that the network can handle all the nine vowels in fairly similar ways. There are no vowels that are specially difficult. Two vowels, "u" and "æ", are a bit easier to handle than the rest of the vowels.

As the data, the vowels, are somewhat specific for each language, it is hard to make comparisons between methods or experiments, analyzing speech data - like the Norwegian steady state vowels. However, one could mention that Waibel et. al [4] report on a recognition experiment of five vowels in Japanese speech using a neural network. Their work include much more extensive preprocessing than reported here (essentially a plain FFT) and a recognition rate of 98.6%, i.e. almost the same as our 99%.

## Acknowledgements

The authors would like to acknowledge comments on the manuscript by Clark Lindsey

## References

1) Richard P. Lippmann, "Review of Neural Networks for Speech Recognition", *Neural Computation,* vol 1, pp 1-38, 1989.

2) David J. Burr, "Experiments on Neural Net Recognition of Spoken and Written Text", *IEEE Trans. Acoust. Speech, Signal Processing*, vol 36, no 7, pp 1162 - 1168, July 1988.

3) Alexander Waibel, Toshiyuki Hanazawa, Geoffrey Hinton, Kiyohiro Shikano, and Kevin J.Lang, "Phonem Recognition Using Time-delay Neural Networks", *IEEE Trans. Acoust. Speech, Signal Processing*, vol 37, no3, pp 328-339, March 1989.

4) Alexander Waibel, Hidefumi Sawai, and Kiyohiro Shikano, " Modularity and Scaling in Large Phonemic Neural Networks", *IEEE Trans. Acoust. Speech, Signal Processing*, vol 37, no 12, pp1888-1898, December 1989.

5) Alex Waibel, "Modular Construction of Time-Delay Neural Networks for Speech Recognition", *Neural Computation*, vol 1, pp 39-46, 1989.

6) John B. Hampshire, II, and Alexander H. Waibel, "A Novel Objective Function for Improved Phoneme Recognition Using Time-Delay Neural Networks", *IEEE Trans. Neural Networks*, vol 1, no 2, pp 216 -228, June 1990.

7) L. Bottou, F.Fogelman Soulié, P.Blanchet, and J.S.Liénard, "Speaker-Independent Isolated Digit Recognition: Multilayer Perceptron vs. Dynamic Time Warping", *Neural Networks,* vol 3, pp453-465,1990.

8) Kevin J. Lang, Alex H. Waibel, and Geoffrey E. Hinton, "A Time-Delay Neural Network Architecture for Isolated Word Recognition", *Neural Networks*, vol 3, pp 23-43,1990.

9) J.M.Holtzman, "Automatic Speech Recognition Error/No Decission Tradeoff Curves", *IEEE Trans. Acoust. Speech, Signal Processing*, vol ASSP-32, no 6, pp 1232 - 1235, December 1984.

10) George J. Vysotsky, "A Speaker-Independent Discrete Utterance Recognition System, Combining Deterministic and Probabilistic Strategies", *IEEE Trans. Acoust. Speech, Signal Processing*, vol ASSP-32, no 3, pp 489 - 499, June 1984.

11) Lawrence R. Rabiner, and Stephen E. Levinson, "A Speaker-Independent, Syntax-Directed, Connected Word Recognition Systemm Based on Hidden Markov Models and Level Building", *IEEE Trans. Acoust. Speech, Signal Processing*, vol ASSP-33, no 3, pp 561-573, June 1985.

12) Gary E. Kopec, and Marcia A. Bush, "Network-Based Isolated Recognition Using Vector Quantization", *IEEE Trans. Acoust. Speech, Signal Processing*, vol ASSP-33, no 4, pp850-867, August 1985.

13) Youshiaki Kitazume, Eiji Ohira, and Takeyuki Endo, " LSI Implementation of a Pattern Matching Algorithm for Speech Recognition", *IEEE Trans. Acoust. Speech, Signal Processing*, vol ASSP-33, no 1 pp1-4, February 1985.

14) Demetri Terzopoulos, "Co-Occurrence Analysis of Speech Waveforms", *IEEE Trans. Acoust. Speech, Signal Processing*, vol ASSP-33, no 1, pp 5 - 30, February 1985.

15) Hy Murveit, and Robert W. Brodersen, "An Integrated-Circuit-Based Speech Recognition System", *IEEE Trans. Acoust. Speech, Signal Processing*, vol Assp-34, no 6, pp 1465 - 1472, December 1986.

16) Enrico L. Bocchieri, and George R. Doddington, "Frame-Spesific Statistical Features Speaker Independent Speech Recognition, *IEEE Trans. Acoust. Speech, Signal Processing*, vol ASSP-34, no 4, pp 755 - 764, August 1986.

17) Marcia A. Bush, and Gary E. Kopec, "Network-Based Connected Digit Recognition", *IEEE Trans. Acoust. Speech, Signal Processing*, vol ASSP-35, no 10 , pp 1401 - 1413, October 1987.

18) Yoh'ichi Tohkura, "A Weighted Cepstral Distance Measure for Speech Recognition", *IEEE Trans. Acoust. Speech, Signal Processing*, vol ASSP-35, no 10, pp 1414 - 1422, October 1987.

19) Richard M. Stern, and Moshé J. Lasry, "Dynamic Speaker Adaption for Feature-Based Isolated Word Recognition", *IEEE Trans. Acoust. Speech, Signal Processing*, vol ASSP-35, no 6 ,pp 751 - 763, June 1987.

20) David K. Burton, "Text-Dependent Speaker Verification Using Vector Quantization Source Coding", *IEEE Trans. Acoust. Speech, Signal Processing*, vol ASSP-35, no 2, pp 133 - 143, February 1987.

21) David Mansour, and Bing Hwang Juang, "The Short-Time Modified Coherence Representation and Noisy Speech Recognition", *IEEE Trans. Acoust. Speech, Signal Processing*, vol 37, no 6, pp 795- 804, June 1989.

22) Luciano Fissore, Pietro Laface, Giorgio Micca, and Roberto Pieraccini, "Lexical Access to Large Vocabularies for Speech recognition", *IEEE Trans. Acoust. Speech, Signal Processing*, vol 37, no 8, pp 1197 - 1213, August 1989.

23) David J. Pepper and Mark A. Clement, "Phonemic Recognition Using a Large Hidden Markov Model", *IEEE Trans. Signal Processing*, vol 40, no 6, pp 1590 - 1595, June 1992.

24) X.D.Huang, "Phonem Classification Using Semicontinous Hidden Markov Models", *IEEE Trans. Signal Processing*, vol 40, no 5, pp 1062 - 1067, May 1992.

# Learning incremental case assignment based on modular connectionist knowledge sources[1]

Stefan Wermter, Ulf Peters
Department of Computer Science
University of Hamburg
22765 Hamburg, Federal Republic of Germany

Email: wermter@nats2.informatik.uni-hamburg.de
peters@nats2.informatik.uni-hamburg.de

## Abstract

This paper describes techniques for designing appropriate hybrid connectionist architectures in real world language environments. We argue that for dealing with arbitrary real world corpora we can identify the underlying constraints for a task but the integration and interaction of these constraints cannot be predicted in general for arbitrary unrestricted language bases. Therefore flexible automatic learning and incremental parallel integration of various constraints are particularly important for scaling up in real world environments. As a particular example we will focus on a hybrid connectionist architecture for semantic case assignment to support automatic learning and incremental parallel constraint integration.

## 1  Introduction

In the past there have been a few attempts to represent semantic case assignment in restricted domains using connectionist networks [2] [4]. However, it has not been examined (1) to what extent such monolithic network architectures could scale up in a real world environment of language processing and (2) to what extent such models could interact with other modules.

Our underlying motivation is that a semantic case for a certain word should depend on the general distribution of words and semantic cases in a corpus. For instance, for the city "Hamburg" the TO or FROM case is much more significant than the INSTRUMENT case. For the word "with" the INSTRUMENT case is more significant than the case TO or FROM. We will call the impact of this distribution of certain words for certain cases the "case semantics constraint".

Both, content words (e.g. nouns like "Hamburg") and function words (e.g. prepositions like "with") can be significant and their distribution across various cases should contribute to semantic case assignment. For instance, consider the phrases "in a computer" and "with a computer". If we simply rely on the case plausibility of individual words the word "computer" might have a preference for INSTRUMENT if it occurred more often in this case role. However, in spite of a possible general preference for INSTRUMENT the phrase "in the computer" would rather belong to the AT case due to the context of the preposition "in". We will call this sequential preceding influence "case context constraint".

While content nouns are usually at the end of a phrase group, function words are at the beginning of a phrase group. For instance, if we assume that content words are a primary source for correct case assignments, one

---

[1]This research was supported in part by the Federal Secretary for Research and Technology under contract #01IV101A0.

simple constraint would be to emphasize the nouns at the right phrase group boundaries as in "a ticket from Hamburg for a senior". Here "ticket", "Hamburg", and "senior" represent the right boundaries of the phrase groups "a ticket", "from Hamburg", and "for a senior" respectively. This syntactic additional knowledge might further improve case assignment. We will call this constraint "case syntax constraint".

In order to test a modular organization of knowledge sources in accordance with the interactive incremental and parallel processing of this knowledge we designed a modular hybrid connectionist architecture. This architecture is regarded as a test bed for the interactions in even more complex architectures. The goal of building such a hybrid connectionist architecture was (1) to explore a single connectionist network for semantic case assignment, (2) to compare this monolithic connectionist network with a modular hybrid connectionist architecture for the same task, and (3) to examine the incremental interactions of a syntactic and a semantic module for assigning semantic cases to phrases.

# 2 Towards a parallel incremental modular architecture

## 2.1 Training and testing using a real world corpus

Natural language phrases occur particularly often in book titles. Therefore we took advantage of a large number of real world phrases from a library corpus which also had been used for a different domain filtering task [5]. For examining the learning of different constraints for case assignment in phrases we used a corpus of 795 phrases covering areas like mathematics, music, chemistry, theology, art, computer science, history/politics, materials, electrical engineering and law. Then, each word was represented as a vector of 10 real values where the 10 components represented the normalized plausibility based on the relative occurrence of the basic cases for the specific word in the corpus (e.g., (0.1 0.05 0.05 0 0.2 0 0 0.2 0.4 0)). The basic cases were Head-start, Patient, Instrument, Modifier, At-location, At-value, To-location, To-value, From-location, and From-value. To each word of a phrase a more abstract case was associated:

```
HEAD-START      Properties
PATIENT         (Properties) of a computer
INSTRUMENT      (Solutions) with a computer
MODIFIER        (Solutions with a computer) for children
AT              in the airport, in 1993
TO              to Hamburg, to December 1993
FROM            from Hamburg, from December 1993
```

The basis corpus was divided into a training corpus and a test corpus. 277 of the 795 phrases were taken as a training set. From the remaining 518 phrases we only accepted the 132 phrases for the test set whose representations were different from the training phrases in order to put a very strong restriction on the evaluation of the generalization results (this test set restriction is harder than the real world!).

## 2.2 Representing case semantics constraint and case context constraint

During our subsequent description of architectures we will test different variations of the recurrent plausibility networks (see figure 1 a). Recurrent plausibility networks [6] contain feedforward networks and simple recurrent networks with the backpropagation learning rule [3] as special cases and generalize the backpropagation learning rule to an arbitrary fixed number of recurrent connections.

Here we summarize briefly the general properties of recurrent plausibility networks [6]. Let $L_i(t)$ denote the set of indices of the $ith$ layer at time $t$ with $i \in \{0, \cdots, n\}, L_0(t) = Inputlayer(t)$, and $L_n(t) = Outputlayer(t)$. Then, the input to a unit $j$ is given as:

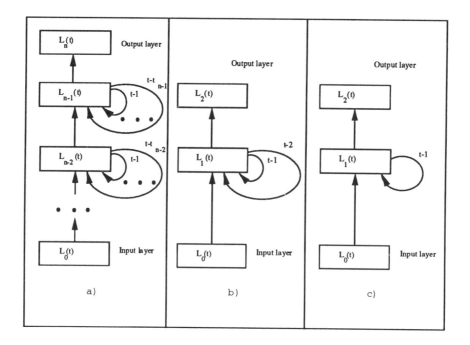

Figure 1: General plausibility network (a) and two special networks H8C1C2 (b) and H8C1 (c)

$$net_j(t) = \sum_z \sum_i w_{ij} y_i(t - z) \tag{1}$$

for $z \in \{0, \cdots, t_x\}$, $t_x$ is the maximum time step of context layers for $L_x$, unit $j \in L_x$ and $x > 0$. Furthermore, $w_{ij}$ is the weight from unit $i$ to unit $j$, $y_i(t)$ is the current computed output value of unit $i$ at time $t$. Finally let $d_{pj}$ denote the desired output value of a unit at the output layer, $\delta_k(t)$ the computed error at hidden unit $k$, function $f$ is a semilinear function, that is, the function $f$ is non-decreasing and differentiable, and $CL_{x-1}(t - z) = L_x(t - z - 1)$. Then, the update rule for a general recurrent plausibility network can be specified as:

$$\Delta w_{ij}(t) \equiv \begin{cases} (d_j(t) - y_j(t)) \, f_j'(net_j(t)) \, y_i(t) & \text{if } i \in L_{n-1}(t), j \in L_n(t) \\[2mm] \left(\sum_k \delta_k(t) \, w_{jk}\right) f_j'(net_j(t)) \, y_i^*(t) & \text{otherwise} \end{cases} \tag{2}$$

$$y_i^*(t) = \begin{cases} y_i(t) & \text{if } i \in L_{x-1}(t) \\ y_i(t-1) & \text{if } i \in CL_{x-1}(t-1) \\ \vdots & \vdots \\ y_i(t - t_x) & \text{if } i \in CL_{x-1}(t - t_x) \end{cases} \tag{3}$$

This learning rule for plausibility networks applies to hidden layers that can have an arbitrary but fixed number of distributed recurrent connections. This way, the internal dynamic states of a plausibility network over time can be used to introduce incremental context and sequentiality in a general manner. In this paper we will examine plausibility networks for case assignment. We first represented the case semantics constraint in a recurrent plausibility network which has the task to associate cases to words of a phrase. That is, input to the network is a plausible significance vector for the word representation as described above and output is a vector for 7 abstract cases. Only the one unit of the output vector which represents the particular abstract case is set to 1, all other units are set to 0. The task of this network is to associate abstract cases to word representations. Recurrent connections should enable the network to integrate the preceding context of a phrase in order to make a case assignment. Figure 1 b and c show two of the various possible architectures which were examined using learning rates between 0.1 to 0.000001 of the backpropagation learning rule. Several other architectures with more context were used as well.

Using just the two constraints, the performance of two representative network architectures with 8 hidden units for the learning rate 0.1 was 81.0% for training and 63.7% for testing a H8C1 network and 82.2% for training and 60.4% for testing H8C1C2. In this corpus the content nouns are far more significant for case role assignment than function words. Therefore, the assignments at function words get somewhat disturbed by strong preceding assignments of content words and content words get disturbed by weakening influence of preceding function words[2].

## 2.3 Balancing context with the case syntactic constraint

The use of additional syntactic knowledge is motivated by an analysis of the current performance with respect to basic syntactic categories. For each word in a phrase we determined basic syntactic categories and abstract syntactic categories in order to examine sources for remaining errors. The performance is weak for the start of a group (preposition 69.7%, conjunction 73.0%) compared to the end (noun 83.3%). This examination further supported the integration of a learning syntactic module which emphasized the importance of right group borders rather than left group borders.

We determined the syntactic representation of a word as a normalized plausibility vector of 7 units where each unit represented the occurrence significances across the corpus. The basic syntactic categories were noun, determiner, adjective, adverb, verb, conjunction, preposition. Then for each word we associated the abstract syntactic categories for the word as the output representation. The abstract syntactic categories were: noun group, verb group, genitive group, prepositional group, conjunctional group. Then different architectures and parameters were tested and a recurrent plausibility network H6C1 trained for 3000 epochs with a learning rate of 0.01 was used as the best syntactic network. The overall performance for the same phrases as for the semantic module was 96.6% on the syntactic training set and 92.9% on the test set. The syntactic network is now used as a filter in order to identify these right phrase boundaries.

## 2.4 Coupling syntactic and semantic networks

Both networks work incrementally and independently generating case hypotheses and abstract syntactic hypotheses for each word. At the beginning of a phrase group both syntactic and semantic hypotheses might still be wrong. However, particularly towards the end of abstract syntactic groups these hypotheses will be much better. The syntactic module runs one word ahead of the semantic module in order to provide the knowledge about a subsequent group boundary. If the syntactic module signals that the next word for the semantic module will be the start of a new phrase group we have identified a right phrase group and an appropriate point where the semantic case hypothesis is particularly reliable. This control knowledge is realized in a symbolic control module (see figure 2).

The influence of having a additional syntactic hypotheses about phrase boundaries was tested based on many different semantic recurrent plausibility networks. In all analyzed network architectures the addition of a module for syntactic hypotheses for phrase boundaries compared favorably to a monolithic architecture. For instance, the H8C1 network improved from 81.0% to 83.9% and a H8C1C2C3 network from 80.0% to 83.1% by adding syntactic to the semantic and contextual constraints.

---

[2]Of course this result does not suggest to use non-recurrent networks since they can not represent context in general and for arbitrary other corpora.

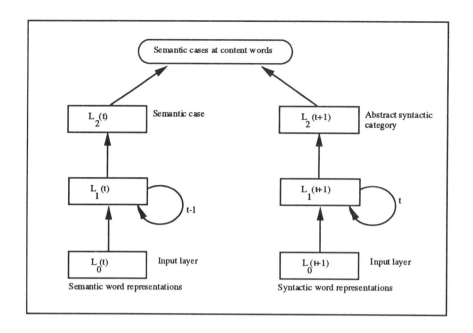

Figure 2: Modular system architecture for learning semantic case assignment

Below we show examples of the incremental generation of semantic and syntactic hypotheses for the cases and the syntactic phrase boundaries as well as the finally assigned case. As we can see incorrect semantic hypotheses occur particularly at the left start of phrase groups so that the emphasis of the right end of phrase groups using the syntactic hypotheses can filter out initial errors.

| Words of Phrase | Semantic Hypothesis | Syntactic Hypothesis | Assigned Case |
|---|---|---|---|
| Extremes | HEAD-START | <- | HEAD-START |
| and | HEAD-START | | |
| related | HEAD-START | | |
| properties | HEAD-START | <- | HEAD-START |
| of | PATIENT | | |
| random | PATIENT | | |
| sequences | PATIENT | <- | PATIENT |
| and | *HEAD-START | | |
| processes | PATIENT | <- | PATIENT |
| Supercharging | HEAD-START | | |
| C | PATIENT | <- | PATIENT |
| with | *PATIENT | | |
| assembly | *HEADSTART | | |
| language | INSTRUMENT | <- | INSTRUMENT |

# 3  Summary and conclusions

We have described a hybrid architecture for assigning cases to phrases. Assigning semantic cases to parts of phrases is an important problem since semantic cases are needed for a semantic interpretation of phrases and since isolated phrases occur very frequently across various domains. In contrary to many previous symbolic approaches for assigning cases in sentences we have examined the *learning* of case roles based on connectionist networks. From a viewpoint of connectionist architectures we have shown that a modular architecture based on additional syntactic hypotheses performed better than a monolithic architecture based on only semantic and contextual hypotheses although case assignment is basically a semantic process. The clear formulation of the constraints and the performance evaluation of the different classes of architectures allowed to improve the overall performance. The best learned performance with recurrent plausibility networks was 83.9%. We have not identified a clear comparative learning system in the literature. The closest learning case role system reaches 67% using a more complex architecture for a more complex sentence analyzing problem [1].

We have introduced a three step technique: (1) Training semantic recurrent plausibility networks with case semantics constraint and case context constraint. (2) Analysis of the influence of function words versus contents words. (3) Balancing this influence with an additional training using a syntactic recurrent plausibility network. This technique can be used independently of the particular underlying semantic and structural categories and independently of the used corpus. Such general and learning techniques should be particularly useful for providing robust parsing results in real world environments and for interacting with faulty text or speech bases.

# References

[1] A. N. Jain. A connectionist learning architecture for parsing spoken language. Technical Report CMU-CS-91-208, Carnegie Mellon University, Pittsburgh, PA, 1991.

[2] J. L. McClelland and A. H. Kawamoto. Mechanisms of sentence processing: assigning roles to constituents. In J. L. McClelland and D. E. Rumelhart, editors, *Parallel Distributed Processing*, volume Vol. 2, pages 272–326. MIT Press, Cambridge, MA, 1986.

[3] D. E. Rumelhart, G. E. Hinton, and R. J. Williams. Learning internal representations by error propagation. In D. E. Rumelhart and J. L. McClelland, editors, *Parallel Distributed Processing*, volume Vol. 1, pages 318–362. MIT Press, Cambridge, MA, 1986.

[4] M. F. St. John and J. L. McClelland. Learning and applying contextual constraints in sentence comprehension. *Artificial Intelligence*, 46:217–257, 1990.

[5] S. Wermter. Connectionist context processing for phrase filtering. In *Proceedings of the World Congress on Neural Networks*, pages 100–103, Portland, USA, 1993.

[6] S. Wermter. A hybrid connectionist approach for a scanning understanding of natural language phrases. Technical Report Doctoral thesis, University of Hamburg, Hamburg, FRG, 1993.

# Self-organising maps in synthetic speech

A J D Cohen and M J Bishop

Department of Cybernetics, University of Reading, Whiteknights, Reading, RG5 2AY, United Kingdom.

cybadc@cyber.reading.ac.uk

## Abstract

The goal of the research presented here is to apply neural network learning methods to some of the lower-level problems in formant synthesis currently performed by Synthesis-by-Rule (SBR) systems. These systems tend to be strongly influenced by notations developed by linguists (see review in Klatt, 1987), which were primarily devised to deal with written rather than spoken language. One aim is to evolve different (sub-symbolic) phonetic codings or representations from the rather abstract symbolic ones used by linguists, though the latter can be a useful formula to measure success against. By providing a distance metric in an ordered 2D space of speech sounds, a bridge between symbolic and acoustic data is established. It is commonplace in designing symbolic expert systems that representations matter more than the rules which operate on them. Hence the approach described here might also be useful in the design of a hybrid neural/symbolic system to operate in the speech synthesis domain.

## 1. Application of the SOM to phoneme data

It is known from Kohonen's use of the Self-Organising Map (SOM) that it has a use in speech, where it may form the famous 'phonotopic map' (Kohonen, 1988). In outline the SOM approximates to the probability density function of the input pattern space, by representing the N-dimensional pattern vectors on a 2D array of reference vectors in such a way that the resulting clusterings conform to an elastic surface, where neighbouring units share similar reference vectors. This procedure has not so far been applied to speech synthesis, and is seen as a recognition technology only, perhaps because of its roots in pattern recognition. In fact, it can be applied to problems in many different domains. The SOM can be applied to any feature or pattern space to determine if n-dimensional data may be represented in 2-dimensions at any level of abstraction. Figs 1a and 1b show a map resulting from applying the algorithm to phoneme feature data. In this case, the point is not to do feature extraction (since the features are already known), but to provide a statistical clustering in 2D which can indicate whether the features chosen provide a good basis for analysis. The maps in Fig 1a and b suggest that phoneticians have 'got it right' in that the features do result in a clustering of similar sounds such as stops, fricatives and nasals, as well as the more obvious separation between vowels and consonants. It is worth pointing out that both the Self-Organising Map (SOM) and Learning Vector Quantisation (LVQ) algorithms do not handle raw data (such as waveform values or image intensity values), but operate on data such as spectral components or Linear Predictive Coding (LPC) coefficients which are themselves the output of a significant processing stage, and can justifiably be called features.

The phoneme map is produced by a single Kohonen layer which self-organises using the standard algorithm (Kohonen, 1990), taking as input 9 articulatory features which are commonly used by phoneticians to describe the possible speech sounds. The features used were all encoded by a single binary digit except for vowel height. Two features were used for height simply because there are three possibilities: open, mid and closed, which cannot be encoded by a binary bit[1]. Fig 1 shows a 12x8 map created (as are all the following maps) with hexagonal connections in the lattice indicating units which are topographically close. A monotonically shrinking 'bubble' neighbourhood was used in all the maps shown here. Kohonen refers to this type of kernel as a bubble because it relates to certain kinds of activity bubbles in laterally connected networks (see Kohonen, 1989).

Fig 1 shows a 8x12 map created (as were all the maps shown) with hexagonal connections in the lattice indicating units which are topographically close. A monotonically shrinking 'bubble' neighbourhood was used in all the maps shown here. Kohonen refers to this type of kernel as a bubble because it relates to certain kinds of activity bubbles in laterally connected networks (see Kohonen, 1989).

The analysis of fig 1 is at a phonemic level of description, which is a very abstract level compared to the phonetic descriptions standardly used, which take into account much more of the context. The abstractness of phonemes makes them more difficult candidates for basic units, even though most recognition and synthesis systems use a phoneme stage. However, the essential point is that trajectory across the map provides a bridge between the symbolic way of describing the data space and the data itself, which is sensitive to its structure. All current SBR systems use a phoneme representation at some point, and therefore might benefit from this type of

---

[1] Thanks to John Local for supplying the phoneme data.

representation (see comments in part 3 below). Robustness of the mappings (Eg from text to phonemes) could be increased in a system based on NETtalk (Sejnowski and Rosenberg, 1986), since similar sounds (words) will have similar trajectories across the map. Suppose the following means of training a Multi-Layer Perceptron (MLP) on 8x12 SOM co-ordinates were adopted: 20 binary outputs in two groups of 8 and 12 units are used. Within each group each unit has an inhibitory connections to every other unit and an excitatory connection to itself, in a 'winner-take-all' scheme. In the first group each winning unit refers to an x-coordinate, in the second group each unit refers to a y-coordinate so that any possible output of the network refers to a location on the SOM. Assuming the MLP has learnt to generalise (ie has not been over-trained) then if an incorrect location is output, it should lie close to the correct output. This will in turn point to a similar (or possibly identical) diphone to the desired output, because of the SOM clustering of similar patterns. A conclusive account of generalisation is not yet available, but Ogawa and Yamasaki (1992) give one solution from the point of view of function approximation.

```
f    .    s    .    sh   .    ch   .

.    .    .    .    .    .    .    j

v    .    z    .    dh   .    .    .

.    .    .    .    .    th   .    nch

r    .    l    .    .    .    .    .

.    y    .    .    m    .    nk   .

.    .    .    n    .    b    .    g

w    .    .    .    .    .    .    .

.    u    .    i    .    d    .    .

.    .    .    .    .    .    .    .

o    .    e    .    t    .    p    .

.    @    .    a    .    ^    .    k
```

Fig 1: Clustering of phoneme data (8x12)

This result shows that the underlying dimensionality of the phoneme feature data was 2D, thus allowing a perspicuous but non-symbolic representation to be developed: the trajectory across the 2D phoneme space. If it is further considered that the unlabelled nodes on fig 1 above can be used to represent intermediate sounds to their neighbours, the map is able to provide a representation for unclassified sounds in terms of similarity to the existing ones. The labelled nodes have the strongest activation for a given input, but neighbouring nodes may in some cases have nearly as strong an excitation; thus the map may be interpreted as representing a continuum rather than a discrete set of symbols. The SOM has even been integrated with the high-level symbolic logic language PROLOG (Ultsch, 1992)

Clearly, it would be interesting to repeat the process with diphone formant data to see if a similar 2D map can be formed. Formants are known to be important in perception, but do not in general correspond to a particular vocal tract configuration. This map could then form the basis of a simple synthesis strategy, as outlined in section 3 below. By grouping similar diphones a simple distance metric may be established in the diphone address space which would allow similar words to have similar representations. In the case of a split decision matters are more complicated than with the phoneme map, for which the training vectors were themselves (articulatory) features, in that it is not so obvious as to how formant vectors can be combined.

## 2. Application of the SOM to diphone data

The diphone data was obtained in the standard manner (Miller and Isard, 1986) using pitch-synchronous LPC analysis on nonsense words[2] digitised at 10Khz, applying the covariance method in nearly all cases to

---

2 Thanks to Stephen Isard for supplying nonsense words.

calculate the LPC coefficients (in the other cases the autocorrelation procedure was used). The formant data obtained ( F1, F2, F3, and F4 -formant bandwidths were discarded) in each frame were passed as a single vector to the SOM. (For a description of the SOM algorithm see Kohonen, 1990; 1989). Some diphones would run over more frames than others, so shorter vectors were padded with zeros to make them up to the length of the longest. The average length of a diphone (unpadded) was about 30 frames; the bulk of this would naturally consist of steady-state rather than transitional data. However, the training sets in the maps shown were chosen so that the significant variance would lie in the transitional parts of the input vector, rather than in the less interesting steady-state portions.

A similar type of experiment to that in section 1 can be carried out on diphone formant data. However, some more sophisticated methods need to be used in dealing with larger amounts of data. This involves some more pre-processing of the input vectors, as well a more thorough training and testing process. A number of maps showing clustering of similar sounds (formant vectors) have been obtained (fig 2a and 2b show examples). Larger maps containing up to 945 diphones have also been created. In contrast to the one- and three-point representations used in Huang (1992) for vowels, the entire diphone is presented to the network for classification. The frame length (not more than 10ms) should mean that all perceptually relevant information is captured in the formant trajectories.

To factor out the influence of the initial configuration of the network (the reference vectors are initialised to small random values) 15 trials were run on each data set, and the map with the lowest quantisation error (QE) selected as the best. The QE is simply the mean error over the N pattern vectors in the set,

$$QE = \frac{\sum_{t=1}^{N} \|x(t) - m_c(t)\|}{N}$$

where $x(t)$ is the input vector and $m_c$ the best matching reference vector for $x(t)$. In order to compare QEs the topology (form of lateral connections) and adaptation functions must be the same, as the amount of lateral interaction determines the degree of elasticity of the network (see Kohonen, 1989, pp.123-157). In the simplest case of competitive learning the neighbourhood contains only one unit, so a QE of zero may be achieved, but in this case there is no self-organising power as lateral interaction has been eliminated.

Schematically then, resynthesis would take place on the basis of a trajectory across a diphone map. The trajectory may be stored simply as a vector of coordinates which are 'lit up' on the map. These vectors would occupy little storage space, and can be passed as input to a further SOM layer to try to cluster similar sounding words, providing a distance measure for large-vocabulary systems. The time-varying, sequential properties of speech which are difficult for neural nets to handle can thus be modelled as a spatial pattern in an accessible and straightforward manner. The ordering of components in a vector can capture the direction taken by the trajectory. This can resolve any potential confusion of phonetically reversed strings such as '-k','ka', 'at', 't-' and '-t', 'ta', 'ak', 'k-', where individual sounds tend to have similar locations on the map. These vectors of addresses would be completely different (Eg the endpoints would be far apart), although the closeness of the individual segments which are similar is maintained in 'diphone space' on the map.

```
   .      .      .      .     aar   .    aag   .    aam   .
   .      .     aaw    .      .     .    .     .    aap   .
   .      .      ʻ     .     aay   .    .     .     .    aak
   .      .     aazh   .      .     .    .    aat   .     .
   .      .      .     .      .     .    .     .     .    aas
   .     aash   .     aaj    .      .   aath   .     .     .
   .      .      .     .     aal    .    .     .     .     .
 aaz    aad     .     aah    .      .    .     .     .     .
   .      .      .     aaf    .    aang  .    aan   .    aadh
 aab    aach   aav    .      .      .    .     .     .     .
```
Key: /aa/ "bad", /ng/ "bang", /zh/"azure", /dh/ "than"

Fig 2a: Clustering of diphone data for aa-C

It is not possible to pass the formant vectors which would be referenced by each address directly to the synthesizer. The formant trajectories obtained by LPC do not match the overall spectral envelope because poles with a wide bandwidth are discarded. (These poles usually represent source or radiation characteristics, and are not traceable to the vocal tract). In addition, there may be inaccurate formant labelling where two formants cross. Improved methods of parameter extraction are the subject of research (de Veth et al, 1990) , but in their absence there are basically two possibilities:

(a) Store the diphones as LPC coefficients. In standard diphone synthesis (such as Isard and Miller, 1986) the diphones are analysed as LPC reflection coefficients, and then converted to a representation of the vocal tract as a series of equal length tubes (Atal and Hanauer, 1971) to allow further manipulation. Smoothing can then take place on the log area functions of these tubes. The separation of source and filter information allows new F0 and intensity contours to be synthesized when a new word is generated. If this is not done the results are highly unnatural. However, detailed control over formant values is naturally impossible, as the waveforms are stored in the time domain. Each coefficient affects a wide range of frequencies in a complex manner. A limited amount of control is available over durations, but normally only of the steady state portions, as shortening/lengthening of transitions may not be done in a linear fashion. An advantage of this method is its simplicity -all the spectral information apart from F0 is included in the coefficients, which have to be calculated during the analysis process in any case.

(b) Store the diphones as formants and combine the formant values to generate formant tracks -in this case only filter information is stored. However, there are advantages in storing the diphones as frames of formants (vocal tract information only). The source information is then generated by the artificial larnyx of the synthesiser. The Klatt synthesiser offers three models of the glottal source: the basic impulsive voicing source, and two more sophisticated sources - the LF model (Fant, Liljencrants and Lin, 1985) and KLGLOTT (Klatt and Klatt, 1990). In addition, smoothing of the other formant tracks to eliminate pops and crackles is necessary. As with (a) control of both pitch (F0) and intensity (amplitude) is available, to synthesize a new intonation contour. This can be assisted by the understanding of formant behaviour at segment boundaries which exists in the rule-based tradition (Eg. Allen et al, 1987). Control over durations is possible by insertion/deletion of frames. Therefore, higher quality speech is potentially available with the more complex formant synthesis.

```
daa  .       aab  .      aap  .      aach aaf
 .   .       aag  .       .   aah   .     .
gaa  .        .   aaj  .       .    aas  aash
 .   baa  .        .    .      aaz   .     .
 .   .        .   aad  aadh .        .    aazh
 .   faa  .        .    .      aam   .     .
saa  .        .   paa  .       .     .    aal
 .   haa  .        .    .      aay   .     .
 .   .        .   jaa  .       .     aan   .
 .   .        .    .    .      naa   .    aar
waa  .       zaa  ngaa laa    .      .     .
maa  .        .    .    .      .     raa   .
 .   .       dhaa .    .      chaa  .     vaa
taa  .        .   kaa  .       .     .    thaa
```

Fig 2b: Clustering of data for aa-C and C-aa

The creation of a 'diphone space' in 2D may assist in both choosing the correct (best matching) segments and in interpolation at segment boundaries. In a text-to-speech application, when mapping from text onto diphones, then it is clearly an easier task for an MLP to map neighbouring regions of input space onto neighbouring regions of output space. In joining segments the amount of distance travelled across the map is evidence as to how different the two segments are in perceptual terms, and so to the amount and type of smoothing of formant values needed. The maps also suggest an approach to the problem of calculating segment durations, which is currently under investigation. For example, consider the sequence 'aalaa'. This can be made up of the diphones 'aal' and 'laa', which are close in diphone space. This suggests a shorter duration for 'aalaa' than for 'aalpaa', where there is a transition into a consonant, which is acoustically very different (and further away on the SOM). These considerations are of course subject to modification by other factors, such as the need to stress a particular word.

## 3. Related systems

Scordilis (1991) and Scordilis and Gowdy (1990) describe work which aims to learn the rules which relate phonemic information to synthesizer control values. The view taken here is that such rules do not exist because the phonemic representations are too abstract for the job, and so there is no point trying to learn them -by whatever means. The author makes use of the text-to-phoneme approach, inspired by NETtalk, in contrast to the diphones used here. NETtalk (Sejnowski and Rosenberg, 1986) really proved that even with a powerful statistical learning technique in a network of 25000 weights, you cannot learn a mapping from text to phonemes. Performance on its 20000 word training set reached %90, but this is substantially surpassed by typical rule-based systems. On the other hand, there have been many successful SBR programs based on diphones (see Klatt, 1987 for a review). Scordilis (1991) notes that a very large training database will be needed, but that its creation will be a slow procedure due to the difficulties in accurate formant extraction, which require hand-checking and a lot of adjustment. In the absence of good automatic formant extraction procedures this is a problem faced by all neural-net based formant synthesizers.

Cawley and Noakes (1992) describe an application of backpropagation to learning the formant transitions of particular diphones. Their training data was supplied by the JSRU SBR system, which is one solution to the data shortage problem mentioned above. They thus rely on the generalisation properties of the MLP to out-perform the lower-level functions of the prosodic and phonetic modules of a conventional SBR system. However, it is difficult to test this hypothesis on the basis of artificial data, as the network is only exposed to rule-generated data which means it is unlikely to out-perform the SBR system.

In the small vocabulary systems that are currently feasible for both synthesis and recognition, on theoretical grounds using diphones rather than phones for recognition might offer several advantages. Modelling of transitions is the most difficult part of synthesis, just as recognition of the same phoneme in different coarticulation contexts is the most difficult part of phoneme recognition. In both cases the same type of compromise between huge memories for whole word templates and poor performance due to coarticulation for phone templates can be made. Diphones represent a good middle-ground for many applications. If a diphone map were trained on multiple tokens of each diphone it could perform the discriminative function of a recognition system, whilst the more sequential, time-varying aspects of the speech signal could be dealt with by HMMs (Bourlard and Wellekens, 1990, discuss combined methods of this type).

## 4. Summary and conclusion

The outline of a conventional SBR system (fig 3a) has a series of symbolic stages before the final low-level stage ('synthesis routines') calculates the synthesizer parameters. The essential feature is the 'abstract linguistic description' which must be derived before any attempt is made to calculate parameter values. In the proposed system of fig 5a this middle stage is replaced by the SOM stage, which also passes values for distance between segments to the next two stages. Generation of an intonation contour, though this has been implemented with neural nets, is probably best handled with rules as it is almost purely a prosodic (ie sentence level) matter. (Minute variations in F0 from frame to frame as occurs in natural speech are a separate issue handled by the synthesizer source model).

The SOM coding replaces the linguistic description, and leads to direct access of formant values for that diphone, which then become default values for the next stage to operate on (fig 3b). In conclusion, arguments have been presented for the use of non-symbolic codings as the central stage of a text-to-speech system. These codings are both closer to the acoustic domain and offer a more flexible means of integrating neural and symbolic systems.

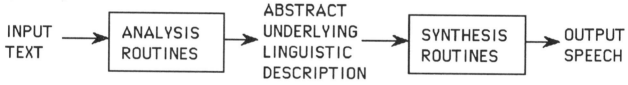

Fig 3a: Conventional SBR system (after Klatt (1987) fig 1)

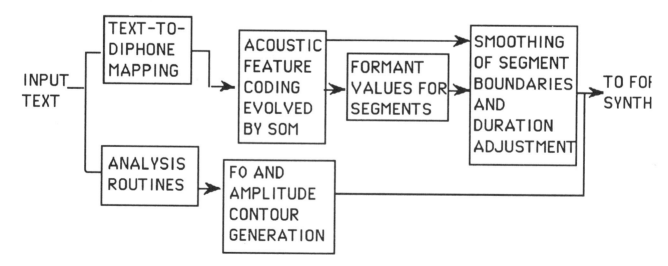

Fig 3b: Proposed hybrid neural/symbolic system.

Allen, J, Hunnicutt, M S, and Klatt, D H, (1987), "From text to speech: The MITalk system", Cambridge University Press.

Atal, B S, and Hanauer, S L, (1971), "Speech Analysis and Synthesis by Linear Prediction of the Speech Wave", JASA 50, pp.637-655.

Bourlard, H, and Wellekens, C J, (1990), "Links between Markov models and multilayer perceptrons", IEEE Trans. Pattern Analysis and Machine Intelligence, PAMI-12, pp.1167-1178.

Cawley, G C, and Noakes, P D, (1992), "Diphone Synthesis using a Neural Network", in Aleksander, I, and Taylor, J G, (Eds), "Artificial Neural Networks, Volume 2", 1992 Elsevier Science Publishers B.V.

Fant, G, Liljencrants, J, and Lin, Q G, (1985), "A Four-Parameter Model of Glottal Flow", Speech Transmission Labs QPSR 4, Royal Institute of Technology, Stockholm, pp.1-13.

Huang, C B, (1990), "Modelling Human Vowel Identification Using Aspects of Formant Trajectory and Context", in Tohkura, Y, Vatikiotis-Bateson, E, and Sagisaka, Y, (Eds), "Speech Perception, Production and Linguistic Structure", Proceedings of the ATR workshop held in Kyoto, Japan, November 1990, IOS press, Oxford, UK.

Isard, S D, and Miller, D A, (1986), "Diphone Synthesis Techniques", Proceedings IEEE Speech Input/Output Conference, pp.78-82.

Klatt, D H, (1987), "Review of text-to-speech conversion for English", JASA 82(3), pp.737-793.

Klatt, D H, and Klatt, L C, (1990), "Analysis, Synthesis and Perception of Voice Quality Variations among Female and Male Talkers", JASA, 87, pp.820-857.

Kohonen, T, (1988), "The 'neural' phonetic typewriter", IEEE Computer 21, pp.11-22, 1988

Kohonen, T, (1989), "Self-Organisation and Associative Memory", Springer Verlag, 3rd Edition.

Kohonen, T, (1990), "The Self-Organising Map", IEEE Proc. 78, 9, pp.1464-1480.

Ogawa, H, and Yamasaki, K, (1992), "A Theory of Over-Learning", in Aleksander, I, and Taylor, J G, (Eds), "Artificial Neural Networks, Volume 2", 1992 Elsevier Science Publishers B.V.

Scordilis, M S, (1991), "A Neural Network Cluster for the Control of a Speech Synthesiser", in Tzafestas, S G, (Ed), "Engineering Systems with Intelligence", Kluwer Academic Press, pp.229-235.

Scordilis, M S, and Gowdy, J N, (1990), "Neural network control for a cascade/parallel formant synthesizer", IEEE ICASSP-90, pp.297-300.

Sejnowski, T J, and Rosenberg, C R, (1986), "NETtalk: a parallel network that learns to read aloud", John Hopkins University Electrical Engineering and Computer Science Technical Report JHU/EECS-86/01, and reprinted in Anderson, J A, and Rosenfeld, E, (Eds), "Neurocomputing: Foundations of Research", 1988 MIT Press.

Ultsch, A, (1992), "Knowledge Acquisition with Self-Organizing Neural Networks", in Aleksander, I, and Taylor, J G, (Eds), "Artificial Neural Networks, Volume 2", 1992 Elsevier Science Publishers B.V.

de Veth, J, Brouwers, W, Loman, H, Boves, L, (1990), "Robust ARMA Analysis as an aid in developing parameter control rules for a pole-zero cascade speech synthesizer", IEEE ICASSP-90, pp.305-308

# INTEGRATING SYMBOLIC AND PARALLEL DISTRIBUTED PROCESSES IN A JIGSAW NEURAL NETWORK

Roman Pozarlik

Technical University of Wroclaw, Institute of Engineering Cybernetics
Janiszewskiego Str. 11-17, PL 50-372 Wroclaw, Poland
email: rpoz@plwrtu11.bitnet

Parallel Distributed Processing models may exhibit a lawful behavior without using explicit rules and structured representations. A content-sensitive representation introduced here provides a novel paradigm of information processing natural for PDP models. This representation allows designing a modular PDP network called Jigsaw Neural Network that copes with syntax of a natural language. It is shown how a grammatically well-defined sequential behavior may be observed on a macrolevel of the whole network whilst a neural microlevel is operating in a parallel manner on distributed data. The model presents an iterative approach to sentence processing but it does not cause any limitations in terms of a normally performed language. It is suggested that information processing in PDP models may be practically not reducible to a symbolic level of description that can only approximate their performance.

## 1. Introduction

Classical symbolic descriptions of a problem such as syntax of natural language result in compositionally structured data and special symbols-manipulating techniques. They are not adequate for PDP models which do not exhibit explicit capabilities of representing structured data. Connectionist models that demonstrate promising account of some aspects of language (e.g. Elman, 1991) rely on learning scenarios but are not analytically derived from a description of the problem. Thus an explanation of their performance in terms of structural representations is not fully justified although such representations seem to be the only ones we currently know. The inadequacy of the representations creates the gap between symbolism and connectionism. The paper proposes a novel type of representation which is not structured (in the ordinary meaning of the word) and is straightforwardly interpretable in terms of parallel distributed processes.

A content-sensitive representation (CSR) introduced here accounts as well for syntax of natural language as classical approaches do. It explores the notion of a set and simple set operations. It is sensitive only to the content of information (the presence or absence of some neurons' firing but not their structural relationships) represented by a distributed activity in the network. The CSR assumes that information processing in PDP models will have a form of a succession of patterns of activity in the whole network. Such an iterative processing does not cause any limitations in terms of syntactic complexity of a normally performed language. Moreover, it is not just an implementation of a "low-level" serial algorithm. Patterns of activity in the consecutive time steps can represent much higher-level stages in information processing.

Implementation of the CSR in a neural network is natural when a coarse-coding method is used. The achieved network is modular and is called the Jigsaw Neural Network (JNN). Modularity is an important feature of real biological circuits and has some advantages over homogeneous networks (Jacobs & Jordan, 1992; Mumford, 1992). Hierarchical modularity is not, as yet, well understood (but see Sutton et al., 1988, 1991; Sutton, 1991; for study on neural networks with hierarchical nested modules). The JNN is defined in this paper in terms of parallel interactions between modules.

In this paper a small fragment of English grammar is analysed. At first, the idea of the JNN model for this grammar is presented. At second, the main features of the CSR are explained. Finally, a discussion on a constraint imposed on information processing by the model and conclusions close the paper. Results for a more elaborated version of the English grammar and a detailed description of these ideas may be found in (Pozarlik, 1994).

## 2. The idea of a Jigsaw Neural Network

The name for the network stems from an analogy of its performance to a jigsaw puzzle completion task. The JNN is supposed to have a modular architecture. It is composed from several groups of neurons called modules (nine in the example below) that interact with each other in a parallel manner. A configuration of their activities emerging from such interactions should be one from a set of predetermined configurations (that is the analogy to a jigsaw puzzle completion task) and thus may represent an informational entity. Moreover, the network should have capabilities to proceed through a sequence of such possible configurations in a well-defined manner (i.e. according to a set of rules). Such a formulation of the problem of sequential processing of information is the most general one and should not be mistaken with an implementation of classical symbolic methods in neural networks because PDP models may offer a quite new paradigm of information processing.

Natural language processing may be considered as a landmark problem of the so called well-defined sequential behavior. This paper investigates syntax of natural language. Details presented below concern the grammar described in the next section. The configurations of the JNN in the consecutive time steps form a sequence that may reflect one of possible sentences accepted (or produced) by the grammar. This sentence is presented as a sequence of nonterminal symbols that can be easily instantiated by particular words.

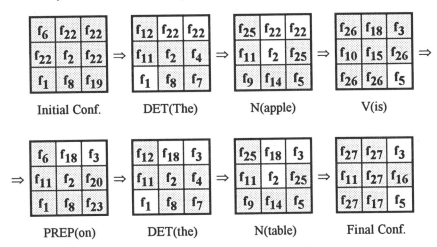

**Figure 1.** The sequence of configurations of the JNN may be interpreted as the sequence of nonterminal symbols (the exemplary instantiation of this sequence is presented in brackets). There are nine modules in the network represented by small squares and numbered from left to right. Symbols $f_i$ indicate modules' activities. Shaded modules represent specific activity in a configuration. The symbols Initial Conf. and Final Conf. indicate initial and final configurations respectively.

Configurations may have univocal interpretations due to a specific activity indicated by shaded modules in figure 1 (not shaded ones represent activity depending on context). The main problem addressed in the paper is how parallel and distributed interactions between modules may result with such a well-defined sequential behavior (with, for example, a well-defined sequence of nonterminal symbols).

This problem was solved by means of a content-sensitive representation. A representation of this type, which is equivalent for a small grammar defined by a set of production rules, is presented in the next section. The exemplary performance of the JNN for this grammar is presented in figure 1 (for all details concerning the transformation from the representation to the JNN model see Pozarlik, 1994). The network is composed of nine modules $M_i$ numbered from left to right (figure 1). Each module's activity at a time is indicated by a symbol $f_i$. Modules may exhibit the following possible activities

$M1 = (f_{12}, f_6, f_{13}, f_{25}, f_{26}, f_{27})$,     $M4 = (f_{11}, f_{10}, f_{22}, f_{24})$,     $M7 = (f_9, f_1, f_{21}, f_{26}, f_{27})$,

$M2 = (f_{18}, f_{22}, f_{27})$,     $M5 = (f_{15}, f_2, f_{27})$,     $M8 = (f_8, f_{14}, f_{17}, f_{26})$,

$M3 = (f_3, f_{22}, f_{24})$,     $M6 = (f_{16}, f_4, f_{20}, f_{22}, f_{25}, f_{26})$,     $M9 = (f_7, f_5, f_{19}, f_{23}, f_{24})$.

For the problem being considered here the configurations in figure 1 present in a way patterns of activity of all neurons in the network observed from the outside. It must be emphasised that the interpretation of every configuration as a nonterminal symbol serves as a criterion of how well-defined a sequence of such configurations has been (the observed sequences of configurations are supposed to illustrate the very paradigm of what is called Parallel Distributed Processing (with special emphasis on natural language processing) but the model is not a completely defined network with input-output capabilities and a precisely defined architecture and dynamics).

The predetermined configurations $C_i$ are identified with nonterminal symbols in the grammar and two configurations called *Initial Conf.* and *Final Conf.* They are defined as the following vectors of the successive modules' activities

| | | | | | | | | | |
|---|---|---|---|---|---|---|---|---|---|
| **Initial Conf.,** | $C1 = [$ | $f_6,$ | $f_{22},$ | $f_{22},$ | $f_{22},$ | $f_2,$ | $f_{22},$ | $f_1,$ | $f_8,$ | $f_{19}$ ], |

Initial Conf., $C1 = [\ f_6,\ f_{22},\ f_{22},\ f_{22},\ f_2,\ f_{22},\ f_1,\ f_8,\ f_{19}\ ]$,

DET, $C2 = [\ f_{12},\ *,\ *,\ f_{11},\ f_2,\ f_4,\ *,\ f_8,\ f_7\ ]$,

PREP, $C3 = [\ f_6,\ *,\ *,\ f_{11},\ f_2,\ f_{20},\ f_1,\ f_8,\ f_{23}\ ]$,

ADJ, $C4 = [\ f_{13},\ *,\ f_{24},\ f_{24},\ f_2,\ *,\ f_{21},\ f_8,\ f_{24}\ ]$,

N, $C5 = [\ f_{25},\ *,\ *,\ f_{11},\ *,\ f_{25},\ f_9,\ f_{14},\ f_5\ ]$,

V, $C6 = [\ f_{26},\ f_{18},\ f_3,\ f_{10},\ f_{15},\ f_{26},\ f_{26},\ f_{26},\ *\ ]$,

Final Conf., $C7 = [\ f_{27},\ f_{27},\ *,\ f_{11},\ f_{27},\ f_{16},\ f_{27},\ f_{17},\ *\ ]$,

where an asterisk indicates any activity in that place. The network's evolution in time is specified by associative interactions between two configurations possibly adjacent in time. The list of all associations, written in the notation $C_i(t) \Rightarrow C_j(t+1)$, is the following

$[\ f_6,\ f_{22},\ f_{22},\ f_{22},\ f_2,\ f_{22},\ f_1,\ f_8,\ f_{19}\ ]\ \Rightarrow\ [f_{12},\ *,\ *,\ f_{11},\ f_2,\ f_4,\ *,\ f_8,\ f_7\ ]$,

$[\ f_6,\ f_{22},\ f_{22},\ f_{22},\ f_2,\ f_{22},\ f_1,\ f_8,\ f_{19}\ ]\ \Rightarrow\ [f_{25},\ *,\ *,\ f_{11},\ *,\ f_{25},\ f_9,\ f_{14},\ f_5\ ]$,

$[f_{12},\ *,\ *,\ f_{11},\ f_2,\ f_4,\ *,\ f_8,\ f_7\ ]\ \Rightarrow\ [f_{25},\ *,\ *,\ f_{11},\ *,\ f_{25},\ f_9,\ f_{14},\ f_5\ ]$,

$[f_{12},\ *,\ *,\ f_{11},\ f_2,\ f_4,\ *,\ f_8,\ f_7\ ]\ \Rightarrow\ [f_{13},\ *,\ f_{24},\ f_{24},\ f_2,\ *,\ f_{21},\ f_8,\ f_{24}\ ]$,

$[\ f_6,\ *,\ *,\ f_{11},\ f_2,\ f_{20},\ f_1,\ f_8,\ f_{23}\ ]\ \Rightarrow\ [f_{12},\ *,\ *,\ f_{11},\ f_2,\ f_4,\ *,\ f_8,\ f_7\ ]$,

$[\ f_6,\ *,\ *,\ f_{11},\ f_2,\ f_{20},\ f_1,\ f_8,\ f_{23}\ ]\ \Rightarrow\ [f_{25},\ *,\ *,\ f_{11},\ *,\ f_{25},\ f_9,\ f_{14},\ f_5\ ]$,

$[f_{13},\ *,\ f_{24},\ f_{24},\ f_2,\ *,\ f_{21},\ f_8,\ f_{24}\ ]\ \Rightarrow\ [f_{25},\ *,\ *,\ f_{11},\ *,\ f_{25},\ f_9,\ f_{14},\ f_5\ ]$,

$[f_{25},\ f_{18},\ *,\ f_{11},\ *,\ f_{25},\ f_9,\ f_{14},\ f_5\ ]\ \Rightarrow\ [f_{27},\ f_{27},\ *,\ f_{11},\ f_{27},\ f_{16},\ f_{27},\ f_{17},\ *\ ]$,

$[f_{25},\ *,\ *,\ f_{11},\ *,\ f_{25},\ f_9,\ f_{14},\ f_5\ ]\ \Rightarrow\ [f_{26},\ f_{18},\ f_3,\ f_{10},\ f_{15},\ f_{26},\ f_{26},\ f_{26},\ *\ ]$,

$[f_{26},\ f_{18},\ f_3,\ f_{10},\ f_{15},\ f_{26},\ f_{26},\ f_{26},\ *\ ]\ \Rightarrow\ [f_{12},\ *,\ *,\ f_{11},\ f_2,\ f_4,\ *,\ f_8,\ f_7\ ]$,

$[f_{26},\ f_{18},\ f_3,\ f_{10},\ f_{15},\ f_{26},\ f_{26},\ f_{26},\ *\ ]\ \Rightarrow\ [\ f_6,\ *,\ *,\ f_{11},\ f_2,\ f_{20},\ f_1,\ f_8,\ f_{23}\ ]$,

$[f_{26},\ f_{18},\ f_3,\ f_{10},\ f_{15},\ f_{26},\ f_{26},\ f_{26},\ *\ ]\ \Rightarrow\ [f_{25},\ *,\ *,\ f_{11},\ *,\ f_{25},\ f_9,\ f_{14},\ f_5\ ]$,

$[f_{26},\ f_{18},\ f_3,\ f_{10},\ f_{15},\ f_{26},\ f_{26},\ f_{26},\ *\ ]\ \Rightarrow\ [f_{27},\ f_{27},\ *,\ f_{11},\ f_{27},\ f_{16},\ f_{27},\ f_{17},\ *\ ]$,

where an asterisk indicates any activity from the previous configuration. An association $C_i(t) \Rightarrow C_j(t+1)$ means that the configuration $C_i(t)$ implies another configuration $C_j(t+1)$ in the next time step. Starting from the initial configuration the JNN can proceed through different sequences of configurations, which sequences may be identified with nonterminal symbol sequences satisfying the appropriate grammatical rules. However, these rules are not explicitly written anywhere in the network. The informational entities that are considered here, namely, the nonterminal symbols, are represented in a distributed way by whole configurations of the modules' activities. The network is operating in a parallel manner proceeding from one configuration to another. Note that the defined network is nondeterministic just as the grammar is.

## 3. The content-sensitive representation

The CSR is a result of a content-sensitivity analysis of neural networks' performance. The main feature of this analysis is that it assumes a holistic and iterative mode of information processing in neural networks. As a result, only the content of information represented by a network's pattern of activity at a time (which content is regarded to be unstructured because it is available in a holistic manner) is important in processing of this type. This content may be represented by a set of the smallest portions of information called *features* and designated by symbols $f_i$. A feature may represent some activity of a group of neurons. Then a set of features will represent a pattern of activity of the whole network. All details concerning this analysis and the representation may be found in (Pozarlik, 1994). Only the results are presented in this paper.

The CSR is composed of two components. The first one is a list of predetermined patterns of activity $P_i$ representing symbols used to form possible sentences. They are defined by sets of features in the form

$$P_i = \{ \text{Cont}_i , \text{Spec}_i \} \quad \text{where} \quad \text{Cont}_i = \{ \text{context features} \}, \text{ and } \text{Spec}_i = \{ \text{specific features} \}.$$

Every set is composed of two subsets including *context features* and *specific features* respectively. Context features represent those aspects of a pattern $P_i$ which depend on a temporal context. The subset $\text{Cont}_i$ represents all possible contexts in which this pattern $P_i$ may appear. Specific features represent activity always observed in that pattern $P_i$. In a given sequence of patterns and in a given time step a pattern $P_i(t)$ is represented by one set of features composed of all its specific features and some of its context features (depending on context). The second element of the representation is the list of associations in the notation

$$L_k \Rightarrow R_k, \quad \text{where} \quad L_k, \text{ and } R_k = \{ \text{context features} \} \cup \{ \text{specific features} \}.$$

Using the sum of two subsets instead of one set in the association above has only an illustrative function. Every association describes a transition from one pattern $P_i(t)$ to another $P_j(t+1)$ in a reduced manner (a full description gives a list of associations in the form presented in the previous section). The left side of the k-th association $L_k$ includes only some of the features that are present in a pattern $P_i(t)$ and that are necessary for the transition to a pattern $P_j(t+1)$. Similarly the right side of the k-th association $R_k$ includes some of the features that will be present in the next pattern $P_j(t+1)$ and that will somehow indicate this pattern. The pattern $P_j(t+1)$ may be identified by means of $R_k$ features and is then completed by its specific features and some of its context features (depending on context). The figure 2 illustrates the idea of how associations are encoded.

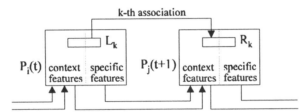

**Figure 2.** The two patterns $P_i(t)$ and $P_j(t+1)$ are illustrated by bigger squares divided into two parts (they represent sets of features ascribed to every pattern). The small squares illustrate features that form the k-th association. The arrow between them indicates transition that is encoded by this association. The other arrows illustrate that context features in the next pattern $P_j(t+1)$ are formed from the contextual and specific activity in the previous pattern.

Any sequence of patterns can be formed iteratively in this way with a constraint described in the next section. The CSR will be presented for the simple grammar defined by the following production rules.

| | | |
|---|---|---|
| S | → | NP VP |
| NP | → | DET ADJ N \| DET N \| N |
| VP | → | V NP \| V \| V PP |
| PP | → | PREP NP |

The grammar has five nonterminal symbols. There must be defined patterns for those symbols and two additional ones called Initial Pat. and Final Pat. The CSR achieved for the grammar has the following form

The list of patterns:

|  |  |
|---|---|
| **Initial Pat.,** | $P_1 = \{\{ \ \}, \{ f_{19}, f_6, f_1, f_8, f_2 \}\},$ |
| **DET,** | $P_2 = \{\{ f_1, f_3, f_{18} \}, \{ f_{12}, f_8, f_2, f_4, f_{11}, f_7 \}\},$ |
| **PREP,** | $P_3 = \{\{ f_3, f_{18} \}, \{ f_{20}, f_6, f_1, f_8, f_2, f_{11} \}\},$ |
| **ADJ,** | $P_4 = \{\{ f_4, f_{18} \}, \{ f_{21}, f_8, f_2, f_{13} \}\},$ |
| **N,** | $P_5 = \{\{ f_2, f_3, f_{18} \}, \{ f_{14}, f_5, f_{11}, f_9 \}\},$ |
| **V,** | $P_6 = \{\{ f_5 \}, \{ f_{10}, f_{18}, f_3, f_{15} \}\},$ |
| **Final Pat.,** | $P_7 = \{\{ f_3, f_5 \}, \{ f_{17}, f_{16}, f_{11} \}\}.$ |

The list of associations:

| | | | |
|---|---|---|---|
| 1: | $\{ f_{18}, f_{14}, f_5 \}$ | $\Rightarrow$ | $\{ f_5, f_{16} \},$ |
| 2: | $\{ f_{18}, f_{10}, f_3 \}$ | $\Rightarrow$ | $\{ f_3, f_{18}, f_{11} \},$ |
| 3: | $\{ f_6, f_1 \}$ | $\Rightarrow$ | $\{ f_1, f_7 \},$ |
| 4: | $\{ f_8, f_2 \}$ | $\Rightarrow$ | $\{ f_2, f_9 \},$ |
| 5: | $\{ f_{12}, f_4 \}$ | $\Rightarrow$ | $\{ f_4, f_{13} \},$ |
| 6: | $\{ f_{14}, f_5 \}$ | $\Rightarrow$ | $\{ f_5, f_{15} \},$ |

The CSR above can be used to recognize grammatical correctness of a given sentence or to produce the set of sentences generated by the grammar (note that parsing is not the same what is called natural language processing but it is a method being used in many classical approaches to deal with this problem). For example, in order to produce a sentence the following steps must be carried out.

At first for a given pattern $P_i(t)$ there must be found an association $L_k \Rightarrow R_k$ whose part $L_k$ has features present in that pattern. The condition $P_i(t) \cap L_k = L_k$ must be satisfied. Associations that have more $L_k$ features must be considered first. At second, the next possible pattern $P_j$ pointed to by $R_k$ features must be found. This pattern must satisfy the condition $R_k \cap ( Cont_j \cup Spec_j ) = R_k$. Finally, the next pattern $P_j(t+1)$ must be formed from its specific features and appropriate context features using the equation $P_j(t+1) = R_k \cup ( P_i(t) \cap Cont_j ) \cup Spec_j$. Starting from the initial pattern $P_1$ these steps are repeated up to the pattern $P_7$ where no association can be found. The sentence in figure 1 has the following sequence of patterns in the CSR (numbers indicate applied associations).

$$\{ f_{19}, f_6, f_1, f_8, f_2 \}_{P1} \overset{3}{\Rightarrow} \{ f_1, f_{12}, f_8, f_2, f_4, f_{11}, f_7 \}_{P2} \overset{4}{\Rightarrow} \{ f_2, f_{14}, f_5, f_{11}, f_9 \}_{P5} \overset{6}{\Rightarrow}$$

$$\{ f_5, f_{10}, f_{18}, f_3, f_{15} \}_{P6} \overset{2}{\Rightarrow} \{ f_3, f_{18}, f_{20}, f_6, f_1, f_8, f_2, f_{11} \}_{P3} \overset{3}{\Rightarrow}$$

$$\{ f_1, f_3, f_{18}, f_{12}, f_8, f_2, f_4, f_{11}, f_7 \}_{P2} \overset{4}{\Rightarrow} \{ f_2, f_3, f_{18}, f_{14}, f_5, f_{11}, f_9 \}_{P5} \overset{1}{\Rightarrow} \{ f_3, f_5, f_{16}, f_{11} \}_{P7}$$

The CSR can be implemented in a neural network using, for example, a coarse-coding method, which assumes that features are represented by groups of neurons later called modules. This implementation of the CSR requires to define which features will be represented by which modules; this means satisfying some constraints (for example, features that can appear in a pattern at the same time should not be represented by the same neurons). As a result, a model of the JNN is achieved and patterns $P_i$ become configurations $C_i$. The JNN for the CSR above is presented in the previous section.

A JNN was defined for a more elaborated version of the English grammar (Pozarlik, 1994). This grammar captures in a way the following problems: noun phrase consistency, subject-verb agreement, verbal group consistency in all tenses, passive verb usage, and transitive-intransitive verbs usage. The achieved network has twenty two modules.

## 4. A constraint resulting from the presented paradigm of information processing

The presented model copes with syntax of natural language and operates iteratively along sentences. Limited resources of the JNN imply that language accepted by the model does not have a self-embedding property. Many authors claim that natural language has this property (e.g. Moll et al., 1988). All arguments that support the claim stem from the assumption that there are sentences which can exhibit infinite numeric agreement between some constituents and in order to describe such unlimited agreement there must be used a recursive procedure, which fact implies a self-embedding property. But normally performed language does not exhibit such a property. Human cognitive limitation (Miller, 1956) implies that sentences with a very limited number of central nested clauses can be processed. This fact is not important for classical symbolic approaches because descriptions they provide are free from this limitation and it would be strange to impose any artificial constraints on them. It may however be an important and inherent feature of a paradigm of information processing in neural networks. Thus, this constraint is not considered to be a limitation but seems to be consistent with human cognitive capabilities. How severe this constraint is, depends on architectural and dynamic features of a network and processed sentences themselves.

The CSR achieves systematicity because informational entities that exhibit the same property are represented in a similar manner and inherit the same features in the representation (finally, they are ascribed to very similar patterns of activity). As a result, the so called binding problem is reduced to a quantitative problem of memorizing fully distributed patterns that are somehow correlated. The problem of compositionality, central for connectionism, does not have to be connected with structured representations. The CSR does not exhibit structural compositionality (see van Gelder, 1990, for extensive discussion) but sentences described by it can have an interpretation of being compositional expressions.

## 5. Conclusions

In this paper a novel paradigm of information processing has been introduced, which is based on a content-sensitive representation. The representation makes it possible to design a modular neural network that captures sequential behavior defined according to some rules and that operates in a parallel manner on distributed data. It seems to promise to be capable of bridging the gap between symbolism and connectionism.

PDP models accomplish regularities in their performance via self-organizing mechanisms and that regularities are very difficult to be described by hard rules. The CSR could offer flexible enough level of description of the performance. However, the whole designing process of the JNN is not easy to be done backwards from a given network to the CSR. It is theoretically possible but would be burdened by an enormously high computational cost. This suggests that a given JNN may be practically not reducible to a CSR that would describe its behavior. A symbolic level of description (especially, classical rule-driven descriptions) can offer only an approximation of information processing taking place in PDP models.

The author wishes to thank Tomasz Pelc for reading of the paper and helpful comments. The technical report cited in references is available from the author by a surface or electronic mail.

## References

Elman, J.L. (1991), Distributed Representations, Simple Recurrent Networks, and Grammatical Structure, *Machine Learning*, 7, 195-225.

van Gelder, T. (1990), Compositionality: A Connectionist Variation on a Classical Theme, *Cognitive Science*, 14, 355-384.

Jacobs, R.A. and Jordan, M.I. (1992) Computational Consequences of a Bias toward Short Connections, *Journal of Cognitive Neuroscience*, 4-3, 323-336.

Miller, G.A. (1956), The magical number seven, plus or minus two : Some limits on our capacity for processing information, *The Psychological Review*, 63-2, 81-97.

Moll, R.N., Arbib, M.A., and Kfoury, A.J. (1988), *An Introduction to Formal Language Theory*, Springer-Verlag, New York.

Mumford, D. (1992), On the computational architecture of the neocortex : The role of cortico-cortical loops, *Biological Cybernetics*, 66, 241-251.

Pozarlik, R. (1994) A Connectionist Approach to Natural Language Processing, *Technical Report*, Institute of Engineering Cybernetics, Wroclaw.

Sutton, J.P., Beis, J.S., and Trainor, L.E.H. (1988), Hierarchical model of memory and memory loss, *J. Phys. A: Math. Gen.*, 21, 4443-4454.

Sutton, J.P., Trainor, L.E.H. (1991), Information Processing in Multi-Levelled Neural Architectures, in *Proceedings Intern. AMSE Conference Neural Networks*, San Diego (USA), vol. 1, pp. 59-66.

Sutton, J.P. (1991), Mean Field Theory of Nested Neural Clusters, in *Proceedings Intern. AMSE Conference Neural Networks*, San Diego (USA), vol. 1, pp. 47-58.

# Spoken Word Recognition
## using
## Adder Neurons
## and
## Ear Filter Model

Janko Mrsic-Flogel    John E.T. Shaw

Department of Computing
Imperial College of Science, Technology and Medicine
180, Queen's Gate
London SW7 2BZ
e-mail: jmf@doc.ic.ac.uk

## Abstract

*A system for spoken word recognition has been proposed, based on Adder Neuron recognisers [Mrsic-Flogel 1992]. The Adder neuron is not computationally intensive, requiring no multiplication or division instructions for operation. An Ear Filter Feature Detection System (EFFDS) has been designed, as pre-processing module for the Adder Neuron recognisers. A simulation of the system has been implemented. Using basic training algorithms a correct recognition rate of 75% was achieved for speaker-dependent word recognition (numbers 'zero' to 'nine') in continuous speech under normal noise conditions.*

## Introduction

Human speech recognition can be considered in two phases: extraction of features from the speech signal in the inner ear and auditory nerve, and recognition of words, phrases and sentences in the brain. In both cases the processing is carried out by the massively parallel system of vast numbers of simple 'processing units' (neurons) that makes up the human brain. The information received in the speech signal is often incomplete and ambiguous. There is not always a clear distinction between different vowels and consonants, even when spoken by the same speaker. Interpretation of words and phrases is highly dependent on the context in which they are spoken. Speech is a very difficult stochastic process, and its elements are not unique at all.

However, traditional approaches to creating automatic speech recognisers (ASRs) have involved complex software systems on serial computers that consider speech as a clearly defined, ordered process. These approaches have proved moderately successful. The most widely used methods consist of a feature detection phase for extracting frequency component information from the speech signal (e.g. Fourier analysis or filter-bank analysis) and a pattern matching phase where input frequency patterns are compared with trained frequency patterns using statistical techniques (e.g. hidden Markov models) [Deller 1993].

Because ASR's need to be approaching real-time for most practical applications, these serial computer based approaches tend to sacrifice accuracy for efficiency. Although some efficiency gains can be made using parallel processor computers, the algorithms of these traditional approaches are essentially serial and centralised in nature. These approaches are also not well suited to dealing with the stochastic, ambiguous nature of the speech signal.

In the mid 1980's there was a resurgence of interest in neural networks as an alternative computing paradigm. Neural networks are massively parallel networks of simple nodes that are intended to resemble the structure and functionality of the human brain (although there is not enough understanding about how the human brain works). They are well suited to recognising patterns in disordered stochastic data sets. One of the main areas in which neural networks have been applied is ASR's. Various neural network - based approaches have been reasonably successful in small speech recognition tasks.

However there have been two main problems with neural network approaches so far: firstly the massive number of overlapping connections between nodes in most networks makes them very difficult to implement in hardware, so the networks are usually only simulated on serial computers and are therefore very computationally inefficient [Lipman 1989]. Secondly most neural network techniques cannot cope with recognising patterns that vary in time, so that their utility is limited to isolated word recognition, where the beginnings and ends of trained and input patterns must be clearly identified and matched [Paping 1992].

For the potential of neural network approaches to be realised in the field of speech recognition, these problems must be overcome. One approach that does overcome both these problems very effectively was proposed [Mrsic- Flögel 1992]. This approach is based on the concept of the Adder Neuron. The basic Adder Neuron is a simple 'neural' node, similar to the perceptron node used in most neural networks, see figure 1. It is designed to be connected with other nodes in a linear 'chain' to make a recogniser (figure 2). Each neuron in the sequence can add to a score that is passed along the Adder Neuron chain. The linear nature of the recognisers makes them easy to implement in hardware.

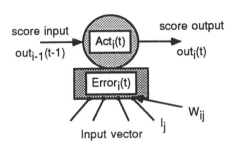

**Figure 1:** The basic Adder Neuron

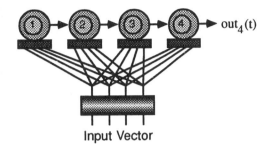

**Figure 2:** Adder Chain Structure

**Node Function**

i) Input Pattern Detection

A node $i$ is trained to a particular input pattern by setting its weights $W_{ij}$ to the actual input values $I_j$. The detection/recognition involves taking the error between the trained weight vector $W_i$ and the input vector I, and triggering node activation if this error is less than $\theta_t$ (the error threshold). The error and activation are calculated as described below:

$$\text{Error}_i = \Sigma(I_j - W_{ij}) \; ; \text{calculating error for the i-th node}$$

if $\text{Error}_i < \theta_i$ then $\text{act}_i = 1$   ; if error is less than threshold activate adder

ii) Activation decay

It is proposed that the activation of the adder node decays exponentially in time by the equation

$$\text{act}_i(t) = \theta_i * \text{act}_i(t-1)$$

where $\theta_i$ is the decay constant of adder node i. This decay has the effect of continuing (spreading) the activation of the node over a longer period in time after initial activation. While the activation value of the node is greater than the activity threshold ($f_i$), the node will keep the adder process active:

if $\text{act}_i(t) > f_i$ then activate adder function in node i at time(cycle) t

The exponential decay of the activation serves as a local short term memory mechanism for the activation of adder nodes.

iii) Adder function

Once the adder process is active in a node, the result from the previous adder node in the chain is incremented by one and is output to the next chain element. If the adder is not active the value of the previous node is just passed on:

if $\text{act}_i(t) > f_i$ then $\text{out}_i(t) = \text{in}_i(t) + 1$
else $\text{out}_i(t) = \text{in}_i(t)$      (where $\text{in}_i(t) = \text{out}_{i-1}(t-1)$)

These recognisers can be used to recognise temporal sequences such as sequences of feature vectors of a speech signal. They can cope automatically with matching similar patterns that vary in duration, and identifying sequences that are sub sequences of the input (i.e. identifying words within continuous spoken sentences). They can be very simple to train, requiring only one reference pattern per recogniser.

## iv) Adder Chain Operation

Figures 2 and 3 show the operation of a four element adder chain trained to recognise the sequence 1 3 2 4. In this example we have set the decay constant of the activation function so that each neuron remains active for three cycles after firing. The numbers in the circles represent the score for each of the four nodes at time t. The time warping is realised by the sustained activation function.

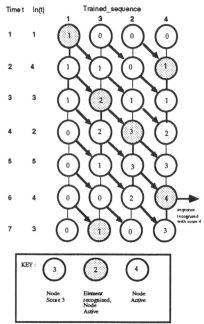

**Figure 3**: Adder Neuron Recogniser Chain : recognising the sequence 1-3-2-4.

Voting systems of Adder Node recognisers were simulated in C++ on an Apple Macintosh. The simulation used separate objects for each of the Adder Nodes, and overall control functions for implementing the voting system.

### Word Recognisers using Ear Filters.

The approach adopted to using Adder Node voting techniques in speech recognition was to train recognisers on the speech signals of individual words using the vector outputs of the Ear Filter Feature Detection System (EFFDS) at successive time windows. The recognisers would then be fed an input speech signal, via the EFFDS, consisting of continuously uttered sequences of the trained words. These recognisers would act as a small vocabulary, continuous speech word detection system.

In the experiments the recognisers were trained on a single English male speaker uttering ten numbers, and fed test input signals consisting of the same speaker uttering sequences of those numbers in a natural, continuous voice, with a normal level of background noise. This system was simulated in software on an Apple Macintosh computer.

Very promising results were achieved by the various versions of the system - between 60% and 100% of words were correctly identified in the correct place in time. Although this level of performance is not yet sufficient for practical applications, it is extremely promising given the number of permutations of possible word recognitions in continuous speech (words must be correctly identified in time as well as from a vocabulary).

Speech signals were taken at a sampling rate of 11 kHz, and the EFFDS was run with a window size of 110 samples (i.e. 10 ms). The variations on the system tried for these experiments were in four main areas: the parameters for the Membrane Nodes in the EFFDS, the output of the Normaliser in the EFFDS, the error function used in the Adder Nodes, and the parameters of the voting control system.

We discuss below the simulation of the EFFDS, the output of the EFFDS, the simulation of the recognisers, and the results of the tests.

## Ear Filter Feature Detection System

An Ear Filter Feature Detection System (EFFDS) is constructed using Membrane Nodes, Hair Nodes and Normalisers to convert an input sampled sound (speech) wave into a sequence of consolidated feature vectors (over time windows) for input to a word or lexical recogniser. The basilar membrane has a continuously varying characteristic frequency across its length. It is simulated using a (small) finite number of Membrane Nodes acting as bandpass filters accepting a range of characteristic frequencies.

The human inner ear has c. 5000 inner hair cell/ neurons which have a binary output ( either 'fire' or 'not fire'). It is not computationally feasible on a serial computer to simulate directly 5000 hair cells (and therefore have at least 5000 membrane nodes and 5000 hair nodes). Instead the EFFDS has a smaller number (16 - 32) of Hair Nodes and Membrane Nodes which correspond to the 'critical bands' [Shaw 1993]. The hair node simulates a collection of $n$ binary hair cells by outputting a number between 0 and $n$ that represents the total number of firings of the $n$ cells.

The output of the Hair Nodes representing the inner hair cells is passed through a Normaliser as discussed above. In addition the EFFDS has a single Hair Node that represents the outer hair cells attached to the tectorial membrane. It takes its input directly from the speech signal, and its output is passed through a special normaliser that records the proportional increase/decrease in the firings of the outer Hair Node. The normalised output of the outer Hair Node represents changes in the energy of the total speech wave and is useful in consonant recognition. It is passed to the consolidator along with the output vector of the main Normaliser.

An example EFFDS with 8 Membrane Nodes and hair Nodes is shown in figure 4 below.

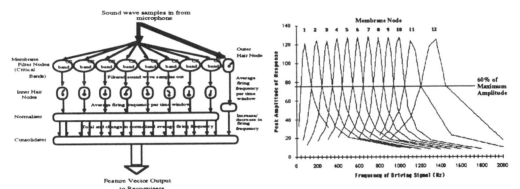

**Figure 4**: System Design diagram of EFFDS   **Figure 5**: Response ranges of filter in EFFDS filter bank

| Node | Range (Hz) | Driving Frequency (Hz) | Damping (sec$^{-1}$) | Input Power (sec$^{-1}$) |
|---|---|---|---|---|
| 1 | 240 - 340 | 282 | 455 | 5000 |
| 2 | 340 - 440 | 382 | 455 | 5000 |
| 3 | 440 - 540 | 481 | 455 | 5000 |
| 4 | 540 - 640 | 579 | 455 | 5000 |
| 5 | 640 - 740 | 677 | 455 | 5000 |
| 6 | 740 - 840 | 774 | 455 | 5000 |
| 7 | 840 - 940 | 870 | 440 | 5000 |
| 8 | 940 - 1040 | 966 | 435 | 5000 |
| 9 | 1040 - 1200 | 1080 | 700 | 7445 |
| 10 | 1200 - 1450 | 1260 | 1050 | 11000 |
| 11 | 1450 - 1850 | 1515 | 1700 | 15000 |
| 12 | 1850 - 2500 | 1900 | 2600 | 20000 |
| 13 | 2500 - 3500 | 2400 | 3300 | 20000 |
| 14 | 3500 - 5000 | 2850 | 4000 | 15000 |

**Table 1**: Membrane node values

## Output Of The EFFDS

The EFFDS output at every time window (defined by the firing frequency of the hair cells) is a vector consisting of normalised values between 0 and 100 representing the outputs of the inner hair cells, values between -100 and 100 representing the change in these normalised values from the previous time step, and a normalised value between 0 and 20 representing the output of the outer hair cell. The EFFDS output vector has 31 elements - 15 normalised values of the absolute hair response, 15 values representing the change in normalised hair response from the last window, and 1 value representing the percentage change in outer hair cell response (corresponding to change in total energy of the speech signal).

To make the output of the EFFDS easy to appreciate it can be transformed into a 3-dimensional colour (figures 6 and 7) spreadsheet chart, similar in the nature of information displayed to a spectrogram. This chart shows each of the absolute normalised inner hair cell values and the normalised outer hair cell value as lines plotted for each time window.

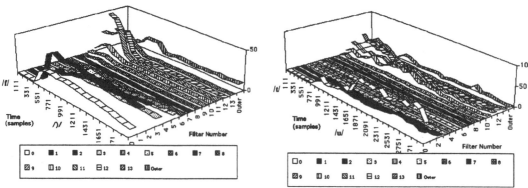

**Figure 6**:Response of EFFDS to the Word "four"    **Figure 7**:Response of EFFDS to the Word "two"

The EFFDS was simulated in C++ on an Apple Macintosh. The simulation used separate objects for each of the membrane nodes and hair nodes, and a separate function for the normaliser.

### Experiments and Results

Experiments were conducted using many variations of the parameters in the EFFDS and recognisers, In each case ten simulated recognisers were trained on ten words spoken by the same male speaker. These recognisers were then tested on input speech samples of the speaker uttering short random sequences of the words continuously and in a natural voice with normal background noise levels (see figure 8).

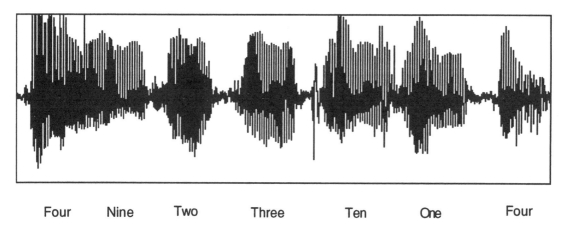

**Figure 8**:Input speech signal for "4 9 2 3 10 1 4"

The following parameters were set:
- A window size of 110 samples;
- Hair node firing threshold of 5000 per window (N.B. much higher powered membrane nodes);
- Error threshold for nodes in each recogniser of 35 - 50 (N.B. absolute error);
- 10 decay steps per recogniser;
- Voting threshold of 60% with minimum margin 10%

The results obtained from the simulations were between 60% and 100% recongition rates, with avereage correct word recognition rate of 75% and proportion of incorrect calssifications at 8%. The average rank of the recogniser for correct word was 1.2 on average (between 1.0 and1.6).

**Further Work**

There are several enhancements to the Adder Neuron model that we propose should be investigated. These are:

- Experimenting and adapting training set specific error weightings: the current system achieving 75% overall correct recognition result made little use of specific knowledge about the training set. By weighting the Adder Neuron error function for each recogniser to be biased towards hair node outputs that are known to be significant in distinguishing the trained word, and by biasing error thresholds and scores towards nodes in the recogniser that are important in the same sense, the performance of the recognisers could be significantly improved. Using such techniques we aim to make any two training classes as close to being two bi-orthogonal (in vector bases sense) as possible. Making pattern bi-orthogonal would give optimal performance in the model. [Weigl 1993]
- Developing, implementing and testing multi-file training: Words are often not recognised because of the diversity of pronunciations of the same word in different context. The recognisers in the developed simulation only allow training based on a single utterance of a word and are not based on several samples of that word. Training based on a set would emphasise the common features more strongly and thus performance should improve. In addition the should system become more successful in speaker-independent speech recognition.
- Implementing and testing of bi-directional time-warping in the model: some words have not been recognised due to the trained word being longer in length (time) that test word. So far Adder Neurons only allow for dynamic time expansion and not contraction. A way to cope with warping time in both directions has been proposed [Shaw 1993]

Based on the above improvements we expect the system to achieve much higher successful recognition rates.

**Conclusion**

The research conducted on Adder nuerons applied to word rectognition has resulted in the following

- implementation of Adder Neurons in software (C++) and a basic training system for speech signals
- an Ear Filter Feature Detection System (EFFDS) was proposed and implemented in software, as pre-processing module for the Adder Neuron recognisers.
- Using basic training algorithms a correct recognition rate of 75% was achieved for speaker-dependent word recognition (numbers 'zero' to 'nine') in continuous speech under normal noise conditions. This result is regarded as very encouraging as base result, for such a short period of research using only basic training methods.
- several improvements have been identified that could significantly improve recognition rate, while keeping the node a very simple processing element (no multiplications or division operations involved in processing of the node's activation function).

**References**

[Deller 1993] Deller J.R., Jr., et al., Discrete-time Processing of Speech Signals, Macmillan Publishing Company, 1993

[Kohonen 1988] Kohonen T. (1988), "The neural phonetic typewriter," Computer Vol 21(3) pp.11-22.

[Lipman 1989] R.P. Lipmann (1989) "Review of Neural Networks for Speech Recognition" in "Readings in Speech Recognition"eds. Waibel and Lee 1990 Morgan Kauffmann.

[Mrsic-Flogel 1992] Mrsic-Flogel J., Temporal Sequence Recognition with Adder Nodes, In Artificial Neural Networks 2, Proc. International Conference on Artificial Neural Networks - Brighton 1993, Eds. I.Aleksander and J.Taylor, Insert, Elsevier Science Publishers, 1992

[Mrsic-Flogel 1993] Mrsic-Flogel J., A Review of RAM-based Weightless Nodes, Proc. Workshop on Neural Networks, Ed. H.Hunning et al., Verlag der Augustinus Buchhandlung, p.130-144

[Paping 1992] Paping M., Strube H.E., "Ein gehoerorientierter Spracherkenner, der robust ist gegen zeitliche Schwankungen im Silben- und Phonembereich," DAGM - Symposium Mustererkennung 1992, 14 Sept 1992, Techn. Univ. Dresden.

[Rabiner 1989] Rabiner L. R.. (1989) "A tutorial on hidden Markov models and selected applications in speech recognition," Proceedings of the IEEE, vol. 77, pp. 257-285

[Rabiner 1990] L.R. Rabiner and S.E. Levinson (1981) "Isolated and Connected Word Recognition - Theory and Selected Applications" in "Readings in Speech Recognition"eds. Waibel and Lee 1990 Morgan Kauffmann.

[Schafer 1974] R.W. Schafer and L.R. Rabiner (1974) "Digital Representations of Speech Signals" in "Readings in Speech Recognition"eds. Waibel and Lee 1990 Morgan Kauffmann.

[Shaw 1993] Shaw J.E.T., Automatic Speech Recognition Using Neural Nodes and Novel Voting Techniques, MSc Thesis, Imperial College, 1993

[Weigl 1993] Weigl K., Metric Tensors and Non-orthogonal Functional Bases, Proc. Workshop on Neural Networks, Ed. H.Hunning et al., Verlag der Augustinus Buchhandlung, p. 96-104

# Person Identification by Neural Networks and Speech Processing

by

Arne Wold[§] and Jørn Wroldsen[#],

Gjovik College of Engineering,[*]

P.O. Box 191, N-2801 GJØVIK,

Norway

## Abstract

It is shown how a simple BP neural network can be successful in recognizing different people by using their speech. We use continous speech from persons reading from a book. Preprocessing consists of calculating the average of 256-points cepstra from 16 Hamming windows of length 32ms. The 40 lowest cepstral coefficients are used as input to a MLP net with configuration 40:5:2. Before performing the person-identification experiments we also show how it is easy to perform speaker independent vowel classification.

[§] email : arnew@linnea.gih.no
[#] email : jorn.wroldsen@gih.no
[*] Gjøvik Ingeniørhøgskole

## 1. Introduction

Speech processing technology has made remarkable progess in the recent years ( see e.g. Mariani, 1989, Furui, 1989 and 1992). However, the ultimate goal of providing machines with the same spoken language skills as humans is still many years ahead of us. With a voice-operated system humans would get a more natural interface with the computer. One can think about such systems for many different purposes, e.g. simultanous translation from one language to another, automatic inquiry of information databases (Kurematsu, 1988; Young and Proctor, 1989; Zue et al., 1990; Woodland, 1992), controlling complex machinery in industry, controlling lighting and recording devices in broadcasting systems (Nunn et al., 1992), entrance control etc.

A full speech processing system is normally broken down into five major components (see e.g. Fallside, 1991). These components are:
- *speech recognition*: acoustic processing (eg spectra), sub-word classification (eg phonemes), lexical access
- *spoken language analysis*: language processing (sentences),semantic processing (meaning)
- *interaction with machine* (eg inquiry of database)
- spoken language generation: message generation (sentences), language processing (words & sentence)
- *speech synthesis*: lexical egress (phonemes & duration), synthesiser controller, terminal synthesiser (speech)

We might also consider adding other components to the system above. It would e.g. in some applications be of vital interest to *recognize* or *identify* the speaker in one of the first modules, and proceedie *only* if the person is accepted. Such systems could of course use a code-word, and as such use only module 1 above. Another approach would be to use some kind of spectral information uniquely *identifying the person independent of the text spoken*. This kind of "voice prints" would be more user-friendly than systems using code-words, and would also more easily be accepted by the users than systems utilizing e.g. finger-prints or retinal features.

Most existing "speech processing" systems only implement component 1 and 3, 3 and 5 or both 1,3 and 5. These are  fairly simple systems compared to the kind of systems one is aiming at.

In this paper we will only deal with the speech-recognition component of a speech processing systems, showing how simple features from the speech signal can be used to identify persons independent of the text spoken. As a test example we first show  how our classifier works to classify vowels. Our classifier will always be based on a backpropagation neural network.

## 2. Classification systems

A general classification system is often thought of as a two-stage process where step one extracts features from the input signal, and step two is the classification based on the extracted features:

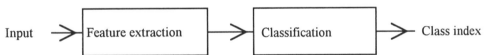

The input may be a speech sample, an image etc. The features to be used varies from problem to problem. In speech processing one often uses FFT spectra or cepstra, or more complicated features based on statistical averages and covariances of the input signal (Neelekantan and Gowdy, 1992). The classifiers used  are usually simple pattern matching, statistical models (e.g. Hidden markov Models) or artificial neural nets.

## 3. Acoustic processing and feature extraction

We performed two different types of experiment, classification of vowels and identification of persons. In both experiments the input data is sampled at 8012 Hz[1].

Classification of vowels.

The samples are grouped in data sets containing 64 samples. Each set is overlapped 50 % as shown, and the time for one set is 64/8012 ≈ 8 msec.

---

[1]The default sampling rate on the NeXT.

| Set no.1 | Set no.3 | Set no.5 | Set no.7 | Set no.9 | Set no.11 |
| Set no.2 | Set no.4 | Set no.6 | Set no.8 | Set no.10 | |

t [msec]

0    4    8    12    16    20    24    28    32    36    40    44

Every dataset is multiplied by a Hanning window given by: $w_i = 0,5 + 0,5 \cdot \sin\left(\frac{\pi \cdot i}{64}\right)$

The resulting dataset is transformed to frequency spectrum using the Hartley transform. Output is 32 frequency components with frequencies given by: $i \cdot \frac{8012}{64} \approx i \cdot 125 \, Hz$

Identification of persons.

Two persons read the same text in a text book for approx. 5 minutes. Long pauses for breathing is removed, and that's the only preprocessing. Then the samples are grouped in data-set containing 256 samples. Each set is overlapped 50 % as shown, and the time for one set is $256/8012 \approx 32$ msec.

| Set no.1 | Set no.3 | Set no.5 | Set no.7 | Set no.9 | Set no.11 |
| Set no.2 | Set no.4 | Set no.6 | Set no.8 | Set no.10 | |

t [msec]

0    16    32    48    64    80    96    112    128    144    160    176

Every dataset is multiplied by a Hamming window given by: $w_i = 0,54 + 0,46 \cdot \sin\left(\frac{\pi \cdot i}{256}\right)$

where i=1,2,...,256. The datasets are used to compute the cepstrum. This will be described in more detail below. The resulting dataset is transformed to frequency spectrum using the Hartley transform. Output is 128 frequency components with frequencies given by: $i \cdot \frac{8012}{256} \approx i \cdot 31,3 \, Hz$

This is expanded to a symmetrical set with 256 components using: Spect[i]:=Spect[256-i].

Before an inverse FFT, we compute the log magnitude of the frequency components. But as we only are interested in the power cepstrum, we use the Hartley transform once more for the inverse FFT, after a scaling, and a test to avoid the log magnitude of very small numbers. The cepstrum components are time samples at:

$t_i = i \cdot \frac{256}{8012 \cdot 128} \sec \approx i \cdot 0,25 \, m\sec.$

To minimize the influence of tiny pauses, 16 sets of cepstrum components are averaged for one input to the neural net.

The cepstrum is a time function, and is the sum of the cepstra of the sound excitation and the vocal tract impulse response, (Rabiner and Gold, p 689). The cepstrum serves to separate the sound excitation from the vocal tract response. Thus the cepstrum of the excitation signal should consist of pulses around $i = 0$, T, 2T, ..., where T is the pitch period. The vocal tract impulse response is a sequence that generally is non.negligible for about 20 to 30 msec. Consequently we decided to try the 40 first (or lowest) cepstral lines as the features given to the neural net (other choices than 40 might be better).

## 4. Neural nets

In our work we used a traditional backpropagation neural network with one input layer, one hidden layer and one output layer (see Rumelhart, Hinton and Williams, 1986). The number of nodes in each layer varied from problem to problem (see below). The nodes only have connections to the previous layer.

The neural net minimise the MSE between the actual output and the target output from each pattern. To decide whether a given pattern is in a given class we have the possibility to set different cuts. A MSE cut of 0.01 would e.g. mean that

$$\sum_{i \in output-nodes} ( \ target(i) \ - output(i) \ )^2 \leq 0.01$$

if the actual pattern is to be classified in the class defined by target(i).

In our network we used the activation function tanh(z) on all nodes in all layers. This means that the output of the network can never exceed $\pm 1.0$. If we set the target values to be vectors composed of $\pm 1.0$ this can lead to weights growing out of reasonable bounds. This can be avoided by setting letting the target vectors be composed of the numbers $\pm 0.9$. Furthermore, it turns out that if we scale the components of the input vectors such that every component fed into the network was in the interval [-1.0, 1.0] we can increse the convergence rate. For all our neural network simulations we used the program NNApp (see appendix A). The manual of NNApp (Drougge and Wroldsen, 1992) also contains further discussion of the back-propagation algoritm, and different tricks and rules of the thumb.

## 5. Experiments and results

We performed two different types of experiment, classification of vowels and identification of persons.

### Vowel experiment:

The data were taken from one person singing the 9 different norwegian vowels a, e, i, o, u, y, æ, ø and å, samplet at 8012Hz[2]. The sound were transformed using a 64 point Hartley transform using a hanning window. We saved the spectrum from every 3. window to the files used for training and testing. Alltogether we saved ~200 patterns from every vowels, and divided the data into 2 datasets, one for training and one for testing (~900 patterns in each). We used all the spectral components as input to the net, giving 32 input nodes[3]. Furthermore we used 10 nodes in the hidden layer and 9 output nodes. The target output for the vowel 'a' was {+1, -1, -1, -1, -1, -1, -1, -1, -1}, for 'e' it was {-1, +1, -1, -1, -1, -1, -1, -1, -1} etc.

In this net we have 32*10*9 = 2880 weights. The chance of overfitting is therfore present. We avoided this by running very few training iterations. Actually the network showed a good generalization when applied to testdata. After only 23 (!) iterations the MSE error was down to 0.0079. The results were:

TABLE 1:

| Dataset: Training set (~900 patterns) | | | |
|---|---|---|---|
| MSE cut | %correct | %wrong | %unclassified |
| 0.01 | 93.6 | 0.2 | 6.2 |
| 0.70 | 99.8 | 0.2 | 0.0 |

TABLE 2:

| Dataset: Test set (~900 patterns) | | | |
|---|---|---|---|
| MSE cut | %correct | %wrong | %unclassified |
| 0.01 | 93.8 | 1.3 | 4.9 |
| 0.70 | 98.7 | 1.3 | 0.0 |

### Person identification experiment:

Encouraged by the success of the simple experiment above we went on to the task of classifying speakers. Our aim was to find a simple neural network based on a few features from continous speech to separate two speakers. The signalprocessing should not be too complicated. After different trials and errors (as explained in the section on signalprocessing above) it turned out that we could manage quite well using the lowest 40 components of a 256 points cepstrum sampled at 8012Hz.

The procedure we used was the following: Two different persons read 5 minutes each from the same pages in a book[4]. We manually edited away the long pauses produced when we had to breath. The small micropauses (~0.1s) that is present in the speech *was left* in the sound-samples. We then calculated 256 point cepstra in 32ms Hamming windows, and averaged over 16 consecutive windows to make one pattern for input to the neural net. Therefore each pattern used in the neural net is based on 0.256s of the original sound sample.

---

[2]The sampling rate is the default sampling rate on the NeXT.

[3]A further analysis could possibly eliminate some of these inputs.

[4]We read from the book "Byens uttrykksformer" by Thomas Thiis Evensen

In this way we made 750 patterns from each person for the training-file, and the rest was put into the test-file (344 + 438 patterns from person A and B respectively). We used 40 input nodes, 5 nodes in the hidden layer, and 2 output nodes. The target output was now taken to be {+0.9 , -0.9 } for person A and {-0.9 , +0.9} for person B[5]. It turned out to be a hard task for the backpropagation network to learn this task. The net starts out with MSE of ~0.9 (naturally, since the weights are randomly initialised, and the target-vector is given as above). After only a few iterations (~10) the MSE is ~0.65, after 100 iterations it was ~0.5. After this it converges more slowly. After 1000 iterations we have MSE = 0.37. From now on it goes slowly down to 0.29 after 5000 iterations. We can summarize the results in the following tables:

TABLE 3:

| Dataset: Training set (1500 patterns), 5000 iter. | | | |
|---|---|---|---|
| MSE cut | %correct | %wrong | %unclassified |
| 0.2 | 71.9 | 3.5 | 24.5 |
| 0.5 | 82.1 | 7.7 | 10.3 |
| 0.8 | 87.5 | 12.4 | 0.1 |

TABLE 4:

| Dataset: Test set (782 patterns) , 5000 iterations | | | |
|---|---|---|---|
| MSE cut | %correct | %wrong | %unclassified |
| 0.2 | 61.6 | 10.2 | 28.1 |
| 0.5 | 71.6 | 16.2 | 12.1 |
| 0.8 | 77.4 | 22.1 | 0.5 |

Other runs produced simuilar results. We even ran for 20000 iterations without getting signinficantly better classification. Actually, a run with 20000 iterations gave MSE=0.31 (worse than above!) and very similar classification results (see table 3 and 4).

TABLE 5:

| Dataset: Training set (1500 patterns), 20000 iter. | | | |
|---|---|---|---|
| MSE cut | %correct | %wrong | %unclassified |
| 0.2 | 72.9 | 5.6 | 21.5 |
| 0.5 | 84.1 | 9.3 | 6.6 |
| 0.8 | 87.7 | 12.3 | 0.1 |

TABLE 6:

| Dataset: Test set (782 patterns) , 20000 iterations | | | |
|---|---|---|---|
| MSE cut | %correct | %wrong | %unclassified |
| 0.2 | 62.1 | 11.3 | 26.6 |
| 0.5 | 74.3 | 17.4 | 8.3 |
| 0.8 | 79.2 | 20.5 | 0.4 |

It should be noted that the experiments above was performed with very limited preprocessing of the data. We only took the cepstrum. Small pauses were left in the data, no normalization was done, etc. As a last experiment we transformed the data with a Z-transform before we fed them into the neural network. The data is the same as above, but on each input vector x(i) we performed the transformation $z(i) = \dfrac{x(i) - \overline{x}}{\sigma_x}$

which acts as a normalization of the data. This actually lead to a faster learning, but the final classification results were not better. The results below (table 7 and 8) were gotten after only 500 iterations, when the MSE was down to 0.32.

TABLE 7:

| Dataset: Training set (1500 patterns), 500 iter. | | | |
|---|---|---|---|
| MSE cut | %correct | %wrong | %unclassified |
| 0.2 | 70.4 | 5.1 | 24.5 |

---

[5]To avoid weigths wandering off it turned out to be useful to use this instead of {1,-1} and {-1,1}

| 0.5 | 81.5 | 9.1 | 9.4 |
| 0.8 | 85.4 | 14.3 | 0.1 |

TABLE 8:

| Dataset: Test set (782 patterns) , 500 iterations | | | |
|---|---|---|---|
| MSE cut | %correct | %wrong | %unclassified |
| 0.2 | 61.0 | 10.4 | 28.6 |
| 0.5 | 71.4 | 17.0 | 11.6 |
| 0.8 | 77.7 | 22.3 | 0.0 |

As can be seen from this, one can expect improvements with more preprocessing and/or postprocessing. We noted e.g. that in the experiment leading to table 3 and 4 above one could improve the results by a simple postprocessing in the following way: Take a sequence of 5 outputs of the net and take a simple majority vote between these 5 results. If we say the class decided by the net should be the class voted by the majority of the 5 outputs, we would get a 91% correct and 9.0% wrong classification of the testdata with a cut of 0.8.[6]

## 6. Conclusions

We have shown how it is possible to build a simple neural network based system which can be used to classify speakers independently of the text spoken. Our aim was to build such a system with as little as possible preprocessing. Further pre- and/or post-processing of the data could possibly improve the results.

## Appendix A: SOFTWARE

All signalprocessing was done on a NeXT station, using a microphone directly hooked up to the standard NeXT microphone input. The software used was a modified and extended version of *Spectro, version 2.102,* developed by P.R. Cook at Stanford Center for Computer Research in Music and Acoustics (CCRMA) (prc@ccrma.stanford.edu). We modified the original Spectro program to have better facilities for saving and loading sounds and spectra, and included a larger selection of transformations.

The neural net si,ulations were also done on the NeXT. We used the the program NNApp, ver.1.0., developed by Drougge and Wroldsen at Gjøvik College of Engineering (see Drougge and Wroldsen, 1992). This program is written in Objective-C (Cox, 1986) for the NeXT computer using the NeXT Interface Builder.

## References

**Cox, B.** (1986): Object Oriented Programming: An Evolutionary Approach, Addison-Wesley, Menlo Park, CA.

**Drougge, E. & Wroldsen, J.** (1992): Neural Network Simulations on the NeXT, *GIH preprint GIH9201.*

**Fallside, F.** (1991): Neural Networks in Spoken Language, *Proc. Neural Network Summer School, April, 1991.*

**Furui, S** (1989) : Digital Speech Processing, Synthesis, and Recognition, *Marcel Dekker, New York.*

**Furui, S** (1992) : Recent advances in speech recog. tech. at NTT laboratories, *Speech Comm. 11 (1992), 195-204.*

**Kurematsu, A.** (1988): Prospect of a basic study for automatice telephone interpretation, *Proc. Int. Conf. Advanced Man-Machine Interface, Tokyo.*

**Mariani, J.** (1989): Recent advances in speech processing, *Proc. IEEE Internat. Conf. Acoust. Speech Signal Process., Glasgow, Scotland, 57.S6.3.*

**Neelekantan, V. & Gowdy, J.N.** (1992): A Comparative Study of Using Different Speech Parameters in The Design of a Discrete Hidden Markov Model, *Proc. of the IEEE, SOUTHEASTCON '92, Birmingham, Alabama.*

**Nunn, J.S., King, J.S. & Spencer, R.H.** (1992): 'Run VT' Voice Control of Broadcast Systems, *International Broadcasting Convention (1992, Amsterdam), RAI Congress and Exhibition, 358, 172-176.*

**Rumelhart, D.E., Hinton, G.E. & Williams,R.J.** (1986): Learning Representations by Error Propagation, *in Parallell Distributed Processing (eds. McClelland, J.L. & Rumelhart, D.E.), MIT Press, Cambridge, USA (1986).*

**Woodland, P.C.** (1992): Spoken Alphabet Recognition Using Multilayer Perceptrons, *Neural networks for vision, speech, and natural language (eds. Lingaard, R., Myers, D.J. & Nightingale, C.), BT telecommunications series.*

**Young, S.J.Y & Proctor, C.E.** (1989): The design and implementation of dialogue control in voice operated database inquiry system, *Computer Speech & Language, 3, 329-353.*

**Zue, V.W., Glass, J., Goodine, D., Leung, H., Philips, M., Poldfroni, J. & Seneff, S.** (1990): The VOYAGER speech understanding system, preliminary development and evaluation, *Proc. ICAASP-90, 73-76.*

---

[6]Actually person A is classified correctly in 83.8% of the cases while person B is classified correctly in 91.0% of the cases.

# Speaker Independent Digit Recognition
# with Reduced Representations for Neural Network VLSI Chip*

Ki-Chul Kim, Il-Song Han†, Jun-Hee Lee, and Hwang-Soo Lee

Department of Information and Communication Engineering
Korea Advanced Institute of Science and Technology
207-43, Cheongryangri-dong, Dongdaemun-gu, Seoul 130-012, KOREA

†Korea Telecom Research Center
17, Woomyun-dong, Suhcho-ku, Seoul 137-140, KOREA

## Abstract

In this paper, we explore the possibility of URAN(Universally Reconstructable Artificial Neural-network) VLSI chip for speech recognition. URAN, a newly developed analog-digital hybrid neural chip, is discussed in respects to its input, output, and weight accuracy and their relations to its performance on speaker independent digit recognition. Multi-layer perceptron(MLP) nets including a large input layer are used to recognize a digit syllable at a forward retrieval in clean and additive white noise conditions. The simulation results using the reduced representations for the input, output, and weight variables of the network give the comparable performance to the ones obtained by the full precision computations. An MLP with the piecewise linear units using low accuracy computation provides good trainability and comparable performance to the networks with the sigmoidal units.

## 1 Introduction

The large computational requirements of the neural networks and their massively parallel architectures have led to a number of hardware implementations [1,2]. Though hardware implementation of the neural networks has many advantages, it involves practical difficulties in speed, scale, and accuracy implementation.

In this paper, URAN, the new analog-digital hybrid VLSI neural network, is described with digital interface to conventional computers. The implementation of the Back Propagation(BP) algorithm employing limited accuracy available to URAN chip is considered and applied to speaker independent digit recognition in clean and additive white noise conditions. Though various kinds of neural network models have been proposed and showed distinct performance in speech recognition areas, we examine simple MLPs to find their adaptability to reduced representations and the linear output function which are available to URAN.

The simulation results show that the performance of speaker independent digit recognition is not degraded for the limited floating point precision equivalent to 8 bit accuracy for input, output, and weight as in the previous works[3]. The MLP used in our simulations has a large number of input units to allow even the largest input pattern to be applied to input neurons at once as a whole. The temporal acoustic contexts are modeled inherently without time normalization by padding silence (zeros) for the words shorter than the size of the input units, which yields the investigation of the fundamental issues related to BP implementation on URAN chip.

In addition, we perform a simulation of on-chip learning by employing a piecewise linear function for hidden and output units instead of sigmoidal activation function. The BP simulations using linear hidden and output units gave similar performance to those using sigmoidal units, once training is completed with sigmoidal units. In addition, an MLP with piecewise linear hidden and output units is trained successfully and shows comparable performance to the ones trained with sigmoidal units in white noise conditions.

## 2 URAN–Universally Reconstructable Artificial Neural-network

### 2.1 Chip Architecture

In general, most of digital, analog, or analog-digital mixed neuro-chips are constrained in accuracy, speed, size or flexibility. There has been made new advancement in those aspects with the suggested analog-digital hybrid neural network circuit. The accuracy is improved by the linear voltage-controlled MOSFET linear resistance circuit for the synapse emulation. The speed is increased by the digital neural state. The general

---

*Sponsored in part by Korea Telecom

| Speed | $200 \times 10^9$ connections/s |
|---|---|
| Synaptic connections | 135,424 |
| Weight accuracy | 8 bit |
| Organization (synapses/neuron) | $92 \times n$, n=1 to 16 (electrically programmable) |
| Function of interchip expansion | Fully asynchronous and direct electrical wired-OR at output |
| Supply voltage | 3 V, -3 V |
| Chip size | $13 \times 13 \ mm^2$ |
| Technology | $1.0\mu$ digital CMOS |
| PGA package | 257 pin |

Table 1: URAN-I features

flexibility is realized by the inherent electrical characteristic of each synapse cell and modular architecture of chip.

Chip features are summarized in Table 1. As in Table 1, the chip performs under the flexible control, that is, the various mode of synaptic connection per neuron, the extendible weight accuracy and the unlimited asynchronous/direct interchip expansion in size and speed. In fact, 16 fully connected module is selected from external and independently - either one by one selection or all at one selection is possible as shown in Fig. 1. Additionally, the speed or modularity of each module is improved by introducing the individual external weight input. The neural hardware of huge size and high speed is straightforwardly implementable with chips in the same way as the chip is with module. Considering the operation of the circuit itself, all circuits over the chip except digital decoder unit are operated in analog. And as they are almost virtually static except switching transistor controlled by neural input, the computation speed is high and even can be improved substantially with the advance of memory production technology. As a basic cell, 9 transistors are used per cell including weight memory. The cell size including interconnection area for URAN-I is reduced to less than 40 $\mu$m in diameter.

With the linear voltage-controlled bipolar current source of each synapse cell, the synaptic function of multiplication is done with the switching transistor, i.e, half-in-analog and half-in-digital. The use of bipolar pulse improved stray effect from switching. Pulse of neural input for switching are not limited in style, time and numbers, that is, they are fully independent from each other.

The linearity is based on the compensated channel resistance of balanced configuration in the triode region, and proved to have more than 8 bit if necessary. The accuracy extendibility and flexible modularity are inherent in electrical wired-OR characteristics from each independent bipolar current source. NO clocking or any synchronous operation is needed in this case, while it is indispensable in most of conventional digital neural hardware of analog-digital neural chip. Any size of network can be integrated of implemented by merely placing the cell in 2 dimensional array without considering the timing requirement of digital or the load effect of analog. In the case of URAN-I, the delay of control signal is considered in designing the logic interface due to the long path on the chip. Off-chip digital interface is depicted in Fig. 2.

## 2.2 The Critical Issues of BP Implementations on URAN Chip

A fundamental limitation of the use of the BP in the training of an MLP is the high degree of required computational accuracy. Three critical issues must be addressed in the parallel implementation of BP on efficient hardware[2]. These are availability of weight values for back propagating the error, the scaling and precision of computations, and the efficient implementation of output transfer function. Among them weight accuracy and output function are considered. URAN can be used for retrieval if low weight accuracy and linear output function are allowed.

The weight accuracy of URAN chip is 8 bit. To perform BP simulations using the weight accuracy available to URAN chip, we first do retrieval tests using the reduced floating point weight values which are saved after normal training phase. We also evaluate an extremely efficient feature vector for input, peak-weighted binary spectrum, to exploit fully URAN chip architecture[4].

As the exact analysis of the non-linear output transfer function on the analog hardware is not possible, the output of the neuron chip is devised to provide linear function. We second perform retrieval tests with the linear output function for the synapse trained with non-linear output function. Finally, we perform training and retrieving using the piecewise linear function for the learning equation derived from the sigmoid output function.

# 3 Experiments with Reduced Representations

## 3.1 Speech Database and Preprocessing

The speaker independent digit recognition experiments have been performed to recognize isolated 10 Korean digits. The speech database was recorded in a silent office room from 10 male and 10 female speakers. Each digit was pronounced 10 times by each speaker. There were thus 2000 tokens in total. Among them 5 repetitions of each digit from 5 male and 5 female speakers ( 5 *repetitions* × 10 *digits* × 10 *speakers* = 500 *tokens* ) were used for training, and the other data set ( 500 tokens ) from the training speakers was used for multi-speaker recognition test, and the remaining 10 speakers' data ( 10 *repetitions* × 10 *digits* × 10 *speakers* = 1000 *tokens*) were used for speaker independent test.

Each utterance was low-pass filtered up to 4.7 kHz, then digitized at a 10 kHz sampling rate with 12 bit quantization. Manually endpointed speech data were preemphasized with a transfer function $H(z) = 1 - 0.98z^{-1}$. After passing through a 20 ms Hamming window at a rate of 10 ms, 17-channel critical-band filter bank analysis was performed to get a 17 dimensional feature vector for each frame. The 17-channel critical-band filter-bank was simulated by 512 point FFT. The data presented to the networks were simply scaled so that the range of the largest coefficient was approximately from -1 to 1.

A binary feature vector which is consisted of only 17 bits for each frame was also used for input. The binary spectrum was obtained by thresholding the second derivative of the normalized LPC spectrum, that is, by clamping spectral peaks above threshold as 1's and the others as 0's [4]. We have not performed word length normalization by using a large input frame buffer. Variable size of input feature vectors are applied to the input layer as a whole by padding zeros for the words shorter than the input layer.

To simulate the effect of noise disturbance, white Gaussian noise were added to the clean speech. The noise was generated to have Gaussian distribution by applying a simple type of smoothing, i.e., averaging over 12 samples, to the computer generated random data. The signal-to-noise ratio (SNR) is defined as the ratio of the speech power level (averaged over the whole test word) to the added noise power.

A zero mean, white Gaussian noise was added to the test utterance to generate noisy speech at each specified SNR, i.e., every 10 dB from 0 dB to 30 dB. An eighth-order Butterworth infinite impulse response (IIR) low pass digital filter with a cutoff frequency of 4.7 kHz was applied to the noise added speech to eliminate the high frequency components caused by the added white noise. The training patterns for all tests were taken from clean speech, and the recognition experiments were performed for each SNR.

## 3.2 MLP Architecture and Training Algorithm

All MLPs trained have 17 × 70 input neurons, 30 hidden neurons, and 10 output neurons. The network architecture used is illustrated in Fig. 3. In general, MLP consists of weighted-sum with sigmoidal output functions. The activation value of output neuron k is defined as follows.

$$O_k = \frac{1}{1 + e^{-\sum_k w_{kj}O_j}} \tag{1}$$

where $O_j$ is the activation value of hidden neuron j, and $w_{kj}$ is the weight from hidden neuron j to output neuron k. The activation value of hidden neuron is also defined by the same function using the activation value of input neuron and weights from input to hidden neurons.

During the training process of MLP, the total-sum-of-squared-error defined by equation (2) to be propagated between the target and the output values are calculated after every feedforward of the input pattern.

$$E = \frac{1}{2} \sum_{\text{all patterns}} \sum_k (Target_k - O_k)^2 \tag{2}$$

Changing the weights by a small amount in the direction of steepest descent minimizes the error and adjusts the internal parameters so as to better model the target input/output pairs.

To accelerate the learning speed a momentum $\gamma$ is used in the weight changes.

$$w_{kj}(t) = \eta \Delta w_{kj} + \gamma w_{kj}(t-1) \tag{3}$$

where $\eta$ is the learning rate, and t is the learning step. The learning rate $\eta$ and the momentum $\gamma$ are set to 0.1 and 0.9, respectively.

The initial strength of the weights are distributed uniformly and randomly from -0.5 to 0.5. The learning procedure was repeated until the total-sum-of-squared-error of the network reaches at 0.01. The recognition phase employs a winner-take-all rule which allows the network to keep the most highly activated neuron in output layer.

## 3.3 Speaker Independent Digit Recognition Results

First, we performed simulations of BP training and testing with reduced accuracy of four, two, and one decimal and binary representations for input, and two decimal places for the weight and output using the sigmoid output function. The training phase of the MLP with reduced floating point input is confined to 200 learning steps, and the MLP with binary input to 500 steps. The speaker independent digit recognition results for the various SNR conditions are listed in Table 2. As shown in the table, the reduced input accuracy does not affect the recognition performance, while the binary feature vector gives somewhat degraded performance.

| SNR | floating point input | | | binary input |
|---|---|---|---|---|
| ratio | 4 decimal | 2 decimal | 1 decimal | 1 bit |
| clean | 97.3 % | 97.1 % | 97.2 % | 90.8 % |
| 30 dB | 96.2 % | 96.2 % | 96.7 % | 90.9 % |
| 20 dB | 88.9 % | 88.8 % | 89.8 % | 87.5 % |
| 10 dB | 60.2 % | 60.4 % | 60.3 % | 67.2 % |
| 0 dB | 29.5 % | 29.8 % | 29.7 % | 38.4 % |

Table 2: Performance of sigmoid output function with reduced input representations

Second, we performed recognition tests using the linear output function as in equation (4) with the weight values trained above.

$$y = a(\sum_k w_{kj}O_j) + b, \quad -A \leq \sum_k w_{kj}O_j \leq A \quad (4)$$

The results were not sensitive to $a$ and $b$ if the domain of the linear function broadly covers the sum-of-weighted-input distributions. The simulation results listed in Table 3, in which $a = 0.1$, $b = 0.5$, and $A = 5$, show similar performance to the ones obtained by sigmoidal units.

We can conclude that the BP retrieval is not affected from the accuracy of weight, input, and output, when training is completed. In addition, training was also possible with two or one decimal places for input and output, which are equivalent to 8 bit or 4 bit precisions.

| SNR | floating point input | | | binary input |
|---|---|---|---|---|
| ratio | 4 decimal | 2 decimal | 1 decimal | 1 bit |
| 30 dB | 96.4 % | 96.2 % | 96.6 % | 90.5 % |
| 20 dB | 90.2 % | 90.1 % | 91.3 % | 86.6 % |
| 10 dB | 59.8 % | 59.8 % | 59.9 % | 68.0 % |
| 0 dB | 30.0 % | 30.8 % | 29.5 % | 38.5 % |

Table 3: Performance of linear output function with reduced input representations

Finally, we performed training using linear output functions. As the training using the simple linear functions such as equation (4) was not accomplished, we used piecewise linear functions combined with three linear functions. By minimizing the mean squared error(MSE) between the sigmoid and piecewise linear functions, a piecewise linear function is found as in equation (5). The MSE becomes zero when we calculate it up to 3 decimal places.

$$\begin{cases} y = 0.0, & x < -7.6 \\ y = 0.0087x + 0.066, & -7.7 \leq x < -2.2 \\ y = 0.206x + 0.5, & -2.2 \leq x < 2.2 \\ y = 0.0087x + 0.934, & 2.2 \leq x < 7.6 \\ y = 1.0, & x > 7.6 \end{cases} \quad (5)$$

The total-sum-of-squared-error after 200 learning steps are compared in Table 4. The piecewise linear units converge well, though the speed is somewhat slow. The recognition results, of which MLPs are trained and tested using the piecewise linear function with two decimal places of output resolution, are listed in Table 5. All MLPs have 30 hidden neurons, and the training phase was the same as the previous simulations.

The influence of the additive white noise is investigated in Table 6 which lists the recognition results of the training patterns in various SNR conditions. The influence of the output function is negligible as shown in the table, and the binary input results in improved performance in the low SNR conditions.

| Output function | floating point input | | | binary input |
|---|---|---|---|---|
| | 4 decimal | 2 decimal | 1 decimal | 1 bit |
| sigmoid | 0.017396 | 0.017363 | 0.017382 | 0.018188 |
| piecewise linear | 0.021355 | 0.021398 | 0.021000 | 0.022862 |

Table 4: Comparison of the total-sum-of-squared-error after 200 learning steps

| SNR ratio | floating point input | | | binary input |
|---|---|---|---|---|
| | 4 decimal | 2 decimal | 1 decimal | 1 bit |
| clean | 97.2 % | 97.1 % | 96.6 % | 90.1 % |
| 30 dB | 96.4 % | 96.4 % | 95.9 % | 89.9 % |
| 20 dB | 91.3 % | 91.3 % | 90.9 % | 86.4 % |
| 10 dB | 61.5 % | 61.6 % | 58.8 % | 65.2 % |
| 0 dB | 32.5 % | 32.6 % | 34.6 % | 37.7 % |

Table 5: Performance of piecewise linear output function with reduced input representations

| SNR ratio | sigmoidal units | | piecewise linear units | |
|---|---|---|---|---|
| | 4 decimal | 1 bit | 4 decimal | 1 bit |
| clean | 100 % | 100 % | 100 % | 100 % |
| 30 dB | 100 % | 99.6 % | 100 % | 100 % |
| 20 dB | 94.0 % | 96.2 % | 94.8 % | 97.8 % |
| 10 dB | 68.0 % | 78.8 % | 70.4 % | 76.4 % |
| 0 dB | 37.0 % | 43.2 % | 40.2 % | 42.6 % |

Table 6: Comparison of the effects of white noise added to the training patterns

## 4 Conclusions

In this paper, we describe the simulation results of the BP algorithms adapted for URAN chip, and show that the reduced weight accuracy using the linear output function is enough to obtain high performance in speaker independent digit recognition, once training was completed. We also illustrate that the piecewise linear output functions is useful for training when the learning equation is derived from the sigmoid output function. The reduced input representation such as the binary input shows improved performance in very low SNR conditions, which seems to be very useful for the input of a real-time speech recognition system using VLSI neural network chip. We are now developing a real-time speech recognition system using URAN chip with the simulated BP algorithms employing the reduced input representations. The reduced representations for the initial weight values, the amount of weight changes, and the total-sum-of-squared-error will be investigated for the complete on-chip training.

## References

[1] Il-Song Han and Ki-Hwan Ahn, "Neural Network VLSI Chip Implementation of Analog-Digital Mixed Operation for more than 100,000 Connections," in *Proc. of MICRONEURO'93*, Apr. 1993, pp. 159-162.

[2] H. McCarter, "Back Propagation Implementation on the Adaptive Solutions CNAPS Neurocomputer Chip," in *Advances in Neural Information Processing Systems 3*, R.P. Lippman, J.E. Moody, and D.S. Touretzky, Eds. Dan Mateo, CA: Morgan Kaufman, 1991, pp. 1028-1030.

[3] J.L. Holt and T.E. Baker, "Back Propagation Simulations Using Limited Precision Calculations," in *Proc. of IJCNN'91*, Vol. II, 1991, pp. 121-126.

[4] K.C. Kim and J.W. Cho, "Robust Speech Recognition Using Frequency Weighted All-Pole Model Spectrum," *Computer Processing of Chinese & Oriental Languages*, Vol. 5, No. 3 & 4, Nov. 1991, pp. 203-216.

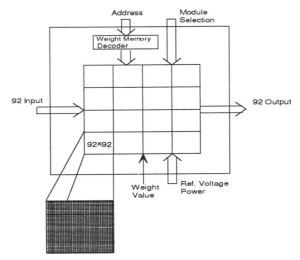

Address     Module Selection

Weight Memory Decoder

92 Input        92 Output

92×92

Weight Value     Ref. Voltage Power

**Fig. 1. URAN-1 block diagram**

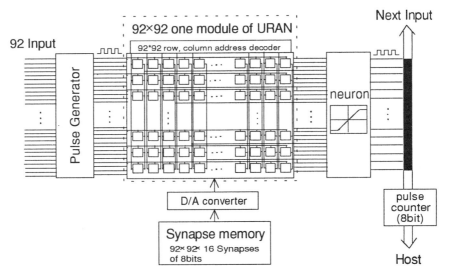

92 Input

92×92 one module of URAN

92*92 row, column address decoder

Pulse Generator

neuron

Next Input

pulse counter (8bit)

Host

D/A converter

Synapse memory
92× 92× 16 Synapses of 8bits

**Fig. 2. Off-chip digital interface**

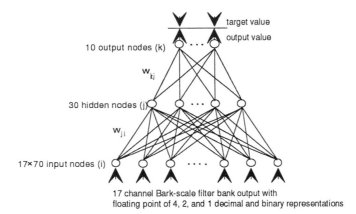

target value

output value

10 output nodes (k)

$w_{kj}$

30 hidden nodes (j)

$w_{ji}$

17×70 input nodes (i)

17 channel Bark-scale filter bank output with floating point of 4, 2, and 1 decimal and binary representations

**Fig. 3. MLP architecture**

# Speech and Language

**Session Chairs: David Rumelhart**
**Richard Peterson**

## POSTER PRESENTATIONS

# Intelligent Judge Neural Network for Speaker Independent Isolated Word Recognition

Dou-Suk Kim, Kyu-Woong Hwang*, and Soo-Young Lee
Department of Electrical Engineering
Korea Advanced Institute of Science and Technology
373-1 Kusong-dong, Yusong-ku, Taejon 305-701, Korea
Tel: +82-42-869-3431; Fax: +82-42-869-3410; E-mail: sylee@ee.kaist.ac.kr
* Currently at the Electronics and Telecommunications Research Institute, P.O. Box 8, Taejon, Korea.

## Abstract

An "intelligent judge" neural network (IJNN) is developed to make decisions out of contradictory arguments, which may come from different classifiers with different characteristics and/or features. For speaker independent isolated word recognition applications multi-layer perceptron (MLP) and hidden-control neural networls (HCNN) are selected for the lower-level classifiers and trained separately. The MLP classifies the word as a spectro-temporal pattern, while the HCNN relies on dynamic nature of the speech signal. The "judge" accepts input values from the lower-level neural network classifiers and provides ruling verdicts. Two intelligent judges have been investigated. The "neuro-judge" rules by extracting decision rules from training data, i.e. disputes between the two classifiers, while the "fuzzy-judge" just utilizes min-max operations. The combined network utilizes both spectro-temporal pattern and dynamic nature of speech, and demonstrates better recognition rate. More importantly its performance is much less sensitive to the choice of training data.

## 1. Introduction

Classification of complex patterns by adaptive learning makes neural networks very attractive for speech recognition applications. Also, due to its inherent parallelism, neural networks can take advantage of special hardwares for real-time applications.

A number of neural network models has been successfully applied to speech recognition problems [1]. Many of them regard the speech signal as spectro-temporal pattern, and utilize classification function of neural networks with proper time alignment, while only a few utilizes dynamic nature of speech signal. The former includes multi-layer perceptron(MLP) [2,3], Self-Organizing Feature Map[4], Learning Vector Quantization[5], and Time-Delay Neural Networks[6]. These approaches assume that separate utterances of the same word should follow similar paths in the feature space, and only the time taken to traverse the path should differ. The most successful time alignment methods include trace segmentation, dynamic time warping (DTW), and hidden Markov models. The latter regards speech signal as output of nonlinear dynamic system, and tries to model the system with recurrent neural networks. Recurrent connections may come from hidden layer [7,8] or output layer [9]. This time dynamics may also be modelled by hidden-control neural networks (HCNN), which combines MLP with state-transition of hidden-Markov model. [10,11]

Although both approaches have been quite successful, they had started with different nature of speech signal and showed advantages and disadvantages. It has been shown that spectro-temporal pattern approaches are better for certain phonemes, while dynamic "temporal flow" approaches provide better results for the others.    In this paper we report a hierachial neural network approach, which combines both nature of the speech signal and demonstrates improved performance both in recognition rates and on robustness to training data.    Although it shares some common background with recent modular neural network architecture based on Pandemonium [12], instead of selecting the lower-level module with the loudest shout, our judge network is adaptively trained for minimum error or utilize min-max logic [13] to make decision based on **combined features** of the lower-level classifier outputs.    Also, unlike other modular neural networks which utilize sub-modules with identical architecture for different sets of patterns [12,13], each lower-level classifier submodule here has unique architecture to look at the problem with **different insights.**

## 2.  Intelligent Judge Neural Network Architecture

The Intelligent Judge Neural Network (IJNN) is composed of a lower-level classifier module and an upper-level verdict module.    The lower-level classifier module consists of several neural network submodules, which try to classify the input patterns based on different aspects and features.    For the speaker-independent isolated-word recognition applications we choose only two classifier submodules, i.e. multi-layer perceptron (MLP) [2,3] and hidden-control neural networks (HCNN) [10,11].    The MLP classifies the speech signal as spectro-temporal pattern, while the HCNN consider it as output of a nonlinear dynamic system.    As shown in Fig.1 output values of these two neural network classifiers are fed to the verdict module to combine both characteristics.

The lower-level MLP submodule classifies input speech signals into M words.    One bipolar output neuron with Sigmoidal nonlinearity is assigned to each word.    For time alignment we adopted simple trace segmentation scheme [14], which provides reasonable performance without serious computation time.    For each isolated word cumulative distances of input features are calculated at each time, and an overall trace, T, of the feature is defined as the cumulative distance at the end point.    To generate normalized features with N time frames, the trace is then divided into (N-1), representing equivalent amounts of feature changes between each normalized time interval.    New input features may be formed by interpolation to provide the equivalent amounts of change between adjacent time frames.    This simple time normalization procedure removes variations of speech periods, especially for steady long-pronounced vowels.

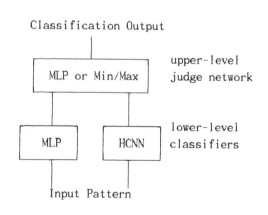

Fig.1   IJNN architecture

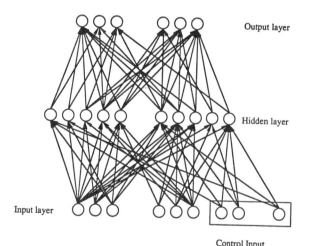

Fig.2   HCNN architecture

Hidden control neural network (HCNN) is a feed-forward neural network with Viterbi segmentation and quite similar to HMM. Basic architecture of the HCNN is shown in Fig.2. It is a recurrent neural network, where output signals at time t are fed back to input for time t+1. The neural value $\mathbf{x}(t)$ is representing a state of speech signal at time t, and the network may provide transition from one state to another at each time interval. To control the state transitions, another vector $\mathbf{c}(t)$ is added in the input layer and consists of "hidden-control" neurons. Provided the hidden-control vector $\mathbf{c}(t) = \mathbf{F}_i$ at time t, $\mathbf{c}(t+1)$ is restricted to be either $\mathbf{F}_i$ or $\mathbf{F}_{i+1}$. For isolated word recognition applications one HCNN is trained to identify dynamics of one word category. Since the identification error is a function of both the synaptic weights and control vector $\mathbf{c}(t)$, the adaptive learning for minimum identification error consists of "re-estimation" of the synaptic weights and "segmentation" of the control vector at each iteration epoch. The "re-estimation" process is the same as error back-propagation learning of standard multi-layer Perceptron, while the "segmentation" process involves Viterbi algorithm. When an unknown word is presented, an optimum control sequence $\mathbf{c}(t)$ and corresponding error are determined by the Viterbi algorithm for each HCNN, and the word is categorized by the HCNN with minimum error.

Provided each classifying submodule had small misclassifing rate, possibility of misclassification by both submodules becomes much smaller. The upper-module serves as an "intelligent judge" and provides verdict for disputes between the classifier submodules. Two different intelligent judges are investigated. The "neuro-judge" itself is an MLP to extract the decision rules from dispute cases. The "fuzzy-judge" first gets smaller values from the two classifier modules for each pattern class, and then selects the class with maximum values. The output values of the lower-level classifiers are fed to the input of the upper-level "judge" MLP. For recognition of M words the "judge" modules have 2M inputs and M outputs. However, to provide similar output values to those of classifying MLP, we map the error output of the HCNN into (-1,1) region.

## 3. Experiments for Korean Digit Recognition

We had applied the IJNN for Korean digit recognition application. Although only 10 words, from "0" to "9", are aimed for recognition, it turned out to be very tough problem. All the Korean digits have only one syllable, which does not have enough features for accurate classification. To make things worse, some of them are very close to each other. For example, number "1" (pronounced as "il") and number "7" ("chil") are only different at the initial consonant. Number "1" ("il") and number "2" ("i"), and also number "3" ("sam") and number "4" ("sa") are only different at the last consonant.

For the input features we use 14 delta-Cepstrum coefficients and 1 delta-power magnitude. Therefore numbers of input neurons for the lower-level MLP and HCNN are 15. Number of input for the upper-level "judge" is 20. All 3 neural modules have 10 outputs. Number of neurons for hidden layer is set to 10.

We had collected 60 sets of speech data from 12 speakers (5 sets each), and used 30 sets (6 speakers) for training and the other 30 sets for testing. This small number of training data also poses very tough generalization problem, which we are trying to prove anyway. To check sensitivities of the recognition system on training data, 3 experiments are conducted by randomly selecting different training data sets. For the training data both the lower-level MLP and HCNN classifiers show 100% correct recognition after training at all the 3 experiments. However, as shown in Table 1, the lower-level MLP and HCNN classifiers show 98.4% and 92.1% correct

Table 1. Recognition Rates for Korean Digit Recognition Experiments

unit: %

|  | Set I | Set II | Set III | Average | Max-Min |
|---|---|---|---|---|---|
| MLP only | 98.7 | 99.3 | 97.3 | 98.4 | 2.0 |
| HCNN only | 95.3 | 93.0 | 88.0 | 92.1 | 5.3 |
| IJNN (neuro-judge) | 99.0 | 99.3 | 98.0 | 98.8 | 1.3 |
| IJNN (fuzzy-judge) | 99.0 | 99.7 | 98.0 | 98.9 | 1.7 |

average recognition rates for the test data, respectively. The relative low recognition rates of the HCNN may be contributed from two stage process, which first segments the word into intervals and later calculates error at the subregions. Errors at the segmentation stage can never be corrected in this model. Although several schemes may be employed to overcome this problem, no specific attempt was made here.

Before applied to the inputs of the upper-level "judge", the HCNN output values were mapped into (-1,+1) region. Also the slope value of the Sigmoid function for the lower-level MLP is set to much smaller value to avoid saturation. The "neuro-judge" MLP is trained by error back-propagation with the same training data used for the lower-level classifiers. After training the "judge" MLP the recognition rates increase to 98.8% in average. Although the reduction of misclassification rate is 25% only, it clearly demonstrates usefulness of the proposed IJNN. The "fuzzy-judge" does better jobs than "neuro-judge", i.e. 98.9% average recognition rate, but the difference is too small to come into conclusion. Actually the MLP alone has very small (1.6%) misclassification rate, and it is difficult to increase the recognition rate in this range. It is also worth noting that deviations of the recognition rates among different training sets become much smaller for the IJNNs. We believe this lower sensitity to trainingg data comes from higher generalization capability due to combination of spectro-temporal pattern aspects and dynamic characteristics of speech signal. In practical applications training data sets are always limited and no a priori knowledge is given to the validity of the data, this low sensitivity to training data is extremely important.

Confusion tables for Data Set III are shown in Tables 2, 3 and 4. Although experiments with Data Set III have the lowest recognition rates, they also show the best performance improvement by the IJNNs. Many of the confusions shown in Tables 2 and 3 are corrected by the "judge" in Table 4. The remaining confusions are common to both the lower-level classifiers, and the "judge" was not able to correct these common confusions.

Performance of this IJNN may be further improved by several techniques. First, performance of the lower-level classifiers can be improved by using more training data. For example, by using 12 training sets instead of 30 sets, the lower-level MLP alone was able to recognize 94.7% correct only. The lower-level classifier networks and the upper-level "judge" network may also be trained with different data, which actually generates disputes among lower-level classifiers during training of the "judge" network. Most importantly, to avoid common confusions among lower-level classifiers, the IJNN can take advantage of different input features and large number of lower-level classifiers. At the previous experiments both the lower-level MLP and HCNN use same delta-Ceptsrum coefficients for input features, which may get rid of important features in original speech signal. Provided quite different input features were used instead of the

Table 2. Confusion Table of the First MLP for Data Set III

| Output<br>Input | 0 | 1 | 2 | 3 | 4 | 5 | 6 | 7 | 8 | 9 |
|---|---|---|---|---|---|---|---|---|---|---|
| 0 | 27 | 1 | 0 | 1 | 0 | 0 | 1 | 0 | 0 | 0 |
| 1 | 0 | 30 | 0 | 0 | 0 | 0 | 0 | 0 | 0 | 0 |
| 2 | 0 | 0 | 30 | 0 | 0 | 0 | 0 | 0 | 0 | 0 |
| 3 | 0 | 0 | 0 | 30 | 0 | 0 | 0 | 0 | 0 | 0 |
| 4 | 0 | 0 | 0 | 0 | 30 | 0 | 0 | 0 | 0 | 0 |
| 5 | 0 | 0 | 2 | 0 | 0 | 30 | 0 | 0 | 0 | 0 |
| 6 | 0 | 0 | 0 | 0 | 0 | 0 | 30 | 0 | 0 | 0 |
| 7 | 0 | 1 | 0 | 0 | 0 | 0 | 0 | 29 | 0 | 0 |
| 8 | 0 | 0 | 0 | 0 | 0 | 0 | 0 | 0 | 30 | 0 |
| 9 | 0 | 0 | 0 | 0 | 0 | 4 | 0 | 0 | 0 | 26 |

Table 3. Confusion Table of the HCNN for Data Set III

| Output<br>Input | 0 | 1 | 2 | 3 | 4 | 5 | 6 | 7 | 8 | 9 |
|---|---|---|---|---|---|---|---|---|---|---|
| 0 | 17 | 0 | 0 | 0 | 0 | 4 | 1 | 0 | 8 | 0 |
| 1 | 0 | 25 | 0 | 0 | 0 | 0 | 0 | 5 | 0 | 0 |
| 2 | 0 | 4 | 26 | 0 | 0 | 0 | 0 | 0 | 0 | 0 |
| 3 | 0 | 0 | 0 | 30 | 0 | 0 | 0 | 0 | 0 | 0 |
| 4 | 0 | 0 | 0 | 0 | 30 | 0 | 0 | 0 | 0 | 0 |
| 5 | 1 | 0 | 0 | 0 | 0 | 23 | 0 | 0 | 1 | 5 |
| 6 | 0 | 0 | 0 | 0 | 0 | 1 | 28 | 0 | 1 | 0 |
| 7 | 0 | 0 | 0 | 0 | 0 | 0 | 0 | 30 | 0 | 0 |
| 8 | 0 | 0 | 0 | 0 | 0 | 0 | 0 | 0 | 30 | 0 |
| 9 | 0 | 0 | 0 | 0 | 0 | 5 | 0 | 0 | 0 | 25 |

Table 4. Confusion Table of the IJNN with for Set III

| Output<br>Input | 0 | 1 | 2 | 3 | 4 | 5 | 6 | 7 | 8 | 9 |
|---|---|---|---|---|---|---|---|---|---|---|
| 0 | 29 | 0 | 0 | 0 | 0 | 0 | 1 | 0 | 0 | 0 |
| 1 | 0 | 30 | 0 | 0 | 0 | 0 | 0 | 0 | 0 | 0 |
| 2 | 0 | 0 | 30 | 0 | 0 | 0 | 0 | 0 | 0 | 0 |
| 3 | 0 | 0 | 0 | 30 | 0 | 0 | 0 | 0 | 0 | 0 |
| 4 | 0 | 0 | 0 | 0 | 30 | 0 | 0 | 0 | 0 | 0 |
| 5 | 0 | 0 | 0 | 0 | 0 | 30 | 0 | 0 | 0 | 0 |
| 6 | 0 | 0 | 0 | 0 | 0 | 0 | 30 | 0 | 0 | 0 |
| 7 | 0 | 1 | 0 | 0 | 0 | 0 | 0 | 29 | 0 | 0 |
| 8 | 0 | 0 | 0 | 0 | 0 | 0 | 0 | 0 | 30 | 0 |
| 9 | 0 | 0 | 0 | 0 | 0 | 4 | 0 | 0 | 0 | 26 |

delta-Cepstrum coefficients, one may have much better improvement from this IJNN. Neural networks based on different concepts and statistical classifiers such as HMM may also be incorporated for the lower-level classifiers.

## 4. Conclusion

In this paper we have proposed a new hierachial neural network for speech recognition, and demonstrated improved performance for Korean digit recognition application. By combining different neural network classifiers, i.e. MLP as a spectro-temporal pattern classifier and NPM as nonlinear dynamic system identifier, we were able to improve recognition rate as well as sensitivity to training data. Another MLP serves as a "judge", which extractes decision rules by learning and provides verdicts on disputes between the lower-level classifiers. Much more performance improvement is expected by using different input features and increasing number of neural network models for the lower-level classifiers.

**Acknowledgement**: This research was supported by Korea Advanced Institute of Science and Technology.

## References

[1] R.P. Lippmann, "Review of neural networks for speech recognition," Neural Computation, vol.1, pp. 1-38, 1989.

[2] B. Gold and R.P. Lippmann, "Neural-net classifiers useful for speech recognition," Proc. IEEE First Int. Conf. Neural Networks, 1987.

[3] R. Gemello and F. Mana, "A neural approach to speaker independent isolated word recognition in an uncontrolled environment," Proc. ICNN-Paris, July 1990, pp. 163-166.

[4] T. Kohonen, " The 'neural' phonetic typewriter," IEEE Computer, pp. 11-12, March 1988.

[5] T. Kohonen, "An introduction to neural computing," Neural Networks, vol.1, pp.3-16, 1988.

[6] A. Waibel, T. Hanazawa, G. Hinton, K. Shikano, and K. Lang, "Phoneme recognition using Time-Delay Neural Networks," Proc. ICASSP, May 1989.

[7] R.L. Watrous, L. Shastri, and A.H. Waibel, "Learned phonetic discrimination using connectionist networks," Proc. European Conf. Speech Tech, Edinburgh, Sept. 1987, pp. 377-380.

[8] D. Albesano, R. Gemello, and F. Mana, "Word recognition with recurrent network automata," Proc. IJCNN, Baltimore, June 1992, pp. II-308-313.

[9] K. Iso and T. Watanabe, "Speaker-independent word recognition using a neural prediction model," Proc. ICASSP, Albuquerque, April 1990, pp. 441-444.

[10] E. Levin, "Modeling time varying systems using hidden control neural architecture," Proc. NIPS-3, Denver, 1991, pp. 147-154.

[11] D.S. Kim and S.Y. Lee, "Weighted distance measure for speaker-independent digit recognition with hidden-control neural network," Proc. ICANN, Amsterdam, 1993.

[12] F.J. Smieja and H. Mühlenbein, "Reflective modular neural network systems," Technical Report 633, GMD, Sankk Augustin, March 13, 1992.

[13] B.T. Zhang and G. Veenker, "Distributed parallel cooperative problem-solving with a voting and election system of neural learning networks," in *Parallel Processing in Neural Systems and Computers*, R. Eckmiller et al. Ed., North Holland, 1990, pp. 513-516.

[14] H.F. Silverman and N.R. Dixon, "State constrained dynamic programming for discrete utterance recognition," Proc. ICASSP, Denver, 1980, pp. 169-172.

# Dynamic Adaptation to Speaking Rate

Mai H. Nguyen     Garrison W. Cottrell
Department of Computer Science & Engineering
Institute for Neural Computation
University of California, San Diego
La Jolla, CA 92093–0114
mnguyen@cs.ucsd.edu

December 1993

**Abstract.** Accounting for acoustic variation is an essential element in automatic speech recognition (ASR). One source of acoustic variation is speaking rate, which can vary by 31% to as much as 60% in conversational speech. Psycholinguistic studies have shown that speaking rate affects speech perception, suggesting that listeners must be sensitive to rate changes and process speech in a rate-dependent manner.

We present a technique to incorporate such rate-dependent processing into an ASR system using a recurrent network to automatically estimate and dynamically adapt to the rate of a signal. We argue that incorporating this technique into a speech recognition system allows for robust classification with respect to rate *without* having to train the system on many different rates. We have applied our method to several signals: sets of sine waves differing in frequency and in phase, a multidimensional signal representing the walking gait of children, and the energy contour of a simple speech utterance. Our experimental results show that the system's time constant rapidly and appropriately reflects rate changes in these signals. We propose to apply this technique to speech, with the goal of building recognizers that are robust to speaking rate variation.

## 1   Introduction

Accounting for acoustic variation is an essential element in automatic speech recognition (ASR). Variation in the acoustic signal arises from physiological differences between talkers, coarticulatory effects in speech production, and external factors such as background noise and channel distortions. Speaking rate is another source of acoustic variation, and although it has received relatively little attention in the ASR literature, it it known that speaking rate varies substantially in conversational speech, across speakers as well as within the speech of a single speaker. It has been shown that variation in rate during the course of a conversation averages about 31% [7] and can be as much as 60% [5]. Obviously, human listeners are not severely affected by such wide variations in speaking rate. Thus, it can be argued, there must be some process of adaptation by which the listener adjusts to the rate of the incoming speech signal. In fact, several psycholinguistic studies (*e.g.,* [9] [4]) have shown that speech rate, as determined from the surrounding context, biases interpretation of a phonetic segment. For example, a rapidly articulated long vowel is frequently interpreted as a short vowel if embedded in a sentence spoken at a slower rate [6]. Given the wide and frequent variation of speaking rate in conversational speech, this suggests that listeners must be sensitive to rate changes and process speech in a rate-dependent manner. It makes sense, then, that such rate-dependent processing is also necessary to produce good results in an ASR system.

Conventional ASR techniques, such as Dynamic Time Warping (DTW) and Hidden Markov Models (HMM), have attempted to address the issue of acoustic changes caused by speaking rate variation. However, the solutions offered by these techniques do not take advantage of the additional information on rate provided by the surrounding context. DTW minimizes the effects of rate by normalizing each segment to its "normal," standard length by warping the time axis of a speech pattern so that, temporally, it matches the reference template, *i.e.,* long versions of a word or phoneme are compressed, while short versions are stretched to a standard length. But in doing so, all timing information that may convey rate information is essentially eliminated. HMMs incorporate a statistical duration model which allows for some temporal differences between a test segment and its prototypical form. However, HMMs do not interpret any temporal differences such as duration *relative* to rate. In fact, neither DTW nor HMM provides any mechanism for treating acoustic changes due to rate variation as anything other than noise. Any variations in acoustic features that are manifestations of rate changes are normalized segment by segment, without reference to the rate of the surrounding context. Any variations in acoustic features that are manifestations of rate changes are interpreted segment by segment, without reference to the We claim that this rate-*ind*ependent processing cannot yield 100% correct classification. In contrast, our approach is to treat acoustic variations caused by rate as additional information that should be accounted for in order to achieve good recognition.

## 2 Dynamic Rate Adaptation

Our technique for rate adaptation is similar to the temporal auto-association technique [3]. A recurrent network is trained to be a model of the input signal by predicting the signal at some delay. In order to have a way of adjusting the speed of the network, we use the Delta-Net technique [10]. The Delta-Net is simply a finite-difference approximation of a continuous time network.

The real-time recurrent learning algorithm [11] is used to train the network to predict the signal for a particular delay ($\delta$) and a particular time constant ($\tau$). The weights are then fixed, and the network is presented the signal at a different rate. The network adapts to the new rate by adjusting its time constant using gradient descent. The network equations are

$$
\begin{aligned}
y_k(t + \Delta t) &= (1 - \frac{1}{1 + \exp^{-\alpha_k}}) \cdot y_k(t) + \frac{1}{1 + \exp^{-\alpha_k}} \cdot f(s_k(t)) \\
s_k(t) &= \sum_j w_{kj} y_j(t),
\end{aligned}
\tag{1}
$$

where $\alpha$ parameterizes the time constant $\tau$: $\tau_k = 1 + \exp^{-\alpha_k}$.

The time constant update rule is given as:

$$
\Delta \alpha_i(t) = -\eta \frac{\partial E}{\partial \alpha_i(t)} = -\eta \sum_i \frac{\partial E}{\partial y_k(t)} \frac{\partial y_k(t)}{\partial \alpha_i},
\tag{2}
$$

where, by defining $q_i^k(t + \Delta t) \equiv \frac{\partial y_k}{\partial \alpha_i}(t + \Delta t)$ and $g_i \equiv \frac{1}{1 + \exp^{-\alpha_i}}$, we have

$$
q_i^k(t + \Delta t) = q_i^k(t) + g_i \cdot \left[ f'(s_k(t)) \sum_j w_{kj} q_i^j(t) - q_i^k(t) \right] + \delta_{ik} \cdot g_i(1 - g_i) \cdot [f(s_k(t)) - y_k(t)].
\tag{3}
$$

The complete derivation of these equations is given in [1].

## 3 Experimental Results

### 3.1 Sine Waves

Our first set of experiments were to see if the method would work for simple sine waves. We trained a network to predict two sine waves, $sin(x)$ and $sin(2x)$, with a phase delay of 36 degrees. Then, with the weights fixed, the time constant $\tau$ is allowed to change from its initial value of 1 according to Equation 2. We should note here that the problem posed to the system is exacerbated by the fact that we did not start the system at the original rate and slowly adjust it; we simply presented it with the fast signal abruptly. The system adjusted to the rate of the new input within three cycles for this two-frequency problem. We had similar results with another network trained to predict four sine waves with four different phases. The four-phase network needed only a single cycle to adapt to the rate of the new input.

## 3.2 Gait Data

To test DRA on a more complex signal, we used a 24-dimensional time-varying signal representing the average walking cycle for a seven-year-old. The data, produced at the Motion Analysis Laboratory at the Children's Hospital in San Diego, was extracted from free-speed, level-walking subjects. Each vector of data consists of 24 floating point numbers to represent the joint angles in both legs at each time step. Since we did not have data for children walking at different rates, we simulated different rates by sampling the signal at different intervals: normal rate refers to every other time step; fast rate refers to every third time step for a speedup of 1.5; and slow rate refers to every time step for a speedup of 0.5 relative to the normal rate.

As with the sine wave experiments, results obtained here show that even though the network did not learn to predict the original signal perfectly, it was still able to adjust the time constant in order to adapt to the rate of the new signal. For the slow signal, rate adaptation was completed within four cycles; similar results were obtained for the fast signal.

## 3.3 Energy Contour

To apply our method of dynamic rate adaptation to speech, we used a similar network to predict the acoustic energy contour of a speech signal. The simple utterance *"ba ba...ba"* was used as data for this experiment. The utterance was recorded at three rates: 4 *ba*'s per second (fast), 3 *ba*'s per second (medium), and 2 *ba*'s per second (slow). The energy contour was computed for the utterance spoken by the same speaker at fast, medium, and slow rates, using 20-msec frames, 10 msec apart. The $log_{10}$ of the energy function was taken, and the results are scaled to $[0, 1]$ and smoothed using a moving average for input to the recurrent network. Energy functions of the three different rates are shown in Figure 1.

For this experiment, we let the time constant adapt along with the weights in the first training phase. The idea is allow the time constant to settle to some optimal value for the medium rate before it is adapted to accommodate for other rates. As in previous experiments, the network was trained to predict the energy of the medium-rate utterance. To test how well the time constant can reflect rate changes, a "new" utterance was created by concatenating the three utterances in this order: medium, fast, medium, slow, medium. With the weights fixed, the network was given this concatenated utterance as input, and the time constant was adjusted. Figure 2 shows how the time constant changes to reflect rate variation for this test utterance. Five other test utterances were constructed in a similar fashion. For all six utterances, the time constant appropriately reflects the direction of rate change; that is, the time constant increases when the rate of the signal increases, and vice versa, for all rate transitions.

# 4   Application to Speech

The dynamic rate adaptation technique described above can be applied to speech in the following way. Each subword recognizer will be implemented as a recurrent network using the Delta-Net update equations presented in Section 2. Each recognizer will be trained to track the parameters associated with a specific subword using a prediction task in the same manner that the networks in Section 3.1 were trained to track sine waves. During recognition, each recognizer's time constant will be adapted as needed to minimize prediction error. The essential part of this setup is that the time constant provides each recognizer an extra degree of freedom to adapt to changes in the speech signal due to rate variation. All recognizers will be used to recognize the input speech signal, and the recognizer with the lowest prediction error will determine the classification.

It is important to make use of context to constrain processing rates. As described above, each model would have an independent time constant. However, in order to capture the "rate of speech", the time constants of different recognizers should constrain each other. Different recognizers should adjust their time constants in relatively the same manner, *i.e.,* if one recognizer adjusts its time constant to indicate a faster rate, then recognizers for succeeding subwords should follow. Thus, we would want to implement a constraint on the direction of change for all time constants dependent on the time constant value of the recognizer with the lowest error for the current subword.

One way to achieve this would be to use a single global rate. However, the fact that changes due to rate are nonlinear in the speech signal makes this idea of constraining time constants not so simple. Vowels

IV-585

are much more elastic than consonants, for example, and this must be modeled by the recognizers. This nonlinearity can be modeled by allowing different types of recognizers to change their time constants by different amounts. For example, vowel recognizers can change their time constants by twice the amount as consonant recognizers. One way to implement this is to have different time constant learning rates for different classes of recognizers. However, this still does not address the issue of mutual constraint.

An alternative is to take a cue from elastic networks [2]. The idea is shown in Figure 3. Recognizers' time constants will be tied with elastic constraints so that when the recognizer with the lowest prediction error changes its time constant, all other time constants will also change proportionally. The nonlinearity in compression of speeded speech can be modeled by encoding the constraints between the classes. A "class" might be all recognizers with central vowels, for example. Then the time constant of central consonant models can be loosely tied to the vowel one with an elastic constraint. Under this view, there is no "rate box", rather, there is a global view of the rate only through the interactions of all of the modules. We can also include the energy prediction module described in the previous section, with elastic constraints between it and the other time constants. Vowels are the speech sounds with the strongest intensities; thus, acoustic energy peaks can be used to indicate vocalic segments in the speech signal. Since the rate at which vocalic segments occur is comparable to the syllable rate in speech production [8], acoustic energy can be used to give a reasonable estimate of speaking rate. Acoustic energy may not be a sufficiently reliable source of vowel rate, however, since speaker characteristics such as pitch can alter the energy profile. Allowing constraints to flow both ways should allow the subword models to overcome the errors in the global rate box.

Another issue is how to model spectral changes due to rate variation. Although recent psycholinguistic results (e.g., [6]) suggest that most changes due to rate affect the temporal characteristics of the speech signal, some researchers have shown some effects on the spectral characteristics as well, albeit spectral changes are less dramatic and not very consistent. If it turns out that spectral changes do occur, we would be able to model this by simply feeding the time constant as direct input into the recognizer, allowing changes in rate, as captured by changes in the time constant, to alter the mapping from acoustics to phonetics.

# References

[1] Garrison W. Cottrell, Fu-Sheng Tsung, and Mai Huong T. Nguyen. Dynamic rate adaptation. *AI Journal*, 1992.

[2] Richard Durbin and David Willshaw. An analogue approach to the travelling salesman problem using an elastic net method. *Nature*, 326:689–691, 1987.

[3] Jeffrey L. Elman. Finding structure in time. *Cognitive Science*, 14:179–211, 1990.

[4] Terry L. Gottfried, Joanne L. Miller, and Paula E. Payton. Effect of speaking rate on the perception of vowels. *Phonetica*, 47:155–172, 1990.

[5] Jacques Mehler, Emmanuel Dupoux, and Juan Segui. Constraining models of lexical access: the onset of word recognition. In Gerry T. M. Altmann, editor, *Cognitive models of speech processing*. MIT Press, 1990.

[6] Joanne L. Miller. Effects of speaking rate on segmental distinctions. In Peter D. Eimas and Joanne L. Miller, editors, *Perspectives on the study of speech*. Lawrence Erlbaum Associates, 1981.

[7] Joanne L. Miller, Francois Grosjean, and Concetta Lomanto. Articulation rate and its variability in spontaneous speech: a reanalysis and some implications. *Phonetica*, 41:215–225, 1984.

[8] Lawrence R. Rabiner and Ronald W. Schafer. *Digital processing of speech signals*. Prentice-Hall, 1978.

[9] Q. Summerfield, P.J. Bailey, J. Seton, and M. F. Dorman. Fricative envelope parameters and silent intervals in distinguishing 'slit' and 'split'. *Phonetica*, 38:181–192, 1981.

[10] Fu-Sheng Tsung. Learning in recurrent finite difference networks. In D. S. Touretzky, J. L. Elman, T. J. Sejnowski, and G. E. Hinton, editors, *Proceedings of the 1990 Connectionist Models Summer School*. Morgan Kaufmann, 1991.

[11] Ron Williams and Dave Zipser. A learning algorithm for continually running fully recurrent neural networks. *Neural Computation*, 1:270–280, 1989.

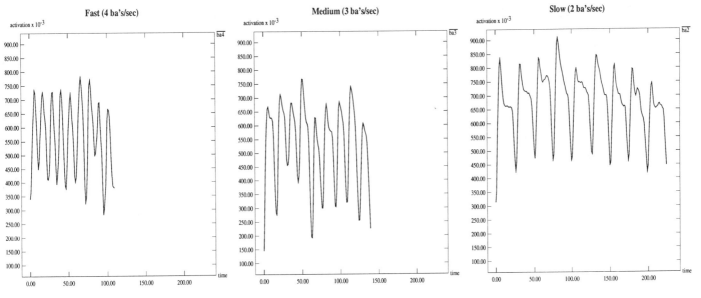

Figure 1: *Energy contours of the utterance "ba ba ... ba," spoken by a single talker at three different rates: fast, medium, and slow.*

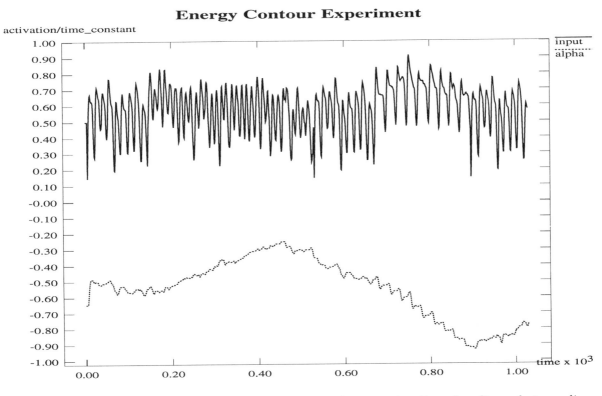

Figure 2: *Energy contour experiment — The test utterance is a concatenation of medium-, fast-, medium-, slow-, and medium-rate utterances. The bottom curve illustrates how α changes along with the rate of the utterance.*

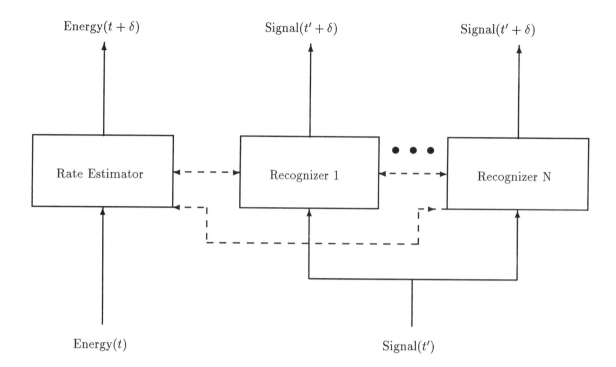

Figure 3: *Using dynamic rate adaptation for recognition — The rate estimator module estimates global rate by predicting the energy contour of the speech signal, and the recognizers track the speech signals by predicting their parameters. Both rate module and recognizers adjust their time constant with respect to prediction errors to adapt to the rate. Dashed lines indicate inter-module rate constraints.*

# Recognition of CV Segments using Fuzzy Neural Networks

B.Yegnanarayana, S.R.Prakash and C.Chandra Sekhar
Department of Computer Science and Engineering,
Indian Institute of Technology, Madras - 600036, India.

## ABSTRACT

This paper reports studies on recognition of CV segments using fuzzy neural networks. The CV segments in continuous speech are characterized by the dynamics of the vocal tract system during the production of these sounds. The dynamics is captured by a set of formant contours derived from the speech data. Due to the variable nature of speech production, the derived features like formants can be viewed as fuzzy data. Likewise, the class label for a given feature data is usually fuzzy rather than crisp. When the fuzzy nature of input data and output class label is incorporated into a neural network classifier, the classification performance improves significantly. Results are given for a set of 9 classes of CV segments to demonstrate the significance of fuzzy neural networks for speech recognition.

## 1. INTRODUCTION

The objective of this study is to demonstrate that using fuzzy neural networks it is possible to obtain good recognition accuracy for Consonant-Vowel (CV) segments in continuous speech. Reliable spotting of CV segments in continuous speech can significantly improve the performance of a speech-to-text system [1]. CV segments also form the basic production units in most languages, and as such carry significant information content about the message in the speech utterance [2]. The training and test sets of data for CV segments can be collected using manual or semiautomatic identification of CV regions in continuous speech. The training set is used to train a neural network classifier under supervised mode. The recognition performance of the neural network classifier is· studied by making the input features and output class labels as fuzzy membership function values, thus reflecting the fuzzy nature of the speech data in the design of the classifier. In the next section we discuss the fuzzy nature of speech data and the choice of formants as features representing the CV segments. The fuzzy neural network classifier is based on the ideas proposed by Pal and Mitra in [3]. We discuss the details of the fuzzy neural network classifier in Section 3. Studies on recognition of CV segments using the fuzzy neural network classifier are described in Section 4.

## 2. FUZZY NATURE OF SPEECH DATA

In continuous speech the same CV may occur in different contexts. Therefore there may be variability in the features of the utterance due to variability in speech production as well as due to context. Moreover, there will also be variability in speech production due to different speakers. All these factors lead to feature data that can best be described in linguistic terms , such as 'low', 'medium' and 'high', which in turn can best be expressed as values of membership functions of fuzzy sets.

It is necessary to represent the information in speech signal in suitable parameters or features for input to a classifier. parameters like spectral coefficients, cepstral coefficients, etc., are likely to be influenced by the nature of signal processing as well , besides the natural variations in the production process. The variations due to signal processing operations contribute to distortion and noise, rather than fuzziness. Therefore it is preferable to consider articulatory or related acoustic parameters like formants as features representing the CV segments. Formants are relatively easier to extract compared to articulatory parameters. Formant features also reflect the dynamics of the vocal tract system in the form of formant trajectories. Therefore the formants were selected as parameters to represent the CV segments in this study.

Speaker variability is caused due to differences in the dimensions of the vocal tract systems. In order to compensate this to some extent, ratios of formants may be considered as features. Since we are considering only two speakers data in this study, we have decided to consider only the formant values as features. Formant data is collected for successive frames of speech signal data in each CV segment.

Formants are resonances of the vocal tract system, and hence any natural variations in the shape of the vocal tract are reflected in these resonances as well. Since variability due to speech, context and speaker are all preserved in the formant trajectories, the formant data can be assumed fuzzy, and the data is fuzzified before feeding it to a neural network classifier for training and testing.

Fuzzification of formant data involves several issues. For example, one could fuzzify the features individually in the frequency and time domains. But it appears more logical if the fuzzification could be done knowing that the three formants should occur together as a set in each frame. Also the formants in successive frames are not independent. Hence this dependency should also be considered in fuzzifying the input data to the neural network classifier.

It is natural to expect that the class labels will not be crisp either, due to significant overlap of features across the different classes of CV segments. Therefore, for effective classification, it is preferable that the output classes are fuzzy. In the next section we describe a fuzzy neural network classifier that takes fuzzy input data.

### 3. FUZZY NEURAL NETWORK CLASSIFIER

It was shown in [3] that fuzzification of input data and the output class label data improves the classification performance of a multilayer perceptron network for recognition of vowels using formants as features. The network takes as input the values of fuzzy membership functions for each of the three formants. Each input feature $F_j$ in quantitative form is expressed in terms of membership values to each of the three linguistic properties 'low', 'medium' and 'high'. The $\pi$ membership function is used to assign membership values for the input features. The $\pi$ membership function in one-dimensional form, with range [0,1], is defined as

$$\pi(x:\ c,r) = \begin{cases} 2(1 - (|x-c|/r))^2, & \text{for } r/2 \leq |x-c| \leq r, \\ 1 - 2(|x-c|/r)^2, & \text{for } 0 \leq |x-c| \leq r/2, \\ 0, & \text{otherwise,} \end{cases}$$

where x is a pattern point, r is the radius of the function and c is the central point.

The fuzzy sets for the linguistic properties 'low', 'medium' and 'high' for each formant are represented by $\pi$ functions. The parameters of $\pi$ functions are defined below.

Let $F_{jmax}$ and $F_{jmin}$ be the upper and lower bounds of feature $F_j$ in all pattern points. For the three linguistic property sets, parameters are defined as

$$r_{medium}(F_j) = 0.5\ (F_{jmax} - F_{jmin})$$

$$c_{medium}(F_j) = F_{jmin} + r_{medium}(F_j)$$

$$r_{low}(F_j) = (c_{medium}(F_j) - F_{jmin})/fdenom$$

$$c_{low}(F_j) = c_{medium}(F_j) - 0.5\ r_{low}(F_j)$$

$$r_{high}(F_j) = (F_{jmax} - c_{medium}(F_j))/fdenom$$

$$c_{high}(F_j) = c_{medium}(F_j) + 0.5\ r_{high}(F_j)$$

where 'fdenom' is a parameter controlling the extent of overlapping. A 9-dimensional vector is derived for the three formants using these membership functions and is given as input to the multilayer perceptron network.

During the training phase, the desired output vector is expressed as the desired membership values, lying in the range [0,1]. To obtain these values, the weighted distance of an n-dimensional training pattern $\mathbf{F}_i$ from the kth class is defined as

$$z_{ik} = \sum_{j=1}^{n} \left[ \frac{F_{ij} - o_{kj}}{v_{kj}} \right]^2$$

where $F_{ij}$ is the value of the jth component of the ith pattern, $o_{kj}$ and $v_{kj}$ are the mean and standard deviation, respectively, of the $F_j$s of the training data for the kth class. The membership

value for the ith pattern to the kth class is defined as

$$d_k(\mathbf{F}_i) = \cfrac{1}{1 + \left(\cfrac{z_{ik}}{f_d}\right)^{f_e}}$$

where the positive constants $f_d$ and $f_e$ control the amount of
fuzziness in the class-membership set. The desired output vector
for a training pattern is obtained by computing the membership
values for the pattern to each of the classes.

In the next section, we describe recognition studies on
classification of CV segments using the fuzzy neural networks.

## 4. RECOGNITION STUDIES

Speech data for the studies described in this section was
collected from utterances of several sentences in Hindi (an
Indian language) spoken by two male speakers. From these utterances, occurrences of CV segments are manually excised by visual
inspection of the speech signal waveform and by careful listening
of the segmented data. Only consonant-vowel (CV) segments are
considered. Consonant clusters followed by a vowel were not
considered in this study. Data for the following 9 CV classes
have been collected: /ka/, /ke/, /ko/, /ga/, /ta/, /to/, /dha/,
/pa/ and /ba/. The choice of these classes was mostly dictated by
the availability of sufficient numbers of these segments in the
speech data collected for several sentences.

For each CV segment only a fixed 40 msec portion from the
vowel onset point was considered. This portion generally reflects
the transition of the vocal tract system from the place of artic-
ulators corresponding to the consonant position to the shape of
the vocal tract corresponding to the following vowel, including
some steady vowel part. Formants were extracted using linear
prediction analysis for each frame of size 128 samples at 10 kHz
sampling rate, with a·shift of 32 samples. The formant contours
were hand edited and smoothed to remove spurious peaks. From the
resulting smooth contours the first three formants were obtained
for each of the 10 frames in a CV segment.

The formant data is fuzzified using the membership functions
discussed in Section 3. Thus for each CV segment, a 90-
dimensional vector of membership values is generated. This representation is used as input to the classifier in various recognition studies reported in this section. The desired output data is
also fuzzified as discussed in Section 3 for training the neural
network classifier.

The classifier is a multilayer feedforward network trained
using back propagation algorithm. Three hidden layers were used
in the network. The number of input nodes, output nodes and the
hidden layer nodes vary depending on the study. Several recognition studies were conducted to understand the significance of
fuzzification of individual frames and sequence of frames as well
as the number of frames for CV classification.

## 4.1 Classification of vowels

First we have considered the task of classification of vowels and the significance of fuzzification of input data and output data. The vowel formant data was collected from the 9th frame of each CV segment for the five vowels /a/, /e/, /i/, /o/ and /u/. Since there is only one frame of data, there are three formants and hence 9 membership values for input to the classifier. The network consists of an input layer with 9 nodes, three hidden layers each with 20 nodes and an output layer with 5 nodes corresponding to the 5 vowel classes. A total of 90 training patterns and 90 test patterns were used for all classes. The classification accuracy was 58% for the case when the output data was crisp and 74% for the case when the output data was fuzzified. The result shows that fuzzification of output significantly improves the classification accuracy.

## 4.2 Classification of CV segments using 2 frames of data

For CV classification we have studied the performance using only two frames of data for each CV segment, one in the initial part (2nd frame) and the other in the final part (9th frame). Now the number of input membership values is 18. The network has 18 nodes in the input layer, 20 nodes in each of the three hidden layers and 9 nodes in the output layer corresponding to the 9 CV classes. A total of 90 training patterns and 90 test patterns were used for all classes. Using fuzzification of both input and output data, we have obtained a recognition accuracy of 63%. The correct output in the first two choices gives a recognition accuracy of 72%.

## 4.3 Classification of CV segments using all the 10 frames of data

In this study, all the 10 frames of data were used as input for each CV segment. Now the number of input membership values is 90. Correspondingly the number of nodes in each of the three hidden layers was increased to 50. The number of nodes in the output layer was 9 corresponding to the 9 CV classes. The recognition accuracy in this case is 62% when the best single output was considered and it is 78% when the best two outputs are considered. It may be noted that in this case the input formant data for each frame was fuzzified independently. On the other hand, there is a sequence of frames in each CV segment, and the data in each frame depends to some extent on the adjacent frames. If this fact was used in determining the membership values for each frame, the recognition accuracy has improved. In fact by reducing the fuzziness in the formant data in subsequent frames in a data dependent manner and using the resultant 90 membership values as input, the recognition accuracy obtained is 73% for the single best choice case and 85% for the best two choices case.

## 5. CONCLUSIONS

The studies reported in this paper show that fuzzification of input and output data improves the recognition accuracy of CV segments. In particular, fuzzification of input data taking into account the fact that the formant data is for a sequence of frames, improves the recognition of CV segments significantly. In these studies only a simple method was used to implement the dependence of fuzziness on the sequence. But a more sophisticated data dependent approach for determining the fuzzy membership values for data both along frequency and along time may improve the recognition performance still further.

REFERENCES:

1. H.Sawai, A.Waibel, M.Miyatake and K.Shikano, "Spotting Japanese CV-syllables and phonemes using time-delay neural networks," Proceedings of ICASSP'89, pp.25-28, May 1989.

2. A.M.Liberman, P.C.Delattre, F.C.Cooper and L.J.Gerstman, "The role of consonant-vowel transitions in the perception of the stop and nasal consonants," in D.B.Fry (Ed.), Acoustic Phonetics, Cambridge University Press, pp.315-331, 1976.

3. Sankar K. Pal and Sushmita Mitra, "Multilayer perceptron, fuzzy sets and classification," IEEE Trans. on Neural Networks, vol.3, no.5, pp.683-697, September 1992.

# A Speaker Recognition System Based on Auditory Model

Xin Jiang, Zhengyu Gong, Fan Sun and Huisheng Chi
National Laboratory on Machine Perception
Center for Information Sciences
Peking University, Beijing 100871, China

## Abstract

A speaker recognition system based on auditory path model and auditory cortex model is presented. The auditory path model is a multi-layer feedforward neural network with partial connections. The auditory cortex model is a multilayer SOM-like neural network with local connections. Some commonly acknowledged facts of auditory system are reflected in the model. Simulation results show the effectiveness of the model in speaker recognition.

## I. Introduction

In recent years many researchers working on speech processing are greatly in terested in auditory systems, for a model based on the human auditory system, which is nearly perfect, has great potential in improving the performance of speech recognition or speaker recognition. Although building a model embedding all the principles of auditory system is currently impossible, the model that could showsome of its properties would be more adaptive and robust. In this paper, a speaker recognition system based on the hybrid neural network model which simulates some of the process of auditory path and auditory cortex is presented. Because many important aspects of auditory path and auditory cortex are still not clear, the model presented is simple and just tries to embed facts commonly acknowledged about the auditory system.

As we know, speech signal is transformed to the firings of inner hair cells through the mechanic vibration of basilar membrane in cochlea. The neural firings are then transmitted to auditory cortex through auditory path. Physiological experiments show that along basilar membrane from oval window to apex of cochlea the characteristic frequencies are arranged with a tonotopical structure, i.e. from higher frequency to lower frequency. The auditory path is composed of neural fibres linked by synapes and some information in neural firings is processed along the path[2]. The neural branchs from cochlea, through cochlear nucleus, get to the superior complex olivary, which is the first stop of auditory path. From there they go up through lateralis thalamus system to the interior colliculus in mesencephalon. The last stop before reaching auditory cortex is medial geniculuts body in thalamus. There they are connected to cortex. Cortex appears generally to have six-layer structure and large amount of intra-layer and inter-layer synapses. Nearer neurons are mutually excited and the farther neurons are mutually inhibited. Research shows that about 40% neurons in the auditory cortex do not respond to pure tone and just respond to complex sound such as noise and "ka ta" sound. The other 60% neurons respond to pure tone but they do not react in a simple manner.

\* This work was supported by the National Nature Science Foundation of China Grant No. 960012 and the Climbing Program—National Key Project for Fundamental Research in China Grant No. 92097

Some of the neurons increase firing rate when sound is presented and some decrease their firing rate. Some respond to the on-set of voice and some respond to the off-set. Some are narrowly tuned and other are not. Some just respond to the change of tone. The tonotopic organization is also found in auditory cortex. Because of the limitation of current study of auditory system and artificial neural network, we could only reflect some of the facts in our model. In section I, the auditory path model is presented. Auditory cortex model is presented in section II. Simulation results are presented in section IV. In section V, the conclusions are given.

## II. Auditory Path

Auditory system is the most complex one among all kinds of perceptual systems[1]. The perception of complex voice pattern is the combination of bottom-up process ( data-driven ) and top-down process ( knowledge-driven ). In the bottom-up process, a person extracts perceptual features from speech signal, but does not build fine-tuned feature selector. The auditory path starts from inner hair cells. The neurons agitating from inner hair cells have maximal senstivity to different frequency according to their places, and the property of tonotopic organization is kept to interior colliculus. Some of small neurons in medial geniculuts body are narrowly tuned and do not have plasticity. Some of big neurons respond to a wide range of frequencies are plastic and learned quickly. While the information is passing throught the auditory path, it is somewhat processed. On one hand, this processing keeps the tonotopic organizing property, on the other hand it extracts and enhences features.

Based on these considerations, we designed a feed-forward network to simulate the auditory path. The network is similar structure to a multi-layer perceptron, with an input-layer, a hidden-layers and an output-layer. There are partial connections between the input-layer and hidden-layer and full connections between the hidden-layer and output-layer ( see Fig. 1 ). To reflect the characteristic frequency response arrangement of basilar membrane and mask effect, neurons in the hidden-layer have different number connections to input layer. The left neuron has the least connections. To the right, the number of connections of hidden neuron increases. The right hidden neuron has the biggest number of connections. The output layer gives supervisor while training, which force the network to extract speaker-related features. To deal the dynamics of speech signal, all neurons have time-delayed connections.

## III. Auditory Cortex[5-9]

Auditory cortex can be generally considered as a layered upward structure with complex connections. The information is processed from a lower layer to an upper layer. When neural firings are passing through the layer of neurons, their abstract meanings are transformed. The layers of neurons have different structures and functions. It could be said that this upward structure can successively abstract information and classify patterns and every layer has certain kinds of functions. The input of neurons in cortex mainly comes from two sources: 1. external input from other perceptual organs and other domains; 2. internal input from same domain or same layer. There are many kinds of mutual reaction between neurons, but nearer neurons have one common mode: the nearest neurons are mutually excited and the farther ones are mutually inhibited, and more farther ones are mutually excited again but with weaker stimulations. This form of mutuality is similar to the shape of "Mexican hat".

Based on these considerations, we use a multi-layer SOM-like network to simulate it ( See Fig. 2 ). It has three layers with same size (N×N), but the connections between layers are different.

The neurons in the first layer have full connections with input. The network is trained with Kohonen SOM algorithm[9, 11]. Define the distance between input X (t) and neuron ( i, j ) as:

$$d_{ij}(t) = |W_{ij} - X(t)| \tag{1}$$

where, $W_{ij}$ is the reference vector of neuron $(i, j)$, $i = 0, ....N - 1$, $j = 0, ....N - 1$.

Then the output of the neuron $(i, j)$ is calculated[12],

$$O'_{ij}(t) = \frac{k}{\sqrt{1 + d^2_{ij}(t)}} \tag{2}$$

in which $k$ is a constant. To deal the dynamics of speech signal, the output is delayed[10]. So the real output of first layer is

$$O_{ij}(t) = \alpha \cdot O'_{ij}(t) + (1 - \alpha) \cdot O_{ij}(t - 1) \tag{3}$$

where $\alpha$ is a constant and $0 < \alpha < 1$. The output of first layer is the input to the second layer.

The second layer has local connections with first layer ( see Fig. 3 ). The neuron $(i, j)$ is connected to the neuron $(i, j)$ in first layer and its neighbors. There is no delay in second layer.

The third layer has similar structure with the second one, but it has connections to the first layer, i. e. the neuron $(i, j)$ is connected to the neuron $(i, j)$ in the first layer.

The second layer and the third layer are trained with Kononen SOM algorithm also. To accelerate learning, we make the learning rate in the winner neighborhood different size. As the neuron nears the winner, the learning rate is bigger, while the neuron is far from the winner, the learing rate is small.

## IV. Experiment

### 1) Speech Database and Preprocessing

The database is composed of isolated digits "0", "1", ... "10", spoken by 9 male speakers. Every one speaks every digit 10 times. The first 5 utterance are taken as training set and the other 5 utterance recording one week after are taken as test set. The speech signal is low passed ( 3400Hz ), sampled ( 10KHz ), digitized ( 12bit ), preemphasized ( 1-0.95z ) and framed ( 25.6ms ). LPC power spectrum is taken from every frame, and put to 12 channel with critical bandwidth. Their central frequencies are 227, 342, 467, 604, 754, 917, 1096, 1370, 1712, 2141, 2767, 3345 ( unit Hz ). The entropy of each channel is calculated:

$$P'(i) = P(i) / \sum_{i=1}^{12} P(i) \qquad i = 1, ....12 \tag{4}$$

$$H(i) = -P'(i)logP'(i) \qquad i = 1, ....12 \tag{5}$$

where, $P(i)$ is the energy of each channel, $P'(i)$ is the pecentage of $P(i)$ is total energy and $H(i)$ is the entropy, which used as raw feature. This kind of processing is to simulate the firing of inner hair cells.

### 2) Auditory Path Model

To show the effectiveness of auditory path model, we have done the following experiments.

a) Using DTW only

The reference templates are taken from training set, i. e. for every speaker and digit, there are 5 templates. Each test template is matched with these templates using DTW algorithm, and decision is made upon the minimal distance. Results are shown in Table-1.

Table-1. The recognition rate using DTW only

| text | 1 | 2 | 3 | 4 | 5 | 6 | 7 | 8 | 9 | 10 | average |
|------|------|------|------|------|------|------|------|------|------|------|---------|
| recognition rate | 82.2% | 80.0% | 88.9% | 97.8% | 82.2% | 86.7% | 84.4% | 86.7% | 82.2% | 77.8% | 84.9% |

b) Using auditory path model and DTW

Based on Section **I**, a subnetwork with the structure shown in Fig. 1 is built for every digit. The network has 12 input neurons, 18 hidden neurons and 9 output neurons corresponding to the 9 speakers. The maximal delay of connections is 2. The networks are trained with back-probagation through time algorithm [3]. After training, all speech samples are fed to the networks. The outputs of hidden units for samples in training set are taken as reference templates and the outputs for samples in test set are taken as test templates. The templates are matched with DTW algorithm. Result are shown in Table-2.

Table-2. The recognition rate using auditory path model and DTW

| text | 1 | 2 | 3 | 4 | 5 | 6 | 7 | 8 | 9 | 10 | average |
|---|---|---|---|---|---|---|---|---|---|---|---|
| recognition rate | 84.4% | 84.4% | 84.4% | 93.3% | 84.4% | 86.7% | 88.9% | 93.3% | 88.9% | 88.9% | 87.8% |

We could see in Table-1 and Table-2 that the average recognition rate increases by 2.9% when the auditory path model is used. The variation of recognition rates for different text is reduced as well. This shows that the auditory model trained with the supervised learning algorithm could extract and enhance speaker-related features .

### 3) Cortex model

a) Single layer SOM with raw input

A single layer SOM with $10 \times 10$ ( N=10 ) neurons is employed in the experiment. The input to the network is entropy of each channel in the preprocessing. Results are shown in Table-3.

Table-3. The recognition rate using single layer SOM with raw input

| text | 1 | 2 | 3 | 4 | 5 | 6 | 7 | 8 | 9 | 10 | average |
|---|---|---|---|---|---|---|---|---|---|---|---|
| recognition rate | 84.4% | 82.2% | 77.8% | 88.7% | 73.3% | 86.7% | 86.7% | 80.0% | 88.7% | 82.2% | 83.1% |

b) Single layer SOM with output from auditory path model

The neural network is the same as the one in the expriment a). But the input is the output of the auditory path model. Results are shown in Table-4.

Table-4. The recognition rate using single layer SOM with output from auditory path model

| text | 1 | 2 | 3 | 4 | 5 | 6 | 7 | 8 | 9 | 10 | average |
|---|---|---|---|---|---|---|---|---|---|---|---|
| recognition rate | 86.7% | 86.7% | 88.7% | 93.3% | 82.2% | 95.5% | 91.1% | 84.4% | 88.7% | 88.7% | 88.5% |

c) Multi-layer SOM with output from auditory path model

The model is three layer SOM with the structure shown in Fig. 2. The input to the network is the same as in experiment b). Results are shown in Table-5.

Table-5. The recognition rate using three layer SOM with output from auditory path model

| text | 1 | 2 | 3 | 4 | 5 | 6 | 7 | 8 | 9 | 10 | average |
|---|---|---|---|---|---|---|---|---|---|---|---|
| recognition rate | 88.7% | 86.7% | 93.3% | 91.1% | 88.7% | 93.3% | 91.1% | 88.7% | 93.3% | 95.6% | 91.1% |

From experiment a) and b), we could see the effect of auditory path model for improving the average recognition rate and reducing variation of recognitionrates for different text. In experiment c) we see further improvement in averagerecognition rate and reduction in recognition rates for different text by usingmulti-layer SOM with local connections. This shows that as patterns are transformed from layer to layer, they are getting more and more stable and high level feature are extracted.

## V. Conclusion

We presented a speaker recognition system using a simple auditory model inthis paper. In the model the tonotopical structure is kept by partial connections and the mask effect is reflected. The layered structure of cortex is simulated by a multi-layer SOM with local connections. Although the model is too simple, but it does improve the performance of our speaker recognition system. Compared with the conventional DTW algorithm, average recognition rate increases by 6.1%. As we know, auditory system is a complex system with bottom-up and top-down perceptual process. If we could reflect more aspects in the model, we would make the model more reasonable and further improve the performance. That will be our future work.

## Reference

[1]  H. Chi, On the Aritificial Neural Network Auditory Model, Proc. of CCNN-90, 1990, pp43-53.

[2]  P. B. Deres, E. N. Pinson, The Speech Chain—The Physics and biology of Spoken Language, ANCHOR PRESS, NEW YORK, 1973.

[3]  P. J. Werbs, Backpropogadion Through Time: What It Does and How to Do it, Proc. of IEEE Vol 78., No. 10, Oct. 1990, pp. 1550-1560.

[4]  L. R. Rabiner, A. E. Resenberg and S. E. Livinson, Consideration in Dynamic Warping Algorithms for Discrete Word Recognition, IEEE trans. on ASSP, Vol. 26, 1978, pp. 575-582.

[5]  P. H. Lindsay, D. A. Norman, Human Information Processing: An Introduction to Psychology, second edtion, Academic Press, 1977.

[6]  P. Yan, etc., Artifical Neural Networks: Model, Analysis and Application, Anhui Educational Press, 1993.

[7]  T. L. Bennett, The Sensory World: An Introduction to Sensation and Perception, Wadsworth Publishing Company, 1978.

[8]  S. W. Kuffler, J. G. Nicholls, A. R. Martin, From Neuron to Brain, Sinauer Associates Inc., 1984

[9]  T. Kohonen, The Self-Organizing Map, Proc. of IEEE, Vol. 78, No. 9, Sept. 1990, pp. 1464-1480.

[10]  Jari Kangas, Time-delayed Self-Organizing Maps, Proc. of IJCNN'90—San Diego, Vol. I, 1990, pp. 313-318.

[11]  A. Ghosh, N. R. Pal, Self-Organizing for Object Extraction Using a Multilayer Neural Network and Fuzziness Measures, IEEE trans. on Fuzzy Systems, Vol. 1, No. 1, pp. 54-68, Feb. 1993

[12]  K. Hsieh, W. Chen, A Neural Network Model Which Combines Unsupervised and Supervised Learning, IEEE trans. on Neural Networks, Vol. 4, No. 2, pp. 357-360, Mar. 1993

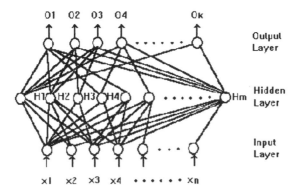

Fig. 1. Network Structure Based on Auditory Path

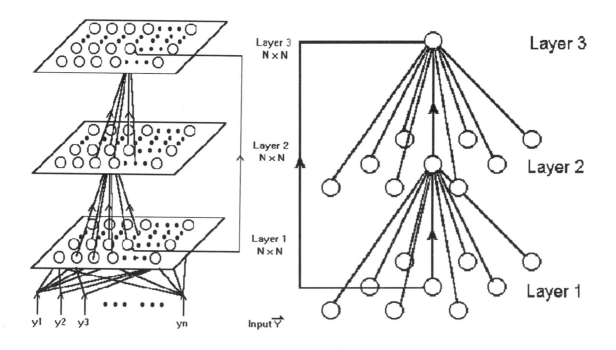

Fig. 2. Network Structure of Multi—layer SOM

Fig. 3. Local Connections of Multi—layer SOM

# ADEQUACY OF NEURAL PREDICTORS FOR SPEAKER IDENTIFICATION

## T. Artières, P. Gallinari

LAFORIA-IBP UA CNRS 1095
Tour 46-00 Boite 169
Université Paris 6, 4 place Jussieu
75252 Paris cedex 05 France
gallinari@laforia.ibp.fr
artieres@laforia.ibp.fr

## Abstract

We analyse in this paper neural prediction systems for automatic speaker identification (A.S.I.) and links between models complexity and their performances. We develop two ideas for enhancing such systems : we first reconsider the validity of standard hypothesis underlying the use of predictive models, we then propose different techniques for incorporating a-priori knowledge in our models. We illustrate the different points by providing results on 15 talkers from the TIMIT database.

## 1. Introduction

Recently, speaker identification has been tackled by different methods which have been developed and used successfully for speech recognition tasks. This is the case for example with Hidden Markov Models (HMM) [Rosenberg], Vectorial Autoregressive Models (VAM) [Bimbot, Montacié], and Neural Networks (NN) [Bennani, Oglesby, Artieres 91].

HMMs or VAMs methods for ASI are based on a modelization of the conditional class probability for each talker, and parameters estimation is usually performed independently for each model. The main benefit of these production systems is that they allow incremental modifications of the speaker database, which is an essential requirement for most ASI systems. However, speech utterance modelization being an indirect way to perform classification, only a small part of the information contained in the models will be relevant for classification. Direct classification methods [Bennani] or discriminant criteria for production systems [Mellouk] synthesize more efficiently such information, but suffer from other limitations and are not adequate for ASI when the population may change and is not limited in size [Artieres 93].

These two approaches being apparently intrinsically limited, it is important to find alternatives to existing systems for such applications. We will explore here the potential of neural predictive systems in an attempt to take benefit from the variety of implementations they allow. We present these systems in §2, and put into evidence some of their inherent limitations in §4. We propose in §5 and §6 two main directions to improve such systems for ASI.

## 2. Predictive systems

Linear auto-regressive models have shown good performances on identification tasks. However, most tests for now have been performed on clean speech (e.g. TIMIT), and good performances are reached after seconds of speech. The development of neural networks has made possible the use of non linear predictive models and a few systems have already been proposed for speaker recognition tasks. These systems could be of arbitrary complexity and shape which should allow to by-pass limitations of linear models and to explore in greater depth speaker representation issues.

Predictive systems rely on the hypothesis that an exact modelization of the talkers speech signal will contain the information needed for speaker recognition. Although this should be true in theory, things are not so simple. Whatever the model, speech production is only roughly approximated and the resulting speaker models are often very similar. In addition, training criteria for predictive systems do not aim directly at optimizing the decision criterion and due to the nature of speech, most of the information contained in the models will be useless for identification.

Different approaches have been proposed over the years for the classification of sequences. However, it is difficult to define efficient and robust speaker characteristics which can be automatically extracted from the speech signal. In this sense, speaker identification with production models is an ill posed problem.

### 2.1 Predictive Models

Predictive models are trained to produce frame t, given a prediction context of the frame. The underlying hypothesis when using a predictive model is that speech signal is a stationary autoregressive process, obeying equation (1) :

$$X_t = F(C_t) + \varepsilon_t \ \forall \ t = 1...T \tag{1}$$

where $X_1^T = \{X_1,...,X_T\}$ is a deterministic parameter-vector sequence resulting from the analysis of a speech utterance, $C_t$ is the prediction context for frame $X_t$, $\varepsilon_t$ is a noise independently identically distributed (i.i.d.), and F is a time independent function. Training aims at estimating F parameters so as to reach a minimal residual error $\varepsilon_t$. In the following, we will implicitly use $X_t$ both for the random variable and his realizations in time.

A probabilistic interpretation of the model behavior can be derived by considering that $\varepsilon_t$ obeys a gaussian law $N(\mu,\Sigma)$. The conditional probability density of $X_t$ given $C_t$ is then :

$$P(X_t/F(C_t))=P(\varepsilon_t)=\frac{1}{(2\pi)^{\frac{d}{2}}|\Sigma|^{\frac{1}{2}}}\exp[-\frac{1}{2}D(x_t-F(C_t))] \qquad \text{with } D(x_t-F(C_t)) = [x_t-F(C_t)-\mu]^t\,\Sigma^{-1}[x_t-F(C_t)-\mu] \qquad (2)$$

### 2.2 Utterance probability

Let us consider an utterance $X_1^T$ and an order p autoregressive model whose context is $C_t = X_{t-p}^{t-1} = (X_{t-p},...,X_{t-1})$.

The probability of the whole utterance $X_1^T$ is : 
$$P(X_1^T)=[\prod_{t=p+1}^T P(X_t/F(C_t))]\,.P(X_1, X_2,.., X_p)$$

Usually, the initial probability $P(X_1, X_2,.., X_p)$ is ignored so that :

$$P(X_1^T) \propto \prod_{t=p+1}^T P(X_t/F(C_t)) \quad \text{and} \qquad -\log(P(X_1^T) \propto \sum_t[D(X_t-F(C_t)) + \log(|\Sigma|)]$$

Furthermore, assuming $(\mu,\Sigma) = (0,I)$ , we have : 
$$D(X_t-F(C_t)) = \|X_t- F(C_t)\|^2$$

and 
$$-\log(P(X_1^T)) \propto \sum_t \|X_t - F(C_t)\|^2$$

Under this hypothesis, maximizing the utterance probability is equivalent to minimizing the standard quadratic cost.

# 3. Experiments and data-base

All the experiments presented in this paper have been performed on a small set of 15 female speakers from the first dialect of the TIMIT database. This base being very clean and recorded in a single session, speaker identification is easy when the test utterance is long enough. In order to test our methods, we have used short segments from different lengths. The 5 SX sentences have been used for training, and the five remaining sentences (3 SI + 2 SA) for testing. Input data for the models are vectors resulting from a 16-order LPCC analysis, using 25,6 ms Hamming windows, with an overlap of 15,6 ms. The duration of an n-frame-length utterance is thus $\frac{n}{100}$ seconds. The neural nets used in the experiments reported here are Multi-Layer Perceptrons (MLP), with one hidden layer, trained to produce frame $X_t$, given a prediction context of the frame. In all the experiments we used the two preceding frames $X_{t-1}$ and $X_{t-2}$ as the prediction context for the frame $X_t$, as explained later in §5.

# 4. Complexity and identification

When performing tests with predictive neural nets of increasing complexity, for example by varying the number of hidden cells, the following behavior may be observed up to a certain complexity of the models (figure 1) :
    - the mean square error decreases both on the testing and training sets.
    - the identification rate reaches a peak and then slowly decreases.

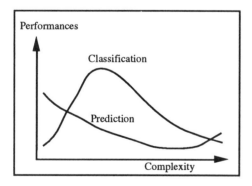 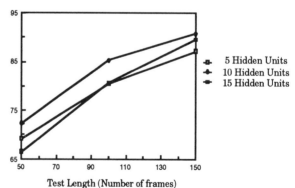

Figure 1 : typical identification rate of predictive NNs as a function of their complexity : the optimum classification rate is reached before square error increase on the test set indicates over-training.

Figure 2 : identification performances of NNs with different complexities (5, 10, 15 hidden units) and $(\mu,\Sigma)$ = (0,I), as a function of the test sequence length.

However this is not a classical over-training phenomenon, optimum classification is reached largely before over training (figure 1), this complicates noticeably the problem.

Figure 2 illustrates the complexity adequacy problem for three models, the intermediate model (10 hidden cells) providing the best classification performances. Results in table 1, illustrate the phenomenon for the three models from fig. 2. The training criterion of the whole system is such that, beyond a given complexity, the predictive nets still learn speech production, but this is useless for speaker identification. Similar results with NNs and HMMs have been observed respectively by [Hattori] and [Matsui]. Table 1 shows that the problem is more complicated since mean speaker separation go on increasing with model complexity, while classification performances decrease.

| Complexity | 5 | 10 | 15 |
|---|---|---|---|
| Training MSE | 0,097 | 0,067 | 0,056 |
| Test MSE | 0,109 | 0,076 | 0,061 |
| Others MSE | 0,150 | 0,102 | 0,070 |
| Separation Ratio | 0,72 | 0,74 | 0,81 |
| Indententification % | 69,3 | 72,4 | 66,5 |

Table 1 : mean euclidean error (MSE) of models with different complexities (5, 10 , 15 hidden cells) for training and  test. "Others" represents the mean euclidean error of  a model computed over the data of the other speakers. Separation is the ratio "Test MSE / Others MSE" which is a mean speaker separability measure of the models.

These models are thus intrinsically limited when used for classification. In order to improve their performances, one can follow two directions. The first one is to develop more appropriate models of the speech signal. Message and identity being deeply intermingled in the signal one will try to better modelize both informations simultaneously, a compromise must then be found for choosing the models which give the best identification results. The second consists in separating as much as possible speaker information from the other information sources, by incorporating a-priori knowledge in the models. These two directions may be combined. However, for simplicity, we have studied them independently and will present the corresponding results in the next two sections.

# 5.  Modelization

The inadequacy of modelization training criteria for identification makes the choice of an optimal architecture complicated. However, performance increases can be obtained by improving the adequacy of the models. We examine in §5.1 the influence of a weight decay term during training, and discuss in §5.2 the importance of different assumptions upon the stochastic part of signal modelization or equivalently on the prediction error. We discuss in §5.3 the importance of the stationarity hypothesis.

The fit between a predictive model and an identification task depends on the order and the form of the predictor. Some authors have reported experiments on different implementations of predictive models. [Kawabata] has proposed three types of predictions : forward, backward and interpolation which correspond respectively to a past context, a future context, and a mixed past and future context. Most of the experiments reported in the literature have been performed using order 1 to 3 [Bimbot,Mellouk, Hattori, Levin, Iso] causal models.

We have performed some experiments in order to determine the model nature and found that forward models are reasonable compromises between task and model complexities. We will present experiments performed with past-context and order 2 predictive models. The prediction context for frame t is thus the two preceding frames at time t-2 and t-1, our predictive models will have 32 input units and 16 outputs.

## 5.1   Tuning   the   complexity

Several approaches have been proposed for tuning the model complexity in order to increase its generalization abilities [Le Cun, Hinton]. One of the most popular relies on the use of regularizing terms in the cost function corresponding to constraints on the transfer function of the network. The general form of these cost functions is :

$$C = C1 + \alpha\, C2 \tag{3}$$

where C1 measures the fit to the data and C2 constrains the range of the weights so as to reduce the influence of useless parameters.

| Nb hidden cells | Weight decay | Test length (in frames) | | | |
|---|---|---|---|---|---|
| | | 50 | 100 | 150 | Sentences |
| 5 | No | 69,3 | 80,4 | 87,2 | 93,3 |
| 5 | Yes | 69,8 | 81,8 | 88,6 | 97,3 |
| 10 | No | 72,4 | 85,4 | 90,7 | 93,3 |
| 10 | Yes | 73,7 | 86,4 | 92,2 | 97,3 |
| 15 | No | 66,5 | 80,6 | 89,5 | 84 |
| 15 | Yes | 72,1 | 85,2 | 92,1 | 96 |

Table 2 : performances of different models with and without a weight decay term during training. Prediction error is supposed gaussian with zero mean and identity covariance matrix.

IV-603

We have used here :

$$C1 = \sum_t \|X_t - F(C_t)\|^2 \quad \text{and} \quad C2 = \sum_{i,j} \|w_{ij}\|^2 \quad \text{where } w_{ij} \text{ are the net weights.}$$

More sophisticated regularizers have been proposed [Weigend, Hinton], however probably because of the complexity of the data, the simple form (3) has been found among the most efficient here.
Results in table 2 show the increased identification rate when using a weight decay. Of course the increase is larger when the net is more complex. One can see however that, even for simpler models, training data introduce a bias into the solution. Thus the soft constraints of (3) are useful for this problem eventhough the training criterion is not directly related to the classification goal.

## 5.2  Error modelization

The i.i.d. assumption according to which successive prediction errors are uncorrelated is clearly not correct. [Petek] proposed a method relaxing this hypothesis by modelizing the dependence of the successive errors, leading to some improvements in identification. Beside, the gaussian hypothesis is justified by the central limit theorem. We focus here on different modelizations of the prediction error but still consider it as a gaussian i.i.d. process $N(\mu,\Sigma)$.

A predictive NN, trained to minimize the square error criterion : $C = \sum_{(X_{t-2}, X_{t-1}, X_t)} \|X_t - F(X_{t-2}, X_{t-1})\|^2$

approximates the function $F_{opt}$:

$$F_{opt}(x,y) = \int_z z \cdot p(X_t = z / X_{t-1} = y, X_{t-2} = x) dz$$

where the sum is over the data space. The vectorial average of the prediction errors, on the learned signal, is an estimate of the following null sum (4). Practically, with limited databases, this sum is not exactly null, and it may be useful to estimate the mean $\mu$ for each model.

$$< (\varepsilon_t)^{opt} > = \sum_{X_t} [F_{opt}(X_{t-1}, X_{t-2}) - X_t] p(X_t / X_{t-1}, X_{t-2}) dX_t = 0 \tag{4}$$

The underlying assumption on the noise dispersion when using euclidean distance is clearly restrictive. Table 3 shows the improvements obtained from different modelizations of the prediction error. Results are given for NNs with 10 hidden cells. Similar results have been obtained with other architectures. Using a non isotropic noise, i.e. a full covariance matrix allows to improve significantly the performances. The combined use of a weight decay and a full covariance matrix gives even better results.

| Error | Decay | 50 | 100 | 150 | Sentences |
|-------|-------|------|------|------|-----------|
| (0,I) | no | 72,4 | 85,4 | 90,7 | 93,3 |
| (μ,D) | no | 72,2 | 84,9 | 91,8 | 97,3 |
| (μ,Σ) | no | 75,4 | 88,6 | 93,5 | 97,3 |
| (μ,Σ) | yes | 78 | 89,2 | 93,5 | 100 |

Table 3 : Effect of the error modelization on the identification performance with 10 hidden cells neural nets. (0,I) is a white noise, μ means that the mean is estimated from training data, D and Σ that the covariance matrix is estimated respectively as diagonal or full.

## 5.3  Multi-state models

The models presented up to now modelize the speech signal as a stationary autoregressive process. It is reasonable to assume that, whatever the nature of speaker information may be, this does not correspond to the reality. As for HMMs, model adequacy may be improved by introducing non stationarity. We make the hypothesis that the process is locally stationary autoregressive, and may be described with a finite number of states, each corresponding to a different prediction function. Every talker will be modelized by N multi-layer perceptrons, each of them being specialized on different parts of the speech signal. These nets play the role of states in HMMs. We consider here ergodic models, with equal transition probabilities between states. Estimation of transition probabilities is useless for speaker identification [Tishby, Matsui], at least when the number of states is small.
The models are initialized according to a data clustering. It is clear that the initialization is important, but other choices did not led to better performances. Optimization is then realized simultaneously on the signal segmentation and on the models parameters. For each training pattern, the N prediction errors are computed, but only the parameters of the winner, the one with minimum error, are modified according to a gradient descent method. Error characteristics $(\mu,\Sigma)$ for every states are recomputed after each presentation of the whole training set. During recognition, the score of a model is computed along the lower cost state sequence, using a Viterbi-like algorithm. Let $F_i$ denotes the prediction function associated to the $i^{th}$ state, due to ergodicity, the score for a talker model $(F_1, ..., F_N)$ is computed by:

$$\text{Min}_{c_1...c_T} \left[ \sum_t D_{c_t}(x_t - F_{c_t}(C_t)) + \log|\Sigma_{c_t}| \right] = \sum_t \text{Min}_i [D_i(x_t - F_i(C_t)) + \log|\Sigma_i|]$$

where $D_i$ is defined according to (2), and $c_1...c_T$ is the state sequence with : $\forall t = 1...T \; c_t \in \{1,...,N\}$.

This corresponds to an approximation of the maximum likelihood criterion (MLE) [Levin]. Note that the optimization of the pure MLE criterion could be easily realized by considering all the state sequences.

| nb States | nb hidden cells | Error | nb Param | 50 frames | 100 frames | 150 frames | Sentences |
|---|---|---|---|---|---|---|---|
| 1 | 10 | (0,I) | 506 | 72,4 | 85,4 | 90,7 | 93,3 |
| 1 | 10 + Decay | (μ,Σ) | 650 | 78 | 89,2 | 93,5 | 100 |
| 1 | 5 | (0,I) | 261 | 69,3 | 80,4 | 87,2 | 93,3 |
| 3 | 5 | (0,I) | 783 | 74,8 | 86,7 | 91 | 100 |
| 3 | 5 + Decay | (0,I) | 783 | 75,1 | 87 | 91,6 | 98,7 |
| 3 | 5 | (μ,D) | 879 | 76,3 | 88,3 | 93,6 | 100 |
| 3 | 5 | (μ,Σ) | 1215 | 80,8 | 92,7 | 96 | 100 |

Table 4 : performances of one-state and three-state ergodic models combined with different modelizations of the errors. The fourth column gives the number of parameters per speaker model.

Table 4 shows the performances of 3-states models with a 5 hidden cells NN per state. These models give significantly better results than one-state models. This remains true whatever the error modelization is. Multi-state models are not only more complex than one state models, but also more appropriate. The improvement in identification rate comes from a better modelization of the speech signal. Here, as above, a compromise has to be found in order to find the best models for identification.

In the next section, for the sake of simplicity, we go back to one-state models, with an error N(0,I), and examine which kind of a-priori informations we can incorporate in the models.

# 6. Using a-priori knowledge

We discussed in §4 inherent limitations of modelization-based systems. We presented in §5 some ways for improving their performances by changing standard assumptions of predictive modelization. In this section, we discuss how to improve our system by incorporating a-priori information in the system. This information may be added while training as well as while performing recognition or both.

We present two approaches both aiming at detecting relevant information for the ASI task, for the two of them learning may still be performed separately for talker models.

### a. Basis

Speech segments are not equally important for speaker classification. [Anglade] have used a priori knowledge for selecting manually a few frames from each speech utterance. This allows to reach good performances using very short sequences. On TIMIT, we have been able by selecting 10 frames for each sentence to reach the same performances than for whole sentences. [Li] have also proposed a heuristic technique for the selection of speech segments and observed increased performances. The key problem is to propose a robust and automatic feature selection technique.

In the following, a segment will be a series of successive frames whose length may vary between one up to the length of the sentence. A segment is useful for the identification task if the classification error of the correct model is minimum on this segment. Let us assume that it is possible to characterize the errors of the system, and to a certain extent, to predict them. Our aim will be to learn a function of the segments, whose output reflects the discriminative character of this segment. This information may be used either while training or testing : it is possible to focus training on discriminative segments, alternatively computation of a model score should take into account the discriminant ability of the segments. Moreover, the average value over a sentence of such a function is an indication of the discriminative information it contains. It can be used for rejecting sequences whose mean measure are below a given threshold [Artieres 93] or to gather enough data for each talker while training.

We present below two methods for building such a function.

### b. mean speaker

Feature extraction for identification aims at removing from the input signal components which are useless for the classification task. In the present case, speech and speaker components are intricated and do not separate, attempts to factorize message and speaker characteristics [Tishby] have been unsuccessful. Instead of trying directly this separation, we will train a mean speaker NN to modelize speech from a large number of talkers. This NN will average the characteristics of different talkers and modelize well speech segments corresponding to a small variance of the ideal transfer function of the different talkers, while producing an important error on segments corresponding to higher variance in the response of the different talkers. Of course, there are other sources of error such as the non stationarity or the variation rate of the signal. In a first approximation, they could be considered similar for the different talkers. This idea may be implemented in several ways. Here, we first trained a predictive model using the data from several speakers. The components of the error vector of this model were then used for weighting the corresponding components of each talker error. Training is then performed for the different talkers according to this weighted error criterion. A frame accurately predicted by the mean speaker will have few influence for training a talker model, non discriminative information is thus removed from the speech signal. Table 5 shows the performances of this training procedure. This allows to increase the performances of 1 to 2 % depending on the model complexity.

### c. analysis of the system

This method is based on the analysis of the system behavior during test. We have tested two implementations:
    - for the first one, we perform a clustering of the frames and compute for each cluster the proportion of correct decisions on its frames. For each frame, the function will output the proportion associated to its cluster.
    - the other is implemented with a NN which takes as input frames $x_{t-2}$ to $x_t$ and is trained to output a 1 if the system decision based on $x_t$ prediction is correct and 0 otherwise.
The two functions will thus output a real value between 0 and 1 for each frame which represents the confidence into the local decision of the system. Both give similar approximations of the system behavior, the NN implementation approximates more closely the performances of the system and gives a smoother response. We have used these functions to weight the errors in the recognition procedure, as described above. Performances increase only in small proportions (table 6). When examining the behaviour of these systems, it can be observed that these functions do not model accurately enough the system so that there is an imbalance between improvements due to the method and errors. New investigations are currently being performed on these ideas.

| # segments | Test Length (frames) | 5 Hidden Units | | 10 Hidden Units | |
|---|---|---|---|---|---|
| | | normal training | MS training | normal training | MS training |
| 950 | 50 | 69,3 | 71,1 | 72,4 | 73,2 |
| 800 | 100 | 80,4 | 82,7 | 85,4 | 86,1 |
| 650 | 150 | 87,2 | 88,9 | 90,7 | 91,8 |
| 75 | Sentences | 93,3 | 93,3 | 93,3 | 93,3 |

Table 5 : learning with a mean speaker model (MS) as a function of utterance length.

| Test Length (in frames) | 50 | 100 | 150 | whole sentence |
|---|---|---|---|---|
| without G | 69,3 | 80,4 | 87,2 | 93,3 |
| with G | 69,9 | 81,6 | 87,8 | 94,7 |

Table 6 : performances of the system on 15 talkers by weighting the local errors with the NN implementation of the G function. NN with 5 hidden units have been used in this experiment.

## 7. Conclusion

We have pointed out inherent limitations of predictive models. The main one is a consequence of the discrepancy between training and test criteria which makes model selection more difficult than usual. We have explored solutions offered by predictive NNs for these problems and developped two main directions. The first one analyses the links between the model complexity and the performances of the system, the second focuses on the detection of discriminative information. The different methods have been investigated separately and allow improvements up to 8 % compared to standard predictive systems. These first results are promising, we are currently investigating other implementations along the same lines.

### REFERENCES

[Anglade] Anglade Y., Fohr D., Junqua J.C. 93 : speech discrimination in adverse conditions using acoustic knowledge and selectively trained neural networks, ICASSP, II 279-282.
[Artieres 91] Artières T., Bennani Y., Gallinari P., Montacié C. 91 : connectionist and conventional models for free text talker identification, Neuro-Nîmes.
[Artieres 93] Artières T., Gallinari P. 93 : neural models for extracting speaker characteristics in speech modelization systems, Eurospeech, III - 2263-2266.
[Bennani] Bennani Y., Gallinari P. 91 : on the use of TDNN extracted features information for talker identification, ICASSP'91.
[Bimbot] Bimbot F., Mathan L., Lima A., Chollet G. 92 : standard and target driven AR-vector models for speech analysis and speaker recognition, ICASSP, II 5-8.
[Hattori] Hattori H. 92 : text independent speaker recognition using neural networks, ICASSP, II 153-156.
[Hinton] Hinton .G.E, van Camp D. 93 : keeping neural network simple, IEEE ICANN, 11-18.
[Iso] Iso K., Watanabe T. 91, large vocabulary speech recognition using neural prediction model, ICASSP, 57-60.
[Kawabata] Kawabata T. 92 : predictor codebooks for speaker-independent speech recognition, ICASSP, Vol I, 353-356.
[Le Cun] Le Cun Y., Denker J.S., Solla S.A. 90 : optimal brain damage, NIPS, vol 2, 598-605.
[Levin] Levin E. 93 : hidden control neural architecture modeling of non linear time varying systems and its applications, IEEE Trans on NN, vol 4, Jan 93, 109-116.
[Li] Li K. P., Porter J.E. 88 : normalizations and selection of speech segments for speaker recognition scoring, ICASSP, 595-598.
[Matsui] Matsui T., Furui S. 92 : comparison of text-independent speaker recognition methods using vq-distorsion and discrete/continuous HMMs, ICASSP, 157-160.
[Mellouk] Mellouk A., Gallinari P. 93 : a discriminative neural predictive system for speech recognition, ICASSP, Vol 2,533-536.
[Montacié] Montacie C., Le Floch J.L. 92 : AR-Vector models for free text speaker identification, ICSLP.
[Oglesby] Oglesby J., Mason J.S. 91 : radial basis function networks for speaker recognition, ICASSP, 393-396.
[Petek] Petek B., Ferligoj A. 93: exploiting prediction error in a predictive-based connectionist speech recognition system, ICASSP, Vol II, 267-270.
[Rosenberg] Rosenberg A.E., Lee C, Soong F. K. 90 : sub-word unit talker verification using hidden Markov models, ICASSP, 269-272.
[Tishby] Tishby N. 88 : information theoretic factorization of speaker and language in hidden Markov models with application to speaker recognition, ICASSP.
[Weigend] Weigend A.S., Rumelhart D.E., Huberman B.A. 91 : generalization by weight elimination with application to forecasting, NIPS, Vol 3, 875-882.

# THE COCHLEAR NUCLEUS AND PRIMARY CORTEX AS A SEQUENCE OF DISTRIBUTED NEURAL FILTERS IN PHONEME PERCEPTION

JOHN ANTROBUS, CHAIM TARSHISH, SOPHIE MOLHOLM, MACIEJ SAWICKI
CITY COLLEGE OF THE CITY UNIVERSITY OF NEW YORK
NEW YORK, NEW YORK, 10031
and
JEFFREY FOOKSON
NEW YORK UNIVERSITY

Abstract. *The remarkable ability of the human auditory system to learn to recognize the highly variable acoustic representations of each phoneme has not been matched by artificial neural networks - perhaps because they lack representations of the genetically-selected, neural filters that sequentially and in parallel reduce this variability. This paper uses recent neuroperceptual findings to guide the design of putative filters in the cochlear nucleus and primary auditory cortex that support phoneme perception.*

The large variability in intra- and inter-speaker acoustic-phonemic relations has greatly impeded efforts to represent and understand phoneme perception. It is suggested here that this variability is reduced sequentially by parallel subphonemic neural filters. Reducing variability in the acoustic speech signal is a process of sequentially identifying invariant subphonemic features of increasing orders of abstraction. This serial and parallel neural computing process has the advantage of reducing the dimensionality of the categorizing problem computed at each step and thereby, of simplifying the final phoneme identification problem space.

The human speech perception system appears to acquire good generalization of phoneme perception with only one, the mother, or a very few, teachers. The ability to generalize from such a restricted phoneme training set must be credited to genetically acquired auditory filters or preprocessors that reduce the variability in the phoneme "signal" before it reaches the left middle temporal gyrus of the cerebral cortex (LMTG; Mazoyer et al., 1993) where it learns the phonemes of a particular language. By carrying out low level generalization functions, these filters reduce dependence on a large speaker training sample for phoneme generalization used by machine speech recognition systems.

This conception of fixed, followed by a trainable, processor is consistent with genetic models where the more primitive components of complex biological systems were, in an earlier stage of evolution, able to function successfully as complete systems (Holland, 1993). As regions of the cerebral cortex were added in the course of evolution, they took as their "auditory" input, the output of preexisting "hard wired" auditory systems that must have been capable of some generalization functions.

Until recently, the near impossibility of observing the auditory nuclei of unanesthetized animals provided little basis for modelling neural processes beyond the cochlea (Shamma, 1985; Waibel et al., 1988; Kohonen, 1988). But it is now clear that as speech information moves from the cochlea (Sinex et al., 1991) through the cochlear nucleus to the LMTG (Mazoyer et al., 1993), neurons are selectively tuned to successively more abstract phonemic subfeatures. Rhode (1991) has described single units in the **cochlear nucleus** (CN) that respond selectively to subphonemic features. For example, formant transitions are a critical acoustic component of consonants: certain "onset" and "chopper" cells respond selectively to ramp or "swept" frequencies. Duration of a phoneme feature is critical for vowel recognition: "pauser" cells (onset spike -> an OFF interval -> steady firing) respond selectively to different acoustic durations. Dynamic change is a characteristic of all phonemic subfeatures; a variety of "onset" cells are tuned to different classes of dynamic change. Lamina III & IV in A1 further extend this abstract filtering process. A "double on" response to the prevoiced component of a consonant such as /p/ identifies the voice onset time interval that distinguishes it from the voiced consonant, /b/ (Steinschneider et al., 1993).

In order to test the merits of a phoneme perception model based on these neuroperceptual observations, the architectural and computational assumptions are represented in a neural network model, **HEARNET**, which is then evaluated for its ability to simulate the recognition of a small sample of phonemes. HEARNET consists of **FilterSys (See Figure 1)**, a series of parallel interconnected tonotopically and amplitopically ordered artificial neural filters designed to represent selected characteristics of the human auditory filter system that are genetically fixed, and **LearnNet**, a recurrent supervised backpropagation network that takes the output of FilterSys as its input and learns subword features.

**FilterSys**

The conception of the auditory system as a network of genetically fixed filters is borrowed from a similar model of the visual system (Van Essen et al., 1992). Taking their output from more elementary filters that simulate CN output, parallel sets of filters starting with a representation of neurons in the CN (Kiange & Peake, 1988; Sachs & Blackburn, 1991) abstract and compact different auditory characteristics. Successive filters further abstract and compact these characteristics, phonemic subfeatures from which the features of phonemes are eventually computed. The output of these genetically-fixed filters is passed to LearnNet, that learns to select and use the filtered subfeatures to classify the continuous input into a sequence of overlapping phonemes.

FilterSys carries out parallel sequences of transforms of the power spectra of the acoustic signal (.05 - 4.5 Khz, in 22 ms. Hamming windows in successive 11 ms. steps and passes its output in 22 ms. steps; energy is expressed to the power of 0.6 dynes/cm$^2$ and, within each band, is squashed between 0 & 1 with a sigmoid function. Filters are constructed from networks of discrete units whose links and weights are set by the designer.

Input to FilterSys is scaled by both auditory frequency and pitch. As the filtered information moves up through FilterSys, the output of higher order filters represents increasingly complex context-dependent characteristics of the speech signal. The **Broad Band** filter (5, ordered 2 octave (pitch) band units in 1 octave steps; representing broad band CN neurons described by Sachs &

Blackburn, 1991) produces a **Pitch X Duration X Loudness** filter matrix that appears to be effective for detecting consonant information, but quite useless for categorizing vowels.

The sharp resolution of the Narrow Band units (1/3 octave (pitch) units in 1/6 octave steps to 4.5 Khz.) is designed to resolve the slope and pitch of the individual formant transitions. Using lateral inhibition, **ON**, **OFF**, **Ramp Pitch** and Pauser units, **Center Band Pitch and Duration** and **Slope of Mean Pitch Ramp Bands** networks compute the running center pitch, slope and duration of individual formants. This local pitch information is passed on to a larger **Relative Pitch Band Intervals** filter that represents the pitch intervals as distances from $F_0$.

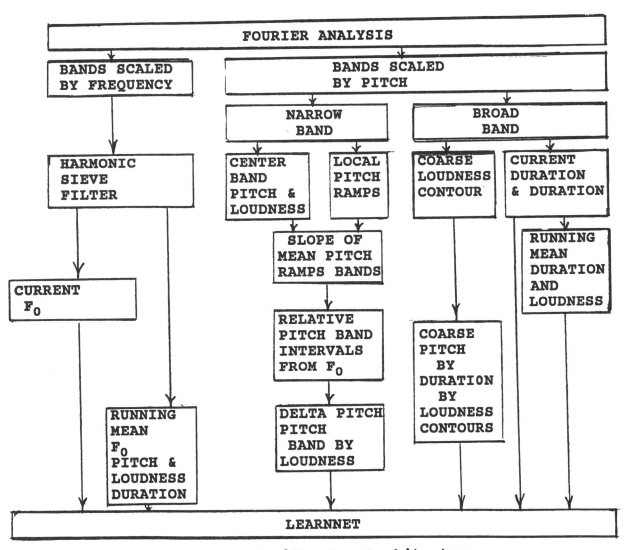

Figure 1. Summary of FilterSys Architecture.

The harmonically ordered units produce the **Harmonic Sieve Filter** (Cohen et al., 1992) that locates values of $F_0$ in the 0.1 - 0.25 Khz range. Later filters use **Pauser** units to time $F_0$. $F_0$ values are used in a **Pitch Band Intervals** net to compute the pitch interval distances between $F_0$ and the formants, whether moving or stationary. LearnNet relies on this matrix for vowel identification. A set of **Echoic** $F_0$ filters, constructed from Pauser Units with slow decay times, provide the system with a running average of both $F_0$ pitch and duration, both of which contribute to a stable speech normalization process.

Recurrent loops within many these filters allow them to sustain their activity until overridden by new information. Simultaneously, lateral inhibition units in the recurrent loops continue to sharpen their outputs. As the accuracy of this output increases over successive iterations, LearnNet is provided with an increasingly distinct basis for discriminating among ambiguous and noise embedded linguistic units. LearnNet not only learns to select the useful contextual information in the output of FilterSys, but it creates and learns to select additional more abstract contextual information on its own.

**LearnNet**

LearnNet is simply a backpropagation network with a recurrent Jordan (1986) type layer that acts as a working memory for the net. The recurrent layer copies the output layer to a state layer and then returns it to the input of the out layer when the next cycle of new information arrives so that new information is always read in one or more temporal contexts. Of the 9 output units, three units each are assigned to the first consonant, vowel, and terminal consonant.

Within this project, the primary role of LearnNet is to evaluate the preprocessing role of FilterSys, and its subnetworks. Phonemes, like other classes of speech, are nonlinear as well as linear functions of phonemic and subphonemic features. Back propagation is the learning model of choice for evaluating the manner in which FilterSys organizes the elementary information in the speech signal because it is highly successful at sorting the useful from the irrelevant information in its input, and at computing the linear and nonlinear transformations necessary to recognize the output classes specified by some external "teacher."

**Compacting and FilterSys-to-LearnNet Sampling Rate**

One guide to maximizing the compacting of the speech signal is provided by the observations of Phillips (1993) and Steinschneider et al. (1993) who find none of the periodic components of speech in the cerebral cortex. Steinschneider et al. show that the periodic representation of $F_0$ is filtered out between the thalamocortical input and lamina 3 and 4b of A1 so that the cortex need only respond to context dependent **changes** in the signal. Their voice onset model for an unvoiced consonant (lamina 4 & 3 pyramidal cell excitation -> hyperpolarization and 2nd depolarization (from voicing) -> 2nd lamina 3 hyperpolarization -> lamina 3 depolarization) accounts for the double ON A1 pattern that describes the voice onset interval. Their model provides an empirical marker for aligning FilterSys filters with the spatial location of human auditory neuro-computations.

## Constraints on Shifting Sampling Rate: FilterSys-to-LearnNet

As acoustic information enters the cochlea and moves through continuous transformations up the auditory pathways, the minimum sampling rate necessary to compute each transformation becomes successively slower. In general, as information moves from the cochlea to the cortex, the need to resolve high frequency information gives way to the requirement of computing information in low frequency contexts. For example, the Nyquist frequency for resolving the useful high auditory frequencies in the speech of children and female adults is approximately 15 kHz., but once the power in each band is computed, a sampling rate of only 100 Hz. (step sizes of 10 ms.) is sufficient to resolve the slope of a formant transition in a "chirp," a component of an initial consonant. Once a 30 - 50 ms. slope is compacted and represented in a filter as a single ON, the sampling rate can be further reduced for input to LearnNet. The current sampling rate of LearnNet is 30.3 Hz. with a window size of 33 msec. Mean syllable length is reduced from 97 frames to 32.4 after compacting.

The standard AI response to the analysis of the serially-ordered speech signal is to wait until all the information relevant to a particular linguistic unit, such as a word, is collected, and then process it. But the nervous system cannot use this strategy because it cannot store long sequences of raw data. It must, therefore, successively transform and, in so doing, compact the information in the acoustic signal. Because the early nuclei have no way of knowing when a higher level unit is completed, they must transform information in a continuous fashion. While each neural entity, $n_{j-1} \ldots n_{j-v}$ , has its own form of "echoic" memory, the memory of their individual inputs to $n_j$ is implicit in the state of $n_j$ as well as any echoic memory associated with $n_j$. As each successive nucleus, $n_k \ldots n_m$, carries out its particular transformation of its input, the lower level nuclei, $n_{j-1} \ldots n_{j-v}$, are freed to receive new data.

## Recognition Accuracy of the Current HEARNET Model

We are in the process of collecting speech samples of isolated CVCs, training the model and testing it for generalization.

## References

Cohen, M. A., Grossberg, S. & Wyse L. (1992). A neural network model of pitch detection and representation. Technical Report CAS/CNS-92-024, Boston University Center for Adaptive Systems.

Holland, J. (1993). Can there be a unified theory of complex adaptive systems? Presented at the conference on The mind, brain and complex adaptive systems, The Krasnow Institute of Advanced Study and the Santa Fe Institute, May 24-26, Fairfax Virginia.

Jordan, M. (1986). Serial order: A parallel distributed approach. ICS Report 8604. La Jolla: University of California, San Diego.

Kiange, N. Y-s., & Peake, W. T. (1988). Physics and physiology of hearing. In Atkinson, R. C., Herrnstein, R. J., Lindzey, G., & Luce, D. R. Steven's handbook of experimental psychology. pp. 277-326, N. Y. Wiley Interscience.

Kohonen, T. (1988). The "neural" phonetic typewriter. Computer, 21, 11-22.

Mazoyer, B. M., Tzourio, N., Syrota, V., Frak, V., Murayama, N., Levier, O., Salamon, G., Dehaene, S., Cohen, L., & Mehler, J. (1993). The cortical representation of speech. Journal of Cognitive Neuroscience, 5, 467-479.

Phillips, D. P. (1993). Representation of acoustic events in the primary auditory cortex. Journal of Experimental Psychology: Human Perception and Performance, 19, 203-216.

Rhode, W. S. (1991) Physiological-Morphological properties of the cochlear nucleus. In R. A. Altschuler, R. P. Bobbin, B. M. Clopton, & D. W. Hoffman, D. W. (Eds.) The neurobiology of hearing (pp. 47-77). N. Y.:Raven.

Rumelhart, D. E., Hinton, G. E. & Williams, R. J. (1986). Learning internal representations by error propagation. (pp 318-362). In J. L. McClelland, D. E. Rumelhart (Eds.) Parallel distributed processing: Explorations in the microstructure of cognition. Cambridge, MA.: MIT Press.

Sachs, M. B., & Blackburn, C. C. (1991). Processing of complex sounds in the cochlear nucleus. In R. A. Altschuler, R. P. Bobbin, B. M. Clopton, & D. W. Hoffman (Eds.) (1991). The neurobiology of hearing. N. Y.: Raven.

Shamma, S. (1985) Speech processing in the auditory system I. Representation of speech sounds in the responses of the auditory nerve, Journal of the Acoustical Society of America, 78, 1612-1621.

Sinex, D. G., McDonald, L. P., & Mott, J. B. (1991). Neural correlates of nonmonotonic temporal acuity for voice onset time. Journal of the Acoustical Society of America, 90, 2441-2449.

Steinschneider, M., Schroeder, C. E., Arezzo, J. C. & Vaughan Jr., H. G. (1993). Speech evoked activity in primary auditory cortex: Effects of voice onset time. Submitted for publication.

Van Essen, D. C., Anderson, C. H. & Fellerman, D. J. (1992). Information processing in the primate visual system: An integrated systems perspective. Science, 255, 419-422.

Waibel A., Hanazawa T., Hinton G., Shikano K. & Lang K. (1988) Phoneme recognition using Time-Delay Neural Networks, Proc. ICASSP-88, NY.

*Poster presented at the World Congress on Neural Networks, San Diego, June 4-9, 1993.*

# BEHAVIORAL AND ELECTROPHYSIOLOGICAL CORRELATES OF READING PROCESSES.

Margaret Niznikiewicz, Ph.D.,* Nancy K. Squires, Ph.D.
State University of New York at Stony Brook, Stony Brook, NY 11790
* Harvard Medical School, Brockton VAMC, Psychiatry 116A, Belmont St., Brockton, MA 02401

## ABSTRACT

Phonological processing in silent reading was explored in a paradigm in which homophones were presented both in the word pairs and the sentence condition. Reaction times, error data and Evoked Potentials were recorded to the target words. Both behavioral and the EP data suggested the phonological codes were activated in SILENT reading and the two measures provided complementary information on the reading processes. EP data suggested that the phonological codes were accessed early in the reading processes, as indexed by the N200, and were separate from semantic processes, as indexed by the N400. The behavioral data highlighted the interaction of the orthographic, phonological and semantic information, which was modulated by a task-relevant strategy and lead to the final decision and the behavioral response.

## INTRODUCTION

To arrive at a meaning of a written word, a reader must go through several cognitive operations including perceptual, orthographic, phonological and lexical processing. Most models of reading assume that readers rely on orthographic information to get at the meaning of a word. However, the extent to which phonological information may be used in silent reading has been the subject of a protracted debate (see Van Orden, 1991). Some authors posit that phonological processing is obligatory ("mediation hypothesis", Huey, 1908) while others see its role as a back-up system that may be used in reading difficult texts, or by non-fluent readers (e.g., Adams, 1990). In fact, it has been demonstrated that as children become more proficient readers rely more on the orthographic information (e.g., Doctor and Coltheart, 1980). On the other hand, phonological coding in silent reading has been demonstrated in a number of experiments. In some studies, accessing the phonological code was demonstrated at a prelexical stage, i.e., before lexicon is accessed (e.g., Van Orden, 1987, Perfetti, Bell, Delaney, 1988); while in others this effect has been demonstrated at the postlexical stage, i.e., after lexicon and meaning were activated (e.g. Treiman, Freyd, and Baron, 1983).

One of the more popular methods of demonstrating the effects of the phonological processing in reading has employed homophones, i.e., words that sound alike but have different spelling and meaning (e.g., "rose" vs "rows"), as probes. The rationale is that if homophones activate the phonological code along with the graphemic code, there should be activation of two lexical entries (or two different meanings). Consequently, it would be more difficult to reject an incorrect homophonic word (e.g., "rows" belonging to the category: "flower"), leading on occasion to an incorrect lexical decision. Thus, in lexical decision tasks, longer RTs and/or higher error rates to homophones (the "homophonic effect") could be regarded as evidence for the activation of a phonological code.

One of the challenges in exploring the role of phonological processing in reading is the use of proper control condition (Van Orden, 1991) that would enable one to conclude that observed effects are solely due to the phonological identity of the stimuli and not to the orthographic or semantic processing. Working memory load is another factor that can influence the way in which phonological information is used in reading. An incorrect homophone in a sentential context will be more likely processed as its correct counterpart than when it appears in a word-pair context because of the biasing sentential context and the larger extent to which the memory system is taxed (e.g. Treiman, Freyd, and Baron, 1983, Kinsch and Van Dijk, 1978; Just and Carpenter, 1980; Baddeley, 1989). Presumably, memory would be taxed more while processing sentences than single words. Accordingly, this study used four stimulus types to explore the relative contributions of the 1) phonological, 2) orthographic and 3) semantic processing in reading using both pairs of words and sentences. Also, reading sentences seemed to be closer to real-life reading situations. Based on past research longer reaction times (RTs) and/or error rates were predicted to target homophones than to other stimuli. Also, longer RTs and more errors were predicted in the sentence than in the word condition due to a larger processing load imposed on the memory system. Simultaneously, Evoked Potentials (EPs) were recorded to target stimuli. The Evoked potential technique allows for recording brain activity time-locked to stimulus presentation providing important information about the neuronal processes underlying cognitive operations as they happen on-line thus complementing global measures such as RTs and error data. It has been demonstrated that EP data (especially N400 component, peaking about 400 msec after stimulus presentation) are sensitive to different aspects of language processing. (e.g., Kutas and Hillyard, 1984; 1988; Neville, 1985; Smith et al., 1986; Holcomb and

Neville, 1990; Rugg and Barnett, 1989; Garsney et al., 1989). Some previous ERP studies have explored the involvement of phonological processing in reading (Kramer and Donchin, 1987; Rugg, 1984; Polich et al., 1983). However, this is the first ERP study to investigate the use of phonological information in a task requiring processing of meaning. Three main questions were addressed: 1) what is the role of phonological processing in silent reading? 2) what is a temporal course of activation of the phonological codes? 3) how might phonological processing in reading depend on the type of reading material? The joint analysis of behavioral and ERP data was conducted to help relate the cognitive constructs used in describing reading processes (based on behavioral data) to underlying electrophysiological events, thus yielding new insights about cognitive functioning in reading.

**METHOD**

Subjects.

Twenty seven male and twenty four female, English speaking, undergraduate students (ages 19-29) of the State University of New York at Stony Brook participated in the study. To ensure that the subjects did not differ in their reading abilities and to exclude dyslexic and learning-delayed individuals, only the individuals with a score higher than 80 on the Wide Range Achievement Test (WRAT) - Reading, 90 on the WRAT-Spelling, and 80 on the Woodcock Johnson Phonological, were included in the study.

Experimental Conditions.

Word and sentence conditions were used to compare RT and ERP data across different linguistic tasks. Four types of stimuli were constructed for each condition to assess the relative contributions of phonological and orthographic codes in reading for meaning. A lexical-decision task in which subjects decided if the two words were semantically related, was used in the word condition, and a sentence- acceptability judgment task in which the subjects decided if a sentence made sense, in the sentence condition.

Stimuli.

Thirty high and medium frequency (Kutzera and Francis, 1967) homophone pairs were used in each condition. In the word condition, each member of a homophonic pair (e.g., plain-plane) was used as a target stimulus in order to control for the potential differences in word frequency and/or graphemic structure between the two words. For each target homophone two control word pairs were constructed to control for the effects 1) graphemic similarity between two homophonic words 2) absence of a semantic relationship between two homophonic words and 3) a semantically related word-pair foil was developed. The control words were always in the target position, and are referred to as graphemic, semantic, or unrelated targets, depending on the features shared with a nodal homophone (i.e., the one for which they were developed as control stimuli). An example below shows a homophonic word pair plain-plane and its control stimuli is:

homophonic:   plain-plane       plane-plain
graphemic:    plane-place       plain-plaid
semantic:      plane-jet          plain-dull
unrelated:     plane-host       plain-fast

The thirty homophonic word pairs gave a total of 120 word pairs generated with the the first homophone in a pair, and 120 word pairs generated with the second item, forming two word-pair lists which, randomized twice, gave four word-pair lists.

The same 30 homophonic pairs were used in the sentence condition to create 2 sets of 120 sentences which, randomized twice, gave four lists of sentences. Each word of a homophonic pair was placed in the target position (target homophone) at the end of a sentence. For example, for bore-boar two homophonic, the two semantically correct sentences were: The movie was such a bore, and The hunter had shot a huge boar. (semantic manipulation). In the homophonic manipulation, correct homophones were replaced with incorrect ones: The movie was such a boar, and The hunter had shot a huge bore. The other two sentence types (both semantically incongruent) were used to test for 1) the graphemic similarity of the two homophones (graphemic manipulation): The movie was such a bone and The hunter had shot a huge boat.2) the effects of incongruence not related to orthographic structure ('unrelated' manipulation): The movie was such a rope. and The hunter had shot a huge desk. Since the four sentential manipulations differed solely in their target words, with the sentences providing identical context across a set, the experimental effects are discussed in respect to a type of the control word: semantic, homophonic, graphemic, and unrelated.

In both conditions the words were presented over an IBM, VGA computer monitor, one word at a time, from a distance of 160 cm. Stimulus duration was 475 msec, the interstimulus interval (ISI) was 100 msec, and the intertrial interval (ITI) 1800 msec. Subjects responded "yes" or "no" by pushing one of two response buttons as soon as possible. The use of the right and left hands was counterbalanced across the subjects. Reaction times (RTs) longer than two seconds were excluded from the analysis. Half of the subjects were exposed to the sentence condition first and the other half to the word condition first. The target words did not repeat between conditions. The ERP, RT, and error data were collected only for the target words. Only RTs to correct items were used in the analysis. In each condition an average RT was calculated for each subject, and each stimulus type, by dividing an overall RT per stimulus type by the number of correct responses.

The EEG activity was recorded from Fz, Cz, and Pz, over 975 msec with 100 msec baseline and averaged on-line separately for the four different types of stimulus words. The bandpass was .1 Hz to 100 Hz. A neck electrode was used as reference and the right mastoid as ground. Eye movements were monitored from an electrode under the right eye. Two components were selected for analysis; N200 was defined as the most negative component between the post-stimulus latencies of 200 and 400 msec, and N400 was defined as the most negative going component between the post-stimulus latencies of 300 and 700 msec. The components were selected at Cz, where they were most readily observable.

Figure 3: Grand average waveforms.

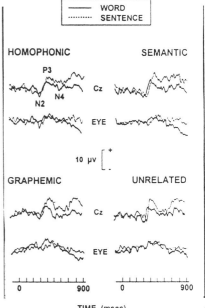

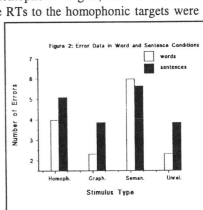

Statistical Analyses.

For RTs and errors, the effects of experimental condition and four different stimulus types were assessed by a two (experimental condition: word vs sentence condition) x four (stimulus type: homophonic, graphemic, semantic, and unrelated) ANOVA. The effects of experimental condition and stimulus type on the latency and amplitude of the N200 and N400 components were assessed by means of two (experimental condition: word vs sentence) x three (electrode site: Fz, Cz, Pz) x four (stimulus type: homophonic, graphemic, semantic, unrelated) ANOVAs.

## RESULTS

### Behavioral Results.

The reaction times were analyzed for the correct items only. Reaction times in the sentence condition averaged 817 msec, while in the word condition they averaged 643 msec. The ANOVA on RTs showed significant main effects of condition [F(1,46) = 37.861; p = .001] and target type [F(3,138) = 4.981; p = .006], and a significant interaction between condition and target type [F(3,138) = 3.552; p = .03].

In the word condition, the shortest RTs were to the homophonic target, followed by the graphemic and then the semantic targets. The longest RTs were to the unrelated targets. Planned comparisons revealed that the RTs to the homophonic targets were significantly shorter than the RTs to the unrelated (p =.001), and semantic targets (p = .05), but were not significantly shorter than the RTs to graphemic targets (see Figure 1).

In the sentence condition the longest RTs were to the incorrect homophonic targets, and the shortest RTs were to the semantic targets. Planned comparisons revealed that the RTs to the homophonic targets were significantly longer than the RTs to the graphemic targets (p = .05) and semantic targets (p = .01) but did not differ significantly from the RTs to the unrelated targets.

Error rates were analyzed as the number of false positive decisions to incongruous words ( homophonic, graphemic and unrelated targets) and the number of negative decisions to semantic targets. The ANOVA on the

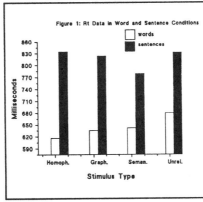

IV-615

number of errors revealed significant main effects of condition [F(1,45) = 4.691; p = .04] and target type [F(3,135) = 11.491; p = .0001]. More errors were committed in the sentence condition (mean = 4.6) than in the word condition (mean = 3.6). The same pattern of error distribution across the four target types was found in the word and the sentence conditions (see Fig. 2). The largest number of errors was committed to the semantic targets in both conditions. The second highest number of errors was to the homophonic targets. Planned comparisons revealed that the number of errors to the homophonic targets was significantly higher than the number of errors to the graphemic and unrelated targets in both the word and the sentence conditions (p = .001).

ERP Results

N200 and P300 were well defined peaks, while N400 took a form of a broad negativity spanning the latency of 400 to 750 msec poststimulus (see Figure 3).

0 latency (mean = 293, +/- 40 msec) was 20 msec longer in the sentence condition than in the word condition, as indicated by a main effect of condition [F(1,35) = 19.662; p = .0002]. Similarly, N400 latency ( mean = 593 msec, +/- 74 msec), was 21 msec longer in the sentence than in the word condition indicated by a main effect of condition [F(1,27) = 5.036; p = .033]. The ANOVA on N200 amplitude revealed a

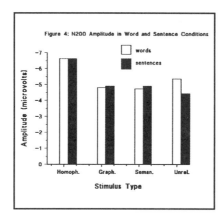

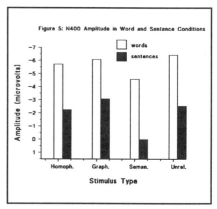

significant main effect of target type [F(3,105) = 3.951; p = .01] and a significant interaction between condition and electrode site [F(2,70) = 3.75; p = .03]. For N200, the most negative amplitudes were in response to the homophonic targets in both the word and the sentence condition (see Fig.4). The ANOVA on N400 amplitude showed main effects of condition [F(1,26) = 34.451; p = .0001) and target type [F(3,78) = 4.681; p = .005], and a significant interaction of condition and electrode site. N400 amplitude was more negative in the word than in the sentence condition for all types of targets. As seen in Figure 5, in both conditions larger negativities were observed for all the targets that did not make sensible endings (i.e., to homophonic, graphemic, and unrelated targets). The N400 amplitude was smallest in response to words that made sensible endings in the sentence condition, and to words that were semantically related in the word condition (semantic targets).

**DISCUSSION**

The results of this study indicate that phonological codes can be activated in silent reading, at least under some conditions. They suggest that the way people use phonological information depends on the task at hand. The phonological effect measured behaviorally manifested itself differently in the word and the sentence conditions. The ERP data indicate activation of phonological codes (as indexed by N200) at the early stages of word processing, thus lending support for the prelexical hypotheses of phonological code activation. The effect of activating a semantic representation were observed later, as indexed by the N400 component, and did not interact with the effects of processing the more physical aspects of words, such as their phonological and graphemic codes.

Behavioral Results

In the word condition, the shortest RTs were to the homophonic targets. Also, most errors were committed to these words. These fast responses suggest that subjects did not need to analyze the meaning of the homophonic word pairs to decide about their semantic relatedness. Apparently, both phonological and graphemic codes were routinely activated. In the case of a homophonic word pair, the comparison between the outcome of the phonological analysis (e.g., pour and poor) - the two items sound identical, and of the graphemic analysis (the two items look different), could lead to a correct, negative decision about the two words' semantic unrelatedness without accessing a semantic store. (In English, two words that have different spelling and sound identical never have the same meaning.) However, the error data indicate that on some occasions, phonological information activated a semantic store, which resulted in a higher proportion of false positive errors to the homophonic targets (deciding that two words were related when they were not) than to unrelated targets.

In the sentence condition, the RTs to homophonic incongruent words (e.g., The hunters shot a huge bore) were longer than to any other stimuli. Also, most errors were committed to these items. These results are in agreement with the earlier studies (e.g., Cohen, 1980; Treiman et al., 1983) suggesting that the phonological code was activated in this task. The structural differences between the word and sentence conditions influenced the way the phonological code was utilized. In the sentence condition, neither the phonological nor orthographic features of the word preceding the target could aid in making a semantic decision about a sentence. Instead, the target word had to be incorporated into the preceding context. In the case of homophones, the conflict between two different semantic outputs caused an increase in RTs, and, in some cases, was resolved in favor of the results of phonological analysis - as the high number of errors attests. Since the conflict between two competing semantic interpretations could arise only if the competing phonological and orthographic codes were activated before accessing the lexicon, the phonological information in the sentence condition must have been activated prelexically. Heavy dependence on the working memory system could another factor that contributed to the activation of the phonological codes given the evidence that memory for linguistic material in the working memory is phonologically based (e.g., Baddeley, Vallar and Wilson; 1987; Ellis and Henneley, 1984).

In summary, the RTs and error data reveal the complexity of reading processes. Eighty percent of homophonic targets were responded to correctly, suggesting that readers do rely on orthographic information. Significantly shorter RTs to the homophonic targets in the word condition and longer RTs and more errors to homophonic items in the sentence condition demonstrated the flexibility in using a phonological code which is dependent on the structure and demands of the task. These results suggest that in describing reading processes it may be useful to adopt an interactive framework (McClelland and Rumelhart, 1981; and Seidenberg et al., 1984) in which familiar multi-letter and multi-phone strings activate word candidates and the one that is most activated is selected. Feedback loops exist between the letter units, the phonemes units, and the semantic units and the activation of the phonological code is more a matter of degree. The use of homophonic words in the sentences and word pairs underscored this flexibility of the cognitive system.

## ERP Results

### The N200

The fronto/central N200 in the present study may be a variety of the mismatch negativity or N2b identified by Renault and Lesevre (1982) although it differs in significant ways. An N200 was recorded to all types of stimuli. No N200 amplitude difference was observed between the word and sentence conditions for any type of stimulus suggesting that it was not sensitive to memory demands. Similar amplitudes were recorded to the graphemic, semantical, and unrelated targets and significantly larger amplitude was recorded to the homophonic stimuli. These results suggest the N200 amplitude was sensitive to the registration of certain physical aspects of stimuli, but did not distinguish between different graphemic or semantic relationships between the target word and the preceding context. The larger N200 amplitude to homophonic items cannot be attributed to the physical properties of homophonic stimuli; in the word condition, the orthographic features of the homophonic and graphemic targets were equally similar to the preceding context. The result cannot also be explained by the semantic incongruity between the homophonic words and the preceding stimuli. In both the word and the sentence condition, graphemic and unrelated targets were semantically as unrelated to the preceding context as the homophonic targets were, and yet the N200 amplitude to these stimuli was significantly smaller than to the homophonic targets. Apparently, the N200 to the homophonic targets reflected the processes of simultaneous access of phonological as well as graphemic codes and possibly the forming of lexical representations, which were separate from semantic analysis. The increased N200 amplitude to homophones could have been related to the detection of conflict between the outputs of the phonological and orthographic analyses. Thus, the ERP data suggest that the earlier stages of processing were dominated by sensory processes, i.e., the analyses of phonological and graphemic information, and, perhaps, to the forming of a lexical representation. More abstract, semantically dominated, processing was conducted at later stages and was indexed by the N400.

### The N400

The processes of evaluating the semantic relationships between the stimuli contributed to an N400-like component that was primarily sensitive to semantic incongruities in both the word and sentence conditions regardless of whether the target stimuli were homophonic, graphemic, or unrelated. Larger N400 amplitude was recorded in the word than in the sentence condition. Based on theories of lexical memory (e.g., Collins and

Loftus, 1975; Posner and Snyder, 1975; Neely, 1977), many authors (e.g., Bentin, McCarthy, and Wood, 1985; Stuss, Picton, and Cerri, 1988) have suggested that the N400 recorded to semantically incongruous items indexes priming effects. In electrophysiological studies using word pairs, larger amplitudes have been reported to "unexpected" words (e.g., Stuss et al., 1988 Bentin, McCarthy, and Wood, 1985) and Bentin et al. suggested that the amplitude of the N400 was proportional to the amount of lexical search. Researchers exploring sentential processes have emphasized the role of context (Kutas and Hillyard ,1984; Kutas and Van Petten, 1990) arguing that the N400 amplitude was related to the degree of the contextual constraint for a given word in a sentence. Thus, words that are poorly predicted by the context could elicit substantial N400s even though they form a semantically acceptable sentence. The N400 in the word condition was frontally distributed, and in the sentence condition, it was centrally distributed. It is therefore possible that the two types of priming might involve related, although not identical, cognitive and physiological mechanisms. Larger amplitudes in the word condition confirmed earlier hypotheses about the relationship between the N400 amplitude and the strength of priming effects: single words provided less contextual constraint than did whole sentences for a target in the final position.

The processes of reading as evidenced by behavioral and ERP data.

Both the behavioral and ERP data suggested that phonological processes were activated in silent reading. Analyzed jointly, the two data sets provide for revealing comparisons and demonstrate the utility of using traditional measures such as RT and error data in conjunction with on-line measures. In this study, the behavioral data, as a composite measure, suggested a highly parallel and interactive process: the responses seemed to be influenced by a task-related strategy and the memory load, and there was evidence that both semantic and sensory information was considered. The ERP data suggested more sequential processing where information about the physical structure of words seemed to be analyzed first, as indexed by the N200, and semantic information second, as indexed by the N400. Speculations on the nature of the processes that provided for these differences may include postulating information about orthographic, phonological and semantic features is stored in the way that it be readily accessed and the different types of information can interact. It is feasible that these operations are influenced strategic processes, understood as a high level cognitive operation or as a result of bottom-up driven learning processes that operate by modulation of weights at the neuronal nodes, to yield the final decision about a stimulus. For example, in the word condition, perceptual evidence was sufficient to make a decision. Thus, other sources of information did not enter into the decision making process to the same extent as they did in the case of other stimuli. On the other hand, in the sentence condition, both perceptual and semantic information had to be considered in making decisions about the homophonic items. The working memory system might be conceptualized here as serving the function of maintaining excitation of the areas that contain information pertinent to the task, thus providing a unifying "space" for the cognitive operations to be performed and distributed over different structures.

## REFERENCES

Adams, M. J. 1990. Beginning to Read. Thinking and Learning about print. The MIT Press, Cambridge, MA.Paul, London. 26-64.

Barnard, P. 1985. Interacting Cognitive Subsystems. A Psycholinguistic Approach to Short Term Memory. In: Ellis, A. (Ed.). Progress in the Psychology of Language. vol. 2. 197-258. Lawrence Erlbaum, London.

Baddeley, A. D., Vallar, G., Wilson, B. 1987. Sentence Comprehension and Phonological Memory: Some Neuropsychological Evidence. In: Coltheart, M. (Ed.). Attention and Performance XII, The Psychology of Reading. Lawrence Erlbaum Assoc., Publishers, Hove and London. Hillsdale.

Baddeley, A. D. 1989. Broadbent, D., McGough, . L., Kosslyn, M., Mackintosh, N., Tulving, E., Weiskrantz, L. (eds). Working Memory. Claredon Press, Oxford.

Bentin, S., McCarthy, G., Wood, C. (1985). Event Related Potentials, Lexical Decision, and Semantic Priming. Electroencephalography and Clinical Neurophysiology, 60, 343-355.

Doctor, E. A. and Coltheart, M. 1980. Children's Use of Phonological Encoding When Reading for Meaning. Memory and Cognition, 8(3), 195-209.

Collins, A. M., Loftus, E. F. (1975). A Spreading Activation Theory of Semantic Processing. Psychological Review, 83, 407-428.

Ellis, N. C., and Henneley, R. A. 1984. A Bilingual Word-Length Effect: Implications for Intelligence Testing and the Relative Ease of Mental Calculation in Welsh and English. British Journal of Psychology, 71, 43-52.

Garsney, S., Tanenhaus, M and Chapman, R. 1989. Evoked Potentials and the Study of Sentence

Comprehension. Journal of Psycholinguistic Research, vol. 18, 1, 51-50.

Huey, E.B. (1908). The psychology and pedagogy of reading. New York, MacMillan.

Kinsch, W. and van Dijk, T. A. 1978. Towards the Model of Text Comprehension and Production. Psychological Review, 85, 363-394.

Kramer, A. F., Donchin, E. 1987. Brain Potentials as Indices of Orthographic and Phonological Interaction During Word Matching. Journal of Experimental Psychology: Learning, Memory and Cognition, 13, 76-86.

Kutas, M. & Hillyard, M. 1982. The Lateral Distribution of Event-Related Potentials During Sentence Processing. Neuropsychologia, 20, 579-590.

Kutas, M., & Hillyard, S. 1984. Brain Potentials During Reading Reflect Word Expectancy and Semantic Association. Nature, 307, 12, 161-163.

Kutas, M., Van Petten, C. 1990. Electrophysiological Perspectives on Comprehending Written Language. New Trends and Advances techniques in Clinical Neurophysiology (EEG Suppl.41). 155-167.

Kutzera, H. & Francis, W.N. 1967. Computational Analysis of Present Day American-English. Providence, RI: Brown University Press.

McLelland J. L. Rumelhart, D. E. 1981. An Interactive Activation Model of the Effect of Context on Perception. Part 1: An Account of Basic Findings. Psychological Review, 88, 375-407.

Neely, J. H. (1977). Semantic Priming and Retrieval from Lexical Memory: Roles of Inhibitionless Spreading Activation and Limited-Capacity Attention. Journal of Experimental Psychology: General, 106, 226-234.

Neville, H. 1985. Biological Constraints on Semantic Processing: a Comparison of Spoken and Signed Languages. Psychophysiology, 22, 576.

Perfetti, C. A., Bell, L. C., Delaney, S. M., 1988. Automatic (Prelexical) Phonetic Activation in Silent Reading: Evidence from Backward Masking. Journal of Memory and Language , 27, 1-22.

Polich, J., McCarthy, G., Wang, W. S., Donchin, E. 1983. When Words Collide: Orthographic and Phonological Inference During Word Processing. Biological Psychology, 16, 155-180.

Posner, M. & Snyder, C. 1975. Information Processing and Cognition. In: Solso, R.(Ed.), The Loyola Symposium. Erlbaum, Hillsdale, New Jersey.

Renualt, B., Lesevre, N. 1982. Topographical Study of the Emitted Potential Obtained After Omission of an Expected Visual Stimulus. In: Multidisciplinary Perspectives in Event-Related Brain Potentials Research. U.S. Government Printing Office, Washington, DC.

Rugg, M. 1984. Event Related Potentials in Phonological Matching Tasks. Brain and Language, 23, 225-240.

Stuss, D., Picton, T., & Cerri, A. 1986. Searching for the Names of Pictures: An Event Related Potential Study. Psychophysiology, 23 (2), 215-223.

Treiman, R., Freyd, J., Baron, J. 1983. Phonological Recording and Use of Spelling Sound Rules in Reading of Sentences. Journal of Verbal Learning and Verbal Behavior, 22, 682-700.

Van Orden, G. C. 1987. A ROWS is a Rose: Spelling Sound and Reading. Memory and Cognition, 15,

Van Orden, G. C. 1991. Phonological mediationis fundamental to reading. In D. Besner & G. Humphreys (Eds), Basic Processes in Reading: Visual Word Recognition. (pp 238-255). Hillsdale, NJ: Erlbaum.

# A Neural Network for Speech Encryption and Filtering

Jean ROUAT, Fang HE and Daniel AUDET,
Dépt. des Sc. Appl., Univ. du Québec à Chicoutimi,
Chicoutimi, Québec, Canada, G7H 2B1

## Abstract

We propose a speech encryption system based on a neural network "filter". In previous work [3], we have demonstrated that it is possible to filter speech with a feedforward architecture even when the training has been performed on sinusoidal signals. The same network is used to perform speech encryption and decoding. We report simulation results in floating and fixed point arithmetics. Transmission experiments through noisy channels and attempts to decipher the encoded speech by foreign decoders are also reported. The preliminary results show that such encryption technique might be possible trough digital transmission channels.

## 1.    INTRODUCTION

The feedforward network is one of the most widely used neural network in pattern recognition and for discriminative tasks [4][6]. It is known to be static, with respect to processing, since no recursion is involved, but is able to generalize very easily. Feedforward neural networks have been succesfully applied to noisy speech filtering [7], to the estimation of noisy sinusoidal signals [1] and to multi-tone estimation [5].

Usually, the learning process of a feedforward neural network using backpropagation is a long and tedious task when training is carried out using long speech sentences. Furthermore, the performance depends on the training corpus. In order to alleviate these problems, we present a network which is trained on specific tone sequences to filter noisy speech and we show how such network can be used for speech encryption.

In section 2 we present the network and the training phase. In section 3 we present VLSI simulations of the neural network filter. In section 4, we propose a speech encryption technique based on the neural network filter and section 5 is the conclusion.

## 2. THE NEURAL NETWORK FILTER ARCHITECTURE AND TRAINING

The system is a three-layer feedforward neural network trained using backpropagation technique. The first (input signal) and third (output signal) layers are composed of 20 units. The hidden layer contains 18 nonlinear units having a sigmoidal transfer function. The output units ar similar to the the hidden layer units.

In a previous paper we have demonstrated that such network is capable of generalizing in amplitude and frequency. Therefore, a suitable sequence of sinusoidal signals allows to train nonlinear filters, which can then be used to process noisy speech even though training has never been done on speech [3].

### 2.1 Learning phase

A twenty samples rectangular window is positioned on the input signal. After each iteration the window is shifted by ten samples. This means that, during the learning phase, the overlap between successive windows is equal to ten samples. Since the sampling frequency is 16 kHz, the window size is 1.25 ms (20 samples).

The number of iterations required to train the network depends on the kind of filtering that has to be done by the network. A typical autoassociative training of the network used in the encrytion task lasts 150000 iterations. The error obtained with this training is $0.12 \; 10^{-4}$. However, if one considers $0.26 \; 10^{-4}$ as an acceptable error (that is if a low periodic noise is present in the output signal), then 20000 iterations are sufficient.

Depending on the task which has to be performed by the network, a different training is used. We list some of the possible applications (see [2] [3] for more details).

### • A noise "remover"

Noisy sinusoidal signals are fed into the network and they are associated to the corresponding clean signals at the output (heteroassociation).

### • A "low-pass" filter

Two identical sequences of low-frequency sinusoidal signals are placed at the input and output units (autoassociation).

- **"Standard" filters**

The network is able to perform "high-pass", "band-pass", etc. "filtering" depending on the signal sequences used during training.

### 2.2 The filtering

For filtering, a 1.25 ms window in combination with an equal size shift is used. This yields a non-overlapping filtering of the speech signal. Depending on the type of filter to be used, one can select among a number of networks (noise "remover", "low-pass", "band-pass", etc.).

Since the filtering is nonlinear, distorsions (in the linear connotation) are introduced by the network. Surprisingly, those distorsions are not disagreeable to the human ear and the quality of the speech is perceived as being very good [2] [3].

### 3. FIXED POINT ARITHMETIC SIMULATION

A fixed point arithmetic simulation has been carried out in order to study the potential of a VLSI implementation of the neural network filter. It has been trained on a Sparc2 workstation using floating-point arithmetic whereas the filtering (recall) has been performed using fixed point arithmetic. The connection weights and the input/output data have been tested under various precision (ranging from 7 to 15 bits). In these experiments, allocating 14 bits to the weights as well as to the input/output data of the network yielded the same auditory quality as the original network using full precision. Allocating 10 bits to the weights and to the input/output data yielded a good telephone speech quality containing a small periodic noise. This noise depends on the width of the adjacent window and it is a characteristic of an uncompletely trained network. An 8-bit precision yielded, of course, a stronger noise but the speech remained very intelligible.

To summarize, a 14 bits precision for the weights and data gives a very good speech quality without any noise. With a 10-bit precision, the speech remains very good, but a weak noise is present. With an 8-bit precision, the noise is not acceptable to the listeners. It is important to note that the training has been carried out using full floating-point precision. Therefore, the recall of the network (performed using fixed-point arithmetic) introduces a mismatch between the trained network and the recalled network. It should be possible to improve the performance by performing the training using fixed-point arithmetic. Consequently, allocating 10 to 8 bits to the weights should yield satisfactory results, without periodic noise in the synthesized speech.

## 4.    THE SPEECH ENCRYPTION

A three layer nonlinear feedforward neural network can define a mapping f between an input space X and an output space Z. Therefore, it is possible to find the mapping such that $\forall$ x $\varepsilon$ X, then $\exists$ z $\varepsilon$ Z and z = f(x) by learning through a sufficient number of (x,z) examples. The learning is usually done via the backpropagation algorithm. Different weight distributions can define the same mapping function f. In other words there are multiple solutions to the problem of defining the mapping of a given function f. Furthermore, the backpropagation can lead to a convergence on a local minimum of the error surface, still giving a satisfactory approximation of the f mapping. As the convergence of the backpropagation depends on the initial configuration, two different sets of initial weights should generate a different combination of weight vectors if the sets are "far" enough when expressed in the gradient space.

In the paper, we exploit the "weakness" of the training technique in order to create different versions of the neural network (different weight sets) that implement the same mapping function.

### 4.1 The speech coder
It is made of the input and the hidden layers of a trained neural network filter. A vector (y) containing 18 values, each corresponding to one of the 18 nonlinear hidden node outputs, is generated every 1.25 ms when speech is fed into the coder.

### 4.2 The decoder
It comprises the corresponding output layer of the same trained neural network filter. The decoder receives a vector y every 1.25 ms and synthesizes the associated twenty speech samples.

In order to evaluate the validity of such an approach, two sets of experiments have been conducted. In the first set, the transmission of the coded signal through a noisy channel was simulated. In the second set, a foreign decoder was tested.

### 4.3 Noisy channel transmission

Let us consider the vector y whose components are the output of the hidden nodes. Since the components are highly decorrelated by the transformation performed by the coder, it is difficult to correct potential errors occuring during the transmission based on the predictability of the y vector components. Therefore it is important to evaluate the impact of such transmission errors.

In a first experiment a white gaussian noise has been added during the wideband transmission between the coder and the decoder. A male speaker was asked to read the following french sentence: "Quand ils ont vu un voyageur, la bise et le soleil se disputaient". Three listeners have estimated the subjective quality of the synthesized speech for Signal to Noise Ratios (SNRs) of 57dB, 37 dB, 31 dB, 23 dB and 17dB between the informative signal (signal y) and the noise. According to the listeners the SNR should not be less than 31 dB. In fact, for a SNR of 17dB during the transmission, the synthesized speech is very noisy and difficult to understand. A SNR of 31 dB yields an acceptable quality (telphone quality).

Digital transmission errors have also been simulated. The average transmission error probability was set to 0,0001, assuming an ideal distorsion-less channel. The listeners found that the speech "is of very good quality, with some distorsions coming from the amplifier", "The distorsion does not bother me since the speech is of a very good quality", "Sometimes the amplifier saturates, but we have to pay attention to perceive it".

Those results suggest that the transmission should be digital and a PCM-TDM transmission system might be adequate.


### 4.4 Decryption test

Another set of experiments has been performed in order to evaluate the capacity of a network to decipher a message encoded by a "foreign" network. Preliminary results show that the initial weight configuration is crucial. In fact, decoders could not decipher the information sent from coders designed using a neural network with different initial weight configurations (we used a random generator). The only decoder that was able to decipher the information had 70% of the initial weights of the network filter equal to those of the network filter associated to the encoder (for the same node connections). The same experiment has been performed using a different percentage (25% instead of 70%). In this case, the decoder failed to synthesize intelligible speech. It is important to notice that further experiments have to be carried out to evaluate the exact limits of the algorithm.

## 5    DISCUSSION

A coder/decoder system based on a neural network filter has been proposed. The preliminary results indicate that the approach exhibits an interesting potential. However, before using such a system in a real life environment, more experiments are required to estimate its robustness against foreign decoders.

## 6    ACKNOWLEDGMENTS

This work has been supported by NSERC of Canada, by the Canadian Microelectronic Corporation, by the FCAR of Québec and by the Fondation de l' Université du Québec à Chicoutimi. Many thanks are due to Nicolas Gagnon and Jérôme Collin for providing us with the VLSI simulator.

## 7    REFERENCES

[1] Cichocki A. and Lobos T. (1992) "A Neural network for online estimation of parameters of noisy sinusoidal signals", Proceedings of the EUSIPCO 1992, vol. 6, pp. 831-834.
[2] Ennaji A. (1992). "Analyse et conception d'un réseau de neurones formels pour le filtrage d'un signal dynamique", Master thesis, Université du Québec à Chicoutimi, Canada.
[3] Ennaji A. and Rouat J. (1992). "Conception of Speech Filters Based on a Neural Network", Proceedings of the International Conference on Spoken Language Processing, Banff, october 12 to 16, Vol. 2, pp 1387-1390.
[4] Pao Y.-H. (1989). "Adaptive Pattern Recognition and Neural Networks", Addison-Wesley.
[5] Rao S. S. and Sethuraman (1991). "A Neural Network Pre-processor for Multi-tone Detection and Estimation", in Neural Networks for Signal Processing, proceedings of the 1991 IEEE Workshop, pp. 580-588.
[6] Schalkoff R. (1992). "Pattern Recognition, statistical, structural and neural approaches", John Wiley & sons, Inc.
[7] Tamura S. and Waibel A. (1988). "Noise reduction using connectionist models", Proceedings of the I.E.E.E. International Conference on Acoustics Speech and Signal Processing, vol.S, pp. 553-556.

# Phoneme Learning as a Feature Selection Process

Gabriele Scheler
Forschungsgruppe KI/Kognition
Institut für Informatik
Technical University Munich
80290 München, Germany
e-mail: scheler@informatik.tu-muenchen.de

**Abstract**

In this paper it is argued that phonological units are created from phonetic representations mainly as a process of feature selection. Feature selection can be implemented as a computationally very simple procedure. It consists of reducing the dimensionality of feature vectors to very few distinctive features, which are then generalized and applied to the classification of all phonetic representations. Feature selection can be modelled for instance by supervised learning methods, where two patterns are being compared and parameters which code the influence (or "weight") of a specific position are being set. Applying this method to a phonetic representation of German vowels, we find that indeed very few phonetic features are being used to mark the class boundaries. These correspond to the distinctive features arrived at in classical structural phonology. However, there may exist phonemes which cannot be characterised by a combination of major distinctive features. Rather than extending the feature selection model it seems justified to treat these cases as "exceptions", which are a common occurence in linguistic functions. Exception handling is incorporated into a learned classification function by pointwise additions of Boolean functions for individual pattern combinations. An interesting side result is thus a differentiation of generalizable and stored patterns, i.e. rules and exceptions.

## 1 Phonetic features and Phonemes

The goal in this paper is to show how the classification of patterns of phonetic features (=phones) to phonemes can be acquired. In every language a number of differentiable phones belong to one phoneme. To learn the phonemic pattern of a language amounts to learn a classification of all naturally occurring phones to a phoneme.

The continuum of articulatory places or acoustically defined frequency formants for a single phone can be cut up into a set of descriptive features ([BaF92]). The phonetic representation chosen in this example is a rather conservative one, based on the IPA-notation. Similar results should be obtainable with other phonetic representations, derived more directly from acoustic speech analysis. At least motor representations usually contain all the features that are necessary to distinguish phoneme classes.

Phonetic features for German vowels, the corresponding patterns and their intended classification are shown in Table 1. Only tense vowels are shown. Non-segmental features such as length,syllabicity, nasalization, rhotacization, diphthongs have also been excluded. Note that increasing the number of features does not affect the analysis, as further distinctions will simply be ignored during learning of the classification.

| | front rounded | front unrounded | central unrounded | back unrounded | back rounded |
|---|---|---|---|---|---|
| high | ue | i | | | u |
| mid-high | oe1 | e1 | e2 | | o1 |
| mid-low | oe1 | ae1 | | a2 | o2 |
| low | | ae2 | a1 | a3 | o3 |

Table 1: Phonetic feature descriptions for allophonic variations of German vowels

As has been noted by phonologists for a long time ([Tru58]), the grouping of phones to phonemes gives rise to phonological systems, which are organized by few phonetic contrasts, and consist of phonemes with more or less systematicity.

This classificational process is modelled here by a supervised feature selection method, i.e. classification by a subset of the original features which is based on a training set of classified patterns.

In general, feature selection means to find a set of relevant features for classification in contrast to feature extraction where features are extracted as linear combinations of existing features (cf. [Dud73],p.246-248, [Dev82],p.187-190). I.e. in this case features are not constructed by the phonological analysis component (which is cognition rather than perception) after the phonetic representation has been established.

We are using a parametrized distance function as an adaptive measure of similarity and a corresponding training scheme to set its parameters in order to synthesize a specific distance function (cf. [Sche93] for a detailed analysis of the learning scheme, cf. also [Sche92]).

# 2   Classification of German vowels

Input patterns have been encoded as binary feature vectors of length 9, where each position marks the absence or presence of a phonetic feature from Table 1.

E.g., "i"

| Front | Central | Back | Rounded | Unrounded | High | Mid-High | Mid-Low | Low |
|---|---|---|---|---|---|---|---|---|
| 1 | 0 | 0 | 0 | 1 | 1 | 0 | 0 | 0 |

The distance function scheme for feature selection is a weighted Hamming distance called $d_\lambda$ and defined as:

$$d_\lambda(pattern1, pattern2) = \sum_i^n \lambda_i \times |pattern1_i - pattern2_i|$$

IV-627

For each of the target classes a single exemplar is given in order to achieve a nearest-neighbor classification with the learned distance function for all other patterns.

Learning (or "adapting") a distance function is achieved by setting values to the parameters $\lambda_i$.

All $\lambda_i$ that occur (as a sum) in the distance equation for patterns of the same class are set to 0, and an arbitrary free variable $\lambda_i$ of those occuring in the sum for patterns of different classes is set to 1.

This very simple learning method has certain advantages:

1. $\lambda_i$ corresponding to irrelevant features are set to 0 or left unset. Accordingly the size of the feature set does not affect learning or generalization.

2. For a certain unknown parameter $\lambda_i$ we can define a training pattern $x$ that gives a value to it, by changing the $i$'th position in a classified pattern $p$: $d_\lambda(x,p) = \lambda_i$.

3. By monitoring conflicts in parameters settings, we can make a list of patterns not representable by the distance function scheme.

This is useful because we can make a list of exceptions while learning, and we notice when patterns to set a parameter are not within the problem space. Minimal training sets can be generated from the classified patterns(cf. 2). Here we used a training set consisting of 3 patterns (oe1, a2, a3).

The values for the parameters after training are :

| $\lambda_1$ | $\lambda_2$ | $\lambda_3$ | $\lambda_4$ | $\lambda_5$ | $\lambda_6$ | $\lambda_7$ | $\lambda_8$ | $\lambda_9$ |
|---|---|---|---|---|---|---|---|---|
| 1 | 0 | 0 | 1 | $\lambda_5$ | 1 | 0 | 0 | 0 |

There are no patterns available to set $\lambda_5$.

In applying the distance function we find that patterns for the phoneme 'e' (e1,e2) are not correctly classified, all others are.

These results are closely related to equivalent terms of classical structural phonology:

- Certain phonetic contrasts are "neutralized", namely center/back, mid-high/mid-low/low. The phonological contrasts are front vs. (center,back) and high vs. (mid-high, mid-low, low).

- Rounded/Unrounded form a 'privative' pair,i.e. it is sufficient to mark one of them.

- The phoneme 'e' has less systematicity, therefore secondary phonological contrasts have to be introduced to characterize it in addition to the fully systematical vowel phonemes.

The result of the learning process can also easily be transformed into a classical phoneme definition operating with distinctive (phonological) features.

Distinctive features of the German vowel system are according to this analysis, (cf. also [Wae83])

$$\begin{bmatrix} +-front \\ +-rounded \\ +-high \end{bmatrix}$$

When we apply a learning procedure, in some cases we are content with a certain percentage of correctness. In this case, 13 of 15 patterns are correctly classified, which is

86,7%. But at least in the context of linguistic abilities we need a method which allows to acquire a certain faculty completely.

# 3   Exception Handling

By using $d_\lambda$ as the basis for classification, we have imposed a specific classification and generalization scheme. I.e. only certain classifications can be learned with $\lambda$-parameters, and the generalization principle from training examples to a whole pattern set is also fixed.

When a training set is not fully representable with $\lambda$-parameters, there is the option of representing conflicting training patterns explicitly and separately as "exceptions" within the overall distance function. In comparison to the option of choosing a distance function scheme with higher representational power (a more universal function approximator) this has the advantage that learning effort can be kept low, rule abstraction is still simple, and generalization restricted to the "regular patterns" rather than the examples.

In a situation, where all exceptions can be listed as training examples, 100% correctness of the learned pattern classificator can be achieved.

There are two cases of misclassifications of two patterns $a$ and $b$ without exception handling:

- $d_\lambda(a, b) = 1$ where it should be $= 0$.

  The goal is to multiply the distance function by a term, which yields 0 when a and b are compared and 1 otherwise.

  The simplest expression for the multiplication term is the Boolean function $f_{\neg(ab)}$ which is $= 0$ iff $x = <ab>$ and which can be written as

  $$f_{\neg(ab)}(x) = \neg(\bigwedge_i^n \chi_i \wedge \bigwedge_i^n \epsilon_i)$$

  $$
  \begin{array}{llll}
  \chi_i = x_i & \text{if } a_i = 1 & \epsilon_i = y_i & \text{if } b_i = 1 \\
  \chi_i = \neg x_i & \text{if } a_i = 0 & \epsilon_i = \neg y_i & \text{if } b_i = 0
  \end{array}
  $$

  By substituting $\neg x$ by $(1 - x)$ and $\wedge$ by $\times$ we can translate this function into an arithmetic expression. The Boolean function $f_{\neg(e1e2)}$ requires $2n$ (n=patternlength, here: 18) variables.

- $d_\lambda(a, b) = 0$ where it should be $= 1$.

  Here we want to add a term to the distance function which is 1 for a and b as input and 0 otherwise. Again the simplest expression is a function $f_{ab}$, defined like $f_{\neg(ab)}$ above.

  For the given problem, this would require to add the functions ($f_{ae1e1}, f_{ae2e1}, f_{a1e2}, f_{a2e2}, f_{a3e2}$) with a total of 5*18 variables.

Result:
$$d_\lambda^{excep}(x, y) = d_\lambda(x, y) \times \prod_{\forall a,b} f_{\neg(ab)}(<xy>) + \sum_{\forall a,b} f_{ab}(<xy>)$$

There are several possibilities of simplifying this expression (multiplicational as well as additional terms) based on the following observation: Each individual Boolean function $f$ may be represented by another function $f^*$ as long as the following equations hold:

$f^*_{ab}(< xy >) = 1 = f_{ab}(< xy >)$ for patterns $a = x, b = y$

$f^*_{ab}(< xy >) = 0 = f_{ab}(< xy >)$ for patterns $x, y$ such that $class(x) = class(y)$

$f^*_{ab}(< xy >) =$ arbitrary value, for all other patterns $(class(x) \neq class(y)$ or $x, y$ do not occur in problem space)

In a similar vein we can define $f^*_{\neg(xy)}$. From this observation it follows that simplifications (i.e. using fewer variables in the definition of the Boolean function) have to be performed dependent on the actual classes that exist.

The following strategy has been used for the implemented function definition:

1. find a position $i$ where a and b differ.
2. for all patterns $x$, $class(x) = class(a)$: are all $x$ equal at position $i$?
   If not, go to 1.
3. for all patterns $y$, $class(y) = class(b)$: are all $x$ equal at position $i$?
   If not, go to 1.
4. position $i$ found.

The strategy fails, when all positions have been tried and step 4 is not reached. Otherwise a positional differential criterion $i$ for the exceptional patterns has been found. Then we can define an additional term for $d(a, b)$ as:

$$+|x_i - y_i| * desc(a)$$

$$desc(a) = \neg x_1 \wedge \neg x_4 \wedge \neg x_6$$

$desc(a)$ is a description for exactly all patterns in $class(a)$, which is given by the result of the learning of $d_\lambda$.

Simplifications of Boolean functions allow in principle the introduction of 'secondary rules', i.e. a generalization from the exceptions. Because such a simplified function is not maximally constrained, it incorporates by itself a certain limited generalization. For instance, the new positional criterion $i$ can be the basis for a secondary rule schema.

This possibility has not been further pursued here.

The complete distance function for the classification of phonetic feature vectors to German vowel phonemes, gained by this method is:

$$
\begin{aligned}
d^{excep}_\lambda(x, y) = \quad & \sum_i^n \lambda_i * |x_i - y_i| * \\
& 1 - (x_1(1 - x_2)(1 - x_3)(1 - x_4)x_5(1 - x_6)x_7(1 - x_8)(1 - x_9)* \\
& (1 - y_1)y_2(1 - y_3)(1 - y_4)y_5(1 - y_6)y_7(1 - y_8)(1 - y_9)) + \\
& x_1(1 - x_4)(1 - x_6)|x_7 - y_7| + (1 - x_1)(1 - x_4)(1 - x_6)|x_7 - y_7|
\end{aligned}
$$

# 4   Results of analysis

In the processing of speech, acoustic input is transformed into a phonetic representation, consisting of individual phonetic features. This process is also known as categorical perception. The task of phonology consists of relating these universal phonetic representations to the language–specific phonological units, e.g. phonemes, which operate as true symbols in the language process.

In particular, we use the observation made in structural phonology that few phonetic contrasts are actually needed to determine the phonemic class.

A classification using a feature selection technique shows which phonetic features are employed as phonological contrasts.

With the indicated encoding and the distance function scheme $d_\lambda$ we achieve a separation as required. However, certain patterns may not be classifiable with this type of generalization. Rather than extending the feature selection model it seems justified to treat these cases as "exceptions", which are a common and real occurence in linguistic functions.

After parameters in the distance function scheme have been set, exceptional cases are defined and can be recognized by the classifier.

The distance classifier can then be automatically enhanced to cover all the exceptional cases that occur.

In contrast to prevailing methods of learning from examples (e.g. function approximation by back-propagation [RHW86] or machine learning techniques [DiM84]), this method provides a way of distinguishing between generalizable features which form the basis of the distance function scheme and additionally stored patterns, which are added as deviating function values. Thus one possibility of distinguishing rules from exceptions within a pattern classification framework is presented.

# References

[BaF92] Barry,W.J. and A.J. Fourcin: Levels of labelling. *Computer Speech and Language* 6(1992) :1-14.

[Dev82] Devijfer,P.A. and J.Kittler: *Pattern Recognition. A statistical approach.* Prentice Hall 1982.

[DiM84] Dietterich,T. and R. Michalski: A Comparative Review of selected Methods for Learning from Examples. In: Michalski,R.,J.Carbonell and T. Mitchell: *Machine Learning. An Artificial Intelligence Approach.* Springer 1984.

[Dud73] Duda,Richard O. and Peter E. Hart: *Pattern Classification and Scene Analysis.* John Wiley 1973.

[RHW86] Rumelhart,D.,G.Hinton and R. Williams: Learning Internal Representations by Error Propagation. In: McClelland,J. and D.Rumelhart: *Parallel Distributed Processing.* MIT Press 1986.

[Sche92] Scheler, G.: The Use of an Adaptive Distance Measure in Generalizing Pattern Learning. *Proceedings of ICANN92*, Elsevier 1992,pp. 131-134.

[Sche93] Scheler, G.: *Pattern Classification with Adaptive Distance Measures.* forthcoming 1993.

[Tru58] Trubetzkoy,N.S.: *Grundzüge der Phonologie.* Vandenhoeck und Ruprecht 1958, 6th ed. 1977.

[Wae83] Waengler,H.-H.: *Grundriss einer Phonetik des Deutschen.* Marburg, 4th ed. 1983.

# Learning Image Motion Fields of 3D Objects in Motion

Robert K. Cunningham and Allen M. Waxman[1]
Machine Intelligence Technology Group
MIT Lincoln Laboratory
Lexington, MA 02173

An architecture that learns projected, two dimensional image motion of silhouettes of three dimensional objects is proposed and simulated. It is argued that first order velocity terms (divergence, curl and deformation) are more representative of the object than zeroth order (translational) or second order motion terms, and thus these terms are learned as a pattern. Simulations are presented for a rotating prolate spheroid whose silhouette is viewed from thirty different elevations in perspective projection, learning both the movement and the aspects of the object. Processing begins by extracting edges from the silhouette of the object; these are used to compute the neighborhood flow for each view angle. Several different flow representations are considered. These are then input to an unsupervised ART2A network (Carpenter et al., 1991a) which serves to cluster the input flow. The results of this clustering are depicted on a "motion viewing sphere" which indicates which view angles have the same motion cluster. Classes of learned, characteristic motion are related to learned, characteristic (aspect) views (Seibert & Waxman, 1992).

**INTRODUCTION**  Recently Perrett and his colleagues provided physiological evidence for neurons which code the conjunction of form and motion (Perrett et al., 1990), when they discovered cells in macaque temporal cortex that responded to specific forms (eg., a human hand) in selected motion (e.g., bringing food to the monkey).

Before this, there had been psychophysical evidence for a process sensitive to patterns of motion. Johansson (1973) had discovered that the motion of an actor's ankles, knees, hips, shoulders, elbows and wrists alone could be used to discriminate real human motion from random motion. In these experiments, static presentation of lights locating the principle joints were indistinguishable from random light patterns, but a short sequence of images could differentiate the two. Subsequent work indicated that humans could discern a surprising amount of information from these sparse displays, including the gender or even the identity of the actor (Cutting, 1978; Cutting and Kozlowski 1977).

Although this early psychophysical work suggests that form-and-motion cells may exist, modeling has focused on recovering *structure from motion* (Waxman & Wohn, 1988). This is due in part to history: the earliest psychophysical experiments used wire figures that were unknown to the subjects (Wallach, 1953). This approach has proven to be sensitive to image noise and local velocity estimates, so we propose instead a system which learns the two-dimensional characteristic motions of an object and associates these with a learned static, view-based representation of the object. We call the resulting problem a *structure and motion* problem to emphasize that in most situations both types of information are available and each can be used to cue the other.

In this paper, the structure and motion problem is explored by examining the motion required to pass from one aspect, or characteristic view (Kooenderink & van Doorn, 1979) of an object to another, and by comparing this with intra-aspect motion. To make the results easy to interpret, a non-articulating object is simulated undergoing rotation about a single axis. In this case the object is a prolate spheroid rendered in perspective projection and rotating about one of its shorter axes, but the processing demonstrated here could also be used to learn and recall the characteristic motions of an aerobatic plane viewed from the ground. It is hoped that the ellipsoid shape reminds the reader of the fuselage of an airplane.

---

[1]The authors would like to acknowledge the support of the Air Force Office of Scientific Research.

**SYSTEM ARCHITECTURE: AN OVERVIEW**  A major goal of the modeling work presented here is that it lays the foundation for a later neural model of the human and monkey ability to learn objects and their characteristic motions. All objects have a limited set of motions that they typically perform: limbs cannot bend in opposition to their joints, cars cannot move vertically, and planes cannot fly perpendicular to their fuselage. In a living, adapting system, learning must occur on-line, and new inputs must either activate existing, previously coded motion patterns or generate new patterns. In this preliminary work, neural models are used to understand the difficulties encountered when coding motion, but where analytical methods provide greater insight, they are used instead. This work emphasizes higher level visual processes, so difficult low-level vision tasks such as figure-ground separation will be avoided by constraining system input to images with sufficient figure-ground contrast to permit segmentation by image thresholding techniques. The resulting images will therefore be silhouettes. The input will be further restricted to single-part objects, although the system must be designed so as to permit extention to learning the motions of articulated objects.

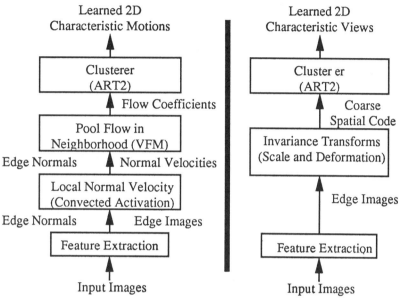

Figure 1. Left: Architecture for learning the characteristic image motions of an object. Right: Architecture used by Seibert and Waxman (1992) to learn the characteristic views of an object.

With these restrictions in mind, characteristic motions of objects can be adaptively learned by the system illustrated on the left of in Figure 1. The first processing step extracts features, which for the simulations presented here are edges, from previously segmented objects. Sequences of the resulting edge images are then compared to obtain projected local, normal velocity estimates. These normal velocity estimates are pooled within a neighborhood (currently the entire image, but eventually defined either by static cues or by the degree of fit with other points already in the neighborhood), and image flow coefficients are obtained. These coefficients are complement-coded (Carpenter et al., 1991b) and the six element vector is clustered by ART2A (Carpenter et al., 1991a), which learns and recognizes the characteristic 2D object motions. To meet the requirement that the system model an adapting system, the architecture is designed to continuously learn new characteristic motions of objects or recognize old motion patterns. The ability to stably perform on-line learning is the chief advantage of ART2A over other neural network models which might be suitable for this task.

On the right of Figure 1 is an overview of the initial processing stages of a model designed to learn characteristic views of three dimensional objects (Seibert & Waxman, 1992). The high curvature features typically used in that system have been replaced by edge features to increase the number of inputs to the unsupervised classifier. The input features are then made scale invariant by a log-polar transform (which is used to convert changes in scale to translations in log space) followed by an averaging in the log radius dimension. These scale invariant images are then sampled by broad receptive fields (which provide some invariance to deformation), and their outputs are then clustered by ART2A. The invariances greatly enhance code compression of the characteristic views. Although similar motion invariances are desirable, the same techniques can not be used, in part because translation, rotation and scaling *are* the characteristic motions being learned. Some insight and partial solutions will be discovered when a detailed description of projected motion is undertaken in the next section. Later processing stages (not shown) of the characteristic view learning system learn image transitions and accumulate evidence for a known or novel object. Future work will integrate this high level view-transition learning with a high level motion-transition learning module; this preliminary work examines the relationship between learned characteristic motions and learned characteristic views.

**MEASURING NEIGHBORHOOD MOTION** Next we consider the type of image motion learned by the network. The analysis will follow the order of a Taylor series expansion of the motion in a neighborhood which contains the object. Zeroth-order motion is pure translation, and indicates the direction and rate at which the entire object moves across the visual field. It is useful for tracking the object via smooth pursuit eye motion (Goldberg et al., 1991), but does provide information about the local image geometry. Thus the zeroth-order image motion will not be used in learning motion patterns induced by the object moving in 3D.

The first-order terms of image motion describe how the local image geometry is changing, due to the time-varying silhouette of the moving object. Furthermore, physiological evidence exists for first-order flow detectors, following the work of Koenderink and van Doorn (1976) relating visual optical flow to divergence (div), curl and deformation (def) tensors of the local velocity field. In this work, these quantities replace the first order terms of the Taylor series, in part because they can be geometrically described. The divergence describes the rate at which a surface patch expands as a whole, while the curl describes the rate at which the patch rotates in the image plane. The def indicates the amount a neighborhood is compressed or stretched. Finally, the def only takes on positive values indicating where deformation is occurring, whereas the other quantities take on positive and negative values, to differentiate between expansion and contraction in the case of div, or clockwise and counterclockwise in the case of curl.

Psychophysical and physiological evidence for sensitivity to the zeroth (translational) and first-order terms is widely reported. The work of Regan and Beverly (1979) indicated that humans are sensitive to divergence and curl. Tanaka and Saito (1986,1989a,1989b) and Duffy and Wurtz (1991a,1991b) located cells in the dorsomedial region of the medial superior temporal area (MSTd) which could measure constant translational motion, divergence and curl. Tanaka and Saito discovered cells that were tuned to speed, and divergent cells which were more tuned to divergence than deformation. Duffy and Wurtz noted that some neurons responded to one of the three components, while others responded to the combinations of translation and curl, translation and divergence, or translation and curl, but never curl and divergence. However, Andersen et al. (1993) report that some cells in MST are sensitive to spiraling motion (i.e., a combination of div and curl).

Second order motion flow is next considered. Waxman and Wohn (1988) argue strongly for computing second-order motion flow by noting that first order flow exactly describes the motion of planar surface patches, but surface curvature does not influence image flow until second-order terms are introduced. Notwithstanding this strong computational argument, psychophysical evidence suggests that some second-order motion is invisible to humans. Todd (1992) generated movies of rigid orbs in pure second-order motion which appear to deform rather than move rigidly, indicating that humans favor the non-rigid interpretation to the veridical second-order motion interpretation. Todd believes that second-order motion may be represented and perceived, but only at a very coarse grain (Todd 1992, personal communication). Furthermore, there is yet to be supporting physiological evidence for "second-order flow neurons".

In conclusion, the physiological, psychophysical, and analytical results suggest the orders of image motion that should be learned. Zeroth-order terms, while clearly neurally represented and perceptually available, are dependent on the distance to the viewed object. For this first series of simulations, they will therefore be ignored. First-order terms, also represented by neurons and perceived by humans will be included in the simulations, in the form of the div, curl and def quantities. Second-order terms are not yet widely supported by physiological and psychophysical evidence, even though they are analytically valuable. These terms will be used to help recover the flow field, but will not provide input to the motion learning module.

**MODEL SIMULATIONS** A prolate spheroid is rendered in perspective projection using *rayshade*, a public domain, constructive solid geometry raytracer. The prolate spheroid rendered here is a ``cigar'' shaped object whose long axis is three times longer than the short axis and is seen rotating about one of its short axes. In the first "movie", the observer is perpendicular to the axis of rotation; this is called elevation angle 0. Viewing from above and along the axis of rotation will be called elevation angle 90, while viewing from below and along the axis of rotation is labeled elevation angle -90. The second movie is of the same motion taken from five degrees of elevation, and movies were made every five degrees up to an elevation of sixty degrees. Azimuth is defined with respect to the long axis of the prolate spheroid: when this axis is perpendicular to the line of sight, the spheroid is said to be at azimuth angle 0. These images are then converted into silhouettes, so all image shading information is removed. Although in more complicated objects internal structure would be obscured, this renders later processing invariant to illumination differences and the motion of highlights. Edges are then extracted (currently using Sobel edge detectors, eventually using a minimal version of the Boundary Contour System (Grossberg & Mingolla, 1985). Next, local normal velocity estimates are obtained using the Convected Activation Method (Waxman et al., 1988). Although the simulations employ an analytical version of the model, a later neural model was developed by Fay and Waxman (1992). In the early model, a series of spatiotemporal gaussian waves ride along (are convected) on top of edges or feature points as a function of time. These wave profiles maintain their shape, and it is simple to extract their phase velocities, which correspond to the normal velocities along edges. Next the velocity functional method (VFM) is used to pool the normal velocity estimates in a neighborhood (Waxman & Wohn, 1988), and generate the first-order flow field quantities needed to determine the div, curl and def. These three terms are then complement coded (Carpenter et al., 1991b) to represent the presence of large negative or positive values of the div and curl terms, and the presence and absence of a large def term. These six terms are then clustered by an ART2A unsupervised classifier, and the templates generated by this network are fed to a second ART2A network. The cascaded networks tend to reduce order effects and further compress the motion categories.

If the ART2A categories are combined with knowledge of the initial view angle, they can be mapped onto a sphere which encircles the object. Figure 2 shows from above, the *motion view sphere* (Seibert and Waxman, 1992) for the prolate spheroid when its long axis is oriented vertically and the vigilance of the first ART2A is 0.70, while the vigilance of the second ART2A is 0.6. The shaded dots indicate the learned motion categories, and are arranged in concentric circles which represent a complete rotation of the prolate spheroid as viewed from each elevation. Zero degrees of azimuth is on the left side of this sphere, which means that categories on this side represent motions of the prolate spheroid when viewed broadside.

The darkest category in the figure represents the motion of the object when the object is viewed from different elevations end-on, and the next darkest category (positioned laterally on the diagram) is situated along the azimuths where the object is viewed broadside. The darkest category represents the motion of a narrower range of azimuths than the next-darkest category, because the same perturbation of the 3D prolate spheroid results in a smaller perturbation of the projection of the broadside motion than of the end-on motion. The category patterns exhibit symmetries as expected. Each ring (elevation) is approximately symmetric because the object silhouette's motion is identical when viewed from in front or behind, so the motion category on either side of the view sphere is identical.

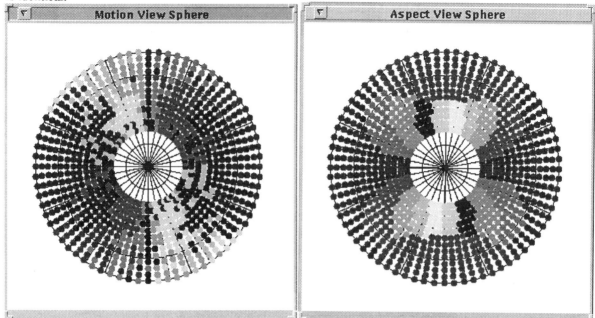

Left: Motion View Sphere seen from above. The shaded dots represent ten categories formed by ART2A when presented with complement coded inputs representing the div, curl and def of the motion field as a function of azimuth and elevation. The view sphere can be considered to surround the prolate spheriod with its long axis oriented vertically. Right: Aspect View Sphere. Nine shape categories formed by ART2A (with a vigilance of 0.7) as a function of azimuth and elevation when presented with log-polar mapped inputs representing the edges of the prolate spheroid.

If the analysis depicted on the right side of Figure 1 is performed, then the aspect view sphere depicted on the right of Figure 2 results. In this case the shaded dots indicate categories of the spatial layout of edges. The aspect view sphere also should be symmetric, and in this case is more consistent than the Motion View Sphere. The broad lateral regions continue all the way into the center, because the view of the prolate spheroid from zero degrees of azimuth and sixty degrees of elevation is identical to the view from zero degrees of azimuth and elevation. The central rings of the sphere, corresponding to views from above, contain many patterns because the image projection of the ends of the spheroid enter new receptive fields as it rotates below the observer. The outer rings, corresponding to views from the side of the object, are more coarsely encoded because the projection of the silhouette travels back and forth across the same few receptive fields.

**CONCLUSIONS** We have shown that objects in 3D motion induce image motion pathways that can be learned by an unsupervised classifier network. Image motion categories can represent an object motion, from a viewer-centered coordinate system. The learned motion categories provide a complementary representation to the learned shape categories (aspects), and future work will relate these two representations further. It is tempting to interpret our motion categories in the context of complex pattern motion cells observed in MST (Andersen et al., 1993).

**REFERENCES**
Andersen, R. A., Treue, S., Graziano, M., Snowden, R. J., & Quin, N. (1993). From direction of motion to patterns of motion: Heirarchies of motion analysis in the visual cortex. In Ono, T., Squire, L., Raichle, M., Perrett, D., & Fukuda, M., *Brain Mechanisms of Perception and Memory, From Neuron to Behavior*,183-199.

Carpenter, G. A., Grossberg, S., & Rosen, D. B. (1991a). ART2A: An adaptive resonance algorithm for rapid category learning and recognition. *Neural Networks*, 4(4), 493-504.

Carpenter, G. A., Grossberg, S., & Rosen, D. B. (1991b). Fuzzy ART: Fast stable learning and categorization of analog patterns by an adaptive resonance system. *Neural Networks*, 4(6), 759--772.

Duffy, C. J. & Wurtz, R. H. (1991a). Sensitivity of MST neurons to optic flow stimuli. I. A Continuum of response selectivity to large-field stimuli. *Journal of Neurophysiology*, 65(6), 1346--1359.

Duffy, C. J. & Wurtz, R. H.(1991b). Sensitivity of MST neurons to optic flow stimuli. II. Mechanisms of response selectivity revealed by small-field stimuli. *Journal of Neurophysiology*, 65(6), 1346--1359.

Fay, D. & Waxman, A. M. (1992). Neurodynamics of real-time image velocity extraction. In Carpenter, G. A. & Grossberg, S., *Neural Networks for Vision and Image Processing*, 9, 221--246. MIT Press, Cambridge, MA.

Goldberg, M. E., Eggers, H. M., & Gouras, P. (1991). The Ocular Motor System In Kandel, E. R., Schwartz, J. H., Jessell, T. M., *Principles of Neural Science (3rd Edition).*,43, 467--480. Elsevier, New York.

Grossberg, S. & Mingolla, E. (1985). Neural dynamics of form perception: Boundary completion, illusory figures, and neon color spreading. *Psychological Review*, 92(2), 173--211.

Johansson, G. (1973). Visual perception of biological motion and a model for its analysis. *Perception and Psychophysics*, 14, 201--211.

Johansson, G. (1975). Visual motion perception. *Scientific American*, 232(6), 76--88.

Koenderink, J. J. & van Doorn, A. J. (1976). Local structure of movement parallax of the plane. *Journal of the Optical Society of America*, 66, 717--723.

Kooenderink, J. J. & van Doorn, A. J. (1979). The internal representation of solid shape with respect to vision. *Biological Cybernetics*, 32, 211--216.

Marr, D. (1982). Vision - A Computation Investigation into the Human Representation and Processing of Visual Information. W. H. Freeman and Company, New York, U.S.A.

Nakayama, K. (1985). Biological image motion processing: A review. *Vision Research*, 25(5), 625--660.

Perrett, D. I., Harries, M. H., Benson, A. J., Chitty, A. J., Mistlin, A. J. (1990). Retreival of structure from rigid and biological motion: An analysis of the visual responses of neurones in the macaque temporal cortex. In Blake, A. Troscianko, T., AI and the Eye, 8, 181--199. John Wiley & Sons, Ltd.

Regan, D. & Beverley, K. I. 1979. Visually guided locomotion: Psychophysical evidence for a neural mechanism sensitive to flow patterns. *Science*, 205, 311--313.

Saito, H., Yukie, M., Tanaka, K., Hikosaka, K., Fukada, Y., & Iwai, E. (1986). Integration of direction signals of image motion in the superior temporal sulcus of the Macaque monkey. *Journal of Neuroscience*, 6, 145--157.

Seibert, M. Waxman, A. (1992). Adaptive 3D-Object Recognition from Multiple Views. *IEEE Transactions on Pattern Analysis and Machine Intelligence*,14(2), 107--124.

Tanaka, K., Fukada, Y., Saito, H.-A. (1989). Underlying mecanisms of the response dpecificity of expansion/contraction and rotation cells in the dorsal part of the medial superior temporal area of the macaque monkey. *Journal of Neurophysiology*, 62(3), 642--656.

Tanaka, K. Saito, H.-A. (1989). Analysis of motion of the visual field by direction, expansion/contraction, and rotation cells clustered in the dorsal part of the medial superior temporal area of the macaque monkey. *Journal of Neurophysiology*, 62(3), 626--641.

Todd, J. (1992). Evidence against second order flow. Boston University CN730 Lecture.

Wallach, H. & O'Connell, D. N. (1953). The kinetic depth effect. *Journal of experimental Psychology*, 45, 360--368.

Waxman, A. M. & Wohn, K. (1988). Image Flow Theory: A framework for 3D inference from time-varying imagery. In Brown, C., Advances in Computer Vision, 1, 165--224. Earlbaum, Hillsdale, NJ.

Waxman, A. M., Wu, J., and Bergholm, F. 1988. Convected activation profiles and the measurement of visual motion. In *Proceedings of the IEEE Conference on Computer Vision and Pattern Recognition*, 717--723 Ann Arbor, MI.

# Cognitive Neuroscience

**Session Chairs: Daniel Alkon**
**David Fong**

**ORAL PRESENTATIONS**

# Primacy Effects in Sequential Task Performance

Raju S. Bapi and Daniel S. Levine

Department of Mathematics, University of Texas at Arlington, Arlington, TX 76019-0409

## Abstract

An avalanche model of motor sequence encoding is presented. The aim is to reproduce data showing that monkeys with frontal lobe damage can learn an invariant sequence of movements if it is rewarded, but cannot learn to perform any one of several variations of a sequence if all are rewarded. We present simulations of the primary learning of sequences, and demonstrate parameters that can lead to a primacy effect in recalling items of this sequence from long term memory. Two different versions of the avalanche network and their simulations are presented, of which the second version includes a layer of sequence detectors. Suggestions are made for including yet another layer to classify these temporal sequences and group them together based on reward. Analogies are drawn between the classifier layer and the frontal lobes, and between the avalanche module and part of the basal ganglia.

(A longer version of this article has been submitted to *Neural Networks* for publication in a special issue.)

## Introduction and Background

The frontal lobes have been implicated in forming strategies for goal-directed behavior [8, 21]. This general function seems to involve co-ordination of subsystems that integrate motivational and cognitive information [20, 25] with other subsystems that link past events or actions across time [3, 8, 24] and anticipate future events or actions [15]. The motivational-cognitive linkages involving the frontal lobes have previously been simulated in neural networks by [17, 18]. In this article, we look at an example of linking events across time.Specifically, we discuss networks that model data of Brody and Pribram [3] and Pinto-Hamuy and Linck [24] on the performance of movement sequences by frontally damaged monkeys. These data, to be described below, show that intact frontal lobes are not necessary for primary learning of invariant sequences, but are necessary for learning sequences whose order is flexible. This is a prime example of the importance of the prefrontal cortex for complex behavioral rule formation, which is a necessary component of planning. Hence, frontally damaged people or animals tend to be distractible and unable to stick to plans [13, 29].

Grossberg [9, 10] developed the *outstar avalanche* for spatiotemporal pattern storage and performance. A space-time pattern is sliced into a sequence of $n$ spatial patterns separated by equal time intervals. Each of the spatial patterns is stored in an outstar $O_i$ and the signal from $O_i$'s source node $v_i$ arrives at $v_{i+1}$ with a delay. So, given an input signal at $v_1$, the entire pattern is reproduced sequentially from outstars $O_1, O_2, O_3,..., O_n$. Grossberg [11, pp. 265-269] modified the basic avalanche architecture to make sequence performance less ritualistic and more sensitive to external feedback. The resulting network is shown in Fig. 1. Each one of a sequence of movements has three representations, and these are stored in layers $\mathcal{F}^1$, $\mathcal{F}^2$, and $\mathcal{F}^3$.During performance of one of the movements, its representation is kept active via reverberation between $\mathcal{F}^1$ and $\mathcal{F}^3$. The $\mathcal{F}^2$ representation of that movement inhibits the reverberation in the same column once the movement is performed, and excites the representation of the next movements via a learnable connection. The arousal node controls starting and stopping of the sequence based on external feedback, and also regulates the speed of performance. Our network will build on this basic model, extending it to include a sequence detector layer and a classification mechanism.

Various authors [1, 2, 5, 19, 22, 27] have attempted to use the insights developed in [11]. An essential feature of all these attempts is to build an STM layer that preserves the order of item presentations in the amplitudes of node activations. They use an LTM invariance principle [11] which guarantees the preservation of the order of past events as new events are perturbing the system. Other authors [7, 16, 28] have used different types of architectures for spatiotemporal pattern processing. Our architecture differs from all of these as it is proposed to model frontal lobe data on sequential performance. The requirements for learning to perform a sequence of motor patterns are slightly different from those for learning to encode a sequence of sensory patterns. Some design issues are discussed in the next section. Experimental data will then be presented with a view to motivating the architecture and to discuss general issues raised by the data.

INPUT

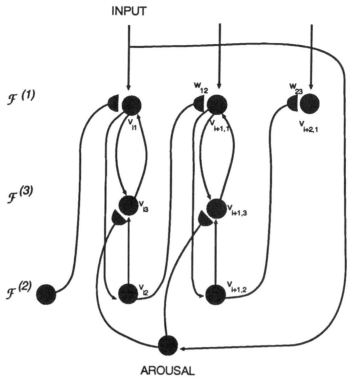

**Fig. 1.** Avalanche network for sequence generation. (Adapted from [11] with the permission of Academic Press.)

## Experimental Data

Effects of frontal lesions on performance of sequential tasks were studied by Pinto-Hamuy and Linck [24] and Brody and Pribram [3] in macaque monkeys. Postoperative retention was assessed in two types of test: one, in which the subjects were to respond in such a way that they had to push all of several cued panels without repetitions but in any order (*internally ordered* or flexible sequence test), and another in which they had to respond in an exact order by pushing a series of panels based on given cues (*externally ordered* or invariant sequence test). Monkeys were trained on a four-by-four array of stimulus-response panels. The training and test patterns used in [3] included three externally ordered sequence (E-O-Sq) tasks comprising "red-green" (large solidly colored circles); "0"-"2"; and "0"-"2"-"6" (white number patterns against a dark field); three internally ordered sequence (I-O-Sq) tasks consisting of "blue"-"yellow" (a blue filled plus sign and a yellow filled triangle); "4"-"5"; and "4"-"5"-"7" (white patterns against a dark field). On each trial in the E-O-Sq case, the stimuli appeared in randomly placed locations on the four-by-four panel array. In order to receive a reward the monkey pressed first the red and then the green panel irrespective of their location. The stimuli disappeared after each press within a trial and reappeared immediately in a new random configuration. The trial ended if the first panel pressed was not red, or if the second press was incorrect or if the subject was successful. Only successful completions were rewarded. The internally ordered sequence was presented in exactly the same manner except that the monkey was permitted to choose different orders from trial to trial as long as any given sequence contained no repetitions. Brody and Pribram [3] obtained similar qualitative results, but observed that impairment in performance depended on the level of experience achieved with the test apparatus. These experimental results on sequences are generally in line with the observations of Fuster [8] that the frontal lobes are not involved in the representation of externally ordered sequences but are needed if a flexible reply is needed, as in the case of internally ordered sequence performance. In the next section, a network architecture to model these data will be described.

## Network Architecture

Our network is in two stages (see Fig. 2). Stage 1 represents the sequence itself and transitions between items in the sequence. To simplify the model, we assume that all items are of equal duration and have identical inter-item intervals. Also, we assume that spatial aspects of stimuli are preprocessed and the network receives sequential inputs of items. Hence, our network has to deal only with order aspects of a sequence. Stage 2 adds sequence detector nodes, and the next stage will add a classification mechanism. The first stage is as shown in Fig. 1. This network keeps the order information in STM as a spatial pattern of monotone decreasing activities. This is called *primacy* in item activation, that is, the first item seen by the network has the largest activation. Grossberg [11] suggested that as items are presented serially, STM tends to store them with a *recency* gradient in activations. However, a primacy gradient is useful to store the sequence in LTM, to enable the network to recall the sequence in the correct order. He suggested that order reversal from recency to primacy can be achieved by interactions among item activities in STM combined with LTM-STM interactions. Hence our network includes a layer of sequence detectors ($\mathscr{F}^4$), analogous to that in [28], and two-way learnable connections between $\mathscr{F}^3$ and $\mathscr{F}^4$. It also includes on-center off-surround interactions within each of the layers $\mathscr{F}^3$ and $\mathscr{F}^4$. With the right choice of parameters and signal function (faster-than-linear), a sequence can be encoded only by one detector.

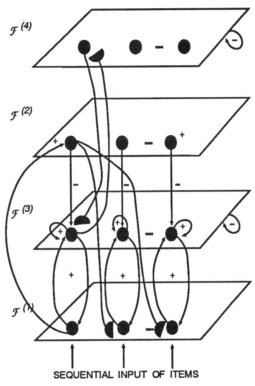

**Fig. 2.** Second stage of the sequence network, including a sequence detector layer.

The movements in a sequence are presented to the $\mathscr{F}^1$ layer in order. The input node $v_{i,1}$ receives unit activation. The node $v_{i,1}$ excites nodes $v_{i,2}$ (in the $\mathscr{F}^2$ layer) and $v_{i,3}$ (in the $\mathscr{F}^3$ layer) in the same column. Activity reverberates between $v_{i,1}$ and $v_{i,3}$. When $v_{i,2}$ receives enough excitation, it inhibits reverberation in its column and excites all the $v_{j,1}$ for $j \neq i$. When a new movement is performed by the network at $v_{i+1,1}$, the weight from $v_{i,2}$ to $v_{i+1,1}$ is strengthened by a Hebbian learning rule representing transition between movements. Thus when the network performs a movement sequence, transitions between movements are stored in this chain of weights. While the item activations are reverberating in the $\mathscr{F}^3$ layer, a sequence detector at the $\mathscr{F}^4$ layer samples the order information in the spatial pattern of activities. This order information is stored in the distribution of top-down weights from $\mathscr{F}^4$ to $\mathscr{F}^3$. The first sequence detector is chosen randomly and rewarded for the length of sequence presentation.

### Simulation and Results
Simulations of the Stage 1 network shown in Fig. 1 were conducted. Items of a three-element sequence were presented in succession for 5 time units each, followed by 10 time units with no input. We observed a primacy effect in weight distribution after only 5 presentations of the three-element sequence (i.e., 100 time steps). The results are not shown here but are shown in our longer article. The second stage of simulation was based on the network of Fig.

2. We had decided to add the layer of sequence detectors ($\mathcal{F}^4$) to aid in future extensions involving sequence classification and reordering. Consequently, we needed to test whether the above primacy effect could be preserved with this addition. The items of the sequence were presented in succession for 5 time units each, followed by a pause that was also 5 time units long. After item presentations, a detector node (chosen randomly at first, then fixed) received a reward. Again, after only about five presentations (90 time steps), there was clear indication that the network was showing the expected primacy effect. Figs. 3 and 4 show the results.

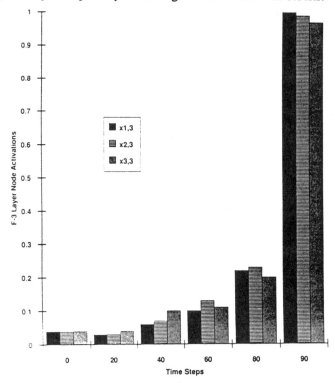

**Fig. 3.** In the network of Fig. 2, STM activations in $\mathcal{F}^3$ nodes (scaled by their maximum) show a primacy effect.

Fig. 3 shows the node activations in the $\mathcal{F}^3$ layer. In the first stage of simulations, STM activity in this layer had always shown a recency distribution.Now, however, the activities show a primacy distribution. This shows the effect of competition among $\mathcal{F}^3$ nodes and also the STM-LTM interactions helping to enhance the activity of the first item in preference to others. We observed (the graphs are not shown here) that the actual transitions from items 1 to 2 and items 2 to 3 are represented in differentially enhanced weights $w_{1,2}$ and $w_{2,3}$ respectively. In the first stage, only the weights $w_{1,2}$ and $w_{2,3}$ were present. So this stage shows that even if all the items are initially connected, order between items can be learned via differential enhancement of the appropriate interitem weights. This represents the invariant order between items in an externally ordered sequence.

For an internally ordered sequence, order must be recalled flexibly, based on the context of earlier movements. In order to achieve this, order information has to be stored and reorganized based on context. We have seen in Fig. 3(a) that the order is organizing itself into a primacy distribution of STM activities. This information is further captured in the distribution of top-down ($\mathcal{F}^4$ to $\mathcal{F}^3$) and bottom-up ($\mathcal{F}^3$ to $\mathcal{F}^4$) weights, as shown in Figs. 4(a) and 4(b) respectively. The bottom-up weights from $\mathcal{F}^3$ to the remaining detectors and the top-down weights from the remaining detectors to $\mathcal{F}^3$ have not shown any tendency to store the sequence in their distribution, which is a desirable effect. Since these other weights have not shown any preference to store this sequence, we have not shown the graphs for these. Thus, if this sequence is presented or performed again, bottom-up weights prime the first detector with greater strength, and in turn the first detector can more readily strengthen this sequence at $\mathcal{F}^3$.

### Discussion
Resonance between bottom-up input and top-down expectation will be useful in extending our model to include a classifier of sequences involving a mechanism similar to ART [4] or ARTMAP [5]. For reordering the

sequence as in the data of [3, 24], we need to introduce a mechanism that can reorder the sequences to establish resonance. For example, in modeling learning of an internally ordered sequence, one might add to the network a supervised ARTMAP mechanism [5], so that if several variations on a sequence are all rewarded, the tendency to perform any of the variations is increased. The network would also need to keep track of which movements have already been performed, in order to engage the appropriate exemplar of such a class of sequences. Based on the results of [3, 24], these classifying mechanisms would seem to involve the prefrontal cortex. Detailed anatomical ascription for the rest of our network may be premature, but there are grounds for gross hypotheses. The first three layers shown in the avalanche network of Fig. 1 may be analogous to parts of the corpus striatum, since that subcortical motor control area is involved in the initiation of willed movements and is strongly influenced by feedback connections with the frontal lobes [26]. The arousal node in those figures may be analogous to the nucleus accumbens, a "gateway" from limbic motivational areas to the striatum [14]. These hypotheses should become more detailed and sharper as the work herein is integrated with other work in progress on the role of specific cortical-subcortical circuits and neural transmitters in cognitive tasks (e.g., [23]).

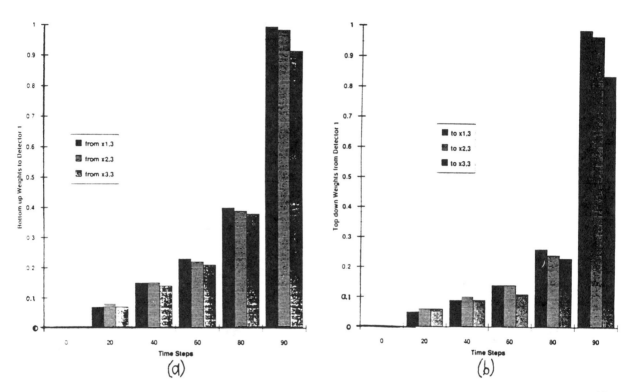

**Fig. 4.** (a) Weights from the $\mathscr{F}^3$ layer nodes to Detector 1 capture the order information in the sequence with a primacy distribution. (b) Weights from Detector 1 to $\mathscr{F}^3$ nodes (scaled by their maximum) have a primacy distribution to enable the network to recall the first item with the largest activation.

## References

[1] Banquet, J.P., & Contreras-Vidal, J. (1993). *World Congress on Neural Networks, Portland, Oregon* (Vol. 2). Hillsdale, NJ: Erlbaum.

[2] Bradski, G., Carpenter, G.A., and Grossberg, S. (1991). *International Joint Conference on Neural Networks, Seattle* (Vol. I). Piscataway, NJ: IEEE.

[3] Brody, B.A., & Pribram, K.H. (1978). *Brain*, 101, 607-633.

[4] Carpenter, G.A., & Grossberg, S. (1987). *Computer Vision, Graphics, and Image Processing*, 37, 54-115.

[5] Carpenter, G.A., Grossberg, S., & Reynolds, J.H. (1991). *Neural Networks*, 4, 565-588.

[6] Cohen, M.A., & Grossberg, S. (1986). *Human Neurobiology*, 5, 1-22.

[7] Dehaene, S., Changeux, J-P., & Nadal, J.P. (1987). *Proceedings of the National Academy of Sciences USA*, 84, 2727-2731.

[8] Fuster, J.M. (1989). *The prefrontal cortex*. New York: Raven.

[9] Grossberg, S. (1969). *Journal of Mathematics and Mechanics*, **19**, 53-91.

[10] Grossberg, S. (1970). *Studies in Applied Mathematics*, **49**, 135-166.

[11] Grossberg, S. (1978). In R. Rosen & F. Snell (Eds.), *Progress in Theoretical Biology* (Vol. 5).

[12] Grossberg, S., & Merrill, J.W.L. (1992). *Cognitive Brain Research*, **1**, 3-38.

[13] Grueninger, W.E., & Pribram, K.H. (1969). *Journal of Comparative and Physiological Psychology*, **15**, 195-240.

[14] Hestenes, D.O. (1992). In D.S. Levine & S.J. Leven (Eds.), *Motivation, emotion, and goal direction in neural networks*. Hillsdale, NJ: Erlbaum.

[15] Ingvar, D. (1985). *Human Neurobiology*, **4**, 124-136.

[16] Jordan, M.I. (1986). Technical Report ICS 8604, Institute for Cognitive Science, University of California, San Diego.

[17] Leven, S.J., & Levine, D.S. (1987). In M. Caudill and C. Butler (Eds.), *Proceedings of the First International Conference on Neural Networks* (Vol. II). San Diego: IEEE/ICNN.

[18] Levine, D.S., & Prueitt, P.S. (1989). *Neural Networks*, **2**, 103-116.

[19] Mannes, C. (1992). In *International Joint Conference on Neural Networks, Baltimore, Maryland, June 7-11, 1992* (Vol. 4). Piscataway, NJ: IEEE.

[20] Milner, B. (1964). In J.M. Warren & K. Akert (Eds.), *The frontal granular cortex and behavior* (pp. 313-334). New York: McGraw-Hill.

[21] Nauta, W.J.H. (1971). *Journal of Psychiatric Research*, **8**, 167-187.

[22] Nigrin, A.L. (1990). In *Proceedings of the IJCNN-90, Washington, DC* (Vol. 1). Hillsdale, NJ: Erlbaum.

[23] Parks, R.W., & Levine, D.S. (submitted). Neural network modeling of verbal fluency in Alzheimer's disease.

[24] Pinto-Hamuy, T., & Linck, P. (1965). *Experimental Neurology*, **12**, 96-107.

[25] Pribram, K.H. (1961). *Experimental Neurology*, **3**, 432-466.

[26] Rolls, E.T., & Williams, G.V. (1987). In J.S. Schneider & T.I. Kidsky (Eds.), *Basal ganglia and behavior: Sensory aspects and motor functioning*. Toronto: Hans Huber.

[27] Vogh, J. (1993). *World Congress on Neural Networks, Portland, Oregon* (Vol. II). Hillsdale, NJ: Erlbaum.

[28] Wang, D.L., and Arbib, M.A. (1990). *Proceedings of the IEEE*, **78**, 1536-1543.

[29] Wilkins, A.J., Shallice, T., & McCarthy, R. (1987). *Neuropsychologia*, **25**, 359-365.

## Appendix

Following are equations and parameters used in simulation of Stage 2 (cf. Fig. 2.) Equations for Stage 1 are similar.

$$\dot{x}_{i,1} = -ax_{i,1} + \left( \sum_{i \neq j, j \in \mathscr{F}^{(2)}} w_{j,i} x_{j,2} + I_i \right)(r - x_{i,1})$$

$$\dot{x}_{i,3} = -bx_{i,3} + \{cx_{i,1} + gw_{A,i}[x_A - \Gamma]^+\}(r - x_{i,3}) - d[x_{i,2} - \Theta]^+ x_{i,3}; \quad where [w]^+ = \begin{cases} w & if\ w > 0 \\ 0 & if\ w \leq 0 \end{cases}$$

$$\dot{x}_{i,2} = -ex_{i,2} + fx_{i,1}(r - x_{i,2})$$

$$\dot{x}_A = -ax_A + (\sum_i I_i + R)(r - x_A)$$

Transition weights: $\dot{w}_{i,j} = x_{i,2}(-lw_{i,j} + mx_{j,1})$

Weights from arousal node to $\mathscr{F}^3$ layer: $\dot{w}_{A,i} = (-lw_{A,i} + mx_{i,3})[x_A - \Gamma]^+$

$$\dot{x}_{i,3} = -bx_{i,3} + \{cx_{i,1} + gw_{A,i}[x_A - \Gamma]^+ + n \sum_{j \in \mathscr{F}^{(4)}, i \in \mathscr{F}^{(3)}} w_{j,i} x_{j,4} + ch(x_{i,3})\}(r - x_{i,3}) - d[x_{i,2} - \Theta]^+ x_i$$

$$- d(x_{i,3} - s) \sum_{k \neq i} h(x_{k,3}); \quad where\ h(y) = \frac{1}{1 + e^{(\Phi - y)}}\ (sigmoid\ function).$$

$$\dot{x}_{i,4} = -ax_{i,4} + \{n \sum_{j \in \mathscr{F}^{(3)}} w_{j,i} x_{j,3} + pj(x_{i,4}) + R\}(r - x_{i,4}) - p(x_{i,4} - s) \sum_{k \neq i} j(x_{k,4}); \quad j(y) = y^2$$

Bottom up weights from $\mathscr{F}^3$ to $\mathscr{F}^4$: $\dot{w}_{i,j} = x_{i,3}(-lw_{i,j} + mx_{j,4})$

Top down weights from $\mathscr{F}^4$ to $\mathscr{F}^3$: $\dot{w}_{i,j} = x_{i,4}(-lw_{i,j} + mx_{j,3})$

**Parameters:** a=10, b=5, c=1, d=22, e=10, f=1, g=0.2, k=3, l=0.9, m=3, n=0.3, p=0, r=6.1, s=0.1, $\Theta$=0.2, $\Gamma$=0.1, $\Phi$=0.3, R=1.

# MEDIUM and LONG-TERM MEMORY in CONTEXT PROCESSING: A NETWORK MODEL of CORTEX-HIPPOCAMPUS RELATIONS

Jean Paul Banquet [1] and José L. Contreras-Vidal [2]

CREARE Universite Pierre et Marie Curie Paris

and

Center for Adaptive Systems and Cognitive and Neural Systems
Boston University
Boston , MA 02215 USA

and

Motor Control Laboratory
Department of Exercise Science and Physical Education
Arizona State University
Tempe, AZ 85287-0404 USA

**Abstract**

A neural network model of cortico-hippocampal relations designed to meet principles and constraints mainly derived from cognitive psychophysiology (Event-related-potentials, ERPs) and behavior is found to present key characteristics of hippocampal function:

(1) Extension of short-term memory into an intermediate range register; (2) Correlation of simultaneous events (in space) or successive events (in time) for creating complex entities or chunks. These two functions are tightly related in a twoway fashion, bottom-up and top-down: -The persitence of information beyond the duration of short-term memory is necessary for binding multimodal or multilocal informations together; -Once the binding is learned it allows priming of temporal patterns or completion of spatial patterns. A theory is presented on how this binding process could take place.

## 1 FROM BRAIN PROCESSING TO MODEL DESIGN

Temporal context processing were analysed in simplified paradigms preserving temporal context quintessential features, without life situation complexities, as in speech or writing. Namely, the information to be extracted and learned by the subjects during complex cognitive discrimination tasks concerned time intervals, temporal sequences and event- category probability. Distinct components of the cognitive ERPs reflected these different functions along with memory.

## 2 HIERARCHY of SELF-SIMILAR PROCESSES

Self-similar match-based coding-categorization processes repeat at different levels of complexity. ERPs point to at least three levels: single events, event sequences, and probability.

1. The system performing identification-categorization of single events, possibly by linking multiple features into a single percept, is reflected by an N200-P300 complex (Banquet and Grossberg, 1987).

2. The system grouping multiple events into unitized chunks of event short sequences is reflected by the N400-P300 complex. These chunks are stored in short (STM) and long (LTM) term memory.

3. Event Probability is amplitude encoded by P300.

In spite of the differences in information complexity pattern recognition processes seem to be based on similar match-mismatch pattern comparisons in different neural structures. This functional uniformity could correspond to cortex uniform columnar organization whatever the areas considered.

This structural characteristic is implemented in the system by similar two-level cooperative-competitive structures inspired from ART. The most relevant characteristics of ART here are: - A feature layer presenting

---

[1] Supported by INSERM, NATO, and DGA/DRET Grant # 911470/A000/DRET/DS/DR

[2] On leave from Monterrey Institute of Technology, México.

a distributed activation pattern close to input physical reality; -A code layer operating a maximal code compression and providing a similar code whatever information complexity to be coded. In this compression, information loss is minimized and learning stability is secured by top-down adaptive filters which compute a LTM average of the patterns which selected the correspoding codes for their representation.

# 3   STABILITY - PLASTICITY DILEMMA

The system is still another illustration of the stability-plasticity dilemma (Banquet and Grossberg, 1987). P300 shows how the brain monitors moment-to-moment fluctuations in local probabilities and sequential dependencies by short-range memory registers, yet simultaneously extracts longer range prior probability trends.

Along with top-down filters and orienting system for stability and plasticity respectively, the importance of systems with multiple dynamical range is emphasized by simulations.

Recent electromagnetic evidence reveals different "life-times" in primary and association cortex (Lü et al. 1992). These dynamical ranges determine the level of complexity at which an information can be processed and integrated.

# 4   CONTEXT EFFECTS on PATTERN RECOGNITION

Once context has been learned, contextual effects are implemented by top-down intersystemic long-range interactions.

Top-down interactions take place within (short-range) or between (long-range) systems. The meaning of top-down is functional (not anatomical), from more complex to simpler processing levels. Thus it could correspond either to cortico-subcortical relations (e.g. from cortex to thalamus), or to cortico-cortical relations (e.g. from secondary to primary cortex).

Brain uses anticipation, priming and preparation to take into account contextual probabilistic or deterministic regularities during cognitive task performance. Different types of temporal contexts at various levels of complexity and/or integration are learned during sequentially delivered Bernoulli series. Contextual learning can be considered as a particular case of *associative learning*.

Perceptual-motor preparation could correspond to either advance performance of some processing steps or to preset steps such that threshold activity is reached faster after stimulus delivery. A close correspondance exists between temporal contexts and priming-preparation modes.

### 4.0.1   Timing and Anticipation

A pair of events forms the simplest context. With constant ISI time intervals are rapidly learned. Time interval evaluation between two stimuli induces the most elementary type of priming, a non-specific increase in arousal prior to and peaking at stimulus delivery expected time. This anticipation predicts when, not which event will appear in close future time.

These properties are implemented by nonspecific priming effects from timing system to the different category codes of ART F2 layer.

### 4.0.2   Probability Context and Weighted Preparation

At a higher integration level, probability relations are rapidly encoded by P300. (less than 10 stimuli). Yet, after 10 stimuli subjects have not learned the prior probability rule, but rather a local sample of this prior probability.

Priming corresponding to this probability context could be made available to lower order processing stages only after about 150 events (Banquet and Grossberg, 1987 ). This priming is category-specific and results from learning a subjective probability for each event category. Briefly, top-down signaling shows up in ERP activity in two possibly related ways, anticipatory negativity prior to stimulus and amplitude and chronology changes of early negative components (Banquet and Grossberg, 1987).

Why probability-related top-down priming and preparation manifest only after about 150 events when corresponding information is available as early as after 10 events? Brain seems to need evidence accumulation in favor of a probability law in order to overcome inherent local frequency fluctuations. A more mechanistic interpretation in terms of transient and asymptotic behavior, and supra-threshold activity will be provided by the model.

### 4.0.3 Sequential Dependencies and Specific Priming

The more complex temporal context results from event temporal ordering or sequential dependencies. ERPs show sequential dependency tracking, in STM, back at least to the sixth order . This amplitude coding can be displayed as a tree diagram representing amplitude response mapping to the last element of a sequence (root element of the tree), as a function of preceding stimuli organisation.

Beyond temporary sequential dependency coding in STM subjects learn and store in LTM at least the most typical sequences corresponding to a particular probability condition . The further a sequence deviates from the expectations for a given probability condition, the larger the corresponding P300 amplitude. This increment could result from a *sequential mismatch* between the current sequence and chunk prototypes stored in medium or long-term memory.

Sequential dependencies in STM, and corresponding prototypical sequences or chunks in LTM, constitute the third type and certainly the most informative temporal context. As such it puts constraints on anticipatory processes similar to the constraints that the first words of a sentence impose on possible ways to terminate it.

# 5   NEURAL NETWORK ARCHITECTURE

The architecture of the system (Fig 1) reflects this hierarchy of self-similar modules found in the brain organization. Indeed, besides the categorization level which is an ART module accepting continuous inputs, choice, chunk and probability networks can be viewed as variations of ART. They have a structure similar to a F2 categorial layer of ART. But instead of receiving features, they receive categorized events. Instead of coding single events, they code complex categories such as chunks or probabilities. Only the timing module and the temporal order module (TOM) have specific structures which have been described elsewhere (Banquet and Contreras-Vidal 1993). The timing module inspired from Grossberg and Merrill (1992) is formed of a battery of nodes which react to the stimuli with different speeds. LTM weights learn during the window of activation the different levels of node activity. The integrated response of the system pics at the time corresponding to a learned interstimulus interval.

The TOM module performs a coding of events temporal order by a spatially distributed amplitude gradient. It is based on the principles of invariance and pseudonormalization developped by Grossberg (1978). The core architecture of the network is similar to that developped by Bradski et al. (1992). Several parts of this architecture are relevant to hippocampal function. First in the TOM there is a buffer layer whose function is to maintain the pattern of activation during the free interval between stimuli. As such it can be compared to an extended short-term memory (STM) or an "implicit" working memory. Second the chunk network has a function similar to that of a temporal correlator, in that it binds together several successive repetitive events presenting a specific sequence. Finally, probability layer has in the present implementation more a function of integration of repetitions of occurrences. The slow dynamics of the nodes of this layer, and even more the LTM weights afferents to the nodes correspond to the hippocampal function of extension of the STM range of cortical systems to an intermediate range allowing integration of information on a longer time span . The simulation results will confirm the importance of this intermediate range in between the short and long-permanent yf the cortical networks.

# 6   SIMULATION RESULTS

The presentation is focused on the effects resulting from the interaction between TOM and probability networks. The simulations explicit how the combination of a short, intermediate and long-range memory capacity is necessary to emulate the performance of the sole P300 ERP system.

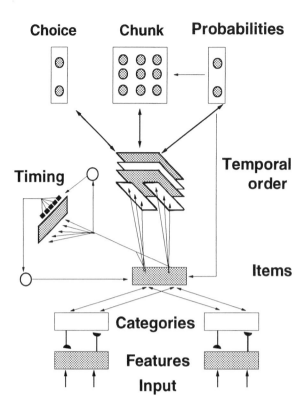

Figure 1: Architecture of the multiple-module system for (1) categorization of events with two modality features, (2) Timing, and (3) Temporal order with its three outcomes: Choice, probability, and chunks.

Simulation results demonstrate how the function performed by probability nodes proper concern more local probability and sequential dependency short-term evaluation than prior probability computation. Prior probability coding per se is devoted to long-term memory weights of bottom-up adaptive filters. Intact LTM weights are necessary if the activity level of the system is to asymptote to a correct level (Fig 2). A microsurgery suppressing LTM weight gating of the probability nodes does not prevent node activation to reach a stable state but induces a bias in amplitude prior probability coding (Fig. 2). A slow-down in probability node dynamics can partially compensate for the absence of LTM weights. Nevertheless, the stable level of activity reached by the system is biased toward a intermediate value for both low and high probability, and therefore does not provide a correct coding. Furthermore, slow nodes lose their sensitivity to local frequency fluctuations. Three parameters are important for inducing a satisfactory balance between short-term and long-term sensitivity in the behavior of probability nodes, the two time constants controlling node and LTM dynamics, $\epsilon_1$ and $\epsilon_2$, plus the shape of node autoactivation function. A correct balance between the two time constants allows simultaneous coding of probability and at same time sequential dependencies. A linear feedback function systematically biases amplitude coding towards an intermediate value. Only a sigmoid function allows the system to asymptotically tend towards a correct code.

In Figure 2, the left column presents linear (a) or sigmoidal(b,c,d) feedback functions. Furthermore from b to d probability node dynamics become faster. Then the system presents larger oscillations in response to sequential dependencies and local probability fluctuations. The experimental relation between local fluctuations and steady state amplitude is better fitted by (d).

Middle column has same parameters as left one, except that LTM weights are absent suppressing LTM learning. Oscillations and asymptotic value still exist, but amplitude probability coding is biased towards intermediate values.

Right column features responses to probability changes at different point of the sequence (arrows): after 400 stimuli in i and k, and after 200 and 400 in j and l. The system adaptability to new conditions depends

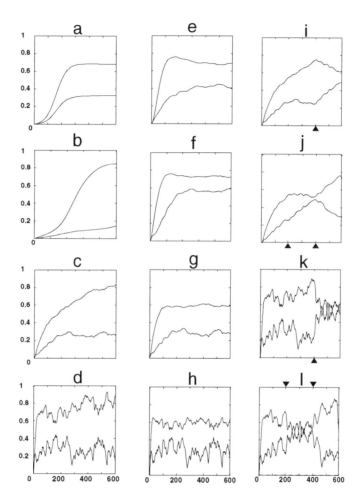

Figure 2: Activation of the probability layer for two categories A and B of 600 events (500 in b and f). In left and middle columns P(A) = .2, P(B) = .8. In right column one or two probability shifts occur at times indicated by arrows, from .2/.8 to .5/.5 or reverse.

on previous sequence duration and on probability node dynamics, faster tracking associated with faster dynamics.

# 7   FITTING the DATA

Probability layer presents several desirable characteristics:

1. Probability nodes adapt to a new probability condition in less than 10 stimuli, in agreement with results by Johnson and Donchin (1982). However, this early coding is dependent on local probability fluctuations. A stable regime which overcomes these local fluctuation is reached after between 100-200 stimuli. This number of events corresponds approximately to the delay necessary for the manifestation of top-down probability context effects.

2. Due to slower dynamics, probability system encodes local probability and temporal order in its amplitude fluctuations. If events are sorted out according to their previous history subclasses of events are created which are preceded by the same subsequences. The amplitude distribution of probability node responses to these subclasses forms a tree diagram similar to experimental results.

3. Probability node activity level at steady state correctly encodes probability relation between item categories. Thus probability nodes apparently encode simultaneously two types of information, temporal order and prior probability, as does indeed P300 system (Squires et al., 1976; Johnson and Donchin, 1982). But microsurgery supressing the LTM weights induces an increase in local fluctuations of node activity. A steady state is still reached between 100 and 200 stimuli due to stimulus repe tition. However, there is no correct prior probability encoding by node activity amplitude at steady state. Therefore, probability nodes by themselves are more adapted to coding stimulus frequency local fluctuations and sequential dependencies than probability per se. The apparent encoding of two types of information at two levels of integration by the same system is due to probability node gating by the adaptive filter LTM weights. These results shed some light on the concept of attentional memory trace (Näätänen, 1982) that could correspond in this case to probability nodes disconnected from LTM weight modulation. In the absence of adequate registers, event repetion is not sufficient to encode such a time-distributed information as probability.

## CORTEX-HIPPOCAMPUS RELATIONSHIP and DECLARATIVE MEMORY

The cortico-subcortical cooperativity illustrated in TOM-Probability modules is not necessarily akin to the link between cortex and hippocampus involved in declarative long-term memory consolidation. Nevertheless, two features of our system are relevant to this function: (1) The same information, event temporal order, has a spatially distributed transient representation at "cortical" level (choice network) and a compressed more stable coding at "hippocampal" level (chunk and probability nodes); (2) A long-loop top-down mechanism from probability layer (hippocampus) to ART (cortex) is required in the system to implement anticipation-priming. This along with classical assumptions on hippocampal function suggests an hypothesis on hippocampal role in laying down long-term declarative memory traces in cortex.

At present a few strong but very general quasicertitudes exist on hippocampal function related to LTM consolidation. A mechanistic interpretation of this function is elaborated in the model framework. (1) Hippocampus and related structures are essential for laying down a long-term memory trace for dated events in episodic memory, as evidenced by anterograde amnesia in man. (2) Prospective studies in monkeys have demonstrated the limited duration (weeks or months) of this hippocampal involvement. The integrity of older memories ipso facto demonstrates that hippocampus per se does not serve as a permanent repository for these traces supposedly located in cortex. (3) Long Term Potentiation (LTP) induces transient synaptic facilitation at different levels of hippocampus and cortex which could be a basis for the memory consolidation function of hippocampus .

Yet this hippocampal function is difficult to express in terms of information *storage* or *retrieval*. Several authors agree that hippocampus temporarily *binds* together distributed sites in neocortex whose reactivation will support a holistic memory.

In a different direction of research, some authors (Gray et al., 1989) have interpreted local synchronization as a mean for the brain to bind features together. Long distance intra or inter hemispheric synchronization has also been documented both in animals (Singer, 1993) and humans (Banquet, 1973, 1983). There must be specific long distance cortico-cortical connections at the basis of this long range synchronizations. Some of them like the callosal connections are hardwired, or early established. They connect mostly homotopic cortical regions. Connections involved in LTM trace consolidation must be plastic by definition, and either intrahemispheric or between heterotopic or homotopic regions of the two hemispheres. In EEG signal correlation or coherence analysis during different brain states, a high level of coherence between spectral activities of different brain regions can be achieved in two ways: (1) Corpus callosum induces an interhemispheric binding; in this case there is frequency synchronisation, but an hemisphere may lead the other inducing a phase shift. (2) A deeply located center controls the activity and sets the pace in different cortical regions (Banquet, 1983).

Putting these facts together hippocampus, (and related structures) because of its compactness, the close connection between its right and left parts, its two-way connections to the entire cortex could be this deeply located structure that repetitively synchronizes during consolidation phase the electrical activity of once-coactivated cortical regions. Henceforth, it would compensate, in episodic memory consolidation, for multiple event-repetition inducing procedural or semantic storage in the absence of hippocampus. This repetitious automatic coactivation could be implemented in different ways and in particular be due to that only a fragment of the original memory pattern is a sufficient cue to reactivate the entire original pattern. This reactivation should not necessarily lead to a conscious rememberance of the original memory. Several networks in hippocampus could play this function of pattern binding and retrieval. This class of architectures has been the object of earliest and most successful modelling (Grossberg, 1972; Kohonen, 1984).

The system structure with its short and long loop feedback mechanisms suggests that resonnant activity inside the loops could operate the synchronization of different cortical modal activities together. These repeated synchronous activation will pave the way for the creation of long-distance weighted cortico-cortical connections, which could thus be established even in the case of a single occurrence of a complex event. Once established, these cortico-cortical connectivity would supress cortical dependency on hippoca mpus for episodic memory recall. The schematic connectivity pattern at hippocampal le vel would have been transfered on a larger scale cortical network.

Thus, this view of the instauration of declarative memories integrates three classical assumptions on brain function: (1)Resonnant activity in reciprocally connected structures as a basis for LTM storage (Grossberg, 1976a, b); (2) Cortical synchronization as a feature binding factor (Gray et al. 1989); (3) Hippocampus as a correlator for multimodal cortical areas. Our hypothesis can possibly be tested in animals or even in humans after hippocampal surgery. In particular, intra and interhemispheric coherence of cortical EEG activity should be decreased in surgical subjects, mostly in response to complex multimodal stimuli.

This model of episodic memory consolidation is complementary to another model of cortico-hippocampal interactions (Carpenter and Grossberg, 1993) related to the vigilance parameter of ART orienting subsystem and its effects on category formation. This model operates in a recognition learning paradigm and seems optimally suited to explain "semantic" memory consolidation.

# References

Banquet, J.P. (1973). Spectral analysis of the EEG in altered states of consciousness. *Electroencephalography and Clinical Neurophysiology*, **35**, 143-151.

Banquet, J.P. (1983). Inter and intra-hemispheric relationships of the EEG during sleep in man. *Electroencephalography and Clinical Neurophysiology*, **55**, 51-59.

Banquet, J.P. and Grossberg, S. (1987). Probing cognitive processes through the structure of event-related potentials during learning: An experimental and theoretical analysis. *Applied Optics*, **26**, 4931-4946.

Bradski, G., Carpenter, G., Grossberg, S. (1992). Working memory network for learning temporal order with application to three-dimensional visual object recognition. *Neural Computation*, **4**, 270-286.

Carpenter, G.A. and Grossberg, S. (1993). Normal and amnesic learning, recognition, and memory by a neural model of cortico-hippocampal interactions. *Trends in Neuroscience*, **16**, 131-137.

Gray, C.M., König, P., Engel, A.K., Singer, W. (1989). Oscillatory responses in cat visual cortex exhibit intercolumnar synchronization which reflect global stimulus properties. *Nature*, **338**, 334-37.

Grossberg, S. (1972c). Neural expectation: Cerebellar and retinal analogs of cells fired by learnable and unlearned pattern classes. *Kybernetik*, **10**, 49-57.

Kohonen, T. (1984). Self-Organization and Associative Memory. Berlin: Springer-Verlag. 312 p.

Grossberg, S. (1976a). Adaptive pattern classification and universal recoding, I: Parallel development and coding of neural feature detectors. *Biological Cybernetics*, **23**, 121-134.

Grossberg, S. and Merrill, J.(1992). A neural network model of adaptively timed reinforcement learning and hippocampal dynamics. *Cognitive Brain Research*,**1**, 3-38.

Johnson, R. Jr. and Donchin E. (1982). Sequential expectancies and decision making in a changing environment: an electrophysiological approach, *Psychophysiology*, **19**, 183-199.

Lü, Z.L., Williamson, S. J., Kaufman, L. (1992). Human auditory primary and association cortex have differing lifetimes for activation traces. *Brain research*, **572**, 236-241.

Näätänen, R. (1982). Processing Negativity: an evoked-Potential reflection of selective attention, *Psychological Bulletin*, **92**, 605-640.

Singer, W. (1993). Oral communication. World Congress on Neural Networks. Portland: Oregon.

Squires, K.C., Wickens, C., Squires, N.C. and Donchin, E., (1976) The effect of stimulus sequence on the waveform of cortical event-related potential, *Science*, **193**, 1142-1146.

# SYNCHRONIZED NEURAL ACTIVITIES: A MECHANISM FOR PERCEPTUAL FRAMING

Stephen Grossberg* and Alexander Grunewald[†]
Center for Adaptive Systems and Department of Cognitive and Neural Systems
Boston University, 111 Cummington Street, Boston, MA 02215

**Abstract**

Variability in retinal and geniculate processing rate that is dependent on stimulus properties suggests that some later process can put parts corresponding to the same retinal image back into register. This resynchronization process is called perceptual framing. Here a neural network model of emergent boundary segmentation is used to show that synchronized cortical activities can subserve this role. Psychophysical results about the minimum delay between two visual stimuli that leads to the perception of temporal order can be explained and replicated with this model.

## 1 Introduction

The image that impinges on the retina is continuously transduced into neural signals. Subsequent processing in the lateral geniculate nucleus (LGN) occurs equally continuously. So long as all parts of the retinal image are processed at the same rate, this poses no problem. However, when the retinal image changes very quickly, for example during self motion or the motion of an object, then problems in processing can arise. The source of these problems lies in the fact that there is no guarantee that all parts of the retinal image are processed at the same rate, and in fact large variabilities dependent on stimulus parameters such as contrast and spatial frequency have been observed in both the retina (Bolz, Rosner, & Wässle, 1982) and the LGN (Sestokas & Lehmkuhle, 1986). Many real life images that we process in our lives contain a large number of different contrasts and spatial frequencies. How then does the visual system ensure that cortical representations of an image processed at any given time, for example for recognition, really correspond to the same retinal image? Why do wrong correspondences occur only under extreme viewing conditions (Intraub, 1985)?

A simple passive process based on convergence of signals in striate cortex does not suffice. Such a passive process could be based on slowly discriminating neurons in striate cortex, which is against current physiological evidence (Celebrini, Thorpe, Trotter, & Imbert, 1993). Another passive mechanism would be to have neurons with very fast time constants, which again is not supported by current data (Mason, Nicoll, & Stratford, 1991; Softky & Koch, 1993). Hence an active process is required, and this process is called *perceptual framing* (Varela, Toro, John, & Schwartz, 1981).

*Supported in part by AFOSR F49620-92-J-0499, ONR N00014-92-J-4015, and ONR N00014-91-J-4100.
†Supported in part by AFOSR F49620-92-J-0225 and AFOSR F49620-92-J-0334.

## 2    Perceptual Framing

Perceptual framing is the process of binding together parts of neural representations corresponding to the same image that may have come temporally out of register due to early processing. A possible mechanism for this would be some clocking device. Here we propose that synchronization of distributed cortical activities can temporally realign out-of-phase image parts. It has been found that cortical activities synchronize in the cat and in the monkey when a stimulus is present in the visual field (Eckhorn, Bauer, Jordan, Brosch, Kruse, Munk, & Reitboeck, 1988; Gray & Singer, 1989), even when the receptive fields of the units recorded do not overlap.

A way to test this notion of perceptual framing has been to link it to the perception of simultaneity and of temporal order of two separate visual stimuli. Perceptual framing suggests that there is a definite nonzero lower bound for the time between two such stimuli that they be perceived as sequential, rather than simultaneous. Indeed such a lower bound has been found (Hirsch & Sherrick, 1961).

## 3    A model for perceptual framing

Grossberg and Mingolla (1985a, 1985b) developed a model called the Boundary Contour System (BCS) for the generation of emergent boundaries by the visual cortex. This model was later adapted to show that cortical synchronization of neural activities does not require the presence of a central clocking mechanism (Grossberg & Somers, 1991). In the present study, we further develop and modify this model. There are two layers, one consisting of fast-slow neural oscillators (Ellias & Grossberg, 1975), and the other of bipole cells, that receive input to two separate lobes, in addition to receiving direct bottom-up input. In the present simulations, bipole cells fire if at least two of its three receptive zones are activated. The model is shown in Figure 1.

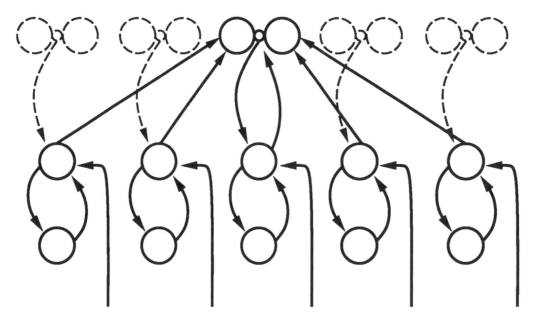

Figure 1: The architecture of the model proposed. A layer of fast–slow oscillators is coupled via a layer of bipole cells. In contrast to previous versions of the model, there is a direct signal from each oscillator to its corresponding bipole cell which facilitates boundary completion.

To test the model it was necessary to find out how much time difference between neural representations of visual stimuli smeared out across time in the early processing stages (corresponding to retinal and geniculate processing) could be resynchronized. A summary of these simulations is shown in Figure 2. Representations as much as 10 ms offset can be easily framed. In these simulations it was assumed that a 5 ms visual pulse gets smeared out to 25 ms of geniculate activity, which agrees with the variability of LGN responses (Sestokas & Lehmkuhle, 1986).

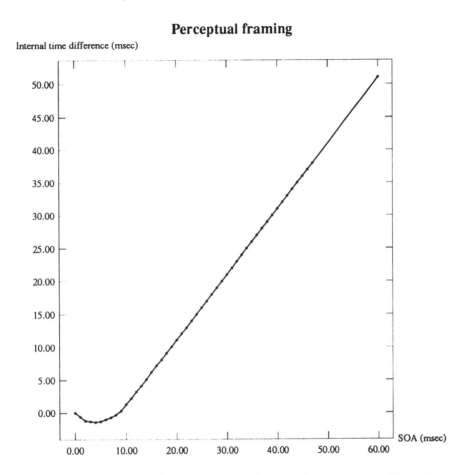

**Perceptual framing**

Figure 2: The effect of perceptual framing. The abscissa indicates the SOA (in simulated ms) between two stimuli, and the ordinate gives the resulting time difference (in simulated ms) between peaks of activity in the internal representations of the two stimuli.

To compare these results to psychophysical findings we transformed them to probabilities. From recent data (Maunsell & Gibson, 1992) it can be calculated that the standard deviation $\sigma$ of the response onset latency in striate cortex within a single layer is about 6 ms. The probability that two neural events that are separated by $t$ ms is then given by

$$P(\text{Perceive as two events}) = \Phi\left(\frac{t}{2\sigma}\right)$$

where $\Phi$ is the normal distribution function. Since identical stimuli were used in the simulation as in Hirsch and Sherrick (1961) the comparison between the two is most appropriate, and this is shown in Figure 3. The fit is very close.

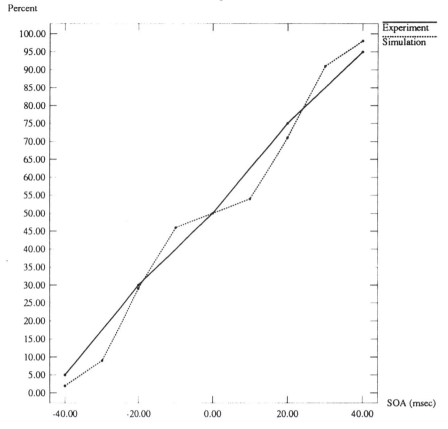

**Visual temporal order**

Figure 3: Accuracy of temporal order perception as a function of SOA. Comparison between experimental results and the model proposed. SOA indicates the time by which stimulus one (e.g. the "right stimulus") leads the other stimulus in a two stimulus presentation task. The ordinate gives the percent responses that stimulus one appeared first. Solid line: results from experimental study. Dotted line: results from simulation of the model.

## 4   Simulations

In the simulations of the model there were 64 oscillators arranged along a ring. Each oscillator consisted of two nodes each, one fast and one slow. The activity of the fast node is denoted by $x_i$, of the corresponding slow node by $y_i$. The index $i$ denotes the position of the oscillator, and ranges from 1 to 64. Oscillators with indices differing by one are neighbors. Since the oscillators are arranged as a ring, units indexed by 1 and 64 respectively are also neighbors. This structure was chosen to avoid edge effects. Care was taken to ensure that input was sufficiently far removed from the wrap around position to avoid undesirable side effects. The input to the network is denoted by $I_i$ and it is position specific. Associated with every oscillator there is a bipole cell, whose activity is denoted by $z_i$. The equations governing the oscillators are:

$$\frac{dx_i}{dt} = -Ax_i + (B - x_i)(Cf_o(x_i) + C\alpha f_o(z_i) + I_i) - Dx_i f_o(y_i) \tag{1}$$

$$\frac{dy_i}{dt} = E(x_i - y_i) \tag{2}$$

where the signal function $f_o$ is given by

$$f_o(x) = \frac{x^{n_o}}{Q_o^{n_o} + x^{n_o}} \tag{3}$$

and $A, B, C, D, E$ and $\alpha$ are parameters of the network. The parameters $n_o$ and $Q_o$ determine the signal function of the oscillator. The equation governing the bipole cells is:

$$z_i = [Pf_b(L_i) + Pf_b(R_i) + P^*f_b(C_i) - \Gamma_{cpl}]^+ \tag{4}$$

where

$$[x]^+ = \max(x, 0) \tag{5}$$

and the bipole signal function is

$$f_b(x) = \frac{x^{n_b}}{Q_b^{n_b} + x^{n_b}}. \tag{6}$$

Where $P, P^*$ and $\Gamma_{cpl}$ are parameters. The parameters $n_b$ and $Q_b$ determine the signal function of the bipole cell. The kernels are given by

$$L_i = \frac{1}{w} \sum_{j=1}^{w} f_o(x_{i-j}) \tag{7}$$

$$R_i = \frac{1}{w} \sum_{j=1}^{w} f_o(x_{i+j}) \tag{8}$$

$$C_i = f_o(x_i) \tag{9}$$

where $w$ is the halfwidth of the kernel. The initial conditions of the network where chosen to be $x_i = 0.2, y_i = 0.4,$ and $z_i = 0$ for all $i$. The initial value of the slow variable is maintained by tonic input, which is quenched when an input comes on. Scaling of time was done by taking into account that the period of oscillations should be about 40 ms. Thus it was found that putting a timestep of 1 unit in the model equal to 1 ms yields good results. Thus the integration stepsize used was $H = 0.1$ ms. The parameters used throughout this report are $A = 1, B = 1, C = 20, D = 33.3, E = 0.05, \alpha = 0.05, n_o = 4, Q_o = 0.9, n_b = 5, Q_b = 0.006, P = 1, P^* = 0.5, \Gamma_{cpl} = 1, w = 6$. Each node received a constant level of background activity ($I_i = 0.2$). Two nodes received an input ($I_i = 0.5$). The first input ($i = 30$) comes at simulation onset, the second input ($i = 34$) comes on later by an amount specified with SOA.

# 5   Discussion

Perceptual framing can be modeled as the synchronization of cortical activities. Synchronization may play other roles than to define the coherent spatial patterns processed by short term memory. Long-term potentiation (LTP) is the change of synaptic efficacy due to pre- or postsynaptic activity (Bliss & Collingridge, 1993). LTP has been linked to learning. LTP occurs reliably when converging input is synchronized. Thus perceptual framing may subserve the additional role of providing synchronized activities for perceptual learning, which has been shown to occur rapidly, but to have long lasting effects (Karni & Sagi, 1993) In this broader context, synchronization sets up a resonant state that drives the learning process, as in Adaptive Resonance Theory (Grossberg, 1976).

# Reference

Bliss, T. V. P., & Collingridge, G. L. (1993). A synaptic model of memory: long-term potentiation in the hippocampus. *Nature, 361*, 31–39.

Bolz, J., Rosner, G., & Wässle, H. (1982). Response latency of brisk-sustained (X) and brisk-transient (Y) cells in the cat retina. *Journal of Physiology (London), 328*, 171–190.

Celebrini, S., Thorpe, S., Trotter, Y., & Imbert, M. (1993). Dynamics of orientation coding in area V1 of the awake primate. *Visual Neuroscience, 10*, 811–825.

Eckhorn, R., Bauer, R., Jordan, W., Brosch, M., Kruse, W., Munk, M., & Reitboeck, H. J. (1988). Coherent oscillations: a mechanism of feature linking in the visual cortex? *Biological Cybernetics, 60*, 121–130.

Ellias, S. A., & Grossberg, S. (1975). Pattern formation, contrast control, and oscillations in the short term memory of shunting on-center off-surround networks. *Biological Cybernetics, 20*, 69–98.

Gray, C. M., & Singer, W. (1989). Stimulus-specific neuronal oscillations in orientation columns of cat visual cortex. *Proceedings of the National Academy of Sciences USA, 86*, 1698–1702.

Grossberg, S. (1976). Adaptive pattern classification and universal recoding, II: feedback, expectation, olfaction, illusions. *Biological Cybernetics, 23*, 187–202.

Grossberg, S., & Mingolla, E. (1985a). Neural dynamics of form perception: boundary completion, illusory figures, and neon color spreading. *Psychological Review, 92*, 173–211.

Grossberg, S., & Mingolla, E. (1985b). Neural dynamics of perceptual grouping: Textures, boundaries, and emergent segmentations. *Perception & Psychophysics, 38*(2), 141–171.

Grossberg, S., & Somers, D. (1991). Synchronized oscillations during cooperative feature linking in a cortical model of visual perception. *Neural Networks, 4*, 453–466.

Hirsch, I. J., & Sherrick, C. E. (1961). Perceived order in different sense modalities. *Journal of Experimental Psychology, 62*(5), 423–432.

Intraub, H. (1985). Visual dissociation: an illusory conjunction of pictures and forms. *Journal of Experimental Psychology: Human Perception and Performance, 11*(4), 431–442.

Karni, A., & Sagi, D. (1993). The time course of learning a visual skill. *Nature, 365*, 250–252.

Mason, A., Nicoll, A., & Stratford, K. (1991). Synaptic transmission between individual pyramidal neurons of the rat visual cortex in vitro. *Journal of Neuroscience, 11*(1), 72–84.

Maunsell, J., & Gibson, J. R. (1992). Visual response latencies in striate cortex of the macaque monkey. *Journal of Neurophysiology, 68*(4), 1332–1343.

Sestokas, A. K., & Lehmkuhle, S. (1986). Visual response latency of X- and Y-cells in the dorsal lateral geniculate nucleus of the cat. *Vision Research, 26*(7), 1041–1054.

Softky, W. R., & Koch, C. (1993). The highly irregular firing of cortical cells is inconsistent with temporal integration of random EPSPs. *Journal of Neuroscience, 13*(1), 334–350.

Varela, F. J., Toro, A., John, E. R., & Schwartz, E. L. (1981). Perceptual framing and cortical alpha rhythm. *Neuropsychologia, 19*(5), 675–686.

# Unification of Hippocampal Function via Computational Considerations

William B Levy
Department of Neurosurgery
University of Virginia
Charlottesville, VA 22908

## Abstract

This paper discusses a minimal computational model to unify the functions of the hippocampus. In this model, the sparse recurrent connectivity of CA3 produces recodings that are suitable for sequence learning, cognitive mapping, and context formation. This context formation is actually a compressed code that is suitable for instructing the cerebral cortex. Furthermore, by virtue of its recurrent connectivity and learned sequences, the CA3 region spontaneously produces sequence fragments that may act as the input that produces long-term storage in cerebral cortex.

## I.    Introduction

The thesis of this paper is that we can unify the cognitive functions of the hippocampus, and its related paralimbic structures, by considering the computations performed by the hippocampus and related structures. There are several functions of the hippocampus which we would like to understand including its ability to teach the cortex, cognitive mapping, and its ability to mix signals and remove redundancy from cortical codes. A central idea is that the sparse recurrence of CA3 and of several other, less direct feedback systems leads to an ability to learn and to compress sequences.

### IA.    Why Teach the Cortex?

The combined requirements of fast learning across time and spatially disparate cortical encodings necessitate the dependence of cerebral cortex on the hippocampus and related structures.

When synaptic modification rate constants are large enough, the hippocampus functions as a fast learning, intermediate-term storage device suitable for teaching a long-term storage device as would be found in cerebral cortex. There is an advantage accrued by separating fast and slow learning, that is the efficiency of encoding. Fast learning systems will have a very low capacity. Thus, in order to have a one-trial learning ability and a large memory capacity, two systems are necessary. Another important reason for cerebral cortex to depend on another structure for its learning is the ultimately sparse connectivity of cerebral cortex. Most of the cortical connections are with neighboring regions, and just the fact that there are $10^{10}$ neurons and only $10^{14}$ connections rather than $10^{20}$ connections, implies that, of all possible connections, only one in a million actually exist. Thus, in order to produce associations between disparate sensory systems, higher order systems are needed to bridge the activity patterns (Fig. 1). Apparently Nature has created a hierarchy of such systems which eventually ends with the hippocampus. Presumably this hierarchy saves on the number of interconnections and leaves the burden of finding the proper pathway of interconnections to higher order regions. As the highest order of all such regions, i.e. the furthest from both sensory and motor cortices, the hippocampus is in a unique position to mediate those associations which could not be efficiently bridged by any lower region. Indeed, the bridging of associations that we picture are not simple static associations, but actually bridging sequences (Mitchison, 1988; Levy, 1989).

Because the hippocampus has both recurrence and a relatively higher level of interconnections than cerebral cortex, it is highly suited for finding rather disparate sensory associations over time and/or space.

### 1B.    Cognitive Mapping

Our theory of cognitive mapping is simple. From codes of individual places, sequences are

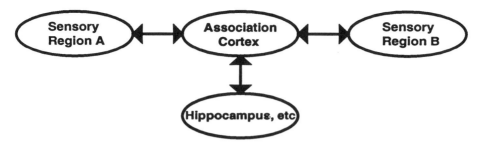

**Figure 1.** The primary function of the human hippocampus is twofold. First, it acts as a fast learning system that later teaches the slower learning cerebral cortex and associated cortical regions. Second, the hippocampus must discover short paths to associate sensory regions not directly interconnected. The bidirectional arrows are meant to indicate a crude reciprocity of connectivity between regions.

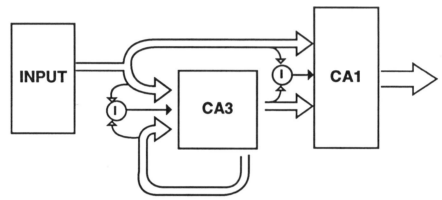

**Figure 2.** A simplified hippocampal model that learns sequences. The learning can be used for sequence completion, including disambiguation of overlapping sequences, fast learning that is automatically rebroadcast so as to mediate slow learning, and jump ahead that allows predictive decisions that occur faster than real time.

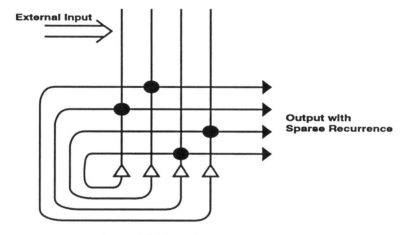

**Figure 3.** The sparse recurrent connections of CA3 produce an asymmetric connectivity.

produced via concatenation. It is from the learning of these sequences that an organism gains the ability to navigate through its world. That is, from previously learned sequences of places, the organism can predict the paths that will carry it from one place to another.

### IC.    Compressed Codes

The nature of the compressed codes that maintain information has been discussed previously (Levy, 1989). There we emphasized that the signal mixing and recurrence properties of the hippocampus and related structures are critical to code compression and redundancy reduction. The nature of the compression is simple to understand. Essentially, just consider a sequence A,B,C that is recoded by hippocampal region CA3 into A',B',C'. Then the new code is compressed if the Hamming distances among A', B', and C' are less than those among the original representation A, B, and C.

### II.    Computational Architecture

We have tried to identify the minimal computational architecture for the problems mentioned above. The computational architecture is made up of two essential parts (Fig. 2): 1) a recoder that is inspired by the CA3 region of the hippocampus, and 2) a decoder of the recoded signals inspired by the CA1 region of the hippocampus.

There are four essential aspects to the performance of the CA3 portion of the network. The first aspect is a connectivity of sparse recurrence (Fig. 3). The second is a neuronal delay of at least one time step in converting an input to an output. The third feature is an associative modification rule that spans at least one time step, and the fourth is some generic feedback inhibition that narrowly bounds total activity. Other characteristics that might add to the performance of the network, but seem nonessential, include the use of neurons whose excitation is continuous in time by virtue of an RC (resistance capacitance)-based time constant, the use of a multiplicity of axonal delays interconnecting various neurons in the network, the use of a longer time-spanning associative modification rule, and the use of a theta rhythm-like process to reset the network.

The sparse recurrence of the connectivity in the CA3 region produces an essentially asymmetric network (Fig. 3). This asymmetry makes it more difficult for the network to fall into asymptotically stable points (Minai & Levy, 1993a,c,d). Although asymptotically stable states are desirable in typical pattern recognition situations, here we desire networks that can learn to reproduce sequences and learn to jump ahead in sequences. Thus, the asymmetry of the recurrent connections propels the network to construct stable sequence modes rather than single, asymptotically stable states. These learned sequences are useful for sequence problems in general, but they have another use. Specifically, these stable modes of learned sequences are also useful in training the cerebral cortex (Minai & Levy, 1993b). After fast learning, initiation of network dynamics from random starting points will produce network states that tend to drift into a stable mode or a portion of a stable mode because the learned sequence mode is an attractor. As a result, a sequence or sequence fragment is often produced (Minai & Levy, 1993b). Such sequence fragments might correspond to the observations of Pavlides & Winson (1989) and of Wilson & McNaughton (1993). Moreover, these spontaneously produced sequence fragments are obvious candidates for the hippocampus to use as a slow teaching method for the edification of cerebral cortex.

The CA1 decoder is a simple reinforced learning system that performs pattern recognition on the new codes created by CA3.

### III.    Computational Abilities

The computational abilities of the hippocampal network include sequence learning (Minai et al., submitted to this conference) and code compression (Prepscius & Levy, submitted to this conference). We should also point out that sequence learning will correspond to cognitive mapping and fast prediction (ibid). In particular, as an animal moves through its environment, a sequence is created. Such a sequence is then recoded in a way that is compressed. The overlapping parts of the compressed code can be seen as the context created by the sequence. In terms of coding, this context is essentially the shared coding elements of the compressed sequence (Levy, 1989). It is this context (or overlap in the compressed code) that we hypothesize provides the mapping by which the hippocampus creates, or biases, the shorter bridging pathways between distant cortical regions that need to be associated.

In viewing sequence learning as part of cognitive mapping, we need only realize that an organism exists in time. Thus, any series of inputs are, in fact, elements of a sequence. Such elements of a sequence are, in fact, encodings of the animal's input environment, including the physical space in which the animal exists, but also any internally generated predictions about where it is or will be.

Because the environment includes both local cues and distal cues, neighboring events in time will tend to be coded similarly by virtue of being neighboring in space. Even more important, however, is that the network will try to compress this coding to one of greater similarity when prediction across time is valid. That is, even in the cases where successive events have very different encodings, so long as one event is a good predictor of another event, then these two events should be coded similarly. This coding method has the advantage of allowing the animal to do rapid, approximate inference. For example, consider an extreme case where A usually implies B, and B actually implies C. If the coding of predictable representations becomes more similar, i.e. if A is very, very reliable in its ability to predict B, and if B is perfectly reliable in its ability to predict C, then A should also predict C, and it does so based on recoding B and A into C. (Of course, bypassing B might be conceived of as a loss of information, but we should recognize that the brain is able to maintain a multiple coding system so that B is, in fact, being represented somewhere.)

## IV.    Problems to Solve

By self-admission there is one aspect of this theory that I find most troublesome. Inherent in the proposal that the hippocampus teaches the entorhinal cortex and that the entorhinal cortex teaches the structures that innervate it, etc., is a requirement for accurate reciprocal innervations between areas and mechanisms that realign successive recodings to initial codings.

It is questionable whether cortical associative innervation, at the detailed level required by such a teaching operation (i.e. the recoding-decoding), actually exists. Thus, there seems to be a need for synaptogenesis rules that will appropriately implement this teaching, including what must be viewed as a decoding [in the same sense that we propose a CA1-like region to decode the new representations of CA3 (see Minai et al., 1993)].

Because both the cerebral cortical codes and the hippocampal codes will change with time, there is also a requirement that some type of consistency be maintained between regions. Such parallel realignment of connectivity may require a reorganization of connections between regions on a neuron by neuron basis.

## V.    Possible Objections

Doubtlessly the ideas presented here will require a great deal of research to understand their full implications and parametric limitations. More detailed anatomical and physiological knowledge will naturally help restrict the many free variables which must be specified to implement this model. But whether such facts are critical to the generic functions of the model seems unlikely.

A second and more serious objection is that our system lacks a mismatch detector. Such a detector must exist as shown by the many experiments on the P300 wave. However, the neural structures and computations underlying the P300 are a matter of conjecture. Even so, models with mismatch detection exist (Grossberg, 1982) and would be useful here. In particular, to account for the discriminability of similar patterns (see O'Reilly & McClelland, 1993; Gluck & Myers, 1993) a mismatch detector may be needed to produce a distinctive coding for initially similar events.

Another issue is the functional and computational similarities between this model of the hippocampus and models of other brain structures, particularly parahippocampal and association cortices. In fact, such functional and computational similarities are not an accident and are inherent in any approach that attempts to abstract cortical function. That is, abstracted cortical function will be the same in different cortical regions. What will differ among cortical regions is the specific nature of the inputs to each region and each region's computational characteristics that are undoubtedly matched to the statistics of the particular input signals. To be more specific, signal mixing and the reduction of redundancy by association are recapitulated throughout association cortices. Moreover, if we conceptualize mammalian cortical evolution as successive refinements of a single theme (e.g. something resembling dorsal cortex of reptiles), then we will expect and even find desirable such similarities. That is, the evolution of much of cerebral cortex came from a hippocampal-like structure and, therefore, the evolved, abstracted function will be similar.

A sparsely recurrent connectivity occurs throughout cortex, at least in the form of reciprocally innervated cortical regions (e.g. VI to V2 and V2 to VI) if not in the local architecture of these regions (e.g. interconnected pyramidal neurons of layers II and III within a given cortical region). What is different about such regions (apart from the details of the cell types themselves) is: (1) the density of connectivity and the distances spanned by such recurrence, and (2) the nature of the inputs reaching each region. Thus, it is altogether acceptable if the entorhinal cortex and its associated structures - without the hippocampus - actually perform computations similar to those performed by the hippocampus per se.

Finally, by using a hierarchy of regions to produce signal mixing, redundancy reduction, compressed coding, context encodings, and generic associative encoding, Nature may have solved two problems. First, it avoided the need for an excessively large hippocampus (i.e., a little mixing occurs in successive regions in proportion to the probability of finding associations between the areas being mixed so that overall connectivity is minimized). Second, an additional property is produced for free. This property is our ability to keep distinct nearly identical events that happen at different times. The idea is that in the backward cascade by which higher order associative regions teach lower order ones, we have encodings that maintain temporally distinguished, but nearly identical, events. Thus, the gradients of limbically induced retrograde amnesia and the existence of longer gradients of retrograde amnesia in higher mammals suggest the slow, successive teaching of memories down the hierarchy. It is this successive hierarchical teaching that preserves the ordering, over days and months, of the representations being taught by the higher, more associative cortices to the lower order, more sensory cortices.

## Acknowledgements

This work was supported by NIH MH48161, MH00622, RR07864, NSF MSS-9216372 and EPRI RP8030-08 to WBL, and by the Department of Neurosurgery, Dr. John A Jane, Chairman. This paper benefitted from discussions with Bruce McNaughton, James McClelland, and Mark Gluck.

## References

Gluck, M.A. & Myers, C.E. (1993) Adaptive stimulus representations: a computational theory of hippocampal-region function. In: Advances in Neural Information Processing Systems 5. (S.J. Hanson, J.D. Cowan, & C.L. Giles, Eds.), San Mateo: Morgan Kaufmann, pp. 937-944.

Grossberg, S. (1982) Studies of Mind and Brain. Dordrecht: D. Reidel.

Levy, W. B (1989) A computational approach to hippocampal function. In: Computational Models of Learning in Simple Neural Systems. (R.D. Hawkins and G.H. Bower, Eds.), New York: Academic Press, pp. 243-305.

Minai, A.A. & Levy, W.B (1993a) Predicting complex behavior in sparse asymmetric networks. In: Advances in Neural Information Processing Systems 5. (S.J. Hanson, J.D. Cowan, & C.L. Giles, Eds.), San Mateo: Morgan Kaufmann, pp. 556-563.

Minai, A.A. & Levy, W.B (1993b) Sequence learning in a single trial. World Congress on Neural Networks II, 505-508.

Minai, A.A. & Levy, W.B (1993c) Setting the activity level in sparse random networks. Neural Computation, in press.

Minai, A.A. & Levy, W.B (1993d) The dynamics of sparse random networks. Biol. Cyber., in press.

Minai, A.A., Barrows, G.L. & Levy, W. B (1993) Disambiguation of pattern sequences with recurrent networks. Submitted.

Mitchison, G. (1988) The organization of sequential memory: sparse representations and the targetting problem. In: Organization of Neural Networks. (W.V. Seelen, G. Shaw, A. Leinhos, Eds.), VCH-Verlag, Weinheim, pp. 347-67.

O'Reilly, R.C. & McClelland, J.L. (1993) Hippocampal conjunctive encoding, storage, and recall: avoiding a tradeoff. Submitted.

Pavlides, C. & Winson, J. (1989) Influences of hippocampal place cell firing in the awake state on the activity of these cells during subsequent sleep episodes. J. Neurosci. 9:2907-2918.

Prepscius, C. & Levy, W.B (1993) Sequence prediction and cognitive mapping by a biologically plausible neural network. Submitted.

Wilson, M.A. & McNaughton, B.L. (1993) Persistence of behaviorally induced correlation in place cell activity during sleep. Soc. Neurosci. Abstr. 19:795.

# NEURAL SCALE INVARIANCE:
# AN INTEGRATIVE MODEL WITH IMPLICATIONS FOR
# NEUROPATHOLOGY

Jeffrey P. Sutton [1,2] and Hans C. Breiter [1,3]

[1] Department of Psychiatry, Harvard Medical School, Building 149 13th Street, Charlestown MA USA 02129
[2] Center for Biological and Computational Learning, E25-201, MIT, Cambridge MA USA 02139
[3] NMR Center, Massachusetts General Hospital, Building 149 13th Street, Charlestown MA USA 02129

email: sutton@ai.mit.edu, hansb@nmr-r.mgh.harvard.edu

Neural scale invariance is a proposition that describes different levels of neural dynamics. We suggest that scale invariance, while an approximation to real neural dynamics, is a helpful concept in integrating different levels of organization and in predicting alterations present in a variety of disorders affecting the nervous system. We discuss the notion's theoretical basis and outline how new experimental techniques are potentially useful in validating the model.

## 1. Introduction

In basic neuroscience, there is a trend to examine phenomena within a single level of neural organization. This approach has led to many interesting discoveries, especially in the reductionistic realms of cellular signaling and molecular neurobiology. While it is generally acknowledged that integrative or systems neuroscience is an important area of investigation, it is not clear how to best bridge different levels of understanding. Researchers in neural networks and psychophysics are cognizant of this situation, and have been somewhat successful in applying computational methods to link the levels of neuron, distributed networks and cognitive neuroscience (figure 1). However, there are few unifying principles that relate the structural and dynamical features within and between levels of neural systems.

The situation in clinical neuroscience is possibly worse. Neurology and psychiatry both profess a comprehensive view of nervous system homeostasis and pathology. The triad of biology, psychology and sociology as fundamental components of illness are standard dogma, yet the ability to integrate these three domains is sub-optimal. Within each domain, including the biological sphere, large hiatuses exist between levels of description of pathophysiological mechanisms.

For example, cognitive impairments are an important feature of many disorders, including Alzheimer's disease and depression. Presumably there are strong biological underpinnings to cognitive dysfunction, and in the case depression, the neural substrate is remarkably responsive to current medication treatment. Although considerable insights into the effects of anti-depressants on synaptic modulation and cognitive performance exist, little is known about the intermediate levels of neural functioning that mediate cognition and that may be altered in disease processes.

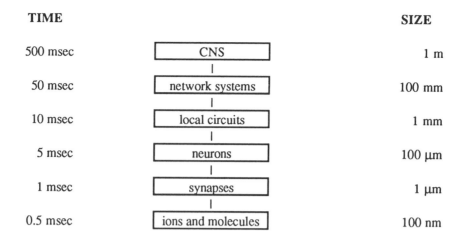

| TIME | | SIZE |
|------|--|------|
| 500 msec | CNS | 1 m |
| 50 msec | network systems | 100 mm |
| 10 msec | local circuits | 1 mm |
| 5 msec | neurons | 100 μm |
| 1 msec | synapses | 1 μm |
| 0.5 msec | ions and molecules | 100 nm |

Figure 1. Standard model of central nervous system (CNS) hierarchical organization. Each level is scaled according to approximate measures of time and size.

## 2. Neural Scale Invariance

In this paper, we outline a novel and potentially useful way of viewing neural behavior at multiple levels of organization. The idea is speculative, remarkably simple and has direct implications for modeling nervous system dysfunction. We suggest that, to first approximation, the dynamic principles governing neural activity at one level of organization are applicable to many levels of organization. With some liberty, we have termed this notion *neural scale invariance*. The concept differs from standard experimental (e.g. Morris et al., 1988) and system-theoretical (e.g. Erdi, 1984) views of stratified neural systems by including but transcending notions of structural hierarchy (figure 1). In our model, we propose (i) a framework for bridging multiple structural levels using nested distributed networks, (ii) a quasi-rigorous mathematical description of how to express the dynamics at any level in terms of dimensionless variables, and (iii) a means of predicting alterations at many levels in disorders affecting the nervous system. Our proposal is motivated by three considerations. These are briefly outlined below.

### 2.1 Modern Theories of Dimensionality

The seminal works of Widom, Kadanoff and Wilson on scaling laws and renormalization group theory provide a groundwork for describing complex physical systems using dimensionless variables (see Balescu, 1975 for a good overview). There is enormous power in being able to reduce many important features of a system, regardless of the level of phenomenology, to a discussion of a few critical measures. While the theoretical treatment of dimensionality in these systems has been largely confined to equilibrium phenomena, it may be possible to extract the principle of universality to describe multi-level and dynamic neural architectures.

In examining principles of neural systems, it is important to distinguish between these systems and the systems in statistical physics. Neurobiological systems are not likely to be scale invariant in a strict mathematical sense. Whereas all the components (e.g. molecules) in a physical system are treated the same, neurons are heterogeneous in structure, connectivity patterns and excitability. Averages performed over neural activity at one level, to yield a scalar measure of network activity at another level, may factor out essential information. Nevertheless, there are degrees of similarity, aside from scale, in the relationships between a collection of neurons in a distributed network and an ensemble of local neural networks within a brain region. Both have sparse but relatively widely propagating connections, and both have some autonomous functioning capabilities.

## 2.2 Hierarchical Cluster Networks

One approach to detailing the topology of neural scale invariance is to use nested hierarchies (Sutton et al., 1988). This scheme posits that a particular level of neural organization, such as a region of cortex, is composed of networks that cluster together based on functional connectivity patterns. Each network is comprised of adaptive sub-networks (figure 2), and the outputs from the sub-networks collectively make up the output of a larger network. Multiple levels of distributed nesting give rise to an interesting parallel architecture wherein the vector relationships between any pair of neurons is preserved. Correlations among the networks are maintained at all levels, and averaging takes into account neural heterogeneity in activity patterns (Sutton, 1991). A prediction of the model is that different levels of network organization, whether they be small local networks or large regional systems, obey similar computational principles. Another prediction is that alterations at one level affect all levels in some manner. This feature has been demonstrated in a simulation of neural dysfunction in a model of Alzheimer's disease (Sutton et al., 1988).

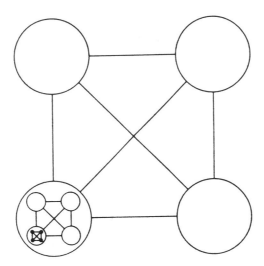

Figure 2. Schematic illustration of neural network clustering. Four levels of organization are shown, commencing with four neural units (bottom left hand corner) that interconnect to form a small network. In turn, this network links to other networks to form larger scale networks, and so on. While the figure is suggestive of self-similar structures (i.e. fractals), there is considerable heterogeneity in connectivities. Moreover, the connections are not fixed in time since the system is adaptive at all levels. Modified from Sutton et al. (1988).

## 2.3 Intermediate Level Functional Recordings

Until recently, it has proved extremely difficult to obtain experimental data to test whether or not neural scale invariance is a viable proposition. With the advent of multi-cellular *in vivo* recordings and functional magnetic resonance imaging (fMRI), the capability to test hypotheses regarding intermediate level networks (1-100 mm, 100-500+ msec; figure 1) is becoming feasible. These levels of neural organization are made up of networks where standard techniques have not provided adequate spatial and temporal resolution simultaneously.

fMRI is a non-invasive technique which is sensitive, in part, to real-time changes in the magnetic properties of hemoglobin as it moves between its oxygenated and de-oxygenated states (Kwong et al., 1992). These changes correlate with neural activation. It has been our experience that the patterns of fMRI activation within and between human brain regions are intuitively reminiscent of the spectrum of responses observed in excitable neural membranes. Brain regions are relatively quiescent and then activate transiently. The responses vary in magnitude and duration, and although the data are preliminary and require further analysis, different combinations of overlapping networks appear to be recruited and respond in a manner that is both stimulus and state dependent (Breiter et al., 1993).

## 3. Dynamic Formulation

At the levels of single neurons and small networks, response properties have been well described by mathematical and computational formulations, including the Hodgkin and Huxley equations (1952) and Genesis simulations. Do the dynamics applicable at these levels lend themselves to higher levels of neural description? Certainly many approaches have been taken to describe higher levels of functioning, and some deal with scale-like notions. For instance, Wilson and Cowan (1972) built on a Hodgkin and Huxley format, but they made approximations that reduced their model to general populations of excitatory and inhibitory neurons. Any intermediate biological structure was lost. It may be that scale invariance has not been considered as a possible organizational principle because biological details about intermediate levels of function have simply not been available.

What form would a general model of scale invariance take? One possibility is to look at simple response dynamics of units within a network. The units may correspond to ion channels, neurons or networks of varying degrees of complexity as described in the nested cluster model (section 2.2). While the goal is to delineate general principles, it is understood that the details of the units and responses are important for characterizing each level of description. A simple version of the model is shown in figure 3.

Perhaps the most studied mathematical description of interacting units is captured in the Hodgkin and Huxley equations. A simplified but representative format is given by:

$$C\frac{dV}{dt} + I(V, W_1, ..., W_n) = I(t) \tag{1}$$

$$\frac{dW_i}{dt} = \phi \frac{\left[W_{i,\infty}(V) - W_i\right]}{\tau_i(V)}. \tag{2}$$

The variables represent the potential (deviation from a "resting" state) $V$, capacitance $C$, current $I$, conducting variables $W_1, ..., W_n$, time constant $\tau_i$ and temperature-like, time scale factor $\phi$.

Equations (1) and (2) are very general. While they describe excitable membrane responses given certain constraints, we suggest that they may also be similar to universal equations that are pertinent for describing dynamics at multiple levels within the neural hierarchy. This assertion treats the variables as dimensionless entities and assumes that there are measures that operate as electrical circuit analogues at multiple levels. There is support for this stance in some artificial neural networks, wherein the electrical properties of the network as a whole share features with the membrane-like properties of the network's components.

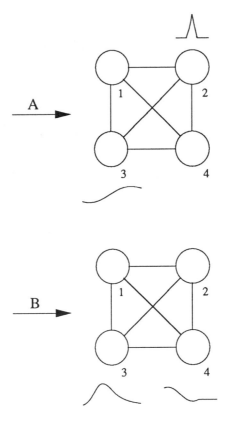

Figure 3. Highly simplified representation of neural scale invariance. Interconnected units have similar dynamic properties regardless of the level of neural organization. In the conditions of paradigm A, units 2 and 3 are activated in different ways. Units 1 and 4 are quiescent. Unit 3 is also activated under the conditions in B, but the response pattern differs from that in A. Unit 4 switches off, and units 1 and 2 are inactive. By adjusting the parameters of the system, the model may describe events at multiple levels, including the dynamics among ion channels, single neurons, small neural networks or local brain regions (c.f. Breiter et al., 1993).

Experimental verification of the hypothesis of neural scale invariance is viewed as a two step process. In the first stage, a determination needs to made as to whether or not the response patterns at multiple levels obey universal equations. This endeavor involves mathematical constructs and is not dependent on the requirement that the variables actually be observable quantities. The second step of the process evaluates the possibility that the variables are experimentally measurable. If this turns out to be the case, then we suggest that strong scale invariance exists. A purely mathematical description, without confirmation that the variables are observable, corresponds to weak scale invariance.

## 4. Implications for Neuropathology

According to the notion of neural scale invariance, dysfunction is not confined to a single level of the neural architecture (for example, Breiter et al., manuscript submitted). Each level is linked by complex connections such that the behavior at one level is not merely the average behavior of its collective parts. In fact, changes in relatively small numbers of widely projecting neurons, such as those cell populations involved in neuromodulation, potentially impact many levels simultaneously.

We suggest that finding a disturbance at one level implies that other levels are also altered. If neural scale invariance is a viable principle, the nature of the disturbance will also share characteristic properties across different scales of activity. However, it is unreasonable to assert that a complete description of a disorder could be given at all levels based on this notion since each level has unique structural and functional details.

An oversimplified example of how this schema might work concerns some subjects with attention problems. Consider a set of dynamic equations wherein the temperature-like parameter $\phi$ is changed, resulting in an increase in network fluctuations. At the single neuron level, there would be diminished fidelity of signal transmission across synapses. Decreased aminergic modulation has been implicated in this process and in inattention. Intermediate level networks with increased fluctuations would yield less averaged activation during functional neuroimaging (e.g. PET scanning). Cognitive testing would reveal significant scatter among subtest scores, although the performance on any given subtest might be excellent. All of the aforementioned measures have been observed! However, a multi-level or integrative view of attention disorders is rarely adopted. Scale invariance may be applicable to attention deficit disorder and many other disorders, and it has considerable potential for synthesizing complex pathophysiological mechanisms that are generally present in nervous system dysfunction.

## 5. Summary

In this paper, we have outlined a novel way of viewing neural organization and dynamics. By utilizing the notion of scale invariance, we suggest that multiple levels of neural function share common features and that these features are relevant to normal as well as abnormal processes. A rigorous development of scale invariance is required before its veracity can be fully determined.

The support of NSF, grant ASC 9217041 to the CBCL at MIT, NARSAD and NIH, for a fellowship in NMR research (HCB), is gratefully acknowledged.

## References

Balescu R. *Equilibrium and Nonequilibrium Statistical Mechanics*. 1975. Wiley: New York.

Breiter HC, Filipek PA, Savage CR, et al. Brain morphology in patients with obsessive-compulsive disorder. Submitted.

Breiter HC, Kwong KK, Baker JR, et al. Functional magnetic resonance imaging of symptom provocation in obsessive-compulsive disorder. *SMRM, 12th Annual Meeting Proceedings*. 1993.

Erdi P. System-theoretical approach to the neural organization: Feed-forward control of the ontogenetic development. In Trappl R (ed.) *Cybernetics and Systems Research 2*. 1984. Elsevier: North-Holland.

Hodgkin AL, Huxley AF. A quantitative description of membrane current and its application to conduction and excitation in nerve. *J. Physiol. (London)*. 1952;**117**:500-544.

Kwong KK, Belliveau JW, Chesler DA, et al. Dynamic magnetic resonance imaging of human brain activity during primary sensory stimulation. *Proc Natl Acad Sci USA*. 1992;**89**:5675-5679.

Morris RGM, Kandel ER, Squire LR. The neuroscience of learning and memory: cells, neural circuits and behavior. *TINS*. 1988;**11**(4):125-127.

Sutton JP. Mean field theory of nested neural clusters. *Proceedings Intern. AMSE Conference Neural Networks, Vol. 1*. 1991:47-58.

Sutton JP, Beis JS, Trainor LEH. Hierarchical model of memory and memory loss. *J. Phys. A: Math. Gen.* 1988;**21**:4443-4454.

Wilson HR, Cowan JD. Excitatory and inhibitory interactions in localized populations of model neurons. *Biophys. J.* 1972;**12**:1-24.

# Neurodynamics and Chaos

**Session Chairs: Harold Szu**
**Mona Zaghloul**

**ORAL PRESENTATIONS**

# Multi-Resolution Analyses of Fuzzy Membership Functions by means of Chaotic Neural Networks

Harold Szu, Joe Garcia, Lotfi Zadeh[#],

NSWCDD, Code B44, Silver Spring MD 20903

[#]Dept. of EE &CS., Univ. of California-Berkeley, Berkeley CA 94720

**Charles Hsu, Joseph DeWitte, Jr., Mona Zaghloul**

EE&CS GWU, Wash. DC 20052

## Abstract

An application of two-scale multiresolution analysis to the Fuzzy Membership Function (FMF) is suggested by the bifurcation route to chaos, which is generated by our chaotic neuron model. Two applications are given. (1) The mean synaptic weight field plays an important role for fast pattern recognition capability in examples of both habituation and novelty detections [WCNN-93]. (2) Another novel usage of the Chaotic Neural Network and Fuzzy Logic is that of sharpening of FMF, say for the representation of the peak of Cherry Blossoms. Comparisons among the Artificial (ANN), Biological (BNN) and Chaotic Neural Networks (CNN) are given.

**Keywords:** Chaos, Chaotic Neuron, Chaotic Neural Networks, Multiple Resolution, Bifurcation, Habituation, Novelty, Chips, SPICE

## 1. Multi-Resolution Fuzzy Logic and Bifurcation to Chaos

Fuzzy Logic (FL) is useful in industrial engineering because it is simple (if-then rule-based) and provides us with the capability to "explore the tolerance of imprecision", according to L. Zadeh [1]. But just "like any other mathematical or computer model, FL falls prey to the 'curse of dimensionality'" [2]. We wish to point out that Artificial Neural Networks (ANN) have helped the FL in four areas, and where and when the Chaotic Neural Networks (CNN) can do it more efficiently.

(1) Determination of Fuzzy Rule Set: ANNs have been used to learn the classifier variances having major and minor axes with respect to the (If-Input, Then-Output) rule domain, which when projected along the output and input axses give respectively the Fuzzy Membership Functions (FMF)[3]. To change the rule is more important to change FMF[4].

(2) Determination of the FMF: For example, it is often assumed that such membership functions are described by triangles with obvious centroids (rather than a crisp rectangle for numerical value)[5,6]. Automatic optimal splitting and combing of membership functions, as well as the shape of those functions, can be determined from data fed into a neural network. This paper addresses such a possibility via bifurcation.

(3) Determination of Fuzzy Inference Engine: A system is a distribution of parameters, of which an ANN is one that is useful for fuzzy logic control (Yamakawa[7]), e. g., truck-backing [8].

(4) Contribution to fast learning of ANN: Applying the Min-Max operations respectively for Fuzzy rule and defuzzification, both Carpenter et al [9] and Simpson [10] have achieved fast learning.

(5) Determination of Efficient Representation of Fuzzy Dynamics: Recently, a self-reference fuzzy liar paradox dynamics [11] and nonlinear spatiotemporal phenomena are efficiently described by chaotic maps or flows. This paper touches upon whether or not the underlying choatic maps are useful for some applications of the FL via the CNN [12].

We envision that both ANNs and CNNs can someday be used to embed such distributed representations into fuzzy logic inference engines. Why chaos? Only chaos is exponentially fast in switching from one attractor basin to another in terms of the ANN energy landscape, and yet the unpredictable outcome is always bounded within the possible membership set. Such a set is an open set of possibly infinite logic values, as opposed to binary logic, and therefore escapes the normalization requirement of the traditional probability theory.

A motivation for chaotic fuzzy neural networks is to develop systems that can efficiently represent or predict events in chaotic processes. For various reasons, given by [11-16], we wish to study a biologically meaningful neuron model that is "simple enough but not any simpler (A. Einstein)" yet can produce a bifurcation cascade toward chaos. The model must be easily fabricated as a learnable neural network on electronic chips. Therefore, an implementable neuron model should have no delay in neuron input-output, should not require expensive sample-and-hold circuitry and should not have any inductance coil element. Indeed, such a Chaotic Neural Network (CNN) has been designed [14,15] based on the 1-D N-shaped sigmoidal function $\sigma_N$ that has a portion near the input threshold value associated with a negative-slope logic which has been derived for a Markovian mean field approximation of the Cainainello refractory delay model [17]. It was further pointed out by [15] that chaos may provide us a dynamical basis for fuzzy reasoning. In this paper we explore such a practical bridge between CNNs and fuzzy logic and hope to achieve a learnable fuzzy membership function (FMF).

For instance, as long as one can vaguely recollect from the past decades (in the spirit of "exploiting the tolerance of imprecision"), the Japanese embassy in Washington D.C. usually fails to predict the peak weekend for the annual Cherry Blossoms (CB). Since D. C. is located close to the Appalachian ridge in an unstable region where weather systems from Canada and the Gulf of Mexico converge, the weather chaotically fluctuates from year to year. Compounding this is the modulation by the 11-year period solar cycle. Cherry trees are not cooperating with the embassy planning, but with Mother Nature---the species genetics and the weather (conceivably the Winter snowfall, the Spring rainfall, and the Solar activity play some roles). These complex conditions drive the underlying chaotic dynamics of the CB making long range forecasting especially difficult for this part of the United States. Since the full CB does not last long (having a life span $\Delta t$ about five to ten days), it is difficult to predict the exact peak. How does one then treat such a chaotic time series?

It is intuitively clear that chaos provides a deterministic possibility useful for fuzzy logic. A computational basis of fuzzy logic is the rule and the FMF, which is often chosen in the shape of a triangle for a clear centroid at its tip t =0 shown in Fig. 1 (a):

$$\Phi(t) \quad = \quad 1 \quad -|t|; \qquad 0 \le |t| \le 1, \qquad\qquad (1)$$
$$0; \qquad\qquad \text{otherwise.}$$

It turns out that the triangle is equivalent to a low-pass scaling function used for the multiple resolution high-pass wavelet analysis:

$$\Phi(t) \quad = \quad \Phi(2t+1)/2 \quad + \quad \Phi(2t) \quad + \quad \Phi(2t-1)/2 \qquad\qquad (2)$$

shown in Fig. 1 (b) for the two-scale scaling relationship [20] illustrating a special case of the Collage Theorem [21].

If the underlying fuzzy dynamics are the bifurcation route toward chaos, then we can expand the chaotic data set efficiently on this set of nesting triangular membership functions (MF), regressing from an non-overlapping crisp MF becoming overlapping fuzzy MF as schematically shown in Fig. 2. The Analogy between the bifurcation route to chaos (left of Fig. 2) and the crisp route to fuzzy overlapping membership function (right of Fig. 2). Note that Fig. 2 has taken into account of the standard FMF overlapping & complementing characterisitics, but without the details of the CB ratio $\Delta T/\Delta t$ shown in next Fig. 3.

If we assume [19] the triangle envelop covering a typical bifurcation cascade spectrum as the Fuzzy Membership Function (FMF), then the bifurcation to chaos suggests a multi-resolution FMF analysis as follows. We introduce an average life span $\Delta t$, say $< \Delta t > = 7$ days, with a standard deviation $\sigma_t$ of 3 days. We also introduce the time resolution scale length $\Delta T$ in the analysis of the periodic CB event. One can trivially forecast every year with the absolute certainty, "crisp or sharp" that the CB will surely peak sometime during the $\Delta T^{(o)}$ = Spring time of the year. A factor 2 increase in the precision, $\Delta T^{(1)} = \Delta T^{(o)}/2$, corresponds to a decrease in the certainty of the event: CB peak during March or April. Likewise, for $\Delta T^{(2)} = \Delta T^{(1)}/2$, still less certainty in the unit of a two week period at the end of March or at the beginning of April. However, this non-overlapping membership function can not be extended indefinitely. This is because of $\Delta T^{(3)} = \Delta T^{(2)}/2$ the sub-triangle becomes overlapping, thus marking the onset of the FMF when the resolution scale $\Delta T^{(3)}$ for a week approaches the average CB event span $<\Delta t >$.

Eq(2) gives the contribution due to the sharpening of the uncertainty FMF indicated by the dashed triangle having a narrowed range as shown in Fig. 3.

$$\Phi(2t) = \Phi(t) - \Phi(2t+1)/2 - \Phi(2t-1)/2 \qquad (3)$$

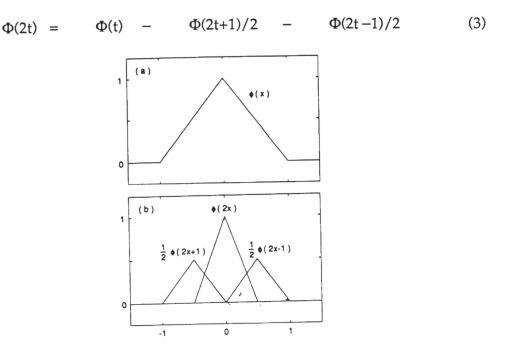

Fig. 1  A Hat Scaling Function Relation Useful for Fuzzy Membership Functions

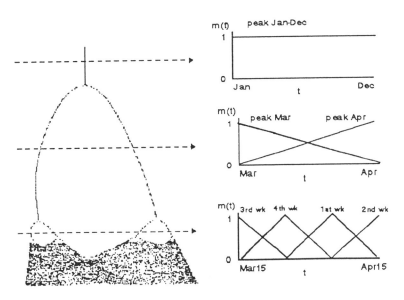

Fig. 2  Analogy between the bifurcation route to chaos (left) and the crisp route to fuzzy overlapping membership function (right)

When actual data of the CB becomes available, we can apply the standard discrete wavelet analysis via Quadrature Mirror Filter Bank [31],

$$t \dashrightarrow t' = t - b / a$$
$$b = I; \quad I = 0, \pm 1, \pm 2, \pm 3,$$

where b is the shift parameter by days to catch the exact CB day defined with a FMF of width $\Delta T^{(3)}$ to train a classical artificial neural networks (ANN) to predict the CB event. A more efficient way is to combine a wavelet network with an ANN into a so-called "wavenet"[45], of which each neuron assumes a daughter wavelet transfer function having a single value of $a = 2^I$.

In this paper, we wish to emphasize that a CNN has intrinsically combined an ANN with the multiresolution scale analysis via bifurcations. Since the bifurcation output of a $\sigma_N$ neuron realizes a member of the FMF, then such cooperative chaotic neurodynamics determines a collective resolution scale $<\Delta T>$ which in turn may provide us with the possibility of a learnable fuzzy logic reasoning concerning when a quasi-periodic event will occur with respect to the dyadic scale.

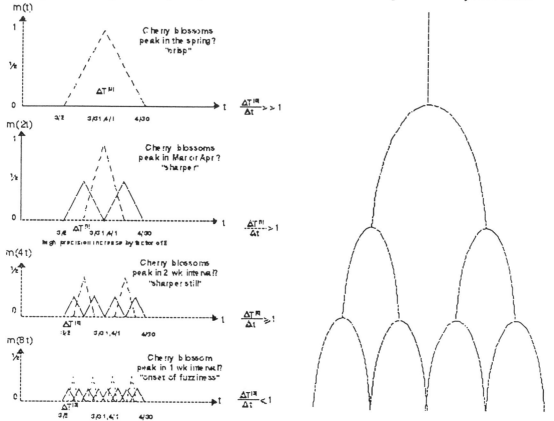

Fig. 3 The dashed triangles indicate the differences between two adjacent resolutions of the bifurcated membership functions in terms of the resolution scales $\Delta T^{(n)}$ toward overlap with the mean event life span $<\Delta t>$.

We have pointed out the parallel route from "crisp" to "fuzzy" as "bifurcation" to "chaos". It is thus interesting to exam how a minimum change of the traditional sigmoidal neuron transfer function can generate the bifurcation to chaos in Sect. 2.

## 2. Review of Single Chaotic Neuron $\sigma_N$ Models

The Nagumo-Sato (1972) model [33] of a neuron was originally biologically motivated by Fitzhugh (1961) [32], developed mathematically by Caianiello (1961)[31] and implemented with tunneling diodes and an inductance element by Harmon(1961) [34]. The inductor has a magnetic field which produces cross talk in an IC implementation. Recently, this challenge has been circumvented by Chua's Circuit[22], implemented by Yamakawa's chip [35] and Aihara circuit.[30,38]. Various mathematical models of chaotic neurons are: (i) one-dimensional (1-D) recursive maps without delay; the single neuron via Feigenbaum-like cascaded bifurcation spectrum that were demonstrated mathematically for the first time by Szu *et. al.* (ii) 1-D class of delayed maps include Caianiello & Nagumo models, and Aihara, and Yamakawa which is shown to be 2-D map without the delay.

This class of 1-D delayed map can map 2-D $(x_n, y_n)$ to 2-D $(x_{n+1}, y_{n+1})$ without any delay.

$$X_{n+1} = f(X_n) - aY_n$$
$$Y_{n+1} = X_n$$

In the sense of Poincare chaos, the sensitivity to the initial condition might be due to the fact that in this delayed map all the previous data history is required to determine the present value , so that a slight change in data will perturb the outcome. This conjecture is easily seen by solving it formally:

$$X_{n+1} = \Sigma^{\infty}_{k=0} (-a)^k f(X_{n-2k}); \text{ equivalently} \qquad X_{n+1} = f(X_n) - aX_{n-1}$$

where $f(X_n)$ is the piecewise-linear discrete function in the cases of Yamakawa and Aihara, and is a smooth quadratic function, $f(X_n) = X_n^2 - 1$ for Henon map. Thus we have demonstrated that the set of 1-D delayed map is mathematically equivalent to a 2-D map without the delay of the Henon type attractor. Then the question remains what is computationally efficient while truly being a 1-D map without the delay?

To stay within the time scale of the classical McCulloch-Pitts (M-P) model of ANN we have modified the instantaneous input-output mapping:

$$v_i(t_{n+1}) = \sigma(u_i(t_n)) = (1 + \exp(-u_i(t_n)))^{-1} \qquad (4)$$

The net neuron input is an instantaneously weighted sum from other neurons,

$$u_i(t_n) \qquad = \qquad \Sigma_{j \neq i} W_{ij}(t_n) v_j(t_n) \qquad + \theta_i(t_n) \qquad (5)$$

which is the original M-P model. The modified neuron is similar to a squid axon measured under normal physiological conditions [37,38] but differs in the delay, given by Szu *et. al.* [17,18], as a piecewise negative logic (i.e. an abnormal or sick neuron having less output with more input near the threshold) which is chosen to be a zero threshold value shown in Fig. 4. This single neuron model is called $\sigma_N$, containing a piecewise negative logic section[13-19]. Heuristically speaking , the negative slope region represents axonal fatigue. In other words, due to the high output pulse rate, the cell can no longer support the housekeeping functions, and it cannot maintain a constant threshold $\theta$. Therefore, $\theta$ is proportional to how rapid the output changes: $\theta \approx d\sigma/du = 4\lambda v(1-v)$, which is the chaos logistic function [13-16]. In the linear region of $\sigma$, $v = \sigma(u-\theta) \approx \sigma(u - 4\lambda v(1-v)) \approx \sigma(u) - \sigma(4\lambda v(1-v)) \approx \sigma_N(u)$. The subtraction of $\theta$ from the input is the source of the dip in the $\sigma_N$ function. Rigorously [16,19], we derive the $\sigma_N$ function from a mean field approximation of the net input $u_i$ that satisfies a recursion relationship $u_i(t_{n+1}) = k u_i(t_n) + [a(t_n) - \alpha \sigma(u_i(t_n))]$ for the refractory delay. The net input $u_i(t_{n+1})$ depends only on the current state $u_i(t_n)$ and no longer on the entire past history, which indicates a *Markovian* chain. We can sum up the refractory delay effect and construct, a pre-squashed N-shape sigmoidal function $v_i(t_{n+1}) = \sigma_N(u_i(t_{n+1}))$ with *no delay*, by means of a graphical method [20]. The function $\sigma_N$ is numerically modeled as follows ( see Fig. 3)

    if ( $u_i <= -1.0$)  return $(1/(1+\exp(-(u_i+1))))$

    else if ($u_i < 1.0$)       return $(-(u_i-1)/4)$

    else               return $(2/(1+\exp(-(u_i-1))))$.      (6)

To avoid the discontinuity points of $\sigma_N$, we have approximated $\sigma_N$ as a cubic map:

$$v_n \qquad = \qquad P_3(u_n) = u_n (u_n + a)(u_n - b)(1/c^2) \qquad (7a)$$
$$u_{n+1} = \qquad v_n \qquad (7b).$$

The cubic map has one attractor at $u=0$, and <u>two</u> repellers of positive slopes at $u = -a$, $u = +b$. It differs from the quadratic logistic or Feigenbaum map of one attractor at and one repeller defined as

$$v_n = P_2(u_n) = 4\lambda u_n (1-u_n) \qquad (8a)$$
$$u_{n+1} = \qquad v_n. \qquad (8b)$$

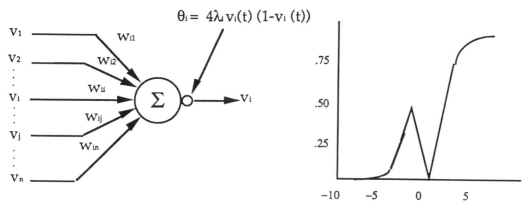

$$\theta_i = 4\lambda v_i(t) (1-v_i(t))$$

## Fig. 4 Biological Conjecture for Piecewise Negative Logic $\sigma_N$ Neuron Model

A class of polynomials $P_N$ similar to Eqs(7,8) can be considered as the complexity increases. In the a=b case, Feigenbaum's peak value at $u_n=1/2$, the λ-knob, is related to the cubic roots (u=±a, u=0) at its maximum location: u=-a/√3 and λ=$a^3$/√3. Aihara et al. changed the shape of $\sigma_N$ (denoted by a smaller letter before the sigmoidal squash) in the parameter space of k and a, and then squashed it further with the sigmoidal σ after a delay, i.e. $\sigma(\sigma_N)\equiv\sigma_N$ after a delay , in order to produce the chaos. The bifurcation route to chaos is through the "square dance"[40] supported (in Fig. 5 Cubic map) on a dotted curve as the second iterate.

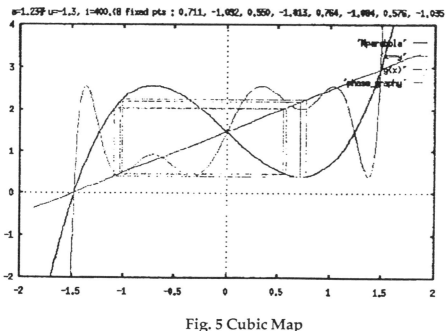

## Fig. 5 Cubic Map

Here, the neuron output is plotted versus the left cubic root, a, and b=0.9, $1/c^2=3/2$. The first bifurcation occurs for a>0.72. From these displays, we conclude that the 1-D map without delay can produce chaos via a bifurcation cascade. This fact is due to the instability of the feedback baseline intersecting the $\sigma_N$ curve when the slope of the baseline changes. As the feedback gain ω increases beyond the absolute value of the slope of the function $\sigma_N$, i.e. 1/4.

Our model has nevertheless produced a Feigenbaum-like bifurcation cascade, which will be shown to belong to the infinite-value, or fuzzy, logic. Our model can learn the synaptic weights, via fixed-point Hebbian dynamics that determine the "mean-weight" governing the iterative feedback between.(i) a fixed-point Hebbian synaptic weight dynamic: $dW_{ij}/dt = -(W_{ij} - [x_i x_j - \delta_{ij}])$ with $x_i \equiv 2v_i - 1$; (ii) an instantaneous input $u_i = \Sigma_j W_{ij} v_j$; and (iii) a piecewise negative logic output

$v_i = \sigma_N(u_i)$. Rather than a single neuron with direct feedback ($y=x$, or $v_i=u_i$), which behaves like a dog that bites its own tail, a modification of the baseline slope $y \neq x$ occurs because the main input $u_i$ must be weighted by the synaptic junctions of all neuron outputs. Thus, the mean weight and its variance characterize an "average" baseline, that provides insight about *collective* chaos [20].

## 4. Conclusion

We compare among Artificial, Biological, and Chaotic NN [23-29] on (i) models, (ii) architectures, (iii) learning methods, and (iv) memory mechanisms as follows:

•Neuron Models

| | |
|---|---|
| ANN | •Simplicity for stable engineering |
| | •Analog or Binary coding |
| | •M.-P. monotonic single-value logic $v_i = \sigma(u_i)$ |
| BNN | •Exploring noise and instability advantages |
| | •Pulse coding for long distance broadcasting, |
| | •Potentiation for short distance synaptic junction |
| | •Refractory delay, bursting, plateau, rebound |
| CNN | •Piecewise negative logic $v_i = \sigma_N(u_i)$ |
| | •Infinite value logic but with a bounded range of outputs |
| | •Markovian instantaneous mapping without refractory delay |
| | •Massive Parallel Chip Implementation without coils. |
| | •Neural chaos dictates fuzzy reasoning dynamics |

•Network Architectures: net input $u_i = \Sigma_j W_{ij} v_j - \theta_i$

| | |
|---|---|
| ANN | •Fixed & Layered Architectures |
| BNN | •Dynamical interconnect networks |
| CNN | •Global interconnection within a functional unit. |

•Learning Methodologies

| | |
|---|---|
| ANN | •Fixed-point (f.p.) dynamics & small perturbation learning: |
| | •Energy landscape concept |
| | (1) Input dynamics (Hopfield) |
| | $$du_i/dt = -\partial H/\partial v_i = -(u_i - \Sigma_j W_{ij} v_j + \theta_i) = 0 \text{ (f.p.)} \Rightarrow \text{M.-P.}$$ |
| | (2) Output dynamics(Cohen-Grossberg) |
| | $$dv_i/dt = -(v_i - \sigma(u_i)) = 0 \text{ (f.p.)} \Rightarrow \text{M.-P.}$$ |
| | (3) Gradient descent dynamics (weight error Backprop.) |
| | $$\partial W_{ij}/\partial t = -\partial E/\partial W_{ij}$$ |
| BNN | •Coherence for adaptation & Synchronicity for consciousness |
| CNN | •Fuzzy dynamics exploring the tolerance of imprecision. |

•Memory Mechanism

| | |
|---|---|
| ANN | •Outer Products, Neighbor Classifiers, Adaptive Resonances |
| BNN | •Long Term, & Short Term Traces Matched Filtering |
| CNN | •Habituation pattern formation and fast Novelty storage. |

• Collective Behaviors in Biological NN and Artificial NN

| | BNN, | ANN |
|---|---|---|
| • Consciousness to mind---Simultaneity to Coherence | yes ? | not yet |
| • Associative Memory---Attractor Basins | yes | yes |
| • Habituation to Novelty ---Bifurcation to Chaotic Orbits | yes ? | yes? |
| • Noisy effects----correlation enhancement for optimization | yes ? | yes |

In order to make a systematic departure to the classical McCulloch-Pitts neuron model that have already extensively been used in the ANN community with, we have previously produced with a minimum change, a pulse coding for periodic and quasiperiodic spikes, as well as irregular to chaotic spikes trains [13,14,15].

Recently, Yanai & Amari showed an increased memory capacity for non-monotonic neurons [41]. For the CNN this is not meant to increase the associative memory capacity, but rather implement pattern recognition dynamics that can efficiently explore the tolerance of imprecisio

In summary, for biological single neuron relationships, we consider incoherence or coherence phenomena, but the community still needs to quantify the degree of synchronicity such as those of partial coherence measure in optics. For collective behaviors, we wish to differentiate the bounded measure of chaotic nonlinear dynamics versus those linear unbounded stochastic noise effect. It is known by the name of the central limit theorem in the probability theory that any noise distribution, constant density or not, so long as the second moment is bounded, in the limit of large sampling, it becomes a Gaussian distribution function (which is extended to the finite domain). While linear noise may be good for the global optimization by the simulated annealing strategy [42,43], nonlinear chaos may be useful for fuzzy reasoning.

(i) All chaotic outputs (of such a single $\sigma_N$-neuron up to $10^5$ $\sigma_N$-neurons) are unpredictable but always bounded. The open chaotic set forms a naturally Fuzzy Membership Function (FMF) of which its time evolution is governed by the CNN. The chaotic output states., unlike the unbounded noise effect, can be dynamically evolving through learning in time.

(ii) The fuzzy characteristics are just the statistical aspect of dynamical chaos that can change the fuzziness by input data to CNN given a desirable imprecision.

The CNN can provide a dynamic Fuzzy Logic learning and reasoning.

Acknowledgement: The authors (Szu & Garcia) acknowledge the support of NSWCDD S. & V. Fund, and (Szu & Rogers) for NSWCDD IR Fund. Discussion with M. Feigenbaum is acknowledged

**References**

[1] L. Zadeh, "Fuzzy Sets," Info & Control , V. 8, pp338-353, 1965.

[2] B. Kosko & S. Isaka, "Fuzzy Logic,"Sci. Am. ,pp. 76-81, July 1993.

[3] J. Dickerson, B. Kosko, "Fuzzy Function Approximation with Supervised Ellipsoidal Learning, WCNN-93 Vol. II, pp.9-17, Portland July 1993.

[4] P. Werbos, "Elastic Fuzzy Logic : A better way to combine Neural and Fuzzy Capabilities,"WCNN, V.II, pp.623-626, 1993.

[5] E. Cox, "Fuzzy Fundamantals,"IEEE Spectrum, pp. 58-61, Ocb. 1992.

[6] E. Cox, "Adaptive Fuzzzy Systems,"IEEE Spectrum, pp. 27-31, Feb 1993.

[7] T. Yamakawa, "A Fuzzy Inference Engine in nonlinear analog mode and its application to a fuzzy logic control""Trans IEEE NN V.4, pp.496-522, May 1993.

[8] S. Kong, B. Kosko, "Adap. Fuz. Sys. for Backing up a truck-&-tailer," T. IEEE V.3, 211-223, 1992.

[9] G. Carpenter, S. Grossberg, D. B. Rosen,"Fuzzy ART: Fast Learning & Categorization of Analog Patterns by An Adaptive Resonanc Systems, V. 4, p. 759-771, 1991.

[10] P. Simpson, "Fuzzy Min-Max N.N.--Part 1: Classification," Trans. IEEE NN, V.3, pp. 776-786, Sep. 1992;"Fuzzy Min-Max N.N.--P. 2: Clustering,"TRans IEEE Fuzzy Sys. V.1, pp32-45, Feb 1993.

[11] P. Grim, "Self-Reference and Chaos in Fuzzy Logic", Trans IEEE Fuzzy S. V.1, pp.237-253, 1993.

[12] H. Szu, L. Zadeh, C. Hsu, J. DeWitte, Jr., G. Moon, D. Gobovi, M. Zaghloul," Chaotic Neurochips for Fuzzy Computing," SPIE Prooceedings, Vol. 2037, (Wisniewski ), pp. 11-16 , July, San Diego 1993.

[13] H. Szu, G. Rogers,"Single Neuron Chaos," IJCNNBaltimore, V.III,pp103-108.

[14] H. Szu, G. Rogers,"Generalized McCullouch-Pitts Neuron Model with Threshold Dynamics,"IJCNN-92 Baltimore, Vol. III, pp.535-540 (June 7-11,92)

[15] H. Szu, B. Telfer, G Rogers, Kyoung Lee, Gyu Moon, M.Zaghloul, M. Loew," Collective Chaos in Neural,Networks," Int'l Joint Conf. Neural Networks, IJCNN-92 Beijing China, Nov 1-6, 1992.

[16] H. Szu, B. Telfer, G. Rogers, D. Gobovic, C. Hsu,M. Zaghloul, W. Freeman, "Spatiotemporal Chaos Information Processing in Neural Networks --Elect.Implent.," WCNN-93, Port. OR, July 1993.

[17] H. Szu,R. Yentis, C. Hsu, D. Gobovic, M. Zaghloul,"Chaotic Models and Artificial Neural Networks,"IJCNN-93 Nagoya, pp. 1473-1476, Nagoya, Oct. 1993.

[18] D. Gobovic, C.C. Hsu, M. Zaghloul, H. Szu, "Chaotic Neuron Models & Their Elect.Circ. Implem.," to appear in Trans IEEE Circuit.

[19] H. Szu, J. Garcia, G. Roger, L. Zadeh, C. Hsu, J. DeWitte, Jr., G. Moon, D. Gobovic, M. Zaghloul, "Neural Network Models for Chaotic-Fuzzy Information Processing," In: Proc. of 2nd Appalancian Conf. on Neurodynamics (Radford U., Sept. 1993 ) (ed. K Pribran, INNS Press, LEA, 1994)

[20] I. Daubechies, " Ten Lectures on Wavelets," SIAM Publ. 1992. p. 146.

[21] M. Barnsley, L. Hurd, "Fractal Image Compression,"AK Peters, Wellesley MA 1993. p. 100

[22] Leon O. Chua, editor of special issue on"Chaotic Systems," Proc. IEEE, V. 75, no.8, 1987;

[23] A. Rodriguez-Vazquez, et al, "Chaos from switched-capacitor circuits: discrete maps," Proc. IEEE v. 75, pp.1109-1106, 1987.

[24] M.Y. Choi, "Dynamic Model of Neural Networks,"Phys. Rev. Lett. V. 61, 2809,1988.

[25] Lipo Wang, E. Pichler, J. Ross,"Oscillations and Chaos in neural networks: An Exactly solvable model," Proc. Natl, Acad. Sci. USA, Vol. 87, pp 9467-9471, 1990

[26] D. Hansel, H. Sompolinky, "Synchronization and Computation in a Chaotic Neural Network," Phys. R. Lett. 68, pp718-721, 92.

[27] E. K. Blum and Xin Wang, "Stability of Fixed Points and Periodic Orbits and Bifurcations in Analog Neural Networks," Neural Networks, V.5, pp. 557-587, 1992.

[28] G. Basti, A. Perrone, V. Cimagalli, M.Giona,E. Pasero, G. Morgavi,"A Dynamic Approach to invariant Feature Extraction from Time-Varying Inputs by Using Chaos in Neural Networks,"IJCNN-91 San Diego,-92 Vol. III, pp505-510.

[29] J. C. Principle, P. Lo."Chaotic Dynamics of Time-Delay Neural Networks," IJCNN-91 San Diego, Vol. II, pp403-409.

[30] K. Aihara, T. Takabe, M Yoyoda,"Chaotic Neural Network,"Phys. Lett A.144,333,1990

[31] E. R. Caianiello,A. Deluca, "Decision equation for binary systems. Application to neural behavior,"Kybernetik Vol. 3 , pp.33-40,1966.

[32] R. Fitzhugh, "Impulses and Physiological states in theoretical models of nerve membrane", Biophysics Vol. 1, pp. 445-466, 1961.

[33] J.Nagumo, S. Sato, "On a response characteristic of a mathematical neuron model," Kybernetik V. 10, pp. 155, 1972

[34] L.D.Harmon,"Studies with artificial neuron I: Propertied and functions of an artificial neuron"Kybernetik V.1,89-101,1961

[35] T. Yamakawa, T. Miki, E. Uchino,"A Chaotic Chip for Analyzing Nonlinear Discrete Dynamica Network Systems," Proc. 2nd. Int'l Conf. Fuzzy Logic & NN, Iizuka, Japan, 1992, pp563-566.

[36] N. Kanou, Y. Herio, K. Aihara, S. Nakamura,"A current-mode circuit of a chaotic neuron model," IEEE Circuit & System Conf. Proceedings, 1993

[37] S.Yoshizawa, H. Osada, J. Nagumo,"Pulse sequence generated by a degenerate Analog neuron model," Bio Cyb. Vol. 45, pp.23-33, 1982.

[38] K. Aihara, G. Matsumoto,"Chaotic oscillations and bifurcations in squid giant axons,"In; Chaos, A.V. Holden (ed), In: Princeton Univ . Press, Ch. 12, p. 257 1986

[39] Gen Matsumoto, K. Aihara, Y. Hanyu, N. Takahashi, S. Yoshizawa, J. Nagumo,"Chaos and Phase Locking in Normal Squid Axons,"Phys. Lett. A123, 162-166, 1987.

[40] D.R. Hofstadter, "Metamagical Themas:Questing for the Essence of Mind and Pattern," Chapter 16 ("Mathematical Chaos and Strange Attractors"), Basic Books : N.Y. 1985, pp364-395

[41] H. Yanai,S. Amari, "A Theory on N.N. with Non-monotone Neurons," ICNN, 1385, 1993.

[42] H. Szu, R. Hartley, "Fast Simulated Annealing," Phys. Letters V. A22, pp.157-162, June 8, 1987.

[43] H. Szu, R. Hartley," Nonconvex Optimization by Simulated Annealing," Proc. IEEE, V. 75, pp. 1538-1540, 1987.

[44] H. Szu & B, Telfer, "Mathematical Theorems of Adaptive Wavelet Transforms," to appear in: Adaptive Wavelet Transforms, 2nd special issue of Optical Engineering, June 1994.

[45] H. Szu, B. Telfer, S. Kadame, "Neural Network Adaptive Wavelets for Signal representation and Classification," In: Wavelet Transforms, special issue of Optical Engineering, Vol. 31, pp. 1907-1916, Sept. 1992.

# CMOS Circuit Implementation to Control Chaotic Neuron

Charles C. Hsu, Mona Zaghloul, Harold Szu*
Department of Electrical Engineering and Computer Science,
The George Washington University, Washington, DC. 20052
* NSWCDD, Code R44, Silver Spring 20903

## Abstract

A chaotic neuron is implemented by a piece wise linear N-shape function as the transfer function of the neuron. The baseline, mapping function, is interpreted as a type of weights between neurons. It can be controlled to drive the neuron into chaos or out of chaos. A voltage-mode CMOS circuit to implement the chaotic neural model is proposed. The existence of chaotic dynamics in a prototype circuit is demonstrated by SPICE simulations. The proposed circuit is applicable to implement a chaotic neural network composed of such neurons on a VLSI chip.

## 1. Introduction

Recently, studies on nonlinear dynamics of artificial neural network and the implementation of the analog circuit have attracted the attention of many authors. Most of the neurons are built up with simple neuron model such as sigmoid function. However, we have to notice that the real neurons are more dynamical than such conventional neurons. Chaotic response of real nerve membranes were reported in electrophysiological experiments with squid giant axons[1]. It shows that a simple dynamical neuron model can easily describe the chaotic dynamics in real neurons. Sufficient evidence also exists to strongly support the hypothesis that the chaos constitutes the basic form of collective neural activity for all perceptual processes[2]. In response to these discoveries that come from neurobiology new models of neural networks composed of chaotic neurons have recently been proposed.[3,4,5,6,7].

In this paper, we propose a model of a chaotic neuron using a PWL N-shape function. The concept of baseline will be introduced and analyzed. The control of this baseline will be developed to drive the neuron into or out of chaos. In addition, the PWL N-shape function composed of an inverter function and a linear function can be changed through this linear function or the power supply of the CMOS inverter. A voltage mode chaotic circuit that implements this chaotic neuron model is proposed. SPICE simulation is demonstrated.

## 2. Chaotic Neuron Model

The history of one of the most prominent models of biological neurons starts with McCulloch-Pitts neuron[8] and Caianiello's description[9]. The neurotic equations are further modified by Nagumo and Sato[1]. Next, Aihara[3] suggested that the output function of the artificial neuron which is a step function in Nagumo and Sato model can be replaced by a continuous increasing function. A chaotic neuron model that has been proposed by Aihara, et. al [3] and derived from McCulloch-Pitts neuron model is defined by the following equations:

$$x(n+1) = kx(n) - \beta f( x(n) ) + B$$
$$y(n+1) = f( x(n+1) ) \tag{1}$$

where $x(n+1)$ is the internal state and $y(n+1)$ is the output of the neuron at the discrete time $n+1$; f is a sigmoid continuous nonlinear output function of the chaotic neuron; B is the sum of all input excitations; $\beta$ is parameters for refractoriness, and k is the damping factor of the refractoriness.

We propose a chaotic neuron model using PWL N-shape function as the following equation:
$$y(n+1) = F( x(n) )$$
$$= h( x(n) ) + \alpha x(n)$$
$$x(n+1) = a y(n+1) + c$$
$$= g( y(n+1) ) \tag{2}$$

where h( x(n) ) is a piecewise linear function in $x_n$, defined as shown in Fig.1. The function g(x) is what refer to as baseline, where the parameters a and c are scalar factors.

The model derived by Aihara differs from the proposed model by the proposed baseline function g(x). Fig.2 shows the comparison between the two models, where g(x) is considered as the "weights" relating to the connection of each neuron to other neurons.

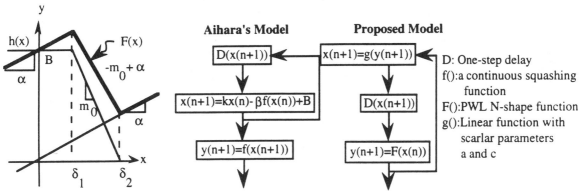

Fig.1 Graphic Composition of N-shape Function    Fig.2 Comparison between Aihara's Model and Proposed Model

To simplify the analysis, we approximate the PWL N-shape function by the following expression:

$$F(x) = \begin{cases} m_1 x + b_1 & x \le \delta_1 \\ m_2 x + b_2 & \delta_1 \le x \le \delta_2 \\ m_3 x + b_3 & \delta_2 \le x \end{cases} \tag{3}$$

The mapping F(x) of equation (2) has two critical turning points and represents the piece wise linear mapping which is well studied in [10,11]. Corollary 2.1 in [11] states the conditions for the existence of the chaotic behavior of equation (2) when a = 1, and c = 0. The results in [11] conclude that the mapping F(x) is chaotic in a region defined by the following set of inequalities, assuming $m_2 < 0$, and a =1, c=0 in equation (2):

*Set A*                                         or        *Set B*

i)    $m_3(1 + m_2) \le -1$              i)    $m_1(1 + m_2) \le -1$        (4)

ii)   $(1 - m_2)b_3 < (1 - m_3) b_2$      ii)   $(1 - m_1)b_2 < (1 - m_2)b_1$

iii)  $\dfrac{m_2^2 b_3 + m_2 b_2 + b_2}{1 - m_2^2 m_3} \le \dfrac{m_2 b_1 - m_1 b_2}{m_2 - m_1}$      iii)  $\dfrac{m_2^2 b_1 + m_2 b_2 + b_2}{1 - m_2^2 m_1} \ge \dfrac{m_3 b_2 - m_2 b_3}{m_3 - m_2}$

Fig.1 is the graphical composition of N-shape function where the mapping function F(x) can be expressed as :

$m_1 = \alpha,$          $m_2 = -m_0 + \alpha,$          $m_3 = \alpha$

$b_1 = B,$          $b_2 = B + m_0 \delta_1,$          $b_3 = 0$          (5)

Therefore, the piece wise linear function that is realized by the proposed circuit can be approximated by the following expression:

$$F(x) = \begin{array}{ll} \alpha x + B & x < \delta_1 \\ (-m_0 + \alpha )x + B + m_0 \delta_1 & \delta_1 \le x < \delta_2 \\ \alpha x & \delta_2 \le x \end{array} \tag{6}$$

The first two conditions from equation (4) guarantee that the baseline crossed the descreasing part of the N function, and that at least one period-three oscillations exists in the unimodal map. These conditions can be expressed in terms of a and c as:

$$\alpha (a - m_0 + \alpha) \le -a^2$$

$$(a + m_0 - \alpha) c > (a - \alpha) ( c - B - m_0 \delta_1)$$

$$(a - \alpha) (c - B - m_0 \delta_1) < (a + m_0 - \alpha) (B - c) \tag{7}$$

Assume for a moment that c=0 (i.e., the sum of contributions of the neurons and external inputs is zero). From condition (7) for the proposed neuron ($\alpha$=0.65, $m_0$=3.65) it can be found that the neuron displays chaos for $0.65 < a < 1.108$. This condition can be observed also from the bifurcation diagram of this case (c=0) shown in Fig.3. However, condition (7) do not cover the chaotic region, $1.108 < a < \sim 1.45$, that is obtained by period doubling. Thus, the chaotic region of a neuron without contribution of other neurons or external inputs (c=0) is $0.65 < a < 1.45$. This is very useful result for learning weights in the neural network. Assume for a moment that the baseline slope is fixed as 1 ( a=1). Then from the conditions given in (7), it can be obtained that the neuron is chaotic if $-0.944 < c < 0.737$, and $2.85 < c < 4.53$. These result also can be observed in Fig. 4 where the full region of chaos of map(2) in the space of parameters a and c is shown. Another simulation in Fig. 5 for fixed Baseline (i.e., a=1 and c=0), to find the bifurcation diagram in function of $\alpha$ (the ration of the linear function of PWL N-shape) is critical.

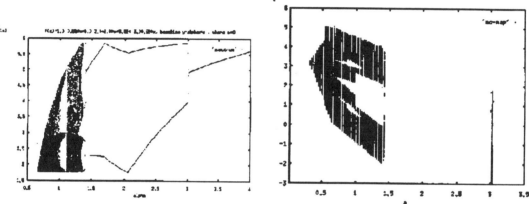

Fig. 3 Cascade spectrum for F(x) vs. a when c=0    Fig.4 Chaotic region of map in space of a and c

As an example, we selected a set of parameters: $\alpha$=0.65, $m_0$=-3.65, B=5, $\delta_1$=1.33, $\delta_2$=2.7, a=1, and c=0. We find out those parameters drive the system into chaos shown in Fig.6.

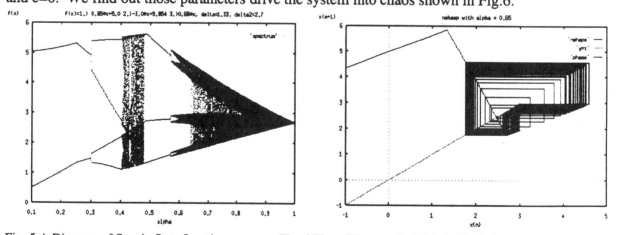

Fig. 5 A Diagram of Steady State Iteration    Fig. 6 Phase Diagram for F(x), PWL N-shape

# 3. Electronic Implementation of the Chaotic Neuron

From the previous section, we can control parameters $\alpha$, a, and c to drive the system. A voltage mode circuit is proposed in this section to implement the chaotic neuron. The neuron model of equation (2) expressed in terms of the PWL N-shape function F(x) and the Baseline function is represented in the block diagram of Fig. 7. The inverter function can be implemented by a CMOS inverter. The voltage divider using two resistors ( one is passive, another is active.) can act as the linear function. The summing circuit , and sample and hold circuit can be implemented by Op amps. The circuit block is shown in Fig.8. The Circuit realization is shown in Fig.9.

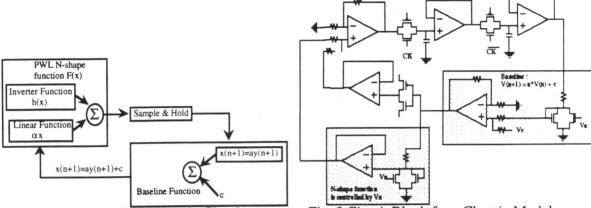

Fig. 7 Block Diagram for a Chaotic Circuit          Fig. 8 Circuit Block for a Chaotic Model

The linear function is implemented by a voltage divider with one passive resistor and one active resistor. Vn is the parameters to control the active resistors. When the Vn increases, the resistance of active resistor decreases. The output voltage is equal to $R_a V_{in}/(R_a + R_p)$ which also decreases, where $R_a$ is the active resistor, and $R_p$ is the passive resistor. Therefore, Vn can be the parameter to control the ratio between these two resistors which can act as the linear function. The SPICE simulations are shown in three cases. 1). When Vn=6.2V, the ratio of the linear function function in the PWL N-shape is o.65, and Vc=0.0 (a=1 is assumed), from Fig.5 we know that the result is chaotic. Fig.10a and Fig.10b show the time series and the phase diagram for chaotic result. 2). When Vn=8.5V, the reatio of the linear function function in the PWL N-shape is 0.5, and Vc=0.0 (a=1 is assumed), from Fig.5 we know that the result is three fixed points. Fig.11a and Fig.11b show the time series and the phase diagram for three fixed points. 3). When Vn=6.2V, the ratio of the linear function function in the PWL N-shape is 0.65, and Vc=1.0 (a=1 is assumed), from Fig.3 we know that the result is convergent. Fig.12 shows the phase diagram for convergent result.

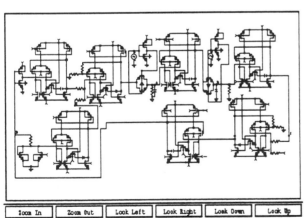

Fig. 9 Circuit Realization for a Chaotic Neuron          Fig.10a SPICE simulation for chaotic result

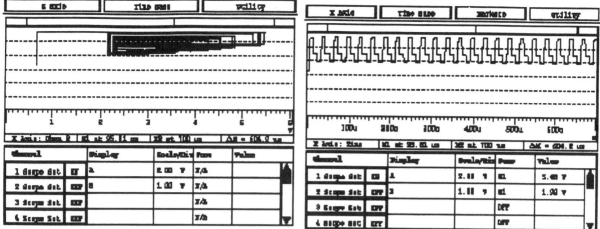

Fig.10b SPICE simulation for chaotic result    Fig.11a SPICE simulation for three fixed points

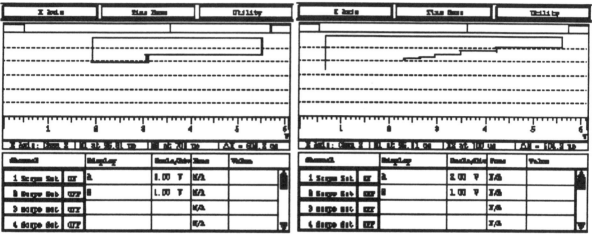

Fig.11b SPICE simulation for three fixed points  Fig.12 SPICE simulation for convergent result

## 4.    Conclusion

A neuron model that displays chaos is introduced.  The model is derived and compared from the well-known Nagumo-Sato and Aihara's neuron model.  The neuron dynamics is described by one-dimensional nonlinear mapping.  Conditions for the chaotic behavior are also given.  The numerical behavior of chaotic neuron is simulated.  An electronic circuit is proposed.  The SPICE simulation is demonstrated.  The proposed circuit model gives a wide hardware-wise flexibility for building different transfer characteristic of a single neuron and for supporting any neural network structure.

## Reference
[1]    G. Matsumoto, K. Aihara, Y. Honyu, N. Takahashi, S. Yoshizawa, J. Naguma, "Chaos and Phased Lockin in Normal Squid Axon," *Phys. Lett. A, vol.* 123, no. 4, pp. 162-166, Aug. 1987
[2]    Christine A. Skarda and Walter J. Freeman, "How brains make chaos in order to make sense of the world," Behavior and Brain Science(1987) pp161-195, Combridge Unversity Press
[3]    K. Aihara, T. Takabe, and M.Toyoda, "Chaotic neural networks," *Phys. Lett. A*, vol. 144, no. 6,7, pp. 333-340, Mar. 1990

[4]    H. Szu, R.Yentis, C. Hsu, D.Gobovic, and M.Zaghloul, "Chaotic Neuron Model and Neural Networks," Accepted to appear in the Proc. of IJCNN, Nagoya, Japan, Oct. 1993

[5]    H. Szu, C. Hsu, J.Dewitte, G. Moon, D. Gobovic, M Zaghloul, "Chaotic Neurochip fro Fuzzy Computing," Invited Paper, SPIE vol. 2037-18, San Diego, July, 1993

[6]    H.Szu, D. Gobovic, C. Hsu, M. Zaghloul, "Spatiotemporal Chaos Information Processing in Neural Networks - Electronic Implementation," WCNN, pp 719-734, Portland, Oregan, July, 1993

[7]    D. Gobovic, C. Hsu, M. Zaghloul, H.Szu, "Chaotic Neuron Models and their Electronic Circuri Implementation," Submitted by Trans Systems IEEE

[8]    W.S. McCulloch, W. H. Pitts, *Bull, Math. Biophys.* 5, pp 115, (1943)

[9]    E.R. Caianiello, "outline of a Theory of Thought-Process and Thinking Machines," *J. Theor. Biol.*, 2, pp. 204-235, 1962

[10]   D. Veitch, "Windows of Stability in Control Chaos, "*IEEE Transcations on Circuits and Systems, vol.* 38, no.38, pp. 808-819, Oct. 1992

[11]   J. Bailieul, R. W. Brocket, R.B. Washburn, "Chaotic Motion in Nonlinear Feedback Systems," *IEEE transcations on Circuits and Systems, vol.* CAS-27, no. 11, pp. 990-997, Nov. 1980

# Switched-Capacitor Chaotic Neural Networks for Traveling Salesman Problem

Y. Horio, [†] K. Suyama, [†] A. Dec, [†] and K. Aihara [‡]

[†]Department of Electrical Engineering and
Center for Telecommunications Research
Columbia University, New York, NY 10027, USA

[‡]Department of Mathematical Engineering and
Information Physics
University of Tokyo, Tokyo, Japan

## ABSTRACT

A 4-city traveling salesman problem is used to demonstrate the capability of switched-capacitor chaotic neural networks. The switched-capacitor neurons used in the network were integrated using a standard 2-$\mu$m, double-poly, double-metal, n-well CMOS technology. The optimum solutions for different sets of network parameters were repeatedly observed from the experiments. *Transient chaos*, a phenomenon needed to achieve global convergence through *chaotic simulated annealing*, is demonstrated using the neuron. This suggests the feasibility of using switched-capacitor neural networks as a hardware optimization engine with efficient global convergence property.

## 1  INTRODUCTION

The application of neural networks to global optimization problems such as the Traveling Salesman Problem (TSP) [1, 2] have been plagued by notorious "local minima" problems although such networks do have a desirable property to converge to a stable equilibrium solution. Neural networks can also provide a hardware solution to optimization problems whose complexity demands high computational efficiency. Nonlinearity is an essential ingredient for the operation of neural networks. Sigmoidal or threshold functions are normally used for the nonlinear function.

Chaotic neural networks, which have recently been proposed by [3], are based on a neuron model with rich nonlinear dynamics including chaotic, periodic, and fixed point responses. The model is a consequence of experimental observations from biological neurons, which exhibit far more complex dynamics than conventional neuron models with "static" response [4]. An important attribute of a chaotic neural network is chaotic search ability [5]. That is, its solution is capable of leaping out from local minima spontaneously and to effectively "visit" the global minimum. This was successfully demonstrated by simulation for the TSP [6, 7] and the dynamic associative memory [8].

Switched-capacitor (SC) circuit technique has been used to design an integrated circuit (IC) chip for chaotic neural networks [9, 10, 11]. This paper demonstrates a 4-city TSP as an application of the IC chip. Empirical explanations are given for a condition to reach the global solution. *Transient chaos*, which is a crucial phenomenon to achieve global convergence through an approach called *chaotic simulated annealing* [12, 13], is also demonstrated using the SC chaotic neuron.

# 2  SWITCHED-CAPACITOR CHAOTIC NEURAL NETWORK

A SC implementation of chaotic neuron with self-feedback strength control is shown in Fig. 1 [9, 10, 11]. The circuit realizes a modified version [12, 13] of the chaotic neuron model [3] as follows:

$$y(t_{n+1}) = ky(t_n) - \alpha T(t)f(y(t_n)) + U(t_n) + \theta \tag{1}$$
$$x(t_{n+1}) = f(y(t_{n+1})) \tag{2}$$

where $y(t_n)$ is the internal state of the neuron at discrete time $t_n$, $U(t_n)$ is the sum of all inputs from other neurons, $\theta$ is an external bias constant, $T(t)$ is the self-feedback strength, $\alpha$ is a parameter for refractoriness, $k$ is the damping factor of the refractoriness, $f(\cdot)$ is a continuous nonlinear function, and $x(t_n)$ is the analog output of the neuron. $h(\cdot)$ in Fig. 1 is a threshold function, which imitates waveform shaping dynamics of axon [3]. $T(t)$ is used to demonstrate transient chaos as shown in Sec. 4. Various design issues, such as the relationships between capacitor ratios and the above parameters, the nonidealities associated with the operational amplifier and nonlinear output function, etc., are discussed in [11].

Figure 2 shows a photomicrograph of the switched-capacitor chaotic neuron. A 2-$\mu m$, double-poly, double-metal, n-well CMOS technology was used to fabricate nine neurons in a chip. No effort was carried out to "pack" as many neurons as possible for this test chip.

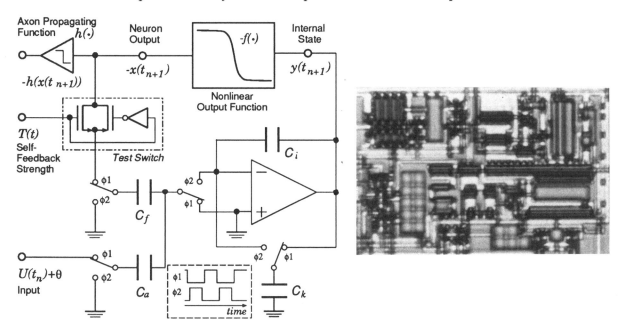

Figure 1: Switched-capacitor chaotic neuron.    Figure 2: Photomicrograph of the chaotic neuron.

# 3  TRAVELING SALESMAN PROBLEM

The TSP is a popular optimization problem for demonstrating the effectiveness of newly proposed algorithms. In this paper, we use 16 SC chaotic neurons to represent a 4-city TSP problem. The representation scheme using a permutation matrix proposed in [1] is used here. Notable difference from [1] is obviously the use of SC chaotic neurons.

Figure 3 describes the experimental setup for the TSP network. OUT $ij$ is interpreted as an $i$th row and $j$th column entry of an $4 \times 4$ square array. "1" at OUT $ij$ means that $j$th city visited

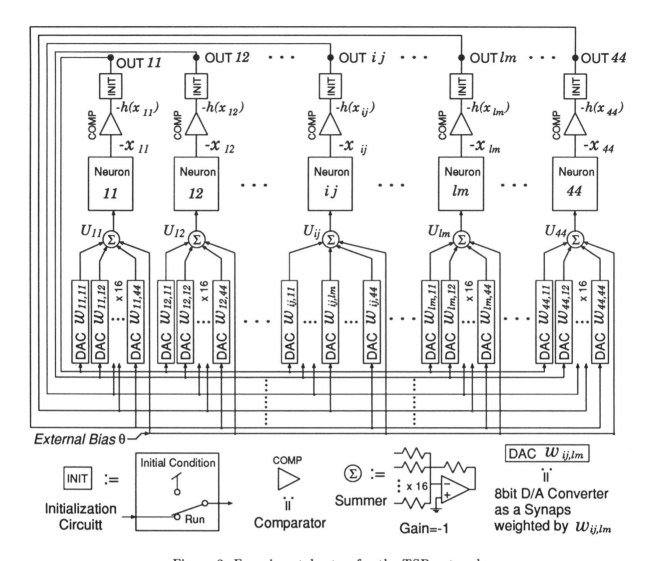

Figure 3: Experimental setup for the TSP network.

is city $i$. The neuron is the integrated SC chaotic neuron whose output, $-x_{ij}(t_n)$ in (1), is an analog value at the output of the nonlinear function shown in Fig. 1. The comparators are used to shape the output to extract the polarity of the signal. The use of the polarity information is appealing in a VLSI environment since the information can be transmitted over a long distance without much degradation in a large IC chip. Synaptic weights $w_{ij,lm}$ are implemented by 256 8-bit Digital-to-Analog converters (DACs) where each weight is set sequentially by a PC through a data acquisition board. Summers are implemented by inverting summers using op amps and precision resistors (0.1 percent tolerance). Initial conditions can be specified through INIT blocks, which consist of switches as shown in the inset of Fig. 3. During an initialization phase, the network is put through a large number of iterations with a given initial condition. Thus, the network is allowed to settle to a consistent state with the given initial condition. The whole network is operated with a 100 kHz clock, which amounts to 100,000 iterations per second.

The energy function to be minimized is defined using the polarity information as follows:

$$E^h(t_n) = \frac{A}{2} \sum_{i=1}^{N} \left\{ \sum_{j=1}^{N} (h(x_{ij}(t_n)) - 1) \right\}^2 + \frac{B}{2} \sum_{j=1}^{N} \left\{ \sum_{i=1}^{N} (h(x_{ij}(t_n)) - 1) \right\}^2$$

$$+ \frac{D}{2} \sum_{i=1}^{N} \sum_{l=1}^{N} \sum_{j=1}^{N} d_{il} h(x_{ij}(t_n)) \times \{h(x_{l,j+1}(t_n)) + h(x_{l,j-1}(t_n))\} \quad (3)$$

where $A$, $B$, and $D$ are positive constants, $d_{il}$ is the distance between cities $i$ and $l$, $x_{ij}(t_n)$ represents the case when city $i$ is visited $j$th at a discrete time $t_n$, and $N$ is the number of cities. As was done in [1], the first and second terms on the right hand side of the above equation represent constraints such that each row and column, respectively, has only one nonzero entry. The third constraint is to minimize the total distance.

The synaptic weights and the bias value $\theta$ can be obtained by:

$$w_{ij,lm} = -A\delta_{il}(1 - \delta_{jm}) - B\delta_{im}(1 - \delta_{il}) - Dd_{il}(\delta_{m,j+1} + \delta_{m,j-1}) \quad (4)$$

and

$$\theta = R(A + B) \quad (5)$$

where $w_{ij,lm}$ is a synaptic weight from neuron $lm$ to neuron $ij$, $\delta_{ij} = 1$ if $i = j$ and $\delta_{ij} = 0$ otherwise, and $R$ is the firing rate parameter. $R$ is a scaling factor which can modify the bias value $\theta$ for a given set of $A$ and $B$ in order to adjust the performance of the network, as will be explained in Sec. 4.

## 3.1 Experimental Results

After the DACs (see Fig. 3) are programmed using the weights computed by (4) for a given problem and an appropriate value of $R$ was chosen (see Sec. 4), we tested the performance of the network by setting initial conditions randomly. For each initial condition, the outputs were observed for the first 10,000 iterations. The collected data is stored in a computer where various analyses are possible. Figure 4 shows a plot of the energy function $E^h(t_n)$ from 300th to 800th iteration when $R = 0.490$ (this corresponds to $\theta = 1.469$ V). Within 10,000 iterations, the network visited local minima 3 times and the global minimum 5 times. From the figure, we can observe that the global minimum was reached even *after* the network reached a local minimum. Although the local minimum shown in the figure suggests that its energy and that of the global minimum differ only slightly, the network can differentiate them distinctly.

Table 1 shows a preliminary result of the statistical performance of the network with 100 initial conditions that are randomly generated. The results suggest a good ability to reach the global minimum though no effort was done, due to time constraint for this publication, to search for a value of $R$ for the best performance.

## 4   DISCUSSION

In a VLSI environment, unavoidable deviations of circuit components due to nonideal effects cause variations in neuron characteristics. However, measurements of the neurons used in the network have shown that their response characteristics are found to be similar. Detail characteristics of a typical SC chaotic neuron from the chip are shown in Fig. 5. The top plot is the bifurcation diagram of the neuron. The second plot shows the Lyapunov exponent $\lambda$ that is computed from

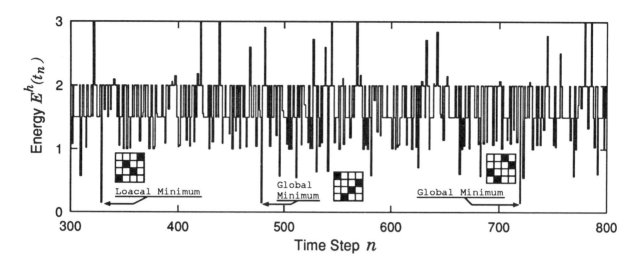

Figure 4: The energy function $E^h(t_n)$ vs. time step for $\theta = 1.469$

the mapping of $y(t_n)$ and $y(t_{n+1})$. The average firing rate $\rho$ is plotted next by computing $\rho = \frac{1}{9000} \sum_{k=1}^{9000} h(x(t_k))$. If $h(\cdot)$ is replaced by the identity function, the average firing rate $\rho_A$ becomes the Angel's staircase [7], as shown in the fourth plot.

The Angel's staircase is valuable to determine the correlation between the average firing rate and the external bias while it is difficult to enumerate a corresponding value for a given external bias using the other plots. This is due to a relatively smooth nature of $\rho_A$. Figure 5 indicates the values of $\rho_A$ and $\theta$ for the three cases shown in Table 1. For each case, the nonlinear map using the measured data is plotted to show the qualitative difference among chaotic attractors. It is premature to draw any conclusions with the limited amount of data. However, the average firing rate and the behavior of chaotic attractor appear to be important parameters to influence the performance of the the network. More detailed experiments are being conducted and the results will be published in [14].

As the plot of $E^h(t_n)$ in Fig. 4 clearly demonstrated, the network has an ability to escape from local minima. However, it is also obvious that the network does not "converge" to the global minimum due to the chaotic dynamics that allow the network to avoid the local minimum traps. Chaotic simulated annealing [12, 13] has been proposed to solve this problem. This takes advantage of a phenomenon called transient chaos, which brings the network into a chaotic state first. Then, by decreasing the self-feedback strength $T(t)$ gradually, the network converged to the global minimum robustly [13] in numerical simulation. Using the test switch shown in Fig. 1, we have demonstrated transient chaos [11]. Figure 6 shows an example of the phenomenon. $\theta$ was 2.006 V and $T(t)$ was decreased from 0.75 V to -0.25 V. Thus, we postulate that SC chaotic neural networks are capable of realizing a physical circuit for chaotic simulated annealing with global convergence property.

## Acknowledgement

The authors thank T. Ikeguchi from Science University of Tokyo for his help with Lyapunov exponent calculations.

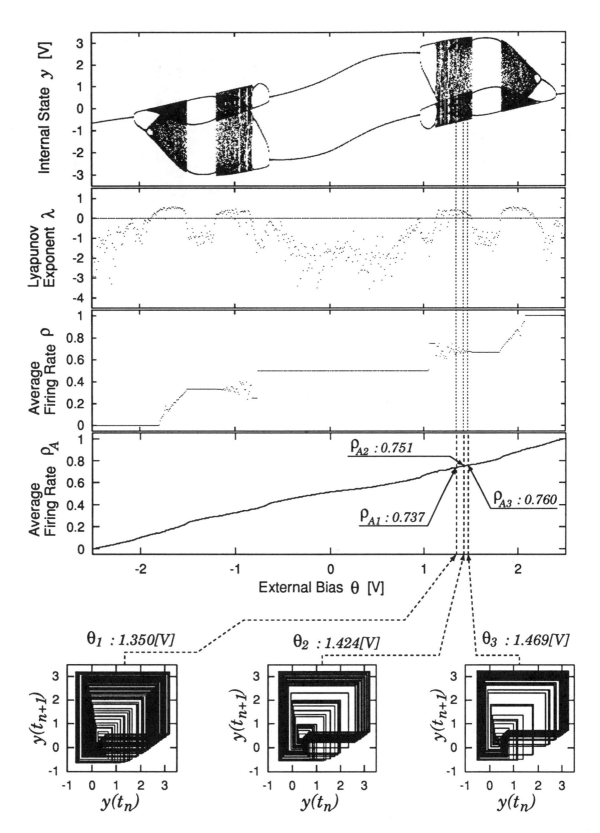

Figure 5: Characteristics of the SC chaotic neuron.

Table 1: Performance of the network

| $\rho_A$ | 0.737 | 0.751 | 0.760 |
|---|---|---|---|
| $R$ | 0.450 | 0.475 | 0.490 |
| Hit Rate to the Global Minimum | 21% | 67% | 71% |
| Hit Rate to Possible Solutions | 72% | 100% | 99% |

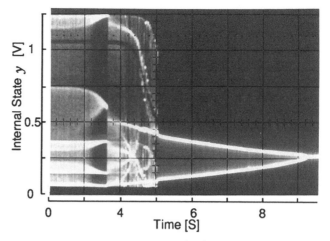

Figure 6: Time evolution of $y(t_n)$ when $\theta = 2.006$V

# References

[1] J. J. Hopfield and D. W. Tank, ""Neural" computation of decisions in optimization problems" *Biol. Cybern.*, 52, pp. 141-152, 1985.

[2] G. V. Wilson and G. S. Pawley, "On the stability of the travelling salesman problem algorithm of Hopfield and Tank," *Biol. Cybern.*, 58, pp. 63-70, 1988.

[3] K. Aihara, T. Takabe, and M. Toyoda, "Chaotic neural networks," *Phys. Lett. A*, vol. 144, no. 6,7, pp. 333-340, Mar. 1990.

[4] G. Matsumoto, K. Aihara, Y. Hanyu, N. Takahashi, S. Yoshizawa, and J. Nagumo, "Chaos and phase locking in normal squid axons," *Phys. Lett. A*, vol. 123, no. 4, pp. 162-166, 1987.

[5] S. Nara, P. Davis, and H. Totsuji, "Memory search using complex dynamics in a recurrent neural network model," *Neural Networks,* vol. 6, no. 7, pp. 963-973, 1993.

[6] H. Nozawa, "A neural network model as a globally coupled map and applications based on chaos," *Chaos,* vol. 2, no. 3, pp. 377-386, American Institute of Physics, 1992.

[7] T. Yamada, K. Aihara, and M. Kotani, "Chaotic neural networks and the traveling salesman problem," *Proc. IEEE Joint Conf. Neural Network '93*, pp. 1549-1552, Nagoya, Japan, Oct. 1993.

[8] M. Adachi, K. Aihara, and M. Kotani, "Nonlinear associative dynamics in chaotic neural networks," in *Proc. 2nd Int. Conf. Fuzzy Logic and Neural Networks*, pp. 947-950, Iizuka, Japan, July 1992.

[9] Y. Horio and K. Suyama, "Switched-capacitor chaotic neuron for chaotic neural networks," in *Proc. IEEE Int. Symp. Circuits Syst.* pp. 1018-1021, Chicago, IL, May 1993.

[10] Y. Horio and K. Suyama, "IC implementation of switched-capacitor chaotic neuron," submitted to *IEEE Int. Symp. Circuits Syst.* 1994.

[11] Y. Horio and K. Suyama, "IC implementation of switched-capacitor chaotic neuron for chaotic neural networks," submitted to *IEEE Trans. Neural Networks.*

[12] L. Chen and K. Aihara, "Transient chaotic neural networks and chaotic simulated annealing," in *Towards the Harnessing of Chaos - Proc. 7th Toyota Conf.*, edited by M. Yamaguchi, Shizuoka, Japan, Nov. 1993.

[13] L. Chen and K. Aihara, "Chaotic simulated annealing by a neural network model with transient chaos," submitted to *Neural Networks.*

[14] Y. Horio, K. Suyama, A. Dec, and K. Aihara, "Engineering applications of switched-capacitor chaotic neural networks," to be published.

# APPEARANCE OF DEVIL'S STAIRCASE IN INTRACELLULAR CALCIUM SPIKES IN RESPONSE TO PULSATILE RELEASE OF NEUROTRANSMITTERS FROM THE BRAIN

Teresa Ree Chay
Department of Biological Sciences, University of Pittsburgh
Pittsburgh, Pennsylvania 15260 USA

## ABSTRACT

The brain releases hormones and neurotransmitters in a pulsatile manner. In response to this, some nerve cells release calcium ions from the intracellular calcium stores (*e.g.*, endoplasmic recticulum). Using a mathematical model presented in this paper, we show that the $Ca^{2+}$ released from the calcium store follows N:M patterns where there are M releases of $Ca^{2+}$ in response to N applications of neurotransmitters. From these patterns, we construct a devil's staircase and then show that the rules governing this staircase are indeed universal. This work thus provides a theoretical explanation for the appearance of blocked and delayed responses of $[Ca^{2+}]_i$ spikes in response to pulsed agonists and demonstrates the existence of universality in such a phase-locking system.

## 1. INTRODUCTION

A wide variety of cells generate repetitive changes in their intracellular $Ca^{2+}$ concentration, $[Ca^{2+}]_i$, when neurotransmitters and hormones that engage in the phospholinositide- (PI-)signalling pathway are applied steadily. Under *in vivo* conditions, however, neurotransmitters and hormones are not released steadily but are released in a pulsatile fashion (Kriebel *et al.*, 1990; Brabant *et al.*, 1992). Thus, how $[Ca^{2+}]_i$ responds to a pulsatile application of agonists is of physiological interest. Using the model presented in Sec. 2, we investigate the effect of a pulsatile application of the agonist on the $[Ca^{2+}]_i$ responses. In Sec. 3, we show that as the frequency of pulse intervals is increased, the system will pass through N:M phase locked regimes, where N is the number of stimuli and M is the number of responses (N>M). By following the method which was designed for the heart rhythms (Shrier *et al.*, 1987), we further show how to predict this type of rhythm using a simple recurrence relationship that relates two successive stimulus durations. Using the predicted N:M rhythms thus obtained, we plot the ratio M/N versus the simulus frequency. Such a plot is given the name "Devil's staircase," because between any two steps there is an infinity of steps, and only the devil is able to climb such stairs. Our staircase, indeed, follows the universal rules of phase-locking nonlinear dynamical systems.

## 2. THE MODEL

The model presented in this section is modified from Example 2 of Cuthbertson and Chay (1991) to accommodate the scheme proposed by Bourne and Stryer (1992). The essence of this model is that a build-up of guanosine-5'-triphosphate-binding proteins ($G_\alpha$-GTP) leads to a sudden activation of phospholipase C (PLC) when four moles of $G_\alpha$-GTP is combined with one mole of PLC. The activated form of PLC (PLC*) is the GTPase activating protein (GAP). GAP is an effector which can produce inositol (1,4,5) triphosphate ($InsP_3$) and diacylglycerol (DAG) from phosphatidyl inositol (4,5) biphosphate ($PIP_2$). $InsP_3$, in turn, can release $Ca^{2+}$ from the endoplasmic reticulum (ER) by activting the $InsP_3$-sensitive $Ca^{2+}$-releasing channel in ER. We assume that the rate of appearance and that of disappearnce of PLC* are enhanced by a DAG-dependent protein (*e.g.*, protein kinase C). The production of DAG and $IP_3$ by PLC* is also enhanced by the same protein.

According to the mechanisms discussed above, the following four simultaneous differential equations provide the core of the model. The first equation describes the dynamic change of $[G_\alpha\text{-GTP}]$,

$$\frac{d[G_\alpha\text{-GTP}]}{dt} = k_g[G_\alpha\text{-GDP}] - 4k_p[G_\alpha\text{-GTP}]^4[\text{PLC}] - h_g[G_\alpha\text{-GTP}] \tag{1}$$

where the first term on the right is an increase of $[G_\alpha\text{-GTP}]$ due to the conversion of $G_\alpha\text{-GDP}$ to $G_\alpha\text{-GTP}$, the second term is a loss of $[G_\alpha\text{-GTP}]$ to form the activated form of PLC, and the third term is due to the hydrolysis of $G_\alpha\text{-GTP}$ back to $G_\alpha\text{-GDP}$.

The second differential equation involves the dynamic change of DAG and InsP$_3$:

$$\frac{d[\text{DAG}]}{dt} = k_d\frac{[\text{DAG}]^2}{K_D^2 + [\text{DAG}]^2}[\text{PLC*}] - h_d[\text{DAG}] + \ell_d \tag{2}$$

where the first term is the production of DAG from PIP$_2$ by the action of PLC*, the second term is a loss of DAG due to other chemical reactions, and $\ell_d$ is a leak term which keeps [DAG] at the basal level. For simplicity, it is assumed that [DAG] and [InsP$_3$] increase with the same rate such that $[\text{DAG}]=[\text{InsP}_3]$.

The third differential equation describes the dynamic change of $[\text{Ca}^{2+}]_i$:

$$\frac{d[\text{Ca}^{2+}]_i}{dt} = k_c\frac{[\text{InsP}_3]^3}{K_s^3 + [\text{InsP}_3]^3} - h_c[\text{Ca}^{2+}]_i + \ell_c \tag{3}$$

where the first term is an increase of $[\text{Ca}^{2+}]_i$ due to the release of Ca$^{2+}$ from the Ca$^{2+}$ store, and the second term is a loss of $[\text{Ca}^{2+}]_i$ due to the Ca$^{2+}$-ATPase pumps, and the third term is a leak which keeps the cell at its basal level of Ca$^{2+}$ in the absence of external stimuli.

The hypothesis that PLC* is GAP gives the following differential equation for the g-protein-PLC complex:

$$\frac{d[\text{PLC*}]}{dt} = \frac{[\text{DAG}]^2}{K_D^2 + [\text{DAG}]^2}\left\{k_p[G_\alpha\text{-GTP}]^4[\text{PLC}] - h_p[\text{PLC*}]\right\} \tag{4}$$

where the first term inside the curly brackets is the formation of PLC* from PLC by the action of $G_\alpha\text{-GTP}$, and the second term is a loss of PLC* due to the hydrolysis of the complex back to $G_\alpha\text{-GDP}$.

In the above equations, $[G_\alpha\text{-GDP}]$ can be related to $[G_\alpha\text{-GTP}]$ by the relation

$$[G_\alpha\text{-GDP}] = G_0 - [G_\alpha\text{-GTP}] - 4[\text{PLC*}] \tag{5}$$

where $G_0$ is the total concentration of the g-proteins. Likewise, [PLC] is related to [PLC*] by the relation,

$$[\text{PLC}] = P_0 - [\text{PLC*}] \tag{6}$$

where $P_o$ is the total concentration of PLC.

In this model, the agonist concentration is equated to $k_g$ (see eqn. 1), whose value increases as the agonist concentration increases. Periodic stimulation was performed under a nonoscillating condition (*i.e.*, $k_g$=0.005) where the cell is quiescent at the resting level of $[Ca^{2+}]_i$=200 nM. Other parameters used for the simulations (unless otherwise stated) are: $h_g$=0.0 s$^{-1}$, $k_d$=700 s$^{-1}$, $h_d$ =100 s$^{-1}$, $\ell_d$=250 nM·s$^{-1}$, $k_c$ = 9.0x10$^4$ nM·s$^{-1}$, $h_c$ = 1.0 s$^{-1}$, $\ell_c$ = 200 nM·s$^{-1}$, $k_p$=2x10$^{-7}$nM$^{-4}$·s$^{-1}$, $h_p$'0.5 s$^{-1}$, $K_s$=300 nM, $K_D$=25 nM, $G_o$=200nM, and $P_o$=10nM.

## 3. RESULTS

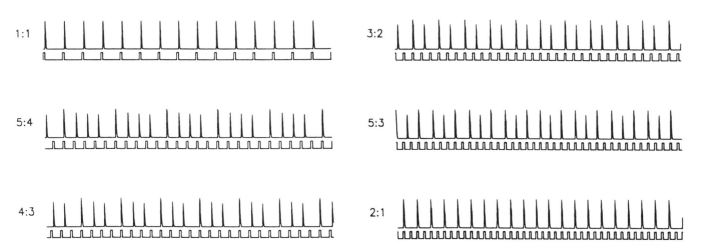

**Figure 1:** $[Ca^{2+}]_i$ spikes (the upper traces) in response to the agonist pulses (lower traces).

The four simultaneous differential equations were solved by an ODE solver. Figure 1 shows phase locking patterns of $[Ca^{2+}]_i$ (the upper trace) in response to repetitve agonist stimuli (the lower traces). As shown in the lower traces, the stimulus is a square in shape with a base of $k_g$=0.005 sec$^{-1}$, a height of $k_g$=0.04 sec$^{-1}$, and a duration of 10 seconds. Here, the 1:1, 5:4, 4:3, 3:2, 5:3, and 2:1 rhythms were obtained by progressively decreasing SS to 70, 54, 52, 45, 38, and 35 seconds. We note that the 5:4 and 4:3 rhythms shown in this figure also occurs in heart patients and is known as Wenckebach periodicity or Mobitz Type I block. The Mobitz type II block (which occurs in abnormal heart rhythms) can also be seen in the 3:2 and 2:1 rhythms. A complex 5:3 reverse Wenckebach rhythm composed of alternating 3:2 and 2:1 cycles can also be seen between the 3:2 and 2:1 rhythms (see the second frame from the bottom). The rhythms shown in this figure also resemble those seen experimentally in squid axons (Hayashi *et al.*, 1982; Matsumoto *et al.*, 1987) and theoretically (Holden and Muhamad, 1984; Aihara and Matsumoto, 1987) using the Hodgkin-Huxley model (1952). The delay and blocking observed here can be explained as follows: According to this model, Ca$^{2+}$ can only be released from the Ca$^{2+}$ stores when $[G_\alpha$-GTP] reaches a critical level. The build-up of $[G_\alpha$-GTP] is slow, and during this build-up $[Ca^{2+}]_i$ remains at its resting level. The response is blocked because not enough $[G_\alpha$-GTP] is created when the agonist is pulsed prematurely.

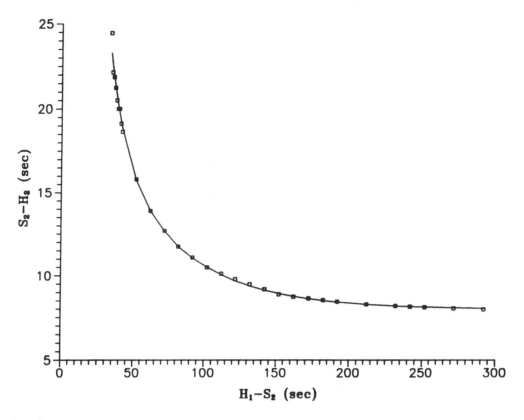

$$SH = 8.0 + 135.19 \ Exp(-9.23 \times 10^{-2} \times HS) + 18.27 \ Exp(-1.95 \times 10^{-2} \times HS)$$

**Figure 2:** **Response time $(S_2\text{-}H_2)$ as a function of the preceding recovery time $(H_1\text{-}S_2)$.**

Figure 2 shows a recovery curve where the response time $(S_2\text{-}H_2)$ is plotted as a function of the preceding recovery time $(H_1\text{-}S_2)$. This curve was constructed from the following scheme. A train of stimuli $(S_1)$ is periodically delivered to the cell at a regular interval of 500 sec. For each stimulus follows a $Ca^{2+}$ response (H) at some later time, where H is recorded when the upstroke of $[Ca^{2+}]_i$ becomes 0.4 µM. We then introduce a premature stimulus $(S_2)$ at the end of the train at intervals less than 500 sec. As in Fig. 1, $S_1$ and $S_2$ are square stimuli consisting of a base of $k_g$=0.005 sec$^{-1}$, a height of $k_g$=0.04 sec$^{-1}$, and a duration of 10 seconds.

The recovery curve shown in Fig. 2 can be fitted to two exponential functions,

$$SH = SH_{min} + \alpha_1 \exp\left[\frac{-HS}{\tau_1}\right] + \alpha_2 \exp\left[\frac{-HS}{\tau_2}\right] \qquad (7)$$

where SH stands for $S_2\text{-}H_2$, HS stands for $H_1\text{-}S_2$, and $HS_{min}$ is $S_1\text{-}H_1$ (the interval between the response and the primary pulse at the steady state), and $\alpha_1$, $\alpha_2$, $\tau_1$, and $\tau_2$ are the parameters to be fitted from the curve. The curve shown by the solid line in the same figure was fitted with the following parametric values: $SH_{min}$=8.0 sec, $\alpha_1$=135.2 sec, $\alpha_2$=18.3 sec, and $\tau_1$=10.8 sec, and $\tau_2$=51.3 sec. Note that in this model it takes at least 8 seconds to respond to an external stimulus, i.e., $SH_{min}$ is equal to 8 seconds.

The recovery curve data can then be used to find the steady-state path on the $SH_{i+1}\text{-}SH_i$ plane (i.e., a plane consisting of two successive responses). This can be done by formulating an iterative function; this function is formulated from eqn. 7 by noting $HS_i = SS - SH_i$ and substituting this equality into eqn. 7,

$$SH_{i+1} = SH_{min} + \alpha_1 \exp\left[\frac{-K(SS)+SH_i}{\tau_1}\right] + \alpha_2 \exp\left[\frac{-K(SS)+SH_2}{\tau_2}\right] \tag{8}$$

where K takes integer values of 1, 2, 3, ..., as discussed in Shrier *et al.* (1987).

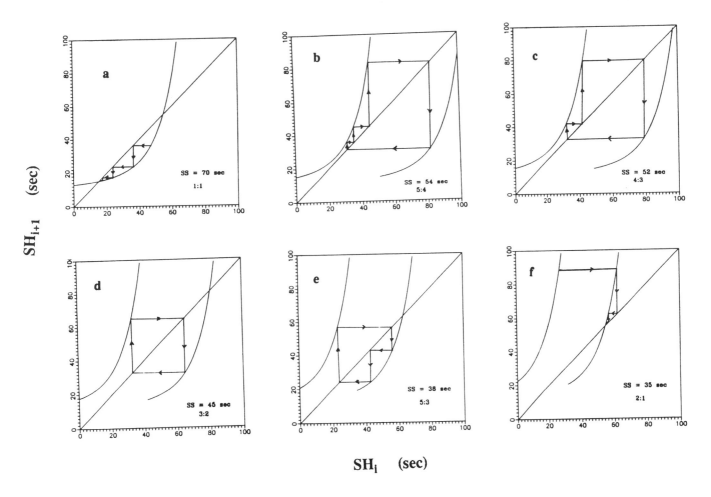

Figure 3: The response time $(S_{i+1}-H_{i+1})$ versus the preceding response time $(S_i-H_i)$.

Figure 3 shows iterative maps of solving eqn. 8 at six different values of the pacing cycle length SS. The diagonal line is the line which lies on $SH_{i+1}=SH_i$. The pacing cycle lengths are given on the figure. The arrowed lines are the steady state paths. The curve shown in Fig. 3 is obtained using K=1 from the above iterative function starting from $SH_i=SH_{min}$, and the upper and lower curves in the remaining figures are obtained using K=1 and K=2, respectively. In these figures, the straight line is a 45-degree line which is obtained using the equation $SH_{i+1}= SH_i$. Here, the SS values decrease progressively from 70 sec, 54 sec, 52 sec, 45 sec, 38 sec, 35 sec. The arrowed lines are obtaining using the following recipe: (i) Starting from any point in the 45-degree line, move vertically until the trajectory hits the curve, (ii) then move horizontally until it hits the diagonal line, (iii) repeat the above two steps over and over again, and finally (iv) stop the process when the trajectory repeats the same path over and over (*i.e.*, when the trajectory enters the steady state path). These iterative maps can generate the N:M patterns shown Fig. 1, and indeed this figure was reproduced by solving the differential equations given in Sec. 2.

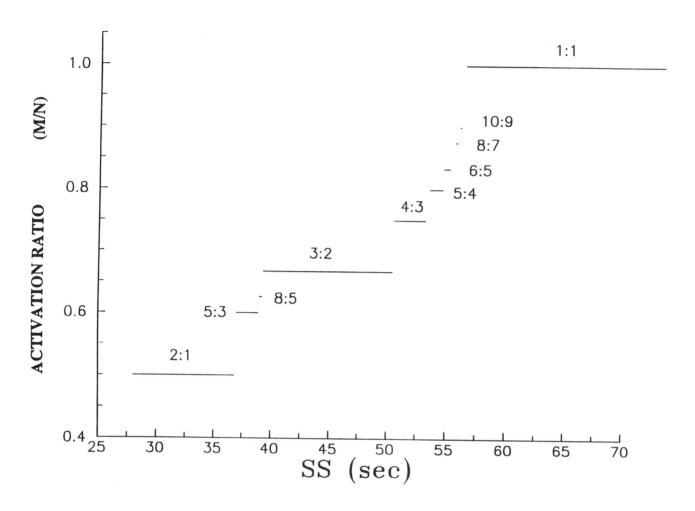

**Figure 4:** **Devil's staicase which shows the ratio (M/N) as a function of stimulus intervals.**

Figure 4 is the theoretically computed M/N ratio (known as the activation ratio) plotted as a function of pacing interval SS, where M number of $Ca^{2+}$ spikes are generated by N agonist pulse stimulation. Here, SS varies between 25 sec and 70 sec. This range covers from 1:1 to 2:1 rhythms. Below 25 seconds exist alternating Wenckebach rhythms and higher grade blockes. Note a close similarity between this figure and that obtained for the heart rhythm of a patient (Shrier et al., 1988). This feature is common in many of phase-locking systems whether they are biological or physical. There are some interesting features associated with this figure. One of these features is the addition rule: It has been shown mathematically that between any two adjacent steps of N:M and N':M' patterns, it is possible to find an additional smaller step whose rhythmic pattern is N+N':M+M' (Keener, 1981). Thus, between the 1:1 and 2:1 rhythms one expects to find an infinity of steps, and the name devil's staircase was derived for this reason. Consistent with this rule, the iterative equation given in eq. 8 gave rise to many steps, as shown in this figure. Other interesting features of this staircase as stated by Peitgen et al. (1992) are: i) It is borderline fractal because it is not self-similar, ii) it has a fractal dimension of 1.0, iii) it has the area equal to 1/2, and iv) its boundary of curve is exactly 2.

## 4. DISCUSSION

We have demonstrated in this paper that the model presented in Sec. 2 exhibits many interesting types of rhythms when the agonists are pulsed periodically. At certain frequency ranges we find phase-locked N:M responses similar to those found in the Hodgkin-Huxley system driven by a train of electrical pulses and types of arrhythmias usually seen in the heart. An interesting aspect of the present study is that Wenckebach-like rhythms in the receptor-operated model follows the devil's staircase. This staircase has the property that between two adjacent steps there are many other types of steps with shorter transition zones. It also follows the addition rule such that between N:M and N':M' rhythms, there is (M+M'):(N+N') rhythm (Keener, 1981). This staircase is boderline fractal in that it has a fractal dimension of unity but is not self-similar (Peitgen et al., 1992). Since the devil's staircase is fractal in nature, it is universal at the transition to chaos (Bak, 1977).

The devil's staircase has been observed in various phase-locked physical systems and its significance has been well recognized (see the discussion by Bak, 1977). However, this paper is the first theoretical demonstration that such a staircase also arises in the calcium release mechanism by the endoplasmic reticulum in response to neurotransmitter pulses from the brain. In addition, we have illustrated a feasibility of observing such a staircase experimentally using a two-pulse protocol. We have also shown that this staircase follows the universal rule in chaos theory. Universality that exists in chaos theory is an interesting subject (Peitgen et al., 1992). This is a contribution to what expect to be an entertaining and enlighting future in cellular $Ca^{2+}$ dynamics.

The work of TRC was supported by the Pennsylvania Chapter of the American Heart Association.

## REFERENCE

Aihara K. and G. Matsumoto. 1987. Forced oscillations and routes to chaos in the Hodgkin-Huxley axons and squid giant axons. In: *Chaos in Biological Systems.* Eds. H. Degn, Holden, A.V. and Olsen, L.F. Plenum, New York, N.Y.

Bak, P. 1986. The Devil's staircase. Physics Today: **22**: 38-45.

Bourne, H. R. and L. Stryer. The target sets the tempo. Nature **358**: 541-543.

Brabant, G., K. Prank, C. Schofl. 1990. Trends Endocrinol. Metab. **3**: 181-188.

Cuthbertson, K. S. R. and T. R. Chay. 1991. Modelling receptor-controlled intracellular calcium oscillators. Cell Calcium. **12**: 97-108.

Hayashi, H., M. Nakao, and K. Hirakawa. 1982. Chaos in the self-sustained oscillation of an excitable biological membrane under sinusoidal stimulation. Phys. Lett. **88A**: 265-266.

Hodgkin, A. and A. F. Huxley. 1952. A quantitative description of membrane current and application to conduction and excitation in nerve. J. Physiol. (London), **117**: 500-544.

Holden, A. V. and M. A. Muhamad. 1984. J. Electrophysiol. Tech. **11**: 135-147.

Keener, J. P. 1981. On cardiac arrhythmias: AV conduction block. J. Math. Biol. **12**: 215.

Kriebel, M. E., J. Vautrin, and J. Holsapple (1990). Brain Res. Rev. **15**: 167-178.

Matsumoto, G., K. Aihara, Y. Hanyu, N. Takahashi, S. Yoshizawa, and J-I Nagumo. 1987. Chaos and phase locking in normal squid axon. Phys. Lett. A. **123**: 162-166.

Peitegen, H-O, H. Jurgens, and D. Saupe. 1992. Chaos and Fractals. New Frontier of Science. Springer-Verlag. New York. pp 220-228.

Shrier, A., H. D. Dubarsky, M Rosengarten, M. R. Guevara, S. Nattel, and L. Glass. 1987. Prediction of complex atrioventricular conduction rhythms in humans with use of the atrioventricular nodal recovery curve. Circulation **76**: 1196-1205.

# BIFURCATIONS AND CHAOS IN PULSING Si NEURONS

A. G. U. Perera, S. R. Betarbet and S. G. Matsik
Department of Physics and Astronomy
Georgia State University
Atlanta, GA 30303.

ABSTRACT—An iterative map is derived from the device equations for a silicon $p^+$-n-$n^+$ diode, which emulates a biological neuron. This map is extended to a coupled neuron circuit which could be used as a single channel of a parallel asynchronous processor. The extended map output is studied under different driving conditions, showing fixed points (both stable and unstable) and limit cycles. The modeling outputs are compared with the experimental outputs which show a Hopf bifurcation. Also shown are the periodic and chaotic responses of a network corresponding to recognition or lack of recognition of IR signals.

A hardware neural network has been constructed. The active element of this artificial neuron is a nonlinear integrate-and-fire $p^+$-n-$n^+$ diode, which acts as a parametrically modulated time series generator. In our previous work, we have described the operation of the diodes which offer promise in terms of providing components for systems which simulate networks of real neurons.[1,2] A spiketrain can be regarded as a physical representation of a time series $T_1, T_2, T_3, \ldots$. We developed a device physics model to explain the pulse output of these devices. By converting this model to a form of an iterative map $T_{n+1} = f(T_n, \{\text{device parameters}, <\text{inputs}>\})$ we can see the nonlinear behavior of the system which include summed and temporally integrated inputs ($<\text{inputs}>$). This can convert spiketrain inputs (as well as graded signal inputs) from other neurons into an analog signal which can exercise parametric control over the generation of a new time series in a network situation. The explicit form of $f$ is associated with the dynamical system (real or artificial neuron, etc).

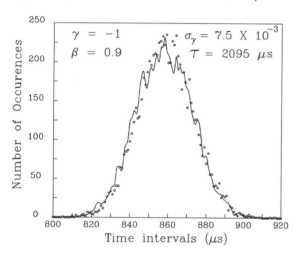

Figure 1: Interpulse time interval histograms for a single pulsing diode. The circles indicate the experimental points and the line is from the iterative map model. The values for parameters used are also given. The space charge noise in $\gamma$ is denoted by $\sigma_\gamma$.

Our model to predict the successive interpulse time intervals (IPTIs) gives an iterative map:

$$T_{n+1} = f(T_n) = \left(1 - [1 - T_n]^{-\beta} e^{\gamma}\right)$$

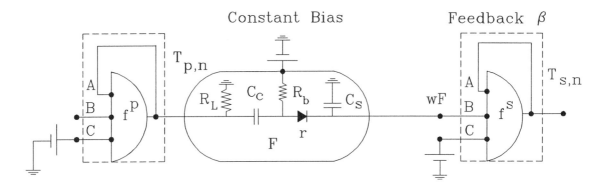

Figure 2: The circuit diagram used in both the experiment and the model, showing the coupling of two pulsing diodes. The dashed areas represent the pulsing diodes in the experimental circuit. B and C terminals refer to the transient and constant inputs to the circuit. The transfer functions of the secondary and primary pulsing diodes are denoted by $f^s$ and $f^p$. The transfer function of the filter circuit used in the coupling is $F$ and $wF$ is weighted output of the filter. The filter values are $R_L = 310K\Omega$, $C_c{=}0.01\mu F$, $R_b{=}150K\Omega$ and $C_s{=}0.07\mu F$.

where $\beta$ is the feedback gain and $\gamma$ is the dynamical space charge variation noise factor. The time interval from the model is a dimensionless ratio of the real time interval between spikes and a factor $\tau$. The parameters depend on the inputs and device parameters. The results obtained using this model for a single pulsing diode are shown in Fig. 1 as a fit to the experimental data obtained.

If a secondary pulsing diode unit is connected (see Fig. 2) to a primary pulsing diode ($f^p$), through a filter ($F$), the iterative map of the secondary unit ($f^s$) becomes

$$T_{s,n+1} = f^s\big(wF(T_{p,n-1}) + T_{s,n}\big) \quad \text{where} \quad T_{p,n-1} = f^p(T_{p,n-2})$$

where

$$f^a(T_{a,n}) = 1 - e^{\gamma_a}\big(1 - T_{a,n}\big)^{-\beta_a} = T_{a,n+1} \quad (a = \text{s or p}) \quad \text{and} \quad F(T_{p,n}) = \frac{T_{p,n}\tau_p}{2\pi r C_s}$$

For the primary diode with a constant input $\beta_p = \lambda/T_{p,n}^2$ is a constant as $T_{p,n}$ stabilizes to a constant time interval which is the mean of a normal distribution due to noise (Fig. 1). For time varying inputs (e.g. with another pulsing diode as input) the mean time interval $T_{s,n}$ varies. Hence $\beta_{s,n} = \lambda/T_{s,n-2}^2$ where the delay (from $n$ to $n-2$) is due to signal transmission delays of a single pulse in the primary diode, the filter circuit and the secondary diode.

To simplify the map we we remove the subscripts for the secondary and primary units and substitute $(1 - T_n) = X_n$, $K_1 = 1/wF$ and $K_2 = wF\exp(\gamma)$. We can consider the feedback $\beta_n$ to be a phase parameter similar to the map parameter $T_n$, as it is physically responsible for transferring a portion of the device output back to the input after a delay. Our map is equivalent to a third order difference equation. Hence we can convert it into a second order planar map [3]. The resulting delayed map has the form

$$X_{n+1} = K_2\big(X_n - K_1\big)^{-\lambda/(1-X_{n-1})^2}. \tag{1}$$

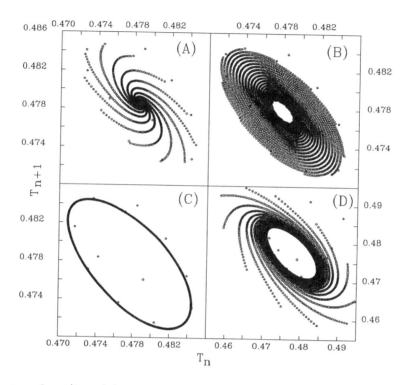

Figure 3: Model output for $\gamma/\lambda =$ (A) 8.18, (B) 8.159, (C) 8.1567, and (D) 8.14. We can observe a Hopf bifurcation from (A) to (C). At (D) the limit cycle has grown so that only the unstable fixed point is visible. The successive points do not move along the spirals seen but instead jump between the branches (skipping three branches) around the pattern moving steadily inward or outward. The other parameters are $\gamma_s$=-1, $\gamma_p$=-1, $\beta_p$=0.125, $T_{n,1} = 0.5$.

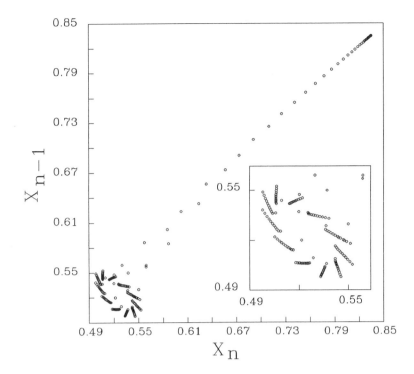

Figure 4: The unstable fixed point obtained by the time reversal of Eqn. 1 for the parameters shown in Fig. 3D. The inset shows the unstable limit cycle has 11 arms corresponding to the $11^{th}$ root of -1 for a nearby value of the control parameter.[3] $X_n = 1 - T_n$, $X_{n-1} = 1 - T_{n-1}$.

The series obtained by time reversal of the map in Eqn. 1 converges to a fixed point as seen Fig 4, indicating an unstable fixed point in the original map.

Using the embedding $X_1^n = X_n$, $X_2^n = X_{n-1}$, $X_3^n = X_{n-2}$ we obtain the following form for the map in Eqn. 1

$$X_1^{n+1} = K_2 (X_1^n - K1)^{-\lambda/(1-X_3^n)}$$
$$X_2^{n+1} = X_1^n$$
$$X_3^{n+1} = X_2^n.$$

This has a fixed point at (0.83507, 0.83507, 0.83507). Constructing the Jacobian matrix for this map we obtain the following expression for the eigenvalues

$$\mu^3 + \frac{\lambda K_2}{(1-X_3)^2}(X_1 - K_1)^{-1-\lambda/(1-X_3)^2}\lambda^2 - \frac{2K_2\lambda}{(1-X_3)^3}(X_1 - K_1)^{-\lambda/(1-X_3)^2} = 0$$

Evaluating this at the fixed point (0.83507) we obtain eigenvalues of -3.41875 and -3.967±3.41875$i$. Since these all have modulus greater than 1 the fixed point is unstable. This confirms the fixed point shown in Fig. 4 for the time reversed map.

The network output is extremely sensitive to changes in the $\gamma/\lambda$ ratio which is equivalent to the diode bias. This is illustrated in Fig 3, where a small change in the ratio, (in absence of noise) results in the stable fixed point being converted to a limit cycle (Hopf bifurcation). As the control parameter is decreased the limit cycle grows until only the

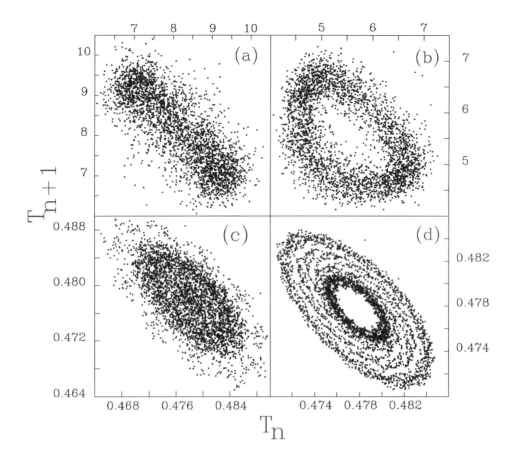

Figure 5: Experimental interpulse time interval ($T_n$) data for constant bias of (a) 4.7 V and (b) 4.8 V. The model output from the circuit in Fig. 2, with (c) $\gamma_s/\lambda = 8.17$ and (d) $\gamma_s/\lambda = 8.1567$. We observe a Hopf bifurcation from a stable fixed point (a,c) to a limit cycle (b, d). The common parameters are $\beta_p = 0.125$, $\gamma_s = \gamma_p = -1$, the noise $\sigma_s^\gamma = \sigma_p^\gamma = 10^{-3}$ and the coupling $w = 10^{-4}$.

unstable fixed point at its center is visible in Fig. 3(D). Dynamic noise in a diode can be a stabilizing factor and may produce a limit cycle. The two diode experimental circuit gives a rich spectrum of nonlinear behavior depending on the driving parameters. For example under a constant sub-threshold bias (to C terminal in Fig. 2) and a transient input B (the pulse output $T_p$ through a filter, equivalent to a weighted ($w$) transfer function $F$ in the model) the 2-D return map shows a stable fixed point as indicated in Fig. 5 (a). A stable fixed point is seen for the experimental data at a constant bias of 4.7 V in Fig. 5 (a). As the constant bias is increased to 4.8 V a Hopf bifurcation[3] occurs producing the limit cycle in Fig. 5 (b). A similar effect is seen for the model results in Fig. 5 (c) and (d).

When this device is used as an IR detector, the output time series $T_n$ with $n = 1, 2, 3 \ldots$ can create patterns which can be called mode locked when the output follows a periodic pattern of pulsing such that $T_n$ is a periodic function of $n$. In Fig. 6 we illustrate 'recognition' of color temperature 220K via period-9 mode locking. This is similar to the suggestion made by Skarda and Freeman[4] saying recognition corresponds to periodic (oscillatory) network response and novelty or lack of recognition corresponds to nonperiodic, chaotic response.

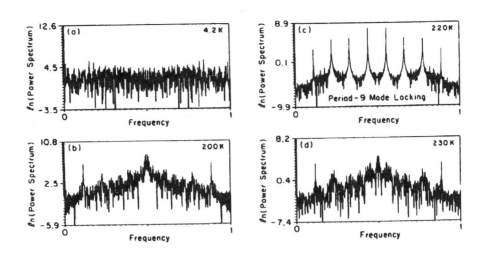

Figure 6: Power spectra obtained by Fourier analysis of 1024 measured interpulse time intervals at 9.138V bias for different blackbody source temperatures: a) 4.2K b) 200K c) 220K d) 230K. The vertical axis has a logarithmic scale. The frequency variable on the horizontal axis is the inverse of the time series periodicity.[2]

Acknowledgment: This work was supported in part by the U.S. NSF under contract # ECS-9296238.

# References

[1] D. D. Coon and A. G. U. Perera, Int. J. Electronics **63**, 61 (1987).

[2] D. D. Coon and A. G. U. Perera, *Photon Detection with Parallel Asynchronous Processing* in **Visual Communications and Image Processing '90 - SPIE Volume 1360**, SPIE, 1990, pp. 1620-1630.

[3] J. Hale and H. Koçak, *Dynamics and Bifurcations*, Springer-Verlag, New York, 1991.

[4] C. A. Skarda and W. J. Freeman, Behavioral and Brain Sciences **10**, 161 (1987).

# Developing Multiple Attractors in a Recurrent Neural Network

Judith E. Dayhoff*, Peter J. Palmadesso**, Fred Richards**

* University of Maryland
College Park, MD 20742

.

** Plasma Physics Division
Naval Research Laboratory
Washington, D.C. 20375

February 15, 1994

### Abstract

Neural networks with recurrent connections and nonlinear squashing functions are capable of dynamic activity, including periodic and quasi-periodic oscillations, and chaotic attractors. Here we explore the development of attractors by changing the neural network's weights according to a perturbation schedule that depends on previous success in developing attractors. The networks were rewarded for developing multiple attractors. The resulting networks demonstrate capacity that could ultimately be tapped for pattern classification and optimization tasks.

## 1  Introduction

Recurrent neural networks are capable of rich dynamic behavior that can potentially be used for recognition, optimization, and control applications. Unlike feed-forward networks, which are static, networks with recurrent connections can exhibit periodic oscillations, quasi-periodic oscillations, and chaotic attractors as well as fixed point attractors. In applications, these attractors could represent pattern classes, memories, optimization solutions, or control actions. Different sets of initial states or initial spatiotemporal stimuli could drive the network into these different final attractors. Thus, it is key to develop networks with multiple attractors that can be triggered by known initial conditions.

When attractors are not limited to fixed point stable states, new attractors are possible, including quasi-periodic oscillations and chaotic attractors as well as periodic oscillations. In the computational paradigm suggested by Hopfield, optimization and memory recall is performed when the network settles into a fixed point attractor, but the capacity is highly limited and the basins of attraction are not adjusted to cover the desired regions. A key to overcoming these limitations is to explore networks with multiple higher-order (non-fixed-point) attractors and to vary these attractors with weight changes.

In this paper we report observations on networks with recurrent connections, positive and negative activation values, non-linear squashing functions, and asymmetric weights. With random weights and initial states, a single attractor was usually observed. To generate multiple attractors, we developed a perturbation method that successively perturbs weights and saves values that led to increased numbers of attractors.

## 2  Network Structure

The neural networks were single layer networks with recurrent connections. Each pair of units had bidirectional connections; weights on these reciprocal connections did not have to be the same (e.g. $w_{ij} = w_{ji}$ or $w_{ij} \neq w_{ji}$). The networks were fully connected or sparsely connected, with some weights set to zero. Activation levels were determined by the following equation:

$$a_j(t+1) = f(\sum_{i=1}^{N} g w_{ji} a_i(t)) \tag{1}$$

where $a_j(t)$ = activation of unit j at time t, $w_{ji}$ = weight to unit j from unit i, $N$ = the number of processing units, the function $f$ is a squashing function, and $g$ a multiplier, set to 1.0 during our perturbation experiments. Although a variety of functions may be used for $f$, we have used a symmetric sigmoid (tanh) function as follows in our simulations, $f(x) = (1/(1 + e^{-x}) - 0.5) * 2.0$, which allows activation values to vary from -1.0 to 1.0.

## 3  Attractors

Neural networks were generated with random weights in fully and sparsely connected configurations. Configurations were denoted (N,K), meaning N units and K incoming connections to each unit. Source units for the K non-zero incoming connections were chosen at random. Weights and initial states were generated at random from a uniform distribution (-1.0:1.0].

Transitions from fixed point attractors to chaotic attractors were observed as g was increased starting from numbers below 1.0, with N=64 and K=16 or 64. The average activation at time t ($\bar{a}(t)$) was calculated, and $\bar{a}(t+1)$ versus $\bar{a}(t)$ was graphed. Transients were not included in the graphs, thus attractors projected to $\bar{a}(t)$ were shown. As noted by Doyon et al [1], increasing factor g caused a progression of graphs to be generated, starting with a single fixed point and bifurcating into limit cycles and eventually to a chaotic attractor [2]. Transition to chaos happened rapidly, with changes in the first to fourth decimal place of g.

Figure 1 shows an attractor projected as $\bar{a}(t+1)$ versus $\bar{a}(t)$. This attractor occurred after 1000 initial steps were skipped, to avoid transients. The network had N=64, K=16. Factor g=1.3, which was above the region with only a fixed point attractor and lower than the region where a chaotic attractor appears. The attractor in Figure 1 is symmetric, as inclusion of point (x,y) always occurs with inclusion of point (-x,-y). This there is a $180°$ rotational symmetry about (0,0). This symmetry results from the symmetry in the squashing function, which allows both negative and positive activation values.

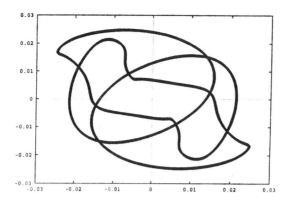

Figure 1: Symmetric attractor, $\bar{a}(t+1)$ versus $\bar{a}(t)$. This structure represents a quasi-periodic oscillation and is produced from a dense set of dots.

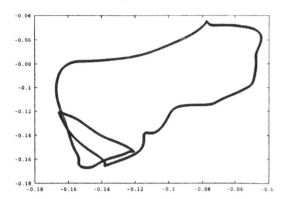
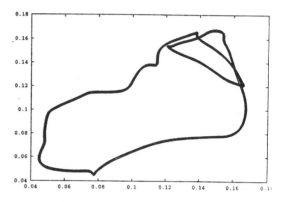

Figure 2: Two attractors, symmetric, from same network. These structures represent quasi-periodic oscillations.

Figure 2 shows a pair of attractors found in a network with N=64 and K=64. Taken together, they possess the same symmetry as the single attractor in Figure 1 - $180^o$ rotation about (0,0). They result from different initial states of the same network. As before, 1000 steps were skipped to avoid transients. In this network, g=1.5, which is between the fixed point and chaotic regions.

Experiments were done to see whether different attractors resulted from different initial conditions in the same network (e.g. with the same weights fixed). Initial conditions were generated from a uniform random distribution for each entry, (-1:1], and used as initial states in the network. Iterations forward passed through transients, and the attractors reached after the transients were graphed. Usually different initial states produced the same attractor (as projected onto $\bar{a}(t)$) or the attractor's inverse, in which each point of the attractor was multiplied by -1.0 (e.g. Figure 2). Rarely could we find situations where different initial states produced different attractors for a randomly selected set of weights and initial activations. In the case of Figure 1, all initial states resulted in the same (symmetric) attractor. In the case of Figure 2, some initial states resulted in the attractor in Figure 2(a) and other initial states resulted in the attractor in Figure 2(b), its symmetric counterpart.

Thus multiple dynamic attractors did not usually appear to occur in a neural network built from random weights with random initial conditions. This result motivates the development of paradigms that find weights that produce multiple dynamic attractors that can be accessed from different initial states.

# 4 Perturbation

A training schedule was devised with the goal of developing multiple attractors within the same network, accessed by different initial states. Attractors were not limited to fixed points and reciprocal weights were not limited to equal values.

A perturbation schedule is applied to the weights in which random numbers are added to a randomly selected subset of weights in the network. In each iteration a set of $q$ weights, $(w_1, w_2, ..., w_q)$ is selected at random and perturbed as $w_i = w_i + m\epsilon_i$ where $\epsilon_i$ is a random variable and $m$ a multiplier. The new network is then tested with a set of initial states $\mathbf{B_i}$ ($i = 1, 2, ..., n_B$). For each initial state, the network is iterated forwards past transients, using (1), until an attractor or final set of states is reached and the attractor is classified as fixed point ("order 0"), an $n$-cycle oscillator ("order $n$"), or a final state with no observed repeats. Performance is then evaluated according to one of the following: (1) number of distinct attractors, or (2) number of distinct $n$-cycle attractors ($2 < n < max$). At each perturbation, if performance is better with the perturbed weights, then the new weights are saved. Otherwise the perturbations are discarded.

Thus, each perturbation is governed by the following parameters: the quantity of weights $q$ and the multiplier $m$. A perturbation schedule is proposed, to vary these parameters. The user choses an initial value for each parameter. A parameter is changed incrementally whenever a perturbation fails to increase performance, and is also changed whenever a perturbation succeeds in increasing performance. Parameters that dictate the amount of change in the values are chosen by the user. These parameters are: $m_f$ = the amount added to $m$ upon failure, $m_s$ = the amount added to $m$ upon success, $q_f$ = the amount added to $q$ upon failure, and $q_s$ = the amount added to $q$ upon success. Either parameter or both may be adjusted for the perturbation schedule. At any point the user may manually reset these parameters.

Typically, the initial value for $m$ and $q$ are chosen to be so low that early perturbations do not increase performance. Changes upon failure would be small positive numbers. Changes upon success would be larger negative numbers, so that the successful region would be scanned again. Alternatively, the parameters can be started large and changes scan downwards to smaller numbers during perturbation, until successful regions for change are found.

With the perturbation schedule, the network explores values of $q$ and $m$ that tend to produce more attractors or more n-cycle attractors ($n > 1$). Preliminary explorations showed that particular ranges of each of these values are auspicious for increasing performance of the network.

The results of the perturbation analysis depend on the set of initial states $\mathbf{B_i}$ used. This set should include a representative sample of initial states needed for typical applications. In our test cases we generated initial states from a uniform random distribution.

Initially the weights are set at small random numbers, but can be set deterministically,

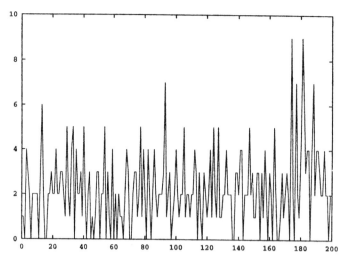

Figure 3: Number of attractors as a function of iteration.

also. For example, initial weights calculated from a Hopfield associative memory [3] starts the network with multiple fixed-point attractors.

# 5 Results

Figure 3 shows the results from a 10-neuron network that was subjected to 200 perturbations taken from a uniform random distribution [-1:1]. The network was fully interconnected, and initial weights were small random numbers from a uniform distribution [-1:1]. The number of attractors is plotted for each iteration of weight perturbations. Only when the number of attractors exceeded the previous maximum were the weight perturbations saved. The perturbation schedule had $q = 50$, $m = 1$, with no changes in $m$ and $q$ over time. Iterations reported as 0 attractors usually had exceedingly long transients and thus only transients were found.

The final number of attractors developed in this example was nine, and all were of order 2 (2-cycles). Some 2-cycles were inverses of others (e.g. multiplied by -1). Thus at least 5 distinct attractors were present. This contrasts with the Hopfield Network memory, which produces approximately 0.15n memories for n processing units, which would limit the system to under 2 usable attractors for 10 units. Thus it appears that new paradigms are possible with the more flexible networks used here.

Figure 4 shows results from another 10-neuron network subjected to 200 perturbations. Parameters $q = 20$, $m = 1$ initially, $m_f = 0.1$ and $m_s = -2.0$. On iteration 30, 12 attractors were found and on iteration 185, 13 attractors were found. The 12-attractor network had all 2-cycle oscillator attractors, whereas the 13-attractor network had twelve 4-cycle oscillators and one 2-cycle oscillator.

# 6 Discussion

To exploit the rich dynamic behavior of neural networks for computational purposes, we must first be able to build dynamic attractors into a network through weight adjustment.

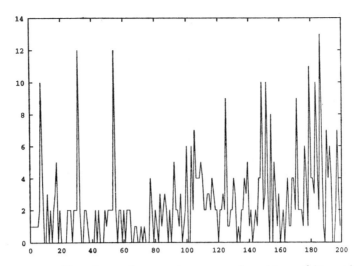

Figure 4: Number of attractors as a function of iteration.

Although previous work by Doyon et al [1] demonstrated transitions from fixed-point to chaotic attractors, it did not show how multiple distinct attractors were developed and accessed through unique initial states. In this paper we have used the number of attractors as the performance criterion when developing weights in a recurrent neural network. A perturbation schedule changed groups of weights randomly, and networks with increased numbers of distinct attractors were saved. Attractors can be fixed point or $n$-cycle oscillators and the number of attractors was increased in an accretional fashion by the network. The number of attractors developed exceeds the capacity of the Hopfield network associative memory. In associative memory applications, the dynamic networks used here offer a wide repertoire of differing basins of attraction with complex boundaries, and, as a result, exceed the limited set of boundary basins available in the Hopfield associative memory.

# 7   References

1. B. Doyon, B. Cessac, M. Quoy, and M. Samuelides, 1993. Control of the transition of chaos in neural networks with random connectivity. Int'l J. Bifurcation and Chaos 3(2): 279-291.

2. H. Sompolinsky, A. Crisanti, and H. J. Sommers, 1988. Chaos in random neural networks. Phys. Rev. Lett. 61: 259-262.

3. J. J. Hopfield, 1984. Neurons with graded response have collective computational properties like thos of two-state neurons. Proc. Natl. Acad. Sci. USA, Biophysics 81: 3088-3092.

**Acknowledgements** The first author was supported by the Naval Research Laboratory (Special Project on Nonlinear Systems and Contract N00014-90K-2010), and the National Science Foundation (Grants CDR-88-03012 and BIR9309169). The other authors acknowledge support from the Office of Naval Research. Thanks to Ira Schwartz and Ed Ott for stimulating discussion of related topics. Fred Richards is currently at Entropic Research Laboratory, Inc., 600 Pennsylvania Ave. S.E., Suite 202, Washington, D. C. 20003.

# Chaos as a Network Mechanism
# for Endogenous Generation of Variability in Behavior

John Fiala, Steve Olson

Department of Cognitive and Neural Systems, Boston University
111 Cummington St., Rm. 244, Boston, MA 02215

## Abstract

A neural network is presented which exhibits random variability as an emergent property of the network. The chaotic dynamic of the network provides endogenous random generation useful for learning sensorimotor kinematics of visually-guided arm movements. The network is a variant of the gated dipole with feedback which, in contrast to previous models, does not rely on large amplitude noise for random behavior.

## 1. Introduction

Many recent authors have noted the importance of self-generated behavioral variability to adaptation (Conrad, 1986; Gaudiano & Grossberg, 1990, 1991; Kelso & Dung, 1993; Mpitsos, et al, 1988). In order to find and learn the most successful behavior, an organism must be able to internally generate a spectrum of possible behaviors from which to choose. In the absence of familiar stimuli for which an appropriate response has been learned, the organism must have an internal mechanism which introduces variability in behavior. If the organism relies only on external stimuli to determine behavior, then the set of possible actions is limited and therefore the adaptability of the organism is also limited. Endogenous (or internal) mechanisms for random generation allow exploration of a behavioral domain to improve adaptation. Such themes are familiar, of course, in theories of evolution by natural selection. What has been suggested, however, is that if variability improves the adaptive process then it is in the interest of the organism to be able to generate that variability internally, by mechanisms which it can regulate, rather than relying on externally imposed randomness (Conrad, 1986).

In the behavioral domain, an important theoretical question is how a plausible neural network can generate random behavior useful for adaptation. Models of endogenous random generation rely on built-in sources of noise to provide variability. This noise, as will be described for the model of Gaudiano and Grossberg below, is generally an assumed source of randomness which introduces the property of variability into the model equations. It is possible, however, to construct a neural network which has random variability as an emergent property of the network equations themselves, without input from external sources of randomness. An example of a network with this type of emergent property is the subject of this paper.

Many neural networks which exhibit chaotic dynamics have been described (King, 1991; Basar, 1990). Chaos has been known to arise in feedback gated dipole networks for at least a decade (Carpenter & Grossberg, 1983). In the gated pacemaker model, Carpenter and Grossberg found that for a certain shape of neural transmission function the system could exhibit an irregular oscillation indicative of chaos. The functional role of chaos has not been resolved, however, despite much speculation as to possible roles for chaos in biological systems (Conrad, 1986; King, 1991; Skarda & Freeman, 1987). We show how chaos in neural networks can be used to generate randomness useful for adaptation. An example is given of how the chaotic dynamic of a particular network may provide endogenous random generation of sample training vectors useful in learning the sensorimotor kinematics of visually-guided arm movements. We begin by describing the original endogenous random generator model of Gaudiano and Grossberg (1990). Our model is a simple modification of their basic circuit, the gated dipole with feedback.

## 2. The ERG Circuit

In the vector associative map (VAM) model of motor learning (Gaudiano & Grossberg, 1991), the kinematic map relating the visually perceived position of the hand and the arm muscle contractions which realize that position is learned by sampling the relationship throughout the workspace of the arm. In other words, the hand is viewed at a number of different locations and the associated muscle contractions which correspond to that hand position are learned. In order to sample the workspace, the endogenous random generator (ERG) circuit was proposed. This cir-

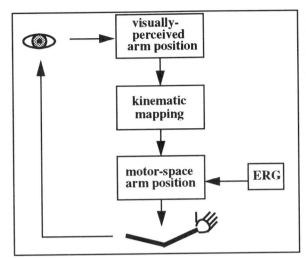

**Figure 1.** Application of Endogenous Random Generator (ERG) to motor learning problem.

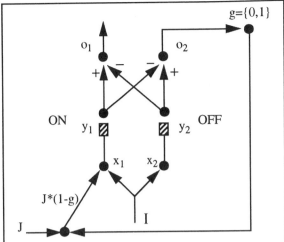

**Figure 2.** The basic ERG circuit.

cuit automatically creates a random velocity signal which is used as a movement command to generate a new arm position. By generating a sequence of such movement commands followed by quiescent periods in which learning could take place, the circuit serves as a basic component in a real-time model of unsupervised learning. The basic system components are depicted in Figure 1.

The ERG circuit has also been used in other models of motor learning, such as the DIRECT model of Bullock, et al (1993). In this model, the kinematic relationship between visually-perceived hand velocities and joint angle rotation rates is learned by sampling the workspace with arm movements. In contrast to the VAM model, the DIRECT model learns during the arm movements rather than during the periods of non-movement. However, the same ERG circuit can be used to support this model of self-organizing motor control.

The ERG circuit is depicted in Figure 2. The basic circuit design is that of the gated dipole (Grossberg, 1972), which has been the basis of models of endogenous rhythm generation (Carpenter & Grossberg, 1983). In the ERG, the opponent ON/OFF states of the dipole are coupled with slow transmitter dynamics and feedback to produce an endogenous generator of spontaneous activity (Gaudiano and Grossberg, 1990). Variability in the ERG circuit is induced by large amplitude noise present in the phasic input signal $J$. In the original ERG simulations this noise is modeled by the equation

$$J = \begin{cases} max\,(0, J \in \left[\mu - \dfrac{\sigma}{2}, \mu + \dfrac{\sigma}{2}\right]), & \text{with probability} \quad \dfrac{1}{p} \\[2mm] \mu, & \text{with probability} \quad (1 - \dfrac{1}{p}) \end{cases} \qquad \text{(EQ 1)}$$

Thus, $J$ consists of random noise spikes distributed in amplitude around an average level $\mu$. The term $p$ represents the average time between spikes. Typical values are $\mu=0.05$, $\sigma=1$, $p=0.5$, with the $x_1$ and $x_2$ variables restricted to [0,1].

## 3. Chaotic Dynamics

Certain continuous-time dynamical systems exhibit complicated behavior, characterized by irregular (non-periodic) oscillations. In a dissipative dynamical system, the state of the system is attracted to a localized region of the state space within which this irregular or *chaotic* motion is demonstrated perpetually. An important property of systems with chaotic dynamics is ergodic movement on this region of the state space, the attractor. Although each orbit of the system remains within the attractor, the motion is unpredictable in the long run. Thus chaotic systems exhibit *sensitive dependence on initial conditions*—trajectories starting close together diverge exponentially with time. Any orbit will eventually cover a dense region of the state space.

Chaotic dynamics can be best characterized by certain empirical measures. For example, it has been recognized that the strange attractors of chaotic systems are fractal objects, and thus have a fractal dimension, which is strictly less than their topological dimension. The dimension D of the attractor can be estimated from a time series by box-counting algorithms such as the one proposed by Liebovitch and Toth (1989). Another important invariant of chaotic systems is their Lyapunov exponents. Lyapunov exponents measure the amount of expansion (or contraction) in a given direction of the state space over time. Chaotic systems, which undergo dynamical analogs of stretching and folding in discrete maps, have at least one positive Lyapunov exponent, indicating that nearby trajectories are diverging along some direction over time. Greene and Kim (1987) describe a technique for determining the Lyapunov exponents of a system of autonomous differential equations. Both fractal dimension and Lyapunov exponents can be used to help differentiate between (high-dimensional) noise and (low-dimensional) chaos in the real world. We will make use of estimates of both invariants to help motivate the fact that the system which we describe is indeed chaotic.

## 4. A Chaotic ERG

The success of the ERG circuit of the previous section depends on the presence of external noise in the signal $J$. A slight modification of the circuit leads to a system with a chaotic dynamic in the absence of large amplitude noise. The chaotic dynamic has the proper characteristics for endogenous random generation. A random amplitude output signal is produced at an irregular rate, with long quiescent intervals in between for learning.

Figure 3 shows the modified ERG circuit. The ON- and OFF-channels feed back to themselves rather than only having the OFF-channel feedback to the ON-channel. In addition, this feedback is a continuous rather than a binary signal. Each channel forms an oscillator, and by choosing different parameters for the channels the circuit becomes that of two coupled oscillators. Coupled oscillators of different frequencies can give rise to chaotic dynamics. This allows the elimination of the noisy phasic input $J$.

The equations of the modified ERG circuit are of the same form as the original ERG. The input channel activations are given by

$$\dot{x}_i = -\alpha x_i + (\beta_i - x_i)\,(I + [o_i]^+)\;;i \in \{1,2\} \tag{EQ 2}$$

The transmitter dynamics are given by

$$\dot{y}_i = \gamma(\lambda_i - y_i) - h(x_i)\,y_i \tag{EQ 3}$$

where

$$h(x) = \delta x^2 \tag{EQ 4}$$

The output activations are given by the differential equations

$$\dot{o}_1 = \varepsilon\,(x_1 y_1 - x_2 y_2 - o_1) \tag{EQ 5}$$

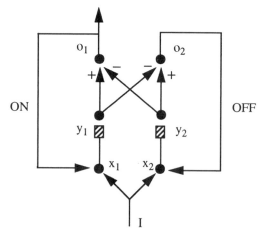

**Figure 3.** The chaotic ERG circuit.

$$\dot{o}_2 = \varepsilon\,(x_2 y_2 - x_1 y_1 - o_2) \tag{EQ 6}$$

To get the desired dynamical behavior we chose the parameters $\alpha$=0.5, $\beta_1$=3.0, $\beta_2$=7.0, $\gamma$=0.1, $\lambda_1$=3.0, $\lambda_2$=7.0, $\delta$=0.5, and $\varepsilon$=5.0. As the arousal signal parameter $I$ is varied, the system exhibits different behaviors. For $I$ greater than about 0.11 or $I$ less than about 0.06 the network has a fixed point attractor. For $I$ in the range (0.06,0.1), the system exhibits an irregular oscillation indicative of chaos.

We simulate the equations (EQ 2) - (EQ 6) using the above parameters. For all simulations shown, a fourth-order Runga-Kutta integration routine was used with a fixed step size. Similar results were obtained using fourth-order Runga-Kutta with an adaptive step size or the Kaps-Rentrap algorithm for stiff systems. Figure 4 shows the irregular oscillations in the ON-channel for $I$=0.086. The step size for this simulation was chosen to be 0.01. The $(x_1,y_1)$ state of the ON-channel dwells at the point $A$ for a long time, then makes a rapid excursion in $x_1$ and $y_1$, returning to $A$. During the dwell at $A$ in the ON-channel, the OFF-channel is slowly spiraling outward from a point repeller. As the OFF-channel oscillation grows it interacts with the ON-channel, causing an excursion in $(x_1,y_1)$. The ON-channel activity sends the OFF-channel state $(x_2,y_2)$ back very near the unstable repelling point. This activity repeats endlessly and the system is attracted to this mode of oscillation from arbitrary non-zero initial conditions. If $I$ is decreased from $I$=0.086, the duration of the dwell period lengthens and the variation in the excursions decreases, until finally the system becomes unable to escape from point $A$.

We have analyzed the chaotic nature of the attractor at $I$=0.086 by using standard measures as described in Section 3. The fractal dimension $D_0$ of the attractor in Figure 4 is about 1.29, as measured using an implementation of the box-counting algorithm called FD3, written by John Sarraille and Peter DiFalco of CSU Stanislaus. We also estimated the Lyapunov spectrum of the system using an implementation of the algorithm described by Greene and Kim (1987). For the above parameters the Lyapunov exponents in bits/second of the 6 degree-of-freedom system are {0.041817, 0.009283, -0.287593, -0.957049, -7.214060, -10.752373}. Since a continuous-time system will have one zero Lyapunov exponent, there appears to be one small positive exponent which is indicative of chaos. The small magnitude of this exponent correlates with the observed slowly growing oscillation as the OFF-channel leaves the vicinity of the repeller.

## 5. Generation of Random Training Vectors

Each excursion in the $(x_1,y_1)$ plane is of variable size and duration. In addition, these excursions come at irregular times, although each excursion is always followed by a long quiescent period. Figure 5 depicts the rectified output of the ON-channel for a simulation of 400 seconds. Each output excursion lasts for approximately 3 seconds, while the silent intervals in between excursions last for approximately 70 seconds. This output can be used to provide random

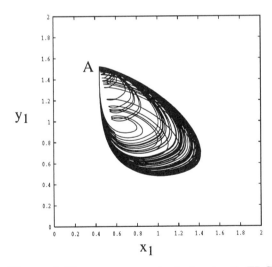

**Figure 4.** The strange attractor in the chaotic ERG ON-channel oscillations.

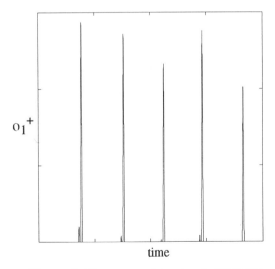

**Figure 5.** The output of the chaotic ERG ON-channel.

training positions to the system of Figure 1 as in Gaudiano & Grossberg (1991).

We demonstrate this procedure by examining the behavior of an idealized model in which the position of a joint is controlled by push-pull inputs from a pair of ERG circuits, termed *agonist* and *antagonist*. The joint command position is updated from ERG outputs by the differential equation

$$\dot{p}_i = 2\frac{(1-p_i)}{(2-p_i)}g(o_{ag}) - \frac{2p_i}{(1+p_i)}g(o_{antag})$$
(EQ 7)

where *g(z)* is a threshold-linear function given by

$$g(z) = max(0, z - \eta)$$
(EQ 8)

Thus, $p_i$ is a normalized representation $(0,1)$ of the joint position. Each excursion of an ON-channel results in a movement of the joint from the current position to a new position. Since the outputs of the ERGs are randomly-varying, the joint will be moved to a set of positions over time which randomly sample the workspace. The quiescent periods between motions are used for learning the kinematic relationship at the sampled locations.

To demonstrate the randomness of the resulting training set and afford comparison with the results obtained by Gaudiano and Grossberg (1990, 1991), simulations were performed for a two-joint arm model, such that $i=1,2$ in (EQ 7). There is a pair of independent ERGs for each joint in this model, one with the ON-channel connected to $o_{ag}$ and another with the ON-channel connected to $o_{antag}$. Following Gaudiano and Grossberg (1991), the resulting joint position values are mapped to the joint range $(-\pi, \pi)$ using linear interpolation.

The previously stated parameters of the model were used along with $I=0.086$, $\eta=0.20$, and an integration step size of 0.01. The initial joint position variables were set to $p_1=p_2=0.5$. To demonstrate the sensitive dependence on initial condition in the chaotic ERG, the states of the four ERGs were initially set to zero in all variables except $x_1$, which was almost the same for all ERGs. The four different $x_1$ initial conditions were within 0.0005 of 0.1. Despite the closeness of the starting conditions the activities of the ERGs become completely different as the system evolves due to the chaotic nature of the dynamics. The outputs of the ON-channels of the ERGs exhibit unrelated patterns of activity over time.

Figure 6 depicts the random arm positions attained during the quiescent periods in a simulation of 20,000 seconds. As shown in Figure 7, the distribution of phase, measured by counting occurrences in sixteen evenly-spaced sectors of Figure 6, is approximately uniform throughout the workspace. Likewise, there is a regular distribution of radially measured distances of the random vectors from (0,0). The variability demonstrated by these results is comparable to

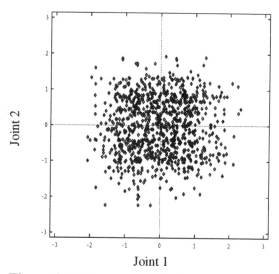

**Figure 6.** Training vectors obtained using chaotic ERG output.

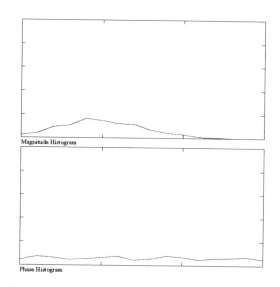

**Figure 7.** Distribution of the training vectors of Figure 6.

that achieved in the original ERG driven by a random phasic input.

## 6. Conclusion

A modification of the basic gated dipole circuit with feedback, as used in the original ERG model, can result in a neural network which has a chaotic dynamic. This chaotic dynamic can be used for endogenous random generation. The chaotic ERG network has randomness as an emergent property, rather than by the injection of large amplitude noise.

The chaotic ERG network was designed so as to retain the form of the original ERG circuit. One can imagine myriad other dynamical systems may exhibit similar properties. Indeed, circuits with superior properties for endogenous random generation may well be devised. We merely demonstrate that chaotic dynamics can serve a system as a mechanism for the internal generation of random variability.

## Acknowledgments

John Fiala was supported under grants from the Office of Naval Research (ONR N00014-92-J-1309). Steve Olson was supported in part by the Air Force Office of Scientific Research (AFOSR F49620-92-J-0334), British Petroleum (BP 89A-1204), the National Science Foundation (NSF IRI-90-24877), and the Office of Naval Research (ONR N00014-91-J-4100). The authors thank Paolo Gaudiano for helpful discussions on this topic and the manuscript.

## 7. References

Basar, E., (ed.), (1990). *Chaos in Brain Function*. Berlin: Springer-Verlag.

Bullock, D., Grossberg, S., Guenther, F. H., (1993). A self-organizing neural model of motor equivalent reaching and tool use by a multijoint arm. Submitted to *Journal of Cognitive Neuroscience*

Carpenter, G. A., Grossberg, S., (1983). A neural theory of circadian rhythms: The gated pacemaker. *Biological Cybernetics* **48**:35-59.

Conrad, M., (1986). What is the use of chaos? In *Chaos*, Holden, A. V., (ed.), pp. 3-14. Princeton University Press.

Gaudiano, P., Grossberg, S., (1990). A self-regulating generator of sample-and-hold random training vectors. Proceedings of the Intl. Joint Conf. on Neural Networks, Caudill, M., (ed.), Vol. 2, pp. 213-216 Hillsdale, NJ: Erlbaum.

Gaudiano, P., Grossberg, S., (1991). Vector associative maps: Unsupervised real-time error-based learning and control of movement trajectories. *Neural Networks* **4**:147-183.

Greene, J. M., Kim, J-S, (1987). The calculation of Lyapunov spectra. *Physica D* **24**:213-225.

Grossberg, S., (1972). A neural theory of punishment and avoidance. II. Quantitative theory. *Mathematical Biosciences* **15**:39-67.

Kelso, J. A. S., Dung, M., (1993). Fluctuations, intermittency, and controllable chaos in biological coordination. In Variability and Motor Control, Newell, K., Corcos, D., (eds.), pp. 291-316. Champaign, Ill: Human Kinetics Press.

King, C. C., (1991). Fractal and chaotic dynamics in nervous systems. *Progress in Neurobiology* **36**:279-308.

Liebovitch, L. S., Toth, T. (1989) A fast algorithm to determine fractal dimensions by box counting. *Physics Letters A* **141**:386-390.

Mpitsos, G. J., Creech, H. C., Cohan, C. S., Mendelson, M., (1988). Variability and chaos: Neurointegrative principles in self-organization of motor patterns. In *Dynamic Patterns in Complex Systems*, Kelso, J. A. S., Mandell, A. J., Shesinger, M. F., (eds.), pp. 162-190. World Scientific Pub.

Skarda, C. A., Freeman, W. J., (1987). How brains make chaos in order to make sense of the world. *Behavioral and Brain Sciences* **10**:161-195. (See also subsequent commentaries.)

# Learning the Dynamical Invariants of Chaotic Time Series by Recurrent Neural Networks

G. Deco and B. Schürmann

*Siemens AG, Corporate Research and Development, ZFE ST SN 41*
*Otto-Hahn-Ring 6, 81739 Munich, Germany*

## Abstract

One way to analyse chaotic systems is to calculate the dynamical invariants which characterize the chaotic attractor. The two most important invariants are the largest Lyapunov exponent which contains information on how far in the future predictions are possible, and the Correlation or Fractal Dimension which indicates how complex the dynamical system is. In this paper, we formulate a recurrent network that is able to learn chaotic maps, and investigate whether the neural model also captures the dynamical invariants of a chaotic time series. We discover a novel type of overtraining which corresponds to the forgetting of the largest Lyapunov exponent during learning. We call this phenomenon "dynamical overtraining". Furthermore, we introduce a penalty term that involves a dynamical invariant of the network and avoids the "dynamical overtraining". As example we use the Henon map and a real world chaotic series that corresponds to the concentration of one of the chemicals as a function of time in experiments on the Belusov-Zabotinskii reaction in a well-stirred flow reactor.

## 1.0 Introduction

The use of nonlinear models like neural networks offers a tool for studying the prediction of chaotic time series. In recent years an appreciable amount of literature dealt with this subject (e.g. Farmer and Sidorovich, 1987; Lapedes and Farber, 1989; Weigend et al., 1990; Albano et al., 1992) but the comparisons performed therein are restricted to the comparisons of predictors (error functions). Recently Principe et al. (1992) analysed the modeling of chaotic time series with feedforward neural networks as well as the dynamical invariants of the real time series and of the trained model. The authors affirmed that the backpropagation learning rule employed to train the neural network by minimizing the prediction error does not consistently indicate that the neural network based model has indeed captured the dynamics of the system. They demonstrated empirically for the Henon map that the largest Lyapunov exponent and the Correlation Dimension are not captured by the neural model.

In this paper we also analyse neural network models of chaotic time series by comparing the dynamical invariants which characterize the chaotic attractor, the invariants being the largest Lyapunov exponent and the Correlation Dimension. Feedforward and two different recurrent neural architectures are used and analysed. The trained network is employed as a recurrent model that generates a "learnt" time series. Only if the dynamics of the original data were captured the dynamic invariants resulting from these data are obtained. Poincare maps and Fourier power spectra are employed for dynamical comparison between model and data as well. A stable learning algorithm for the recurrent architecture is presented for modeling of chaotic time series. A recurrent architecture is introduced that captures very efficiently the dynamics of strange attractors. As a special case of the recurrent models we recover the traditional feedforward model of Principe et al. (1992). We show for various examples, contrary to the affirmation of Principe et al. (1992) that the dynamics is indeed captured by this feedforward model if enough hidden units and enough training data are used. A novel penalty term is introduced in the cost function that involves the Lyapunov exponent of the network and eliminates the "dynamical overtraining" (forgetting of the Lyapunov exponent) discovered in this study. A thorough empirical study is performed on the Henon map, and for the Belousov-Zhabotinskii chemical reaction.

## 2.0 Theoretical Formulation

Given is a chaotic dynamic system

$$\vec{y}(t+1) = g(\vec{y}(t)) \tag{2.1}$$

Let us define an observable measurement

$$x(t) = f(\vec{y}(t)) \tag{2.2}$$

The Takens-Theorem assures that for an embedding

$$\vec{\xi}(t) = (x(t), x(t-\tau), ..., x(t-d\tau)) \tag{2.3}$$

a map

$$\vec{\xi}(t+1) = F[\vec{\xi}(t)] \tag{2.4}$$

exists and has the same dynamical characteristics as the original system $\vec{y}(t)$ if $d = 2D + 1$, where D is the dimension of the strange attractor.

In this paper we introduce two different recurrent architectures. The essential idea is to reproduce the recurrency of the equations above by the structures of the net. The two architectures are presented graphically in Figure 1.

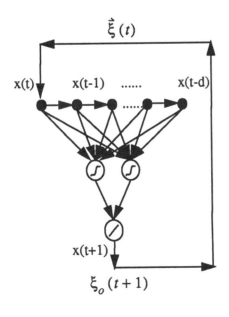

Figure 1-a

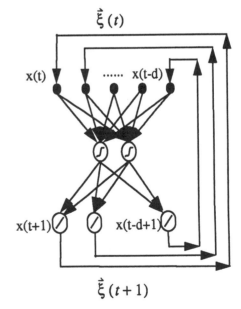

Figure 1-b

The update equations for the architecture of Figure 1-a may be written as

$$\vec{\xi}_o(t+1) = \sum_i W_i \cdot \tanh\left(\sum_k \omega_{ik} \cdot \vec{\xi}_k(t)\right) \tag{2.5}$$

$$\vec{\xi}_j(t+1) = \vec{\xi}_{j-1}(t) \quad , (j > 0) \tag{2.6}$$

For the architecture of figure 1-b, the update equations are

$$\vec{\xi}_j(t+1) = \sum_i W_{ji} \cdot \tanh\left(\sum_k \omega_{ik} \cdot \vec{\xi}_k(t)\right) \tag{2.7}$$

For training the networks we use a modified version of Backpropagation Trough Time (BTT) (Pearlmutter, 1989). Two modifications are introduced in this paper: 1) *Stochastic Sampling of Orbits* and 2) *Lyapunov Weighted Backpropagation Trough Time*. Due to the fact that the series to be learned is chaotic, only short term predictions are possible. We generate samplings of sequences,

$$S(t) = \vec{\xi}(t), \vec{\xi}(t+1), \dots \vec{\xi}(t+\Delta) \tag{2.8}$$

of the embedding vector and use this sampling for training the recurrent neural network with BTT through $\Delta$ cycles. The value of $\Delta$ depends on the largest Lyapunov coefficient. The samplings at different initial time t are presented stochastically during training. The update of the weights has been done "Sampling-by-Sampling". Also due to the chaotic character of the sequence to be learned the meaning of the backpropagated error $\delta_T$ is progressively deteriorated during iteration. The distortion in each iteration is given by $exp(\lambda)$ (with the largest Lyapunov exponent $\lambda$). Therefore, we introduce a forgetting function in the update of the weights in the learning rule of BTT that takes into account the distortion of the errors,

$$\delta_i(t) = \sigma'_i(t-1)\left(E_i(t)e^{\lambda(\hat{t}-t)} + \sum_j w_{ji}\delta_j(t+1)\right) \quad ; \quad t = \hat{t} + 1 + \Delta, \dots \hat{t} \tag{2.9}$$

The learning is in this way stable.

## 3.0 Results and Simulations

We analyse two different chaotic series, namely
1) the 2-D Henon Map,

$$x_{n+1} = 1 - 1.4x_n^2 + y_n \tag{3.1}$$

$$y_{n+1} = 0.3x_n \tag{3.2}$$

2) 1-D Belousov-Zhabothinskii
An acid bromate solution oxidises malonic acid in the presence of a metal ion catalyst and more than 30 chemical constituents in a well-stirred reactor (Roux et al., 1983).

The concentration of the bromide ion was measured and parametrized with the map

$$c_{n+1} = a \cdot e^{-bc_n} \tag{3.3}$$

Multiplicative noise was added. Correlation Dimension, Lyapunov exponent, Poincare maps and spectral power spectrum of the modeled series were compared with the values corresponding to the true strange attractor.

The influences of dimension of input space, number of hidden units and number of training patterns in feedforward architectures were studied. Contrary to the affirmation of Principe et al. (1992) a feedforward net is able to learn the Lyapunov exponent and Correlation Dimension if the numbers of input dimension, hidden units and training data are large enough.

Recurrent networks may be trained for learning chaos. The multi-delayed architecture introduced here yields very good results. Dynamical invariants were learned and long term prediction was improved.

A "dynamical overtraining" was observed. A novel penalty term is introduced in order to solve this problem. The cost function is defined by the sum of the squared error and the squared difference between the true largest Lyapunov exponent and the Lyapunov exponent of the network. In the one-dimensional case for a neural network $f(x)$, the cost function reads

$$E = \left( \sum_{p=1}^{N} \| O - f(x) \|^2 \right) + \left( \lambda_{true} - \frac{1}{N} \sum_{p=1}^{N} ln \left| \frac{\partial f}{\partial x}(x) \right| \right)^2 \tag{3.4}$$

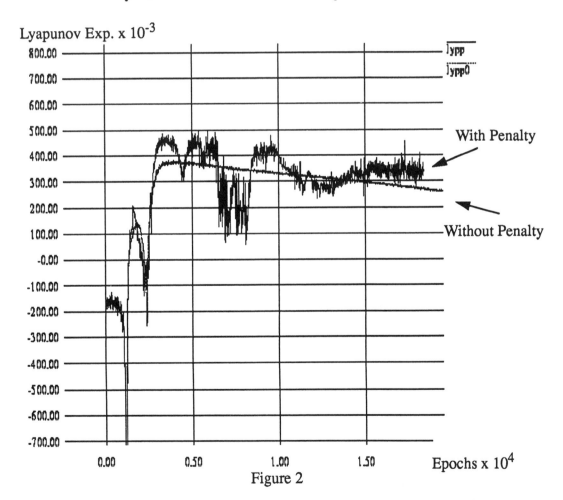

Figure 2

In Figure 2, a typical result for dynamical overtraining and its remedy by introducing the penalty term of (3.4) is displayed, the reaction considered being 1-D Belousov-Zhabothinskii. According to Roux et al., the largest Lyapunov exponent $\lambda = 0, 3 \pm 0.1$. It is seen that without penalty term, $\lambda$ does not saturate whereas with penalty term a plateau is reached after a sufficient number of epochs.

References:

- Albano A., Passamante A., Hediger T. and Mary Eileen Farell, 1992, "Using neural nets to look for chaos", Physica D 58, 1.

- Farmer J. and Sidorowich J., 1987, "Predicting chaotic time series", Phys. Rev. Letters 59, 845.

- Grassberger P. and Procaccia I., 1983, "Characterization of strange attractors", Phys. Rev. Lett. 50, 346.

- Lapedes A and Farber R., 1987, "Nonlinear signal processing using neural networks: Prediction and system modelling", Tech. Rep. n LA-UR-87-2662, Los Alamos National Laboratory, Los Alamos, NM.

- Pearlmutter B., 1989, "Learning State Space Trajectories in Recurrent Neural Networks", Neural Computation 1, 239-269.

- Principe J., Rathie A. and Kuo J., 1992, "Prediction of chaotic time series with neural networks and the issue of Dynamic modeling", Bifurcation and Chaos 2, n.4, 989.

- Weigend A., Rumelhart D. and Huberman B., 1990, "Back-Propagation, weight elimination and time series prediction", in Connectionist Models, Proc. 1990, eds. Touretzky, Elman, Sejnowski and Hinton, 105-116.

- Roux J.-C., Simoyi R. H. and Swinney H. L., 1983, "Observation of Strange Attractor", Physica D 8, 257-266.

- Wolf A., Swift J. B., Swinney H. L. and Vastano J. A., 1985, "Determining Lyapunov Exponents from a Time Series", Physica D 16, 285-317.

# Decision Boundaries of the Complex Valued Neural Networks

Tohru Nitta

Electrotechnical Laboratory,

1-1-4 Umezono, Tsukuba Science City, Ibaraki, 305 Japan.

**Abstract :**
This paper presents some results of an analysis on the decision boundaries of the complex valued neural networks. The main results may be summarized as follows. (a) Weight parameters of a complex valued neuron have a restriction which is concerned with two-dimensional motion. (b) The decision boundary of a complex valued neuron consists of two hypersurfaces which intersect orthogonally, and divides a decision region into four equal sections. The decision boundary of a three-layered complex valued neural network has this as a basic structure, and its two hypersurfaces intersect orthogonally if net inputs to each hidden neuron are all sufficiently large.

## 1   Introduction

The back-propagation algorithm (called here, "Real-BP") [5] is an adaptive procedure which is widely used in training a multilayer perceptron for a number of classification applications in areas such as speech and image recognition. The "Complex-BP" algorithm [3, 4] is a complex valued version of the "Real-BP". This algorithm enables the network to learn complex valued patterns naturally, and has the ability to learn 2D motion as its inherent property [3, 4].

This paper makes clear the differences between the Real-BP and the Complex-BP by analyzing their fundamental properties from the view of network architectures. The main results may be summarized as follows. (a) Weight parameters of a complex valued neuron have a restriction which is concerned with two-dimensional motion, and learning proceeds under this restriction. (b) The decision boundary of a complex valued neuron consists of two hypersurfaces which intersect orthogonally, and divides a decision region into four equal sections. The decision boundary of a three-layered complex valued neural network has this as its basic structure, and its two hypersurfaces intersect orthogonally if net inputs to each hidden neuron are all sufficiently large. It seems that the complex valued neural network and the related Complex-BP algorithm are natural for learning of complex valued patterns for the above reasons. Hereafter, we will refer to a real valued (usual) neural network as a "Real-BP network", a complex valued neural network as a "Complex-BP network", a neuron used in the Real-BP network as a "real valued neuron", and a neuron used in the Complex-BP network as a "complex valued neuron".

## 2   The "Complex-BP" Algorithm

This section briefly describes the Complex-BP algorithm [3, 4]. It can be applied to multi-layered neural networks in which weights, threshold values, input and output signals are all complex numbers, and the output function $f_C$ of a neuron is defined to be

$$f_C(z) = f_R(x) + i f_R(y), \tag{1}$$

where $z = x + iy$, $i$ denotes $\sqrt{-1}$ and $f_R(u) = 1/(1 + \exp(-u))$, that is, the real and imaginary parts of the output of a neuron mean the sigmoid functions of the real part $x$ and imaginary part $y$ of the net input $z$ to neuron, respectively. The learning rule has been obtained by using a steepest descent method.

Note that there is another formulation of the complex valued version [1] in which the output function is a complex valued function $f_C(z) = 1/(1 + \exp(-z))$, where $z = x + iy$.

# 3 Structure of Decision Boundaries in the Complex-BP Network

In this section, we analyze the properties of decision boundaries in the Complex-BP network.

## 3.1 Weight Parameters of a Real Valued Neuron

We first examine the basic structures of weights of a real valued neuron. Consider a real valued neuron with $n$-inputs, weights $w_k \in \mathbf{R}$ $(1 \leq k \leq n)$, and a threshold value $\theta \in \mathbf{R}$, where $\mathbf{R}$ denotes the set of real numbers. Let an output function $f_R : \mathbf{R} \to \mathbf{R}$ of the neuron be $f_R(u) = 1/(1 + \exp(-u))$. Then, for $n$ input signals $x_k \in \mathbf{R}$ $(1 \leq k \leq n)$, the real valued neuron generates $f_R(\sum_{k=1}^{n} w_k x_k + \theta)$ as an output. This may be interpreted as follows: a real valued neuron moves a point $x_k$ on a real line (i dimension) to another point $w_k x_k$ whose distance from

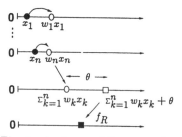

Fig. 1 An image of the processing in a real valued neuron.

the origin is $w_k$ times as long as that of the point $x_k$ $(1 \leq k \leq n)$, and regarding $w_1 x_1, \ldots, w_n x_n$ as vectors $\boldsymbol{w}_1 \boldsymbol{x}_1, \ldots, \boldsymbol{w}_n \boldsymbol{x}_n$, the real valued neuron adds them, resulting in a 1-dimensional real valued vector $\sum_{k=1}^{n} \boldsymbol{w}_k \boldsymbol{x}_k$, and finally, moves the end point of the vector $\sum_{k=1}^{n} \boldsymbol{w}_k \boldsymbol{x}_k$ to another point $(\sum_{k=1}^{n} w_k x_k) + \theta$ (Fig. 1). The output value of the real valued neuron can be obtained by applying a nonlinear transformation $f_R$ to the value $(\sum_{k=1}^{n} w_k x_k) + \theta$. Thus, a real valued neuron basically administers the movement of points on a real line (1 dimension), and its weight parameters $w_1, \ldots, w_n$ are completely independent of one another.

## 3.2 Weight Parameters of a Complex Valued Neuron

Next, we examine the basic structures of weights of a complex valued neuron. Consider a complex valued neuron with $n$-inputs, weights $w_k = w_k^r + i w_k^i \in C$ $(1 \leq k \leq n)$, and a threshold value $\theta = \theta^r + i\theta^i \in C$, where $C$ denotes the set of complex numbers. Then, for $n$ input signals $x_k + iy_k \in C$ $(1 \leq k \leq n)$, the complex valued neuron generates

$$X + iY = f_C\left(\sum_{k=1}^{n}(w_k^r + i w_k^i)(x_k + i y_k) + (\theta^r + i\theta^i)\right)$$

$$= f_R\left(\sum_{k=1}^{n}(w_k^r x_k - w_k^i y_k) + \theta^r\right) + i f_R\left(\sum_{k=1}^{n}(w_k^i x_k + w_k^r y_k) + \theta^i\right) \quad (2)$$

as an output. Hence, a complex valued neuron with $n$-inputs is equivalent to two real valued neurons with $2n$-inputs in Fig. 2. We shall refer to a real valued neuron corresponding to the real part $X$ of an output of a complex valued neuron as a "Real-Part Neuron", and a real valued neuron corresponding to the imaginary part $Y$ as an "Imaginary-Part Neuron".

Note here that

$$\begin{bmatrix} X \\ Y \end{bmatrix} = F\left(\left[\begin{array}{cc|c|cc} w_1^r & -w_1^i & \cdots & w_n^r & -w_n^i \\ w_1^i & w_1^r & \cdots & w_n^i & w_n^r \end{array}\right]\left[\begin{array}{c} x_1 \\ y_1 \\ \hline \vdots \\ \hline x_n \\ y_n \end{array}\right] + \begin{bmatrix} \theta^r \\ \theta^i \end{bmatrix}\right)$$

$$= F\left(|w_1|\begin{bmatrix} \cos\alpha_1 & -\sin\alpha_1 \\ \sin\alpha_1 & \cos\alpha_1 \end{bmatrix}\begin{bmatrix} x_1 \\ y_1 \end{bmatrix} + \cdots + |w_n|\begin{bmatrix} \cos\alpha_n & -\sin\alpha_n \\ \sin\alpha_n & \cos\alpha_n \end{bmatrix}\begin{bmatrix} x_n \\ y_n \end{bmatrix} + \begin{bmatrix} \theta^r \\ \theta^i \end{bmatrix}\right),$$

$$(3)$$

where, $F\left(\begin{bmatrix} x \\ y \end{bmatrix}\right) = \begin{bmatrix} f_R(x) \\ f_R(y) \end{bmatrix}$, $\alpha_k = \arctan(w_k^i / w_k^r)$ $(1 \leq k \leq n)$. In equation (3), $|w_k|$ means reduction or magnification of the distance between a point $(x_k, y_k)$ and the origin in the complex plane, $\begin{bmatrix} \cos \alpha_k & -\sin \alpha_k \\ \sin \alpha_k & \cos \alpha_k \end{bmatrix}$ the counterclockwise rotation by $\alpha_k$ degrees about the origin, and ${}^t[\theta^r \;\; \theta^i]$ translation. Thus, we find that a complex valued neuron with $n$-inputs applies a linear transformation called "2D motion" to each input signal (complex number), that is, equation (3) basically involves "2D motion" (Fig. 3).

As seen in the previous subsection, a real valued neuron basically administers the movement of points on a real line (1 dimension), and its weight parameters are completely independent of one another. On the other hand, as we have seen, a complex valued neuron basically administers 2D motion on the complex plane, and we may also interpret that the learning means adjusting 2D motion. This structure imposes the following restrictions on a set of weight parameters of a complex valued neuron (Fig. 2).

(Weight for the <u>real part</u> $x_k$ of an input signal to "<u>Real-Part Neuron</u>")

$=$ (Weight for the <u>imaginary part</u> $y_k$ of an input signal to "<u>Imaginary-Part Neuron</u>"),

(4)

(Weight for the <u>imaginary part</u> $y_k$ of an input signal to "<u>Real-Part Neuron</u>")

$= -$ (Weight for the <u>real part</u> $x_k$ of an input signal to "<u>Imaginary-Part Neuron</u>"). (5)

Learning is carried out under these restrictions. From a different angle, we can see that "Real-Part Neuron" and "Imaginary-Part Neuron" influence each other via their weights.

Thus, we find that extending the Real-BP to complex numbers has varied the structure from <u>1 dimension</u> to <u>2 dimensions</u>. The structures of weight parameters described above will appear as orthogonality of decision boundaries in the next subsection.

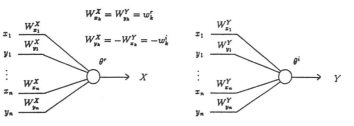

Fig. 2 Two real valued neurons which are equivalent to a complex valued neuron.

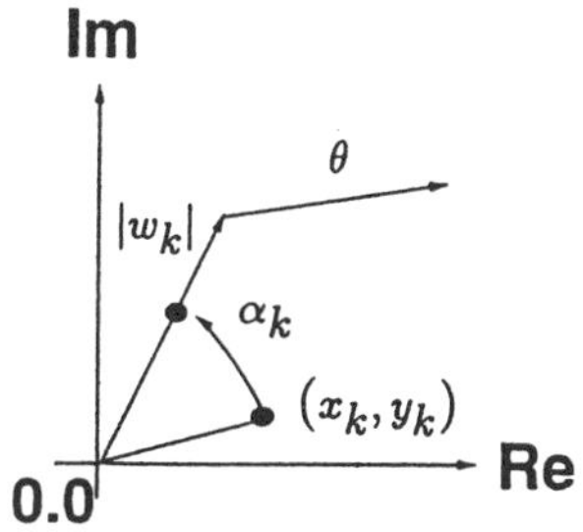

Fig. 3 An image of the two-dimensional motion for complex valued signals.

## 3.3 Orthogonality of Decision Boundaries in the Complex-BP Network

The decision boundary is a border by which pattern classifiers such as the Real-BP classify patterns, and generally consists of hypersurfaces. Decision boundaries of neural networks of real valued neurons have been examined empirically by Lippmann [2]. This subsection mathematically analyzes decision boundaries of neural networks of complex valued neurons.

### 3.3.1 A Case of a Single Neuron

We first analyze the decision boundary of a single complex valued neuron.

Let the weights denote $\boldsymbol{w} = {}^t[w_1 \cdots w_n] = \boldsymbol{w}^r + i\boldsymbol{w}^i$, $\boldsymbol{w}^r = {}^t[w_1^r \cdots w_n^r]$, $\boldsymbol{w}^i = {}^t[w_1^i \cdots w_n^i]$, and let the threshold denote $\theta = \theta^r + i\theta^i$. Then, for $n$ input signals (complex numbers) $z = {}^t[z_1 \cdots z_n] = x + iy$, $x = {}^t[x_1 \cdots x_n]$, $y = {}^t[y_1 \cdots y_n]$, the complex valued neuron generates

$$X + iY = f_R\left(\begin{bmatrix} {}^t w^r & -{}^t w^i \end{bmatrix} \begin{bmatrix} x \\ y \end{bmatrix} + \theta^r\right) + i f_R\left(\begin{bmatrix} {}^t w^i & {}^t w^r \end{bmatrix} \begin{bmatrix} x \\ y \end{bmatrix} + \theta^i\right) \quad (6)$$

as an output. Here, for any two constants $C^R, C^I \in (0,1)$, let

$$X(x,y) = f_R\left(\begin{bmatrix} {}^t w^r & -{}^t w^i \end{bmatrix} \begin{bmatrix} x \\ y \end{bmatrix} + \theta^r\right) = C^R, \quad (7)$$

$$Y(x,y) = f_R\left(\begin{bmatrix} {}^t w^i & {}^t w^r \end{bmatrix} \begin{bmatrix} x \\ y \end{bmatrix} + \theta^i\right) = C^I. \quad (8)$$

Note here that expression (7) is the decision boundary for the <u>real part</u> of an output of the complex valued neuron with $n$-inputs. That is, input signals $(x,y) \in R^{2n}$ are classified into two decision regions $\{(x,y) \in R^{2n} | X(x,y) \geq C^R\}$ and $\{(x,y) \in R^{2n} | X(x,y) < C^R\}$ by the hypersurface given by expression (7). Similarly, expression (8) is the decision boundary for the <u>imaginary part</u>. The normal vectors $H^R(x,y)$ and $H^I(x,y)$ of the decision boundaries ((7), (8)) are given by

$$H^R(x,y) = \left(\frac{\partial X}{\partial x_1} \cdots \frac{\partial X}{\partial x_n} \frac{\partial X}{\partial y_1} \cdots \frac{\partial X}{\partial y_n}\right) = f_R'\left(\begin{bmatrix} {}^t w^r & -{}^t w^i \end{bmatrix} \begin{bmatrix} x \\ y \end{bmatrix} + \theta^r\right) \cdot \begin{bmatrix} {}^t w^r & -{}^t w^i \end{bmatrix},$$
$$(9)$$

$$H^I(x,y) = \left(\frac{\partial Y}{\partial x_1} \cdots \frac{\partial Y}{\partial x_n} \frac{\partial Y}{\partial y_1} \cdots \frac{\partial Y}{\partial y_n}\right) = f_R'\left(\begin{bmatrix} {}^t w^i & {}^t w^r \end{bmatrix} \begin{bmatrix} x \\ y \end{bmatrix} + \theta^i\right) \cdot \begin{bmatrix} {}^t w^i & {}^t w^r \end{bmatrix}. \quad (10)$$

Noting that the inner product of expressions (9) and (10) is zero, we can find that the decision boundary for the real part of an output of a complex valued neuron and that for the imaginary part <u>intersect orthogonally</u>.

Generally, a real valued neuron classifies input real-valued signals into two classes (0, 1). On the other hand, a complex valued neuron classifies input complex-valued signals into four classes (0, 1, $i$, $1 + i$). As described above, the decision boundary of a complex valued neuron consists of two hypersurfaces which intersect orthogonally, and divides a decision region into four equal sections. Thus, a complex valued neuron can be considered to have a natural decision boundary for complex valued patterns.

### 3.3.2 A Case of a Three-Layered Network

Next, we examine the decision boundary of a three-layered Complex-BP network. Consider a three-layered Complex-BP network with $L$ input neurons, $M$ hidden neurons, and $N$ output neurons. We use $w_{ji} = w_{ji}^r + iw_{ji}^i$ for the weight between the input neuron $i$ and the hidden neuron $j$, $v_{kj} = v_{kj}^r + iv_{kj}^i$ for the weight between the hidden neuron $j$ and the output neuron $k$, $\theta_j = \theta_j^r + i\theta_j^i$ for the threshold of the hidden neuron $j$, $\gamma_k = \gamma_k^r + i\gamma_k^i$ for the threshold of the output neuron $k$. Then, for $L$ input signals $z = {}^t[z_1 \cdots z_L] = x + iy$, $x = {}^t[x_1 \cdots x_L]$, $y = {}^t[y_1 \cdots y_L]$, the net input $U_j$ to the hidden neuron $j$ is given by

$$U_j = U_j^r + iU_j^i = \left[\sum_{i=1}^{L}(w_{ji}^r x_i - w_{ji}^i y_i) + \theta_j^r\right] + i\left[\sum_{i=1}^{L}(w_{ji}^i x_i + w_{ji}^r y_i) + \theta_j^i\right]. \quad (11)$$

Hence, the output $H_j$ of the hidden neuron $j$ is given by $H_j = H_j^r + iH_j^i = f_R(U_j^r) + if_R(U_j^i)$. Furthermore, the net input $S_k$ to the output neuron $k$ is given by

$$S_k = S_k^r + iS_k^i = \left[\sum_{j=1}^{M}(v_{kj}^r H_j^r - v_{kj}^i H_j^i) + \gamma_k^r\right] + i\left[\sum_{j=1}^{M}(v_{kj}^i H_j^r + v_{kj}^r H_j^i) + \gamma_k^i\right]. \quad (12)$$

Hence, the output $O_k$ of the output neuron $k$ is given by $O_k = O_k^r + iO_k^i = f_R(S_k^r) + if_R(S_k^i)$. Here, for any two constants $C^R, C^I \in (0,1)$, let

$$O_k^r(\boldsymbol{x}, \boldsymbol{y}) = C^R, \quad (13)$$
$$O_k^i(\boldsymbol{x}, \boldsymbol{y}) = C^I. \quad (14)$$

The expressions (13), (14) are the decision boundaries for the real and imaginary parts of the output neuron $k$ in the 3-layered Complex-BP network, respectively. The normal vectors $H^R(\boldsymbol{x}, \boldsymbol{y})$, $H^I(\boldsymbol{x}, \boldsymbol{y})$ of these hypersurfaces ((13), (14)) are given by

$$H^R(\boldsymbol{x}, \boldsymbol{y}) = \left(\frac{\partial O_k^r}{\partial x_1} \cdots \frac{\partial O_k^r}{\partial x_L} \frac{\partial O_k^r}{\partial y_1} \cdots \frac{\partial O_k^r}{\partial y_L}\right), \quad (15)$$

$$H^I(\boldsymbol{x}, \boldsymbol{y}) = \left(\frac{\partial O_k^i}{\partial x_1} \cdots \frac{\partial O_k^i}{\partial x_L} \frac{\partial O_k^i}{\partial y_1} \cdots \frac{\partial O_k^i}{\partial y_L}\right), \quad (16)$$

and their inner product is given by

$$H^R(\boldsymbol{x}, \boldsymbol{y}) \cdot {}^t H^I(\boldsymbol{x}, \boldsymbol{y})$$
$$= \frac{\partial O_k^r}{\partial x_1} \cdot \frac{\partial O_k^i}{\partial x_1} + \cdots + \frac{\partial O_k^r}{\partial x_L} \cdot \frac{\partial O_k^i}{\partial x_L} + \frac{\partial O_k^r}{\partial y_1} \cdot \frac{\partial O_k^i}{\partial y_1} + \cdots + \frac{\partial O_k^r}{\partial y_L} \cdot \frac{\partial O_k^i}{\partial y_L}. \quad (17)$$

Note here that, for any $1 \le i \le L$,

$$\frac{\partial O_k^r}{\partial x_i} \cdot \frac{\partial O_k^i}{\partial x_i} + \frac{\partial O_k^r}{\partial y_i} \cdot \frac{\partial O_k^i}{\partial y_i}$$
$$= \frac{\partial f_R(S_k^r)}{\partial S_k^r} \cdot \frac{\partial f_R(S_k^i)}{\partial S_k^i} \cdot \left[\sum_{j=1}^{M}\left(v_{kj}^r w_{ji}^r \cdot \frac{\partial f_R(U_j^r)}{\partial U_j^r} - v_{kj}^i w_{ji}^i \cdot \frac{\partial f_R(U_j^i)}{\partial U_j^i}\right)\right]$$
$$\cdot \left[\sum_{j=1}^{M}\left(v_{kj}^i w_{ji}^r \cdot \frac{\partial f_R(U_j^r)}{\partial U_j^r} + v_{kj}^r w_{ji}^i \cdot \frac{\partial f_R(U_j^i)}{\partial U_j^i}\right)\right]$$
$$- \frac{\partial f_R(S_k^r)}{\partial S_k^r} \cdot \frac{\partial f_R(S_k^i)}{\partial S_k^i} \cdot \left[\sum_{j=1}^{M}\left(v_{kj}^r w_{ji}^r \cdot \frac{\partial f_R(U_j^i)}{\partial U_j^i} - v_{kj}^i w_{ji}^i \cdot \frac{\partial f_R(U_j^r)}{\partial U_j^r}\right)\right]$$
$$\cdot \left[\sum_{j=1}^{M}\left(v_{kj}^i w_{ji}^r \cdot \frac{\partial f_R(U_j^i)}{\partial U_j^i} + v_{kj}^r w_{ji}^i \cdot \frac{\partial f_R(U_j^r)}{\partial U_j^r}\right)\right]. \quad (18)$$

Hence, the inner product of the normal vectors is not always zero. Therefore, we can not conclude that the decision boundaries (hypersurfaces) for the real and imaginary parts of the output neuron $k$ in the 3-layered Complex-BP network intersect orthogonally. However, paying enough attention to expression (18), we can find that if $f_R'(U_j^r) = f_R'(U_j^i)$ for any $1 \le j \le M$, then the inner product is zero. In general, if both $|u_1|$ and $|u_2|$ are sufficiently large, we can consider that $f'_R(u_1)$ is nearly equal to $f'_R(u_2)$. Hence, if, for any $1 \leq j \leq M$, there exist sufficiently large positive real numbers $K_1, K_2$ such that

$$|U_j^r| = \left| \sum_{i=1}^{L}(w_{ji}^r x_i - w_{ji}^i y_i) + \theta_j^r \right| = \left| \sum_{i=1}^{L} |w_{ji}||z_i|\cos(\alpha_{ji} + \beta_i) + \theta_j^r \right| > K_1, \qquad (19)$$

$$|U_j^i| = \left| \sum_{i=1}^{L}(w_{ji}^i x_i + w_{ji}^r y_i) + \theta_j^i \right| = \left| \sum_{i=1}^{L} |w_{ji}||z_i|\sin(\alpha_{ji} + \beta_i) + \theta_j^i \right| > K_2, \qquad (20)$$

where $\tan(\alpha_{ji}) = w_{ji}^i/w_{ji}^r$, $\tan(\beta_i) = y_i/x_i$, then the two decision boundaries ((13), (14)) intersect orthogonally. That is, if both the absolute values of the real and imaginary parts of the net input (complex number) to the hidden neuron $j$ are sufficiently large for any $1 \leq j \leq M$, then the decision boundaries intersect orthogonally. In other words, there is a very strong possibility that the two decision boundaries in $(\boldsymbol{x}, \boldsymbol{y})$ intersect orthogonally, when $|\boldsymbol{z}| = \sqrt{|z_1|^2 + \cdots + |z_L|^2}$ is sufficiently large. Therefore, the following theorem and corollary can be obtained.

**Theorem**  If both the absolute values of the real and imaginary parts of the net inputs to all hidden neurons are sufficiently large, then the decision boundaries for the real and imaginary parts of an output neuron in the 3-layered Complex-BP network intersect orthogonally.

**Corollary**  There is a very strong possibility that the decision boundaries for the real and imaginary parts of an output neuron in the 3-layered Complex-BP network in $(\boldsymbol{x}, \boldsymbol{y})$ such that $|\boldsymbol{z}|$ is sufficiently large, intersect orthogonally.

# 4  Conclusions

We have clarified the differences between the Real-BP and the Complex-BP through theoretical analyses of their fundamental properties from the perspective of network architectures. In particular, we discovered that the Complex-BP network had some inherent properties on decision boundary. The orthogonality property of decision boundary is well suited to the classification of complex valued patterns into four classes 0, 1, $i$, and $1 + i$. The Complex-BP algorithm might well be a natural method to learn complex valued patterns in this sense, and is expected to be effectively used in fields dealing with complex numbers.

## Acknowledgements

The author would like to give special thanks to Drs. S.Akaho, Y.Akiyama and M.Asogawa for valuable comments. He also expresses his thanks to Drs. T.Yuba, K.Ohta, T.Furuya and T.Higuchi for providing the opportunity for this study.

# References

[1] Kim, M. S. et al. (1990). Modification of Backpropagation Networks for Complex-Valued Signal Processing in Frequency Domain. *Proc. IJCNN*, Vol.3, June, pp.27-31.

[2] Lippmann, R. P. (1987). An Introduction to Computing with Neural Nets. *IEEE Acoustic, Speech and Signal Processing Magazine*, April, pp.4-22.

[3] Nitta, T. and Furuya, T. (1991). A Complex Back-Propagation Learning. *Transactions of Information Processing Society of Japan*, Vol.32, No.10, pp.1319-1329 (in Japanese).

[4] Nitta, T. (1993). A Complex Numbered Version of the Back-Propagation Algorithm. *Proc. WCNN*, Portland, July, Vol.3, pp.576-579.

[5] Rumelhart, D. E. et al. (1986). *Parallel Distributed Processing*, Vol.1, MIT Press.

# Discrete Chaotic Processes and Recurrent Neural Networks

Edward M. Corwin, Antonette M. Logar
Department of Mathematics and Computer Science,
South Dakota School of Mines and Technology
Rapid City, SD 57701
William B.J. Oldham
Computer Science Department
Texas Tech University
Lubbock, TX 79409

## Abstract

Several techniques have been applied to the problem of mimicing the behavior of chaotic systems. In particular, recurrent neural networks have been used to learn time series known to be chaotic. However, there exists a class of problems for which the most popular algorithms may be inappropriate. A recurrent neural network learning algorithm based on continuous mathematics will not be appropriate for some chaotic sequences generated by discrete processes. This paper explores the underlying cause of the unsuitabilty and proposes a direction for learning rule development based on discrete mathematics.

## Introduction

The exploration and exploitation of the properties of chaotic systems has become a topic of great interest. One aspect of that research has been the pursuit of neural network architectures capable of predicting, albeit for finite periods of time, the behavior of chaotic systems. For example, if, as many people believe, the stock market is chaotic, great gains can be made by a mechanism which can perform relatively short term predictions accurately. Other natural phenomena, such as weather patterns and heart beat rhythms also exhibit chaotic behavior[4][8][10]. The advantages produced by improving weather predictions or predicting imminent heart beat irregularities, even over a relatively small time period, are equally obvious. It has been shown that recurrent neural networks with as few as one neuron are capable of producing chaos[12], but the question of whether networks can learn a chaotic behavior, either by producing a close approximation for some finite period of time or by capturing the chaotic dynamics in the network equations, is still a topic of great interest.

A variety of techniques have been applied to the problem of predicting chaotic time series, including recurrent networks [2][3][5][6][7]. However, existing recurrent network learning rules [9][11][13] were developed using continuous mathematics and assume that the trajectory to be matched is continuous with a bounded derivative that is independent of time. We present an argument that continuous models are not appropriate for neural networks that are to learn sequences generated by some discrete chaotic processes. We also present an example of a continuous model with unbounded derivative that is one direction for modification of current architectures. We end with what we feel is a better alternative, that of developing learning algorithms based on discrete mathematics rather than continuous mathematics.

## Continuous Models of Discrete Chaotic Sequences

In this section we will demonstrate that there exist discrete time chaotic dynamical systems for which a continuous model with a bounded derivative would be inappropriate. We consider the well-known logistic map difference equation and whether or not the behavior of this discrete time system can be modeled as a sampling of a continuous time system. The logistic map considered here is given by $x_{n+1} = 4x_n ( 1 - x_n )$. This map is known to exhibit chaotic behavior. If we use the most simplistic method for creating a differential equation model we would get the following :

$$x(t+1) = 4 \, x(t)(1 - x(t))$$

Using :

$$x(t+h) \approx x(t) + hx'(t)$$

and a step size of one, gives :

$$x(t+1) \approx x(t) + x'(t)$$

The most straightforward next step would be to change the approximations to equalities. This yields:

$$\begin{aligned}
x'(t) &= x(t+1)\text{-}x(t) \\
&= 4 \, x(t)(1\text{-}x(t))\text{-}x(t) \\
&= 3x(t)\text{-}4[x(t)]^2 \\
&= x(t)[3\text{-}4x(t)] \ .
\end{aligned}$$

This last differential equation clearly has an attracting fixed point at $\alpha = 3/4$ since at $\alpha$ we have $x'(t) = 0$ and $x'(t) > 0$ for any $0 < x < \alpha$ and $x'(t) < 0$ for any $x > \alpha$. Therefore, the most obvious differential equation model cannot produce chaos since a starting value of zero remains at zero, a starting value of one maps to zero and remains at zero, and all other starting values approach $\alpha$.

Now we turn toward the possibility that another model exists. Assume there is a continuous model with bounded derivative $y(t)$ such that $x_n = y(n\Delta t + c_0)$ for all $n$ and all choices of $x_0$, where $c_0$ is a constant that depends on the choice of $x_0$. If such a function does exist, we can normalize the time scale so that $\Delta t = 1$. This gives $x_n = y(n+c_0)$. We can also pick any point we wish for $y(0)$, so we pick $y(0) = 1$. This choice leads to $y(1) = 0$ and since $y$ must be continuous, every possible value will be covered in the interval $t \in [0,1]$.

Solving for points $x_n$ that map to a constant $k$ gives :

$$x_n = \frac{1 \pm \sqrt{1-k}}{2}$$

This gives two distinct points which map to $k$ for all $k$ values other than $k = 1$. We now show by contradiction that for $k \le 1$, the smaller of these points is at most $k/2$.

$$\frac{1-\sqrt{1-k}}{2} > \frac{k}{2} \Rightarrow 1-\sqrt{1-k} > k \Rightarrow 1-k > \sqrt{1-k} \Rightarrow k^2-2k+1 > 1-k \Rightarrow k^2 > k \Rightarrow k > 1$$

Since 1/2 maps to 1 which in turn maps to 0, there will be a sequence of $t$ values for which $y(t) = 1$ that get arbitrarily close to integer $t$ values at which $y(t) = 0$. Thus, such a function would have an unbounded derivative. This proves that there is no continuous model with bounded derivative of the logistic map.

We now generalize this argument. Let $x_{n+1} = g(x_n)$ describe a chaos-producing difference equation in a bounded range. Assume that there is a differentiable model $y(t)$ such that $x_n = y(n\Delta t + c_0)$ for all $n$ and all choices of $x_0$ as above and $y'(t)$ is bounded. Further assume there is a fixed point $\alpha$, that is, if $x_n = \alpha$ then $x_{n+1} = \alpha$. We can normalize the range to be $[0,1]$. We can translate the time axis so that $f(0) = \alpha$, and normalize the time axis so that, $f(n) = \alpha$ for all integers $n$. Without loss of generality, we assume that $\alpha < 1$. If $\alpha = 1$, consider the system $z(t) = 1 - x(t)$ and use the following to show there is no model for $z$ and therefore no model for $x$. Also, we may assume that our continuous model is increasing for small positive $t$ values since if the model is flat we can translate the time axis until it is not, and if the model is decreasing we can again let $z(t) = 1 - x(t)$ and take $1 - y(t)$ as our model to be sampled. Let $M$ be a fixed positive real number. We claim that $y'(t) \ge M$ for some value of $t$. This will show that the derivative is unbounded and yield a contradiction showing that there is no model with the assumed features. Fix $\gamma$ with $\alpha < \gamma < 1$. Let $\varepsilon > 0$ be such that $y(t)$ is increasing on $[\alpha, \varepsilon]$ and

$$\frac{\gamma - \alpha}{\varepsilon} \geq M.$$

By the property of topological transitivity, there must be a point $f(\delta)$ in the interval $(\alpha, f(\varepsilon))$ that has an iterate in the interval $(\gamma, 1)$. This gives $f(n + \delta) > \gamma$ for some integer $n$. Let $m$ be the slope of the line from the point $(n, \alpha)$ to the point $(n+\delta, f(n+\delta))$. This gives :

$$m = \frac{f(n+\delta) - \alpha}{\delta} \geq \frac{\gamma - \alpha}{\varepsilon} \geq M.$$

By the mean-value theorem, there is a point in the interval $(n, n + \delta)$ at which $y'(t) = m$ and hence where $y'(t) \geq M$. This completes the proof that $y'(t)$ is unbounded. Thus there cannot be a continuous model with a bounded derivative of a discrete time system with a bounded range that produces chaos and has a fixed point.


**A Continuous Model for the Logistic Map**

In this section we will demonstrate that, if we abandon the requirement that the derivative of the model is bounded, then a continuous model of the logistic map does exist.

Let :

$$x(t) = 1 - \frac{1 + \cos(2^{\lfloor t \rfloor} 2\pi t)}{2}$$

We claim that this generates a continuous map that can be used to give the logistic map $x(t+1) = 4x(t)(1 - x(t))$. Clearly this function is continuous since the only possible problem is the floor function and

$$\lim_{t \to n} x(t) = x(n) = 0$$

for all integers $n$. Thus, there are no discontinuities at the discontinuities of the floor function and, therefore, no discontinuities anywhere. In fact, it is differentiable since it is differentiable at all nonintegral values and the derivative approaches zero from both sides of all integers. However, this is not a counterexample to previous claims about the lack of a model since the derivative is unbounded.

We now show that the above function can be sampled to generate the logistic map. For simplicity, let $u(t) = 2^{\lfloor t \rfloor} 2\pi t$, then $x(t) = 1 - [1 + \cos(u(t))]/2$. It can be shown that $u(t+1) = 2(u(t) + 2^{\lfloor t \rfloor} 2\pi)$. Thus, $\cos(u(t+1)) = \cos(2u(t))$.

Substituting this into the definition of $x(t+1)$ and simplifying gives :

$$\begin{aligned}
x(t+1) &= 1 - [1 + \cos(2u(t))]/2 \\
&= 1 - [1 + (2\cos^2(u(t)) - 1]/2 \\
&= 1 - \cos^2(u(t))
\end{aligned}$$

Next, we compute the value of $x(t+1)$ using the logistic map :

$$x(t+1) = 4x(t)(1-x(t))$$
$$= 4[1-(1+\cos(u(t)))/2][1-(1-(1+\cos(u(t)))/2)]$$
$$= [2-1-\cos(u(t))][1+\cos(u(t))]$$
$$= [1-\cos(u(t))][1+\cos(u(t))]$$
$$= 1-\cos^2(u(t))$$

Thus, the above definition of $x(t)$ does indeed give a continuous map that can be sampled to generate the logistic map. This can be used to predict the logistic map far into the future without the same roundoff problems that iteratively computing the map directly would have. However, it will suffer from some numerical error since the curve will be very steep for large $t$ values.

**A Proposed Class of Learning Rules for Recurrent Neural Networks**

The network presented in [1] by Aihara, Takabe and Toyoda was used as the basis for the following derivation. Experiments with that network have shown it can produce chaos and that parameters can be adjusted to allow dynamic shifts into and out of chaotic regimes[6]. The network's ability to "learn" chaos through parameter alteration made it a promising vehicle for our learning rule development.

Given that continuous models are not always appropriate for discrete chaotic sequences, we turn toward the development of discrete-time training algorithms for recurrent neural networks. From our above discussion, it is unreasonable for a network to learn an arbitrary discrete-time chaotic sequence by learning a continuous trajectory that can be sampled to produce the sequence. We now present a class of training algorithms that do not assume an underlying continuous model. Our experiments to date, while not extensive, indicate that these algorithms are more effective than those developed using traditional continuity assumptions for learning discrete-time chaotic sequences.

*The "One-Time-Step" Rule*

As a starting point, consider the simplified network dynamics equations given in [1] :

$$y_i(t+1) = ky_i(t) + (k-1)\theta_i + \sum_j w_{ij} f(y_j(t)) + \sum_j v_{ij} I_j(t)$$

where $y_i$ is the output from node $i$, $I_i$ is the $i^{th}$ externally applied input, $k$ is a damping factor which implements exponentially decreasing effects from previous time steps, $\theta_i$ is a threshold value analogous to the threshold value used in feed forward networks, $w_{ij}$ is the weight on the connection from node $j$ to node $i$, $v_{ij}$ is the weight on the connection from the $j^{th}$ external input to node $i$, and $f$ is a continuous node activation function. The error at time $t$ at an output node $i$ with desired output $\hat{y}_i(t)$ is :

$$E = (y_i(t) - \hat{y}_i(t))^2$$

From now on, assume node $n$ is the only output node. This gives :

$$\frac{\partial E}{\partial w_{ij}}(t+1) = 2(y_n(t) - \hat{y}_n(t))\frac{\partial y_n(t)}{\partial w_{ij}}$$

For weights into node $n$, there is a direct impact of changing the weight on the error for the next time step.

$$\frac{\partial E}{\partial w_{ij}}(t+1) = 2(y_n(t) - \hat{y}_n(t))f(y_j(t))$$

For a weight into a node $i$ that is not the output node, the first impact on the error is seen in two time steps. Using the chain rule to determine this impact gives :

$$\frac{\partial E}{\partial w_{ij}}(t+1) = 2(y_n(t) - \hat{y}_n(t))w_{ni}f'(y_i(t))f(y_j(t-1))$$

Similar rules can be derived for updating the input weights and the $\theta$'s.

### *Extension to more than one time step*

We now introduce some notation to simplify the necessary calculation. Let $\partial_1$ indicate the partial derivative using the dynamics equation for one time step as used in the one-step-method. Now let $\partial_r$ indicate the partial if the given $y$ variable is expanded in terms of $y$ values from $r$ time steps back. Using this notation we have that the change made to weight $w_{ab}$ for an $r$-time-step algorithm will be a multiple of :

$$\frac{\partial_r E}{\partial_r w_{ab}}(t+r+1) = 2(y_n(t+r) - \hat{y}_n(t+r))\frac{\partial_r}{\partial_r w_{ab}}y_n(t+r)$$

Applying the chain rule to the definition of $y_i(t)$ gives a method for computing $\partial_{r+1}$ in terms of $\partial_r$ :

$$\frac{\partial_{r+1} y_i(t+r+1)}{\partial_{r+1} w_{ab}} = k\frac{\partial_r y_i(t+r)}{\partial_r w_{ab}} + \sum_j \frac{\partial_r}{\partial_r w_{ab}} w_{ij} f(y_j(t+r))$$

$$= k\frac{\partial_r y_i(t+r)}{\partial_r w_{ab}} + \delta_{ia} f(y_b(t+r)) + \sum_j w_{ij} \frac{\partial_r}{\partial_r w_{ab}} f(y_j(t+r))$$

$$= k\frac{\partial_r y_i(t+r)}{\partial_r w_{ab}} + \delta_{ia} f(y_b(t+r)) + \sum_j w_{ij} f'(y_j(t+r))\frac{\partial_r}{\partial_r w_{ab}} y_j(t+r)$$

Note that $\delta_{ab}$ is the Kronecker delta, 1 if $a = b$ and 0 otherwise. This gives a recursive formula that can be used to create a weight update algorithm based on any number of time steps. The derivations for the input weights and the $\theta$'s are similar and are omitted.

### Conclusion

Chaotic sequences can be generated by continuous or discrete processes. A common approach to predicting the future behavior of either type of sequence has been to train a recurrent neural network using a learning rule based on continuous mathematics. We have shown that chaotic sequences generated by discrete processes cannot be adequately modeled with the continuous learning rule approach. We have also presented a learning rule for the Aihara, Takabe and Toyoda network which is based on discrete mathematics and can be used to learn sequences generated by discrete chaotic processes. We have not yet explored the implications Takens' theorem on embedding dimension would have for this research. This will be a matter for future exploration.

### Bibliography

[1] Aihara, K., T. Takabe, and M. Toyoda, "Chaotic Neural Networks", *Physics Letters A*, Volume 144, Number 6,7, March 12, 1990.

[2] Casdagli, Martin, "Nonlinear Prediction of Chaotic Time Series", *Physica D*, p. 335, 1989.

[3] Farmer, Doyne and John Sidorowich, "Exploiting Chaos to Predict the Future and Reduce Noise", LA-UR-88-901, 1988.

[4] Gulick, Denny, *Encounters with Chaos*, McGraw Hill Publishers, New York, 1992.

[5] Lapedes, Alan and Robert Farber, "Nonlinear Signal Processing Using Neural Networks : Prediction and System Modeling", LA-UR-87-2662, 1987.

[6] Logar, Antonette, *Recurrent Neural Networks and Time Series Prediction*, Ph.D. Dissertation, Texas Tech University, 1991.

[7] Mead, W.C., R.D. Jones, Y.C. Lee, C.W. Barnes, G.W. Flake, L.A. Lee, M.K. O'Rourke, "Prediction of Chaotic Time Series Using CNLS-Nets : Example - The Mackey-Glass Equation", LA-UR-91-720, 1991.

[8] Nicolis, C and G. Nicolis, "Reconstruction of the Dynamics of the Climatic System from Time Series Data", *Proceedings of the National Academy of Science*, USA, Volume 83, pp. 536-540, Geophysics, February 1986.

[9] Pearlmutter, Barak, "Dynamic Recurrent Neural Networks" , Technical Report, CMU-CS-90-196, December 1990.

[10] Peterson, Ivars, and Carol Ezzell, "Crazy Rhythms: Confronting the Complexity of Chaos in Biological Systems", *Science News*, Volume 142, No. 10, pp. 145-160, September 5, 1992.

[11] Sun, Guo-Zheng, Hsing-Hen Chen, and Yee-Chung Lee, "Green's Function Method for Fast On-Line Learning Algorithm for Recurrent Neural Network", *Advances in Information Processing Systems 4*, John E. Moody, Steven J. Hanson, and Richard P. Lippmann, editors, 1992.

[12] Szu, Harold and George Rogers, "Single Neuron Chaos", *Proceedings of the International Joint Conference on Neural Networks*, Volume I, pp.103-108, Baltimore, Maryland, June 1992.

[13] Williams, R.J. and D. Zipser, "A Learning Algorithm for Continually Running Fully Recurrent Neural Networks", *Neural Computation*, Volume 1 (2) , 1989.

# Percolation on a Feed-Forward Network

R. Deaton, P. Shah, and M. J. Bartz
Department of Electrical Engineering
Memphis State University
Memphis, TN 38152
(901)678-3250

## Abstract

The relationship between a feed-forward neural network's performance, and the number of layers and the number of neurons in each layer is unknown. Work in complex systems has shown that a spatial arrangement that is poised between order and disorder might enhance system adaptability and reliability. A process that establishes a spatial arrangement between order and disorder is percolation. Percolation is the study of the formation of a conducting path through an array or network. In percolation, a site in a lattice is connected to another site if a uniform random number is less than a predetermined probability. The value of the probability at which a cluster of connected sites just spans the lattice is the percolation threshold. In this work, percolation on a feed-forward network was simulated with Monte Carlo techniques. The percolation threshold on the directed graph of a feed-forward network decreased as the width of the network increased, and increased as the length of the network increased. The average Shannon entropy per vertex, and the average mutual information between input and output layers were calculated. These results indicated that the information capacity of the network was concentrated in the vicinity of the percolation transition.

## Introduction

Artificial neural networks are composed of relatively simple, highly-interconnected processing units. The individual processing units form the weighted sum of their inputs, where the weights are associated with the connections between units, and pass this sum through a threshold function to determine the state of the unit. Because of the strong, long-range interactions between processing units, artificial neural networks, are capable of performing complicated computational and pattern recognition tasks. Numerous forms of neural networks exist, and continue to be developed. In recurrent networks, feedback or loops are allowed among processing units. Feed-forward neural networks do not have loops or feedback among processing units. A diagram of a typical feed-forward neural network is shown in Figure 1. The network shown in Figure 1 is by convention a two-layer network, because the units in the input layer (solid circles) do no computation, and has one hidden or intermediate layer and an output layer. In this work, however, the input layer has been counted, so that the network in Figure 1 is a 3 by 3 network.

Others[1,2] have shown that multi-layer, feed-forward networks are capable of approximating any non-linear mapping arbitrarily closely. The number of layers, other than the input and output layers, that is required is one or greater for any continuous mapping, and in general, is at most two, where the quality of the approximation increases as the number of units in the hidden layers grows arbitrarily. Moreover, there is no proof that network performance will not benefit by increasing the number of hidden layers beyond two.[3] Therefore, one can say that the number of hidden layers for a given task should be greater than or equal to one, but that for a given problem, the exact size and configuration of the network for best performance is not known.

In addition, it is desirable for neural networks to generalize to patterns for which they have not been explicitly trained, and to do reasonable computations in novel situations. For generalization, a rule of thumb is to use the smallest network that will produce a reasonable fit to the training data.[4] Too small of a network will not be able to learn a solution to the problem. With too large a network, learning may be slow and sensitive to small changes in the input. The network may eventually memorize the training data, and fit it well. The network, however, will have no flexibility or adaptability, and will not be able to perform adequately when presented with new situations or inputs. To produce a minimum network for maximum generalization, parts of the network, connections or neurons, are pruned. This produces a more sparsely connected graph than before. Pruning is done on a heuristic basis, and the optimum size of a network for generalization is not in general known.

Work in complex systems and emergent computation has indicated that dynamic systems composed of simple, fully-interacting units, like neural networks, are more robust and adaptive when they operate at the edge between order and randomness.[5,6] This edge is like a phase transition, which has been observed in neural networks,[7] and has been termed a self-organized critical state.[8] In this state, the system may be more adaptive to perturbation, and robust to damage, such as missing weights and neurons. Spatially, the transition between order and randomness may be modeled as a percolation transition. Percolation[9] is a model for the random formation of a conducting or percolating cluster across an array. Sites on the array are filled or connected by comparing a uniform random number with a probability. The probability that generates a connected cluster spanning the array is called the percolation threshold. At the percolation threshold, the cluster which is just spanning the array has a fractal structure. There are two types of percolation problem. In the site problem, vertices on the array are either occupied or empty. The percolating cluster consists of those occupied sites that span the array. In the bond problem, connections or edges are placed between vertices on the array. The percolating cluster consists of those vertices which are connected and which span the array. Kauffman has shown a correspondence between adaptability of a complex system, and the percolation threshold.[5] According to Langton,[6] existence at the transition from order to disorder allows a complex system to perform complicated computations by allowing the simultaneous transmission, storage, and modification information.

In this work, percolation on the directed graph of a feed-forward network, and some of its information transmission capabilities were simulated with Monte Carlo techniques.[10] The percolation threshold for the network increased as the number of layers in the network increased, and decreased as the number of neurons in a layer increased. The average entropy per vertex and the average mutual information between input and output layers were concentrated in the vicinity of the percolation transition. This result supports some of the ideas from complex systems theory. In addition, as the size of the network increased, the average entropy and mutual information were more localized, corresponding to a sharper percolation transition for larger arrays. The mutual information also decreased as the size of the network increased.

**Methods**

The percolation problem on the directed graph of a feed-forward network was simulated using Monte Carlo methods. In the simulations, the primary goal was to determine the value of the percolation probability, $P_\infty$. $P_\infty$ is the order parameter for the percolation problem, and is the probability that a given vertex on the graph belongs to the percolating cluster. For an infinite size graph, it is expressed as

$$P_\infty(p) = \begin{cases} 0 & \text{if } p < p_c \\ > 0 & \text{if } p > p_c \end{cases}, \tag{1}$$

where $p$ is the probability that a given connection is present, or the concentration of connections on the network, and $p_c$ is the percolation threshold, or the concentration of connections on the network which produces a spanning cluster.[9] For a finite graph, finite-size effects cause the graph to percolate before $P_\infty$.[9] This is because on a finite graph, there is a finite probability that it will percolate before $P_\infty$ is reached. As the size of the graph is increased, the percolation transition becomes sharper, and closer to the true $P_\infty$.

The connections between vertices on the graph were made randomly in Bernoulli trials with a probability $p$. The parameter $p$ is the probability that two given vertices are connected, and also, the concentration of connections in the network. It was incremented from 0 to 1. A uniform random number was generated for each connection in the network, and compared to the given $p$. If the random number was less than $p$, then a connection was made; otherwise no connection was made. After all the connections in the network had been set, the entire graph was checked for a percolating cluster. If a percolating cluster was found, then, the number of vertices or neurons connected in the cluster was counted, and $P_\infty$ calculated as the fraction of vertices on the spanning cluster. This was done several times for each value of $p$, and the results averaged. For purposes of simulation, all the inputs were set to 1. The weight, associated with a given connection, was either unity or zero. The neurons did an OR of their inputs which consisted of sequences of zeroes and ones. If the OR produced a one, then, the outgoing connections from that neuron were made with probability $p$. If the OR produced a zero, then, all outgoing connections were set to zero.

To investigate the information processing capability of the network, and its connection to the percolation problem on the network's graph, the Shannon entropy and mutual information were calculated.[11]

The Shannon entropy is given by

$$H(A) = -\sum_{i=1}^{K} p_i \log_2 p_i, \qquad (2)$$

where $A$ is a random variable with $K$ states, which are taken with a discrete probability $p_i$. The logarithm is taken in base 2 so that $H(A)$ is in units of bits. The Shannon entropy is a measure of the uncertainty in a random variable, and is the number of bits that are necessary to describe the random variable.[12] In this work, the average entropy of the vertices in the network was computed. This was done by calculating the probability that a given vertex was on the spanning cluster, and averaging over the entire network. Therefore, the state of the vertices was either a 1 if on the spanning array, or 0 if not.

The average mutual information between a vertex in the input layer and the output layer was also calculated, and is given by

$$I(A, B) = H(A) + H(B) - H(A, B), \qquad (3)$$

where $H(A, B)$ is the joint entropy given by

$$H(A, B) = -\sum_{i=1}^{K} \sum_{j=1}^{L} p_{ij} \log_2 p_{ij}, \qquad (4)$$

and where $A$ is a random variable with $K$ states, and $B$ is a random variable with $L$ states which are taken with a discrete joint probability $p_{ij}$. The mutual information is a measure of the correlation between two random variables, or the amount of information one random variable reveals about another.[12] In this work, the average mutual information between vertices in the input layer and output layer was calculated. This was done by calculating the average individual and joint probabilities that a vertex in the input layer and a vertex in the output layer were on the spanning cluster, and all combinations thereof.

**Results**

The percolation probability for networks as the length (number of layers) increased is shown in Figure 2 for networks of size 2 rows by 2 columns ($2 \times 2$), $5 \times 2$, $10 \times 2$, $100 \times 2$, and $1000 \times 2$. As seen in Figure 2, the percolation threshold increased as the length of the network increased. As the length became large, the threshold appeared to go toward 1, which is the threshold for one-dimensional percolation.[9]

In Figure 3, the percolation behavior is shown as the width (number of neurons per layer) increased for networks of size $2 \times 2$, $2 \times 5$, $2 \times 10$, and $2 \times 100$. The percolation probability decreased as the width of the network increased, and appeared to approach 0, which is the percolation threshold for an infinite dimensional tree.[9]

In Figures 4 and 5, the average entropy of a vertex in the graph is shown as the length and width increased, respectively. In Figures 6 and 7, the average mutual information between vertices in the input layer and the output layer is shown as the length and width increased, respectively.

**Discussion**

As the length of the network or number of layers increased, the percolation threshold increased (Figure 2). The percolation threshold seemed to be going toward $p = 1$, which would correspond to one-dimensional percolation.[9] Along each branch of a tree in a Bethe lattice,[9] new vertices will always be reached. As the distance from the originating vertex increases, the number of new vertices increases exponentially,[9] and therefore, so do possibilities for continuation of the percolation cluster. In the feed-forward network in this paper, the number of new vertices only increased as (number of layers)$^d$, where $d$ is the dimension or number of vertices in a layer. The number of possibilities for percolating branches was constant at each layer, $(d^2)$, and therefore, the threshold concentration of connections, $p$, that is needed for percolation increased.

The fact that the percolation threshold on the directed graph of a feed-forward neural network changed as the size of the network changed is similar to the percolation behavior of a Bethe lattice where the percolation threshold is[9]

$$p_c = \frac{1}{z - 1}, \qquad (5)$$

where $p_c$ is the percolation threshold, and $z$ is the number of neighbors for each vertex. As the number of neighbors or dimensionality of the lattice increases, the percolation threshold decreases. This was the type of behavior that was observed as the width of the neural network increased. Since each vertex in a given layer is possibly connected to all vertices in the previous and subsequent layers, the number of neighbors of each site is equal to the 2 times the number of vertices in each layer. As the number of neighbors increased, the percolation threshold decreased, as seen in Figure 3.

Computation in a neural network depends on the ability to communicate information through the network. For this reason, the entropy and mutual information of vertices in relation to the percolation cluster were investigated. If a vertex is not a member of the spanning or percolating cluster, then, by definition, it cannot transmit information through the network. Therefore, the average entropy per vertex is a measure of the information processing capacity of a network. Langton[6] has used similar measures for cellular automata. For the feed-forward graph, the average entropy was concentrated in the vicinity of the percolation transition (Figures 4 and 5). As the size of the network increased, the average entropy became more sharply peaked, as does the percolation transition region (Figures 2 and 3). The same holds for the average mutual information between input and output layers. The average mutual information is a measure of the correlation between vertices in the input and output layers. These results support the theory that complex systems have their greatest computational capability in the vicinity of a transition from order to disorder.[5,6] Also suggestive, is the narrowing of the average entropy, and the narrowing and decrease of the mutual information as the size, width and length, of the network increases. For smaller networks, the optimum processing size may extend over a wider range of the network's connection configurations than for larger networks. The larger networks, however, are capable of many more configurations which involve a larger number of processing units. Further investigation is needed to establish the connection among network topology, percolation, and computation. Further work along these lines may lead to a better understanding of the optimum network size for both accuracy and adaptability.

## Conclusion

Percolation on the directed graph of a feed-forward neural network was investigated. The percolation threshold, or concentration of connections to span the network, decreased as the number of neurons increased per layer, and increased as the number of layers increased. The information capacity and transmission properties were investigated by calculating the average entropy of sites in relation to the percolating cluster, and the mutual information between the input and output layers. These quantities were found to be concentrated in the percolation transition region, and in general, were relatively broader and larger for smaller networks. These results have implications for the determination of the optimum network size for both generalization and accuracy of solution, and support the theory that a complex system performs better near a transition between order and disorder.

## References

[1] G. Cybenko, "Approximation by superpositions of a sigmoidal function," *Mathematics of Control, Signals, and Systems*, vol. 2, pp. 303-314, 1989.

[2] K. M. Hornik, M. Stinchcombe, and H. White, "Multilayer feedforward networks are universal approximators," *Neural Networks*, vol. 2, pp. 359-366, 1989.

[3] D. R. Hush and B. G. Horne, "Progress in supervised neural networks," *IEEE Signal Processing Magazine*, pp. 8-39, January 1993. [4] R. Reed, "Pruning algorithms–A survey", *IEEE Trans. Neural Nets.*, vol. NN-4, pp. 740-747, 1993.

[5] S. A. Kauffman, *Origins of Order*, New York: Oxford University Press, 1993.

[6] C. G. Langton, "Computation at the edge of chaos: Phase transitions and emergent computation," *Physica D*, vol. 42, pp. 12-37, 1990.

[7] K. E. Kurten, "Critical Phenomena in model neural networks," *Phys. Lett.* A, vol. 129, p.157, 1988.

[8] P. Bak, C. Tang, and K. Wiesenfeld, "Self-organized criticality," *Phys. Rev.* A, vol. 38, pp. 364-374, 1988.

[9] D. Stauffer and A. Aharony, *Introduction to Percolation Theory*, London: Taylor and Francis, 1992.

[10] K. Binder and D. W. Heermann, *Monte Carlo simulation in statistical physics*, Berlin: Springer-Verlag, 1988.

[11] C. E. Shannon, "A mathematical theory of communication," *Bell Sys. Tech. Journal*, vol. 27, pp. 379-423, 1948.

[12] T. M. Cover and J. A. Thomas, *Elements of Information Theory*, New York: John Wiley and Sons, Inc., 1991.

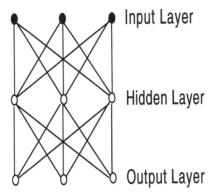

Figure 1: Graph of feed-forward neural network

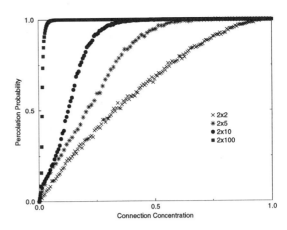

Figure 3: Percolation Probability versus connection concentration as width of network increased.

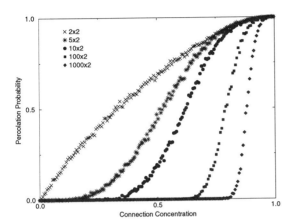

Figure 2: Percolation Probability versus connection concentration as length of network increased.

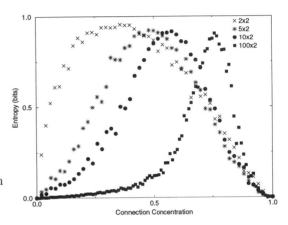

Figure 4: Average Entropy versus bond concentration as length of network increased.

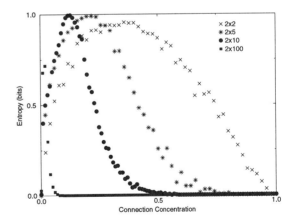

Figure 5: Average Entropy versus connection concentration as width of network increased.

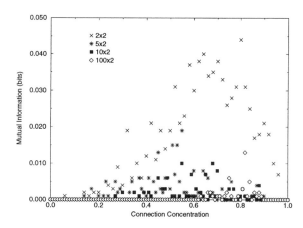

Figure 6: Average Mutual Information of input and output layers versus connection concentration as length of network increased.

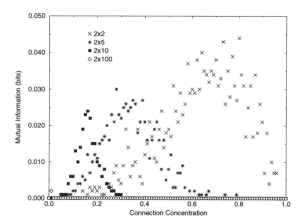

Figure 7: Average Mutual Information of input and output layers versus connection concentration as width of network increased.

# Locally Excitatory Globally Inhibitory Oscillator Networks

DeLiang Wang[†] and David Terman[‡]

[†]Department of Computer and Information Science and Center for Cognitive Science
[‡]Department of Mathematics
The Ohio State University, Columbus, Ohio 43210, USA

## Abstract

*An novel class of locally excitatory, globally inhibitory oscillator networks (LEGION) is proposed and investigated analytically and by computer simulation. The model of each oscillator corresponds to a standard relaxation oscillator with two time scales. The network exhibits a mechanism of selective gating, whereby an oscillator jumping up to its active phase rapidly recruits the oscillators stimulated by the same pattern, while preventing other oscillators from jumping up. We show analytically that with the selective gating mechanism the network rapidly achieves both synchronization within blocks of oscillators that are stimulated by connected regions and desynchronization between different blocks. Computer simulations demonstrate LEGION's promising ability for segmenting multiple input patterns in real time. This model lays a physical foundation for the oscillatory correlation theory of feature binding, and may provide an effective computational framework for pattern segmentation and figure/ground segregation.*

## 1. Introduction

A basic attribute of perception is its ability to group elements of a perceived scene or sensory field into coherent clusters (objects). This ability underlies perceptual processes such as figure/ground segregation, identification of objects, and separation of different objects, and it is generally known as pattern segmentation or perceptual organization. Despite the fact that humans perform it with apparent ease, the general problem of pattern segmentation remains unsolved in the engineering of sensory processing, such as computer vision and auditory processing.

Fundamental to pattern segmentation is the grouping of similar sensory features and the segregation of dissimilar ones. Theoretical investigations of brain functions and feature binding point to the mechanism of temporal correlation as a representational framework [11, 12]. In particular, the correlation theory of von der Malsburg [11] asserts that an object is represented by the temporal correlation of the firing activities of the scattered cells coding different features of the object. A natural way of encoding temporal correlation is to use neural oscillations, whereby each oscillator encodes some feature (maybe just a pixel) of an object. In this scheme, each segment (object) is represented by a group of oscillators that shows synchrony (phase-locking) of the oscillations, and different objects are represented by different groups whose oscillations are desynchronized from each other. Let us refer to this form of temporal correlation as *oscillatory correlation*. The theory of oscillatory correlation has received direct experimental support from the cell recordings in the cat visual cortex [1, 2] and other brain regions. The discovery of synchronous oscillations in the visual cortex has triggered much interest from the theoretical community in simulating the experimental results and in exploring oscillatory correlation to solve the problems of pattern segmentation (see among others [14, 4, 8, 9, 5, 7, 13]). While several demonstrate synchronization in a group of oscillators using local (lateral) connections [4, 7, 13], most of these models rely on long range connections to achieve phase synchrony. It has been pointed out that local connections in reaching synchrony may play a fundamental role in pattern segmentation since long-range connections would lead to indiscriminate segmentation [9, 13].

There are two aspects in the theory of oscillatory correlation: (1) synchronization within the same object; and (2) desynchronization between different objects. Despite intensive studies on the subject, the question of desynchronization has been hardly addressed. The lack of an efficient mechanism for desynchronization greatly limits the utility of oscillatory correlation to perceptual organization. In this paper, we propose a new class of oscillatory networks, LEGION, and show that it can rapidly achieve both synchronization within each object and desynchronization between a number of simultaneously presented objects. LEGION is composed of the following elements: (1) A new model of a basic oscillator; (2) Local excitatory connections to produce phase synchrony within each object; (3) A global inhibitor that receives inputs from the entire network and feeds back with inhibition to produce desynchronization of the oscillator groups representing different objects. In other words, the mechanism of

LEGION consists of local cooperation and global competition, thus fully encoding oscillatory correlation. This surprisingly simple neural architecture may provide an elementary approach to pattern segmentation and a computational framework for perceptual organization.

## 2. Model Description

The building block of LEGION, a single oscillator $i$, is defined in the simplest form as a feedback loop between an excitatory unit $x_i$ and an inhibitory unit $y_i$:

$$\frac{dx_i}{dt} = 3x_i - x_i^3 + 2 - y_i + \rho + I_i + S_i \qquad (1a)$$

$$\frac{dy_i}{dt} = \varepsilon \left( \gamma (1 + tanh(x_i/\beta)) - y_i \right) \qquad (1b)$$

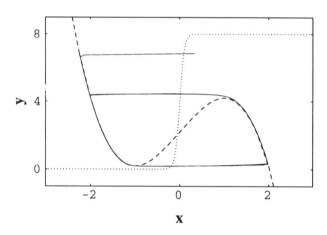

**Figure 1**. Nullclines and periodic orbit of a single oscillator as shown in the phase plane. The $x$-nullcline ($dx/dt = 0$) is shown by the dashed curve and the $y$-nullcline ($dy/dt = 0$) is shown by the dotted curve. In a simulation when the oscillator starts at a randomly generated point (upper middle position in the figure) in the phase plane, it quickly converged to a stable trajectory of a limit cycle. The parameters for this simulation are $I = 0.2$, $\rho = 0.02$, $\varepsilon = 0.02$, $\gamma = 4.0$, $\beta = 0.1$.

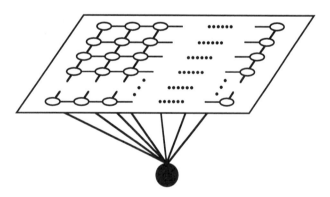

**Figure 2**. Architecture of a two dimensional LEGION with nearest neighbor coupling. The global inhibitor is indicated by the black circle.

where $\rho$ denotes the amplitude of a Gaussian noise term. $I_i$ represents external stimulation to the oscillator, and $S_i$ denotes coupling from other oscillators in the network. The noise term is introduced both to test the robustness of the system and to actively desynchronize different input patterns. The parameter $\varepsilon$ is chosen to be small. In this case (1), without any coupling or noise, corresponds to a standard relaxation oscillator. The x-nullcline of (1) is a cubic curve, while the y-nullcline is a sigmoid function, as shown in Fig. 1. If $I > 0$, these curves intersect along the middle branch of the cubic, and (1) is oscillatory. The periodic solution alternates between the silent and active phases of near steady state behavior. The parameter $\gamma$ is introduced to control the relative times that the solution spends in these two phases. If $I < 0$, then the nullclines of (1) intersect at a stable fixed point along the left branch of the cubic. In this case the system produces no oscillation. The oscillator model (1) may be interpreted as a model of spiking behavior of a single neuron, or a mean field approximation to a network of excitatory and inhibitory neurons.

The LEGION we study here in particular is two dimensional. However, the results can easily be extended to other dimensions. Each oscillator in the LEGION is connected to only its four nearest neighbors, thus forming a 2-D grid. This is the simplest form of local connections. The global inhibitor receives excitation from each oscillator of the grid, and in turn inhibits each oscillator. This architecture is shown in Fig. 2. The intuitive reason why the LEGION gives rise to pattern segmentation is the following. When multiple connected objects are mapped onto the grid, local connectivity on the grid will group together the oscillators covered by each object. This grouping will be reflected by phase synchrony within each object. The global inhibitor is introduced for desynchronizing the oscillatory responses to different objects. We assume that the coupling term $S_i$ in (1) is given by

$$S_i = \sum_{k \in N(i)} W_{ik}\, S_\infty(x_k,\, \theta_x) - W_z\, S_\infty(z,\, \theta_{xz}) \qquad (2)$$

$$S_\infty(x,\, \theta) = \frac{1}{1 + exp[-K(x - \theta)]} \qquad (3)$$

where $W_{ik}$ is a connection (synaptic) weight from oscillator $k$ to oscillator $i$, and $N(i)$ is the set of the neighoring oscillators that connect to $i$. In this model, $N(i)$ is the four immediate neighbors on the 2-D grid, except on the boundaries where $N(i)$ may be either 2 or 3 immediate neighbors. $\theta_x$ is a threshold (see the sigmoid function of Eq. 3) above which an oscillator can affect its neighbors. $W_z$ (positive) is the weight of inhibition from the global inhibitor $z$, whose activity is defined as

$$\frac{dz}{dt} = \phi\, (\sigma_\infty - z) \qquad (4)$$

where $\sigma_\infty = 0$ if $x_i < \theta_{zx}$ for every oscillator, and $\sigma_\infty = 1$ if $x_i \geq \theta_{zx}$ for at least one oscillator $i$. Hence $\theta_{zx}$ represents a threshold. If the activity of every oscillator is below this threshold, then the global inhibitor will not receive any input. In this case $z \to 0$ and the oscillators will not receive any inhibition. If, on the other hand, the activity of at least one oscillator is above the threshold $\theta_{zx}$ then, the global inhibitor will receive input. In this case $z \to 1$, and each oscillator feels inhibition when $z$ is above the threshold $\theta_{zx}$. The parameter $\phi$ determines the rate at which the inhibitor reacts to such stimulation.

In summary, once an oscillator is active, it triggers the global inhibitor. This then inhibits the entire network as described in Eq. 1. On the other hand, an active oscillator spreads its activation to its nearest neighbors, again through (1), and from them to its further neighbors. Thus, the entire dynamics of LEGION is a combination of local cooperation through excitatory coupling among neighboring oscillators and global competition via the global inhibitor. In the next section, we give a number of properties of this system.

Besides boundaries, the oscillators on the grid are basically symmetrical. Boundary conditions may cause certain distortions to the stability of synchrous oscillations. Recently, Wang [13] proposed a mechanism called *dynamic normalization* to ensure that each oscillator, whether it is in the interior or on a boundary, has equal overall connection weights from its neighbors. The dynamic normalization mechanism is adopted in the present model to form effective connections. For binary images (each pixel being either 0 or 1), the outcome of dynamic normalization is that an effective connection is established between two oscillators if and only if they are neighbors and both of them are activated by external stimulation. The network defined above can readily be applied for segmentation of binary images. For gray-level images (each pixel being in a certain value range), the following slight modification suffices to make the network applicable. An effective connection is established between two oscillators if and only if they are neighbors and the difference of their corresponding pixel values is below a certain threshold.

## 3. Analytical Results

We have formally analyzed the LEGION. Due to space limitations, we can only list the major conclusions without proofs. The interested reader can find the details in Terman and Wang [10]. Let us refer to a *pattern* as a connected region, and a *block* be a subset of oscillators stimulated by a given pattern. The following results are about singular solutions in the sense that we formally set $\varepsilon = 0$. However, as shown in [10], the results extend to the case $\varepsilon > 0$ sufficiently small.

**Theorem 1.** (*Synchronization*). The parameters of the system can be chosen so that all of the oscillators in a block always jump up simultaneously (synchronize). Moreover, the rate of synchronization is exponential.

**Theorem 2.** (*Pattern Separation*) The parameters of the system and a constant $T$ can be chosen to satisfy the following. If at the beginning all the oscillators of the same block synchronize with each other and the temporal distance between any two oscillators belonging to two different blocks is greater than $T$, then (1) Synchronization within each block is maintained; (2) The blocks activate with a fixed ordering; (3) At most one block is in its active phase at any time.

**Theorem 3.** (*Desynchronization*) If at the beginning all the oscillators of the system lie not too far away from each other, then the condition of Theorem 2 will be satisfied after some time. Moreover, the time it takes to satisfy the condition is no greater than $N$ cycles, where $N$ is the number of patterns.

The above results are true with arbitrary number of oscillators. In summary, LEGION exhibits a mechanism, referred to as *selective gating*, which can be intuitively interpreted as follows. An oscillator jumping to its active phase opens a gate to quickly recruit the oscillators of the same block due to local connections. At the same time, it closes the gate to the oscillators of different blocks. Moreover, segmentation of different patterns is achieved very rapidly in terms of oscillation cycles.

## 4. Computer Simulation

To illustrate how LEGION is used for pattern segmentation, we have simulated a 20x20 LEGION as defined by (1)-(4). We arbitrarily selected four objects (patterns): two **O**'s, one **H**, and one **I**; and they form the word **OHIO**. These patterns were simultaneously presented to the system as shown in Figure 3A. Each pattern is a connected region, but no two patterns are connected to each other.

All the oscillators stimulated (covered) by the objects received an external input $I = 0.2$, while the others have $I = -0.02$. Thus the oscillators under stimulation become oscillatory, while those without stimulation remain silent. The amplitude $\rho$ of the Gaussian noise is set to 0.02. Thus, compared to the external input, a 10% noise is included in every oscillator. Dynamic normalization results in that only two neighboring oscillators stimulated by a single pattern have an effective connection. The differential equations were solved numerically with the following parameter values: $\varepsilon = 0.02$, $\phi = 3.0$; $\gamma = 6.0$, $\beta = 0.1$, $K = 50$, $\theta_x = -0.5$, and $\theta_{zx} = \theta_{xz} = 0.1$. The total effective connections were normalized to 6.0. The results described below were robust to considerable changes in the parameters. The phases of all the oscillators on the grid were randomly initialized.

Fig. 3B-3F shows the instantaneous activity (snapshot) of the network at various stages of dynamic evolution. The diameter of each black circle represents the $x$ activity of the corresponding oscillator. That is, if the range of $x$ values of all the oscillators are given by $x_{min}$ and $x_{max}$, then the diameter of the black circle corresponding to an oscillator is proportional to $(x-x_{min})/(x_{max}-x_{min})$. Fig. 3B shows a snapshot of the network a few steps after the beginning of the simulation. In Fig. 3B, the activities of the oscillators were largely random. Fig. 3C shows a snapshot after the system had evolved for a short time period. One can clearly see the effect of grouping and segmentation: all the oscillators belonging to the left **O** were entrained and had large activities. At the same time, the oscillators stimulated by the other three patterns had very small activities. Thus the left **O** was segmented from the rest of the input. A short time later, as shown in Fig. 3D, the oscillators stimulated by the right **O** reached high values and were separated from the rest of the input. Fig. 3E shows another snapshot after Fig. 3D. At this time, pattern **I** had its turn to be activated and separated from the rest of the input. Finally in Fig. 3F, the oscillators representing **H** were active and the rest of the input remained silent. This successive "pop-out" of the objects continued in a stable periodic fashion. To provide a complete picture of dynamic evolution, Fig. 3G shows the temporal evolution of each oscillator. Since the oscillators receiving no external input were inactive during the entire simulation process, they were excluded from the display in Fig. 3G. The activities of the oscillators stimulated by each object are combined together in the figure. Thus, if they are synchronized, they appear like a single oscillator. In Fig. 3G, the four upper traces represent the activities of the four oscillator blocks, and the bottom trace represents the activity of the global inhibitor. The synchronized oscillations within each object are clearly shown within just three cycles of dynamic evolution.

The exact shapes and positions of the patterns in Fig. 3 do not matter for pattern segmentation. In fact, this 2-D LEGION provides a general solution to segmentation of planar connected patterns.

## 5. Discussion

Besides neural plausibility, oscillatory correlation has a unique feature as an computational approach to the engineering of pattern segmentation and figure/ground segregation. Due to the nature of oscillations, no single object can dominate and suppress the perception of the rest of the image permanently. The current dominant object has to give way to other objects being suppressed, and let them have a chance to be spotted. Although at most one object can dominant at any time instant, due to rapid oscillations, a number of objects can be activated over a short time period. This intrinsic dynamic process provides a natural and reliable representation of multiple segmented patterns.

The basic principles of selective gating are established for LEGION with lateral connections beyond nearest neighbors. Indeed, in terms of synchronization, more distant connections even help expedite phase entrainment. In this sense, synchronization with all-to-all connections is an extreme case of our system. With nearest-neighbor connectivity (Fig. 2), any isolated part of an image is considered as a segment. In an noisy image with many tiny regions, segmentation would result in too many small fragments. More distant connections would also provide a solution to this problem. Lateral connections typically take on the form of Gaussian distribution, with the connection strength between two oscillators falling off exponentially. Since global inhibition is superimposed to local excitation, two oscillators positively coupled may be desynchronized if global inhibition is strong enough. Thus, it is unlikely that all objects in an image form a single segment as the result of extended connections.

Due to its critical importance for computer vision, pattern segmentation, or perceptual organization as known in computer vision, has been studied quite extensively. Many techniques have been proposed in the past [3, 6]. Despite these techniques, as pointed out by Haralick and Shapiro [3], there is no underlying theory of image segmentation, and the techniques tend to be adhoc and emphasize some aspects while ignoring others. Compared to the traditional techniques for pattern segmentation, the oscillatory correlation approach offers many unique advantages. The dynamical process is inherently parallel. While conventional computer vision algorithms are based on descriptive criteria and many adhoc heuristics, LEGION as exemplified in this paper performs computations based on only connections and oscillatory dynamics. The organizational simplicity renders LEGION particularly feasible for VLSI implementation. Also, continuous-time dynamics allows real time processing, desired by many engineering applications.

**Acknowledgments**. DLW is supported in part by the NSF grant IRI-9211419 and the ONR grant N00014-93-1-0335. DT is supported in part by the NSF grant DMS-9203299LE.

# References

[1] R. Eckhorn, et al., "Coherent oscillations: A mechanism of feature linking in the visual cortex?" *Biol. Cybern.*, vol. 60, pp. 121-130, 1988.

[2] C.M. Gray, P. König, A.K. Engel, and W. Singer, "Oscillatory responses in cat visual cortex exhibit inter-columnar synchronization which reflects global stimulus properties," *Nature*, vol. 338, pp. 334-337, 1989.

[3] R.M. Haralick and L.G. Shapiro, "Image segmentation techniques," Comput. Graphics Image Process., vol. 29, pp. 100-132, 1985.

[4] P. König and T.B. Schillen, "Stimulus-dependent assembly formation of oscillatory responses: I. Synchronization," *Neural Comput.*, vol. 3, pp. 155-166, 1991.

[5] T. Murata and H. Shimizu, "Oscillatory binocular system and temporal segmentation of stereoscopic depth surfaces," *Biol. Cybern.*, vol. 68, pp. 381-390, 1993.

[6] S. Sarkar and K.L. Boyer, "Perceptual organization in computer vision: a review and a proposal for a classificatory structure," IEEE Trans. Syst. Man Cybern., vol. 23, 382-399, 1993.

[7] D. Somers, and N. Kopell, "Rapid synchronization through fast threshold modulation," *Biol. Cybern,* vol. 68, pp. 393-407, 1993.

[8] H. Sompolinsky, D. Golomb, and D. Kleinfeld, "Cooperative dynamics in visual processing," *Phys. Rev. A,* vol. 43, pp. 6990-7011, 1991.

[9] O. Sporns, G. Tononi, and G.M. Edelman, "Modeling perceptual grouping and figure-ground segregation by means of active reentrant connections," *Proc. Natl. Acad. Sci. USA*, vol. 88, pp. 129-133, 1991.

[10] D. Terman and D.L. Wang, "Global competition and local cooperation in a network of neural oscillators," Submitted, 1993.

[11] C. von der Malsburg, "The correlation theory of brain functions," Internal Report 81-2, Max-Planck-Institut for Biophysical Chemistry, Göttingen, FRG, 1981.

[12] C. von der Malsburg and W. Schneider, "A neural cocktail-party processor," *Biol. Cybern.*, vol. 54, pp. 29-40, 1986.

[13] D.L. Wang, "Modeling global synchrony in the visual cortex by locally coupled neural oscillators," *Proc. 15th Ann. Conf. Cognit. Sci. Soc.*, pp. 1058-1063, 1993.

[14] D.L. Wang, J. Buhmann, and C. von der Malsburg, "Segmentation in associative memory," *Neural Comput.*, vol. 2, pp. 94-106, 1990.

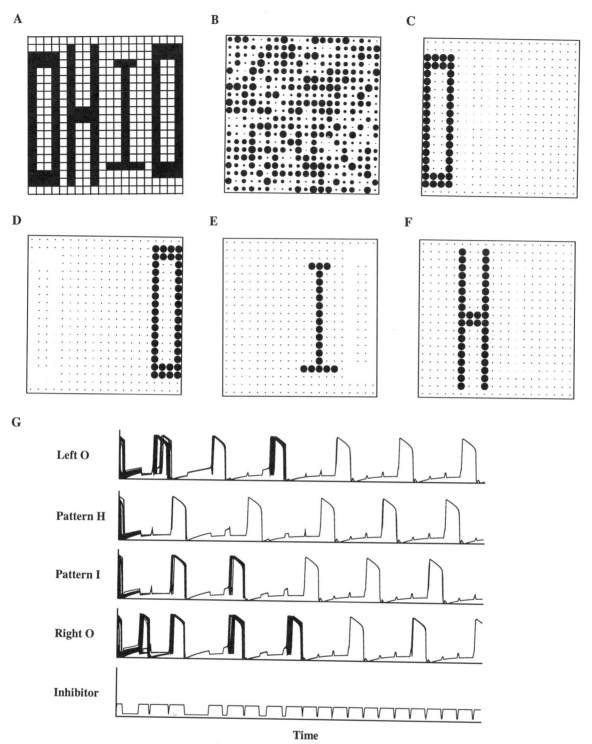

**Figure 3. A** An image composed of four patterns which were presented (mapped) to a 20x20 grid of oscillators. **B** A snapshot of the activities of the oscillator grid at the beginning of dynamic evolution. **C** A snapshot taken shortly after the beginning. **D** Another snapshot taken shortly after **C**. **E** Another snapshot taken shortly after **D**. **F** Another snapshot taken shortly after **E**. **G** The upper four traces show the combined temporal activities of the oscillator blocks representing the four patterns, respectively, and the bottom trace shows the temporal activity of the global inhibitor. The simulation took 8,000 integration steps.

# Dynamics of an integrate-and-fire neuron without dendritic potential reset.

Paul C. Bressloff

*Department of Mathematical Sciences, Loughborough University of Technology,
Loughborough, Leicestershire LE11 3TU*

**Abstract.** The dynamics of a compartmental model integrate-and-fire neuron is analysed. The neuron is taken to consist of a single dendritic compartment coupled to a single somatic compartment; only the latter resets when the neuron fires. The compartmental model equations are shown to reduce to a scalar Volterra integral equation thus allowing an iterative solution for the firing-times of the neuron to be derived. In the case of constant external inputs, the steady-state of the neuron is found to satisfy a Fredholm integral equation from which the firing-frequency of the neuron can be obtained. The firing-frequency is determined as a function of the membrane time constants of the neuron. The analysis presented here can be generalized to more general compartmental models.

## 1. Compartmental model integrate-and-fire neuron.

At the simplest level of description, a neuron fires whenever the membrane potential $\phi$ at the axon hillock (point of exit of axon from cell body or soma) exceeds some threshold h, and provided that the neuron is outside its relative refractory period $t_R$. The firing times of the neuron satisfy the iterative equation

$$T_{k+1} = \inf\{t|\phi(t) \geq h; t \geq T_k + t_R\}, \quad k \geq 0 \tag{1}$$

where $T_k$ is the time at which the neuron fires for the $k^{th}$ occasion since the initial time $T_0$. (We shall assume that the neuron also fires at $t = T_0$). When the neuron fires there is a rapid depolarisation of the membrane potential at the axon hillock followed by a hyperpolarisation due to delayed potassium rectifier currents. This process can be modelled by assuming that the membrane potential $\phi$ is simply reset to some resting level $\overline{\phi}$ whenever the neuron fires; details of the firing-mechanism and the pulse shape of a nerve impulse are ignored in these so called *integrate-and-fire* models [1,2]. Suppose for the moment that any dendritic structure is neglected. The state of the neuron can then be described in terms of the single membrane potential $\phi$, which satisfies the leaky-integrator equation

$$\frac{d\phi}{dt} = -\frac{\phi}{\tau} + I(t), \quad t \in (T_k, T_{k+1}), \quad k = 0, 1,.. \tag{2a}$$

$$\lim_{\delta \to 0} \phi(T_k - \delta) = h, \quad \lim_{\delta \to 0} \phi(T_k + \delta) = \overline{\phi}, \quad \delta > 0 \tag{2b}$$

The solution to equation (2a) is given by

$$\phi(t) = e^{-(t-T_k)/\tau}\overline{\phi} + \int_{T_k}^{t} e^{-(t-t')/\tau}I(t')dt' \tag{3}$$

Therefore, given the firing-time $T_k$, the subsequent firing-time $T_{k+1}$ may be determined from equations (1) and (3). It follows that the complete set of firing-times are generated by iteration [1,2].

An implicit assumption of this model is that the whole neuron resets on firing, which means that the neuron's behaviour after the occurrence of a nerve impulse is independent of the post-synaptic potentials across the dendritic tree prior to spike generation. (For a discussion of this point within the context of temporal signal processing see [3]). In order to avoid such an unrealistic scenario it is necessary to take into account the spatial structure of a neuron so that one can differentiate between axonal and dendritic potentials.

A simple solution is to divide the neuron into two compartments [4,5]. The first, which represents the dendritic tree and soma, receives multiple synaptic inputs. The output from this compartment is taken to be the input current to the second compartment, which represents the axon hillock or trigger zone of nerve impulse generation. The dendro-somatic membrane potential V evolves according to a standard leaky-integrator equation without any influence from the nerve impulse generation process. Meanwhile, the membrane potential $\phi$ at the trigger zone satisfies equation (2a) with $I(t) \approx dV/dt$, and is reset each time the neuron fires as described by equation (2b). This model can also take into account a more detailed description of the geometry of the neuron by representing the dendro-somatic system using a multi-compartmental model [5].

A limitation of the above model is that it takes reset to be localized at a point (the trigger zone) rather than extended over a region of the neuron. Here we shall consider an intermediate situation in which reset occurs across the whole soma but does not enter directly into the dendrites. In a similar fashion to [4], we divide the neuron into two compartments but now one corresponds to the dendritic tree and the other to the soma (including the trigger zone). The associated compartmental model equations are

$$C\frac{dV}{dt} = -\frac{V}{R} + \frac{\phi - V}{r} + I \tag{4}$$

$$C_\phi \frac{d\phi}{dt} = -\frac{\phi}{R_\phi} + \frac{V - \phi}{r} \quad t \in (T_k, T_{k+1}), \quad k = 0, 1,.. \tag{5}$$

where V is the membrane potential of the dendritic compartment and $\phi$ is the membrane potential of the soma, which resets according to equation (2b). The parameters C, R and $C_\phi$, $R_\phi$ are the leakage capacitance and resistance of the dendrites and soma respectively whilst r is the junctional resistance between the two compartments. In contrast to the models of Ref. [4,5], when the membrane potential $\phi$ resets there is feedback into the dendritic system due to the coupling between $\phi$ and the potentials V.

The dendritic membrane potentials V can be eliminated from equations (4) and (5) to give a scalar integro-differential equation for $\phi(t)$. Taking the $\phi$-dependent term on the right-hand side of (4) as an additional input, we can use a variations of parameter formula to obtain

$$V(t) = e^{-(t-T_0)/\tau}V(T_0) + \int_{T_0}^{t} e^{-(t-t')/\tau}\left[I(t') + \frac{1}{\hat{\gamma}_0}\phi(t')\right]dt', \tag{6}$$

where a factor of $C^{-1}$ has been absorbed into I(t) and

$$\frac{1}{\tau} = \frac{1}{RC} + \frac{1}{rC}, \frac{1}{\hat{\tau}} = \frac{1}{R_\phi C_\phi} + \frac{1}{rC_\phi}, \hat{\gamma}_0 = rC, \hat{\gamma} = rC_\phi \tag{7}$$

If equation (6) is now substituted into equation (5), we obtain an integro-differential equation for $\phi$,

$$\frac{d\phi}{dt} = -\frac{\phi}{\hat{\tau}} + \frac{1}{\hat{\gamma}_0\hat{\gamma}}\int_{T_0}^{t} e^{-(t-t')/\tau}\phi(t')dt' + F(t), \quad t \in (T_k, T_{k+1}) \quad k \geq 0 \tag{8}$$

with

$$F(t) = \frac{1}{\hat{\gamma}} e^{-(t-T_0)/\tau} V(T_0) + \frac{1}{\hat{\gamma}} \int_{T_0}^{t} e^{-(t-t')/\tau} I(t')dt' \qquad (9)$$

Equation (8) must be supplemented by the reset condition (2b). This means that $\phi$ evolves according to a *nonlinear* integral equation, where the nonlinearity is due to the discontinuity associated with reset. Equation (8) can be represented schematically as the feedback system shown in figure 1. That is, the model neuron is equivalent to a standard leaky integrate-and-fire neuron with external input F(t) and an additional feedback contribution that takes into account the coupling of $\phi$ with the underlying dendritic potential. The feedback transfer function is $G(t) = \alpha e^{-t/\tau}$, $\alpha = (\hat{\gamma}_0 \hat{\gamma})^{-1}$

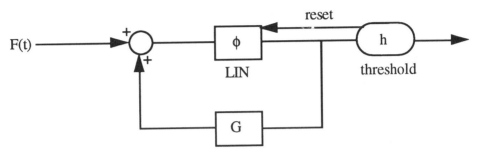

Figure 1.

## 2. Iterative solution for the firing-times.

We shall now construct a unique iterative solution to equations (8) and (2b) that generalizes the solution found for the point-like model, equation (3). The first step is to introduce a set of continuous functions $\phi_k: [0, \infty] \to \Re$, $k \geq 0$, where $\phi_k(0) = \bar{\phi}$, and to write the solution as

$$\phi(t+T_k) = \phi_k(t), \ t \in (0, \Delta_k), \qquad \Delta_k = T_{k+1} - T_k \qquad (10)$$

$$\lim_{\delta \to 0} \phi(T_k + \delta) = \phi_k(0) = \bar{\phi}, \lim_{\delta \to 0} \phi(T_k - \delta) = \phi_{k-1}(T_k) = h \qquad (11)$$

Assume that $T_j$, $\phi_j(t)$, $j = 0, 1, ..., k-1$ and $T_k$ are known and that we wish to determine $\phi_k$ and $T_{k+1}$. The function $\phi_k$ satisfies the linear Volterra integro-differential equation

$$\frac{d\phi_k}{dt} = -\frac{\phi_k}{\hat{\tau}} + G(t-t')\phi_k(t')dt' + F_k(t), \ t \geq 0, \ k \geq 0 \qquad (12)$$

where $F_0(t) = F(t)$ and

$$F_k(t) = F(t) + \sum_{j=0}^{k-1} \int_0^{\Delta_j} G(t - t' + T_k - T_j)\phi_j(t')dt', k \geq 1 \qquad (13)$$

Note that there is no reset of $\phi_k$. We shall show below that one can uniquely solve equation (12) for any given k. Thus the complete solution $\phi(t)$ is generated by iteration. First we determine $\phi_0$ using the initial conditions on $\phi$ and $V_\alpha$ at $t = T_0$. The firing-time $T_1$ is then obtained by finding when the solution $\phi_0(t)$ first crosses the threshold h (equation (1)). Proceeding inductively, we solve $\phi_k$, $k \geq 1$ in terms of $\{\phi_j, T_j, j = 0, 1, ..., k-1\}$ and $T_k$, and then calculate the firing-time $T_{k+1}$ using equation (1).

It remains to prove that there exists a unique solution to equation (12). First note that both the convolution kernel G(t) and the function $F_k$ are continuous on $[0,\infty)$. Therefore, we can apply the following result.

*Variation of parameters formula* [6]: Consider a linear Volterra equation of convolution type having the form of equation (12) in which $\hat{\tau}$ is a real constant, and $F_k$ and B are both real continuous functions on $[0,\infty)$. If $Z(t)$ is the solution of the homogeneous equation

$$\frac{dZ}{dt} = -\frac{Z}{\hat{\tau}} + \int_0^t G(t-t')Z(t')dt', \quad Z(0) = 1 \tag{14}$$

and if $\phi_k(t)$ is a solution of equation (12) on $[0,\infty)$ then

$$\phi_k(t) = Z(t)\bar{\phi} + \int_0^t Z(t-t')F_k(t')dt' \quad t \geq 0, \tag{15}$$

Thus $\phi_k$ is uniquely determined by the initial condition $\phi_k(0) = \bar{\phi}$.

Equation (14) may be solved using Laplace transforms, that is,

$$Z(t) = \mathcal{L}^{-1}\left(\frac{1}{s+\hat{\tau}^{-1}-\tilde{G}(s)}\right)(t) \tag{16}$$

where $\mathcal{L}^{-1}$ indicates the inverse Laplace transform and $\tilde{G}(s) = \alpha/(s+\varepsilon)$, with $\varepsilon = 1/\tau$. Substituting into equation (16) gives

$$\tilde{Z}(s) = \frac{s+\varepsilon}{(s+\varepsilon)(s+\hat{\varepsilon})-\alpha}, \quad \hat{\varepsilon} = \hat{\tau}^{-1} \tag{17}$$

The poles of $\tilde{Z}(s)$ are the roots of the denominator on the right-hand side of equation (17). These roots are real and are equal to $-\varepsilon_\pm$ where

$$\varepsilon_\pm = \frac{1}{2}\left[\varepsilon + \hat{\varepsilon} \pm \sqrt{(\varepsilon+\hat{\varepsilon})^2 - 4\varepsilon\hat{\varepsilon} + 4\alpha}\right] \tag{18}$$

We note from equations (7) that $\varepsilon\hat{\varepsilon} > \alpha$ so that $\varepsilon_\pm > 0$, i.e. both poles lie in the left-hand complex plane. We now apply the expansion theorem of Laplace Transforms to obtain

$$Z(t) = \left(\frac{\varepsilon - \varepsilon_-}{\varepsilon_+ - \varepsilon_-}\right)e^{-\varepsilon_- t} + \left(\frac{\varepsilon_+ - \varepsilon}{\varepsilon_+ - \varepsilon_-}\right)e^{-\varepsilon_+ t} \tag{19}$$

## 3.    Steady-state firing rate.

Having found the general solution to the compartmental model equations of an integrate-and-fire neuron without dendritic potential reset, we are now in a position to determine the output of the neuron, i.e. the sequence of firing-times, in response to various inputs. Suppose for simplicity that the input to the neuron is constant and that $k \gg 1$, $T_k \gg T_0$. We can use the latter condition to eliminate any transients. First observe that equation (9) becomes $F(t) \approx I\tau/\hat{\gamma}$ for $t > T_k \gg T_0$. Thus all dependence on the initial value of the dendritic potential $V(T_0)$ vanishes. We now make the following *ansatz*: The neuron relaxes to a unique steady-state $\psi(t)$ characterised by a regular firing-pattern of period $\Delta$ where $\lim_{k\to\infty}\Delta_k \to \Delta$ and $\lim_{k\to\infty}\phi_k(t) \to \psi(t)$. Taking the limit $k \to \infty$ in equation (12), it can be shown that $\psi(t)$ satisfies the self-consistency condition

$$\psi(t) = f(t) + \int_0^\Delta K(t,t')\psi(t')dt', \quad t \geq 0 \tag{20}$$

with

$$K(t,t') = \int_0^t Z(t-t'')\sum_{m=1}^\infty G(t''-t'+m\Delta)dt'', \quad f(t) = Z(t)\overline{\phi} + \frac{I\tau}{\hat{\gamma}}\int_0^t Z(t-t')dt' \tag{21}$$

and $\Delta$ is determined self-consistently according to $\psi(\Delta) = h$

Equation (20) is a Fredholm integral equation of the second kind [7]. This equation can be solved explicitly in the special case of a single dendritic compartment. Substituting equation (19) into (21) and performing the summation over m gives

$$K(t,t') = \frac{\alpha}{\varepsilon_+ - \varepsilon_-}\frac{e^{-\Delta\varepsilon}}{1-e^{-\Delta\varepsilon}}e^{\varepsilon t'}\left[e^{-\varepsilon_- t} - e^{-\varepsilon_+ t}\right] \tag{22}$$

Thus the kernel K is *degenerate* in the sense that it can be decomposed as $K(t,t') = a(t)b(t')$. Choosing $b(t') = e^{\varepsilon t'}$, equations (22) and (20) then yield

$$\psi(t) = f(t) + a(t)\int_0^\Delta e^{\varepsilon t'}\psi(t')dt', \quad a(t) = \frac{\alpha}{\varepsilon_+ - \varepsilon_-}\frac{e^{-\Delta\varepsilon}}{1-e^{-\Delta\varepsilon}}\left[e^{-\varepsilon_- t} - e^{-\varepsilon_+ t}\right] \tag{23}$$

which implies that the solution $\psi(t)$ has the form $\psi(t) = f(t) + \eta a(t)$ for some constant coefficient $\eta$. Substitution into (20) now shows that

$$\eta = \int_0^\Delta e^{\varepsilon t'}\left[f(t') + \eta a(t')\right]dt' \tag{24}$$

Evaluate the integrals on the right-hand side of equation (24),

$$A_1 \equiv \int_0^\Delta e^{\varepsilon t'}f(t')dt' = \overline{\phi}\frac{1}{\varepsilon_+ - \varepsilon_-}\left[e^{-\Delta\varepsilon_-} - e^{-\Delta\varepsilon_+}\right] + \frac{I\tau}{\hat{\gamma}}\frac{e^{\Delta\varepsilon}}{\varepsilon_+ - \varepsilon_-}\left[\frac{1-e^{-\Delta\varepsilon_-}}{\varepsilon_-} - \frac{1-e^{-\Delta\varepsilon_+}}{\varepsilon_+}\right] \tag{25}$$

$$A_2 \equiv \int_0^\Delta e^{\varepsilon t'}a(t')dt' = \frac{\alpha}{\varepsilon_+ - \varepsilon_-}\frac{e^{-\Delta\varepsilon}}{1-e^{-\Delta\varepsilon}}\left[\left(\frac{e^{(\varepsilon-\varepsilon_-)\Delta}-1}{\varepsilon-\varepsilon_-}\right) - \left(\frac{1-e^{(\varepsilon-\varepsilon_+)\Delta}}{\varepsilon_+-\varepsilon}\right)\right] \tag{26}$$

If $A_2 \neq 1$ then there is a unique solution for $\eta$ given by $\eta = A_1/(1-A_2)$. Finally, the period $\Delta$ can be obtained from the self-consistency condition,

$$h = f(\Delta) + \frac{A_1(\Delta)}{1-A_2(\Delta)}a(\Delta) \tag{27}$$

Equation (27) is a transcedental equation that has to be solved numerically. For simplicity we assume that the reset level $\overline{\phi} = 0$. Then both $f(\Delta)$ and $A_1(\Delta)$ are proportional to $I\tau/\hat{\gamma}$ so that equation (27) can be written in the form $h\hat{\gamma}/I = \mu(\Delta,\varepsilon,\hat{\varepsilon},\alpha)/\varepsilon$. That is, the function $\mu$ is independent of the input I. Thus the steady-state firing frequency $\Omega = 1/\Delta$ can be determined as a function of $1/I$ for a range of values of the various time constant parameters $\varepsilon$, $\hat{\varepsilon}$ and $\alpha$. A detailed study across the complete parameter domain will be presented elsewhere. Here we shall briefly consider the particular case of high constant inputs. The interspike time-interval $\Delta$ is then small allowing an expansion of equation (26) in powers of $\Delta$. The leading order terms are

$$\frac{h\hat{\gamma}}{I} = \frac{\Delta}{\varepsilon} + \left(\frac{1}{\varepsilon} - \hat{\varepsilon}\right)\frac{\Delta^2}{2\varepsilon} + O(\Delta^3) \tag{28}$$

Hence, for high inputs the frequency is proportional to the input I. (Note that for very large I, the firing-rate will saturate at $f_{max} = 1/t_R$, where $t_R$ is the absolute refractory period). It is interesting to compare equations (27) and (28) with the corresponding result of Kohn [5]. There the two compartments are in series (without coupling) as described in section 1, and

$$\Delta = -\frac{1}{\hat{\varepsilon}_0}\ln\left[1 - \frac{h}{I}\hat{\varepsilon}_0\varepsilon_0\right], \quad \varepsilon_0 = 1/RC, \quad \hat{\varepsilon}_0 = 1/R_\phi C_\phi \tag{29}$$

with $\Delta \approx h\varepsilon_0/I$ for large inputs. (In the case of the standard integrate-and-fire model of equation (2), $\Delta$ is given by equation (29) for $\hat{\varepsilon}_0 = 1$). Thus there is no dependence on the junctional time constants $\hat{\gamma}$, $\hat{\gamma}_0$. The presence of these time constants in our model has at least two consequences. First, $\varepsilon > \varepsilon_0$ and $\hat{\varepsilon} > \hat{\varepsilon}_0$, in other words, the effective membrane time constants are smaller. Second, the input I is scaled by a factor of $\hat{\gamma}$. Hence, in the high input limit for example our model predicts a higher (lower) firing-rate than the Kohn model if $\varepsilon\hat{\gamma} < \varepsilon_0$ ($\varepsilon\hat{\gamma} > \varepsilon_0$). Differences also emerge in the reponse to small inputs and to time-varying inputs as we shall show elsewhere.

## 4.    Discussion.

Integrate-and-fire models usually assume that reset occurs either across the whole neuron or at a single point (the trigger zone) without interaction with the remainder of the neuron. A more realistic approach is to introduce some compartmental structure and restrict reset to some extended subregion of the neuron, here taken to be the soma. (As far as we are aware the exact extent of the reset domain is currently unknown). Electrical coupling of the soma with the dendrites leads to a feedback signal across the dendrites when the neuron resets. Such a coupling is measured in terms of the junctional time constants $\hat{\gamma}$, $\hat{\gamma}_0$. In this paper we analysed the dynamics of this model using integral equations. There are a number of possible extensions of this work. First, one can incorporate multi-compartmental models that take into account the complex topology of a neuron's dendritic tree. The analysis proceeds in a similar fashion to the two-compartment model except that the convolution kernels G(t) and Z(t) are now constructed from the Green's function of an arbitrary tree. General expressions for such a Green's function have recently been derived [8]. Second, one can consider stochastic versions of the model, which raises interesting issues in stochastic functional equations. Finally, some form of asymptotic analysis is needed for the integral equation (15) to check the validity of our ansatz. (Preliminary numerical work seems to support the ansatz).

## References.

[1] B. W. Knight, *J. Gen. Phys.*, **59**, 734 (1972).
[2] J. P. Keener, F. C. Hoppenstead and J. Rinzel, *SIAM J. Appl. Math.* **41**, 503 (1981).
[3] P. C. Bressloff, *Network* **4**, 155 (1993).
[4] J. P. Rospars and P. Lansky, *Biol. Cybern.*, **69**, 283 (1993).
[5] A. F. Kohn, *IEEE Biomed. Eng.* **36**, 44 (1989).
[6] T. A. Burton, *SIAM Review*, **25**, 343 (1983).
[7] D. Porter and D. S. G. Stirling, *Integral equations* (Cambridge University Press, 1990).
[8] P. C. Bressloff and J. G. Taylor, Biol. Cybern. **69** (1993).

# Neurodynamics and Chaos

**Session Chairs: Harold Szu**
**Mona Zaghloul**

## POSTER PRESENTATIONS

# VLSI Neuromorphs
# Exhibit Wide-Range Dynamics

John G. Elias and David P. M. Northmore

Electrical Engineering &
Neuroscience Program
University of Delaware
Newark, DE. 19716

## ABSTRACT

The impulse response behavior of an analog VLSI neuromorph whose primary computational substrate is a spatially extensive artificial dendritic tree is described. Experimental results are presented that show these silicon neuromorphs can produce impulse responses that last nine orders of magnitude longer than their initiating impulses. The shape and duration of the impulse response is tunable over a wide range through the use of programmable switched-capacitors to simulate the axial and parallel resistances of the dendritic tree. The VLSI implementation of artificial dendrites comprising switched-capacitor resistive elements is briefly described.

## INTRODUCTION

Our neuromorphs are VLSI circuits that comprise a spatially extensive artificial dendritic tree [1], [2], a spike generating soma, and many spike output pathways, each of which imparts a programmable delay to the spikes traveling on it. Figure 1a is a simplified circuit diagram of a short, five-compartment section of silicon dendrite. Each compartment has a capacitor, $C_m$, representing a membrane capacitance, two programmable resistors, $R_m$ and $R_a$, representing a membrane resistance and a cytoplasmic resistance, and several MOS field effect transistors that simulate synapses by enabling transient inward or outward transmembrane current. The resulting potential appearing at the soma, point S in Figure 1b, determines the rate of output spike firing. P-channel transistors (upper) produce excitatory effects on spike firing by increasing the membrane potential. Inhibition is mediated by two interleaved populations of n-channel transistors (lower). Half have their source terminals connected to ground and exert inhibitory effects by lowering membrane potential; the other half have their source terminals connected to a programmable voltage and exert inhibitory effects by pulling the membrane potential towards this voltage. When this voltage is set near the membrane resting voltage these transistors behave like shunting or silent inhibitory synapses [3]-[5]. For the results reported here, all inhibitory transistor sources were set to ground potential to produce only hyperpolarizing membrane potential changes.

The synapse transistors are turned on by an impulse signal applied to their gate terminals. The resultant transmembrane current depends on the conductance of the transistor in the on state, the duration of the gate terminal impulse signal, and the potential difference across the transistor. In most of our VLSI implementations, the dendritic branches have sixteen compartments (32 synapses) which are connected together to form artificial dendritic trees (ADTs) like that shown in Figure 1b.

A neuromorph's dynamics is due in large part to the Nth-order low-pass filter properties of its ADT. The spatial and temporal signal processing capabilities are illustrated in Figure 1c,d by the effects of activating synapses at various positions on an ADT. The impulse responses were measured at the soma (point S in Figure 1b) after activating a single excitatory or inhibitory synapse at 15 different locations on an ADT. Although the synapse transistors were turned on for only 100 nsec, the resulting impulse responses last for hundreds of milliseconds. The peak amplitude of the response is largest for synaptic activation nearest the soma and diminishes rapidly for sites farther away, while the latency to peak increases with distance from the soma. These effects of synapse position mimic those occurring in passive dendrites of biological neurons [6],[7]. They also illustrate how the ADT structure inherently accords different weights to synapses: pulsatile afferent signals exert effects in time and amplitude that depend upon synapse position. In this paper we show how ADT dynamics is easily altered using switched-capacitors to vary impulse response duration by six orders of magnitude

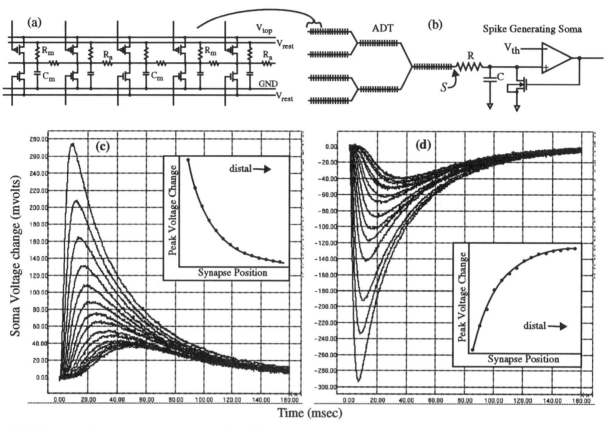

FIGURE 1. a) Five compartment segment of artificial dendrite. b) Diagram of VLSI neuromorph comprising a spatially extensive artificial dendritic tree (ADT) and a spike generating soma. The crosses on the ADT represent synapse locations. c) and d) Measured impulse responses at soma (point S) due to activating a single synapse at different locations for 100 nsec. Note that the response lasts over 1,000,000 times longer than the signal that caused it. Insets show the peak voltage change as a function of synapse position.

In many real systems, the inherent dynamics may span a wide temporal range, from hundreds of microseconds to thousands of milliseconds. The dynamic behavior of our ADT-neuromorphs depends on the relative values of $R_m$, $R_a$, and $C_m$, analogous to biological dendrites [8]. Furthermore, the dynamics of individual branches or individual neuromorphs may need to be considerably different from each other, depending on the application. The ADT fixed-value compartmental capacitor, $C_m$, (see Figure 1a) is purposely made small to conserve silicon real estate (100-2000 fF, depending on the particular chip design), suggesting that a wide range of programmable compartmental resistances (1-1,000,000 megohms) is required to realize the range of expected dynamics.

A programmable well-behaved resistor can be realized by switching one terminal of a grounded capacitor between the terminals of the resistor [9]. The effective resistance depends on the switching frequency and the value of the holding capacitor, C (see Figure 2). In our silicon neuromorphs C has been experimentally determined to be approximately five femtofarads.

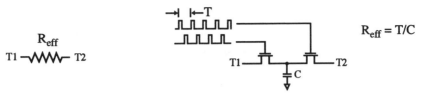

FIGURE 2. Switched-capacitor resistor. A holding capacitor transfers a small amount of charge between the terminals (T1 and T2) every switching period, T. The effective resistance is determined by a programmable switching frequency and the value of the holding capacitor.

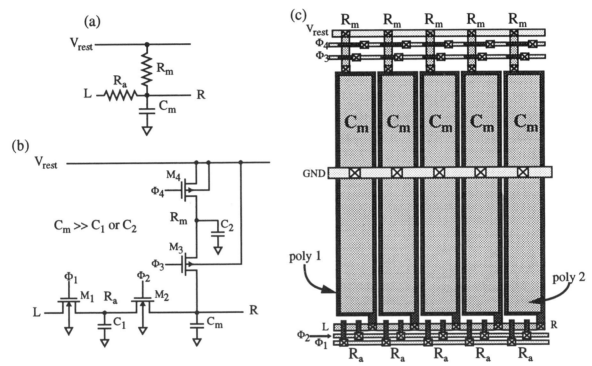

FIGURE 3. a) Compartment circuit diagram *sans* synapse circuitry. b) Switched-capacitor implementation of compartmental resistances. Transistors $M_3$, $M_4$ and capacitor $C_2$ emulate $R_m$. Transistors $M_1$, $M_2$, and capacitor $C_1$ emulate $R_a$. Clock signals, $\phi_1$, $\phi_2$, $\phi_3$, $\phi_4$, permit adjustment of resistance over a wide range. $V_{rest}$ establishes the resting voltage (typically 2.5V). c) Basic VLSI layout. Five compartments are abutted together to form a short dendrite branch section (synapse circuitry not shown). The compartmental capacitor, $C_m$, is implemented with poly1/poly2 plates and varies between 0.1-2.0 pF, depending on the particular chip design. Construction of ADTs is done by placing compartments side-by-side until the desired branch length is reached. Branches are then connected via metal or poly wires to form trees. The spacing between compartments is 2 μm, and they are aligned such that the inputs of one compartment connect to the outputs of the previous compartment.

## VLSI Implementation

Figure 3a shows the circuit diagram of a dendrite compartment *sans* synapse circuitry and Figure 3b shows its switched-capacitor implementation. Capacitor $C_1$ coupled with transistors $M_1$ and $M_2$ emulate the axial resistor, $R_a$, while $C_2$, $M_3$, and $M_4$ emulate the membrane resistor, $R_m$. The switches, $M_1$, $M_2$, $M_3$, and $M_4$, in the open state have a resistance of about $10^{12}$ Ω, and in the closed state their resistance is about 30 KΩ. The gate signals, $\Phi_1/\Phi_2$ and

$\Phi_3/ \Phi_4$ do not overlap in the logic 1 state, ensuring that only one switch of each pair is closed at a time. All chips were fabricated using a 2 μm CMOS double-poly n-well process on a 2mm by 2mm MOSIS Tiny Chip format. Figure 3c illustrates the basic integrated circuit layout of a five compartment VLSI dendrite section, excluding the synapse circuitry.

## RESULTS

The variation in impulse response with changes in dendrite resistances is shown in Figure 4 for a four-branched neuromorph. A single midbranch synapse was activated for 100 nsec and the soma voltage recorded for 160 msec. Figure 4a shows recordings of impulse responses (offset for clarity) obtained with different values of $R_m$ and $R_a$ at a fixed $R_m/R_a$ ratio of 100 to 1. As both $R_m$ and $R_a$ increased by the same factor, the time scale of the impulse response lengthened so that a simple time scaling preserved the shape of the impulse response. By contrast, Figure 4b shows that increasing the Rm/Ra ratio led to an increase in decay time relative to rise time (i.e., impulse response shape was not preserved).

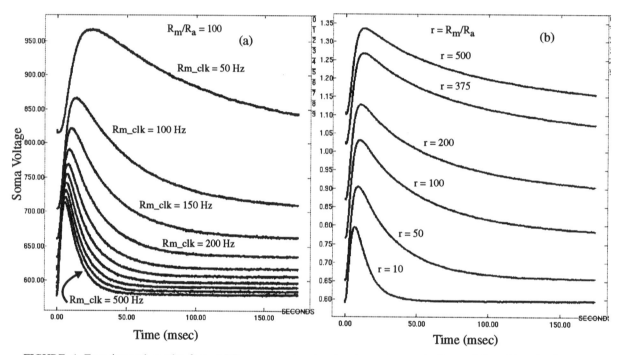

FIGURE 4. Experimental results from ADT-neuromorphs showing how changes in $R_m$ and $R_a$ affect the impulse response. Curves show soma voltage after activating a single ADT synapse for 100 nsec. Curves offset for clarity. a) data for fixed ratio of $R_m/R_a$ (r = 100). Frequency of switched-capacitor, Rm, is shown next to corresponding curve. b) data for fixed $R_a$ and various values of $R_m$, (Rm_clk = 50 Hz).

Figure 5a shows impulse responses generated by a 100 nsec activation of a proximal synapse when the switched-capacitor clocks were set at their lowest frequencies to produce slow dynamics. Thus, when Rm_clk was 5 Hz, the decay time of the impulse response was nearly 20 seconds; the activation of more distal synapses produced even longer decay times (Figure 5b). The effective resistance of $R_m$ at these low switching frequencies is over 1000 GΩ as determined by comparing experimental data to simulation results. With these dynamics, the impulse response lasts over a billion times longer than the impulse that initiated it. At high switching frequency (~10 Mhz), where the ADT-neuromorph's dynamics is much faster, the decay time for the impulse response is approximately 100 μsec.

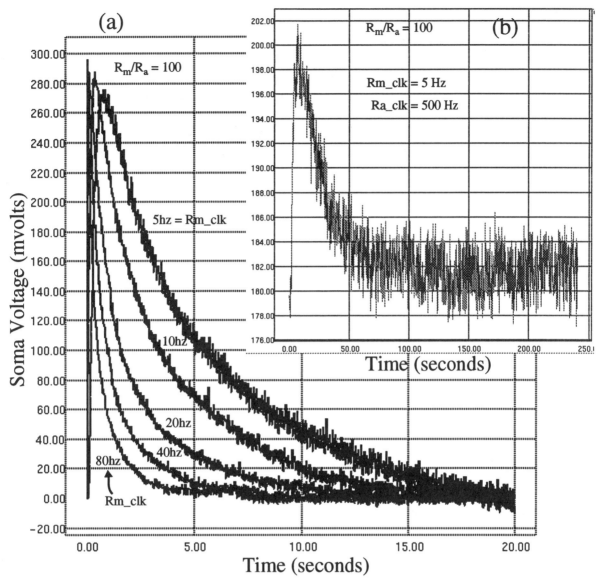

FIGURE 5. Impulse response due to activating a single synapse for 100 nsec. In these experiments, the switched-capacitor clocks were set at their lowest frequencies to produce very slow dynamics. At the lowest end, where Rm_clk was 5 Hz, the decay time was nearly 20 seconds. In each recording, the frequency of Ra_clk was 100 times that of Rm_clk. Activating more distal synapses using these dynamics produce even longer decay times. The effective $R_m$ resistance at the low end of switching frequency is over 1000 G$\Omega$. a) proximal synapse b) midbranch synapse. The impulse response lasts over nine orders of magnitude longer than the initiating impulse.

## SUMMARY

The results presented here demonstrate that a wide range of ADT-neuromorph dynamics is easily obtained by changing the switching frequency of the dendritic tree switched-capacitor transistors. The ability to change the dynamical behavior of a particular ADT-neuromorph or group of neuromorphs provides a way to match temporal response to a specific application or task. We believe that this capability represents a distinct advantage to be exploited. In a companion paper [10], we present some initial work on changing neuromorph dynamics and its effect on neuromorph spiking output as a function of changing temporal patterns of pulsatile inputs.

## ACKNOWLEDGEMENTS

This work was supported by grants from the National Science Foundation (# BCS-9315879) and the University of Delaware Research Foundation.

## REFERENCES

[1]   J. G. Elias, "Artificial dendritic trees," *Neural Computation,* vol. 5, pp. 648-664, 1993.

[2]   J. G. Elias, "Silicon dendritic trees," to appear in *Silicon Implementation of Pulse-Coded Neural Networks,* ed. J. Meador, Chap. 2, 1994, Kluwer Academic Press, Norwell, Mass.

[3]   V. Torre and T. Poggio, "A synaptic mechanism possibly underlying directional selectivity to motion," *Proc. R. Soc. Lond.* B. vol 202, pp. 409-416, 1978.

[4]   C. Koch and T. Poggio, "Biophysics of computation: neurons, synapses, and membranes," in *Synaptic Function* edited by G.M. Edelman, W.E. Gall, W.M. Cowan. Wiley-Liss, New York, pp. 637-697, 1987.

[5]   C. Koch, T. Poggio, and V. Torre, "Nonlinear interactions in a dendritic tree: Localization, timing and role in information processing," *Proc. Natl. Acad. Sci.* vol. 80 pp. 2799-2802.

[6]   W. Rall, "Theoretical significance of dendritic trees for neuronal input-output relations," in *Neural Theory and Modeling,* R. F. Reiss, Ed., Stanford University Press, pp. 73-79, 1964.

[7]    G. M. Shepherd and C. Koch, "Dendritic electrotonus and synaptic integration", in *The Synaptic Organization of the Brain,* ed. G. M. Shepherd, Oxford University Press, appendix, 1990.

[8]   W. Rall, "Cable properties of dendrites and effect of synaptic location," in *Excitatory Synaptic Mechanisms,* P. Andersen and J. K. S. Jansen, eds. Universitetsforlaget, Oslo, 1970.

[9]   P. E. Allen and E. Sanchez-Sinencio, *Switched Capacitor Circuits.* New York: Van Nostrand Reinhold Company, 1984.

[10]   D. P. M. Northmore and J. G. Elias, "Dynamical VLSI neuromorphs," submitted to WCNN-94

# Behavior of the Complex Numbered Back-Propagation Network which has Learned Similar Transformation

Tohru Nitta

Electrotechnical Laboratory,

1-1-4 Umezono, Tsukuba Science City, Ibaraki, 305 Japan.

**Abstract :**

In this paper, the ability of the "Complex-BP" algorithm to learn *similar transformation* is analyzed. A Complex-BP network which has learned *similar transformation*, has the ability to generalize the *similitude ratio* with a distance error which is represented by the sine of the difference between the argument of the test pattern and that of the training pattern.

## 1 Introduction

The "Complex-BP" algorithm [2, 3] is a complex numbered version of the standard back-propagation algorithm, called here, "Real-BP" [4]. This algorithm enables the network to learn complex-valued patterns naturally. It has been shown by computational experiments that the algorithm can transform geometrical figures (whereas, the Real-BP cannot) [2, 3], which is an inherent property of the Complex-BP. In this connection, the Complex-BP algorithm has already been applied to the interpretation of optical flow (motion vector field calculated from images) and estimation of motion which are important tasks in computer vision [5, 6].

This paper presents a mathematical analysis of the behavior of a neural network which has learned the concept of *similar transformation*, using the Complex-BP. The result of this analysis is as follows: a Complex-BP network which has learned a single similitude ratio, has the ability to generalize the similitude ratio with a distance error which is represented by the sine of the difference between the argument of the test pattern and that of the training pattern.

## 2 The "Complex-BP" Algorithm

This section briefly describes the Complex-BP algorithm [2, 3]. It can be applied to multi-layered neural networks in which weights, threshold values, input and output signals are all complex numbers, and the output function $f_C$ of a neuron is defined to be

$$f_C(z) = f_R(x) + i f_R(y), \tag{1}$$

where $z = x + iy$, $i$ denotes $\sqrt{-1}$ and $f_R(u) = 1/(1 + \exp(-u))$, that is, the real and imaginary parts of the output of a neuron mean the sigmoid functions of the real part $x$ and imaginary part $y$ of the net input $z$ to neuron, respectively. The learning rule has been obtained by using a steepest descent method.

Note that there is another formulation of the complex-valued version [1] in which the output function is a complex-valued function $f_C(z) = 1/(1 + \exp(-z))$, where $z = x + iy$.

## 3 An Analysis of the Ability to Learn Similar Transformation

This section presents a mathematical analysis of the behavior of a complex-valued neural network which has learned the concept of similar transformation using the Complex-BP algorithm.

We will introduce a simple 1-1-1 three-layered (complex-valued) network for the analysis. We will use $v \exp[iw] \in C$ for the weight between the input and hidden neurons, $c \exp[id] \in C$ for the weight between the hidden and output neurons, $s \exp[it] \in C$ for the threshold of the hidden neuron, and $r \exp[il] \in C$ for the threshold of the output neuron, where $C$ denotes the set of complex numbers. Let $v^0 \exp[iw^0]$, $c^0 \exp[id^0]$, $s^0 \exp[it^0]$ and $r^0 \exp[il^0]$ denote learning parameters after learning. We will also define in advance the following constants:

$$K = \frac{1}{(1+\sqrt{2})c^0 + 2r^0}, \quad G = \frac{kac^0v^0}{2(kav^0 + s^0)}, \quad A = \frac{c^0s^0}{2(kav^0 + s^0)}, \quad B = \frac{c^0}{\sqrt{2}}, \quad C = r^0,$$

$$H_R = A\cos(t^0 + d^0) + B\cos\left(d^0 + \frac{\pi}{4}\right) + C\cos(l^0),$$

$$H_I = A\sin(t^0 + d^0) + B\sin\left(d^0 + \frac{\pi}{4}\right) + C\sin(l^0),$$

$$M = 2K\sqrt{H_R^2 + H_I^2}. \tag{2}$$

We will use the following learning patterns: $p$ points with equal intervals "$a$" on a straight line which forms an angle $x$ degrees to the real axis, are transformed into the points which can be obtained by the similar transformation on the distance from the origin with the similitude ratio $\beta$ in the complex plane, respectively (Fig. 1). That is, there are $p$ training points; for any $1 \le k \le p$, an input point can be expressed as

$$ka\exp[ix], \tag{3}$$

and the corresponding output point as

$$\frac{1}{2}ka\beta \exp[ix] + \frac{1}{\sqrt{2}}\exp\left[i\frac{\pi}{4}\right], \tag{4}$$

where $k, p \in N$, $a, x, \beta \in R^+$, $0 < pa\beta \le 1$ which limits the values of learning patterns to the range from $-1$ to $1$ in the complex plane ($R^+$ denotes the set of nonnegative real numbers). Note that although the output points take a value $z$ within the range $-1 \le Re[z], Im[z] \le 1$, we transformed them as having a value $z$ within the range $0 \le Re[z], Im[z] \le 1$, because the Complex-BP network generates a value $z$ within the range $0 \le Re[z], Im[z] \le 1$. For this reason, eqn (4) seems to be somewhat complicated.

The following theorem will explain the qualitative properties of the generalization ability of the Complex-BP on a similitude ratio.

THEOREM 1. *Fix $1 \le k \le p$ arbitrarily. To the Complex-BP network which has learned the training points (eqns (3) and (4)), a test point $ka\exp[i(x + \phi)]$ is given which can be obtained by a counterclockwise rotation of an input training point $ka\exp[ix]$ by arbitrary $\phi$ degrees about the origin (Fig. 1). Then, the network generates the following value:*

$$\left[\frac{1}{2}ka\beta \exp[i(x+\phi)] + \frac{1}{\sqrt{2}}\exp\left[i\frac{\pi}{4}\right]\right] + E(\phi) \in C. \tag{5}$$

*The first term of eqn (5) refers to the point which can be obtained by the similar transformation of the test point $ka\exp[i(x+\phi)]$ on the distance from the origin with the similitude ratio $\beta$ in the complex plane (Fig. 1). Note that $\beta$ is the similitude ratio which the network has learned. Also, the second term $E(\phi)$ is a complex number which denotes the error,* and the absolute value called *"Generalization Error on Similitude Ratio"* is given in the following expression:

$$|E(\phi)| = M\left|\sin\left(\frac{\phi}{2}\right)\right|.$$

(6)

The proof will be given in the Appendix.

We can find from Theorem 1 that the "Generalization Error on Similitude Ratio" $|E(\phi)|$ increases as the distance between the test and input training points increases (i.e., $\phi$ becomes larger), and it takes the maximum value $M$ at the point which gives the largest distance ($\phi = 180$). Furthermore, it decreases as the test point approaches the input training point.

## 4    Conclusions

We have analyzed the behavior of a Complex-BP network which has learned the concept of *similar transformation* and cleared the qualitative property of the generalization ability of the Complex-BP on a similitude ratio. A Complex-BP network which has learned a single similitude ratio, has the ability to generalize the similitude ratio with a distance error which is represented by the sine of the difference between the argument of the test pattern and that of the training pattern. The analysis of the behavior of a Complex-BP network which has learned more than one similitude ratio will be presented in a future paper.

### Acknowledgements

We wish to thank Drs. K.Ohta and T.Higuchi for providing the opportunity for this study.

## References

[1] Kim, M. S. and Guest, C. C. (1990). Modification of Backpropagation Networks for Complex-Valued Signal Processing in Frequency Domain. *Proc. IEEE/INNS International Joint Conference on Neural Networks*, San Diego, June, Vol.3, pp.27-31.

[2] Nitta, T. and Furuya, T. (1991). A Complex Back-Propagation Learning. *Transactions of Information Processing Society of Japan*, Vol.32, No.10, pp.1319-1329 (in Japanese).

[3] Nitta, T. (1993). A Complex Numbered Version of the Back-Propagation Algorithm. *Proc. INNS World Congress on Neural Networks*, Portland, July, Vol.3, pp.576-579.

[4] Rumelhart, D. E. et al. (1986). *Parallel Distributed Processing*, Vol.1, MIT Press.

[5] Miyauchi, M. and Seki, M. (1992). Interpretation of Optical Flow through Neural Network Learning. *Proc. IEEE International Conference on Communication Systems /International Symposium on Information Theory and its Applications*, Singapore, pp.1247-1251.

[6] Miyauchi, M., Seki, M., Watanabe, A. and Miyauchi, A. (1992). Interpretation of Optical Flow through Neural Network Learning. *Proc. IAPR Workshop on Machine Vision Applications*, Tokyo, pp.523-528.

# APPENDIX

## Proof of Theorem 1

In order to prove Theorem 1, a technical result is needed:

LEMMA. *For any $1 \le k \le p$, the following approximate equations hold:*

$$K\left[G\cos(x + w^0 + d^0) + H_R\right] + \frac{1}{2} = \frac{1}{2}ka\beta\cos(x) + \frac{1}{2}, \qquad (A-1)$$

$$K\left[G\sin(x + w^0 + d^0) + H_I\right] + \frac{1}{2} = \frac{1}{2}ka\beta\sin(x) + \frac{1}{2}. \qquad (A-2)$$

*Proof.* For any $1 \le k \le p$, by computing the output value of the Complex-BP network for the input training point $ka\exp[ix]$, we find that the real part of the output value is equal to the left side of eqn (A-1), and the imaginary part the left side of eqn (A-2). In the above computations, the sigmoid function in the output function (eqn (1)) of each neuron was approximated by the following piecewise linear functions:

$$g(x) = \begin{cases} \frac{1}{2(kav^0 + s^0)}x + \frac{1}{2} & (-(kav^0 + s^0) \le x \le kav^0 + s^0) \\ 1 & (kav^0 + s^0 < x) \\ 0 & (x < -(kav^0 + s^0)) \end{cases} \qquad (A-3)$$

for the hidden neuron, and

$$h(x) = \begin{cases} \frac{1}{(1+\sqrt{2})c^0 + 2r^0}x + \frac{1}{2} & \left(-(\frac{1+\sqrt{2}}{2}c^0 + r^0) \le x \le \frac{1+\sqrt{2}}{2}c^0 + r^0\right) \\ 1 & \left(\frac{1+\sqrt{2}}{2}c^0 + r^0 < x\right) \\ 0 & \left(x < -(\frac{1+\sqrt{2}}{2}c^0 + r^0)\right) \end{cases} \qquad (A-4)$$

for the output neuron. On the other hand, the real and imaginary parts of the output value of the complex-valued neural network for the input training point should be equal to the real and imaginary parts of the output training point $(1/2)ka\beta\exp[ix] + (1/\sqrt{2})\exp[i(\pi/4)]$, respectively. This concludes the proof of Lemma. ∎

*Proof of Theorem 1.* Theorem 1 will be proved according to the following policy: using eqns (A-1) and (A-2) in Lemma, we compute the output value of the Complex-BP network for the test point $ka\exp[i(x+\phi)]$, and transform it into [ The point which can be generated by the similar transformation of the test point on the distance from the origin with the similitude ratio $\beta$ ] + [ Error ].

First, we compute the <u>real part</u> of the output value when the test point $ka\exp[i(x+\phi)]$ is fed into the Complex-BP network. Using the equation

$$\cos\theta - \lambda\sin\theta = \sqrt{1 + \lambda^2}\cos(\theta + \phi) \qquad (A-5)$$

for any $\theta$, where $\lambda = \tan\phi$, and by computing [ eqn (A-1) ] $- \lambda \cdot$[ eqn (A-2) ], we get

$$K\left[G\cos(x + \phi + w^0 + d^0) + H_R\right] + \frac{1}{2} = \left[\frac{1}{2}ka\beta\cos(x + \phi) + \frac{1}{2}\right] + E_{re}(\phi), \qquad (A-6)$$

where

$$E_{re}(\phi) = 2K\sin\left(\frac{\phi}{2}\right) \cdot \left[A\sin\left(t^0 + d^0 + \frac{\phi}{2}\right) + B\sin\left(d^0 + \frac{\pi}{4} + \frac{\phi}{2}\right) + C\sin\left(l^0 + \frac{\phi}{2}\right)\right] \qquad (A-7)$$

Note that the left side of eqn (A-6) refers to the <u>real part</u> of the output value of the Complex-BP network for the test point, and the first term of the right side of eqn (A-6) the <u>real part</u> of "the point which can be generated by the similar transformation of the test point on the distance from the origin with the similitude ratio $\beta$" $ka\beta \exp[i(x + \phi)]$. Finally, $E_{re}(\phi)$ refers to the <u>real part</u> of a complex number which denotes "Error".

Similarly, using the equation

$$\lambda \cos\theta + \sin\theta = \sqrt{1 + \lambda^2} \sin(\theta + \phi) \qquad (A - 8)$$

for any $\theta$, where $\lambda = \tan\phi$, and by computing $\lambda \cdot [$ eqn (A-1) $] + [$ eqn (A-2) $]$, we get

$$K\left[G\sin(x + \phi + w^0 + d^0) + H_I\right] + \frac{1}{2} = \left[\frac{1}{2}ka\beta\sin(x + \phi) + \frac{1}{2}\right] + E_{im}(\phi), \qquad (A - 9)$$

where

$$E_{im}(\phi) = -2K\sin\left(\frac{\phi}{2}\right) \cdot \left[A\cos\left(t^0 + d^0 + \frac{\phi}{2}\right) + B\cos\left(d^0 + \frac{\pi}{4} + \frac{\phi}{2}\right) + C\cos\left(l^0 + \frac{\phi}{2}\right)\right].$$
$$(A - 10)$$

Note that the left side of eqn (A-9) refers to the <u>imaginary part</u> of the output value of the Complex-BP network for the test point, and the first term of the right side of eqn (A-9) the <u>imaginary part</u> of "the point which can be generated by the similar transformation of the test point on the distance from the origin with the similitude ratio $\beta$" $ka\beta \exp[i(x + \phi)]$. Finally, $E_{im}(\phi)$ refers to the <u>imaginary part</u> of a complex number which denotes "Error".

Hence, it follows from eqns (A-6) and (A-9) that the output value of the Complex-BP network for the test point can be expressed as

$$\left[\frac{1}{2}ka\beta\exp[i(x + \phi)] + \frac{1}{\sqrt{2}}\exp\left[i\frac{\pi}{4}\right]\right] + E(\phi), \qquad (A - 11)$$

where

$$E(\phi) \stackrel{\text{def}}{=} E_{re}(\phi) + iE_{im}(\phi). \qquad (A - 12)$$

That is, the Complex-BP network reduces the test point $ka\exp[i(x + \phi)]$ on the distance from the origin with the learned similitude ratio $\beta$ with the error $E(\phi)$. And eqn (6) follows from eqns (A-7) and (A-10). ∎

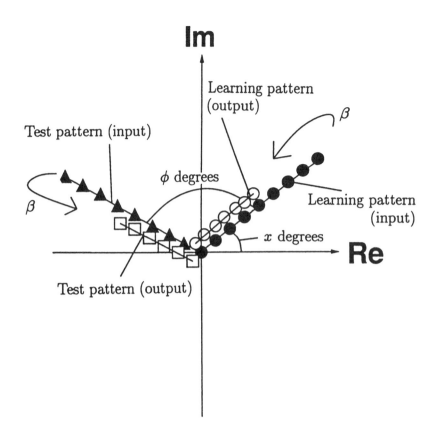

**Fig. 1.** Learning and test patterns used in the mathematical analysis of the behavior of a Complex-BP network which has learned the similar transformation of the points on the distance from the origin with the similitude ratio $\beta$ in the complex plane. A black circle denotes an input training point, a white circle an output training point, a black triangle an input test point, and a white square an output test point generated by the Complex-BP.

# Globally Diagonal Lyapunov Functions for Discrete-Time Analogy Neural Networks

Liang Jin, Peter N. Nikiforuk, Madan M. Gupta

Intelligent Systems Research Laboratory
College of Engineering, University of Saskatchewan
Saskatoon, Saskatchewan, Canada S7N 0W0

## ABSTRACT

*In this paper, some global stability criteria of an equilibrium state for a general class of discrete-time dynamic neural networks are presented using a novel diagonal Lyapunov function approach, and the resultsing criteria are described by the diagonal Lyapunov matrix equations. First, globally diagonal Lyapunov function approaches are applied to a study equilibrium stability problem of a class of discrete-time dynamic neural networks without linear terms. Some novel stability conditions are then obtained for a general class of discrete-time dynamic neural networks.*

## 1. INTRODUCTION

Dynamic neural networks which contain both the feedforward and feedback connections between neural layers play an important role in visual processing, pattern recognition as well as in neural computing and control. However, the complex dynamic structures of such neural networks in computing tasks such as information processing and associative memory present a challenge in regards to stability investigations. The idea of stability of an equilibrium point of a dynamic system is of fundamental importance for the dynamic neural networks. An equilibrium is stable if all nearby solutions stay nearby. It is asymptotically stable if all nearby solutions not only stay nearby, but also tend to the equilibrium point.

*Diagonal Lyapunov function method* was first proposed by *Persidskii* (1969) for studying the absolute stability, which is based on the existence of a diagonal solution of the Lyapunov equation. Recently, *Kaszkurewicz* and *Bhaya* (1993) used this approach to discuss robust stability of a class of continuous-time and discrete-time nonlinear systems, and *Matsuoka* (1992) derived a diagonal Lyapunov function for a Hopfield neural network with an asymmetric weight matrix, and established some absolute stability conditions which were more relax than the previous stability results on dynamic neural networks. In this paper, a novel diagonal Lyapunov function approach is employed to study globally asymptotical stability of a general class of discrete-time analogy neural networks. The resultsing criteria for globally asymptotical stability are described by the diagonal Lyapunov matrix equations.

## 2. DISCRETE-TIME ANALOGY NEURAL NETWORKS

Consider a class of dynamic neural network described by the following set of difference equations

$$\mathbf{x}(k+1) = -A\mathbf{x}(k) + W\sigma(\mathbf{x}(k)) + \mathbf{s} \tag{1}$$

where $\mathbf{x} = [x_1, \ldots, x_n]^T$ is the neuraal state vector, $W = [w_{ij}]_{n \times n}$ is the synaptic weight matrix, $\mathbf{s} = [s_1, \ldots, s_n]^T$ is the constant threshold vector, and the coefficient matrix $A = [\alpha_1, \ldots, \alpha_n]$ with $|\alpha_i| < 1$. The nonlinear neural activation function $\sigma(.)$ may be chosen as a continuous and differentiable nonlinear sigmoidal function satisfying the following conditions: (i) $\sigma(x) \longrightarrow \pm 1$ as $x \longrightarrow \pm\infty$; (ii) $\sigma(x)$ is bounded with the upper bound 1 and the lower bound $-1$; (iii) $\sigma(x) = 0$ at a unique point $x = 0$; (iv) $\sigma'(x) > 0$ and $\sigma'(x) \longrightarrow 0$ as $x \longrightarrow \pm\infty$; (v) $\sigma'(x)$ has a global maximal value $\lambda$.

Typical examples of such a function $\sigma(.)$ are

$$\sigma_1(x) = tanh(\lambda x), \quad \sigma_2(x) = \frac{1 - e^{-\lambda x}}{1 + e^{-\lambda x}}, \quad \sigma_3(x) = \frac{2}{\pi} tan^{-1}(\frac{\pi\lambda}{2}x)$$

where $\lambda > 0$ is a constant which determines the slope of $\sigma(x)$ or the so-called *activation gain*. The above nonlinear activation functions are bounded, monotonic, non-decreasing functions. Define a mapping $\mathbf{g} : R^n \longrightarrow R^n$ as $\mathbf{g}(\mathbf{x}) = (A + I)^{-1}W\sigma(\mathbf{x}) + (A + I)^{-1}\mathbf{s}$. The equilibrium points of the system (1) are then the fixed points of the mapping $\mathbf{g}(\mathbf{x})$. Furthermore, for an arbitrary given constant input $\mathbf{s} \in R^n$, let $\Omega$ be a hypercube defined by $\Omega = \{\mathbf{x} : |\mathbf{x} - (A + I)^{-1}\mathbf{s}| \leq \sqrt{n}/\alpha\|W\|_2\}$, where $\alpha = min\{\alpha_i + 1\}$. Then for an arbitrary $\mathbf{x} \in \Omega$

$$|\mathbf{g}(\mathbf{x}) - (A + I)^{-1}\mathbf{s}| = |(A + I)^{-1}W\sigma(\mathbf{x})| \leq \|(A + I)^{-1}\|_2\|W\|_2|\sigma(\mathbf{x})| \leq \frac{\sqrt{n}}{\alpha}\|W\|_2$$

holds. Hence, $\mathbf{g}(\mathbf{x})$ is a continuous mapping from a bounded and closed set $\Omega$ onto itself; that is, $\mathbf{g}(\mathbf{x}) : \Omega \longrightarrow \Omega$. According to the well-known Brouwer's fixed point theorem, $\mathbf{g}(\mathbf{x})$ has at least one fixed point in $\Omega$.

Let $\mathbf{x}^* = [x_1^*, ..., x_n^*]^T$ be an equilibrium state of system (1), one may introduce a new state vector $\mathbf{z} = [z_1, ..., z_n]^T = \mathbf{x} - \mathbf{x}^*$. Then, system (1) can be rewritten in terms of $\mathbf{z}$ as

$$\mathbf{z}(k + 1) = -A\mathbf{z}(k) + Wf(\mathbf{z}(k)) \tag{2}$$

where $\mathbf{f}(\mathbf{z}) = [f_1(z_1), \vdots, f_n(z_n)]^T$ and $f_i(z_i) \equiv \sigma_i(z_i + x_i^*) - \sigma_i(x_i^*)$. Since $0 < \sigma_i'(z_i + x_i^*) = f_i'(z_i) \leq \lambda$, $i = 1, 2, ..., n$, we have $\lambda z_i \leq f_i(z_i) < 0$, for $z_i < 0$, and $0 < f_i(z_i) \leq \lambda z_i$, for $z_i > 0$.

## 2. GLOBAL STABILITY FOR THE MODEL WITHOUT LINEAR TERMS

### 2.1 The Previously Reported Results

A simplified model of discrete-time analogy neural networks can be obtained by setting all $\alpha_i = 0$ in Eq. (1). In this case, Eq. (1) can be represented as

$$\mathbf{z}(k + 1) = W\mathbf{f}(\mathbf{z}(k)) \tag{3}$$

When the synaptic weight matrix $W$ is symmetric; that is, $W = W^T$, a global convergence condition proposed by *Marcus* and *Westervelt* (1989) is $\lambda_{min}(W) < 1/\lambda$, where $\lambda_{min}(W)$ represents the minumim eigenvalue of the matrix $W$. If this condition is satisfied, the states of the system (1) will always converge to one of their asymptotical stable equilibrium points regardless to the initial values of the states. However, the interesting point of this paper is globally asymptotical stability of the indivdual equilibrium points.

On the other hand, the *Lyapunov's first method or Lyapunov's direct method* may be used to derive the stability conditions of equilibrium point of system (3). To apply this method for stability analysis, the Jacobian $J(\mathbf{z})$ of the system (3) is given by

$$J(\mathbf{z}) = WF(\mathbf{z})$$

where $F(\mathbf{z}) = diag[f_1'(z_1), ..., f_n'(z_n)]$. The system (3) has a unique equilibrium point if all the eigenvalues of the Jacobian are inside the unit circle for all the states $\mathbf{z}$, and a given weight matrix $W$. In this case, where $Wf(\mathbf{z})$ is a contraction mapping, and system (3) has a unique global attractor $\mathbf{z} = \mathbf{0}$ or $\mathbf{x} = \mathbf{x}^*$. Hence, for the arbitrary initial state, the state of system (1) will converge to $x^*$ for a given weight matrix $W$ and input $s$. Note that every eigenvalue of a matrix is not greater than any matrix norm; thatis

$$\lambda_{max}(.) \leq \|.\|$$

one may obtain the following inequality

$$\lambda_{max}(WF(\mathbf{z})) \leq \|WF(\mathbf{z})\| \leq \|W\|\|F(\mathbf{z})\| \leq \lambda\|W\|$$

Hence, a simple norm stability condition for system (3) which was suggested by *Li* (1992) may be direct given as follows

$$\|W\| < \frac{1}{\lambda} \tag{4}$$

where the following several types of matrix norms may be used in calculation

$$\|W\|_1 = \max_j \sum_{i=1}^n |w_{ij}|, \quad \|W\|_\infty = \max_i \sum_{j=1}^n |w_{ij}|, \quad \|W\|_2 = \{\lambda_{max}(W^T W)\}^{1/2}$$

On the other hand, as proposed by *Jin, Nikiforuk*, and *Gupta* (1992), the Ostrowski's theorem [7] may be used for estimating the positions of all eigenvalues of the Jacobian $J()$, then a global stability condition may be given as

$$\max_i \{|w_{ii}| + R_i^\gamma C_i^{1-\gamma}\} < \frac{1}{\lambda} \tag{5}$$

where $R_i$ and $C_i$ denote the deleted row and deleted column sums of $W$, respectively, and are defined by

$$R_i = \sum_{j=1, j \neq i}^n |w_{i,j}|, \quad and \quad C_i = \sum_{j=1, j \neq i}^n |w_{j,i}|$$

The stability condition (5) may provide a better stability estimation than the norm stability condition (4) [10]. Obviously, when $\gamma = 0$ and $\gamma = 1$, the inequality (4) becomes as the norm conditions $\|W\|_1 < 1/\lambda$ and $\|W\|_\infty < 1/\lambda$, respectively.

## 2.2 Diagonal Stability Condition

**Lemma 1.** *The system (3) is globally asymptotically stable, if there exists a positive definite and radially unbounded function* $V(\mathbf{z}(k))$ *which satisfies: (i)* $V(\mathbf{z}(k)) \geq 1/\lambda^2 V(\mathbf{f}(\mathbf{z}(k)))$; *(ii)* $1/\lambda^2 V(\mathbf{f}(\mathbf{z}(k))) > V(W\mathbf{f}(\mathbf{z}((k)))$.

**Proof.** Along the solution of the system (3), one may obtain

$$\begin{aligned} \Delta V(\mathbf{z}(k)) &= V(\mathbf{z}(k+1)) - V(\mathbf{z}(k)) = V(W\mathbf{f}(\mathbf{z}(k)) - V(\mathbf{z}(k)) \\ &= V(W\mathbf{f}(z(k))) - \frac{1}{\lambda^2} V(\mathbf{f}(\mathbf{z}(k))) < 0 \end{aligned}$$

for all $\mathbf{z}(k) \neq 0$ and $\Delta V(\mathbf{z}(k)) = 0$ if and only if $\mathbf{z} = 0$. Therefore, $V(\mathbf{z})$ is a globally Lyapunov function of the system, and $\mathbf{z} = 0$ is globally asymptotically stable. $\square$

**Theorem 1** *The system (3) is globally asymptotically stable if for a* $n \times n$ *positive diagonal matrix* $P = diag[p_1, \ldots, p_n]$ *with* $p_i > 0$ *for all* $1 \leq i \leq n$, *there exists a positive definite matrix* $Q > 0$ *such that*

$$W^T P W - \frac{1}{\lambda^2} P = -Q. \tag{6}$$

**Proof.** Let a function be defined as

$$V(\mathbf{z}(k)) = \sum_{i=1, j=1}^n p_{ij} z_i(k) z_j(k) = \mathbf{z}^T P \mathbf{z} \tag{7}$$

Then, $V(\mathbf{z})$ is a positive definite. Since $P$ is positive diagonal matrix, then

$$\mathbf{z}^T P \mathbf{z} \geq \frac{1}{\lambda^2} \mathbf{f}(\mathbf{z})^T P \mathbf{f}(\mathbf{z})$$

Hence,

$$\Delta V(\mathbf{z}(k)) = \mathbf{z}^T(k+1) P \mathbf{z}(k+1) - \mathbf{z}^T(k) P \mathbf{z}(k)$$

$$\begin{aligned}
&= \mathbf{f}^T(\mathbf{z}(k))W^T PW\mathbf{f}(\mathbf{z}(k)) - \mathbf{z}^T(k)P\mathbf{z}(k) \\
&\leq \mathbf{f}^T(\mathbf{z}(k))W^T PW\mathbf{f}(\mathbf{z}(k)) - \frac{1}{\lambda^2}\mathbf{f}^T(\mathbf{z}(k))P\mathbf{f}(\mathbf{z}(k)) \\
&= \mathbf{f}^T(\mathbf{z}(k))[W^T PW - \frac{1}{\lambda^2}P]\mathbf{f}(\mathbf{z}(k))
\end{aligned} \tag{8}$$

Therefore, the result is obtained. $\square$

Theorem 1 indicates that if there exists a positive definite matrix $Q$ such that the solution $P$ of the matrix equation (6) is positive diagonal matrix, then the system (3) is globally asymptotically stable. In other words, if the synaptic weight matrix $W$ is diagonal stable, the neural system (3) is then globally asymptotical stable. In Section 5, an example will be used to show that the stability condition given in Theorem 1 may provide a better estimation for stability of the system (3) than the previously results.

## 3. GLOBAL STABILITY CONDITIONS FOR THE GENERAL MODEL

### 3.1 The Previously Reported Results

Next, let us consider a more general model of discrete-time dynamic neural network with the form

$$\mathbf{x}(k+1) = -A\mathbf{x}(k) + W\sigma(\mathbf{x}(k)) + \mathbf{I} \tag{9}$$

where $A = diag[\alpha_1,\ldots,\alpha_n]$ with $-1 < \alpha_i < 1$. The new system may be easily obtained as

$$\mathbf{z}(k+1) = -A\mathbf{z}(k) + W\mathbf{f}(\mathbf{z}(k)) \tag{10}$$

For the above neural system, the Gerschgorin's theorem [7] based global stability conditions are easily obtained as follows

$$\sum_{j=1}^{n} |w_{ij}| < \frac{1}{\lambda}(1 - \alpha_i), \quad i = 1,\ldots,n \tag{11}$$

or

$$\sum_{i=1}^{n} |w_{ij}| < \frac{1}{\lambda}(1 - \alpha_j), \quad j = 1,\ldots,n \tag{12}$$

A generalization of the above criteria was proposed by *Jin*, *Nikifourk*, and *Gupta* (1992) using Ostrowski's theorem as follows

$$\max_i \{|w_{ii}| + R_i^\gamma C_i^{1-\gamma}\} < \frac{1}{\lambda}(1 - \alpha_i) \tag{13}$$

### 3.2 Diagonal Lyapunov Function

For the system (10), a Lyapunov function is still defined as Eq. (7), then

$$\Delta V(\mathbf{z}(k)) = \mathbf{z}^T[APA - P]\mathbf{z} - \mathbf{z}^T APW\mathbf{f}(\mathbf{z}) - \mathbf{f}^T(\mathbf{z})W^T PA\mathbf{z} + f^T(\mathbf{z})W^T PWf(\mathbf{z})$$

Since $P$ is a positive diagonal matrix, it is easy to imply

$$\mathbf{z}^T[APA - P]\mathbf{z} \leq \frac{1}{\lambda^2}\langle|\mathbf{f}(\mathbf{z})|\rangle^T[APA - P]\langle|\mathbf{f}(\mathbf{z})|\rangle \leq 0 \tag{14}$$

and

$$\begin{aligned}
-\mathbf{z}^T APW\mathbf{f}^T(\mathbf{z}) &\leq \frac{1}{\lambda}\langle|\mathbf{f}(\mathbf{z})|\rangle^T |A||P||W|\langle|\mathbf{f}(\mathbf{z})|\rangle \\
-\mathbf{f}^T(\mathbf{z})W^T PA\mathbf{z} &\leq \frac{1}{\lambda}\langle|\mathbf{f}(\mathbf{z})|\rangle^T |W|^T P|A|\langle|\mathbf{f}(\mathbf{z})|\rangle
\end{aligned}$$

where the vectorial morm $\langle |.| \rangle$ is defined as $\langle |x| \rangle \equiv (|x_1|, \ldots, |x_n|)^T$ for a vector $\mathbf{x} \in R^n$. Hence

$$
\begin{aligned}
\Delta V(\mathbf{z}(k)) \;\leq\;& \frac{1}{\lambda^2}\langle |\mathbf{f}(\mathbf{z})| \rangle^T [APA - P]\langle |\mathbf{f}(\mathbf{z})| \rangle + \frac{1}{\lambda}\langle |\mathbf{f}(\mathbf{z})| \rangle^T |A|P|W|\langle |\mathbf{f}(\mathbf{z})| \rangle \\
&+ \frac{1}{\lambda}\langle |\mathbf{f}(\mathbf{z})| \rangle^T |W|^T P|A|\langle |\mathbf{f}(\mathbf{z})| \rangle + \langle |\mathbf{f}| \rangle^T (\mathbf{z})W^T PW \langle |\mathbf{f}(\mathbf{z})| \rangle ] \\
=\;& \langle |\mathbf{f}(\mathbf{z})| \rangle^T [\frac{1}{\lambda^2}(APA - P) + \frac{1}{\lambda}(|A|P|W| + |W|^T P|A|) + |W|^T P|W|]\langle |\mathbf{f}(\mathbf{z})| \rangle
\end{aligned}
$$

Therefore, the following theorem may be obtained.

**Theorem 3** *The system (10) is globally asymptotically stable if for a positive diagonal matrix $P$, there exists a positive definite matrix $Q > 0$ such that*

$$
\frac{1}{\lambda^2}(APA - P) + \frac{1}{\lambda}(|A|P|W| + |W|^T P|A|) + |W|^T P|W| = -Q. \tag{15}
$$

The above theorem indictes that if the matrix $(|A| + \lambda|W|)$ is diagonal stable, the neural system (9) is globally asymptotical stable.

## 4. AN EXAMPLE

In this example, it will be shown that if a suitable positive diagonal matrix $P$ is chosen, the stability condition presented in Theorem 1 is more relaxed than the stability conditions (4) and (5) obtained by the norm condition [13] and Ostrowski's theorem [10], respectively. Consider a simple two-neuron system without external inputs with the following form

$$
\begin{cases}
x_1(k+1) &= (\frac{1}{2})tanh(x_1(k)) + (\frac{3}{4})tanh(x_2(k)) \\
x_2(k+1) &= (\frac{1}{3})tanh(x_1(k)) + (\frac{4}{9})tanh(x_2(k))
\end{cases} \tag{16}
$$

where the $2 \times 2$ weight matrix is

$$
W = \begin{pmatrix} w_{11} & w_{12} \\ w_{21} & w_{22} \end{pmatrix} = \begin{pmatrix} \frac{1}{2} & \frac{3}{4} \\ \frac{1}{3} & \frac{4}{9} \end{pmatrix}
$$

In this case

$$
\begin{cases} R_1 = 3/4 \\ R_2 = 1/3 \end{cases}, \qquad \begin{cases} C_1 = 1/3 \\ C_2 = 3/4 \end{cases}
$$

and

$$
\max_i \min_{\gamma \in [0,1]} \{w_{ii} + R_i^\gamma C_i^{1-\gamma}\} = \frac{1}{2} + \left(\frac{3}{4}\right)^{1/2}\left(\frac{1}{3}\right)^{1/2} = 1
$$

Hence, the stability of the system (16) can not be guaranteed using the stability condition (5). The stability of the system (16) can now be tested using the norm stability condition (4) as follows

$$
\begin{aligned}
||W||_1 &= \max_j \sum_{i=1}^{2} |w_{i,j}| = \frac{5}{4} > 1 \\
||W||_\infty &= \max_i \sum_{j=1}^{2} |w_{i,j}| = \frac{43}{36} > 1 \\
||W||_2 &= \{\lambda_{max}(W^T W)\}^{1/2} = 1.065
\end{aligned}
$$

Unfortunately, based on the above choices of the matrix norms, the norm stability conditions can also not ensure the stability of the system (16). Furthermore, the stability condition given in Theorem 1 is used to test the stability of the system. Let $P = diag[p_1, p_2]$ with $p_1 > 0$ and $p_2 > 0$, then

$$W^T PW - P = \begin{pmatrix} \frac{1}{9}p_2 - \frac{3}{4}p_1 & \frac{3}{8}p_1 + \frac{4}{27}p_1 \\ \frac{3}{8}p_1 + \frac{4}{27}p_2 & \frac{9}{16}p_1 - \frac{65}{81}p_2 \end{pmatrix}$$

If let $p_1 = 1$ and $p_2 = 2$, one may obtain

$$W^T PW - P = - \begin{pmatrix} \frac{19}{36} & -\frac{145}{216} \\ -\frac{145}{216} & \frac{1351}{1296} \end{pmatrix} = -Q$$

where

$$Q = \begin{pmatrix} \frac{19}{36} & -\frac{145}{216} \\ -\frac{145}{216} & \frac{1351}{1296} \end{pmatrix}$$

is positive definite. Therefore, the system (16) is globally asymptotically stable.

## 5. CONCLUSIONS

Some novel global stability criteria for a general class of discrete-time neural networks were presented in this paper using globally diagonal Lyapunov function approach. Comparisons between the new stability conditions and previously reported results which were derived using the commonly-used Gerschgorin's theorem indicate that the former may provide the better estimation for the global stability. An example was given for demonstrating the effectiveness of the stability criteria presented.

# References

[1] M.A. Cohen and S. Grossberg, "Absolute Stability of global pattern information and parallel memory storage by competitive neural networks", *IEEE* Trans. on Systems, man, and Cybernetics, SMC-13, pp. 815-826, 1983.

[2] S. Grossberg, " Nonlinear neural networks: Principles, mechanisms and architectures", *Neural Networks*, Vol. 1, No. 1, pp. 17-61, 1988.

[3] A. Guez, V. Protopopsecu and J. Barhen, " On the stability, storage capacity, and design of nonlinear continuous neural networks", *IEEE* Trans. on Systems, man, and Cybernetics, SMC-18, pp. 80-87, 1988.

[4] M.W. Hirsch, "Convergence in neural networks, Proceedings of the IEEE International Conference on Neural Networks, Vol. II, San Diego, CA, 1987.

[5] J. Hopfield,"Neural networks and physical systems with emergent collective computational abilities," in Proc. Nat. Acad. Sci. USA, vol. 79, 1982, pp. 2554-2558.

[6] J. Hopfield,"Neurons with graded response have collective computational properties like those of two state neurons," in Proc. Nat. Acad. Sci. USA, vol. 81, 1984, pp. 3088-3092.

[7] R.A. Horn and C.A. Johnson, *Matrix Analysis*, Cambridge University Press, 1985.

[8] L. Jin, P.N. Nikiforuk and M.M. Gupta, " Dynamics and Stability of Multilayered Recurrent Neural Networks", Proc. of the 1993 IEEE International Conference on Neural networks (ICNN'93), Vol. II, pp. 1135-1140, 1993.

[9] L. Jin, P.N. Nikiforuk and M.M. Gupta, " Equilibrium stability of Discrete-time dynamic neural model," Proc. of the 1993 World Congress on Neural Networks, Vol. IV, pp. 276-279, 1993.

[10] L. Jin, P.N. Nikiforuk and M.M. Gupta, " Absolute Stability Conditions for discrete-Time Recurrent Neural Networks ", *IEEE* Trans. Neural Networks [Accepted], 1992.

[11] E. Kaszkurewicz A. Bahaya, "Roubst Stability and Diagonal Liapunov Functions," *SIAM* J. Matrix Anal. Appl., Vol. 14, No. 2, pp. 508-520, April 1993.

[12] D.G. Kelly, " Stability in contractive nonlinear neural networks", *IEEE* Trans. on Biomedical Engineering, Vol. 37, pp. 231-242, 1990.

[13] L.K. Li, "Fixed Point Analysis For Discrete-Time Recurrent Neural Networks", Proc. *IJCNN*, Vol. IV, pp. 134-139, June, 1992.

[14] C.M. Marcus and R.M. Westervelt , "Dynamics of iterated map neural networks," Physical Review A, Vol. 40, No. 1, pp. 577-587, 1989.

[15] K. Matsuoka, " Stability Conditions for Nonlinear Continuous Neural Networks with Asymmetric Connection Weights", Neural Networks, Vol. 5, pp. 495-500, 1992.

[16] S.K, Persidskil, "Problem of absolute stability," Automat. Remote Control, Vol. 12, pp. 1889,-1895, 1969.

# Dynamical VLSI Neuromorphs

David P. M. Northmore and John G. Elias

Neuroscience Program &
Electrical Engineering
University of Delaware
Newark, DE. 19716

## ABSTRACT

We describe electronic neuromorphs with extensive dendritic trees in which switched capacitor circuits emulate membrane and cytoplasmic resistances. By varying these resistances, and thereby the dendritic dynamics, it is possible to achieve tunable frequency selectivity and rate-invariance of spatiotemporal pattern responses.

## INTRODUCTION

Biological neural systems, especially those that process temporal information such as the auditory system, contain neurons that exhibit filtering characteristics that enable them to respond to specific frequencies of input spikes [1]. If artificial neuronal systems are to be similarly capable of filtering spikes trains, it would be important for individual neurons to have adjustable dynamics.

Our neuromorphs are VLSI circuits that comprise a spatially extensive artificial dendritic tree [2], a spike generating soma, and many spike output pathways, each of which imparts a programmable delay to the spikes traveling on it. Figure 1a is a simplified circuit diagram of a short, five-compartment section of silicon dendrite. Each compartment has a capacitor, $C_m$, representing a membrane capacitance, two programmable resistors, $R_m$ and $R_a$, representing a membrane resistance and a cytoplasmic resistance, and several MOS field effect transistors that simulate synapses by enabling transient inward or outward transmembrane current. The resulting potential appearing at the soma, point S in Figure 1b, determines the rate of output spike firing. P-channel transistors (upper) produce excitatory effects on spike firing by increasing the membrane potential. Inhibition is mediated by two interleaved populations of n-channel transistors (lower). Half have their source terminals connected to ground and exert inhibitory effects by lowering membrane potential; the other half have their source terminals connected to a programmable voltage and exert inhibitory effects by pulling the membrane potential towards this voltage. When this voltage is set near the membrane resting voltage these transistors behave like shunting or silent inhibitory synapses [3]-[5]. For present purposes, all inhibitory transistor sources were set to ground potential to produce only hyperpolarizing membrane potential changes.

The synapse transistors are turned on by an impulse signal applied to their gate terminals. Although synapse transistors are on for only 50 nsec, the resulting impulse response measured at the input to the soma (point S in Figure 1b) may last thousands of milliseconds. The peak amplitude of the response is largest for synaptic activation nearest the soma and diminishes rapidly for sites farther away, while the latency to peak increases with distance from the soma. Thus, as in passive dendrites of biological neurons [6]-[7], location on the dendrite determines the weighting of a synapse in its effects on amplitude and timing of the voltage response at the soma.

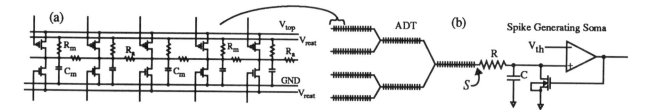

FIGURE 1. a) Five compartment segment of artificial dendrite. b) Diagram of VLSI neuromorph comprising a spatially extensive artificial dendritic tree (ADT) and a spike generating soma, The crosses on the ADT represent synapse locations. In most of our chips, dendritic trees are made of a number of branches each having 32 synapses.

The spike-generating soma (see Figure 1b) is a resettable RC integrator. When the voltage across the capacitor, $C$, exceeds a programmable threshold voltage, $V_{th}$, the comparator generates a spike that discharges $C$ and is captured in a register which is sampled by routing circuitry ("virtual wires," [2]). The spike firing frequency $F_{out}$ is given by

$$ F_{out} = -\left( RC \cdot \log\left( 1 - \frac{V_{th}}{V_s} \right) \right)^{-1} \tag{1} $$

where $V_s$ is the voltage at the soma (point S in Figure 1b).

The dynamic behavior of ADT-neuromorphs depends on the relative values of $R_m$, $R_a$, and $C_m$, as it would in biological dendrites [8]. An important feature of our VLSI neuromorphs is that $R_m$ and $R_a$ are implemented by switched capacitors [9], allowing them to be controlled over wide ranges of resistance values. The soma integrator resistor, R, is also a switched capacitor, permitting the selection of a wide range of spike firing frequencies.

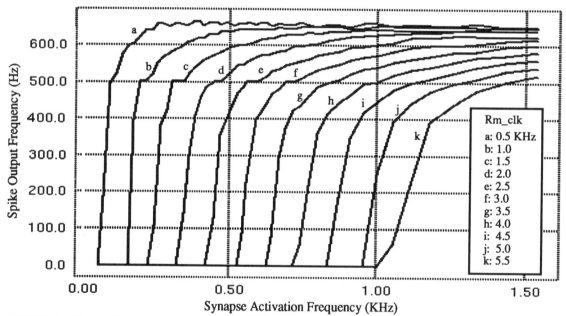

FIGURE 2. Effect of varying dynamics on "high-pass" input-output spike frequency function for an ADT-neuromorph with two equal dendritic branches. Each spike of a constant frequency input train simultaneously activated four excitatory synapses at the distal end of each dendritic branch. Output spike frequency was obtained by averaging the spike intervals in the steady state. Cut-off frequency increased linearly with increasing frequency of Rm_clk. In all cases, Ra_clk frequency = 100 * Rm_clk. Spike generator threshold, $V_{th}$ = 2.65 volts.

## RESULTS

Measurements were made on ADT-neuromorphs possessing various dendritic branching arrangements. Each dendritic branch accommodated 16 excitatory and 16 hyperpolarizing inhibitory synapses. In all experiments, multiple synapses were activated with various temporal patterns through a virtual wire system [2] while recording soma voltage and spike output. Synapse transistors were turned on for 50 - 100 nsec. A common set of switched capacitor (SC) switching signals (Rm_clk and Ra_clk) supplied all the branches of a neuromorph, giving each branch nominally similar dynamics. $R_m$ and $R_a$ (Ohms) are related to Rm_clk and Ra_clk (Hz) by

$$R_x \approx 2 \times 10^{14} / \text{Rx\_clk} \qquad x = m, a \qquad (2)$$

### Tunable Frequency Selectivity

In processing continuous trains of spikes, an ADT-neuromorph can be considered as converting multiple input spike frequencies into an output spike frequency. In the following experiments, an input spike train of constant frequency activated a number of synapses simultaneously. By suitable choice of the synapses activated, and of the spike generator threshold, $V_{th}$, ADT-neuromorphs may be made to exhibit a variety of frequency selectivities that can be tuned by varying the dendritic dynamics. In all experiments, the mean spike frequency of the output was measured in the steady state i.e., 50 ms after the start of the input train.

Figure 2 shows "high-pass" responses obtained by activating a set of eight distal excitatory synapses on a two-branched tree under different dendritic dynamics. Spike output cut-off frequency is a linear function of the SC switching frequency (Rm_clk). Figure 3 shows that our neuromorphs can be made to exhibit a frequency band selectivity when the input spike train activates an appropriate combination of both excitatory and inhibitory synapses. The position of the peak of the band selective response depends on ADT dynamics and is linearly dependent on SC switching rate over the entire range. Spike generator threshold, $V_{th}$, which strongly affects the amplitude of the band-selective function, was adjusted at each SC clock frequency to bring the peak output firing rate to approximately the same level.

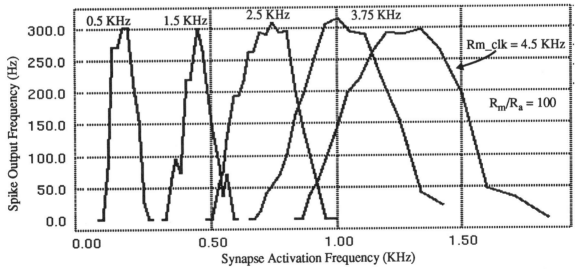

FIGURE 3. Effect of varying dynamics on "band-selective" input-output spike frequency function for an ADT-neuromorph with two dendritic branches. Each input spike simultaneously activated 5 excitatory and 2 inhibitory synapses in the middle of one dendritic branch. Output spike frequency was measured as in Fig. 2. $V_{th}$ was adjusted to equalize the peak output firing frequencies. Results with five different values of Rm_clk are shown, in all cases Ra_clk = 100*Rm_clk. The location of the peak frequency increased linearly with Rm_clk.

## Rate-Invariance of Spatiotemporal Pattern Response

The activation of an arbitrary set of excitatory and inhibitory synapses in a temporal sequence gives rise to a complex waveform at the soma representing the summation (not necessarily linear) of individual impulse responses. The waveform shape depends on the dynamics. For example, as shown in Figure 4, larger values of $R_m$ and $R_a$ result in greater temporal summation between the impulse responses of temporally contiguous input pulses, larger excursions in membrane potential, and more output spikes discharged for a given $V_{th}$.

Similar differences in temporal summation occur for fixed dynamics. Figure 5a shows the response of a neuromorph to the sequential activation of the same set of 16 synapses, with time intervals of 2, 1 and 0.25 msec between activations. Because this pattern of synapses is activated at different temporal rates with fixed dynamics, the response waveforms exhibit very different behavior. However, variable dynamics (Figure 5b) allows a given synaptic pattern activated at different rates to generate soma voltage waveforms that are essentially identical in shape over widely different time scales, analogous to wavelet dilation and contraction [10]. Figure 5b also shows that the number of output spikes remains constant in number and patterning, provided that soma integration time (RC in Eq. 1) is changed in proportion to ADT dynamics. This is readily done by controlling the switched capacitor emulating R.

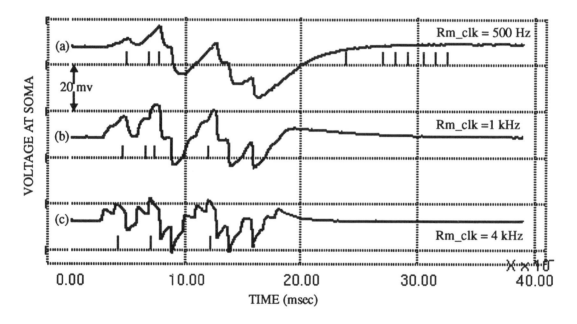

FIGURE 4.    Effect of varying dynamics on voltage changes at soma and the resulting output spikes generated by 16 sequential activations of an arbitrary set of synapses (10 excitatory, 6 inhibitory). The interval between synapse activations was 1 msec. $R_m/R_a = 100$; $V_{th} = 2.60$ volts; spike generator RC = 2.2 msec. Output spikes are shown under its corresponding waveform.

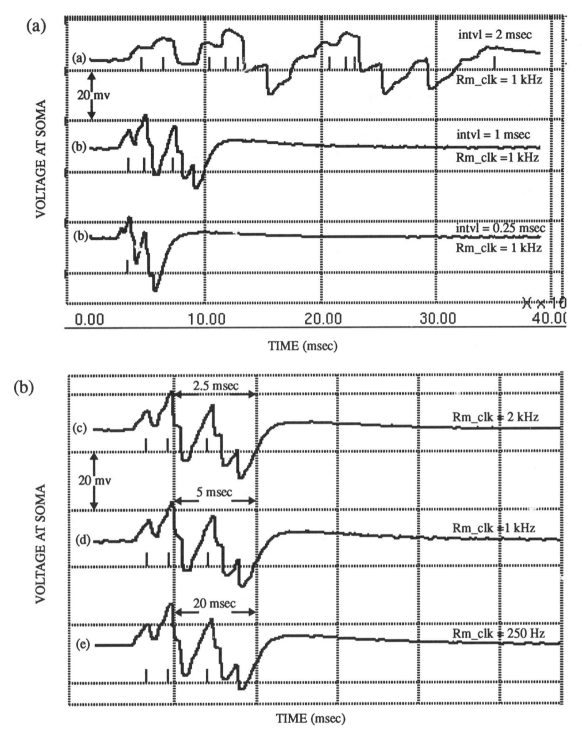

FIGURE 5. a) Effects of varying synapse activation interval (intvl) on soma voltage and spike output. The same sequence of synapses as used in Fig. 4 were activated at 0.25, 1.0 and 2.0 ms intervals, with fixed ADT dynamics ($R_m/R_a$ = 100; Rm_clk = 1 KHz). Spike generator RC = 2.2 msec. b) Changing dynamics in proportion to the rate of synapse activation generates equivalent soma waveforms but on different time scales. The spike generator RC was also changed in proportion to Rm_clk, giving equivalent patterns of output spikes. Output spikes are shown under its corresponding waveform.

IV-781

## DISCUSSION

The results show that a single ADT-neuromorph is capable of processing an input spike train in a variety of ways, depending upon the pattern of synaptic sites activated. Furthermore, the variable dynamics conferred by the use of switched capacitors gives the neuromorph a tuning ability that allows its temporal response to be matched to a specific application or task. For example, to set up a population of neuromorphs each tuned to a preferred frequency, a typical arrangement found in biological sensory systems [1], an appropriate pattern of synaptic connections can be replicated on the dendrites of the population, and different frequency multiples of an SC switching signal distributed to the different members. Because the SC switching signals can be derived from spikes circulating through the virtual-wire system, one can envision a system of self-tuning neuromorphs that could adapt, for example to optimize discrimination of spike trains.

The facility for varying ADT dynamics, allows complex spatio-temporal input patterns presented at different rates to generate identical waveforms at the soma, given appropriate time-scaling. With proportionate adjustment of the spike integrator RC, the number of output spikes is also invariant. This property in a system of neuromorphs could, for example, be useful in the recognition of spatial patterns irrespective of their rate of presentation

## ACKNOWLEDGMENTS

This work was supported by grants from the National Science Foundation (#BCS-9315879) and the University of Delaware Research Foundation.

## REFERENCES

[1]     G. Rose, "A temporal-processing mechanism for all species?" Brain Behav. Evol. vol 28, pp 134-144, 1986.

[2]     J. G. Elias, "Artificial dendritic trees," *Neural Computation*, vol. 5, pp. 648-664, 1993.

[3]     V. Torre and T. Poggio, "A synaptic mechanism possibly underlying directional selectivity to motion," *Proc. R. Soc. Lond.* B. vol 202, pp. 409-416, 1978.

[4]     C. Koch and T. Poggio, "Biophysics of computation: neurons, synapses, and membranes," in *Synaptic Function* edited by G.M. Edelman, W.E. Gall, W.M. Cowan. Wiley-Liss, New York, pp. 637-697, 1987.

[5]     C. Koch, T. Poggio, and V. Torre, "Nonlinear interactions in a dendritic tree: Localization, timing and role in information processing," *Proc. Natl. Acad. Sci.* vol. 80 pp. 2799-2802.

[6]     W. Rall, "Theoretical significance of dendritic trees for neuronal input-output relations," in *Neural Theory and Modeling*, R. F. Reiss, Ed., Stanford University Press, pp. 73-79, 1964.

[7]     G. M. Shepherd and C. Koch, "Dendritic electrotonus and synaptic integration", in *The Synaptic Organization of the Brain*, ed. G. M. Shepherd, Oxford University Press, appendix, 1990.

[8]     W. Rall, "Cable properties of dendrites and effect of synaptic location," in *Excitatory Synaptic Mechanisms*, P. Andersen and J. K. S. Jansen, eds. Universitetsforlaget, Oslo, 1970.

[9]     P. E. Allen and E. Sanchez-Sinencio, *Switched Capacitor Circuits*. New York: Van Nostrand Reinhold Company, 1984.

[10]    I. Daubechies, *Ten Lectures on Wavelets*. Capital City Press, Montpelier, Vermont, 1992.

# CONSCIOUS CONTROL:
# FROM FREUD TO THE  FRONTAL LOBE

**Henrique Schützer Del Nero, M.D.**
**Institute for Advanced Study-University of São Paulo**

**Lucia Maria Argollo Maciel, M.D.**
**Neuroscience and Behavior Program -University of São Paulo**

**Alfredo Portinari Maranca, M.Sc.**
**Polytechnic School-University of São Paulo**

**José Roberto Castilho Piqueira, Ph.D.**
**Polytechnic School-University of São Paulo**

**ADDRESS**: Rua Rubens do Amaral, 346. CEP:05653-010. São Paulo. SP. BRASIL
**E. Mail: SCHUTZER@BRUSPVM.BITNET**

## ABSTRACT

By the end of the last century, when Freud wrote his Project of a Scientific Psychology, the epistemic battle between reductionistic and emergent models of mind were beginning. In this abandoned text, that was published posthumously, the author tries to give a quantitative description, with neurological plausibility, regarding the knowledge of that time, of the processes that might underlie psychic function and dysfunction. Inserted in the flavor of his first topography, in which Freud states that there are three classes of states: *conscious, pre-conscious and unconscious*, the Project proposes a model based upon quantities of energy that flow through three main types of neurons. The interplay between perception, memory and consciousness, in spite of the highly and dated metaphorical aspect of the work, are still plausible, mainly if one looks to biochemical aspects of *hebbian* memories, to neuropsychologycal aspects of the relation between the hippocampus and the frontal lobes functions and to the tentative models that treat neurons as oscillators, extracting from  dynamical systems analysis of their connections a rich source of lessons that must enlighten the process by which conscious control may appear as an adaptive interpreter of states in the state-space of a very complex non-linear system that uses bifurcations as a source of topological variability, linearizing automatic control and partitioning endeavors through non-linearities and maybe chaos. Artificial models of mind will be incomplete if they don't face the problem of voluntary-conscious control.

## I. Freud, Neural Networks and Reduction

Our goal here is not to stress Freud's work, but only to use it as a source for an old dilemma that still pervades the cognitive sciences: the role of consciousness and of volition-control of behavior and mentation (manipulation of "mental representations").

Freud's project [1] is an essay written at the end of the century, trying to launch the metaphorical basis for a scientific psychology based upon neural processes. It postulates that there are three types of neurons in the Central Nervous System, connected or not by contact-barriers (an equivalent to what later would be qualified as the strength of the synapse). These neurons are: $\varphi$-neurons tied to perception, receiving a quantity Q of energy or information from the environment; $\psi$-neurons that store memories and increase or decrease their connectivity through experience and $\omega$-neurons that are tied to consciousness. The scheme works as follows: Environmental information considered as quantity Q of energy reaches the system impressing $\varphi$-neurons. They retransmit these bits of information to $\psi$-neurons. There, memories happen, through modification of the strength of connections and impressed by another quantity Q' that is information that comes from the body (proprioception and pulsions). Finally, this n-$\psi$ informations plus Q' reach $\omega$-neurons that are tied to conscious experiences.

The second Freud, or his second topography moves in a more functionalistic-emergent vein, proposing three classes, *ego, id and super-ego*, as the *loci* of mental functions and its neurotic deviances (Freud worked very litlle with psychotic deviances, maybe reflecting a good intuition of the limits of psychoanalytical theory). According to the tradition of Frege and of the developments of logic in the XX century, mental functions came to be considered as emergent predicates of neural implementations. Mental blocks were to be considered as primitives over which rules apply, creating strings of sentences or thoughts. The models of traditional Artificial Intelligence after Turing, Newell, Simon, Marr among others, followed this prescription: there is not a perfect or complete translation from a mental idiom unto a neural one, hence the level of algorithm and of computation must be dissociated from the level of implementation. This is what is called functionalistic-emergent tradition, endorsing projects of traditional AI and capturing the very essence of the major part of Freud's work on mental functions.[2]

Neural Networks recently became a movement which has surrendered towards putting neurological data among the elements that must be considered if one expects to understand cognition. Initially inspired in a very restricted metaphor of connections, neural nets quickly evolved to a clear separation: a) pragamatically inspired networks, with refined mathematics beneath them, became a powerful tool to manipulate a certain class of theoretical and practical problems where data are known and rules are shadowed. These networks, in spite of the historical commitment to neural-inspiration, may have slim CNS (Central Nervous System) plausibility. b) neuronal networks that try to capture data that come from the neuronal research: these networks are more committed to giving a plausible explanation of what goes on in the CNS, but the problem of what level of the CNS is being considered still remains. If neural nets considered mental representations and interpret nodes and connections with mental categories, they are so functionalistic as traditional AI are, with the exception of the nature of the computations they perform. Briefly, there are two classes of problems involved when one deals with the dichotomy reduction x emergence regarding the relation between mind and brain:

     1. There are semantical aspects of the projectability (in Goodman's terms [3]) of mental blocks unto physical blocks.

     2. There are syntactical, i.e. computational-algorithmic aspects of projectability. Then, one must build the following statements:

* Traditional AI (logical rules of computation) + mental primitives = emergence of the mental regarding the physical (symbolic paradigm - Fodor, Pylyshin, Marr)

* Neural Networks (differential equations, tensors, etc) + mental primitives = emergence of the mental regarding the physical (sub-symbolic paradigm - Rumelhart, Smolensnky)

* Neural Networks + neural signals = reduction of the mental to the physical (anti-representationalism- Freeman, Pribam, Posner)

     From the above said one must see that Neural Networks are not a sufficient condition to consider the mental to be reduceable, or translated, to the physical. Sometimes they may be a necessary condition, considering that the analogy is rich enough to allow some interesting results regarding the presumable way the CNS manipulates information.

     What comes to the arena, recalling Freud's Project, is that there are really two main styles of computation: traditional AI or connectionist AI (neural nets). Freud pursues the second within the Project and the first in his second topography. But is the style of the Project really reductionist in the sense above said? Or it is only a kind of more intimate relation between mind and brain, in spite of the emergence of the semantical categories? One may postulate hysteria as primitive, or as the name for a basin of attraction. Both, however, are emergent regarding the semantical categories, in spite of being different regarding the style of computation.

     Models can pursuit reduction from the syntactical point of view and from the semantical point of view. Syntactically speaking neural nets and Freud's Project are reduction-driven. Semantically speaking they're not, as far as taking advantage of categories that are assumed to exist-- i.e. mental categories (thoughts, feelings, goals, intentions, beliefs, etc). Neural networks represent a serious attempt to face the problem of grasping the so called brain-style of computation, but this is only half of the job. If one doesn't look at the astonishing difference between voluntary-conscious modes of operation of the CNS, one always deals with "automatic" aspects of control and of computation. The crucial aspect of the models must cope with the problem of consciousness and of volition, proposing metaphors for it. In this sense the Project touches an important point: in spite of being emergent, in our definition, from the semantical point of view, Freud sees the importance of putting consciousness in the arena, maybe as an inspiration that any model of mind that doesn't pay attention to it, even being reductionist and quantitative, will soon be doomed to failure.

## II. Consciousness, volition and semantical reduction
The way to cope with the problem of models that are only reduction-driven in the syntactical vein, as Freud's Project and the major part of neural networks, is:

a) to adopt an antirepresentationalistic approach

b) to consider the dichotomy conscious x automatic process

c) to consider voluntary control as a mark of cognitive systems able to display consciousness

d) to consider conscious, hence voluntary, control as a problem of neural structure and function and not as
       a mark of "intentionality" in Brentano's sense, what should imply impossibility of reduction
using laws and bridge-principles that were nomological, too.[4]

e) to propose mathematical tools that can enlighten the style of brain-computation that allows classes of
       different phenomena to exist: automatic and conscious-voluntary ones.

f) to understand that syntactical reduction is tied to the nature of the algorithm and semantical reduction
       is tied to the nature of the way one considers codification to hold in the CNS.

### a. Antirepresentationalism
There are clearly two meanings in the term representation when one deals with cognitive architectures.

* Representation$_1$ can be consider as intentionality, i.e. the mode certains operators, like beliefs, fears,hopes, etc fulfill with real or imaginary objecets, sentences like: "Paul fears that....". Intentionality is the very mark of the mental according to many authors and mainly those that use Traditional Artificial Intelligence to model the mind.

* Representation$_2$ can be considered as a kind of map that connects external stimuli and internal equivalents. This concept is more tied to the neural maps of function, closer to the way neuropsychology works and recalls the mathematical notion of domain and image of a function.

Representation 1 is not compatible with the project of a semantical reduction, contrary to representation 2 that is neutral, not having any peculiarity that precludes this kind of reduction to hold. Anti-representationalism must be considered against type 1. This is a very common misunderstanding in the texts and articles, maybe due to the fact that representation 1 *is the unique meaning for representation.*

### b. Conscious x automatic process
Consciousness has been considered a *taboo* among a lot of serious researchers : either it means a pseudo-concept or it means a distant attribute of the mental that has to wait till more data is known. In our view, this is a misjudgement of the importance of this entity, or class of processes, or states: if one doesn't face the problem of conscious control, one doesn't grasp the most crucial point of cognitive architectures, and of the semantical relevance of the brain structure to the mental function.

Consciousness has to be divided in two different aspects:

a) *conscious phenomenal experience*: this is a mark of a very inner experience, objective regarding the subject, but always subjective regarding reports. It is impossible to treat this inner-experience as an object of science, at least of hard-formal science [5]

b) *conscious control*: this a mark of a kind of attitudes that can be overtly considered as a different way of processing information, opposed to automatic- unconscious control. Conscious control can be regarded as a scientific object , being able to occur in third-person statements with public verifiability.

Some authors state that consciousness is the phenomenal, first-person's experience (e.g. Searle in [5]). We don't deny that these kinds of experiences exist, but we have serious doubts, as Searle, if there is a way to build a science of these inner-private experiences. Science is a way to write declarative and normative sentences that can be publicly verified or refuted. Inner-private experiences can become public throughout the meanings of language. If this happens to work regarding everyday problems with a degree of accuracy compatible with common-sense reasoning and knowledge, this doesn't imply that this kind of reasoning and knowledge can, or must, be transferred to the scientific style of stating things. One of the mistakes of current programs is the effort to capture the process by which common-sensical reasoning works, as if it were a well-succeeded strategy. It is well succeeded in terms of predictions of a very restricted amplitude. The more sophisticated knowledge gets, the more formal tools are recruited, the more counter-intuitive statements are set, the more resistance or ignorance common people show regarding the issue. If one accepts a theory of motion based upon the Aristotelian *impetus* one is prepared to do research on a phenomenal common-sensical approach of consciousness. If, otherwise, one needs something less impregnated of anthropomorphism, then consciousness, despite the presumed depth and certainty of your experience now while reading this page, should be considered as one possible mode cognitive architecture deals with inputs and outputs taking advantage of two ways of processing internal information: an automatic one and a conscious one. Consider, for example, driving a car: the first steps of learning are very hard, slow and conscious. The well-learned task, except for risky moments, becomes more and more automatic. In this sense, automatic (hence not-conscious, well learned, pre-wired or well-represented) means a kind of optimal solution for a problem that has, perhaps, two sets of variables that show bijective and inversible functions among their elements. The richer the task the more partitions have to be built in terms of getting optimal relations. For simple, trivial and old domains, it is better to have a way of processing information quickly and in an optimal way. Creativity and judgment are not problems of optimality. They don't have to be solved in seconds, but they have to be well solved, or at least in a way apt to be justified.

Conscious control, contrary to the shadows that preclude phenomenal experience to be an object of a scientific inquiry of cognitive systems, means a way of manipulating information in a highly complicated way, semantically loaded and slowly computed. The interplay between syntactical automatic memories in the hippocampus and *semantically-conscious* frontal lobes must enlighten these differences. This difference must be in the core of a renewed Project, where neuropsychologycal aspects play a role, as old inpirations did when Freud wrote and shelved his suggestions.

In a recent work Moscovitch and Umilta revisited some concepts and proposed a model of a highly modular system that processes low-level information (in our terms, syntactically loaded) in the hippocampus through working-memories and that recruits frontal lobes as a source of interpretation of these shallow-outputs to create a goal-purposeful device. Information in the frontal lobes would be more semantically loaded, interpreted, and more tied to consciousness [6].

In another classical series of experiments, Libet showed a slow negative potential that precedes "voluntary action before a subject mentally decides that he intends to make a movement."[7]. These experiments, showed, in our opinion, that there is a preliminary event of conscious control and then a phenomenal experience. In spite of looking counter-sensical, what defines conscious control is not *ipso factu* the subject's report of conscious awareness (since we put in doubt the publicly objective status of this statement) but the style, function and structures involved in computing as such, and not in the automatic mode.

Voluntary control, consciousness and semantics are to be considered in a solid block of relations, regarding the type of structures that are involved in some complex tasks, to launch good metaphors that inspire what we call semantical reduction.

### c. Voluntary control

What may characterize conscious control is the recruitment of large areas of the neocortex mainly located in the frontal lobes and to have a highly interpreted, hence semantically loaded, way of handling information. The underlying mechanisms that must be in the core of these processes are biochemical changes in the rate of quantal liberation of vesicles of neurotransmitter at the synaptic clefts, as proposed by Eccles [8], a capacity that would be evolutionary tied to the new areas of the brain, and that occur in a non-causal domain. Measures of information in this case would require an apparatus that is closer to the quantum formalisms, being the measure of probability a Gabor function and not a Shannon one.[9] Classical ways of seeing probabilities at the neuronal level as they proposed by Freeman through the tools of the Theory of Dynamical Systems, or Quantum Fields, as proposed by Pribam, using dipole oscillations at the dendritic branches, are two ways of searching for the low-level mechanisms that subsume the voluntary-conscious mode of computation. In both approaches the basic formalism that lies in beneath is the synchronism of oscillations: in Pribam's works there is an oscillatory field of dipole molecules, in Freeman's work there is a classical transformation of pulse at the neuronal level to frequencies at the assemblies level, letting non-linearities to produce bifurcations and chaos as a source of novelty, learning and categorization. Each bifurcation would constitute a branch in a strange Rossler's attractor and that would be the core mechanism of high-level processing. [10]

Volitions in this functional view could be the process that occurs in new structures of the brain, in a complex way that is semantically loaded, since it manipulates shallow outputs from the hippocampus and from other areas. Of course, in this sense, voluntary control is a concept firmly tied to consciousness. Freud's work induces a misjudgment of the term volition, because unconscious voluntary wishes are assumed to exist. In the phenomenal aspect of consciousness this may be true, but in the computational-control inspired aspect it is not possible.

To be conscious it has to be potentially voluntary-driven. To be voluntary- driven means to be highly interpreted (semantically loaded). To be semantically loaded means to recruit large areas of neocortex and to be computationally slow and sparse, but creative in terms of rearranging representations (in the sense 2 above defined). Maybe the process by which some aversive memories allow avoidance subsumes the best example of conscious computation without consciousness awareness. But to accept that the psychoanalytical work through memories, recollection and interpretation can allow relief of neurotic symptoms is a tacit acceptance that one thing is the phenomenal-conscious experience and other is the highly interpreted and sparsed conscious encoding. In this sense, Freud could be correct had he stated the clear separation, but of course the nature of volition in the control-computational view (maybe as non-causal in the "quantum interpretation", or not-predicatable in the dynamical systems interpretation) is far from the deterministic aspect of the will of Freud's unconscious. Freud could be redeemed regarding the misjudgment of the very status of consciousness in a scientific project, but the status of volitions as purposeful must be rechecked in order to adapt recent and old metaphors about the psychic system.

### III. Outline of a semantical reduction throughout formalisms and brain mechanisms.

Genuine reduction from the semantical point of view would be a kind of constraint the brain level imposes over the cognitive level. Neural networks are the first step regarding the brain-style of computation. But are they the last model? Moreover, are there models that can have the virtues of being syntactically (level of algorithm) and semantically (level of codification) reduction-driven?

Neurons are oscillators in the Hodking-Huxley models: be it in the classical transformations that allow to consider assembles of neurons governed by van der Pol equations, be it in the "quantum field" approach, there are some fundamental facts:

a) frequencies and time are essential to understanding dynamical computation and codification in the Central Nervous System

b) learning, consciousness and the will are evolutionary gains that allow the system to program itself in different environments and in on-line situations. These evolutionary traits are essential to cope with complex situations, but pay the cost of lacking robustness and globality of solutions.

Then: one must suggest that more primitive systems and automatic computations are closer to linear operations and linear codes. This guarantees invariance of solutions and quick responses to environmental stimuli. But, novelty, learning and creativity are all handled by systems that escape in certain structures of the well-behaved style of linear systems and codes. The neocortex structures, both in the macro as in the micro function, may display the complexity of behavior a conscious-voluntary controller needs. There the space is partitioned according to the underlying physical-chemical reactions (e.g. the rate of change of quantal liberation of vesicles in the synapse, the control of memories through long term potentials and its pre-synaptic control through CO and NO, the slow oscillation that pervades the cortex, etc) described by complicated mathematical structures. Non-linearities with central manifolds that indicate to non-linearizable systems (or quantum described systems with uncertainty aggregated, or dissipative systems far from the equilibrium point), are possible candidates to explain a real dynamical system, that behaves linearly where representations 2 are well formed, allowing speed and certainty to be an adaptive trait and behaves non-linearly when representations must be sought, rearranging the elements in new domains and with new relations. Bifurcations in the classical realm must be the mathematical expression of the most powerful structures of CNS, the Nature carefully selected allowing consciousness to appear: the possibility that quantitative variation of parameters allows dramatic change on the qualiatative domain. Topologically, bifurcations are the source of qualitative variations in the space of states. One must not confuse the level of iteration in an equation and its phase portrait, power spectrum, flux, etc. The former deals with an interval of numbers that feed an equation allowing other numbers to appear as results. The latter are qualitative partitions in the topological space where things may look alike or not, but where the concept that governs similarity and difference is that of homeomorphism. Given this brief concepts of the Theory of Dynamical Systems, one may suggest that:

1. Linear systems don't require an excessive amount of semantics.

2. Non-linear systems are the source of conscious control.

3. From the Neuropsychological data, one may risk saying that information is iterated in a syntanctical way in the hippocampus and other functionally equivalent places. Whenever a bifurcation occurs, changing abruptly the topological behavior of the space of states, another system of neurons tries to grasp the variation from the topological point of view, and not the process by which this variation was created. This implies creating an interpretation that names each new topological branch of the space, handling it with simpler structures from the computational and encoding point of view. This may be the source of the progressive appearance of conscious control, and of the apparent distance, henceforth, "emergence", of the level of symbol manipulation and the level of implementation.

Shortly, a genuine model of semantical and syntactical reduction would have to:

4. have a neural networks style of computation but with genuine dynamics, maybe as coupled oscillators, or through the formalisms of solitons, etc

5. have a neural codification that grasps the richness of non-linearities or of other mathematical tools of description (non-linear codes, and maybe codes closer to Gabor table of frequencies *versus* time)

6. have a way to compare the supposed primitives of logically inspired architectures of cognition, intelligence and emotion and the multiple spaces build through the labor of non-linearities, dissipation, uncertainty, etc, that might be the essence of voluntary-control: the mark of cognition, of Culture, of mankind and of a legitimate science of the mind.

## REFERENCES

[1] **Freud,S**. (1953-74) *The Standard Edition of the Complete Psychologycal Works of Sigmund Freud.* Ed. J.Strachey London: Hogarth

[2] **Flanagan, O.** (1984) *The Science of the Mind.* MIT Press

[3] **Goodman,N**. (1951) *The Structure of Appearance.* The Bobbs-Merril Company,Inc.

[4] **Fodor,J**. (1975) *The Language of Thought.* Harvard University Press

[5] **Searle,J**. (1992) *The Rediscovery of the Mind.* MIT Press.

[6] **Moscovitch,M. and Umilta,C.** (1991) "Conscious and Nonconscious Aspects of Memory: a Neuropsychological Framework of Modules and Central Systems" in **Lister,R. and Weigartner,H**. (ed) *Perspectives on Cognitive Neuroscience.* Oxford University Press.

[7] **Libet.B. et al.** (1983) "Time of conscious intention to act in reaction to onset of cerebral activity(readiness-potential).The unconscious iniatation of a freely voluntary act"*in Brain* 106

[8] **Eccles,J**. (1993) "Evolution of Complexity of the Brain with the Emergence of Consciousness" in **Pribam, K**. (ed) *Rethinking Neural Networks: Quantum Fields and Biological Data.* INNS Press. Lawrence Erlbaum Asssociates Publishers

[9] **Gabor, D.** (1946) "Theory of communication". *Journal Of The Institution of Electrical Engineers,* III, 93: 429-457

[10] **Freeman, W.** (1992) "Tutorial on Neurobiology: From single neurons to brain chaos" *in International Journal of Bifurcation and Chaos,* vol.2, No.3

# NETWORKS OF COUPLING OSCILLATORS:
## The case for a "Math" Psychiatry

**Henrique Schützer Del Nero, M.D.**
Institute for Advanced Study- University of São Paulo
**Lucia Maria Argollo Maciel, M.D.**
Neuroscience and Behavior Program- University of São Paulo

ADDRESS: Rua Rubens do Amaral, 346 CEP:05653-010 São Paulo SP Brasil
E. Mail: schutzer@bruspvm.bitnet

## ABSTRACT

*The problem of mental emergence in complex architecture has dominated the field of Cognitive Science and of Neural Networks in the past decades. Several algorithms and ways for processing information have been invented, but it still remains a problem concerning the gap between mental function and dysfunction: are neural networks an adequate way to*
*explain psychiatric disorders? Talking about Math Psychiatry means a common search for meta-foundations, theoretical inspirations that might enlighten the frontiers and limitations of such "discipline". Freud wrote his Metapsychology but, nowadays Psychiatry is closer to the brain than to the mother. Brain mechanisms, however, are meaningless if one doesn't scaffold the way information is codified in semantical nets, subserving function and deviance.*
*Dynamical nets of van der Pol's oscillators can display lots of topological variations, due mainly to non-linearities and sensitivity to the initial conditions. This doesn't want to be a model of the brain a but a source of inspiration to a Math Psychiatry that uses Mathematics as foundation and not as tool to cope with data.*

### I. Psychiatry

It is difficult to characterize in very few words what is the very object of Psychiatry. Common-sensical approaches confuse the clinical and pharmacological practice with psychotherapies, mainly psychoanalysis. The Babel that results from this confusion is due mainly to a strict difficulty to define the object, the relations and their deviances. In this way, Cognitive Science, Neuropsychology and the formalisms of Artificial Intelligence can be very welcome, if they are preceded by a careful conceptual analysis of the potential mistakes that crowd the field.

Psychology can be seen in different ways:

a) as a doctrine of intentional states: beliefs, intentions, desires, goals, etc. This usage of the psychic, mental, etc. is common to a certain field that culminated with the logical style of seeing the mind: traditional Artificial Intelligence. Mind here is a program with its own primitives and rules. Inference rules will guide the formation of strings of primitive atoms. These atoms are not to be confused with the neuronal atoms that underlie mental activity.

b) as a doctrine of faculties: memories, judgments, imagination, perception, consciousness, critics, conation, affects, humor, temperament, personality, etc.

The history of Psychiatry, of Psychotherapeutic approaches(e.g. Psychoanalysis), of Cognitive Science in its reaction against Behaviorism and of Neural Networks has much more in common, as one can imagine at first sight. Mind has been the Mecca of the models and searching for Mecca one may, sometimes, abandon meta-models, i.e. theoretical foundations.

Psychology as intentionality pervaded a lot of arguments of the traditional models based upon rules that grasp inspiration from Logics and that manipulates semantical blocks that are supposed to exist. Two extreme reactions supervened: either common-sensical knowledge was elected as the source of mental categories (e.g. theories of epistemic utility using programs that contain "beliefs", "desires, etc.)  or mental blocks were denied even to exist (eliminative materialism of Churchland among others )

Psychology as faculties pervaded Neruropsychology and still impresses this kind of mitigated-modern phrenology. Localization of brain function, being mental derivates epiphenomenal, is the root of today's sophisticated models based upon PET-scan (positron emission tomography), MRT (magnet resonance tomography) etc. Neurophysiology in another extreme through careful dissecation of ionic channels through intracellular patch-clamp techniques seeks the very nature of the flow of energy in the Central Nervous System (CNS). Models try to grasp at the same time ionic plausible  biological candidates for back-propagation algorithms (e.g. micro-tubular antidromical movement) and for memories and learning and purpose. Everything sometimes has the influence of well-known behavioral "laws", allowing conditioning to hold and reward and punishment to complete the mess.

May one be confident about the future of such theoretically empty strategies? Or is data something that must be accumulated until it reaches a critical value and allows phase-transition to occur? While many of us search for the Grail or wait till  glasses become crystals, let us put more ingredients in the field.


Psychiatry deals with mental disjunction. The mental is a certain kind of processes that happen in highly complex structures like the human-neocortex. The most important traits of the mental are: consciousness, language, "free-will", judgment and responsibility. Then: Psychiatry deals with dysfunction of consciousness in its phenomenal form (and not mechanical like stupor, coma, drowsiness, etc.), of language in its "symbolic" form (and not in the mechanical aphasic form), of "free-will" in its compulsive-obsessive forms (and not with bad choices), of judgment in its psychopathic and psychotic deviances (amoral disorders and delusions for example) and of responsibility (aging and mental retardation with preclusion of imputability from the juridical point of view).

Emotions are a very special part of the mental subserving mood disorders and anxiety but the commitment of these syndromes with more primitive neuronal systems might suggest that there are equivalents of them in other animals.

It may look easy to define things as above done and then persecute, without any caution principle, models of very sort. Hybrid models that have neural nets and expert systems, carefully handled by external heuristics and exhausting supervised training sets sometimes relax unto stable configurations that mimic a deviant episode. In this syncretic run, biochemistry and will, neurons and subjects, bifurcations and choices, all treated at the same level. In Psychiatry the situation is no more gratifying: drugs that act at the synaptic cleft are used conjointly with hugs to establish a rich "cross-talk" between signals and symbols. Is Freudian mother still present, are the primitives of mankind so simple, is it love that cures or is there something still hidden from our simple minded brains?

## II. Semantics and Mathematics

What place does semantics occupy in formal systems? This is the core of the problems mentioned above. There are several conceptions of formalisms. One states that categories only substitute bounded-variables, being dissociated from them. Others defend that there is a more essential relationship between mathematical structures and the domains of interpretation of the variables and parameters.

This must be stressed because:

a) every mature science gets more and more formalisms in its statements

b) Psychiatry and Psychology are, in this sense, immature sciences

Then : either more data must be waited until formalisms can hold or formalisms must precede data, orienting research.

This way of looking at things is not universal. Many people deny that Psychology and Psychiatry can be formalized, hence they are not immature. The very nature of these disciplines preclude formalisms to do a lot of work because they are firmly tied to first person's experiences: acquaintance, inner-feelings, etc. This would be a realm of phenomenology and Mathematical and Physical tools would be useless here.

I assume that this is not true, because phenomenal experience, in spite of being direct must be a mistake from the realistic point of view: as our senses may deceive us (e.g. phantom limb pain) so may it happen with our inner phenomenological experiences. In other words, the way our mental screen seems to see the world is only a perspective, theoretically loaded, of the world. It assumes a lot of boundaries that don't really exist, or at least that are denied in several branches of hard sciences.

What characterizes the mental blocks, be it in their semantical boundaries, be it in their rules of connection, must be the new facts that appear with the neocortex in humans. What kind of novelty could have happened that allowed the mind to emerge and everything else, like neurotic and psychotic disorders?

The cue must stay in the very nature of neuronal computations that at the same time create a rich syntax and a rich semantics. Postulating a dissociation between semantical blocks and rules of connecting them must be the last mistake of a dualistic tradition. This still pervades our models, creating a fragile scheme that is not apt to answer problems like the Searle's Chinese room. (Briefly, if a computer manipulates chinese symbols with the appropriate rules, it can give right outputs that look like a chinese-speaker, but that in fact don't mean comprehension of chinese.) [1]

Searle proposes that the genuine model of a cognitive architecture must mimic the real powers of the human brain. This must seem elliptical and obscure if one doesn't pay attention to the basic proposals that stay in beneath:

a) consider computation as the very essence of mindful architectures

b) consider mathematical analysis as the broad sense of computation

c) consider what kind of highly complex events that happen in the CNS and mainly in the neocortex areas that can endorse a physically complex system to exist

d) consider the mathematical description of such complexity

e) try to translate the complexity at the processing level to the complexity at the semantical level, trying to find a homeomorphism between them (bijective, sobrejective inversible function).


Of course these statements are very general and vacuous in a certain sense. How can Psychiatry be firmly impressed by them?

Psychiatry stays exactly in the privileged place: it has a branch in the biochemistry of the brains and another in the subject's experience, personal story and phenomenal experience. Moreover, consciousness must be the very essence of humankind, be it in its physiology be it in its pathology.

Then one may look at a model that shows:

a) real dynamical properties

b) self organizing algorithms (insofar as there is a lot of supervised learning)

c) that shows the capacity to change dramatically from past conducts and habits.

d) that can exhibit learning through the presence of only one case

e) that have a way to process quantities and to analyze qualities.

What does it mean? It means that the conscious mode of computation and the emergence of the mental must be a kind of reprocessing of information in new domains. There is a primitive chain of information processing that is apt to give all animals but humans fantastic strategies of survival. In humans however, these signals must be converted unto symbols which means a kind of reinterpretation or second codification. Quantities at the first level must become qualities at the new levels. What is the plausibility of this proposal?

1. The hipoccampus process information at the first level and the neocortex areas reprocess giving new kinds of interpretation with a highly semantical character. But what does it mean to have a highly semantical character? It means to have a kind of analyzer that grasps only topological variations in the first module.

Then, the mind would be a kind of codifying-manipulating engine that analyses states in space of states and not he structure of the equations that generated these states.

There would be a kind of logic in the system: inputs must be converted and analyzed through the "first layer" regarding state-variables and parameters. Solutions of the first level would constitute the flux, the phase portrait, the power spectrum, etc. The second interpreter would be interested only in the saliences from the topological point of view that came from the first level. Suppose just for example that a linear equation is iterated at the first level. The second level would have only one state that could define the first: in other words the richer the non-linear system in the first level is the more information (in Shannon's terms) the second level would grasp. Each bifurcation, i.e. a qualitative change in the system's behavior regarding a quantitative variation of a parameter would double the information in bits of the system at the second level.

Mind and consciousness, and also its deviances would be in this scheme a way to map and rename, using for it the blocks of experience with its natural intersections and ambiguities, topological variations at the first level;

1) primitive low-level systems ; first level linear computation

2) intermediate systems : first level non-linear computation

3) mental systems: first level non-linear computation sensitive to the initial conditions.

The following prescriptions would complete a way to see Psychiatry as a branch of Cognitive Science in its highly and broad computational (hence formal character.

a) consider neurons as oscillators (e.g. van der Pol)

b) connect them through a kind of hebbian synapse

c) build an architecture of three layers: the first receives the signal, the second processes it the third analyses the topological character of the processing mechanisms of the second (through Fourier series, flux, phase portrait etc.)

d) consider this interplay when dealing with quantitative measurements and qualitative inference about the clinical status of the patient.

e) relate qualitative variability from the sematical point of view with topological variability in the equations (non-linearities, bifurcations, chaos, etc.)

f) consider learning, memories and categorization (dream algorithms, for example) as modification of friction coefficients, connections, and natural frequencies of each oscillator.

g) consider the source for creativity and for deviance that such systems have and mainly, the possibility that, in spite of the immense difficulties from the analytical point of view, this is the "geometry of mind", what may reallocate mind as kind of complex "two layers computation" and not a kind of dissociation between processing and encoding, syntax and semantics, drugs and hugs.

### III. Conclusions

The main suggestions of this article are that mathematical analysis cannot be out of the study of the brain, be it in Neurology be it in Psychiatry. Neural Networks deserve the merits for having illuminated the absence of a solid knowledge of Math among those that intend to model the brain and its major predicate: the mind.

Deviances in the Psychiatric domain, be they biochemical, be they "communications disorders"as many like to call neuroses nowadays, must be reviewed with an acute sense that Dynamical Systems Theory, for example, can furnish us a lot of inspirations to understand psychopathology, if the way the mental emerges from the non-linearities of the brain becomes conceptually well understood.

Bifurcations, quantum fields, holograms, Gabor functions, deterministic chaos, oscillations, solitons, etc are key concepts if one wants to see the new metaphors for the next century, candidates to be new paradigms for a legitimate science of the mind and of psychiatric deviances.

Neurons, assemblies and even lobes may use the formalism of oscillations that is rich enough to subsume bottom-up strategies to hold, like the comprehension of vision, but also top-down strategies like understanding delusional aspects of a depressed patient that change dramatically from the qualitative point of view with slight quantitative variations in synaptic parameters (gain functions, capture range of frequencies in Phase Locker Loop -PLL, etc)

Mathematics and Physics associated with Neurosciences and with careful analysis of the conceptual basis can lead Psychiatry to a respectful realm with the status of a mature science of the mind. Cognitive Science and Neural Networks must pay attention to this extreme of mentation: it suffers, it inflicts pain, it destroys, it commits suicide, it cries it waits a lot from us. Maybe Math is the only mad idea to redeem a couple of Psychiatrists that see the knowledge that come from the orthodoxical medical approaches not sufficient to cope with insanity.

## REFERENCES

**Stein,D. and Young,J**. (1992) *Cognitive Science and Clinical Disorders*. Academic Press Inc.

**Lister,R and Weigartner,J**.(ed) (1991) *Perspectives on Cognitive Neuroscience*. Oxford Univ.Press

**Ono,T, Squire,L, Raichle,M, Perret,D. Fukuda,M**.(ed) (1993) *Brain Mechanisms of Perception and Memory*. Oxford University Press

**Levine,D and Leven,S**. (ed) (1992) *Motivation, Emotion and Goal Direction in Neural Networks*. Lawrence Erlbaum Associates.

**Pribam,K** (1993) *Rethinking Neural Networks: Quantum fields and Biological Data*. INNS Press

**Freeman,W**.(1992) "Tutorial on Neurobiology:From single neurons to brain chaos" *in International Journal of Bifurcations and Chaos vol.2 No.3*

**Del Nero,H. e Piqueira,J** (1993) Cognitive Science and the Failure of Behaviorism : quantum, classical and mind indeterminacies. *IEEE SMC Conference 1993*. Le Touquet

**Del Nero,H. e Piqueira,J** (1993) Dreams and consciousness: what do they have to do with neural networks? *WCNN'1993*. Portland

**Del Nero, H. e Piqueira,J**. (1992) Consciousness and Cognitive Science. *IEEE SMC Conference 1992*. Chicago

**Piqueira,J and Del Nero,H**. (1992) Cognition: chaos, determinism and emergence. *IEEE SMC Conference 1992* Chicago

# Probabilities of Transitions Between Stable States of Neural Networks

Vladimir Chinarov

Scientific Research Center "Vidhuk",
Vladimirskaya Str. 61-b, 252033 Kiev, Ukraine

**Abstract.** Dynamic behavior of neural networks with heterogeneous connections between neurons is analyzed. The algorithm for the optimal trajectory connecting distinct basins of attraction is proposed. The trajectory starts near the stable state at some point with coordinates determined by the procedure based on the minimum action principle, passes in the small vicinity of a saddle point and goes into the domain of attraction of other stable state. The transition probability is determined by the flux over the saddle point.

## 1 Introduction

Several papers have appeared in recent years dealing with the problem of noise influence on the dynamics of neural system [1,2,5]. The important characteristics of dynamic systems with coexisting attractors are probabilities of transitions between them. Usually these attractors are associated with memories stored by the neural network [6,7].

Studying the properties of stochastic effects in the network may have an important functional significance for the understanding of mechanisms of the processing information by neural networks. The questions which arise here are as those: what type of interaction between different neural structures may ensure the activity phases synchronization for providing the necessary control function for the system, how must self-organize corresponding neural network for generation of the activity pattern with preassigned parameters, what is the nature of dependence of transition probabilities between attractors in neural networks on the system parameters.

In this work we study the dynamic behavior of neural network driven by external noise. The network consists of nets with spatially heterogeneous synaptic connections between neurons. The proposed scheme may generate the stable rhythmic activity and possesses the temporal and phase characteristics existing in real systems such as movement activity generators. The problem is actual for many neurophysiological systems, in particular, for olfactory bulb of mammals [1,4,8] and system controlling movement activity [9]. We have used the Wilson-Cowan [10] type equations for the excitatory and inhibitory activities with some modifications.

An approach to determine the transition probabilities between different attractors of the network is developed.

## 2 Neural network model

Let us consider the neural network with its dynamic state to be described by a point on the phase space of a system. The evolution of this point (system's trajectory) is described by the following system of equations

$$dX_i/dt = -X_i + S(\alpha_i X_i + f_i(t)) + U(\sum_{k=1}^{n} c_{ik}X_k), \qquad (1)$$

$$T\, dU/dt = -U + \sum_{k=1}^{n} \beta_k X_k, \qquad (i=1,..,n) \qquad (2)$$

where the activities $\{X_i\}$ are the proportions of excitatory and inhibitory cells, respectively, firing per unit time, $f_i(t)$ are the input signals to the excitatory and inhibitory populations, and the coefficients $\alpha_i$ describe the average strength of excitatory ($\alpha_i > 0$) and inhibitory ($\alpha_i < 0$) synapses [6,10], the sigmoid function $S(x)$ in (1) represents the neuron response to the inputs from the adjacent neurons.

The function U has a property of a control function due to presence of a feedback loop in the system. It connects different subpopulations of neurons summarizing their outputs. The corresponding evolution equation (2) may be considered as one that describes the change of average membrane potential of terminal's fibers along which the excitatory and inhibitory influences on the network are entered [2]. Parameter T and coefficients $\beta_k$ characterize, respectively, the corresponding membrane time constant and average action of the excitatory and inhibitory outputs on the terminals.

It can be easily shown using an affine transformation of the form $\vec{Y} = \hat{C}\, \vec{X}$, that system (1) will be a standard Wilson-Cowan (for the average neural activity) model [10] or the Grossberg additive model [9] (for i=1,2,...,n):

$$dy_i/dt = -b_i y_i + \sum_{j=1}^{n} S_j (\prod_{k=1}^{n} r_{jk} y_j + d_j), \qquad (3)$$

in the limiting case when $T \longrightarrow 0$. The subpopulations of excitatory and inhibitory neurons will be then interconnected via the elements $r_{jk}$.

Simulations on the base of Eqs. (1)-(3) show that this network possesses complex dynamic behavior with different coexisting attractors such as limit cycles and fixed points. Moreover, one can also observe a synchronization of activity patterns in ensembles with only excitatory neurons ($\alpha_i > 0$).

3  Noisy dynamics of neural net

We are interested here in a case when the values of parameters $\alpha_i$, $f_i(t)$, $c_{ik}$ are such that system (1) has several steady states. These states may be either focuses (nodes), or limits cycles. The steady state may be characterized by the domains (or basins) of attraction on the phase plane (with the boundary in a form of unstable limit cycle), or may possess the separatrix passing through the saddle point (unstable steady state) and dividing different basins of attraction.

We assume that fluctuations of dynamic variables $X_i$ are determined by fluctuations of synaptic activity of dendritic tree enclosing neurons and its topology. Fluctuations of averaged non-equilibrium potential are calculated taking into account the fact that characteristic dendritic scale of the "dressed" neuron which define the damping length of fluctuations (diffusion length), is much less than the mean inter-neuron distance and therefore the fluctuations of the membrane potential for each neuron are independent.

Due to the possible large-scale fluctuations of activities in (1) there may occur, besides the relaxation to steady states, relatively large rare fluctuations causing the transitions between them. We will assume that characteristic probabilities W of such transitions are much less than the reciprocal relaxation times $\tau_r$ to the steady state. In result of transitions between steady states some stationary distribution over the system states is worked out and dependence of statistical characteristics of a system on its parameters becomes single-valued. In this case the summary activity of neural network (or rather its ensemble average ) uniquely depends on the input signals $f_i$. We will have then the following inequality when the network is to be used as a memory unit

$$\tau_r \leq \tau_{sw} \sim (1/f_i)|df_i/dt|, \; \tau_0 < W^{-1}, \qquad (4)$$

where $\tau_{sw}$ is switching time and $\tau_0$ is a characteristic time between switchings.

The size of minimal characteristic scale of the switching time is $\tau_r$ ($\tau_{sw} \geq \tau_r$) for arbitrarily fast changing of control parameter $f_i$. The times $W^{-1}$ define "the safety limit" for the storing of information by neural network. Thus, for the reliable performance of the switching element in the working range of parameters the following condition must be fulfilled

$$W \ll \tau_r^{-1}. \qquad (5)$$

Practically this is a condition on the relative weakness of noise. It leads to the situation when "activation energy" (this definition is of conditional nature because in the non-equilibrium system transitions are not described by the standard Arrhenius law) of the escape from the steady state is much greater than the noise intensity and exponential factor determines, to logarithmic accuracy, the nature of dependence of transition probabilities W on system parameters. In this case it has sharp exponential dependence on the control parameters $f_i$. However, in the vicinity of bifurcation points, (the condition (5) is not fulfilled there), "the safety limit" for the storing of information sharply decreases as the working range of control parameter becomes nearer to the bifurcation point. On the other hand, the closer the system approaches to the bifurcation point, the smaller is the characteristic work of the switching and energy expenditure in memory units. The existence of these alternative demands for performance of optimal ratio between reliability and memory storage capacity of the network makes the problem of determination of the transition probability W as a function of system's parameters  to be of great importance.

## 4  Fluctuational transitions between attractors of the network

To study the noise influence on the network  dynamics  we consider first the simple case of the additive noise  in  Eqs. (1)-(2). Rewrite them in a form

$$dX_i/dt = K_i(X_i) + \xi_i(t), \qquad (6)$$

$$T \, dU/dt = L(X_i) + \xi_U(t), \qquad (7)$$

where

$$K_i(X_i) = - X_i + S(\alpha_i X_i + f_i(t)) + U(\sum_{k=1}^{n} c_{ik} X_k), \qquad (8)$$

$$L(X_i) = -U(X_i) + \sum_{k=1}^{n} \beta_k X_k, \qquad (9)$$

where $\xi_i(t)$ is the  Gaussian zero  mean  random  process  with correlation function $B_{ik}(\tau)$ defined by equation

$$< \xi_i(t)\xi_k(t-\tau)> = 2 \, D\delta(\tau) \, B_{ik}(\tau), \qquad (10)$$

where D is the noise intensity.

In the case of the low intensity noise limit ($D \ll 1$), the system with overwhelming probability approaches one or another stable state, while the transitions between steady  states  do not happen practically within such a time. At larger  times  $\tau$ ($\tau \gg W$) in the small vicinity of one of the stable states the quasistationary distribution is formed. For the times $\tau \gg \tau_r$ under the large (and, respectively,  with  small  probability) "outburst" of the noise, the system went out from the vicinity of this stable state and went into the vicinity of  the  point of  observation  $X_i(t), U(X_i(t))$.  The  problem  we  deal  with consists  of  the  obtaining  of  such  a  distribution  and calculation of  corresponding  escape  probabilities.  In  the general case the considered network must be viewed as part  of a larger system — the network and its environment. This  gives the network a memory, rendering the activity process $X_i(t)$  by itself non-Markovian. However, the  joint  process  $(X_i, U)$  is Markovian.

For the case of white noise  in  Eqs.  (6)-(7)  the  most simple approach to consider the transition probability density $\rho(x_i, u; t)$ for the joint stochastic process $(X_i, U)$ consists  of in seeking for the  solution  of  corresponding  Fokker-Planck equation. The quasistationary solution for this  equation  can be found in  the  form  $\rho \propto \exp(-R/D)$,  where  $R = R(X_i, U)$ satisfies the nonlinear equation (for the purpose  to  clarify the ideas of developed approach we  consider  below  only  the case of single compartment neural net ($i = 1$))

$$H\big(R_x, R_u; x, u\big) = 0, \qquad (11)$$

where

$$H = \frac{1}{2}\left[B_{xx}R_x^2 + 2B_{xu}R_xR_u + B_{uu}R_u^2\right] + K_1R_x + LR_u, \quad (12)$$

$$R_x = \partial R/\partial x, \quad R_u = \partial R/\partial u. \quad (13)$$

The function $R(x,u)$ can be associated with a mechanical action of a two-dimensional auxiliary system with the coordinates $x,u$, and Eq. (11) is then a Hamilton-Jacobi equation. The related Hamiltonian equations for the "coordinates" $x,u$ and "momenta" $R_x$, $R_u$ describe the extreme paths of the system. The probability of the escape from a stable state f is given, to logarithmic accuracy, by the expression [3]

$$W = \text{const} \cdot \exp\left[-R/D\right], \quad R \equiv R(x_s,u_s), \quad (R(x_f,u_f) = 0), \quad (14)$$

where $x_{f,s}$, $u_{f,s}$ are the values of the activity X and control function U of the initial system in the stable state f and in the saddle point s. Function R satisfies the conditions: $R(x_f,u_f) \cong 0$, $\partial R/\partial x\big|_f = \partial R/\partial u\big|_f = 0$; the point $x_f,u_f$ (on the phase plane) is the global minimum of R.

An approach to the calculation of activation energies R of fluctuational transitions is based on numerical analysis of the Hamiltonian equations for an auxiliary system (11)–(13) or the corresponding equations for the "coordinates" $x$, $u$ and momenta $R_x$, $R_u$ of this system

$$\dot{x} = \partial H/\partial R_x, \quad \dot{u} = \partial H/\partial R_u, \quad \dot{R}_x = -\partial H/\partial x, \quad \dot{R}_u = -\partial H/\partial u. \quad (15)$$

The extreme paths starting from a fixed point f make a single-parameter set. This can be easily verified by noting that in the immediate vicinity of a point f Eqs. (15) can be linearized in

$$x_1 = x - x_f, \quad x_2 = u - u_f \quad (16)$$

and the solution of (15) is of the form

$$R(x,u) = \frac{1}{2} \sum_{i,j=1,2} A_{ij}x_ix_j, \quad |x_{1,2}| \to 0. \quad (17)$$

The coefficients of the matrix $\|A_{ij}\|$ are given by the equations

$$\frac{1}{2}\sum_{m,n}\left(\frac{\partial^2 H}{\partial R_{x_m}\partial R_{x_n}}\right)_f A_{mi}A_{nj} + \sum_m \left(\frac{\partial^2 H}{\partial x_i \partial R_{x_m}}\right)_f A_{mj} = -\frac{1}{2}\left(\frac{\partial^2 H}{\partial x_i \partial x_j}\right)_f,$$

$$(i,j=1,2) \quad (18)$$

where the subscript f means that the derivatives are calculated for $x_1 = x_2 = R_{x_1} = R_{x_2} = 0$. The initial conditions for Eqs. (15) can be chosen at finite $x_1$, $x_2$ and finite $t = t_0$. For $t \to -\infty$ a path parameterized in this way approaches $x_1$

$= x_2 = 0$ (i.e., $x \rightarrow x_f$, $u \rightarrow u_f$), and all points $(x_1, x_2)$ already passed can be equally chosen as the initial ones for the same path. Hence, the problem of calculating an activation energy comes to finding the value of the parameter for which the extreme path arrives to a saddle point to a given accuracy.

## 5  Summary

We have studied the dynamical behavior of neural networks with spatially heterogeneous synaptic connections between neurons. The proposed scheme may provide generation of the stable rhythmic activity possessing temporal characteristics which exist in the real movement activity generators and can explain phase dependent switching over their parameters under the influence of noise inputs. The algorithm for searching of the optimal trajectory which connects distinct basins of attraction is proposed.

## References

[1]  C.M. Ahn & W.J.Freeman: Neural dynamics under noise in the olfactory system. Biol. Cybern., 17, pp. 165-168 (1975).

[2]  V.A. Chinarov, A.M. Degtyarenko & M.A. Feldman: Dynamic behaviour of neural networks driven by colored noise. In: A.V. Holden & V.I. Kryukov (Eds.) Neurocomputers and Attention, University Press, Manchester, II, pp. 479-487 (1991).

[3]  V.A. Chinarov, M.I. Dykman & V.N. Smelanski: Dissipative corrections to escape probabilities of thermally — nonequilibrium systems. Phys. Rev. E47, pp. 2448-2461 (1993).

[4]  W.J. Freeman: EEG Analysis gives model of neuronal template matching mechanism for sensory search with olfactory. Bulb. Biol. Cybern. 35, pp. 221-234 (1979).

[5]  D. Gorse & J.G. Taylor: An analysis of noisy RAM and neural nets. Physica D 34, pp. 90-114 (1989).

[6]  S. Grossberg: Nonlinear neural networks: principles, mechanisms, and architectures. Neural Network. 1, pp. 17-61 (1988).

[7]  T. Kohonen: Self-organization and associative memory. Springer, Berlin, (1984).

[8]  Z. Li & J.J. Hopfield: Modeling the olfactory bulb and its neural oscillatory processing. Biol. Cybern. 61, pp. 379-392 (1989).

[9]  K. Matsuoka: Mechanisms of frequency and pattern control in the neural rhythm generators. Biol. Cybern. 56, pp. 345-353 (1987).

[10] H.R. Wilson & J.D. Cowan: Excitatory and inhibitory interactions in localized populations of model` neurons. Biophys. J. 12, pp. 1-24 (1972).

# Phase Transitions in Neurodynamics

## Richard T. Gordon

Computational Intelligence Laboratory
Information Services Research and Development Group
Chubb Group of Insurance Companies
120 Fifth Avenue, Suite 2200, Pittsburgh, PA 15222-3008

### Abstract

Most current approaches to the mechanisms of the brain fail to address the fundamental physics at work. In this paper work on phase transitions, and specifically critical phase transitions, and attractors are presented as a theory toward the physical mechanisms of the brain. Examples are presented demonstrating these mechanisms in olfactory and visual systems, as well as in cognitive contexts.

### Introduction

Many approaches have been taken to explain the mechanisms responsible for the workings of the human brain. Whether one takes early models utilizing a homunculus; current rule based cognitive models; or biological models of neurons, axons and synapses; these models all fail to address the fundamental physics at work in the brain. In this paper, the mechanisms of the brain are presented within a connectionist framework in the context of phase transitions, and specifically second order or "critical" phase transitions, and the existence of attractors.

### Cognitive Aspects

If one looks at a local neighborhood structure in the brain. The trajectory of the dynamics will change until such time as a critical state is reached. At this state the local neighborhood will undergo a phase transition creating or recalling a memory state.

Performing this task requires simultaneously satisfying many constraints. In such problems, it is often the case that it is easy to find "local" solutions that satisfy some of the constraints but very difficult to find a global solution that simultaneously satisfies the maximum number of constraints. Often there are many completions of the input that are local maxima, in which some knowledge associations are activated, but fewer completions that are global maxima, in which many local neighborhoods become simultaneously activated.[1] At high temperatures, the structures occupy states that are local solutions, but at low temperatures, the structures occupy only states that are global solutions.

Thus the process of solving corresponds to the passage of the dynamical system from a high temperature phase to a low temperature phase. If there is a sharp transition between these phases major decisions are made that can only be undone at lower temperatures by waiting for a very long time.[1] Thus it becomes important to cool slowly through phase transitions. This will maximize the probability that the decisions are made properly, with the system finding the global maximum relatively quickly without getting stuck for long times in local maxima.[1] A previous analysis of this premise suggests that phase transitions do exist in models of decision making.[1]

With the concept of attention, we have a psychophysiological process consisting simultaneously of two components. The first component takes one of several simultaneously possible trains of thought with focalization and concentration at its essence. The second component is a process combining several distinct modalities into a single train of thought.[2]

The main functional element is the model of an assembly of nonformal neurons which serves as a single submodule for the system model of attention.[2] During active perception of external stimuli, separate modules and the whole of the system work near points of an unstable equilibrium resembling the physical effect of metastability of phase transitions. It is proposed that this property reflects the existence phase transitions in the brain[2] and is supported by low-frequency EEG oscillations.

Phase-frequency-space coding is universal for all sensory modalities and is probably the same for thinking and moving. Attention is unstable, or at most, metastable. Due to noise, each "stationary state" has a finite lifetime depending upon the parameters and initial states of the system.[2] Breakdown of attention may be abrupt or gradual. In the latter case models show an interesting nonlinear effect of cycle slipping, which can be described as a jumping of the phase difference.[2]

Complex neuromodulatory effects of acetylcholine depend upon the location and types of receptors and channels present in the different neurons. One main effect is facilitory excitation. In facilitory excitation the phasic release of acetylcholine, involving the bursting of PGO cells in the brainstem, coupled with tonic aminergic demodulation, induces bifurcations in information sequencing at the module level.[3]

### Physical Models

Patterns of 40 to 80 Hz oscillation have been observed in the large scale activity of the olfactory bulb and cortex[4], and the visual neocortex.[5,6] These patterns have been found to predict the olfactory and visual pattern recognition responses of trained animals.

The observed physiological activity in the olfactory cortex may be idealized mathematically as a "cycle", $rx_j e^{i(\theta j + wt)}$, with $j = 1, 2, \ldots, n$. Such a cycle is a periodic attractor if it is stable. The global amplitude r is just a scaling factor for the pattern x, and the global phase w in $e^{iwt}$ is a periodic scaling that scales x by a factor between $\pm 1$ at the frequency w as t varies.[7]

The same vector x or pattern of relative amplitudes can appear in space as a standing wave, like that seen in the olfactory bulb, if the relative phase $\theta_{i+1}=\theta_i$, or as a traveling wave, like that seen in the prepyriform cortex, if the relative phase components of $\theta$ form a gradient in space, $\theta_{i+1}=1/a\theta_i$. The traveling wave will sweep out the amplitude pattern x in time, but the root mean square amplitude measured experimentally will be the same x, regardless of the phase pattern. For an arbitrary phase vector, these simple single frequency cycles can make very complicated spatio-temporal patterns. From the mathematical point of view, the relative phase pattern $\theta$ is a degree of freedom in the type of patterns which can be stored. Patterns of uniform amplitude x which differ only in the phase locking pattern $\theta$ could be stored as well.[7]

Recall has been defined as the ability to retrieve an item from a list of items originally presented during a previous learning period, given an appropriate cue, or spontaneously. Similarly, recognition has been defined as the ability to successfully acknowledge that a certain item has or has not appeared in the tutorial list learned before.[8] The Hopfield model[9] provides a framework for examining these ideas.

The dynamics of this model are composed of a nonlinear, iterative, asynchronous transformation of the state of the system. Stochastic noise, analogous to the temperature T from statistical mechanics, may also be included in the process. Let the state of neuron i be a binary variable $S_i$, which takes the values $\pm 1$ corresponding to either a firing or resting state. Further take a local neighborhood's state S to be a vector specifying the values of all its neurons, with $J_{ij}$ being the synaptic strength between neurons i and j. It then follows that the input field h of neuron i is given by

$$h_i = \sum_{j \neq i}^{N} J_{ij} S_j \tag{1}$$

The dynamic behavior of the neuron can then be described by:

$$S_i(t+1) = \begin{cases} 1, & with\ probability\ \frac{1}{2}(1+tgh(\frac{h_i}{T})) \\ -1, & with\ probability\ \frac{1}{2}(1-tgh(\frac{h_i}{T})) \end{cases} \tag{2}$$

A new memory pattern $\xi^\mu$ is stored by modifying every ij element of the synaptic connection matrix according to:

$$J^{new}_{ij} = J^{old}_{ij} + \frac{1}{N}\xi^\mu_i \xi^\mu_j \tag{3}$$

In this model every stored memory is an attractor with an associated local neighborhood corresponding to its basin of attraction.[8]

A longitudinal examination of the learning process illustrates a new form of mechanical inference: induction by phase transition. As such, a small adjustment in activation causes a bifurcation in the limit behavior. This phase transition corresponds to the onset of the capacity for generalizing to arbitrary length strings. A study of the automata resulting from the acquisition of previously published languages indicates that while the architecture is not guaranteed to find a minimal finite automata consistent with the exemplars, this model does appear capable of generating non-regular languages by exploiting fractal and chaotic dynamics.[10]

The model undergoes a bifurcation, where a small change in activation leads to a phase transition from a fixed point to a limit cycle. This phase transition is so adaptive to the classification task that the model rapidly exploits it. This is a new and interesting form of mechanical induction. Before the phase transition, the model is in principle not capable of performing the serial parity task, after the phase transition it is.[10] The link between work in complex dynamical systems and neural networks is well established both on the neurobiological level[11] and on the mathematical level[1,12-14], and is established to a lesser extent on the cognitive level.[10,15]

There is an interesting formal question, which has been brought out on the universality of cellular automata and on the descriptive complexity of bifurcating systems.[16] That is, what is the relationship between the complex dynamics of neural systems and traditional measures of computational complexity?[10] The hypothesis can be proposed that the state space limit of a dynamical recognizer, as $\sum^* \to \sum^\infty$, is an attractor, which is cut by a threshold function. The complexity of the language recognized is regular if the cut falls between disjoint limit points, context free if it cuts a recursive region, and context sensitive if it cuts a chaotic region.[10]

To describe the use-dependent self-organization of neural connections[17,18], it has been proposed that a set of coupled equations involving the electrical activities and neural connection density[19], can be physiologically supported given that:

(1) Modifiable synapses grow or collapse due to the competition among themselves for some trophic factors, which are secreted retrogradely from the postsynaptic side to the presynaptic side.[20]

(2) Synapses also sprout or retract according to the occurrence of presynaptic spike activity and postsynaptic local membrane depolarization.[20]

(3) There already exist lateral connections within the layer, into which the modifiable nerve fibers are destined to project, before the synaptic modification begins.[20]

Given the above, it can be shown that nearly all the physiological experimental results concerning the ocular dominance patterns of cats and monkeys reared under normal or various abnormal visual conditions can be explained from a viewpoint of the phase transition phenomena.[20] Considering the statements above, a set of coupled equations involving the electrical activities and the neural connection density can be constructed. In these equations the time scale of electrical activities is much smaller than the time course necessary for synapses to grow or retract. This allows use of an adiabatic approximation to the equations. The firing frequency elicited from neurons in the projecting neuronal layer is identified with a stochastic process which is specialized by the spatial correlation function $C_{k\mu;k'\mu'}$. Where k and k' are the positions of the neurons in the projecting layer and $\mu$ is the different pathways such as ipsilateral or contralateral, on-center or off-center, color specific or nonspecific, etc.[20]

Taking the equilibrium solution to the equations as a set of Potts spin variables $\sigma_{jk\mu}$, then if neuron k in the projecting layer sends an axon to position j in the target layer $\sigma_{jk\mu}=1$, and if not $\sigma_{jk\mu}=0$, with the spin variable having the property:

$$\sum_{k\mu} \sigma_{jk\mu}=1 \tag{4}$$

Limiting the discussion to equilibrium solutions we can reduce the problem to the thermodynamics of the spin system. We can describe the equilibrium behavior of the modifiable nerve terminals in terms of the Hamiltonian H and a temperature T given by:

$$H=-q\sum_{jk\mu} \eta_{k\mu}\sigma_{jk\mu}-\sum_{jk\mu}\sum_{j'k'\mu'} V_{jj'}C_{k\mu;k'\mu'}\sigma_{jk\mu}\sigma_{j'k'\mu'} \tag{5}$$

$$T\propto \left(\frac{\tau_c}{\tau_s}\right)^{1/2} \tag{6}$$

where k and $C_{k\mu;k'\mu'}$ are the averaged firing frequency and correlation function respectively. The interaction between the synapses in the target layer are given by $V_{jj'}$, and q is the ratio of the total averaged membrane potential to the average membrane potential induced through the modifiable synapses from the projecting layer. The terms $\tau_c$ and $\tau_s$ represent the correlation time of the electrical activities and the time course for synapses to grow and collapse.[20] Specific cortical map structure is determined by the correlation function and the synaptic interaction function. Neglecting the k dependence of the correlation function and taking only ipsilateral and contralateral pathways given by $\mu$, the Potts spin variable can be reduced to the Ising spin by:

$$S_j=\sum_{k\mu} \mu\sigma_{jk\mu} \tag{7}$$

where j is the position in layer 4 of the primary visual cortex and $S_j$ takes the value +1 or -1 corresponding to ipsilateral or contralateral dominance. This system can then be described by the Hamiltonian:

$$H = -h\sum_{j} S_j - \frac{J}{2}\sum_{j}\sum_{j'\neq j} V_{jj'} S_j S_{j'}$$

(8)

This reduction to the Ising spin then returns us to the basis of the Hopfield model.

## References

1. P. Smolensky, in " Parallel Distributed Processing: Exploring the Microstructure of Cognition, Vol. 1, (MIT Press, Cambridge, MA, 1986)
2. V.I. Kryukov, in "Advances in Neural Information Processing Systems 1", (Morgan Kaufmann, San Mateo, CA, 1989)
3. J.P. Sutton, A.N. Mamelak, J.A. Hobson, in "Advances in Neural Information Processing Systems 4",(Morgan Kaufmann, San Mateo, CA, 1992),
4. W.J. Freeman, B. Baird, Behavioral Neuroscience (1986).
5. W.J. Freeman, B.W. van Dijk, Brain Research, 422, 267 (1987).
6. C.M. Grey, W. Singer, PNAS (1988).
7. B. Baird, in "Advances in Neural Information Processing Systems 1", (Morgan Kaufmann, San Mateo, CA, 1989)
8. E. Ruppin, Y. Yeshurun, in "Advances in Neural Information Processing Systems 3", (Morgan Kaufmann, San Mateo, CA, 1991)
9. J.J. Hopfield, Proceedings of the National Academy of Sciences, 79, 2554 (1982).
10. J.B. Pollack, in "Advances in Neural Information Processing Systems 3", (Morgan Kaufmann, San Mateo, CA, 1991).
11. C.A. Skarda, W.J. Freeman, Brain & Behavioral Science, 10 (1987).
12. B. Derrida, R. Meier, Physical Review A, 38 (1988).
13. B.A. Hubberman, T. Hogg, Artificial Intelligence, 33, 155 (1987).
14. K.E. Kurten, in "Institute of Electrical and Electronics Engineers First International Conference on Neural Networks", II-197-20 (1987).
15. J.B. Pollack, in "Advances in Neural Information Processing Systems 1", (Morgan Kaufmann, San Mateo, CA, 1989)
16. J.P. Crutchfield, K. Young, in "Complexity, Entropy and the Physics of Information", (Addison-Wesley, Redwood City, CA, 1990)
17. E. Frank, Trends in Neuroscience, 10, 188 (1987).
18. W. Singer, in "The Neural and Molecular Basis of Learning", (Wiley & Sons, New York, 1987)
19. S. Tanaka, in "The Proceedings of SICE '88", ESS2-5, (1988).
20. S. Tanaka, in "Advances in Neural Information Processing Systems 1", (Morgan Kaufmann, San Mateo, CA, 1989)

# CHAOS, ADAPTATION AND NEURAL NETWORKS

James A. Shine

4218 Alcott St

Alexandria, VA 22309

## ABSTRACT

Biological neural systems show behavior which can be described by chaotic models and equations. Some of these equations show similarities to both classical neural network paradigms and newer models of complex adaptive systems. This paper attempts to define unifying principles in these three separate mathematical models.

# NEURAL FEATURE EXTRACTION / COMPRESSION FOR ORIENTATION-INVARIANT UNDERWATER TARGET RECOGNITION USING MULTI-SPARSE-SENSORS

C. X. TAN,    Y. L. MA

Institute of Acoustic Engineering, Northwestern Polytechnic University

Xi'an 710072, P. R. China

**ABSTRACT:**    Feature extraction for orientation-invariant underwater target recognition is an important problem in acoustic information processing. It has not yet been solved by conventional pattern recognition or expert systemsbecause a) The received signal characteristics vary violently with the orientation of targets; b) Resolution of sound is too lower than that of radar and optical signals. Satisfactory neural network approach to the problem has also not been reported.

The paper demonstrates a novel neural approach both to extract features automatically and reduce feature dimension up to 24 times for orientation-invariant underwater target recognition. The transmitted signal is narrow band Linearly-Frequency-Modulated(LFM) chirp. Multi-sparse-sensors are used to receive return signal from targets. Our neural processor directly maps signals in space domain and time domain to a very low dimension of adaptive feature space. Its every neuron divides input space by a adaptive hyperspheroidal or hyperboloidal boundary. The stability and distribution of the features are studied in detail according to the Euclidean distance. The effect of the sensor interval on the performance is also studied. Recognition results using the proposed processor with less than ten bits of quantization are presented for 4-class underwater target orientation-invariant case study. For the case study, the new method is shown to give better recall accuracy with fewer weights than other neural networks tested

**Keywords:**    Feature extraction, Acoustic informatiom processing, Neural networks, Automatic target recognition, Orientation-invariant, Pattern recognition.

## 1. INTRODUCTION

Feature extraction plays a dominant role in target recognition, especially for underwater targets in remote acoustic fields.There has not yet existed a satisfactory approach to extract feature with fewer dimension for orientation-invariant underwater target recognition by the conventional methods, although it has received considerable attention because of its increasingly importance in many ocean engineering applications. As sound energy has least propagation loss in a ocean and other high frequency signals can not propagate distantly in water, the sound has been used as predominant carrier of target information, which makes feature extraction more difficult than by radar or optical signals. As far as active sonar concerned, the characteristics of sonar returns from a target vary violently for different depth, range, target movement, hydrothermal environment, especially for different orientation which is the main changing factor for general distant targets. Additionally, the signal resolution and information on targets themslves provided by underwater acoustic systems most in use are more limited than provided by radar and optical systems.

Traditional pattern recognition requires some assumptions( e.g. simplifying assumptions about the structure of signals in order to reduce the computation required to reach accurate classification) and priori knowledge ( e.g. the explicit knowledge of data distributions). For many applications the former can hardly keep valid and the latter is not always available[1]. Another difficulty is the computational burden particularly for the traditional nonparametric pattern recognition. The most difficulty is how to extract features for orientation-invariant classification.

The expert system approach is also troubled with knowledge acquisition and chaos problems under the situation.

The development of artificial neural networks(ANN) has provided potential solutions to these problems[2][3][4][5]. They need neither restrictive assumptions about the structure of the input patterns[1], nor the explicit knowledge of data distributions[2]. However, seldom were the conventional feedforward nets seen to be used to extract and compress feature for orientation—invariant target recognition. Unsupervised learning nets, e.g. ART net, Cohenen net, Counter—propagation net, may be used for feature mapping, but not optimal for our problem because they localize the computational power of the network according to the distribution of input signals( which scatter sparsely and intermix among different targets) rather than localizing this power according to where it is needed for performing the mapping, resulting in EXPLOSION of processing units and weights.

The work presented in the paper differs from previous ones by the following points:
— It directly use neural network to extract/compress automatically feature for orientation—invariant recognition.
— It directly adopt information in space domain and in time domain together.High performance with small processor and few sensors.
— Its every neuron divides input space by an adaptive hyperspheroidal or hyperboloidal boundary.
Its performance is studied by extensive computer simulations for 4 artificial underwater targets, together with a comparative study with conventional BP, ART, CPN networks. The effect of the interval distance among sensors on its performance is also studied.

## 2. ARCHITECTURE and GENERAL IDEA

The schematic of the proposed architecture is shown in Figure 1.
The LFM chirp is transmitted. The multi—sparse—sensor array, whose setup may be arbitrary and distances between adjacent sensors may be much larger than half wavelength, is used to receive return waves from targets in distant fields. Among the preprocessing are noise cancellation ( for instance, adaptive noise cancellation for linear noise and neural noise cancellation[6] for nonlinear situation. ), complex envelope demodulation, matched filtering for pulse compression, removing the effect of propagation delay and other factors, sampling modulus of the matched filters and unit normalization of them in parallel, etc. Then the signals flow in a set of Time—Delayed Units corresponding to sensors. The neural network directly uses the 2—dimension signals in space domain and in time domain to extract/compress automatically feature for orientation—invariant recognition. The top layer(s) of the network classify these pattern and map them to a meaning space giving the target index.

The feature extraction and compression are achieved in one step at the same time by a single neural layer whose processing units are especially designed as shown in Figure 2. The dimension in the layer is ever less. The neuron contains 2 order moments in its input interface, resulting in that before the nonlinear activation function, a 2 order hypersurface decision boundary (e.g. the hyperspheroid, the hyperboloid, etc.) is automatically generated according to the needed mapping. An attractive aspect of it is that it automatically determines a "reject" class region outside of the class regions. The "image" is further compressed after the nonlinear activation. The neuron demonstrates highly ability of fusion and cluster.

The modified BP algorithm[5]is adopted to train the neural network, which dynamically learns multi—patterns in parallel with limited dynamic range of weights and adaptively adjusts the learning

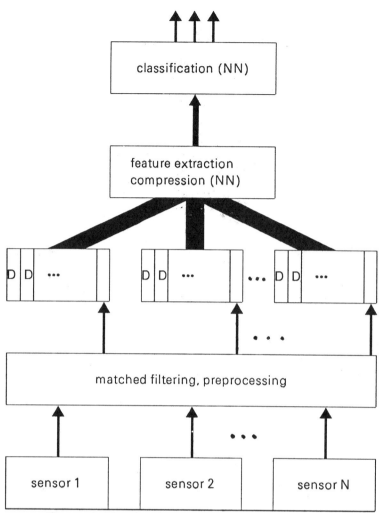

**Figure 1   The Architecture of the Proposed System**

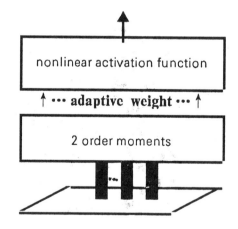

**Figure 2   The Neural Processing Unit**

rates.

## 3 TARGETS and INPUT PATTERNS

Previous reseaches have shown that Apart from target itself, the target orientation related to the incident waves playes the predominant effect on the reflection characteristics of underwater targets for the high aspect ratio (length divided by width ) targets [6].

We consider recognizing and discriminating 4 targets of return waves with a wide range of distortions present. These targets themselves are very much alike in architecture. Orientation, or the incident angle from transmitted waves to the targets, changes from $+80°$ to $-80°$ for each target. Target distance related to the sensors is 20 KM. The impinging pulse used in the study is narrow band LFM chirp whose duratoin time is 1.6 seconds, centeral frequency is 1 KHz, bandwidth is 100Hz. In order to study the effect of intervals between sensors on recognition, two 3-sensor horizontal line arrays are used to receive returns from targets. their intervals are half wavelength ( ARRAY I ) and 10-wavelength (ARRAY II) respectively. For the arrays, The DOAs keep at 30°. 2000 returns per array, half for training and half for testing, are obtained for the 4 targets at different orientations from $-80°$ to $80°$, whose SNRs are between 5dB and 10 dB.

Signals from every sensor flow through matched filters in parallel. The modulus of EACH matched filter output is independently normalized in time domain according to the Euclidean norm. The sampling frequency for matched filter outputs is 300Hz.

The preprocessed input patterns are of $3 \times 37$ dimensions ( space domain $\times$ time domain ) for ARRAY I (SET A), and $3 \times 40$ dimensions for ARRAY II (SET B) respectively. We have studied the distribution of the normalized input patterns in the learning data base using Array I in detail. This data base includes 1000 patterns corresponding with 4 targets at 250 orientations from $-80°$ to 80°. According to the Euclidean distances, the numbers of nearest neighbors necessary for fully correct recognition are shown in Table 1. Many neighbor regions contain only one or two patterns due to the intermix of patterns among different targets. The pattern space distributions appear to be very complicated. For the same target, these exist a very wide range of distortions among these patterns because of the change of orientations. At the same time, many pattern vectors  for different targets are much closer than those for the same target according to their Euclidean distances. The same situations are demonstrated by the frequency domain anlysis on the database. There are no obvious features for classification.

### TABLE 1
**Nearest Neighbor Numbers in Normalized Input Pattern Space of Learning Database I Based on the Euclidean distance**

| Target | Total Number of Neighbors | Number of Neighbors closing above 10 vectors | Number of Neighbors closing less than 3 vectors |
|--------|--------|--------|--------|
| A | 153 | 4 | 95 |
| B | 146 | 6 | 91 |
| C | 127 | 4 | 82 |
| D | 131 | 7 | 75 |

# 4. RESULTS and DISCUSSIONS

For the convenience of implementations, the accuracies of all the input data and computations in the work reported are limited to 10 bits of quantization.

Table 2 gives recognition accuracies for the 4 target using 4 different methods. For Set A, $N = 3 \times 37$ input neurons were used for all methods. For Set B, $N = 3 \times 40$. The size of each network is determined mainly by the dimension of the layer next to the input because of the higher input dimension.

The ART 2, CPN and the standard BP net are too large to be practical for the application. Their classification accuracies are also too limited for the case. Among the 4 methods considered, the proposed method performs best orientation—invariant recognition with very small net size. The dimension of the feature extracted automatically by it is only 5. The compressions of dimensions from the normalized input space to the feature space are up to 24 for Set B and 22 for Set A, respectively.

**Table 2** Ststistics of Recognition Accuracies

| Processor | Training Set A $P_c(\%)$ | Test Set A $P_c(\%)$ | Training Set B $P_c(\%)$ | Test Set B $P_c(\%)$ | Processor Size, $S$ |
|---|---|---|---|---|---|
| Standard BP | 67.5 | 65 | 71.8 | 73.2 | $40 \times 4$ |
| ART 2 | 66 | 65.4 | 68.8 | 67.9 | $4 \times 100$ |
| CPN | 63.4 | 64.5 | 68 | 68.4 | $400 \times 4$ |
| The Proposed Net | 84.4 | 85.8 | 100 | 92.5 | $5 \times 4$ |

Where Set As are acquired with the half—wavelength array and Set Bs with the 10—wavelength array. $S$ means ( dimension of the hidden layer $\times$ dimension of its output) for BP,CPN and the proposed method. for ART 2 it is the output dimension. $P_c$ means the correct classification probability.

Extensive observation and anlysis on the internal connections and mappings of the proposed net demonstrate that over a wide range of target orientations, its feature vectors extracted by the net clusters stably in the hypersphere(s) only corresponding with the target, for each target. Table 3 gives the numbers of hypersphere for the 4 targets.

**Table 3 The Number of Hyperspherical Regions in the Feature Space Needed for Classification**

| Target | Test Set A | | Test Set B | |
|---|---|---|---|---|
| | $N_h$ | $M_p(\%)$ | $N_h$ | $M_p(\%)$ |
| A | 5 | 62 | 4 | 68 |
| B | 7 | 43 | 3 | 62 |
| C | 12 | 24 | 3 | 68 |
| D | 18 | 22 | 4 | 43 |

where $N_h$ and $M_p$ are the number of hyperspheres and the maximum ratio of the pattern number included in one hypersphere to the tatol pattern number of the corresponding class.

Statistics indicate that for the same number sensors, with the increase of the distances among sensors, the feature fusion performance improves very much over a larger range of orientations. The classification accuracies increase also with larger sensor array.

## 5. CONCLUSIONS

We have demonstrated a new approach to automatic extraction / compression feature for orientation—invariant underwater target recognition. For a 4—target case study,we have obtained recognition accuracy on test data of 92.5% with the orientation from $-80^\circ$ to $80^\circ$, while our processor works with less than ten bits of quantization and it automatically extracts only 5 dimensions of relatively stable features with 3 sensors. In addition to its specific neuron, it is attractive in that it directly uses signals in space domain and time domain to extract / compress automatically features for orientation—invariant recognition, with small processor size and fewer sensors which may be separated distantly one another. Both the architecture simplification and high performance of the proposed method encourage practical engineering applications, particularly to the mechanical failure diagnosis, flaw detection, sonar, radar, ultrasonic and seismic information processing, industrial automation, etc.

**REFERENCES**
1  R. Paul Gorman et al, " Learned Classification of Sonar Targets Using a Massively Parallel Network ", IEEE Trans. on ASSP,Vol.36, NO.7,1988
2  Fogelman Soulie,"Neural Networks for Pattern Rcognition",Proc. of IJCNN—91, Seattle.
3  C. X. Tan and Y. L. Ma,"Compound Artificial Neural Network Based Classifiers With Applications to High Resolution Signal Recognition", Proc. of IEEE Symposium on Industrial Electronics, 1992.
4  Y. L. Ma, "Advances in Acoustic Signal Processing", Keynote address to WESTPAC'IV, 1991, Australia
5  C. X. Tan, Y. L. Ma, "Rapid Signal Classification Using Hybrid ANNs " Proc. of $C^2N^2$ '91.
6  C. X. Tan, et al, "A Neural Network for Improvement of Wdeband and Coloured Noise Cancellation ", Proc. of IJCNN'92.